THE BANKNOTE BOOK

2014

EDITOR
Owen W. Linzmayer

BanknoteNews.com
San Francisco, California
United States of America
www.BanknoteBook.com

SUBSCRIBE TODAY!

THE BANKNOTE BOOK

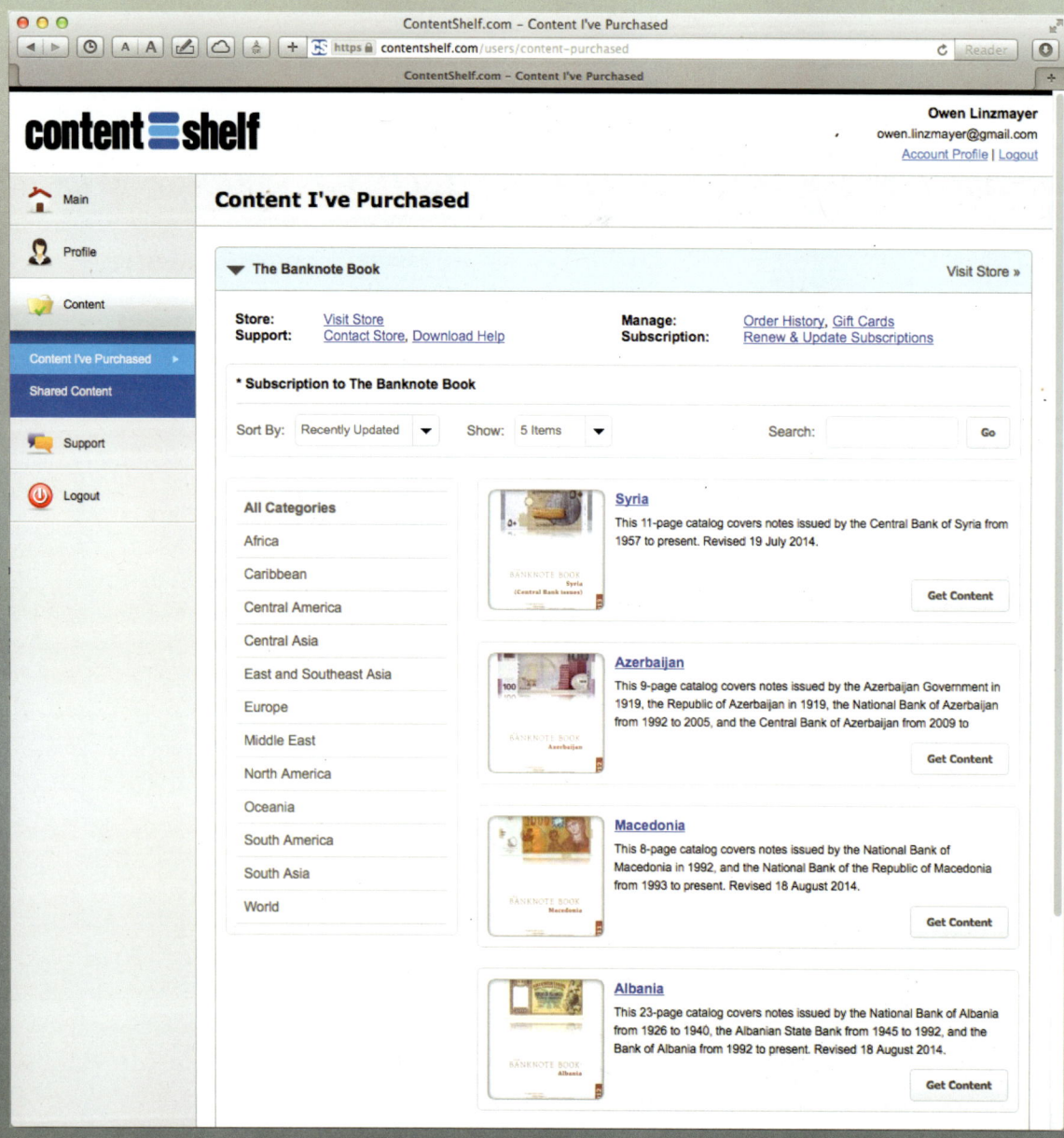

The print edition of The Banknote Book belongs in every numismatic reference library, but for the very latest pricing and note issues, a subscription to the online edition is essential because it entitles you to all newly published and revised chapters during your subscription period. Country-specific chapters can be downloaded as PDFs for use on computers, tablets, and smartphones.

The Banknote Book in print and online…an unbeatable combination!

www.BanknoteBook.com

Contents

Nigeria	1565
(North) Korea	1584
Oceania	1607
Oman	1609
Pakistan	1621
Palestine	1649
Panama	1653
Papua New Guinea	1655
Paraguay	1674
Poland	1693
Qatar	1722
Qatar & Dubai	1731
Republic of the Congo	1734
Rhodesia	1740
Rhodesia and Nyasaland	1745
Russia	1749
Rwanda	1759
Rwanda and Burundi	1772
Saar	1775
Saint Helena	1778
Saint Lucia	1782
Samoa	1783
Sao Tome and Principe	1790
Sarawak	1799
Saudi Arabia	1808
Senegal	1819
Serbia	1822
Serbian Krajina	1829
Seychelles	1839
Sierra Leone	1855
Singapore	1865
Slovakia	1885
Slovenia	1899
Solomon Islands	1912
Somalia	1921
Somaliland	1932
South Arabia	1939
(South) Korea	1942
South Sudan	1959
(South) Vietnam	1962
Sri Lanka	1977
Straits Settlements	1990
Sudan	2001
Suriname	2025
Swaziland	2039
Syria	2052
Tajikistan	2063
Tangier	2071
Tanzania	2074
Tonga	2088
Trans-Dniester	2094
Trinidad and Tobago	2109
Tunisia	2124
Turkey	2135
Turkmenistan	2173
Turks & Caicos Islands	2183
Uganda	2186
Ukraine	2204
United Arab Emirates	2219
Upper Senegal and Niger	2231
Uruguay	2232
Uzbekistan	2253
Vanuatu	2261
Vietnam	2269
Yemen	2282
Zaïre	2291
Zambia	2308
Zanzibar	2326
Zimbabwe	2329

The Banknote Book

Volume 3. Nigeria to Zimbabwe

© Owen W. Linzmayer, 2014

The contents of this catalogue, including the numbering system and illustrations are protected by copyright.

Owen W. Linzmayer has asserted his rights under the Copyright, Designs and Patents Act, 1988, to be identified as Author of this Work

All rights reserved. No part of this publication may be reproduced, stored in a retrieval system, or transmitted, in any form or by any means, electronic, mechanical, photocopying, recording or otherwise, without the prior written permission of the copyright holder.

ISBN: 978-1-907427-42-8

Printed and bound in Malta
by Gutenberg Press Ltd.

For the publishers:

SPINK & SON LTD.
69 Southampton Row
Bloomsbury
London WC1B 4ET

www.spink.com

Nigeria

For earlier issues, see British West Africa.

Contents

Government of Nigeria (GON).............................. 1565
Central Bank of Nigeria (CBN) 1565

Monetary System
01.07.1959: 1 Nigerian pound = 20 shillings
01.01.1973: 1 Nigerian naira (NGN) = 100 kobo = 0.50 pound

Government of Nigeria

1918 WWI Emergency Issues

These notes were printed locally to alleviate a shortage of silver coins after World War I. They were issued under ordinance XXII of 1918.

GON B1 (P1): 1 shilling — Good / Fine / XF
Green. Front (uniface): Text. No security thread. Watermark: Unknown. Printer: (Unknown, Nigeria). 130 x 67 mm.
    a. December 1918. Sig: David Sliman MacGregor.   400   1,200   2,500

GON B2 (P1A): 10 shillings — Good / Fine / XF
Red. Front (uniface): Text. No security thread. Watermark: Unknown. Printer: (Unknown, Nigeria). Unknown dimensions.
    a. December 1918. Sig: David Sliman MacGregor.   —   —   —

No image available
GON B3 (P1B): 20 shillings — Good / Fine / XF
Black. Front (uniface): Text. No security thread. Watermark: Unknown. Printer: (Unknown, Nigeria). Unknown dimensions.
    a. December 1918. Sig: David Sliman MacGregor.   —   —   —

Central Bank of Nigeria

The Central Bank of Nigeria (CBN) was established by the Central Bank Act of 1958 and commenced operations on 1 July 1959.

For more information, visit www.cbn.gov.ng.

CBN Signature Varieties

1

GOVERNOR
Roy Pentelow Fenton
(24.07.1958 - 24.07.1963)

DIRECTOR	DIRECTOR	DIRECTOR
Mallam Yakubu Wanka	F. Ola Awosika	Jabin Asidishor Obahor

2

GOVERNOR
Alhaji Aliyu Mai-Bornu
(25.07.1963 - 22.06.1967)

DIRECTOR	DIRECTOR	DIRECTOR
E. A. Iyanda	Mallam Yakubu Wanka	Jabin Asidishor Obahor

3

GOVERNOR
Clement Nyong Isong
(15.08.1967 - 22.09.1975)

GENERAL MANAGER
M. A. Adejoro

GOVERNOR	CHIEF OF BANKING OPERATIONS

4

Clement Nyong Isong
(15.08.1967 - 22.09.1975)

Francis Anegbode Ijewere

5

Mallam Adamu Ciroma
(24.09.1975 - 28.06.1977)

Alhaji Amusa Oladimeji Gbadamosi Otiti

6

Ola Vincent
(28.06.1977 - 28.06.1982)

Alhaji Amusa Oladimeji Gbadamosi Otiti

CBN Signature Varieties

	GOVERNOR	DIRECTOR OF DOMESTIC OPERATIONS
7	 Ola Vincent (28.06.1977 - 28.06.1982)	 A. Bamidele A. Obilana
8	 Ola Vincent (28.06.1977 - 28.06.1982)	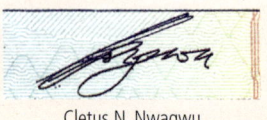 Cletus N. Nwagwu
9	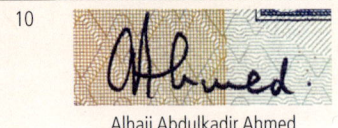 Alhaji Abdulkadir Ahmed (28.06.1982 - 30.09.1993)	 Cletus N. Nwagwu

	GOVERNOR	DIRECTOR OF CURRENCY OPERATIONS
10	 Alhaji Abdulkadir Ahmed (28.06.1982 - 30.09.1993)	 Unknown
11	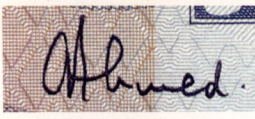 Alhaji Abdulkadir Ahmed (28.06.1982 - 30.09.1993)	 Alhaji Monsuru Adetoro
12a	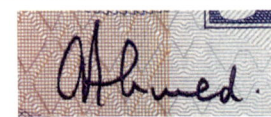 Alhaji Abdulkadir Ahmed (28.06.1982 - 30.09.1993)	 Alhaji Muhammad Abubakar Sadiq
12b	 Alhaji Abdulkadir Ahmed (28.06.1982 - 30.09.1993)	 Alhaji Muhammad Abubakar Sadiq
13	 Paul Agbai Ogwuma (01.10.1993 - 29.05.1999)	 Alhaji Muhammad Abubakar Sadiq
14	 Joseph Oladele Sanusi (29.05.1999 - 29.05.2004)	 Alhaji Muhammad Abubakar Sadiq
15	Joseph Oladele Sanusi (29.05.1999 - 29.05.2004)	Patrick I. C. Anene

CBN Signature Varieties

16	 Chukwuma "Charles" Soludo (29.05.2004 - 06.03.2009)	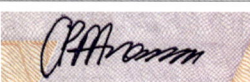 Patrick I. C. Anene

	GOVERNOR	DIRECTOR OF CURRENCY AND BRANCH OPERATIONS
17	 Chukwuma "Charles" Soludo (29.05.2004 - 06.03.2009)	Benjamin Chuks Onyido
18	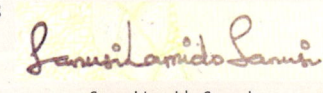 Sanusi Lamido Sanusi (06.04.2009 - present)	 Benjamin Chuks Onyido

	GOVERNOR	DIRECTOR OF CURRENCY OPERATIONS
19	Sanusi Lamido Sanusi (06.04.2009 - present)	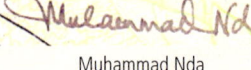 Muhammad Nda
20	 Sanusi Lamido Sanusi (06.04.2009 - present)	 Mahmoud K. Umar

1958 Issues

On 1 July 1959, the Central Bank of Nigeria exchanged old West African Currency Board (see British West Africa) notes and coins at par for the new Nigerian currency, all dated 15TH SEPTEMBER, 1958.

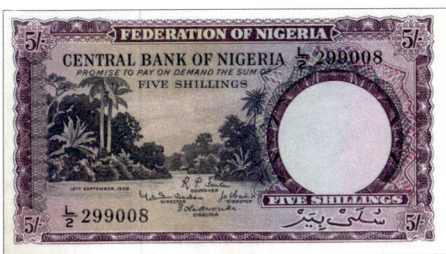

CBN B1 (P2): **5 shillings** (withdrawn 1965)   VG   VF   UNC
Purple and dark green. Front: Niger River scene with palm trees. Back: Palm trees. Solid security thread. Watermark: Lion head. Printer: (W&S). 120 x 65 mm.

		VG	VF	UNC
☐ a.	15TH SEPTEMBER, 1958. Signature 1. Intro: 01.07.1959.	35	100	400
☐ as1.	Diagonal red *SAMFUR* overprint on front; punched. Uniface.	—	—	—
☐ as2.	Diagonal red *SAMFUR* ovpt on back. Uniface.	—	—	—
☐ as3.	Diagonal red *SPECIMEN* overprint; punched.	—	—	600
☐ as4.	Diagonal purple *SPECIMEN* handstamp; horizontal *SPECIMEN* perforation; punched.	—	—	—
☐ at.	Color trial: Brown.	—	—	120

CBN B2 (P3): **10 shillings** (withdrawn 1965)   VG   VF   UNC
Green and brown. Front: Niger River scene with palm trees. Back: Men sowing crops; mountain; man holding groundnuts (peanuts); straw huts. Solid security thread. Watermark: Lion head. Printer: (W&S). 138 x 76 mm.

		VG	VF	UNC
☐ a.	15TH SEPTEMBER, 1958. Signature 1. Intro: 01.07.1959.	50	200	800
☐ as1.	Diagonal red *SAMFUR* overprint on front; punched. Uniface.	—	—	—
☐ as2.	Diagonal red *SAMFUR* ovpt on back. Uniface.	—	—	—
☐ as3.	Diagonal red *SPECIMEN* overprint; punched.	—	—	750
☐ as4.	Diagonal red *SPECIMEN* overprint; normal s/n.	—	—	—
☐ as5.	Horizontal *SPECIMEN* perforation; punched; no serial numbers.	—	—	—
☐ as6.	Diagonal purple *SPECIMEN* handstamp; horizontal *SPECIMEN* perforation; punched.	—	—	—
☐ at.	Color trial: Red.	—	—	375

CBN B3 (P4): **1 pound** (withdrawn 1965) VG VF UNC
Red and brown. Front: Niger River scene with palm trees. Back: Five workers harvesting cocoa pods from trees with machetes and basket. Solid security thread. Watermark: Lion head. Printer: (W&S). 153 x 83 mm.

		VG	VF	UNC
☐	a. 15TH SEPTEMBER, 1958. Signature 1. Intro: 01.07.1959.	2.50	10	65
☐	as1. Diagonal red *SAMFUR* overprint on front; punched. Uniface.	—	—	—
☐	as2. Diagonal red *SAMFUR* ovpt on back. Uniface.	—	—	—
☐	as3. Diagonal red *SPECIMEN* overprint; punched.	—	—	750
☐	as4. Diagonal red *SPECIMEN* overprint; normal s/n.	—	—	—
☐	as5. Horizontal *SPECIMEN* perforation; punched; no serial numbers.	—	—	—
☐	as6. Diagonal purple *SPECIMEN* handstamp; horizontal *SPECIMEN* perforation; punched.	—	—	—
☐	at. Color trial: Blue.	—	—	275

CBN B4 (P5): **5 pounds** (withdrawn 1965) VG VF UNC
Dark green and purple. Front: Niger River scene with palm trees. Back: Palm trees; storage shed; three men harvesting palm fruit. Solid security thread. Watermark: Lion head. Printer: (W&S). 166 x 100 mm.

		VG	VF	UNC
☐	a. 15TH SEPTEMBER, 1958. Signature 1. Intro: 01.07.1959.	25	100	450
☐	as1. Diagonal red *SAMFUR* overprint on front; punched. Uniface.	—	—	—
☐	as2. Diagonal red *SAMFUR* ovpt on back. Uniface.	—	—	—
☐	as3. Diagonal red *SPECIMEN* overprint; punched.	—	—	900
☐	as4. Horizontal *SPECIMEN* perforation; punched; no serial numbers.	—	—	—
☐	as5. Diagonal purple *SPECIMEN* handstamp; horizontal *SPECIMEN* perforation; punched.	—	—	—
☐	at. Color trial: Green.	—	—	450

1967 Issues

In 1965, Nigeria's legal tender was changed to reflect the country's republican status, which had been declared in 1963. As such, the title on the front of the new notes was changed from *FEDERATION OF NIGERIA* to *FEDERAL REPUBLIC OF NIGERIA*. Additionally, the Niger River scene was replaced by the bank's headquarters building in Lagos, since moved to Abuja.

CBN B5 (P6): **5 shillings** (withdrawn 1968)   VG   VF   UNC
Lilac and blue. Front: Central Bank of Nigeria building in Lagos. Back: Log raft on river; two men cutting log with chain saw. Solid security thread. Watermark: Lion head. Printer: Unknown. 126 x 73 mm.

   ☐ a. No date. Signature 2. Intro: 1967.   5   25   200
   ☐ as1. Diagonal red *SPECIMEN* overprint; all-zero s/n.   —   —   375
   ☐ as2. Diagonal red *SPECIMEN* overprint; normal s/n.   —   —   —
   ☐ as3. Diagonal red *SPECIMEN* overprint on front only; normal serial numbers.

CBN B6 (P7): **10 shillings** (withdrawn 1968)   VG   VF   UNC
Green and brown. Front: Central Bank of Nigeria building in Lagos. Back: Two men carrying groundnut sacks on their heads. Solid security thread. Watermark: Lion head. Printer: Unknown. 138 x 76 mm.

   ☐ a. No date. Signature 2. Intro: 1967.   25   100   450
   ☐ as1. Diagonal red *SPECIMEN* overprint; all-zero s/n.   —   —   450
   ☐ as2. Diagonal red *SPECIMEN* overprint; normal s/n.   —   —   —
   ☐ as3. Diagonal red *SPECIMEN* overprint on front only; normal serial numbers.

CBN B7 (P8): **1 pound** (withdrawn 1968)   VG   VF   UNC
Red and brown. Front: Central Bank of Nigeria building in Lagos. Back: Man with machete beating cluster from date palm. Solid security thread. Watermark: Lion head. Printer: Unknown. 153 x 83 mm.

   ☐ a. No date. Signature 2. Intro: 1967.   0.75   2   6
   ☐ as1. Diagonal red *SPECIMEN* overprint; all-zero s/n.   —   —   300
   ☐ as2. Diagonal red *SPECIMEN* ovpt on front and back; normal serial numbers.
   ☐ as3. Diagonal red *SPECIMEN* overprint on back only; normal serial numbers.
   ☐ as4. Diagonal red *SPECIMEN* overprint on front only; normal serial numbers.

1968 Issues

In 1968, during the Nigerian-Biafra War, Nigeria changed the colors of its notes and demonetized the older issues in an attempt to cripple Biafra's finances.

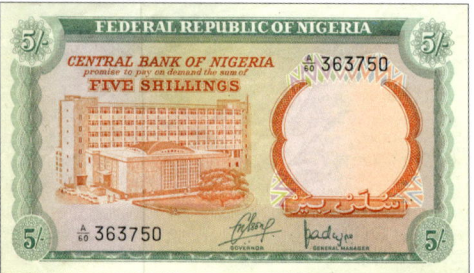

CBN B8 (P9): **5 pounds** (withdrawn 1968)   VG   VF   UNC
Green and brown. Front: Central Bank of Nigeria building in Lagos. Back: Four people removing cocoa beans from pods into two baskets. Solid security thread. Watermark: Lion head. Printer: (TDLR). 158 x 89 mm.

		VG	VF	UNC
a.	No date. Signature 2. Intro: 1967.	20	125	420
as1.	Diagonal red *SPECIMEN* overprint; all-zero s/n.	—	—	1,000
as2.	Diagonal red *SPECIMEN* overprint; normal s/n.	—	—	—
as3.	Diagonal *CANCELLED* perforation; all-zero s/n.	—	—	—
as4.	Diagonal red *SPECIMEN* overprint on back only; normal serial numbers.	—	—	150
as5.	Diagonal red *SPECIMEN* and DLR oval ovpts; horizontal red *SPECIMEN* Nº # ovpt at lower left; punched.	—	—	335

CBN B9 (P10): **5 shillings** (withdrawn 1973)   VG   VF   UNC
Green and orange. Front: Central Bank of Nigeria building in Lagos. Back: Log raft on river; two men cutting log with chain saw. Solid security thread. Watermark: Lion head. Printer: Unknown. 128 x 72 mm.

		VG	VF	UNC
a.	No date. Signature 3. Intro: 1968.	10	50	150
b.	Signature 4.	10	50	150
as1.	Diagonal red *SPECIMEN* overprint; all-zero s/n.	—	—	25
as2.	Diagonal red *SPECIMEN* overprint on front only; normal serial numbers.	—	—	150
as3.	Diagonal red *SPECIMEN* overprint on back only; normal serial numbers.	—	—	150
bs.	Diagonal red *SPECIMEN* overprint; normal s/n.	—	—	150

CBN B10 (P11): **10 shillings** (withdrawn 1973)   VG   VF   UNC

Violet and brown. Front: Central Bank of Nigeria building in Lagos. Back: Two men carrying groundnut sacks on their heads. Solid security thread. Watermark: Lion head. Printer: Unknown. 138 x 76 mm.

		VG	VF	UNC
☐	a. No date. Signature 3. Intro: 1968.	15	50	200
☐	b. Signature 4.	20	80	350
☐	as1. Diagonal red *SPECIMEN* overprint; all-zero s/n.	—	—	25
☐	as2. Diagonal red *SPECIMEN* overprint; normal s/n.	—	—	150
☐	as3. Diagonal red *SPECIMEN* overprint on back only; normal serial numbers.	—	—	—

CBN B12 (P13): **5 pounds** (withdrawn 1973)   VG   VF   UNC

Brown and blue. Front: Central Bank of Nigeria building in Lagos. Back: Coat of arms; Four people removing cocoa beans from pods into two baskets. Solid security thread. Watermark: Lion head. Printer: Unknown. 158 x 89 mm.

		VG	VF	UNC
☐	a. No date. Signature 3. Intro: 1968.	20	75	500
☐	b. Signature 4.	20	75	500
☐	as1. Diagonal red *SPECIMEN* overprint; all-zero s/n.	—	—	25
☐	as2. Diagonal red *SPECIMEN* overprint; normal s/n.	—	—	—

CBN B11 (P12): **1 pound** (withdrawn 1973)   VG   VF   UNC

Brown and purple. Front: Central Bank of Nigeria building in Lagos. Back: Man with machete beating cluster from date palm; coat of arms. Solid security thread. Watermark: Lion head. Printer: Unknown. 153 x 83 mm.

		VG	VF	UNC
☐	a. No date. Signature 3. Intro: 1968.	20	75	300
☐	b. Signature 4.	25	125	600
☐	as1. Diagonal red *SPECIMEN* overprint; all-zero s/n.	—	—	25
☐	as2. Diagonal red *SPECIMEN* overprint; normal s/n.	—	—	—
☐	as3. Diagonal red *SPECIMEN* overprint on back only; normal serial numbers.	—	—	—

1973-1977 Decimal Issues

Nigeria changed to decimal currency on 1 January 1973. The major currency unit is the naira, equivalent to 10 shillings: the minor unit is the kobo; 100 of which make one naira. The naira replaced the pound at the rate of 2 naira = 1 pound. Nigeria was the last country to abandon the pound/shilling/pence system.

These notes are printed on paper manufactured by Portals, UK.

CBN B13 (P14): **50 kobo** (withdrawn 1991)   VG   VF   UNC
Blue, purple, and brown. Front: Central Bank of Nigeria building in Lagos. Back: Coat of arms; log raft on river; two men cutting log with chain saw. Solid security thread. Watermark: Eagle. Printer: Unknown. 127 x 73 mm.

		VG	VF	UNC
a.	No date. Signature 4. Intro: 01.01.1973.	0.50	2	10
b.	Signature 5.	1.25	5	30
c.	Signature 6.	0.50	2	10
d.	Signature 7.	0.50	2	10
e.	Signature 8.	0.50	2	10
f.	Signature 9.	0.50	2	10
g.	Signature 10.	—	—	3
h.	Signature 11.	1.25	5	30
i.	Signature 12a.	0.50	2	10
as1.	Diagonal red *SPECIMEN* overprint on front only.	—	—	—
as2.	Diagonal red *SPECIMEN* overprint on back only.	—	—	—
bs1.	Diagonal red *SPECIMEN* ovpt on front and back.	—	—	—
bs2.	Diagonal red *SPECIMEN* overprint on front only.	—	—	—
cs.	Diagonal red *SPECIMEN* overprint on back only; no serial numbers.	—	—	—

Replacement notes: Prefix numerator DZ.

CBN B14 (P15): **1 naira** (withdrawn 1977)   VG   VF   UNC
Red and brown. Front: Central Bank of Nigeria building in Lagos. Back: Coat of arms; two men carrying groundnut sacks on their heads. Solid security thread. Watermark: Eagle. Printer: (TDLR). 137 x 78 mm.

		VG	VF	UNC
a.	No date. Signature 4. Intro: 01.01.1973.	1.25	5	15
b.	Signature 5.	1.25	5	15
c.	Signature 6.	1.25	5	15
d.	Signature 7.	5	15	50
as1.	Diagonal red *SPECIMEN* overprint on front only.	—	—	—
as2.	Diagonal red *SPECIMEN* overprint on back only.	—	—	—
as3.	Horizontal *SPECIMEN OF NO VALUE* perf; horizontal black *PROOF N°* # ovpt at lower left.	—	—	—
as4.	Diagonal red *SPECIMEN* and DLR oval ovpts; horizontal red *SPECIMEN N°* # ovpt at lower left; punched.	—	—	125
bs.	Diagonal red *SPECIMEN* overprint.	—	—	—
ds1.	Diagonal red *SPECIMEN* overprint on back only; no serial numbers.	—	—	—
ds2.	Diagonal red *SPECIMEN* overprint on front only.	—	—	—

Replacement notes: Prefix numerator DZ.

CBN B15 (P16): **5 naira** (withdrawn 1977)   VG   VF   UNC

Blue-gray and olive green. Front: Central Bank of Nigeria building in Lagos. Back: Coat of arms; man with machete beating cluster from date palm. Solid security thread. Watermark: Eagle. Printer: (TDLR). 151 x 84 mm.

		VG	VF	UNC
☐	a. No date. Signature 4. Intro: 01.01.1973.	5	20	70
☐	b. Signature 5.	5	15	50
☐	c. Signature 6.	15	60	275
☐	d. Signature 7.	20	75	600
☐	as1. Diagonal red *SPECIMEN* overprint on front only.	—	—	—
☐	as2. Diagonal red *SPECIMEN* overprint on back only.	—	—	—
☐	as3. Horizontal *SPECIMEN OF NO VALUE* perf; horizontal black *PROOF Nº #* ovpt at lower left.	—	—	200
☐	as4. Diagonal red *SPECIMEN* and DLR oval ovpts; horizontal red *SPECIMEN Nº #* ovpt at lower left; punched.	—	—	200
☐	bs. Diagonal red *SPECIMEN* overprint.	—	—	—
☐	ds1. Diagonal red *SPECIMEN* overprint on back only; no serial numbers.	—	—	—
☐	ds2. Diagonal red *SPECIMEN* overprint on front only.	—	—	—

Replacement notes: Prefix numerator DZ.

CBN B16 (P17): **10 naira** (withdrawn 1977)   VG   VF   UNC

Carmine and dark blue. Front: Central Bank of Nigeria building in Lagos. Back: Coat of arms; Kainji dam spillway on River Niger. Solid security thread. Watermark: Eagle. Printer: (TDLR). 157 x 90 mm.

		VG	VF	UNC
☐	a. No date. Signature 4. Intro: 01.01.1973.	7.50	25	250
☐	b. Signature 5.	5	20	85
☐	c. Signature 6.	35	125	450
☐	d. Signature 7.	35	125	500
☐	as1. Diagonal red *SPECIMEN* overprint on front only.	—	—	—
☐	as2. Diagonal red *SPECIMEN* overprint on back only.	—	—	—
☐	as3. Diagonal red *SPECIMEN* and DLR oval ovpts; horizontal red *SPECIMEN Nº #* ovpt at lower left; punched.	—	—	200
☐	bs. Diagonal red *SPECIMEN* overprint.	—	—	—
☐	cs1. Diagonal red *SPECIMEN* overprint on back only; no serial numbers.	—	—	—
☐	cs2. Diagonal red *SPECIMEN* overprint on front only.	—	—	—

Replacement notes: Prefix numerator DZ.

1977-1979 Issues

Unlike the preceding series with notes of graduating sizes, all of the denominations in this series are the same dimension. The notes bear the portraits of eminent Nigerians who were declared national heroes on 1 October 1978. The backs of the notes reflect cultural aspects of Nigeria. The 20-naira note was issued first, in 1977, while the three lower denominations followed two years later.

CBN B17 (P19): **1 naira** (withdrawn 1984)　　　　VG　VF　UNC
Red and orange. Front: Herbert Macaulay. Back: Coat of arms; carved ivory Bini mask. Solid security thread. Watermark: Eagle. Printer: Unknown. 151 x 78 mm.

☐ a.　No date. Signature 7. Intro: 02.07.1979.　　0.25　2　7.50
☐ b.　Signature 8.　　　　　　　　　　　　　　　1.50　6　25
☐ c.　Signature 9.　　　　　　　　　　　　　　　—　0.75　3
☐ as.　Diagonal red *SPECIMEN* overprint.　　　　—　—　—

Replacement notes: Prefix numerator DZ.

CBN B18 (P20): **5 naira** (withdrawn 1984)　　　　VG　VF　UNC
Green and blue. Front: Alhaji Sir Abubakar Tafawa Balewa. Back: Coat of arms; four Nkpokiti dancers with drums. Solid security thread. Watermark: Eagle. Printer: (TDLR). 151 x 78 mm.

☐ a.　No date. Signature 7. Intro: 02.07.1979.　　1　5　15
☐ b.　Signature 8.　　　　　　　　　　　　　　　5　20　60
☐ c.　Signature 9.　　　　　　　　　　　　　　　0.50　2.50　10
☐ as1.　Diagonal red *SPECIMEN* overprint.　　　—　—　—
☐ as2.　Diagonal red *SPECIMEN* and DLR oval ovpts;　—　—　350
　　　horizontal red *SPECIMEN Nº* # ovpt at lower left; punched.

Replacement notes: Prefix numerator DZ.

CBN B19 (P21): **10 naira** (withdrawn 1984)　　　VG　VF　UNC
Maroon and tan. Front: Alvan Ikoku. Back: Coat of arms; two Fulani milk maids carrying bowls on their heads. Solid security thread. Watermark: Eagle. Printer: Unknown. 151 x 78 mm.

☐ a.　No date. Signature 7. Intro: 02.07.1979.　　2.50　10　30
☐ b.　Signature 8.　　　　　　　　　　　　　　　5　20　70
☐ c.　Signature 9.　　　　　　　　　　　　　　　5　20　70
☐ as1.　Diagonal red *SPECIMEN* overprint on back only;　—　—　—
　　　no serial numbers.
☐ as2.　Diagonal red *SPECIMEN* overprint on front only.　—　—　—

Replacement notes: Prefix numerator DZ.

1984-2006 Issues

In April 1984, these four notes were issued with new colors as a tactical measure by the military administration which took power in December 1983. The move was intended to arrest the alarming rate of currency trafficking going on at the time. Several of the denominations have been observed with both 4.5- and 6.25-mm tall prefix varieties, as well as single- and double-letter numerators.

CBN B20 (P18): **20 naira** (withdrawn 1984)   VG   VF   UNC
Multicolor. Front: General Murtala Ramat Muhammed. Back: Coat of arms. Solid security thread. Watermark: Eagle. Printer: Unknown. 151 x 78 mm.

		VG	VF	UNC
a.	No date. Signature 5. Intro: 11.02.1977.	50	200	400
b.	Signature 6.	20	60	200
c.	Signature 7.	8	20	65
d.	Signature 8.	6	25	70
e.	Signature 9.	4	10	35
bs.	Diagonal red *SPECIMEN* overprint.	—	—	—
cs1.	Diagonal red *SPECIMEN* overprint on back only; no serial numbers.	—	—	—
cs2.	Diagonal red *SPECIMEN* overprint on front only.	—	—	—

Replacement notes: Prefix numerator DZ.
The note was issued on the first anniversary of the assassination of General Murtala Ramat Muhammed.

CBN B21 (P23): **1 naira** (withdrawn 1991)   VG   VF   UNC
Violet and green. Front: Herbert Macaulay. Back: Coat of arms; carved ivory Bini mask. Solid security thread. Watermark: Eagle. Printer: (TDLR). 151 x 78 mm.

		VG	VF	UNC
a.	No date. Signature 9. Intro: April 1984.	0.25	1	3
b.	Signature 10.	0.25	1	3
c.	Signature 11.	1	5	15
d.	Signature 12a.	1	5	15
as.	Diagonal red *SPECIMEN* and DLR oval ovpts; horizontal red *SPECIMEN Nº* # ovpt at lower left; punched.	—	—	125

Replacement notes: Prefix numerator DZ.

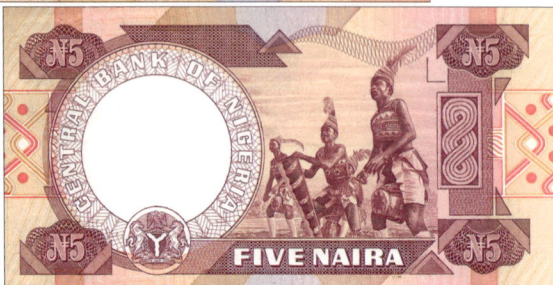

CBN B22 (P24): **5 naira** (withdrawn February 2007)   VG   VF   UNC

Violet and orange. Front: Alhaji Sir Abubakar Tafawa Balewa. Back: Coat of arms; four Nkpokiti dancers with drums. Solid security thread. Watermark: Eagle. Printer: Unknown. 151 x 78 mm.

			VG	VF	UNC
☐	a.	No date. Signature 9. Intro: April 1984.	—	4	15
☐	b1.	Signature 10.	—	2.50	10
☐	b2.	UV printing in green, not orange; latent image added to left of portrait; *CENTRAL BANK OF NIGERIA* microprinted above signatures.	—	2.50	10
☐	c.	Signature 11.	—	—	2
☐	d.	Signature 12a.	—	—	2
☐	e.	Signature 13.	—	—	1
☐	f.	Signature 14.	—	—	5
☐	g.	2001.	—	—	1
☐	h.	2002.	—	—	1
☐	i.	2004. Signature 15.	—	—	1
☐	j.	2005. Signature 16.	—	—	1
☐	k.	Signature 17.	—	—	1

Replacement notes: Prefix numerator DZ.

CBN B23 (P25): **10 naira** (withdrawn May 2007)   VG   VF   UNC

Red and orange. Front: Alvan Ikoku. Back: Coat of arms; two Fulani milk maids carrying bowls on their heads. Solid security thread. Printer: (TDLR). 151 x 78 mm.

			VG	VF	UNC
☐	a.	No date. Intro: April 1984. Signature 9. Diagonal lines in watermark area on front.	2.50	10	40
☐	b.	Signature 10. Fine lines in watermark area on front; *CENTRAL BANK OF NIGERIA* microprinted above signatures.	—	5	15
☐	c.	Signature 11.	—	—	3
☐	d1.	Signature 12a.	—	—	3
☐	d2.	Signature 12b.	—	—	3
☐	e.	Signature 13.	—	—	3
☐	f.	Signature 14.	—	—	2
☐	g.	2001.	—	—	2
☐	h.	2002.	—	—	6
☐	i.	2003. Printed date near embossed *2002*.	—	—	2
☐	j.	Signature 15.	—	—	2
☐	k.	2004.	—	—	2
☐	l.	2005.	—	—	2
☐	m.	Signature 16.	—	—	2
☐	n.	Signature 17.	—	—	2
☐	as.	Diagonal red *SPECIMEN* and DLR oval ovpts; horizontal red *SPECIMEN Nº #* ovpt at lower left; punched.	—	—	150

Replacement notes: Prefix numerator DZ.

The 5-naira note with signature 10 is available in two varieties with several differences, the easiest of which to distinguish is the addition of microprinting. On earlier issues, the parallelogram surrounding the denomination in Arabic script above the signatures has a solid bottom line (CBN B22b1, top), whereas on later issues the line consists of the words *CENTRAL BANK OF NIGERIA* repeated in microprint (B22b2, bottom).

CBN B24 (P26): **20 naira** (withdrawn May 2007)   VG   VF   UNC

Green and tan. Front: General Murtala Ramat Muhammed. Back: Coat of arms. Solid security thread. Watermark: Eagle. Printer: (TDLR). 151 x 78 mm.

		VG	VF	UNC
☐ a.	No date. Intro: April 1984.	15	30	60
	Signature 9.			
	Diagonal lines in watermark area on front.			
☐ b.	Signature 10.	—	—	6
	Fine lines in watermark area on front; latent image added on portait; *CENTRAL BANK OF NIGERIA* microprinted above signatures.			
☐ c.	Signature 11.	—	—	4
☐ d1.	Signature 12a.	—	—	4
☐ d2.	Signature 12b.	—	—	4
☐ e.	Signature 13.	—	—	2
☐ f.	Signature 14.	—	—	2
☐ g.	2001.	—	—	2
☐ h.	2002.	—	—	2
☐ i.	2003. Printed date near embossed *2002*.	—	—	2
☐ j.	Signature 15.	—	—	2
☐ k	2004.	—	—	2
☐ l.	2005. Signature 16.	—	—	2
☐ m.	Signature 17.	—	—	2
☐ n.	2006.	—	—	2
☐ as.	Diagonal red *SPECIMEN* and DLR oval ovpts; horizontal red *SPECIMEN Nº* # ovpt at lower left; punched.	—	—	200

Replacement notes: Prefix numerator DZ.

CBN B25 (P27): **50 naira** (withdrawn May 2007)   VG   VF   UNC

Violet and purple. Front: Eagle; three men and a woman; map of Nigeria; eagle as registration device. Back: Eagle; drum; two workers with baskets picking tea leaves; boy digging cassava with hoe; coat of arms; cowrie shells. Windowed security thread with demetalized *CBN*. Watermark: Eagle. Printer: Unknown. 151 x 78 mm.

		VG	VF	UNC
☐ a.	No date. Signature 11. Intro: October 1991.	1	5	15
☐ b.	Signature 12b.	—	—	6
☐ c.	Signature 13.	—	—	6
☐ d.	Signature 14.	0.50	2.50	10
☐ e.	2001.	—	—	6
☐ f.	2004. Signature 15.	—	—	6
☐ g.	2005. Signature 16.	—	—	6
☐ h.	Signature 17.	—	—	6

Replacement notes: Prefix numerator DZ.

1999-2014 Issues

CBN B26 (P28): **100 naira** (US$0.70)   VG   VF   UNC

Rust. Front: Chief Obafemi Awolowo, former Premier of Western Region. Back: Zuma Rock in Niger State; coat of arms. Windowed security thread with demetalized *CBN*. Watermark: Chief Obafemi Awolowo and electrotype *100 CBN*. Printer: Unknown. 151 x 78 mm.

☐	a.	1999. Signature 14. Intro: 01.12.1999. ZUMA ROCK FCT, ABUJA (error) on back.	FV	FV	5
☐	b.	ZUMA ROCK (corrected) on back.	FV	FV	3
☐	c.	2001.	FV	FV	3
☐	d.	2004. Signature 15.	FV	FV	3
☐	e.	2005. Signature 16.	FV	FV	3
☐	f.	Signature 17.	FV	FV	7
☐	g.	2006.	FV	FV	3
☐	h.	2007.	FV	FV	3
☐	i.	2008.	FV	FV	3
☐	j.	2009.	FV	FV	3
☐	k.	Signature 18.	FV	FV	3
☐	l.	2010.	FV	FV	3
☐	m.	Signature 19.	FV	FV	3
☐	n.	2011.	FV	FV	3
☐	o.	2012.	FV	FV	3
☐	p.	Signature 20.	FV	FV	3
☐	q.	2013.	FV	FV	3

Replacement notes: Prefix numerator DZ.

This note caused a controversy because Zuma Rock pictured on back is in Niger State, not the Federal Capital Territory of Abuja, as the caption originally indicated.

CBN B27 (P29): **200 naira** (US$1.45)   VG   VF   UNC

Brown, orange, and green. Front: Alhaji Sir Ahmadu Bello, the Sarduana of Sokoto and the first Premier of Northern Nigeria. Back: Two cattle; sacks of groundnuts; cocoa pods; date palms; corn; coat of arms. Windowed security thread with demetalized *CBN*. Watermark: Alhaji Sir Ahmadu Bello and electrotype *200 CBN*. Printer: Unknown. 151 x 78 mm.

☐	a.	2000. Sig. 14. Prefix A/39. Intro: 01.11.2000.	FV	FV	7.50
☐	b.	2001. Prefix G/3.	FV	FV	7.50
☐	c.	2002. Prefix G/64.	FV	FV	15
☐	d.	2003. Signature 15. Prefix I/74.	FV	FV	7.50
☐	e.	2004. Prefix J/67.	FV	FV	7.50
☐	f.	Signature 16. Prefix M/3.	FV	FV	7.50
☐	g.	2005. Prefix N/53 - Q/20.	FV	FV	7.50
☐	h.	Signature 17. Prefix R/65.	FV	FV	7.50
☐	i.	2006. Prefix DZ/18.	FV	FV	7.50
☐	j.	2007. Prefix S/70.	FV	FV	7.50
☐	k.	2008. Prefix DB/2.	FV	FV	7.50
☐	l.	2009. Prefix DZ/4.	FV	FV	7.50
☐	m.	Signature 18. Prefix AB/29.	FV	FV	7.50
☐	n.	2010. Prefix AD/21.	FV	FV	7.50
☐	o1.	Signature 19. 9-mm tall *Two* in denomination at front center. Prefix AG/66.	FV	FV	7.50
☐	o2.	11-mm tall *Two* in denomination at front center. Prefix AG/88 - AH/67.	FV	FV	7.50
☐	p.	2011. Prefix AC/84.	FV	FV	7.50
☐	q.	2012. Prefix AH/6.	FV	FV	7.50
☐	r.	Signature 20. Prefix AC/15.	FV	FV	7.50
☐	s.	2013. Prefix AD/64.	FV	FV	7.50
☐	t.	2014. Prefix AE/5.	FV	FV	7.50

Replacement notes: Prefix numerator DZ.

Both of the above scans are of 200-naira notes dated 2010, signed by Sanusi Lamido Sanusi and Muhammad Nda, with prefix numerators AG. However, on CBN B27o1 (left), the spelled out denomination "Two Hundred Naira" and the signatures are located higher up than on CBN B27o2 (right), the word "Two" is 9-mm tall versus 11-mm tall, and Sanusi's signature is equal in width to that of Nda.

CBN B28 (P30): **500 naira** (US$3.60) VG VF UNC

Orange, purple, and red. Front: Dr. Nnamdi Azikiwe, first President of the Federal Republic of Nigeria. Back: Off-shore oil platform; coat of arms. Windowed security thread with demetalized *CBN*. Watermark: Dr. Nnamdi Azikiwe and electrotype *500 CBN*. Printer: Unknown. 151 x 78 mm.

			VG	VF	UNC
☐	a.	2001. Signature 14. Prefix A/4 - C/81. Intro: 04.04.2001.	FV	FV	10
☐	b.	2002. Prefix C/89 - F/84.	FV	FV	10
☐	c.	2004. Signature 15. Prefix G/41 - H/79.	FV	FV	10
☐	d.	2005. Signature 16. Prefix I/91 - K/41.	FV	FV	10
☐	e.	Signature 17. Prefix L/2 - L/74.	FV	FV	10
☐	f.	2006. Prefix G/39 - G/94.	FV	FV	10
☐	g.	2007. Prefix I/43 - P/38.	FV	FV	10
☐	h.	2008. Prefix R/77.	FV	FV	10
☐	i.	2009. Prefix V/48 - W/66.	FV	FV	10
☐	j.	Signature 18. Prefix X/11 - B/50.	FV	FV	10
☐	k.	2010. Sig. 19. Prefix B/69 - H/42, AB/37 - AD/3.	FV	FV	10
☐	l.	2011. Prefix H/75 - K/53.	FV	FV	10
☐	m.	2012. Signature 20. Prefix L/3, AB/79 - AE/2.	FV	FV	10
☐	n.	2013. Prefix AE/46.	FV	FV	10
☐	o.	2014. Prefix AH/96.	FV	FV	10

Replacement notes: Prefix numerator DZ.

CBN B29 (P36): **1,000 naira** (US$7.15) VG VF UNC

Brown. Front: Alhaji Aliyu Mai-Bornu and Dr. Clement Isong, first and second indigenous governors of the Central Bank of Nigeria; coat of arms holographic patch. Back: Central Bank of Nigeria headquarters building in Abuja; straw huts; rock formation; coat of arms. Windowed security thread with demetalized *CBN*. Watermark: Portraits and electrotype *CBN 1000*. Printer: Unknown. 151 x 78 mm.

			VG	VF	UNC
☐	a.	2005. Signature 17. Prefix A/16 - B/60. Intro: 12.10.2005.	FV	FV	20
☐	b.	2006. Prefix B/94 - B/106.	FV	FV	20
☐	c.	2007. Prefix B/146 - B/671.	FV	FV	20
☐	d.	2009. Signature 18. Prefix C/4.	FV	FV	25
☐	e.	2010. Prefix C/11 - C/92.	FV	FV	20
☐	f.	Signature 19. Prefix G/5 - L/4.	FV	FV	20
☐	g.	2011. Prefix E/2 - E/46.	FV	FV	20
☐	h.	2012. Signature 20. Prefix F/92 - G/50.	FV	FV	20
☐	i.	2013. Prefix R/23.	FV	FV	20
☐	j.	2014. Prefix R/83.	FV	FV	20

Replacement notes: Prefix numerator DZ.

2006-2013 Issues

CBN B30 (P32): **5 naira** (<US$0.05) VG VF UNC
Mauve. Front: Prime Minister Alhaji Sir Abubakar Tafawa Balewa; bank logo. Back: Map of Nigeria; four Nkpokiti dancers with drums; coat of arms. Solid security thread with demetalized *CBN*. Watermark: Coat of arms and electrotype *CBN*. Printer: Unknown. 130 x 72 mm.

☐	a.	2006. Signature 17. 6-digit s/n. Intro: 28.02.2007.	FV FV	1
☐	b.	7-digit serial numbers.	FV FV	1
☐	c.	2007. 6-digit serial numbers.	FV FV	5
☐	d.	2008.	FV FV	1

Replacement notes: Prefix numerator DZ.

CBN B31 (P33): **10 naira** (US$0.05) VG VF UNC
Red. Front: Alvan Ikoku; bank logo. Back: Map of Nigeria; two Fulani milk maids carrying bowls on their heads; coat of arms. Solid security thread with demetalized *CBN*. Watermark: Coat of arms and electrotype *CBN*. Printer: Unknown. 130 x 72 mm.

☐	a.	2006. Signature 17. 7-digit s/n. Intro: 28.02.2007.	FV FV	1.50
☐	b.	2007.	FV FV	1.50
☐	c.	2008.	FV FV	1.50
☐	d.	2009. 6-digit serial numbers.	FV FV	1.50

Replacement notes: Prefix numerator DZ.

CBN B32 (P34): **20 naira** (US$0.15) VG VF UNC
Green. Front: General Murtala Ramat Muhammed; bank logo. Back: Map of Nigeria; Ladi Kwali, a renowned potter, with bowls and vases; coat of arms. No security thread. Watermark: *CBN*. 130 x 72 mm. Polymer.

☐	a.	2006. Signature 17. Intro: 28.02.2007. 6-digit serial numbers. Printer: (NSP&M).	FV FV	2
☐	b.	7-digit serial numbers. Printer: (G&D).	FV FV	2
☐	c.	2007. 6-digit serial numbers. Printer: (NSP&M).	FV FV	2
☐	d.	7-digit serial numbers. Printer: (G&D).	FV FV	2
☐	e.	2008. 6-digit serial numbers. Printer: (NSP&M).	FV FV	2
☐	f.	2009.	FV FV	2
☐	g.	2010. Signature 18.	FV FV	2
☐	h.	Signature 19.	FV FV	2
☐	i.	2011.	FV FV	2
☐	j.	7-digit serial numbers.	FV FV	2
☐	k.	2012. Signature 20.	FV FV	2
☐	l.	2013.	FV FV	2
☐	bs.	Diagonal red *SPECIMEN* overprint; horizontal red *SPECIMEN* Nº # ovpt at lower left.	— —	950

Replacement notes: Prefix numerator DZ.
This is the first polymer note issued by Nigeria.

2009-2013 Issues

On 30 September 2009, the bank introduced 5-, 10-, and 50-naira notes printed on polymer. 1.3 billion notes were printed by Giesecke & Devrient (identified by 7-digit serial numbers), while 615 million notes were printed by Nigeria Security Printing and Minting (identified by 6-digit serial numbers).

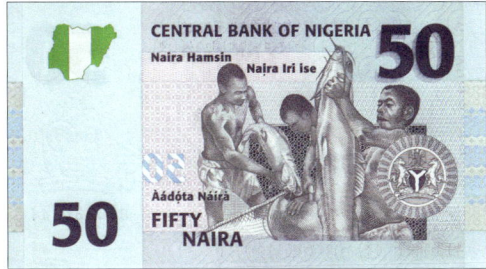

CBN B33 (P35): **50 naira** (US$0.35)   VG   VF   UNC

Blue. Front: Three men and a woman; bank logo. Back: Map of Nigeria; three men with two fish; coat of arms. Solid security thread with demetalized *CBN*. Watermark: Coat of arms and electrotype *CBN*. Printer: Unknown. 130 x 72 mm.

☐ a.	2006. Signature 17. 7-digit s/n. Intro: 28.02.2007.	FV	FV	2.50
☐ b.	2007. 6-digit serial numbers.	FV	FV	2.50
☐ c.	7-digit serial numbers.	FV	FV	3.50
☐ d.	2008. 6-digit serial numbers.	FV	FV	2.50
☐ cs.	Diagonal red *SPECIMEN* overprint; horizontal red *SPECIMEN N°* # ovpt at lower left.	—	—	—

Replacement notes: Prefix numerator DZ.

CBN B34 (P38): **5 naira** (<US$0.05)   VG   VF   UNC

Mauve. Front: Prime Minister Alhaji Sir Abubakar Tafawa Balewa; bank logo. Back: Map of Nigeria; four Nkpokiti dancers with drums; coat of arms. No security thread. Watermark: *CBN*. 130 x 72 mm. Polymer.

☐ a.	2009. Signature 17. Intro: 30.09.2009. 6-digit serial numbers. Printer: (NSP&M).	FV	FV	1
☐ b.	7-digit serial numbers. Printer: (G&D).	FV	FV	1
☐ c.	Signature 18.	FV	FV	1
☐ d.	2011. Signature 19.	FV	FV	1
☐ e.	2013. Signature 20.	FV	FV	1
☐ bs.	Diagonal red *SPECIMEN* overprint; horizontal red *SPECIMEN N°* # ovpt at lower left.	—	—	750

Replacement notes: Prefix numerator DZ.

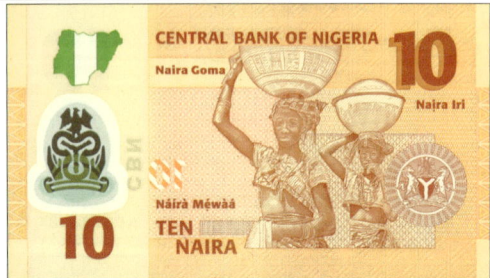

2010 Commemorative Issues

This 50-naira note commemorates the nation's 50th anniversary of independence. It is like the preceding issue, but with a 50th anniversary logo.

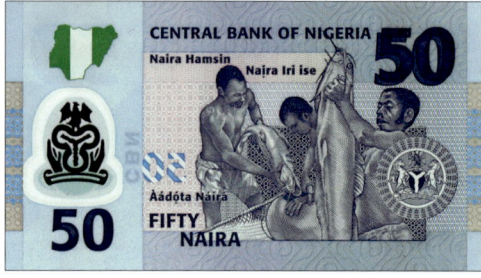

CBN B35 (P39): **10 naira** (US$0.05)   VG   VF   UNC
Red. Front: Alvan Ikoku; bank logo. Back: Map of Nigeria; two Fulani milk maids carrying bowls on their heads; coat of arms. No security thread. Watermark: *CBN*. 130 x 72 mm. Polymer.

☐ a.	2009. Intro: 30.09.2009. Signature 17. 7-digit s/n. Printer: (G&D).	FV	FV	1.50
☐ b.	Signature 18. 6-digit s/n. Printer: (NSP&M).	FV	FV	1.50
☐ c.	7-digit serial numbers. Printer: (G&D).	FV	FV	1.50
☐ d.	2010. Signature 18. 6-digit serial numbers.	FV	FV	1.50
☐ e.	Signature 19.	FV	FV	1.50
☐ f.	2011. 6-digit serial numbers.	FV	FV	1.50
☐ g.	7-digit serial numbers. Varnish coating.	FV	FV	1.50
☐ h.	2013. Signature 20.	FV	FV	1.50
☐ hs.	Diagonal red *SPECIMEN* overprint; horizontal red *SPECIMEN N°* # ovpt at lower left.	—	—	950

Replacement notes: Prefix numerator DZ.

CBN B37 (P37): **50 naira** (US$0.35)   VG   VF   UNC
Blue. Front: Three men and a woman; Nigeria's 50th Independence logo; bank logo. Back: Map of Nigeria; three men with two fish; coat of arms. No security thread. Watermark: *CBN*. Printer: Unknown. 130 x 72 mm. Polymer.

☐ a.	2010. Signature 19. Intro: 29.09.2010.	FV	FV	2.50

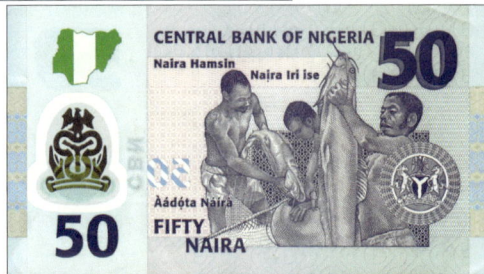

CBN B36 (P40): **50 naira** (US$0.35)   VG   VF   UNC
Blue. Front: Three men and a woman; bank logo. Back: Map of Nigeria; three men with two fish; coat of arms. No security thread. Watermark: *CBN*. 130 x 72 mm. Polymer.

☐ a.	2009. Intro: 30.09.2009. Signature 17. 7-digit s/n. Printer: (G&D).	FV	FV	2.50
☐ b.	Signature 18. 6-digit s/n. Printer: (NSP&M).	FV	FV	2.50
☐ c.	7-digit serial numbers. Printer: (G&D).	FV	FV	2.50
☐ d.	2010. 6-digit serial numbers. Printer: (NSP&M).	FV	FV	2.50
☐ e.	2011. Signature 19.	FV	FV	2.50
☐ f.	7-digit serial numbers. Printer: (G&D).	FV	FV	2.50
☐ g.	2013. Signature 20.	FV	FV	2.50

Replacement notes: Prefix numerator DZ.

Looking Forward

- According to an article in Leadership dated 13 May 2012, the Central Bank of Nigeria is contemplating introducing 2,000- and 5,000-naira notes, as well as replacing the 10-, 20-, and 50-naira notes with coins.

- According to an article on WorldStage dated 23 August 2012, the Central Bank of Nigeria has announced plans to introduce a new 5,000-naira banknote in the first quarter of 2013. The restructuring exercise, code-named Project Cure, will change the naira currency structure to 12, comprising of six coins and six banknote denominations. "Under the structure, the existing denominations of N50, N100, N200, N500 and N1,000 will be designed with added security features. It is our pleasure to inform you that a new high currency denomination will also be introduced. It is the N5,000 note. In the same vein, the lower banknote denominations of N5, N10 and N20 will be coined," said the governor of the bank, Mallam Sanusi Lamido Sanusi.

The new 5,000-naira banknote will have pictures of three Nigerian heroine and nationalists, namely Funmilayo Ransome-Kuti, Margaret Ekpo, and Alhaja Sawaba Gambo on the front while the National Assembly pictures would be the illustrations at its back.

- According to an article in allAfrica dated 12 September 2012, the Central Bank of Nigeria plans to no longer print banknotes on polymer due to higher costs (a result of Australia-based Securency's monopoly on the substrate) and environmental issues. Currently the bank issues polymer notes in its lowest denominations of 5, 10, 20, and 50 naira. All but the 50-naira denomination will be replaced by coins when the bank restructures the currency as expected in 2013.

Museum

The Currency Museum of the Central Bank of Nigeria was commissioned on 6 May 2009, as part of activities marking the 50th anniversary of the bank.

For more information, visit www.cenbank.org/museum.

Acknowledgements

This chapter was compiled with the generous assistance of Sejin Ahn, Mohammed el-Arabi, Thomas Augustsson, Arigo Avbovbo, Aleksey Avdeev, Abdullah Beydoun, Jean-Michel Engels, Mike Jowett, Thomas Krause, Wally Myers, Rafal Nogowczyk, Mikhail "Mike" Prizov, Nazir Rahemtulla, Andrew Roberts, Norman Schmidt (www.brunos-weltbanknoten.de), Mel & Jeremy Steinberg (www.banknotes-steinberg.com), Bill Stubkjaer, Christoph Thomas, Tristan Williams, Christof Zellweger, and others.

Sources

Cuhaj, George S. *Standard Catalog of World Paper Money, General Issues, 1368-1960*. 14th edition. 2012. ISBN 978-1-4402-3090-5. Krause Publications (www.krausebooks.com), 700 East State St., Iola, WI, 54990-0001.

Cuhaj, George S. *Standard Catalog of World Paper Money, Modern Issues, 1961-Present*. 19th edition. 2013. ISBN 978-1-4402-3571-9. Krause Publications (www.krausebooks.com), 700 East State St., Iola, WI, 54990-0001.

Eu, Peter, Ben Chiew, and Stane Straus. *World Polymer Banknotes: A Standard Reference*. 2nd edition. 2006. ISBN 983-43038-2-3. Eureka Metro, P. O. Box 30, Jalan Kelang Lama, Kuala Lumpur, 57000, Malaysia.

Feller, Rachel. "Rachel Notes: Nigeria." *IBNS Journal*. Volume 44 Number 1. p.47.

Kelly, Richard. "Early Paper Money in British West Africa." *IBNS Journal*. Volume 16 Number 3. p.151.

Kelly, Richard. "Blue Books and Bank Histories." *IBNS Journal*. Volume 16 Number 4. p.224.

Krause, Thomas and Peter Bauer. *Specialized Catalogue of World Plastic Money*. 5th edition. 2009. www.polymernotes.de.

Symes, Peter. *The Banknotes of Biafra*. December 2006. David White, 7 Burraneer Close, Ferntree Gully, Victoria 3156, Australia.

Symes, Peter. "The Bank Notes of Biafra." *IBNS Journal*. Volume 36 Number 4. p.27.

Share Your Input, Info, and Images

This catalog is believed to be complete and correct as of the time of publication. Prices and face values were last updated 9 September 2011. Please report errors or omissions so that corrections may be made. If you can more precisely identify the name or location of anything depicted on a note, please share that information. Furthermore, if you own an unlisted type or variety, please submit scans of the front and back of the note so that it can be documented. Scans should be 300 dots per inch, 100% actual size, 24-bit color, saved as *uncompressed* JPEG files, and sent to owen@banknotenews.com. Be sure to fully describe all attributes of the note which are not apparent upon visual inspection of the images alone, such as physical dimension, watermark, and security thread.

(North) Korea

For earlier issues, see Korea.

Contents

Red Army Headquarters (RAH) 1584
Central Bank of North Korea (CBNK).................. 1585
Central Bank of the Democratic People's
Republic of Korea (DPRK) 1587
Trade Bank of DPRK (TB) 1603

Monetary System
06.12.1947: 1 North Korean won (KPW) = 100 jeon

붉은군대 사령부
(Red Army Headquarters)

Following Japan's defeat in World War II, in August 1945 Korea was divided into a Soviet-occupied zone north of the 38th parallel and an American-occupied zone in the south. In 1948, Korea was divided into two separate countries (the Democratic People's Republic of Korea in the north, and the Republic of Korea in the south), each with their own currencies, both called won, and both of which replaced the yen at par.

1945 Military Payment Certificates

The Red Army Headquarters (RAH) abolished Bank of Korea notes and put these notes into circulation instead. The denomination is expressed in Hanja (logographic Chinese characters) at center, with the year in Western digits below; all other text is in Hangul, the native alphabet of the Korean language.

RAH B1 (P1): 1 원 (won)   VG   VF   UNC
Green and brown. Front: Floral design. Back: Floral design. No security thread.
Watermark: Unknown. Printer: Unknown. 126 x 69 mm.
☐ a. 1945.   10   50   125

RAH B2 (P2): 5 원 (won)   VG   VF   UNC
Brown and blue. Front: guilloche patterns. Back: Floral design. No security thread.
Watermark: Star pattern. Printer: Unknown. 135 x 74 mm.
☐ a. 1945.   15   60   150

RAH B3 (P3): 10 원 (won)   VG   VF   UNC
Purple and green. Front: Floral design. Back: Guilloche patterns. No security thread.
Watermark: Unknown. Printer: Unknown. 153 x 83 mm.
☐ a. 1945.   15   75   200

RAH B4 (P4): 100 원 (won)   VG   VF   UNC

Pink and green. Front: Floral design. Back: Guilloche patterns. No security thread. Printer: Unknown. 153 x 83 mm.

- a. 1945. Watermark: Unknown.   25   85   225
- b. Watermark: None.   25   85   225

北朝鮮 中央 銀行券
(Central Bank of North Korea)

The Central Bank of North Korea (CBNK) was established in 1947 by the People's Committee of North Korea, led by Kim Il Sung.

1947 Issues

The won became the currency of North Korea on 6 December 1947, replacing the Soviet won and Korean yen that were still in circulation. The notes without watermarks were printed on white paper many years after the watermarked notes on buff paper, reportedly by corrupt officials who attempted to sell them to neighboring countries.

CBNK B1 (P5): 15 전 (jeon)   VG   VF   UNC

Brown. Front: Text. Back: Guilloche patterns. No security thread. Printer: Unknown. 88 x 44 mm.

- a. 1947.   0.75   2.50   10
  Buff paper. Watermark: Star pattern.
- b. White paper. Watermark: None.   —   —   1.75

CBNK B2 (P6): 20 전 (jeon)   VG   VF   UNC

Green. Front: Text. Back: Guilloche patterns. No security thread. Printer: Unknown. 90 x 45 mm.

- a. 1947.   1   3   12
  Buff paper. Watermark: Star pattern.
- b. White paper. Watermark: None.   —   —   1

CBNK B3 (P7): 50 전 (jeon)   VG   VF   UNC

Blue and green. Front: Text. Back: Guilloche patterns. No security thread. Printer: Unknown. 104 x 52 mm.

- a. 1947.   0.50   2   6.50
  Buff paper. Watermark: Star pattern.
- b. White paper. Watermark: None.   —   —   1.50

CBNK B4 (P8): 1 원 (won)   VG   VF   UNC

Brown and green. Front: Smokestacks; farmer with hoe; man with sledgehammer; bank seal. Back: Highest peak of Mount General in the Baekdu (white-headed) Mountain range; trees. No security thread. Printer: Unknown. 115 x 61 mm.

- a. 1947.   0.75   2.50   10
  Buff paper. Watermark: Star pattern.
- b. White paper. Watermark: None.   —   —   2

CBNK B5 (P9): **5 원 (won)**　　　　　　　　　　　　　**VG　VF　UNC**
Blue, green, and red. Front: Smokestacks; farmer with hoe; man with sledgehammer; bank seal. Back: Highest peak of Mount General in the Baekdu (white-headed) Mountain range; trees. No security thread. Watermark: Pattern. Printer: Unknown. 130 x 70 mm.
　☐　a.　1947.　　　　　　　　　　　　　　　　　—　—　2

While there are several other minor differences between CBNK B5 (left) and B6 (right), one of the easiest ways to distinguish between the two notes is by comparing the lower character in the rosette at right on the back of the notes.

CBNK B6 (P10): **5 원 (won)**　　　　　　　　　　　　　**VG　VF　UNC**
Blue, green, and red. Front: Smokestacks; farmer with hoe; man with sledgehammer; bank seal. Back: Highest peak of Mount General in the Baekdu (white-headed) Mountain range; trees. No security thread. Printer: Unknown. 130 x 70 mm.
　☐　a.　1947.　　　　　　　　　　　　　　　　1　2.50　10
　　　　Buff paper. Watermark: Star pattern.
　☐　b.　White paper. Watermark: None.　　　　　—　—　2

CBNK B7 (P10A): **10 원 (won)**　　　　　　　　　　　　**VG　VF　UNC**
Green and red. Front: Smokestacks; farmer with hoe; man with sledgehammer; bank seal. Back: Highest peak of Mount General in the Baekdu (white-headed) Mountain range; trees. No security thread. Printer: Unknown. 133 x 73 mm.
　☐　a.　1947.　　　　　　　　　　　　　　　　2　6　20
　　　　Buff paper. Watermark: Star pattern.
　☐　b.　White paper. Watermark: None.　　　　　—　—　2.50

CBNK B8 (P11): **100 원 (won)**　　　　　　　　　　　　**VG　VF　UNC**
Red. Front: Bank seal; smokestacks; farmer with hoe; man with sledgehammer. Back: Highest peak of Mount General in the Baekdu (white-headed) Mountain range; trees. No security thread. Printer: Unknown. 169 x 95 mm.
　☐　a.　1947.　　　　　　　　　　　　　　　　4　15　50
　　　　Buff paper. Watermark: Star pattern.
　☐　b.　White paper. Watermark: None.　　　　0.50　2　8
This note was widely counterfeited for use by United Nations forces operating behind enemy lines in North Korea. Genuine notes are typically off-center, whereas fakes are perfectly centered.

조선민주주의인민공화국 조선중앙은행
(Central Bank of the Democratic People's Republic of Korea)

On 9 September 1948, the country formally changed its name to the Democratic People's Republic of Korea (DPRK), and the name of the central bank was similarly altered. Hangul, the native alphabet of the Korean language, is used for all text.

1959 Issues

In 1959, the won was revalued at a rate of 100:1, and new banknotes were issued. The red circle on the front of each note is the seal of the chairman of the bank.

DPRK B1 (P12): 50 전 **(jeon)**   VG   VF   UNC
Blue and orange. Front: Hoe and hammer; coat of arms. Back: Guilloche patterns. No security thread. Watermark: Geometric pattern. Printer: Unknown. 131 x 59 mm.
- [ ] a. 1959.   0.50   2   10
- [ ] as. Diagonal red 견본 overprint.   —   —   30

DPRK B2 (P13): 1 원 **(won)**   VG   VF   UNC
Red and green. Front: Coat of arms; fishing boat with net and flag. Back: Guilloche patterns. No security thread. Watermark: Geometric pattern. Printer: Unknown. 149 x 65 mm.
- [ ] a. 1959.   0.50   2.50   10
- [ ] as. Diagonal red 견본 overprint.   —   —   —

DPRK B3 (P14): 5 원 **(won)**   VG   VF   UNC
Blue and green. Front: Coat of arms; Kim Il Sung University building in Pyongyang, trees, and people. Back: Guilloche patterns. No security thread. Watermark: Geometric pattern. Printer: Unknown. 154 x 68 mm.
- [ ] a. 1959.   1   4   15
- [ ] as. Diagonal red 견본 overprint.   —   —   —

DPRK B4 (P15): 10 원 **(won)**   VG   VF   UNC
Red. Front: Coat of arms; Liberation Monument in Pyongyang; Taedong Gate in Pyongyang. Back: Woman with basket picking fruit from tree; mountains. No security thread. Watermark: Geometric pattern. Printer: Unknown. 160 x 71 mm.
- [ ] a. 1959.   1   4   15
- [ ] as. Diagonal black 견본 overprint.   —   —   —

1978 Issues

With the exception of the 100-won denomination, the following notes were issued over the years in five different varieties with different color serial numbers on front and overprints on back to distinguish between their intended use. Notes with no overprint and red and black serial numbers were issued by the central bank for general circulation. In 1979, the Bank of Trade issued notes with green seals and black serial numbers to be used as foreign exchange certificates (FECs) by socialist visitors buying from locals, but notes with blue guilloches and black serial numbers were to be used when buying from foreigners. Conversely, when capitalist visitors bought from locals, notes with red seals and red serial numbers were used, but notes with red guilloches and red serial numbers were used when buying from fellow foreigners.

DPRK B5 (P16): 50 원 **(won)**   VG   VF   UNC
Purple and green. Front: Coat of arms; Taedong Bridge over Taedong River in Pyongyang; buildings; mountain. Back: Mountains; woman in field holding wheat. No security thread. Watermark: Geometric pattern. Printer: Unknown. 193 x 89 mm.

☐ a. 1959.   3   10   40
☐ as. Diagonal red 견본 overprint.   —   —   —

The seals (top row) and guilloches (bottom row) were overprinted on the backs of the 1978 notes to distinguish between their intended use as foreign exchange certificates.

DPRK B6 (P17): 100 원 **(won)**   VG   VF   UNC
Green and lilac. Front: Coat of arms; factory with smokestacks; railroad steam train. Back: Craggy cliffs; river. No security thread. Watermark: Geometric pattern. Printer: Unknown. 204 x 94 mm.

☐ a. 1959.   5   20   75
☐ as. Diagonal red 견본 overprint.   —   —   —

DPRK B7 (P18): 1 원 **(won)**   VG   VF   UNC
Green, blue, and purple. Front: Coat of arms; mongnan (Seibold's magnolia) flowers; boy with bugle, girl with bouquet of flowers, soldier, and dancer with hoop; banner with Korean slogan 세상에부럼없어라 (Nothing to envy in the world); city buildings. Back: Scenes from "Sea of Blood" opera: soldier with uplifted rifle; woman with basket of flowers; woman with pistol; city buildings. No security thread. Watermark: None. Printer: Unknown. 132 x 64 mm.

☐ a. 1978. No overprint on back.   —   —   2
☐ b. Green seal on back. Intro: 1979.   —   —   1.50
☐ c. Red seal on back. Intro: 1979.   —   —   1.50
☐ d. Red guilloche with 1 on back. Intro: 1984.   —   —   1.50
☐ e. Blue guilloche with 1 on back. Intro: 1984.   —   —   1.50
☐ as. Horizontal red 견본 overprint on front only; —   —   1
      all-zero serial numbers

DPRK B8 (P19): **5** 원 **(won)**   VG   VF   UNC

Blue and green. Front: Coat of arms; industrial city with smokestacks, factories, bridge, electrical towers, and trucks; man with large gear holding Book of Kim Il-Sung Collected Works; woman holding wheat. Back: Mongnan (Seibold's magnolia) flowers; Mount Kumgang; trees. No security thread. Watermark: None. Printer: Unknown. 142 x 70 mm.

☐	a.	1978. No overprint on back.	— —	1.50
☐	b.	Green seal on back. Intro: 1979.	— —	1.50
☐	c.	Red seal on back. Intro: 1979.	— —	1.50
☐	d.	Red guilloche with *5* on back. Intro: 1984.	— —	1.50
☐	e.	Blue guilloche with *5* on back. Intro: 1984.	— —	1.50
☐	as.	Horizontal red 견본 overprint on front only; all-zero serial numbers	— —	1

DPRK B9 (P20): **10** 원 **(won)**   VG   VF   UNC

Brown and green. Front: Coat of arms; statue of woman with wheat and man with book riding Chollima (thousand-mile horse) on Mansu Hill in Pyongyang. Back: Sail boats; waterfront factories with smokestacks. No security thread. Watermark: None. Printer: Unknown. 150 x 75 mm.

☐	a.	1978. No overprint on back.	— —	4
☐	b.	Green seal on back. Intro: 1979.	— —	1.50
☐	c.	Red seal on back. Intro: 1979.	— —	1.50
☐	d.	Red guilloche with *10* on back. Intro: 1984.	— —	1.50
☐	e.	Blue guilloche with *10* on back. Intro: 1984.	— —	1.50
☐	as.	Horizontal red 견본 overprint on front only; all-zero serial numbers	— —	1

DPRK B10 (P21): **50** 원 **(won)**   VG   VF   UNC

Green and brown. Front: Coat of arms; helmeted soldier with rifle; woman with wheat; man holding torch aloft; factory worker holding Book of Kim Il-Sung Collected Works overhead; 주체 (Juche). Back: Fir trees; Samjiyon lake; Baekdu (white-headed) Mountain. No security thread. Watermark: None. Printer: Unknown. 162 x 79 mm.

☐	a.	1978. No overprint on back.	— —	1.50
☐	b.	Green seal on back. Intro: 1979.	— —	1.50
☐	c.	Red seal on back. Intro: 1979.	— —	1.50
☐	d.	Red guilloche with *50* on back. Intro: 1984.	— —	1.50
☐	e.	Blue guilloche with *50* on back. Intro: 1984.	— —	1.50
☐	as1.	Horizontal red 견본 overprint on front only; all-zero serial numbers	— —	1
☐	as2.	Horizontal red 견본 overprint on front only; normal serial numbers	— —	1

DPRK B11 (P22): **100** 원 **(won)**   VG   VF   UNC

Tan, pink, brown, and green. Front: Coat of arms; flowers; Kim Il Sung. Back: Flowers; trees; houses (birthplace of Kim Il Sung) in Mangyongdae. No security thread. Watermark: Winged horse (Chollima). Printer: Unknown. 169 x 84 mm.

☐	a.	1978.	— —	2
☐	as.	Vertical red 견본 overprint on front only; all-zero serial numbers	— —	1

1992 Issues

These reduced-size notes were issued to halt the massive export of the 1978 series during the economic chaos caused by the dissolution of the Soviet Union. The watermarks on these and later issues sometimes appear to be missing, but in reality are present, just not in the correct position.

DPRK B12 (P39): 1 원 (won) VG VF UNC
Green, brown, and blue. Front: Coat of arms; actress Hong Yonhi with basket of flowers. Back: Mount Kumgang; waterfalls; Samseonam (Three Taoist hermit) rock formation; flying woman playing flute. No security thread. Watermark: Winged horse (Chollima). Printer: Unknown. 115 x 55 mm.
- ☐ a. 1992. — — 1
- ☐ as1. Boxed horizontal red 견본 ovpt on front only; — — 1
  all-zero serial numbers; 23- or 25-mm wide box.
- ☐ as2. Boxed horizontal red 견본 ovpt on front only; — — 1
  normal serial numbers; 25-mm wide box.

DPRK B13 (P40): 5 원 (won) VG VF UNC
Blue and green. Front: Coat of arms; atomic symbol; factory building; students; boy holding book with hand on globe; buildings. Back: Grand People's Study House building on Namsan Hill in Pyongyang. No security thread. Watermark: Winged horse (Chollima). Printer: Unknown. 125 x 60 mm.
- ☐ a. 1992. — — 2
- ☐ as1. Boxed horizontal red 견본 ovpt on front only; — — 1.50
  all-zero serial numbers.
- ☐ as2. Boxed horizontal red 견본 ovpt on front only; — — 1.50
  normal serial numbers; 30-mm wide box.

DPRK B14 (P41): 10 원 (won) VG VF UNC
Brown and olive green. Front: Coat of arms; worker pressing button; statue of woman with wheat and man with book riding Chollima (thousand-mile horse) on Mansu Hill in Pyongyang; factory buildings with smokestacks. Back: West Sea Barrage flood gates in Nampho. No security thread. Watermark: Winged horse (Chollima). Printer: Unknown. 135 x 65 mm.
- ☐ a. 1992. — — —
- ☐ as1. Boxed horizontal red 견본 ovpt on front only; — — 1.50
  all-zero serial numbers.
- ☐ as2. Boxed horizontal red 견본 ovpt on front only; — — 1.50
  normal serial numbers; 30-mm wide box.

DPRK B15 (P42): 50 원 (won) VG VF UNC
Brown and olive green. Front: Tower of Juche Idea monument with flame in Pyongyang; man in suit, man in overalls, woman with headscarf; olive branch; coat of arms. Back: Fir trees and Baekdu (white-headed) Mountain. No security thread. Watermark: Juche monument torch. Printer: Unknown. 145 x 70 mm.
- ☐ a. 1992. — — 1.50
- ☐ as1. Boxed horizontal red 견본 ovpt on front only; — — 1.50
  all-zero serial numbers; 26- or 34-mm wide box.
- ☐ as2. Boxed horizontal red 견본 ovpt on front only; — — 1.50
  normal serial numbers; 34-mm wide box.

1998 Issues

These notes are like the preceding issues, but with new date (expressed as the Korean year of the era 주체 [Juche, self-reliance] 87 above the western date in parentheses), cruder engravings, and lithographed printing. The new 500-won note was initially put into circulation only in the Lajin-Sonbong Free Trade Zone (later called the Lason FTZ), but by 2002 it was used throughout the country.

DPRK B16 (P43): **100 원 (won)**   VG   VF   UNC

Brown. Front: Coat of arms; flowers; Kim Il Sung. Back: Trees; houses (birthplace of Kim Il Sung) in Mangyongdae. No security thread. Watermark: Arch of Triumph. Printer: Unknown. 155 x 75 mm.

- a. 1992. Watermark: Head-on view. — — 1.50
- b. Watermark: 3/4 view. — — 1.50
- as. Boxed horizontal red 견본 ovpt on front only; all-zero serial numbers; 26- or 34-mm wide box. — — 2
- bs. Boxed horizontal red 견본 ovpt on front only; all-zero serial numbers; 26-mm wide box. — — 2

The Arch of Triumph watermark comes in two varieties: head-on view (DPRK B16a, left), and 3/4 view (B16b, right)

DPRK B17 (P40): **5 원 (won)**   VG   VF   UNC

Blue and green. Front: Coat of arms; atomic symbol; factory building; students; boy holding book with hand on globe; buildings. Back: Grand People's Study House building on Namsan Hill in Pyongyang. No security thread. Watermark: Winged horse (Chollima). Printer: Unknown. 125 x 60 mm.

- a. 1998. — — 1.50
- as. Boxed horizontal red 견본 ovpt on front only; all-zero serial numbers. — — 1.50

DPRK B18 (P41): **10 원 (won)**   VG   VF   UNC

Brown and olive green. Front: Coat of arms; worker pressing button; statue of woman with wheat and man with book riding Chollima (thousand-mile horse) on Mansu Hill in Pyongyang; factory buildings with smokestacks. Back: West Sea Barrage flood gates in Nampho. No security thread. Watermark: Winged horse (Chollima). Printer: Unknown. 135 x 65 mm.

- a. 1998. — — 1.50
- as. Boxed horizontal red 견본 ovpt on front only; all-zero serial numbers. — — 1.50

2000 Worker's Party 55th Anniversary Numismatic Products

DPRK BNP1 (PCS3): 1 원 (won)   UNC

☐ a. DPRK B7 with black *The 55th Anniversary of Foundation of the Worker's Party of Korea 10th. 10. Juche 89 (2000)* overprint.   3

DPRK BNP2 (PCS4): 5 원 (won)   UNC

☐ a. DPRK B8 with red *The 55th Anniversary of Foundation of the Worker's Party of Korea 10th. 10. Juche 89 (2000)* overprint.   3

☐ b. DPRK B8 with red 조선로동당창건 55돐 주체89(2000)년 10월 10일 overprint.   3

DPRK B19 (P44): 500 원 (won)   VG   VF   UNC

Light blue, green, and purple. Front: Coat of arms; Kumsusan Memorial Palace (Kim Il Sung Mausoleum) in Pyongyang; flowers. Back: Rungna bridge over the Daedong river in Pyongyang; olive branch. No security thread. Printer: Unknown. 155 x 75 mm.

☐ a. 1998. Watermark: Arch of Triumph. Fine lines in clouds around palace.   —   —   1.50

☐ b. Watermark: Winged horse (Chollima).   —   —   1.50

☐ c. Lines blurred around palace. Intro: 2002. Watermark: Arch of Triumph.   —   —   1.50

☐ bs1. Boxed horizontal red 견본 ovpt on front only; all-zero serial numbers.   —   —   3

☐ bs2. Boxed horizontal red 견본 ovpt on front only; normal serial numbers.   —   —   3

DPRK BNP3 (PCS5): 10 원 (won)   UNC

☐ a. DPRK B10 with black *The 55th Anniversary of Foundation of the Worker's Party of Korea 10th. 10. Juche 89 (2000)* overprint.   3

The clouds surrounding the palace on the front of the note are clearly defined on earlier 500-won notes (DPRK B19a/b, left), but are blurred on later issues (B19c, right).

DPRK BNP4 (PCS6, PCS7, PCS8): 50 원 (won)   UNC

☐ a1. DPRK B11 with red *The 55th Anniversary of Foundation of the Worker's Party of Korea 10th. 10. Juche 89 (2000)* overprint.   3

☐ a2. DPRK B11 with black *The 55th Anniversary of Foundation of the Worker's Party of Korea 10th. 10. Juche 89 (2000)* overprint.   3

☐ b. DPRK B11 with red 조선로동당창건 55돐 주체89(2000)년 10월 10일 overprint.   —   3

2002 Sun's Day 90th Anniversary Numismatic Products

This note was issued to celebrate "Sun's Day," which is the birthday of Kim Il Sung.

DPRK BNP5 (PNL): **5** 원 **(won)**
- a. DPRK B8 with black *Sun's Day, Celebration, 90th Anniversary 15th. 4. Juche 91 (2002)* overprint.

2002 Issues

These two notes were issued following the July 2002 devaluation of the official exchange rate of the won from 2.15 won to 151 won per dollar, which was close to the then black market rate.

UNC
—

DPRK B20 (P45a): **1,000** 원 **(won)**　　　　　　VG　VF　UNC

Green and light blue. Front: Coat of arms; flowers; Kim Il Sung. Back: Trees; houses (birthplace of Kim Il Sung) in Mangyongdae. No security thread. Watermark: Arch of Triumph. Printer: Unknown. 155 x 75 mm.

- a. 2002. Watermark: Head-on view.　　　　—　—　5
- b. Watermark: 3/4 view.　　　　—　—　5
- as. Boxed horizontal red 견본 ovpt on front only; all-zero serial numbers.　　　　—　—　25
- bs. Boxed horizontal red 견본 ovpt on front only; normal serial numbers.　　　　—　—　25

DPRK B21 (P46): 5,000 원 (won)   VG   VF   UNC

Purple. Front: Coat of arms; flowers; Kim Il Sung. Back: Trees; houses (birthplace of Kim Il Sung) in Mangyongdae. No security thread. Watermark: Arch of Triumph. Printer: Unknown. 155 x 75 mm.

- ☐ a. 2002. Intro: October 2002. — — 3
  Watermark: Head-on view.
- ☐ b. Watermark: 3/4 view. — — 3
- ☐ as. Boxed horizontal red 견본 ovpt on front only; — — 30
  all-zero serial numbers.
- ☐ bs. Boxed horizontal red 견본 ovpt on front only; — — 30
  normal serial numbers.

2005 Issues

This 200-won note is a new denomination.

DPRK B22 (P48): 200 원 (won)   VG   VF   UNC

Blue, green, and brown. Front: Coat of arms; mongnan (Seibold's magnolia) flowers. Back: Stars and denomination. No security thread. Printer: Unknown. 140 x 72 mm.

- ☐ a. 2005. — — 1
  With security fibers in paper.
  Watermark: Large winged horse (Chollima).
- ☐ b. Without security fibers in paper. — — 1
  Watermark: Small winged horse (Chollima).
- ☐ as1. Boxed horizontal red 견본 ovpt on front only; — — 1
  all-zero serial numbers.
- ☐ as2. Boxed horizontal red 견본 ovpt on front only; — — 1
  normal serial numbers.

1998-2005 Commemorative Issues

These overprinted notes were issued in 2005 to commemorate the 60th anniversary of the country's liberation on 15 August 1945.

The English translation of the Korean overprint is "Democratic People's Republic Of Korea 60th foundation anniversary."

DPRK B23 (PNL): 200 원 (won)   VG   VF   UNC

Blue, green, and brown. Front: 60th anniversary overprint; coat of arms; mongnan (Seibold's magnolia) flowers. Back: Stars and denomination. No security thread. Watermark: Winged horse (Chollima). Printer: Unknown. 140 x 72 mm.

- ☐ a. 2005. Intro: 2005. — — 15

Overprinted on DPRK B22.

DPRK B24 (PNL): 500 원 (won)   VG   VF   UNC

Light blue, green, and purple. Front: 60th anniversary overprint; coat of arms; Kumsusan Memorial Palace (Kim Il Sung Mausoleum) in Pyongyang; mongnan (Seibold's magnolia) flowers. Back: Rungna bridge over the Daedong river in Pyongyang; olive branch. No security thread. Watermark: Winged horse (Chollima). Printer: Unknown. 155 x 75 mm.

- ☐ a. 1998. Intro: 2005. — — 15

Overprinted on DPRK B19.

DPRK B25 (PNL): **1,000** 원 (won)　　　　　　　VG　VF　UNC
Green and light blue. Front: 60th anniversary overprint; coat of arms; mongnan (Seibold's magnolia) flowers; Kim Il Sung. Back: Trees; houses (birthplace of Kim Il Sung) in Mangyongdae. No security thread. Watermark: Arch of Triumph. Printer: Unknown. 155 x 75 mm.

　☐　a.　2002. Intro: 2005.　　　　　　　　　—　—　20
　☐　as.　Boxed horizontal red 견본 ovpt on front only;　—　—
　　　　all-zero serial numbers.
Overprinted on DPRK B20.

DPRK B26 (PNL): **5,000** 원 (won)　　　　　　　VG　VF　UNC
Purple. Front: 60th anniversary overprint; coat of arms; mongnan (Seibold's magnolia) flowers; Kim Il Sung. Back: Trees; houses (birthplace of Kim Il Sung) in Mangyongdae. No security thread. Watermark: Arch of Triumph. Printer: Unknown. 155 x 75 mm.

　☐　a.　2002. Intro: 2005.　　　　　　　　　—　—　40
Overprinted on DPRK B21.

2006-2007 Issues

These notes are like the preceding issues, but new date and the banner beneath the denomination on the bottom right and left front does not extend to note's edge.

DPRK B27 (PNL): **500** 원 (won)　　　　　　　VG　VF　UNC
Green and purple. Front: Coat of arms; Kumsusan Memorial Palace (Kim Il Sung Mausoleum) in Pyongyang; mongnan (Seibold's magnolia) flowers. Back: Rungna bridge over the Daedong river in Pyongyang; olive branch. No security thread. Watermark: Arch of Triumph. Printer: Unknown. 155 x 75 mm.

　☐　a.　2007.　　　　　　　　　　　　　　　—　—　1.50
　☐　as.　Boxed horizontal red 견본 ovpt on front only;　—　—
　　　　all-zero serial numbers.

DPRK B28 (P45b): **1,000** 원 (won)　　　　　　　VG　VF　UNC
Green and light blue. Front: Coat of arms; mongnan (Seibold's magnolia) flowers; Kim Il Sung. Back: Trees; houses (birthplace of Kim Il Sung) in Mangyongdae. No security thread. Watermark: Arch of Triumph. Printer: Unknown. 155 x 75 mm.

　☐　a.　2006.　　　　　　　　　　　　　　　—　—　2
　☐　as.　Boxed horizontal red 견본 ovpt on front only;　—　—
　　　　all-zero serial numbers.

DPRK B29 (PNL): **5,000 원 (won)**   VG   VF   UNC
Purple. Front: Coat of arms; mongnan (Seibold's magnolia) flowers; Kim Il Sung. Back: Trees; houses (birthplace of Kim Il Sung) in Mangyongdae. No security thread. Watermark: Arch of Triumph. Printer: Unknown. 155 x 75 mm.
    ☐ a.   2006.   —   —   1.50
    ☐ as. Boxed horizontal red 견본 ovpt on front only; all-zero serial numbers.

1992-2007 Commemorative Issues

These overprinted notes were issued in 2007 to commemorate the 95th birthday of Kim Il Sung, who was born on 15 April 1912.

The English translation of the Korean overprint is "Great leader Kim Il Sung comrade birth 95th."

DPRK B30 (P49): **1 원 (won)**   VG   VF   UNC
Green, brown, and blue. Front: 95th birthday overprint; coat of arms; actress Hong Yonhi with basket of flowers. Back: Mount Kumgang; waterfalls; flying woman playing flute. No security thread. Watermark: Winged horse (Chollima). Printer: Unknown. 115 x 55 mm.
    ☐ a.   1992. Intro: 2007.   —   —   1
Overprinted on DPRK B12.

DPRK B31 (P50): **5 원 (won)**   VG   VF   UNC
Blue and green. Front: 95th birthday overprint; coat of arms; atomic symbol; factory building; students; boy holding book with hand on globe; buildings. Back: Grand People's Study House building on Namsan Hill in Pyongyang. No security thread. Watermark: Winged horse (Chollima). Printer: Unknown. 125 x 60 mm.
    ☐ a.   1998. Intro: 2007.   —   —   3
Overprinted on DPRK B17.

DPRK B32 (P51): **10 원 (won)**   VG   VF   UNC
Brown and olive green. Front: 95th birthday overprint; coat of arms; worker pressing button; statue of woman with wheat and man with book riding Chollima (thousand-mile horse) on Mansu Hill in Pyongyang; factory buildings with smokestacks. Back: West Sea Barrage flood gates in Nampho. No security thread. Watermark: Winged horse (Chollima). Printer: Unknown. 135 x 65 mm.
    ☐ a.   1998. Intro: 2007.   —   —   4
Overprinted on DPRK B18.

DPRK B33 (P52): **50 원 (won)** VG VF UNC

Brown and olive green. Front: 95th birthday overprint; Tower of Juche Idea monument with flame in Pyongyang; man in suit, man in overalls, woman with headscarf; olive branch; coat of arms. Back: Fir trees and Baekdu (white-headed) Mountain. No security thread. Watermark: Juche monument torch. Printer: Unknown. 145 x 70 mm.

    ☐ a. 1992. Intro: 2007. — — 5

Overprinted on DPRK B15.

DPRK B34 (P53): **100 원 (won)** VG VF UNC

Brown. Front: 95th birthday overprint; coat of arms; mongnan (Seibold's magnolia) flowers; Kim Il Sung. Back: Trees; houses (birthplace of Kim Il Sung) in Mangyongdae. No security thread. Watermark: Arch of Triumph. Printer: Unknown. 155 x 75 mm.

    ☐ a. 1992. Intro: 2007. — — 4

Overprinted on DPRK B16.

DPRK B35 (P54): **200 원 (won)** VG VF UNC

Blue, green, and brown. Front: 95th birthday overprint; coat of arms; mongnan (Seibold's magnolia) flowers. Back: Stars and denomination. No security thread. Watermark: Winged horse (Chollima). Printer: Unknown. 140 x 72 mm.

    ☐ a. 2005. Intro: 2007. — — 6

Overprinted on DPRK B22.

DPRK B36 (P55): **500 원 (won)** VG VF UNC

Green and purple. Front: 95th birthday overprint; coat of arms; Kumsusan Memorial Palace (Kim Il Sung Mausoleum) in Pyongyang; mongnan (Seibold's magnolia) flowers. Back: Rungna bridge over the Daedong river in Pyongyang; olive branch. No security thread. Watermark: Arch of Triumph. Printer: Unknown. 155 x 75 mm.

    ☐ a. 2007. Intro: 2007. — — 10

Overprinted on DPRK B27.

2002-2008 (2009) Issues

The North Korean central bank revalued and replaced the national currency as of 30 November 2009. With the exchange rate of 100:1, the formerly largest denomination of 5,000 won is now equivalent to 50 new won. There are nine new won notes ranging from 5 to 5,000 won, which matches the previous currency structure with the exception that the 1-won note has been replaced by a coin and the 2,000-won denomination is new.

There is little concrete information on the reason for this move. Speculation is that the government hopes to dampen inflation, harm the black market, or uncover large caches of hidden cash. The official exchange rate of the won had been 140 to the US dollar, but on the black market it traded at closer to 3,000 to one.

The government had planned to allow each household to exchange up to 100,000 won for new banknotes, but in the face of public protests, the exchangeable amount was increased, initially to 150,000 won, then later to 500,000 won. These limitations apply only to cash; won deposited in banks can be converted, but only after officials investigate the source of funds over one million won. Citizens had from between 30 November and 6 December to exchange currency. New notes started circulating from 7 December.

DPRK B37 (P56): **1,000 원 (won)**   VG   VF   UNC
Green and light blue. Front: 95th birthday overprint; coat of arms; mongnan (Seibold's magnolia) flowers; Kim Il Sung. Back: Trees; houses (birthplace of Kim Il Sung) in Mangyongdae. No security thread. Watermark: Arch of Triumph. Printer: Unknown. 155 x 75 mm.
     ☐ a.   2006. Intro: 2007.   —   —   3
Overprinted on DPRK B28.

DPRK B38 (PNL): **5,000 원 (won)**   VG   VF   UNC
Purple. Front: 95th birthday overprint; coat of arms; mongnan (Seibold's magnolia) flowers; Kim Il Sung. Back: Trees; houses (birthplace of Kim Il Sung) in Mangyongdae. No security thread. Watermark: Arch of Triumph. Printer: Unknown. 155 x 75 mm.
     ☐ a.   2006. Intro: 2007.   —   —   6
Overprinted on DPRK B29.

DPRK B39 (P58): **5 원 (won)**   VG   VF   UNC
Blue, green, and purple. Front: Coat of arms; atomic symbol; man with glasses; boy with cap. Back: Dam. No security thread. Watermark: Mongnan (Seibold's magnolia) flowers. Printer: Unknown. 145 x 65 mm.
     ☐ a.   2002. Intro: 30.11.2009.   —   —   0.50

DPRK B40 (P59): **10 원 (won)** VG VF UNC

Blue, green, and purple. Front: Coat of arms; star; pilot, sailor, and soldier. Back: Korean War Victory Monument in Pyongyang with soldier holding flag. No security thread. Watermark: Mongnan (Seibold's magnolia) flowers. Printer: Unknown. 145 x 65 mm.

☐ a. 2002. Intro: 30.11.2009. — — 1

DPRK B41 (P60): **50 원 (won)** VG VF UNC

Purple. Front: Coat of arms; flame atop Juche Idea monument in Pyongyang; man in business suit, man in overalls, and woman wearing blouse. Back: Party Foundation Monument in Pyongyang with hands holding hammer, paint brush, and sickle. No security thread. Watermark: Mongnan (Seibold's magnolia) flowers. Printer: Unknown. 145 x 65 mm.

☐ a. 2002. Intro: 30.11.2009. — — 1

DPRK B42 (P61): **100 원 (won)** VG VF UNC

Green. Front: Coat of arms; mongnan (Seibold's magnolia) flowers. Back: Denomination and guilloche pattern. Solid security thread with printed text. Watermark: Mongnan (Seibold's magnolia) flowers. Printer: Unknown. 145 x 65.

☐ a. 2008. Intro: 30.11.2009. — — 1.50

DPRK B43 (P62): **200 원 (won)** VG VF UNC

Violet. Front: Coat of arms; statue of woman with wheat and man with book riding Chollima (thousand-mile horse) on Mansu Hill in Pyongyang. Back: Denomination and guilloche pattern. Solid security thread with printed text. Watermark: Mongnan (Seibold's magnolia) flowers. Printer: Unknown. 145 x 65.

☐ a. 2008. Intro: 30.11.2009. — — 2

DPRK B44 (P63): **500 원 (won)**   VG   VF   UNC

Gray and purple. Front: Coat of arms; Arch of Triumph. Back: Denomination and guilloche pattern. Solid security thread with printed text. Watermark: Mongnan (Seibold's magnolia) flowers. Printer: Unknown. Dimensions 145 x 65 mm.

☐ a. 2008. Intro: 30.11.2009.   —   —   1.75

DPRK B46 (P65): **2,000 원 (won)**   VG   VF   UNC

Light blue and gray. Front: Coat of arms; Jong Il Peak, trees, and cabin (birthplace of Kim Jong Il). Back: Fir trees and Baekdu (white-headed) Mountain. Solid security thread with printed text. Watermark: Mongnan (Seibold's magnolia) flowers. Printer: Unknown. 145 x 65 mm.

☐ a. 2008. Intro: 30.11.2009.   —   —   4
☐ as. Boxed horizontal red 견본 ovpt on front only.   —   —   4

DPRK B45 (P64): **1,000 원 (won)**   VG   VF   UNC

Pink. Front: Coat of arms; house (birthplace of Kim Jong Suk, Kim Il Sung's first wife and Kim Jong Il's mother) in Hoeryong. Back: Birch trees on shore of Lake Samji; mountain. Solid security thread with printed text. Watermark: Mongnan (Seibold's magnolia) flowers. Printer: Unknown. 145 x 65 mm.

☐ a. 2008. Intro: 30.11.2009.   —   —   7
☐ as. Boxed horizontal red 견본 ovpt on front only.   —   —   5

DPRK B47 (P66): **5,000 원 (won)**   VG   VF   UNC

Brown and pink. Front: Coat of arms; star; Kim Il Sung; mongnan (Seibold's magnolia) flowers. Back: Trees; houses (birthplace of Kim Il Sung) in Mangyongdae. Solid security thread with printed text. Watermark: Mongnan (Seibold's magnolia) flowers. Printer: Unknown. 145 x 65 mm.

☐ a. 2008. Intro: 30.11.2009.   —   —   7
☐ as. Boxed horizontal red 견본 ovpt on front only.   —   —   5

2014 Commemorative Issues

These overprinted notes were issued in 2014 to commemorate the 100th birthday of Kim Il Sung, who was born on 15 April 1912.

The English translation of the Korean overprint is "Great leader Kim Il Sung comrade birth 100th."

DPRK B48 (PNL): **5 원 (won)**   VG   VF   UNC
Blue, green, and purple. Front: 100th birthday overprint; coat of arms; atomic symbol; man with glasses; boy with cap. Back: Dam. No security thread. Watermark: Mongnan (Seibold's magnolia) flowers. Printer: Unknown. 145 x 65 mm.
    ☐ a. 2002. Intro: 2014. — — 0.50
Overprinted on DPRK B39.

DPRK B49 (PNL): **10 원 (won)**   VG   VF   UNC
Blue, green, and purple. Front: 100th birthday overprint; coat of arms; star; pilot, sailor, and soldier. Back: Korean War Victory Monument in Pyongyang with soldier holding flag. No security thread. Watermark: Mongnan (Seibold's magnolia) flowers. Printer: Unknown. 145 x 65 mm.
    ☐ a. 2002. Intro: 2014. — — 1
Overprinted on DPRK B40.

DPRK B50 (PNL): **50 원 (won)**   VG   VF   UNC
Purple. Front: 100th birthday overprint; coat of arms; flame atop Juche Idea monument in Pyongyang; man in business suit, man in overalls, and woman wearing blouse. Back: Party Foundation Monument in Pyongyang with hands holding hammer, paint brush, and sickle. No security thread. Watermark: Mongnan (Seibold's magnolia) flowers. Printer: Unknown. 145 x 65 mm.
    ☐ a. 2002. Intro: 2014. — — 1
Overprinted on DPRK B41.

DPRK B51 (PNL): **100 원 (won)**   VG   VF   UNC
Green. Front: 100th birthday overprint; coat of arms; mongnan (Seibold's magnolia) flowers. Back: Denomination and guilloche pattern. Solid security thread with printed text. Watermark: Mongnan (Seibold's magnolia) flowers. Printer: Unknown. 145 x 65.
    ☐ a. 2008. Intro: 2014. — — 1.50
Overprinted on DPRK B42.

DPRK B52 (PNL): **200 원 (won)** VG VF UNC

Violet. Front: 100th birthday overprint; coat of arms; statue of woman with wheat and man with book riding Chollima (thousand-mile horse) on Mansu Hill in Pyongyang. Back: Denomination and guilloche pattern. Solid security thread with printed text. Watermark: Mongnan (Seibold's magnolia) flowers. Printer: Unknown. 145 x 65.

☐ a. 2008. Intro: 2014.   — — 2

Overprinted on DPRK B43.

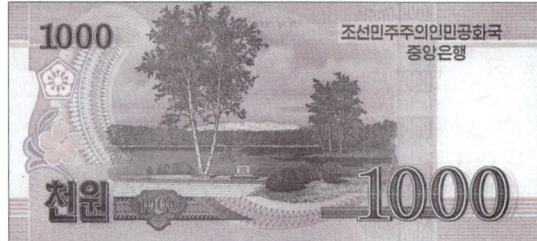

DPRK B54 (PNL): **1,000 원 (won)** VG VF UNC

Pink. Front: 100th birthday overprint; coat of arms; house (birthplace of Kim Jong Suk, Kim Il Sung's first wife and Kim Jong Il's mother) in Hoeryong. Back: Birch trees on shore of Lake Samji; mountain. Solid security thread with printed text. Watermark: Mongnan (Seibold's magnolia) flowers. Printer: Unknown. 145 x 65 mm.

☐ a. 2008. Intro: 2014.   — — 7

Overprinted on DPRK B45.

DPRK B53 (PNL): **500 원 (won)** VG VF UNC

Gray and purple. Front: 100th birthday overprint; coat of arms; Arch of Triumph. Back: Denomination and guilloche pattern. Solid security thread with printed text. Watermark: Mongnan (Seibold's magnolia) flowers. Printer: Unknown. Dimensions 145 x 65 mm.

☐ a. 2008. Intro: 2014.   — — 1.75

Overprinted on DPRK B44.

DPRK B55 (PNL): **2,000 원 (won)** VG VF UNC

Light blue and gray. Front: 100th birthday overprint; coat of arms; Jong Il Peak, trees, and cabin (birthplace of Kim Jong Il). Back: Fir trees and Baekdu (white-headed) Mountain. Solid security thread with printed text. Watermark: Mongnan (Seibold's magnolia) flowers. Printer: Unknown. 145 x 65 mm.

☐ a. 2008. Intro: 2014.   — — 4

Overprinted on DPRK B46.

DPRK B56 (PNL): **5,000 원 (won)**   VG   VF   UNC
Brown and pink. Front: 100th birthday overprint; coat of arms; star; Kim Il Sung; mongnan (Seibold's magnolia) flowers. Back: Trees; houses (birthplace of Kim Il Sung) in Mangyongdae. Solid security thread with printed text. Watermark: Mongnan (Seibold's magnolia) flowers. Printer: Unknown. 145 x 65 mm.
    ☐ a. 2008. Intro: 2014.   —   —   7
Overprinted on DPRK B47.

조선민주주의인민공화국무역은행
(Trade Bank of DPRK)

1988 Capitalist Issues

These foreign currency exchange notes (외화와바꾼돈표) were issued by the Trade Bank of DPRK (TB) for use by capitalist visitors exchanging hard currency. They were used until 1999, then officially abolished in 2002, in favor of foreign currencies.

TB B1 (P23): **1 전 (jeon)**   VG   VF   UNC
Blue and purple. Front: Coat of arms. Back: Guilloche pattern. No security thread. Watermark: None. Printer: Unknown. 100 x 45 mm.
    ☐ a. 1988.   —   —   1

TB B2 (P24): **5 전 (jeon)**   VG   VF   UNC
Blue and purple. Front: Coat of arms. Back: Guilloche pattern. No security thread. Watermark: None. Printer: Unknown. 100 x 45 mm.
    ☐ a. 1988.   —   —   1

TB B3 (P25): **10 전 (jeon)**   VG   VF   UNC
Blue, green, and yellow. Front: Coat of arms. Back: Guilloche pattern. No security thread. Watermark: None. Printer: Unknown. 100 x 45 mm.
    ☐ a. 1988.   —   —   2

TB B4 (P26): **50 전 (jeon)**   VG   VF   UNC
Blue, green, and yellow. Front: Coat of arms. Back: Guilloche pattern. No security thread. Watermark: None. Printer: Unknown. 100 x 45 mm.
    ☐ a. 1988.   —   —

TB B5 (P27): **1 원 (won)** VG VF UNC
Green. Front: Statue of woman with wheat and man with book riding Chollima (thousand-mile horse) on Mansu Hill in Pyongyang; coat of arms. Back: Guilloche pattern. No security thread. Watermark: None. Printer: Unknown. 110 x 55 mm.
☐ a. 1988. — — 1

TB B6 (P28): **5 원 (won)** VG VF UNC
Green. Front: Statue of woman with wheat and man with book riding Chollima (thousand-mile horse) on Mansu Hill in Pyongyang; coat of arms. Back: Guilloche pattern. No security thread. Watermark: None. Printer: Unknown. 120 x 60 mm.
☐ a. 1988. — — 3.50

TB B7 (P29): **10 원 (won)** VG VF UNC
Green. Front: Statue of woman with wheat and man with book riding Chollima (thousand-mile horse) on Mansu Hill in Pyongyang; coat of arms. Back: Guilloche pattern. No security thread. Watermark: None. Printer: Unknown. 130 x 65 mm.
☐ a. 1988. — — 4

TB B8 (P30): **50 원 (won)** VG VF UNC
Green. Front: Statue of woman with wheat and man with book riding Chollima (thousand-mile horse) on Mansu Hill in Pyongyang; coat of arms. Back: Guilloche pattern. No security thread. Watermark: None. Printer: Unknown. 140 x 70 mm.
☐ a. 1988. — — 2

1988 Socialist Issues

These foreign currency exchange notes were issued by the Trade Bank of DPRK for use by visitors exchanging currency from socialist countries. They were used until 1999, then officially abolished in 2002, in favor of foreign currencies.

TB B9 (P31): **1 전 (jeon)** VG VF UNC
Red. Front: Coat of arms. Back: Guilloche pattern. No security thread. Watermark: None. Printer: Unknown. 100 x 45 mm.
☐ a. 1988. — — 1

TB B10 (P32): **5 전 (jeon)** VG VF UNC
Red and purple. Front: Coat of arms. Back: Guilloche pattern. No security thread. Watermark: None. Printer: Unknown. 100 x 45 mm.
☐ a. 1988. — — 1

TB B11 (P33): 10 전 (jeon)   VG   VF   UNC
Red and green. Front: Coat of arms. Back: Guilloche pattern. No security thread. Watermark: None. Printer: Unknown. 100 x 45 mm.
☐ a. 1988.   —   —   2

TB B12 (P34): 50 전 (jeon)   VG   VF   UNC
Red and brown. Front: Coat of arms. Back: Guilloche pattern. No security thread. Watermark: None. Printer: Unknown. 100 x 45 mm.
☐ a. 1988.   —   —   1

TB B13 (P35): 1 원 (won)   VG   VF   UNC
Red. Front: International Friendship Exhibition building in Myohyang-san; trees; globe with olive sprig; coat of arms. Back: Globe with olive sprig; guilloche pattern. No security thread. Watermark: None. Printer: Unknown. 110 x 55 mm.
☐ a. 1988.   —   —   2.25

TB B14 (P36): 5 원 (won)   VG   VF   UNC
Red. Front: International Friendship Exhibition building in Myohyang-san; trees; globe with olive sprig; coat of arms. Back: Globe with olive sprig; guilloche pattern. No security thread. Watermark: None. Printer: Unknown. 120 x 60 mm.
☐ a. 1988.   —   —   2

TB B15 (P37): 10 원 (won)   VG   VF   UNC
Red. Front: International Friendship Exhibition building in Myohyang-san; trees; globe with olive sprig; coat of arms. Back: Globe with olive sprig; guilloche pattern. No security thread. Watermark: None. Printer: Unknown. 130 x 65 mm.
☐ a. 1988.   —   —   2.50

TB B16 (P38): 50 원 (won) VG VF UNC
Red. Front: International Friendship Exhibition building in Myohyang-san; trees; globe with olive sprig; coat of arms. Back: Globe with olive sprig; guilloche pattern. No security thread. Watermark: None. Printer: Unknown. 140 x 70 mm.
☐ a. 1988. — — 2

Looking Forward

According to an article in The Hindu Business Line dated 11 August 2014, the portrait of Kim Il Sung, the founder of North Korea, has been removed from the new 5,000-won note in favor of the birthplace of Kim Il Sung in Mangyongdae, with the back depicting the International Friendship Exhibition building in Myohyang-san.

Acknowledgements

This chapter was compiled with the generous assistance of Darius Alejunas, Thomas Augustsson, Robert Bethea, Jim W.-C. Chen, Donald Cleveland, Jim Copeland, Jean-Michel Engels, Alberto Fochi, Torsten Fuhlendorf, Wonsik Kang, Vitali Khaletski, Kevin Klauss, Jason Lee, Wally Myers, Rui Manuel Palhares, Alexandr Petrov, Rudolf L. van Renesse, John Sandrock, Alexey Semakov, Bill Stubkjaer, Jan Stuller, Vincent Tan, Christoph Thomas, Frank van Tiel, Tristan Williams, Ömer Yalcinkaya, and others.

Sources

Boon, K. N. *World Paper & Polymer Uncut Banknotes.* 1st edition. 2012. ISBN 978-983-43313-4-4. Trigometric Sdn.Bhd. (www.3833.com), Lot 327, Amcorp Mall, 18 Jalan Persiaran Barat, off Jalan Timur, Petaling Jaya, 46050 Selangor D.E., Malaysia.

Cuhaj, George S. *Standard Catalog of World Paper Money, General Issues, 1368-1960.* 14th edition. 2012. ISBN 978-1-4402-3090-5. Krause Publications (www.krausebooks.com), 700 East State St., Iola, WI, 54990-0001.

Cuhaj, George S. *Standard Catalog of World Paper Money, Modern Issues, 1961-Present.* 18th edition. 2012. ISBN 978-1-4402-2956-5. Krause Publications (www.krausebooks.com), 700 East State St., Iola, WI, 54990-0001.

Friedman, Herbert A. "United Nations Counterfeits of the North Korean 100 Won Bank Note." *IBNS Journal.* Volume 40 Number 4. p.14.

Heath, Henry B. "Personalities on the Bank Notes of Korea." *IBNS Journal.* Volume 39 Number 3. p.39.

Tomita, Masahiro. "Destiny of the North Korean Won." *IBNS Journal.* Volume 41 Number 4. p.14.

Yi, Yin (editor). *Contemporary China's Banknote Printing & Minting for Foreign Countries.* March 2000. ISBN 7-5049-2116-5. China Financial Publishing House.

Share Your Input, Info, and Images

This catalog is believed to be complete and correct as of the time of publication. Prices and face values were last updated 26 October 2012. Please report errors or omissions so that corrections may be made. If you can more precisely identify the name or location of anything depicted on a note, please share that information. Furthermore, if you own an unlisted type or variety, please submit scans of the front and back of the note so that it can be documented. Scans should be 300 dots per inch, 100% actual size, 24-bit color, saved as *uncompressed* JPEG files, and sent to owen@banknotenews.com. Be sure to fully describe all attributes of the note which are not apparent upon visual inspection of the images alone, such as physical dimension, watermark, and security thread.

Oceania

For earlier issues, see Gilbert and Ellice Islands.

Monetary System
1 Oceanian pound = 20 shillings

The Japanese Government

1942 Issues

These four notes, officially "Foreign Denomination Military Certificates," were issued by Japanese forces soon after they invaded New Britain on 23 January 1942, and New Guinea on 8 March, and were declared the sole legal tender in the British South Pacific territories (Gilbert Islands, New Britain, New Guinea, and Solomon Islands) on 14 March 1943. All of these notes have block letters starting with the letter O. These notes are often collectively referred to as "JIM" for Japanese Invasion Money.

1/4-shilling notes have been reported but are fakes. Souvenir copies of the official notes were printed in Australia during World War II with red *REPLICA* overprinted on the back, so be on the lookout for evidence of erasures.

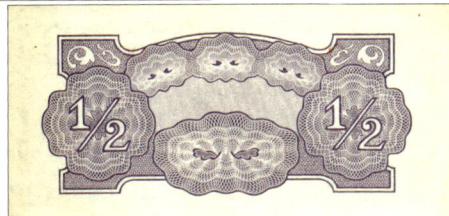

JG B1 (P1): 1/2 shilling   VG   VF   UNC
Purple. Front: Coat of arms; palm trees at shore. Back: Guilloche patterns. No security thread. Watermark: Pattern. Printer: (Printing Bureau, Japan). 121 x 58 mm.
- a. No date. Intro: Mid-1942.   1.50   6   25
  Block letters (OA, OB, OC) 45 mm apart.
- b. Block letters (OC) 35 mm apart.   1   4   15
- bs. Vertical red 見本 overprint on front.   —   —   150

JG B2 (P2): 1 shilling   VG   VF   UNC
Blue and light green. Front: Breadfruit tree; coat of arms; palm trees at shore. Back: Guilloche patterns. No security thread. Watermark: Pattern. Printer: (Printing Bureau, Japan). 141 x 68 mm.
- a. No date. Intro: Mid-1942.   1   3   12
  Block letters OA, OB, OC.
- as. Vertical red 見本 overprint on front.   —   —   150

JG B3 (P3): 10 shillings   VG   VF   UNC
Brown. Front: Palm trees with coconuts; coat of arms; palm trees at shore; coconuts. Back: Guilloche patterns. No security thread. Watermark: Pattern. Printer: (Printing Bureau, Japan). 151 x 71 mm.
- a. No date. Intro: Mid-1942. Block letters OA.   6   25   100
- as. Two vertical red 見本 overprints on front.   —   —   200

JG B4 (P4): **1 pound**   VG   VF   UNC
Green and light blue. Front: Tree with fruit; coat of arms; palm trees at shore. Back: Guilloche patterns. No security thread. Watermark: Pattern. Printer: (Printing Bureau, Japan). 163 x 77 mm.

		VG	VF	UNC
☐	a. No date. Intro: Mid-1942. Block letters OA.	2	8	30
☐	as1. Two vertical red 見本 overprints on front; no overprint on back.	—	—	175
☐	as2. Two vertical red 見本 overprints on front; diagonal red script *Specimen* 115-mm wide overprint on back; punched.	—	—	175
☐	as3. Two vertical red 見本 overprints on front; horizontal red script *Specimen* 70-mm wide overprint on back.	—	—	175

Looking Forward
For later issues, see Papua New Guinea and Solomon Islands.

Acknowledgements
This chapter was compiled with the generous assistance of Mark Irwin, Wally Myers, Stack's Bowers & Ponterio (www.StacksBowers.com), and others.

Sources
Cuhaj, George S. *Standard Catalog of World Paper Money, General Issues, 1368-1960*. 14th edition. 2012. ISBN 978-1-4402-3090-5. Krause Publications (www.krausebooks.com), 700 East State St., Iola, WI, 54990-0001.

Fujita, Kazuya. "Japanese Military Currency (1937-1945): Quantities Printed And Issued." *IBNS Journal*. Volume 42 Number 2. p.18.

James, Tony. "Australian Army Claimed JIM Replicas as Proof of Invasion Plan." *IBNS Journal*. Volume 51 Number 4. p.39.

Nader, A. F. and Barry Kessell. "Updating the JIM Series: Burma and Oceania." *IBNS Journal*. Volume 16 Number 2. p.71.

Tan, Steven. *Standard Catalogue of Malaysia Singapore Brunei Coin & Paper Money*. 18th edition. 2007. ISBN 983-9650-02-05. International Stamp & Coin Sn. Bhd., 2.4 & 2.5, Pertama Shopping Complex, 2nd Floor, Jalan Tuanku Abdul Rahman, 50100 Kaula Lumpur, Malaysia.

Share Your Input, Info, and Images
This catalog is believed to be complete and correct as of the time of publication. Prices and face values were last updated 5 October 2012. Please report errors or omissions so that corrections may be made. If you can more precisely identify the name or location of anything depicted on a note, please share that information. Furthermore, if you own an unlisted type or variety, please submit scans of the front and back of the note so that it can be documented. Scans should be 300 dots per inch, 100% actual size, 24-bit color, saved as *uncompressed* JPEG files, and sent to owen@banknotenews.com. Be sure to fully describe all attributes of the note which are not apparent upon visual inspection of the images alone, such as physical dimension, watermark, and security thread.

Oman

For earlier issues, see Muscat and Oman.

Contents

Oman Currency Board (OCB) 1609
Central Bank of Oman (CBO) 1611

Oman, officially the Sultanate of Oman, is a country in southwest Asia on the southeast coast of the Arabian Peninsula. It borders the United Arab Emirates on the northwest, Saudi Arabia on the west and Yemen on the southwest. The coast is formed by the Arabian Sea on the south and east and the Gulf of Oman on the northeast. The country also contains Madha, an exclave enclosed by the United Arab Emirates, and Musandam, an exclave also separated by Emirati territory.

Monetary System

11.11.1972: rial Saidi changed name to rial Omani
1 Omani rial (OMR) = 1,000 baisa (also written baiza)

Arabic Numbers

0	1	2	3	4	5	6	7	8	9
٠	١	٢	٣	٤	٥	٦	٧	٨	٩

Oman Currency Board

On 23 July 1970, Qaboos bin Said, son of the sultan of Muscat and Oman, staged a coup d'état in the Salalah palace and subsequently renamed the country the Sultanate of Oman. This led to the creation of the Oman Currency Board (OCB) as the new note-issuer in the country.

OCB Signature Varieties

1	
	(Chairman)
	Mahmood Muhammad Murad

1972 Issues

These issues are identical to the 1970 notes issued by the Sultanate of Muscat and Oman, with the exception that they bear a new signature and title on the front, as well as the name of the new note-issuing authority on the back, and the name of the currency has changed.

OCB B1 (P7): **100 baiza** (demonetized 09.03.1979)   VG   VF   UNC
Brown and turquoise. Front: Coat of arms with crossed swords and khanjar (dagger). Back: Geometric designs. Solid security thread. Watermark: Coat of arms. Printer: (BWC). 114 x 52 mm.
- a. No date. Signature 1. Intro: 18.11.1972.   1   4   10
- as. Diagonal red نموذج overprint on front; — — 125
  diagonal red hollow *SPECIMEN* overprint on back;
  horizontal *SPECIMEN* perforation.
- t. Color trial: Violet-brown.   —   —   100

OCB B2 (P8): **1/4 rial Omani** (demonetized 09.03.1979)   VG   VF   UNC
Blue and brown. Front: Coat of arms with crossed swords and khanjar (dagger). Back: Jalali Fort in Muscat. Solid security thread. Watermark: Coat of arms. Printer: (BWC). 128 x 58 mm.
- a. No date. Signature 1. Intro: 18.11.1972.   2.50   10   40
- as. Diagonal red نموذج overprint on front; — — 125
  diagonal red hollow *SPECIMEN* overprint on back;
  horizontal *SPECIMEN* perforation.
- t. Color trial: Green.   —   —   100

OCB B3 (P9): **1/2 rial Omani** (demonetized 09.03.1979)   VG   VF   UNC

Green and purple. Front: Coat of arms with crossed swords and khanjar (dagger). Back: Sumail Fort. Solid security thread. Watermark: Coat of arms. Printer: (BWC). 134 x 67 mm.

- ☐ a. No date. Signature 1. Intro: 18.11.1972.   3   11   45
- ☐ as. Diagonal red نموذج overprint on front;   —   —   150
  diagonal red hollow *SPECIMEN* overprint on back; horizontal *SPECIMEN* perforation.
- ☐ t. Color trial: Black and purple.   —   —   100

OCB B4 (P10): **1 rial Omani** (demonetized 09.03.1979)   VG   VF   UNC

Red and olive green. Front: Coat of arms with crossed swords and khanjar (dagger). Back: Sohar Fort. Solid security thread. Watermark: Coat of arms. Printer: (BWC). 145 x 78 mm.

- ☐ a. No date. Signature 1. Intro: 18.11.1972.   4   12   70
- ☐ as. Diagonal red نموذج overprint on front;   —   —   150
  diagonal red hollow *SPECIMEN* overprint on back; horizontal *SPECIMEN* perforation.
- ☐ t. Color trial: Blue.   —   —   125

OCB B5 (P11): **5 rials Omani** (demonetized 09.03.1979)   VG   VF   UNC

Purple and blue. Front: Coat of arms with crossed swords and khanjar (dagger). Back: Nizwa Fort. Solid security thread. Watermark: Coat of arms. Printer: (BWC). 151 x 85 mm.

- ☐ a. No date. Signature 1. Intro: 18.11.1972.   12   50   200
- ☐ as. Diagonal red نموذج overprint on front;   —   —   200
  diagonal red hollow *SPECIMEN* overprint on back; horizontal *SPECIMEN* perforation.
- ☐ t. Color trial: Red and blue.   —   —   240

OCB B6 (P12): **10 rials Omani** (demonetized 09.03.1979)   VG   VF   UNC

Brown and blue. Front: Coat of arms with crossed swords and khanjar (dagger). Back: Mirani Fort in Muscat. Solid security thread. Watermark: Coat of arms. Printer: (BWC). 157 x 91 mm.

- ☐ a. No date. Signature 1. Intro: 18.11.1972.   50   200   400
- ☐ as. Diagonal red نموذج overprint on front;   —   —   250
  diagonal red hollow *SPECIMEN* overprint on back; horizontal *SPECIMEN* perforation.
- ☐ t. Color trial: Blue-green.   —   —   350

Central Bank of Oman

The Central Bank of Oman commenced operations on 1 April 1975. For more information, visit www.cbo-oman.org.

CBO Signature Varieties

1
(Chairman)
Tarik bin Taimur

2
(Sultan of Oman)
Sultan Qaboos bin Said

1976-1985 Issues

CBO B1 (P13): **100 baisa** (US$0.25)   VG   VF   UNC
Light brown and yellow. Front: Coat of arms with crossed swords and khanjar (dagger). Back: Aerial view of Port Qaboos at Muttrah with ships. Solid security thread. Watermark: Coat of arms. Printer: (BWC). 121 x 63 mm.
- ☐ a. No date. Signature 1. Intro: 18.11.1976.   FV   FV   2.25
- ☐ as. Five diagonal red نموذج overprints on front;   —   —   600
five diagonal red *SPECIMEN* overprints on back; black # overprint at upper left on back.

CBO B2 (P14): **200 baisa** (US$0.50)   VG   VF   UNC
Purple. Front: Coat of arms with crossed swords and khanjar (dagger). Back: Rustaq Fort. Solid security thread. Watermark: Coat of arms. Printer: (TDLR). 132 x 65 mm.
- ☐ a. No date. Signature 2. Intro: 01.01.1985.   FV   FV   3.50

CBO B3 (P15): **1/4 rial** (US$0.65)   VG   VF   UNC
Blue and brown. Front: Coat of arms with crossed swords and khanjar (dagger). Back: Jalali Fort in Muscat. Solid security thread. Watermark: Coat of arms. Printer: (BWC). 129 x 68 mm.
- ☐ a. No date. Signature 1. Intro: 18.11.1976.   FV   3   12
- ☐ as. Five diagonal red نموذج overprints on front;   —   —   100
five diagonal red *SPECIMEN* overprints on back; black # overprint at upper left on back.

CBO B4 (P16): **1/2 rial** (US$1.30)   VG   VF   UNC
Green. Front: Coat of arms with crossed swords and khanjar (dagger). Back: Sumail Fort. Solid security thread. Watermark: Coat of arms. Printer: (BWC). 137 x 73 mm.
- ☐ a. No date. Signature 1. Intro: 18.11.1976.   FV   6   25
- ☐ as. Five diagonal red نموذج overprints on front;   —   —   100
five diagonal red *SPECIMEN* overprints on back; black # overprint at upper left on back.

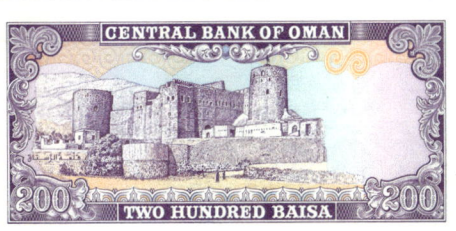

OMAN 1976-1985 ISSUES | THE BANKNOTE BOOK

CBO B5 (P17): **1 rial** (US$2.60)   VG   VF   UNC
Red and olive green. Front: Coat of arms with crossed swords and khanjar (dagger). Back: Sohar Fort. Solid security thread. Watermark: Coat of arms. Printer: (BWC). 145 x 78 mm.

- a. No date. Signature 1. Intro: 18.11.1976.   FV   8   30
- as. Five diagonal red نموذج overprints on front;   —   —   100
  five diagonal red *SPECIMEN* overprints on back;
  black # overprint at upper left on back.

CBO B7 (P19): **10 rials** (US$26)   VG   VF   UNC
Brown and blue. Front: Coat of arms with crossed swords and khanjar (dagger). Back: Mirani Fort in Muscat. Solid security thread. Watermark: Coat of arms. Printer: (BWC). 165 x 78 mm.

- a. No date. Signature 1. Intro: 18.11.1976.   FV   FV   100
- as. Five diagonal red نموذج overprints on front;   —   —   100
  five diagonal red *SPECIMEN* overprints on back;
  black # overprint at upper left on back.

CBO B6 (P18): **5 rials** (US$13)   VG   VF   UNC
Lilac and blue. Front: Coat of arms with crossed swords and khanjar (dagger). Back: Nizwa Fort. Solid security thread. Watermark: Coat of arms. Printer: (BWC). 155 x 78 mm.

- a. No date. Signature 1. Intro: 18.11.1976.   FV   FV   60
- as. Five diagonal red نموذج overprints on front;   —   —   75
  five diagonal red *SPECIMEN* overprints on back;
  black # overprint at upper left on back.

CBO B8 (P20): **20 rials** (US$52)   VG   VF   UNC
Gray-blue and orange. Front: Sultan Qaboos bin Said. Back: Central Bank of Oman headquarters building. Solid security thread. Watermark: Coat of arms. Printer: (BWC). 175 x 78 mm.

- a. No date. Signature 1. Intro: 18.11.1976.   FV   100   200
- as. Five diagonal red نموذج overprints on front;   —   —   150
  five diagonal red *SPECIMEN* overprints on back;
  black # overprint at upper left on back.

CBO B9 (P21): **50 rials** (US$130) VG VF UNC
Olive green and brown. Front: Sultan Qaboos bin Said. Back: Jabreen Fort. Solid security thread. Watermark: Coat of arms. Printer: (TDLR). 185 x 78 mm.

☐	a.	No date. Signature 2. Intro: 23.07.1982.	FV	200	475
☐	as.	Five diagonal red نموذج overprints on front; five diagonal red *SPECIMEN* overprints on back; black # overprint at upper left on back; punched.	—	—	600

1985-1994 Issues

CBO B10 (P22): **100 baisa** (US$0.25) VG VF UNC
Light brown. Front: Sultan Qaboos bin Said. Back: Aerial view of Port Qaboos at Muttrah with ships. Solid security thread printed with Arabic text. Watermark: Sultan. Printer: (BABN). 121 x 63 mm.

☐	a.	١٩٨٧ (1987). Signature 2.	0.75	2.50	10
☐	b.	١٩٨٩ (1989).	FV	1	4
☐	c.	١٩٩٢ (1992).	1.25	5	20
☐	d.	١٩٩٤ (1994).	FV	0.75	3

CBO B11 (P23): **200 baisa** (US$0.50) VG VF UNC
Purple. Front: Sultan Qaboos bin Said. Back: Rustaq Fort. Solid security thread. Watermark: Sultan. Printer: (TDLR). 132 x 65 mm.

☐	a.	١٩٨٧ (1987). Signature 2.	FV	1.25	5
☐	b.	١٩٩٣ (1993).	FV	2.50	10
☐	c.	١٩٩٤ (1994).	FV	1.25	5

CBO B12 (P24): **1/4 rial** (US$0.65) VG VF UNC
Blue. Front: Sultan Qaboos bin Said. Back: Modern fishing industry with two men cleaning fish; large ship. Solid security thread printed with Arabic text. Watermark: Sultan. Printer: (TDLR). 135 x 69 mm.

☐	a.	١٩٨٩ (1989). Signature 2.	FV	1.25	5

CBO B13 (P25): **1/2 rial** (US$1.30) VG VF UNC
Green. Front: Sultan Qaboos bin Said. Back: Sultan Qaboos University campus buildings. Solid security thread printed with Arabic text. Watermark: Sultan. Printer: (TDLR). 140 x 74 mm.

    a. ١٩٨٧ (1987). Signature 2. FV 1.75 6.50

CBO B15 (P27): **5 rials** (US$13) VG VF UNC
Red. Front: Sultan Qaboos bin Said. Back: Nizwa Fort. Solid security thread printed with Arabic text. Watermark: Sultan. Printer: (TDLR). 155 x 78 mm.

    a. ١٩٩٠ (1990). Signature 2. FV FV 50

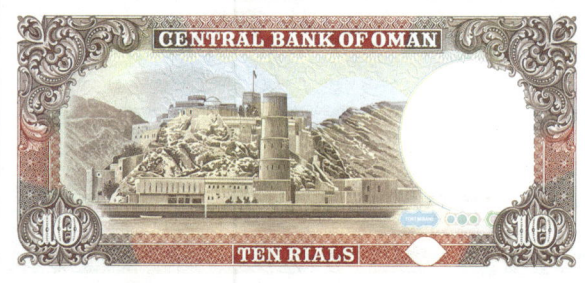

CBO B14 (P26): **1 rial** (US$2.60) VG VF UNC
Red. Front: Sultan Qaboos bin Said. Back: Sohar Fort. Solid security thread printed with Arabic text. Watermark: Sultan. Printer: (TDLR). 145 x 78 mm.

    a. ١٩٨٧ (1987). Signature 2. FV 8 30
    b. ١٩٨٩ (1989). FV 5 20
    c. ١٩٩٤ (1994). FV 5 20

CBO B16 (P28): **10 rials** (US$26) VG VF UNC
Dark brown. Front: Sultan Qaboos bin Said. Back: Mirani Fort in Muscat. Solid security thread printed with Arabic text. Watermark: Sultan. Printer: (TDLR). 165 x 78 mm.

    a. ١٩٨٧ (1987). Signature 2. FV 40 120
    b. ١٩٩٣ (1993). FV 40 120

1995 Issues

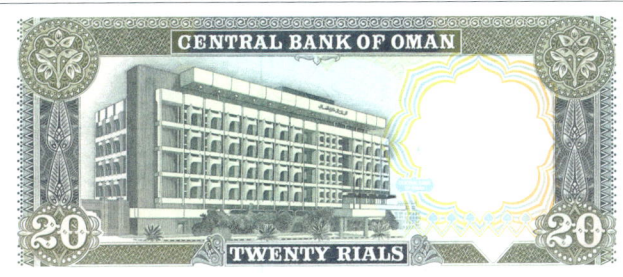

CBO B17 (P29): **20 rials** (US$52)   VG   VF   UNC
Green. Front: Sultan Qaboos bin Said. Back: Central Bank of Oman headquarters building. Solid security thread printed with Arabic text. Watermark: Sultan. Printer: (TDLR). 175 x 78 mm.

  ☐ a. ١٩٨٧ (1987). Signature 2.   FV   75   300
  ☐ b. ١٩٩٤ (1994).   FV   FV   150

CBO B18 (P30): **50 rials** (US$130)   VG   VF   UNC
Green. Front: Sultan Qaboos bin Said. Back: Jabreen Fort. Solid security thread printed with Arabic text. Watermark: Sultan. Printer: (TDLR). 185 x 78 mm.

  ☐ a. ١٩٨٥ (1985). Signature 2.   FV   400   1,000
  ☐ b. ١٩٩٢ (1992).   FV   FV   300
  ☐ as. Five diagonal red نموذج overprints on front;   —   —   320
      five diagonal red SPECIMEN overprints on back;
      black # overprint at upper left on back.

CBO B19 (P31): **100 baisa** (US$0.25)   VG   VF   UNC
Green. Front: Coat of arms; falaj (irrigation channel) with palm trees; Sultan Qaboos bin Said. Back: Birds; Verreaux's eagle; white oryx. Solid security thread. Watermark: Sultan. Printer: (G&D). 121 x 64 mm.

  ☐ a. ١٩٩٥/1995. Signature 2. Intro: 01.11.1995.   FV   FV   1
  ☐ as. Five diagonal red نموذج overprints on front;   —   —   —
      red # overprint at lower center on front;
      five diagonal red SPECIMEN overprints on back.

Replacement notes: Prefix denominator ٩٩.

CBO B20 (P32): **200 baisa** (US$0.50)   VG   VF   UNC
Dark blue. Front: Coat of arms; Seeb (MCT) and Salalah (SLL) airports with jet; Sultan Qaboos bin Said. Back: Marine Science & Fisheries Centre building; Raysut Port. Solid security thread. Watermark: Sultan. Printer: (G&D). 128 x 64 mm.

  ☐ a. ١٩٩٥/1995. Signature 2. Intro: 01.11.1995.   FV   FV   3
  ☐ as. Five diagonal red نموذج overprints on front;   —   —   —
      red # overprint at lower center on front;
      five diagonal red SPECIMEN overprints on back.

CBO B21 (P33): **1/2 rial** (US$1.30)   VG   VF   UNC

Brown. Front: Coat of arms; Bahla Fort; Sultan Qaboos bin Said. Back: Nakhl Fort and Al-Hazm Fort. Solid security thread. Watermark: Sultan. Printer: (G&D). 135 x 64 mm.

☐ a. ١٩٩٥/1995. Signature 2. Intro: 01.11.1995.   FV   FV   2
☐ as. Five diagonal red نموذج overprints on front;   —   —   —
       red # overprint at lower center on front;
       five diagonal red *SPECIMEN* overprints on back.

Replacement notes: Prefix denominator ٩٩.

CBO B22 (P34): **1 rial** (US$2.60)   VG   VF   UNC

Purple. Front: Coat of arms; highways; Sultan Qaboos Sports Centre stadium; Sultan Qaboos bin Said. Back: Three dhows on stilts; khanjar (dagger); jewellery. Solid security thread printed with Arabic text. Watermark: Sultan. Printer: (G&D). 146 x 76 mm.

☐ a. ١٩٩٥/1995. Signature 2. Intro: 01.11.1995.   FV   FV   3
☐ as. Five diagonal red نموذج overprints on front;   —   —   —
       red # overprint at lower center on front;
       five diagonal red *SPECIMEN* overprints on back.

CBO B23 (P35): **5 rials** (US$13)   VG   VF   UNC

Red. Front: Coat of arms; Sultan Qaboos University building with clock tower; Sultan Qaboos bin Said. Back: Nizwa buildings. Solid security thread printed with Arabic text. Watermark: Sultan. Printer: (BDF). 153 x 76 mm.

☐ a. ١٩٩٥/1995. Signature 2. Intro: 01.11.1995.   FV   20   35
☐ b. Reflective pattern of khanjars (daggers) on back.   FV   20   35
☐ as. Five diagonal red نموذج overprints on front;   —   —   —
       red # overprint at lower left on front;
       five diagonal red *SPECIMEN* overprints on back.

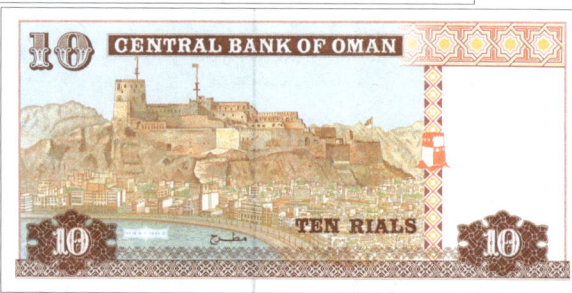

CBO B24 (P36): **10 rials** (US$26)   VG   VF   UNC

Brown. Front: Coat of arms; Salalah Tower; palm trees; Sultan Qaboos bin Said. Back: Muttrah Fort and town with harbor. Solid security thread printed with Arabic text. Watermark: Sultan. Printer: (BDF). 160 x 76 mm.

☐ a. ١٩٩٥/1995. Signature 2. Intro: 01.11.1995.   FV   FV   60
☐ as. Five diagonal red نموذج overprints on front;   —   —   —
       red # overprint at lower left on front;
       five diagonal red *SPECIMEN* overprints on back.

2000 Issues

These notes are like the preceding issues, but with holographic stripes at right front, and new dates.

CBO B25 (P37): **20 rials** (US$52)   VG VF UNC

Light blue. Front: Coat of arms; Central Bank of Oman headquarters building; Sultan Qaboos bin Said; broadcasting tower in Ruwi. Back: Muscat Securities Market; Rysayl industrial area; Oman Chamber of Commerce and Industry building. Solid security thread printed with Arabic text. Watermark: Sultan. Printer: (BDF). 167 x 76 mm.

- ☐ a. ١٩٩٥/1995. Signature 2. Intro: 01.11.1995.   FV FV 100
- ☐ as. Five diagonal red نموذج overprints on front; red # overprint at lower left on front; five diagonal red SPECIMEN overprints on back.   — — —

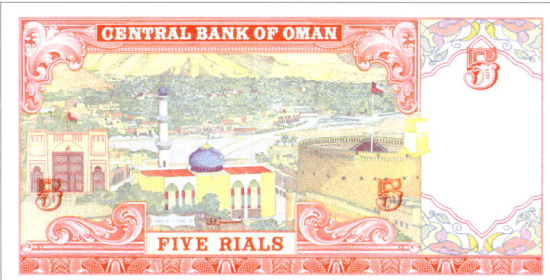

CBO B27 (P39): **5 rials** (US$13)   VG VF UNC

Red. Front: Coat of arms; Sultan Qaboos University building with clock tower; Sultan Qaboos bin Said. Back: Nizwa buildings. Solid security thread printed with Arabic text. Holographic stripe. Watermark: Sultan. Printer: Unknown. 153 x 76 mm.

- ☐ a. ٢٠٠٠/2000. Signature 2.   FV FV 25

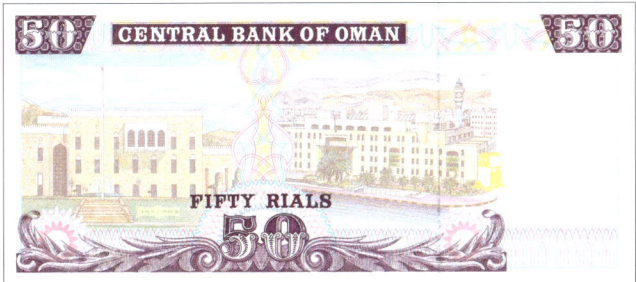

CBO B26 (P38): **50 rials** (US$130)   VG VF UNC

Purple. Front: Coat of arms; Ministry of Finance and Economy building; Sultan Qaboos bin Said; Mirani Fort. Back: Cabinet building; Ministry of Commerce and Industry building. Solid security thread printed with Arabic text. Watermark: Sultan. Printer: (BDF). 174 x 76 mm.

- ☐ a. ١٩٩٥/1995. Signature 2. Intro: 01.11.1995.   FV FV 250
- ☐ as. Five diagonal red نموذج overprints on front; red # overprint at lower left on front; five diagonal red SPECIMEN overprints on back.   — — —

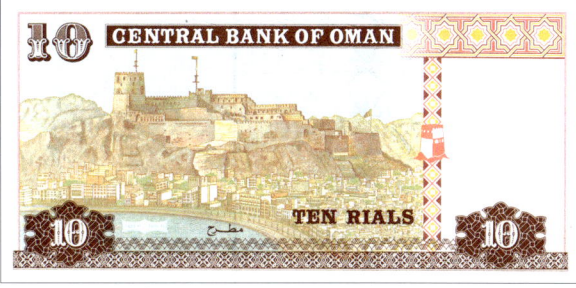

CBO B28 (P40): **10 rials** (US$26)   VG VF UNC

Brown. Front: Coat of arms; Salalah Tower; palm trees; Sultan Qaboos bin Said. Back: Muttrah Fort and town with harbor. Solid security thread printed with Arabic text. Holographic stripe. Watermark: Sultan. Printer: Unknown. 160 x 76 mm.

- ☐ a. ٢٠٠٠/2000. Signature 2.   FV FV 50

2005 Commemorative Issues

This colorful 1-rial note commemorates the 35th National Day (18 November), the day Sultan Qaboos bin Said overthrew the restrictive rule of his father in 1970. It is also the sultan's birthday.

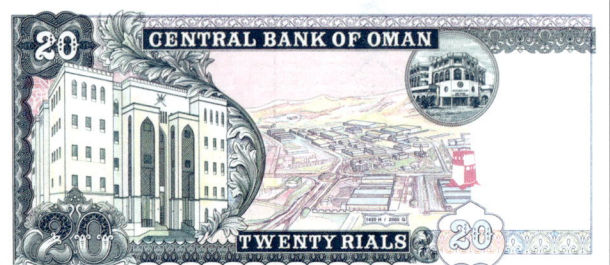

CBO B29 (P41): **20 rials** (US$52)   VG   VF   UNC
Light blue. Front: Coat of arms; building; Sultan Qaboos bin Said; Broadcasting Tower in Ruwi. Back: Muscat Security Market; Rysayl industrial area; Oman Chamber of Commerce and Industry building. Solid security thread printed with Arabic text. Holographic stripe. Watermark: Sultan. Printer: Unknown. 167 x 76 mm.
    a. ٢٠٠٠/2000. Signature 2.   FV   FV   100

CBO B31 (P43): **1 rial** (US$2.60)   VG   VF   UNC
Purple. Front: Coat of arms with crossed swords and khanjar (dagger); incense burner; Sultan Qaboos bin Said. Back: Shabab Oman sailing ship; birds; 35th National Day logo; mosque minaret; jewellery; Jalali Fort. Solid security thread. Watermark: Sultan and Cornerstones. Printer: (TDLR). 145 x 76 mm.
    a. ٢٠٠٥/2005. Signature 2.   FV   FV   7
Replacement notes: Prefix denominator ٩٩.

CBO B30 (P42): **50 rials** (US$130)   VG   VF   UNC
Purple. Front: Coat of arms; Ministry of Finance and Economy building; Sultan Qaboos bin Said; Mirani Fort. Back: Cabinet building; Ministry of Commerce and Industry building. Solid security thread printed with Arabic text. Holographic stripe. Watermark: Sultan. Printer: Unknown. 174 x 76 mm.
    a. ٢٠٠٠/2000. Signature 2.   FV   FV   200

2010 Commemorative Issues

These notes commemorate the 40th National Day (18 November), the day Sultan Qaboos bin Said overthrew the restrictive rule of his father in 1970. It is also the sultan's birthday.

CBO B33 (PNL): **5 rials** (US$13)   VG   VF   UNC

Red. Front: Khanjar (dagger); crown as registration device; Sultan Qaboos University building with clock tower; Sultan Qaboos bin Said; coat of arms with crossed swords and khanjar (dagger); main entrance of the CBO headquarters. Back: Nizwa buildings; 40th National Day logo; crown. varifeye thread and windowed security thread with demetalized *5 RIALS*. Watermark: Sultan and electrotype *5*. Printer: (G&D). 153 x 76 mm.

- ☐ a.   1431 H / 2010 G. Signature 2. Intro: Feb. 2012.   FV   FV   25
- ☐ as.   Five diagonal red نموذج overprints on front;
  red # overprint at lower left on front;
  five diagonal red *SPECIMEN* overprints on back.   —   —   —

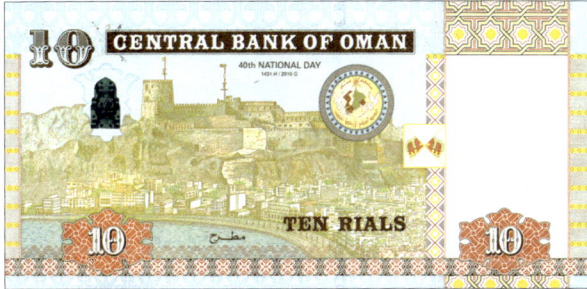

CBO B34 (PNL): **10 rials** (US$26)   VG   VF   UNC

Brown. Front: Urn; crown as registration device; Salalah Tower; palm trees; Sultan Qaboos bin Said coat of arms with crossed swords and khanjar (dagger); main entrance of the CBO headquarters. Back: Muttrah Fort and town with harbor; 40th National Day logo; crown. varifeye thread and windowed security thread with demetalized *10 RIALS*. Watermark: Sultan and electrotype *10*. Printer: (G&D). 160 x 76 mm.

- ☐ a.   1431 H / 2010 G. Signature 2. Intro: Feb. 2012.   FV   FV   50
- ☐ as.   Five diagonal red نموذج overprints on front;
  red # overprint at lower left on front;
  five diagonal red *SPECIMEN* overprints on back.   —   —   —

Replacement notes: Prefix denominator ٩٩.

CBO B32 (P44): **20 rials** (US$52)   VG   VF   UNC

Blue, olive green, and purple. Front: Crown as registration device; Sultan Qaboos Grand Mosque in Bausher; coat of arms with crossed swords and khanjar (dagger); Sultan Qaboos bin Said; main entrance of the CBO headquarters. Back: Coat of arms; Royal Opera House building in Muscat; 40th National Day logo; crown. varifeye thread and windowed security thread with demetalized *20 RIALS*. Watermark: Sultan and electrotype *20*. Printer: (G&D). 167 x 76 mm.

- ☐ a.   1431 H / 2010 G. Signature 2. Intro: 22.11.2010.   FV   FV   80

Replacement notes: Prefix denominator ٩٩.

CBO B35 (PNL): **50 rials** (US$130) VG VF UNC
Purple. Front: Crown; crown as registration device; Ministry of Finance and Economy building; Sultan Qaboos bin Said; Mirani Fort; coat of arms with crossed swords and khanjar (dagger); main entrance of the CBO headquarters. Back: Cabinet building; Ministry of Commerce and Industry building; 40th National Day logo; crown. varifeye thread and windowed security thread with demetalized *50 RIALS*. Watermark: Sultan and electrotype *50*. Printer: (G&D). 174 x 76 mm.

- a. 1431 H / 2010 G. Signature 2. Intro: Feb. 2012. — FV — FV — 200
- as. Five diagonal red نموذج overprints on front; red # overprint at lower left on front; five diagonal red *SPECIMEN* overprints on back. — — —

Replacement notes: Prefix denominator ۹۹.

Museum

The Central Bank of Oman operates a Currency Museum in its headquarters building

Acknowledgements

This chapter was compiled with the generous assistance of Thomas Augustsson, Hartmut Fraunhoffer (www.banknoten.de), Wally Myers, David Murcek (www.themonetaryunit.com), Laurence Pope, Stefan Rombaut, Gergely Scheidl (banknoteshop@gmx.net), Peter Symes, Christoph Thomas, Frank van Tiel, Tristan Williams, Christof Zellweger, and others.

Sources

Cuhaj, George S. *Standard Catalog of World Paper Money, Modern Issues, 1961-Present*. 18th edition. 2012. ISBN 978-1-4402-2956-5. Krause Publications (www.krausebooks.com), 700 East State St., Iola, WI, 54990-0001.

Darley-Doran, Robert E. *History of Currency in the Sultanate of Oman*. 1990. ISBN 0-907605-33-8. Spink and Son (for the Central Bank of Oman), London.

Symes, Peter. "The Note Issues of the Sultanate of Oman." *IBNS Journal*. Volume 34 Number 2. p.22.

Symes, Peter. Reference Site for Islamic Banknotes (www.islamicbanknotes.com)

Share Your Input, Info, and Images

This catalog is believed to be complete and correct as of the time of publication. Prices and face values were last updated 1 July 2011. Please report errors or omissions so that corrections may be made. If you can more precisely identify the name or location of anything depicted on a note, please share that information. Furthermore, if you own an unlisted type or variety, please submit scans of the front and back of the note so that it can be documented. Scans should be 300 dots per inch, 100% actual size, 24-bit color, saved as *uncompressed* JPEG files, and sent to owen@banknotenews.com. Be sure to fully describe all attributes of the note which are not apparent upon visual inspection of the images alone, such as physical dimension, watermark, and security thread.

Pakistan

Contents

Government of Pakistan (GOP) 1621
State Bank of Pakistan (SBP) 1628
Haj Issues (SBP) 1646

Monetary System
1947: 1 Pakistani rupee (PKR) = 16 anna = 64 paisa
1961: 1 Pakistani rupee (PKR) = 100 paisa

In August 1947, India and Pakistan declared independence from the United Kingdom. At the time, Pakistan consisted of the predominantly Muslim regions of West Pakistan and East Bengal (renamed East Pakistan in 1955), geographically separated by India, which was largely Hindu.

Initially, brand new notes were delivered to banks stapled together in bundles of 100. However, at some point this practice was discontinued. As such staple holes are to be expected even in uncirculated condition.

Government of Pakistan

The issuance of 1-rupee notes is the responsibility of the Government of Pakistan, whereas higher denomination notes are issued by the State Bank of Pakistan. However, some of the earlier issues of higher denominations are inscribed as Government of Pakistan because they were designed prior to the establishment of the State Bank of Pakistan.

GOP Signature Varieties
(Secretary, Ministry of Finance)

1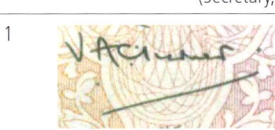
Victor A. Turner
(16.05.1948 - 31.01.1950)

2
Abdul Qadir
(01.02.1950 - 25.07.1952)

3
Mumtaz Hasan
(28.07.1952 - 07.07.1953)

4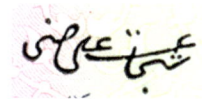
Shujaat Ali Hasnie
(unknown)

5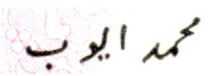
Mohammed Ayub
(unknown - October 1958)

6
Hafiz Abdul Majeed
(01.11.1958 - 19.06.1961)

7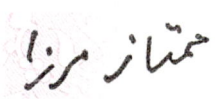
Mumtaz Mirza
(20.06.1961 - 28.02.1963)

8
Mirza Muzaffar Ahmad
(06.03.1963 - 31.05.1966)

GOP Signature Varieties
(Secretary, Ministry of Finance)

9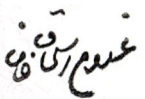
Ghulam Ishaq Khan
(01.06.1966 - 08.09.1970)

10
Aftab Ghulam Nabi Kazi
(09.09.1970 - 19.08.1973)

11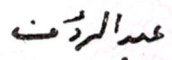
Abdul Rauf Shaikh
(20.08.1973 - 06.10.1977)

12
Aftab Ahmad Khan
(09.10.1977 - 30.07.1979)

13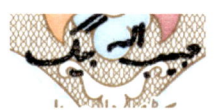
Habibullah Baig
(01.08.1979 - 07.06.1987)

14
Izharul Haq
(08.06.1987 - 14.08.1988)

15
Saeed Ahmad Qureshi
(15.08.1988 - 21.01.1989)
(23.08.1990 - 31.07.1991)

16
Rafique A. Akhund
(22.01.1989 - August 1990)

17
Qazi Alimullah Marfi
(01.08.1991 - 24.09.1992)
(28.10.1993 - 29.06.1994)

18
Khalid Javed
(25.09.1992 - 24.04.1993)

19
Javed Talat
(30.06.1994 - 01.03.1996)

20
Mian Tayyab Hasan
(02.03.1996 - 31.10.1996)

21
Mueen Afzal
(01.11.1996 - 30.06.1998)

22
Mohammed Younus Khan
(01.07.1998 - unknown)

1948 Provisional Issues

On 1 April 1948, these notes were issued by the Reserve Bank of India and the Government of India on behalf of the Government of Pakistan (GOP), for use exclusively within Pakistan, without the possibility of redemption in India. Printed by the India Security Press (ISP) in Nasik, these notes consist of Indian note plates engraved (not overprinted) with the words *GOVERNMENT OF PAKISTAN* in English and "Hukumat-e-Pakistan" in Urdu added at the top and bottom, respectively, of the watermark area on the front only; the signatures on these notes remain those of Indian banking and finance officials.

The Reserve Bank of India ceased to function in Pakistan as of 30 June 1948, though Indian notes without inscriptions continued to circulate until 30 September 1948, after which time they were withdrawn.

India Signature Varieties

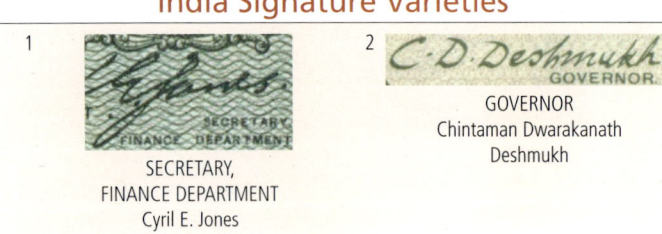

1 — SECRETARY, FINANCE DEPARTMENT, Cyril E. Jones

2 — GOVERNOR, Chintaman Dwarakanath Deshmukh

GOP B1 (P1): **1 rupee** (demonetized 01.01.1952)   Good   Fine   XF
Blue-gray. Front: Obverse of Indian 1-rupee silver coin with King George VI. Back: Reverse of Indian 1-rupee silver coin dated 1940. No security thread. Watermark: King George VI. Printer: (ISP). 101 x 63 mm.
- a. 1940. Signature Jones. Intro: 01.04.1948.   50   150   500
  Prefix Q, R, S.
- as. Horizontal red *SPECIMEN* overprint.   —   —   —

Like India P25c, but with *GOVERNMENT OF PAKISTAN* engraved in watermark area.

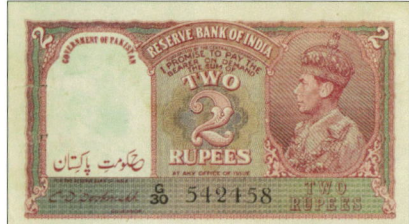

GOP B2 (P1A): **2 rupees** (demonetized 01.01.1952)   Good   Fine   XF
Lilac. Front: King George VI. Back: Reserve Bank of India logo. No security thread. Watermark: King George VI. Printer: (ISP). 114 x 63 mm.
- a. No date. Signature Deshmukh. Intro: 01.04.1948.   —   1,250   —
  Prefix G.
- as. Horizontal red *SPECIMEN* overprint.   —   —   —

Like India P17b, but with *GOVERNMENT OF PAKISTAN* engraved in watermark area.

GOP B3 (P2): **5 rupees** (demonetized 01.01.1952)   Good   Fine   XF
Green. Front: King George VI. Back: Reserve Bank of India logo; three antelope. Solid security thread. Watermark: King George VI. Printer: (ISP). 126 x 73 mm.
- a. No date. Signature Deshmukh. Intro: 01.04.1948.   75   250   1,000
  Prefix A, B.
- as. Horizontal red *SPECIMEN* overprint.   —   —   —

Like India P23a, but with *GOVERNMENT OF PAKISTAN* engraved in watermark area.

1948 Emergency Issues

Prior to the establishment of the State Bank of Pakistan on 12 May 1948, the Government of Pakistan anticipated the need for notes to replace the Reserve Bank of India issues which were to be withdrawn on 30 September 1948. As such, Thomas De La Rue prepared an emergency issue of 5-, 10-, and 100-rupee notes bearing the name of the Government of Pakistan, although they were actually issued by the State Bank of Pakistan on 1 October. All of these notes are signed by Ghulam Mohammed, who served as the minister of the treasury from 1948 to 1951.

GOP B4 (P3): **10 rupees** (demonetized 01.01.1952)   Good   Fine   XF
Violet, red, brown, green, and orange. Front: King George VI. Back: Dhow boat; Reserve Bank of India logo. Solid security thread. Watermark: King George VI. Printer: (ISP). 146 x 80 mm.

☐ a. No date. Signature Deshmukh. Intro: 01.04.1948.   15   200   900
     Prefix H, J.
☐ as. Horizontal red *SPECIMEN* overprint.   —   UNC   11,500

Like India P24, but with GOVERNMENT OF PAKISTAN engraved in watermark area.

GOP B6 (P5): **5 rupees** (demonetized 01.10.1955)   VG   VF   UNC
Blue. Front: Crescent moon and star. Back: Guilloche patterns. No security thread. Watermark: None. Printer: (TDLR). 128 x 72 mm.

☐ a. No date. Signature Ghulam Mohammed.   40   150   600
     Intro: 01.10.1948. Prefix: None, 1- or 2-letter.
☐ as1. Diagonal red *SPECIMEN* overprint.   —   —   —
☐ as2. Diagonal black DLR oval overprint;   —   XF   1,100
     horiz. black *SPECIMEN NO* # ovpt at lower left.

GOP B5 (P3A): **100 rupees** (demonetized 01.01.1952)   Good   Fine   XF
Green, violet, and orange. Front: King George VI. Back: Roaring tiger; Reserve Bank of India logo. Solid security thread. Watermark: King George VI. Printer: (ISP). 170 x 107 mm.

☐ a. No date. Signature Deshmukh. Intro: 01.04.1948.   200   800   3,000
     Prefix B.
☐ as. Horizontal red *SPECIMEN* overprint.   —   UNC   16,500

Like India P20k, but with GOVERNMENT OF PAKISTAN engraved in watermark area.

1949 Issues

Beginning with this 1949 note, the inscription "Government of Pakistan" in Urdu appears on 1-rupee notes only. All higher denominations are issued by the State Bank of Pakistan.

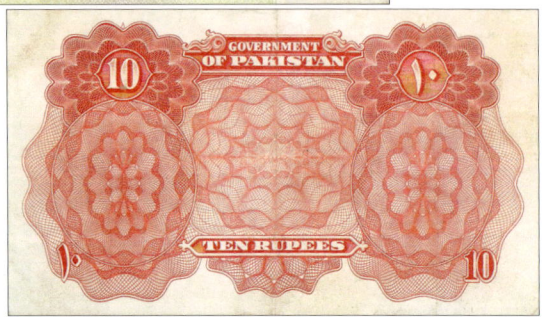

GOP B7 (P6): 10 rupees (demonetized 01.08.1956)   VG   VF   UNC
Red. Front: Crescent moon and star. Back: Guilloche patterns. No security thread. Watermark: None. Printer: (TDLR). 146 x 82 mm.
- ☐ a. No date. Signature Ghulam Mohammed.   30   125   500
  Intro: 01.10.1948. Prefix: None, 1- or 2-letter.
- ☐ as1. Diagonal black *SPECIMEN* overprint.   —   —   —
- ☐ as2. Diagonal black *SPECIMEN* and DLR oval ovpts;   —   XF   1,150
  horiz. black *SPECIMEN NO #* ovpt at lower left.

GOP B9 (P4): 1 rupee (demonetized)   VG   VF   UNC
Green, orange, and pink. Front: Crescent moon and star. Back: Naulakha Pavilion in Shahi Qila (Lahore Fort), viewed through archway. No security thread. Watermark: Crescent moon and star. Printer: (BWC). 102 x 63 mm.
- ☐ a. No date. Signature 1. Intro: 01.03.1949.   50   100   400
- ☐ as1. Diagonal red *SPECIMEN* overprint; punched.   —   —   —
- ☐ as2. Horizontal *SPECIMEN* perforation.   —   —   —

1952 Issues

This note is like the preceding issues, but the front is blue, the back is purple, and the orientation of the crescent moon and star is flipped. These notes were printed by Thomas De La Rue.

GOP B8 (P7): 100 rupees (demonetized 01.08.1956)   VG   VF   UNC
Green. Front: Crescent moon and star. Back: Guilloche patterns. No security thread. Watermark: None. Printer: (TDLR). 166 x 90 mm.
- ☐ a. No date. Signature Ghulam Mohammed.   100   600   1,000
  Intro: 01.10.1948. Prefix: None, 1- or 2-letter.
- ☐ as1. Diagonal red *SPECIMEN* overprint.   —   —   —
- ☐ as2. Diagonal red or black DLR oval overprint;   —   XF   1,700
  horiz. red or black *SPECIMEN NO #* ovpt at lower left.
- ☐ as3. Diagonal *CANCELLED* perforation.   —   XF   2,800

GOP B10 (P8): 1 rupee (demonetized)   VG   VF   UNC
Blue, red, green, and purple. Front: Crescent moon and star. Back: Naulakha Pavilion in Shahi Qila (Lahore Fort), viewed through archway. No security thread. Watermark: Crescent moon and star. Printer: (TDLR). 102 x 63 mm.
- ☐ a. No date. Intro: 01.02.1952.   60   175   300
  Signature 1. Without line in fractional prefix.
- ☐ b. Signature 2. With line in fractional prefix.   60   175   300
- ☐ as1. Black DLR oval overprint;   —   —   —
  horiz. black *SPECIMEN NO #* ovpt at lower left.
- ☐ as2. Diagonal red *SPECIMEN* overprint;   —   —   —
  black DLR oval ovpt; .
  horiz. black *SPECIMEN NO #* ovpt at lower left.

1953-1961 Issues

In 1953, the Pakistan Security Printing Corporation (PSPC) took over production of all notes issued by Pakistan. This note is like the preceding issues, but the back is blue.

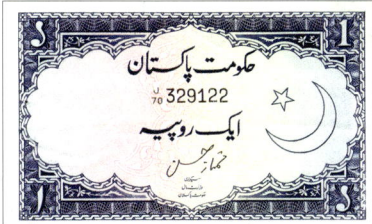

GOP B11 (P9): **1 rupee** (demonetized)   VG   VF   UNC
Blue, red, and green. Front: Crescent moon and star. Back: Naulakha Pavilion in Shahi Qila (Lahore Fort), viewed through archway. No security thread. Watermark: Crescent moon and star. Printer: (PSPC). 102 x 63 mm.

			VG	VF	UNC
☐	a.	No date. Signature 2. Intro: 31.01.1953.	10	25	50
☐	b.	Signature 3. With line in fractional prefix.	25	50	100
☐	c.	Without line in fractional prefix.	1	4	15
☐	d.	Signature 4. Intro: 1955.	1	4	15
☐	e.	Signature 5. Intro: 1956.	1	4	15
☐	f.	Signature 6. Intro: 1958.	1	4	15
☐	g.	Signature 7. Intro: 1961.	1	4	15

For notes with Bangladesh stamp, see Bangladesh PRB B1.

1964-1972 Issues

In 1964, the State Bank of Pakistan began printing the 1-rupee notes with purple backs, like the earlier notes printed by TDLR. They can be distinguished by the signatures on front.

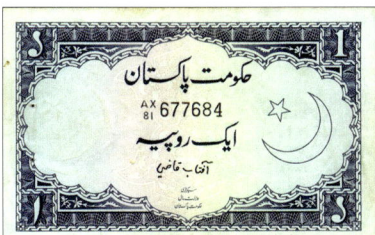

GOP B12 (P9A): **1 rupee** (demonetized)   VG   VF   UNC
Blue, red, green, and purple. Front: Crescent moon and star. Back: Naulakha Pavilion in Shahi Qila (Lahore Fort), viewed through archway. No security thread. Watermark: Crescent moon and star. Printer: (SBP). 103 x 63.5 mm.

			VG	VF	UNC
☐	a.	No date. Signature 8. Intro: 14.07.1964.	0.50	2	8
☐	b.	Signature 9. Intro: 1966.	0.50	2	8
☐	c.	Signature 10. Intro: 1972.	0.50	2	8

Replacements: Prefix 1/X. For notes with Bangladesh stamp, see Bangladesh PRB B2.

1972-1973 Issues

Following the 1972 civil war between East and West Pakistan, the Government of Pakistan issued these new notes which are like the preceding issues, but changed in color so that the earlier notes could be demonetized.

GOP B13 (P10): **1 rupee** (US$0.01)   VG   VF   UNC
Brown, yellow, blue, pink, and violet. Front: Crescent moon and star. Back: Naulakha Pavilion in Shahi Qila (Lahore Fort), viewed through archway. No security thread. Watermark: Crescent moon and star. Printer: (PSPC). 102 x 63 mm.

			VG	VF	UNC
☐	a.	No date. Signature 10. Intro: 20.12.1972.	0.75	1.50	3
☐	b.	Signature 11. Intro: 1973.	0.75	1.50	3
☐	as.	Diagonal red Urdu overprint on front; diagonal red *SPECIMEN* overprint on back; horiz. black *SPECIMEN* № # ovpt at upper right.	—	—	800

Replacement notes: Prefix denominator X.

1974 Issues

This 1-rupee note has "One rupee" written in four regional languages (Punjabi, Sindhi, Pushto, and Baluchi) in the panel at bottom front. An unissued 5-rupee note with the same four languages is on display at the Museum of the State Bank of Pakistan in Karachi, so it's likely that an entire series was planned using the theme of four languages. These plans were apparently abandoned because it was felt that the inclusion of these four languages would promote provincialism.

GOP B14 (P24): 1 rupee (US$0.01)   VG   VF   UNC
Blue-gray, yellow, purple, and pink. Front: Crescent moon and star. Back: Minar-e-Pakistan monumental minaret in Iqbal Park, Lahore. No security thread. Watermark: Crescent moon and star. Printer: (PSPC). 102 x 64 mm.

☐ a. No date. Signature 11. Intro: 16.05.1974.   4   15   50

Replacement notes: Prefix denominator X.

1975-1979 Issues

This 1-rupee note is like the preceding issues, but has a decorative panel at bottom front without regional text.

GOP B15 (P24A): 1 rupee (US$0.01)   VG   VF   UNC
Blue-gray, yellow, purple, and pink. Front: Crescent moon and star. Back: Minar-e-Pakistan monumental minaret in Iqbal Park, Lahore. No security thread. Watermark: Crescent moon and star. Printer: (PSPC). 102 x 64 mm.

☐ a. No date. Signature 11. Intro: 15.04.1975.   —   0.25   1.50
       1-letter numerator in fractional prefix.
☐ b. Sig. 12. Intro: 1977. 1- or 2-letter numerator.   —   0.25   1.50
☐ c. Sig. 13. Intro: 1979. 1- or 2-letter numerator.   —   0.25   1.50
☐ as. Diagonal red Urdu overprint on front;   —   —   900
       diagonal red *SPECIMEN* overprint on back;
       horiz. black *SPECIMEN No.#* ovpt at upper right.
☐ bs. Diagonal red *SPECIMEN* and DLR oval ovpts;   —   —   800
       horiz. red *SPECIMEN No.#* ovpt at lower left;
       punched.

Replacement notes: Prefix denominator X or *.

1981 Issues

This 1-rupee note features an entirely new design and greater use of color.

GOP B16 (P25): **1 rupee** (US$0.01)   VG   VF   UNC

Brown, light blue, orange, and lilac. Front: Crescent moon and star. Back: Tomb of Allama Muhammad Iqbal in Lahore, without Urdu inscription below. No security thread. Watermark: Crescent moon and star. Printer: (PSPC). 95 x 60 mm.

- ☐ a. No date. Signature 13. Intro: 24.03.1981.   —   0.25   1.50
- ☐ as. Horizontal red Urdu overprint on front;   —   —   600
      diagonal red *SPECIMEN* overprint on back;
      horiz. black *SPECIMEN No.#* ovpt at upper right.

Like subsequent issues, but without Urdu inscription at bottom center on back.
Replacement notes: Prefix denominator X.

1982 Issues

These notes are like the preceding issues, but with an Urdu inscription on the back (at bottom center) which can be translated as "Legal livelihood is equal to prayer."

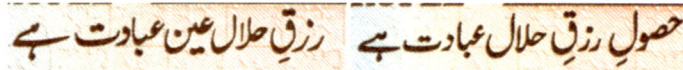

The 1-rupee notes are available with two different Urdu inscriptions on back. The original inscription (GOP B17, left) appears on notes issued in 1982, whereas the revised inscription (GOP B18, right) appears on notes issued in 1984 and after.

GOP B17 (P26): **1 rupee** (US$0.01)   VG   VF   UNC

Brown, light blue, orange, and lilac. Front: Crescent moon and star. Back: Tomb of Allama Muhammad Iqbal in Lahore, with Urdu inscription below. No security thread. Watermark: Crescent moon and star. Printer: (PSPC). 95 x 60 mm.

- ☐ a. No date. Signature 13.   —   0.25   1.50
      Serial number at upper center. Intro: 20.01.1982.
- ☐ b. Serial number at lower right.   —   0.25   1.50
- ☐ bs. Diagonal red Urdu overprint on front;   —   —   475
      diagonal red *SPECIMEN* overprint on back;
      horiz. black *SPECIMEN No.#* ovpt at upper right.

Like preceding issues, but with Urdu inscription added at bottom center on back.
Replacement notes: Prefix denominator X.

PAKISTAN 1984-2001 ISSUES

1984-2001 Issues

These notes are like the preceding issues, but with a revised Urdu inscription on the back (at bottom center) which can be translated as "Earning legal livelihood is equal to prayer."

The 1-rupee note was replaced by a coin in the 1990s, but was reissued temporarily in 2001 to use up the remaining stock of unissued notes.

GOP B18 (P27): **1 rupee** (US$0.01)

Brown, light blue, orange, and lilac. Front: Crescent moon and star. Back: Tomb of Allama Muhammad Iqbal in Lahore, with revised Urdu inscription below. No security thread. Watermark: Crescent moon and star. Printer: (PSPC). 95 x 60 mm.

		VG	VF	UNC
☐ a.	No date. Signature 13. Intro: 07.02.1984. 1- or 2-letter numerator in fractional prefix. Serial number at upper center.	—	0.25	1.50
☐ b.	Serial number at lower right. 2-letter numerator.	—	0.25	1.50
☐ c.	Signature 14. Serial number at upper center.	—	0.25	1.50
☐ d.	Serial number at lower right.	—	0.25	1.50
☐ e.	Signature 15. Serial number at upper center.	—	0.25	1.50
☐ f.	Serial number at lower right.	—	0.25	1.50
☐ g.	Signature 16. Serial number at upper center.	—	0.25	1.50
☐ h.	Serial number at lower right.	—	0.25	1.50
☐ i.	Signature 17. Serial number at upper center.	—	0.25	1.50
☐ j.	Serial number at lower right.	—	0.25	1.50
☐ k.	Signature 18. Intro: 1992.	—	0.25	1
☐ l.	Signature 19. Intro: 1994. 1- or 2-letter prefix.	—	0.25	1
☐ m.	Signature 20. Intro: 1996.	—	0.25	1
☐ n.	Signature 21. Intro: 1996.	—	0.25	1
☐ o.	Signature 22. Intro: 2001.	—	0.25	1

Replacement notes: Prefix denominator X.

State Bank of Pakistan

The State Bank of Pakistan Order was issued on 12 May 1948. The issuance of 1-rupee notes is the responsibility of the Government of Pakistan, whereas higher denomination notes are issued by the State Bank of Pakistan (SBP).

For more information, visit www.sbp.org.pk.

SBP Signature Varieties
(Governor)

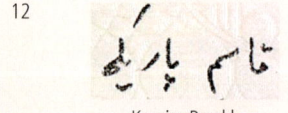
Kassim Parekh
(05.09.1989 - 30.08.1990)

* (Acting Governor)
Mukhtar Nabi Qureshi
(06.11.1999 - 23.11.1999)

Muhammad Yaqub
(20.07.1993 - 05.11.1999)

14
Ishrat Hussain
(02.12.1999 - 01.12.2005)

SBP Signature Varieties

(Governor)

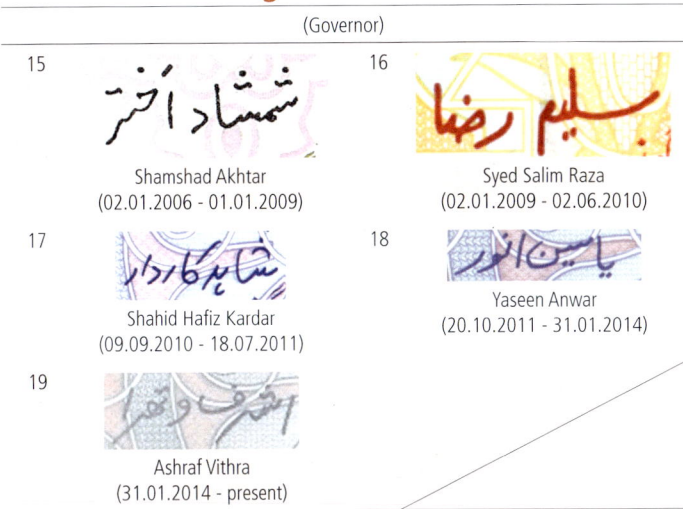

15	Shamshad Akhtar (02.01.2006 - 01.01.2009)	16	Syed Salim Raza (02.01.2009 - 02.06.2010)
17	Shahid Hafiz Kardar (09.09.2010 - 18.07.2011)	18	Yaseen Anwar (20.10.2011 - 31.01.2014)
19	Ashraf Vithra (31.01.2014 - present)		

* This official is not known to have signed any notes.

The 100- and 500-rupee notes from 1953 to 1966 were printed or overprinted with the name of the administrative region of the State Bank of Pakistan in which they were issued: Dhaka (capital of East Pakistan), Karachi, or Lahore. On the 100-rupee notes, the name in Urdu appears at lower center on the front. On the 500-rupee notes, the name in Bengali appears at lower left and in Urdu at lower right.

Administrative Region Varieties

City	Bengali	Urdu
Dhaka	ঢাকা	ڈھاکہ
Karachi	করাচী	کراچی
Lahore	লাহোর	لاہور

1949-1967 Issues

SBP B1 (P11): **2 rupees** (demonetized) VG VF UNC
Brown, blue, pink, and green. Front: One of four minarets at the tomb of Mughal Emperor Jahangir near the town of Shahdara Bagh in Lahore. Back: Badshahi mosque (Royal mosque) in Lahore. No security thread. Watermark: Crescent moon and star. Printer: (BWC). 112 x 62 mm.

- a. No date. Signature 1. Fractional prefix. — 1,300 —
  Intro: 01.03.1949.
- as1. Diagonal red *SPECIMEN* overprint; punched. — — 2,500
- as2. Horizontal *SPECIMEN* perforation. — — —

SBP B2 (P12): **5 rupees** (demonetized 05.06.1972) VG VF UNC
Purple. Front: Village; river with boat carrying bales of jute; bank logo. Back: Road through the mountainous Khyber Pass. Solid security thread. Watermark: Crescent moon and star. Printer: (TDLR). 128 x 72 mm.

- a. No date. Intro: 01.09.1951. 2 10 40
  Signature 1. Prefix: 1- or 2-letter.
- b. Signature 2. Prefix: 2-letter. Intro: 1953. 2 10 40
- c. Signature 3. Intro: 1960. — — —
- d. Prefix: Fractional. 2 10 40
- as1. Red DLR oval overprint; — XF 850
  horiz. red *SPECIMEN NO #* ovpt at lower left.
- as2. Diagonal red *SPECIMEN* and DLR oval ovpts; — — 1,500
  horiz. red *SPECIMEN NO #* ovpt at lower left.
- t. Color trial: Blue. — — 1,500

For notes with Bangladesh stamp, see Bangladesh PRB B3.

SBP B3 (P13): **10 rupees** (demonetized 05.06.1972) VG VF UNC
Brown. Front: Shalimar Gardens in Lahore; bank logo. Back: Tombs near Thatta. Solid security thread. Watermark: Crescent moon and star. 146 x 82 mm.

		VG	VF	UNC
☐ a.	No date. Intro: 01.09.1951. Printer: (TDLR). Signature 1. Prefix: 1- or 2-letter.	1	5	40
☐ b.	Signature 2. Printer: (PSPC). Intro: 1953. Prefix: 2-letter.	1	5	40
☐ c.	Prefix: Fractional.	1	5	40
☐ d.	Signature 3. Red serial numbers. Intro: 1960.	1	5	40
☐ e.	Maroon serial numbers.	1	5	40
☐ f.	Signature 5. Red serial numbers. Intro: 1967.	1	5	40
☐ as.	Red DLR oval overprint; horiz. red *SPECIMEN NO* # ovpt at lower left.	—	XF	1,200
☐ bs.	Diagonal red Urdu overprint.	—	—	4,000
☐ ds.	Diagonal black *SPECIMEN* and DLR oval ovpts; horiz. black *SPECIMEN NO* # ovpt at lower left.	—	500	—
☐ fs.	Diagonal red Urdu overprint.	—	XF	1,400

For notes with Bangladesh stamp, see Bangladesh PRB B4.

SBP B4 (P14): **100 rupees** (withdrawn 08.06.1971) VG VF UNC
Violet and orange. Front: Guilloche patterns. Back: Guilloche patterns. Solid security thread. Watermark: Crescent moon and star. 166 x 92 mm.

		VG	VF	UNC
☐ a.	No date. Intro: 15.09.1953. Signature 1. Printer: (TDLR). Dhaka printed in Urdu at lower center.	10	75	150
☐ b.	Karachi printed in Urdu at lower center.	10	75	150
☐ c.	Signature 2. Printer: (PSPC). Intro: 1954. Dhaka printed in Urdu at lower center.	10	75	150
☐ d.	Karachi printed in Urdu at lower center.	10	75	150
☐ as.	Diagonal black Urdu overprint.	—	XF	1,350
☐ bs1.	Black DLR oval overprints; horiz. black *SPECIMEN Nº* # ovpt at lower left.	—	XF	1,500
☐ bs2.	Diagonal black Urdu overprint; horizontal red *No.* # overprint at upper right.	—	AU	1,250
☐ ds.	Diagonal black Urdu overprint; horizontal red *No.* # overprint at upper right.	—	—	—
☐ t.	Color trial: Green uniface back mounted on card.	—	—	—

The serial numbers on 100-rupee notes printed by TDLR use a variable-weight font (left), whereas notes printed by PSPC use a monoweight font (right).

1957-1971 Issues

These notes are the first to feature a portrait of Mohammed Ali Jinnah, also known as Quaid-e-Azam (Great Leader), a tradition maintained on all subsequent issues by the State Bank of Pakistan.

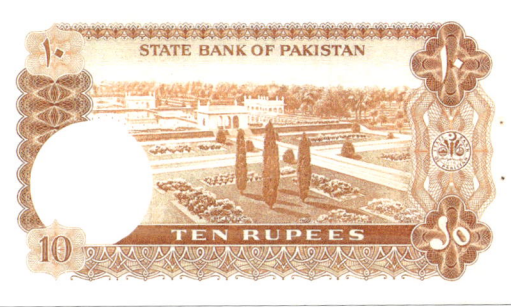

SBP B5 (P15): **5 rupees** (demonetized 05.06.1972)   VG   VF   UNC

Purple, light blue, and pink. Front: Mohammed Ali Jinnah wearing jacket and tie. Back: Bank logo; terraced hillside; branch with tea leaves. Solid security thread. Watermark: Mohammed Ali Jinnah. Printer: (PSPC). 128 x 72 mm.

☐	a.	No date. Intro: 19.09.1966. Signature 4. 1- or 2-letter prefix.	0.50	2.50	8
☐	b.	Signature 5. 2-letter prefix. Intro: 1967.	0.50	2.50	8
☐	c.	Fractional prefix.	0.50	2.50	8
☐	d.	Signature 6. Intro: 1971.	5	25	80
☐	as.	Horizontal red Urdu overprint on front; diagonal red *SPECIMEN* overprint on back.	—	AU	1,200

For notes with Bangladesh stamp, see Bangladesh PRB B5.

SBP B6 (P16): **10 rupees** (demonetized 05.06.1972)   VG   VF   UNC

Brown, blue, green, pink, and orange. Front: Mohammed Ali Jinnah wearing jacket and tie; flowers. Back: Shalimar Gardens in Lahore; bank logo. Solid security thread. Watermark: Mohammed Ali Jinnah. Printer: (PSPC). 148 x 82 mm.

☐	a.	No date. Intro: 16.11.1970. Signature 5. 1- or 2-letter prefix.	1.25	5	20
☐	b.	Signature 6. 2-letter prefix. Intro: 1971.	2	8	30
☐	as.	Diagonal red Urdu overprint on front only; horiz. black *SPECIMEN No.* # ovpt at lower left.	—	—	1,350

For notes with Bangladesh stamp, see Bangladesh PRB B6.

SBP B7 (P17): **50 rupees** (demonetized 01.03.1972)　　VG　VF　UNC

Green and orange. Front: Mohammed Ali Jinnah wearing jacket and tie. Back: Bank logo; palm trees and jute drying on riverbank; river with three boats carrying bales of jute. Solid security thread. Watermark: Mohammed Ali Jinnah. Printer: (PSPC). 155 x 82 mm.

			VG	VF	UNC
☐	a.	No date. Signature 4. Intro: 12.06.1964. 5-mm wide prefix. 1- or 2-letter prefix.	1	4	15
☐	b.	4-mm wide prefix. 2-letter prefix.	1	4	15
☐	c.	Signature 5. 5-mm wide prefix. Intro: 1967.	1	4	15
☐	d.	Signature 6. Intro: 1971.	20	80	200
☐	as.	Horizontal red Urdu overprint on front only.	—	—	1,200

For notes with Bangladesh stamp, see Bangladesh PRB B7.

Some of the 50-rupee notes with Shujaat Ali Hasnie's signature have 5-mm wide prefixes (SBP B7a, left), and some have 4-mm wide prefixes (B7b, right).

SBP B8 (P18): **100 rupees** (withdrawn 08.06.1971)　　VG　VF　UNC

Green, purple, and orange. Front: Mohammed Ali Jinnah; bank logo. Back: Badshahi mosque (Royal mosque) in Lahore. Solid security thread. Watermark: Mohammed Ali Jinnah. Printer: (PSPC). 166 x 92 mm.

			VG	VF	UNC
☐	a.	No date. Intro: 24.12.1957. Sig. 2. Dhaka overprint in Urdu at lower center.	2	8	25
☐	b.	Karachi overprint in Urdu at lower center.	2	8	25
☐	c.	Lahore overprint in Urdu at lower center.	2	8	25
☐	d.	Signature 3. Intro: 1960. Dhaka overprint in Urdu at lower center.	2	8	25
☐	e.	Karachi overprint in Urdu at lower center.	2	8	25
☐	f.	Lahore overprint in Urdu at lower center.	2	8	25
☐	g.	No overprint. 4.25-mm wide prefix.	2	8	25
☐	h.	5.5-mm wide prefix.	2	8	25
☐	i.	Signature 5. Intro: 1967.	2	8	25
☐	bs.	Horizontal red Urdu overprint.	—	—	1,250

For notes with Bangladesh stamp, see Bangladesh PRB B8.

1972-1975 Issues

East Pakistan declared war on West Pakistan on 25 March 1971, and declared its independence as Bangladesh on 17 April 1971, though victory wasn't achieved until 16 December 1971. During the civil war, many banks in East Pakistan were looted and large quantities of notes stolen. It was an unofficial practice of some Bengalis to protest Pakistani rule by stamping banknotes with *BANGLA DESH* as two words in either Bengali or English. On 8 June 1971, the Pakistani government declared that all banknotes bearing such stamps ceased to be legal tender. Furthermore, to prevent looted high-denomination notes from disrupting the Pakistani economy, the government also withdrew the legal tender status of all 100- and 500-rupee notes.

Following the civil war, the State Bank of Pakistan issued these new notes which are like the preceding issues—with the exception of the slightly redesigned 100-rupee note—but changed in color so that the older notes could be demonetized. No new 500-rupee note was issued in this family.

SBP B9 (P19): **500 rupees** (withdrawn 08.06.1971)   VG   VF   UNC

Red, yellow, pink, and light green. Front: Mohammed Ali Jinnah wearing jacket and tie. Back: State Bank of Pakistan headquarters building in Islamabad; bank logo. Solid security thread with printed *PAKISTAN*. Watermark: Mohammed Ali Jinnah. Printer: (PSPC). 176 x 92 mm.

		VG	VF	UNC
☐ a.	No date. Signature 4. Intro: 28.10.1964. Dhaka overprints in Bengali and Urdu.	15	25	60
☐ b.	Karachi overprints in Bengali and Urdu.	10	20	40
☐ c.	Lahore overprints in Bengali and Urdu.	10	20	40
☐ d.	Signature 5. Intro: 1967. Karachi overprints in Bengali and Urdu.	10	20	40
☐ as.	Horizontal black Urdu overprint on front; two diagonal black *SPECIMEN* ovpts on back.	—	—	1,475

For notes with Bangladesh stamp, see Bangladesh PRB B9.

SBP B10 (P20): **5 rupees** (US$0.05)   VG   VF   UNC

Orange, green, and blue. Front: Mohammed Ali Jinnah wearing jacket and tie. Back: Bank logo; terraced hillside; branch with tea leaves. Solid security thread. Watermark: Mohammed Ali Jinnah. Printer: (PSPC). 128 x 72 mm.

		VG	VF	UNC
☐ a.	No date. Signature 6. Intro: 05.06.1972.	0.50	2	7
☐ b.	Signature 7. 1- or 2-letter prefix. Intro: 1972.	0.25	1	4
☐ c.	Fractional prefix.	0.50	2	7
☐ d.	Signature 8. Intro: 1975.	0.50	2	7
☐ as.	Horizontal red Urdu overprint on front; diagonal red *SPECIMEN* overprint on back; horiz. black *SPECIMEN No. #* ovpt at lower left.	—	—	1,125

PAKISTAN 1972-1975 ISSUES

SBP B11 (P21): **10 rupees** (US$0.10)   VG   VF   UNC

Green, blue, and pink. Front: Mohammed Ali Jinnah wearing jacket and tie. Back: Shalimar Gardens in Lahore; bank logo. Solid security thread. Watermark: Mohammed Ali Jinnah. 148 x 82 mm.

		VG	VF	UNC
☐ a.	No date. Intro: 05.06.1972. Signature 6. Printer: (PSPC).	2.50	5	10
☐ b.	Signature 7. 2-letter prefix. Intro: 1972. Monoweight serial number font.	0.50	2	5
☐ c.	Variable-weight s/n font. Printer: (TDLR).	5	10	20
☐ d.	Double asterisk prefix (not replacement notes).	75	225	—
☐ e.	Fractional prefix. Monoweight serial number font. Printer: (PSPC).	5	10	20
☐ as.	Diagonal red Urdu overprint on front; diagonal red *SPECIMEN* overprint on back; horiz. black *SPECIMEN No.* # ovpt at lower left.	—	—	1,475
☐ cs.	Diagonal red *SPECIMEN* and DLR oval ovpts; horiz. red *SPECIMEN NO* # ovpt at lower left.	—	XF	950

TDLR printed ten million 10-rupee notes, identifiable by the unique serial number font. Notes with the monoweight serial number font (left) have been verified before and after the variable-weight serial number font (right) used by TDLR.

SBP B12 (P22): **50 rupees** (US$0.55)   VG   VF   UNC

Blue and orange. Front: Mohammed Ali Jinnah wearing jacket and tie. Back: Bank logo; palm trees and jute drying on riverbank; river with three boats carrying bales of jute. Solid security thread. Watermark: Mohammed Ali Jinnah. Printer: (PSPC). 155 x 82 mm.

		VG	VF	UNC
☐ a.	No date. Signature 6. Intro: 01.03.1972.	2.50	10	45
☐ b.	Signature 7. Intro: 1972.	1.50	7	25
☐ c.	Signature 8. Intro: 1975.	2	8	30
☐ bs.	Diagonal red Urdu overprint on front; diagonal red *SPECIMEN* overprint on back; horiz. black *SPECIMEN No.* # ovpt at lower left.	—	—	2,600

SBP B13 (P23): **100 rupees** (US$1.10)   VG   VF   UNC

Gray-blue, pink, and light green. Front: Mohammed Ali Jinnah wearing jacket and tie. Back: Bank logo; Badshahi mosque (Royal mosque) in Lahore. Solid security thread. Watermark: Mohammed Ali Jinnah. Printer: (PSPC). 166 x 92 mm.

		VG	VF	UNC
☐ a.	No date. Signature 7. Intro: 01.03.1972.	4	15	65
☐ b.	Signature 8. Intro: 1975.	—	1,600	
☐ as.	Horizontal red Urdu overprint on front; diagonal red *SPECIMEN* overprint on back; horiz. black *SPECIMEN No.* # ovpt at lower left.	—	—	2,250

1976-1982 Issues

Following the East Pakistan's independence as Bangladesh, these new Pakistani notes no longer have Bengali text nor scenes reflecting the former eastern region, such as tea plantations and jute harvesting.

SBP B14 (P28): **5 rupees** (US$0.05)   VG   VF   UNC
Brown, pink, orange, and purple. Front: Mohammed Ali Jinnah wearing jacket and tie. Back: Bank logo; railroad tracks entering Khojak Tunnel (aka Sheilla Bagh Tunnel) in Killa Abdullah district of Balochistan; without Urdu inscription beneath bank name. Solid security thread. Watermark: Mohammed Ali Jinnah. Printer: (PSPC). 128 x 72 mm.

- ☐ a. No date. Intro: 12.07.1976.   —   0.50   2
  Signature 8. 1- or 2-letter prefix.
- ☐ b. Signature 9. 2-letter prefix. Intro: 07.03.1982.   —   0.50   2
- ☐ c. 1-letter numerator in fractional prefix.   —   0.50   2
- ☐ as. Horizontal red Urdu overprint on front;   —   —   675
  diagonal red *SPECIMEN* overprint on back;
  horiz. black *SPECIMEN No.* # ovpt at lower left.

SBP B15 (P29): **10 rupees** (US$0.10)   VG   VF   UNC
Olive green, yellow, purple, and pink. Front: Mohammed Ali Jinnah wearing jacket and tie. Back: Bank logo; Mohen-Jo-Daro (Mound of the Dead) archeological site in Larkana; without Urdu inscription beneath bank name. Solid security thread. Watermark: Mohammed Ali Jinnah. Printer: (PSPC). 140 x 73 mm.

- ☐ a. No date. Intro: 12.07.1976.   —   0.50   2
  Signature 8. 1- or 2-letter prefix.
- ☐ b. Signature 9. 2-letter prefix. Intro: 01.04.1982.   —   0.50   2
- ☐ c. 1- or 2-letter numerator in fractional prefix.   —   0.50   2
- ☐ as. Diagonal red Urdu overprint on front;   —   —   850
  diagonal red *SPECIMEN* overprint on back;
  horiz. black *SPECIMEN No.* # ovpt at lower left.

SBP B16 (P30): **50 rupees** (US$0.55)   VG   VF   UNC
Burgundy, purple, orange, blue, brown, and pink. Front: Mohammed Ali Jinnah wearing jacket and tie. Back: Trees and main gate to Shahi Qila (Lahore Fort); without Urdu inscription beneath bank name; bank logo. Solid security thread. Watermark: Mohammed Ali Jinnah. Printer: (PSPC). 154 x 73 mm.

- ☐ a. No date. Intro: 29.12.1977.   1   3   12
  Signature 8. 1- or 2-letter prefix.
- ☐ b. Signature 9. 2-letter prefix. Intro: 07.03.1982.   —   2   7
- ☐ as. Diagonal red Urdu overprint on front;   —   —   1,050
  diagonal red *SPECIMEN* overprint on back;
  horiz. black *SPECIMEN No.* # ovpt at lower left.

PAKISTAN 1982 ISSUES

SBP B17 (P31): **100 rupees** (US$1.10)   VG   VF   UNC

Red, orange, and tan. Front: Mohammed Ali Jinnah wearing jacket and tie. Back: Bank logo; trees, clock tower, and buildings at Islamia College University in Peshawar; without Urdu inscription beneath bank name. Solid security thread. Watermark: Mohammed Ali Jinnah. Printer: (PSPC). 164 x 73 mm.

☐ a. No date. Intro: 12.07.1976.   —   2.50   10
       Signature 8. 1- or 2-letter prefix.
☐ b. Signature 9. 2-letter prefix without asterisk.   —   2.50   10
       Intro: 11.07.1982.
☐ c. Asterisk preceding prefix.   —   2.50   10
☐ as. Horizontal red Urdu overprint on front;   —   —   1,050
       diagonal red *SPECIMEN* overprint on back;
       horiz. black *SPECIMEN No. #* ovpt at lower left.
☐ bs. Diagonal red *SPECIMEN* and DLR oval ovpts;   —   XF   625
       horiz. red *SPECIMEN NO #* ovpt at lower left.

100-rupee notes with asterisks preceding the prefix are not replacement notes. The asterisk was added because the prefix range was reused.

1982 Issues

These notes are like the preceding issues, but with a line of Urdu inscription on the back (below the bank's name) which can be translated as "Legal livelihood is equal to prayer."

The 5- through 100-rupee notes are available with two different Urdu inscriptions on back. The original inscription (left) appears on notes issued in 1982, whereas the revised inscription (right) appears on notes issued in 1984 and after.

SBP B18 (P33): **5 rupees** (US$0.05)   VG   VF   UNC

Brown, pink, orange, and purple. Front: Mohammed Ali Jinnah wearing jacket and tie. Back: Bank logo; railroad tracks entering Khojak Tunnel (aka Sheilla Bagh Tunnel) in Killa Abdullah district of Balochistan; with Urdu inscription beneath bank name. Solid security thread. Watermark: Mohammed Ali Jinnah. Printer: (PSPC). 128 x 72 mm.

☐ a. No date. Signature 9. Intro: 1982.   —   0.50   2.50
☐ as. Diagonal red Urdu overprint on front;   —   —   775
       diagonal red *SPECIMEN* overprint on back;
       horiz. black *SPECIMEN No. #* ovpt at upper right.

SBP B19 (P34): **10 rupees** (US$0.10)   VG   VF   UNC

Olive green, yellow, purple, and pink. Front: Mohammed Ali Jinnah wearing jacket and tie. Back: Bank logo; Mohen-Jo-Daro (Mound of the Dead) archeological site in Larkana; with Urdu inscription beneath bank name. Solid security thread. Watermark: Mohammed Ali Jinnah. Printer: (PSPC). 140 x 73 mm.

☐ a. No date. Signature 9. Intro: 1982.   —   0.50   2.50
       Urdu inscription overprinted.
☐ b. Urdu inscription engraved.   —   0.50   2.50
☐ as. Diagonal red Urdu overprint on front;   —   —   700
       diagonal red *SPECIMEN* overprint on back;
       horiz. black *SPECIMEN No.#* ovpt at upper right.

1984-2006 Issues

The 5- through 100-rupee notes are like the preceding issues, but with a revised Urdu inscription on the back (below the bank's name) which can be translated as "Earning legal livelihood is equal to prayer."

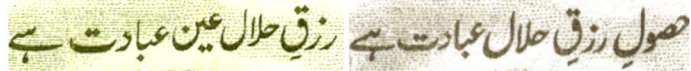

The 5- through 100-rupee notes are available with two different Urdu inscriptions on back. The original inscription (left) appears on notes issued in 1982, whereas the revised inscription (right) appears on notes issued in 1984 and after.

SBP B20 (P35): **50 rupees** (US$0.55) VG VF UNC

Burgundy, purple, orange, blue, brown, and pink. Front: Mohammed Ali Jinnah wearing jacket and tie. Back: Trees and main gate to Shahi Qila (Lahore Fort); with Urdu inscription beneath bank name; bank logo. Solid security thread. Watermark: Mohammed Ali Jinnah. Printer: (PSPC). 154 x 73 mm.

☐	a.	No date. Signature 9. Intro: 1982.	2	8	20
☐	b.	Fractional prefix.	—	—	—
☐	as.	Diagonal red Urdu overprint on front; diagonal red *SPECIMEN* overprint on back; horiz. black *SPECIMEN No.#* ovpt at upper right.	—	—	875

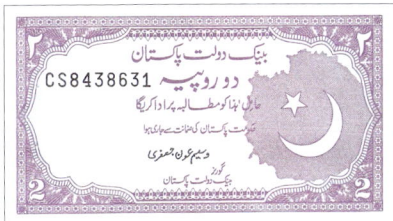

SBP B22 (P37): **2 rupees** (<US$0.05) VG VF UNC

Purple, blue, and pink. Front: Crescent moon and star. Back: Badshahi mosque (Royal mosque) in Lahore. No security thread. Watermark: Crescent moon and star. Printer: (PSPC). 108 x 60 mm.

☐	a.	No date. Intro: 24.08.1985. Signature 9. 1- or 2-letter prefix.	FV	FV	1
☐	b.	Signature 10. Intro: 10.07.1986. 2-letter prefix.	FV	FV	1
☐	c.	Signature 11. Intro: 1988.	FV	FV	0.75
☐	d.	Signature 12. Intro: 1990.	FV	FV	0.75
☐	e.	Signature 13. Intro: 1993.	FV	FV	0.75
☐	as.	Diagonal red Urdu overprint on front; diagonal red *SPECIMEN* overprint on back; horiz. black *SPECIMEN No.#* ovpt at lower right.	—	—	475

Replacement notes: Prefix 1/X.

SBP B21 (P36): **100 rupees** (US$1.10) VG VF UNC

Red, orange, and tan. Front: Mohammed Ali Jinnah wearing jacket and tie. Back: Bank logo; trees, clock tower, and buildings at Islamia College University in Peshawar; with Urdu inscription beneath bank name. Solid security thread. Watermark: Mohammed Ali Jinnah. Printer: (PSPC). 164 x 73 mm.

☐	a.	No date. Signature 9. Intro: 1982. Urdu inscription overprinted. 2-letter prefix.	—	4	15
☐	b.	1- or 2-letter numerator in fractional prefix.	—	4	15
☐	c.	Urdu inscription engraved. Prefix GZ/1 - JM/1.	—	5	20
☐	as.	Diagonal red Urdu overprint on front; diagonal red *SPECIMEN* overprint on back; horiz. black *SPECIMEN No.#* ovpt at upper right.	—	—	1,000

SBP B23 (P38): **5 rupees** (US$0.05)   VG   VF   UNC

Brown, pink, orange, and purple. Front: Mohammed Ali Jinnah wearing jacket and tie. Back: Bank logo; railroad tracks entering Khojak Tunnel (aka Sheilla Bagh Tunnel) in Killa Abdullah district of Balochistan; with revised Urdu inscription beneath bank name. Solid security thread. Watermark: Mohammed Ali Jinnah. Printer: (PSPC). 128 x 72 mm.

		VG	VF	UNC
☐ a.	No date. Signature 9. Intro: 01.04.1984. 1- or 2-letter numerator in fractional prefix.	FV	FV	1
☐ b.	Signature 10. Intro: 1986.	FV	FV	1
☐ c.	Signature 11. Intro: 1988.	FV	FV	1
☐ d.	Signature 12. Intro: 1989.	FV	FV	1
☐ e.	Signature 13. Intro: 1993.	FV	FV	1
☐ f.	3-letter prefix.	FV	FV	1
☐ g.	Signature 14. Intro: 1999.	FV	FV	1

Replacement notes: Prefix denominator X.

SBP B24 (P39): **10 rupees** (US$0.10)   VG   VF   UNC

Olive green, yellow, purple, and pink. Front: Mohammed Ali Jinnah wearing jacket and tie. Back: Bank logo; Mohen-Jo-Daro (Mound of the Dead) archeological site in Larkana; with revised Urdu inscription beneath bank name. Solid security thread. Watermark: Mohammed Ali Jinnah. Printer: (PSPC). 140 x 73 mm.

		VG	VF	UNC
☐ a.	No date. Signature 9. Intro: 1984. Partial intaglio. 1- or 2-letter numerator in fractional prefix.	FV	FV	1.50
☐ b.	Entirely lithograph.	FV	FV	1.50
☐ c.	Signature 10. Intro: 1986.	FV	FV	1.50
☐ d.	Signature 11. Intro: 1988.	FV	FV	1.50
☐ e.	Signature 12. Intro: 1989.	FV	FV	1.50
☐ f.	Signature 11. 3-letter prefix. Intro: 1990.	FV	FV	1.50
☐ g.	Signature 13. Intro: 20.07.1993.	FV	FV	1.50
☐ h.	Watermark: Smaller Jinnah's portrait. Prefix: SAA - TAZ.	FV	FV	6
☐ i.	Signature 14. Intro: 24.11.1999.	FV	FV	1.50
☐ j.	Signature 15. Intro: 2006.	FV	FV	1.50
☐ js.	Vertical *SPECIMEN* perforation.	—	—	—

Replacement notes: Prefix X or denominator X.

SBP B25 (P40): **50 rupees** (US$0.55)   VG   VF   UNC

Burgundy, purple, orange, blue, brown, and pink. Front: Mohammed Ali Jinnah wearing jacket and tie. Back: Trees and main gate to Shahi Qila (Lahore Fort); with revised Urdu inscription beneath bank name; bank logo. Solid security thread. Watermark: Mohammed Ali Jinnah. Printer: (PSPC). 154 x 73 mm.

☐ a.	No date. Intro: 01.04.1986. Signature 9. 2-letter prefix.	FV	FV	3
☐ b.	1- or 2-letter numerator in fractional prefix.	FV	FV	3
☐ c.	Signature 10. Intro: 10.07.1986.	FV	FV	3
☐ d.	Signature 11. 3-letter prefix. Intro: 1988.	FV	FV	3
☐ e.	Signature 12. Intro: 1989.	FV	FV	3
☐ f.	Signature 13. Intro: 20.07.1993.	FV	FV	3
☐ g.	Signature 14. Intro: 1999.	FV	FV	3
☐ h.	Signature 15. Intro: 2006.	FV	FV	3
☐ hs.	Vertical *SPECIMEN* perforation.	—	—	—

SBP B26 (P41): **100 rupees** (US$1.10)   VG   VF   UNC

Red, orange, and tan. Front: Mohammed Ali Jinnah wearing jacket and tie. Back: Bank logo; trees, clock tower, and buildings at Islamia College University in Peshawar; with revised Urdu inscription beneath bank name. Solid security thread. Watermark: Mohammed Ali Jinnah. Printer: (PSPC). 164 x 73 mm.

☐ a.	No date. Intro: 1986. Signature 9. 2-letter numerator in fractional prefix.	FV	FV	5.75
☐ b.	Signature 10. Intro: 1986. 1- or 2-letter numerator in fractional prefix.	FV	FV	5.75
☐ c.	3-letter prefix.	FV	FV	5.75
☐ d.	Signature 11. Intro: 1988, 1990.	FV	FV	5.75
☐ e.	Signature 12. Intro: 1989.	FV	FV	5.75
☐ f.	Signature 13. Intro: 20.07.1993.	FV	FV	5.75
☐ g.	Signature 14. Intro: 24.11.1999.	FV	FV	5.75
☐ h.	Signature 15. Intro: 2006.	FV	FV	5.75
☐ hs.	Vertical *SPECIMEN* perforation.	—	—	—

SBP B27 (P42): **500 rupees** (demonetized 01.10.2012) VG VF UNC
Blue-green, olive green, pink, and orange. Front: Mohammed Ali Jinnah wearing jacket and tie. Back: State Bank of Pakistan headquarters building in Karachi; bank logo. Solid security thread with printed *STATE BANK OF PAKISTAN*. Watermark: Mohammed Ali Jinnah. Printer: (PSPC). 175 x 72 mm.

			VG	VF	UNC
☐	a.	No date. Intro: 01.04.1986. Signature 9. 1-letter prefix.	FV	FV	30
☐	b.	Signature 10. Intro: 1986.	FV	FV	30
☐	c.	Signature 11. 1- or 2-letter prefix. Intro: '88, '90.	FV	FV	30
☐	d.	Signature 12. 2-letter prefix. Intro: 1989.	FV	FV	30
☐	e.	Signature 13. Intro: 20.07.1993.	FV	FV	30
☐	f.	Signature 14. Intro: 24.11.1999.	FV	FV	30
☐	g.	Signature 15. Intro: 2006.	FV	FV	30
☐	as.	Diagonal red Urdu overprint on front; diagonal red *SPECIMEN* overprint on back; horiz. black *SPECIMEN No.#* ovpt at lower left.	—	—	1,000
☐	gs.	Vertical *SPECIMEN* perforation.	—	—	—

SBP B28 (P43): **1,000 rupees** (US$11) VG VF UNC
Dark blue, green, blue, and orange. Front: Mohammed Ali Jinnah wearing jacket and tie. Back: tomb of Mughal Emperor Jahangir near the town of Shahdara Bagh in Lahore; bank logo. Solid security thread with printed *STATE BANK OF PAKISTAN*. Watermark: Mohammed Ali Jinnah. Printer: (PSPC). 174 x 73 mm.

			VG	VF	UNC
☐	a.	No date. Signature 10. Intro: 18.07.1988. 1-letter prefix.	FV	FV	40
☐	b.	Signature 11. Intro: 1988, 1990.	FV	FV	55
☐	c.	Sig. 13. Intro: 20.07.1993. 1- or 2-letter prefix.	FV	FV	30
☐	d.	Signature 14. Intro: 24.11.1999. 2-letter prefix.	FV	FV	50
☐	e.	Signature 15. Intro: 2006.	FV	FV	50
☐	as.	Diagonal red Urdu overprint on front; diagonal red *SPECIMEN* overprint on back; horiz. black *SPECIMEN No.#* ovpt at lower left.	—	—	1,125
☐	es.	Vertical *SPECIMEN* perforation.	—	—	—

1997 Commemorative Issues

Five million 5-rupee notes with prefix COM were issued to commemorate the Golden Jubilee (50th anniversary) of independence. At left front is a starburst design with the Urdu phrase "Pachas Sala Jashan-e-Azadi" (Fifty Year Anniversary of Freedom) above 50 in Urdu numerals at center and 1947-1997 in Western numerals below.

SBP B29 (P44): **5 rupees** (US$0.05)　　　　　　　　VG　VF　UNC
Purple, light green, and orange. Front: Mohammed Ali Jinnah. Back: Trees and tomb of Shah Rukn-e-Alam in Multan; bank logo. Solid security thread. Watermark: Mohammed Ali Jinnah. Printer: (PSPC). 130 x 72 mm.

☐	a.	1997. Signature 13. Intro: 13.08.1997.	— —	1
☐	p.	No signature; no serial number; horizontal *SPECIMEN* perforation.	— —	100

2005-2014 Issues

These notes feature entirely new designs and vibrant colors.

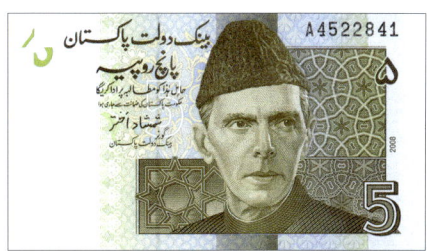

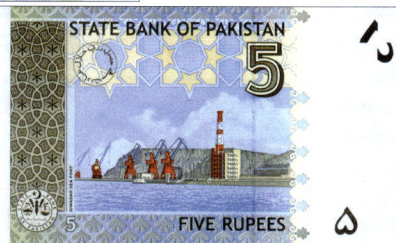

SBP B30 (P53): **5 rupees** (demonetized 01.01.2012)　　VG　VF　UNC
Greenish gray, blue, yellow, and red. Front: Mohammed Ali Jinnah wearing national dress (sherwani). Back: Bank logo; gantry cranes at Gwadar Sea Port. Solid security thread with printed *STATE BANK OF PAKISTAN 5*. Watermark: Mohammed Ali Jinnah and electrotype *5*. Printer: (Pakistan Security Printing Corporation). 115 x 65 mm.

☐	a.	2008. Signature 15. 1- or 2-letter prefix. Intro: 08.07.2008.	FV FV	1
☐	b.	2009. Signature 16. 2-letter prefix. Intro: 15.05.2009.	FV FV	1
☐	c.	2010.	FV FV	1
☐	as.	Horizontal *SPECIMEN* perforation.	— —	50
☐	bs.	Horizontal *SPECIMEN* perforation.	— —	50

Replacement notes: Prefix X.

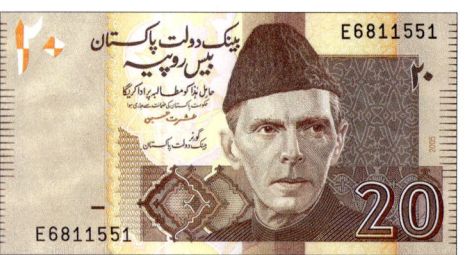

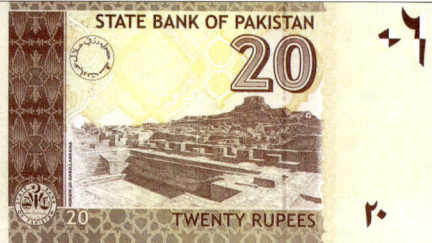

SBP B31 (P45 & P54): **10 rupees** (US$0.10)   VG   VF   UNC

Olive green, orange, and violet. Front: Mohammed Ali Jinnah wearing national dress (sherwani). Back: Bank logo; flag atop Khyber Pass stone gateway in Peshawar. Solid security thread with printed *STATE BANK OF PAKISTAN 10*. Watermark: Mohammed Ali Jinnah and electrotype *10*. Printer: (Pakistan Security Printing Corporation). 115 x 65 mm.

		VG	VF	UNC
☐ a.	2006. Signature 15. 1- or 2-letter prefix. Prefix S-W notes have glossy anti-soiling varnish; prefix Y onwards have semi-matte varnish.	FV	FV	1
☐ b.	2007. 2-letter prefix.	FV	FV	1
☐ c.	2008.	FV	FV	1
☐ d.	2009. Signature 16. Intro: 15.05.2009.	FV	FV	1
☐ e.	2010.	FV	FV	1
☐ f.	Signature 17. Intro: 03.01.2011.	FV	FV	1
☐ g.	2011.	FV	FV	1
☐ h.	Signature 18.	FV	FV	1
☐ i.	2012.	FV	FV	1
☐ j.	2013.	FV	FV	1
☐ k.	2014.	FV	FV	1
☐ l.	Signature 19.	FV	FV	1
☐ as.	Horizontal *SPECIMEN* perforation.	—	—	55
☐ ds.	Horizontal *SPECIMEN* perforation.	—	—	55
☐ fs.	Horizontal *SPECIMEN* perforation.	—	—	55
☐ hs.	Horizontal *SPECIMEN* perforation.	—	—	55

Replacement notes: Prefix X.

SBP B32 (P46): **20 rupees** (US$0.20)   VG   VF   UNC

Brown, yellow, and orange. Front: Mohammed Ali Jinnah wearing national dress (sherwani). Back: Bank logo; Mohen-Jo-Daro (Mound of the Dead) archeological site in Larkana. Solid security thread with printed *STATE BANK OF PAKISTAN 20*. Watermark: Mohammed Ali Jinnah and electrotype *20*. Printer: (Pakistan Security Printing Corporation). 123 x 65 mm.

		VG	VF	UNC
☐ a.	2005. Signature 14. 1- or 2-letter prefix. Intro: 13.08.2005.	FV	FV	1.50
☐ b.	2006. Signature 15. 2-letter prefix.	FV	FV	1.25
☐ c.	2007.	FV	FV	1.25
☐ as.	No overprint or perforation; all-zero s/n.	—	—	100
☐ bs.	Vertical *SPECIMEN* perforation.	—	—	—

Replacement notes: Prefix X.

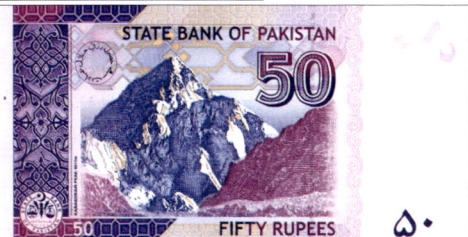

SBP B33 (P55): **20 rupees** (US$0.20)　　　　　　　　VG　VF　UNC

Orange, green, and yellow. Front: Mohammed Ali Jinnah wearing national dress (sherwani). Back: Bank logo; Mohen-Jo-Daro (Mound of the Dead) archeological site in Larkana. Solid security thread with printed *STATE BANK OF PAKISTAN 20*. Watermark: Mohammed Ali Jinnah and electrotype *20*. Printer: (Pakistan Security Printing Corporation). 123 x 65 mm.

			VG	VF	UNC
☐	a.	2007. Signature 15. 1- or 2-letter prefix. Intro: 22.03.2008.	FV	FV	1
☐	b.	2008. 1- or 2-letter prefix.	FV	FV	1
☐	c.	2009. Signature 16. 2-letter prefix. Intro: 15.05.2009.	FV	FV	1
☐	d.	2010.	FV	FV	1
☐	e.	Signature 17. Intro: 03.01.2011.	FV	FV	1
☐	f.	2011.	FV	FV	1
☐	g.	Signature 18.	FV	FV	1
☐	h.	2012.	FV	FV	1
☐	i.	2013.	FV	FV	1
☐	j.	2014. Signature 19.	FV	FV	1
☐	as.	Horizontal *SPECIMEN* perforation.	—	—	—
☐	cs.	Horizontal *SPECIMEN* perforation.	—	—	—
☐	es.	Horizontal *SPECIMEN* perforation.	—	—	—
☐	gs.	Horizontal *SPECIMEN* perforation.	—	—	—

Like preceding issues, but colors changed to avoid confusion with 5,000-rupee note.
Replacement notes: Prefix X.

SBP B34 (P47 & P56): **50 rupees** (US$0.55)　　　　　　　　VG　VF　UNC

Purple, violet, and orange. Front: Mohammed Ali Jinnah wearing national dress (sherwani). Back: Bank logo; K2 peak in Karakorum Mountains between Pakistan and China. Solid security thread with printed *STATE BANK OF PAKISTAN 50*. Watermark: Mohammed Ali Jinnah and electrotype *50*. Printer: (Pakistan Security Printing Corporation). 131 x 65 mm.

			VG	VF	UNC
☐	a.	2008. Signature 15. 1- or 2-letter prefix. Intro: 08.07.2008.	FV	FV	2
☐	b.	2009. Sig. 16. 2-letter prefix. Intro: 15.05.2009.	FV	FV	1.50
☐	c.	2010.	FV	FV	1
☐	d.	Signature 17. Intro: 03.01.2011.	FV	FV	1
☐	e.	2011.	FV	FV	1
☐	f.	Signature 18.	FV	FV	1
☐	g.	2012.	FV	FV	1
☐	h.	2013.	FV	FV	1
☐	i.	2014. Signature 19.	FV	FV	1
☐	as.	Horizontal *SPECIMEN* perforation.	—	—	50
☐	bs.	Horizontal *SPECIMEN* perforation.	—	—	50
☐	ds.	Horizontal *SPECIMEN* perforation.	—	—	50
☐	fs.	Horizontal *SPECIMEN* perforation.	—	—	50

SBP B35 (P48 & P57): **100 rupees** (US$1.10)   VG   VF   UNC

Red, brown, and orange. Front: Mohammed Ali Jinnah wearing national dress (sherwani). Back: Bank logo; trees and Quaid-e-Azam (Great Leader, i.e. Mohammed Ali Jinnah) residency in Ziarat-Quetta. Windowed security thread with demetalized *100*. Watermark: Mohammed Ali Jinnah and electrotype *100*. Printer: (Pakistan Security Printing Corporation). 140 x 65 mm.

☐	a.	2006. Sig. 15. 1-letter prefix. Intro: 10.11.2006.	FV	FV	5
☐	b.	2007. 1- or 2-letter prefix.	FV	FV	4.50
☐	c.	2008. 2-letter prefix.	FV	FV	4
☐	d.	2009. Signature 16. Intro: 15.05.2009.	FV	FV	4
☐	e.	2010.	FV	FV	2
☐	f.	Signature 17. Intro: 03.01.2011.	FV	FV	2
☐	g.	2011.	FV	FV	2
☐	h.	Signature 18.	FV	FV	2
☐	i.	2012.	FV	FV	2
☐	j.	2013.	FV	FV	2
☐	as.	Horizontal *SPECIMEN* perforation.	—	—	—
☐	ds.	Horizontal *SPECIMEN* perforation.	—	—	—
☐	fs.	Horizontal *SPECIMEN* perforation.	—	—	—
☐	hs.	Horizontal *SPECIMEN* perforation.	—	—	—

SBP B37 (P49): **500 rupees** (US$5.50)   VG   VF   UNC

Aqua, olive green, and light blue. Front: Mohammed Ali Jinnah wearing national dress (sherwani); OVI flag. Back: Bank logo; Badshahi mosque (Royal mosque) in Lahore. Windowed security thread with demetalized *500*. Watermark: Mohammed Ali Jinnah and electrotype *500*. Printer: (Pakistan Security Printing Corporation). 149 x 65 mm.

☐	a.	2009. Sig. 16. 1-letter prefix. Intro: 25.01.2010.	FV	FV	18
☐	b.	2010.	FV	FV	15
☐	c.	Signature 17. Intro: 03.01.2011.	FV	FV	15
☐	d.	2011. 1- or 2-letter prefix.	FV	FV	15
☐	e.	Signature 18. 2-letter prefix.	FV	FV	15
☐	f.	2012.	FV	FV	15
☐	g.	2013.	FV	FV	15
☐	h.	2014.	FV	FV	15
☐	as.	Horizontal *SPECIMEN* perforation.	—	—	—
☐	cs.	Horizontal *SPECIMEN* perforation.	—	—	—
☐	es.	Horizontal *SPECIMEN* perforation.	—	—	—

Like preceding issues, but with flag in green-to-magenta OVI added at right on the front.

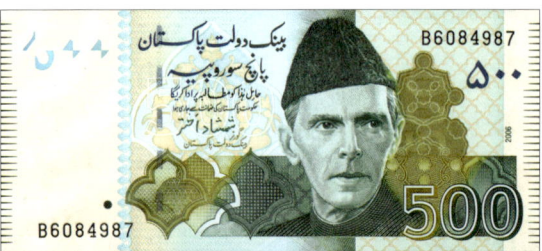

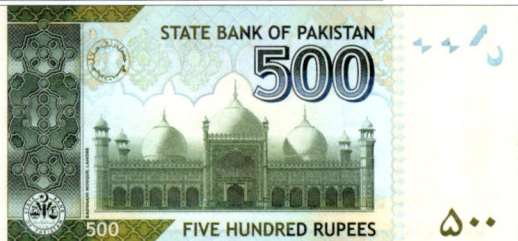

SBP B36 (P49): **500 rupees** (US$5.50)   VG   VF   UNC

Aqua, olive green, and light blue. Front: Mohammed Ali Jinnah wearing national dress (sherwani). Back: Bank logo; Badshahi mosque (Royal mosque) in Lahore. Windowed security thread with demetalized *500*. Watermark: Mohammed Ali Jinnah and electrotype *500*. Printer: (Pakistan Security Printing Corporation). 149 x 65 mm.

☐	a.	2006. Sig. 15. 1-letter prefix. Intro: 10.11.2006.	FV	FV	25
☐	b.	2007. 1- or 2-letter prefix.	FV	FV	20
☐	c.	2008. 2-letter prefix.	FV	FV	20
☐	as.	Horizontal *SPECIMEN* perforation.	—	—	—

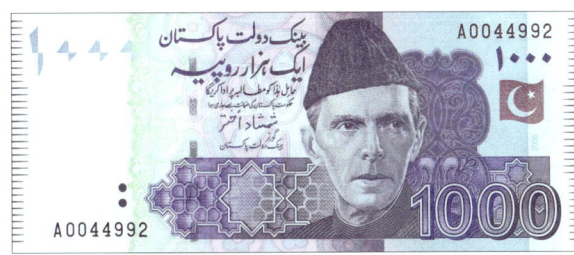

SBP B38 (P50): **1,000 rupees** (US$11)   VG   VF   UNC

Purple, light green, and light blue. Front: Mohammed Ali Jinnah wearing national dress (sherwani); OVI flag. Back: Bank logo; trees, clock tower, and buildings at Islamia College University in Peshawar. Windowed security thread with demetalized *1000*. Watermark: Mohammed Ali Jinnah and electrotype *1000*. Printer: (Pakistan Security Printing Corporation). 155 x 65 mm.

		VG	VF	UNC
☐ a.	2006. Sig. 15. 1-letter prefix. Intro: 26.02.2007.	FV	FV	45
☐ b.	2007.	FV	FV	50
☐ c.	2008. 1- or 2-letter prefix.	FV	FV	35
☐ d.	2009. Sig. 16. 2-letter prefix. Intro: 15.05.2009.	FV	FV	30
☐ e.	2010.	FV	FV	30
☐ f.	Signature 17. Intro: 03.01.2011.	FV	FV	30
☐ g.	2011.	FV	FV	25
☐ h.	Signature 18. Intro: 10.02.2012.	FV	FV	25
☐ i.	2012.	FV	FV	25
☐ j.	2013.	FV	FV	25
☐ k.	2014.	FV	FV	25
☐ l.	Signature 19.	FV	FV	25
☐ as.	Horizontal *SPECIMEN* perforation.	—	—	150
☐ ds.	Horizontal *SPECIMEN* perforation.	—	—	150
☐ fs.	Horizontal *SPECIMEN* perforation.	—	—	150
☐ hs.	Horizontal *SPECIMEN* perforation.	—	—	150

This note caused a controversy because the flag at right front is lilac rather than green, and packs of note were bound with a paper band, not stapled as in the past. The bank explained that the Pakistani flag does not appear on any SBP notes; the crescent and five-pointed star is merely a security feature printed with magenta-to-green OVI. Furthermore, stapling was halted to increase the longevity of the notes.

SBP B39 (P51): **5,000 rupees** (US$55)   VG   VF   UNC

Orange, brown, and red. Front: Mohammed Ali Jinnah wearing national dress (sherwani); OVI flag. Back: Bank logo; Faisal mosque in Islamabad. Windowed security thread with demetalized *5000*. Watermark: Mohammed Ali Jinnah and electrotype *5000*. Printer: (Pakistan Security Printing Corporation). 165 x 65 mm.

		VG	VF	UNC
☐ a.	2006. Signature 15. Intro: 27.05.2006.	FV	FV	200
☐ b.	2007.	FV	FV	200
☐ c.	2008.	FV	FV	200
☐ d.	2009. Signature 16. Intro: 15.05.2009.	FV	FV	200
☐ e.	2012. Signature 18.	FV	FV	200
☐ f.	2013.	FV	FV	200
☐ as.	Horizontal *SPECIMEN* perforation.	—	—	—
☐ ds.	Horizontal *SPECIMEN* perforation.	—	—	—
☐ es.	Horizontal *SPECIMEN* perforation.	—	—	—

Haj Issues

In an effort to control the foreign exchange of its currency, Pakistan issued special notes for use only by Muslims making the pilgrimage, called the Haj, to Mecca in Saudi Arabia, as well as other holy sites in Iraq. The Haj notes were not legal tender in Pakistan, but they could be used in Saudi Arabia to purchase Saudi riyals and were then remitted to Pakistan via Saudi Arabian banks.

1950 Haj Issues

The first so-called "Haj note" issued by the government was the 100-rupee note using the same design as the existing Government of Pakistan note of that denomination, but red in color instead of green, and with an overprint on the front.

SBP BR1 (PR1): 100 rupees (withdrawn April 1994)   VG   VF   UNC
Red. Front: Guilloche patterns; horizontal black *FOR PILGRIMS FROM PAKISTAN FOR USE IN SAUDI ARABIA AND IRAQ* overprint. Back: Guilloche patterns. No security thread. Watermark: Crescent moon and star. Printer: (TDLR). 166 x 92 mm.

- ☐ a. No date. Sig. hulam Mohammed. Intro: 1950.
- ☐ as. Black DLR oval overprint; horiz. black *SPECIMEN NO. #* ovpt at lower left.   —   XF   20,000

1951 Haj Issues

The introduction of the first Haj note cut down considerably on the illicit exportation and repatriation of Pakistani currency, so a 10-rupee Haj note was subsequently authorized, based upon the same design as the new regular State Bank of Pakistan note issued on 1 September 1951, but green in color instead of brown. The overprint on the front of this and subsequent Haj notes is slightly different than that used on the first 100-rupee Haj note in that it specifies that the notes are for use in Saudi Arabia only, thereby excluding Iraq.

A 100-rupee note with the same overprint as this 10-rupee note is referenced in an undated press release by the Bank of Pakistan, but no such note has been confirmed to exist.

SBP BR2 (PR2): 10 rupees (withdrawn April 1994)   VG   VF   UNC
Green. Front: Shalimar Gardens in Lahore; bank logo; horizontal black *FOR HAJ PILGRIMS FROM PAKISTAN FOR USE IN SAUDI ARABIA ONLY* overprint. Back: Tombs near Thatta. Solid security thread. Watermark: Crescent moon and star. Printer: (TDLR). 146 x 82 mm.

- ☐ a. No date. Signature 1. Intro: 1951.   —   1,000   —
- ☐ b. Signature 2. Unconfirmed.   —   —   —
- ☐ c. Signature 3. Intro: 1960.   —   1,000   —
- ☐ d. Signature 5. Intro: 1967.   —   1,000   —
- ☐ as. Diagonal red hollow *SPECIMEN* overprint.   —   XF   8,500
- ☐ bs. Horizontal *SPECIMEN OF NO VALUE* perf.   —   —   6,250

1970-1972 Haj Issues

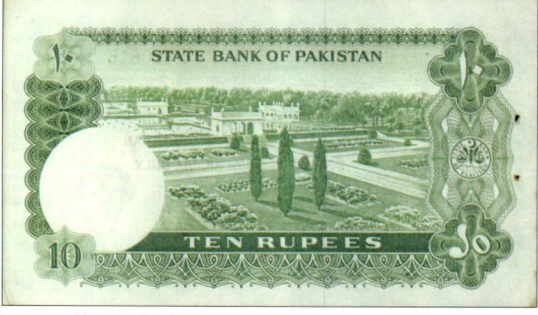

SBP BR3 (PR3): 10 rupees (demonetized 1972)   VG   VF   UNC
Green. Front: Mohammed Ali Jinnah wearing jacket and tie; horizontal black *FOR HAJ PILGRIMS FROM PAKISTAN FOR USE IN SAUDI ARABIA ONLY* overprint. Back: Shalimar Gardens in Lahore; bank logo. Solid security thread. Watermark: Mohammed Ali Jinnah. Printer: (PSPC). 148 x 82 mm.

- ☐ a. No date. Signature 5. Intro: 1970.   250   1,000   3,000
- ☐ b. Signature 6. Intro: 1971.   125   500   2,000

1975-1978 Haj Issues

SBP BR4 (PR4): **10 rupees** (withdrawn April 1994)   VG   VF   UNC
Purple. Front: Mohammed Ali Jinnah wearing jacket and tie; horizontal black *FOR HAJ PILGRIMS FROM PAKISTAN FOR USE IN SAUDI ARABIA ONLY* overprint. Back: Shalimar Gardens in Lahore; bank logo. Solid security thread. Watermark: Mohammed Ali Jinnah. Printer: (PSPC). 148 x 82 mm.
   ☐ a. No date. Signature 7. Intro: 1972.   100   150   200

SBP BR6 (PR6): **10 rupees** (withdrawn April 1994)   VG   VF   UNC
Blue. Front: Mohammed Ali Jinnah wearing jacket and tie; horizontal black *FOR HAJ PILGRIMS FROM PAKISTAN FOR USE IN SAUDI ARABIA ONLY* overprint. Back: Bank logo; Mohen-Jo-Daro (Mound of the Dead) archeological site in Larkana; without Urdu inscription beneath bank name. Solid security thread. Watermark: Mohammed Ali Jinnah. Printer: (PSPC). 140 x 73 mm.
   ☐ a. No date. Signature 9. Intro: 1978.   —   —   —

SBP BR5 (PR5): **100 rupees** (withdrawn April 1994)   VG   VF   UNC
Brown. Front: Mohammed Ali Jinnah wearing jacket and tie; horizontal black *FOR HAJ PILGRIMS FROM PAKISTAN FOR USE IN SAUDI ARABIA ONLY* overprint. Back: Bank logo; Badshahi mosque (Royal mosque) in Lahore. Solid security thread. Watermark: Mohammed Ali Jinnah. Printer: (PSPC). 166 x 92 mm.
   ☐ a. No date. Signature 7. Intro: 1972.   500   1,100   2,500

SBP BR7 (PR6): **10 rupees** (withdrawn April 1994)   VG   VF   UNC
Blue. Front: Mohammed Ali Jinnah wearing jacket and tie; horizontal black *FOR HAJ PILGRIMS FROM PAKISTAN FOR USE IN SAUDI ARABIA ONLY* overprint. Back: Bank logo; Mohen-Jo-Daro (Mound of the Dead) archeological site in Larkana; with Urdu inscription beneath bank name. Solid security thread. Watermark: Mohammed Ali Jinnah. Printer: (PSPC). 140 x 73 mm.
   ☐ a. No date. Signature 9. Intro: 1978.   4   7   20

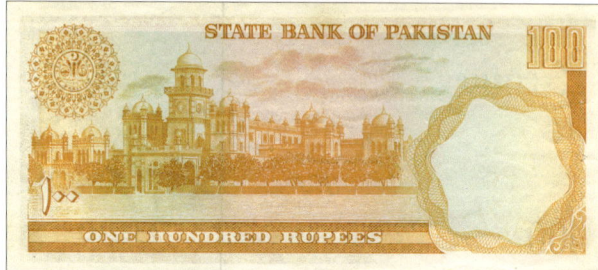

SBP BR8 (PR7): **100 rupees** (withdrawn April 1994)   VG VF UNC
Orange. Front: Mohammed Ali Jinnah wearing jacket and tie; horizontal black *FOR HAJ PILGRIMS FROM PAKISTAN FOR USE IN SAUDI ARABIA ONLY* overprint. Back: Bank logo; trees, clock tower, and buildings at Islamia College University in Peshawar; without Urdu inscription beneath bank name. Solid security thread. Watermark: Mohammed Ali Jinnah. Printer: (PSPC). 164 x 73 mm.

☐	a. No date. Signature 8. Intro: 1975.	30	60	125
☐	b. Signature 9. Intro: July 1978.	5	10	20

The use of Haj notes continued until 1994, although the signatures were not always updated to reflect the current governor of the State Bank of Pakistan. All Haj notes were withdrawn in April 1994.

Acknowledgements

This chapter was compiled with the generous assistance of Sejin Ahn, Brent Arthurson, Thomas Augustsson, Jim W.-C. Chen, Jean-Michel Engels, Chris Hall, Murray Hanewich, Jarno Komulainen, Takis Kouvatseas, Claudio Marana, Qaisar Miana, Victor M. González Miguel, Peter Mosselberger (www.banknote.ws), Hans-Dieter Müeller, Sam Nakhjavani (www.foreignpapermoney.com), Alexander Petrov, George Provencal, Yahya Qureshi, Jürg Rindlisbacher, Gergely Scheidl (banknoteshop@gmx.net), Stack's Bowers & Ponterio (www.StacksBowers.com), Bill Stubkjaer, Peter Symes, Frank van Tiel, Ludek Vostal, Tristan Williams, and others.

Sources

Bohora, Anil R. "The Indian Rupee: Used Around the World." *IBNS Journal*. Volume 48 Number 4. p.43.

Bokhari, Jamal and Anil R. Bohora. "Banknotes of Early Pakistan: Payment Refused in India." *IBNS Journal*. Volume 50 Number 3. p.40.

Cuhaj, George S. *Standard Catalog of World Paper Money, General Issues, 1368-1960*. 14th edition. 2012. ISBN 978-1-4402-3090-5. Krause Publications (www.krausebooks.com), 700 East State St., Iola, WI, 54990-0001.

Cuhaj, George S. *Standard Catalog of World Paper Money, Modern Issues, 1961-Present*. 18th edition. 2012. ISBN 978-1-4402-2956-5. Krause Publications (www.krausebooks.com), 700 East State St., Iola, WI, 54990-0001.

Hessler, Gene. "Joseph Lawrence Keen—British Engraver—1919-2004." *IBNS Journal*. Volume 43 Number 2. p.12.

Hessler, Gene. "Stanley Doubtfire, British Engraver." *IBNS Journal*. Volume 44 Number 1. p.21.

Joiya, Dr. Malik Aftab Maqbool. "Letters to the Editor." *IBNS Journal*. Volume 50 Number 4. p.8.

Kasbati, Rafiq and Yahya Qureshi. *Bank Notes & Coins Catalogue of Pakistan (1948-2003)*. 1st edition. 2003. Rafiq Kasbati & Yahya Qureshi, 7-Cochiwala Market, Karachi, 74000, Pakistan.

Symes, Peter. "The Haj Notes of Pakistan." *IBNS Journal*. Volume 38 Number 3. p.34.

Symes, Peter. "The Banknotes of Bangladesh—The First Ten Years." *IBNS Journal*. Volume 51 Number 1. p.20.

Symes, Peter. Reference Site for Islamic Banknotes (www.islamicbanknotes.com).

Symes, Peter. "The Bank Notes of Pakistan-1947 to 1972." *IBNS Journal*. Volume 38 Number 4. p.6.

Symes, Peter. "The Pakistan Overprints of Bangladesh." *IBNS Journal*. Volume 39 Number 3. p.14.

Symes, Peter. "The Bank Notes of Pakistan 1972-2000." *IBNS Journal*. Volume 39 Number 4. p.6.

Symes, Peter. "Bangladesh Overprints - An Update." *IBNS Journal*. Volume 44 Number 1. p.32.

Share Your Input, Info, and Images

This catalog is believed to be complete and correct as of the time of publication. Prices and face values were last updated 24 August 2012. Please report errors or omissions so that corrections may be made. If you can more precisely identify the name or location of anything depicted on a note, please share that information. Furthermore, if you own an unlisted type or variety, please submit scans of the front and back of the note so that it can be documented. Scans should be 300 dots per inch, 100% actual size, 24-bit color, saved as *uncompressed* JPEG files, and sent to owen@banknotenews.com. Be sure to fully describe all attributes of the note which are not apparent upon visual inspection of the images alone, such as physical dimension, watermark, and security thread.

Palestine

For earlier issues, see Egypt.

Monetary System
27.02.1927: 1 Palestine pound = 1,000 mils

Palestine Currency Board

The Palestine Currency Board (PCB) was formed in London on 15 June 1926. The passage of the Palestine Currency Order of His Majesty in council on 7 February 1927 declared as legal tender the Palestine pound, equal in value to the British pound sterling and divided into 1,000 mils.

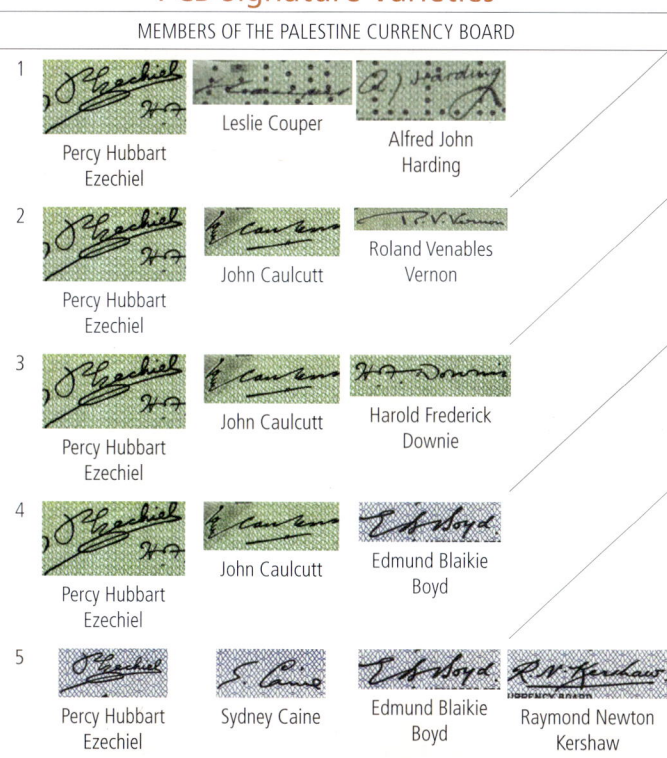

PCB Signature Varieties
MEMBERS OF THE PALESTINE CURRENCY BOARD

1. Percy Hubbart Ezechiel — Leslie Couper — Alfred John Harding
2. Percy Hubbart Ezechiel — John Caulcutt — Roland Venables Vernon
3. Percy Hubbart Ezechiel — John Caulcutt — Harold Frederick Downie
4. Percy Hubbart Ezechiel — John Caulcutt — Edmund Blaikie Boyd
5. Percy Hubbart Ezechiel — Sydney Caine — Edmund Blaikie Boyd — Raymond Newton Kershaw
6. Percy Hubbart Ezechiel — Sydney Caine — Christopher Gilbert Eastwood — Raymond Newton Kershaw

1927--1945 Issues

On 1 November 1927 the banknotes of the Palestine Currency Board were placed into circulation. These notes carry text in the three official languages of Palestine: Arabic, English, and Hebrew. Prior to this release, Egyptian notes were legal tender in Palestine and remained so until 31 March 1928. British Treasury 1-pound notes and Bank of England 5-pound notes were also legal tender in those areas of Palestine occupied by the British in 1918.

PCB B1 (P6): **500 mils** (demonetized 16.09.1948)   Good Fine XF
Purple and green. Front: Rachel's Tomb on the West Bank near Bethlehem. Back: Tower of David (Migdal David) citadel in Jerusalem. No security thread. Watermark: Olive sprig. Printer: *THOMAS DE LA RUE & COMPANY, LIMITED, LONDON*. 127 x 76 mm.

a.	1st September 1927. Signature 1. Prefix A.	1,500	2,500	5,000
b.	30th September, 1929. Signature 2. Prefix A - D.	1,000	2,000	3,500
c.	20th April, 1939. Signature 3. Prefix D - J. Different serial number font.	300	650	2,500
d.	15th August, 1945. Signature 6. Prefix J - K. Prefix L notes were unissued.	400	500	1,750
as.	Horizontal *CANCELLED* perforation.	—	—	—
bs.	Horizontal *CANCELLED* perforation.	—	—	—
ds.	Horizontal *CANCELLED* perforation.	—	—	—
t.	Color trial: Red dated 1st September 1927	—	—	—

PCB B2 (P7): **1 pound** (demonetized 16.09.1948) **Good Fine XF**

Green. Front: Dome of the Rock on the Temple Mount in Jerusalem. Back: Tower of David (Migdal David) citadel in Jerusalem. No security thread. Watermark: Olive sprig. Printer: *THOMAS DE LA RUE & COMPANY, LIMITED, LONDON*. 165 x 89 mm.

☐	a.	1st September, 1927. Signature 1. Prefix A - B.	500	1,000	3,500
☐	b.	30th September, 1929. Signature 2. Prefix B - H.	350	750	3,000
☐	c.	20th April, 1939. Signature 3. Prefix H - Z. Different serial number font.	250	700	1,500
☐	d.	1st January, 1944. Signature 5. Prefix A/1 - C/1. Prefix D/1 notes were unissued.	350	750	2,000
☐	as.	Horizontal *CANCELLED* perforation.	—	—	—
☐	bs.	Horizontal *CANCELLED* perforation.	—	—	—
☐	ds.	Horizontal *CANCELLED* perforation.	—	—	—
☐	t.	Color trial: Orange dated 30th September, 1929.	—	XF	21,000

PCB B3 (P8): **5 pounds** (demonetized 16.09.1948) **Good Fine XF**

Red and green. Front: Crusader's Tower in Ramleh. Back: Tower of David (Migdal David) citadel in Jerusalem. No security thread. Watermark: Olive sprig. Printer: *THOMAS DE LA RUE & COMPANY, LIMITED, LONDON*. 192 x 101 mm.

☐	a.	1st September, 1927. Signature 1. Prefix A.	—	45,000	—
☐	b.	30th September, 1929. Signature 2. Prefix A - B.	1,000	2,250	5,000
☐	c.	20th April, 1939. Signature 3. Prefix B - D. Different serial number font.	650	1,500	3,000
☐	d.	1st January, 1944. Signature 5. Prefix D - F.	750	1,750	3,500
☐	as.	Horizontal *CANCELLED* perforation.	—	—	—
☐	bs.	Horizontal *CANCELLED* perforation.	—	—	—
☐	t.	Color trial: Green dated 30th September, 1929.	—	XF	25,500

PCB B4 (P9): **10 pounds** (demonetized 16.09.1948)　　**Good　Fine　XF**

Blue and green. Front: Crusader's Tower in Ramleh. Back: Tower of David (Migdal David) citadel in Jerusalem. No security thread. Watermark: Olive sprig. Printer: *THOMAS DE LA RUE & COMPANY, LIMITED, LONDON*. 192 x 101 mm.

			Good	Fine	XF
☐	a.	1st September,1927. Signature 1. Prefix A.	—	60,000	—
☐	b.	30th September,1929. Signature 2. Prefix A.	1,000	3,000	6,000
☐	c.	7th September,1939. Signature 3. Prefix A - B. Different serial number font.	750	1,500	4,000
☐	d.	1st January,1944. Signature 5. Prefix B - C.	1,000	3,000	6,000
☐	as.	Horizontal *CANCELLED* perforation.	—	—	—
☐	ds.	Horizontal *CANCELLED* perforation.	—	—	13,500
☐	t1.	Color trial: Brown dated 30th September,1929.	—	XF	22,000
☐	t2.	Color trial: Brown and green dated 7th September,1939.	—	—	—

PCB B5 (P10): **50 pounds** (demonetized 16.09.1948)　　**Good　Fine　XF**

Purple. Front: Crusader's Tower in Ramleh. Back: Tower of David (Migdal David) citadel in Jerusalem. No security thread. Watermark: Olive sprig. Printer: *THOMAS DE LA RUE & COMPANY, LIMITED, LONDON*. 192 x 101 mm.

			Good	Fine	XF
☐	a.	1st September,1927. Signature 1. Prefix A.	—	—	—
☐	b.	30th September,1929. Signature 2. Prefix A.	—	—	65,000
☐	c.	7th September,1939. Signature 3. Prefix A. Different serial number font.	—	—	75,000
☐	as.	Horizontal *CANCELLED* perforation.	—	—	—
☐	bs.	Horizontal *CANCELLED* perforation.	—	—	100,000
☐	cs.	Horizontal *CANCELLED* perforation.	—	—	—
☐	t.	Color trial: Orange dated 30th September,1929.	—	—	—

All but 82 of these notes were redeemed by the Bank of England.

PCB B6 (P11): **100 pounds** (demonetized 16.09.1948)   Good   Fine   XF
Purple. Front: Crusader's Tower in Ramleh. Back: Tower of David (Migdal David) citadel in Jerusalem. No security thread. Watermark: Olive sprig. Printer: THOMAS DE LA RUE & COMPANY, LIMITED, LONDON. 192 x 101 mm.

☐	a.	1st September, 1927. Signature 1. Prefix A.	—	—	—
☐	b.	30th September, 1929. Signature 2. Prefix A.	—	—	—
☐	c.	10th September, 1942. Signature 4. Prefix A. Unconfirmed.	—	—	—
☐	as.	Horizontal CANCELLED perforation.	—	—	—
☐	bs.	Horizontal CANCELLED perforation.	—	—	125,000
☐	cs.	Horizontal CANCELLED perforation.	—	—	—

All but 8 of these notes were redeemed by the Bank of England.

Looking Forward

For later issues, see Israel and Jordan.

Acknowledgements

This chapter was compiled with the generous assistance of Mahdi Bseiso (www.jordancurrency.com), Heritage Auctions (HA.com), Wally Myers, Ibrahim Salem, Udi Sarfati, Bill Stubkjaer, Shlomo Tepper, Tristan Williams, Avish Yeshurun, and others.

Sources

Arkin, Yigal. *Banknotes and Coins of Israel 1927-2006*. 2006. ISBN 965-90754-2-1. Bank of Israel Currency Department. Jerusalem.

Cuhaj, George S. *Standard Catalog of World Paper Money, General Issues, 1368-1960*. 14th edition. 2012. ISBN 978-1-4402-3090-5. Krause Publications (www.krausebooks.com), 700 East State St., Iola, WI, 54990-0001.

Dabbah, Raphael. *Currency Notes of the Palestine Currency Board*. ISBN 965-90650-1-9. www.palestinecurrency.com.

Dabbah, Raphael. "Currency Note of the Palestine Currency Board - an Unknown 1939 £P50 Variety." *IBNS Journal*. Volume 51 Number 4. p.13.

Fisher, Jack H. "The Influence of King Abdullah ibn Hussein al-Hashemi on the Paper Money of the Hashemite Kingdom of the Jordan." *IBNS Journal*. Volume 32 Number 1. p.28.

Fisher, Jack H. "Where are the Regular Issue (not the Canceled and Specimen) 1927 Ten-Pound Palestine Currency Board Notes?" *IBNS Journal*. Volume 33 Number 1. p.7.

Fisher, Jack H. "Palestine Currency Board Coins and Paper Money" *IBNS Journal*. Volume 9 Number 2. p.52.

Frankl, Franz. "The Holy Land: People and Mandate Money." *IBNS Journal*. Volume 14 Number 3. p.123.

Frankl, Franz. "The Palestine Currency Board Banknotes." *IBNS Journal*. Volume 15 Number 1. p.24.

Frankl, Franz. "Promissory Notes—Lifeblood of Palestine's Trade." *IBNS Journal*. Volume 17 Number 1. p.28.

Haffner, Sylvia. *The History of Modern Israel's Money From 1917 to 1967*. First edition. San Diego, California.

Katt, M. E. "Egyptian Government Currency Notes used in Palestine." *IBNS Journal*. Volume 15 Number 1. p.51.

Shneydor, N. A. "Evolving Policies in the Dating of Banknotes of the Near-East." *IBNS Journal*. Volume 53 Number 2. p.9.

Tepper, Shlomo. "News about the Palestine Currency Notes." *IBNS Journal*. Volume 42 Number 4. p.41.

Tepper, Shlomo. "Pinchas Rotenberg and the New Currencies in Palestine." *IBNS Journal*. Volume 43 Number 1. p.18.

Tepper, Shlomo. *The Unissued Banknotes of Palestine and Israel*. November 2009. ISBN 965-90661-1-2. Jerusalem, Israel.

Share Your Input, Info, and Images

This catalog is believed to be complete and correct as of the time of publication. Prices and face values were last updated 8 July 2011. Please report errors or omissions so that corrections may be made. If you can more precisely identify the name or location of anything depicted on a note, please share that information. Furthermore, if you own an unlisted type or variety, please submit scans of the front and back of the note so that it can be documented. Scans should be 300 dots per inch, 100% actual size, 24-bit color, saved as *uncompressed* JPEG files, and sent to owen@banknotenews.com. Be sure to fully describe all attributes of the note which are not apparent upon visual inspection of the images alone, such as physical dimension, watermark, and security thread.

Panama

For earlier issues, see United States.

Contents

Republica de Panama (RDP) 1653
Banco Central de Emision (BCE) 1653

Monetary System

1 Panamanian balboa (PAB) = 100 centésimos

Republica de Panama (Republic of Panama)

Article 117 of the Panamanian constitution of 1904 stated that no paper money would be issued by the new republic. Instead, United States dollars circulated in Panama.

1933 "Sosa" Issues

In 1933, Comptroller General Don Martin Sosa introduced a bill proposing the issue of 2 million balboas in different denominations of paper money, but the National Assembly did not pass the bill. An unissued 10-balboa note dated 1933 has been reported, but remains unconfirmed.

No image available.

RDP B1 (P21): **1 balboa** Good Fine XF
Front: Coat of arms; Vasco Núñez de Balboa standing with sword and flag. Back: Unknown. No security thread. Watermark: Unknown. Printer: Unknown. Unknown dimensions.
   ☐ a. 05.08.1933. Signature TK. Unissued. — — —

Banco Central de Emision de la Republica de Panama (Central Bank of Issue of the Republic of Panama)

In 1941, President Dr. Arnulfo Arias pushed the government to enact Article 156 to the constitution, authorizing official and private banks to issue paper money. As a result, on 30 September 1941, El Banco Central de Emision de la Republica de Panama (BCE) was established.

BCE Signature Varieties

1
   CONTRALOR GENERAL   MINISTRO DE HACIENDA Y TESORO
   Augusto Guillermo Arango   Enrique Linares Jr.

1941 "Arias Seven Day" Issues

The bank was authorized to issue up to 6,000,000 balboas worth of paper notes, but only 2,700,000 balboas were issued on 2 October 1941. A week later, Dr. Ricardo Adolfo de la Guardia replaced Arias as president in a coup supported by the United States. The new government immediately closed the bank, withdrew the issued notes, and burned all unissued stocks of same. Very few of these so-called "Arias Seven Day" notes escaped incineration.

BCE B1 (P22): **1 balboa** (withdrawn 09.10.1941) Good Fine XF
Purple, red, and green. Front: Vasco Núñez de Balboa wearing helmet. Back: Coat of arms. No security thread. Watermark: None. Printer: HAMILTON BANK NOTE NEW YORK. 158 x 67 mm.
   ☐ a. 1941. Signature 1. Intro: 02.10.1941. 250 600 1,350
   ☐ as. Horizontal blue SPECIMEN overprint; punched. — UNC 1,000

BCE B2 (P23): **5 balboas** (withdrawn 09.10.1941)   Good Fine XF

Black, blue, purple, and orange. Front: Indigenous Panamanian chieftain, Urracá, holding crude ax and banner. Back: Coat of arms. No security thread. Watermark: None. Printer: *HAMILTON BANK NOTE NEW YORK*. 158 x 67 mm.

- ☐ a. 1941. Signature 1. Intro: 02.10.1941.   1,000 2,750 5,000
- ☐ as. Horizontal blue *SPECIMEN* overprint; punched.   —   UNC 1,500

BCE B3 (P24): **10 balboas** (withdrawn 09.10.1941)   Good Fine XF

Black, brown, green, and orange. Front: Panama Viejo (Old Panama) vignette with palm tree and ruins of tower and buildings. Back: Coat of arms. No security thread. Watermark: None. Printer: *HAMILTON BANK NOTE NEW YORK*. 158 x 67 mm.

- ☐ a. 1941. Signature 1. Intro: 02.10.1941.   1,500 4,500 7,500
- ☐ as. Horizontal blue *SPECIMEN* overprint; punched.   —   UNC 2,500

BCE B4 (P25): **20 balboas** (withdrawn 09.10.1941)   Good Fine XF

Black, orange, red, and purple. Front: Carreta de bueyes (ox cart) with sugar cane and standing farmer. Back: Coat of arms. No security thread. Watermark: None. Printer: *HAMILTON BANK NOTE NEW YORK*. 158 x 67 mm.

- ☐ a. 1941. Signature 1. Intro: 02.10.1941.   5,000 15,000 25,000
- ☐ as. Horizontal blue *SPECIMEN* overprint; punched.   —   UNC 3,500

Looking Forward

For later issues, see United States.

Acknowledgements

This chapter was compiled with the generous assistance of Heritage Auctions (HA.com), Don Cleveland, Don Ludwig, Wally Myers, and others.

Sources

Beresiner, Yasha. "Panama - The City Under Tall Trees." *IBNS Journal*. Volume 15 Number 3. p.123.

Cuhaj, George S. *Standard Catalog of World Paper Money, General Issues, 1368-1960*. 14th edition. 2012. ISBN 978-1-4402-3090-5. Krause Publications (www.krausebooks.com), 700 East State St., Iola, WI, 54990-0001.

Loeb, Dr. Walter M. "The 1941 Issue of Panamanian Paper Money." *IBNS Journal*. Volume 4 Number 3. p.11.

Share Your Input, Info, and Images

This catalog is believed to be complete and correct as of the time of publication. Prices and face values were last updated 2 May 2011. Please report errors or omissions so that corrections may be made. If you can more precisely identify the name or location of anything depicted on a note, please share that information. Furthermore, if you own an unlisted type or variety, please submit scans of the front and back of the note so that it can be documented. Scans should be 300 dots per inch, 100% actual size, 24-bit color, saved as *uncompressed* JPEG files, and sent to owen@banknotenews.com. Be sure to fully describe all attributes of the note which are not apparent upon visual inspection of the images alone, such as physical dimension, watermark, and security thread.

Papua New Guinea

For earlier issues, see Australia and Oceania.

Monetary System
19.04.1975: 1 Papua New Guinean kina (PGK) = 100 toea

Bank of Papua New Guinea

On 1 November 1973, soon after self-government and almost two years before independence, the Bank of Papua New Guinea (BPNG) was established as the nation's central bank.

For more information, visit www.bankpng.gov.pg.

BPNG Signature Varieties

	GOVERNOR	SECRETARY DEPARTMENT OF FINANCE
1	Henry ToRobert (1973 - 1993)	Mekere Morauta
2	Henry ToRobert (1973 - 1993)	John Vulupindi
3	Henry ToRobert (1973 - 1993)	Morea Vele
4*	Henry ToRobert (1973 - 1993) Mekere Morauta** (31.07.1993 - 15.09.1994)	 Gerae Aopi
5*	 Koiari Tarata (15.09.1994 - 08.04.1998)	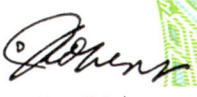 Gerae Aopi
6	 Koiari Tarata (15.09.1994 - 08.04.1998)	 Rupa Mulina
	GOVERNOR	SECRETARY DEPARTMENT OF TREASURY

BPNG Signature Varieties

7	 John Vulupindi (1998)		 Morea Vele
8	 Morea Vele (1998 - 1999)		 Brown Bai
9	 Leonard Wilson Kamit (1999 - 2009)		 Koiari Tarata
10	 Leonard Wilson Kamit (1999 - 2009)		 Simon Tosali
11	 Loi Martin Bakani (09.12.2009 - present)		 Simon Tosali

* On B9a/b only, title is SECRETARY DEPARTMENT OF FINANCE AND PLANNING.

1975 Issues

On 19 April 1975, Papua New Guinea introduced its own currency, the kina and toea. The designs of these notes were rendered from photographs, drawings, and actual objects by Willie Stevens, a Papua New Guinea artist working with another artist from the Reserve Bank of Australia. To reduce public confusion, the color schemes are similar to the Australian notes they replaced at par. Until the end of 1975, both currencies circulated, but as of 1 January 1976, the dollar was withdrawn and was no longer legal tender.

BPNG B1 (P1): **2 kina** (demonetized June 2013) VG VF UNC
Green. Front: Coat of arms with bird of paradise perched on Kundu drum and ceremonial spear. Back: Mount Hagan axe; Kula arm band from Milne Bay Province; engraved dogs' tooth necklace from Bougainville; Sepik clay pot; tapa cloth patterns. Solid security thread. Watermark: Bank logo. Printer: (NPA). 140 x 70 mm.
- a. No date. Signature 1. Intro: 19.04.1975. — — 3
- as1. Two diagonal red hollow *SPECIMEN* overprints; — — 120
  horizontal red *NO VALUE* overprint at center left;
  horiz. red *SPECIMEN No.* # overprint at lower right.
- as2. No overprint; all-zero serial numbers. — — 250

BPNG B2 (P2): **5 kina** (demonetized June 2013) VG VF UNC
Violet. Front: Coat of arms with bird of paradise perched on Kundu drum and ceremonial spear. Back: Primitive currencies; Hombuli mask used for bridal payments in Sepik region; kina shell used in Highlands; shell necklace from Milne Bay; necklace interwoven with New Ireland seeds; tapa cloth patterns. Solid security thread. Watermark: Bank logo. Printer: (NPA). 145 x 73 mm.
- a. No date. Signature 1. Intro: 19.04.1975. 3 8.50 25
- as1. Two diagonal red hollow *SPECIMEN* overprints; — — 120
  horizontal red *NO VALUE* overprint at center left;
  horiz. red *SPECIMEN No.* # overprint at lower right.
- as2. No overprint; all-zero serial numbers. — — 250

BPNG B3 (P3): **10 kina** (demonetized June 2013) VG VF UNC
Blue. Front: Coat of arms with bird of paradise perched on Kundu drum and ceremonial spear. Back: Tami bowl; bird of paradise skin; Tambu shell money from New Britain; boar tusks from the Highlands; tapa cloth patterns. Solid security thread. Watermark: Bank logo. Printer: (NPA). 150 x 75 mm.
- a. No date. Signature 1. Intro: 19.04.1975. 7.50 20 60
- as1. Two diagonal red hollow *SPECIMEN* overprints; — — 130
  horizontal red *NO VALUE* overprint at center left;
  horiz. red *SPECIMEN No.* # overprint at lower right.
- as2. No overprint; all-zero serial numbers. — — 250

1977-1980 Issues

These notes are like the preceding series, but instead of white spaces near the sides, they now have subtle patterns in the background. This change made the notes more resistant to soiling common in the tropical conditions of Papua New Guinea. The 20-kina denomination is new.

BPNG B4 (P5): **2 kina** (demonetized June 2013)   VG   VF   UNC
Green. Front: Coat of arms with bird of paradise perched on Kundu drum and ceremonial spear. Back: Mount Hagan axe; Kula arm band from Milne Bay Province; engraved dogs' tooth necklace from Bougainville; Sepik clay pot; tapa cloth patterns. Solid security thread. Watermark: Bank logo. Printer: (NPA). 140 x 70 mm.
- a. No date. Signature 1. Intro: 01.06.1980.   —   —   3
- b. Signature 2.   —   10   30
- c. Signature 3.   —   —   2

See B8 for 2-kina note with signature 3 and lighter shading around bird.

BPNG B5 (P6): **5 kina** (demonetized June 2013)   VG   VF   UNC
Violet. Front: Coat of arms with bird of paradise perched on Kundu drum and ceremonial spear. Back: Primitive currencies; Hombuli mask used for bridal payments in Sepik region; kina shell used in Highlands; shell necklace from Milne Bay; necklace interwoven with New Ireland seeds; tapa cloth patterns. Solid security thread. Watermark: Bank logo. Printer: (NPA). 148 x 73 mm.
- a. No date. Signature 1. Intro: 01.06.1980.   —   10   30
- b. Signature 2.   —   10   30

BPNG B6 (P7): **10 kina** (demonetized June 2013)   VG   VF   UNC
Blue. Front: Coat of arms with bird of paradise perched on Kundu drum and ceremonial spear. Back: Tami bowl; bird of paradise skin; Tambu shell money from New Britain; boar tusks from the Highlands; tapa cloth patterns. Solid security thread. Watermark: Bank logo. Printer: (NPA). 150 x 75 mm.
- a. No date. Signature 1. Intro: 01.06.1980.   —   —   6

BPNG B7 (P4): **20 kina** (demonetized June 2013)   VG   VF   UNC
Red-brown. Front: Coat of arms with bird of paradise perched on Kundu drum and ceremonial spear. Back: boar head; toea (cowrie shell) necklace from Madang; Toa armband from Central Province; shell ornament from Western Province; tapa cloth patterns. Solid security thread. Watermark: Bank logo. Printer: (NPA). 150 x 75 mm.
- a. No date. Signature 1. Intro: 19.04.1977.   10   25   80
- as1. Two diagonal red hollow *SPECIMEN* overprints; horizontal red *NO VALUE* overprint at center left; horiz. red *SPECIMEN No. #* overprint at lower right.   —   —   130
- as2. No overprint; all-zero serial numbers.   —   —   170

1977 Numismatic Products

The Bank of Papua New Guinea produced 500 sets of notes for sale to collectors at face value of 37 kina.

BPNG BNP1 (PNL): **2-20 kina**   UNC
- a. BPNG B1-B3 and B7 (4 notes) with matching serial numbers.   190

1981-1999 Issues

These 2- and 5-kina notes are like the same denominations of the preceding issues, but with slightly lighter design elements (most noticeable in the shading around the bird on front) and serial numbers with darker and thicker type faces. The 10-kina note has a new design on the front; the 20-kina note has subtle changes to the underprint pattern; and the 50-kina denomination is entirely new.

BPNG B8 (P12A): **2 kina** (demonetized June 2013)   VG   VF   UNC
Green. Front: Coat of arms with bird of paradise perched on Kundu drum and ceremonial spear. Back: Mount Hagan axe; Kula arm band from Milne Bay Province; engraved dogs' tooth necklace from Bougainville; Sepik clay pot; tapa cloth patterns. Solid security thread. Watermark: Bank logo. Printer: (TDLR). 140 x 70 mm.
     a.   No date. Signature 3. Intro: 1992.   —   —   4.50

See B4 for 2-kina note with signature 3 and darker shading around bird.

BPNG B9 (P13 & P14): **5 kina** (demonetized June 2013)   VG   VF   UNC
Violet. Front: Coat of arms with bird of paradise perched on Kundu drum and ceremonial spear. Back: Primitive currencies; Hombuli mask used for bridal payments in Sepik region; kina shell used in Highlands; shell necklace from Milne Bay; necklace interwoven with New Ireland seeds; tapa cloth patterns. Watermark: Bank logo. Printer: (TDLR). 148 x 73 mm.

     a.   No date. Intro: 1992.   —   —   10
         Signature 3. Solid security thread.
     b.   Signature 4. Windowed security thread. Intro: 1993.   —   —   5.50
     c.   Signature 5.   —   —   10
     d.   Signature 6.   —   —   10
     e.   Signature 8.   —   —   10
     f.   Signature 9.   —   —   10
     as.   Diagonal red *SPECIMEN* overprint.   —   —   100
     cs.   Diagonal red *SPECIMEN* overprint.   —   —   100
     ds.   Diagonal red *SPECIMEN* overprint.   —   —   100
     fs.   Diagonal red *SPECIMEN* overprint.   —   —   100

BPNG B10 (P9): **10 kina** (demonetized June 2013)   VG   VF   UNC

Blue. Front: Coat of arms with bird of paradise perched on Kundu drum and ceremonial spear; National Parliament building in Port Moresby. Back: Tami bowl; bird of paradise skin; Tambu shell money from New Britain; boar tusks from the Highlands; tapa cloth patterns. Solid security thread. Watermark: Bank logo. Printer: (NPA). 150 x 75 mm.

☐	a.	No date. Signature 2. Intro: 01.04.1985.	—	—	6.50
☐	b.	Signature 3.	—	—	5.50
☐	c.	Signature 5.	—	—	7.00
☐	d.	Signature 6.	—	—	4.50
☐	e.	Signature 7.	—	—	6.50
☐	as.	Two diagonal red hollow *SPECIMEN* overprints; horizontal red *NO VALUE* overprint at center left; horiz. red *SPECIMEN No.* # overprint at lower right.	—	—	55
☐	cs.	No overprint; all-zero serial numbers.	—	—	170

This note was issued to mark the 10th anniversary of independence and the 1984 opening of the National Parliament building, which appears as the new background on the front.

BPNG B12 (P11): **50 kina** (demonetized June 2013)   VG   VF   UNC

Orange. Front: Coat of arms with bird of paradise perched on Kundu drum and ceremonial spear; National Parliament building in Port Moresby. Back: Prime Minister Michael Somare; spears from Sepik; shield and mask from New Ireland; leaf and pointed Tubuan face mask from New Britain; headdress from the Highlands; mask and costume from Sepik River. Solid security thread printed *PAPUA NEW GUINEA*. Watermark: Bank logo. Printer: (NPA). 150 x 75 mm.

☐	a.	No date. Signature 3. Intro: 01.08.1988.	—	—	20
☐	as.	Horizontal red *SPECIMEN* # ovpt at center right.	—	—	90

BPNG B11 (P10): **20 kina** (demonetized June 2013)   VG   VF   UNC

Red-brown. Front: Coat of arms with bird of paradise perched on Kundu drum and ceremonial spear. Back: boar head; toea (cowrie shell) necklace from Madang; Toa armband from Central Province; shell ornament from Western Province; tapa cloth patterns. Solid security thread. Watermark: Bank logo. Printer: (NPA). 150 x 75 mm.

☐	a.	No date. Signature 3. Intro: 1981.	—	—	7
☐	b.	Signature 5.	—	—	5.50
☐	c.	Signature 6.	—	—	45
☐	d.	Signature 7.	—	—	5.50
☐	e.	Signature 9.	—	—	45
☐	as.	Specimen.	—	—	—
☐	bs.	No overprint; all-zero serial numbers.	—	—	180

1991 "South Pacific Games" Commemorative Issues

This 2-kina note was issued to commemorate the hosting of the 9th South Pacific Games, which ran from 7-21 September 1991 in the cities of Port Moresby and Lae. In addition to the South Pacific Games logo (a stylized bird of paradise in national colors, designed by art student Miria Miria), the note features *SPG 9* printed at lower left on front where a second serial number would normally appear. This is Papua New Guinea's first polymer note.

BPNG B13 (P12): **2 kina** (US$0.80) VG VF UNC
Green. Front: Logo of *9th SOUTH PACIFIC GAMES, PAPUA NEW GUINEA 1991*; coat of arms with bird of paradise perched on Kundu drum and ceremonial spear. Back: Mount Hagan axe; Kula arm band from Milne Bay Province; engraved dogs' tooth necklace from Bougainville; Sepik clay pot; tapa cloth patterns. No security thread. Watermark: None. Printer: (NPA). 140 x 70 mm. Polymer.
- a. 1991. Signature 3. Introduced July 1991. — — 4.50
- as1. Horizontal red *SPECIMEN* overprint. — — 250
- as2. No overprint; all-zero serial numbers. — — 100

SPG prefix stands for "South Pacific Games."

1991 "South Pacific Games" Numismatic Products

BPNG BNP2 (PNL): **2 kina** UNC
- a. BPNG B13 in folder. 25

1995 "PNG 20th Anniversary" Commemorative Issues

This 2-kina note was issued to commemorate the 20th anniversary of independence on 16 September 1995. In addition to the logo, the note features *PNG 20* printed in the lower left corner on front where a second serial number would normally appear.

BPNG B14 (P15): **2 kina** (US$0.80) VG VF UNC
Green. Front: 20th anniversary logo; coat of arms with bird of paradise perched on Kundu drum and ceremonial spear. Back: Mount Hagan axe; Kula arm band from Milne Bay Province; engraved dogs' tooth necklace from Bougainville; Sepik clay pot; tapa cloth patterns. No security thread. Watermark: Bank logo. Printer: (NPA). 140 x 70 mm. Polymer.
- a. No date. Signature 5. Intro: September 1995. — — 7
- as1. No overprint; all-zero serial numbers. — — 250
- as2. Horizontal red *SPECIMEN No. #* overprint on back; all-zero serial numbers. — — 250

1995 "PNG 20th Anniversary" Numismatic Products

BPNG BNP3 (PNL): **2 kina** UNC
- a. BPNG B14 in folder. 25

1996-2002 Issues

This 2-kina note is like the preceding issue (BPNG B8), but it is now printed on polymer, not paper.

BPNG B15 (P16): **2 kina** (US$0.80) VG VF UNC

Green. Front: Coat of arms with bird of paradise perched on Kundu drum and ceremonial spear. Back: Mount Hagan axe; Kula arm band from Milne Bay Province; engraved dogs' tooth necklace from Bougainville; Sepik clay pot; tapa cloth patterns. No security thread. Watermark: Bank logo. Printer: (NPA). 140 x 70 mm. Polymer.

a.	No date. Signature 5. Intro: 1996.	—	—	5
b.	Signature 6. Intro: 1999.	—	—	1.50
c.	Signature 9. Intro: 2002.	—	—	3.50
as.	No overprint; all-zero serial numbers.	—	—	170

1998 "Bank Silver Jubilee" Commemorative Issues

This 10-kina note was issued to commemorate the 25th anniversary of the Bank of Papua New Guinea. In addition to the blue-on-silver logo, the note features *SJ XXV* (Silver Jubilee 25) printed at lower center on front where a second serial number would normally appear.

BPNG B16 (P17): **10 kina** (demonetized June 2013) VG VF UNC

Blue. Front: Silver jubilee logo; coat of arms with bird of paradise perched on Kundu drum and ceremonial spear; National Parliament building in Port Moresby. Back: Tami bowl; bird of paradise skin; Tambu shell money from New Britain; boar tusks from the Highlands; tapa cloth patterns. Solid security thread. Watermark: Bank logo. Printer: (NPA). 150 x 75 mm.

a.	1998. Signature 7. Intro: 1998.	—	—	4.50
as.	Horizontal red *SPECIMEN No. #* overprint; all-zero serial numbers.	—	—	130

1998 Numismatic Products

BPNG BNP4 (PNL): **10 kina** UNC
  a. BPNG B16 in folder. —

1999-2002 Issues

These notes are like the preceding issues of the same denominations, but they are now printed on polymer, not paper. The 50-kina note is the first in which the first two digits of the serial number represent the last two digits of the year of printing. However, this system of dating notes has not been consistently applied on subsequent issues of other denominations.

BPNG B17 (P26): **10 kina** (US$4.05) VG VF UNC
Blue. Front: Coat of arms with bird of paradise perched on Kundu drum and ceremonial spear; National Parliament building in Port Moresby. Back: Tami bowl; bird of paradise skin; Tambu shell money from New Britain; boar tusks from the Highlands; tapa cloth patterns. No security thread. Watermark: Bank logo. Printer: (NPA). 150 x 75 mm. Polymer.

☐ a.	Signature 9. Intro: 2000.	— —	15
☐ as1.	No overprint; all-zero serial numbers.	— —	250
☐ as2.	Horizontal red *SPECIMEN No.* # overprint; all-zero serial numbers.	— —	110

BPNG B18 (P18): **50 kina** (US$20) VG VF UNC
Orange. Front: Coat of arms with bird of paradise perched on Kundu drum and ceremonial spear; National Parliament building in Port Moresby. Back: Prime Minister Michael Somare; spears from Sepik; shield and mask from New Ireland; leaf and pointed Tubuan face mask from New Britain; headdress from the Highlands; mask and costume from Sepik River. Simulated security thread with *50PNG*. Watermark: Bank logo. Printer: (NPA). 150 x 75 mm. Polymer.

☐ a.	(19)99. Signature 8. Intro: 28.06.1999.	— —	70
☐ b.	Signature 9.	— —	60
☐ c.	(20)02.	— —	60
☐ as1.	No overprint; all-zero serial numbers.	— —	180
☐ as2.	Horizontal red *SPECIMEN No.* # overprint; all-zero serial numbers.	— —	200

The MV prefix on (19)99-dated notes stands for "Morea Vele," governor of the BPNG.

2000 "Year 2000" Commemorative Issues

This 5-kina note was issued to commemorate the new millennium. It is like the preceding note (B9), but has a golden *Year 2000*.

BPNG B19 (P19): **5 kina** (demonetized June 2013) VG VF UNC

Violet. Front: *Year 2000* gold stamp; coat of arms with bird of paradise perched on Kundu drum and ceremonial spear. Back: Primitive currencies; Hombuli mask used for bridal payments in Sepik region; kina shell used in Highlands; shell necklace from Milne Bay; necklace interwoven with New Ireland seeds; tapa cloth patterns. Windowed security thread. Watermark: Bank logo. Printer: (TDLR). 148 x 73 mm.

- ☐ a. 2000. Signature 8. Intro: 2000.   — — 12
- ☐ as. No *Year 2000* overprint; *PNG 002000* s/n.   — — 140

PNG prefix stands for "Papua New Guinea."

2000 "Currency" Commemorative Issues

This 5-kina note was issued to commemorate the 25th anniversary of the kina and toea currency. It is like B9, but has *PNGCSJ 1942000* (Papua New Guinea Currency Silver Jubilee 19.04.2000) printed in red, and a silver foil flag patch.

BPNG B20 (P20): **5 kina** (demonetized June 2013) VG VF UNC

Violet. Front: Red *PNGCSJ 1942000* overprint; coat of arms with bird of paradise perched on Kundu drum and ceremonial spear; silver foil flag overprint. Back: Primitive currencies; Hombuli mask used for bridal payments in Sepik region; kina shell used in Highlands; shell necklace from Milne Bay; necklace interwoven with New Ireland seeds; tapa cloth patterns. Windowed security thread. Watermark: Bank logo. Printer: (TDLR). 148 x 73 mm.

- ☐ a. 1942000. Signature 9. Intro: 19.04.2000.   — — 20
- ☐ as. Diagonal red *SPECIMEN* overprint.   — — 110

2000 "PNG Silver Jubilee" Commemorative Issues

These notes were issued to commemorate the 25th anniversary of independence. They are like preceding issues, but with silver jubilee logos on front.

BPNG B21 (P21): **2 kina** (US$0.80) VG VF UNC
Green. Front: *25 Papua New Guinea Silver Jubilee* logo; coat of arms with bird of paradise perched on Kundu drum and ceremonial spear. Back: Mount Hagan axe; Kula arm band from Milne Bay Province; engraved dogs' tooth necklace from Bougainville; Sepik clay pot; tapa cloth patterns. No security thread. Watermark: Bank logo. Printer: (NPA). 140 x 70 mm. Polymer.
☐ a. (20)00. Signature 9. Intro: 2000. — — 5

BPNG B22 (P22): **5 kina** (demonetized June 2013) VG VF UNC
Violet. Front: Coat of arms with bird of paradise perched on Kundu drum and ceremonial spear; *25 Papua New Guinea Silver Jubilee* logo. Back: Primitive currencies; Hombuli mask used for bridal payments in Sepik region; kina shell used in Highlands; shell necklace from Milne Bay; necklace interwoven with New Ireland seeds; tapa cloth patterns. Windowed security thread. Watermark: Bank logo. Printer: (TDLR). 148 x 73 mm.
☐ a. No date. Signature 9. Intro: 2000. — — 8.50
☐ as. Diagonal red *SPECIMEN* overprint. — — 60
ISJ prefix stands for "Independence Silver Jubilee."

BPNG B23 (P23): **10 kina** (US$4.05) VG VF UNC
Blue. Front: *25 Papua New Guinea Silver Jubilee* logo; coat of arms with bird of paradise perched on Kundu drum and ceremonial spear; National Parliament building in Port Moresby. Back: Tami bowl; bird of paradise skin; Tambu shell money from New Britain; boar tusks from the Highlands; tapa cloth patterns. No security thread. Watermark: Bank logo. Printer: (NPA). 150 x 75 mm. Polymer.
☐ a. (20)00. Signature 9. — — 40

BPNG B24 (P24): **20 kina** (demonetized June 2013) VG VF UNC
Red-brown. Front: *25 Papua New Guinea Silver Jubilee* logo; coat of arms with bird of paradise perched on Kundu drum and ceremonial spear. Back: boar head; toea (cowrie shell) necklace from Madang; Toa armband from Central Province; shell ornament from Western Province; tapa cloth patterns. Solid security thread. Watermark: Bank logo. Printer: (NPA). 150 x 75 mm.
☐ a. (20)00. Signature 9. — — 35

BPNG B25 (P25): **50 kina** (US$20)   VG VF UNC
Orange. Front: Coat of arms with bird of paradise perched on Kundu drum and ceremonial spear; *25 Papua New Guinea Silver Jubilee* logo; National Parliament building in Port Moresby. Back: Prime Minister Michael Somare; spears from Sepik; shield and mask from New Ireland; leaf and pointed Tubuan face mask from New Britain; headdress from the Highlands; mask and costume from Sepik River. Simulated security thread with *50PNG*. Watermark: Bank logo. Printer: (NPA). 150 x 75 mm. Polymer.
☐ a.   (20)00. Signature 9.   —   —   65

2002-2005 Issues

These notes are like the preceding issues, but the format of the serial number has changed to a two-character prefix followed by an eight-digit number, with the exception of the 5-kina note dated 2005, which uses initials of the bank's officers as a three-character prefix.

BPNG B26 (P16d): **2 kina** (US$0.80)   VG VF UNC
Green. Front: Coat of arms with bird of paradise perched on Kundu drum and ceremonial spear. Back: Mount Hagan axe; Kula arm band from Milne Bay Province; engraved dogs' tooth necklace from Bougainville; Sepik clay pot; tapa cloth patterns. No security thread. Watermark: Bank logo. Printer: (NPA). 140 x 70 mm. Polymer.
☐ a.   (20)02. Signature 9.   —   —   4

BPNG B27 (P13): **5 kina** (demonetized June 2013)   VG VF UNC
Violet. Front: Coat of arms with bird of paradise perched on Kundu drum and ceremonial spear. Back: Primitive currencies; Hombuli mask used for bridal payments in Sepik region; kina shell used in Highlands; shell necklace from Milne Bay; necklace interwoven with New Ireland seeds; tapa cloth patterns. Windowed security thread with demetalized *5 BPNG*. Watermark: Bank logo. Printer: (TDLR). 148 x 73 mm.
☐ a.   (20)02. Signature 9.   —   —   7
☐ b.   (20)05. Signature 10.   —   —   8
☐ as. Diagonal red *SPECIMEN* overprint.   —   —   60
☐ bs. Diagonal red *SPECIMEN* overprint.   —   —   60
STK prefix on B27b stands for "Simon Tosali - Kamit," the two signatories on the note.

BPNG B28 (P26b): **10 kina** (US$4.05)   VG VF UNC
Blue. Front: Coat of arms with bird of paradise perched on Kundu drum and ceremonial spear; National Parliament building in Port Moresby. Back: Tami bowl; bird of paradise skin; Tambu shell money from New Britain; boar tusks from the Highlands; tapa cloth patterns. No security thread. Watermark: Bank logo. Printer: (NPA). 150 x 75 mm. Polymer.
☐ a.   (20)02. Signature 9.   —   —   10
☐ as. No overprint; no perforation; all-zero serial numbers.   —   —   —

BPNG B29 (P10e): **20 kina** (demonetized June 2013) VG VF UNC
Red-brown. Front: Coat of arms with bird of paradise perched on Kundu drum and ceremonial spear. Back: boar head; toea (cowrie shell) necklace from Madang; Toa armband from Central Province; shell ornament from Western Province; tapa cloth patterns. Windowed security thread with demetalized *20 BPNG*. Watermark: Bank logo. Printer: (NPA). 150 x 75 mm.
    ☐ a. (20)02. Signature 9. — — 40
    ☐ as. Diagonal red *SPECIMEN* overprint. — — —

2003 "Bank's 30th Anniversary" Commemorative Issues

These notes were issued to commemorate the 30th anniversary of the founding of the Bank of Papua New Guinea.

BPNG B30 (PNL): **5 kina** (demonetized June 2013) VG VF UNC
Violet. Front: Coat of arms with bird of paradise perched on Kundu drum and ceremonial spear; golden overprint of bank logo between *1973 2003*. Back: Primitive currencies; Hombuli mask used for bridal payments in Sepik region; kina shell used in Highlands; shell necklace from Milne Bay; necklace interwoven with New Ireland seeds; tapa cloth patterns. Windowed security thread with demetalized *5 BPNG*. Watermark: Bank logo. Printer: (TDLR). 148 x 73 mm.
    ☐ a. (20)03. Signature 9. — — 60
    ☐ as. Diagonal red *SPECIMEN* overprint. — — 110
LWK prefix stands for "Leonard Wilson Kamit," governor of the BPNG.

BPNG B31 (P27): **20 kina** (US$8.15) VG VF UNC
Red-brown. Front: 30th anniversary logo; coat of arms with bird of paradise perched on Kundu drum and ceremonial spear. Back: boar head; toea (cowrie shell) necklace from Madang; Toa armband from Central Province; shell ornament from Western Province; tapa cloth patterns. No security thread. Watermark: Bank logo. Printer: (NPA). 150 x 75 mm. Polymer.
    ☐ a. No date. Signature 9. Intro: 03.11.2003. — — 30
    Serial number looks like it starts with last two digits of year, but it's not a date code.
LK prefix stands for "Leonard Kamit," governor of the BPNG.

2006 Issues

BPNG B32 (PNL): **20 kina** (US$8.15) VG VF UNC
Red-brown. Front: Coat of arms with bird of paradise perched on Kundu drum and ceremonial spear. Back: boar head; toea (cowrie shell) necklace from Madang; Toa armband from Central Province; shell ornament from Western Province; tapa cloth patterns. No security thread. Watermark: Bank logo. Printer: (NPA). 150 x 75 mm. Polymer.
    ☐ a. No date. Signature 10. Intro: 2006. — — 30
    Serial number looks like it starts with last two digits of year, but it's not a date code.
    ☐ as. Diagonal red *SPECIMEN* overprint. — — 55
BP prefix stands for "Benny Popoitai," deputy governor of the BPNG.

2007 "South Pacific Games" Commemorative Issues

BPNG B33 (P34): **5 kina** (demonetized June 2013)   VG   VF   UNC

Violet. Front: *2007 XIII South Pacific Games* logo; coat of arms with bird of paradise perched on Kundu drum and ceremonial spear. Back: Primitive currencies; Hombuli mask used for bridal payments in Sepik region; kina shell used in Highlands; shell necklace from Milne Bay; necklace interwoven with New Ireland seeds; tapa cloth patterns. Windowed security thread with demetalized 5 BPNG. Watermark: Bank logo. Printer: (TDLR). 148 x 73 mm.

- a. 2007. Signature 10. Intro: 20.06.2007. — — 6
- as. Diagonal red *SPECIMEN* overprint. — — —

2005-2014 Issues

These notes mark the completion of the transition to polymer for Papua New Guinea. This series began with the 2005 introduction of the 100-kina note and finished with the 2008 introduction of the 50-kina note, which marked the 35th anniversary of the bank.

BPNG B34 (P28): **2 kina** (US$0.80)   VG   VF   UNC

Green. Front: Coat of arms with bird of paradise perched on Kundu drum and ceremonial spear; National Parliament building in Port Moresby. Back: Mount Hagan axe; Kula arm band from Milne Bay Province; engraved dogs' tooth necklace from Bougainville; Sepik clay pot; tapa cloth patterns. No security thread. Watermark: Bank logo. Printer: (NPA). 140 x 70 mm. Polymer.

- a. (20)07. Signature 10. Intro: 19.04.2007. — — 2
- b. (20)08. — — 1.50
- c. (20)13. Signature 11. — — 1.50
- d. (20)14. — — 4

BPNG B34 (P28): **2 kina** (US$0.80)   VG   VF   UNC

- as. Diagonal red *SPECIMEN* overprint. — — 20
- cs. Diagonal red *SPECIMEN* overprint. — — 130
- ds. Diagonal red *SPECIMEN* overprint. — — 130

BPNG B35 (P29): **5 kina** (US$2.05)   VG   VF   UNC

Violet. Front: Coat of arms with bird of paradise perched on Kundu drum and ceremonial spear; National Parliament building in Port Moresby. Back: Primitive currencies; Hombuli mask used for bridal payments in Sepik region; kina shell used in Highlands; shell necklace from Milne Bay; necklace interwoven with New Ireland seeds; tapa cloth patterns. No security thread. Watermark: Bank logo. Printer: (NPA). 148 x 73 mm. Polymer.

- a. (20)08. Signature 10. Intro: 18.04.2008. — — 4.50
- b. (20)09. — — 4
- as. Diagonal red *SPECIMEN* overprint. — — 35

BPNG B36 (P30): **10 kina** (US$4.05)   VG   VF   UNC

Blue. Front: Coat of arms with bird of paradise perched on Kundu drum and ceremonial spear; National Parliament building in Port Moresby. Back: Tami bowl; bird of paradise skin; Tambu shell money from New Britain; boar tusks from the Highlands; tapa cloth patterns. No security thread. Watermark: Bank logo. Printer: (NPA). 150 x 75 mm. Polymer.

- a. (20)08. Signature 10. Intro: 18.04.2008. — — 8
- b. (20)13. Signature 11. — — 10
- as. Diagonal red *SPECIMEN* overprint. — — 40
- bs. Diagonal red *SPECIMEN* overprint. — — 150

BPNG B37 (P31): **20 kina** (US$8.15)   VG   VF   UNC

Red-brown. Front: Coat of arms with bird of paradise perched on Kundu drum and ceremonial spear; National Parliament building in Port Moresby. Back: boar head; toea (cowrie shell) necklace from Madang; Toa armband from Central Province; shell ornament from Western Province; tapa cloth patterns. No security thread. Watermark: Bank logo. Printer: (NPA). 150 x 75 mm. Polymer.

☐	a.	(20)07. Signature 10. Intro: 05.11.2007.	—	—	20
☐	b.	(20)13. Signature 11.	—	—	20
☐	c.	(20)14.	—	—	20
☐	as.	Diagonal red *SPECIMEN* overprint.	—	—	90
☐	bs.	Diagonal red *SPECIMEN* overprint.	—	—	160
☐	cs.	Diagonal red *SPECIMEN* overprint.	—	—	160

BPNG B38 (P32): **50 kina** (US$20)   VG   VF   UNC

Orange. Front: Coat of arms with bird of paradise perched on Kundu drum and ceremonial spear; National Parliament building in Port Moresby. Back: Prime Minister Michael Somare; spears from Sepik; shield and mask from New Ireland; leaf and pointed Tubuan face mask from New Britain; headdress from the Highlands; mask and costume from Sepik River. No security thread. Watermark: Bank logo. Printer: (NPA). 150 x 75 mm. Polymer

☐	a.	(20)08. Signature 10. Intro: 31.10.2008.	—	—	45
☐	b.	(20)12. Signature 11.	—	—	45
☐	as.	Diagonal red *SPECIMEN* overprint.	—	—	120
☐	bs.	Diagonal red *SPECIMEN* overprint.	—	—	85

BPNG B39 (P33): **100 kina** (US$41)   VG   VF   UNC

Green and gold. Front: Coat of arms with bird of paradise perched on Kundu drum and ceremonial spear; National Parliament building in Port Moresby. Back: Palm tree; cowrie shells; fish; timber; cargo ship; oil rig; bird; jumbo jet; dump truck; microwave tower. No security thread. Watermark: Bank logo. Printer: (NPA). 150 x 75 mm. Polymer.

☐	a.	(20)05. Signature 10. Intro: 02.11.2005.	—	—	85
☐	b.	(20)07.	—	—	110
☐	c.	(20)14. Signature 11.	—	—	110
☐	as.	Diagonal red *SPECIMEN* overprint.	—	—	200
☐	cs.	Diagonal red *SPECIMEN* overprint.	—	—	200

2008 "Bank's 35th Anniversary" Commemorative Issues

This 2-kina note commemorates the 35th anniversary of the Bank of Papua New Guinea. It is like the preceding issue, but the front has a special logo celebrating the bank's 35th anniversary.

BPNG B40 (P35): **2 kina** (US$0.80)   VG   VF   UNC

Green. Front: Coat of arms with bird of paradise perched on Kundu drum and ceremonial spear; National Parliament building in Port Moresby; BPNG 35th anniversary logo. Back: Mount Hagan axe; Kula arm band from Milne Bay Province; engraved dogs' tooth necklace from Bougainville; Sepik clay pot; tapa cloth patterns. No security thread. Watermark: Bank logo. Printer: (NPA). 140 x 70 mm. Polymer.

☐	a.	(20)08. Signature 10. Intro: 31.10.2008.	—	—	1.50

2008 Numismatic Products

6,000 of the 2-kina commemorative notes were packaged in folders with 2-kina commemorative coins, for sale at 30 kina each.

BPNG BNP4.5 (PNL): **2 kina** UNC
☐ a.   BPNG B40 in folder with 2-kina coin.   20

2009 "Kina & Toea Day" Commemorative Issues

Although dated 2008, these notes were issued to commemorate the 2009 Kina & Toea Day (19 April 2009), and are similar to the preceding polymer notes, but they are printed on paper and carry a logo celebrating the bank's 35th anniversary. Three million 20-kina notes were printed, and one million five hundred 100-kina notes were printed.

BPNG B41 (P36): **20 kina** (demonetized June 2013)   VG   VF   UNC
Red-brown. Front: BPNG 35th anniversary logo; coat of arms with bird of paradise perched on Kundu drum and ceremonial spear; National Parliament building in Port Moresby. Back: boar head; toea (cowrie shell) necklace from Madang; Toa armband from Central Province; shell ornament from Western Province; tapa cloth patterns. Windowed security thread with demetalized *BPNG*. Watermark: Bank logo, electrotype *BPNG,* and Cornerstones. Printer: (TDLR). 150 x 75 mm.
  ☐ a.   2008. Signature 10. Intro: 04.23.2009.   —   —   1
  ☐ as. Diagonal red *SPECIMEN* overprint.   —   —   35
Replacement notes: Prefix ZZZZ.
BPNG prefix stands for "Bank of Papua New Guinea."

BPNG B42 (P37): **100 kina** (demonetized June 2013)   VG   VF   UNC

Green and gold. Front: BPNG 35th anniversary logo; coat of arms with bird of paradise perched on Kundu drum and ceremonial spear; National Parliament building in Port Moresby. Back: Palm tree; cowrie shells; fish; timber; cargo ship; oil rig; bird; jumbo jet; dump truck; microwave tower. Optiks security thread with demetalized *BPNG 100*. Watermark: Bank logo and Cornerstones. Printer: (TDLR). 150 x 75 mm.

☐	a.	2008. Signature 10. Intro: 04.23.2009.	— —	25
☐	as1.	Diagonal red *SPECIMEN* overprint.	— —	85
☐	as2.	No overprint; all-zero serial numbers.	— —	475

Replacement notes: Prefix ZZZZ.
BPNG prefix stands for "Bank of Papua New Guinea."

2009 Numismatic Products

500 sets of notes with matching serial numbers were produced for sale at 300 kina each, although the bank reserved the first 10 sets.

BPNG BNP5 (PNL): **20 kina** and **100 kina**   UNC

☐	a.	BPNG B41 and B42 (2 notes) with matching s/n in folder.	200

2010 Commemorative Issues

On 15 September 2010 the Bank of Papua New Guinea introduced new polymer notes to commemorate the 35th anniversary of independence from Australia. These notes are like the preceding issues, but the fronts have a special logo celebrating the nation's 35th anniversary, along with the text *35th Anniversary 1975 – 2010*. Also, the design of the 100-kina note has been modified slightly, with some elements rearranged.

BPNG B43 (P38): **2 kina** (US$0.80)   VG   VF   UNC

Green. Front: Coat of arms with bird of paradise perched on Kundu drum and ceremonial spear; 35th anniversary logo; National Parliament building in Port Moresby. Back: Mount Hagan axe; Kula arm band from Milne Bay Province; engraved dogs' tooth necklace from Bougainville; Sepik clay pot; tapa cloth patterns. No security thread. Watermark: Bank logo. Printer: (NPA). 140 x 70 mm. Polymer.

☐	a.	(20)10. Signature 10. Intro: 15.09.2010.	FV FV	2

BPNG B44 (P39): **5 kina** (US$2.05)   VG   VF   UNC

Violet. Front: Coat of arms with bird of paradise perched on Kundu drum and ceremonial spear; 35th anniversary logo; National Parliament building in Port Moresby. Back: Primitive currencies; Hombuli mask used for bridal payments in Sepik region; kina shell used in Highlands; shell necklace from Milne Bay; necklace interwoven with New Ireland seeds; tapa cloth patterns. No security thread. Watermark: Bank logo. Printer: (NPA). 148 x 73 mm. Polymer.

☐	a.	(20)10. Signature 10. Intro: 15.09.2010.	FV FV	5

BPNG B45 (P40): **10 kina** (US$4.05)   VG   VF   UNC

Blue. Front: Coat of arms with bird of paradise perched on Kundu drum and ceremonial spear; 35th anniversary logo; National Parliament building in Port Moresby. Back: Tami bowl; bird of paradise skin; Tambu shell money from New Britain; boar tusks from the Highlands; tapa cloth patterns. No security thread. Watermark: Bank logo. Printer: (NPA). 150 x 75 mm. Polymer.

    ☐ a.   (20)10. Signature 10. Intro: 15.09.2010.   FV   FV   8

BPNG B46 (P41): **20 kina** (US$8.15)   VG   VF   UNC

Red-brown. Front: Coat of arms with bird of paradise perched on Kundu drum and ceremonial spear; 35th anniversary logo; National Parliament building in Port Moresby. Back: boar head; toea (cowrie shell) necklace from Madang; Toa armband from Central Province; shell ornament from Western Province; tapa cloth patterns. No security thread. Watermark: Bank logo. Printer: (NPA). 150 x 75 mm. Polymer.

    ☐ a.   (20)10. Signature 10. Intro: 15.09.2010.   FV   FV   18

BPNG B47 (P42): **50 kina** (US$20)   VG   VF   UNC

Orange. Front: Coat of arms with bird of paradise perched on Kundu drum and ceremonial spear; 35th anniversary logo; National Parliament building in Port Moresby. Back: Prime Minister Michael Somare; spears from Sepik; shield and mask from New Ireland; leaf and pointed Tubuan face mask from New Britain; headdress from the Highlands; mask and costume from Sepik River. No security thread. Watermark: Bank logo. Printer: (NPA). 150 x 75 mm. Polymer.

    ☐ a.   (20)10. Signature 10. Intro: 15.09.2010.   FV   FV   45

BPNG B48 (P43): **100 kina** (US$41)   VG   VF   UNC

Green and gold. Front: 35th anniversary logo; coat of arms with bird of paradise perched on Kundu drum and ceremonial spear; 35th anniversary logo; National Parliament building in Port Moresby. Back: Coffee beans; cardamom seeds; coconut palm tree; fish; timber; cargo ship; oil rig; bird; jumbo jet; dump truck; microwave tower. No security thread. Watermark: Bank logo. Printer: (NPA). 150 x 75 mm. Polymer.

    ☐ a.   (20)10. Signature 10. Intro: 15.09.2010.   FV   FV   75

2012 Issues

BPNG B49 (PNL): **100 kina** (US$41)   VG   VF   UNC
Green and gold. Front: Coat of arms with bird of paradise perched on Kundu drum and ceremonial spear; National Parliament building in Port Moresby. Back: Coffee beans; cardamom seeds; coconut palm tree; fish; timber; cargo ship; oil rig; bird; jumbo jet; dump truck; microwave tower. No security thread. Watermark: Bank logo. Printer: (NPA). 150 x 75 mm. Polymer.

     ☐ a. (20)12. Signature 11.   FV   FV   80
     ☐ as. Diagonal red *SPECIMEN* overprint.   —   —   150

Like BPNG B48, but without the 35th anniversary logo.

2013 Commemorative Issues

These notes commemorate the 40th anniversary of the Bank of Papua New Guinea. They are like the preceding issue, but the front has a special logo celebrating the bank's 40th anniversary.

BPNG B50 (PNL): **2 kina** (US$0.80)   VG   VF   UNC
Green. Front: Coat of arms with bird of paradise perched on Kundu drum and ceremonial spear; National Parliament building in Port Moresby; 40th anniversary logo. Back: Mount Hagen axe; Kula arm band from Milne Bay Province; engraved dogs' tooth necklace from Bougainville; Sepik clay pot; tapa cloth patterns. No security thread. Watermark: Bank logo. Printer: (NPA). 140 x 70 mm. Polymer.

     ☐ a. 2013. Signature 11. Intro: 04.11.2013.   FV   FV   1.50

BPNG B51 (PNL): **100 kina** (US$41)   VG   VF   UNC
Green and gold. Front: Coat of arms with bird of paradise perched on Kundu drum and ceremonial spear; National Parliament building in Port Moresby; 40th anniversary logo. Back: Coffee beans; cardamom seeds; coconut palm tree; fish; timber; cargo ship; oil rig; bird; jumbo jet; dump truck; microwave tower. No security thread. Watermark: Bank logo. Printer: (NPA). 150 x 75 mm. Polymer.

     ☐ a. 2013. Signature 11. Intro: 04.11.2013.   FV   FV   75

Acknowledgements

This chapter was compiled with the generous assistance of Brent Arthurson, Thomas Augustsson, Kee Hong Boon (Tigerson), Donald Cleveland, Kai Hwong, Mark Irwin, Thomas Krause, Manfred Krüger, Don Ludwig, Claudio Marana, Frederick Martin, Leszek Porowski, Andrew Randall, Sean Rooney, Eberhard Siegele, Stane Štraus (www.polymernotes.org), Bill Stubkjaer, Christoph Thomas, Frank van Tiel, Allan Tilley, David White, Trevor Wilkin (www.polymernotes.com), and others.

Sources

Boon, K. N. *World Paper & Polymer Uncut Banknotes.* 1st edition. 2012. ISBN 978-983-43313-4-4. Trigometric Sdn.Bhd. (www.3833.com), Lot 327, Amcorp Mall, 18 Jalan Persiaran Barat, off Jalan Timur, Petaling Jaya, 46050 Selangor D.E., Malaysia.

Cuhaj, George S. *Standard Catalog of World Paper Money, Modern Issues, 1961-Present.* 18th edition. 2012. ISBN 978-1-4402-2956-5. Krause Publications (www.krausebooks.com), 700 East State St., Iola, WI, 54990-0001.

Cleveland, Donald R. "The Bank Notes of Papua New Guinea Part I—The Pre-Independence Years." *IBNS Journal.* Volume 31 Number 2. p.7.

Cleveland, Donald R. "The Bank Notes of Papua New Guinea — Part II Issues After Independence." *IBNS Journal.* Volume 31 Number 3. p.13.

Eu, Peter, Ben Chiew, and Stane Straus. *World Polymer Banknotes: A Standard Reference.* 2nd edition. 2006. ISBN 983-43038-2-3. Eureka Metro, P. O. Box 30, Jalan Kelang Lama, Kuala Lumpur, 57000, Malaysia.

Krause, Thomas and Peter Bauer. *Specialized Catalogue of World Plastic Money.* 5th edition. 2009. www.polymernotes.de.

Krause, Thomas. "Die Banknoten von Papua Neuguinea." www.papuanotes.de

Mira, William John Dickson. *From Cowrie to Kina: The coinages, currencies, badges, medals, awards, and decorations of Papua New Guinea.* 1986. ISBN 978-0959320305. Spink & Son (Australia) Pty. Ltd., APA Chambers, 53 Martin Place, Sydney, NSW 2000.

Share Your Input, Info, and Images

This catalog is believed to be complete and correct as of the time of publication. Prices and face values were last updated 15 August 2014. Please report errors or omissions so that corrections may be made. If you can more precisely identify the name or location of anything depicted on a note, please share that information. Furthermore, if you own an unlisted type or variety, please submit scans of the front and back of the note so that it can be documented. Scans should be 300 dots per inch, 100% actual size, 24-bit color, saved as *uncompressed* JPEG files, and sent to owen@banknotenews.com. Be sure to fully describe all attributes of the note which are not apparent upon visual inspection of the images alone, such as physical dimension, watermark, and security thread.

Paraguay

Earlier Issues

Prior to the establishment of the Banco Central del Paraguay on 25 March 1952, banknotes were issued by El Tesoro Nacional, La Tesoreria General, Caja de Conversión, Tesoro Nacional, República del Paraguay, El Banco de la República del Paraguay, and Banco del Paraguay. These issues will be added to this chapter in the future.

Monetary System

05.10.1943: 1 Paraguayan guaraní (PYG) = 100 cents

Spanish Months of the Year

Enero (January)	Febrero (February)	Marzo (March)
Abril (April)	Mayo (May)	Junio (June)
Julio (July)	Agosto (August)	Septiembre (September)
Octubre (October)	Noviembre (November)	Diciembre (December)

Banco Central del Paraguay (Central Bank of Paraguay)

The Banco Central del Paraguay (BCP) was established by law 18 on 25 March 1952. It took over operations from the Banco del Paraguay. For more information, visit www.bcp.gov.py.

BCP Signature Varieties

	GERENTE	PRESIDENTE
1	Hermógenes González Maya	Epifanio Méndez Fleitas
2	Pedro Alcantara Caballero	Epifanio Méndez Fleitas
3	Pedro Ramón Chamorro (different width signatures exist)	Gustavo Storm
4	Pedro Ramón Chamorro	César Romeo Acosta (Sept. 1960 - Feb. 1989)
5	Óscar Stark Rivarola (different width signatures exist)	César Romeo Acosta (Sept. 1960 - Feb. 1989)

BCP Signature Varieties

6
Augusto Colmán Villamayor — César Romeo Acosta (Sept. 1960 - Feb. 1989)

7
Alberto Cáceres Ferreira — César Romeo Acosta (Sept. 1960 - Feb. 1989)

8
Óscar Rodríguez — Crispiniano Sandoval (Feb. 1989 - Mar. 1991)

9
Rubén Falcón Silva — José Enrique Paéz (Mar. 1991 - Aug. 1993)

10
Carlos Aquino Benítez — Jacinto Estigarribia Mallada (Aug. 1993 - June 1995)

11
Carlos Aquino Benítez — Dionisio Coronel

12
Edgar Isidro Cáceres Vera — Dionisio Coronel

13
Edgar Isidro Cáceres Vera — Hermes Aníbal Gómez Ginard (June 1995 - Aug. 1998)

14
Edgar Isidro Cáceres Vera — Washington Aswhell (Apr. 1999 - May 2001)

BCP Signature Varieties

	GERENTE GENERAL	PRESIDENTE
15	 Gilberto Rodríguez Garcete	 Raúl José Vera Bogado (May 2001 - Nov. 2002)
16	 Gilberto Rodríguez Garcete	 Juan Antonio Ortiz Vely (Nov. 2002 - 2007)
17	 Gilberto Rodríguez Garcete	 Ángel Gabriel González Cáceres
18	 Darío Rolando Arréllaga Yaluk	 Mónica Pérez Dos Santos
19	 Darío Rolando Arréllaga Yaluk	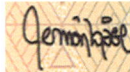 Germán Hugo Rojas Irigoyen (2007 - 2008)
20	Jorge Aurelio Villalba Leguizamón	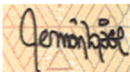 Germán Hugo Rojas Irigoyen (2007 - 2008)
21	Jorge Aurelio Villalba Leguizamón	 Jorge Raúl Corvalán Mendoza (different signatures exist) (2008 - 2013)
22	Jorge Aurelio Villalba Leguizamón	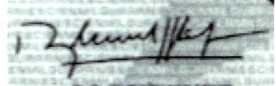 Carlos Fernández Valdovinos (October 2013 - present)

1952 Issues

These notes are like the preceding issues of 1943, but carry the name of the new bank, as well as the new authorizing law date of 25 March 1952, and they have solid security threads (as well as colored fibers on later issues).

BCP B1 (P185): 1 guaraní   VG   VF   UNC

Green and brown. Front: Soldado paraguayo (Paraguayan soldier) with machete and rifle; Ministry of Finance oval shield with lion and cap. Back: Banco Central del Paraguay headquarters building in Asunción. Solid security thread. Watermark: None. Printer: *THOMAS DE LA RUE & COY. LTD. LONDRES, INGLATERRA.* 120 x 60 mm.

		VG	VF	UNC
☐ a.	25 DE MARZO DE 1952. Signature 2. One red serial number. Serie A.	0.75	2.50	10
☐ b1.	Signature 3. 42-mm wide *GERENTE* signature.	0.75	2.50	10
☐ b2.	18-mm wide *GERENTE* signature. Serie A, B.	0.75	2.50	10
☐ c.	Signature 4. Serie B. Security fibers added at right front.	0.75	2.50	10
☐ d.	Signature 5.	0.75	2.50	10
☐ e.	Two black serial numbers.	0.50	1.50	6
☐ s1.	Diagonal black *SPECIMEN* and DLR oval ovpts; horiz. black *SPECIMEN No.* # ovpt at lower left.	—	—	—
☐ s2.	Diagonal *SPECIMEN* perforation.	—	—	—
☐ s3.	Horizontal *CANCELLED* perforation.	—	—	100

BCP B2 (P186): **5 guaraníes** VG VF UNC
Blue and red. Front: General José Eduvigis Díaz; Ministry of Finance oval shield with lion and cap. Back: Banco Central del Paraguay headquarters building in Asunción. Solid security thread. Watermark: None. Printer: *THOMAS DE LA RUE & COY. LTD. LONDRES, INGLATERRA*. 124 x 64 mm.

		VG	VF	UNC
☐ a.	25 DE MARZO DE 1952. Signature 1. One red serial number. Serie A.	1.50	5	20
☐ b1.	Signature 3. 42-mm wide *GERENTE* signature.	1	4	15
☐ b2.	18-mm wide *GERENTE* signature.	1.50	5	20
☐ c.	Security fibers added at right front.	1.50	5	20
☐ d.	Signature 5. Two black serial numbers. Prefix A.	1	4	15
☐ s1.	Diagonal black *SPECIMEN* and DLR oval ovpts; horiz. black *SPECIMEN No.* # ovpt at lower left.	—	—	—
☐ s2.	Diagonal *SPECIMEN* perforation.	—	—	—
☐ s3.	Horizontal *CANCELLED* perforation.	—	—	100

BCP B3 (P187): **10 guaraníes** VG VF UNC
Red and purple. Front: Don Carlos Antonio López; Ministry of Finance oval shield with lion and cap. Back: Banco Central del Paraguay headquarters building in Asunción. Solid security thread. Watermark: None. Printer: *THOMAS DE LA RUE & COY. LTD. LONDRES, INGLATERRA*. 125 x 70 mm.

		VG	VF	UNC
☐ a.	25 DE MARZO DE 1952. Signature 1. One black serial number. Serie A.	1	4	17
☐ b.	Signature 2.	1.25	5	23
☐ c1.	Signature 3. 42-mm wide *GERENTE* signature.	1.25	5	23
☐ c2.	18-mm wide *GERENTE* signature. Security fibers added at right front.	0.75	2.50	11
☐ d.	Signature 4.	1.25	5	23
☐ e.	Signature 5.	1	4	15
☐ f.	Two black serial numbers. Prefix B.	0.75	2.50	11
☐ s1.	Diagonal black *SPECIMEN* and DLR oval ovpts; horizon. red *SPECIMEN No.* # ovpt at lower left.	—	—	150
☐ s2.	Diagonal *SPECIMEN* perforation.	—	—	—
☐ s3.	Horizontal *CANCELLED* perforation.	—	—	100

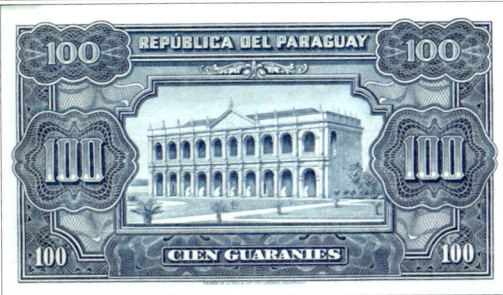

BCP B4 (P188): **50 guaraníes**   VG   VF   UNC

Brown and olive green. Front: Dr. José Gaspar Rodríguez de Francia; Ministry of Finance oval shield with lion and cap. Back: Banco Central del Paraguay headquarters building in Asunción. Solid security thread. Watermark: None. Printer: *THOMAS DE LA RUE & COY. LTD. LONDRES, INGLATERRA.* 125 x 75 mm.

		VG	VF	UNC
☐ a.	25 DE MARZO DE 1952. Signature 1. One black serial number. Serie A.	2.50	10	40
☐ b.	Signature 2.	2.50	10	40
☐ c1.	Signature 3. 42-mm wide *GERENTE* signature.	2.50	10	40
☐ c2.	18-mm wide *GERENTE* signature.	2.50	10	40
☐ d.	Signature 5. Security fibers added at right front.	2	8	35
☐ s1.	Diagonal black *SPECIMEN* and DLR oval ovpts; horiz. black *SPECIMEN No. #* ovpt at lower left.	—	—	—
☐ s2.	Diagonal *SPECIMEN* perforation.	—	—	—
☐ s3.	Horizontal *CANCELLED* perforation.	—	—	130

BCP B5 (P189): **100 guaraníes**   VG   VF   UNC

Green and blue. Front: Mariscal José Félix Estigarribia; Ministry of Finance oval shield with lion and cap. Back: Palacio Legislativo (Legislative Palace) building in Asunción. Solid security thread. Watermark: None. Printer: *THOMAS DE LA RUE & COY. LTD. LONDRES, INGLATERRA.* 140 x 80 mm.

		VG	VF	UNC
☐ a.	25 DE MARZO DE 1952. Signature 1. One black serial number. Serie A.	4	15	60
☐ b.	Signature 2.	4	15	60
☐ c1.	Signature 3. 42-mm wide *GERENTE* signature.	4	15	60
☐ c2.	18-mm wide *GERENTE* signature. Security fibers added at right front.	4	15	60
☐ d.	Signature 4.	4	15	60
☐ e.	Signature 5.	2.50	10	45
☐ s1.	Diagonal black *SPECIMEN* and DLR oval ovpts; horiz. black *SPECIMEN No. #* ovpt at lower left.	—	—	—
☐ s2.	Diagonal *SPECIMEN* perforation.	—	—	—

PARAGUAY 1963 ISSUES

BCP B6 (P190): **500 guaraníes**   VG   VF   UNC

Blue, red, pink, and light green. Front: Mariscal Francisco Solano López; Ministry of Finance oval shield with lion and cap. Back: Oratorio de la Virgen de la Asunción y Panteón Nacional de los Héroes (Oratory of Our Lady of the Assumption and the National Pantheon of Heroes. Solid security thread. Watermark: None. Printer: *THOMAS DE LA RUE & COY. LTD. LONDRES, INGLATERRA.* 148 x 83 mm.

		VG	VF	UNC
☐ a.	25 DE MARZO DE 1952. Signature 1. One red serial number. Serie A.	50	175	—
☐ b.	Signature 2.	50	175	—
☐ c1.	Signature 3. 42-mm wide *GERENTE* signature.	50	175	—
☐ c2.	Security fibers added at right front.	50	175	—
☐ c3.	18-mm wide *GERENTE* signature.	50	175	—
☐ d.	Signature 5.	50	175	—
☐ s1.	Diagonal red *SPECIMEN* and DLR oval ovpts; horiz. red *SPECIMEN No.* # ovpt at lower left.	—	—	475
☐ s2.	Diagonal *SPECIMEN* perforation.	—	—	—
☐ s3.	Diagonal *CANCELLED* perforation.	—	—	200

BCP B7 (P191): **1,000 guaraníes**   VG   VF   UNC

Violet and orange. Front: Men standing around table with overturned chair, declaring independence from Spain on 14 de Mayo de 1811; Ministry of Finance oval shield with lion and cap. Back: Building in Asunción. Solid security thread. Watermark: None. Printer: *THOMAS DE LA RUE & COY. LTD. LONDRES, INGLATERRA.* 160 x 85 mm.

		VG	VF	UNC
☐ a.	25 DE MARZO DE 1952. Signature 1. One black serial number. Serie A.	60	250	—
☐ b.	Signature 2.	60	250	—
☐ c1.	Signature 3. 42-mm wide *GERENTE* signature.	60	250	—
☐ c2.	Security fibers added at right front.	60	250	—
☐ c3.	18-mm wide *GERENTE* signature.	60	250	—
☐ d.	Signature 5.	60	250	—
☐ s1.	Diagonal black DLR oval ovpts; horiz. black *SPECIMEN No.* # ovpt at lower left.	—	—	—
☐ s2.	Diagonal *SPECIMEN* perforation.	—	—	—

1963 Issues

These notes, and all subsequent issues, are all the same size (157 x 67 mm) and have two serial numbers on front, though the position of the left serial number moved from the lower corner to the upper corner on some denominations.

BCP B8 (P192): 1 guaraní   VG   VF   UNC

Green. Front: Ministry of Finance oval shield with lion and cap; soldado paraguayo (Paraguayan soldier) with machete and rifle. Back: Banco Central del Paraguay headquarters building in Asunción; trees. Solid security thread. Watermark: None. Printer: *THOMAS DE LA RUE & COMPANY, LIMITED.* 157 x 67 mm.

- ☐ a. 25 DE MARZO DE 1952. Intro: 15.08.1963.   0.25   1   4
  Signature 5. Prefix A.
- ☐ as. Diagonal red *SPECIMEN* overprint.   —   —   —

Replacement notes: Prefix Z.

BCP B9 (P193): 1 guaraní   VG   VF   UNC

Green. Front: Ministry of Finance oval shield with lion and cap; soldado paraguayo (Paraguayan soldier) with machete and rifle. Back: Palacio Legislativo (Legislative Palace) building, trees, statue and flag poles in Asunción. Solid security thread. Watermark: None. Printer: *THOMAS DE LA RUE & COMPANY, LIMITED.* 157 x 67 mm.

- ☐ a1. 25 DE MARZO DE 1952.   0.25   1   4
  Signature 5. Prefix A.
  Left serial number at lower corner.
  20-mm wide *GERENTE* signature.
- ☐ a2. 30-mm wide *GERENTE* signature.   0.25   1   4
- ☐ b. Signature 6.   0.25   1   4
- ☐ c. Left serial number at upper corner.   0.25   1   4
- ☐ s1. Diagonal red *SPECIMEN* overprint.   —   —   —
- ☐ s2. Diagonal black *SPECIMEN* and DLR oval ovpts;   —   —   —
  horizon. black *SPECIMEN Nº #* ovpt at lower left;
  punched; no sigs; left s/n at lower corner.
- ☐ cs. Diagonal red *MUESTRA SIN VALOR* overprint.   —   —   —
  No signature. Serial number at upper left.

Replacement notes: Prefix Z.

BCP B10 (P194): 5 guaraníes   VG   VF   UNC

Blue. Front: Ministry of Finance oval shield with lion and cap; La Mujer Paraguaya (Paraguayan woman) holding vase. Back: Hotel Guaraní building. Solid security thread. Watermark: None. Printer: *THOMAS DE LA RUE & COMPANY, LIMITED.* 157 x 67 mm.

- ☐ a. 25 DE MARZO DE 1952. Intro: 15.08.1963.   1   4   15
  Signature 5. Prefix A.
- ☐ as1. Diagonal red *SPECIMEN* overprint.   —   —   —
- ☐ as2. Diagonal red *MUESTRA SIN VALOR* overprint.   —   —   —
  No signature. Serial number at upper left.

Replacement notes: Prefix Z.

BCP B11 (P195): 5 guaraníes   VG   VF   UNC

Black. Front: Ministry of Finance oval shield with lion and cap; La Mujer Paraguaya (Paraguayan woman) holding vase. Back: Hotel Guaraní building. Solid security thread. Watermark: None. Printer: *THOMAS DE LA RUE & COMPANY, LIMITED.* 157 x 67 mm.

- ☐ a1. 25 DE MARZO DE 1952.   1   4   15
  Signature 5. Prefix A.
  Left serial number at lower corner.
  42-mm wide *GERENTE* signature.
- ☐ a2. 30-mm wide *GERENTE* signature.   1   4   15
- ☐ b. Signature 6.   1   4   15
- ☐ c. Left serial number at upper corner.   0.25   1   4
- ☐ cs. Diagonal red *MUESTRA SIN VALOR* overprint;   —   —   50
  no signatures.

Replacement notes: Prefix Z.

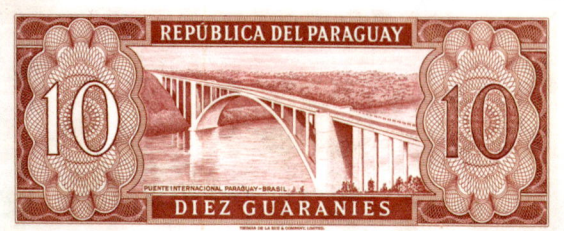

BCP B12 (P196): **10 guaraníes** VG VF UNC

Red. Front: Ministry of Finance oval shield with lion and cap; General Eugenio A. Garay. Back: Puente Internacional Paraguay-Brasil (International Bridge of Friendship) over Paraná River between Paraguay and Brazil. Solid security thread. Watermark: None. Printer: *THOMAS DE LA RUE & COMPANY, LIMITED*. 157 x 67 mm.

			VG	VF	UNC
☐	a1.	25 DE MARZO DE 1952. Intro: 15.08.1963. Signature 5. Prefix A. Left serial number at lower corner. 42-mm wide *GERENTE* signature.	1.50	6	25
☐	a2.	30-mm wide *GERENTE* signature.	1.50	6	25
☐	b.	Signature 6.	0.50	1.25	5
☐	c.	Left serial number at upper corner. With or without UV pattern of *10* at front center.	0.25	1	4
☐	s1.	Diagonal black *SPECIMEN* overprint.	—	—	25
☐	s2.	Diagonal black *SPECIMEN* and DLR oval ovpts; horizon. black *SPECIMEN Nº #* ovpt at lower left; punched; no sigs; left s/n at lower corner.	—	—	70
☐	cs.	Diagonal red *MUESTRA SIN VALOR* overprint; no signatures.	—	—	—

Replacement notes: Prefix Z.

BCP B13 (P197): **50 guaraníes** VG VF UNC

Brown. Front: Ministry of Finance oval shield with lion and cap; Mariscal José Félix Estigarribia. Back: Ruta Trans-Chaco; hut, palm trees, road, bridge, stream, men on horseback, and cattle. Solid security thread. Watermark: None. Printer: *THOMAS DE LA RUE & COMPANY, LIMITED*. 157 x 67 mm.

			VG	VF	UNC
☐	a1.	25 DE MARZO DE 1952. Intro: 15.08.1963. Signature 5. Prefix A. Left serial number at lower corner. 42-mm wide *GERENTE* signature.	2.50	10	40
☐	a2.	30-mm wide *GERENTE* signature.	2.50	10	40
☐	b.	Signature 6.	1.50	5	20
☐	c.	Left serial number at upper corner. With or without UV pattern of *50* at front center.	0.75	2.50	10
☐	s1.	Diagonal red *SPECIMEN* overprint.	—	—	25
☐	s2.	Diagonal red *SPECIMEN* and DLR oval ovpts; horizontal red *SPECIMEN Nº #* ovpt at lower left; punched; no sigs; left s/n at lower corner.	—	—	70
☐	cs.	Diagonal red *MUESTRA SIN VALOR* overprint; no signatures.	—	—	—

Replacement notes: Prefix Z.

BCP B14 (P198): **100 guaraníes** VG VF UNC

Green. Front: Ministry of Finance oval shield with lion and cap; General José Eduvigis Díaz. Back: Ruinas de Humaitá 1865/70 (ruins of St. Charles Borromeo Church in Humaitá). Solid security thread. Watermark: None. Printer: *THOMAS DE LA RUE & COMPANY, LIMITED*. 157 x 67 mm.

			VG	VF	UNC
☐	a.	25 DE MARZO DE 1952. Intro: 15.08.1963. Signature 5. Prefix A.	1.25	5	20
☐	as.	Diagonal red *SPECIMEN* overprint.	—	—	25

Replacement notes: Prefix Z.

BCP B15 (P199): **100 guaraníes**   VG   VF   UNC

Orange. Front: Ministry of Finance oval shield with lion and cap; General José Eduvigis Díaz. Back: Ruinas de Humaitá 1865/70 (ruins of St. Charles Borromeo Church in Humaitá). Solid security thread. Watermark: None. Printer: THOMAS DE LA RUE & COMPANY, LIMITED. 157 x 67 mm.

- a. 25 DE MARZO DE 1952.   1.50   6   25
  Signature 5. Prefix A.
  Left serial number at lower corner.
- b. Signature 6.   1   4   16
- c. Left serial number at upper corner.   0.75   3   14
  With or without UV pattern of 100 at front center.
- cs. Diagonal red MUESTRA SIN VALOR overprint;   —   —   —
  no signatures.

Replacement notes: Prefix Z.

BCP B16 (P200): **500 guaraníes**   VG   VF   UNC

Blue. Front: Ministry of Finance oval shield with lion and cap; General Bernardino Caballero; column. Back: Flota Mercante del Estado (state merchant fleet) ships in port with cranes. Solid security thread. Watermark: None. Printer: THOMAS DE LA RUE & COMPANY, LIMITED. 157 x 67 mm.

- a. 25 DE MARZO DE 1952. Intro: 15.08.1963.   2.50   10   40
  Signature 5. Prefix A.
  Left serial number at lower corner.
- b. Signature 6.   2.50   10   40
- c. Left serial number at upper corner.   2.50   10   40
- bs. Diagonal red MUESTRA SIN VALOR overprint;   —   —   25
  no signatures.

Replacement notes: Prefix Z.

BCP B17 (P201): **1,000 guaraníes** (demonetized 06.01.2014)   VG   VF   UNC

Purple. Front: Ministry of Finance oval shield with lion and cap; Mariscal Francisco Solano López; column. Back: Oratorio de la Virgen de la Asunción y Panteón Nacional de los Héroes (Oratory of Our Lady of the Assumption and the National Pantheon of Heroes). Solid security thread. Watermark: None. Printer: THOMAS DE LA RUE & COMPANY, LIMITED. 157 x 67 mm.

- a1. 25 DE MARZO DE 1952. Intro: 15.08.1963.   2.50   10   40
  Signature 5. Prefix A.
  Left serial number at lower corner.
  42-mm wide GERENTE signature.
- a2. Narrower GERENTE signature.   2.50   10   40
- b. Signature 6.   2.50   10   40
- c. Left serial number at upper corner.   2.50   10   40
- s1. Diagonal red MUESTRA SIN VALOR overprint;   —   —   25
  no signatures.
- s2. Diagonal red SPECIMEN ovpt; no signatures;   —   —   25
  left serial number at lower corner.

Replacement notes: Prefix Z.

BCP B18 (P202): **5,000 guaraníes** (US$1.10)   VG   VF   UNC

Red. Front: Ministry of Finance oval shield with lion and cap; Don Carlos Antonio López. Back: Palacio de los López (Lopez Palace) building in Asunción. Solid security thread. Watermark: None. Printer: THOMAS DE LA RUE & COMPANY, LIMITED. 157 x 67 mm.

- a1. 25 DE MARZO DE 1952. Intro: 15.08.1963.   8   30   120
  Signature 5. Prefix A.
  Left serial number at lower corner.
  42-mm wide GERENTE signature.
- a2. 30-mm wide GERENTE signature.   8   30   120
- b. Signature 6.   8   30   120
- c. Left serial number at upper corner.   8   30   120
- s. Diagonal red SPECIMEN overprint.   —   —   25
- bs. Diagonal red MUESTRA SIN VALOR overprint;   —   —   25
  no signatures.

Replacement notes: Prefix Z.

BCP B19 (P203 & P204): **10,000 guaraníes** (US$2.25) VG VF UNC
Olive green. Front: Ministry of Finance oval shield with lion and cap; Dr. José Gaspar Rodríguez de Francia. Back: Men standing around table with overturned chair, declaring independence from Spain on 14 de Mayo de 1811. Solid security thread. Watermark: None. Printer: *THOMAS DE LA RUE & COMPANY, LIMITED*. 157 x 67 mm.

☐ a. 25 DE MARZO DE 1952. Intro: 15.08.1963. 8 30 120
    Signature 5. Prefix A.
    Left serial number at lower corner.
    Portrait title as *DR. JOSÉ CASPAR...* (error).
☐ b. Signature 6. 10 40 150
    Portrait title as *DR. JOSÉ GASPAR...* (correct).
☐ c. Left serial number at upper corner. 10 40 150
☐ as1. Diagonal red *SPECIMEN* overprint. — — 25
☐ as2. Diagonal red *MUESTRA SIN VALOR* overprint. — — 25
    No signature. Serial number at upper left.
Replacement notes: Prefix Z.

1978 Numismatic Products

Thomas De La Rue created "official presentation sets of specimen banknotes from around the world" for The Franklin Mint, a private company that mailed the sets every six weeks to subscribers from 1978 to 1979. Each set of notes with matching serial numbers originally cost $14 and came in an envelope with a numbered and dated certificate of authenticity and an index card describing the notes in detail. Based upon serial numbers observed, at least 10,440 sets were produced, and a complete collection comprises 15 sets with a total of 73 notes from 16 issuing authorities. Rarely available in the original small brown storage box, the notes are usually sold by country set, but are sometimes sold individually. Do not mistake these numismatic products for the specimen varieties listed separately, which the security printer created for its note-issuing clients.

BCP BNP1 (PCS1): **100 - 10,000 guaraníes** UNC
☐ a. BCP B15-B19 (5 notes) with diagonal *SPECIMEN* overprint and 25
    Maltese cross prefix. Intro: 28.03.1979.

1982-1990 Bilingual Issues

These notes are like the preceding issues, but with the denomination spelled in Spanish on the front and Guaraní on the back.

BCP B20 (P205): **100 guaraníes** VG VF UNC
Green. Front: Ministry of Finance oval shield with lion and cap; General José Eduvigis Díaz. Back: Ruinas de Humaitá 1865/70 (ruins of St. Charles Borromeo Church in Humaitá). Solid security thread. Watermark: None. Printer: *THOMAS DE LA RUE & COMPANY, LIMITED*. 157 x 67 mm.

☐ a. 25 DE MARZO DE 1952. Intro: 1982. 0.25 0.75 3.50
    Signature 6. Prefix A.
☐ b. Signature 7. 0.25 0.75 3.50
☐ c. Signature 8. 0.25 0.75 3.50
☐ d. Signature 9. 0.25 0.75 3.50
Replacement notes: Prefix Z.

BCP B21 (P206): **500 guaraníes** VG VF UNC
Blue. Front: Ministry of Finance oval shield with lion and cap; General Bernardino Caballero; column. Back: Flota Mercante del Estado (state merchant fleet) ships in port with cranes. Solid security thread. Watermark: None. Printer: *THOMAS DE LA RUE & COMPANY, LIMITED*. 157 x 67 mm.

☐ a. 25 DE MARZO DE 1952. Intro: 1982. 0.50 2 7
    Signature 6. Prefix A.
☐ b. Signature 7. 0.50 2 7
☐ c. Signature 8. 0.50 2 7
☐ d. Signature 9. 0.50 2 7
☐ e. Signature 10. 0.50 2 7
☐ f. Signature 11. 0.50 2 7
Replacement notes: Prefix Z.

BCP B22 (P207): **1,000 guaraníes** (demonetized 06.01.2014)   VG   VF   UNC
Purple. Front: Ministry of Finance oval shield with lion and cap; Mariscal Francisco Solano López; column. Back: Oratorio de la Virgen de la Asunción y Panteón Nacional de los Héroes (Oratory of Our Lady of the Assumption and the National Pantheon of Heroes). Solid security thread. Watermark: None. Printer: *THOMAS DE LA RUE & COMPANY, LIMITED*. 157 x 67 mm.

- ☐ a. 25 DE MARZO DE 1952. Intro: 1982.   1   3   13
  Signature 6. Prefix A.
- ☐ b. Signature 7.   1   3   13
- ☐ c. Signature 8.   1   3   13
- ☐ d. Signature 9.   1   3   13
- ☐ e. Signature 10.   1   3   13
- ☐ f. Signature 11.   1   3   13

Replacement notes: Prefix Z.

BCP B23 (P208): **5,000 guaraníes** (US$1.10)   VG   VF   UNC
Red. Front: Ministry of Finance oval shield with lion and cap; Don Carlos Antonio López. Back: Palacio de los López (Lopez Palace) building in Asunción. Solid security thread. Watermark: None. Printer: *THOMAS DE LA RUE & COMPANY, LIMITED*. 157 x 67 mm.

- ☐ a. 25 DE MARZO DE 1952. Intro: 1982.   4   15   70
  Signature 6. Prefix A.
- ☐ b. Signature 7.   4   15   70
- ☐ c. Signature 8.   4   15   70
- ☐ d. Signature 9.   4   15   70
- ☐ e. Signature 10.   4   15   70
- ☐ f. Signature 11.   4   15   70
- ☐ g. Signature 12.   4   15   70
- ☐ h. Signature 13.   4   15   70

Replacement notes: Prefix Z.

BCP B24 (P209): **10,000 guaraníes** (US$2.25)   VG   VF   UNC
Olive green. Front: Ministry of Finance oval shield with lion and cap; Dr. José Gaspar Rodríguez de Francia. Back: Men standing around table with overturned chair, declaring independence from Spain on 14 de Mayo de 1811. Solid security thread. Watermark: None. Printer: *THOMAS DE LA RUE & COMPANY, LIMITED*. 157 x 67 mm.

- ☐ a. 25 DE MARZO DE 1952. Intro: 1982.   —   —   —
  Signature 6. Prefix A.
- ☐ b. Signature 7.   —   —   —
- ☐ c. Signature 8.   —   —   —
- ☐ d. Signature 10.   —   —   —
- ☐ e. Signature 11.   —   —   —
- ☐ f. Signature 12.   —   —   —
- ☐ g. Signature 13.   —   —   —
- ☐ h. Signature 15. Intro: 2001.   —   —   —

Replacement notes: Prefix Z.

BCP B25 (P210): **50,000 guaraníes** (demonetized 04.10.2012)   VG   VF   UNC
Blue, green, and orange. Front: Cap as registration device; round coat of arms with star; stylized map of Paraguay; round emblem with lion and cap; soldado paraguayo (Paraguayan soldier) with machete and rifle. Back: Casa de la Independencia (Independence House) museum building in Asunción. Solid security thread. Watermark: Soldier. Printer: *THOMAS DE LA RUE AND COMPANY LIMITED*. 157 x 67 mm.

- ☐ a. 25 DE MARZO DE 1952. Intro: 1990.   —   —   —
  Signature 8. Prefix A.
- ☐ b. Signature 9.   —   —   —
- ☐ c. Signature 10.   —   —   —

Replacement notes: Prefix Z.

1994 Issues

These notes are like the preceding issues, but with windowed security threads instead of solid threads, horizontal serial number in green, not black, and a gray geometric overprint on the map at center front.

BCP B26 (P211): **50,000 guaraníes** (demonetized 04.10.2012)   VG   VF   UNC

Blue, green, and orange. Front: Cap as registration device; round coat of arms with star; stylized map of Paraguay; round emblem with lion and cap; soldado paraguayo (Paraguayan soldier) with machete and rifle. Back: Casa de la Independencia (Independence House) museum building in Asunción. Windowed security thread. Watermark: Soldier. Printer: THOMAS DE LA RUE AND COMPANY LIMITED. 157 x 67 mm.

- [ ] a. 25 DE MARZO DE 1952. Intro: 1994. — — —
        Signature 10. Prefix A.
- [ ] b. Signature 11. — — —
- [ ] c. Signature 12. — — —
- [ ] d. Signature 13. — — —

1995 Issues

These notes are like the preceding issues, but with slightly modified engravings and new printer imprints.

BCP B27 (P212): **500 guaraníes**   VG   VF   UNC

Blue. Front: Ministry of Finance oval shield with lion and cap; General Bernardino Caballero; column. Back: Flota Mercante del Estado (state merchant fleet) ships in port with cranes. Solid security thread. Watermark: None. Printer: FRANÇOIS-CHARLES OBERTHUR. 157 x 67 mm.

- [ ] a. 25 DE MARZO DE 1952. Intro: 1995.   0.25   1.25   6
        Signature 12. Prefix A.
- [ ] b. Signature 13.   0.25   1.25   6

BCP B28 (P213): **1,000 guaraníes** (demonetized 06.01.2014)   VG   VF   UNC

Purple. Front: Ministry of Finance oval shield with lion and cap; Mariscal Francisco Solano López; column. Back: Oratorio de la Virgen de la Asunción y Panteón Nacional de los Héroes (Oratory of Our Lady of the Assumption and the National Pantheon of Heroes). Solid security thread. Watermark: None. Printer: FRANÇOIS-CHARLES OBERTHUR. 157 x 67 mm.

- [ ] a. 25 DE MARZO DE 1952. Intro: 1995.   0.50   2   8
        Signature 12. Prefix A.
- [ ] b. Signature 13.   0.50   2   8

1997-2003 Issues

These notes all bear the authorizing law (489/95) date of 29 June 1995 in the lower border, but they also bear the series year on front.

BCP B29 (P214): 1,000 guaraníes (demonetized 06.01.2014)   VG   VF   UNC
Purple. Front: Round coat of arms with star; round emblem with lion and cap; Mariscal Francisco Solano López; column. Back: Oratorio de la Virgen de la Asunción y Panteón Nacional de los Héroes (Oratory of Our Lady of the Assumption and the National Pantheon of Heroes). Solid security thread. Watermark: None. Printer: *CICCONE CALCOGRAFICA S.A.* 157 x 67 mm.
  a. 1998. Signature 13. Prefix B.   0.50   2   8

BCP B30 (P215): 5,000 guaraníes (US$1.10)   VG   VF   UNC
Red. Front: Ministry of Finance oval shield with lion and cap; Don Carlos Antonio López. Back: Palacio de los López (Lopez Palace) building in Asunción. Windowed security thread with demetalized *G5000*. Watermark: None. Printer: *THOMAS DE LA RUE & COMPANY, LIMITED*. 157 x 67 mm.
  a. 1997. Signature 13. Prefix B.   —   —   —

BCP B31 (P216a): 10,000 guaraníes (US$2.25)   VG   VF   UNC
Olive green. Front: Round coat of arms with star; round emblem with lion and cap; Dr. José Gaspar Rodríguez de Francia. Back: Men standing around table with overturned chair, declaring independence from Spain on 14 de Mayo de 1811. Windowed security thread with demetalized *G10000*. Watermark: None. Printer: *CICCONE CALCOGRAFICA S.A.* 157 x 67 mm.
  a. 1998. Signature 13. Prefix B.   FV   6   25
  as. Diagonal red *SPECIMEN* overprint.   —   —   —

BCP B32 (P217): 50,000 guaraníes (demonetized 04.10.2012)   VG   VF   UNC
Blue, green, and orange. Front: Cap as registration device; round coat of arms with star; stylized map of Paraguay; round emblem with lion and cap; soldado paraguayo (Paraguayan soldier) with machete and rifle. Back: Casa de la Independencia (Independence House) museum building in Asunción. Windowed security thread with demetalized *G50000*. Watermark: Soldier's head. Printer: *THOMAS DE LA RUE AND COMPANY LIMITED*. 157 x 67 mm.
  a. 1997. Signature 13. Prefix B.   10   20   80
  as. Diagonal red *MUESTRA SIN VALOR* overprint.   —   —   —

BCP B33 (P218): **50,000 guaraníes** (demonetized 04.10.2012) VG VF UNC
Blue, green, and orange. Front: Staircase OVI patch; cap as registration device; round coat of arms with star; stylized map of Paraguay; round emblem with lion and cap; soldado paraguayo (Paraguayan soldier) with machete and rifle. Back: Casa de la Independencia (Independence House) museum building in Asunción. Windowed security thread with demetalized *G50000*. Watermark: Soldier's head. Printer: *DE LA RUE.* 157 x 67 mm.

☐	a.	1998. Signature 13. Prefix B.	2	8	30
☐	as.	Diagonal red *MUESTRA SIN VALOR* overprint.	—	—	—

Like preceding issue, but with staircase OVI patch, shortened printer imprint, and *GERENTE GENERAL* title for left signature.

BCP B34 (P219): **100,000 guaraníes** (US$22) VG VF UNC
Green, blue, and yellow. Front: Holographic patch; round coat of arms with star; round emblem with lion and cap; San Roque González de Santa Cruz. Back: Represa de Itaipu (Itaipu hydroelectric dam) on the Parana River. Windowed security thread with demetalized *G100000*. Watermark: San Roque González de Santa Cruz. Printer: *DE LA RUE.* 157 x 67 mm.

☐	a.	1998. Signature 13. Prefix A.	—	—	—
☐	as.	Diagonal red *MUESTRA SIN VALOR* overprint.	—	—	—

2000-2003 Issues

These notes are like preceding issues, but with intaglio symbols for the blind at lower left front.

BCP B35 (P214): **1,000 guaraníes** (demonetized 06.01.2014) VG VF UNC
Purple. Front: Square symbol for blind; round coat of arms with star; round emblem with lion and cap; Mariscal Francisco Solano López; column. Back: Oratorio de la Virgen de la Asunción y Panteón Nacional de los Héroes (Oratory of Our Lady of the Assumption and the National Pantheon of Heroes). Solid security thread. Watermark: None. 157 x 67 mm.

☐	a.	2001. Signature 15. Prefix B. Printer: *DE LA RUE.*	0.75	2.50	10
☐	b.	2003. Signature 16. Printer: *FRANÇOIS-CHARLES OBERTHUR.*	0.75	2.50	10
☐	as.	Diagonal red *MUESTRA SIN VALOR* overprint.	—	—	—

BCP B36 (P220a): **5,000 guaraníes** (US$1.10) VG VF UNC
Red. Front: Diamond symbol for blind; round coat of arms with star; round emblem with lion and cap; Don Carlos Antonio López. Back: Palacio de los López (Lopez Palace) building in Asunción. Windowed security thread with demetalized *G5000*. Watermark: None. Printer: *CICCONE CALCOGRAFICA S.A.* 157 x 67 mm.

☐	a.	2000. Signature 14. Prefix C. With or without UV *5000* to left of portrait.	0.75	3	12
☐	as.	Diagonal black *SPECIMEN* overprint.	—	—	—

BCP B37 (P220b): **5,000 guaraníes** (US$1.10)　　　　VG　VF　UNC
Red. Front: Diamond symbol for blind; round coat of arms with star; round emblem with lion and cap; Don Carlos Antonio López. Back: Palacio de los López (Lopez Palace) building in Asunción. Windowed security thread with demetalized *G5000*. Watermark: None. Printer: *CICCONE CALCOGRAFICA S.A.* 157 x 67 mm.
- a. 2003. Signature 16. Prefix C.　　　　　FV　2　8
- as. Diagonal red hollow *SIN VALOR* overprint.　—　—　—

Like preceding issue, but diamond symbol for blind at extreme lower left corner.

BCP B38 (P216b): **10,000 guaraníes** (US$2.25)　　　VG　VF　UNC
Olive green. Front: Triangle symbol for blind; round coat of arms with star; round emblem with lion and cap; Dr. José Gaspar Rodríguez de Francia. Back: Men standing around table with overturned chair, declaring independence from Spain on 14 de Mayo de 1811. Windowed security thread with demetalized *G10000*. Watermark: None. Printer: *CICCONE CALCOGRAFICA S.A.* 157 x 67 mm.
- a. 2003. Signature 17. Prefix B.　　　　　FV　FV　10

2002 Commemorative Issues

This note commemorates the 50th anniversary of the Banco Central del Paraguay. Below the date at center front is the text *CINCUENTENARIO DEL BANCO CENTRAL DEL PARAGUAY*.

BCP B39 (P221): **1,000 guaraníes** (demonetized 06.01.2014)　VG　VF　UNC
Purple. Front: Square symbol for blind; round coat of arms with star; round emblem with lion and cap; Mariscal Francisco Solano López; column. Back: Oratorio de la Virgen de la Asunción y Panteón Nacional de los Héroes (Oratory of Our Lady of the Assumption and the National Pantheon of Heroes). Solid security thread. Watermark: None. Printer: *FRANÇOIS-CHARLES OBERTHUR.* 157 x 67 mm.
- a. 2002. Signature 15. Prefix B.　　　　　—　—　2
- as. Diagonal red *MUESTRA SIN VALOR* overprint.　—　—　—

2004-2005 Issues

These notes are like preceding issues, but with full bleed designs, and novel serial numbers printed vertically and horizontally, except the 20,000-guaraní note, on which the vertical serial numbers are all the same size.

BCP B40 (P222): **1,000 guaraníes** (demonetized 06.01.2014)　VG　VF　UNC
Purple. Front: Square symbol for blind; round coat of arms with star; round emblem with lion and cap; Mariscal Francisco Solano López; column. Back: Oratorio de la Virgen de la Asunción y Panteón Nacional de los Héroes (Oratory of Our Lady of the Assumption and the National Pantheon of Heroes). Windowed security thread with demetalized *G1000*. Watermark: Cornerstones. Printer: *DE LA RUE.* 157 x 67 mm.
- a. 2004. Signature 17. Prefix C.　　　　　—　—　1.75
- b. 2005. Signature 18. Prefix D.　　　　　—　—　1.75

BCP B41 (P223a): **5,000 guaraníes** (US$1.10) VG VF UNC

Red. Front: Diamond symbol for blind; round coat of arms with star; round emblem with lion and cap; Don Carlos Antonio López. Back: Palacio de los López (Lopez Palace) building in Asunción. Windowed security thread with demetalized *G5000*. Watermark: Cornerstones. Printer: *DE LA RUE*. 157 x 67 mm.

☐ a.   2005. Signature 18. Prefix D.   FV   FV   5

BCP B42 (P224a): **10,000 guaraníes** (US$2.25) VG VF UNC

Olive green. Front: Triangle symbol for blind; round coat of arms with star; round emblem with lion and cap; Dr. José Gaspar Rodríguez de Francia. Back: Men standing around table with overturned chair, declaring independence from Spain on 14 de Mayo de 1811. Windowed security thread with demetalized *G10000*. Watermark: Cornerstones. Printer: *DE LA RUE*. 157 x 67 mm.

☐ a.   2004. Signature 17. Prefix C.   FV   FV   4

BCP B43 (P225): **20,000 guaraníes** (US$4.50) VG VF UNC

Blue and green. Front: Circle symbol for blind; BCP registration device; round coat of arms with star; round emblem with lion and cap; La Mujer Paraguaya (Paraguayan woman) holding vase. Back: Modern Banco Central del Paraguay headquarters building in Asunción. Windowed security thread with demetalized *G20000*. Watermark: None. Printer: *Giesecke & Devrient*. 157 x 67 mm.

☐ a.   2005. Signature 18. Prefix A.   FV   FV   12
☐ as. Diagonal red *MUESTRA SIN VALOR* overprint.   —   —   —

BCP B44 (P226): **100,000 guaraníes** (US$22) VG VF UNC

Green, blue, and yellow. Front: Semicircle symbol for blind; lion and cap registration device; holographic patch; round coat of arms with star; round emblem with lion and cap; San Roque González de Santa Cruz. Back: Represa de Itaipu (Itaipu hydroelectric dam) on the Parana River. Windowed security thread with demetalized *G100000*. Watermark: San Roque González de Santa Cruz. Printer: *DE LA RUE*. 157 x 67 mm.

☐ a.   2004. Signature 17. Prefix B.   FV   FV   40

BCP B45 (P227): **100,000 guaraníes** (US$22)　　VG　VF　UNC

Green, blue, and yellow. Front: Semicircle symbol for blind; lion and cap registration device; OVI patch; round coat of arms with star; round emblem with lion and cap; San Roque González de Santa Cruz. Back: Represa de Itaipú (Itaipú hydroelectric dam) on the Parana River. Windowed security thread with demetalized *G100000*. Watermark: San Roque González de Santa Cruz. Printer: *FRANÇOIS-CHARLES OBERTHUR*. 157 x 67 mm.

　☐ a.　2005. Signature 18. Prefix C.　　FV　FV　40

Like preceding issue, but with OVI patch instead of hologram and new printer imprint.

2005-2011 Issues

BCP B46 (P228): **2,000 guaraníes** (US$0.45)　　VG　VF　UNC

Purple and green. Front: Open book; round coat of arms with star; round emblem with lion and cap; Adela and Celsa Speratti; BCP registration device. Back: Parade of young men waving flags. No security thread. Watermark: None. 157 x 67 mm. Polymer.

　☐ a.　2008. Signature 21. Intro: 18.12.2009.　FV　FV　2.25
　　　　Printer: *OBERTHUR TECHNOLOGIES*. Prefix A.
　☐ b.　2009. Printer: *Giesecke & Devrient*. Prefix B.　FV　FV　2.50
　☐ c.　2011. Printer: *CANADIAN BANK NOTE*　FV　FV　2.50
　　　　COMPANY, LIMITED. Prefix C.

BCP B47 (P223b): **5,000 guaraníes** (US$1.10)　　VG　VF　UNC

Red. Front: Diamond symbol for blind; round coat of arms with star; round emblem with lion and cap; Don Carlos Antonio López. Back: Palacio de los López (Lopez Palace) building in Asunción. Wide color-changing windowed security thread. Watermark: None. Printer: *Giesecke & Devrient*. 157 x 67 mm.

　☐ a.　2008. Signature 20. Prefix E.　　FV　FV　2

BCP B48 (P224b/c): **10,000 guaraníes** (US$2.25)　　VG　VF　UNC

Olive green. Front: Triangle symbol for blind; round coat of arms with star; round emblem with lion and cap; Dr. José Gaspar Rodríguez de Francia. Back: Men standing around table with overturned chair, declaring independence from Spain on 14 de Mayo de 1811. Watermark: None. 157 x 67 mm.

　☐ a.　2005. Signature 18. Prefix D.　　FV　FV　10
　　　　Narrow windowed security thread with
　　　　demetalized *G10000*. Printer: *DE LA RUE*.
　☐ b.　2008. Signature 21. Prefix E.　　FV　FV　12
　　　　Wide color-changing windowed security thread.
　　　　Printer: *OBERTHUR TECHNOLOGIES*.

Like preceding issue, but with *10 MIL* in upper right corner on front.

BCP B49 (P230a): **20,000 guaraníes** (US$4.50)   VG   VF   UNC

Blue and green. Front: Circle symbol for blind; BCP registration device; round coat of arms with star; round emblem with lion and cap La Mujer Paraguaya (Paraguayan woman) holding vase. Back: Modern Banco Central del Paraguay headquarters building in Asunción. Windowed security thread with demetalized *BCP 20000*. Watermark: La Mujer Paraguaya and electrotype *20 MIL*. Printer: *CRANE CURRENCY*. 157 x 67 mm.

☐ a. 2007. Signature 20. Prefix B. Intro: 10.12.2008.   FV   FV   10

BCP B50 (P225A & P231): **50,000 guaraníes**   VG   VF   UNC

Blue, green, and orange. Front: Staircase OVI patch; star symbol for blind; cap as registration device; round coat of arms with star; stylized map of Paraguay; round emblem with lion and cap; soldado paraguayo (Paraguayan soldier) with machete and rifle. Back: Casa de la Independencia (Independence House) museum building in Asunción. Windowed security thread with demetalized *G50000*. Watermark: Soldier. Printer: *FRANÇOIS-CHARLES OBERTHUR*. 157 x 67 mm.

☐ a. 2005. Signature 18. Prefix C. Unissued.   —   —   75

Six boxes containing 250,000 new 50,000-guaraní notes were stolen during shipment by sea between France and Uruguay. They were intended to enter circulation in early December 2006, but in response to the theft, the bank canceled the emission.

BCP B51 (P232a): **50,000 guaraníes** (US$11)   VG   VF   UNC

Purple, peach, and green. Front: Pentagon symbol for blind; map; guitar registration device; guitarist and composer Agustín Pío Barrios (also known as Mangoré) in tuxedo; round coat of arms with star; round emblem with lion and cap. Back: Guitar. Windowed security thread with demetalized *G50000*. Watermark: Agustín Pío Barrios. Printer: *FRANÇOIS-CHARLES OBERTHUR*. 157 x 67 mm.

☐ a. 2007. Signature 19. Prefix D. Intro: 12.05.2008.   FV   FV   15

2007-2013 Issues

These notes are like the preceding issues, but with Motion security threads instead of windowed threads, and other changes to the engravings due to a switch in printers.

BCP B52 (P230b): **20,000 guaraníes** (US$4.50)   VG   VF   UNC

Blue and green. Front: Circle symbol for blind; BCP registration device; round coat of arms with star; round emblem with lion and cap La Mujer Paraguaya (Paraguayan woman) holding vase. Back: Modern Banco Central del Paraguay headquarters building in Asunción. Motion windowed security thread. Watermark: La Mujer Paraguaya and electrotype *20 MIL*. Printer: *Giesecke & Devrient*. 157 x 67 mm.

☐ a. 2009. Signature 21. Prefix C.   FV   FV   10
☐ b. 2011. Prefix D.   FV   FV   10

BCP B53 (P232b/c): **50,000 guaraníes** (US$11)   VG   VF   UNC

Purple, peach, and green. Front: Pentagon symbol for blind; map; guitar registration device; guitarist and composer Agustín Pío Barrios (also known as Mangoré) in tuxedo; round coat of arms with star; round emblem with lion and cap. Back: Guitar. Motion windowed security thread. Watermark: Agustín Pío Barrios. Printer: *Giesecke & Devrient*. 157 x 67 mm.

☐	a.	2009. Signature 21. Prefix E. Intro: Dec. 2010.	FV	FV	20
☐	b.	2011. Prefix F. Wmk: Electrotype *50 MIL* added.	FV	FV	20

BCP B54 (P233): **100,000 guaraníes** (US$22)   VG   VF   UNC

Green, blue, and yellow. Front: Semicircle symbol for blind; round coat of arms with star; lion and cap registration device; round emblem with lion and cap; San Roque González de Santa Cruz. Back: Represa de Itaipu (Itaipu hydroelectric dam) on the Parana River. Motion windowed security thread. Watermark: San Roque Gonzalez de Santa Cruz and electrotype *100 MIL*. 157 x 67 mm.

☐	a.	2007. Signature 20. Intro: 10.12.2008. Printer: *CRANE CURRENCY*. Prefix D.	FV	FV	40
☐	b.	2008. Intro: January 2011. Prefix E.	FV	FV	40
☐	c.	2011. Signature 21. Prefix F. Printer: *OBERTHUR TECHNOLOGIES*.	FV	FV	30
☐	d.	2013. Signature 22. Printer: *CRANE CURRENCY*.	FV	FV	30

2010 Issues

BCP B55 (P223c): **5,000 guaraníes** (US$1.10)   VG   VF   UNC

Red. Front: Diamond symbol for blind; round coat of arms with star; round emblem with lion and cap; Don Carlos Antonio López. Back: Palacio de los López (Lopez Palace) building in Asunción. Wide color-changing windowed security thread with demetalized lion and *BCP G5000*. Watermark: None. Printer: *CASA DE MOEDA DO BRASIL*. 157 x 67 mm.

☐	a.	2010. Signature 21. Prefix F.	FV	FV	2

BCP B56 (PNL): **10,000 guaraníes** (US$2.25)   VG   VF   UNC

Olive green. Front: Triangle symbol for blind; round coat of arms with star; round emblem with lion and cap; Dr. José Gaspar Rodríguez de Francia. Back: Men standing around table with overturned chair, declaring independence from Spain on 14 de Mayo de 1811. Wide color-changing windowed security thread with demetalized star and *REPUBLIC DEL PARAGUAY 10000*. Watermark: None. Printer: *CASA DE MOEDA DO BRASIL*. 157 x 67 mm.

☐	a.	2010. Prefix F. Signature 21.	FV	FV	6

2011 Issues

BCP B57 (P234): **5,000 guaraníes** (US$1.10)   VG   VF   UNC
Red. Front: Locomotive steam engine; round coat of arms with star; round emblem with lion and cap; Don Carlos Antonio López. Back: Palacio de los López (Lopez Palace) building in Asunción; locomotive steam engine. No security thread. Watermark: None. Printer: (CBN). 157 x 67 mm. Polymer.
   ☐ a.   2011. Signature 21. Prefix G. Intro: 14.01.2013.   FV   FV   3

BCP B58 (PNL): **10,000 guaraníes** (US$2.25)   VG   VF   UNC
Olive green. Front: Triangle symbol for blind; round coat of arms with star; round emblem with lion and cap; Dr. José Gaspar Rodríguez de Francia. Back: Men standing around table with overturned chair, declaring independence from Spain on 14 de Mayo de 1811. Wide color-changing windowed security thread with demetalized star and *REPUBLIC DEL PARAGUAY 10000*. Watermark: None. Printer: *PWPW S.A*. 157 x 67 mm.
   ☐ a.   2011. Prefix G. Signature 21.   FV   FV   6
Like BCP B56, but new printer imprint and revised engravings, plus blank area to right of portrait.

Looking Forward

On 21 October 2009, the Banco Central de Paraguay announced it would remove three zeroes from the guaraní in 2011 in an attempt to simplify economic transactions. The revised currency was to be called the new guaraní for a two-year period. As of mid-2013, such notes have yet to be issued.

Acknowledgements

This chapter was compiled with the generous assistance of Thomas Augustsson, Robert Breslin, David Burns, Fernando Chilavert, David F. Cieniewicz (www.banknotestore.com), Compagnie Generale De Bourse (www.CGB.fr), Mirsad Delic, Arnoldo Efron (Monetary Research Institute), Alberto Fochi, Hartmut Fraunhoffer (www.banknoten.de), Heritage Auctions (HA.com), Tomasz Jazwinski, Vygandas Kadzys, Claudio Marana, Andrés Michelfelder, Victor Manuel González Miguel, Richard Miranda, Peter Mosselberger (www.banknote.ws), Wally Myers, George Provencal, Bill Stubkjaer, Christoph Thomas, Frank van Tiel, Ludek Vostal, and Didier Wiot, others.

Sources

Cuhaj, George S. *Standard Catalog of World Paper Money, General Issues, 1368-1960*. 14th edition. 2012. ISBN 978-1-4402-3090-5. Krause Publications (www.krausebooks.com), 700 East State St., Iola, WI, 54990-0001.

Cuhaj, George S. *Standard Catalog of World Paper Money, Modern Issues, 1961-Present*. 20th edition. 2014. ISBN 978-1-4402-4037-9. Krause Publications (www.krausebooks.com), 700 East State St., Iola, WI, 54990-0001.

Mayans, Miguel Ángel Pratta. *Billetes del Paraguay Año 1851 - 2012*. 3rd edition. 2012. ISBN 978-99953-2-544-2. Numismatica Independencia S.R.L. (www.nisa.com.py), 14 de Mayo 221, Asunción, Paraguay.

Share Your Input, Info, and Images

This catalog is believed to be complete and correct as of the time of publication. Prices and face values were last updated 13 September 2013. Please report errors or omissions so that corrections may be made. If you can more precisely identify the name or location of anything depicted on a note, please share that information. Furthermore, if you own an unlisted type or variety, please submit scans of the front and back of the note so that it can be documented. Scans should be 300 dots per inch, 100% actual size, 24-bit color, saved as *uncompressed* JPEG files, and sent to owen@banknotenews.com. Be sure to fully describe all attributes of the note which are not apparent upon visual inspection of the images alone, such as physical dimension, watermark, and security thread.

Poland

For earlier issues, see Russia.

Earlier Issues

Prior to the establishment of the Narodowy Bank Polski (National Bank of Poland) in 1945, notes were issued by the Bank Polski (Bank of Poland), the Polska Krajowa Kasa Pożyczkowa (Polish National Loan Office), the Ministerstwo Skarbu (Ministry of Finance), and the Bank Emisyjny w Polsce (Emission Bank in Poland). These notes will be added to this catalog in the future.

Monetary System

1916-1924: 1 marka polska = 100 fenigów
1924: 1 Polish złoty = 100 groszy
1950: 1 Polish złoty (PLZ) = 100 groszy
1995: 1 Polish złoty (PLN) = 100 groszy

Polish Months of the Year

Stycznia (January)	Lutego (February)	Marca (March)
Kwietnia (April)	Maja (May)	Czerwca (June)
Lipca (July)	Sierpnia (August)	Września (September)
Października (October)	Listopada (November)	Grudnia (December)

Narodowy Bank Polski (National Bank of Poland)

The Narodowy Bank Polski (NBP) started its operation in 1945 as a state-owned bank supervised by the minister of treasury. For more information, visit www.nbp.pl.

NBP Signature Varieties

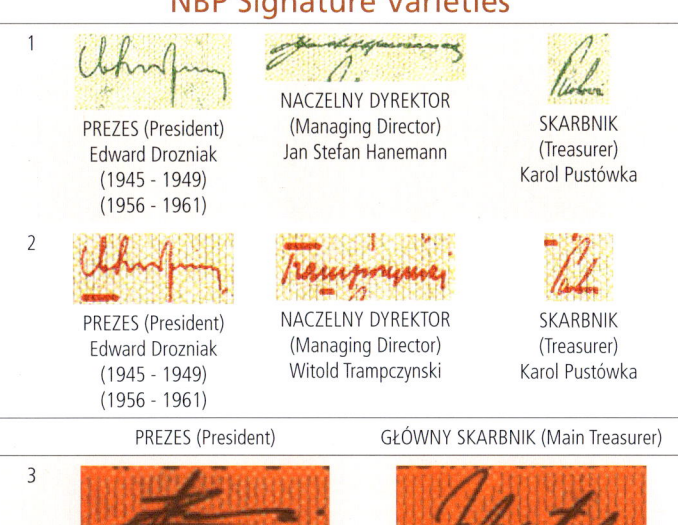

	PREZES (President)	GŁÓWNY SKARBNIK (Main Treasurer)
4	 Stanisław Majewski (1965 - 1968)	 Jan Bartosik
*	Leonard Siemiatkowski (1968 - 1972)	
5	 Witold Bień (1973 - 1980)	 Czesław Kaminski
6	 Witold Bień (1973 - 1980)	 Edmund Banasiak
7	 Witold Bień (1973 - 1980)	 Jerzy Lasocki
8	 Stanisław Majewski (1981 - 1985)	 Jerzy Lasocki
*	Zdzisław Pakuła (1985)	
9	 Władysław Baka (1985 - 1988) (1989 - 1991)	 Zbigniew Marski
10	 Zdzisław Pakuła (1988 - 1989)	 Zbigniew Marski

	PREZES (President)	GŁÓWNY SKARBNIK (Main Treasurer)
11	 Władysław Baka (1985 - 1988) (1989 - 1991)	 Jerzy Lasocki
12	 Grzegorz Wójtowicz (1991)	 Jerzy Lasocki
*	Andrzej Topinski (1991 - 1992)	
13a	 Hanna Gronkiewicz-Waltz (1992 - 2001)	 Wiesław Biernatowicz
13b	 Hanna Gronkiewicz-Waltz (1992 - 2001)	 Wiesław Biernatowicz
14	 Leszek Balcerowicz (2001 - 2007)	 Mariusz Mastalerz
15	 Sławomir Skrzypek (2007 - 2010)	 Monika Nowosielska
*	Piotr Wiesiołek (2010)	
16	 Marek Belka (2010 - present)	 Jerzy Stopyra
17	 Marek Belka (2010 - present)	 Marek Oles

* This official is not known to have signed any notes.

Prefixes

In some of the following listings, the earliest and latest prefixes which have been verified are shown. In other listings, only the prefix format is listed. Be advised that not all prefixes within the range shown have been verified; it's possible that the printer skipped some letters for unknown reasons. Also, there have been some confirmed cross-overs (i.e. the same prefix appears on different types or varieties), therefore the prefix itself can't be used as the sole determining factor in identifying a note.

1944-1945 Issues

On 10 January 1945, the 1940- and 1941-dated notes issued by the Bank Emisyjny w Polsce (Emission Bank in Poland) ceased to be legal tender and were exchanged at par for these 1944-dated notes issued by the Narodowy Bank Polski (National Bank of Poland), but only for three days and up to very modest limit of 500 złotych per person.

These notes were designed and initially printed by Goznak in Moscow, Russia with a grammatical error in the legal clause, which was corrected when production of the notes was subsequently transferred to Poland.

For reproductions of these notes with overprints issued in 1974 and 1979, see NBP BNP3 and BNP5, respectively.

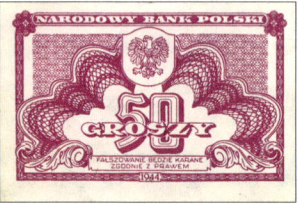 

NBP B1 (P104): **50 groszy** (withdrawn 08.11.1950)   VG   VF   UNC
Violet. Front: Coat of arms with eagle. Back: Guilloche pattern. No security thread. Watermark: Six-pointed star pattern. Printer: (Goznak). 81 x 52 mm.
    a. 1944. No signature. No serial numbers.   2   8   30
        Intro: 29.02.1945.

NBP B2 (P105): **1 złoty** (withdrawn 08.11.1950)   VG   VF   UNC
Green and orange. Front: Coat of arms with eagle. Back: Guilloche pattern. No security thread. Watermark: Six-pointed star pattern. Printer: (Goznak). 136 x 66 mm.
    a. 1944. No signature. Prefix format *XX*.   3   12   45
        Intro: 18.09.1944.

NBP B3 (P106 & P107): **2 złote** (withdrawn 08.11.1950)   VG   VF   UNC
Brown and blue. Front: Coat of arms with eagle. Back: Guilloche pattern. No security thread. Watermark: Six-pointed star pattern. 137 x 67 mm.

- a. 1944. No signature.   4   15   60
  OBOWIĄZKOWYM (error). Printer: (Goznak).
  Prefix format *XX, Xx, xX*. Intro: 18.09.1944.
- b. *OBOWIĄZKOWE* (corrected). Printer: (PWPW).   20   80   300
  Prefix format *XX, Xx, xX*. Intro: 12.04.1945.

NBP B4 (P108 & P109): **5 złotych** (withdrawn 08.11.1950)   VG   VF   UNC
Violet-brown and green. Front: Coat of arms with eagle. Back: Guilloche pattern. No security thread. Watermark: Six-pointed star pattern. 142 x 71 mm.

- a. 1944. No signature.   10   20   80
  OBOWIĄZKOWYM (error). Printer: (Goznak).
  Prefix format *XX*. Intro: 18.09.1944.
- b. *OBOWIĄZKOWE* (corrected). Printer: (PWPW).   10   20   80
  Prefix format *XX, xX*. Intro: 19.10.1945.

NBP B5 (P110 & P111): **10 złotych** (withdrawn 08.11.1950)   VG   VF   UNC
Blue and green. Front: Coat of arms with eagle. Back: Guilloche pattern. No security thread. Watermark: Six-pointed star pattern. 160 x 80 mm.

- a. 1944. No signature.   10   40   160
  OBOWIĄZKOWYM (error). Printer: (Goznak).
  Prefix format *XX*. Intro: 27.08.1944.
- b. *OBOWIĄZKOWE* (corrected). Printer: (PWPW).   10   40   160
  Prefix format *Xx*. Intro: 22.03.1945.
- bs. Diagonal red *WZÓR* overprint.   —   —   —

NBP B6 (P112 & P113): **20 złotych** (withdrawn 08.11.1950)   VG   VF   UNC
Blue-black and lilac. Front: Coat of arms with eagle. Back: Guilloche pattern. No security thread. Watermark: Six-pointed star pattern. 170 x 83 mm.

- a. 1944. No signature.   20   50   200
  OBOWIĄZKOWYM (error). Printer: (Goznak).
  Prefix format *XX*. Intro: 27.08.1944.
- b. *OBOWIĄZKOWE* (corrected). Printer: (PWPW).   10   25   100
  Prefix format *XX, Xx, xX*. Intro: 19.10.1945.
- bs. Diagonal red *WZÓR* overprint.   —   —   —

NBP B7 (P114 & P115): **50 złotych** (withdrawn 08.11.1950) VG VF UNC
Violet and lilac. Front: Coat of arms with eagle. Back: Guilloche pattern. No security thread. Watermark: Six-pointed star pattern. 180 x 95 mm.

- a. 1944. No signature. 25 100 350
  OBOWIĄZKOWYM (error). Printer: (Goznak).
  Prefix format *XX*. Intro: 27.08.1944.
- b. *OBOWIĄZKOWE* (corrected). Printer: (PWPW). 15 60 250
  Prefix format *XX, Xx*. Intro: 24.10.1945.
- bs. Diagonal red *WZÓR* overprint. — — —

NBP B8 (P116 & P117): **100 złotych** (withdrawn 08.11.1950) VG VF UNC
Red. Front: Coat of arms with eagle. Back: Guilloche pattern. No security thread. Watermark: Six-pointed star pattern. 188 x 100 mm.

- a. 1944. No signature. 25 100 350
  OBOWIĄZKOWYM (error). Printer: (Goznak).
  Prefix format *XX*. Intro: 27.08.1944.
- b. *OBOWIĄZKOWE* (corrected). Printer: (PWPW). 15 60 250
  Prefix format *XX, Xx, xX*. Intro: 24.11.1945.
- bs. Diagonal black *WZÓR* overprint. — — —

1946 Issues

NBP B9 (P118 & P119): **500 złotych** (withdrawn 16.09.1946)   VG   VF   UNC
Black and orange. Front: Coat of arms with eagle. Back: Guilloche pattern. No security thread. Watermark: Six-pointed star pattern. 193 x 102 mm.
- ☐ a. 1944. No signature.   60   250   1,000
  OBOWIĄZKOWYM (error). Printer: (Goznak).
  Prefix format XX. Intro: 27.08.1944.
- ☐ b. OBOWIĄZKOWE (corrected). Printer: (PWPW).   50   150   600
  Prefix format XX, Xx. Intro: 10.10.1945.
- ☐ bs. Diagonal red WZÓR overprint.   —   —   —

Withdrawn from circulation after only two years due to a large number of counterfeits.

NBP B10 (P120): **1,000 złotych** (withdrawn 08.11.1950)   VG   VF   UNC
Brown. Front: Coat of arms with eagle. Back: Guilloche pattern. No security thread. Watermark: Six-pointed star pattern. Printer: (PWPW). 182 x 97 mm.
- ☐ a. 1945. No sig. Ser. A, B, Dh. Intro: 01.09.1945.   60   250   1,000
- ☐ as. Diagonal red WZÓR overprint;   —   —   450
  vertical red BEZ WARTOŚCI overprint.

NBP B11 (P123): **1 złoty** (withdrawn 08.11.1950)   VG   VF   UNC
Dark red. Front: Guilloche patterns. Back: Guilloche patterns. No security thread. Watermark: Six-pointed star pattern. Printer: (PWPW). 98 x 54 mm.
- ☐ a. 15 MAJA 1946. Signature 2. No serial numbers.   1   3   8
  Intro: 02.12.1946.
- ☐ as. Horizontal red SPECIMEN overprint and large X.   —   —   —

NBP B12 (P124): **2 złote** (withdrawn 08.11.1950)   VG   VF   UNC
Green. Front: Guilloche patterns; flowers; coat of arms with eagle. Back: Guilloche patterns. No security thread. Watermark: Six-pointed star pattern. Printer: (PWPW). 104 x 57 mm.
- ☐ a. 15 MAJA 1946. Signature 2. No serial numbers.   1   4   10
  Intro: 15.03.1947.
- ☐ as. Horizontal red SPECIMEN overprint and large X.   —   —   —

NBP B13 (P125): **5 złotych** (withdrawn 08.11.1950) VG VF UNC
Gray-blue. Front: Guilloche patterns; flowers. Back: Guilloche patterns; coat of arms with eagle. No security thread. Watermark: Geometric pattern with *W*. Printer: (PWPW). 122 x 66 mm.

- ☐ a. 15 MAJA 1946. Signature 2. No serial numbers. 1 8 20
  Intro: 05.02.1948.
- ☐ as. Horizontal red *SPECIMEN* overprint and large *X*. — — —

NBP B14 (P126): **10 złotych** (withdrawn 08.11.1950) VG VF UNC
Reddish-brown, green, and yellow. Front: Guilloche patterns; coat of arms with eagle. Back: Guilloche patterns. No security thread. Watermark: Geometric *W* pattern. Printer: (PWPW). 128 x 70 mm.

- ☐ a. 15 MAJA 1946. Signature 2. No serial numbers. 2 10 30
  Intro: 18.08.1947.
- ☐ as. Horizontal red *SPECIMEN* overprint and large *X*. — — —

NBP B15 (P127): **20 złotych** (withdrawn 08.11.1950) VG VF UNC
Green, brown, and violet. Front: Guilloche patterns; coat of arms with eagle. Back: Guilloche patterns; airplane engine; Lisunov Li-2 airplanes. No security thread. Watermark: Geometric *W* pattern. Printer: (PWPW). 158 x 84 mm.

- ☐ a. 15 MAJA 1946. Signature 2. Prefix A - G. 10 40 150
  Intro: 01.07.1948.
- ☐ as. Horizontal red *SPECIMEN* overprint and large *X*. — — —

NBP B16 (P128): **50 złotych** (withdrawn 08.11.1950) VG VF UNC
Brown, gold, purple, and blue. Front: Sailing ship; coat of arms with eagle; modern ocean freighter. Back: Sailboat and two larger ships. No security thread. Watermark: Geometric *W* pattern. Printer: (PWPW). 164 x 87 mm.

- ☐ a. 15 MAJA 1946. Signature 2. Prefix A - S. 12 50 200
  Intro: 22.09.1947.
- ☐ as. Horizontal red *SPECIMEN* overprint and large *X*. — — —

NBP B17 (P129): **100 złotych** (withdrawn 08.11.1950)   **VG**   **VF**   **UNC**

Red and yellow. Front: Woman holding flowers and sickle; coat of arms with eagle; man holding scythe and sheaf of wheat. Back: Sheaves of wheat; man plowing field with tractor; flowers. No security thread. Watermark: Geometric *W* pattern. Printer: (PWPW). 170 x 91 mm.

- ☐ a. 15 MAJA 1946. Signature 2. Prefix A - R, Mz.   12   50   200
  Intro: 02.12.1946.
- ☐ as1. Horizontal black *SPECIMEN* overprint.   —   —   —
- ☐ as2. Horizontal red *SPECIMEN* overprint and large *X*.   —   —   —

NBP B19 (P122): **1,000 złotych** (withdrawn 08.11.1950)   **VG**   **VF**   **UNC**

Brown and purple. Front: Miner holding pick and lantern; coat of arms with eagle; man holding hammer and wrench with gear and railroad ties at his feet. Back: Smokestacks, railroad cars, and factory buildings in Łódź. No security thread. Watermark: Geometric *W* pattern. Printer: (PWPW). 182 x 97 mm.

- ☐ a. 15 STYCZNIA 1946. Signature 1.   25   100   400
  Prefix format *X, XX, Xx* (with and w/o period).
  Intro: 16.08.1946.
- ☐ as. Horizontal red *SPECIMEN* overprint and large *X*.   —   —   —

NBP B18 (P121): **500 złotych** (withdrawn 08.11.1950)   **VG**   **VF**   **UNC**

Black and green. Front: Man holding ship with anchor at his feet; coat of arms with eagle; man holding fish and rope. Back: Ships in Motława River and city buildings in Gdańsk. No security thread. Watermark: Geometric *W* pattern. Printer: (PWPW). 176 x 94 mm.

- ☐ a. 15 STYCZNIA 1946. Signature 1.   25   100   400
  Prefix format *X, Xx*. Intro: 15.07.1946.
- ☐ as. Horizontal red *SPECIMEN* overprint and large *X*.   —   —   —

1947 Issues

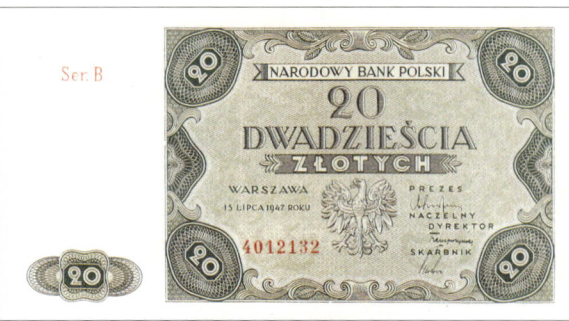

NBP B20 (P130): **20 złotych** (withdrawn 08.11.1950)   VG   VF   UNC
Olive green and light green. Front: Coat of arms with eagle. Back: Hammer, railroad ties, gear, laurel branch, globe, open book, and triangle. No security thread. Watermark: Geometric *W* pattern. Printer: (PWPW). 158 x 84 mm.

- ☐ a.   15 LIPCA 1947. Signature 2. Ser. A - E.   15   50   200
  Intro: 11.06.1949.
- ☐ as.   Horizontal red *SPECIMEN* overprint and large *X*.   —   —   275

NBP B21 (P131): **100 złotych** (withdrawn 08.11.1950)   VG   VF   UNC
Red and gray. Front: Coat of arms with eagle; standing woman holding sheaf of wheat and basket of fruit. Back: Five horses in field with wooden fence. No security thread. Watermark: Geometric *W* pattern. Printer: (PWPW). 170 x 91 mm.

- ☐ a.   15 LIPCA 1947. Signature 2. Ser. A - H.   20   60   225
  Intro: 21.02.1949.
- ☐ p.   Proof dated 1 LIPCA 1948.   —   —   1,500
- ☐ as1. Diagonal black *SPECIMEN* overprint.   —   —   —
- ☐ as2. Horizontal red *SPECIMEN* overprint and large *X*.   —   —   475

NBP B22 (P132): **500 złotych** (withdrawn 08.11.1950)   VG   VF   UNC
Blue and tan. Front: Coat of arms with eagle; standing woman holding anchor and oar with sailing ship at her feet. Back: Crane and trams on Gdynia dock; tug boat and ship. No security thread. Watermark: Geometric diamond pattern. Printer: (Tiskárna platidel Národní banky Československé, Prague). 176 x 94 mm.

- ☐ a.   15 LIPCA 1947. Sig. 2. Seria A - Z, A2 - S4.   30   125   500
  Intro: 20.01.1949.
- ☐ as.   Horizontal red *SPECIMEN* overprint and large *X*.   —   —   500

1948 Issues

On 30 October 1950, the preceding notes dated 1944-1947 were exchanged at a ratio of 100:1 for new 1948-dated notes. Prices and bank account holdings were revalued at 100:3.

Up until 2004, the bank sold uncirculated notes to collectors. These remainders are fairly common and less expensive than notes which were actually issued into circulation.

NBP B23 (P133): **1,000 złotych** (withdrawn 08.11.1950) VG VF UNC
Brown and olive green. Front: Coat of arms with eagle; standing man holding hammer and wrench with gear and railroad engine at his feet. Back: Smokestacks and factory buildings. No security thread. Watermark: Geometric *W* pattern. Printer: (PWPW). 182 x 97 mm.

- a. 15 LIPCA 1947. Signature 2. Ser. A - L. 15 60 250
     Intro: 01.12.1948.
- as1. Diagonal red *SPECIMEN* overprint. — — 920
- as2. Horizontal red *SPECIMEN* overprint and large *X*. — — 375

NBP B24 (P134): **2 złote** (withdrawn 30.09.1960) VG VF UNC
Gray. Front: Coat of arms with eagle. Back: Narodowy Bank Polski building. No security thread. Printer: (PWPW). 120 x 58 mm.

- a. 1 LIPCA 1948. Intro: 30.10.1950. 1 6 15
     Signature 2.
     Watermark: Small interlocking circles pattern.
     Prefix A - Z, AA - AZ, BA - BP, CA - CT.
- b. Watermark: Large interlocking circles pattern. 2 8 20
     Prefix BR-BZ.

NBP B25 (P135): **5 złotych** (withdrawn 31.12.1959) VG VF UNC
Crimson and light brown. Front: Coat of arms with eagle. Back: Farm buildings; man plowing field with tractor. No security thread. Watermark: Woman's head. Printer: (PWPW). 142 x 67 mm.

- a. 1 LIPCA 1948. Signature 2. Intro: 30.10.1950. 15 60 250
     Prefix A - I, AA - AW, BA - BR.
- as. Diagonal red *SPECIMEN* overprint and large *X*. — — —

NBP B26 (P136): **10 złotych** (withdrawn 31.12.1965)   VG   VF   UNC
Brown and green. Front: Coat of arms with eagle; man with moustache. Back: Woman and two men loading hay onto horse-drawn cart. No security thread. Watermark: Woman's head. 147 x 70 mm.

			VG	VF	UNC
☐	a.	1 LIPCA 1948. Signature 2. Intro: 30.10.1950. Prefix A - T. Printer: (Pénzjegynyomda a Magyar Nemzeti Bank, Budapest).	10	40	120
☐	b.	Prefix AA - AZ, BA - BR. Printer: (PWPW).	2	8	30
☐	as.	Diagonal red *SPECIMEN* overprint and large *X*.	—	—	—

Prefix AW notes are remainders sold to collectors.

NBP B28 (P138): **50 złotych** (withdrawn 30.06.1978)   VG   VF   UNC
Green. Front: Coat of arms with eagle; sailor wearing hat. Back: Cranes, trams, ship, and tug boat in port of Gdynia. No security thread. Watermark: Woman's head. 164 x 78 mm.

			VG	VF	UNC
☐	a.	1 LIPCA 1948. Signature 2. Intro: 30.10.1950. Prefix A - Z, C2 - Z3 with 6-digit serial numbers. Printer: (Tiskárna bankovek Státní banky Ceskoslovenské, Prague).	50	200	700
☐	b.	Prefix A with 7-digit serial numbers. Printer: (Riksbankens Sedeltryckeri, Stockholm).	30	125	500
☐	c.	Prefix format *XX*. Printer: (PWPW).	5	15	65
☐	as1.	Diagonal red *SPECIMEN* overprint; ladder s/n.	—	—	—
☐	as2.	Diagonal red *SPECIMEN* overprint; normal s/n.	—	—	—
☐	cs.	Diagonal red *WZÓR* overprint; normal s/n.	—	—	—
☐	p.	Separate front/back proof on oversized paper.	—	—	—

Prefix EL notes are remainders sold to collectors.

NBP B27 (P137): **20 złotych** (withdrawn 30.06.1977)   VG   VF   UNC
Light blue, bluish-black, and pink. Front: Coat of arms with eagle; woman wearing headscarf. Back: Cloth Hall (Sukiennice) building in Kraków. No security thread. Watermark: Man's head. 160 x 76 mm.

			VG	VF	UNC
☐	a.	1 LIPCA 1948. Signature 2. Intro: 30.10.1950. Prefix A - E. Printer: (Pénzjegynyomda a Magyar Nemzeti Bank, Budapest).	30	125	500
☐	b.	Prefix AA - BB. Printer: (BABN).	25	100	400
☐	c.	Prefix BC - KF. Printer: (PWPW).	2.50	10	40
☐	as.	Diagonal red *SPECIMEN* overprint and large *X*.	—	—	—
☐	cs.	Diagonal red *SPECIMEN* overprint.	—	—	—

Prefix KE notes are remainders sold to collectors.

NBP B29 (P139): **100 złotych** (withdrawn 30.06.1977)   VG   VF   UNC

Red. Front: Coat of arms with eagle; man. Back: Smokestacks and factory buildings. No security thread. Watermark: Woman's head. 172 x 82 mm.

		VG	VF	UNC
☐ a.	1 LIPCA 1948. Signature 2. Intro: 30.10.1950. Prefix A - U. Printer: (Tiskárna bankovek Státni banky Ceskoslovenské, Prague).	50	150	600
☐ b.	Prefix format XX. Printer: (PWPW). 100 in guilloche at center front with outline.	5	15	60
☐ c.	100 in guilloche at center front without outline. Prefix FP, FU - FZ, GA - GZ, HA.	15	50	200
☐ bs.	Diagonal red WZÓR overprint; normal s/n.	—	—	55

Prefix KR notes are remainders sold to collectors.

NBP B30 (P140): **500 złotych** (withdrawn 31.12.1977)   VG   VF   UNC

Brown and orange. Front: Coat of arms with eagle; miner wearing helmet and holding pick. Back: Miners with picks and shovels digging coal. No security thread. Watermark: Woman's head. 178 x 85 mm.

		VG	VF	UNC
☐ a.	1 LIPCA 1948. Signature 2. Intro: 30.10.1950. Prefix A - D. Printer: (Tiskárna bankovek Státni banky Ceskoslovenské, Prague).	60	250	1,000
☐ b.	Prefix format XX. Printer: (PWPW).	15	60	250
☐ bs1.	Diagonal red WZÓR ovpt on front; normal s/n.	—	—	50
☐ bs2.	Diagonal red SPECIMEN overprint and large X; normal serial numbers.	—	—	—

Prefix CC notes are remainders sold to collectors.

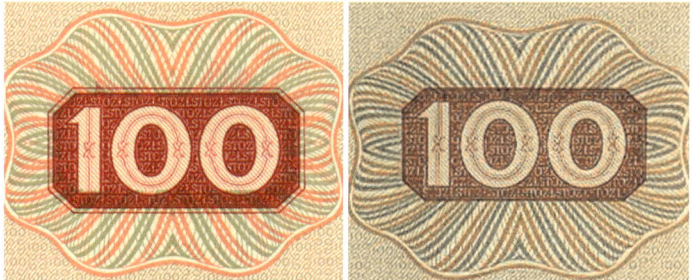

On the 100-złoty note, the guilloche pattern at center front contains the denomination *100* within a box with (NBP B29b, left) and without (B29c, right) a thin outline.

1962-1965 Issues

NBP B31 (P141): **1,000 złotych** (withdrawn 31.12.1978) VG VF UNC

Green, brown, red, and yellow. Front: Nicolaus Copernicus; coat of arms with eagle. Back: Signs of the Zodiac in sphere with earth and planets orbiting the sun. No security thread. Watermark: Nicolaus Copernicus. Printer: (PWPW). 150 x 74 mm.

- a. 29 PAZDZIERNIKA 1965. Signature 4.   10   20   80
  Prefix A - S. Intro: 01.06.66.
- as1. Diagonal red *WZÓR* overprint; normal s/n.   —   —   80
- as2. Diagonal *WZÓR* perforation; low serial numbers.   —   —   —
- as3. Horizontal red or blue *SPECIMEN* ovpt on front;   —   —   —
  horizontal red or blue *WZÓR* ovpt on back;
  all-zero serial numbers.
- s. No ovpt; no perforation; all-zero serial numbers.   —   —   3,350
  Dated 24 MAJA 1962. Signature 3. Unissued.

Prefix S notes are remainders sold to collectors.

1965 Numismatic Products

No image available.
NBP BNP1 (PCS1): **20, 50, 100, 500, and 1,000 złotych**   UNC
- a. NBP B27 - B32 (5) notes with normal serial numbers overprinted   75
  WZÓR.

1967 Numismatic Products

These notes commemorate the 50th anniversary of the Socialist revolution of 1917.

NBP BNP2 (PCS2): **1, 3, 5, and 10 chevonetz**   UNC
- a. Russia P202-205 (4) notes overprinted *WYSTAWA PIENIEDZY*   50
  RADZIECHICH - LISTOPAD 1967 and *50 LAT WIELKIEGO*
  PADZIERNIKA.

1974 Numismatic Products

These notes commemorate the 30th anniversary of the Polish People's Republic.

NBP BNP3 (PCS3): **50 groszy - 500 złotych**   UNC
- a. Reprints of NBP B1 - B9 (9) notes with horizontal   20
  red *EMISJA PAMIĄTKOWA - ODBITA W 1974 r. Z*
  ORYGINALNYCH KLISZ overprint. Each denomination
  has a different serial number, but all notes of a given
  denomination have the same serial numbers.

1978 Numismatic Products

These notes commemorate the 150th anniversary of Polish banknotes.

NBP BNP4 (PCS4): **20 and 100 złotych**   UNC
- a. NBP B27 and B29 (2 notes) with horizontal black *150 LAT BANKU*   20
  POLSKIEGO 1828-1978 overprint.

1979 Numismatic Products

These notes commemorate the 35th anniversary of the Polish People's Republic.

NBP BNP5 (PCS5): **50 groszy - 500 złotych**   **UNC**
- a. Reprints of NBP B1 - B9 (8) notes dated *1979* and overprinted *XXXV - LECIE PRL. 1944-1979*.   25

This note commemorates the 60th anniversary of the modern Polish bank.

NBP BNP6 (PCS6): **100 marek**   **UNC**
Violet and green. Front: General Tadeusz Kościuszko. Back: Coat of arms with crowned eagle. No security thread. Printer: Various. 182 x 108 mm.
- a. Reprint of Poland P17b overprinted *60 LECIE POLSKIEGO BANKNOTU PO ODZYSKANIU NIEPODLEGŁOŚCI 1919-1979*.   15

These notes commemorate a numismatic exposition.

No image available.
NBP BNP7 (PCS7): **2 złotych**   **UNC**
- a. NBP B24 overprinted *WYSTAWA WSPOLCZESNE MONETY / BANKNOTY POLSKIE / OBCE NBP 1979*.   10

1974-1992 Issues

While these notes were issued over time, with ever larger denominations being required due to inflation, they were all withdrawn from circulation on 31 December 1996, but remained exchangeable at the NBP until 31 December 2010, at which time they were demonetized.

NBP B32 (P148): **10 złotych** (demonetized 31.12.2010)　　VG　VF　UNC
Green and blue. Front: General Józef Bem; coat of arms with eagle. Back: Guilloche pattern. No security thread. Watermark: Circle in square pattern. Printer: (PWPW). 138 x 63 mm.

- a. 1 CZERWCA 1982. Signature 8. Prefix A - T. Intro: 11.06.1982. — — 1.50
- as. Diagonal red *WZÓR* overprint on front; diagonal red *SPECIMEN* overprint on back; horizontal black № # and star ovpt at left. — — 80

NBP B33 (P149): **20 złotych** (demonetized 31.12.2010)　　VG　VF　UNC
Brown, and purple. Front: General Romuald Traugutt; coat of arms with eagle. Back: Guilloche pattern. No security thread. Watermark: Circle in square pattern. Printer: (PWPW). 138 x 63 mm.

- a. 1 CZERWCA 1982. Sig. 8. Prefix A - Z, AA - AU. Intro: 11.06.1982. — — 1.50
- as. Diagonal red *WZÓR* overprint on front; diagonal red *SPECIMEN* overprint on back; horizontal black № # and star ovpt at left. — — 80

NBP B34 (P142): **50 złotych** (demonetized 31.12.2010)　　VG　VF　UNC
Green and tan. Front: General Karol Wacław Świerczewski in military uniform; coat of arms with eagle. Back: Cross of Grunwald military decoration with shield and two swords. No security thread. Watermark: Eagle. Printer: (PWPW). 138 x 63 mm.

- a. 9 MAJA 1975. Sig. 6. Prefix A - Z, AA - BU. Intro: 25.11.1975. — 2 14
- b. 1 CZERWCA 1979. Sig. 7. Prefix BW - CY. Intro: 19.07.1979. — — 6
- c. 1 CZERWCA 1982. Sig. 8. Prefix CZ - EF. Intro: 11.06.1982. — — 4
- d. 1 CZERWCA 1986. Sig. 9. Prefix EG - GA. Intro: June 1986. — — 1
- e. 1 GRUDNIA 1988. Sig. 10. Prefix GB - KH. Intro: Dec. 1988. — — 1
- as. Diagonal red *WZÓR* overprint on front; diagonal red *SPECIMEN* overprint on back; horizontal black № # and star ovpt at left. — — 45
- bs. Diagonal red *WZÓR* overprint on front; diagonal red *SPECIMEN* overprint on back; horizontal black № # and star ovpt at left. — — 25
- cs. Diagonal red *WZÓR* overprint on front; diagonal red *SPECIMEN* overprint on back; horizontal black № # and star ovpt at left. — — 150
- ds. Diagonal red *WZÓR* overprint on front; diagonal red *SPECIMEN* overprint on back; horizontal black № # and star ovpt at left. — — 40
- es. Diagonal red *WZÓR* overprint on front; diagonal red *SPECIMEN* overprint on back; horizontal black № # and star ovpt at left. — — 40

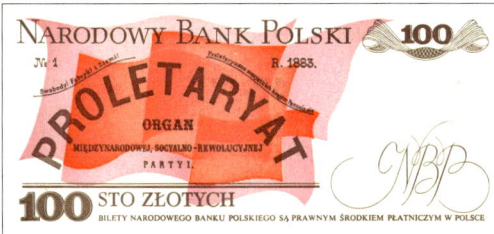

NBP B35 (P143): **100 złotych** (demonetized 31.12.2010)　　VG　VF　UNC

Brown, red, and yellow. Front: Coat of arms with eagle; socialist activist Ludwik Waryński. Back: Proletaryat (Proletariat) flag. No security thread. Watermark: Eagle. Printer: (PWPW). 138 x 63 mm.

		VG	VF	UNC
☐ a.	15 STYCZNIA 1975. Sig. 6. Prefix A - Z, AA-AC. Intro: 01.07.1975.	2	10	25
☐ b.	17 MAJA 1976. Prefix AD - ET. Intro: 01.07.1976.	1	2	8
☐ c.	1 CZERWCA 1979. Sig. 7. Prefix EU - HF. Intro: 19.07.1979.	—	—	5
☐ d.	1 CZERWCA 1982. Sig. 8. Prefix HG - LN. Intro: June 1982.	—	—	1.25
☐ e.	1 CZERWCA 1986. Sig. 9. Prefix LP - NM. Intro: June 1986.	—	—	0.75
☐ f.	1 GRUDNIA 1988. Sig. 10. Prefix TB - TT. Intro: Dec. 1988.	—	—	1
☐ as.	Diagonal blue WZÓR overprint on front; diagonal blue SPECIMEN overprint on back; horizontal black № # and star ovpt at left.	—	—	300
☐ bs1.	Diagonal red WZÓR overprint on front; diagonal red SPECIMEN overprint on back; horizontal black № # and star ovpt at left.	—	—	40
☐ bs2.	Diagonal red SPECIMEN overprint on front; diagonal red WZÓR overprint on back; horizontal black № # and star ovpt at left.	—	—	30
☐ cs.	Diagonal red WZÓR overprint on front; diagonal red SPECIMEN overprint on back; horizontal black № # and star ovpt at left.	—	—	20
☐ ds.	Diagonal red WZÓR overprint on front; diagonal red WZÓR overprint on back; horizontal black № # and star ovpt at left.	—	—	150

NBP B36 (P144): **200 złotych** (demonetized 31.12.2010)　　VG　VF　UNC

Purple, light blue, and yellow. Front: Coat of arms with eagle; nationalist Jarosław Dąbrowski. Back: Bare-breasted woman with arms outstretched against wall carved with faces, from Paul Moreau-Vauthier's sculpture, Victimes des Révolutions, in Père Lachaise Cemetery, Paris, France. No security thread. Watermark: Eagle. Printer: (PWPW). 138 x 63 mm.

		VG	VF	UNC
☐ a.	25 MAJA 1976. Sig. 6. Prefix A - Z, AA - AR. Intro: 19.07.1976.	—	—	30
☐ b.	1 CZERWCA 1979. Sig. 7. Prefix AS - BP. Intro: 19.07.1979.	—	—	20
☐ c.	1 CZERWCA 1982. Sig. 8. Prefix BR - CP. Intro: June 1982.	—	—	4.50
☐ d.	1 CZERWCA 1986. Sig. 9. Prefix CR - EA. Intro: June 1986.	—	—	2.50
☐ e.	1 GRUDNIA 1988. Sig. 10. Prefix EB - EP. Intro: Dec. 1988.	—	—	1
☐ as.	Diagonal red WZÓR overprint on front; diagonal red SPECIMEN overprint on back; horizontal black № # and star ovpt at left.	—	—	35
☐ bs.	Diagonal red WZÓR overprint on front; diagonal red SPECIMEN overprint on back; horizontal black № # and star ovpt at left.	—	—	30
☐ cs.	Diagonal red WZÓR overprint on front; diagonal red SPECIMEN overprint on back; horizontal black № # and star ovpt at left.	—	—	120
☐ ds.	Diagonal red WZÓR overprint on front; diagonal red SPECIMEN overprint on back; horizontal black № # and star ovpt at left.	—	—	40

NBP B37 (P145): **500 złotych** (demonetized 31.12.2010)   VG VF UNC
Brown and yellowish-green. Front: General Tadeusz Kościuszko; coat of arms with eagle. Back: Coat of arms with crowned eagle; Żywią i Bronią (Feed and Defend) banner with spear, laurels, and wheat. No security thread. Watermark: Eagle. Printer: (PWPW). 138 x 63 mm.

- ☐ a. 16 GRUDNIA 1974. Sig. 5. Prefix A - Z, AA - AD. Intro: 01.01.1975. — — 30
- ☐ b. 15 CZERWCA 1976. Sig. 6. Prefix AE - AY. Intro: 01.09.1976. — — 20
- ☐ c. 1 CZERWCA 1979. Sig. 7. Prefix AZ - CC. Intro: 19.07.1979. — — 10
- ☐ d. 1 CZERWCA 1982. Sig. 8. Prefix CD - GM. Intro: June 1982. — — 1
- ☐ as. Diagonal blue *WZÓR* № # and star ovpt at left; diagonal blue *SPECIMEN* overprint on back. — — 50
- ☐ bs. Diagonal red *WZÓR* overprint on front; diagonal red *SPECIMEN* overprint on back; horizontal black № # and star ovpt at left. — — 50
- ☐ cs. Diagonal red *WZÓR* overprint on front; diagonal red *SPECIMEN* overprint on back; horizontal black № # and star ovpt at left. — — 25
- ☐ ds. Diagonal red *WZÓR* overprint on front; diagonal red *SPECIMEN* overprint on back; horizontal black № # and star ovpt at left. — — 80

NBP B38 (P146): **1,000 złotych** (demonetized 31.12.2010)   VG VF UNC
Blue, yellowish-green, and violet. Front: Coat of arms with eagle; Nicolaus Copernicus. Back: Signs of the Zodiac with earth and planets orbiting the sun. No security thread. Watermark: Eagle. Printer: (PWPW). 138 x 63 mm.

- ☐ a. 2 LIPCA 1975. Sig. 6. Prefix A - Z, AA - BL. Intro: 01.09.1975. — — 25
- ☐ b. 1 CZERWCA 1979. Sig. 7. Prefix BM - DB. Intro: 19.07.1979. — — 7.50
- ☐ c. 1 CZERWCA 1982. Sig. 8. Prefix DC - KN. Intro: June 1982. — — 2
- ☐ as. Diagonal blue *WZÓR* № # and star ovpt at left; diagonal blue *SPECIMEN* overprint on back. — — 40
- ☐ bs. Diagonal red *WZÓR* overprint on front; diagonal red *SPECIMEN* overprint on back; horizontal black № # and star ovpt at left. — — 30
- ☐ cs. Diagonal red *WZÓR* overprint on front; diagonal red *SPECIMEN* overprint on back; horizontal black № # and star ovpt at left. — — 120

NBP B39 (P147): **2,000 złotych** (demonetized 31.12.2010)　　　VG　VF　UNC

Brown, deep purple, orange, and light blue. Front: Coat of arms with eagle; Prince Mieszko I. Back: Sword; King Bolesław I Chrobry. No security thread. Watermark: Eagle. Printer: (PWPW). 138 x 63 mm.

- a. 1 MAJA 1977. Signature 6. Prefix A - R.　　　—　—　20
  Intro: 11.07.1977.
- b. 1 CZERWCA 1979. Sig. 7. Prefix S - Z, AA - BN.　　—　—　15
  Intro: 19.07.1979.
- c. 1 CZERWCA 1982. Sig. 8. Prefix BP - CE.　　　—　—　10
  Intro: June 1982.
- as. Diagonal red *WZÓR* overprint on front;　　　—　—　40
  diagonal red *SPECIMEN* overprint on back;
  horizontal black Nº # and star ovpt at left.
- bs. Diagonal red *WZÓR* overprint on front;　　　—　—　25
  diagonal red *SPECIMEN* overprint on back;
  horizontal black Nº # and star ovpt at left.
- cs. Diagonal red *WZÓR* overprint on front;　　　—　—　25
  diagonal red *SPECIMEN* overprint on back;
  horizontal black Nº # and star ovpt at left.

NBP B40 (P150): **5,000 złotych** (demonetized 31.12.2010)　　　VG　VF　UNC

Green, yellow, light blue, and purple. Front: Coat of arms with eagle; musician Frédéric François Chopin. Back: Score of Polonaise. No security thread. Watermark: Eagle. Printer: (PWPW). 138 x 63 mm.

- a. 1 CZERWCA 1982. Sig. 8. Prefix A - Z, AA - DP.　　—　—　20
  Intro: 11.06.1982.
- b. 1 CZERWCA 1986. Sig. 9. Prefix AY - BT.　　　—　—　30
  Intro: June 1986.
- c. 1 GRUDNIA 1988. Sig. 10. Prefix CP - EA.　　　—　—　25
  Intro: Dec. 1988.
- as. Diagonal red *WZÓR* overprint on front;　　　—　—　160
  diagonal red *SPECIMEN* overprint on back;
  horizontal black Nº # and star ovpt at left.
- bs. Diagonal red *WZÓR* overprint on front;　　　—　—　80
  diagonal red *SPECIMEN* overprint on back;
  horizontal black Nº # and star ovpt at left.

NBP B41 (P151): **10,000 złotych** (demonetized 31.12.2010)　　VG　VF　UNC

Green, black, and violet. Front: Flower; writer and painter Stanisław Wyspiański; flowers; coat of arms with eagle. Back: Wyspiański's painting, Planty o świcie (Planty Park at Dawn), with trees and buildings. No security thread. Watermark: Eagle. Printer: (PWPW). 138 x 63 mm.

- a. 1 LUTEGO 1987. Signature 9. Prefix A - U.　　—　—　25
  Intro: 26.02.1987.
- b. 1 GRUDNIA 1988. Sig. 10. Prefix W - Z, AA - DT.　—　—　6
  Intro: Dec. 1988.
- as. Diagonal red *WZÓR* overprint on front;　　　—　—　70
  diagonal red *SPECIMEN* overprint on back;
  horizontal black Nº # and star ovpt at left.
- bs. Diagonal red *WZÓR* overprint on front;　　　—　—　50
  diagonal red *SPECIMEN* overprint on back;
  horizontal black Nº # and star ovpt at left.

NBP B42 (P152): **20,000 złotych** (demonetized 31.12.2010)　　VG　VF　UNC

Brown, yellow, and orange. Front: Coat of arms with eagle; atomic symbol; physicist Marie Skłodowska Curie. Back: First Polish nuclear reactor, EWA (Eksperymentalny Wodny Atomowy = Experimental Water Atomic). No security thread. Watermark: Eagle. Printer: (PWPW). 138 x 63 mm.

- a. 1 LUTEGO 1989. Sig. 10. Prefix A - Z, AA - AR.　—　—　18
  Intro: 26.02.1989.
- as. Diagonal red *WZÓR* overprint on front;　　　—　—　30
  diagonal red *SPECIMEN* overprint on back;
  horizontal black Nº # and star ovpt at left.

NBP B43 (P153): **50,000 złotych** (demonetized 31.12.2010) VG VF UNC
Green and brown. Front: Quill; writer Stanisław Staszic; coat of arms with eagle. Back: Pałac Staszica (Staszic Palace - Polish Academy of Sciences) building in Warsaw. No security thread. Watermark: Eagle. Printer: (PWPW). 138 x 63 mm.
- ☐ a. 1 GRUDNIA 1989. Sig. 9. Prefix A - Z, AA - BU. Intro: 17.12.1989. — — 25
- ☐ as. Diagonal red *WZÓR* overprint on front; diagonal red *SPECIMEN* overprint on back; horizontal black № # and star ovpt at left. — — 50

NBP B45 (P155): **200,000 złotych** (demonetized 31.12.2010) VG VF UNC
Purple, tan, and red. Front: Coin of Sigismund III; coat of arms with eagle. Back: Shield of Warszawa; buildings in Warsaw. No security thread. Watermark: Circle in square pattern. Printer: (PWPW). 135 x 63 mm.
- ☐ a. 1 GRUDNIA 1989. Signature 9. Prefix A - R. Intro: 07.12.1989. — — 200
- ☐ as. Diagonal red *WZÓR* overprint on front; diagonal red *SPECIMEN* overprint on back; horizon. black № # and star ovpt at lower center. — — 140

NBP B44 (P154): **100,000 złotych** (demonetized 31.12.2010) VG VF UNC
Light blue, black, purple, orange, and green. Front: Plant; coat of arms with eagle; composer Stanisław Moniuszko. Back: Teatr Wielki (Grand Theatre - National Opera) building in Warsaw. No security thread. Watermark: Eagle. Printer: (PWPW). 138 x 63 mm.
- ☐ a. 1 LUTEGO 1990. Sig. 9. Prefix A - Z, AA - CM. Intro: 26.02.1990. — 15 60
- ☐ as. Diagonal red *WZÓR* overprint on front; diagonal red *SPECIMEN* overprint on back; horizontal black № # and star ovpt at left. — — 90

NBP B46 (P156): **500,000 złotych** (demonetized 31.12.2010) VG VF UNC
Green, orange, and purple. Front: Novelist Henryk Sienkiewicz; coat of arms with crowned eagle. Back: Flags, swords, helmet, spear, and shield with three open books. No security thread. Watermark: Eagle. Printer: (PWPW). 138 x 63 mm.
- ☐ a. 20 KWIETNIA 1990. Signature 11. Prefix A - Z, AA - AD. Intro: 01.08.1990. — 40 150
- ☐ as. Diagonal red *WZÓR* overprint on front; diagonal red *SPECIMEN* overprint on back; horizontal black № # and star ovpt at left. — — 180

NBP B47 (P157): **1,000,000 złotych** (demonetized 31.12.2010)　　VG　　VF　　UNC

Brown, olive green, and purple. Front: Flowers; coat of arms with crowned eagle; novelist Władysław Reymont. Back: Farm houses and trees. No security thread. Watermark: Eagle. Printer: (PWPW). 138 x 63 mm.

☐ a.	15 LUTEGO 1991. Signature 12. Prefix A - G. Intro: 22.04.1991.	—	—	175
☐ as.	Diagonal red *WZÓR* overprint on front; diagonal red *SPECIMEN* overprint on back; horizontal black *№* # and star ovpt at left.	—	—	270

NBP B48 (P158): **2,000,000 złotych** (demonetized 31.12.2010)　　VG　　VF　　UNC

Black, purple, orange, green, and blue. Front: Laurels; Prime Minister Ignacy Jan Paderewski; coat of arms with crowned eagle. Back: Laurels; coat of arms with crowned eagle. No security thread. Watermark: Eagle. Printer: (PWPW). 138 x 63 mm.

☐ a.	14 SIERPNIA 1992. Sig. 13a. Intro: 10.11.1992. Prefix A. *Konstytucyjy* (error) on back.	—	—	400
☐ b.	Prefix B. *Konstytucyjny* (corrected) on back.	—	—	300
☐ as.	Diagonal red *WZÓR* overprint on front; diagonal red *SPECIMEN* overprint on back; horizontal black *№* # and star ovpt at left.	—	—	700
☐ bs.	Diagonal red *WZÓR* overprint on front; diagonal red *SPECIMEN* overprint on back; horizontal black *№* # and star ovpt at left.	—	—	450

1990 Numismatic Products

NBP BNP8 (PNL): **50 złotych**　　UNC

Green. Front: Black *NUMIZMATYKA I KOSMOS * PIERWSZY CZLOWIEK W KOSMOSIE * J. GAGARIN ZSRR 1961 r. KNF — WARSZAWA 1990* overprint on watermark area; coat of arms with eagle; sailor wearing hat. Back: Cranes and trams in port; ship and tug boat; circular black *1961 - 1981* overprint on watermark area. No security thread. Watermark: Woman's head. Printer: Unknown. 164 x 78 mm.

☐ a.　NBP B28 overprinted.　　—

1992 Numismatic Products

These notes were originally sold in a folder by Pekao Trading Company from its offices in New York and Warsaw.

NBP BNP9 (PCS8): **50 złotych - 1,000,000 złotych**　　UNC

☐ a.　NBP B32, B34 - B47 (15 notes) specimens in folder.　　—

1993 Issues

These notes are like the preceding issues, but the denominations at lower left front are in red, they have security threads, the watermark is different, and there are other changes, too.

NBP B49 (P159): **50,000 złotych** (demonetized 31.12.2010)   VG   VF   UNC
Green and brown. Front: Quill; writer Stanisław Staszic; coat of arms with crowned eagle. Back: Palac Staszica (Staszic Palace - Polish Academy of Sciences) building in Warsaw. Solid security thread with demetalized *NBP*. Watermark: Crowned eagle and *RP*. Printer: (PWPW). 138 x 63 mm.

- ☐ a.   16 LISTOPADA 1993. Sig. 13a. Prefix A - T.   —   —   30
Intro: 11.04.1994.
- ☐ as.   Diagonal red *WZÓR* overprint on front;   —   —   50
diagonal red *SPECIMEN* overprint on back;
horizontal black *No* # overprint at lower left front.

NBP B50 (P160): **100,000 złotych** (demonetized 31.12.2010)   VG   VF   UNC
Light blue, black, purple, orange, and green. Front: Plant; coat of arms with crowned eagle; composer Stanisław Moniuszko. Back: Teatr Wielki (Grand Theatre - National Opera) building in Warsaw. Solid security thread with demetalized *NBP*. Watermark: Crowned eagle and *RP*. Printer: (PWPW). 138 x 63 mm.

- ☐ a.   16 LISTOPADA 1993. Signature 13a.   —   15   60
Prefix A - Z, AA - AE. Intro: 11.04.1994.
- ☐ as.   Diagonal red *WZÓR* overprint on front;   —   —   90
diagonal red *SPECIMEN* overprint on back;
horizontal black *No* # overprint at lower left front.

NBP B51 (P161): **500,000 złotych** (demonetized 31.12.2010)   VG   VF   UNC
Green, orange, and purple. Front: Novelist Henryk Sienkiewicz; coat of arms with crowned eagle. Back: Flags, swords, helmet, spear, and shield with three open books. Solid security thread with demetalized *NBP*. Watermark: Crowned eagle and *RP*. Printer: (PWPW). 138 x 63 mm.

- ☐ a.   16 LISTOPADA 1993. Signature 13a.   —   40   150
Prefix A - Z, AA, AB. Intro: 24.01.1994.
- ☐ as.   Diagonal red *WZÓR* overprint on front;   —   —   180
diagonal red *SPECIMEN* overprint on back;
horizontal black *No* # overprint at lower left front.

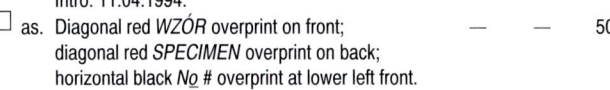

NBP B52 (P162): **1,000,000 złotych** (demonetized 31.12.2010)   VG   VF   UNC
Brown, olive green, and purple. Front: Flowers; coat of arms with crowned eagle; novelist Władysław Reymont. Back: Farm houses and trees. No security thread. Watermark: Crowned eagle. Printer: (PWPW). 138 x 63 mm.

- ☐ a.   16 LISTOPADA 1993. Sig. 13a. Prefix A - N.   —   —   200
Intro: 24.01.1994.
- ☐ as.   Diagonal red *WZÓR* overprint on front;   —   —   300
diagonal red *SPECIMEN* overprint on back;
horizontal black *No* # overprint at lower left front.

NBP B53 (P163): **2,000,000 złotych** (demonetized 31.12.2010)   VG   VF   UNC
Black, purple, orange, green, and blue. Front: Laurels; Prime Minister Ignacy Jan Paderewski; coat of arms with crowned eagle. Back: Laurels; coat of arms with crowned eagle. No security thread. Watermark: Crowned eagle. Printer: (PWPW). 138 x 63 mm.
- ☐ a. 16 LISTOPADA 1993. Sig. 13a. Prefix A, B.   —   —   300
  Intro: 11.04.1994.
- ☐ as. Diagonal red *WZÓR* overprint on front;   —   —   450
  diagonal red *SPECIMEN* overprint on back;
  horizontal black *No* # overprint at lower left front.

1995 Numismatic Products

The Polska Wytwórnia Papierów Wartościowych (Polish Security Printing Works) designed this 5-million-zloty note dated 1995, but it was never produced due to the currency revaluation which took place that year. In 2006, a private firm contracted with PWPW to produce a limited number of replicas never intended for circulation, as indicated by the small line of Polish text at the lower right front. These numismatic products are included in this catalog to inform collectors of their true nature.

NBP BNP11 (PNL): **5,000,000 złotych**   UNC
Green, brown, yellow, and blue. Front: Coat of arms with crowned eagle; Commander Józef Klemens Piłsudski wearing military uniform. Back: Eagle badge of the Polish Legions; Grand Cross (with Star) of the Order of Virtuti Militari; badge of the First Brigade of the Polish Legions. No security thread. Watermark: Crowned eagle and *RP*. Printer: (PWPW). 138 x 63 mm.
- ☐ a. 12 MAJA 1995. Signature 13a. Prefix AA - AB. Unissued.   30
- ☐ as. Diagonal red *WZÓR* overprint on front;   30
  diagonal red *SPECIMEN* overprint on back;
  horizontal black *No* # overprint at lower left front.

1990 Numismatic Products

In 1989, communism collapsed in Poland and the newly elected government prepared a new currency (printed by Giesecke & Devrient in Munich) to be issued in 1992. Due to inadequate security features, continuing inflation, and a lack of national identity, these notes were never issued and almost all of the notes were destroyed. However, some notes were overprinted *NIEOBIEGOWY* which means "not for circulation," then sold to collectors, along with 1,000 sets of specimen notes. 1- and 2-złoty notes without overprints have been confirmed and other denominations may also exist, but none are legal tender and were never issued for circulation.

NBP BNP10.001 (P164): **1 złoty**   UNC
Light blue and brown. Front: Crowned eagle; Maritime Passenger Terminal building in Gdynia. Back: Dar Pomorza (The Gift of Pomerania) three-masted sailing ship. Solid security thread. Watermark: Eagle. Printer: (G&D). 138 x 63 mm.
- ☐ a. 1 MARCA 1990. Sig. 11. Prefix B. Unissued.   —
- ☐ as1. Diagonal red *WZÓR* overprint on front;   100
  diagonal red *SPECIMEN* overprint on back;
  prefix A.
- ☐ as2. Horizontal red *NIEOBIEGOWY* ovpt; prefix C.   10

NBP BNP10.002 (P165): **2 złote** UNC
Tan. Front: Crowned eagle; mining conveyor tower at Katowice coal mine. Back: Gustaw Zemła's Pomnik Powstańców Śląskich (Silesian Insurgents monument) in Katowice. Solid security thread. Watermark: Eagle. Printer: (G&D). 138 x 63 mm.

- a. 1 MARCA 1990. Sig. 11. Prefix A. Unissued. —
- as1. Diagonal red *WZÓR* overprint on front; diagonal red *SPECIMEN* overprint on back; prefix A. 100
- as2. Horizontal red *NIEOBIEGOWY* ovpt; prefix B. 10

NBP BNP10.010 (P167): **10 złotych** UNC
Red. Front: Crowned eagle; King's Castle building in Warsaw. Back: Ludwika Nitschowa's Syrenka (Little Mermaid) statue of bare-breasted woman with sword near River Vistula in Warsaw. Solid security thread. Watermark: Eagle. Printer: (G&D). 138 x 63 mm.

- a. 1 MARCA 1990. Sig. 11. Prefix A. Unissued. —
- as1. Diagonal red *WZÓR* overprint on front; diagonal red *SPECIMEN* overprint on back; prefix A. 100
- as2. Horizontal red *NIEOBIEGOWY* ovpt; prefix D. 10

NBP BNP10.005 (P166): **5 złotych** UNC
Green. Front: Crowned eagle; Zamość city hall building. Back: Order of the Cross of Grunwald military decoration with shield and two swords. Solid security thread. Watermark: Eagle. Printer: (G&D). 138 x 63 mm.

- a. 1 MARCA 1990. Sig. 11. Prefix A. Unissued. —
- as1. Diagonal red *WZÓR* overprint on front; diagonal red *SPECIMEN* overprint on back; prefix A. 100
- as2. Horizontal red *NIEOBIEGOWY* ovpt; prefix E. 10

NBP BNP10.020 (P168): **20 złotych** UNC
Yellow. Front: Crowned eagle; cargo handling facility at Motlawa River in Gdańsk. Back: Abraham van den Blocke's statue of Neptune with trident and seahorse at Court of Artus in Gdańsk. Solid security thread. Watermark: Eagle. Printer: (G&D). 138 x 63 mm.

- a. 1 MARCA 1990. Sig. 11. Prefix A. Unissued. —
- as1. Diagonal red *WZÓR* overprint on front; diagonal red *SPECIMEN* overprint on back; prefix A. 100
- as2. Horizontal red *NIEOBIEGOWY* ovpt; prefix A, E. 10

NBP BNP10.050 (P169): **50 złotych** UNC
Purple and brown. Front: Crowned eagle; Wrocław city hall building. Back: 16th-century seal of Wrocław. Solid security thread. Watermark: Eagle. Printer: (G&D). 138 x 63 mm.

- a. 1 MARCA 1990. Sig. 11. Prefix A. Unissued. —
- as1. Diagonal red *WZÓR* overprint on front; diagonal red *SPECIMEN* overprint on back; prefix A. 100
- as2. Horizontal red *NIEOBIEGOWY* ovpt; prefix H. 10

NBP BNP10.200 (P171): **200 złotych** UNC
Light blue and purple. Front: Crowned eagle; Wawel (king's residence) in Kraków. Back: Seal of Kraków with Piast's crowned eagle. Solid security thread. Watermark: Eagle. Printer: (G&D). 138 x 63 mm.

- a. 1 MARCA 1990. Sig. 11. Prefix A. Unissued. —
- as1. Diagonal red *WZÓR* overprint on front; diagonal red *SPECIMEN* overprint on back; prefix A. 100
- as2. Horizontal red *NIEOBIEGOWY* ovpt; prefix D. 10

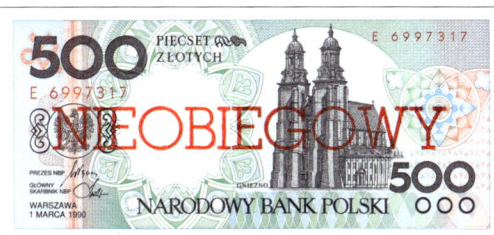

NBP BNP10.100 (P170): **100 złotych** UNC
Orange. Front: Crowned eagle; Poznań city hall building. Back: Seal of Poznań. Solid security thread. Watermark: Eagle. Printer: (G&D). 138 x 63 mm.

- a. 1 MARCA 1990. Sig. 11. Prefix A. Unissued. —
- as1. Diagonal red *WZÓR* overprint on front; diagonal red *SPECIMEN* overprint on back; prefix A. 100
- as2. Horizontal red *NIEOBIEGOWY* ovpt; prefix H. 10

NBP BNP10.500 (P172): **500 złotych** UNC
Green and brown. Front: Crowned eagle; Gniezno cathedral. Back: Seal of Gniezno. Solid security thread. Watermark: Eagle. Printer: (G&D). 138 x 63 mm.

- a. 1 MARCA 1990. Sig. 11. Prefix A. Unissued. —
- as1. Diagonal red *WZÓR* overprint on front; diagonal red *SPECIMEN* overprint on back; prefix A. 100
- as2. Horizontal red *NIEOBIEGOWY* ovpt; prefix E. 10

1994 Issues

Beginning 1 January 1995, the preceding notes dated 1974-1993 were exchanged without limit for 1994-dated notes at a ratio of 10,000:1.

NBP B54 (P173): **10 złotych** (US$3.30)   VG   VF   UNC
Brown and green. Front: Coat of arms with crowned eagle; two stylized Romanesque rosettes; Prince Mieszko I; crown as registration device; decorative floral ornamentation. Back: Crown; fragments of Romanesque columns; silver denar coin. Solid security thread with demetalized *10 ZŁ*. Watermark: Prince Mieszko I. 120 x 60 mm.

- a. 25 MARCA 1994. Sig. 13b. Intro: 01.01.1995.   FV   FV   5
  Prefix AA - BZ. Printer: (TDLR).
- b. Prefix DA. Printer: (PWPW).   FV   FV   5
- as. Diagonal red *WZÓR* overprint on front;   —   —   150
  horizontal red *WZÓR Nr #* overprint at lower left;
  diagonal red *SPECIMEN* overprint on back.

Replacement notes: Prefix YB to YF (PWPW) or ZA (TDLR).

NBP B55 (P174): **20 złotych** (US$6.55)   VG   VF   UNC
Violet and pink. Front: Coat of arms with crowned eagle; Romanesque portal; King Bolesław I Chrobry; crown as registration device; stylized oak tree. Back: Crown; rotunda; silver denar coin; lion rampant on floral osier. Solid security thread with demetalized *20 ZŁ*. Watermark: King Bolesław I Chrobry. 126 x 63 mm.

- a. 25 MARCA 1994. Sig. 13b. Intro: 01.01.1995.   FV   FV   11
  Prefix AA - BF. Printer: (TDLR).
- b. Prefix DA. Printer: (PWPW).   FV   FV   11
- as. Diagonal red *WZÓR* overprint on front;   —   —   150
  horizontal red *WZÓR Nr #* overprint at lower left;
  diagonal red *SPECIMEN* overprint on back.

Replacement notes: Prefix YB to YF (PWPW) or ZA (TDLR).

NBP B56 (P175): **50 złotych** (US$16)   VG   VF   UNC
Navy blue, blue, and light green. Front: Coat of arms with crowned eagle; stylized Gothic rosette; King Casimir III the Great; crown as registration device; monogram of crowned letter *K*. Back: Crown; panorama of Kazimierz; eagle on royal seal of Casimir III the Great; royal insignia, orb, and scepter; panorama of Cracow. Solid security thread with demetalized *50 ZŁ*. Watermark: King Casimir III the Great. 132 x 66 mm.

- a. 25 MARCA 1994. Sig. 13b. Intro: 01.01.1995.   FV   FV   25
  Prefix AA - CJ. Printer: (TDLR).
- b. Prefix DA. Printer: (PWPW).   FV   FV   25
- as. Diagonal red *WZÓR* overprint on front;   —   —   180
  horizontal red *WZÓR Nr #* overprint at lower left;
  diagonal red *SPECIMEN* overprint on back.

Replacement notes: Prefix YA to YE (PWPW) or ZA (TDLR).

NBP B57 (P176): **100 złotych** (US$33)   VG   VF   UNC
Green, olive green, light violet, and blue. Front: Coat of arms with crowned eagle; stylized Gothic ornamentation; King Ladislaus II Jagiello; crown as registration device. Back: Crown; castle of Teutonic Knights at Malbork; eagle on shield from tombstone of Ladislaus II Jagiello; two swords, Teutonic Knight's helmet, and cape. Solid security thread with demetalized *100 ZŁ*. Watermark: King Ladislaus II Jagiello. 138 x 69 mm.

- a. 25 MARCA 1994. Sig. 13b. Intro: 01.06.1995.   FV   FV   45
  Prefix AA - BS. Printer: (TDLR).
- b. Prefix DA. Printer: (PWPW).   FV   FV   45
- as. Diagonal red *WZÓR* overprint on front;   —   —   300
  horizontal red *WZÓR Nr #* overprint at lower left;
  diagonal red *SPECIMEN* overprint on back.

Replacement notes: Prefix YA to YL (PWPW) or ZA (TDLR).

2006 Numismatic Products

This note—designed by Andrzej Heidrich and engraved by Maciej Kopecki—was issued 16 October 2006, the 28th anniversary of Karol Wojtya's election to the papacy. Two million notes were issued in folders for 90 złotych each.

NBP B58 (P177): **200 złotych** (US$65) VG VF UNC

Brown, light yellow, and olive green. Front: Coat of arms with crowned eagle; wreath interwoven with ribbon; holographic patch in shape of Renaissance cartouche; King Sigismund I the Old; crown as registration device; wreath. Back: Crown; Wawel Castle courtyard; eagle within hexagon from the Sigismund Chapel in cathedral on Wawel Hill. Solid security thread with demetalized *200 ZŁ*. Watermark: King Sigismund I the Old. 144 x 72 mm.

☐	a.	25 MARCA 1994. Sig. 13b. Intro: 01.06.1995. Prefix AA - AR. Printer: (TDLR).	FV FV 120
☐	b.	Prefix DA. Printer: (PWPW).	FV FV 110
☐	as.	Diagonal red *WZÓR* overprint on front; horizontal red *WZÓR Nr #* overprint at lower left; diagonal red *SPECIMEN* overprint on back.	— — 500

Replacement notes: Prefix YA or YB (PWPW) or ZA (TDLR).

NBP BNP12 (P178): **50 złotych** (US$16) UNC

Blue, brown, and green. Front: Coat of arms with crowned eagle; world map; John Paul II holding crucifix-topped staff; Peter's keys. Back: Peter's keys; inauguration of John Paul II with cardinal Stefan Wyszynski; quotation from Letter to Poles; Jasna Góra Monastery and church in Częstochowa, Poland. Solid security thread with printed *50 ZL*. Watermark: Papal seal. Printer: *PWPW S.A.* 144 x 72 mm.

☐ a. 16 PAŹDZIERNIKA 2006. Signature 14. Prefix JP.   35

2008 Numismatic Products

On 21 October 2008, the National Bank of Poland announced that it would issue a 10-złoty note to commemorate the 90th anniversary of regaining independence. The front of the note depicts Commander Józef Piłsudski and the front façade of the Belweder Palace. The back of the note contains the Emblem of the Polish Republic—the White Eagle—as designed in 1919, as well as the Monument of the Heroic Deed of Polish Legions in Kielce. On 3 November 2008, the National Bank of Poland introduced the new 10-złoty note. 80,000 notes were packaged in a folder and sold for 15 złotych each. The note was engraved by Maciej Kopecki.

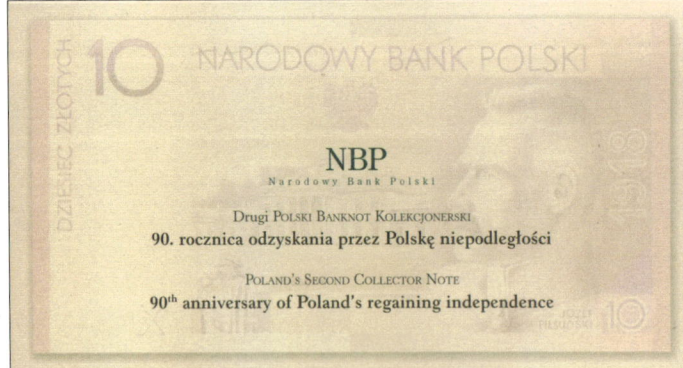

NBP BNP13 (P179): **10 złotych** (US$3.30) UNC
Pink and orange. Front: Belweder Palace in Warsaw; coat of arms with crowned eagle; Commander Józef Klemens Piłsudski wearing military uniform. Back: White eagle; Monument of the Heroic Deed of Polish Legions in Kielce. Solid security thread with microprinted *10 Zł*. Watermark: Piłsudski and electrotype denomination. Printer: *PWPW S.A.* 138 x 69 mm.
☐ a.   4 CZERWCA 2008. Signature 15. Prefix ON. Intro: 03.11.2008.   20

2009 Numismatic Products

To commemorate the 200th anniversary of the birth of the poet Julius Slowacki, the National Bank of Poland issued new 20-złoty notes on 23 September 2009. 80,000 notes were packaged in a folder and sold for 29 złotych each. The note was designed by Maciej Kopecki and engraved by Przemyslaw Krajewski.

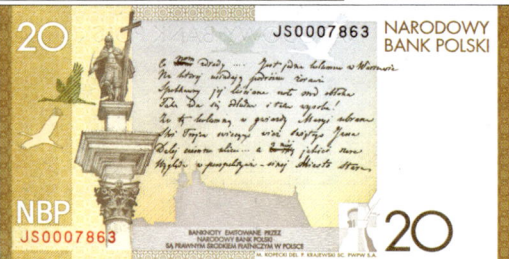

NBP BNP14 (P180): **20 złotych** (US$6.55) UNC
Brown. Front: Quill and inkwell; Krzemieniec chalet in Ukraine; coat of arms with crowned eagle; poet Julius Slowacki. Back: Flying cranes birds; statue of Sigismund III Vasa at Castle Square in Warsaw; handwritten poem "Sedation." Solid security thread with microprinted *20 Zł*. Watermark: Julius Slowacki and electrotype denomination. Printer: *PWPW S.A.* 138 x 69 mm.
☐ a.   8 STYCZNIA 2009. Signature 15. Prefix JS. Intro: 23.09.2009.   20

The National Bank of Poland honored the 200th birthday of musician Frédéric François Chopin with a new commemorative 20-złoty banknote. This note went on sale 26 February 2010 at a price of 50 złoty each.

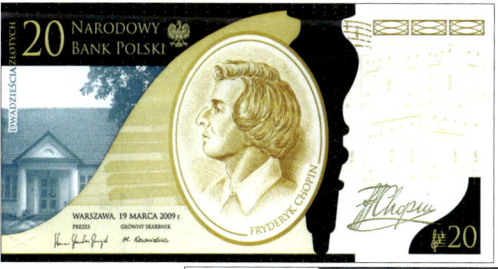

NBP BNP15 (P181): **20 złotych** (US$6.55) **UNC**
Black, tan, and blue. Front: Chopin birthplace mansion in Zelazowa Wola; coat of arms with crowned eagle; musician Frédéric François Chopin; score of Mazurka in B minor, Op. 7; Chopin signature. Back: Masovian willow trees; score of étude in F minor, Op. 10. Solid security thread with microprinted *20 Zł*. Watermark: Frédéric Chopin and electrotype denomination. Printer: *PWPW S.A.* 138 x 69 mm.

☐ a. 19 MARCA 2009. Signature 15. Prefix FC. Intro: 26.02.2010. 20

2011 Numismatic Products

To commemorate the 100th anniversary of the Nobel Prize in chemistry being awarded to Marie Curie, the National Bank of Poland issued new 20-złoty notes on 9 December 2011. 60,000 notes were packaged in a folder and sold for 47 złotych each.

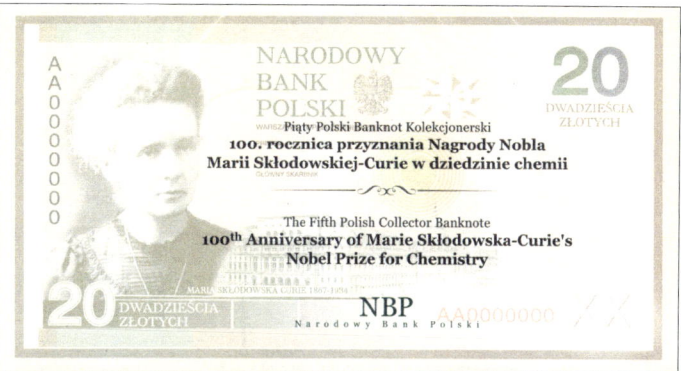

NBP BNP16 (P182): **20 złotych** (US$6.55) **UNC**
Brown and green. Front: Physicist Marie Skłodowska Curie; Sorbona w Paryżu (Sorbonne school building in Paris); coat of arms with crowned eagle; *Ra* (atomic symbol for radium) in SPARK patch of concentric circles. Back: Curie quotation; Instytut Radowy w Warszawie (Radium Institute building in Warsaw); Nobel Prize medal for chemistry. Solid security thread with microprinted *20 Zł*. Watermark: Marie Skłodowska Curie and electrotype denomination. Printer: *PWPW S.A.* 138 x 69 mm.

☐ a. 20 KWIETNIA 2011. Signature 16. Prefix MS. Intro: 09.12.2011. 20

POLAND 2012 ISSUES

2012 Issues

These notes are like earlier issues, but with improved security features, including Omron rings and SPARK patches.

NBP B59 (PNL): **10 złotych** (US$3.30) VG VF UNC

Brown and green. Front: Coat of arms with crowned eagle; two stylized Romanesque rosettes; Prince Mieszko I; crown as registration device; decorative floral ornamentation. Back: Crown; fragments of Romanesque columns; silver denar coin. Solid security thread with demetalized *10 ZŁ*. Watermark: Prince Mieszko I and electrotype *10*. Printer: *PWPW*. 120 x 60 mm.

   ☐ a. 5 STYCZNIA 2012. Signature 16.   FV FV 5
        Prefix AA - AC. Intro: 07.04.2014.
   ☐ as. Diagonal red *WZÓR* overprint on front;   — — 250
        horizontal red *WZÓR Nr #* overprint at lower left;
        diagonal red *SPECIMEN* overprint on back.

NBP B60 (PNL): **20 złotych** (US$6.55) VG VF UNC

Violet and pink. Front: Coat of arms with crowned eagle; Romanesque portal; King Bolesław I Chrobry; crown as registration device; stylized oak tree. Back: Crown; rotunda; silver denar coin; lion rampant on floral osier. Solid security thread with demetalized *20 ZŁ*. Watermark: King Bolesław I Chrobry and electrotype *20*. Printer: *PWPW*. 126 x 63 mm.

   ☐ a. 5 STYCZNIA 2012. Signature 16.   FV FV 10
        Prefix AA - AB. Intro: 07.04.2014.
   ☐ as. Diagonal red *WZÓR* overprint on front;   — — 275
        horizontal red *WZÓR Nr #* overprint at lower left;
        diagonal red *SPECIMEN* overprint on back.

NBP B61 (PNL): **50 złotych** (US$16) VG VF UNC

Navy blue, blue, and light green. Front: Coat of arms with crowned eagle; stylized Gothic rosette; King Casimir III the Great; crown as registration device; SPARK monogram of crowned letter *K*. Back: Crown; panorama of Kazimierz; eagle on royal seal of Casimir III the Great; royal insignia, orb, and scepter; panorama of Cracow. Solid security thread with demetalized *50 ZŁ*. Watermark: King Casimir III the Great and electrotype *50*. Printer: *PWPW*. 132 x 66 mm.

   ☐ a. 5 STYCZNIA 2012. Signature 16.   FV FV 35
        Prefix AA - AD. Intro: 07.04.2014.
   ☐ as. Diagonal red *WZÓR* overprint on front;   — — 275
        horizontal red *WZÓR Nr #* overprint at lower left;
        diagonal red *SPECIMEN* overprint on back.

NBP B62 (PNL): **100 złotych** (US$33) VG VF UNC

Green, olive green, light violet, and blue. Front: Coat of arms with crowned eagle; stylized Gothic ornamentation; King Ladislaus II Jagiello; crown as registration device; SPARK Gothic ornament. Back: Crown; castle of Teutonic Knights at Malbork; eagle on shield from tombstone of Ladislaus II Jagiello; two swords, Teutonic Knight's helmet, and cape. Solid security thread with demetalized *100 ZŁ*. Watermark: King Ladislaus II Jagiello and electrotype *100*. Printer: *PWPW*. 138 x 69 mm.

   ☐ a. 5 STYCZNIA 2012. Signature 16.   FV FV 55
        Prefix AA - AR. Intro: 07.04.2014.
   ☐ as. Diagonal red *WZÓR* overprint on front;   — — 325
        horizontal red *WZÓR Nr #* overprint at lower left;
        diagonal red *SPECIMEN* overprint on back.

2014 Numismatic Products

To commemorate the 100th anniversary of the Polish Legions, the National Bank of Poland issued a new 20-złoty polymer note on 5 August 2014. 50,000 notes were packaged in a folder and sold for 60 złotych each. This note was designed by Andrzej Heidrich, based upon the unissued 5-million-zloty note dated 1995 (see NBP BNP11).

NBP BNP17 (PNL): **20 złotych** (US$6.55)   UNC
Green, brown, yellow, and blue. Front: Belvedere Palace hologram; coat of arms with crowned eagle; Commander Józef Klemens Piłsudski wearing military uniform. Back: Eagle badge of the Polish Legions; Grand Cross (with Star) of the Order of Virtuti Militari; badge of the First Brigade of the Polish Legions; Belvedere Palace hologram. No security thread. Watermark: None. Printer: (PWPW). 147 x 67 mm. Polymer.
- a. 16 STYCZNIA 2014. Signature 17. Prefix LP. Intro: 05.08.2014.   20

Looking Forward

According to a posting on the bank's web site, to commemorate the 600th anniversary of the birth of Janowi Długoszowi, the National Bank of Poland will issue 30,000 new numismatic products in August 2015.

Acknowledgements

This chapter was compiled with the generous assistance of Brent Arthurson, Thomas Augustsson, Pawel Bohdanowicz, David Burns, Tim Ceney, Jim W.-C. Chen, David F. Cieniewicz (www.banknotestore.com), Donald Cleveland, Krzysztof Czupryński, Heritage Auctions (HA.com), Tomasz Jazwinski, Don Ludwig, Wally Myers, Rafal Nogowczyk, George Provencal, Gary Snover, Menelaos Stamatelos, Bill Stubkjaer, Christoph Thomas, Frank van Tiel, Jacek Tylicki, Ludek Vostal, Tristan Williams, Christof Zellweger, and others.

Sources

Atsmony, David. "Unknown Issues of Poland During World War II." *IBNS Journal*. Volume 1 Number 3. p.17.
Cole, Alan M. "Polish Insurgent Currency of 1794." *IBNS Journal*. Volume 16 Number 4. p.204.
Cuhaj, George S. *Standard Catalog of World Paper Money, General Issues, 1368-1960*. 14th edition. 2012. ISBN 978-1-4402-3090-5. Krause Publications (www.krausebooks.com), 700 East State St., Iola, WI, 54990-0001.
Cuhaj, George S. *Standard Catalog of World Paper Money, Modern Issues, 1961-Present*. 20th edition. 2014. ISBN 978-1-4402-4037-9. Krause Publications (www.krausebooks.com), 700 East State St., Iola, WI, 54990-0001.
Fischer, Andrzej. *Katalog Popularnych Banknotów Polskich (Catalogue of Polish Banknotes)*. 2010. ISBN 83-88352-07-5.
Hansen, Flemming Lyngbeck. "Bon Towarowy—An Element of Socialism in Poland." *IBNS Journal*. Volume 31 Number 1. p.7.
Heath, Henry B. "Portraits of Polish Rulers on Bank Notes." *IBNS Journal*. Volume 38 Number 2. p.6.
Jazwinski, Tomasz. "Letter to the Editor." *IBNS Journal*. Volume 34 Number 4. p.7.
Miłczak, Czesław. *Catalogue of Polish Banknotes 1916-1994*, 2000. Warsaw, Poland. ISBN 83-913361-9-0.
Philipson, F. "Historical Notes of Poland." *IBNS Journal*. Volume 8 Number 2. p.56.
Sluszkiewicz, Tomasz. "'English' Counterfeit Bank Note / 500 złoty 1940 Issued by Bank Emisyjny, Commonly Nicknamed 'Mountaineer.'" *IBNS Journal*. Volume 36 Number 2. p.45.
Tomita, Masahiro. "Bon Towarowy: Foreign Exchange Instruments of Poland." *IBNS Journal*. Volume 25 Number 4. p.107.
Walczak, Krzysztof. "The Stories Behind the Cancelled 'Cities' Series of Polish Banknotes." *IBNS Journal*. Volume 51 Number 4. p.43.
Warszawskie Centrum Numizmatyczne web site (www.wcn.pl).
www.banknoty.republika.pl/glowna.html
www.złotye.ru

Share Your Input, Info, and Images

This catalog is believed to be complete and correct as of the time of publication. Prices and face values were last updated 13 June 2014. Please report errors or omissions so that corrections may be made. If you can more precisely identify the name or location of anything depicted on a note, please share that information. Furthermore, if you own an unlisted type or variety, please submit scans of the front and back of the note so that it can be documented. Scans should be 300 dots per inch, 100% actual size, 24-bit color, saved as *uncompressed* JPEG files, and sent to owen@banknotenews.com. Be sure to fully describe all attributes of the note which are not apparent upon visual inspection of the images alone, such as physical dimension, watermark, and security thread.

Qatar

For earlier issues, see Saudi Arabia and Qatar & Dubai.

Contents

Qatar Monetary Agency (QMA) 1722
Qatar Central Bank (QCB) 1725

Monetary System

19.05.1973: 1 Qatari riyal (QAR) = 100 dirham

Arabic Numbers

0	1	2	3	4	5	6	7	8	9
٠	١	٢	٣	٤	٥	٦	٧	٨	٩

Watermark Varieties

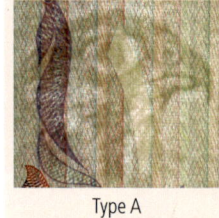  

Type A — Falcon head with overlapping beak
Type B — Falcon head with even beak
Type C — Falcon head and electrotype denomination

Qatar Monetary Agency

The Qatar Monetary Agency (QMA) was established by decree 7 of 1973, and on 9 May 1973, Qatar and Dubai signed an agreement terminating the Qatar-Dubai Currency Agreement of 1966. The agency took over the assets and liabilities of the Qatar-Dubai Currency Board on 19 May 1973, the date when the former issued its first series of notes. Notes from both issuing authorities circulated in parallel for 90 days, after which time the older notes were withdrawn.

QMA Signature Varieties

1	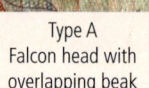
	(Minister of Finance) Abdulaziz al-Thani

1973-1976 Issues

QMA B1 (P1): 1 riyal (demonetized 10.04.1996)   VG   VF   UNC
Red. Front: Coat of arms with dhow and palm trees. Back: Port of Doha with four ships and several smaller boats. Solid security thread. Watermark: Falcon head. Printer: (BWC). 141 x 60 mm.
- a. No date. Signature 1. Prefix ١/١ - ١/١٠٠.   3   12   50
  Intro: 19.05.1973.
- as. Diagonal red *SPECIMEN* overprint; punched.   —   —   2,000

QMA B2 (P2): 5 riyals (demonetized 10.04.1996)   VG   VF   UNC
Brown and purple. Front: Coat of arms with dhow and palm trees. Back: National Museum building (former home of Sheikh Abdullah bin Jassim al-Thani). Solid security thread. Watermark: Falcon head. Printer: (BWC). 146 x 63 mm.
- a. No date. Signature 1. Prefix ١/١ - ١/٤.   6   25   100
  Intro: 19.05.1973.
- as. Specimen.   —   —   300

QMA B3 (P3): **10 riyals** (demonetized 10.04.1996)   **VG   VF   UNC**
Green. Front: Coat of arms with dhow and palm trees. Back: Qatar Monetary Agency headquarters building. Solid security thread. Watermark: Falcon head. Printer: (BWC). 151 x 66 mm.

☐ a. No date. Signature 1. Prefix ١/١ - ١/٦.   15   60   250
     Intro: 19.05.1973.
☐ as. Specimen.   —   —   400

QMA B4 (P4): **50 riyals** (demonetized 10.04.1996)   **VG   VF   UNC**
Blue. Front: Coat of arms with dhow and palm trees. Back: Off-shore oil platform. Solid security thread. Watermark: Falcon head. Printer: (BWC). 156 x 68 mm.

☐ a. No date. Signature 1. Prefix ١/١. Intro:1976.   200   750   2,500
☐ as. Specimen.   —   —   100

QMA B5 (P5): **100 riyals** (demonetized 10.04.1996)   **VG   VF   UNC**
Olive green. Front: Coat of arms with dhow and palm trees. Back: Ministry of Finance building. Solid security thread. Watermark: Falcon head. Printer: (BWC). 161 x 70 mm.

☐ a. No date. Signature 1. Prefix ١/١ - ١/٣.   150   600   2,400
     Intro: 19.05.1973.
☐ as. Specimen.   —   —   1,500

QMA B6 (P6): **500 riyals** (demonetized 10.04.1996)   **VG   VF   UNC**
Olive green. Front: Coat of arms with dhow and palm trees. Back: Mosque of the Sheikhs with minaret. Solid security thread. Watermark: Falcon head. Printer: (BWC). 166 x 72 mm.

☐ a. No date. Signature 1. Prefix ١/١ - ١/٢.   800   3,500   6,000
     Intro: 19.05.1973.
☐ as. Specimen.   —   —   2,000

1981 Issues

The 1981 issues were printed by Thomas De La Rue and feature new designs, a coat of arms that now includes crossed swords, and security threads with the text *QATAR MONETARY AGENCY*.

QMA B7 (P7): **1 riyal** (demonetized 22.06.2006)   VG   VF   UNC
Brown. Front: Coat of arms with dhow, palm trees, and crossed swords. Back: Foreign Ministry building; Mosque of the Sheikhs with minaret; Emiri Palace. Solid security thread with printed *QATAR MONETARY AGENCY*. Watermark: Falcon head. Printer: (TDLR). 134 x 66 mm.
- a. No date. Signature 1. Intro: 25.07.1981.   1   4.75   20

QMA B9 (P9): **10 riyals** (demonetized 22.06.2006)   VG   VF   UNC
Green. Front: Coat of arms with dhow, palm trees, and crossed swords. Back: National Museum building (former home of Sheikh Abdullah bin Jassim al-Thani) with flag and cannon. Solid security thread with printed *QATAR MONETARY AGENCY*. Watermark: Falcon head. Printer: (TDLR). 146 x 69 mm.
- a. No date. Signature 1. Intro: 25.07.1981.   2.50   10   40
- as. Diagonal red *SPECIMEN* overprint; punched.   —   —   300

QMA B8 (P8): **5 riyals** (demonetized 22.06.2006)   VG   VF   UNC
Purple. Front: Coat of arms with dhow, palm trees, and crossed swords. Back: Greenhouses; sheep; field of plants. Solid security thread with printed *QATAR MONETARY AGENCY*. Watermark: Falcon head. Printer: (TDLR). 140 x 67.5 mm.
- a. No date. Signature 1. Intro: 25.07.1981.   1   4   15
  Watermark: Falcon head Type A. Prefix ٥/١-٥/٥.
- b. Watermark: Falcon head Type B. Prefix ٥/٧-٥/١٤.   0.75   2.50   10

QMA B10 (P10): **50 riyals** (demonetized 22.06.2006)   VG   VF   UNC
Blue. Front: Coat of arms with dhow, palm trees, and crossed swords. Back: Worker stoking furnace in steel factory. Solid security thread with printed *QATAR MONETARY AGENCY*. Watermark: Falcon head. Printer: (TDLR). 152 x 70.5 mm.
- a. No date. Signature 1. Intro: 25.07.1981.   10   40   150

1985 Issue

Similarities between the 1-riyal (QMA B7) and 100-riyal (QMA B11) notes of the 1981 issue confused the public, prompting the release of this modified 1-riyal note with clearly different colors and a completely new illustration on back, perhaps from an unused design originally proposed for the 1973 issues.

QMA B11 (P11): **100 riyals** (demonetized 22.06.2006)   VG   VF   UNC
Olive green. Front: Coat of arms with dhow, palm trees, and crossed swords. Back: Qatar Monetary Agency headquarters building. Solid security thread with printed *QATAR MONETARY AGENCY*. Watermark: Falcon head. Printer: (TDLR). 158 x 72 mm.

    a. No date. Signature 1. Intro: 15.05.1981.   40   150   600

QMA B13 (P13): **1 riyal** (demonetized 22.06.2006)   VG   VF   UNC
Brown. Front: Coat of arms with dhow, palm trees, and crossed swords. Back: Dhow; Mosque of the Sheikhs; Foreign Ministry building; Emiri Palace. Solid security thread with printed *QATAR MONETARY AGENCY*. Watermark: Falcon head. Printer: (TDLR). 134 x 66 mm.

    a. No date. Signature 1. Intro: 1985.   0.25   1.25   5
      Wmk: Falcon head Type A. Prefix ٢٥/١١و.
    b. Wmk: Falcon head Type B. Prefix ٥٤/٢٧و.   FV   FV   3.50
    as. Diagonal red *SPECIMEN* overprint; punched.   —   —   525

Qatar Central Bank

The Qatar Central Bank (QCB) was established by decree 15 on 5 August 1993. All coins and notes issued by the Qatar Monetary Agency became the property of the bank but continued to circulate for several years.

For more information, visit www.qcb.gov.qa.

QMA B12 (P12): **500 riyals** (demonetized 22.06.2006)   VG   VF   UNC
Blue and green. Front: Coat of arms with dhow, palm trees, and crossed swords. Back (vertical): Off-shore oil platform. Solid security thread with printed *QATAR MONETARY AGENCY*. Watermark: Falcon head. Printer: (TDLR). 164 x 73.5 mm.

    a. No date. Signature 1. Intro: 25.07.1981.   100   400   800
    as. Specimen.   —   —   1,500

QCB Signature Varieties

	(Governor)	(Minister of Finance)
1	Abdullah Ben Khaled Al-Attiya	Mohammad al-Thani
2	Abdullah Ben Khaled Al-Attiya	Yousef Hussein Kamal
3	Abdullah Saud Al-Thani	Yousef Hussein Kamal

1996 Issues

The newly established QCB issued a new series of notes featuring the name of the new issuer, and slightly reworked designs on front to accommodate two signatures instead of the previous single signature.

QCB B1 (P14): **1 riyal** (demonetized 15.06.2013)   VG   VF   UNC
Brown. Front: Coat of arms with dhow, palm trees, and crossed swords. Back: Dhow; Mosque of the Sheikhs; Foreign Ministry building; Emiri Palace. Solid security thread. Watermark: Falcon head. Printer: (TDLR). 134 x 66 mm.
     a.   No date. Signature 1. Intro: 22.06.1996.   0.25   1   4
          Thread printed *QATAR MONETARY AGENCY* [sic].
     b.   Thread printed *QATAR CENTRAL BANK*.   0.25   0.75   2.75
Replacement notes: Prefix ر٠/ر.

QCB B2 (P15): **5 riyals** (demonetized 15.06.2013)   VG   VF   UNC
Purple. Front: Coat of arms with dhow, palm trees, and crossed swords. Back: Greenhouses; sheep; field of plants. Solid security thread. Watermark: Falcon head. Printer: (TDLR). 140 x 67.5 mm.
     a.   No date. Signature 1. Intro: 22.06.1996.   0.75   2.50   10
          Thread printed *QATAR MONETARY AGENCY* [sic].
     b.   Thread printed *QATAR CENTRAL BANK*.   0.50   2   8

QCB B3 (P16): **10 riyals** (demonetized 15.06.2013)   VG   VF   UNC
Green. Front: Coat of arms with dhow, palm trees, and crossed swords. Back: National Museum building (former home of Sheikh Abdullah bin Jassim al-Thani) with flag and cannon. Solid security thread. Watermark: Falcon head. Printer: (TDLR). 146 x 69 mm.
     a.   No date. Signature 1. Intro: 22.06.1996.   1.50   6   25
          Thread printed *QATAR MONETARY AGENCY* [sic].
     b.   Thread printed *QATAR CENTRAL BANK*.   1.25   5   20

QCB B4 (P17): **50 riyals** (demonetized 15.06.2013)   VG   VF   UNC
Blue. Front: Coat of arms with dhow, palm trees, and crossed swords. Back: Worker stoking furnace in steel factory. Windowed security thread with demetalized text. Watermark: Falcon head. Printer: (TDLR). 152 x 70.5 mm.
     a.   No date. Signature 1. Intro: 22.06.1996.   6   25   100

2003 Issues

All of the 2003 issues use the Type C watermark of the falcon head with electrotype denominations in Arabic and Western numerals.

QCB B5 (P18): **100 riyals** (demonetized 15.06.2013)   VG VF UNC
Olive green. Front: Coat of arms with dhow, palm trees, and crossed swords. Back: Qatar Monetary Agency headquarters building. Windowed security thread with demetalized text. Watermark: Falcon head. Printer: (TDLR). 158 x 72 mm.
☐ a.   No date. Signature 1. Intro: 22.06.1996.   20   75   200

QCB B7 (P20): **1 riyal** (US$0.30)   VG VF UNC
Blue and purple. Front: Coat of arms with dhow, palm trees, and crossed swords. Back: Three native birds: crested lark, Eurasian bee eater, and lesser sand plover. Solid security thread and windowed security thread with demetalized *QCB 1*. Watermark: Falcon head with electrotype ١ over *1*. Printer: (TDLR). 134 x 66 mm.
☐ a.   No date. Signature 2. Intro: 15.06.2003.   FV   FV   1
Replacement notes: Prefix رو/١٠.

QCB B6 (P19): **500 riyals** (demonetized 15.06.2013)   VG VF UNC
Blue and green. Front: Holographic patch; coat of arms with dhow, palm trees, and crossed swords. Back (vertical): Off-shore oil platform. Windowed security thread with demetalized text. Watermark: Falcon head. Printer: (TDLR). 164 x 73.5 mm.
☐ a.   No date. Signature 1. Intro: 22.06.1996.   25   100   400

QCB B8 (P21): **5 riyals** (US$1.40)   VG VF UNC
Green. Front: Coat of arms with dhow, palm trees, and crossed swords. Back: National Museum building; oryx and camel. Solid security thread and windowed security thread with demetalized *QCB 5*. Watermark: Falcon head with electrotype ٥ over *5*. Printer: (TDLR). 140 x 67.5 mm.
☐ a.   No date. Signature 2. Intro: 15.06.2003.   FV   FV   3.50
Replacement notes: Prefix ره/١٠.

QCB B9 (P22): **10 riyals** (US$2.75)   VG   VF   UNC

Orange, brown, and green. Front: Coat of arms with dhow, palm trees, and crossed swords. Back: Dhow; sand dune at Khor al-Udeid. Solid security thread and windowed security thread with demetalized *QCB 10*. Watermark: Falcon head with electrotype ١٠ over *10*. Printer: (TDLR). 146 x 69 mm.

 ☐ a. No date. Signature 2. Intro: 15.06.2003. FV FV 5.75

Replacement notes: Prefix ‏رد/١٠.

QCB B10 (P23): **50 riyals** (US$14)   VG   VF   UNC

Pink, purple, and blue. Front: Silver foil patch; coat of arms with dhow, palm trees, and crossed swords. Back: Qatar Central Bank building; Oyster and Pearl monument. Solid security thread and windowed security thread with demetalized *QCB 50*. Watermark: Falcon head with electrotype ٥٠ over *50*. Printer: (TDLR). 152 x 70.5 mm.

 ☐ a. No date. Signature 2. Intro: 15.06.2003. FV FV 35

Replacement notes: Prefix ‏رج/١٠.

QCB B11 (P24): **100 riyals** (US$27)   VG   VF   UNC

Green, purple, and brown. Front: Holographic patch; coat of arms with dhow, palm trees, and crossed swords. Back: Mosque of the Sheikhs with minaret; al-Shaqab Institute building. Solid security thread and windowed security thread with demetalized *QCB 100* and Arabic text. Watermark: Falcon head with electrotype ١٠٠ over *100*. Printer: (TDLR). 158 x 72 mm.

 ☐ a. No date. Signature 2. Intro: 15.06.2003. FV FV 70

Replacement notes: Prefix ‏رب/١٠.

QCB B12 (P25): **500 riyals** (US$137)   VG   VF   UNC

Blue and violet. Front: Holographic patch; coat of arms with dhow, palm trees, and crossed swords. Back: Royal Palace; Al-Wajbah Fort; falcon head. Solid security thread and windowed security thread with demetalized Arabic text. Watermark: Falcon head with electrotype ٥٠٠ over *500*. Printer: (TDLR). 164 x 73.5 mm.

 ☐ a. No date. Signature 2. Intro: 15.06.2003. FV FV 300

Replacement notes: Prefix ‏را/١٠.

2007 Issues

These two notes are like the preceding issues, but with the designs slightly shifted to make room for Optiks—an 18-mm wide demetalized security thread with a clear polymer oval aperture—which replaces the windowed security thread used on the older notes.

QCB B13 (P26): **100 riyals** (US$27)   VG   VF   UNC
Green and purple. Front: Holographic patch; coat of arms with dhow, palm trees, and crossed swords. Back: Mosque of the Sheikhs with minaret; al-Shaqab Institute building. Solid and Optiks security threads. Watermark: Falcon head with electrotype ٠٠٠ over *100* and Cornerstones. Printer: (TDLR). 158 x 72 mm.
    a.   No date. Signature 3. Intro: 26.09.2007.   FV   FV   60

QCB B14 (P27): **500 riyals** (US$137)   VG   VF   UNC
Blue and violet. Front: Holographic patch; coat of arms with dhow, palm trees, and crossed swords. Back: Royal Palace; Al-Wajbah Fort; falcon head. Solid and Optiks security threads. Watermark: Falcon head with electrotype ٠٠٠ over *500*. Printer: (TDLR). 164 x 73.5 mm.
    a.   No date. Signature 3. Intro: 26.09.2007.   FV   FV   250

2008 Issues

On 15 September 2008, the Qatar Central Bank issued a new series of four notes—1, 5, 10, and 50 riyals—which have symbols along the left front edge that facilitate their use by the sight impaired. New 100- and 500-riyal notes are in the works, but because these denominations were upgraded in 2007 with the addition of the 18-mm wide Optiks security thread, bank officials did not feel the need to update them.

QCB B15 (P28): **1 riyal** (US$0.30)   VG   VF   UNC
Blue and purple. Front: Coat of arms with dhow, palm trees, and crossed swords. Back: Three native birds: crested lark, Eurasian bee eater, and lesser sand plover. Solid security thread and windowed security thread with demetalized *QCB 1*. Watermark: Falcon head with electrotype ٠ over *1*. Printer: (TDLR). 134 x 66 mm.
    a.   No date. Signature 3. Intro: 15.09.2008.   FV   FV   1

QCB B16 (P29): **5 riyals** (US$1.40)   VG   VF   UNC
Green. Front: Coat of arms with dhow, palm trees, and crossed swords. Back: National Museum building; oryx and camel. Solid security thread and windowed security thread with demetalized *QCB 5*. Watermark: Falcon head with electrotype ٠٠ over *50*. Printer: (TDLR). 140 x 67.5 mm.
    a.   No date. Signature 3. Intro: 15.09.2008.   FV   FV   3

Qatar 2008 Issues

QCB B17 (P30): **10 riyals** (US$2.75)   VG VF UNC
Orange and brown. Front: Coat of arms with dhow, palm trees, and crossed swords. Back: Dhow; sand dune at Khor al-Udeid. Solid security thread and windowed security thread with demetalized *QCB 10*. Watermark: Falcon head with electrotype ١٠ over *10*. Printer: (TDLR). 146 x 69 mm.
    ☐ a.   No date. Signature 3. Intro: 15.09.2008.   FV FV 5

QCB B18 (P31): **50 riyals** (US$14)   VG VF UNC
Pink, purple, blue. Front: Holographic patch; coat of arms with dhow, palm trees, and crossed swords. Back: Qatar Central Bank building; Oyster and Pearl monument. Holographic stripe. Windowed security thread with demetalized *QCB 50* in ovals. Watermark: Falcon head, electrotype ٥٠ over *50*, and Cornerstones. Printer: (TDLR). 152 x 70.5 mm.
    ☐ a.   No date. Signature 3. Intro: 15.09.2008.   FV FV 25

Acknowledgements

This chapter was compiled with the generous assistance of Jamal A. Alrefai, Thomas Augustsson, Jim Copeland, Mirsad Delic, Jean-Michel Engels, Tod Hunt, Thomas Krause, Wally Myers, Bill Stubkjaer, Peter Symes, Christoph Thomas, Christof Zellweger, and others.

Sources

Cuhaj, George S. *Standard Catalog of World Paper Money, Modern Issues, 1961-Present*. 20th edition. 2014. ISBN 978-1-4402-4037-9. Krause Publications (www.krausebooks.com), 700 East State St., Iola, WI, 54990-0001.

Eu, Peter, Ben Chiew, and Stane Straus. *World Polymer Banknotes: A Standard Reference*. 2nd edition. 2006. ISBN 983-43038-2-3. Eureka Metro, P. O. Box 30, Jalan Kelang Lama, Kuala Lumpur, 57000, Malaysia.

Krause, Thomas and Peter Bauer. *Specialized Catalogue of World Plastic Money*. 5th edition. 2009. www.polymernotes.de.

Symes, Peter. "The Bank Notes of Qatar." *IBNS Journal*. Volume 39 Number 3. p.6.

Symes, Peter. Reference Site for Islamic Banknotes (www.islamicbanknotes.com).

Share Your Input, Info, and Images

This catalog is believed to be complete and correct as of the time of publication. Prices and face values were last updated 22 July 2011. Please report errors or omissions so that corrections may be made. If you can more precisely identify the name or location of anything depicted on a note, please share that information. Furthermore, if you own an unlisted type or variety, please submit scans of the front and back of the note so that it can be documented. Scans should be 300 dots per inch, 100% actual size, 24-bit color, saved as *uncompressed* JPEG files, and sent to owen@banknotenews.com. Be sure to fully describe all attributes of the note which are not apparent upon visual inspection of the images alone, such as physical dimension, watermark, and security thread.

Qatar & Dubai

For earlier issues, see India and Saudi Arabia.

Monetary System
18.09.1966: 1 Qatar-Dubai riyal = 100 dirham

Arabic Numbers

0	1	2	3	4	5	6	7	8	9
٠	١	٢	٣	٤	٥	٦	٧	٨	٩

Qatar & Dubai Currency Board

From 1959 until 1966, Qatar used the Indian rupee as currency, in the form of Gulf rupees. When India devalued the rupee, Qatar adopted the Saudi riyal from 11 June 1966, until 18 September 1966, at which time the Qatar-Dubai Currency Board (QDCB) introduced the Qatar-Dubai riyal. The Saudi riyal was worth 1.065 rupees, while the Qatar-Dubai riyal was equal to the rupee prior to its devaluation.

QDCB Signature Varieties

1
(Chairman)
Khalifa bin Hamad al-Thani

1966 Issues

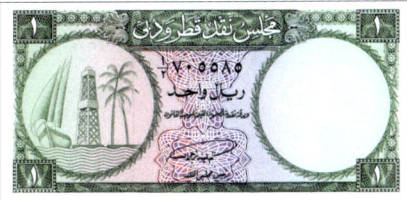

QDCB B1 (P1): 1 riyal (withdrawn 17.08.1973)   VG   VF   UNC
Green. Front: Coat of arms with dhow, oil derrick, and palm trees. Back: Geometric designs. Solid security thread. Watermark: Falcon head. Printer: (BWC). 110 x 55 mm.

- a. No date. Signature 1. Prefix ١/١ - ١/١١.   50   100   550
  Intro: 18.09.1966.
- as. Horizontal red نموذج *SPECIMEN* overprint; punched.   —   —   500
- at. Color trial: Red.   —   —   —

QDCB B2 (P2): 5 riyals (withdrawn 17.08.1973)   VG   VF   UNC
Purple. Front: Coat of arms with dhow, oil derrick, and palm trees. Back: Geometric designs. Solid security thread. Watermark: Falcon head. Printer: (BWC). 120 x 60 mm.

- a. No date. Signature 1. Prefix ١/١ - ١/٦.   250   1,000   4,100
  Intro: 18.09.1966.
- as. Horizontal red نموذج *SPECIMEN* overprint; punched.   —   —   900
- at. Color trial: Brown.   —   —   —

QDCB B3 (P3): 10 riyals (withdrawn 17.08.1973)   VG   VF   UNC
Gray-blue. Front: Coat of arms with dhow, oil derrick, and palm trees. Back: Geometric designs. Solid security thread. Watermark: Falcon head. Printer: (BWC). 130 x 65 mm.

- a. No date. Signature 1. Prefix ١/١ - ١/٩.   400   1,200   4,900
  Intro: 18.09.1966.
- as. Horizontal red نموذج *SPECIMEN* overprint; punched.   —   —   1,300
- at. Color trial: Purple.   —   —   —

QDCB B4 (P4): **25 riyals** (withdrawn 17.08.1973)   VG   VF   XF
Blue. Front: Coat of arms with dhow, oil derrick, and palm trees. Back: Geometric designs. Solid security thread. Watermark: Falcon head. Printer: (BWC). 140 x 70 mm.

☐	a.	No date. Signature 1. Prefix ١/١. Intro: 18.09.1966.	2,000	25,000	56,000
☐	as.	Horizontal red نموذج *SPECIMEN* overprint; punched.	—	UNC	14,000
☐	at.	Color trial: Green.	—	—	—

QDCB B5 (P5): **50 riyals** (withdrawn 17.08.1973)   VG   VF   UNC
Red. Front: Coat of arms with dhow, oil derrick, and palm trees. Back: Geometric designs. Solid security thread. Watermark: Falcon head. Printer: (BWC). 150 x 75 mm.

☐	a.	No date. Signature 1. Prefix ١/١. Intro: 18.09.1966.	2,250	20,000	—
☐	as.	Horizontal black نموذج *SPECIMEN* ovpt; punched.	—	—	6,500
☐	at.	Color trial: Dark brown.	—	AU	10,000

QDCB B6 (P6): **100 riyals** (withdrawn 17.08.1973)   VG   VF   UNC
Olive green. Front: Coat of arms with dhow, oil derrick, and palm trees. Back: Geometric designs. Solid security thread. Watermark: Falcon head. Printer: (BWC). 160 x 80 mm.

☐	a.	No date. Signature 1. Prefix ١/١ - ١/٢. Intro: 18.09.1966.	1,000	4,000	—
☐	as.	Horizontal red نموذج *SPECIMEN* overprint; punched.	—	—	4,000
☐	at.	Color trial: Purple.	—	—	—

On 17 October 2012, the Coin and Medal Department of Bonhams Auctioneers, London auctioned a complete set of notes with matching serial number ١/١ ٠٠٠٠٩ in a blue leather presentation album inscribed *Council For the Currency of Qatar & Dubai*. The set sold for £180,000 (US$279,000) including buyer's premium.

Looking Forward

Following Dubai's entrance into the United Arab Emirates, Qatar began issuing the Qatari riyal separate from Dubai on 19 May 1973. The old notes continued to circulate in parallel for 90 days, at which time they were withdrawn.

For later issues, see Qatar and United Arab Emirates.

Acknowledgements

This chapter was compiled with the generous assistance of Bonhams (www.bonhams.com), Tod Hunt, Mark Irwin, Wally Myers, Hani Rida (http://sababanknotes.6te.net), Jürg Rindlisbacher, Ibrahim Salem, Christof Zellweger, and others.

Sources

Cuhaj, George S. *Standard Catalog of World Paper Money, Modern Issues, 1961-Present*. 17th edition. 2011. ISBN 978-1-4402-1584-1. Krause Publications (www.krausebooks.com), 700 East State St., Iola, WI, 54990-0001.

Fisher, Jack H. "Qatar and Dubai Currency Board Notes." *IBNS Journal*. Volume 33 Number 2. p.26.

Symes, Peter. "The Bank Notes of the Qatar and Dubai Currency Board." *IBNS Journal*. Volume 36 Number 3. p.18.

Symes, Peter. Reference Site for Islamic Banknotes (www.islamicbanknotes.com).

Share Your Input, Info, and Images

This catalog is believed to be complete and correct as of the time of publication. Prices and face values were last updated 15 July 2014. Please report errors or omissions so that corrections may be made. If you can more precisely identify the name or location of anything depicted on a note, please share that information. Furthermore, if you own an unlisted type or variety, please submit scans of the front and back of the note so that it can be documented. Scans should be 300 dots per inch, 100% actual size, 24-bit color, saved as *uncompressed* JPEG files, and sent to owen@banknotenews.com. Be sure to fully describe all attributes of the note which are not apparent upon visual inspection of the images alone, such as physical dimension, watermark, and security thread.

Republic of the Congo

For earlier issues, see French Equatorial Africa.

Contents

Banque Centrale (BC) 1734
Banque des États de l'Afrique Centrale (BEAC) 1735

Monetary System
1971: 1 Congolese franc = 100 centimes

The area north of the Congo River came under French sovereignty in 1880 and was originally known as French Congo. In 1903, the colony's name was officially changed to Middle Congo. In 1908, French Equatorial Africa was formed by combining Middle Congo with Chad, Gabon, and Oubangui-Chari (the modern Central African Republic).

Following the revision of the French constitution that established the Fifth Republic in 1958, French Equatorial Africa dissolved; its constituent parts reformed into autonomous colonies within the French Community. During these reforms, Middle Congo became known as the Republic of the Congo (the neighboring former Belgian colony chose the same name, so they are commonly called Congo-Brazzaville and Congo-Kinshasa, after their respective capitals), and was granted full independence on 15 August 1960.

Banque Centrale (Central Bank)

BC Signature Varieties

1 — LE DIRECTEUR GÉNÉRAL, Claude Panouillot (1955 - 1973) / LE PRÉSIDENT, Georges Gautier

1971 Issue

In 1970, President Marien Ngouabi proclaimed a Marxist-Leninist socialist state. On these notes—and those that follow until 1992—the name of the country is expressed as République Populaire du Congo (People's Republic of the Congo).

BC B1 (P1): 10,000 francs   VG   VF   UNC
Brown and green. Front: Young woman with head scarf; men marching with banner; carved wooden man. Back: Carved wooden statue; man plowing field with tractor; carved wooden mask. No security thread. Watermark: Antelope head. Printer: (BDF). 170 x 92 mm.

☐ a. No date. Signature 1. Intro: 1971.   —   1,500   5,000
☐ as. Vertical *SPECIMEN* perforation;   —   —   1,850
   diagonal black *SPECIMEN* Nº # overprint.

Banque des États de l'Afrique Centrale (Bank of the Central African States)

Originally established by France as the Institut d'Emission de l'Afrique Equatoriale et du Cameroun, in 1972 the bank reorganized and was renamed the Banque des États de l'Afrique Centrale (BEAC).

For more information, visit www.beac.int.

BEAC Signature Varieties

BEAC Signature Varieties

1974-1984 Issues

In 1974, the BEAC issued the first banknotes for its members: Cameroon, Central African Republic, Chad, Gabon, and Republic of the Congo. The backs of the first series are standard in all member states, but the fronts differ from country to country, and include the member state name in French (in this case, République Populaire du Congo).

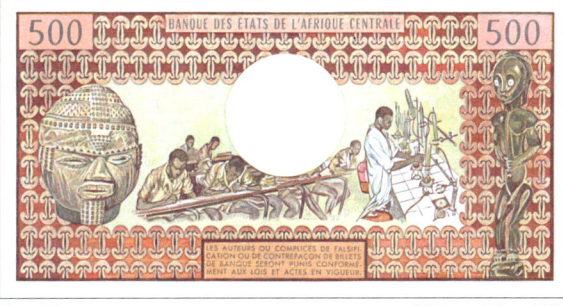

BEAC B1 (P2): **500 francs**   VG   VF   UNC

Brown. Front: Woman; man tossing fishing net in river; trees. Back: Carved wooden mask; male students writing at long desks; student in chemistry lab with beakers; carved wooden statue. No security thread. Watermark: Antelope head. Printer: (FCOF). 158 x 80 mm.

		VG	VF	UNC
☐	a. No date. Signature 2. Intro: 1974.	10	25	100
☐	b. 1-04-1978. Signature 5.	25	50	150
☐	c. 1-07-1980.	3	10	40
☐	d. 1-06-81. Signature 7.	5	20	50
☐	e. 1-01-82.	10	25	100
☐	f. 1-01-83.	5	15	60
☐	g. 1-06-1984.	5	15	50
☐	as. Vertical *SPECIMEN* perforation; diagonal black *SPECIMEN* Nº # overprint.	—	—	—

BEAC B2 (P3): **1,000 francs** VG VF UNC
Blue. Front: Industrial plant with sheds and storage tanks; man with stick in mouth and large ornate collar. Back: Carved wooden mask; mining excavator; tails of two planes; three railroad cars; carved wooden statue. No security thread. Watermark: Antelope head. Printer: (FCOF). 159 x 83 mm.

			VG	VF	UNC
☐	a.	No date. Signature 1. Intro: 1974.	50	100	200
☐	b.	Signature 2.	25	50	150
☐	c.	Signature 4. Intro: 1978.	15	30	35
☐	d.	1-04-1978. Signature 5.	5	20	70
☐	e.	01.06.1981. Signature 7.	15	30	35
☐	f.	1-01-82.	30	60	125
☐	g.	1-01-83.	20	45	90
☐	h.	1-06-1984.	4	15	60

BEAC B3 (P4): **5,000 francs** VG VF UNC
Brown. Front: Man with headdress; waterfall and trees. Back: Carved wooden mask; machinery; building; logs; chains; minaret; carved horse and statue. No security thread. Watermark: Antelope head. Printer: (BDF). 162 x 86 mm.

			VG	VF	UNC
☐	a.	No date. Signature 1. Intro: 1974.	150	300	600
☐	b.	Signature 2.	125	250	550
☐	c.	Signature 6. Intro: 1978.	150	300	600
☐	d.	Signature 7.	125	250	550
☐	as.	Vertical *SPECIMEN* perforation; diagonal black *SPECIMEN Nº #* overprint.	—	—	1,200

BEAC B4 (P5): **10,000 francs** VG VF UNC
Brown and green. Front: Young woman with head scarf; men marching with banner; carved wooden man. Back: Carved wooden statue; man plowing field with tractor; carved wooden mask. No security thread. Watermark: Antelope head. Printer: (BDF). 170 x 90 mm.

			VG	VF	UNC
☐	a.	No date. Signature 2. Intro: 1974.	150	300	600
☐	b.	Signature 3. Intro: 1977.	150	300	600
☐	c.	Signature 6. Intro: 1978.	150	300	600
☐	d.	Signature 7. Intro: 1981.	150	300	600

1983-1991 Issues

BEAC B5 (P6): **5,000 francs**   VG   VF   UNC

Brown and yellow. Front: Carved wooden mask; three houses in village with trees; woman carrying basket of fronds on her back. Back: Stringed musical instrument; man on tractor plowing field; mine conveyor bucket and towers. No security thread. Watermark: Carved mask. Printer: (BDF). 162 x 84 mm

		VG	VF	UNC
☐ a.	No date. Signature 7. Intro: 1984.	10	40	125
☐ b.	Signature 9. Intro: 1991.	7.50	25	100

BEAC B6 (P7): **10,000 francs**   VG   VF   UNC

Green. Front: Five antelope heads; woman. Back: Large group of people loading bananas onto back of truck; various fruits including pineapples and dates. No security thread. Watermark: Woman. Printer: (BDF). 168 x 92 mm.

		VG	VF	UNC
☐ a.	No date. Signature 7. Intro: 1983.	10	40	150

1985-1991 Issues

BEAC B7 (P8): **500 francs**   VG   VF   UNC

Orange and brown. Front: Carved wooden ancestral figure with offering bowl on head; vase. Back: Seated man carving mask; various wooden artifacts. No security thread. Watermark: Carving of seated figure. Printer: (FCOF). 150 x 75 mm.

		VG	VF	UNC
☐ a.	1-01-1985. Signature 7.	1	4	15
☐ b.	1-01-1987.	1	4	15
☐ c.	1-01-1988.	—	—	—
☐ d.	1-01-1989.	1	4	15
☐ e.	1-01-1990. Signature 8.	0.50	2	8
☐ f.	1-01-1991. Signature 9.	0.50	2	8

BEAC B8 (P9): **1,000 francs**   VG   VF   UNC

Blue and violet. Front: Carved wooden animal figures; map with incomplete outline of Chad and various icons, including bird, man poling boat, trees, straw huts, rhinoceros, ship, off-shore oil platform, and elephant. Back: Elephant; antelope; giraffe; carved wooden seated figure. No security thread. Watermark: Carving. Printer: (FCOF). 155 x 78 mm.

		VG	VF	UNC
☐ a.	1-01-1985. Signature 7.	2.50	10	40

Shortly after introduction, Chad's government demanded this note's withdrawal because the map on front omitted Libyan-backed rebel-held territory north of 18° latitude.

1992 Issues

In 1991, *République Populaire du Congo* (People's Republic of the Congo) was renamed *République du Congo* (Republic of the Congo). These notes are like the preceding issues, but have the new country name on the front.

BEAC B10 (P11): **1,000 francs**   VG   VF   UNC
Blue and violet. Front: Carved wooden animal figures; map with complete outline of Chad and various icons, including bird, man poling boat, trees, straw huts, rhinoceros, ship, offshore oil platform, and elephant. Back: Elephant; antelope; giraffe; carved wooden seated figure. No security thread. Watermark: Carving. Printer: (FCOF). 155 x 78 mm.
    a.   1-01-1992. Signature 9.   2   8   25

BEAC B9 is like the preceding issue, but the map of Chad is no longer cut off by the top border, and the icon of a ship has been removed to reveal Equatorial Guinea's Bioko Island, off the west coast of Cameroon.

BEAC B9 (P10): **1,000 francs**   VG   VF   UNC
Blue and violet. Front: Carved wooden animal figures; map with complete outline of Chad and various icons, including bird, man poling boat, trees, straw huts, rhinoceros, ship, offshore oil platform, and elephant. Back: Elephant; antelope; giraffe; carved wooden seated figure. No security thread. Watermark: Carving. Printer: (FCOF). 155 x 78 mm.
    a.   1-01-1987. Signature 7.   2   8   30
    b.   1-01-1988.   2   8   30
    c.   1-01-1989.   —   —   —
    d.   1-01-1990. Signature 8.   1.25   5   20
    e.   1-01-1991. Signature 9.   1.25   5   20

BEAC B11 (P12): **5,000 francs**   VG   VF   UNC
Brown and yellow. Front: Carved wooden mask; three houses in village with trees; woman carrying basket of fronds on her back. Back: Stringed musical instrument; man on tractor plowing field; mine conveyor bucket and towers. No security thread. Watermark: Carved mask. Printer: (BDF). 162 x 84 mm
    a.   No date. Signature 9. Intro: 1992.   15   50   200

BEAC B12 (P13): **10,000 francs**   VG   VF   UNC
Green. Front: Five antelope heads; woman. Back: Large group of people loading bananas onto back of truck; various fruits including pineapples and dates. No security thread. Watermark: Woman. Printer: (BDF). 168 x 92 mm.
- a. No date. Signature 9. Intro: 1992.   20   60   150

Looking Forward
For later issues, see Central African States.

Acknowledgements
This chapter was compiled with the generous assistance of Thomas Augustsson, Andrea Bossi, Compagnie Generale De Bourse (www.cgb.fr), Robin Frost, Heritage Auctions (HA.com), Larry Hirsch (www.aworldcurrency.com), David Jones, Dave Mills (www.frenchbanknotes.com), Wally Myers, Nazir Rahemtulla, Ömer Yalcinkaya (stores.ebay.com/omer-yalcinkaya-store), and others.

Sources
Burson, Weldon. "Signature Combinations of Central African States Banknotes." *IBNS Journal*. Volume 28 Number 2. p.36.

Cuhaj, George S. *Standard Catalog of World Paper Money, General Issues, 1368-1960*. 14th edition. 2012. ISBN 978-1-4402-3090-5. Krause Publications (www.krausebooks.com), 700 East State St., Iola, WI, 54990-0001.

Cuhaj, George S. *Standard Catalog of World Paper Money, Modern Issues, 1961-Present*. 17th edition. 2011. ISBN 978-1-4402-1584-1. Krause Publications (www.krausebooks.com), 700 East State St., Iola, WI, 54990-0001.

Leclerc, Roger and Maurice Kolsky. *Les Billets Africains de la Zone Franc*. Volume 10. 2000. ISBN 2-906602-17-5. Éditions Victor Gadoury (www.gadoury.com). S.C.S. Bouvernon & Cie. 57, rue Grimaldi, MC-98000 Monaco.

Yandesa Mavuzi, Martin. *Numismatique des Monnaies du Congo*. 2010. Brussels, Belgium.

Share Your Input, Info, and Images
This catalog is believed to be complete and correct as of the time of publication. Prices and face values were last updated 11 November 2011. Please report errors or omissions so that corrections may be made. If you can more precisely identify the name or location of anything depicted on a note, please share that information. Furthermore, if you own an unlisted type or variety, please submit scans of the front and back of the note so that it can be documented. Scans should be 300 dots per inch, 100% actual size, 24-bit color, saved as *uncompressed* JPEG files, and sent to owen@banknotenews.com. Be sure to fully describe all attributes of the note which are not apparent upon visual inspection of the images alone, such as physical dimension, watermark, and security thread.

Rhodesia

For earlier issues, see Rhodesia & Nyasaland.

Monetary System
1964: 1 Rhodesian pound = 20 shillings
17.02.1970: 1 Rhodesian dollar (ZWC) = 0.50 pound
1980: 1 Zimbabwe dollar (ZWD) = 1 Rhodesian dollar

Reserve Bank of Rhodesia

RBR Signature Varieties
Governor

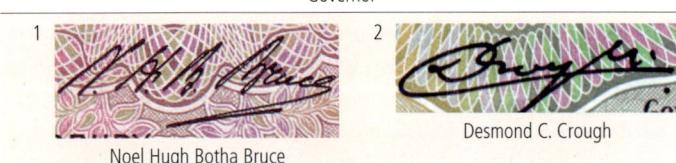

1 — Noel Hugh Botha Bruce
2 — Desmond C. Crough

1964 Issues

RBR B2 (P25): 1 pound — VG VF UNC
Red. Front: Flowers; coat of arms; Queen Elizabeth II. Back: Victoria Falls; trees. Solid security thread. Watermark: Cecil Rhodes. Printer: *BRADBURY, WILKINSON & C⁰ L^D NEW MALDEN, SURREY, ENGLAND*. 150 x 82 mm.

		VG	VF	UNC
a.	3ʳᴰ SEPTEMBER, 1964. Signature 1.	50	125	525
b.	4ᵀᴴ SEPTEMBER, 1964.	50	125	525
c.	7ᵀᴴ SEPTEMBER, 1964.	50	125	525
d.	14ᵀᴴ SEPTEMBER, 1964.	50	125	525
e.	21ˢᵀ SEPTEMBER, 1964.	50	125	525
f.	28ᵀᴴ SEPTEMBER, 1964.	50	125	525
g.	5ᵀᴴ OCTOBER, 1964.	50	125	525
h.	12ᵀᴴ OCTOBER, 1964.	50	125	525
i.	19ᵀᴴ OCTOBER, 1964.	50	125	525
j.	26ᵀᴴ OCTOBER, 1964.	50	125	525
k.	2ᴺᴰ NOVEMBER, 1964.	50	125	525
l.	9ᵀᴴ NOVEMBER, 1964.	50	125	525
m.	16ᵀᴴ NOVEMBER, 1964.	50	125	525
ds.	Horizontal *SPECIMEN* perforation.	—	—	—
t.	Color trial: Green.	—	—	850

RBR B1 (P24): 10 shillings — VG VF UNC
Blue. Front: Zimbabwe bird; leaves; coat of arms; Queen Elizabeth II. Back: Tobacco field. Solid security thread. Watermark: Cecil Rhodes. Printer: *BRADBURY, WILKINSON & C⁰ L^D NEW MALDEN, SURREY, ENGLAND*. 134 x 76 mm.

		VG	VF	UNC
a.	30ᵀᴴ SEPTEMBER, 1964. Signature 1.	75	175	750
b.	7ᵀᴴ OCTOBER, 1964.	75	175	750
c.	14ᵀᴴ OCTOBER, 1964.	75	175	750
d.	21ˢᵀ OCTOBER, 1964.	75	175	750
e.	28ᵀᴴ OCTOBER, 1964.	75	175	750
f.	11ᵀᴴ NOVEMBER, 1964.	75	175	750
g.	16ᵀᴴ NOVEMBER, 1964.	75	175	750
s.	No overprint; punched; all-zero s/n. Dated 5ᵀᴴ NOVEMBER, 1965. Unissued.	—	—	—
t.	Color trial: Brown.	—	—	1,000

1966-1968 Issues

In October 1965, the Salisbury-based board of the Reserve Bank of Rhodesia gave Bradbury, Wilkinson & Co. an order for £20 million worth of banknotes (8 million 10-shilling notes, 11 million 1-pound notes, and 1 million 5-pound notes) for delivery in the second quarter of 1966. However, on 11 November 1965, Rhodesia declared independence, prompting the British government to replace the Salisbury board with a new board in London on 3 December 1965.

The London board allowed Bradbury Wilkinson to complete the print order, which it did in May 1966. However, the Salisbury board refused to pay because it had independently placed an order on 7 April 1966 for a completely new series of banknotes from the German security printer Giesecke & Devrient. A court injunction prevented the G&D banknotes from being sent to Rhodesia, and the entire order was destroyed by the printers. The British government also refused an export licence for the Bradbury Wilkinson notes. In July/August 1967, the BWC notes were transferred to the Bank of England for storage, where they remained until being destroyed in July 1973. To date, only one 10-shilling specimen dated 5 November 1965 has surfaced from the ill-fated BWC order.

Unable to obtain notes printed abroad from an established security printer, the following notes were printed by the bank's own printing works in Salisbury, Rhodesia without imprint. These new notes are like the preceding issues, but feature a new portait of Queen Elizabeth II, red serial numbers, repositioned dates, and revised vignettes on back. These notes circulated in parallel with the preceding issues.

RBR B3 (P26): **5 pounds**   VG   VF   UNC
Purple. Front: Sable antelope; trees; leaves; flowers; coat of arms; Queen Elizabeth II. Back: Trees; Great Zimbabwe ruins. Solid security thread. Watermark: Cecil Rhodes. Printer: *BRADBURY, WILKINSON & C⁰ L^D NEW MALDEN, SURREY, ENGLAND*. 159 x 89 mm.

			VG	VF	UNC
☐	a.	10TH NOVEMBER, 1964. Signature 1.	75	175	750
☐	b.	12TH NOVEMBER, 1964.	75	175	750
☐	c.	16TH NOVEMBER, 1964.	75	175	750
☐	as.	Diagonal red *SPECIMEN* overprint; punched.	—	—	—
☐	cs.	Horizontal *SPECIMEN* perforation.	—	—	—
☐	t.	Color trial: Blue.	—	—	1,200

RBR B4 (P27): **10 shillings**   VG   VF   UNC
Blue. Front: Zimbabwe bird; leaves; coat of arms; Queen Elizabeth II. Back: Tobacco field. Solid security thread. Watermark: Cecil Rhodes. Printer: (RBR, Salisbury). 134 x 76 mm.

			VG	VF	UNC
☐	a.	1ST JUNE, 1966. Signature 1. Intro: 1967.	30	115	450
☐	b.	10TH SEPTEMBER, 1968.	30	115	450
☐	s.	Specimen.	—	—	—

1970-1979 Dollar Issues

The Rhodesian dollar was introduced on 17 February 1970, less than a month before the declaration of the Republic of Rhodesia on 2 March 1970. It replaced the pound at a rate of 2 dollars to 1 pound. These notes are like the preceding issues, but with new currency units, the bank logo replaces the coat of arms, and the coat of arms replaces the portrait of Queen Elizabeth II.

RBR B5 (P28): 1 pound   VG   VF   UNC
Red. Front: Flowers; leaves; coat of arms; Queen Elizabeth II. Back: Victoria Falls; trees. Solid security thread. Watermark: Cecil Rhodes. Printer: (RBR, Salisbury). 150 x 82 mm.

		VG	VF	UNC
☐ a.	15TH JUNE, 1966. Signature 1. Intro: 19.07.1967.	30	115	450
☐ b.	18TH AUGUST, 1967.	30	115	450
☐ c.	1ST SEPTEMBER, 1967.	30	115	450
☐ d.	14TH OCTOBER, 1968.	30	115	450
☐ s.	Specimen.	—	—	—

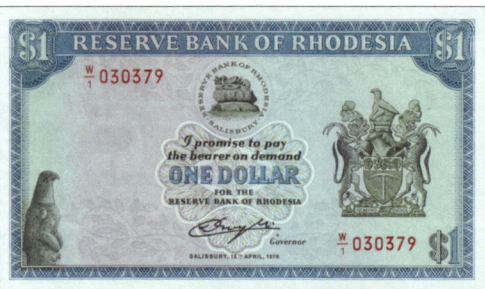
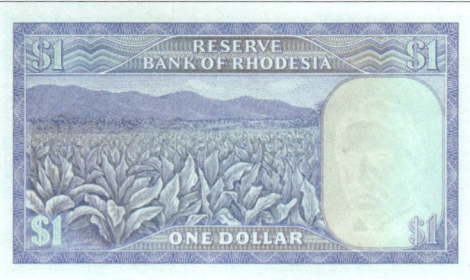

RBR B7 (P30): 1 dollar   VG   VF   UNC
Blue. Front: Zimbabwe bird; leaves; bank logo; coat of arms. Back: Tobacco field. Solid security thread. Printer: (RBR, Salisbury). 134 x 76 mm.

		VG	VF	UNC
☐ a.	17TH FEBRUARY, 1970. Signature 1. Watermark: Cecil Rhodes. Prefix L/19 - L/25.	7	30	85
☐ b.	16TH APRIL, 1971. Prefix L/25 - L/28.	7	30	85
☐ c.	14TH MAY, 1971. Prefix L/28 - L/31.	7	40	85
☐ d.	17TH JUNE, 1971. Prefix L/31 - L/34.	7	30	85
☐ e.	19TH JULY, 1971. Prefix L/34 - L/37.	7	30	85
☐ f.	18TH AUGUST, 1971. Prefix L/37 - L/41.	7	30	85
☐ g.	14TH FEBRUARY, 1973. Prefix L/41 - L/49.	4	15	45
☐ h.	2ND MARCH, 1973. Prefix L/49 - L/57.	4	15	45
☐ i.	12TH AUGUST, 1974. Prefix L/57 - L/64.	4	15	45
☐ j.	2ND SEPTEMBER, 1974. Prefix L/64 - L/71.	4	15	45
☐ k.	15TH OCTOBER, 1974. Prefix L/71 - L/81.	4	15	45
☐ l.	1ST MARCH, 1976. Sig. 2. Prefix L/82 - L/90.	4	15	45
☐ m.	1ST NOVEMBER, 1976. Prefix L/90 - L/97.	4	15	45
☐ n.	18TH APRIL, 1978. Prefix L/97 - L/114.	4	15	45
☐ o.	2ND AUGUST, 1979. Watermark: Zimbabwe bird. Prefix L/115 - L/147.	2.50	10	40
☐ s.	Specimen.	—	—	—

Replacement notes: Prefix W/1.
The 1-dollar note dated 2ND AUGUST, 1979 is remarkable in that it is the only Rhodesian note dated after Rhodesia ceased to exist at midnight 31 May 1979.

RBR B6 (P29): 5 pounds   VG   VF   UNC
Blue and green. Front: Sable antelope; trees; leaves; coat of arms; Queen Elizabeth II. Back: Trees; Great Zimbabwe ruins. Solid security thread. Watermark: Cecil Rhodes. Printer: (RBR, Salisbury). 159 x 89 mm.

		VG	VF	UNC
☐ a.	1ST JULY, 1966. Signature 1. Intro: 1967.	75	275	650
☐ as.	Specimen.	—	—	—

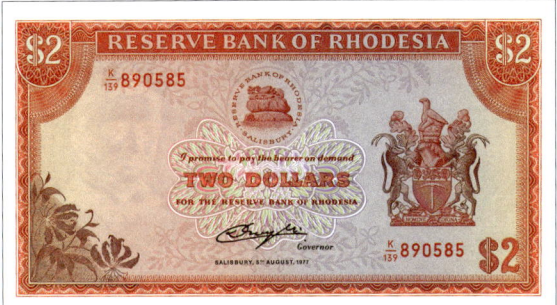

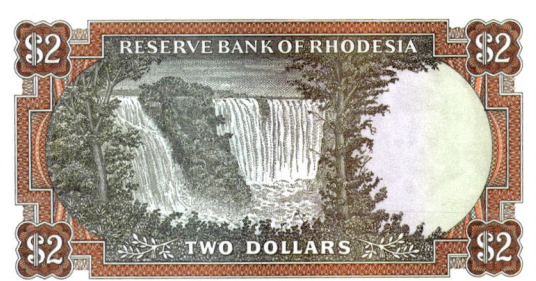

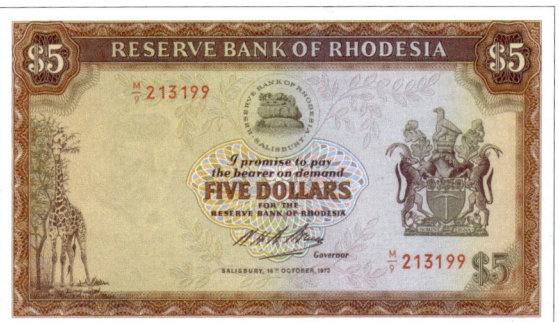

RBR B8 (P31): **2 dollars**   VG   VF   UNC

Red. Front: Flowers; leaves; bank logo; coat of arms. Back: Victoria Falls; trees. Solid security thread. Printer: (RBR, Salisbury). 150 x 82 mm.

		VG	VF	UNC
☐ a.	17TH FEBRUARY, 1970. Signature 1. Watermark: Cecil Rhodes. Prefix K/35 - K/40.	6	25	70
☐ b.	15TH AUGUST, 1970. Prefix K/40 - K/44.	6	25	70
☐ c.	8TH SEPTEMBER, 1970. K/44 - K/49.	6	25	70
☐ d.	10TH NOVEMBER, 1970. Prefix K/49 - K/55.	6	25	70
☐ e.	12TH NOVEMBER, 1971. Prefix K/55 - K/61.	6	25	70
☐ f.	4TH JANUARY, 1972. Prefix K/61 - K/69.	6	25	70
☐ g.	29TH JUNE, 1973. Prefix K/69 - K/78.	5	20	55
☐ h.	10TH JANUARY, 1974. Prefix K/78 - K/89.	5	20	55
☐ i.	20TH JANUARY, 1975. Prefix K/89 - K/101.	5	20	55
☐ j.	4TH MARCH, 1975. Prefix K/101 - K/114.	5	20	55
☐ k.	7TH APRIL, 1975. Prefix K/114 - K/119.	5	20	55
☐ l.	1ST MARCH, 1976. Sig. 2. Prefix K/120 - K/128.	5	20	55
☐ m.	15TH APRIL, 1977. Prefix K/128 - K/139.	5	20	55
☐ n.	5TH AUGUST, 1977. Prefix K/139 - K/148.	5	20	55
☐ o.	10TH APRIL, 1979. Prefix K/148 - K/151.	25	75	300
☐ p.	Watermark: Zimbabwe bird. Prefix K/152 - K/160.	4	12	50
☐ q.	24TH MAY, 1979. Prefix K/161 - K/183.	4	12	50
☐ s.	Specimen.	—	—	—

Replacement notes: Prefix X/1.

RBR B9 (P32): **5 dollars**   VG   VF   UNC

Brown. Front: Giraffe; leaves; bank logo; coat of arms. Back: Male and female lions in bush. Solid security thread. Printer: (RBR, Salisbury). 152 x 86 mm.

		VG	VF	UNC
☐ a.	16TH OCTOBER, 1972. Signature 1. Watermark: Cecil Rhodes. Prefix M/1 - M/10.	7	30	125
☐ b.	1ST MARCH, 1976. Sig. 2. Prefix M/11 - M/14.	8	35	75
☐ c.	20TH OCTOBER, 1978. Prefix M/14 - M/20.	6	28	90
☐ d.	15TH MAY, 1979. Watermark: Zimbabwe bird. Prefix M/21 - M/27.	5	20	85
☐ s.	Specimen.	—	—	—

Replacement notes: Prefix Y/1.

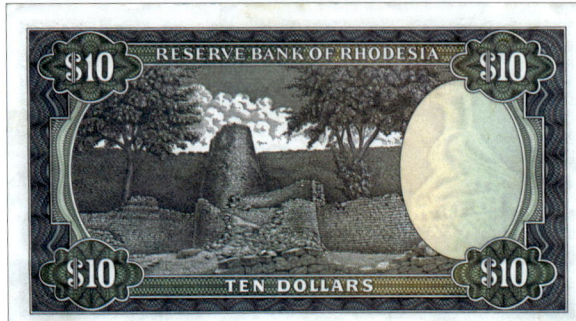

RBR B10 (P33): 10 dollars

Blue and green. Front: Sable antelope; trees; leaves; bank logo; coat of arms. Back: Trees; Great Zimbabwe ruins. Solid security thread. Printer: (RBR, Salisbury). 159 x 89 mm.

			VG	VF	UNC
☐	a.	17TH FEBRUARY, 1970. Signature 1. Watermark: Cecil Rhodes. Prefix J/6 - J/8.	20	85	250
☐	b.	25TH JANUARY, 1971. Prefix J/8 - J/10.	20	85	250
☐	c.	24TH FEBRUARY, 1971. Prefix J/10 - J/11.	20	85	250
☐	d.	8TH MAY, 1972. Prefix J/11 - J/15.	20	100	250
☐	e.	20TH NOVEMBER, 1973. Prefix J/15 - J/20.	9	40	120
☐	f.	15TH DECEMBER, 1973. Prefix J/20 - J/25.	9	40	120
☐	g.	15TH SEPTEMBER, 1975. Prefix J/25 - J/31.	9	40	120
☐	h.	19TH NOVEMBER, 1975. Prefix J/31 - J/37.	9	40	65
☐	i.	3RD DECEMBER, 1975. Prefix J/37 - J/39.	5	20	75
☐	j.	1ST MARCH, 1976. Sig. 2. Prefix J/40 - J/45.	4	15	60
☐	k.	2ND JANUARY, 1979. Watermark: Zimbabwe bird. Prefix J/46 - J/68.	5	20	80
☐	s.	Specimen.	—	—	—

Replacement notes: Prefix Z/1.

Looking Forward

In 1980, the Rhodesian dollar was replaced by the Zimbabwean dollar at par. For later issues, see Zimbabwe.

Acknowledgements

This chapter was compiled with the generous assistance of Arigo Avbovbo, David F. Cieniewicz (www.banknotestore.com), Victor Hasson, Mike Hughes, Steve Milner, Wally Myers, Mikhail "Mike" Prizov, George Provencal, Jefferson Ritson, TDS, Menelaos Stamatelos, Tristan Williams, and others.

Sources

Buczacki, Jerry. "The Currency Notes of Queen Elizabeth II." *IBNS Journal*. Volume 17 Number 2. p.61.

Cuhaj, George S. *Standard Catalog of World Paper Money, Modern Issues, 1961-Present*. 20th edition. 2014. ISBN 978-1-4402-4037-9. Krause Publications (www.krausebooks.com), 700 East State St., Iola, WI, 54990-0001.

Eu, Peter and Ben Chiew. *Queen Elizabeth II*. 1st edition. 2006. ISBN 983-43038-1-5. Eureka Metro, P. O. Box 30, Jalan Kelang Lama, Kuala Lumpur, 57000, Malaysia.

Kantor, M. "Bank Notes of Rhodesia." *IBNS Journal*. Volume 12 Number 3. p.147.

Levius, Harold. "Paper Money Chronicles of African History: Part 2 - The Rhodesias and Nyasaland." *IBNS Journal*. Volume 34 Number 1. p.10.

Levius, Harold. "Paper Money Chronicles of African History: Part 3 - The Rhodesias and Nyasaland." *IBNS Journal*. Volume 34 Number 2. p.30.

Milner, Steve. *Rhodesia-Zimbabwe Banknotes Newsletters*.

Symes, Peter. "The Portraits of Queen Elizabeth II on World Bank Notes." *IBNS Journal*. Volume 44 Number 2. p.8.

Share Your Input, Info, and Images

This catalog is believed to be complete and correct as of the time of publication. Prices and face values were last updated 17 June 2011. Please report errors or omissions so that corrections may be made. If you can more precisely identify the name or location of anything depicted on a note, please share that information. Furthermore, if you own an unlisted type or variety, please submit scans of the front and back of the note so that it can be documented. Scans should be 300 dots per inch, 100% actual size, 24-bit color, saved as *uncompressed* JPEG files, and sent to owen@banknotenews.com. Be sure to fully describe all attributes of the note which are not apparent upon visual inspection of the images alone, such as physical dimension, watermark, and security thread.

Rhodesia and Nyasaland

For earlier issues, see Southern Rhodesia.

Monetary System

1 Rhodesia and Nyasaland pound = 20 shillings

Bank of Rhodesia and Nyasaland

A new currency was created in 1955 to replace the Southern Rhodesian pound which had been circulating in all parts of the federation (Southern Rhodesia, Northern Rhodesia, and Nyasaland). The Rhodesia and Nyasaland pound replaced the Southern Rhodesian pound at par and was pegged at par to the British pound.

BRN Signature Varieties

	Governor
1	A. P. Grafftey-Smith
2	B. C. J. Richards

1956-1961 Issues

Due to the large number of confirmed dates and the possibility that other dates remain to be discovered, instead of assigning unique variety letters to every note based upon a change in the printed date, the banknotes of Rhodesia and Nyasaland have been assigned letters based solely upon the two signature varieties.

BRN B1 (P20): **10 shillings** VG VF UNC
Brown. Front: Fish eagle; coat of arms; Queen Elizabeth II. Back: Trees and boats along river bank. Solid security thread. Watermark: Cecil Rhodes. Printer: *BRADBURY, WILKINSON & C° L^D NEW MALDEN, SURREY, ENGLAND*. 134 x 76 mm.

		VG	VF	UNC
☐ a.	3RD APRIL, 1956. Signature 1.	100	450	1,600
☐ a.	22ND MAY, 1956.	100	450	1,600
☐ a.	4TH AUGUST, 1956.	100	450	1,600
☐ a.	1ST OCTOBER, 1956.	100	450	1,600
☐ a.	20TH NOVEMBER, 1956.	100	450	1,600
☐ a.	15TH JANUARY, 1957.	100	450	1,600
☐ a.	30TH MARCH, 1957.	100	450	1,600
☐ a.	15TH APRIL, 1957.	100	450	1,600
☐ a.	29TH APRIL, 1957.	100	450	1,600
☐ a.	13TH MAY, 1957.	100	450	1,600
☐ a.	27TH MAY, 1957.	100	450	1,600
☐ a.	18TH JULY, 1958.	100	450	1,600
☐ a.	1ST AUGUST, 1958.	100	450	1,600
☐ a.	15TH AUGUST, 1958.	100	450	1,600
☐ a.	19TH JUNE, 1959.	100	450	1,600
☐ a.	3RD JULY, 1959.	100	450	1,600
☐ a.	22ND APRIL, 1960.	100	450	1,600
☐ a.	6TH MAY, 1960.	100	450	1,600
☐ a.	20TH MAY, 1960.	100	450	1,600
☐ a.	3RD JUNE, 1960.	100	300	1,600
☐ a.	17TH JUNE, 1960.	100	450	1,600
☐ b.	30TH DECEMBER, 1960. Signature 2.	100	300	1,700
☐ b.	4TH JANUARY, 1961.	100	300	1,700
☐ b.	6TH JANUARY, 1961.	100	300	1,700
☐ b.	9TH JANUARY, 1961.	100	300	1,700
☐ b.	11TH JANUARY, 1961.	100	300	1,700
☐ b.	13TH JANUARY, 1961.	100	300	1,700
☐ b.	16TH JANUARY, 1961.	100	300	1,700
☐ b.	18TH JANUARY, 1961.	100	300	1,700
☐ b.	20TH JANUARY, 1961.	100	300	1,700
☐ b.	23RD JANUARY, 1961.	100	225	1,700
☐ b.	25TH JANUARY, 1961.	100	300	1,700
☐ b.	27TH JANUARY, 1961.	100	300	1,700
☐ b.	30TH JANUARY, 1961.	100	300	1,700
☐ b.	1ST FEBRUARY, 1961.	100	300	1,700
☐ as1.	Diagonal red *SPECIMEN* overprint; punched. Dated 3RD APRIL, 1956.	—	—	1,000
☐ as2.	Horizontal *SPECIMEN* perforation. Dated 3RD APRIL, 1956.	—	—	—
☐ as3.	Horizontal *SPECIMEN* perforation. Dated 4TH AUGUST, 1956.	—	—	—
☐ as4.	Horizontal *SPECIMEN* perforation. Dated 20TH NOVEMBER, 1956.	—	—	—
☐ as5.	Horizontal *SPECIMEN* perforation. Dated 30TH MARCH, 1957.	—	—	—

BRN B1 (P20): 10 shillings

		VG	VF	UNC
☐	as6. Horizontal *SPECIMEN* perforation. Dated 13TH MAY, 1957.	—	—	—
☐	bs. Horizontal *SPECIMEN* perforation. Dated 27TH JANUARY, 1961.	—	—	—
☐	p. Horizontal *SPECIMEN* perf. No date; no s/n.	—	—	—
☐	t1. Color trial: Blue and orange.	—	—	1,250
☐	t2. Color trial: Green and orange.	—	—	1,250

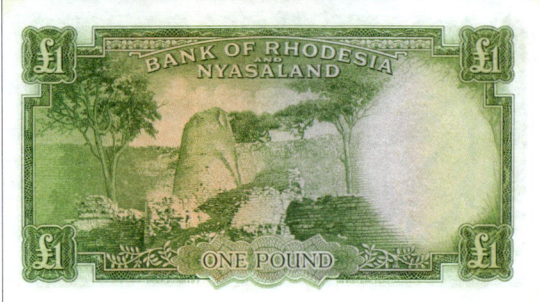

BRN B2 (P21): 1 pound

Green. Front: Leopard; coat of arms; Queen Elizabeth II. Back: Great Zimbabwe ruins. Solid security thread. Watermark: Cecil Rhodes. Printer: *BRADBURY, WILKINSON & CO LD NEW MALDEN, SURREY, ENGLAND*. 150 x 82 mm.

		VG	VF	UNC
☐	a. 3RD APRIL, 1956. Signature 1.	125	575	1,700
☐	a. 22ND MAY, 1956.	125	575	1,700
☐	a. 11TH JUNE, 1956.	125	575	1,700
☐	a. 2ND JULY, 1956.	125	575	1,700
☐	a. 25TH JULY, 1956.	125	575	1,700
☐	a. 17TH AUGUST, 1956.	125	575	1,700
☐	a. 4TH SEPTEMBER, 1956.	125	575	1,700
☐	a. 1ST OCTOBER, 1956.	125	575	1,700
☐	a. 16TH OCTOBER, 1956.	125	575	1,700
☐	a. 5TH NOVEMBER, 1956.	125	575	1,700
☐	a. 20TH NOVEMBER, 1956.	125	575	1,700
☐	a. 6TH DECEMBER, 1956.	125	575	1,700
☐	a. 24TH DECEMBER, 1956.	125	575	1,700
☐	a. 15TH JANUARY, 1957.	125	575	1,700
☐	a. 14TH FEBRUARY, 1957.	125	575	1,700
☐	a. 30TH MARCH, 1957.	125	575	1,700
☐	a. 15TH APRIL, 1957.	125	575	1,700
☐	a. 29TH APRIL, 1957.	125	575	1,700
☐	a. 13TH MAY, 1957.	125	575	1,700
☐	a. 27TH MAY, 1957.	125	575	1,700
☐	a. 11TH JUNE, 1957.	125	575	1,700
☐	a. 24TH JUNE, 1957.	125	575	1,700
☐	a. 6TH JUNE, 1958.	125	575	1,700
☐	a. 20TH JUNE, 1958.	125	575	1,700
☐	a. 4TH JULY, 1958.	125	575	1,700
☐	a. 18TH JULY, 1958.	125	575	1,700
☐	a. 1ST AUGUST, 1958.	125	575	1,700
☐	a. 15TH AUGUST, 1958.	125	575	1,700
☐	a. 26TH MARCH, 1959.	125	575	1,700
☐	a. 9TH APRIL, 1959.	125	575	1,700
☐	a. 23RD APRIL, 1959.	125	575	1,700
☐	a. 8TH MAY, 1959.	125	575	1,700
☐	a. 22ND MAY, 1959.	125	575	1,700
☐	a. 5TH JUNE, 1959.	125	575	1,700

BRN B2 (P21): 1 pound

		VG	VF	UNC
☐	a. 19TH JUNE, 1959.	125	575	1,700
☐	a. 3RD JULY, 1959.	125	575	1,700
☐	a. 29TH JANUARY, 1960.	125	575	1,700
☐	a. 12TH FEBRUARY, 1960.	125	575	1,700
☐	a. 26TH FEBRUARY, 1960.	125	575	1,700
☐	a. 11TH MARCH, 1960.	125	575	1,700
☐	a. 25TH MARCH, 1960.	125	575	1,700
☐	a. 8TH APRIL, 1960.	125	575	1,700
☐	a. 22ND APRIL, 1960.	125	575	1,700
☐	a. 6TH MAY, 1960.	125	575	1,700
☐	a. 20TH MAY, 1960.	125	575	1,700
☐	a. 3RD JUNE, 1960.	125	575	1,700
☐	a. 17TH JUNE, 1960.	125	575	1,700
☐	b. 23RD NOVEMBER, 1960. Signature 2.	135	550	1,850
☐	b. 25TH NOVEMBER, 1960.	135	550	1,850
☐	b. 28TH NOVEMBER, 1960.	135	550	1,850
☐	b. 30TH NOVEMBER, 1960.	135	550	1,850
☐	b. 2ND DECEMBER, 1960.	135	550	1,850
☐	b. 5TH DECEMBER, 1960.	135	550	1,850
☐	b. 7TH DECEMBER, 1960.	135	550	1,850
☐	b. 9TH DECEMBER, 1960.	135	550	1,850
☐	b. 12TH DECEMBER, 1960.	135	550	1,850
☐	b. 14TH DECEMBER, 1960.	135	550	1,850
☐	b. 16TH DECEMBER, 1960.	135	550	1,850
☐	b. 19TH DECEMBER, 1960.	135	550	1,850
☐	b. 21ST DECEMBER, 1960.	135	550	1,850
☐	b. 23RD DECEMBER, 1960.	135	550	1,850
☐	b. 28TH DECEMBER, 1960.	135	550	1,850
☐	b. 30TH DECEMBER, 1960.	135	550	1,850
☐	b. 4TH JANUARY, 1961.	135	550	1,850
☐	b. 6TH JANUARY, 1961.	135	550	1,850
☐	b. 9TH JANUARY, 1961.	135	550	1,850
☐	b. 11TH JANUARY, 1961.	135	550	1,850
☐	b. 13TH JANUARY, 1961.	135	550	1,850
☐	b. 16TH JANUARY, 1961.	135	550	1,850
☐	b. 18TH JANUARY, 1961.	135	550	1,850
☐	b. 20TH JANUARY, 1961.	135	550	1,850
☐	b. 23RD JANUARY, 1961.	135	550	1,850
☐	b. 25TH JANUARY, 1961.	135	300	1,850
☐	b. 27TH JANUARY, 1961.	135	550	1,850
☐	as. Diagonal red *SPECIMEN* overprint; punched. Dated 3RD APRIL, 1956.	—	—	1,100
☐	as. Specimen. Dated 2ND MAY, 1956.	—	—	1,100
☐	bs. Specimen. Dated 29TH DECEMBER, 1961.	135	550	1,850
☐	t. Color trial: Blue and orange.	—	—	1,250

BRN B3 (P22): **5 pounds**   VG   VF   UNC

Blue. Front: Sable antelope; coat of arms; Queen Elizabeth II. Back: Victoria Falls; trees. Solid security thread. Watermark: Cecil Rhodes. Printer: *BRADBURY, WILKINSON & C⁰ L^D NEW MALDEN, SURREY, ENGLAND*. 159 x 89 mm.

☐	a.	3RD APRIL, 1956. Signature 1.	225	750	2,500
☐	a.	1ST OCTOBER, 1956.	225	750	2,500
☐	a.	30TH MARCH, 1957.	225	650	2,500
☐	a.	15TH APRIL, 1957.	225	750	2,500
☐	a.	29TH APRIL, 1957.	225	750	2,500
☐	a.	1ST AUGUST, 1958.	225	750	2,500
☐	a.	15TH AUGUST, 1958.	225	630	2,500
☐	a.	5TH JUNE, 1959.	225	750	2,500
☐	a.	19TH JUNE, 1959.	225	750	2,500
☐	a.	3RD JULY, 1959.	225	1,275	2,500
☐	a.	3RD JUNE, 1960.	225	750	2,500
☐	a.	17TH JUNE, 1960.	225	750	2,500
☐	b.	23RD JANUARY, 1961. Signature 2.	400	1,150	2,800
☐	b.	25TH JANUARY, 1961.	400	1,150	2,800
☐	b.	27TH JANUARY, 1961.	400	1,150	2,800
☐	b.	30TH JANUARY, 1961.	400	1,150	2,800
☐	b.	1ST FEBRUARY, 1961.	400	925	2,800
☐	b.	3RD FEBRUARY, 1961.	400	1,150	2,800
☐	as.	Diagonal red *SPECIMEN* overprint; punched. Dated 3RD APRIL, 1956.	—	—	1,600
☐	t.	Color trial: Red-brown and blue.	—	—	1,800

BRN B4 (P23): **10 pounds**   VG   VF   UNC

Brown. Front: Lion; coat of arms; Queen Elizabeth II. Back: Three elephants; trees. Solid security thread. Watermark: Cecil Rhodes. Printer: *BRADBURY, WILKINSON & C⁰ L^D NEW MALDEN, SURREY, ENGLAND*. 170 x 95 mm.

☐	a.	3RD APRIL, 1956. Signature 1.	1,200	3,225	—
☐	a.	30TH MARCH, 1957.	1,200	3,225	—
☐	a.	15TH APRIL, 1957.	1,200	3,225	—
☐	a.	15TH AUGUST, 1958.	1,200	3,225	—
☐	a.	3RD JULY, 1959.	1,200	3,225	—
☐	a.	3RD JUNE, 1960.	1,200	3,225	—
☐	b.	1ST FEBRUARY, 1961. Signature 2.	1,200	3,225	—
☐	as.	Horizontal *SPECIMEN* perforation. Dated 15TH AUGUST, 1958.	—	—	2,750
☐	bs.	Specimen.	—	—	2,750
☐	p.	Proof.	—	—	—
☐	t.	Color trial: Green.	—	—	3,500

The scene on the back of this note was repurposed for use on Malawi's 200-kwacha note dated 1995 (RBM B35).

Looking Forward

For later issues, see Malawi, Rhodesia, Zambia, and Zimbabwe.

Acknowledgements

This chapter was compiled with the generous assistance of David Burns, Heritage Auctions (HA.com), Larry Hirsch, Steve Milner, Sam Nakhjavani (www.foreignpapermoney.com), Jefferson Ritson, TDS, Tristan Williams, and others.

Sources

Cuhaj, George S. *Standard Catalog of World Paper Money, General Issues, 1368-1960*. 14th edition. 2012. ISBN 978-1-4402-3090-5. Krause Publications (www.krausebooks.com), 700 East State St., Iola, WI, 54990-0001.

Cuhaj, George S. *Standard Catalog of World Paper Money, Modern Issues, 1961-Present*. 17th edition. 2011. ISBN 978-1-4402-1584-1. Krause Publications (www.krausebooks.com), 700 East State St., Iola, WI, 54990-0001.

Eu, Peter and Ben Chiew. *Queen Elizabeth II*. 1st edition. 2006. ISBN 983-43038-1-5. Eureka Metro, P. O. Box 30, Jalan Kelang Lama, Kuala Lumpur, 57000, Malaysia.

Milner, Steve. *Rhodesia-Zimbabwe Banknotes Newsletters*.

Symes, Peter. "The Portraits of Queen Elizabeth II on World Bank Notes." *IBNS Journal*. Volume 44 Number 2. p.8.

Share Your Input, Info, and Images

This catalog is believed to be complete and correct as of the time of publication. Prices and face values were last updated 28 October 2011. Please report errors or omissions so that corrections may be made. If you can more precisely identify the name or location of anything depicted on a note, please share that information. Furthermore, if you own an unlisted type or variety, please submit scans of the front and back of the note so that it can be documented. Scans should be 300 dots per inch, 100% actual size, 24-bit color, saved as *uncompressed* JPEG files, and sent to owen@banknotenews.com. Be sure to fully describe all attributes of the note which are not apparent upon visual inspection of the images alone, such as physical dimension, watermark, and security thread.

Russia

Earlier Issues

Prior to the establishment of the Bank of Russia, the government, treasury, and state bank issued notes. These will be added to this chapter in the future.

Monetary System

1 Russian ruble (RUR) = 100 kopeks
1998: 1 Russian ruble (RUB) = 1,000 Russian ruble (RUR)

Russia is not known to have ever issued replacement notes.

Банк России (Bank of Russia)

The Central Bank of the Russian Federation (Bank of Russia) was founded on 13 July 1990, on the basis of the Russian Republic Bank of the State Bank of the USSR. Accountable to the Supreme Soviet of the RSFSR, it was originally called the State Bank of the RSFSR. On 2 December 1990, the Supreme Soviet of the RSFSR passed a Law establishing the Central Bank of the RSFSR and recognizing the Bank of Russia as a legal entity of the RSFSR accountable to the Supreme Soviet of the RSFSR. The law specified the functions of the bank in organizing money circulation, monetary regulation, foreign economic activity, and regulation of the activities of joint-stock and co-operative banks. In June 1991, the Statute of the Central Bank of the RSFSR (Bank of Russia), accountable to the Supreme Soviet of the RSFSR, was approved.

In November 1991, when the Commonwealth of Independent States was founded and Union structures dissolved, the Supreme Soviet of the RSFSR declared the Central Bank of the RSFSR to be the only body of state monetary and foreign exchange regulation in the RSFSR. The functions of the State Bank of the USSR in issuing money and setting the ruble exchange rate were transferred to it. Prior to 1 January 1992, the Central Bank of the RSFSR was instructed to assume full control of the assets, technical facilities, and other resources of the State Bank of the USSR and all its institutions, enterprises, and organizations.

On 20 December 1991, the State Bank of the USSR was disbanded and all its assets, liabilities, and property in the RSFSR were transferred to the Central Bank of the RSFSR, which several months later was renamed the Central Bank of the Russian Federation (Bank of Russia).

For more information, visit www.cbr.ru.

CBR Signature Varieties

1	
	(Chairman)
	Георгий Матюхин / Georgy Matyukhin
	(25.12.1990 - 01.06.1992)

1992 Issues

CBR B1 (P252): **5,000 рублей (rubles)** — VG VF UNC
Light blue and burgundy. Front: Bolshoi Theatre, Spasskaya (Saviour's Tower), Kremlin buildings, and high-rises in Moscow. Back: Tainitskaya (Secret Tower), First Nameless Tower, Second Nameless Tower, and Petrovskaya (Peter's Tower) on the Moscow Kremlin's southern wall with Bolshoy Moskvoretsky Bridge over Moskva River and Kotelnicheskaya Embankment Apartment building in background. No security thread. Watermark: Star pattern. Printer: (Goznak). 145 x 70 mm.
- a. 1992. Signature 1. Intro: 14.07.1992. — 0.25 1 4
- as. Diagonal red ОБРАЗЕЦ overprint. — — —

CBR B2 (P253): **10,000 рублей (rubles)** — VG VF UNC
Red, brown, orange, and blue. Front: Stylized sun, Russian flag, Senatskaya (Senate Tower), and Senate building in Moscow Kremlin. Back: Spasskaya (Saviour's Tower), Senatskaya (Senate Tower), Nikolskaya (Saint Nicholas Tower), and Uglovaya Arsenalanya (Corner Arsenal Tower) on the Moscow Kremlin's northern wall, with Senate and city buildings in background. No security thread. Watermark: Sun, flag, tower, and senate. Printer: (Goznak). 145 x 70 mm.
- a. 1992. Intro: 29.12.1992. — 0.25 1 5
- as. Diagonal red ОБРАЗЕЦ overprint. — — —

1993 Issues

These notes have the bank's initials in Cyrillic (ЦБР: Центральный Банк России; i.e. Central Bank of Russia) at upper right front.

CBR B3 (P254): **100 рублей (rubles)** (withdrawn 31.12.98)   VG   VF   UNC
Blue, red, and magenta. Front: Stylized sun, Russian flag, Senatskaya (Senate Tower), and Senate building in Moscow Kremlin; bank initials. Back: Kremlin Presidium and Senate dome; Konstantino-Eleninskaya (Konstantine and Elena Tower), Nabatnaya (Alarm Bell Tower), Tsarskaya (Tsar's Tower), and Spasskaya (Saviour's Tower) on the Moscow Kremlin's eastern wall. No security thread. Watermark: Star and wave pattern. Printer: (Goznak). 130 x 57 mm.

     a.   1993. Intro: 26.01.1993.   —   0.25   1.50
         White paper.
     b.   Gray paper.   0.25   1   5
     as. Diagonal red *ОБРАЗЕЦ* overprint.   —   —   —

CBR B4 (P255): **200 рублей (rubles)** (withdrawn 31.12.98)   VG   VF   UNC
Pink, light blue, and green. Front: Stylized sun, Russian flag, Senatskaya (Senate Tower), and Senate building in Moscow Kremlin; bank initials. Back: Kutafya and Troitskaya (Trinity Tower) on the Moscow Kremlin's western wall with State Kremlin Palace in background. No security thread. Watermark: Star and wave pattern. Printer: (Goznak). 130 x 57 mm.

     a.   1993. Intro: 26.01.1993.   0.25   1.50   6
         White paper.
     b.   Gray paper.   0.25   1.50   6
     as. Diagonal red *ОБРАЗЕЦ* overprint.   —   —   —

CBR B5 (P256): **500 рублей (rubles)** (withdrawn 31.12.98)   VG   VF   UNC
Green, blue, purple, and pink. Front: Stylized sun, Russian flag, Senatskaya (Senate Tower), and Senate building in Moscow Kremlin; bank initials. Back: Kremlin Presidium, Spasskaya (Saviour's Tower), and fir trees inside Moscow Kremlin. No security thread. Watermark: Star and wave pattern. Printer: (Goznak). 130 x 57 mm.

     a.   1993. Intro: 20.05.1993.   —   0.50   2.50
         White paper.
     b.   Gray paper.   —   0.50   2.50
     as. Diagonal red *ОБРАЗЕЦ* overprint.   —   —   —

CBR B6 (P257): **1,000 рублей (rubles)** (withdrawn 31.12.98)   VG   VF   UNC
Olive green, brown, and red. Front: Stylized sun, Russian flag, Senatskaya (Senate Tower), and Senate building in Moscow Kremlin; bank initials. Back: Spasskaya (Saviour's Tower) and Senate building in Moscow Kremlin; Saint Basil's Cathedral. No security thread. Watermark: Star pattern. Printer: (Goznak). 152 x 67 mm.

     a.   1993. Intro: 26.01.1993.   0.25   1.25   5
         White paper.
     b.   Gray paper.   1.25   5   20
     as. Diagonal red *ОБРАЗЕЦ* overprint.   —   —   —

CBR B7 (P258): **5,000 рублей (rubles)** (withdrawn 31.12.98)   VG   VF   UNC

Burgundy, purple, and green. Front: Stylized sun, Russian flag, Senatskaya (Senate Tower), and Senate building in Moscow Kremlin; bank initials. Back: Tainitskaya (Secret Tower), First Nameless Tower, Second Nameless Tower, and Petrovskaya (Peter's Tower) on the Moscow Kremlin's southern wall with Bolshoy Moskvoretsky Bridge over Moskva River and Kotelnicheskaya Embankment Apartment building in background. No security thread. Watermark: Flag, tower, and senate. Printer: (Goznak). 152 x 67 mm.

☐	a.	1993. Intro: 26.01.1993. White paper.	5	20	75
☐	b.	1994/1993. Intro: 19.09.1994. Watermark: *5000* added. Pink paper.	5	15	60
☐	as.	Diagonal red *ОБРАЗЕЦ* overprint.	—	—	—
☐	bs.	Diagonal red *ОБРАЗЕЦ* overprint.	—	—	—

CBR B7 - B9 are available in two date varieties (1993 and 1994). Both varieties have a large 1993 date below the watermark area at right front, but the later issue also has the 1994 date vertically at left front in small type (above right).

CBR B8 (P259): **10,000 рублей (rubles)** (withdrawn 31.12.98)   VG   VF   UNC

Purple, green, brown, and blue. Front: Stylized sun, Russian flag, Senatskaya (Senate Tower), and Senate building in Moscow Kremlin; bank initials. Back: Spasskaya (Saviour's Tower), Senatskaya (Senate Tower), Nikolskaya (Saint Nicholas Tower), and Uglovaya Arsenalanya (Corner Arsenal Tower) on the Moscow Kremlin's northern wall, with Senate and city buildings in background. No security thread. Watermark: Flag, tower, and senate. Printer: (Goznak). 152 x 67 mm.

☐	a.	1993. Intro: 12.03.1993. White paper.	5	15	50
☐	b.	1994/1993. Intro: 19.09.1994. Watermark: *10000* added. Blue paper.	5	15	50
☐	as.	Diagonal red *ОБРАЗЕЦ* overprint.	—	—	—
☐	bs.	Diagonal red *ОБРАЗЕЦ* overprint.	—	—	—

CBR B9 (P260): **50,000 рублей (rubles)** (withdrawn 31.12.98)   VG   VF   UNC

Purple, orange, and olive green. Front: Stylized sun, Russian flag, Senatskaya (Senate Tower), and Senate building in Moscow Kremlin; bank initials. Back: Nikolskaya (Saint Nicholas Tower) and Uglovaya Arsenalanya (Corner Arsenal Tower) on the Moscow Kremlin's northern wall. No security thread. Watermark: Flag, tower, and senate. Printer: (Goznak). 152 x 67 mm.

☐	a.	1993. Intro: 20.05.1993.	30	125	500
☐	b.	1994/1993. Intro: 14.07.1994. Watermark: *50000* added.	5	15	60
☐	as.	Diagonal red *ОБРАЗЕЦ* overprint.	—	—	—
☐	bs.	Diagonal red *ОБРАЗЕЦ* overprint.	—	—	—

1995 Issues

On these redesigned issues, the serial numbers appear at left and right front in different colors, a double-headed eagle bank seal appears at upper left front, and the symbols at lower left front are intaglio printed to assist the sight impaired in distinguishing between denominations.

CBR B10 (P261): **1,000 рублей (rubles)** (withdrawn 31.12.98)   VG   VF   UNC
Brown, gray, purple, and green. Front: Bank seal; gantry cranes loading ships at dock in Vladivostok; 1860's military supply ship Manchur atop rostral column commemorating 100th anniversary of Vladivostok's founding. Back: "Two Fingers" rock formation, lighthouse, and cargo ship on the Sea of Japan, Dalnegorsk. 1-mm wide security thread. Watermark: Vertical *1000* (left); Manchur monument (right). Printer: (Goznak). 137 x 61 mm.
 ☐ a. 1995. Intro: 29.09.1995. 0.50 2.50 10
 ☐ as. Diagonal red *ОБРАЗЕЦ* overprint. — — —

CBR B12 (P263): **10,000 рублей (rubles)** (withdrawn 31.12.98)   VG   VF   UNC
Brown, dark green, yellow, and pink. Front: Bank seal; automobile bridge and passenger boat on Yenisei River in Krasnoyarsk; Paraskeva Pyatnitsa Chapel in Krasnoyarsk. Back: Krasnoyarsk hydroelectric dam spillway. 1-mm wide security thread. Watermark: Vertical *10000* (left); Paraskeva Pyatnitsa Chapel (right). Printer: (Goznak). 150 x 65 mm.
 ☐ a. 1995. Intro: 29.09.1995. 2.50 10 55
 ☐ as. Diagonal red *ОБРАЗЕЦ* overprint. — — —

CBR B13 (P264): **50,000 рублей (rubles)** (withdrawn 31.12.98)   VG   VF   UNC
Blue, brown, red, orange, and green. Front: Female figure symbolizing the Neva River at foot of South rostral column on Birzhevaya Square in Saint Petersburg with Peter and Paul Fortress in background. Back: South rostral column and Old Saint Petersburg Stock Exchange building (now a naval museum). Solid security thread. Watermark: Vertical *50000* (left); Peter and Paul Fortress (right). Printer: (Goznak). 150 x 65 mm.
 ☐ a. 1995. Intro: 29.09.1995. 2.50 10 40
 ☐ as. Diagonal red *ОБРАЗЕЦ* overprint. — — —

CBR B11 (P262): **5,000 рублей (rubles)** (withdrawn 31.12.98)   VG   VF   UNC
Green, pink, and brown. Front: Bank seal; Millennium of Russia monument in Novgorod Kremlin; Saint Sophia Cathedral in Novgorod. Back: Palace Tower, Spasskaya (Saviour's Tower), and Knyazhaya (Princess Tower) on the Novgorod Kremlin (Detinets) wall with Volkhov River in background. 1-mm wide security thread. Watermark: Vertical *5000* (left); Saint Sophia Cathedral (right). Printer: (Goznak). 137 x 61 mm.
 ☐ a. 1995. Intro: 29.09.1995. 2 8 35
 ☐ as. Diagonal red *ОБРАЗЕЦ* overprint. — — —

1997-2001 New Ruble Issues

With the exception of the new 1,000-ruble denomination, these notes are like the preceding issues. On 1 January 1998, the ruble was redenominated at a rate of 1:1,000, thereby removing three zeros from all denominations, but doing nothing to address the fundamental economic problems afflicting the country at this time. The currency was subsequently devalued in August 1998. The old 1,000-ruble denomination was replaced by a coin.

CBR B14 (P265): **100,000 рублей (rubles)** (withdrawn 31.12.98)　　VG　VF　UNC
Brown, olive green, and burgundy. Front: Bank seal; bronze sculpture of Apollo in chariot with four horses atop pediment on the Bolshoi Theatre building in Moscow. Back: Bolshoi Theatre building in Moscow. Solid security thread. Watermark: Vertical *100000* (left); Bolshoi Theatre (right). Printer: (Goznak). 150 x 65 mm.
- ☐ a.　1995. Intro: 30.05.1995.　　　　　　　　　　　5　20　70
- ☐ as.　Diagonal red ОБРАЗЕЦ overprint.　　　　　　—　—　—

CBR B15 (P266): **500,000 рублей (rubles)** (withdrawn 31.12.98)　　VG　VF　UNC
Violet and blue. Front: OVI bank seal; Mark Antokolski's statue of Peter the Great in Taganrog; sailing ship in the port of Arkhangelsk. Back: Boat sailing towards Solovetsky Monastery on the Solovetsky Islands in the White Sea. Solid security thread. Watermark: Vertical *500000* (left); Peter the Great (right). Printer: (Goznak). 150 x 65 mm.
- ☐ a.　1995. Intro: 17.03.1997.　　　　　　　　　　　150　500　1,500
- ☐ as.　Horizontal ОБРАЗЕЦ perforation;
　　　two diagonal red ОБРАЗЕЦ ovpts on back.　　—　—　—

CBR B16 (P267): **5 рублей (rubles)** (US$0.15)　　　　VG　VF　UNC
Green, pink, and brown. Front: Bank seal; Millennium of Russia monument in Novgorod Kremlin; Saint Sophia Cathedral in Novgorod. Back: Dvortsovaya (Palace Tower), Spasskaya (Saviour's Tower), and Knyazhaya (Princess Tower) on the Novgorod Kremlin (Detinets) wall with Volkhov River in background. 1-mm wide solid security thread with printed *ЦБР 5*. Watermark: Horizontal *5* (left); Saint Sophia Cathedral (right). Printer: (Goznak). 137 x 61 mm.
- ☐ a.　1997. Intro: 01.01.1998.　　　　　　　　　0.50　2.50　10
- ☐ as1.　ОБРАЗЕЦ perforation.　　　　　　　　　—　—　—
- ☐ as2.　Horizontal ОБРАЗЕЦ perforation;
　　　two diagonal red ОБРАЗЕЦ ovpts on back.　—　—　—

CBR B17 (P268): **10 рублей (rubles)** (US$0.30)　　　VG　VF　UNC
Brown, dark green, yellow, and pink. Front: Bank seal; automobile bridge and passenger boat on Yenisei River in Krasnoyarsk; Paraskeva Pyatnitsa Chapel in Krasnoyarsk. Back: Krasnoyarsk hydroelectric dam spillway. 1-mm wide solid security thread with printed *ЦБР 10*. Watermark: Horizontal *10* (left); Paraskeva Pyatnitsa Chapel (right). Printer: (Goznak). 150 x 65 mm.
- ☐ a.　1997. Intro: 01.01.1998.　　　　　　　　　FV　0.75　3
- ☐ b.　2001/1997. Intro: 01.01.2001. New UV features.　0.50　2　8
- ☐ as.　Horizontal ОБРАЗЕЦ perforation;
　　　two diagonal red ОБРАЗЕЦ ovpts on back.　—　—　—
- ☐ bs.　Horizontal ОБРАЗЕЦ perforation;
　　　two diagonal red ОБРАЗЕЦ ovpts on back.　—　—　—

CBR B17 - B20 are each available in two date varieties (1997 and 2001). Both varieties have a large 1997 date at lower right back, but the later issue also has the 2001 date vertically at left front in small type (above right).

CBR B19 (P270): **100 рублей (rubles)** (US$3.10) VG VF UNC
Brown, olive green, and burgundy. Front: Bank seal; bronze sculpture of Apollo in chariot with four horses atop pediment on the Bolshoi Theatre building in Moscow. Back: Bolshoi Theatre building in Moscow. 1-mm wide solid security thread with printed ЦБР 100. Watermark: Vertical 100 (left); Bolshoi Theatre (right). Printer: (Goznak). 150 x 65 mm.
- a. 1997. Intro: 01.01.1998. 5 15 55
- b. 2001/1997. Intro: 01.01.2001. New UV features. FV 10 40
- as. Horizontal ОБРАЗЕЦ perforation;
  two diagonal red ОБРАЗЕЦ ovpts on back. — — —
- bs. Horizontal ОБРАЗЕЦ perforation;
  two diagonal red ОБРАЗЕЦ ovpts on back. — — —

CBR B18 (P269): **50 рублей (rubles)** (US$1.55) VG VF UNC
Blue, brown, red, orange, and green. Front: Bank seal; female figure symbolizing the Neva River at foot of South rostral column on Birzhevaya Square in Saint Petersburg with Peter and Paul Fortress in background. Back: South rostral column and Old Saint Petersburg Stock Exchange building (now a naval museum). 1-mm wide solid security thread with printed ЦБР 50. Watermark: Horizontal 50 (left); Peter and Paul Fortress (right). Printer: (Goznak). 150 x 65 mm.
- a. 1997. Intro: 01.01.1998. FV 3 12
- b. 2001/1997. Intro: 01.01.2001. New UV features. FV 3 12
- as. Horizontal ОБРАЗЕЦ perforation;
  two diagonal red ОБРАЗЕЦ ovpts on back. — — —
- bs. Horizontal ОБРАЗЕЦ perforation;
  two diagonal red ОБРАЗЕЦ ovpts on back. — — —

CBR B20 (P271): **500 рублей (rubles)** (US$15) VG VF UNC
Violet and blue. Front: OVI bank seal; Mark Antokolski's statue of Peter the Great in Taganrog; sailing ship in the port of Arkhangelsk. Back: Boat sailing towards Solovetsky Monastery on the Solovetsky Islands in the White Sea. 1-mm wide solid security thread with printed ЦБР 500. Watermark: Vertical 500 (left); Peter the Great (right). Printer: (Goznak). 150 x 65 mm.
- a. 1997. Intro: 01.01.1998. FV 25 95
- b. 2001/1997. Intro: 01.01.2001. New UV features. FV FV 55
- as. Horizontal ОБРАЗЕЦ perforation;
  two diagonal red ОБРАЗЕЦ ovpts on back. — — —
- bs. Horizontal ОБРАЗЕЦ perforation;
  two diagonal red ОБРАЗЕЦ ovpts on back. — — —

CBR B21 (P272a): **1,000 рублей (rubles)** (US$31)   VG   VF   UNC

Blue and green. Front: OVI bank seal; statue of Prince Yaroslav the Wise; Our Lady of Kazan Chapel with Yaroslavl Kremlin wall in background; Yaroslavl coat of arms with standing bear carrying halberd. Back: Saint John the Baptist Church and Bell Tower in Yaroslavl. 1-mm wide solid security thread with printed ЦБР 1000. Watermark: Vertical 1000 (left); Prince Yaroslav the Wise (right). Printer: (Goznak). 157 x 69 mm.
- a. 1997. Intro: 01.01.2001.   FV   FV   80
- as. Horizontal ОБРАЗЕЦ perforation;   —   —   —
  two diagonal red ОБРАЗЕЦ ovpts on back.

1997-2004 Issues

With the exception of the new 5,000-ruble denomination (although dated 1997, it was not issued until 2006), these notes are like the preceding issues, but with windowed security threads on back, revised vignettes with color moiré patterns on front, and microperforations on notes 100 rubles and higher. The 5-ruble denomination was replaced by a coin.

CBR B22 (P268c): **10 рублей (rubles)** (US$0.30)   VG   VF   UNC

Brown, dark green, yellow, and pink. Front: Bank seal; automobile bridge and passenger boat on Yenisei River in Krasnoyarsk; Paraskeva Pyatnitsa Chapel in Krasnoyarsk. Back: Krasnoyarsk hydroelectric dam spillway. Windowed security thread. Watermark: Horizontal 10 (left); Paraskeva Pyatnitsa Chapel (right). Printer: (Goznak). 150 x 65 mm.
- a. 2004/1997. Intro: 16.08.2004.   FV   FV   1
- b. Experimental paper with water-repellent finish.   —   —   —
  Prefix фф and ЦЦ.
- as. Horizontal ОБРАЗЕЦ perforation;   —   —   —
  two diagonal red ОБРАЗЕЦ ovpts on back.

CBR B23 (P269c): **50 рублей (rubles)** (US$1.55)   VG   VF   UNC

Blue, brown, red, orange, and green. Front: Bank seal; female figure symbolizing the Neva River at foot of South rostral column on Birzhevaya Square in Saint Petersburg with Peter and Paul Fortress in background. Back: South rostral column and Old Saint Petersburg Stock Exchange building (now a naval museum). Windowed security thread. Watermark: Horizontal 50 (left); Peter and Paul Fortress (right). Printer: (Goznak). 150 x 65 mm.
- a. 2004/1997. Intro: 16.08.2004.   FV   FV   4
- as. Horizontal ОБРАЗЕЦ perforation;   —   —   —
  two diagonal red ОБРАЗЕЦ ovpts on back.

CBR B24 (P270c): **100 рублей (rubles)** (US$3.10)   VG   VF   UNC

Brown, olive green, and burgundy. Front: Bank seal; bronze sculpture of Apollo in chariot with four horses atop pediment on the Bolshoi Theatre building in Moscow. Back: Bolshoi Theatre building in Moscow. Windowed security thread. Watermark: Vertical 100 (left); Bolshoi Theatre (right). Printer: (Goznak). 150 x 65 mm.
- a. 2004/1997. Intro: 16.08.2004.   FV   FV   6
- b. Experimental paper with water-repellent finish.   —   —   —
  Prefix УХ, фф, and ЦЦ.
- as. Horizontal ОБРАЗЕЦ perforation;   —   —   —
  two diagonal red ОБРАЗЕЦ ovpts on back.

CBR B25 (P271c): **500 рублей (rubles)** (US$15) VG VF UNC

Violet and blue. Front: Orange-to-green OVI bank seal; Mark Antokolski's statue of Peter the Great in Taganrog; sailing ship in the port of Arkhangelsk. Back: Boat sailing towards Solovetsky Monastery on the Solovetsky Islands in the White Sea. Windowed security thread. Watermark: Vertical *500* (left); Peter the Great (right). Printer: (Goznak). 150 x 65 mm.

    ☐ a.   2004/1997. Intro: 16.08.2004.   FV FV 35
    ☐ as.   Horizontal *ОБРАЗЕЦ* perforation;
            two diagonal red *ОБРАЗЕЦ* ovpts on back. — — —

CBR B26 (P272b): **1,000 рублей (rubles)** (US$31) VG VF UNC

Blue and green. Front: OVI bank seal; statue of Prince Yaroslav the Wise; Our Lady of Kazan Chapel with Yaroslavl Kremlin wall in background; OVI Yaroslavl coat of arms with standing bear carrying halberd. Back: Saint John the Baptist Church and Bell Tower in Yaroslavl. Windowed security thread. Watermark: Vertical *1000* (left); Prince Yaroslav the Wise (right). Printer: (Goznak). 157 x 69 mm.

    ☐ a.   2004/1997. Intro: 16.08.2004.   FV FV 60
    ☐ as.   Horizontal *ОБРАЗЕЦ* perforation;
            two diagonal red *ОБРАЗЕЦ* ovpts on back. — — —

CBR B27 (P273): **5,000 рублей (rubles)** (US$155) VG VF UNC

Red and brown. Front: OVI bank seal; statue of statesman Nikolay Nikolayevich Muravyov-Amursky; promontory tower in Khabarovsk with commercial ship offshore; Khabarovsk coat of arms in crimson-to-green OVI. Back: Automobile bridge across Amur River (the border between Russia and China negotiated by Muravyov). 3-mm wide windowed security thread with demetalized *5000*. Watermark: Vertical *5000* (left); Nikolay Nikolayevich Muravyov-Amursky and electrotype *5000* (right). Printer: (Goznak). 157 x 69 mm.

    ☐ a.   1997. Intro: 31.07.2006.   FV FV 230
    ☐ as.   Horizontal *ОБРАЗЕЦ* perforation;
            two diagonal red *ОБРАЗЕЦ* ovpts on back. — — —

2010 Issues

These notes are like the preceding issues, but with enhanced security features. In addition, the back of the 500-ruble note was redesigned in response to protests that the preceding issues depicted the Solovetsky Monastery without crosses atop the buildings, dating it to between 1926 and 1938 when the site was used as a special prison and a gulag.

CBR B28 (PNL): **500 рублей (rubles)** (US$15) VG VF UNC

Violet and blue. Front: Bank seal; Mark Antokolski's statue of Peter the Great in Taganrog; sailing ship in the port of Arkhangelsk. Back: Solovetsky Monastery on the Solovetsky Islands in the White Sea. Winged windowed security thread with demetalized *500*. Watermark: Peter the Great and electrotype *500*. Printer: (Goznak). 150 x 65 mm.

    ☐ a.   2010/1997. Intro: 06.09.2011.   FV FV 30

2014 Commemorative Issues

On 30 October 2013, the Bank of Russia began issuing 20 million 100-ruble notes commemorating the XXII Olympic Winter Games and XI Paralympic Winter Games 2014 in Sochi. The new notes are legal tender and will circulate in parallel with existing notes of the same denomination. A private Chinese firm has created a numismatic product by packaging this note in a large folder, but this is not an official issue.

CBR B29 (PNL): **1,000 рублей (rubles)** (US$31) VG VF UNC
Blue and green. Front: Bank seal; statue of Prince Yaroslav the Wise; Our Lady of Kazan Chapel with Yaroslavl Kremlin wall in background; SPARK Yaroslavl coat of arms with standing bear carrying halberd. Back: Saint John the Baptist Church and Bell Tower in Yaroslavl. Winged windowed security thread with demetalized *1000*. Watermark: Prince Yaroslav the Wise and electrotype *1000* (right). Printer: (Goznak). 157 x 69 mm.

    a. 2010/1997. Intro: 10.08.2010. FV FV 55
    as. Horizontal *ОБРАЗЕЦ* perforation; — — —
        two diagonal red *ОБРАЗЕЦ* ovpts on back.

CBR B31 (PNL): **100 рублей (rubles)** (US$3.10) VG VF UNC
Blue, purple, green, and orange. Front (vertical): Holographic flame; snowboarder; mountains; Olympic venues in Sochi. Back (vertical): SPARK bird; Fischt Stadium in Sochi; underprint of athletes including skiers, ski jumper, skaters, hockey player, curler, and bobsled team. Vitrail security thread. Watermark: *sochi.ru 2014* and Olympic rings. Printer: (Goznak). 150 x 65 mm.

    a. 2014. Intro: 30.10.2013. FV FV 12
        Prefix AA, aa, and Aa (reportedly replacement).

CBR B30 (PNL): **5,000 рублей (rubles)** (US$155) VG VF UNC
Red and brown. Front: Bank seal; statue of statesman Nikolay Nikolayevich Muravyov-Amursky; promontory tower in Khabarovsk with commercial ship offshore; SPARK Khabarovsk coat of arms. Back: Automobile bridge across Amur River (the border between Russia and China negotiated by Muravyov). Holographic winged windowed security thread with demetalized *5000*. Watermark: Nikolay Nikolayevich Muravyov-Amursky and electrotype *5000*. Printer: (Goznak). 157 x 69 mm.

    a. 2010/1997. Intro: 06.09.2011. FV FV 225
    as. Horizontal *ОБРАЗЕЦ* perforation; — — —
        two diagonal red *ОБРАЗЕЦ* ovpts on back.

Looking Forward

• On 31 October 2006, the Bank of Russia announced that it intends to replace all 10-ruble banknotes with coins. "Coins serve longer than banknotes," explained deputy chairman Georgy Luntovsky. Coins can circulate for 10 to 15 years, while 10- and 50-ruble notes have a lifetime of approximately half a year.

• On 22 October 2009, the bank announced that it would stop issuing 10-ruble banknotes in 2010 because they wear out quickly and are too expensive to produce. The notes will be replaced by a coin.

• According to an article on AdIndex.ru dated 1 November 2010, Russia's central bank hopes to finalize a new symbol for its currency, the ruble. As of late 2013, no notes have been issued with a ruble symbol.

Acknowledgements

This chapter was compiled with the generous assistance of Brent Arthurson, Aleksey Avdeev, Jim W.-C. Chen, David F. Cieniewicz, Jari Heine, Larry Hirsch, Mikhail Istomin, Peter Kelly, Andrey Kuvaldin, Gianni Lorenzoli, Robert Mol, Wally Myers, George Provencal, Gergely Scheidl (banknoteshop@gmx.net), Menelaos Stamatelos, Bill Stubkjaer, Albert Vokhmin, Tristan Williams, Didier Wiot, Ömer Yalçinkaya, and others.

Sources

Cuhaj, George S. *Standard Catalog of World Paper Money, Modern Issues, 1961-Present*. 19th edition. 2013. ISBN 978-1-4402-3571-9. Krause Publications (www.krausebooks.com), 700 East State Saint, Iola, WI, 54990-0001.

Share Your Input, Info, and Images

This catalog is believed to be complete and correct as of the time of publication. Prices and face values were last updated 26 April 2011. Please report errors or omissions so that corrections may be made. If you can more precisely identify the name or location of anything depicted on a note, please share that information. Furthermore, if you own an unlisted type or variety, please submit scans of the front and back of the note so that it can be documented. Scans should be 300 dots per inch, 100% actual size, 24-bit color, saved as *uncompressed* JPEG files, and sent to owen@banknotenews.com. Be sure to fully describe all attributes of the note which are not apparent upon visual inspection of the images alone, such as physical dimension, watermark, and security thread.

Rwanda

For earlier issues, see Rwanda-Burundi.

Monetary System
1964: 1 Rwandan franc (RWF) = 100 centimes

Banque Nationale du Rwanda (National Bank of Rwanda)

Political, economic, and psychological factors led to the dissolution of the economic union between Rwanda and Burundi on 1 January 1964. The Banque Nationale du Rwanda (BNR), authorized by the Law of 24 April 1964, began operations on 19 May 1964. The Banque d' Emission du Rwanda et du Burundi rights and obligations were ex officio transmitted to the Royal Bank of Burundi and to the National Bank of Rwanda.

For more information, visit www.bnr.rw.

BNR Signature Varieties

1

Le Gouverneur
Jean-Baptiste Habyarimana

2

VICE-GOUVERNEUR
Jean-Baptiste Habyarimana
GOUVERNEUR
Johan A. Brandon
(1964 - 1965)

3

VICE-GOUVERNEUR
Jean-Baptiste Habyarimana
ADMINISTRATEUR
Jean Berchmans Birara

4

VICE-GOUVERNEUR
Jean-Baptiste Habyarimana
GOUVERNEUR
Masaya Hattori
(1965 - 1971)

5

VICE-GOUVERNEUR
Jean Berchmans Birara
GOUVERNEUR
Masaya Hattori
(1965 - 1971)

6

ADMINISTRATEUR
Gaspard Ndandali
GOUVERNEUR
Jean Berchmans Birara
(1971 - 1985)

BNR Signature Varieties

7

ADMINISTRATEUR
Unknown
GOUVERNEUR
Jean Berchmans Birara
(1971 - 1985)

8

ADMINISTRATEUR
Unknown
ADMINISTRATEUR
Jean-Baptiste Ngirabacu

9
 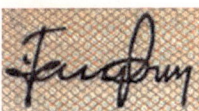
ADMINISTRATEUR
Jean-Baptiste Ngirabacu
GOUVERNEUR
Jean Berchmans Birara
(1971 - 1985)

10

UN ADMINISTRATEUR
Jean-Baptiste Ngirabacu
LE GOUVERNEUR
Jean Berchmans Birara
(1971 - 1985)

11

UN ADMINISTRATEUR
Unknown
UN ADMINISTRATEUR
Jean-Baptiste Ngirabacu

12

UN ADMINISTRATEUR
Unknown
LE GOUVERNEUR
Jean Berchmans Birara
(1971 - 1985)

13

UN ADMINISTRATEUR
Augustin Ruzindana
UN ADMINISTRATEUR
Jean-Baptiste Ngirabacu

14

UN ADMINISTRATEUR
Jean-Baptiste Ngirabacu
LE GOUVERNEUR
Jean Berchmans Birara
(1971 - 1985)

15

2è VICE-GOUVERNEUR
Dominique Munyangoga
1er VICE-GOUVERNEUR
Augustin Ruzindana

16

1ER VICE-GOUVERNEUR
Joseph Habimana
LE GOUVERNEUR
Augustin Ruzindana
(1985 - 1990)

BNR Signature Varieties

* This official is not known to have signed any notes.

1960-1962 (1964) Provisional Issues

In 1964, these provisional notes were created by handstamping (20 to 100 francs) or embossing (500 and 1,000 francs) Rwanda-Burundi notes bearing their original dates and signatures. The stamps consist of the text *BANQUE NATIONALE DU RWANDA* at top, *Le Gouverneur* immediately below, followed by a large facsimile signature of the bank's governor, all in a rectangular box measuring 50 x 40 mm. The color of the ink and the location of the stamp varies from note to note. The 80 x 40 mm embossed seals are similar to the overprints, but can be difficult to detect, especially on worn notes. All original date varieties are listed, but not all have been confirmed with the stamp or embossed.

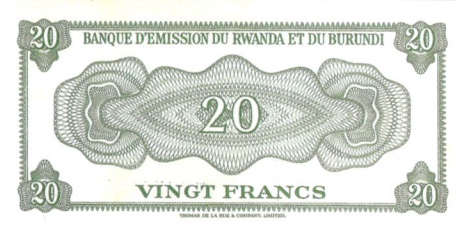

BNR B1 (P1): **20 francs**　　　　　　　　　　**Good　Fine　XF**
Green and pink. Front: Crocodile; river; boxed *BANQUE NATIONALE DU RWANDA* handstamp. Back: Guilloche patterns. No security thread. Watermark: None. Printer: *THOMAS DE LA RUE & COMPANY, LIMITED*. 130 x 64 mm.
　☐ a.　15•09•60. Unconfirmed with stamp.　　　　—　　—　　—
　☐ b.　05•10•60. Signature 1. Intro: 1964.　　　35　125　500
Handstamp on Rwanda-Burundi BERB B3.

BNR B2 (P2): **50 francs**　　　　　　　　　　**Good　Fine　XF**
Red and gray. Front: Lioness; boxed *BANQUE NATIONALE DU RWANDA* handstamp. Back: Guilloche patterns. No security thread. Watermark: None. Printer: (BWC). 140 x 67 mm.
　☐ a.　15.09.60. Signature 1. Intro: 1964.　　　—　　—　　—
　☐ b.　01.10.60.　　　　　　　　　　　　　　　—　200　600
Handstamp on Rwanda-Burundi BERB B4.

BNR B3 (P3): 100 francs   Good   Fine   XF

Blue, green, and orange. Front: Zebu bull; boxed *BANQUE NATIONALE DU RWANDA* handstamp. Back: Guilloche patterns. No security thread. Watermark: None. Printer: (BWC). 150 x 70 mm.

☐	a.	15.09.60. Signature 1. Intro: 1964.	100	400	1,500
☐	b.	01.10.60.	100	400	1,500
☐	c.	31.07.62. Unconfirmed with stamp.	—	—	—

Handstamp on Rwanda-Burundi BERB B5.

BNR B5 (P5): 1,000 francs   Good   Fine   XF

Green and purple. Front: Zebra; embossed *BANQUE NATIONALE DU RWANDA* seal. Back: Guilloche patterns. No security thread. Watermark: None. Printer: (BWC). 170 x 76 mm.

☐	a.	15.09.60. Unconfirmed with embossed seal.	—	—	—
☐	b.	15.05.61.	—	—	—
☐	c.	31.07.62.	—	—	2,000
☐	s.	Specimen.	—	—	—

Embossed Rwanda-Burundi BERB B7.

BNR B4 (P4): 500 francs   VG   VF   UNC

Brown, lilac, and green. Front: Black rhinoceros; forest; embossed *BANQUE NATIONALE DU RWANDA* seal. Back: Guilloche patterns. No security thread. Watermark: None. Printer: *THOMAS DE LA RUE & COMPANY, LIMITED*. 160 x 73 mm.

☐	a.	15•09•60. Unconfirmed with embossed seal.	—	—	—
☐	b.	15•05•61.	—	—	4,000
☐	c.	15•09•61. Unconfirmed with embossed seal.	—	—	—

Embossed Rwanda-Burundi BERB B6.

1964-1976 Issues

BNR B6 (P6): 20 francs

Brown, red, orange, and green. Front: Flag. Back: Three boys and a girl, seated; forest; water pumping station. Watermark: None. Printer: (TDLR). 125 x 70 mm.

		VG	VF	UNC
☐ a.	01-07-64. Signature 2. Solid security thread. Prefix A - E.	2	8	20
☐ b.	01-07-65. Signature 3. Prefix F - H.	2	8	20
☐ c.	31-03-66. Signature 4. Prefix L - P.	1	5	10
☐ d.	15-03-69. Signature 5. Prefix R - Z.	1	5	10
☐ e.	1-09-69. Prefix AB - AC.	2	8	20
☐ f.	1-07-71. Signature 6. Prefix AG - AH.	0.50	2	8
☐ g.	30-10-74. Signature 8. Prefix AQ - AS.	0.50	2	8
☐ h.	1-1-76. Signature 9 w/ black bar over old titles. No security thread. Prefix AX - BC.	0.25	1	4
☐ as1.	Diagonal red *SPECIMEN* overprint.	—	—	15
☐ as2.	Diagonal red *SPECIMEN* and DLR oval ovpts; horizontal red *SPECIMEN Nº* # ovpt at lower left.	—	—	30
☐ bs1.	Diagonal red *SPECIMEN* overprint.	—	—	15
☐ bs2.	Diagonal red *SPECIMEN* and DLR oval ovpts; horizontal red *SPECIMEN Nº* # ovpt at lower left.	—	—	30
☐ cs1.	Diagonal red *SPECIMEN* overprint.	—	—	15
☐ cs2.	Diagonal red *SPECIMEN* and DLR oval ovpts; horizontal red *SPECIMEN Nº* # ovpt at lower left.	—	—	30
☐ ds1.	Diagonal red *SPECIMEN* overprint.	—	—	15
☐ ds2.	Diagonal red *SPECIMEN* and DLR oval ovpts; horizontal red *SPECIMEN Nº* # ovpt at lower left.	—	—	30
☐ fs1.	Diagonal black *SPECIMEN* overprint.	—	—	15
☐ fs2.	Diagonal black *SPECIMEN* and DLR oval ovpts; horizon. black *SPECIMEN Nº* # ovpt at lower left.	—	—	30
☐ gs1.	Diagonal black *SPECIMEN* overprint.	—	—	15
☐ gs2.	Diagonal black *SPECIMEN* and DLR oval ovpts; horizon. black *SPECIMEN Nº* # ovpt at lower left.	—	—	30

Replacement notes: Prefix ZZ.

BNR B7 (P7): 50 francs

Blue, green, and yellow. Front: Map of Rwanda. Back: Underground miners with head lamps and shovels. Watermark: None. Printer: (TDLR). 136 x 70 mm.

		VG	VF	UNC
☐ a.	01-07-64. Sig. 2. Solid security thread. Prefix A.	1	5	20
☐ b.	31-01-66. Signature 4. Prefix D - F.	1	5	20
☐ c.	1-09-69. Signature 5. Prefix L - Q.	1	5	20
☐ d.	1-07-71. Signature 6. Prefix R - T.	0.50	2	8
☐ e.	30-10-74. Signature 7. Prefix V - W.	0.50	2	8
☐ f.	1-1-76. Sig. 9. No security thread. Prefix W - Z.	0.50	2	8
☐ as1.	Diagonal red *SPECIMEN* overprint.	—	—	20
☐ as2.	Diagonal red *SPECIMEN* and DLR oval ovpts; horizontal red *SPECIMEN Nº* # ovpt at lower left.	—	—	30
☐ bs1.	Diagonal red *SPECIMEN* overprint.	—	—	20
☐ bs2.	Diagonal red *SPECIMEN* and DLR oval ovpts; horizontal red *SPECIMEN Nº* # ovpt at lower left.	—	—	30
☐ cs1.	Diagonal black *SPECIMEN* overprint.	—	—	20
☐ cs2.	Diagonal black *SPECIMEN* and DLR oval ovpts; horizon. black *SPECIMEN Nº* # ovpt at lower left; punched.	—	—	35
☐ ds1.	Diagonal black *SPECIMEN* overprint.	—	—	7.50
☐ ds2.	Diagonal black *SPECIMEN* and DLR oval ovpts; horizon. black *SPECIMEN Nº* # ovpt at lower left; punched.	—	—	30
☐ es1.	Diagonal black *SPECIMEN* overprint.	—	—	20
☐ es2.	Diagonal black *SPECIMEN* and DLR oval ovpts; horizon. black *SPECIMEN Nº* # ovpt at lower left; punched.	—	—	30
☐ fs1.	Diagonal black *SPECIMEN* overprint.	—	—	20
☐ fs2.	Diagonal black *SPECIMEN* and DLR oval ovpts; horizon. black *SPECIMEN Nº* # ovpt at lower left; punched.	—	—	—

Replacement notes: Prefix ZZ.

BNR B8 (P8): **100 francs** VG VF UNC

Purple, green, orange, and pink. Front: Map of Rwanda. Back: Woman with woven basket on head; banana trees. Watermark: None. Printer: (TDLR). 144 x 70 mm.

		VG	VF	UNC
☐ a.	01-07-64. Signature 2. Solid security thread. Prefix A - C.	1	5	20
☐ b.	01-07-65. Signature 3. Prefix F - J.	1	4	18
☐ c.	31-03-66. Signature 4. Prefix L - M.	0.75	2.50	10
☐ d.	31-10-69. Signature 5. Prefix R - Y.	1	5	20
☐ e.	1-07-71. Signature 6. Prefix AB - AE.	0.50	2	8.50
☐ f.	30-10-74. Signature 9. Prefix AJ - AM.	0.50	2	8.50
☐ g.	1-1-76. No security thread. Prefix AN - AX.	1	5	20
☐ as1.	Diagonal red *SPECIMEN* overprint.	—	—	25
☐ as2.	Diagonal red *SPECIMEN* and DLR oval ovpts; horizontal red *SPECIMEN Nº* # ovpt at lower left.	—	—	—
☐ bs1.	Diagonal red *SPECIMEN* overprint.	—	—	25
☐ bs2.	Diagonal red *SPECIMEN* and DLR oval ovpts; horizontal red *SPECIMEN Nº* # ovpt at lower left.	—	—	—
☐ cs1.	Diagonal red *SPECIMEN* overprint.	—	—	20
☐ cs2.	Diagonal red *SPECIMEN* and DLR oval ovpts; horizontal red *SPECIMEN Nº* # ovpt at lower left.	—	—	—
☐ ds1.	Diagonal black *SPECIMEN* overprint.	—	—	15
☐ ds2.	Diagonal black *SPECIMEN* and DLR oval ovpts; horizon. black *SPECIMEN Nº* # ovpt at lower left.	—	—	—
☐ es1.	Diagonal black *SPECIMEN* overprint.	—	—	15
☐ es2.	Diagonal black *SPECIMEN* and DLR oval ovpts; horizon. black *SPECIMEN Nº* # ovpt at lower left.	—	—	—
☐ fs1.	Diagonal black *SPECIMEN* overprint.	—	—	25
☐ fs2.	Diagonal black *SPECIMEN* and DLR oval ovpts; horizon. black *SPECIMEN Nº* # ovpt at lower left.	—	—	—

Replacement notes: Prefix ZZ.

BNR B9 (P9): **500 francs** VG VF UNC

Green, orange, and violet. Front: Coat of arms. Back: Man with woven basket on head; trees and crops. Solid security thread. Watermark: None. Printer: (TDLR). 155 x 70 mm.

		VG	VF	UNC
☐ a.	01-07-64. Signature 2. Prefix A.	4	12	50
☐ b.	31-03-66. Signature 4. Prefix A.	4	12	50
☐ c.	31-10-69. Signature 5. Prefix A.	4	12	50
☐ d.	1-07-71. Signature 6. Prefix B.	2	8	30
☐ e.	30-10-74. Signature 7. Prefix C.	2	8	30
☐ f.	1-1-76. Signature 9. Prefix C - D.	1.25	5	20
☐ as1.	Diagonal red *SPECIMEN* overprint.	—	—	25
☐ as2.	Diagonal red *SPECIMEN* and DLR oval ovpts; horizontal red *SPECIMEN Nº* # ovpt at lower left.	—	—	—
☐ bs1.	Diagonal red *SPECIMEN* overprint.	—	—	15
☐ bs2.	Diagonal red *SPECIMEN* and DLR oval ovpts; horizontal red *SPECIMEN Nº* # ovpt at lower left.	—	—	—
☐ cs1.	Diagonal black *SPECIMEN* overprint.	—	—	20
☐ cs2.	Diagonal black *SPECIMEN* and DLR oval ovpts; horizon. black *SPECIMEN Nº* # ovpt at lower left.	—	—	—
☐ ds1.	Diagonal black *SPECIMEN* overprint.	—	—	25
☐ ds2.	Diagonal black *SPECIMEN* and DLR oval ovpts; horizon. black *SPECIMEN Nº* # ovpt at lower left.	—	—	—
☐ es1.	Diagonal black *SPECIMEN* overprint.	—	—	25
☐ es2.	Diagonal black *SPECIMEN* and DLR oval ovpts; horizon. black *SPECIMEN Nº* # ovpt at lower left.	—	—	—

Replacement notes: Prefix ZZ.

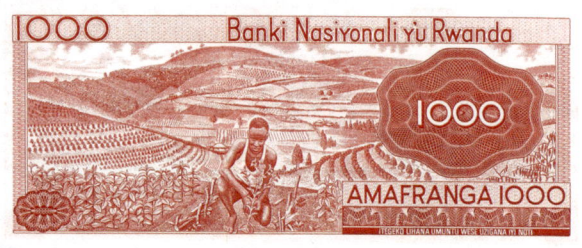

1974 Issues

This 500-franc note features a portrait of Juvénal Habyarimana, who became Rwanda's third president by overthrowing Grégoire Kayibanda on 5 July 1973. Habyarimana remained in power until 6 April 1994, when his airplane, also carrying President Cyprien Ntaryamira of Burundi, was shot down close to Kigali International Airport. His assassination helped spark the Rwandan Genocide.

BNR B10 (P10): **1,000 francs**   VG   VF   UNC
Red, green, and violet. Front: Coat of arms. Back: Man tending plant in terraced hills. Solid security thread. Watermark: None. Printer: (TDLR). 165 x 70 mm.

		VG	VF	UNC
a.	01-07-64. Signature 2. Prefix A.	10	40	150
b.	31-03-66. Signature 4. Prefix A.	10	40	150
c.	15-03-69. Signature 5. Prefix A - B.	10	40	150
d.	1-07-71. Signature 6. Prefix C.	10	40	150
e.	30-10-74. Signature 9. Prefix C.	10	40	150
f.	1-1-76. Prefix E.	10	40	150
as1.	Diagonal red *SPECIMEN* overprint.	—	—	30
as2.	Diagonal red *SPECIMEN* and DLR oval ovpts; horizontal red *SPECIMEN Nº* # ovpt at lower left.	—	—	—
bs1.	Diagonal red *SPECIMEN* overprint.	—	—	30
bs2.	Diagonal red *SPECIMEN* and DLR oval ovpts; horizontal red *SPECIMEN Nº* # ovpt at lower left.	—	—	—
cs1.	Diagonal red *SPECIMEN* overprint.	—	—	25
cs2.	Diagonal red *SPECIMEN* and DLR oval ovpts; horizontal red *SPECIMEN Nº* # ovpt at lower left.	—	—	—
ds1.	Diagonal black *SPECIMEN* overprint.	—	—	35
ds2.	Diagonal black *SPECIMEN* and DLR oval ovpts; horizon. black *SPECIMEN Nº* # ovpt at lower left.	—	—	—
es1.	Diagonal black *SPECIMEN* overprint.	—	—	30
es2.	Diagonal black *SPECIMEN* and DLR oval ovpts; horizon. black *SPECIMEN Nº* # ovpt at lower left.	—	—	—

Replacement notes: Prefix ZZ.

BNR B11 (P11): **500 francs**   VG   VF   UNC
Green, orange, and violet. Front: President Juvénal Habyarimana in military uniform. Back: Man with woven basket on head; trees and crops. Solid security thread. Watermark: None. Printer: (TDLR). 155 x 70 mm.

		VG	VF	UNC
a.	19-4-74. Signature 7. Prefix Z.	1	4	15
as.	Diagonal black *SPECIMEN* overprint.	—	—	50

1978 Issues

The 20- and 50-franc notes were replaced by coins in 1977.

BNR B12 (P12): **100 francs**   VG   VF   UNC
Multicolor. Front: Six zebras; thorny plant. Back: Woman with baby on back; Volcanoes National Park; flowers. No security thread. Watermark: None. Printer: Unknown. 135 x 70 mm.

		VG	VF	UNC
a.	1.01.1978. Signature 10. Prefix AJ - BZ.	1.50	6	25
as.	Diagonal black boxed *SPECIMEN* overprint; diagonal *SPECIMEN* perforation.	—	—	60

BNR B13 (P13): **500 francs**   VG   VF   UNC

Multicolor. Front: Six impalas; trees. Back: Eight drummers; tram car and six miners with picks. No security thread. Printer: Unknown. 145 x 70 mm.

☐	a.	1.01.1978. Signature 11. Watermark: Impala head. Prefix A - B.	3	12	50
☐	b.	Watermark: None. Prefix C.	20	60	150
☐	as.	Diagonal *SPECIMEN* perforation.	—	—	110

BNR B14 (P14): **1,000 francs**   VG   VF   UNC

Green, brown, orange, yellow, and red. Front: Two workers with baskets picking tea leaves; mountains. Back: Woven baskets; mountains; male Intore dancer with spear and shield. No security thread. Watermark: Impala head. Printer: Unknown. 155 x 70 mm.

☐	a.	1.01.1978. Signature 10. Prefix A - E.	4	12	45
☐	as.	Horizontal black boxed *SPECIMEN* handstamp.	—	—	120

BNR B15 (P15): **5,000 francs**   VG   VF   UNC

Green, blue, and brown. Front: Woman with fruit basket on head; workers picking coffee berries in field. Back: Banana tree; lake; mountains. No security thread. Watermark: Impala head. Printer: Unknown. 165 x 70 mm.

☐	a.	1.01.1978. Signature 12. Prefix A - B.	5	20	85
☐	as.	Specimen.	—	—	100

1981-1982 Issues

BNR B16 (P18): **100 francs** (US$0.15)   VG   VF   UNC

Violet, orange, blue, and green. Front: Flower as registration device; coat of arms; five zebras. Back: Woman with baby on back; Volcanoes National Park; flower. No security thread. Watermark: Impala head. Printer: Unknown. 135 x 70 mm.

☐	a.	1•08•1982. Signature 15. Prefix A - H.	0.50	2.50	10

BNR B17 (P16): **500 francs**   VG   VF   UNC

Brown, violet, green, orange, and blue. Front: Coat of arms; three impalas standing in field. Back: 16 men with hoes tending a field. No security thread. Watermark: Crowned crane head. Printer: (TDLR). 145 x 70 mm.

    a. 1•07•1981. Signature 13. Prefix B.   2.50   10   40
    as1. Diagonal *SPECIMEN* overprint.   —   —   20
    as2. Diagonal red *SPECIMEN* and DLR oval ovpts;
        horizontal red *SPECIMEN Nº* # ovpt at lower left.

BNR B18 (P17): **1,000 francs**   VG   VF   UNC

Green, blue, brown, and pink. Front: Coat of arms; man and boy Intore dancers with spears and shields. Back: Two Eastern gorillas; three men in canoe on lake. No security thread. Watermark: Crowned crane head. Printer: (TDLR). 157 x 70 mm.

    a. 1•07•1981. Signature 14. Prefix C.   4   12   30
    as1. Diagonal black *SPECIMEN* overprint.   —   —   15
    as2. Diagonal black *SPECIMEN* and DLR oval ovpts;
        horizon. black *SPECIMEN Nº* # ovpt at lower left.

1988-1989 Issues

These notes are like the preceding issues, but with different dates, signatories, titles, and the denomination spelled *AMAFARANGA* on back, as opposed to *AMAFRANGA*.

BNR B19 (P19): **100 francs** (US$0.15)   VG   VF   UNC

Violet, orange, blue, and green. Front: Flower as registration device; coat of arms; five zebras. Back: Woman with baby on back; Volcanoes National Park; flower. No security thread. Watermark: Impala head. Printer: Unknown. 135 x 70 mm.

    a. 24•04•1989. Signature 17.   0.25   1   4
        Prefix L - Z. 7- or 8-digit serial number.
    as. Diagonal red *SPECIMEN* overprint;   —   —   10
        horizontal red # overprint at lower left.

Replacement notes: Prefix XX.

BNR B20 (P21): **1,000 francs** (US$1.60)   VG   VF   UNC

Green, blue, brown, and pink. Front: Coat of arms; man and boy Intore dancers with spears and shields. Back: Two Eastern gorillas; three men in canoe on lake. No security thread. Watermark: Crowned crane head. Printer: (TDLR). 157 x 70 mm.

    a. 1•01•1988. Signature 16. Prefix D - E.   0.25   1.25   5
    as. Diagonal black *SPECIMEN* overprint.   —   —   30

Replacement notes: Prefix VV.

BNR B21 (P22): **5,000 francs** (US$7.95)   VG   VF   UNC

Green, blue, and brown. Front: Woman with fruit basket on head; workers picking coffee berries in field. Back: Banana tree; lake; mountains. No security thread. Watermark: Impala head. Printer: Unknown. 165 x 70 mm.

- ☐ a. 1.01.1988. Signature 16. Prefix F.   0.50   2   7
- ☐ as. Diagonal black *SPECIMEN* overprint.   —   —   30

Replacement notes: Prefix XX.

1994 Issues

BNR B22 (P23): **500 francs** (US$0.80)   VG   VF   UNC

Blue, pink, and green. Front: Mountains; forest. Back: Female waterbuck standing in grass. Solid security thread. Watermark: Impala head. Printer: (G&D). 130 x 74 mm.

- ☐ a. 1.12.1994. Signature 18. Prefix AA.   —   3   12
- ☐ as. Diagonal black *SPECIMEN* overprint; horizon. black *SPECIMEN N°* # overprint at lower left.   —   —   20

BNR B23 (P24): **1,000 francs** (US$1.60)   VG   VF   UNC

Brown, purple, and red. Front: Mountains; forest. Back: Banana tree; three African buffalo standing in grass. Solid security thread. Watermark: Impala head. Printer: (G&D). 130 x 74 mm.

- ☐ a. 1.12.1994. Signature 18. Prefix AA.   FV   4   15
- ☐ as. Diagonal black *SPECIMEN* overprint; horizon. black *SPECIMEN N°* # overprint at lower left.   —   —   20

BNR B24 (P25): **5,000 francs** (US$7.95)   VG   VF   UNC

Violet, light blue, and brown. Front: Mountains; forest. Back: Trees; male lion lying in grass. Solid security thread. Watermark: Impala head. Printer: (G&D). 130 x 74 mm.

- ☐ a. 1.12.1994. Signature 18. Prefix AA.   20   50   150
- ☐ as. Diagonal black *SPECIMEN* overprint; horizon. black *SPECIMEN N°* # overprint at lower left.   —   —   40

1998 Issues

At some point during the issuance of these notes, the font used for printing the upper left serial numbers changed from wide to narrow.

Font Varieties

BNR B26 (P27): **1,000 francs** (US$1.60)   VG   VF   UNC
Green, blue, and brown. Front: Volcanoes National Park. Back: Ankole-Watusi cattle; workers in tea plantation field. Solid security thread with demetalized *BNR*. Watermark: Intore dancer's head and electrotype *BNR*. Printer: Unknown. 145 x 73 mm.

- ☐ a. 1-12-1998. Signature 20.   FV   FV   5
  Wide font for upper left s/n. Prefix AF - AT.
- ☐ b. Narrow font for upper left s/n. Prefix AW.   FV   FV   5
- ☐ as1. Diagonal red *SPECIMEN* overprint;   —   —   20
  horizontal red *NO #* overprint at lower left.
- ☐ as2. Diagonal red *SPECIMEN* overprint.   —   —   20

BNR B25 (P26): **500 francs** (US$0.80)   VG   VF   UNC
Pink, green, and light blue. Front: Three mountain gorillas. Back: Two boys and a girl seated, reading books; National Museum of Rwanda buildings in Butare (Musée National). Solid security thread with demetalized *BNR*. Watermark: Intore dancer's head and electrotype *BNR*. Printer: Unknown. 136 x 74 mm.

- ☐ a. 1.12.1998. Signature 19.   FV   FV   4
  Wide font for upper left serial number. Prefix AC.
- ☐ b. Narrow font for upper left s/n. Prefix AL.   FV   FV   4
- ☐ as1. Diagonal red *SPECIMEN* overprint;   —   —   10
  horizontal red *NO #* overprint at lower left.
- ☐ as2. Diagonal red *SPECIMEN* overprint.   —   —   10

BNR B27 (P28): **5,000 francs** (US$7.95)   VG   VF   UNC
Red and black. Front: Bird; 11 male and female Intore dancers; circular holographic patch. Back: Coffee plant; Banque Nationale du Rwanda headquarters building in Kigali; coffee berries on branch. Solid security thread with demetalized *BNR*. Watermark: Intore dancer's head and electrotype *BNR*. Printer: Unknown. 158 x 72 mm.

- ☐ a. 1-12-1998. Signature 20.   FV   FV   10
  Wide font for upper left s/n. Prefix AC.
- ☐ b. Narrow font for upper left s/n. Prefix AG.   FV   FV   10
- ☐ as. Diagonal red *SPECIMEN* overprint;   —   —   20
  horizontal red *NO #* overprint at lower left.

Replacement notes: Prefix XX.

2003 Issues

BNR B28 (P29): **100 francs** (withdrawn 31.12.2009)   VG   VF   UNC
Ochre, green, and brown. Front: Two farmers plowing field with Ankole-Watusi cattle; coat of arms. Back: Kibuye landscape and Lake Kivu. No security thread. Watermark: Intore dancer's head and electrotype *BNR*. Printer: Unknown. 130 x 65 mm.

- a. 01-05-2003. Signature 21. Prefix AA - AF.   FV   FV   2
- as. Diagonal red *SPECIMEN* overprint;   —   —   25
  horizontal red # overprint at lower center.

2003-2004 Issues

Whereas preceding issues had the name of the bank in French on the front and Kinyarwanda on the back, these notes have added the name in English.

BNR B29 (P29b): **100 francs** (withdrawn 31.12.2009)   VG   VF   UNC
Ochre, green, and brown. Front: Two farmers plowing field with Ankole-Watusi cattle; coat of arms. Back: Kibuye landscape and Lake Kivu. No security thread. Watermark: Intore dancer's head and electrotype *BNR*. Printer: Unknown. 130 x 65 mm.

- a. 01-09-2003. Signature 21. Prefix AG - AL.   FV   FV   2
- as. Diagonal red *SPECIMEN* overprint;   —   —   25
  horizontal red # overprint at lower center.

BNR B30 (P30): **500 francs** (US$0.80)   VG   VF   UNC
Green. Front: Banque Nationale du Rwanda headquarters building in Kigali. Back: Three workers with baskets picking tea leaves in field. Windowed security thread with demetalized *BNR500*. Watermark: Coat of arms and electrotype *BNR*. Printer: Unknown. 135 x 72 mm.

- a. 01.07.2004. Signature 22. Prefix AA - AC.   FV   FV   5
- as. Diagonal red *SPECIMEN* overprint;   —   —   50
  horizontal red *SPECIMEN Nº* # ovpt at lower left.

BNR B31 (P31a): **1,000 francs** (US$1.60)   VG   VF   UNC
Blue, green, and orange. Front: National Museum of Rwanda buildings in Butare. Back: Golden monkey in Volcanoes National Park. Holographic stripe. Windowed security thread with demetalized *BNR1000*. Watermark: Coat of arms and electrotype *BNR*. Printer: Unknown. 140 x 72 mm.

- a. 01.07.2004. Signature 22. Prefix AA - AE.   FV   FV   10
- as. Diagonal red *SPECIMEN* overprint;   —   —   50
  horizontal red *SPECIMEN Nº* # ovpt at lower left.

BNR B32 (P33): **5,000 francs** (US$7.95) VG VF UNC
Lilac, brown, and orange. Front: Mountain gorilla in the Volcano National Park. Back: two woven baskets. Holographic stripe. Windowed security thread with demetalized *BNR*. Watermark: Coat of arms and electrotype *BNR*. Printer: Unknown. 145 x 72 mm.

    ☐ a. 01-04-2004. Signature 22. Prefix AE - AZ. FV FV 25
       Intro: 12.06.2004.
    ☐ as1. Diagonal red *SPECIMEN* overprint on front only; — — 20
       horizontal red # overprint at lower left.
    ☐ as2. Diagonal red *SPECIMEN* overprint; — — 20
       horizontal red *SPECIMEN Nº* # ovpt at lower left.

Replacement notes: Prefix XX.

2007-2009 Issues

These notes are like the preceding issues, but the indigenous name of the bank now reads *BANKI NKURU Y'U RWANDA*. In 2008 the bank replaced the 100-franc note with a bimetallic coin, and revoked the notes' legal tender status on 31 December 2009.

BNR B33 (PNL): **500 francs** (US$0.80) VG VF UNC
Green. Front: Banque Nationale du Rwanda headquarters building in Kigali. Back: Three workers with baskets picking tea leaves in field. Windowed security thread with demetalized *BNR500*. Watermark: Coat of arms and electrotype *BNR*. Printer: Unknown. 135 x 72 mm.

    ☐ a. 01.02.2008. Signature 22. Prefix AD - AF. FV FV 4

BNR B34 (P31b): **1,000 francs** (US$1.60) VG VF UNC
Blue, green, and orange. Front: National Museum of Rwanda buildings in Butare. Back: Golden monkey in Volcanoes National Park. Holographic stripe. Windowed security thread with demetalized *BNR1000*. Watermark: Coat of arms and electrotype *BNR*. Printer: Unknown. 140 x 72 mm.

    ☐ a. 01.02.2008. Signature 22. Prefix AF - AM. FV FV 7

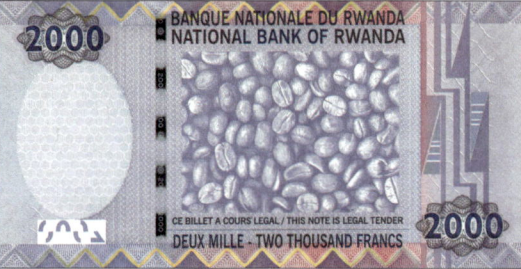

BNR B35 (P32): **2,000 francs** (US$3.20) VG VF UNC
Violet. Front: Hills; communication antenna and parabolic antenna. Back: Coffee beans. Holographic stripe. Windowed security thread with demetalized sun and *2000*. Watermark: Coat of arms, electrotype *BNR*, and Cornerstones. Printer: (TDLR). 142 x 72 mm.

    ☐ a. 31-10-2007. Signature 22. Prefix AA - AJ. FV FV 12
       Intro: mid-Dec. 2007.
    ☐ as. Diagonal red *SPECIMEN* overprint; — — —
       horizontal red # overprint at lower left.

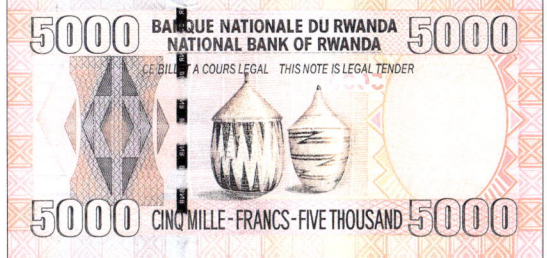

BNR B36 (P33b): **5,000 francs** (US$7.95)   VG   VF   UNC
Lilac, brown, and orange. Front: Mountain gorilla in the Volcano National Park. Back: two woven baskets. Holographic stripe. Windowed security thread with demetalized *BNR*. Watermark: Coat of arms and electrotype *BNR*. Printer: Unknown. 145 x 72 mm.

     a.   01-02-2009. Signature 22. Prefix BD - BP.   FV   FV   20
     as.   Diagonal red *SPECIMEN* overprint;   —   —   —
         horizontal red *SPECIMEN Nº #* ovpt at lower left.

2013 Issues

These notes feature cows on the front reflecting the government's efforts to eradicate malnutrition, and students working with computers on the back reflecting education and technology.

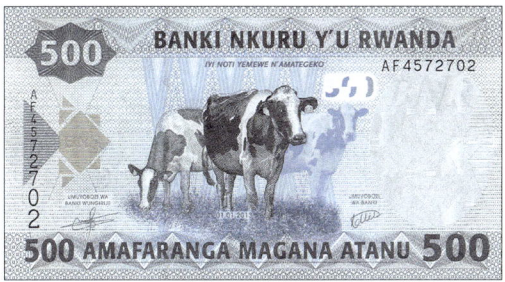

BNR B37 (PNL): **500 francs** (US$0.80)   VG   VF   UNC
Dark blue and gray. Front: Three cows. Back: Four young students with XO computers (from One Laptop Per Child). Windowed security thread with demetalized *BNR500*. Watermark: Coat of arms and electrotype *BNR*. Printer: Unknown. 135 x 72 mm.

     a.   01.01.2013. Signature 23. Prefix AF.   FV   FV   4
         Intro 24.09.2013.

Looking Forward

On 1 July 2010, the East African Community (www.eac.int)—Burundi, Kenya, Rwanda, Tanzania, and Uganda—launched the EAC Common Market for goods, labor, and capital within the region, with the goals of a common currency (the East African shilling) by 2012, and full political federation in 2015. The common currency has yet to come to pass.

Acknowledgements

This chapter was compiled with the generous assistance of Thomas Augustsson, Arigo Avbovbo, Edwin Biersteker, Andrea Bossi, Tim Dinneweth, Hartmut Fraunhoffer (www.banknoten.de), David Jones, Antje Maroussi, Richard Miranda, Rui Manuel Palhares, Alexander Petrov, Ibrahim Salem, Bill Stubkjaer, Christoph Thomas, Frank van Tiel, Ludek Vostal, Sergey Vostrikov, David White, and others.

Sources

August, David and Christian Selvais. *Etat Independant du Congo, Congo Belge, Congo Belge et Ruanda Urundi, Rwanda-Burundi, Katanga 1896 - 1962*. Edition 2002. ISBN 90-9015672-0. Billeta Belgica. Kleit 150 - B-990 Maldegem.

Cuhaj, George S. *Standard Catalog of World Paper Money, General Issues, 1368-1960*. 14th edition. 2012. ISBN 978-1-4402-3090-5. Krause Publications (www.krausebooks.com), 700 East State St., Iola, WI, 54990-0001.

Cuhaj, George S. *Standard Catalog of World Paper Money, Modern Issues, 1961-Present*. 18th edition. 2012. ISBN 978-1-4402-2956-5. Krause Publications (www.krausebooks.com), 700 East State St., Iola, WI, 54990-0001.

Hessler, Gene. "Joseph Lawrence Keen, British Engraver, 1919-2004." *IBNS Journal*. Volume 43 Number 2. p.12.

Share Your Input, Info, and Images

This catalog is believed to be complete and correct as of the time of publication. Prices and face values were last updated 4 January 2013. Please report errors or omissions so that corrections may be made. If you can more precisely identify the name or location of anything depicted on a note, please share that information. Furthermore, if you own an unlisted type or variety, please submit scans of the front and back of the note so that it can be documented. Scans should be 300 dots per inch, 100% actual size, 24-bit color, saved as *uncompressed* JPEG files, and sent to owen@banknotenews.com. Be sure to fully describe all attributes of the note which are not apparent upon visual inspection of the images alone, such as physical dimension, watermark, and security thread.

Rwanda and Burundi

For earlier issues, see Belgian Congo.

Monetary System
1 Rwanda and Burundi franc = 100 centimes

Banque d'Emission du Rwanda et du Burundi
(Issuing Bank of Rwanda and Burundi)

The Banque d'Emission du Rwanda et du Burundi (BERB) was established in 1960.

BERB Signature Varieties

1960-1963 Issues

In 1960, the Belgian Congo franc was replaced by the Rwanda and Burundi franc.

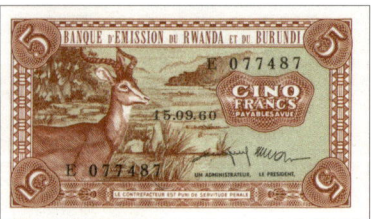

BERB B1 (P1): 5 francs   Good   Fine   XF
Brown and green. Front: Impala; river bank. Back: Guilloche patterns. No security thread. Watermark: None. Printer: (BNdB). 100 x 58 mm.

			Good	Fine	XF
☐	a.	15.09.60. Signature 1. Prefix A - E.	40	90	400
☐	b.	15.05.61. Prefix E - J.	40	100	400
☐	c.	15.04.63. Signature 3. Prefix K.	75	125	450
☐	as.	Diagonal red *SPECIMEN* overprint.	—	—	—

For notes with overprint, see Burundi BDB B1.

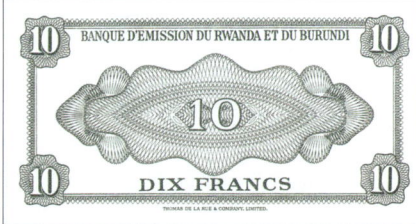

BERB B2 (P2): 10 francs   Good   Fine   XF
Gray, blue, and orange. Front: Hippopotamus; river. Back: Guilloche patterns. No security thread. Watermark: None. Printer: *THOMAS DE LA RUE & COMPANY, LIMITED*. 115 x 61 mm.

			Good	Fine	XF
☐	a.	15•09•60. Signature 1. Prefix A - E.	75	175	575
☐	b.	05•10•60. Prefix F - T.	75	175	575
☐	as1.	Diagonal red *SPECIMEN* overprint.	—	—	—
☐	as2.	Diagonal red *SPECIMEN* and DLR oval ovpts; horizontal red *SPECIMEN N°* # ovpt at lower left; punched.	—	UNC	200

For notes with overprint, see Burundi BDB B2.

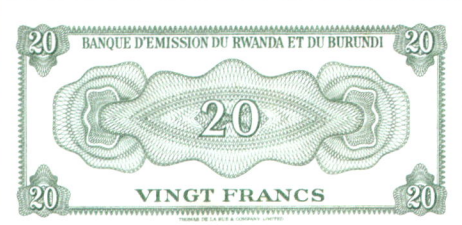

BERB B3 (P3): **20 francs**   Good   Fine   XF

Green and pink. Front: Crocodile; river. Back: Guilloche patterns. No security thread. Watermark: None. Printer: *THOMAS DE LA RUE & COMPANY, LIMITED*. 130 x 64 mm.

		Good	Fine	XF
a.	15•09•60. Signature 1. Prefix A - C.	125	250	750
b.	05•10•60. Prefix D - M.	125	250	750
as1.	Diagonal red *SPECIMEN* overprint.	—	UNC	2,250
as2.	Diagonal red *SPECIMEN* and DLR oval ovpts; horizontal red *SPECIMEN N° #* ovpt at lower left; punched.	—	UNC	400
as3.	Horizontal *CANCELLED* perforation.	—	—	—

For notes with overprint, see Burundi BDB B3.
For notes with handstamp, see Rwanda BNR B1.

BERB B4 (P4): **50 francs**   Good   Fine   XF

Red and gray. Front: Lioness. Back: Guilloche patterns. No security thread. Watermark: None. Printer: (BWC). 140 x 67 mm.

		Good	Fine	XF
a.	15•09•60. Signature 1. Prefix A - E.	50	200	1,800
b.	01•10•60. Prefix F - G.	150	325	650
s1.	Diagonal red *SPECIMEN* overprint.	—	UNC	500
s2.	Horizontal *SPECIMEN* perforation.	—	UNC	500
t.	Color trial: Green and violet. No date; no sig.	—	UNC	750
as.	Diagonal red *SPECIMEN* overprint; punched.	—	—	—

For notes with overprint, see Burundi BDB B4.
For notes with handstamp, see Rwanda BNR B2.

BERB B5 (P5): **100 francs**   Good   Fine   XF

Blue, green, and orange. Front: Zebu bull. Back: Guilloche patterns. No security thread. Watermark: None. Printer: (BWC). 150 x 70 mm.

		Good	Fine	XF
a.	15.09.60. Signature 1. Prefix A - G.	175	350	700
b.	01.10.60. Prefix H.	175	350	700
c.	31.07.62. Signature 2. Prefix L.	175	350	700
as.	Diagonal red *SPECIMEN* overprint; punched. With or without serial numbers.	—	UNC	450
t.	Color trial: Brown and green. No date; no sig.	—	UNC	700

For notes with overprint, see Burundi BDB B5.
For notes with handstamp, see Rwanda BNR B3.

BERB B6 (P6): **500 francs**   Good   Fine   XF

Brown, lilac, and green. Front: Black rhinoceros; forest. Back: Guilloche patterns. No security thread. Watermark: None. Printer: *THOMAS DE LA RUE & COMPANY, LIMITED*. 160 x 73 mm.

		Good	Fine	XF
a.	15•09•60. Signature 1. Prefix A.	500	1,750	4,000
b.	15•05•61.	500	1,750	4,000
c.	15•09•61.	500	1,750	4,000
as1.	Diagonal red *SPECIMEN* overprint.	—	UNC	1,500
as2.	Diagonal red *SPECIMEN* and DLR oval ovpts; horizontal red *SPECIMEN N° #* ovpt at lower left; punched.	—	UNC	1,500
bs1.	Diagonal red *SPECIMEN* and DLR oval ovpts; horizontal red *SPECIMEN N° #* ovpt at lower left; punched.	—	UNC	1,500
bs2.	Horizontal *CANCELLED* perforation.	—	AU	1,200

For notes with overprint, see Burundi BDB B6.
For notes with embossed seal, see Rwanda BNR B4.

BERB B7 (P7): **1,000 francs**
Green and purple. Front: Zebra. Back: Guilloche patterns. No security thread. Watermark: None. Printer: (BWC). 170 x 76 mm.

		Good	Fine	XF
☐ a.	15.09.60. Signature 1. Prefix A.	900	3,750	8,000
☐ b.	15.05.61.	1,000	4,000	8,300
☐ c.	31.07.62. Signature 2.	900	3,750	8,000
☐ as.	Diagonal red *SPECIMEN* overprint; punched. With or without serial numbers.	—	UNC	1,200
☐ t.	Color trial: Purple. No date; no signature.	—	UNC	675

For notes with overprint, see Burundi BDB B7.
For notes with embossed seal, see Rwanda BNR B5.

Looking Forward

In 1964, Rwanda and Burundi introduced their own currencies, the Rwandan franc and the Burundian franc, respectively.

For later issues, see Burundi and Rwanda.

Acknowledgements

This chapter was compiled with the generous assistance of Arigo Avbovbo, David Burns, Tim Dinneweth, Hartmut Fraunhoffer (www.banknoten.de), Robin Frost, Tod Hunt, Mark Irwin, David Jones, Murtaza Karimjee (www.africanbanknotes.blogspot.com), Wally Myers, Laurence Pope, Nizzar Surani (www.nizzarsurani.com), and others.

Sources

August, David and Christian Selvais. *Etat Independant du Congo, Congo Belge, Congo Belge et Ruanda Urundi, Rwanda-Burundi, Katanga 1896 - 1962*. Edition 2002. ISBN 90-9015672-0. Billeta Belgica. Kleit 150 - B-990 Maldegem.

Cuhaj, George S. *Standard Catalog of World Paper Money, Modern Issues, 1961-Present*. 17th edition. 2011. ISBN 978-1-4402-1584-1. Krause Publications (www.krausebooks.com), 700 East State St., Iola, WI, 54990-0001.

Share Your Input, Info, and Images

This catalog is believed to be complete and correct as of the time of publication. Prices and face values were last updated 10 August 2014. Please report errors or omissions so that corrections may be made. If you can more precisely identify the name or location of anything depicted on a note, please share that information. Furthermore, if you own an unlisted type or variety, please submit scans of the front and back of the note so that it can be documented. Scans should be 300 dots per inch, 100% actual size, 24-bit color, saved as *uncompressed* JPEG files, and sent to owen@banknotenews.com. Be sure to fully describe all attributes of the note which are not apparent upon visual inspection of the images alone, such as physical dimension, watermark, and security thread.

Saar

Contents

Mines Domaniales de la Sarre (MDS) 1775
Treasury (TRE) 1776

Monetary System

1919: 1 Saar franc = 100 centimes
1935: 1 Reichsmark =100 Reichspfennig
16.07.1947: 1 Saar mark = 100 pfennig
20.11.1947: 1 Saar franc = 100 centimes
06.07.1959: 1 deutsche mark (DEM) = 100 pfennig

As part of the Treaty of Versailles—signed on 28 June 1919—which ended the state of war between Germany and the Allied Powers, Germany lost its overseas colonies as well as a significant portion of its European territory. The Saar (German: Saarland; French: Sarre)—named after the Saar River—had been part of the German Empire since the Franco-Prussian War of 1870/71, but did not exist as a unified entity until its creation as the Territory of the Saar Basin (formed from southern parts of the German Rhine Province and western parts of the Bavarian Palatinate) by the League of Nations after World War I. Prior to this, some parts of the current entity were Prussian and other parts Bavarian.

Mines Domaniales de la Sarre (State-Owned Mines of the Saar)

The Saar is a heavily-industrialized region with rich coal deposits. As reparations for Germany's destruction of coal mines in Northern France during World War I, France nationalized the Saar's coal mines. During the region's 15 years as an autonomous territory under a League of Nations mandate, it was occupied jointly by Britain and France, and governed by a five-person commission made up of representatives of the occupation forces.

MDS Signature Varieties

1		

LE DIRECTEUR GÉNÉRAL André Louis Joseph Ghislain Defline (1920 - 1929)		LE CAISSIER GÉNÉRAL Unknown

1917 Essays

The Banque de France created essays denominated in 5, 10, 50, 100, and 1,000 francs printed *MINES DOMANIALES FRANÇAISES DE LA SARRE* at top center front. These designs were not adopted and the notes were never issued. The essays are extremely rare and valuable.

1919 Issues

These notes bear redemption clauses in French on the back explaining that while they are equivalent to French currency, they can be redeemed only by the general cashier of the state-owned mines in the Saar if presented prior to 1 January 1930.

MDS B1 (P1): **50 centimes**   VG   VF   UNC
Blue-gray and brown. Front: Round medallion of Roman goddess Minerva wearing helmet. Back: Guilloche pattern; redemption clause in French. No security thread. Watermark: None. Printer: Unknown. 94 x 62 mm.
    a.   No date. Sig. 1. Block letters A, B, C. Intro: 1919.   50   150   500
    as.   Specimen.   —   —   —

MDS B2 (P2): **1 franc**   VG   VF   UNC
Red, orange, and yellow. Front: Round medallion of Roman goddess Minerva wearing helmet. Back: Front and back of French 1-franc coin dated 1919, depicting woman sowing seeds and an olive branch, respectively; caduceus entwined by two snakes; redemption clause in French. No security thread. Watermark: None. Printer: Unknown. 106 x 70 mm.
    a.   No date. Sig. 1. Block letters: A-F. Intro: 1919.   50   150   500
    as.   Specimen.   —   —   —

Treasury

A plebiscite held on 13 January 1935, resulted in the region's reintegration with Germany as the Saarland. However, after World War II, the Saarland again came under French occupation in 1945, and was administered as the Saar Protectorate from 16 February 1946. In 1947, it was united economically with France.

1947 Issues

On 16 July 1947, the Saar mark replaced the Reichsmark as legal tender in the Saar Protectorate. However, these notes were soon replaced following the integration of the Saar into the French currency area. The Saar franc was the currency of the Saar Protectorate and, later, the state of Saarland in the Federal Republic of Germany between 20 November 1947 and 6 July 1959. It was valued at par with the French franc, and French coins and banknotes circulated alongside local issues.

TRE B1 (P3): **1 mark**   VG   VF   UNC
Brown, blue, and yellow. Front: Round medallion of Greek god Zeus wearing crown. Back: Ceres, Roman goddess of the harvest, holding vegetables and cornucopia filled with fruit; counterfeiting warning in French and German. No security thread. Watermark: None. Printer: (BdF). 82 x 52 mm.
- a. 1947. Intro: June 1947.   35   150   250
- as. Horizontal *SPECIMEN* perforation.   —   —   450

TRE B2 (P4): **2 mark**   VG   VF   UNC
Brown, violet, and yellow. Front: Round medallion of Greek god Zeus wearing crown. Back: Ceres, Roman goddess of the harvest, holding vegetables and cornucopia filled with fruit; counterfeiting warning in French and German. No security thread. Watermark: None. Printer: (BdF). 82 x 52 mm.
- a. 1947. Intro: June 1947.   500   900   2,000
- as. Horizontal *SPECIMEN* perforation.   —   —   1,500

TRE B3 (P5): **5 mark**   VG   VF   UNC
Pink, violet, blue, and orange. Front: Round medallion of Greek god Zeus wearing crown. Back: Ceres, Roman goddess of the harvest, holding vegetables and cornucopia filled with fruit; counterfeiting warning in French and German. No security thread. Watermark: None. Printer: (BdF). 82 x 52 mm.
- a. 1947. Intro: June 1947.   100   225   750
- as. Horizontal *SPECIMEN* perforation.   —   —   600

TRE B4 (P6): **10 mark**   VG   VF   UNC
Red, green, yellow, and brown. Front: Roses; woman (symbolizing Peace) holding laurels. Back: Flowers; horse and man; counterfeiting warning in French and German. No security thread. Watermark: Female heads. Printer: (BdF). 130 x 85 mm.
- a. 1947. Intro: June 1947.   150   600   1,500
- as. Diagonal *SPECIMEN* perforation.   —   —   800

TRE B5 (P7): **50 mark**   VG   VF   UNC
Green, red, yellow, and brown. Front: Roses; woman (symbolizing Peace) holding laurels. Back: Flowers; horse and man; counterfeiting warning in French and German. No security thread. Watermark: Female heads. Printer: (BdF). 130 x 85 mm.
- a. 1947. Intro: June 1947.   1,125   2,150   3,000
- as. Diagonal *SPECIMEN* perforation.   —   —   1,800

TRE B6 (P8): **100 mark** VG VF UNC

Yellow, brown, blue, and green. Front: Roses; woman (symbolizing Peace) holding laurels. Back: Flowers; horse and man; counterfeiting warning in French and German. No security thread. Watermark: Female heads. Printer: (BdF). 130 x 85 mm.

			VG	VF	UNC
☐	a.	1947. Intro: June 1947.	2,550	5,600	20,000
☐	as.	Diagonal *SPECIMEN* perforation.	—	—	5,500

Looking Forward

In 1954, a plebiscite rejected the establishment of an independent Saarland. From that point, only French franc banknotes circulated. The state of Saarland became part of the Federal Republic of Germany on 1 January 1957. French notes continued circulating in the Saar until 6 July 1959, after which time German notes circulated. For later issues, see Germany, Federal Republic of.

Acknowledgements

This chapter was compiled with the generous assistance of Compagnie Generale De Bourse (www.cgb.fr), Don Ludwig, Wally Myers, Michel Muszynski, Nikolaj Vladimirov, and others.

Sources

Annales des Mines (http://annales.org).

Cuhaj, George S. *Standard Catalog of World Paper Money, General Issues, 1368-1960*. 14th edition. 2012. ISBN 978-1-4402-3090-5. Krause Publications (www.krausebooks.com), 700 East State St., Iola, WI, 54990-0001.

Fayette, Claude. *Les Billets de la Banque de France et du Trésor 1800 - 2002*. 7th edition. 2007. ISBN 978-2-35058-065-4. Edition Numismatique & Change. Martin Media. 10, avenue Victor-Hugo, 55800 Revigny sur Ornain, France.

Grabowski, Hans L. "1000 Saarfranken (1920)." *Munzen & Sammeln*. October 2011 p.149.

Rosenberg, Holger and Hans-Ludwig Grabowski. *Die deutschen Banknoten ab 1871*. 2009. Battenberg. H. Gietl Verlag & Publikationservice. ISBN 3-924861-96-X.

Share Your Input, Info, and Images

This catalog is believed to be complete and correct as of the time of publication. Prices and face values were last updated 23 December 2011. Please report errors or omissions so that corrections may be made. If you can more precisely identify the name or location of anything depicted on a note, please share that information. Furthermore, if you own an unlisted type or variety, please submit scans of the front and back of the note so that it can be documented. Scans should be 300 dots per inch, 100% actual size, 24-bit color, saved as *uncompressed* JPEG files, and sent to owen@banknotenews.com. Be sure to fully describe all attributes of the note which are not apparent upon visual inspection of the images alone, such as physical dimension, watermark, and security thread.

Saint Helena

For earlier issues, see Great Britain and South Africa.

Monetary System
1 Saint Helena pound = 20 shillings
1971: 1 Saint Helena pound (SHP) = 100 pence

Government of St. Helena

The traditional usage of British and South African currencies in the British dependency of Saint Helena changed with the passage of the Currency Fund Ordinance of 1975 and the Currency Regulations of 1976, which established a currency board and the legal tender status of the new Saint Helena pound.

For more information, visit www.sthelenacurrency.gov.sh.

GOSH Signature Varieties

1976-1985 Issues

In 1976, the currency board of the Government of Saint Helena began issuing 1- and 5-pound notes, followed by 50-pence and 10-pound notes in 1979.

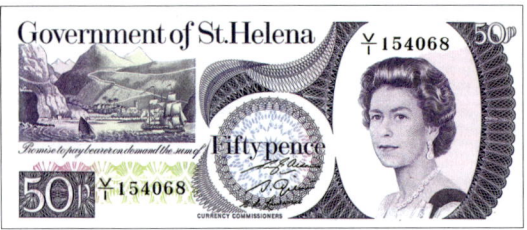

GOSH B1 (P5): **50 pence** (US$0.85)   VG   VF   UNC
Purple. Front: Three sailing ships in Jamestown harbor; Queen Elizabeth II. Back: Coat of arms of the East India Company with lions, flags, shield, and Latin text on banner; St. Helena crest with sailing ship. Solid security thread. Watermark: None. Printer: Unknown. 142 x 59 mm.
   ☐ a. No date. Sig. 2. Prefix V/1. Intro: 29.01.1979.   FV   3   12
   ☐ as. Specimen.   —   —   —
Notes with serial numbers 170,001-200,000 are non-redeemable.

GOSH B2 (P6): **1 pound** (US$1.70)   VG   VF   UNC
Green. Front: Compass rose and seven sailing ships off shore of Saint Helena island; Queen Elizabeth II. Back: Coat of arms of the East India Company with lions, flags, shield, and Latin text on banner (*ANGLÆ* in error); St. Helena crest with sailing ship. Solid security thread. Watermark: None. Printer: Unknown. 151 x 73 mm.
   ☐ a. No date. Sig. 1. Prefix A/1. Intro: 02.02.1976.   FV   15   50
   ☐ as. Diagonal red *SPECIMEN* overprint; punched.   —   —   100

GOSH B3 (P7): **5 pounds** (US$8.55)   VG   VF   UNC

Blue. Front: Sea-level view of sailing ships in Jamestown harbor; Queen Elizabeth II. Back: Coat of arms of the East India Company with lions, flags, shield, and Latin text on banner; St. Helena crest with sailing ship. Solid security thread. Watermark: None. Printer: Unknown. 151 x 73 mm.

		VG	VF	UNC
a.	No date. Signature 1. Incorrect spelling *ANGLÆ* in motto on back. Prefix H/1. Intro: 02.02.1976.	FV	50	100
b.	Signature 2. Corrected spelling *ANGLIÆ* in motto on back. Intro: 1981.	FV	10	40
as.	Diagonal red *SPECIMEN* overprint; punched.	—	—	125
bs.	Diagonal red *SPECIMEN* overprint; punched.	—	—	—

GOSH B4 (P8): **10 pounds** (US$17)   VG   VF   UNC

Red. Front: Five sailing ships anchored in Jamestown harbor; Queen Elizabeth II. Back: Coat of arms of the East India Company with lions, flags, shield, and Latin text on banner. Solid security thread. Watermark: None. Printer: Unknown. 157 x 79 mm.

		VG	VF	UNC
a.	No date. Sig. 2. Prefix P/1. Intro: 29.01.1979.	FV	50	200
b.	Signature 3. Intro: 1985.	FV	FV	25
as.	Diagonal red *SPECIMEN* overprint.	—	—	275
bs.	Diagonal red *SPECIMEN* overprint; punched.	—	—	—
s.	Diagonal red *SPECIMEN* overprint; horizontal red *SPECIMEN OF NO VALUE* ovpt at upper left; punched; no signatures.	—	—	—
r.	Remainder without signatures or serial numbers.	—	—	300

The motto on the back of both the 1- and 5-pound notes issued in 1976 contained the word *ANGLÆ* in error (left). Corrected (right) notes GOSH B5a and B3b were issued in 1981.

1981-1986 Issues

This 1-pound note is smaller than the preceding issue, and it has the corrected spelling of *ANGLIÆ* on the back. The 20-pound denomination is new.

GOSH B5 (P9): **1 pound** (US$1.70)   VG   VF   UNC

Green. Front: Compass rose and seven sailing ships off shore of Saint Helena island; Queen Elizabeth II. Back: Coat of arms of the East India Company with lions, flags, shield, and Latin text on banner (*ANGLIÆ* corrected); St. Helena crest with sailing ship. Solid security thread. Watermark: None. Printer: Unknown. 144 x 66 mm.

    ☐ a. No date. Sig. 2. Prefix A/1. Intro: 1981.   FV   FV   10
    ☐ as. Diagonal red *SPECIMEN* overprint; punched.   —   —   —

Notes with serial numbers 350,000-400,000 are non-redeemable.

GOSH B6 (P10): **20 pounds** (US$34)   VG   VF   UNC

Brown. Front: Three sail boats in Jamestown harbor; Queen Elizabeth II. Back: Coat of arms of the East India Company with lions, flags, shield, and Latin text on banner. Solid security thread. Watermark: None. Printer: Unknown. 164 x 84 mm.

    ☐ a. No date. Signature 4. Prefix A/1. Intro: 1986.   FV   FV   50
    ☐ as. Specimen.   —   —   —

1998 Issues

This 5-pound note is smaller than the preceding issue.

GOSH B7 (P11): **5 pounds** (US$8.55)   VG   VF   UNC

Blue. Front: Sea-level view of sailing ships in Jamestown harbor; Queen Elizabeth II. Back: Coat of arms of the East India Company with lions, flags, shield, and Latin text on banner; St. Helena crest with sailing ship. Solid security thread. Watermark: None. Printer: Unknown. 134 x 70 mm.

    ☐ a. No date. Signature 5. Prefix H/1. Intro: 1998.   FV   FV   14
    ☐ as. Diagonal red *SPECIMEN* overprint; punched.   —   —   110

2004-2012 Issues

These notes feature a new portrait of Queen Elizabeth II, as well as backs redesigned in the style of the other denominations.

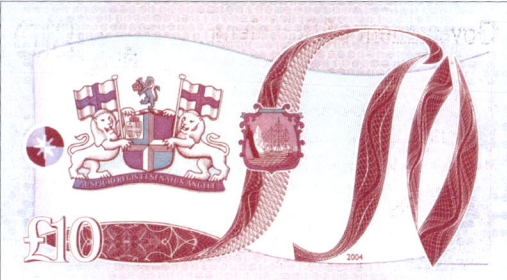

GOSH B8 (P12): **10 pounds** (US$17)   VG   VF   UNC
Red. Front: Five sailing ships anchored in Jamestown harbor; Queen Elizabeth II. Back: Coat of arms of the East India Company with lions, flags, shield, and Latin text on banner; St. Helena crest with sailing ship. Solid security thread. Watermark: None. Printer: (TDLR). 135 x 70 mm.

☐	a.	2004. Signature 6. Prefix P/1.	FV	FV	30
☐	b.	2012. Signature 7. Intro: May 2014.	FV	FV	30
☐	as.	Diagonal red *SPECIMEN* ovpt (300 produced).	—	—	120
☐	bs.	Diagonal red *SPECIMEN* overprint.	—	—	40

GOSH B9 (P13): **20 pounds** (US$34)   VG   VF   UNC
Brown. Front: Three sail boats in Jamestown harbor; Queen Elizabeth II. Back: Coat of arms of the East India Company with lions, flags, shield, and Latin text on banner; St. Helena crest with sailing ship. Solid security thread. Watermark: None. Printer: (TDLR). 135 x 70 mm.

☐	a.	2004. Signature 6. Prefix A/1.	FV	FV	45
☐	b.	2012. Signature 7. Intro: May 2014.	FV	FV	55
☐	as.	Diagonal red *SPECIMEN* ovpt (300 produced).	—	—	150
☐	bs.	Diagonal red *SPECIMEN* overprint.	—	—	55

Buying Notes

The Saint Helena Currency Fund sells banknotes at face value plus 10% commission and postage. For more information, visit www.sthelenacurrency.gov.sh.

Acknowledgements

This chapter was compiled with the generous assistance of David Burns, David F. Cieniewicz (www.banknotestore.com), Mark Irwin, Lawrence W. Keefe, Wally Myers, Mikhail "Mike" Prizov, TDS, Frank van Tiel, and others.

Sources

Bank of St. Helena (www.sainthelenabank.com).
Boon, K. N. *World Paper & Polymer Uncut Banknotes.* 1st edition. 2012. ISBN 978-983-43313-4-4. Trigometric Sdn.Bhd. (www.3833.com), Lot 327, Amcorp Mall, 18 Jalan Persiaran Barat, off Jalan Timur, Petaling Jaya, 46050 Selangor D.E., Malaysia.
Cuhaj, George S. *Standard Catalog of World Paper Money, General Issues, 1368-1960.* 14th edition. 2012. ISBN 978-1-4402-3090-5. Krause Publications (www.krausebooks.com), 700 East State St., Iola, WI, 54990-0001.
Cuhaj, George S. *Standard Catalog of World Paper Money, Modern Issues, 1961-Present.* 17th edition. 2011. ISBN 978-1-4402-1584-1. Krause Publications (www.krausebooks.com), 700 East State St., Iola, WI, 54990-0001.
Eu, Peter and Ben Chiew. *Queen Elizabeth II.* 1st edition. 2006. ISBN 983-43038-1-5. Eureka Metro, P. O. Box 30, Jalan Kelang Lama, Kuala Lumpur, 57000, Malaysia.
Hanke, Steve and Matt Sekerke. "St Helena's forgotten currency board." *Central Banking Journal.* Volume XIII Number 3. February 2003.
Kemp, Brian. "Notes of St. Helena." *IBNS Journal.* Volume 14 Number 3. p.121.
Remick, Jerry. "New Issue for St. Helena." *IBNS Journal.* Volume 17 Number 2. p.96.
Remick, Jerry. "St. Helena's 'Anglae' Errors." *IBNS Journal.* Volume 19 Number 1. p.15.
Rogers, Dr. David. "Island of St. Helena." *IBNS Journal.* Volume 15 Number 3. p.140.
Symes, Peter. "The Portraits of Queen Elizabeth II on World Bank Notes." *IBNS Journal.* Volume 44 Number 2. p.8.

Share Your Input, Info, and Images

This catalog is believed to be complete and correct as of the time of publication. Prices and face values were last updated 21 July 2014. Please report errors or omissions so that corrections may be made. If you can more precisely identify the name or location of anything depicted on a note, please share that information. Furthermore, if you own an unlisted type or variety, please submit scans of the front and back of the note so that it can be documented. Scans should be 300 dots per inch, 100% actual size, 24-bit color, saved as *uncompressed* JPEG files, and sent to owen@banknotenews.com. Be sure to fully describe all attributes of the note which are not apparent upon visual inspection of the images alone, such as physical dimension, watermark, and security thread.

Saint Lucia

Monetary System
1 Saint Lucia pound = 20 shillings

The Government of St. Lucia

From 1851, the British pound circulated in Saint Lucia, replacing the Saint Lucia livre. Sometime after 1882, private banknotes, denominated in dollars, began to be issued on the island. From 1920, some of these notes also bore the value in sterling, with 1 dollar = 4 shillings 2 pence. During this period, no subdivision of the dollar was issued and British coins continued to circulate.

The Government of Saint Lucia issued only two denominations of sterling notes in 1920.

GSL Signature Varieties

	Administrator	Colonial Treasurer
1	Wilfred Bennett Davidson-Houston	George Douglas Mackie

1920 Issues

The English translation of the Latin motto in the coat of arms on the back of these notes is "A Safe Harbor for Ships."

GSL B1 (P1): 5 shillings   Good   Fine   XF
Violet, green, and blue. Front: King George V. Back: Guilloche patterns; coat of arms with flag, pennant, mountainous islands, and banner with motto *SATIO HAUD MALEFIDA CARINIS*. No security thread. Watermark: Geometric pattern. Printer: *THOS. DE LA RUE & C⁰ LTD LONDON*. 140 x 78 mm.
- ☐ a. 1st October 1920. Signature 1.   —   —   —
- ☐ as. Horizontal *CANCELLED* perforation;   —   —   —
horizontal purple *SPECIMEN* ovpt at lower right.

GSL B2 (P2): 10 shillings   Good   Fine   XF
Green, gray, and brown. Front: King George V. Back: Guilloche patterns; coat of arms with flag, pennant, mountainous islands, and banner with motto *SATIO HAUD MALEFIDA CARINIS*. No security thread. Watermark: Geometric pattern. Printer: *THOS. DE LA RUE & C⁰ LTD LONDON*. 140 x 78 mm.
- ☐ a. 1st October 1920. Signature 1.   —   —   —
- ☐ as. Horizontal *CANCELLED* perforation;   —   —   —
horizontal purple *SPECIMEN* ovpt at lower right.

Looking Forward

Three private banks—Barclays Bank, Colonial Bank, and Royal Bank of Canada—issued notes in Saint Lucia, some as late as 1940. For later government issues, see British Caribbean Territories (1950-1964) and East Caribbean States (1965-present).

Acknowledgements

This chapter was compiled with the generous assistance of Arthur Gearing (De La Rue), Andrew Pattison (Spink), and others.

Sources

Cuhaj, George S. *Standard Catalog of World Paper Money, General Issues, 1368-1960*. 14th edition. 2012. ISBN 978-1-4402-3090-5. Krause Publications (www.krausebooks.com), 700 East State St., Iola, WI, 54990-0001.

Share Your Input, Info, and Images

This catalog is believed to be complete and correct as of the time of publication. Prices and face values were last updated 5 July 2013. Please report errors or omissions so that corrections may be made. If you can more precisely identify the name or location of anything depicted on a note, please share that information. Furthermore, if you own an unlisted type or variety, please submit scans of the front and back of the note so that it can be documented. Scans should be 300 dots per inch, 100% actual size, 24-bit color, saved as *uncompressed* JPEG files, and sent to owen@banknotenews.com. Be sure to fully describe all attributes of the note which are not apparent upon visual inspection of the images alone, such as physical dimension, watermark, and security thread.

Samoa

For earlier issues, see Western Samoa.

Monetary System
1967: 1 Samoan tala (WST) = 100 sene

Central Bank of Samoa

Before independence from New Zealand on 1 January 1962, Samoa used British currency issued by the Bank of New Zealand. After independence, currency was initially issued by the Bank of Western Samoa, but that function was taken over by the Monetary Board of Western Samoa in early 1975, and in turn, the Central Bank of Samoa (CBS), which was established in 1984 and headed by W. E. Davies.

For more information, visit www.cbs.gov.ws.

CBS Signature Varieties

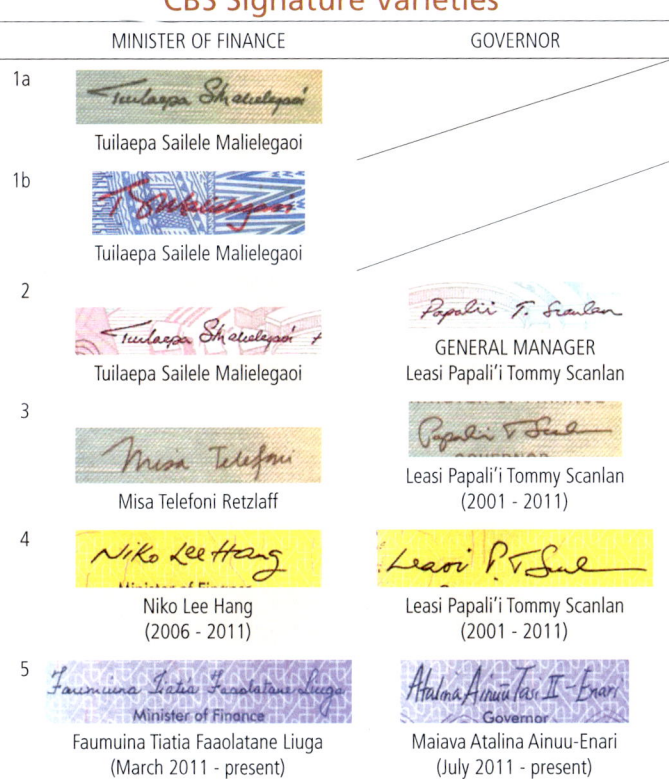

1985-1990 Issues

These notes are like the preceding issue from the Monetary Board of Western Samoa, but with the new issuer's name of the Central Bank of Samoa, in both Samoan and English. The 50- and 100-tala notes are new denominations, and the 1-tala note was discontinued.

CBS B1 (P25): **2 tālā** (demonetized)   VG   VF   UNC
Blue and violet. Front: Flag; sea; mountains; man carving wood. Back: Palm trees; straw hut; sea shore; coat of arms; flag. Solid security thread. Watermark: Malietoa Tanumafili II. Printer: (TDLR). 142 x 72 mm.
- a. No date. Signature 1a. Prefix B - C. Intro: 1985.   —   —   6
- as. Diagonal red *SPECIMEN* overprint.   —   —   60

CBS B2 (P26): **5 tālā** (US$2.15)   VG   VF   UNC
Red. Front: Flag; sea; mountains; boy with pencil writing in workbook. Back: Harbor; coat of arms; flag. Solid security thread. Watermark: Malietoa Tanumafili II. Printer: (TDLR). 142 x 72 mm.
- a. No date. Signature 1a. Prefix A - C. Intro: 1985.   —   —   9
- as. Diagonal red *SPECIMEN* overprint.   —   —   18

CBS B3 (P27): **10 tālā** (US$4.35) VG VF UNC

Brown. Front: Flag; sea; mountains; man harvesting bananas. Back: Palm trees; seashore; coat of arms; flag. Solid security thread. Watermark: Malietoa Tanumafili II. Printer: (TDLR). 142 x 72 mm.

    ☐ a. No date. Signature 1a. Prefix A - C. Intro: 1985. — — 15
    ☐ as. Diagonal red *SPECIMEN* overprint. — — 30

CBS B4 (P28): **20 tālā** (US$8.65) VG VF UNC

Brown and orange. Front: Flag; sea; mountains; man casting fishing net at beach. Back: domed building; coat of arms; flag. Solid security thread. Watermark: Malietoa Tanumafili II. Printer: (TDLR). 142 x 72 mm.

    ☐ a. No date. Signature 1a. Prefix A - B. Intro: 1985. — — 40
    ☐ as. Diagonal red *SPECIMEN* overprint. — — 25

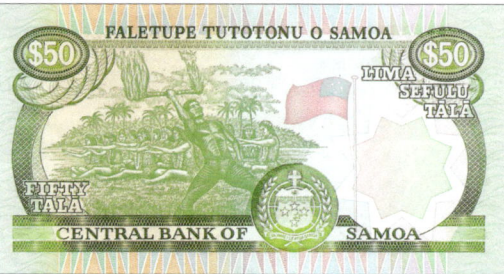

CBS B5 (P29): **50 tālā** (US$22) VG VF UNC

Green. Front: Flag; Robert Louis Stevenson's former house (current residence of head of state) in Vailima; Malietoa Tanumafili II; kava bowl. Back: Man with flaming torch performing Siva Afi (fire dance); female Samoan dance group. Solid security thread. Watermark: Malietoa Tanumafili II. Printer: (TDLR). 142 x 72 mm.

    ☐ a. No date. Signature 2. Prefix A. Intro: 1990. — — 50
    ☐ as. Diagonal red *SPECIMEN* overprint. — — 100

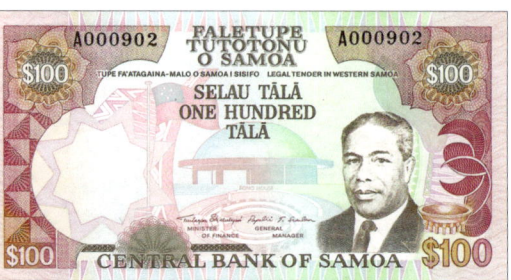

CBS B6 (P30): **100 tālā** (US$43) VG VF UNC

Olive brown and lilac brown. Front: Flag; domed building (Fono House; parliament house) in Apia; Malietoa Tanumafili II; kava bowl. Back: Three workers harvesting cocoa in field; coat of arms; flag. Solid security thread. Watermark: Malietoa Tanumafili II. Printer: (TDLR). 142 x 72 mm.

    ☐ a. No date. Signature 2. Prefix A. Intro: 1990. — — 50
    ☐ as. Diagonal red *SPECIMEN* overprint. — — 100

1991 Commemorative Issues

This 2-tala note was issued to commemorate the Golden Jubilee (50th anniversary) of Malietoa Tanumafili II as head of state. It is the first polymer note issued by Samoa. The ink on the initial intaglio printing (prefix AAA and AAB, the latter used only on uncut sheets of four notes) rubbed off too easily, so the subsequent printings (prefix AAC and AAD) used offset technology before reverting to intaglio (prefix AAE-AAJ). The different prefix ranges have subtly different color schemes.

1991 Numismatic Products

CBS BNP1 (PNL): **2 tala** UNC
- a. CBS B7a in folder. 6

CBS B7 (P31): **2 tala** (US$0.85)   VG VF UNC

Brown, blue, and purple. Front: Village with Straw huts, Mulivai Catholic Cathedral in Apia, buses on Beach Road, and palm trees; Malietoa Tanumafili II; kava bowl. Back: Kava bowl; Samoan family gathered on mats in traditional Samoan fale (house); coat of arms. No security thread. Shadow image: National flag. Printer: (NPA). 140 x 70 mm. Polymer.

- a. No date. Signature 1b. Intaglio. Prefix: AAA-AAB. Intro: 29.09.1991.   — — 7.50
- b. Offset. Prefix: AAC-AAD.   — — 5
- c. Intaglio. Prefix: AAE-AAF. Intro: 1997-2001.   — — 3.50
- d. Intaglio. Prefix: AAH-AAN. Intro: 2003-2009.   — — 3.50
- as. Horizontal red serif *SPECIMEN* overprint at upper center on front; horizontal red serif *SPECIMEN No. #* overprint at lower right on back.   — — 100
- cs. Horizontal red san serif *SPECIMEN* overprint at upper center on front; horizontal red san serif *SPECIMEN No. #* overprint at lower right on back.   — — 200
- ds. Diagonal red *SPECIMEN* overprint. Prefix: AAJ only.   — — 25

The 2-tala note was intaglio and offset printed over the years, resulting in four varieties with subtly different colors in the underprinting (CBS B7a, 7b, 7c, and 7d, left to right).

2002-2005 Issues

These notes are like the preceding issues, but the legal tender notice at top front now refers to Samoa, not Western Samoa. Two signatures, windowed security threads, and Cornerstone watermarks were introduced on later issues.

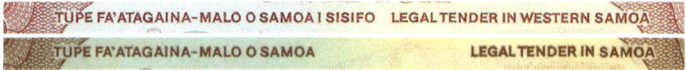

The name of the country differs in the old (top) and new (bottom) legal tender notice.

CBS B8 (P33): **5 tala** (US$2.15)   VG   VF   UNC
Red. Front: Flag; sea; mountains; boy with pencil writing in workbook. Back: Harbor; coat of arms; flag. Watermark: Malietoa Tanumafili II. Printer: (TDLR). 144 x 72 mm.

- ☐ a. No date. Intro: 2002.   —   —   5
  Signature 1a.
  Solid security thread w/o text. Prefix C.
- ☐ b. Solid security thread w/ printed *CBS*. Prefix D-E.   —   —   5
- ☐ c. Signature. 3.   —   —   5
  Windowed security thread with demetalized *CBS*.
  Watermark: Electrotype *CBS* and Cornerstones
  added. Prefix E - F. Intro: April 2005.
- ☐ cs. Diagonal red *SPECIMEN* overprint;   —   —   30
  horizontal red # overprint at lower left.

CBS B9 (P34): **10 tala** (US$4.35)   VG   VF   UNC
Brown. Front: Flag; sea; mountains; man harvesting bananas. Back: Palm trees; seashore; coat of arms; flag. Watermark: Malietoa Tanumafili II. Printer: (TDLR). 142 x 72 mm.

- ☐ a. No date. Intro: 2002.   —   —   10
  Signature 1a.
  Solid security thread w/o text. Prefix C - E.
- ☐ b. Solid security thread w/ printed *CBS*. Prefix F-G.   —   —   10
- ☐ c. Signature 3.   —   —   7
  Windowed security thread with demetalized *CBS*.
  Watermark: Electrotype *CBS* and Cornerstones
  added. Prefix H - J. Intro: April 2005.
- ☐ as. Diagonal red *SPECIMEN* overprint;   —   —   40
  horizontal red # overprint at lower left.
- ☐ cs. Diagonal red *SPECIMEN* overprint;   —   —   40
  horizontal red # overprint at lower left.

CBS B10 (P35): **20 tala** (US$8.65)   VG   VF   UNC
Orange brown. Front: Flag; sea; mountains; man casting fishing net at beach. Back: domed building (Fono House; parliament house) in Apia; coat of arms; flag. Watermark: Malietoa Tanumafili II. Printer: (TDLR). 144 x 72 mm.

- ☐ a. No date. Intro: 2002.   —   —   17
  Signature 1a.
  Solid security thread w/o text. Prefix B - C.
- ☐ b. Solid security thread w/ printed *CBS*. Prefix D-E.   —   —   17
- ☐ c. Signature 3. Windowed security thread with   —   —   15
  demetalized *CBS*. Watermark: Electrotype *CBS*
  and Cornerstones added. Intro: April 2005.
- ☐ as. Diagonal red *SPECIMEN* overprint.   —   —   35
- ☐ cs. Diagonal red *SPECIMEN* overprint;   —   —   40
  horizontal red # overprint at lower left.

2008-2012 Issues

On 1 August 2008, Samoa introduced an entirely new family of notes with bright colors and modern security features. De La Rue designed and printed 9.4 million banknotes at a cost of US$2.8 million.

CBS B11 (P36): **50 tala** (US$22) VG VF UNC
Green. Front: Flag; Robert Louis Stevenson's former house (current residence of head of state) in Vailima; Malietoa Tanumafili II; kava bowl. Back: Man with flaming torch performing Siva Afi (fire dance); female Samoan dance group; palm trees; coat of arms; flag. Windowed security thread with demetalized *CBS*. Watermark: Malietoa Tanumafili II, electrotype *CBS,* and Cornerstones. Printer: (TDLR). 144 x 72 mm.
- a. No date. Sig. 3. Prefix B - C. Intro: April 2005. — — 40
- as. Diagonal red *SPECIMEN* overprint; horizontal red # overprint at lower left. — — 40

CBS B12 (P37): **100 tala** (US$43) VG VF UNC
Olive brown and lilac brown. Front: Flag; domed building (Fono House; parliament house) in Apia; Malietoa Tanumafili II; kava bowl. Back: Three workers harvesting cocoa in field; coat of arms; flag. Windowed security thread with demetalized *CBS*. Watermark: Malietoa Tanumafili II, electrotype *CBS,* and Cornerstones. Printer: (TDLR). 142 x 72 mm.
- a. No date. Signature 3. Prefix B. Intro: April 2005. — — 75
- as. Diagonal red *SPECIMEN* overprint; horizontal red # overprint at lower left. — — 50

CBS B13 (P38): **5 tala** (US$2.15) VG VF UNC
Red. Front: Beach. Back: Robert Louis Stevenson's former house (current residence of head of state) in Vailima; coat of arms. Windowed security thread with demetalized *CBS*. Watermark: Malietoa Tanumafili II, electrotype *CBS,* and Cornerstones. Printer: (TDLR). 139 x 71 mm.
- a. No date. Signature 4. Prefix TK. Intro: 01.08.2008. — — 4
- b. Signature 5. Intro: 2012. — — 4
- as. Diagonal red *SPECIMEN* overprint; horizontal red # overprint at lower left. — — 20

Replacement notes: Prefix ZZ.

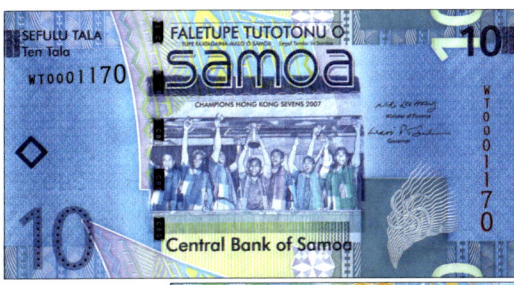
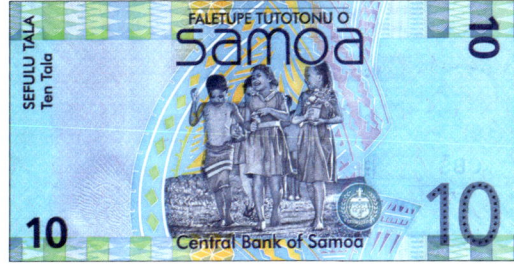

CBS B14 (P39): **10 tala** (US$4.35) VG VF UNC
Blue. Front: Rugby team being crowned champions at the IRB Hong Kong Sevens in 2007. Back: Samoan school children on their way to school; coat of arms. Windowed security thread with demetalized *CBS*. Watermark: Malietoa Tanumafili II, electrotype *CBS,* and Cornerstones. Printer: (TDLR). 139 x 71 mm.
- a. No date. Signature 4. Prefix WT. Intro: 01.08.2008. — — 9
- as. Diagonal red *SPECIMEN* overprint; horizontal red # overprint at lower left. — — 25

Replacement notes: Prefix ZZ.

SAMOA 2008-2012 ISSUES

CBS B15 (P40): **20 tala** (US$8.65)   VG VF UNC

Yellow. Front: Cascading waterfall. Back: Manumea (national bird) and Teuila (national flower); coat of arms. Windowed security thread with demetalized *CBS*. Watermark: Malietoa Tanumafili II, electrotype *CBS* plus Cornerstones. Printer: (TDLR). 139 x 71 mm.

- ☐ a. No date.   —   —   13
  Signature 4. Prefix KT. Intro: 01.08.2008.
- ☐ b. Signature 5. Intro: 2012.   —   —   15
- ☐ as. Diagonal red *SPECIMEN* overprint;   —   —   30
  horizontal red # overprint at lower left.

Replacement notes: Prefix ZZ.

This note was honored as the IBNS Bank Note of the Year 2008.

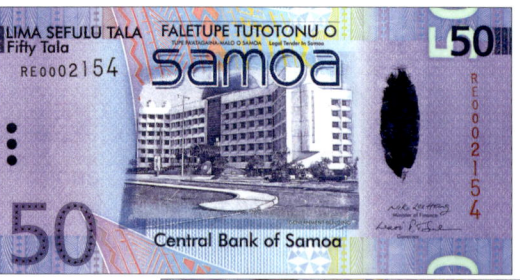

CBS B16 (P41): **50 tala** (US$22)   VG VF UNC

Purple. Front: Government building at Matagialalua. Back: Central Bank of Samoa building; coat of arms. Optiks security thread. Watermark: Malietoa Tanumafili II, electrotype *CBS*. Printer: (TDLR). 139 x 71 mm.

- ☐ a. No date. Signature 4. Prefix RE. Intro: 01.08.2008.   —   —   30
- ☐ as. Diagonal red *SPECIMEN* overprint;   —   —   35
  horizontal red # overprint at lower left.

Replacement notes: Prefix ZZ.

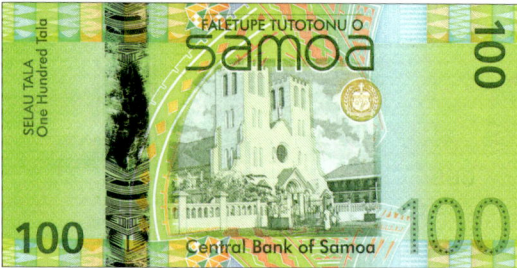

CBS B17 (P42): **100 tala** (US$43)   VG VF UNC

Green. Front: Malietoa Tanumafili II. Back: Mulivai Catholic Cathedral; coat of arms. Optiks security thread. Watermark: Malietoa Tanumafili II, electrotype *CBS*. Printer: (TDLR). 139 x 71 mm.

- ☐ a. No date. Signature 4. Prefix JD. Intro: 01.08.2008.   —   —   70
- ☐ as. Diagonal red *SPECIMEN* overprint;   —   —   40
  horizontal red # overprint at lower left.

Replacement notes: Prefix ZZ.

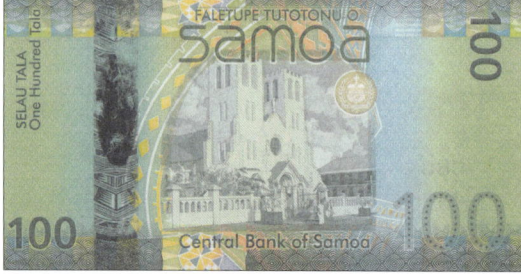

CBS B19 (PNL): **100 tala** (US$43)   VG VF UNC

Green. Front: Malietoa Tanumafili II. Back: Mulivai Catholic Cathedral; coat of arms. Optiks security thread. Watermark: Malietoa Tanumafili II, electrotype *CBS*. Printer: (TDLR). 139 x 71 mm.

- ☐ a. No date. Signature 5. Prefix JD. Intro: 2012.   —   —   35

Like preceding issues, but new signatures and new decorative pattern overprinted on the designs at top and bottom borders on front and back.

2008 Numismatic Products

CBS BNP2 (PNL): **5 - 100 tala** UNC
   ☐ a.   CBS B13as - B17as (5 notes) in folder. —

2012 Commemorative Issues

The Central Bank of Samoa issued two commemorative collectible coins and a limited edition 50-tala banknote for circulation to mark Samoa's 50th Independence Day on 1 June 2012. This note is like the preceding issues, but with *50th ANNIVERSARY OF INDEPENDENCE* below the country's name at upper center on front, darker geometric patterns along the top and bottom edges on both sides, and a new signature combination.

CBS B18 (PNL): **50 tala** (US$22) VG VF UNC
Purple. Front: Government building at Matagialalua; *50th ANNIVERSARY OF INDEPENDENCE*. Back: Central Bank of Samoa building; coat of arms. Optiks security thread. Watermark: Malietoa Tanumafili II, electrotype *CBS*. Printer: (TDLR). 139 x 71 mm.
   ☐ a.   No date. Signature 5. Prefix RE. Intro: 01.06.2012.   —   —   75

Looking Forward

According to a Radio New Zealand International post on 5 April 2011, the Central Bank of Samoa plans to replace the 2-tala (CBS B7) note with a coin, and also plans to reduce the size of its coins in an effort to save money in the face of rising commodities prices.

Buying Notes

The bank sells banknotes at face value plus 10% commission and postage. For more information, visit www.cbs.gov.ws.

Acknowledgements

This chapter was compiled with the generous assistance of Nin Cheun (http://stores.ebay.com/Noteshobby), John Eccles, Jean-Michel Engels, David Hull, Kai Hwong, Mark Irwin, Thomas Krause (www.polymernotes.de), Claudio Marana, Wally Myers, Leszek Porowski, Bill Stubkjaer, Yuri Wierda, Tristan Williams, Aidan Work, and others.

Sources

Boon, K. N. *World Paper & Polymer Uncut Banknotes*. 1st edition. 2012. ISBN 978-983-43313-4-4. Trigometric Sdn.Bhd. (www.3833.com), Lot 327, Amcorp Mall, 18 Jalan Persiaran Barat, off Jalan Timur, Petaling Jaya, 46050 Selangor D.E., Malaysia.

Central Bank of Samoa. *Annual Reports*. 1999-2008.

Cuhaj, George S. *Standard Catalog of World Paper Money, Modern Issues, 1961-Present*. 17th edition. 2011. ISBN 978-1-4402-1584-1. Krause Publications (www.krausebooks.com), 700 East State St., Iola, WI, 54990-0001.

Eu, Peter, Ben Chiew, and Stane Straus. *World Polymer Banknotes: A Standard Reference*. 2nd edition. 2006. ISBN 983-43038-2-3. Eureka Metro, P. O. Box 30, Jalan Kelang Lama, Kuala Lumpur, 57000, Malaysia.

Krause, Thomas and Peter Bauer. *Specialized Catalogue of World Plastic Money*. 5th edition. 2009. www.polymernotes.de.

Krause, Thomas. "Samoan prefixes correspond to date issued." *IBNS Journal*. Volume 47 Number 2. p.4.

Schuler, Kurt. http://users.erols.com/kurrency/ws.htm.

Wierda, Yuri. www.bestbanknotes.com.

Share Your Input, Info, and Images

This catalog is believed to be complete and correct as of the time of publication. Prices and face values were last updated 25 August 2014. Please report errors or omissions so that corrections may be made. If you can more precisely identify the name or location of anything depicted on a note, please share that information. Furthermore, if you own an unlisted type or variety, please submit scans of the front and back of the note so that it can be documented. Scans should be 300 dots per inch, 100% actual size, 24-bit color, saved as *uncompressed* JPEG files, and sent to owen@banknotenews.com. Be sure to fully describe all attributes of the note which are not apparent upon visual inspection of the images alone, such as physical dimension, watermark, and security thread.

Sao Tome and Principe

Contents

Banco Nacional de S. Tomé e Príncipe (BNSTP).... 1790
Banco Central de S. Tomé e Príncipe (BCSTP) 1795

Monetary System
1914: 1 Sao Tome and Principe escudo = 100 centavos
1977: 1 Sao Tome and Principe dobra (STD) = 100 cêntimos

The island of São Tomé was discovered by João de Santarém and Pêro Escobar on 21 December 1470, Saint Thomas Day, hence the name. São Tomé and neighboring Ilha do Príncipe were subsequently claimed as a colony by the Portuguese, who established sugar cane plantations worked by slaves.

Banco Nacional Ultramarino Issues

Prior to the establishment of the Banco Nacional de S. Tomé e Príncipe, banknotes were issued by the Banco Nacional Ultramarino. These notes will be added to this chapter in the future.

Banco Nacional de S. Tomé e Príncipe (National Bank of Sao Tome and Principe)

On 21 July 1975, a year after Portugal's bloodless military coup d'état, known as the Carnation Revolution, São Tomé and Príncipe (Saint Thomas and Prince), a small Portuguese colony in the Gulf of Guinea on the West African coast, became independent. On 24 May 1976, the Banco Nacional Ultramarino (BNU) was nationalized by Decree Law Nº 16/76, and was renamed the Banco Nacional de S. Tomé e Príncipe (BNSTP).

BNSTP Signature Varieties

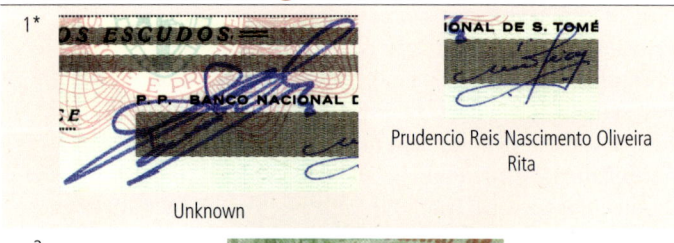

1*
Unknown — Prudencio Reis Nascimento Oliveira Rita

2

Victor Manuel Lopes Correia

BNSTP Signature Varieties

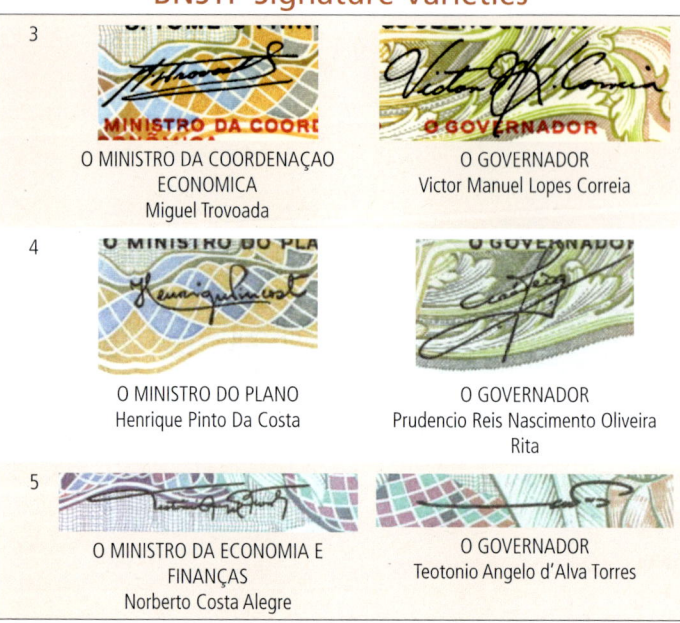

3
O MINISTRO DA COORDENAÇAO ECONOMICA — Miguel Trovoada
O GOVERNADOR — Victor Manuel Lopes Correia

4
O MINISTRO DO PLANO — Henrique Pinto Da Costa
O GOVERNADOR — Prudencio Reis Nascimento Oliveira Rita

5
O MINISTRO DA ECONOMIA E FINANÇAS — Norberto Costa Alegre
O GOVERNADOR — Teotonio Angelo d'Alva Torres

* Notes with these signatures were signed by hand, so variations are to be expected.

1976 Circulating Bearer Cheque Issues

On 21 June 1976, Decree Law Nº 115/76 authorized the Banco Nacional de S. Tomé e Príncipe to issue 15 million escudos worth of the following bearer cheques which were "compulsorily acceptable just as notes for payments of any expenses." The bearer cheques were intended to be used for six weeks, after which time they could be exchanged for banknotes. After three months, the bank began withdrawing the bearer cheques, and they ceased to circulate just six months after introduction.

BNSTP B1 (P50): **500 escudos** (demonetized 21.12.1976)   VG   VF   UNC
Pink on bluish-green. Uniface: Guilloche pattern with bank logo at center; black text. No security thread. Watermark: None. Printer: (Lisbon State Mint). 168 x 75 mm.
☐ a. 21 de Junho de 1976. Signature 1. Unissued.   —   30   85

BNSTP B2 (P51): **1,000 escudos** (demonetized 21.12.1976)   VG   VF   UNC
Pink on bluish-green. Uniface: Guilloche pattern with bank logo at center; red text. No security thread. Watermark: None. Printer: (Lisbon State Mint). 168 x 75 mm.
☐ a. 21 de Junho de 1976. Signature 1.   —   35   100

1976 Provisional Issues

On 15 July 1976, Decree Law Nº 23/76 authorized the overprinting of Banco National Ultramarino notes and created a new national monetary unit, the dobra, to be effective within one year. The red overprint on both the front and back consists of the new bank's logo at left, two lines of text (*BANCO NACIONAL DE S. TOMÉ E PRÍNCIPE / S. Tomé, 1 de Junho de 1976*), and the signature of the bank's governor, Victor Manuel Lopes Correia.

The original BNU notes all come with Francisco J. Vieira Machado signing as BNU's governor at right, and one of seven BNU administrator signatures at left. It is unclear if all seven possible signature combinations exist for each denomination in the original issues. However, some overprinted notes have been confirmed with different original signature varieties on the same denomination.

BNSTP B4 (P45): **50 escudos** (withdrawn 30.09.1977)   VG   VF   UNC
Black, red, green, orange, and blue. Front: BNU seal with sailing ship; Portuguese coat of arms; King Dom Afonso V; red overprint. Back: Woman looking at variety of ancient boats, sailing ships, and modern ocean liner; red overprint. No security thread. Watermark: None. Printer: *BRADBURY, WILKINSON & C⁰ L™ GRAVADORES, NEW MALDEN, SURREY, INGLATERRA*. 157 x 82 mm.
- a. 1 de Junho de 1976. Signature 2 in overprint.   —   10   60
  Confirmed with original Administrator signatures:
  Fernandes, Coutinho.

Overprinted on P37 originally dated 20 de NOVEMBRO de 1958.

BNSTP B3 (P44): **20 escudos** (withdrawn 30.09.1977)   VG   VF   UNC
Brown, orange, red, and green. Front: BNU seal with sailing ship; Portuguese coat of arms; King Dom Afonso V; red overprint. Back: Woman looking at variety of ancient boats, sailing ships, and modern ocean liner; red overprint. No security thread. Watermark: None. Printer: *BRADBURY, WILKINSON & C⁰ L™ GRAVADORES, NEW MALDEN, SURREY, INGLATERRA*. 150 x 80 mm.
- a. 1 de Junho de 1976. Signature 2 in overprint.   —   10   25
  Confirmed with original Administrator signature:
  Fernandes.

Overprinted on P36 originally dated 20 de NOVEMBRO de 1958.

BNSTP B5 (P46): **100 escudos** (withdrawn 30.09.1977)   VG   VF   UNC
Violet, orange, and green. Front: BNU seal with sailing ship; Portuguese coat of arms; King Dom Afonso V; red overprint. Back: Woman looking at variety of ancient boats, sailing ships, and modern ocean liner; red overprint. No security thread. Watermark: None. Printer: *BRADBURY, WILKINSON & C⁰ L™ GRAVADORES, NEW MALDEN, SURREY, INGLATERRA*. 162 x 86 mm.
- a. 1 de Junho de 1976. Signature 2 in overprint.   —   60   100
  Confirmed with original Administrator signatures:
  Fernandes, Coutino, Real.

Overprinted on P38 originally dated 20 de NOVEMBRO de 1958.

SAO TOME AND PRINCIPE 1977 DOBRA ISSUES

1977 Dobra Issues

On 30 September 1977, all BNU overprinted escudo notes were withdrawn and replaced by the following dobra-denominated notes at par, issued by the authorization of *Decreto - Lei Nº 50/76*. The name of the new currency came from the dobra, a Portuguese coin known as a doubloon.

All of these notes feature a portrait of Rei Amador (King Amador) by local artist Protásio Pina (1960-1999). Starting 9 July 1595, Amador led a bloody, unsuccessful slave revolt against the Portuguese colonists, who arrested and hanged Amador on 14 August. He became an emblematic figure of the islanders, and over the centuries a legend arose that Amador was the king of the Angolares (descendants of Angolan slaves) people. Though the myth is unsubstantiated by historical sources, in 2004 the STP General Assembly declared the 4th of January King Amador Day, which is celebrated as a national holiday.

BNSTP B6 (P47): **500 escudos** (withdrawn 30.09.1977)   VG   VF   UNC
Blue, green, and orange. Front: BNU seal with sailing ship; Portuguese coat of arms; King Dom Afonso V; red overprint. Back: Woman looking at variety of ancient boats, sailing ships, and modern ocean liner; Portuguese coat of arms; red overprint. No security thread. Watermark: None. Printer: *BRADBURY, WILKINSON & Cº L^TD GRAVADORES, NEW MALDEN, SURREY, INGLATERRA*. 165 x 86 mm.

☐ a. 1 de Junho de 1976. Signature 2 in overprint.   —   75   200
       Confirmed with original Administrator signatures:
       de Sá, Fernandes, Coutinho.
Overprinted on P39 originally dated 18 de ABRIL de 1956.

BNSTP B8 (P52): **50 dobras** (<US$0.01)   VG   VF   UNC
Red. Front: Coat of arms; African grey parrot (Psittacus erithacus) bird; Rei Amador. Back: Men with fishing nets in small sail boats in harbor; palm trees; Pico Cão Grande (Great Dog Peak) on São Tomé in Obo National Park. Solid security thread. Watermark: Rei Amador. Printer: *BRADBURY, WILKINSON & Cº L^D NEW MALDEN, SURREY, ENGLAND*. 138 x 68 mm.

☐ a.   12 de JULHO de 1977. Signature 3.   0.50   2   8
        Issued: 30.09.1977.
☐ as. Diagonal black *SPECIMEN* overprint;   —   —   180
        horizontal red *SPECIMEN OF NO VALUE*
        overprint at upper left; punched.
☐ p.   Proof.   —   —   —

BNSTP B7 (P48): **1,000 escudos** (withdrawn 30.09.1977)   VG   VF   UNC
Green, blue, and violet. Front: BNU seal with sailing ship; explorer João de Santarém wearing cross; red overprint. Back: Woman looking at variety of ancient boats, sailing ships, and modern ocean liner; red overprint. Solid security thread. Watermark: Coat of arms. Printer: *BRADBURY, WILKINSON & Cº L^TD GRAVADORES, NEW MALDEN, SURREY, INGLATERRA*. 177 x 94 mm.

☐ a. 1 de Junho de 1976. Signature 2 in overprint.   —   120   240
       Confirmed with original Administrator signature:
       Coutinho.
Overprinted on P40 originally dated 11 de MAIO de 1964.

BNSTP B9 (P53): **100 dobras**(<US$0.01) VG VF UNC

Green. Front: Coat of arms; pink ginger lily (Etlingera elatior) flower; Rei Amador. Back: Group of men and women husking coconuts with machete and preparing food. Solid security thread. Watermark: Rei Amador. Printer: *BRADBURY, WILKINSON & C⁰ L^D NEW MALDEN, SURREY, ENGLAND*. 145 x 71 mm.

- a. 12 de JULHO de 1977. Signature 3. 1 4 12
  Issued: 30.09.1977.
- as. Diagonal red *SPECIMEN* overprint; — — 160
  horizontal red *SPECIMEN OF NO VALUE*
  overprint at upper left; punched.
- p. Proof. — — —

BNSTP B10 (P54): **500 dobras** (<US$0.05) VG VF UNC

Purple. Front: Coat of arms; green sea turtle (Chelonia mydas); Rei Amador; flowers. Back: Palm trees; Cascata da Roça Blú-Blú waterfall on São Tomé; flowers. Solid security thread. Watermark: Rei Amador. Printer: *BRADBURY, WILKINSON & C⁰ L^D NEW MALDEN, SURREY, ENGLAND*. 153 x 76 mm.

- a. 12 de JULHO de 1977. Signature 3. 3 10 25
  Issued: 30.09.1977.
- as. Diagonal red *SPECIMEN* overprint; — — 255
  horizontal red *SPECIMEN OF NO VALUE*
  overprint at upper left; punched.
- p. Proof. — — —

BNSTP B11 (P55): **1,000 dobras** (US$0.05) VG VF UNC

Blue and green. Front: Coat of arms; banana stalk; Rei Amador; flowers. Back: Praia das Sete Ondas (Beach of Seven Waves) on São Tomé; man with machete harvesting cocoa pods from tree. Solid security thread. Watermark: Rei Amador. Printer: *BRADBURY, WILKINSON & C⁰ L^D NEW MALDEN, SURREY, ENGLAND*. 162 x 79 mm.

- a. 12 de JULHO de 1977. Signature 3. 8 25 100
  Issued: 30.09.1977.
- as1. Diagonal red *SPECIMEN* overprint; — — 330
  horizontal red *SPECIMEN OF NO VALUE*
  overprint at upper left; punched.
- as2. Diagonal red *ESPÉCIMEN* overprint; punched. — — 330
- p. Proof. — — —

1982 Issues

These notes are like the preceding issues, but the authorization has changed to *Decreto - Lei N⁰ 6/82*, and the titles now appear above the new signatures, not below as had been the case.

BNSTP B12 (P56): **50 dobras** (<US$0.01) VG VF UNC

Red. Front: Coat of arms; African grey parrot (Psittacus erithacus) bird; Rei Amador. Back: Men with fishing nets in small sail boats in harbor; palm trees; Pico Cão Grande (Great Dog Peak) on São Tomé in Obo National Park. Solid security thread. Watermark: Rei Amador. Printer: *BRADBURY, WILKINSON & C⁰ L^D NEW MALDEN, SURREY, ENGLAND*. 138 x 68 mm.

- a. 30 de SETEMBRO de 1982. Signature 4. 0.50 1.50 6

BNSTP B13 (P57): **100 dobras** (<US$0.01)   VG   VF   UNC
Green. Front: Coat of arms; pink ginger lily (Etlingera elatior) flower; Rei Amador. Back: Group of men and women husking coconuts with machete and preparing food. Solid security thread. Watermark: Rei Amador. Printer: *BRADBURY, WILKINSON & C⁰ L⁰ NEW MALDEN, SURREY, ENGLAND*. 145 x 71 mm.

☐ a. 30 de SETEMBRO de 1982. Signature 4.   0.75   2.25   9

BNSTP B14 (P58): **500 dobras** (<US$0.05)   VG   VF   UNC
Purple. Front: Coat of arms; green sea turtle (Chelonia mydas); Rei Amador; flowers. Back: Palm trees; Cascata da Roça Blú-Blú waterfall on São Tomé; flowers. Solid security thread. Watermark: Rei Amador. Printer: *BRADBURY, WILKINSON & C⁰ L⁰ NEW MALDEN, SURREY, ENGLAND*. 153 x 76 mm.

☐ a. 30 de SETEMBRO de 1982. Signature 4.   1   4.25   18

BNSTP B15 (P59): **1,000 dobras** (US$0.05)   VG   VF   UNC
Blue and green. Front: Coat of arms; banana stalk; Rei Amador; flowers. Back: Praia das Sete Ondas (Beach of Seven Waves) on São Tomé; man with machete harvesting cocoa pods from tree. Solid security thread. Watermark: Rei Amador. Printer: *BRADBURY, WILKINSON & C⁰ L⁰ NEW MALDEN, SURREY, ENGLAND*. 162 x 79 mm.

☐ a. 30 de SETEMBRO de 1982. Signature 4.   2   8   26

1989 Issues

These notes are like the preceding issues, but the authorization has changed to *Decreto - Lei Nº 1/88*, the watermark area on front has changed from a basket weave pattern to one comprised of fine lines, and both the printer imprint and the signatures are new. The 50-dobra denomination has been eliminated.

BNSTP B16 (P60): **100 dobras** (<US$0.01)   VG   VF   UNC
Green. Front: Coat of arms; pink ginger lily (Etlingera elatior) flower; Rei Amador. Back: Group of men and women husking coconuts with machete and preparing food. Solid security thread with printed *BNSTP*. Watermark: Rei Amador. Printer: *THOMAS DE LA RUE AND COMPANY LIMITED*. 145 x 71 mm.

☐ a. 4 de JANEIRO de 1989. Signature 5.   0.75   1.75   6.50
☐ as. Diagonal red *SPECIMEN* overprint.   —   —   —

Banco Central de S. Tomé e Príncipe (Central Bank of Sao Tome and Principe)

In the 1980s, São Tomé and Príncipe experienced an economic crisis leading to a lack of confidence in the banking system and the currency. To carry out reforms aimed at macroeconomic stabilization, it was necessary to create a strong and independent institution capable of implementing financial policies and supervising the activities of commercial banks. Through the enactment of Decree Law Nº 8/92, the Banco Central de S. Tomé e Príncipe (BCSTP) was created on 26 August 1992.

For more information, visit www.bcstp.st.

BCSTP Signature Varieties

1	 O MINISTRO DA ECONOMIA E FINANÇAS Arlindo Afonso de Carvalho	 O GOVERNADOR Adelino Santiago Castlo David (1992 - 1994)
2	 MINISTRO DAS FINANÇAS E DE PLANEAMENTO Acácio Elba Bonfim	 GOVERNADOR DO BANCO CENTRAL Carlos Quaresma Batista de Sousa (1995 - 1999)
3	 MINISTRO DAS FINANÇAS E DE PLANEAMENTO Eugénio Lourenço Soares	 GOVERNADORA DO BANCO CENTRAL Maria do Carmo Trovoada Pires de Carvalho Silveira (1999 - 2006)
4	 MINISTRO DO PLANEAMENTO E FINANÇAS Adelino Santiago Castelo David	 GOVERNADORA DO BANCO CENTRAL Maria do Carmo Trovoada Pires de Carvalho Silveira (1999 - 2006)
*		Governor Arlindo Afonso de Carvalho (2006 - 2008)
5	 MINISTRO DAS FINANÇAS E COOPERAÇAO INTERNACIONAL Americo de Oliveira dos Ramos	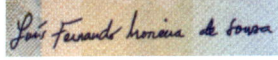 GOVERNADOR DO BANCO CENTRAL Luis Fernando Moreira de Sousa (19.04.2008 - 04.03.2011)
*		Governor Maria do Carmo Trovoada Pires de Carvalho Silveira (04.03.2011 - present)

* This official is not known to have signed any notes.

BNSTP B17 (P61): **500 dobras** (<US$0.05)   VG   VF   UNC

Purple. Front: Coat of arms; green sea turtle (Chelonia mydas); Rei Amador; flowers. Back: Palm trees; Cascata da Roça Blú-Blú waterfall on São Tomé; flowers. Solid security thread with printed *BNSTP*. Watermark: Rei Amador. Printer: *THOMAS DE LA RUE AND COMPANY LIMITED*. 153 x 76 mm.

    ☐ a. 4 de JANEIRO de 1989. Signature 5.   0.50   1.25   5
    ☐ as. Diagonal red *SPECIMEN* overprint.   —   —   —

BNSTP B18 (P62): **1,000 dobras** (US$0.05)   VG   VF   UNC

Blue and green. Front: Coat of arms; banana stalk; Rei Amador; flowers. Back: Praia das Sete Ondas (Beach of Seven Waves) on São Tomé; man with machete harvesting cocoa pods from tree. Solid security thread with printed *BNSTP*. Watermark: Rei Amador. Printer: *THOMAS DE LA RUE AND COMPANY LIMITED*. 162 x 79 mm.

    ☐ a. 4 de JANEIRO de 1989. Signature 5.   0.50   2   8
    ☐ as. Diagonal red *SPECIMEN* overprint.   —   —   —

1993 Issues

The designs of these two notes are like the preceding issues, but the issuer's name has changed, the authorization has changed to *Decreto - Lei Nº 29/93*, the signatures are new, the colorful design is full bleed, and the novel serial numbers are new. The 100-dobra denomination has been eliminated.

BCSTP B1 (P63): **500 dobras** (<US$0.05)   VG   VF   UNC
Purple. Front: Coat of arms; green sea turtle (Chelonia mydas); Rei Amador; flowers. Back: Palm trees; Cascata da Roça Blú-Blú waterfall on São Tomé; flowers. Solid security thread with printed *BCSTP*. Watermark: Rei Amador. Printer: *THOMAS DE LA RUE AND COMPANY LIMITED*. 153 x 76 mm.
   ☐ a.   26 de AGOSTO de 1993. Signature 1.   FV   FV   5

BCSTP B2 (P64): **1,000 dobras** (US$0.05)   VG   VF   UNC
Blue and green. Front: Coat of arms; banana stalk; Rei Amador; flowers. Back: Praia das Sete Ondas (Beach of Seven Waves) on São Tomé; man with machete harvesting cocoa pods from tree. Solid security thread with printed *BCSTP*. Watermark: Rei Amador. Printer: *THOMAS DE LA RUE AND COMPANY LIMITED*. 162 x 79 mm.
   ☐ a.   26 de AGOSTO de 1993. Signature 1.   FV   FV   10

1996-2010 Issues

These colorful notes feature all new designs and new authorization decree law numbers. The 500- and 1,000-dobra denominations have been eliminated.

BCSTP B3 (P65): **5,000 dobras** (US$0.25)   VG   VF   UNC
Purple, green, and orange. Front: Papa figo bird; coat of arms; Rei Amador. Back: Agostinho Neto plantation hospital and bridge. Watermark: Rei Amador. Printer: *THOMAS DE LA RUE LIMITED*. 131 x 67 mm.
   ☐ a.   22 de OUTUBRO de 1996. Signature 2.   FV   FV   4
         Decreto - Lei Nº 42/96.
         One solid thread with demetalized *BCSTP*.
   ☐ b.   Two threads, one with demetalized *BCSTP*.   FV   FV   4
   ☐ c.   26 de AGOSTO de 2004. Signature 3.   FV   FV   4
         Decreto - Lei Nº 10/04.
   ☐ as.   Diagonal red *ESPÉCIME* overprint;   —   —   75
         horizontal red # overprint at lower left.
   ☐ cs.   Diagonal red *ESPÉCIME* overprint;   —   —   75
         horizontal red # overprint at lower left.
Replacement notes: Prefix ZZ.

BCSTP B4 (P66): **10,000 dobras** (US$0.50) VG VF UNC

Green, blue, and purple. Front: Ossobo bird; coat of arms; Rei Amador. Back: Palm trees; Papagaio river bridge in San Antonio; Pico Papagaio (Parrot Peak) on Príncipe. Watermark: Rei Amador. Printer: *THOMAS DE LA RUE LIMITED*. 137 x 67 mm.

☐ a.	22 de OUTUBRO de 1996. Signature 2. *Decreto - Lei Nº 42/96.* One solid thread with demetalized *BCSTP*.	FV	FV	9
☐ b.	Two threads, one with demetalized *BCSTP*.	FV	FV	9
☐ c.	26 de AGOSTO de 2004. Signature 3. *Decreto - Lei Nº 10/04.*	FV	FV	7
☐ as.	Diagonal red *ESPÉCIME* overprint; horizontal red # overprint at lower left.	—	—	75
☐ cs.	Diagonal red *ESPÉCIME* overprint; horizontal red # overprint at lower left.	—	—	75

Replacement notes: Prefix ZZ.

BCSTP B5 (P67): **20,000 dobras** (US$1) VG VF UNC

Red and green. Front: Berries; camussela bird; coat of arms; Rei Amador. Back: City of Santo António; palm trees; beach; buildings along esplanade. Watermark: Rei Amador. Printer: *THOMAS DE LA RUE LIMITED*. 143 x 67 mm.

☐ a.	22 de OUTUBRO de 1996. Signature 2. *Decreto - Lei Nº 42/96.* One solid thread with demetalized *BCSTP*.	FV	FV	15
☐ b.	Two threads, one with demetalized *BCSTP*.	FV	FV	15
☐ c.	26 de AGOSTO de 2004. Signature 3. *Decreto - Lei Nº 10/04.*	FV	FV	13
☐ d.	10 de Dezembro de 2010. Signature 5. *Decreto - Lei No. 12/10.*	FV	FV	13
☐ as.	Diagonal red *ESPÉCIME* overprint; horizontal red # overprint at lower left.	—	—	75
☐ cs.	Diagonal red *ESPÉCIME* overprint; horizontal red # overprint at lower left.	—	—	75

Replacement notes: Prefix ZZ.

BCSTP B6 (P68): **50,000 dobras** (US$2.65) VG VF UNC

Brown, violet, and yellow. Front: Conobia bird; coat of arms; Rei Amador. Back: Banco Central de S. Tome e Príncipe headquarters building. Watermark: Rei Amador. Printer: *THOMAS DE LA RUE LIMITED*. 150 x 67 mm.

☐ a.	22 de OUTUBRO de 1996. Signature 2. *Decreto - Lei Nº 42/96.* One solid thread with demetalized *BCSTP*.	FV	FV	35
☐ b.	Two threads, one with demetalized *BCSTP*.	FV	FV	35
☐ c.	26 de AGOSTO de 2004. Signature 3. *Decreto - Lei Nº 10/04.*	FV	FV	25
☐ d.	10 de Dezembro de 2010. Signature 5. *Decreto - Lei No. 12/10.*	FV	FV	25
☐ as.	Diagonal red *ESPÉCIME* overprint; horizontal red # overprint at lower left.	—	—	75
☐ cs.	Diagonal red *ESPÉCIME* overprint; horizontal red # overprint at lower left.	—	—	75

Replacement notes: Prefix ZZ.

BCSTP B7 (P69): **100,000 dobras** (US$5.30) VG VF UNC

Light blue, green, and dark red. Front: Lines from poem "In Coração em África" (Courage in Africa); Papagaio cinza (gray parrot); leaves; coat of arms; compass rose; poet Francisco José Tenreiro; silver foil open book. Back: Men in costumes with shields standing before monument, celebrating Auto de Floripes in the city of Santo António on the island of Príncipe. Two solid security threads, one with demetalized *BCSTP*. Watermark: Rei Amador. Printer: *DE LA RUE*. 150 x 67 mm.

☐ a.	03 de Junho de 2005. Sig. 4. Intro: 22.12.2008. *Decreto - Lei No. 02/05.*	FV	FV	40
☐ b.	10 de Dezembro de 2010. Signature 5. *Decreto - Lei No. 12/10.*	FV	FV	40
☐ as.	Diagonal red *ESPÉCIME* overprint; horizontal red # overprint at lower left.	—	—	145

Replacement notes: Prefix ZZ.

Acknowledgements

This chapter was compiled with the generous assistance of Thomas Augustsson, Aleksey Avdeev, David F. Cieniewicz (www.banknotestore.com), Compagnie Generale De Bourse (www.cgb.fr), Arthur Gearing (De La Rue), Ian Herford, Heritage Auctions (HA.com), João Loureiro, José Fabrício Macêdo, Robert Mol, David Murcek (www.themonetaryunit.com), Wally Myers, Mikhail "Mike" Prizov, Manuel Pires Horta Rosa, Bill Stubkjaer, Christoph Thomas, António Trigueiros, Tristan Williams, and others.

Sources

Cuhaj, George S. *Standard Catalog of World Paper Money, General Issues, 1368-1960*. 14th edition. 2012. ISBN 978-1-4402-3090-5. Krause Publications (www.krausebooks.com), 700 East State St., Iola, WI, 54990-0001.

Cuhaj, George S. *Standard Catalog of World Paper Money, Modern Issues, 1961-Present*. 18th edition. 2012. ISBN 978-1-4402-2956-5. Krause Publications (www.krausebooks.com), 700 East State St., Iola, WI, 54990-0001.

Fórum de Numismática (www.forum-numismatica.com).

Trigueiros, António and Hugo Antao. "St. Thomas and Prince Cheque-Notes and Overprinted Notes." *IBNS Journal*. Volume 19 Number 1. p.20.

Share Your Input, Info, and Images

This catalog is believed to be complete and correct as of the time of publication. Prices and face values were last updated 13 January 2012. Please report errors or omissions so that corrections may be made. If you can more precisely identify the name or location of anything depicted on a note, please share that information. Furthermore, if you own an unlisted type or variety, please submit scans of the front and back of the note so that it can be documented. Scans should be 300 dots per inch, 100% actual size, 24-bit color, saved as *uncompressed* JPEG files, and sent to owen@banknotenews.com. Be sure to fully describe all attributes of the note which are not apparent upon visual inspection of the images alone, such as physical dimension, watermark, and security thread.

Sarawak

Contents

Sarawak Government Treasury (SGT) 1799
Government of Sarawak (GOS) 1801

Monetary System

1858-1953: 1 Sarawak dollar = 100 cents

Sarawak was part of Brunei until 24 September 1841, when the Sultan of Brunei, Omar Ali Saifuddin II, bestowed upon James Brooke of England the title "Rajah" and a land grant in the southwest near the city of Sarawak (now Kuching). The Kingdom of Sarawak developed and expanded over the decades, growing to occupy much of the north region of the island of Borneo by leasing and annexing land from Brunei.

Sarawak Government Treasury

SGT Signature Varieties

1	*[signature]*
	Treasurer
	George Campbell Gillan
	(1919)

1858-1859 Issues

Each of these uniface notes is printed on hand laid and hand combed paper which bears a rubber-stamped seal of the Sarawak Office of Registry, as well as a handwritten date, serial number, and signature of Charles Adaire Crymble. The value appears at upper right in Jawi and Chinese characters.

SGT B1 (PA1): 5 cents   Good   Fine   XF
Black. Front (uniface): *Treasury Pay Bearer*. No security thread. Watermark: None. Printer: (Unknown, Seychelles). 105 x 80 mm.
   ☐ a.   Handwritten 3/9/58.   —   —   9,500
        Handwritten signature: Charles Adaire Crymble.

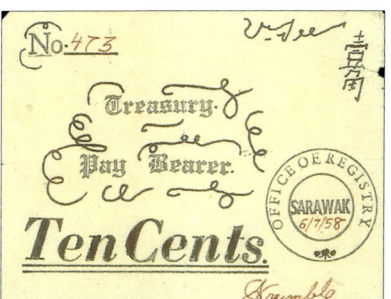

SGT B2 (PA2): 10 cents   Good   Fine   XF
Black. Front (uniface): *Treasury Pay Bearer*. No security thread. Watermark: None. Printer: (Unknown, Seychelles). 105 x 80 mm.
   ☐ a.   Handwritten 6/7/58.   —   VF   9,500
        Handwritten signature: Charles Adaire Crymble.

No image available.

SGT B3 (PA2A): 10 cents   Good   Fine   XF
Black. Front (uniface): *Treasury Pay Bearer*. No security thread. Watermark: None. Printer: (Unknown, Seychelles). 105 x 80 mm.
   ☐ a.   Handwritten 3/9/58.   —   —   —
        Handwritten signature: Charles Adaire Crymble.

SGT B4 (PA3): 20 cents   Good   Fine   XF
Black. Front (uniface): *Treasury Pay Bearer*. No security thread. Watermark: None. Printer: (Government Printing Press, Kuching). 130 x 80 mm.
   ☐ a.   Handwritten 7/5/59.   —   VF   11,000
        Handwritten signature: Charles Adaire Crymble.

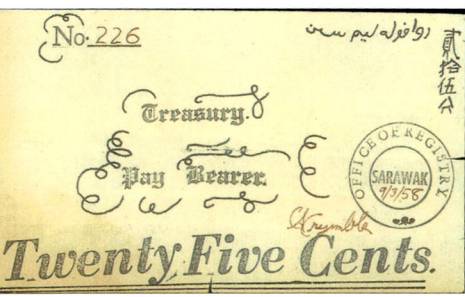

SGT B5 (PA4): 25 cents   Good   Fine   XF
Black. Front (uniface): *Treasury Pay Bearer*. No security thread. Watermark: None. Printer: (Government Printing Press, Kuching). 130 x 80 mm.
   ☐ a.   Handwritten 9/3/58.   —   VF   11,000
        Handwritten signature: Charles Adaire Crymble.

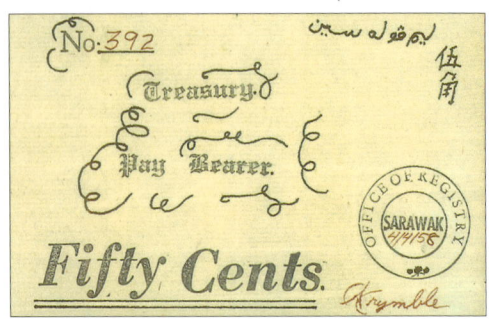

SGT B6 (PA5): 50 cents   Good   Fine   XF

Black. Front (uniface): *Treasury Pay Bearer*. No security thread. Watermark: None. Printer: (Government Printing Press, Kuching). 130 x 80 mm.

- a. Handwritten 4/4/58.   —   VF   13,000
  Handwritten signature: Charles Adaire Crymble.

1862-1863 Issues

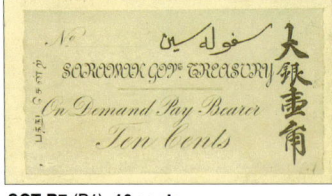

SGT B7 (P1): 10 cents   Good   Fine   XF

Black. Front (uniface): *On Demand Pay Bearer*. No security thread. Watermark: Unknown. Printer: (Unknown, Seychelles). 90 x 45 mm.

- a. Handwritten date.   —   —   —
  Handwritten signature: William M. Crocker or Alfred Robert Houghton.
- p. Proof on card stock.   —   VF   9,600

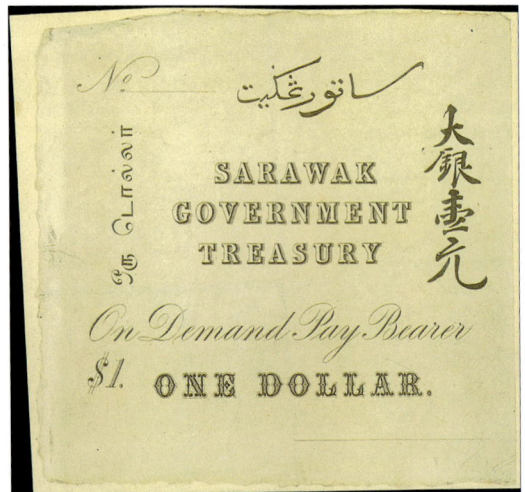

SGT B8 (P1A): 1 dollar   Good   Fine   XF

Black. Front (uniface): *On Demand Pay Bearer*. No security thread. Watermark: Unknown. Printer: (Unknown, Seychelles). 140 x 130 mm.

- a. Handwritten date.   —   —   —
  Handwritten signature: Alfred Robert Houghton.
- p. Proof on card stock.   —   VF   11,000

1919 Issues

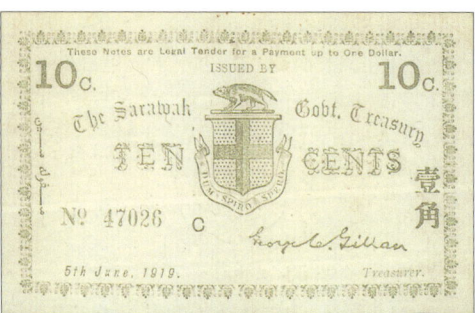

SGT B9 (P7): 10 cents   Good   Fine   XF

Black. Front: Coat of arms. Back: Coat of arms. No security thread. Watermark: Unknown. Printer: (Government Printing Press, Kuching). 130 x 85 mm.

- a. 5th June, 1919. Signature 1. Suffix A - H.   —   650   4,000

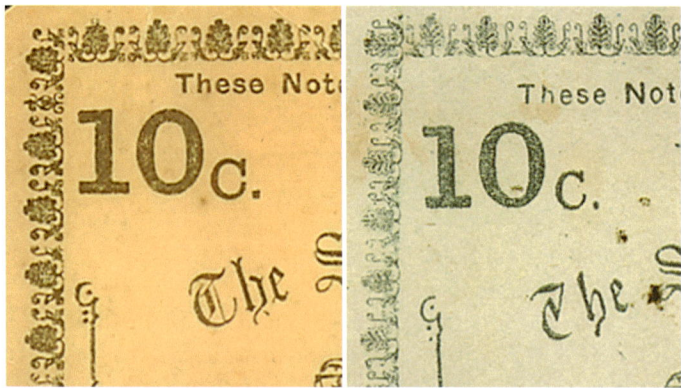

Notes with crude lettering and different border designs than known genuine notes (left) may be counterfeits (right). These suspect notes have been observed with bold suffix B and serial numbers 194xx.

SGT B10 (P8): 25 cents   Good   Fine   XF

Red. Front: Text. Back: Coat of arms. No security thread. Watermark: Unknown. Printer: (Government Printing Press, Kuching). 130 x 90 mm.

- a. 1st July, 1919. Signature 1.   —   —   VF   32,000

Government of Sarawak

GOS Signature Varieties

1
Acc.ᵀ
Joseph Philip Reutens
(1929)

Government Treasurer
George Campbell Gillan
(1935)

2
Treasurer of Sarawak
Arthur A. Rennie
(1929)

3
Treasurer of Sarawak
Edward Parnell
(1935)

4
Treasurer of Sarawak (1937)
Financial Secretary (1938)
Harold Macmillan Calvert

5
Treasurer of Sarawak
Bertram Alfred Trechman
(1940)

1880-1917 Issues

These notes have deckle edges as well as handwritten dates and signatures. They feature a portrait of Charles Johnson Brooke wearing civilian clothes. He became the second "White Rajah" on 3 August 1868 following the death of his uncle, James Brooke, on 11 June 1868. Charles Brooke's facsimile signature appears in the lower left margin with the value in Jawi at lower right, Chinese at center left, and Arabic at center right.

The woman in the central vignette is heiress to the Coutts & Co. banking fortune, Baroness Angelea Georgina Burdett-Coutts. It's likely the ship depicted is The Royalist, the 142-ton schooner owned by James Brooke when he arrived at Kuching, Borneo in 1838.

At right is the Brooke coat of arms with a brock (badger) atop a shield flanked by oak and olive branch laurels.

GOS B1 (P2): 1 dollar   Good   Fine   XF
Black and green. Front (uniface): Charles Johnson Brooke; standing woman with beehive, anchor, and sailing ship; Brooke coat of arms. No security thread. Watermark: Unknown. Printer: *Perkins, Bacon & Cº London*. 180 x 100 mm.

- a. 01.06.1894 - 01.03.1917.   —   10,000   30,000
  Handwritten signatures.
- p. Proof on card stock; punched.   —   —   4,000
- as. Two horizontal red *CANCELLED* overprints.   —   —   —

GOS B2 (P3): 5 dollars   Good   Fine   XF
Black and blue. Front (uniface): Charles Johnson Brooke; standing woman with beehive, anchor, and sailing ship; Brooke coat of arms. No security thread. Watermark: Unknown. Printer: *Perkins, Bacon & Cº London*. 174 x 119 mm.

- a. 01.09.1880 - 27.10.1903.   12,000   —   —
  Handwritten signatures.
- p. Proof on card stock; punched.   —   —   5,200

GOS B3 (P4): 10 dollars   Good   Fine   XF
Black and red. Front (uniface): Charles Johnson Brooke; standing woman with beehive, anchor, and sailing ship; Brooke coat of arms. No security thread. Watermark: Unknown. Printer: *Perkins, Bacon & Cº London*. 174 x 119 mm.

- a. 01.09.1880 - 07.10.1903.   —   —   —
  Handwritten signatures.
- p. Proof on card stock; punched.   —   —   5,600
- as. Two horizontal red *CANCELLED* overprints.   —   VF   43,000

1918-1922 Issues

All of these notes have deckle edges. All but the 1-dollar note have handwritten dates and signatures. They feature a portrait of Charles Vyner Brooke wearing civilian clothes. He became the third "White Rajah" on 24 May 1917 following the death of his father, Charles Johnson Brooke, on 17 May 1917. Vyner Brooke's signature appears in the lower margin.

GOS B4 (P5): 25 dollars — Good / Fine / XF
Black and brown. Front (uniface): Charles Johnson Brooke; standing woman with beehive, anchor, and sailing ship; Brooke coat of arms. No security thread. Watermark: Unknown. Printer: *Perkins, Bacon & Cº Lᵈ London*. 174 x 119 mm.

- a. 19.07.1900 - 07.10.1903. Handwritten signatures. — — —
- p. Proof on card stock; punched. — — —
- as. Two horizontal red *CANCELLED* overprints. — — —

GOS B6 (P9): 1 dollar — Good / Fine / VF
Black and green. Front (uniface): Charles Vyner Brooke; standing woman with beehive, anchor, and sailing ship; Brooke coat of arms. No security thread. Watermark: Unknown. Printer: *Perkins, Bacon & Cº Lᵈ London*. 180 x 100 mm.

- a. 1ˢᵗ July 1919. Printed signature 1. — 5,500 15,000
- as. Two horizontal red *SPECIMEN* overprints. — — 11,200

GOS B5 (P6): 50 dollars — Good / Fine / XF
Black and yellow. Front (uniface): Charles Johnson Brooke; standing woman with beehive, anchor, and sailing ship; Brooke coat of arms. No security thread. Watermark: Unknown. Printer: *Perkins, Bacon & Cº Ld. London*. 174 x 119 mm.

- a. 19.07.1900 - 31.08.1903. Handwritten signatures. — — —
- p. Proof on card stock; punched. — — —

GOS B7 (P10): 5 dollars — Good / Fine / XF
Black and blue. Front (uniface): Charles Vyner Brooke; standing woman with beehive, anchor, and sailing ship; Brooke coat of arms. No security thread. Watermark: Unknown. Printer: *Perkins, Bacon & Cº Lᵈ London*. 167 x 110 mm.

- a. 05.06.1918 - 03.07.1922. Handwritten sigs. — VF 30,000

1929-1940 Issues

These notes feature a portrait of an older Charles Vyner Brooke wearing an ornate uniform with gold braiding and epaulets. The Brooke coat of arms on these notes is no longer flanked by laurels and now has a banner below with the Latin motto *DUM SPIRO SPERO* (While I breathe, I hope).

The 10-cent note was issued to alleviate a shortage of coinage following the outbreak of World War II which cut off Sarawak from receiving shipments from England.

GOS B8 (P11): **10 dollars** Good Fine XF
Black and red. Front (uniface): Charles Vyner Brooke; standing woman with beehive, anchor, and sailing ship; Brooke coat of arms. No security thread. Watermark: Unknown. Printer: *Perkins, Bacon & Cº Lᵈ London*. 167 x 115 mm.
☐ a. 05.06.1918 - 06.10.1922. Handwritten sigs. — — —

No image available.
GOS B9 (P12): **25 dollars** Good Fine XF
Black and brown. Front (uniface): Charles Johnson Brooke; standing woman with beehive, anchor, and sailing ship; Brooke coat of arms. No security thread. Watermark: Unknown. Printer: *Perkins, Bacon & Cº Lᵈ London*. 174 x 119 mm.
☐ a. 19.05.1921 - 06.10.1922. Handwritten sigs. — — —

No image available.
GOS B10 (P13): **50 dollars** Good Fine XF
Black and yellow. Front (uniface): Charles Johnson Brooke; standing woman with beehive, anchor, and sailing ship; Brooke coat of arms. No security thread. Watermark: Unknown. Printer: *Perkins, Bacon & Cº Lᵈ London*. 174 x 119 mm.
☐ a. 19.05.1921 - 06.10.1922. Handwritten sigs. — — —

GOS B11 (P25): **10 cents** VG VF UNC
Red, yellow, and blue. Front (uniface): Brooke coat of arms; Charles Vyner Brooke. No security thread. Watermark: *SDM* (Survey Department Malaya) and map of Malaya. Printer: *SURVEY DEPT. F.M.S.* 120 x 79 mm.
☐ a. 1ˢᵗ August 1940. Signature 5. Prefix A - C. — — 500

GOS B12 (P14): **1 dollar** Good Fine XF
Purple. Front: Palm trees; Charles Vyner Brooke; fronds. Back: Native artifacts; Brooke coat of arms. No security thread. Watermark: None. Printer: *BRADBURY, WILKINSON & Cº Lᵈ ENGRAVERS, NEW MALDEN, SURREY, ENGLAND*. 131 x 83 mm.
☐ a. 1ˢᵗ July 1929. Signature 2. Prefix A/1 - A/3. — 425 1,200
☐ p. Proof. — — 5,600
☐ t. Color trial: Reddish-brown; separate uniface front/back. — — 5,100
☐ as1. Diagonal red *SPECIMEN* overprint. — — —
☐ as2. Red *BWC* circle overprint. — — 10,500

Sarawak 1929-1940 Issues

GOS B13 (P20 & P23): **1 dollar**   Good   Fine   XF

Green. Front: Palm trees; Charles Vyner Brooke; fronds. Back: Native artifacts; Brooke coat of arms. No security thread. Watermark: Unknown. Printer: *BRADBURY, WILKINSON & C⁰ Lᵈ ENGRAVERS, NEW MALDEN, SURREY, ENGLAND*. 131 x 83 mm.

				Good	Fine	XF
☐	a.	1st January 1935. Signature 3. Prefix A/3, A/4.		—	125	400
☐	b.	1st January 1940. Signature 5. Prefix A/5, A/6.		—	UNC	1,200
☐	c.	Red Jawi overprint at center. Prefix A/7, A/8. Unconfirmed as issued.		—	—	—
☐	as.	Red *BWC* circle overprint.		—	UNC	2,400
☐	bs.	Horizontal *CANCELLED* perforation.		—	AU	2,200
☐	cs.	Horizontal *SPECIMEN* perforation.		—	UNC	36,000

In early 1945, the Government of Sarawak ordered a new printing of notes dated 1st January 1940 with serial numbers continuing from the preceding series, but distinguishable from the older issues (GOS B13b, left) by a red overprint of Jawi text on a guilloche rosette at center (B13cs, right).

GOS B14 (P15 & P21): **5 dollars**   Good   Fine   XF

Brown. Front: Brooke coat of arms; palm trees; Charles Vyner Brooke. Back: Native designs. No security thread. Watermark: Unknown. Printer: *BRADBURY, WILKINSON & C⁰ Lᵈ ENGRAVERS, NEW MALDEN, SURREY, ENGLAND*. 144 x 96 mm.

			Good	Fine	XF
☐	a.	1st July 1929. Signature 2. Prefix B/1, B/2. Date and signature printed in brown.	—	400	1,800
☐	b.	1st January 1938. Signature 4. Prefix B/2. Date and signature printed in black with bar obscuring old title.	—	400	2,500
☐	p.	Proof.	—	—	5,500
☐	t.	Color trial: Green.	—	—	5,500
☐	as1.	Diagonal red *SPECIMEN* overprint.	—	—	—
☐	as2.	Horizontal *CANCELLED* perforation.	—	—	—
☐	as3.	Red *BWC* circle overprint.	—	—	13,600
☐	bs.	Horizontal *CANCELLED* perforation.	—	—	—

The 5-dollar notes dated 1st July 1929 have the date and signature printed in brown (GOS B14a, left) whereas those dated 1st January 1938 are printed in black with a bar obscuring the old title (B14b, right).

GOS B15 (P16, P22 & P24): **10 dollars**　　　　　　**Good　Fine　XF**

Red. Front: Brooke coat of arms; palm trees; Charles Vyner Brooke; fronds. Back: Charles Brooke memorial in front of clock tower on Old Court House in Kuching (Sarawak Tourism Complex as of 2003). No security thread. Watermark: Unknown. Printer: *BRADBURY, WILKINSON & C° L*ᵈ *ENGRAVERS, NEW MALDEN, SURREY, ENGLAND*. 158 x 114 mm.

☐	a.	1st July 1929. Signature 2. Prefix C/1. Date and signature printed in red.	—	800　1,600
☐	b.	1st June 1937. Signature 4. Prefix C/2. Date and signature printed in black.	—	750　1,500
☐	c.	1st January 1940. Signature 5. Prefix C/3.	—	900　1,800
☐	p.	Proof.	—	—　6,250
☐	t.	Color trial: Brown-purple.	—	—　5,600
☐	as1.	Diagonal red *SPECIMEN* overprint.	—	—　—
☐	as2.	Red *BWC* circle overprint.	—	—　11,000
☐	cs.	Horizontal *CANCELLED* perforation.	—	—　4,500

GOS B16 (P17): **25 dollars**　　　　　　**Good　Fine　XF**

Blue. Front: Palm trees; Charles Vyner Brooke; Brooke coat of arms; fronds. Back: Government building with flag in Kuching. No security thread. Watermark: Unknown. Printer: *BRADBURY, WILKINSON & C° L*ᵈ *ENGRAVERS, NEW MALDEN, SURREY, ENGLAND*. 170 x 128 mm.

☐	a.	1st July 1929. Signature 2. Prefix D/1 - D/2.	—	6,000　30,000
☐	p.	Proof.	—	—　—
☐	as1.	Two diagonal red *SPECIMEN* overprints.	—	—　—
☐	as2.	Red *BWC* circle overprint; punched.	—	—　15,000
☐	as3.	Horizontal *CANCELLED* perforation.	—	—　—

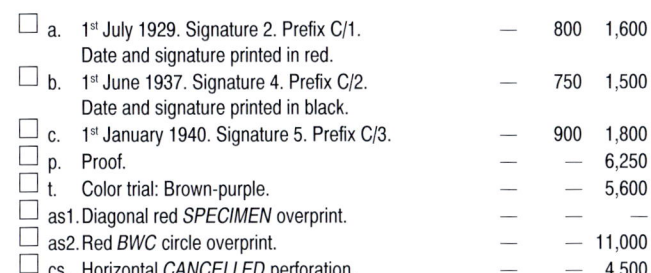

GOS B18 (P19): **100 dollars**   Good   Fine   XF

Purple. Front: Palm trees; Charles Vyner Brooke; Brooke coat of arms; fronds. Back: Native bird and snake artifacts. No security thread. Watermark: Unknown. Printer: *BRADBURY, WILKINSON & C° Ld ENGRAVERS, NEW MALDEN, SURREY, ENGLAND.* 201 x 126 mm.

☐	a.	1st July 1929. Signature 2. Prefix F/1.	—	45,000	—
☐	p.	Proof.	—	—	—
☐	as1.	Two diagonal red *SPECIMEN* overprints.	—	—	—
☐	as2.	Red *BWC* circle overprint; punched.	—	—	27,000

GOS B17 (P18): **50 dollars**   Good   Fine   XF

Green. Front: Palm trees; Charles Vyner Brooke; Brooke coat of arms; fronds. Back: Native designs. No security thread. Watermark: Unknown. Printer: *BRADBURY, WILKINSON & C° Ld ENGRAVERS, NEW MALDEN, SURREY, ENGLAND.* 187 x 133 mm.

☐	a.	1st July 1929. Signature 2. Prefix E/1.	—	15,000	40,000
☐	p.	Proof.	—	—	13,500
☐	t.	Color trial: Brown.	—	—	—
☐	as1.	Two diagonal red *SPECIMEN* overprints.	—	—	—
☐	as2.	Red *BWC* circle overprint; punched.	—	—	25,000

1945 Emergency Issues

These notes were prepared to address a shortage of coinage due to World War II. It is not known if these specimens went into production. No issued notes are known to exist.

GOS B19 (PNL): **1 cent**   VG   VF   UNC
Brown and violet. Front (uniface): Coat of arms. No security thread. Watermark: Unknown. Printer: BRADBURY, WILKINSON & C° L^d NEW MALDEN, SURREY, ENGLAND. 95 x 44 mm.

☐ s. No overprint; no date; no signature; punched. — — 7,500
6.9.45 handwritten in pencil at upper right.

GOS B20 (PNL): **5 cents**   VG   VF   UNC
Blue and orange. Front (uniface): Coat of arms. No security thread. Watermark: Unknown. Printer: BRADBURY, WILKINSON & C° L^d NEW MALDEN, SURREY, ENGLAND. 95 x 44 mm.

☐ s. No overprint; no date; no signature; punched. — — 7,000
6.9.45 handwritten in pencil at upper right.

GOS B21 (PNL): **10 cents**   VG   VF   UNC
Green. Front (uniface): Coat of arms. No security thread. Watermark: Unknown. Printer: BRADBURY, WILKINSON & C° L^d NEW MALDEN, SURREY, ENGLAND. 95 x 44 mm.

☐ s. No overprint; no date; no signature; punched. — XF 18,000
6.9.45 handwritten in pencil at upper right.

Looking Forward

During the occupation period (1942-1945), the Japanese Government issued banknotes in denominations ranging from 1 cent to 1,000 dollars (see Malaya). This currency was fixed at 1 dollar = 1 Japanese yen, compared to a 1:2 pre-war rate. Following the war, the Japanese occupation currency was declared worthless and the previous issues of the Sarawak dollar regained their value relative to sterling (two shillings four pence).

The Board of Commissioners of Currency (BCC), Malaya and British Borneo, was established on 1 January 1952, to provide a common currency for Brunei, the Federation of Malaya, North Borneo, Sarawak, and Singapore. The Malaya and British Borneo dollar replaced (at par) the British North Borneo dollar, Malayan dollar (also used in Brunei and Singapore), and Sarawak dollar. Like its predecessors, it was pegged at one dollar to 2 shillings 4 pence sterling.

For later issues, see Malaya and British Borneo.

Acknowledgements

This chapter was compiled with the generous assistance of Martin Burger, Compagnie Generale De Bourse (www.CGB.fr), Detlef Hilmer (detlef_hilmer@web.de), Larry Hirsch, Don Ludwig, Wally Myers, Andrew Pattison (www.Spink.com), Mikhail "Mike" Prizov, Stack's Bowers & Ponterio (www.StacksBowers.com), Frank van Tiel, and others.

Sources

Boon, K. N. *Malaysia Brunei & Singapore Banknotes & Coins.* 6th edition. 2012. ISBN 978-983-43313-5-1. Trigometric Sdn.Bhd. (www.3833.com), Lot 327, Amcorp Mall, 18 Jalan Persiaran Barat, off Jalan Timur, Petaling Jaya, 46050 Selangor D.E., Malaysia.

Chee, Clement. Odds & Ends of South East Asian Banknotes & Coins. http://clement-oddsends.blogspot.com.

Cuhaj, George S. *Standard Catalog of World Paper Money, General Issues, 1368-1960.* 14th edition. 2012. ISBN 978-1-4402-3090-5. Krause Publications (www.krausebooks.com), 700 East State St., Iola, WI, 54990-0001.

Heath, Henry B. "Notabilities Portrayed on Bank Notes - Part IV." *IBNS Journal*. Volume 44 Number 3. p.30.

Kemp, Brian. "Notes Issued by the White Rajahs of Sarawak." *IBNS Journal*. Volume 14 Number 1. p.17.

Tan, Steven. *Standard Catalogue of Malaysia Singapore Brunei Coin & Paper Money.* 18th edition. 2007. ISBN 983-9650-02-05. International Stamp & Coin Sn. Bhd., 2.4 & 2.5, Pertama Shopping Complex, 2nd Floor, Jalan Tuanku Abdul Rahman, 50100 Kaula Lumpur, Malaysia.

Share Your Input, Info, and Images

This catalog is believed to be complete and correct as of the time of publication. Prices and face values were last updated 13 December 2013. Please report errors or omissions so that corrections may be made. If you can more precisely identify the name or location of anything depicted on a note, please share that information. Furthermore, if you own an unlisted type or variety, please submit scans of the front and back of the note so that it can be documented. Scans should be 300 dots per inch, 100% actual size, 24-bit color, saved as *uncompressed* JPEG files, and sent to owen@banknotenews.com. Be sure to fully describe all attributes of the note which are not apparent upon visual inspection of the images alone, such as physical dimension, watermark, and security thread.

Saudi Arabia

For earlier issues, see Hejaz.

Monetary System
1 Saudi riyal (SAR) = 100 halala

Arabic Numbers

0	1	2	3	4	5	6	7	8	9
.	١	٢	٣	٤	٥	٦	٧	٨	٩

Saudi Arabian Monetary Agency

On 22 October 1952, the Saudi Arabian Monetary Agency (SAMA) opened for business in Jeddah.

For more information, visit www.sama.gov.sa.

SAMA Signature Varieties

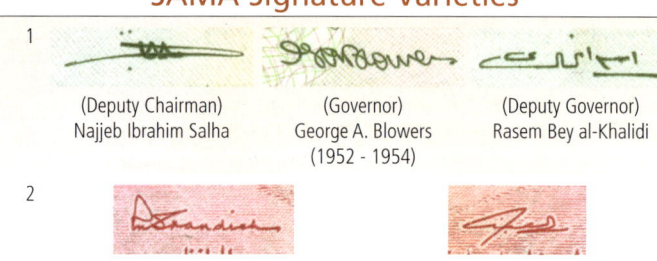

1 (Deputy Chairman) Najjeb Ibrahim Salha | (Governor) George A. Blowers (1952 - 1954) | (Deputy Governor) Rasem Bey al-Khalidi

2 (Governor) Ralph D. Standish (1954 - 1958) | (Chairman) Muhammed Surour al-Saban

(Governor) | (Minister of Finance)

3 Anwar Ali (1958 - 1974) | Tallal bin Abdul Aziz

4 Anwar Ali (1958 - 1974) | Musa'id bin Abdul Rahman

5 Abdul Aziz al-Qurashi (1974 - 1983) | Musa'id bin Abdul Rahman

6 Abdul Aziz al-Qurashi (1974 - 1983) | Muhammad Ali Aba Al-Khail

7a (Acting Governor, signified by small mark at lower right) Hamad Saud al-Sayyari | Muhammad Ali Aba Al-Khail

7b Hamad Saud al-Sayyari (1983 - 2009) | Muhammad Ali Aba Al-Khail

8 Hamad Saud al-Sayyari (1983 - 2009) | Ibrahim bin Abdulaziz bin Abdullah al-Assaf

9 Muhammad Al-Jaser (2009 - 2011) | Ibrahim bin Abdulaziz bin Abdullah al-Assaf

10 Fahad Al-Mubarak (13.12.2011 - present) | Ibrahim bin Abdulaziz bin Abdullah al-Assaf

1953 Haj Pilgrim Receipt Issues

SAMA's charter expressly prohibited it from issuing paper currency, but officials circumvented this restriction by issuing "pilgrim receipts" as a sort of traveler's check to meet the seasonal demand for riyals created by the hundreds of thousands of foreign pilgrims. Originally these receipts were fully backed by silver riyals and were intended for use by pilgrims only, but eventually the backing was degraded and the use of the receipts became widespread throughout the kingdom.

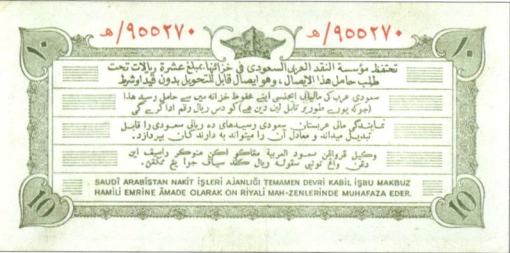

SAMA B1 (P1): **10 riyals** (withdrawn 01.02.1965)   VG   VF   UNC
Green. Front: Coat of arms with palm trees and crossed swords. Back: Text in Malay, Farsi, Arabic, Urdu, and Turkish. Watermark: None. Printer: THOMAS DE LA RUE & CO. LTD. 138 x 66 mm.

- a. ١٣٧٢ (AH1372). Signature 1. Intro: 30.07.1953.   400   1,625   6,000
- as1. Diagonal red *SPECIMEN* and DLR oval overprints; horizontal red *SPECIMEN No.* # ovpt at lower left; punched.   —   —   —
- as2. Diagonal red hollow *SPECIMEN* overprint.   —   —   —

1954 Haj Pilgrim Receipt Issues

SAMA B2 (P4): 10 riyals (withdrawn 01.02.1965)   VG   VF   UNC
Green. Front: Jiddah harbor with two sailing boats. Back: Two coats of arms with palm tree and crossed swords; text in Malay, Farsi, Arabic, Urdu, and Turkish. Solid security thread. Watermark: SAMA repeated. Printer: (TDLR). 172 x 78 mm.

- ☐ a. ١٣٧٣ (AH1373). Signature 1. Intro: 18.05.1954.   20   75   300
- ☐ as. Diagonal red hollow *SPECIMEN* overprint.   —   —   —
- ☐ p. Unissued design on cardboard.   —   —   —

1955 Haj Pilgrim Receipt Issues

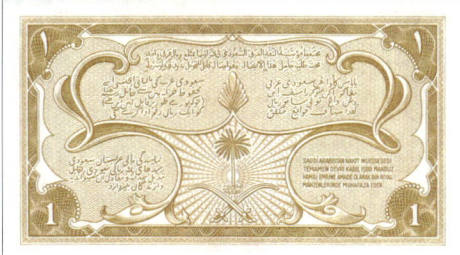

SAMA B3 (P2): 1 riyal (withdrawn 01.02.1965)   VG   VF   UNC
Red and brown. Front: Palace of King Saud, Kassir Khuzam in Jiddah. Back: Text in Malay, Farsi, Arabic, Urdu, and Turkish. Solid security thread. Watermark: SAMA repeated. Printer: (TDLR). 127 x 72 mm.

- ☐ a. ١٣٧٥ (AH1375). Signature 2. Intro: October 1955.   15   70   300
- ☐ as. Horizontal *SPECIMEN* perforation; punched.   —   —   —

1956 Haj Pilgrim Receipt Issues

SAMA B4 (P3): 5 riyals (withdrawn 01.02.1965)   VG   VF   UNC
Blue. Front: Jiddah harbor with one sailing boat. Back: National emblem (two crossed swords with palm tree); text in Malay, Farsi, Arabic, Urdu, and Turkish. Solid security thread. Watermark: SAMA repeated. Printer: (TDLR). 156 x 66 mm.

- ☐ a. ١٣٧٣ (AH1373). Signature 1. Intro: 24.05.1956.   85   350   600
- ☐ as. Diagonal red hollow *SPECIMEN* overprint.   —   —   —

Law of 1.7.AH1379 (1961) "First" Issues

SAMA B5 (P6): 1 riyal (withdrawn 24.06.1971)   VG   VF   UNC
Brown. Front: Jabal an-Nour (The Mountain of Light) near city of Mecca. Back: National emblem (two crossed swords with palm tree). Solid security thread. Watermark: Coat of arms. Printer: (TDLR). 137 x 63 mm.

- ☐ a. ١٣٧٩/٧/١ (AH1379/7/1). Signature 3. Intro: 15.06.1961.   2.50   10   125
- ☐ as. Diagonal black *SPECIMEN* and DLR oval ovpts; punched.   —   —   —

SAMA B6 (P7): **5 riyals** (withdrawn 24.06.1971)   VG   VF   UNC
Blue. Front: Al Mussmack Palace in Riyadh. Back: National emblem (two crossed swords with palm tree). Solid security thread. Watermark: Coat of arms. Printer: (TDLR). 157 x 66 mm.

			VG	VF	UNC
☐	a.	١٣٧٩/٧/١ (AH1379/7/1). Signature 3. Red serial numbers. Intro: 15.06.1961.	15	100	400
☐	b.	Black serial numbers.	20	100	400
☐	c.	Signature 4. Red serial numbers. Intro: 23.09.1963.	—	200	—
☐	as.	Diagonal red *SPECIMEN* and DLR oval overprints; punched.	—	—	—

SAMA B7 (P8): **10 riyals** (withdrawn 24.06.1971)   VG   VF   UNC
Green. Front: Jiddah harbor with two sailing boats. Back: National emblem (two crossed swords with palm tree). Solid security thread. Watermark: Coat of arms. Printer: (TDLR). 165 x 70 mm.

			VG	VF	UNC
☐	a.	١٣٧٩/٧/١ (AH1379/7/1). Signature 3. Intro: 15.06.1961.	20	75	350
☐	b.	Signature 4. Intro: 23.09.1963.	50	200	800
☐	as.	Diagonal red *SPECIMEN* and DLR oval overprints; horizontal red *SPECIMEN Nº* # ovpt at lower left; punched.	—	—	2,800
☐	bs.	Diagonal red *SPECIMEN* and DLR oval overprints; horizontal red *SPECIMEN Nº* # ovpt at lower left; punched.	—	—	—

SAMA B8 (P9): **50 riyals** (withdrawn 24.06.1971)   VG   VF   UNC
Violet. Front: Oil derrick. Back: National emblem (two crossed swords with palm tree). Solid security thread. Watermark: Coat of arms. Printer: (TDLR). 170 x 78 mm.

			VG	VF	UNC
☐	a.	١٣٧٩/٧/١ (AH1379/7/1). Signature 3. Intro: 15.06.1961.	75	250	1,000
☐	b.	Signature 4. Intro: 23.09.1963.	75	250	1,000
☐	as.	Diagonal red *SPECIMEN* and DLR oval overprints; punched.	—	—	—
☐	bs.	Diagonal red *SPECIMEN* and DLR oval overprints; punched.	—	—	1,000

SAMA B9 (P10): **100 riyals** (withdrawn 24.06.1971)   VG   VF   UNC
Orange. Front: Council of Ministers' building, Nasiriyah gate, and Royal Technical Institute, all in Riyadh. Back: Minarets of the Medina Holy Mosque; national emblem (two crossed swords with palm tree). Solid security thread. Watermark: Coat of arms. Printer: (TDLR). 176 x 86 mm.

			VG	VF	UNC
☐	a.	١٣٧٩/٧/١ (AH1379/7/1). Signature 3. Intro: 15.06.1961.	250	1,000	4,000
☐	b.	Signature 4. Intro: 23.09.1963.	225	900	3,750
☐	as.	Diagonal black *SPECIMEN* and DLR oval ovpts; horizontal black *SPECIMEN Nº* # ovpt at lower left; punched.	—	—	4,100

Law of 1.7.AH1379 (1968) "Second" Issues

SAMA B10 (P11): **1 riyal** (withdrawn 16.05.1989)   VG   VF   UNC
Purple. Front: Ministry of Foreign Affairs building in Jiddah. Back: National emblem (two crossed swords with palm tree). Solid security thread. Watermark: Coat of arms. Printer: (TDLR). 128 x 62 mm.

☐ a. ١٣٧٩/٧/١ (AH1379/7/1).   2   8   35
  Signature 4. Intro: 14.02.1968.
☐ b. Signature 5. Intro: 01.03.1976.   3   12   50
☐ as. Specimen.   —   —   —

SAMA B11 (P12): **5 riyals** (withdrawn 16.05.1989)   VG   VF   UNC
Green. Front: Dhahran Airport (DHA) with planes. Back: Al-Dammam sea port; national emblem (two crossed swords with palm tree). Solid security thread. Watermark: Coat of arms. Printer: (TDLR). 146 x 66 mm.

☐ a. ١٣٧٩/٧/١ (AH1379/7/1).   10   40   150
  Signature 4. Intro: 14.02.1968.
☐ b. Signature 5. Intro: 01.03.1976.   10   45   175

SAMA B12 (P13): **10 riyals** (withdrawn 16.05.1989)   VG   VF   UNC
Gray. Front: Holy Mosque in Mecca. Back: al-Massa wall of the Holy Mosque; national emblem (two crossed swords with palm tree). Solid security thread. Watermark: Coat of arms. Printer: (TDLR). 158 x 70 mm.

☐ a. ١٣٧٩/٧/١ (AH1379/7/1). Signature 4.   5   20   80
  Intro: 14.02.1968.

SAMA B13 (P14): **50 riyals** (withdrawn 16.05.1989)   VG   VF   UNC
Brown. Front: National emblem (two crossed swords with palm tree); columns, green dome, and minaret of Al-Masjid al-Nabawi (Prophet's Mosque) in Medina. Back: National emblem (two crossed swords with palm tree); farm in al-Khurg with rows of palm trees. Solid security thread. Watermark: Coat of arms. Printer: (TDLR). 170 x 78 mm.

☐ a. ١٣٧٩/٧/١ (AH1379/7/1).   10   50   340
  Signature 4. Intro: 14.02.1968.
☐ b. Signature 5. Intro: 01.03.1976.   20   200   400
☐ as. Horizontal black *PROOF N°* # ovpt at lower left.   —   —   1,525

SAMA B14 (P15): **100 riyals** (withdrawn 16.05.1989) VG VF UNC
Red. Front: National emblem (two crossed swords with palm tree); Council of Ministers' building in Riyadh. Back: Derricks at Aramco oil refinery. Solid security thread. Watermark: Coat of arms. Printer: (TDLR). 176 x 82 mm.

- a. ١٣٧٩/٧/١ (AH1379/7/1). Signature 4. Intro: 14.02.1968. 40 175 750
- b. Signature 5. Intro: 01.03.1976. 50 200 800

Law of 1.7.AH1379 (1976) "Third" Issues

SAMA B15 (P16): **1 riyal** (US$0.25) VG VF UNC
Brown. Front: Jabal an-Nour (The Mountain of Light) near city of Mecca; King Faisal. Back: National emblem (two crossed swords with palm tree); Lockheed L-1011 jet in Saudia livery in sky over Dhahran Airport (DHA). Solid security thread. Watermark: King Faisal. Printer: (TDLR). 130 x 65 mm.

- a. ١٣٧٩/٧/١ (AH1379/7/1). Signature 6. Intro: 10.10.1976. 1 4 15

SAMA B16 (P17): **5 riyals** (US$1.35) VG VF UNC
Green. Front: Irrigation channel in Hofuf; King Faisal. Back: National emblem (two crossed swords with palm tree); Wadi Gizan dam. Solid security thread. Watermark: King Faisal. Printer: (TDLR). 157 x 70 mm.

- a. ١٣٧٩/٧/١ (AH1379/7/1). Signature 6. Error in "Khamsa" (five) in panel below irrigation channel. Intro: 10.10.1976. 4 15 60
- b. Corrected text. 2 8 35

SAMA B16a: Incorrect panel (top) and B16b: Corrected panel (bottom).

SAMA B17 (P18): **10 riyals** (US$2.65) VG VF UNC
Lilac. Front: Off-shore oil rig; King Faisal. Back: National emblem (two crossed swords with palm tree); Ras Tanoura oil refinery. Solid security thread. Watermark: King Faisal. Printer: (TDLR). 164 x 74 mm.

- a. ١٣٧٩/٧/١ (AH1379/7/1). Signature 6. Intro: 10.10.1976. FV 12 55

SAMA B18 (P19): **50 riyals** (US$13)   VG   VF   UNC

Green. Front: Columns, green dome, and minaret of Al-Masjid al-Nabawi (Prophet's Mosque) in Medina; King Faisal. Back: National emblem (two crossed swords with palm tree); interior columns of Al-Masjid al-Nabawi. Solid security thread. Watermark: King Faisal. Printer: (TDLR). 176 x 84 mm.

		VG	VF	UNC
☐	a. ١٣٧٩/٧/١ (AH1379/7/1). Intro: 10.10.1976. Signature 6, 70 mm apart. Prefix ٦–٤٧.	FV	25	100
☐	b. Signature 6, 60 mm apart. Prefix ٩٩–١٩٩.	FV	25	100
☐	c. Signature 6 (thicker sig. at right). Prefix ٢٠٠–٢٧١.	FV	25	100

Signatures on SAMA B18 are further apart on earlier issues (top) than on later issues (bottom).

SAMA B19 (P20): **100 riyals** (US$27)   VG   VF   UNC

Blue. Front: Holy Mosque in Mecca; King Abdul Aziz ibn Sa'ud. Back: National emblem (two crossed swords with palm tree); al-Massa wall of the Holy Mosque. Solid security thread. Watermark: King Abdul Aziz ibn Sa'ud. Printer: (TDLR). 182 x 86 mm.

		VG	VF	UNC
☐	a. ١٣٧٩/٧/١ (AH1379/7/1). Intro: 10.10.1976. Signature 6, 70 mm apart. Prefix ١٠–٤٧.	FV	40	125
☐	b. Signature 6, 60 mm apart. Prefix ٦١–٣٥٧.	FV	20	85

Law of 1.7.AH1379 (1984) "Fourth" Issues

Cabinet resolution No. 146 dated 7-6-1403AH (21.03.1983) approved the printing of this new series of notes, which are physically smaller than the preceding issues. The 500-riyal denomination is new, as is the use of two new printers—Orell Füssli Security Printing, Switzerland; and Bradbury, Wilkinson & Co., UK—in addition to Thomas De La Rue, which had been solely responsible for producing all of Saudi Arabia's notes to date.

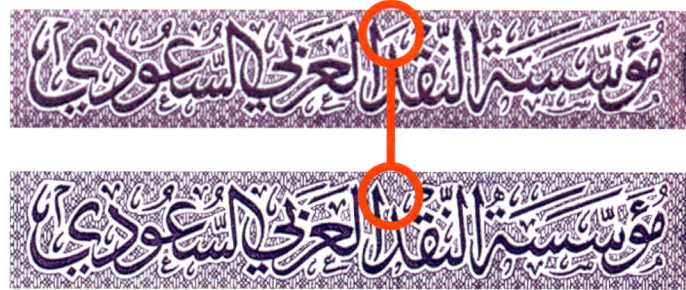

SAMA B20-23 were first issued containing an incorrect accent (top) over the Arabic word for "Monetary" in the panel at upper left front. This was subsequently corrected (bottom).

SAMA B20 (P21): **1 riyal** (US$0.25)   VG   VF   UNC
Brown. Front: 7th century gold Amawi dinar coin; King Fahd. Back: Countryside with flowers; national emblem (two crossed swords with palm tree). Solid security thread. Watermark: King Fahd. Printer: (TDLR). 135 x 62 mm.

- ☐ a. ١٣٧٩/٧/١ (AH1379/7/1). Signature 7a.   FV   FV   4
  Incorrect text. Intro: 05.01.1984.
- ☐ b. Corrected text.   FV   FV   2.50
- ☐ c. Signature 7b.   FV   FV   2
- ☐ d. Signature 8.   FV   FV   1.50

SAMA B21 (P22): **5 riyals** (US$1.35)   VG   VF   UNC
Purple. Front: Traditional boats; King Fahd. Back: Ras Tanoura oil refinery; national emblem (two crossed swords with palm tree). Solid security thread. Watermark: King Fahd. Printer: (TDLR). 145 x 66 mm.

- ☐ a. ١٣٧٩/٧/١ (AH1379/7/1). Signature 7a.   FV   FV   8
  Incorrect text. Intro: 05.01.1984.
- ☐ b. Corrected text.   FV   FV   6
- ☐ c. Signature 7b.   FV   FV   5
- ☐ d. Signature 8.   FV   FV   4.50
  22-mm wide watermark. Prefix ٣٠٥–٤٢٩.
- ☐ e. 24-mm wide watermark. Prefix ٥١٠–.   FV   FV   4.50

SAMA B22 (P23): **10 riyals** (US$2.65)   VG   VF   UNC
Brown. Front: al-Murabah Palace in Riyadh; King Fahd. Back: Palm tree plantation; national emblem (two crossed swords with palm tree). Solid security thread. Watermark: King Fahd. Printer: (BWC). 150 x 68 mm.

- ☐ a. ١٣٧٩/٧/١ (AH1379/7/1). Signature 7a.   FV   FV   20
  Incorrect text. Intro: 05.01.1984.
- ☐ b. Corrected text.   FV   FV   10
- ☐ c. Signature 7b.   FV   FV   10
- ☐ d. Signature 8.   FV   FV   7.50
- ☐ bs. Diagonal red نموذج overprint on front;   —   —   4,000
  diagonal red *SPECIMEN* overprint on back;
  horizontal black # overprint at upper left back.

SAMA B23 (P24): **50 riyals** (US$13)   VG   VF   UNC
Green. Front: Dome of the Rock in Jerusalem; King Fahd. Back: Al-Aqsa Mosque in Jerusalem; national emblem (two crossed swords with palm tree). Solid security thread. Watermark: King Fahd. Printer: (TDLR). 155 x 70 mm.

- ☐ a. ١٣٧٩/٧/١ (AH1379/7/1). Signature 7a.   FV   FV   60
  Incorrect text. Intro: 05.01.1984.
- ☐ b. Corrected text.   FV   FV   30
- ☐ c. Signature 8.   FV   FV   35

SAMA B24 (P25): **100 riyals** (US$27)   VG   VF   UNC

Brown. Front: Green dome and minaret of Al-Masjid al-Nabawi (Prophet's Mosque) in Medina; King Fahd. Back: Al-Masjid al-Nabawi; national emblem (two crossed swords with palm tree). Solid security thread. Watermark: King Fahd. Printer: (OFSP). 160 x 72 mm.

		VG	VF	UNC
☐ a.	١٣٧٩/٧/١ (AH1379/7/1). Signature 7a. Intro: 05.01.1984.	FV	FV	100
☐ b.	Signature 7b.	FV	FV	90
☐ c.	Signature 8.	FV	FV	85

SAMA B25 (P26): **500 riyals** (US$133)   VG   VF   UNC

Brown. Front: Ka'aba (cube) in the courtyard of the Holy Mosque; King Abdul Aziz. Back: Holy Mosque in Mecca; national emblem (two crossed swords with palm tree). Solid security thread. Watermark: King Abdul Aziz. Printer: (OFSP). 166 x 74 mm.

		VG	VF	UNC
☐ a.	١٣٧٩/٧/١ (AH1379/7/1). Signature 7a. Error in "Five Hundred Riyals" in panel below portrait. Intro: 05.01.1984.	FV	FV	400
☐ b.	Corrected text.	FV	FV	325
☐ c.	Signature 7b.	FV	FV	275
☐ d.	Signature 8.	FV	FV	275

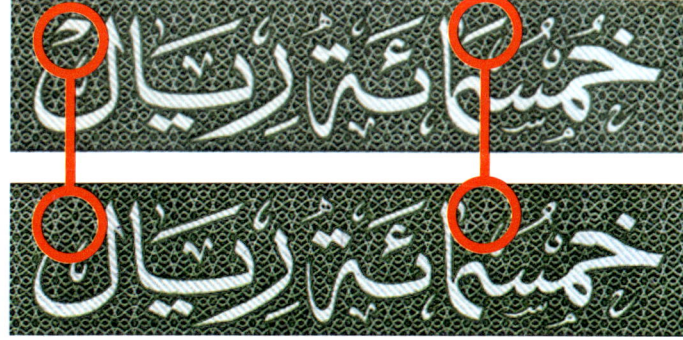

SAMA B25a: Incorrect panel (top) and B25b: Corrected panel (bottom).

1999 Commemorative Issues

These 20- and 200-riyal notes were issued as part of the centenary celebrations of the Kingdom of Saudi Arabia.

SAMA B26 (P27): **20 riyals** (US$5.35)   VG   VF   UNC
Brown. Front: King Abdul Aziz; Quba Mosque in Medina. Back: centenary logo and Jabal an-Nour (The Mountain of Light) near city of Mecca. Holographic patch. Solid security thread and windowed Starwide security thread with demetalized "Saudi Arabian Monetary Authority" in Arabic text. Watermark: King Abdul Aziz with electrotype *20*. Printer: (TDLR). 152 x 69 mm.

    ☐ a. ١٣٧٩/٧/١ (AH1379/7/1). Signature 8.   FV   FV   10
        Intro: 23.01.1999.

SAMA B27 (P28): **200 riyals** (US$53)   VG   VF   UNC
Brown. Front: King Abdul Aziz; gate in western wall of Al Mussmack Palace. Back: Al Mussmack Palace in Riyadh; centenary logo. Holographic patch. Solid security thread and windowed Starwide security thread with demetalized "Saudi Arabian Monetary Authority" in Arabic text. Watermark: King Abdul Aziz with electrotype *200*. Printer: (TDLR). 163 x 73 mm.

    ☐ a. ١٣٧٩/٧/١ (AH1379/7/1). Signature 8.   FV   FV   125
        Intro: 23.01.1999.

2003 Issues

These two notes are similar to the same denominations issued in 1984, but with enhanced security features such as the inclusion of an OVD at front center, a panel of OVI above the portrait, intaglio geometric figures at right front for the visually impaired, and the inclusion of the dates (front and back) in the lower borders.

SAMA B28 (P29): **100 riyals** (US$27)   VG   VF   UNC
Brown. Front: Green dome and minaret of Al-Masjid al-Nabawi (Prophet's Mosque) in Medina; King Fahd. Back: Al-Masjid al-Nabawi; national emblem (two crossed swords with palm tree). OVD. Windowed Starwide security thread with demetalized *100* and Arabic text. Watermark: King Fahd and electrotype *100*. Printer: (TDLR). 160 x 72 mm.

    ☐ a. ١٤٢٤/2003. Signature 8. Intro: 11.10.2003.   FV   FV   60

SAMA B29 (P30): **500 riyals** (US$133)   VG   VF   UNC
Brown. Front: Ka'aba (cube) in the courtyard of the Holy Mosque; King Abdul Aziz. Back: Holy Mosque in Mecca; national emblem (two crossed swords with palm tree). OVD. Windowed security thread with demetalized *500* and Arabic text. Watermark: King Abdul Aziz and electrotype *500*. Printer: (TDLR). 166 x 74 mm.

    ☐ a. ١٤٢٤/2003. Signature 8. Intro: 24.03.2003.   FV   FV   200

2007-2012 "Fifth" Issues

SAMA B30 (P31): **1 riyal** (US$0.25) VG VF UNC
Light green. Front: Front of first Islamic dinar coin; King Abdullah. Back: SAMA headquarters building; national emblem (two crossed swords with palm tree). Windowed security thread with demetalized *SAMA 1*. Watermark: King Abdullah, electrotype *1*, and Cornerstones. Printer: (TDLR). 133 x 63 mm.

☐ a. ١٤٢٨/2007. Signature 8. Intro: 31.12.2007. FV FV 1
☐ b. ١٤٣٠/2009. Signature 9. FV FV 0.50
☐ c. ١٤٣٣/2012. Signature 10. FV FV 0.50

SAMA B31 (P32): **5 riyals** (US$1.35) VG VF UNC
Violet. Front: Ras Tanorah oil refinery; King Abdullah. Back: Jubayl Port in eastern region; national emblem (two crossed swords with palm tree). Windowed security thread with demetalized *SAMA 5*. Watermark: King Abdullah, electrotype *5*, and Cornerstones. Printer: (TDLR). 145 x 66 mm.

☐ a. ١٤٢٨/2007. Signature 8. Intro: 16.07.2007. FV FV 2.50
☐ b. ١٤٣٠/2009. Signature 9. FV FV 2.50
☐ c. ١٤٣٣/2012. Signature 10. FV FV 2.50

SAMA B32 (P33): **10 riyals** (US$2.65) VG VF UNC
Brown. Front: King Abdulaziz's palace in Almoraba area; King Abdullah. Back: King Abdulaziz Historical Center in Riyadh with palm trees; national emblem (two crossed swords with palm tree). Windowed security thread with demetalized *SAMA 10*. Watermark: King Abdullah, electrotype *10*, and Cornerstones. Printer: (TDLR). 150 x 68 mm.

☐ a. ١٤٢٨/2007. Signature 8. Intro: 16.07.2007. FV FV 5
☐ b. ١٤٣٠/2009. Signature 9. FV FV 5
☐ c. ١٤٣٣/2012. Signature 10. FV FV 5

SAMA B33 (P35): **50 riyals** (US$13) VG VF UNC
Dark green. Front: Al Sakhra Dome mosque; King Abdullah. Back: Al Aqsa mosque in Al Quds Al Shareef (Jerusalem); national emblem (two crossed swords with palm tree). Holographic stripe. Windowed security thread with demetalized *50* and Arabic text between wavy lines. Watermark: King Abdullah, electrotype *50*, and Cornerstones. Printer: (TDLR). 155 x 70 mm.

☐ a. ١٤٢٨/2007. Signature 8. Intro: 21.05.2007. FV FV 25
☐ b. ١٤٣٠/2009. Signature 9. FV FV 25
☐ c. ١٤٣٣/2012. Signature 10. FV FV 25

SAMA B34 (P36): **100 riyals** (US$27)　　　　VG　VF　UNC

Red. Front: Green dome and minaret of Al-Masjid al-Nabawi (Prophet's Mosque) in Medina; King Abdullah. Back: Al-Masjid al-Nabawi; national emblem (two crossed swords with palm tree). Holographic stripe. Windowed security thread with demetalized *100* and Arabic text between wavy lines. Watermark: King Abdullah, electrotype *100*, and Cornerstones. Printer: (TDLR). 160 x 72 mm.

    ☐ a. ١٤٢٨/2007. Signature 8. Intro: 21.05.2007.　　FV　FV　45
    ☐ b. ١٤٣٠/2009. Signature 9.　　　　　　　　　　　FV　FV　45

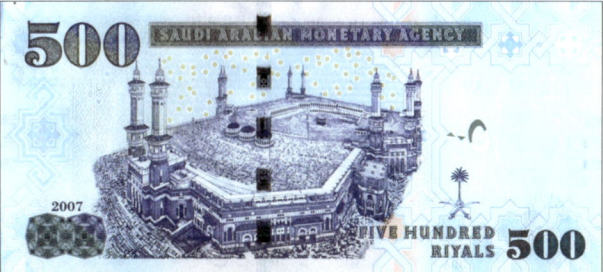

SAMA B35 (P38): **500 riyals** (US$133)　　　VG　VF　UNC

Blue. Front: Ka'aba (cube); King Abdul Aziz. Back: Holy mosque in Makkah Al Mukarramah (Mecca the Honored); national emblem (two crossed swords with palm tree). Holographic stripe. Windowed security thread with demetalized *500* and Arabic text between wavy lines. Watermark: King Abdul Aziz, electrotype *500*, and Cornerstones. Printer: (TDLR). 166 x 74 mm.

    ☐ a. ١٤٢٨/2007. Signature 8. Intro: 17.09.2007.　　FV　FV　235
    ☐ b. ١٤٣٠/2009. Signature 9.　　　　　　　　　　　FV　FV　235
    ☐ c. ١٤٣٣/2012. Signature 10.　　　　　　　　　　FV　FV　235

SAMA Money Museum

The SAMA Money Museum is located in the SAMA Head Office Building at Almazar Street, Riyadh. For more information, write to vaults_issue@sama.gov.sa.

Acknowledgements

This chapter was compiled with the generous assistance of Sejin Ahn, Abdullah Beydoun, Jim Copeland, Yousef Jazzar, Takis Kouvatseas, Wally Myers, Ghassan Samman, Bill Stubkjaer, Richard Sutherland, Peter Symes, Christoph Thomas, Christof Zellweger, and others.

Sources

Cuhaj, George S. *Standard Catalog of World Paper Money, General Issues, 1368-1960*. 14th edition. 2012. ISBN 978-1-4402-3090-5. Krause Publications (www.krausebooks.com), 700 East State St., Iola, WI, 54990-0001.

Cuhaj, George S. *Standard Catalog of World Paper Money, Modern Issues, 1961-Present*. 17th edition. 2011. ISBN 978-1-4402-1584-1. Krause Publications (www.krausebooks.com), 700 East State St., Iola, WI, 54990-0001.

Lott, David. "Security Devices on Saudi Arabian Banknotes." *IBNS Journal*. Volume 25 Number 2. p.45.

Mitchell, John. "Saudi Arabia Aramco Note Issue." *IBNS Journal* Volume 22 Number 1. p.23.

Pugh, Peter. *The Highest Perfection: A History of De La Rue*. 2011. ISBN 978-184831-335-4. Icon Books Ltd. 39-41 North Road, London, N7 9DP.

Said AlHaj Ali, Mohammad. *Saudi Arabian Monetary Agency: A Review of its Accomplishments*. First Print. August 1991. Ayyoubi Printers, Riyahdh.

Shea, Thomas W. "The Riyal: A Miracle in Money." *Saudi Aramco World*. January/February 1969, pp.26-33.

Symes, Peter. "The Bank Notes of Saudi Arabia." *IBNS Journal*. Volume 33 Number 1. p.21.

Symes, Peter. "New Varieties for Old Saudi Notes." *IBNS Journal*. Volume 48 Number 3. p.65.

Symes, Peter. Reference Site for Islamic Banknotes (www.islamicbanknotes.com)

Share Your Input, Info, and Images

This catalog is believed to be complete and correct as of the time of publication. Prices and face values were last updated 17 June 2011. Please report errors or omissions so that corrections may be made. If you can more precisely identify the name or location of anything depicted on a note, please share that information. Furthermore, if you own an unlisted type or variety, please submit scans of the front and back of the note so that it can be documented. Scans should be 300 dots per inch, 100% actual size, 24-bit color, saved as *uncompressed* JPEG files, and sent to owen@banknotenews.com. Be sure to fully describe all attributes of the note which are not apparent upon visual inspection of the images alone, such as physical dimension, watermark, and security thread.

Senegal

Contents

Banque du Sénégal (BDS) 1819
Gouvernement Général de l'A.O.F. (GGAO) 1820

Monetary System
1 franc = 100 centimes

Banque du Sénégal (Bank of Senegal)

Per the decree of 21 December 1853, the Banque du Sénégal (BDS) was the first bank authorized to issue notes in French West Africa. It operated in the capital of Saint-Louis from 1855 until June 1901, at which time the right to issue notes was transferred to the Banque de l'Afrique Occidentale for a 20-year period.

1853-1901 Issues

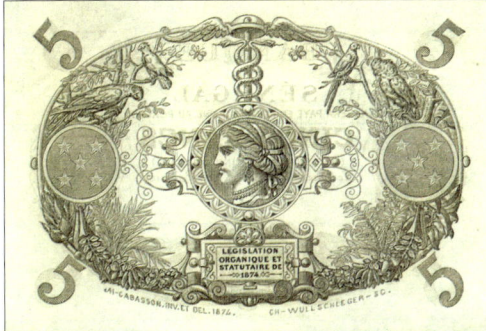

BDS B1 (PA1): 5 francs   VG   VF   UNC
Blue, gray, and black. Front: Head of indigenous man with feathers in hair, earring, and necklace; plants; anchor, barrel, penal code, rudder, and bale; plants; head of indigenous woman with jewelry in hair, earring, and necklace. Back: Five stars in circle; parrots in tree; plants; butterflies; head of woman with ribbons in hair, earring, and necklace; flowers; parrots in tree; five stars in circle. No security thread. Watermark: No. Printer: (BDF). 134 x 92 mm.
     ☐ a. 1874. Handwritten signatures.   —   —   —
     ☐ r. Remainder: No signatures.   —   —   700
     ☐ as. Horizontal black ANNULÉ overprint.   —   XF   2,700
All but 84 of these notes were redeemed by Banque de l'Afrique Occidentale as of 1928.

BDS B2 (PA2): 25 francs   VG   VF   UNC
Black. Front: Border with anchor, flowers, cornstalk, cornucopia, balance scales, sword, snake, mirror, caduceus, and wheat; penal code repeated in two circles. Back: Reverse of front. No security thread. Watermark: 25. Printer: (BDF). 212 x 120 mm.
     ☐ a. No date. Handwritten signatures.   9,500   —   —
     ☐ as. Horizontal ANNULE perf; counterfoil intact.   —   AU   10,000
All but 293 of these notes were redeemed by Banque de l'Afrique Occidentale as of 1928.

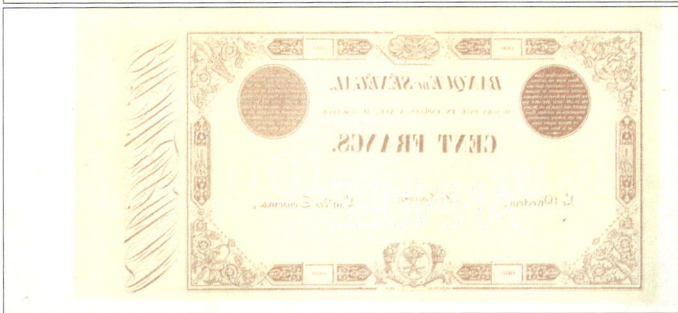

BDS B3 (PA3): 100 francs   VG   VF   UNC
Red. Front: Border with anchor, flowers, cornstalk, cornucopia, balance scales, sword, snake, mirror, caduceus, and wheat; penal code repeated in two circles. Back: Reverse of front. No security thread. Watermark: 100. Printer: (BDF). 212 x 120 mm.
     ☐ a. No date. Handwritten signatures.   —   —   —
     ☐ as. Horizontal ANNULE perf; counterfoil intact.   —   AU   9,500
All but 112 of these notes were redeemed by Banque de l'Afrique Occidentale as of 1928.

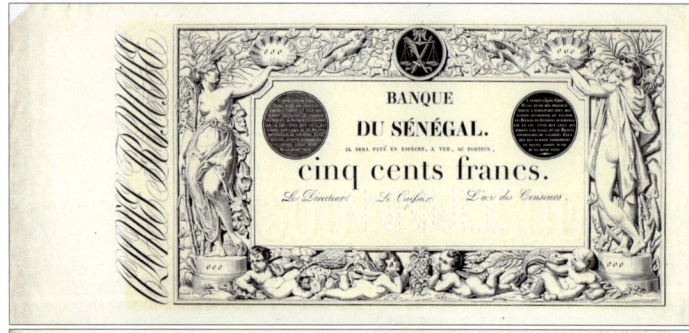

BDS B4 (PA4): 500 francs   VG   VF   UNC

Front: Topless woman (Minerva, symbolizing wisdom) holding cornstalk and seashell; parrots; balance scales; sword; cherubs with turtle, flowers, and fish; Mercury (symbolizing fortune) with anchor holding caduceus and seashell; penal code repeated in two circles. Back: Reverse of front. No security thread. Watermark: *500*. Printer: (BDF). 238 x 135 mm.

☐	a.	Black. No date. Handwritten signatures.	—	—
☐	b.	Blue.	—	—
☐	as.	Horizontal *ANNULE* perf; counterfoil intact.	—	AU 20,000
☐	bs.	No overprint; no perforation; no counterfoil.	—	XF 17,500

All but 19 of these notes were redeemed by Banque de l'Afrique Occidentale as of 1928.

Gouvernement Général de l'A.O.F. - Colonie du Sénégal (General Government of French West Africa - Colony of Senegal)

In 1895 France established Afrique Occidentale Française (French West Africa), a federation of eight territories: Côte d'Ivoire (Ivory Coast), Dahomey (now Benin), French Guinea, French Sudan (now Mali), Mauritania, Niger, Senegal, and Upper Volta (now Burkina Faso).

GGAO Signature Varieties

	Le Trésorier-Payeur (Paymaster)	Le Lt-Gouverneur (Lieutenant Governor)
1	Gustave Duvigneau	Fernand Émile Leveque
2	Auguste-Jacques-Paul Poësson	Pierre Jean Henri Didelot

1917 Emergency Issues

Banque du Sénégal banknotes were in use in French West Africa until 1901 when the Banque de l'Afrique Occidentale was established and began issuing its own notes. Due to the severe shortage of coinage in the colonies due to World War I, on 11 February 1917 a special decree was passed allowing for the issuance of 50-centime, 1-franc, and 2-franc emergency notes, although not all denominations were printed for all of the colonies.

The design of the emergency notes depicted a French coin corresponding to the denomination on the front, and an excerpt of the decree in French on the back. Each colony issued its own notes, distinguished by color, the name of the colony printed below *GOUVERNEMENT GÉNÉRAL DE L'A.O.F.,* and signatures of the colony's paymaster and lieutenant governor.

 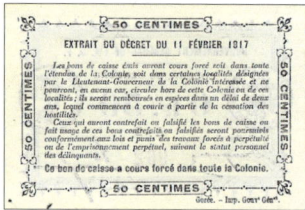

GGAO B1 (P1): 50 centimes   VG   VF   UNC

Blue, green, and black. Front: 50-centime coin. Back: Text. No security thread. Printer: *Gorée. — Imp. Gouv^t Gén^{al}*. 82 x 55 mm.

☐	a.	11 FÉVRIER 1917. Signature 1. Watermark: Bee pattern. 4.5-mm tall serial numbers. 23-mm wide imprint.	50	175	450
☐	b.	3.5-mm tall serial numbers. 26-mm wide imprint.	30	100	250
☐	c.	Watermark: None.	—	—	—
☐	d.	29-mm wide imprint.	—	—	—
☐	e.	Signature 2. 26-mm wide imprint.	45	150	300
☐	r.	Remainder: No serial numbers; punched.	—	—	375

GGAO B2 (P2): 1 franc   VG   VF   UNC

Red, orange, and black. Front: 1-franc coin. Back: Text. No security thread. Printer: *Gorée. — Imp. Gouv^t Gén^{al}.* 102 x 66 mm.

☐	a.	11 FÉVRIER 1917. Signature 1. Watermark: Bee pattern. 4.5-mm tall serial numbers. 23-mm wide imprint.	25	80	375
☐	b.	3.5-mm tall serial numbers. 26-mm wide imprint.	20	75	250
☐	c.	Watermark: None.	20	75	250
☐	d.	Signature 2.	30	115	275
☐	r.	Remainder: No serial numbers; punched.	—	—	—

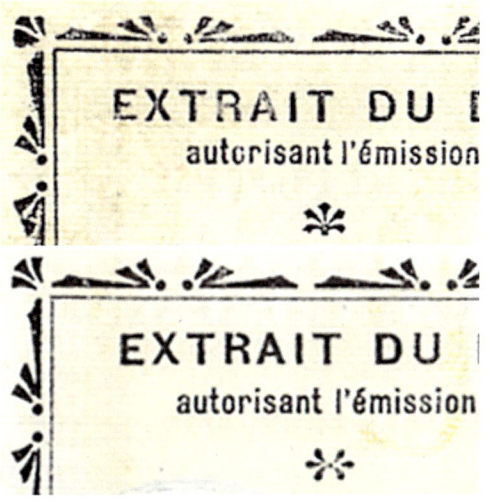

The easiest way to distinguish between the 1-franc varieties is to examine the symbol on the back. On earlier issues, the symbol has five petals (GGAO B2a, top), whereas on later issues it has six petals (GGAO B2b/c/d, bottom).

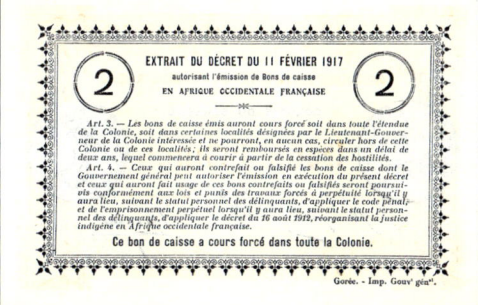

Looking Forward
For later issues, see French West Africa.

Acknowledgements
This chapter was compiled with the generous assistance of Compagnie Generale De Bourse (www.CGB.fr), David Jones, Wally Myers, Mikhail "Mike" Prizov, and others.

Sources
Cuhaj, George S. *Standard Catalog of World Paper Money, General Issues, 1368-1960*. 14th edition. 2012. ISBN 978-1-4402-3090-5. Krause Publications (www.krausebooks.com), 700 East State St., Iola, WI, 54990-0001.

Leclerc, Roger and Maurice Kolsky. *Les Billets Africains de la Zone Franc*. Volume 10. 2000. ISBN 2-906602-17-5. Éditions Victor Gadoury (www.gadoury.com). S.C.S. Bouvernon & Cie. 57, rue Grimaldi, MC-98000 Monaco.

Share Your Input, Info, and Images
This catalog is believed to be complete and correct as of the time of publication. Prices and face values were last updated 25 October 2013. Please report errors or omissions so that corrections may be made. If you can more precisely identify the name or location of anything depicted on a note, please share that information. Furthermore, if you own an unlisted type or variety, please submit scans of the front and back of the note so that it can be documented. Scans should be 300 dots per inch, 100% actual size, 24-bit color, saved as *uncompressed* JPEG files, and sent to owen@banknotenews.com. Be sure to fully describe all attributes of the note which are not apparent upon visual inspection of the images alone, such as physical dimension, watermark, and security thread.

GGAO B3 (P3): 2 francs   VG   VF   UNC

Red, orange, and black. Front: 2-franc coin. Back: Text. No security thread. 130 x 85 mm.

		VG	VF	UNC
☐ a.	11 FÉVRIER 1917. Signature 1. Watermark: Bee pattern. 4.5-mm tall serial numbers. Printer: *Gorée. - Imp. Gouv¹ génᵃˡ*.	—	350	—
☐ b.	3.5-mm tall serial numbers. Printer: *Gorée. — Imp. Gouv¹ Génᵃˡ*.	—	325	—
☐ c.	Watermark: None.	—	—	—
☐ d.	Signature 2.	50	175	600
☐ r.	Remainder: No serial numbers; punched.	—	275	500

Serbia

Earlier Issues

Prior to the establishment of the National Bank of Serbia in 2003, banknotes were issued by various institutions of the forerunner state of Yugoslavia. These issues will be added to this chapter in the future.

Monetary System

1 Serbian dinar (RSD) = 100 para

Народна банка Србије
Narodna Banka Srbija
(National Bank of Serbia)

The National Bank of Serbia (NBS) was established in 2003 by the passage of the Law on the National Bank of Serbia No. 72/2003. For more information, visit www.nbs.rs.

NBS Signature Varieties

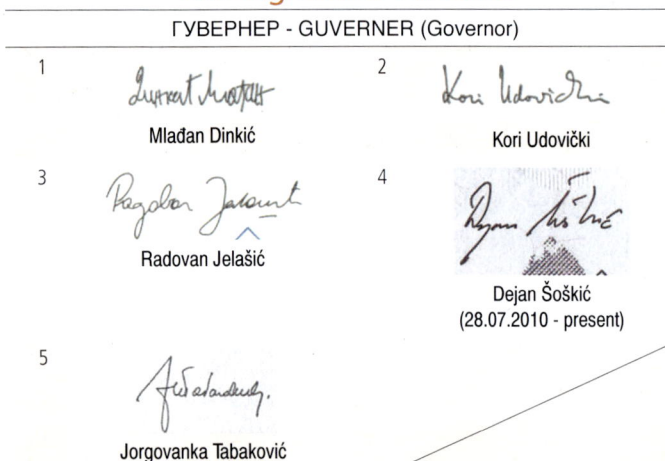

ГУВЕРНЕР - GUVERNER (Governor)

1. Mlađan Dinkić
2. Kori Udovički
3. Radovan Jelašić
4. Dejan Šoškić (28.07.2010 - present)
5. Jorgovanka Tabaković

2003 Commemorative Issues

This 100-dinar note commemorates 120 years of banknote issuance in Serbia.

NBS B1 (P41a): 100 dinara (US$1.20)   VG   VF   UNC

Blue, green, and ochre-yellow. Front: Scientist Nikola Tesla; magnetic induction calculation formula; electrical discharge; Tesla's electric induction device. Back (vertical): National Bank of Serbia seal; Nikola Tesla; Tesla's "White Dove" bird; Tesla's electromagnetic engine. Windowed security thread with demetalized *ДИНАР DINAR*. Watermark: Nikola Tesla. Printer: *NARODNA BANKA SRBIJE - ZAVOD ZA IZRADU NOVČANICA I KOVANOG NOVCA - TOPČIDER*. 143 x 68 mm.

☐ a. 2003. Signature 1. Intro: 02.07.2003.   FV   FV   4.25
☐ as. Specimen.   —   —   —

Replacement notes: Prefix ZA.
Like subsequent issue, but with four lines of text to the left of the signature on back.

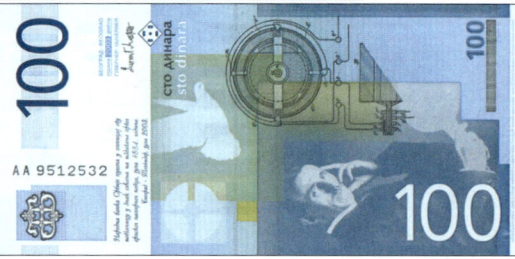

The commemorative text on the back of this note is in Serbian Cyrillic: *Narodna banka Srbije pušta u opticaj ovu novčanicu u znak sećanja na izdavanje prvog srpskog papirnog novca, jula 1884. godine. Beograd-Topčider, jula 2003.* This translates into English as follows: National Bank of Serbia releases to circulation this banknote to commemorate the issuance of the first Serbian paper money, July 1884. Belgrade-Topchider, July 2003.

2003-2004 Issues

All modern Serbian banknotes and coins are produced by the Institute for Manufacturing Banknotes and Coins, a specialized organizational unit of the NBS located in the Belgrade neighborhood of Topčider.

These notes are like the 2000-2002 Yugoslavian notes which they replaced, but they have a different bank seal on back, differences in the text based upon the country's new name, and slight design changes.

The bank seal on the back of Yugoslavian notes dated 2000-2001 (left) is different than that which appears on Serbian notes dated 2003-2004 (right).

NBS B3 (P43): **500 dinara** (US$6.05)   VG   VF   UNC
Blue, green, and yellow. Front: Geographer Jovan Cvijic; globe and map of Serbia. Back (vertical): National Bank of Serbia seal; seated Jovan Cvijic with cane; stylized ethno motives. Holographic patch. Windowed security thread with demetalized *ДИНАР DINAR*. Watermark: Jovan Cvijic. Printer: *NARODNA BANKA SRBIJE - ZAVOD ZA IZRADU NOVČANICA I KOVANOG NOVCA - TOPČIDER*. 147 x 70 mm.
     ☐ a.   2004. Signature 3. Intro: 17.09.2004.   FV   FV   14
     ☐ as. Specimen.   —   —
Replacement notes: Prefix ZA.

NBS B2 (P41b): **100 dinara** (US$1.20)   VG   VF   UNC
Blue, green, and ochre-yellow. Front: Scientist Nikola Tesla; magnetic induction calculation formula; electrical discharge; Tesla's electric induction device. Back (vertical): National Bank of Serbia seal; Nikola Tesla; Tesla's "White Dove" bird; Tesla's electromagnetic engine. Windowed security thread with demetalized *ДИНАР DINAR*. Watermark: Nikola Tesla. Printer: *NARODNA BANKA SRBIJE - ZAVOD ZA IZRADU NOVČANICA I KOVANOG NOVCA - TOPČIDER*. 143 x 68 mm.
     ☐ a.   2004. Signature 3. Intro: 17.09.2004.   FV   FV   7
     ☐ as. Diagonal red hollow *SPECIMEN* overprint;   —   —   250
          black # overprint at lower left.
Replacement notes: Prefix ZA.
Like preceding issue, but without four lines of text to the left of the signature on back.

NBS B4 (P44): **1,000 dinara** (US$12)   VG   VF   UNC
Red, yellow, and gray-blue. Front: Industrialist and bank governor Đorđe Vajfert; Vajfert's brewery in Belgrade. Back (vertical): National Bank of Serbia seal; seated Đorđe Vajfert; interior of the National Bank of Serbia's main building; Saint George slaying dragon. Holographic patch. Windowed security thread with demetalized *ДИНАР DINAR*. Watermark: Đorđe Vajfert. Printer: *NARODNA BANKA SRBIJE - ZAVOD ZA IZRADU NOVČANICA I KOVANOG NOVCA - TOPČIDER*. 151 x 72 mm.
     ☐ a.   2003. Signature 1. Intro: 24.03.2003.   FV   FV   30
     ☐ b.   Signature 2. Intro: 15.09.2003.   FV   FV   25
     ☐ as. Diagonal red hollow *SPECIMEN* overprint;   —   —   275
          black # overprint at lower left.
Replacement notes: Prefix ZA.

NBS B5 (P45): **5,000 dinara** (US$60)   VG   VF   UNC

Green, violet, and gray-yellow. Front: Jurist, historian, sociologist, and journalist Slobodan Jovanovic; sculpture of a woman holding a pigeon on an outstretched hand (detail from the Serbian Academy of Arts and Sciences building). Back (vertical): National Bank of Serbia seal; interior of the Parliament building; Federal Parliament; Slobodan Jovanovic in hat. Holographic patch. Windowed security thread with demetalized *ДИНАР DINAR*. Watermark: Slobodan Jovanovic. Printer: *NARODNA BANKA SRBIJE - ZAVOD ZA IZRADU NOVČANICA I KOVANOG NOVCA - TOPČIDER*. 159 x 76 mm.

- ☐ a. 2003. Signature 1. Intro: 02.07.2003.   FV   FV   120
- ☐ as. Diagonal red hollow *SPECIMEN* overprint;   —   —   300
  black # overprint at lower left.

Replacement notes: Prefix ZA.

2005-2010 Issues

These notes are like the preceding issues, but the bank's seal has been replaced by the national coat of arms on back and several new denominations have been added.

The bank seal on the back of Serbian notes dated 2003-2004 (left) was replaced by the national coat of arms on notes dated 2005-2010 (right).

NBS B6 (P46): **10 dinara** (US$0.10)   VG   VF   UNC

Ochre-yellow, brown, and green. Front: Vuk Stefanovic Karadžic (creator of contemporary Serbian alphabet) as young man; eyeglasses, pen, and open book (exhibits from the standing collection of the Museum devoted to Karadžic and Dositej Obradovic); Karadžic as old man holding sword; bank seal. Back (vertical): Republic of Serbia coat of arms; members of the First Slavic Congress held in Prague in 1848; Serbian characters; Karadžic as seated old man. Windowed security thread with demetalized *ДИНАР DINAR*. Watermark: Vuk Stefanovic Karadžic. Printer: *NARODNA BANKA SRBIJE - ZAVOD ZA IZRADU NOVČANICA I KOVANOG NOVCA - TOPČIDER*. 131 x 62 mm.

- ☐ a. 2006. Signature 3. Intro: 19.05.2006.   FV   FV   1
- ☐ as. Specimen.   —   —   15

Replacement notes: Prefix ZA.

NBS B7 (P47): **20 dinara** (US$0.25)   VG   VF   UNC

Green, ochre-yellow, and black. Front: Petar II Petrovic Njegoš (Serbian Orthodox Prince-Bishop of Montenegro); Cetinje monastery buildings; bank seal. Back (vertical): Republic of Serbia coat of arms; Petar II Petrovic Njegoš; detail from the decorative miniature featured on the first Slavic Octoechos, printed in Cetinje in 1494; Komovi mountain range. Windowed security thread with demetalized *ДИНАР DINAR*. Watermark: Petar II Petrovic Njegoš. Printer: *NARODNA BANKA SRBIJE - ZAVOD ZA IZRADU NOVČANICA I KOVANOG NOVCA - TOPČIDER*. 135 x 64 mm.

- ☐ a. 2006. Signature 3. Intro: 18.07.2006.   FV   FV   1.25
- ☐ as. Specimen.   —   —   15

Replacement notes: Prefix ZA.

NBS B8 (P40): **50 dinara** (US$0.60)   VG   VF   UNC

Violet and ocher. Front: Stevan Stevanovic Mokranjac (composer); scores from the Mokranjac Legacy; violin; keyboards; bank seal. Back (vertical): Republic of Serbia coat of arms; Stevan Stojanovic Mokranjac; motif of Miroslav Gospel illumination scores. Windowed security thread with demetalized *ДИНАР DINAR*. Watermark: Stevan Stevanovic Mokranjac. Printer: *NARODNA BANKA SRBIJE - ZAVOD ZA IZRADU NOVČANICA I KOVANOG NOVCA - TOPČIDER*. 139 x 66 mm.

☐ a. 2005. Signature 3. Intro: 15.11.2005.   FV   FV   3
☐ as. Specimen.   —   —   25

Replacement notes: Prefix ZA.

NBS B10 (P42): **200 dinara** (US$2.40)   VG   VF   UNC

Amber red, brown, and blue. Front: Painter Nadežda Petrovic; Gracanica Monastery sculpture of Petrovic; painter's brush; bank seal. Back (vertical): Republic of Serbia coat of arms; Nadežda Petrovic as nurse in World War I; Gracanica Monastery. Holographic patch. Windowed security thread with demetalized *ДИНАР DINAR*. Watermark: Nadežda Petrovic. Printer: *NARODNA BANKA SRBIJE - ZAVOD ZA IZRADU NOVČANICA I KOVANOG NOVCA - TOPČIDER*. 147 x 70 mm.

☐ a. 2005. Signature 3. Intro: 02.07.2005.   FV   FV   7
☐ as. Specimen.   —   —   25

Replacement notes: Prefix ZA.

NBS B9 (P49): **100 dinara** (US$1.20)   VG   VF   UNC

Blue, green, and ochre-yellow. Front: Scientist Nikola Tesla; magnetic induction calculation formula; electrical discharge; Tesla's electric induction device; bank seal. Back (vertical): Republic of Serbia coat of arms; Nikola Tesla; Tesla's "White Dove" bird; Tesla's electromagnetic engine. Windowed security thread with demetalized *ДИНАР DINAR*. Watermark: Nikola Tesla. Printer: *NARODNA BANKA SRBIJE - ZAVOD ZA IZRADU NOVČANICA I KOVANOG NOVCA - TOPČIDER*. 143 x 68 mm.

☐ a. 2006. Signature 3. Intro: 20.10.2006.   FV   FV   4
☐ as. Specimen.   —   —   25

Replacement notes: Prefix ZA.

NBS B11 (P51): **500 dinara** (US$6.05)   VG   VF   UNC

Blue, green, and yellow. Front: Geographer Jovan Cvijic; globe and map of Serbia; bank seal. Back (vertical): Republic of Serbia coat of arms; seated Jovan Cvijic with cane; stylized ethno motives. Holographic patch. Windowed security thread with demetalized *ДИНАР DINAR*. Watermark: Jovan Cvijic. Printer: *NARODNA BANKA SRBIJE - ZAVOD ZA IZRADU NOVČANICA I KOVANOG NOVCA - TOPČIDER*. 147 x 70 mm.

☐ a. 2007. Signature 3. Intro: 04.06.2007.   FV   FV   15
☐ as. Specimen.   —   —   50

Replacement notes: Prefix ZA.

SERBIA 2011-2014 ISSUES · THE BANKNOTE BOOK

2011-2014 Issues

These notes are like the preceding issues, but the national coat of arms on back is more detailed, in accordance with the Decree on Establishing the Original Great and Small Coat-of-Arms, Flag and National Anthem of the Republic of Serbia, No. 85 of 15 November 2010.

The coat of arms on the back of notes dated 2005-2010 (left) is not as detailed as that which appears on notes dated 2011- (right).

NBS B12 (P52): **1,000 dinara** (US$12) VG VF UNC
Red, yellow, and gray-blue. Front: Industrialist and bank governor Đorđe Vajfert; Vajfert's brewery in Belgrade; bank seal. Back (vertical): Republic of Serbia coat of arms; seated Đorđe Vajfert; interior of the National Bank of Serbia's main building; Saint George slaying dragon. Holographic patch. Windowed security thread with demetalized *ДИНАР DINAR*. Watermark: Đorđe Vajfert. Printer: *NARODNA BANKA SRBIJE - ZAVOD ZA IZRADU NOVČANICA I KOVANOG NOVCA - TOPČIDER*. 151 x 72 mm.

☐ a. 2006. Signature 3. Intro: 18.07.2006.   FV   FV   20
☐ as. Specimen.   —   —   100

Replacement notes: Prefix ZA.

NBS B14 (P54): **10 dinara** (US$0.10) VG VF UNC
Ochre-yellow, brown, and green. Front: Vuk Stefanović Karadžić (creator of contemporary Serbian alphabet) as young man; eyeglasses, pen, and open book (exhibits from the standing collection of the Museum devoted to Karadžić and Dositej Obradović); Karadžić as old man holding sword; bank seal. Back (vertical): Republic of Serbia coat of arms; members of the First Slavic Congress held in Prague in 1848; Serbian characters; Karadžić as seated old man. Windowed security thread with demetalized *ДИНАР DINAR*. Watermark: Vuk Stefanović Karadžić. Printer: *NARODNA BANKA SRBIJE - ZAVOD ZA IZRADU NOVČANICA I KOVANOG NOVCA - TOPČIDER*. 131 x 62 mm.

☐ a. 2011. Signature 4. Intro: 30.09.2011.   FV   FV   1
☐ b. 2013. Signature 5. Intro: 29.05.2013.   FV   FV   1

Replacement notes: Prefix ZA.

NBS B13 (P53): **5,000 dinara** (US$60) VG VF UNC
Green, violet, and gray-yellow. Front: Jurist, historian, sociologist, and journalist Slobodan Jovanović; sculpture of a woman holding a pigeon on an outstretched hand (detail from the Serbian Academy of Arts and Sciences building); bank seal. Back (vertical): Republic of Serbia coat of arms; interior of the Parliament building; Federal Parliament; Slobodan Jovanović in hat. Holographic patch. Windowed security thread with demetalized *ДИНАР DINAR*. Watermark: Slobodan Jovanović. Printer: *NARODNA BANKA SRBIJE - ZAVOD ZA IZRADU NOVČANICA I KOVANOG NOVCA - TOPČIDER*. 159 x 76 mm.

☐ a. 2010. Signature 4. Intro: 26.11.2010.   FV   FV   120

Replacement notes: Prefix ZA.

NBS B15 (P55): **20 dinara** (US$0.25)   VG   VF   UNC

Green, ochre-yellow, and black. Front: Petar II Petrovic Njegoš (Serbian Orthodox Prince-Bishop of Montenegro); Cetinje monastery buildings; bank seal. Back (vertical): Republic of Serbia coat of arms; Petar II Petrovic Njegoš; detail from the decorative miniature featured on the first Slavic Octoechos, printed in Cetinje in 1494; Komovi mountain range. Windowed security thread with demetalized *ДИНАР DINAR*. Watermark: Petar II Petrovic Njegoš. Printer: *NARODNA BANKA SRBIJE - ZAVOD ZA IZRADU NOVČANICA I KOVANOG NOVCA - TOPČIDER*. 135 x 64 mm.

☐ a. 2011. Signature 4. Intro: 30.09.2011.   FV   FV   1.25
☐ b. 2013. Signature 5. Intro: 29.05.2013.   FV   FV   1.25

Replacement notes: Prefix ZA.

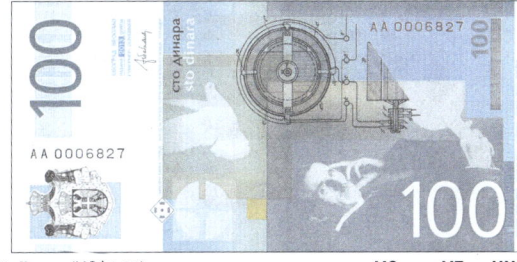

NBS B17 (P49): **100 dinara** (US$1.20)   VG   VF   UNC

Blue, green, and ochre-yellow. Front: Scientist Nikola Tesla; magnetic induction calculation formula; electrical discharge; Tesla's electric induction device; bank seal. Back (vertical): Republic of Serbia coat of arms; Nikola Tesla; Tesla's "White Dove" bird; Tesla's electromagnetic engine. Windowed security thread with demetalized *ДИНАР DINAR*. Watermark: Nikola Tesla. Printer: *NARODNA BANKA SRBIJE - ZAVOD ZA IZRADU NOVČANICA I KOVANOG NOVCA - TOPČIDER*. 143 x 68 mm.

☐ a. 2012. Signature 4. Intro: 11.05.2012.   FV   FV   4
☐ b. 2013. Signature 5. Intro: 29.05.2013.   FV   FV   4

Replacement notes: Prefix ZA.

NBS B16 (P56): **50 dinara** (US$0.60)   VG   VF   UNC

Violet and ocher. Front: Stevan Stevanovic Mokranjac (composer); scores from the Mokranjac Legacy; violin; keyboards; bank seal. Back (vertical): Republic of Serbia coat of arms; Stevan Stojanovic Mokranjac; motif of Miroslav Gospel illumination scores. Windowed security thread with demetalized *ДИНАР DINAR*. Watermark: Stevan Stevanovic Mokranjac. Printer: *NARODNA BANKA SRBIJE - ZAVOD ZA IZRADU NOVČANICA I KOVANOG NOVCA - TOPČIDER*. 139 x 66 mm.

☐ a. 2011. Signature 4. Intro: 20.06.2011.   FV   FV   2
☐ b. 2014. Signature 5. Intro: 28.02.2014.   FV   FV   2

Replacement notes: Prefix ZA.

NBS B18 (P57): **200 dinara** (US$2.40)   VG   VF   UNC

Amber red, brown, and blue. Front: Painter Nadežda Petrovic; Gracanica Monastery sculpture of Petrovic; painter's brush; bank seal. Back (vertical): Republic of Serbia coat of arms; Nadežda Petrovic as nurse in World War I; Gracanica Monastery. Holographic patch. Windowed security thread with demetalized *ДИНАР DINAR*. Watermark: Nadežda Petrovic. Printer: *NARODNA BANKA SRBIJE - ZAVOD ZA IZRADU NOVČANICA I KOVANOG NOVCA - TOPČIDER*. 147 x 70 mm.

☐ a. 2011. Signature 4. Intro: 30.09.2011.   FV   FV   8
☐ b. 2013. Signature 5. Intro: 05.07.2013.   FV   FV   8

Replacement notes: Prefix ZA.

NBS B19 (P51): **500 dinara** (US$6.05) VG VF UNC
Blue, green, and yellow. Front: Geographer Jovan Cvijic; globe and map of Serbia; bank seal. Back (vertical): Republic of Serbia coat of arms; seated Jovan Cvijic with cane; stylized ethno motives. Holographic patch. Windowed security thread with demetalized *ДИНАР DINAR*. Watermark: Jovan Cvijic. Printer: *NARODNA BANKA SRBIJE - ZAVOD ZA IZRADU NOVČANICA I KOVANOG NOVCA - TOPČIDER*. 147 x 70 mm.

☐ a. 2011. Signature 4. Intro: 30.12.2011. FV FV 15
☐ b. 2012. Signature 5. Intro: 07.12.2012. FV FV 15

Replacement notes: Prefix ZA.

NBS B20 (P52): **1,000 dinara** (US$12) VG VF UNC
Red, yellow, and gray-blue. Front: Industrialist and bank governor Đorde Vajfert; Vajfert's brewery in Belgrade; bank seal. Back (vertical): Republic of Serbia coat of arms; seated Đorde Vajfert; interior of the National Bank of Serbia's main building; Saint George slaying dragon. Holographic patch. Windowed security thread with demetalized *ДИНАР DINAR*. Watermark: Đorde Vajfert. Printer: *NARODNA BANKA SRBIJE - ZAVOD ZA IZRADU NOVČANICA I KOVANOG NOVCA - TOPČIDER*. 151 x 72 mm.

☐ a. 2011. Signature 4. Intro: 30.12.2011. FV FV 20

Replacement notes: Prefix ZA.

NBS B21 (PNL): **2,000 dinara** (US$24) VG VF UNC
Orange and brown. Front: Scientist Milutin Milanković; bank seal. Back (vertical): Republic of Serbia coat of arms; seated Đorde Vajfert; interior of the National Bank of Serbia's main building; Milutin Milanković and his scientific works. Holographic patch. Windowed security thread with demetalized *ДИНАР DINAR*. Watermark: Milutin Milanković. Printer: *NARODNA BANKA SRBIJE - ZAVOD ZA IZRADU NOVČANICA I KOVANOG NOVCA - TOPČIDER*. 151 x 72 mm.

☐ a. 2011. Signature 4. Intro: 30.12.2011. FV FV 50
☐ b. 2012. Signature 5. Intro: 07.12.2012. FV FV 45
☐ as. Diagonal *SPECIMEN* perforation. — — —

Replacement notes: Prefix ZA.

Acknowledgements

This chapter was compiled with the generous assistance of Thomas Augustsson, Javier Blake, Jim W.-C. Chen, Alberto Fochi, Kevin Klauss, Claudio Marana, Robert Mol, Wally Myers, Matej Omahen, George Provencal, Bill Stubkjaer, Christoph Thomas, Zlatko Viščević and others.

Sources

Cuhaj, George S. *Standard Catalog of World Paper Money, Modern Issues, 1961-Present*. 19th edition. 2013. ISBN 978-1-4402-3571-9. Krause Publications (www.krausebooks.com), 700 East State St., Iola, WI, 54990-0001.

Friedman, Herb. "Letters to the Editor." *IBNS Journal*. Volume 45 Number 1. p.4.

Viščević, Zlatko. *Coins and Banknotes of Yugoslavia, Slovenia, Croatia, Bosnia and Herzegovina, Serbia, Montenegro and Macedonia*. 2nd edition. 2011. ISBN 978-953-5689-0-3.

Share Your Input, Info, and Images

This catalog is believed to be complete and correct as of the time of publication. Prices and face values were last updated 28 June 2013. Please report errors or omissions so that corrections may be made. If you can more precisely identify the name or location of anything depicted on a note, please share that information. Furthermore, if you own an unlisted type or variety, please submit scans of the front and back of the note so that it can be documented. Scans should be 300 dots per inch, 100% actual size, 24-bit color, saved as *uncompressed* JPEG files, and sent to owen@banknotenews.com. Be sure to fully describe all attributes of the note which are not apparent upon visual inspection of the images alone, such as physical dimension, watermark, and security thread.

Serbian Krajina

For earlier issues, see Croatia and Yugoslavia.

Contents

Republika Srpska Krajina (RSK) 1829
Narodna Banka Republike Srpske Krajine (NB) 1831

Monetary System
1991-1994: 1 Krajina dinar = 100 para

Република Српска Крајина / Republika Srpska Krajina (Republic of Serbian Krajina)

On 1 April 1991, the Republic of Serbian Krajina (RSK), an enclave of Serbian regions, seceded from Croatia (which itself declared independence from Yugoslavia on 25 June 1991) to form its own republic with its capital in Knin. This republic was backed by the Yugoslav People's Army as well as by Serbian militias, but ultimately fell to Croatian forces in August 1995. The many banknotes issued by the Republic of Serbian Krajina between 1991 and 1994 were printed at Yugoslavia's Banknote Printing Works in Belgrade.

RSK Signature Varieties

1	*B. Пеураца*
	МИНИСТАР ФИНАНСИЈА
	(Minister of Finance)
	V. Peuraca

1991 War Loan Certificate Issues

In 1991, three war loan certificates denominated in 10,000-, 20,000-, and 50,000-динара (dinara) were prepared, but never issued. Although these resemble banknotes, they are not banknotes, and therefore are not included in this catalog.

1992 Issues

Bosnia and Herzegovina issued notes identical in color and design to these, but the text on top is different, as is the signature and place of issue (БАЊА ЛУКА = Banja Luka instead of КНИН = Knin).

RSK B4 (PR1): 10 dinara   VG   VF   UNC
Brown and orange. Front: Guilloche patterns; Serbian coat of arms. Back: Serbian coat of arms; Guilloche patterns. Solid security thread with printed *СФРЈ - SFRJ*. Watermark: Head of young girl. Printer: (Banknote Printing Works, Belgrade). 140 x 66 mm.

		VG	VF	UNC
☐	a. 1992. Signature 1. Intro: 14.07.1992.	0.50	1	3
☐	as1. Diagonal red *SPECIMEN* overprint; black # overprint at lower center.	—	—	30
☐	as2. No overprint; all-zero serial number.	—	—	30
☐	r. Remainder: No serial number.	—	—	—

Replacement notes: Prefix ZA.

RSK B5 (PR2): 50 dinara   VG   VF   UNC
Gray and tan. Front: Guilloche patterns; Serbian coat of arms. Back: Serbian coat of arms; Guilloche patterns. Solid security thread with printed *СФРЈ - SFRJ*. Watermark: Head of young girl. Printer: (Banknote Printing Works, Belgrade). 140 x 66 mm.

		VG	VF	UNC
☐	a. 1992. Signature 1. Intro: 14.07.1992.	0.50	1	3.25
☐	as1. Diagonal red *SPECIMEN* overprint; black # overprint at lower center.	—	—	30
☐	as2. No overprint; all-zero serial number.	—	—	30
☐	r. Remainder: No serial number.	—	—	—

Replacement notes: Prefix ZA.

RSK B6 (PR3): **100 dinara**   VG   VF   UNC

Blue and lilac. Front: Guilloche patterns; Serbian coat of arms. Back: Serbian coat of arms; Guilloche patterns. Solid security thread with printed СФРЈ - SFRJ. Watermark: Head of young girl. Printer: (Banknote Printing Works, Belgrade). 140 x 66 mm.

- ☐ a. 1992. Signature 1. Intro: 14.07.1992.   0.50   1   4
- ☐ as1. Diagonal red *SPECIMEN* overprint;   —   —   30
  black # overprint at lower center.
- ☐ as2. No overprint; all-zero serial number.   —   —   30
- ☐ r. Remainder: No serial number.   —   —   —

Replacement notes: Prefix ZA.

RSK B8 (PR5): **1,000 dinara**   VG   VF   UNC

Gray and pink. Front: Guilloche patterns; Serbian coat of arms. Back: Serbian coat of arms; Guilloche patterns. Solid security thread with printed СФРЈ - SFRJ. Watermark: Head of young boy. Printer: (Banknote Printing Works, Belgrade). 145 x 69 mm.

- ☐ a. 1992. Signature 1. Intro: 14.07.1992.   0.50   1   5
- ☐ as1. Diagonal red *SPECIMEN* overprint;   —   —   30
  black # overprint at lower center.
- ☐ as2. No overprint; all-zero serial number.   —   —   30
- ☐ r. Remainder: No serial number.   —   —   —

Replacement notes: Prefix ZA.

RSK B7 (PR4): **500 dinara**   VG   VF   UNC

Blue and pink. Front: Guilloche patterns; Serbian coat of arms. Back: Serbian coat of arms; Guilloche patterns. Solid security thread with printed СФРЈ - SFRJ. Watermark: Head of young boy. Printer: (Banknote Printing Works, Belgrade). 145 x 69 mm.

- ☐ a. 1992. Signature 1. Intro: 14.07.1992.   0.50   1   5
- ☐ as1. Diagonal red *SPECIMEN* overprint;   —   —   30
  black # overprint at lower center.
- ☐ as2. No overprint; all-zero serial number.   —   —   30
- ☐ r. Remainder: No serial number.   —   —   —

Replacement notes: Prefix ZA.

RSK B9 (PR6): **5,000 dinara**   VG   VF   UNC

Violet and lilac. Front: Guilloche patterns; Serbian coat of arms. Back: Serbian coat of arms; Guilloche patterns. Solid security thread with printed СФРЈ - SFRJ. Watermark: Head of young boy. Printer: (Banknote Printing Works, Belgrade). 145 x 69 mm.

- ☐ a. 1992. Signature 1. Intro: 14.07.1992.   0.50   1   4
- ☐ as1. Diagonal red *SPECIMEN* overprint;   —   —   30
  black # overprint at lower center.
- ☐ as2. No overprint; all-zero serial number.   —   —   30
- ☐ r. Remainder: No serial number.   —   —   —

Replacement notes: Prefix ZA.

Narodna Banka Republike Srpske Krajine
(National Bank of the Republic of Serbian Krajina)

NB Signature Varieties

1

ГУВЕРНЕР
(Governor)
Pavao "Pajo" Marjanovic

1992-1993 Issues

Bosnia and Herzegovina issued notes identical in color and design to these, but the text on top is different, as is the signature and place of issue (БАЊА ЛУКА = Banja Luka instead of КНИН = Knin). Rampant inflation required notes of ever-increasing denominations.

NB B1 (PR7): **10,000 dinara**　　　　　　　VG　VF　UNC

Dark green and light blue. Front: Guilloche patterns; Serbian coat of arms. Back: Serbian coat of arms; Guilloche patterns. Solid security thread with printed СФРЈ - SFRJ. Watermark: Head of young boy. Printer: (Banknote Printing Works, Belgrade). 145 x 69 mm.

- a. 1992. Signature 1. — 0.50　1　4
- as1. Diagonal red *SPECIMEN* overprint; black # overprint at lower center. — — 30
- as2. No overprint; all-zero serial number. — — 30
- r. Remainder: No serial number. — — —

Replacement notes: Prefix ZA.

NB B2 (PR8): **50,000 dinara**　　　　　　　VG　VF　UNC

Brown and light brown. Front: Guilloche patterns; Serbian coat of arms. Back: Serbian coat of arms; Guilloche patterns. Solid security thread with printed СФРЈ - SFRJ. Watermark: Head of young boy. Printer: (Banknote Printing Works, Belgrade). 145 x 69 mm.

- a. 1993. Signature 1. 1　5　10
- as1. Diagonal red *SPECIMEN* overprint; black # overprint at lower center. — — 30
- as2. No overprint; all-zero serial number. — — 30
- r. Remainder: No serial number. — — —

Replacement notes: Prefix ZA.

NB B3 (PR9): **100,000 dinara**　　　　　　　VG　VF　UNC

Dark violet and brown. Front: Guilloche patterns; Serbian coat of arms. Back: Serbian coat of arms; Guilloche patterns. Solid security thread with printed СФРЈ - SFRJ. Watermark: Head of woman. Printer: (Banknote Printing Works, Belgrade). 150 x 71 mm.

- a. 1993. Signature 1. 1　5　10
- as1. Diagonal red *SPECIMEN* overprint; black # overprint at lower center. — — 30
- as2. No overprint; all-zero serial number. — — 30
- r. Remainder: No serial number. — — —

Replacement notes: Prefix ZA.

NB B4 (PR10): **1,000,000 dinara** VG VF UNC
Blue-black and yellow. Front: Guilloche patterns; Serbian coat of arms. Back: Serbian coat of arms; Guilloche patterns. Solid security thread with printed CФРJ - SFRJ. Watermark: Head of young girl. Printer: (Banknote Printing Works, Belgrade). 140 x 66 mm.

			VG	VF	UNC
☐	a.	1993. Signature 1.	1	5	25
☐	as1.	Diagonal red *SPECIMEN* overprint; black # overprint at lower center.	—	—	30
☐	as2.	No overprint; all-zero serial number.	—	—	30
☐	r.	Remainder: No serial number.	—	—	—

Replacement notes: Prefix ZA.

NB B6 (PR12): **10,000,000 dinara** VG VF UNC
Dark blue and green. Front: Guilloche patterns; Serbian coat of arms. Back: Serbian coat of arms; Guilloche patterns. Solid security thread with printed CФРJ - SFRJ. Watermark: Head of young girl. Printer: (Banknote Printing Works, Belgrade). 140 x 66 mm.

			VG	VF	UNC
☐	a.	1993. Signature 1.	0.50	1	3
☐	as1.	Diagonal red *SPECIMEN* overprint; black # overprint at lower center.	—	—	30
☐	as2.	No overprint; all-zero serial number.	—	—	30
☐	r.	Remainder: No serial number.	—	—	—

Replacement notes: Prefix ZA.

NB B5 (PR11): **5,000,000 dinara** VG VF UNC
Brown-black and blue. Front: Guilloche patterns; Serbian coat of arms. Back: Serbian coat of arms; Guilloche patterns. Solid security thread with printed CФРJ - SFRJ. Watermark: Head of young girl. Printer: (Banknote Printing Works, Belgrade). 140 x 66 mm.

			VG	VF	UNC
☐	a.	1993. Signature 1.	0.50	1	4
☐	as1.	Diagonal red *SPECIMEN* overprint; black # overprint at lower center.	—	—	30
☐	as2.	No overprint; all-zero serial number.	—	—	30
☐	r.	Remainder: No serial number.	—	—	—

Replacement notes: Prefix ZA.

NB B7 (PR13): **20,000,000 dinara** VG VF UNC
Brown-black and red-orange. Front: Guilloche patterns; Serbian coat of arms. Back: Serbian coat of arms; Guilloche patterns. No security thread. Watermark: Greek key pattern. Printer: (Banknote Printing Works, Belgrade). 140 x 68 mm.

			VG	VF	UNC
☐	a.	1993. Signature 1.	0.50	1.50	5
☐	as1.	Diagonal red *SPECIMEN* overprint; black # overprint at lower center.	—	—	30
☐	as2.	No overprint; all-zero serial number.	—	—	30
☐	r.	Remainder: No serial number.	—	—	—

Replacement notes: Prefix Z.

NB B8 (PR14): 50,000,000 dinara   VG   VF   UNC

Brown-violet and pink. Front: Guilloche patterns; Serbian coat of arms. Back: Serbian coat of arms; Guilloche patterns. No security thread. Watermark: Greek key pattern. Printer: (Banknote Printing Works, Belgrade). 140 x 68 mm.

		VG	VF	UNC
☐	a. 1993. Signature 1.	0.50	1	3
☐	as1. Diagonal red *SPECIMEN* overprint; black # overprint at lower center.	—	—	30
☐	as2. No overprint; all-zero serial number.	—	—	30
☐	r. Remainder: No serial number.	—	—	—

Replacement notes: Prefix Z.

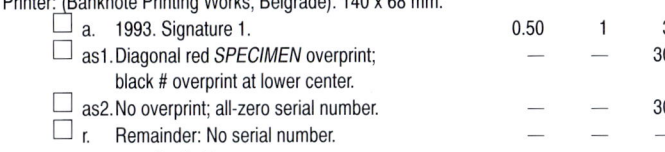

NB B9 (PR15): 100,000,000 dinara   VG   VF   UNC

Dark blue and light blue. Front: Guilloche patterns; Serbian coat of arms. Back: Serbian coat of arms; Guilloche patterns. No security thread. Watermark: Greek key pattern. Printer: (Banknote Printing Works, Belgrade). 140 x 68 mm.

		VG	VF	UNC
☐	a. 1993. Signature 1.	0.50	1	3
☐	as1. Diagonal red *SPECIMEN* overprint; black # overprint at lower center.	—	—	30
☐	as2. No overprint; all-zero serial number.	—	—	30
☐	r. Remainder: No serial number.	—	—	—

Replacement notes: Prefix Z.

NB B10 (PR16): 500,000,000 dinara   VG   VF   UNC

Orange and yellow. Front: Guilloche patterns; Serbian coat of arms. Back: Serbian coat of arms; Guilloche patterns. No security thread. Watermark: Greek key pattern. Printer: (Banknote Printing Works, Belgrade). 140 x 68 mm.

		VG	VF	UNC
☐	a. 1993. Signature 1.	0.50	1	3
☐	as1. Diagonal red *SPECIMEN* overprint; black # overprint at lower center.	—	—	30
☐	as2. No overprint; all-zero serial number.	—	—	30
☐	r. Remainder: No serial number.	—	—	—

Replacement notes: Prefix Z.

NB B11 (PR17): 1,000,000,000 dinara   VG   VF   UNC

Orange-brown and gray. Front: Guilloche patterns; Serbian coat of arms. Back: Serbian coat of arms; Guilloche patterns. No security thread. Watermark: Greek key pattern. Printer: (Banknote Printing Works, Belgrade). 140 x 68 mm.

		VG	VF	UNC
☐	a. 1993. Signature 1.	0.50	1	3
☐	as1. Diagonal red *SPECIMEN* overprint; black # overprint at lower center.	—	—	30
☐	as2. No overprint; all-zero serial number.	—	—	30
☐	r. Remainder: No serial number.	—	—	—

Replacement notes: Prefix Z.

1993 Issues

These notes were issued following the currency reform in Yugoslavia on 1 October 1993, in which six zeroes were removed from the currency, creating a new dinar equal to one million old dinars.

NB B12 (PR18): **5,000,000,000 dinara** VG VF UNC
Purple and gray. Front: Guilloche patterns; Serbian coat of arms. Back: Serbian coat of arms; Guilloche patterns. No security thread. Watermark: Greek key pattern. Printer: (Banknote Printing Works, Belgrade). 140 x 68 mm.

    ☐ a.   1993. Signature 1.   1   2   5
    ☐ as1. Diagonal red *SPECIMEN* overprint;   —   — 30
          black # overprint at lower center.
    ☐ as2. No overprint; all-zero serial number.   —   — 30
    ☐ r.   Remainder: No serial number.   —   —   —

Replacement notes: Prefix Z.

NB B14 (PR20): **5,000 dinara** VG VF UNC
Red-brown and blue-green. Front: Guilloche patterns; Serbian coat of arms. Back: Fortress on hill in Knin. No security thread. Watermark: Greek key pattern. Printer: (Banknote Printing Works, Belgrade). 140 x 66 mm.

    ☐ a.   1993. Signature 1.   0.25 0.50 1.50
    ☐ as1. Diagonal red *SPECIMEN* overprint;   —   — 30
          black # overprint at lower center.
    ☐ as2. No overprint; all-zero serial number. —   — 30
    ☐ r.   Remainder: No serial number.   —   —   —

Replacement notes: Prefix Z.

NB B13 (PR19): **10,000,000,000 dinara** VG VF UNC
Black and red. Front: Guilloche patterns; Serbian coat of arms. Back: Serbian coat of arms; Guilloche patterns. No security thread. Watermark: Greek key pattern. Printer: (Banknote Printing Works, Belgrade). 140 x 68 mm.

    ☐ a.   1993. Signature 1.   0.50 1 3
    ☐ as1. Diagonal red *SPECIMEN* overprint;   — — 30
          black # overprint at lower center.
    ☐ as2. No overprint; all-zero serial number. — — 30
    ☐ r.   Remainder: No serial number.   — — —

Replacement notes: Prefix Z.

NB B15 (PR21): **50,000 dinara** VG VF UNC
Brown and red-orange. Front: Guilloche patterns; Serbian coat of arms. Back: Fortress on hill in Knin. No security thread. Watermark: Greek key pattern. Printer: (Banknote Printing Works, Belgrade). 140 x 66 mm.

    ☐ a.   1993. Signature 1.   0.50 1 3
    ☐ as1. Diagonal red *SPECIMEN* overprint;   — — 30
          black # overprint at lower center.
    ☐ as2. No overprint; all-zero serial number. — — 30
    ☐ r.   Remainder: No serial number.   — — —

Replacement notes: Prefix Z.

NB B16 (PR22): **100,000 dinara**   VG   VF   UNC

Violet and blue-black. Front: Guilloche patterns; Serbian coat of arms. Back: Fortress on hill in Knin. No security thread. Watermark: Greek key pattern. Printer: (Banknote Printing Works, Belgrade). 140 x 66 mm.

- ☐ a. 1993. Signature 1.   1   3   7
- ☐ as1. Diagonal red *SPECIMEN* overprint; black # overprint at lower center.   —   —   30
- ☐ as2. No overprint; all-zero serial number.   —   —   30
- ☐ r. Remainder: No serial number.   —   —   —

Replacement notes: Prefix Z.

NB B18 (PR24): **5,000,000 dinara**   VG   VF   UNC

Dark gray and red-orange. Front: Guilloche patterns; Serbian coat of arms. Back: Fortress on hill in Knin. No security thread. Watermark: Greek key pattern. Printer: (Banknote Printing Works, Belgrade). 140 x 66 mm.

- ☐ a. 1993. Signature 1.   0.50   1   3.50
- ☐ as1. Diagonal red *SPECIMEN* overprint; black # overprint at lower center.   —   —   30
- ☐ as2. No overprint; all-zero serial number.   —   —   30
- ☐ r. Remainder: No serial number.   —   —   —

Replacement notes: Prefix Z.

NB B17 (PR23): **500,000 dinara**   VG   VF   UNC

Brown and dark green. Front: Guilloche patterns; Serbian coat of arms. Back: Fortress on hill in Knin. No security thread. Watermark: Greek key pattern. Printer: (Banknote Printing Works, Belgrade). 140 x 66 mm.

- ☐ a. 1993. Signature 1.   0.25   1   3
- ☐ as1. Diagonal red *SPECIMEN* overprint; black # overprint at lower center.   —   —   30
- ☐ as2. No overprint; all-zero serial number.   —   —   30
- ☐ r. Remainder: No serial number.   —   —   —

Replacement notes: Prefix Z.

NB B19 (PR25): **100,000,000 dinara**   VG   VF   UNC

Gray-brown and dark green. Front: Guilloche patterns; Serbian coat of arms. Back: Fortress on hill in Knin. No security thread. Watermark: Greek key pattern. Printer: (Banknote Printing Works, Belgrade). 140 x 66 mm.

- ☐ a. 1993. Signature 1.   0.50   1   3.50
- ☐ as1. Diagonal red *SPECIMEN* overprint; black # overprint at lower center.   —   —   30
- ☐ as2. No overprint; all-zero serial number.   —   —   30
- ☐ r. Remainder: No serial number.   —   —   —

Replacement notes: Prefix Z.

NB B20 (PR26): **500,000,000 dinara** VG VF UNC
Brown-black and olive gray. Front: Guilloche patterns; Serbian coat of arms. Back: Fortress on hill in Knin. No security thread. Watermark: Greek key pattern. Printer: (Banknote Printing Works, Belgrade). 140 x 66 mm.

☐	a. 1993. Signature 1.	0.25	1	3.75
☐	as1. Diagonal red *SPECIMEN* overprint; black # overprint at lower center.	—	—	30
☐	as2. No overprint; all-zero serial number.	—	—	30
☐	r. Remainder: No serial number.	—	—	—

Replacement notes: Prefix Z.

NB B22 (PR28): **10,000,000,000 dinara** VG VF UNC
Black-blue and red. Front: Guilloche patterns; Serbian coat of arms. Back: Fortress on hill in Knin. No security thread. Watermark: Greek key pattern. Printer: (Banknote Printing Works, Belgrade). 140 x 66 mm.

☐	a. 1993. Signature 1.	1	2	7
☐	as1. Diagonal red *SPECIMEN* overprint; black # overprint at lower center.	—	—	30
☐	as2. No overprint; all-zero serial number.	—	—	30
☐	r. Remainder: No serial number.	—	—	—

Replacement notes: Prefix Z.

NB B21 (PR27): **5,000,000,000 dinara** VG VF UNC
Brown-orange and blue. Front: Guilloche patterns; Serbian coat of arms. Back: Fortress on hill in Knin. No security thread. Watermark: Greek key pattern. Printer: (Banknote Printing Works, Belgrade). 140 x 66 mm.

☐	a. 1993. Signature 1.	1	2	6
☐	as1. Diagonal red *SPECIMEN* overprint; black # overprint at lower center.	—	—	30
☐	as2. No overprint; all-zero serial number.	—	—	30
☐	r. Remainder: No serial number.	—	—	—

Replacement notes: Prefix Z.

NB B23 (PR29): **50,000,000,000 dinara** VG VF UNC
Dark brown and brown. Front: Guilloche patterns; Serbian coat of arms. Back: Fortress on hill in Knin. No security thread. Watermark: Greek key pattern. Printer: (Banknote Printing Works, Belgrade). 140 x 66 mm.

☐	a. 1993. Signature 1.	1	2	7
☐	as1. Diagonal red *SPECIMEN* overprint; black # overprint at lower center.	—	—	30
☐	as2. No overprint; all-zero serial number.	—	—	30
☐	r. Remainder: No serial number.	—	—	—

Replacement notes: Prefix Z.

1994 Issues

These notes were issued in response to another currency reform in Yugoslavia on 1 January 1994, in which nine zeroes were removed from the currency, creating a new dinar equal to 1 billion old dinars.

NB B24 (PR30): **1,000 dinara**　　　　　　　　　　　　　VG　VF　UNC

Blue-black and dark brown. Front: Guilloche patterns; Serbian coat of arms. Back: Fortress on hill in Knin. No security thread. Watermark: Greek key pattern. Printer: (Banknote Printing Works, Belgrade). 140 x 66 mm.

　　☐　a.　1994. Signature 1.　　　　　　　　　　0.25　0.50　2
　　☐　as1.Diagonal red *SPECIMEN* overprint;　　　—　　—　30
　　　　　black # overprint at lower center.
　　☐　as2.No overprint; all-zero serial number.　　—　　—　30
　　☐　r.　Remainder: No serial number.　　　　　—　　—　—

Replacement notes: Prefix Z.

NB B25 (PR31): **10,000 dinara**　　　　　　　　　　　　VG　VF　UNC

Dark brown and dark purple. Front: Guilloche patterns; Serbian coat of arms. Back: Fortress on hill in Knin. No security thread. Watermark: Greek key pattern. Printer: (Banknote Printing Works, Belgrade). 140 x 66 mm.

　　☐　a.　1994. Signature 1.　　　　　　　　　　0.25　0.50　2
　　☐　as1.Diagonal red *SPECIMEN* overprint;　　　—　　—　30
　　　　　black # overprint at lower center.
　　☐　as2.No overprint; all-zero serial number.　　—　　—　30
　　☐	r.　Remainder: No serial number.　　　　　—　　—　—

Replacement notes: Prefix Z.

NB B26 (PR32): **500,000 dinara**　　　　　　　　　　　VG　VF　UNC

Black and dark blue. Front: Guilloche patterns; Serbian coat of arms. Back: Fortress on hill in Knin. No security thread. Watermark: Greek key pattern. Printer: (Banknote Printing Works, Belgrade). 140 x 66 mm.

　　☐　a.　1994. Signature 1.　　　　　　　　　　0.50　1　　3
　　☐　as1.Diagonal red *SPECIMEN* overprint;　　　—　　—　30
　　　　　black # overprint at lower center.
　　☐　as2.No overprint; all-zero serial number.　　—　　—　30
　　☐	r.　Remainder: No serial number.　　　　　—　　—　—

Replacement notes: Prefix Z.

NB B27 (PR33): **1,000,000 dinara**　　　　　　　　　　VG　VF　UNC

Blue-green and dark purple. Front: Guilloche patterns; Serbian coat of arms. Back: Fortress on hill in Knin. No security thread. Watermark: Greek key pattern. Printer: (Banknote Printing Works, Belgrade). 140 x 66 mm.

　　☐　a.　1994. Signature 1.　　　　　　　　　　0.50　1　　3
　　☐　as1.Diagonal red *SPECIMEN* overprint;　　　—　　—　30
　　　　　black # overprint at lower center.
　　☐	as2.No overprint; all-zero serial number.　　—　　—　30
　　☐	r.　Remainder: No serial number.　　　　　—　　—　—

Replacement notes: Prefix Z.

NB B28 (PR34): **10,000,000 dinara**   VG   VF   UNC
Blue-black and red-brown. Front: Guilloche patterns; Serbian coat of arms. Back: Fortress on hill in Knin. No security thread. Watermark: Greek key pattern. Printer: (Banknote Printing Works, Belgrade). 140 x 66 mm.

		VG	VF	UNC
☐ a.	1994. Signature 1.	0.50	1.50	5
☐ as1.	Diagonal red *SPECIMEN* overprint; black # overprint at lower center.	—	—	30
☐ as2.	No overprint; all-zero serial number.	—	—	30
☐ r.	Remainder: No serial number.	—	—	—

Replacement notes: Prefix Z.

Looking Forward

In August 1995, Croatia took control of Serbian Krajina and the Croatian kuna replaced the dinar. For later issues, see Croatia.

Acknowledgements

This chapter was compiled with the generous assistance of Thomas Augustsson, Javier Blake, Robert Breslin, Jim W.-C. Chen, David F. Cieniewicz (www.banknotestore.com), Peter Kelly, Robert Mol, Wally Myers, Menelaos Stamatelos, Bill Stubkjaer, and others.

Sources

Augustsson, Thomas. "The Bank Notes of the Republic of Serbian Krajina." *IBNS Journal*. Volume 39 Number 1. p.15.

Coats, Warren. *One Currency for Bosnia: Creating the Central Bank of Bosnia and Herzegovina*. 2007. ISBN 0-915463-997. Jameson Books (www.jamesonbooks.com).

Cuhaj, George S. *Standard Catalog of World Paper Money, Modern Issues, 1961-Present*. 18th edition. 2012. ISBN 978-1-4402-2956-5. Krause Publications (www.krausebooks.com), 700 East State St., Iola, WI, 54990-0001.

Salem, Farid. "Croatia: What's in a Name?" *IBNS Journal*. Volume 40 Number 4. p.17.

Viščević, Zlatko. *Coins and Banknotes of Yugoslavia, Slovenia, Croatia, Bosnia and Herzegovina, Serbia, Montenegro and Macedonia*. 2nd edition. 2011. ISBN 978-953-5689-0-3.

Share Your Input, Info, and Images

This catalog is believed to be complete and correct as of the time of publication. Prices and face values were last updated 15 June 2012. Please report errors or omissions so that corrections may be made. If you can more precisely identify the name or location of anything depicted on a note, please share that information. Furthermore, if you own an unlisted type or variety, please submit scans of the front and back of the note so that it can be documented. Scans should be 300 dots per inch, 100% actual size, 24-bit color, saved as *uncompressed* JPEG files, and sent to owen@banknotenews.com. Be sure to fully describe all attributes of the note which are not apparent upon visual inspection of the images alone, such as physical dimension, watermark, and security thread.

Seychelles

For earlier issues, see France, India, and Mauritius.

Contents

Government of Seychelles (GOS) 1839
Republic of Seychelles (ROS) 1846
Seychelles Monetary Authority (SMA) 1847
Central Bank of Seychelles (CBS) 1849

Monetary System
1914: 1 Seychellois rupee (SCR) = 100 cents

Government of Seychelles

Seychelles became a separate British colony in 1903, but continued to use banknotes from India and Mauritius as legal tender for several decades.

GOS Signature Varieties

1
Auditor
William Marshall Vaudin
(1914)

2
Governor
Eustace Twisleton-Wykeham-Fiennes
(1918 - 1922)

4
GOVERNOR
de Symons Honey
(1928)

6
GOVERNOR
Arthur Francis Grimble
(19.05.1936 - 1942)

8
GOVERNOR or
OFFICER ADMINISTRATING THE GOVERNMENT
Julian Darrell Bates

9
GOVERNOR
William Addis
(17.10.1953 - 1957)

Treasurer of the Board
Louis Ogilvy Chitty
(1914)

3
GOVERNOR
Joseph Byrne
(26.09.1922 - 1927)

5
GOVERNOR
Gordon James Lethem
(1934)

7
GOVERNOR
William Marston Logan
(30.03.1942 - 1947)

* GOVERNOR
Federick Crawford
(14.05.1951 - 1953)

10
GOVERNOR
John Kingsmill Thorp
(January 1958 - August 1961)

GOS Signature Varieties

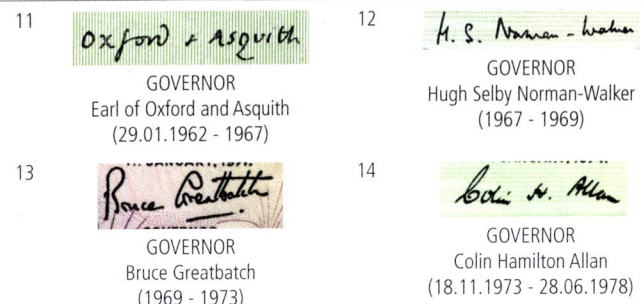

11 GOVERNOR Earl of Oxford and Asquith (29.01.1962 - 1967)
12 GOVERNOR Hugh Selby Norman-Walker (1967 - 1969)
13 GOVERNOR Bruce Greatbatch (1969 - 1973)
14 GOVERNOR Colin Hamilton Allan (18.11.1973 - 28.06.1978)

* This official is not known to have signed any notes.

1914 Emergency Issues

The British Legislative Council authorized the establishment of a Board of Commissioners of Currency through the Paper Currency Ordinance of 1914, which was enacted by C. R. M. O'Brien, the governor of the Colony of the Seychelles on 10 August 1914. As a result, a total of 180,000 rupees in 5- and 10-rupee provisional banknotes was printed locally. The notes were hand-signed by the auditor and treasurer of the board.

No image available.
GOS B1 (PA1): **50 cents**   Good   Fine   XF
Black. Uniface: Text. No security thread. Watermark: None. Printer: (Unknown, Seychelles). Unknown dimensions.
     a.   11th August, 1914. Signature 1.   300   650   1,400

No image available.
GOS B2 (PA2): **1 rupee**   Good   Fine   XF
Black. Uniface: Text. No security thread. Watermark: None. Printer: (Unknown, Seychelles). Unknown dimensions.
     a.   11th August, 1914. Signature 1.   350   750   1,750

No image available.
GOS B3 (PA3): **5 rupees**   Good   Fine   XF
Black. Uniface: Text. Embossed colonial stamp. No security thread. Watermark: None. Printer: (Unknown, Seychelles). 200 x 108 mm.
     a.   11th August, 1914. Signature 1.   950   1,850   4,000

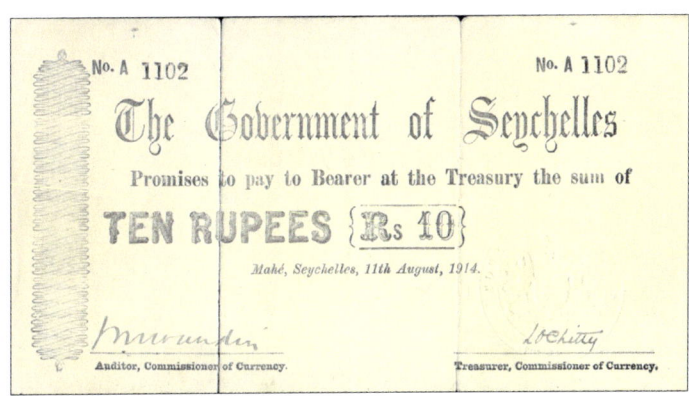

GOS B4 (PA4): **10 rupees**   Good   Fine   XF
Black. Uniface: Text. Embossed colonial stamp. No security thread. Watermark: None. Printer: (Unknown, Seychelles). 200 x 108 mm.
     a.   11th August, 1914. Signature 1.   1,200   3,000   —

1919 Emergency Issues

Through the Paper Currency Ordinance of 1919, a total of 15,000 rupees in 50-cent and 1-rupee provisional banknotes was authorized to replace coins of the same denominations. The notes were hand-signed by the governor, Sir Eustace Twisleton-Wykeham-Fiennes.

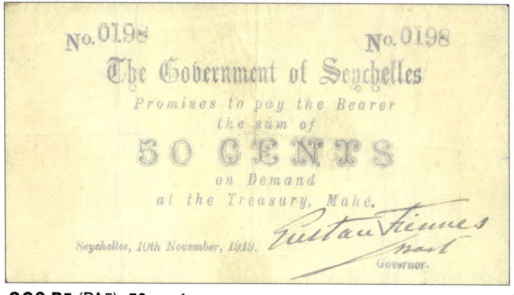

GOS B5 (PA5): **50 cents** Good Fine XF
Black. Uniface: Text and embossed seal. No security thread. Watermark: None. Printer: Unknown. 138 x 75 mm.

☐	a.	10th November, 1919. Signature 2.	450	1,300	—

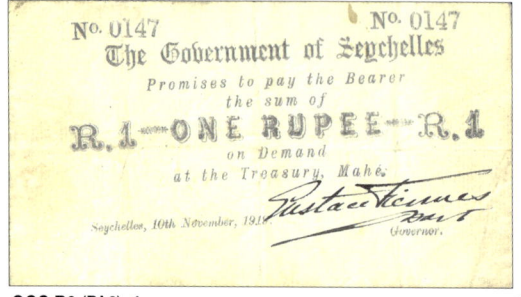

GOS B6 (PA6): **1 rupee** Good Fine XF
Black. Uniface: Text and embossed seal. No security thread. Watermark: None. Printer: Unknown. 138 x 75 mm.

☐	a.	10th November, 1919. Signature 2.	—	—	—

1918-1936 King George V Issues

These notes feature a portrait of King George V facing left. Through the Paper Currency Revised Ordinance of 1928, Governor de Symons Honey authorized a total of 250,000 rupees in banknotes. The Paper Currency (Amendment) Ordinance of 1932 increased the authorization to 500,000 rupees in notes. The Seychelles Currency Notes Ordinance of 1936 repealed all previous enactments on paper currency and established the Seychelles Currency Board. The colonial treasurer was designated as the currency commissioner to administer the currency issue up to 900,000 rupees.

In July 1938, the Colonial Office in Downing Street, London approved the replacement of the "unhygienic" 50-cent and 1-rupee notes with coins. The Coinage Ordinance of 1939 established the Seychelles rupee as legal tender (although other currencies continued to circulate), and authorized the recall of the low-denomination notes.

GOS B7 (P1): **50 cents** (withdrawn 1939) Good Fine XF
Green and violet. Uniface: King George V. No security thread. Watermark: None. Printer: *THOMAS DE LA RUE & COMPANY, LIMITED, LONDON.* 118 x 70 mm.

☐	a.	1st July 1919. Signature 2. Prefix A/1.	125	550	1,500
☐	b.	1st July 1924. Signature 3.	100	500	1,500
☐	c.	6th November 1928. Signature 4.	100	500	1,500
☐	d.	5th October 1934. Signature 5.	100	500	1,250
☐	e.	No date. Signature 6. Intro: 1936.	45	450	1,200
☐	ap.	Proof.	—	—	—

GOS B8 (P2): **1 rupee** (withdrawn 1939) Good Fine XF
Gray and red. Uniface: King George V. No security thread. Watermark: None. Printer: *THOMAS DE LA RUE & COMPANY, LIMITED, LONDON.* 118 x 70 mm.

☐	a.	1918. Signature 2. Prefix A/1.	150	500	1,500
☐	b.	1st July 1919. Signature 2.	150	500	1,350
☐	c.	1st July 1924. Signature 3.	85	350	1,200
☐	d.	6th November 1928. Signature 4.	85	425	1,200
☐	e.	5th October 1934. Signature 5.	50	225	1,000
☐	f.	No date. Signature 6. Intro: 1936.	25	50	500
☐	dp.	Proof.	—	—	—
☐	es.	Vertical *CANCELLED* perforation.	—	—	420

GOS B9 (P3): **5 rupees** Good Fine XF
Brown and green. Uniface: King George V. No security thread. Watermark: None. Printer: *THOMAS DE LA RUE & COMPANY, LIMITED, LONDON.* 160 x 100 mm.

☐	a.	6th November 1928. Signature 4. Prefix A/1.	85	275	850
☐	b.	5th October 1934. Signature 5.	60	200	750
☐	c.	No date. Signature 6. Intro: 1936.	40	180	550
☐	as.	Horizontal *CANCELLED* perforation.	—	—	750
☐	cs.	Horizontal *CANCELLED* perforation.	—	—	750

GOS B10 (P4): **10 rupees**   Good   Fine   XF

Green and red. Uniface: King George V. No security thread. Watermark: None. Printer: THOMAS DE LA RUE & COMPANY, LIMITED, LONDON. 160 x 100 mm.

- a. 6th November 1928. Signature 4. Prefix A/1.   250   700   1,750
- b. No date. Signature 6. Intro: 1936.   90   300   1,000
- p. Proof.   —   —   —

GOS B11 (P5): **50 rupees**   Good   Fine   XF

Orange and blue. Uniface: King George V. No security thread. Watermark: None. Printer: THOMAS DE LA RUE & COMPANY, LIMITED, LONDON. 160 x 100 mm.

- a. 6th November 1928. Signature 4. Prefix A/1.   300   700   1,700
- b. No date. Signature 6. Prefix A/1. Intro: 1936.   200   550   1,750
- t. Color trial: Light brown/olive green and violet.   —   AU   1,250

1942 World War II Emergency Issues

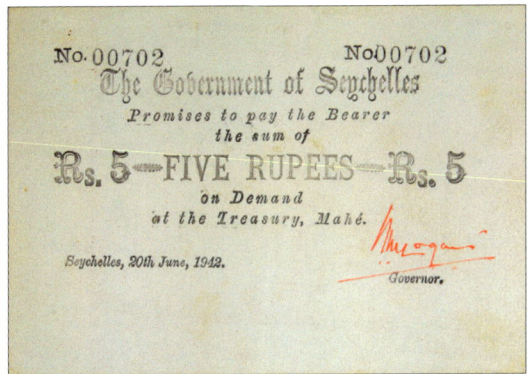

GOS B12 (P5A): **5 rupees**   Good   Fine   XF

Black. Uniface: Text and embossed seal. No security thread. Watermark: None. Printer: Unknown. 141 x 98 mm.

- a. 20th June, 1942. Signature 7.   —   —   12,500

1942-1951 King George VI Issues

The two low-denominations notes feature a portrait of King George VI facing forward, whereas notes 5 rupees and higher show the king facing right. On 3 March 1947, the colonial treasurer declared that all coins and notes from other countries (with the exception of 1-, 2-, and 5-cent coins from Mauritius) ceased to be legal tender in the Seychelles and should be exchanged by 31 March 1947.

GOS B13 (P6): **50 cents**   VG   VF   UNC

Gray-green and violet. Uniface: King George VI. No security thread. Watermark: None. Printer: THOS. DE LA RUE & CO, LTD, LONDON. 120 x 69 mm.

- a. 7th July 1943. Signature 7. Prefix A/1.   125   800   3,000
- b. 6th January 1951.   50   250   750
  Signature 8 with title GOVERNOR.
- c. Signature 8 with title OFFICER   30   165   585
  ADMINISTERING THE GOVERNMENT.
- as. Specimen.   —   —   —
- cs. Horizontal CANCELLED perforation.   —   —   —

GOS B14 (P7): **1 rupee**   VG   VF   UNC

Gray and red. Uniface: King George VI. No security thread. Watermark: None. Printer: THOS. DE LA RUE & CO, LTD, LONDON. 120 x 69 mm.

- a. 7th July 1943. Signature 7. Prefix B/1.   80   300   1,200
- b. 6th January 1951.   80   300   1,200
  Signature 8 with title GOVERNOR.
- c. Signature 8 with title OFFICER   125   475   1,500
  ADMINISTERING THE GOVERNMENT.
- as. No overprint; all-zero serial numbers;   —   —   —
  handwritten 8/11/42 at lower right.

1954-1967 Queen Elizabeth II Issues

These notes feature a portrait of Queen Elizabeth II facing left. Unlike the preceding uniface issues, these notes share a common design on the back.

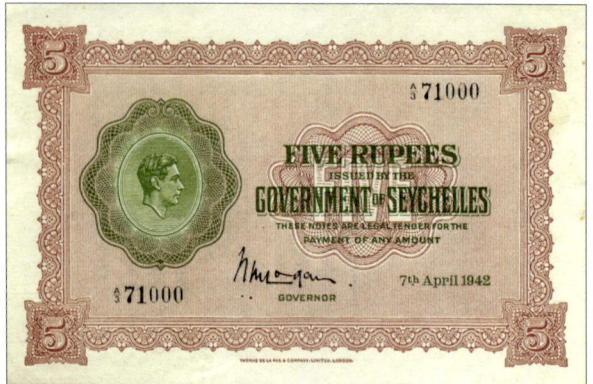

GOS B15 (P8): 5 rupees   VG   VF   UNC
Violet and green. Uniface: King George VI. No security thread. Watermark: None. Printer: *THOMAS DE LA RUE & COMPANY, LIMITED, LONDON.* 160 x 100 mm.
- ☐ a. 7th April 1942. Signature 7. Prefix A/2 - A/3.   80   150   700
- ☐ as. Horizontal *CANCELLED* perforation.   —   —   —

GOS B16 (P9): 10 rupees   VG   VF   UNC
Green and red. Uniface: King George VI. No security thread. Watermark: None. Printer: *THOMAS DE LA RUE & COMPANY, LIMITED, LONDON.* 160 x 100 mm.
- ☐ a. 7th April 1942. Signature 7. Prefix A/1.   200   750   3,200
- ☐ as. Horizontal *CANCELLED* perforation.   —   —   —

GOS B17 (P10): 50 rupees   VG   VF   UNC
Light brown. Uniface: King George VI. No security thread. Watermark: None. Printer: *THOMAS DE LA RUE & COMPANY, LIMITED, LONDON.* 160 x 100 mm.
- ☐ a. 7th April 1942. Signature 7. Prefix A/1.   85   350   1,200
- ☐ as1. Horizontal *CANCELLED* perforation.   —   —   —
- ☐ as2. No overprint; all-zero serial numbers; handwritten *Approved RWC 9/6/42* at lower right.   —   —   —

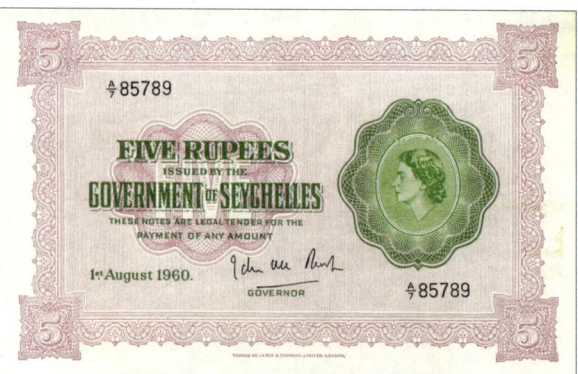

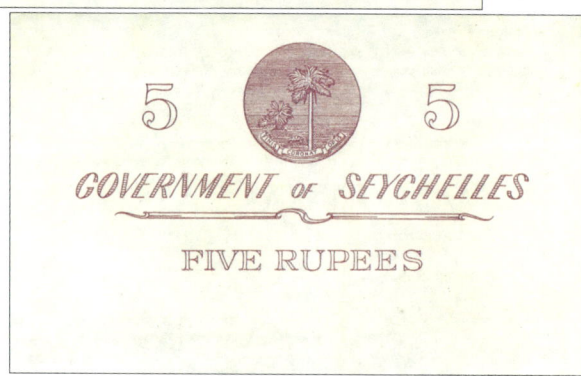

GOS B18 (P11): 5 rupees   VG   VF   UNC
Lilac and green. Front: Queen Elizabeth II. Back: Palm trees and tortoise. No security thread. Watermark: Geometric pattern. Printer: *THOMAS DE LA RUE & COMPANY, LIMITED, LONDON.* 160 x 100 mm.
- ☐ a. 1st August 1954. Signature 9. Prefix A/4 - A/7.   30   125   700
- ☐ b. 1st August 1960. Signature 10. Prefix A/7.   20   100   600

GOS B19 (P12): **10 rupees**   VG   VF   UNC
Green and red. Front: Queen Elizabeth II. Back: Palm trees and tortoise. No security thread. Watermark: Geometric pattern. Printer: *THOMAS DE LA RUE & COMPANY, LIMITED, LONDON*. 160 x 100 mm.

			VG	VF	UNC
☐	a.	1st August 1954. Signature 9. Prefix A/2.	13	250	1,000
☐	b.	1st August 1960. Signature 10. Prefix A/3.	10	150	900
☐	c.	1st May 1963. Signature 11. Prefix A/3.	90	200	900
☐	d.	1st January 1967. Prefix A/4.	7.50	100	850
☐	ds.	Diagonal red *SPECIMEN* and DLR oval ovpts; horizontal red *SPECIMEN N⁰* # ovpt at lower left; punched.	—	—	—

GOS B20 (P13): **50 rupees**   VG   VF   UNC
Black. Front: Queen Elizabeth II. Back: Palm trees and tortoise. No security thread. Watermark: Geometric pattern. Printer: *THOMAS DE LA RUE & COMPANY, LONDON*. 160 x 100 mm.

			VG	VF	UNC
☐	a.	1st August 1954. Signature 9. Prefix A/2.	250	1,000	2,500
☐	b.	1st August 1960. Signature 10. Prefix A/2.	250	1,000	2,500
☐	c.	1st May 1963. Signature 11. Prefix unknown.	250	1,000	2,500
☐	d.	1st January 1967. Prefix unknown.	250	1,000	2,500
☐	cs.	Horizontal *CANCELLED* perforation.	—	—	—
☐	ds.	Diagonal red *SPECIMEN* and DLR oval ovpts; horizontal red *SPECIMEN N⁰* # ovpt at lower left; punched.	—	—	—

1968-1975 Issues

In July 1968, the preceding issues were replaced by notes with new designs featuring the flora and fauna of the islands, and Pietro Annigoni's 1956 portrait of Queen Elizabeth II on the front.

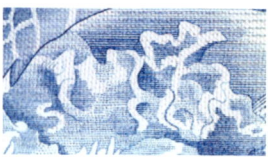

The coral in the lower left front of GOS B22 appears to spell out the word "SCUM."

GOS B21 (P14): **5 rupees** (withdrawn 1972)   VG   VF   UNC
Brown, green, and pink. Front: Coco-de-mer; Seychelles black parrot; palm trees; mountains; Queen Elizabeth II in regalia of Order of the Garter. Back: Guilloche patterns. Solid security thread. Watermark: Black parrot head. Printer: (BWC). 134 x 70 mm.

		VG	VF	UNC
☐ a.	1st JANUARY, 1968. Signature 12. Prefix A/1. Intro: 22.07.1968.	20	75	200
☐ t.	Color trial: Blue-green.	—	—	575
☐ as.	Diagonal SPECIMEN overprint.	—	—	460

GOS B23 (P16): **20 rupees** (demonetized 01.10.1980)   VG   VF   UNC
Mauve and pink. Front: Skink lizard; sooty tern bird; sea shells; coral; Queen Elizabeth II in regalia of Order of the Garter. Back: Guilloche patterns. Solid security thread. Watermark: Black parrot head. Printer: (BWC). 154 x 89 mm.

		VG	VF	UNC
☐ a.	1st JANUARY, 1968. Signature 12. Prefix A/1. Intro: 22.07.1968.	100	300	750
☐ b.	1st JANUARY, 1971. Signature 13. Prefix A/1.	75	150	1,000
☐ c.	1st JANUARY, 1974. Signature 14. Prefix A/1.	50	100	400
☐ t	Color trial: Red.	—	—	—
☐ as.	Diagonal red SPECIMEN overprint; punched.	—	—	630
☐ cs.	Diagonal SPECIMEN overprint.	—	—	—

GOS B22 (P15): **10 rupees** (demonetized 01.10.1980)   VG   VF   UNC
Blue and green. Front: Three men in small boat with harpoon; coral; sea tortoise; Queen Elizabeth II in regalia of Order of the Garter. Back: Guilloche patterns. Solid security thread. Watermark: Black parrot head. Printer: (BWC). 147 x 83 mm.

		VG	VF	UNC
☐ a.	1st JANUARY, 1968. Signature 12. Prefix A/1. Intro: 22.07.1968.	100	250	800
☐ b.	1st JANUARY, 1974. Signature 14. Prefix A/1.	75	150	600
☐ as.	Diagonal red SPECIMEN overprint; punched.	—	—	720

GOS B24 (P17): **50 rupees** (demonetized 01.10.1980)   VG   VF   UNC

Olive green and ochre. Front: Mountain; schooner sail boat; Queen Elizabeth II in regalia of Order of the Garter; palm trees. Back: Guilloche patterns. Solid security thread. Watermark: Black parrot head. Printer: (BWC). 156 x 92 mm.

		VG	VF	UNC
☐ a.	1ˢᵗ JANUARY, 1968. Sig. 12. Prefix A/1. Intro: 22.07.1968.	250	700	1,400
☐ b.	1ˢᵗ JANUARY, 1969.	125	200	1,750
☐ c.	1ˢᵗ OCTOBER, 1970. Signature 13.	125	200	1,300
☐ d.	1ˢᵗ JANUARY, 1972.	125	200	1,300
☐ e.	1ˢᵗ AUGUST, 1973.	100	175	700
☐ t.	Color trial: Bright green.	—	—	1,600
☐ as1.	Diagonal red *SPECIMEN* overprint; punched.	—	—	1,325
☐ as2.	Punched; all-zero serial numbers; no overprint.	—	—	800
☐ as3.	Horizontal *SPECIMEN* perforation.	—	—	—
☐ ds.	Diagonal *SPECIMEN* overprint.	—	—	—

GOS B25 (P18): **100 rupees** (demonetized 01.10.1980)   VG   VF   UNC

Red. Front: Two giant tortoises under a veloutye shrub; Queen Elizabeth II in regalia of Order of the Garter. Back: Guilloche patterns. Solid security thread. Watermark: Black parrot head. Printer: (BWC). 160 x 95 mm.

		VG	VF	UNC
☐ a.	1ˢᵗ JANUARY, 1968. Signature 12. Prefix A/1. Intro: 22.07.1968.	1,250	2,500	6,500
☐ b.	1ˢᵗ JANUARY, 1969.	700	1,500	5,000
☐ c.	1ˢᵗ JANUARY, 1972. Signature 13.	700	1,500	5,000
☐ d.	1ˢᵗ AUGUST, 1973.	700	1,500	5,000
☐ e.	1ˢᵗ JUNE, 1975. Signature 14.	700	1,500	5,000
☐ t.	Color trial: Blue.	—	—	2,750
☐ as.	Diagonal black *SPECIMEN* overprint; punched.	—	—	2,400
☐ ds.	Punched; all-zero serial numbers; no overprint.	—	—	—
☐ s.	Horizontal *CANCELLED* perforation; no date; no serial numbers; handwritten 29.6.67 in top margin.	—	—	—

Bradbury designer Brian Fox altered the original design of the 50-rupee note by artists Wendy Day Veevers-Carter and Mary Hayward in such a way that the fronds in the palm tree at right front spell out the word "SEX" when the note is rotated 90° counterclockwise.

Republic of Seychelles

In 1974, the Currency Commission was established to manage the currency issues for the Republic of Seychelles (ROS). The Seychelles is the smallest nation in the world (approximately 86,000 in 2011) issuing its own currency (i.e., not pegged to a foreign currency and not shared with any other country).

ROS Signature Varieties

1	
	MINISTER FOR FINANCE
	Chamry Chetty

1976 President Mancham Issues

After gaining independence from the United Kingdom on 29 June 1976, the portrait of Queen Elizabeth II on the notes was replaced by that of the first president of the Republic of Seychelles, James Richard Marie Mancham. He was deposed by Prime Minister France-Albert René on 5 June 1977, hence his short tenure on the nation's notes.

ROS B1 (P19): **10 rupees** (demonetized 01.10.1980)   VG   VF   UNC
Blue and pink. Front: Triton seashell; bois rouge flowers; President James Mancham. Back: Palm trees; hut; boats; beach. Solid security thread. Watermark: Black parrot head. Printer: (BWC). 138 x 68 mm.

- a. No date. Signature 1. Prefix A/1. Intro: 1976.   2.50   10   25
- as. Diagonal red *SPECIMEN* overprint; horizontal red *SPECIMEN OF NO VALUE* overprint in upper margin; # overprint at upper left back; punched.   —   —   250

ROS B2 (P20): **20 rupees** (demonetized 01.10.1980)   VG   VF   UNC
Mauve and purple. Front: Turtle; hibiscus flowers; President James Mancham. Back: Island; sailboat. Solid security thread. Watermark: Black parrot head. Printer: (BWC). 144 x 72 mm.

- a. No date. Signature 1. Prefix A/1. Intro: 1976.   4   20   100
- as. Diagonal red *SPECIMEN* overprint; horizontal red *SPECIMEN OF NO VALUE* overprint in upper margin; # overprint at upper left back; punched.   —   —   250

ROS B3 (P21): **50 rupees** (demonetized 01.10.1980)   VG   VF   UNC
Green, pink, and brown. Front: Lion fish; plant; President James Mancham; conus capianeus seashells. Back: Men at Beau Vallon Bay shoreline with fishing net and boat. Solid security thread. Watermark: Black parrot head. Printer: (BWC). 150 x 76 mm.

- a. No date. Signature 1. Prefix A/1. Intro: 1976.   10   75   150
- as. Diagonal red *SPECIMEN* overprint; horizontal red *SPECIMEN OF NO VALUE* overprint in upper margin; # overprint at upper left back; punched.   —   —   250

The Banknote Book

Seychelles 1979-1980 Issues

ROS B4 (P22): **100 rupees** (demonetized 01.10.1980)   VG   VF   UNC
Red and green. Front: Two fairy tern birds; coco-de-mer palm tree; President James Mancham; cypraea mappa seashell. Back: Islands; boats; dock; buildings. Solid security thread. Watermark: Black parrot head. Printer: (BWC). 156 x 80 mm.

- ☐ a. No date. Signature 1. Prefix A/1. Intro: 1976.   20   80   175
- ☐ as. Diagonal red *SPECIMEN* overprint;   —   —   400
  horizontal red *SPECIMEN OF NO VALUE*
  overprint in upper margin;
  # overprint at upper left back; punched.

Seychelles Monetary Authority

The Seychelles Monetary Authority (SMA) was established on 1 December 1978, under the Seychelles Monetary Authority Decree. Simultaneously, the Seychelles Currency Act 1974 was repealed and the Currency Commission abolished.

SMA Signature Varieties

1	*[signature]*
	CHAIRMAN BOARD OF DIRECTORS
	Guy Morel
	(1979 - 1980)

1979-1980 Issues

SMA B1 (P23): **10 rupees** (demonetized 01.07.1993)   VG   VF   UNC
Blue, green, and red. Front: Hibiscus flowers; red-footed booby bird in nest. Back (vertical): Girl picking oleander flowers. Solid security thread. Watermark: Black parrot head. Printer: (BWC). 130 x 65 mm.

- ☐ a. No date. Signature 1. Prefix A. Intro: 30.01.1980.   0.50   2.50   10
- ☐ as. Diagonal red *SPECIMEN* overprint;   —   —   125
  horizontal red *SPECIMEN OF NO VALUE*
  overprint in upper margin;
  # overprint at upper left back; no s/n; punched.

SMA B2 (P24): **25 rupees** (demonetized 01.07.1993)   VG   VF   UNC
Yellow, brown, and green. Front: Coco-de-mer with palm leaves. Back (vertical): Man with machete, baskets, and coconuts. Solid security thread. Watermark: Black parrot head. Printer: (BWC). 140 x 70 mm.

- ☐ a. No date. Signature 1. Prefix A. Intro: 20.02.1980.   2.50   10   40
- ☐ as. Diagonal red *SPECIMEN* overprint;   —   —   175
  horizontal red *SPECIMEN OF NO VALUE*
  overprint in upper margin;
  # overprint at upper left back; no s/n; punched.

Seychelles 1980 Issue

SMA B3 (P25): **50 rupees** (demonetized 01.07.1993)　　　VG　　VF　　UNC

Olive green, brown, and lilac. Front: Turtle; coral. Back (vertical): Seaside buildings; palm trees. Solid security thread. Watermark: Black parrot head. Printer: (BWC). 151 x 75 mm.

　☐　a.　No date. Signature 1. Prefix A. Intro: 11.03.1980.　　4　　15　　60
　☐　as.　Diagonal red *SPECIMEN* overprint;　　　　　　　　　—　　—　　175
　　　　　horizontal red *SPECIMEN OF NO VALUE*
　　　　　overprint in upper margin;
　　　　　# overprint at upper left back; no s/n; punched.

SMA B4 (P26): **100 rupees** (demonetized 25.02.1980)　　VG　　VF　　UNC

Red and light blue. Front: Lion fish; coral. Back (vertical): Fish; man with net; sailfish. Solid security thread. Watermark: Black parrot head. Printer: (BWC). 160 x 80 mm.

　☐　a.　No date. Signature 1. Prefix A. Intro: 02.11.1979.　　15　　30　　125
　☐　as.　Diagonal red *SPECIMEN* overprint;　　　　　　　　　—　　—　　400
　　　　　horizontal red *SPECIMEN OF NO VALUE*
　　　　　overprint in upper margin;
　　　　　# overprint at upper left back; no s/n; punched.

A large shipment of newly printed banknotes was lost in transit when the German coaster Anna Knueppell and the Greek freighter Aeolian Sky collided in the fog near Guernsey in the Channel Islands and the latter sank off the coast of St. Aldhelm's Head, England on 4 November 1979. Only serial numbers A000,000-A300,000 are valid for exchange. Later serial numbers are presumed either salvaged from the wreck or washed ashore.

1980 Issue

This note replaced the preceding 100-rupee notes lost at sea. It features the same design, but with new colors and prefix B.

SMA B5 (P27): **100 rupees** (demonetized 01.07.1993)　　VG　　VF　　UNC

Brown and light blue. Front: Lion fish; coral. Back (vertical): Fish; man with net; sailfish. Solid security thread. Watermark: Black parrot head. Printer: (BWC). 160 x 80 mm.

　☐　a.　No date. Signature 1. Prefix B. Intro: 17.03.1980.　　8　　25　　100
　☐　as1.　Diagonal red *SPECIMEN* overprint;　　　　　　　　—　　—　　175
　　　　　all-zero s/n; # ovpt at upper left back; punched.
　☐　as2.　Diagonal red *SPECIMEN* overprint;　　　　　　　　—　　—　　175
　　　　　horizontal red *SPECIMEN OF NO VALUE*
　　　　　overprint in upper margin;
　　　　　# overprint at upper left back; no s/n; punched.

Central Bank of Seychelles

The Central Bank of Seychelles (CBS) was established on 1 January 1983, when it took over the functions and responsibilities of the Seychelles Monetary Authority.

For more information, visit www.cbs.sc.

CBS Signature Varieties

GOVERNOR

1. Guy Morel (January 1983 - July 1991)
2. Norman Weber (July 1991 - September 1991 and May 1995 - April 2001)
*. Aboo Aumeeroody (September 1991 - April 1995)
3. Francis Chang-Leng (May 2001 - October 2008)
4. Pierre Laporte (02.11.2008 - March 2012)
5. Caroline Abel (March 2012 - present)

* This official is not known to have signed any notes.

1983 Issues

These notes are like the preceding issues, but the name of the issuing authority has changed and the signatory's title is now *GOVERNOR*.

CBS B1 (P28): **10 rupees** (demonetized 01.07.1993) VG VF UNC
Blue, green, and red. Front: Hibiscus flowers; red-footed booby bird in nest. Back (vertical): Girl picking oleander flowers. Solid security thread. Watermark: Black parrot head. Printer: (BWC). 130 x 65 mm.
    a. No date. Signature 1. Prefix C - E. Intro: 1983. — — 7
    as. Diagonal red *SPECIMEN* overprint; — — 185
       horizontal red *SPECIMEN OF NO VALUE*
       overprint in upper margin;
       # overprint at upper left back; no serial numbers.

CBS B2 (P29): **25 rupees** (demonetized 01.07.1993) VG VF UNC
Yellow, brown, and green. Front: Coco-de-mer with palm leaves. Back (vertical): Man with machete, baskets, and coconuts. Solid security thread. Watermark: Black parrot head. Printer: (BWC). 140 x 70 mm.
    a. No date. Signature 1. Prefix C. Intro: 1983. — — 23
    as. Diagonal red *SPECIMEN* overprint; — — 250
       horizontal red *SPECIMEN OF NO VALUE*
       overprint in upper margin;
       # overprint at upper left back; no s/n; punched.

CBS B3 (P30): **50 rupees** (demonetized 01.07.1993) VG VF UNC
Olive green, brown, and lilac. Front: Turtle; coral. Back (vertical): Seaside buildings; palm trees. Solid security thread. Watermark: Black parrot head. Printer: (BWC). 151 x 75 mm.
    a. No date. Signature 1. Prefix C. Intro: 1983. — — 30
    as. Diagonal red *SPECIMEN* overprint; — — 250
       horizontal red *SPECIMEN OF NO VALUE*
       overprint in upper margin;
       # overprint at upper left back; no serial numbers.

CBS B4 (P31): **100 rupees** (demonetized 01.07.1993) VG VF UNC
Brown and light blue. Front: Lion fish; coral. Back (vertical): Fish; man with net; sailfish. Solid security thread. Watermark: Black parrot head. Printer: (BWC). 160 x 80 mm.

- ☐ a. No date. Signature 1. Prefix C - D. Intro: 1983. — 35 75
- ☐ as. Diagonal red *SPECIMEN* overprint; — — 275
  horizontal red *SPECIMEN OF NO VALUE*
  overprint in upper margin;
  # overprint at upper left back; no serial numbers.

1989 Bank Headquarters Issues

These notes feature new designs, but maintain the same dimensions as the preceding issues. Common to the front of all denominations is the new bank headquarters building—on Independence Avenue in Victoria—which opened on 4 June 1984. The notes were issued to mark the Silver Jubilee of the Seychelles People's United Party (now SPPF). The name of the bank and the denominations are now written in both English and Creole.

CBS B5 (P32): **10 rupees** (demonetized 01.12.2000) VG VF UNC
Pink, green, and blue. Front: Four young pioneers saluting; sailfish; Central Bank of Seychelles headquarters building in Victoria; torch; turtle; Bicentennial monument in Victoria; flags; Zonm Lib (Liberation monument) chainbreaker statue. Back: Man with drum; five moutia dancers; dzenze ya shitsuva (chordophone) musical instrument. Solid security thread. Watermark: Black parrot head. Printer: (ABNC). 130 x 65 mm.

- ☐ a. No date. Sig. 1. Prefix A - E. Intro: 01.06.1989. — — 3
- ☐ as. Two diagonal red *SPECIMEN* overprints; — — 110
  red # overprint at lower left back.

CBS B6 (P33): **25 rupees** (demonetized 01.12.2000) VG VF UNC
Pink, purple, and green. Front: Two men with basket husking copra; sailfish; Central Bank of Seychelles headquarters building in Victoria; flowers; island with palm trees; turtle; boy among coco-de-mer fronds. Back: Coconuts; man with ox-drawn copra mill; village building; palm trees; man in hat with coconuts. Solid security thread. Watermark: Black parrot head. Printer: (ABNC). 140 x 70 mm.

- ☐ a. No date. Sig. 1. Prefix A - B. Intro: 01.06.1989. — — 6
- ☐ as. Two diagonal red *SPECIMEN* overprints; — — 120
  red # overprint at lower left back.

CBS B7 (P34): **50 rupees** (demonetized 01.12.2000) VG VF UNC
Green, brown, and orange. Front: Two men in boat; man carrying fish; sailfish; Central Bank of Seychelles headquarters building in Victoria; spiral shell; turtle; prow of wooden boat. Back: Three lesser noddy birds; two fishermen with nets full of tuna fish; ships. Solid security thread. Watermark: Black parrot head. Printer: (ABNC). 151 x 75 mm.

- ☐ a. No date. Sig. 1. Prefix A - B. Intro: 01.06.1989. — — 12
- ☐ as. Two diagonal red *SPECIMEN* overprints; — — 145
  red # overprint at lower left back.

CBS B8 (P35): **100 rupees** (demonetized 01.12.2000)   VG   VF   UNC

Red and orange. Front: People in ox cart; sailfish; Central Bank of Seychelles headquarters building in Victoria; flower; turtle; girl listening to conch shell. Back: Birds; L'Union House buildings on La Digue. Solid security thread. Watermark: Black parrot head. Printer: (ABNC). 160 x 80 mm.

- ☐ a. No date. Sig. 1. Prefix A - B. Intro: 01.06.1989. — — 20
- ☐ as. Two diagonal red *SPECIMEN* overprints; — — 165
  horizontal red # overprint at lower left back.

1998-2013 Issues

These notes feature new designs, a single size, and novel serial numbers, windowed security threads with demetalized text, and turtle watermarks and registration devices.

CBS B9 (P36): **10 rupees** (US$0.75)   VG   VF   UNC

Blue and green. Front: Coat of arms; map; black-spotted trigger fish; coco-de-mer palm tree; turtle as registration device. Back: Cowrie shells; coco-de-mer; two fairy tern birds; hawksbill turtle. Windowed security thread with demetalized *CBS*. Watermark: Turtle. Printer: Unknown. 151 x 75 mm.

- ☐ a. No date. Intro: 18.05.1998. FV FV 2
  Signature 2. Prefix AA - AD.
- ☐ b. Signature 3. Prefix AE - AG. FV FV 2
- ☐ c. 2013. Signature 5. Prefix AH - AK. FV FV 2
- ☐ as. Diagonal red *SPECIMEN* overprint. — — 150
- ☐ bs. Diagonal red *SPECIMEN* overprint; — — 150
  red # overprint at lower left.

CBS B9 (P36): **10 rupees** (US$0.75)   VG   VF   UNC

Replacement notes: Prefix ZZ.

To commemorate its 35th anniversary, the Central Bank of Seychelles overprinted the watermark area on the front of 10-rupee notes (CBS B9c) available only in sheets of 28. Because these notes are not available individually, they have not been assigned their own numbers in this catalog. Collectors should be aware than any such individual notes have been cut from sheets and are not official issues.

CBS B10 (P37): **25 rupees** (US$1.90)   VG   VF   UNC

Purple and lilac. Front: Coat of arms; map; lion fish; Wright's gardenia flower; turtle as registration device. Back: Cowrie shells; buildings and Bicentennial monument in Victoria; coconut crab; blue pigeon bird on a branch. Windowed security thread with demetalized *CBS*. Watermark: Turtle. Printer: Unknown. 151 x 75 mm.

- ☐ a. No date. Intro: 18.05.1998. FV FV 3.50
  Signature 2. Prefix AA - AC.
- ☐ b. Signature 3. Prefix AC - AD. FV FV 3.50
- ☐ as. Diagonal red *SPECIMEN* overprint. — — 160
- ☐ bs. Diagonal red *SPECIMEN* overprint; — — 175
  red # overprint at lower left.

Replacement notes: Prefix ZZ.

2000-2005 Issues

These notes are like the preceding issues, but a foil sailfish has been added at upper right front. Also, on all the notes signed by Francis Chang-Leng, the security threads are 2-mm wide and the vertical serial number is red. The largest denomination is now the 500-rupee note.

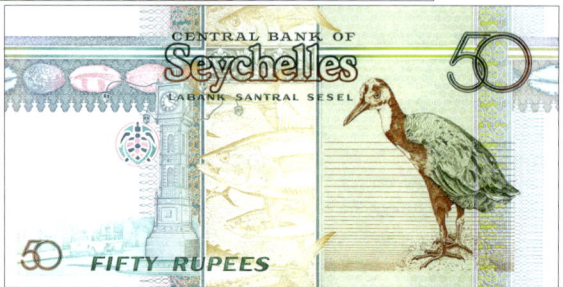

CBS B11 (P38): **50 rupees** (US$3.80)   VG   VF   UNC

Green, brown, and lilac. Front: Coat of arms; map; angel fish; paille en queue orchids; turtle as registration device. Back: Cowrie shells; cars; clock tower in Victoria; yellow-fin tuna fish; tiomitio bird. Windowed security thread with demetalized *CBS*. Watermark: Turtle. Printer: Unknown. 151 x 75 mm.

- ☐ a. No date. Signature 2. Prefix AA – AB.   FV   FV   8
  Intro: 18.05.1998.
- ☐ as. Diagonal red *SPECIMEN* overprint.   —   —   170

Replacement notes: Prefix ZZ.

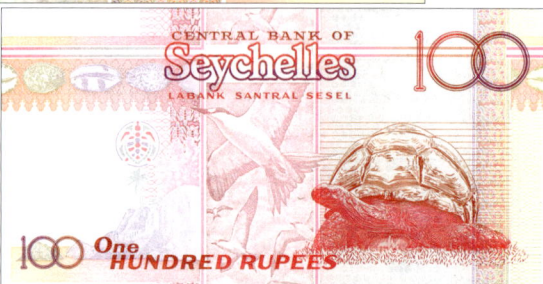

CBS B12 (P39): **100 rupees** (US$7.55)   VG   VF   UNC

Red and orange. Front: Coat of arms; map; vielle babone cecile fish; pitcher plant; turtle as registration device. Back: Cowrie shells; palm tree; bridled tern birds; Seychelles giant tortoise. Windowed security thread with demetalized *CBS*. Watermark: Turtle. Printer: Unknown. 151 x 75 mm.

- ☐ a. No date. Signature 2. Prefix AA – AC.   FV   FV   18
  Intro: 18.05.1998.
- ☐ as. Diagonal red *SPECIMEN* overprint.   —   —   180

Replacement notes: Prefix ZZ.

CBS B13 (PNL): **50 rupees** (US$3.80)   VG   VF   UNC

Green, brown, and lilac. Front: Coat of arms; map; angel fish; paille en queue orchids; turtle as registration device; silver foil sailfish. Back: Cowrie shells; cars; clock tower in Victoria; yellow-fin tuna fish; tiomitio bird. Windowed security thread with demetalized *CBS*. Watermark: Turtle. Printer: Unknown. 151 x 75 mm.

- ☐ a. No date. Signature 3. Prefix AC – AD.   FV   FV   10
  Intro: February 2005.

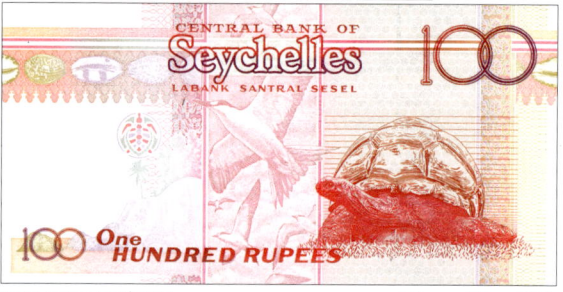

CBS B14 (P40): **100 rupees** (US$7.55)   VG   VF   UNC

Red and orange. Front: Coat of arms; map; vielle babone cecile fish; pitcher plant; turtle as registration device; gold foil sailfish. Back: Cowrie shells; palm tree; bridled tern birds; land tortoise. Windowed security thread with demetalized *CBS*. Watermark: Turtle. Printer: Unknown. 151 x 75 mm.

- ☐ a. No date. Prefix AC – AF. Intro: May 2000.   FV   FV   20
  Purple signature 2. Black vertical serial number.
- ☐ b. Red signature 2. Prefix AF.   FV   FV   20
- ☐ c. Purple signature 3. Red vertical serial number.   FV   FV   20
  Prefix AF – AH.

Replacement notes: Prefix ZZ.

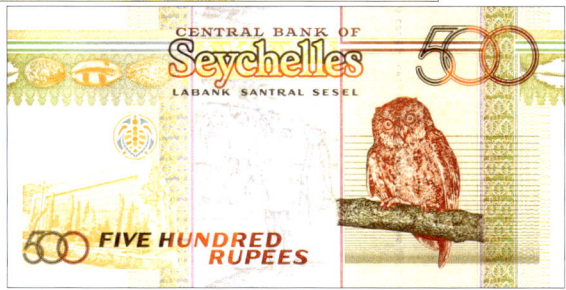

CBS B15 (P41): **500 rupees** (US$38)   VG   VF   UNC

Tan, red, and brown. Front: Coat of arms; map; fish; coco-de-mer palm; turtle as registration device; gold foil sailfish. Back: Cowrie shells; Central Bank of Seychelles headquarters building in Victoria; man with fish on stick; Seychelles scops-owl bird on branch. Windowed security thread with demetalized *CBS*. Watermark: Turtle. Printer: Unknown. 151 x 75 mm.

☐ a. No date. Signature 3. Prefix AA - AB.   FV   FV   65
     Intro: 01.08.2005.

2011-2013 Issues

The Central Bank of Seychelles issued revised 50-, 100-, and 500-rupee banknotes on 7 June 2011. The new notes have enhanced security features, revised colors, and updated designs.

Each of the three new banknotes has a hologram instead of a foil sailfish which appears at upper right front on the preceding issues. On the 50-rupee note, the silver holographic sailfish alternates between the number 50 and an image of the Aldabra rail, a flightless bird. On the 100-rupee note, the gold holographic sailfish alternates between the number 100 and an image of the Seychelles giant tortoise. On the 500-rupee note, the gold holographic sailfish alternates between the number 500 and an image of the Seychelles scops owl.

Additional security upgrades include a 2.5-mm wide fluorescent security thread on the 50-rupee note, a 2.5-mm wide color-shifting security thread on the 100-rupee note, and a 3-mm wide color-shifting security thread on the 500-rupee note. The notes are also protected by De La Rue's unique Gemini technology that fluoresces under ultraviolet light but appears normal in daylight.

The color schemes of the notes have been revised, with the notes being more green, red, and orange, respectively, than the preceding issues. The new notes also carry the year of printing, as well as the signature of Pierre Laporte, the bank's governor. The preceding issues remain legal tender and will be removed from circulation as they wear out.

CBS B16 (P42): **50 rupees** (US$3.80)   VG   VF   UNC

Green, brown, and lilac. Front: Coat of arms; map; angel fish; paille en queue orchids; turtle as registration device; silver holographic sailfish. Back: Cowrie shells; cars; clock tower in Victoria; yellow-fin tuna fish; tiomitio bird. 2.5-mm wide windowed security thread with demetalized *CBS*. Watermark: Turtle. Printer: (TDLR). 151 x 75 mm.

☐ a. 2011. Signature 4. Prefix AE. Intro: 07.06.2011.   FV   FV   10

CBS B17 (P43): **100 rupees** (US$7.55)   VG   VF   UNC

Red and orange. Front: Coat of arms; map; vielle babone cecile fish; pitcher plant; turtle as registration device; gold holographic sailfish. Back: Cowrie shells; palm tree; bridled tern birds; land tortoise. 2.5-mm wide windowed security thread with demetalized *CBS*. Watermark: Turtle. Printer: (TDLR). 151 x 75 mm.

☐ a. 2011. Sig. 4. Prefix AH - AK. Intro: 07.06.2011.   FV   FV   14
☐ b. 2013. Sig. 5. Prefix AL.   FV   FV   14

CBS B18 (P44): **500 rupees** (US$38) VG VF UNC
Tan, red, and brown. Front: Coat of arms; map; fish; coco-de-mer palm; turtle as registration device; gold holographic sailfish. Back: Cowrie shells; Central Bank of Seychelles headquarters building in Victoria; man with fish on stick; Seychelles scops-owl bird on branch. 3.0-mm wide windowed security thread with demetalized *CBS*. Watermark: Turtle. Printer: (TDLR). 151 x 75 mm.

☐ a. 2011. Sig. 4. Prefix AB - AC. Intro: 07.06.2011. FV FV 65

Acknowledgements

This chapter was compiled with the generous assistance of Robin Hughes-d'Aeth, Thomas Augustsson, Donald Cleveland, Ian Gradon (www.worldnotes.co.uk), Owen Griffiths, Gerhard Hoeck, Fergus Hutchison, Mike Jowett (www.africanbanknotes.com), Wally Myers, Thomas Neldner, Noble Numismatics (www.noble.com.au), Laurence Pope, Stefan Rombaut, TDS, Gergely Scheidl (banknoteshop@gmx.net), Stack's Bowers & Ponterio (www.StacksBowers.com), Bill Stubkjaer, Christoph Thomas, Frank van Tiel, Ludek Vostal, David White, Tristan Williams, and others.

Sources

Anonymous. *History of Paper Currency in the Seychelles*. December 2008. 30th anniversary special edition. Central Bank of Seychelles, P.O. Box 701, Victoria, Mahé, Seychelles.

Cuhaj, George S. *Standard Catalog of World Paper Money, General Issues, 1368-1960*. 14th edition. 2012. ISBN 978-1-4402-3090-5. Krause Publications (www.krausebooks.com), 700 East State St., Iola, WI, 54990-0001.

Cuhaj, George S. *Standard Catalog of World Paper Money, Modern Issues, 1961-Present*. 18th edition. 2012. ISBN 978-1-4402-2956-5. Krause Publications (www.krausebooks.com), 700 East State St., Iola, WI, 54990-0001.

Eu, Peter and Ben Chiew. *Queen Elizabeth II*. 1st edition. 2006. ISBN 983-43038-1-5. Eureka Metro, P. O. Box 30, Jalan Kelang Lama, Kuala Lumpur, 57000, Malaysia.

Narbeth, Colin. "Letter to the Editor." *IBNS Journal*. Volume 34 Number 1. p.9.

Symes, Peter. "The Portraits of Queen Elizabeth II on World Bank Notes." *IBNS Journal*. Volume 44 Number 2. p.8.

Share Your Input, Info, and Images

This catalog is believed to be complete and correct as of the time of publication. Prices and face values were last updated 16 November 2012. Please report errors or omissions so that corrections may be made. If you can more precisely identify the name or location of anything depicted on a note, please share that information. Furthermore, if you own an unlisted type or variety, please submit scans of the front and back of the note so that it can be documented. Scans should be 300 dots per inch, 100% actual size, 24-bit color, saved as *uncompressed* JPEG files, and sent to owen@banknotenews.com. Be sure to fully describe all attributes of the note which are not apparent upon visual inspection of the images alone, such as physical dimension, watermark, and security thread.

Sierra Leone

For earlier issues, see British West Africa.

Monetary System
04.08.1964: 1 Sierra Leonean leone (SLL) = 100 cents

Bank of Sierra Leone

Prior to the establishment of the Bank of Sierra Leone (BSL), the West Africa Currency Board was responsible for the issue of currency in Sierra Leone. Following the attainment of independence on 27 April 1961, however, the need was felt for a separate monetary institution controlled by Sierra Leone. Preliminary arrangements for the establishment of a central bank including the drafting of the legislation then commenced. On 27 March 1963, the Bank of Sierra Leone Act became law and the bank began operation on 4 August 1964, the day Sierra Leone changed to the decimal system of currency.

For more information, visit www.bsl.gov.sl.

BSL Signature Varieties

1

GOVERNOR
Gordon E. Hall

DEPUTY GOVERNOR
Sylvanus Bamidele Nicol-Cole

DIRECTORS
McCormack Charles Easmon
Davidson Abioseh Nicol
Claude Nelson-Williams

2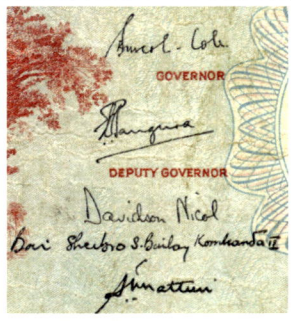

GOVERNOR
Sylvanus Bamidele Nicol-Cole

DEPUTY GOVERNOR
Samuel Lansana Bangura

DIRECTORS
Davidson Abioseh Nicol
Bai Sherbro S. Bailey Kornkanda II
Sahrfillie Matturi

BSL Signature Varieties

3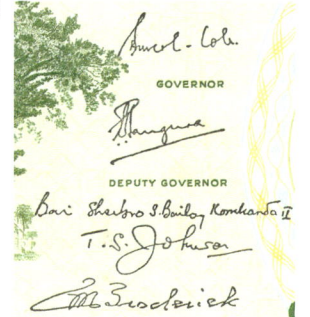

GOVERNOR
Sylvanus Bamidele Nicol-Cole

DEPUTY GOVERNOR
Samuel Lansana Bangura

DIRECTORS
Bai Sherbro S. Bailey Kornkanda II
T. S. Johnson
Sylvester Modupe Broderick

4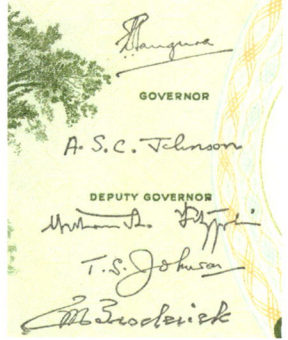

GOVERNOR
Samuel Lansana Bangura

DEPUTY GOVERNOR
Arthur Salaco Christopher Johnson

DIRECTORS
William Henry Fitzjohn
T. S. Johnson
Sylvester Modupe Broderick

5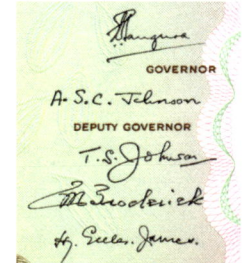

GOVERNOR
Samuel Lansana Bangura

DEPUTY GOVERNOR
Arthur Salaco Christopher Johnson

DIRECTORS
T. S. Johnson
Sylvester Modupe Broderick
H. Eccles-James

6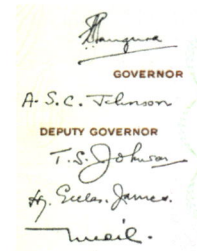

GOVERNOR
Samuel Lansana Bangura

DEPUTY GOVERNOR
Arthur Salaco Christopher Johnson

DIRECTORS
T. S. Johnson
H. Eccles-James
Michael Keili

7

GOVERNOR
Samuel Lansana Bangura

DEPUTY GOVERNOR
Arthur Salaco Christopher Johnson

DIRECTORS
Sheku Siaka Magona
H. Eccles-James
Michael Keili

8

GOVERNOR
Samuel Lansana Bangura

DEPUTY GOVERNOR
Arthur Salaco Christopher Johnson

DIRECTORS
Sheku Siaka Magona
H. Eccles-James
George Lawrence Valentine Williams

BSL Signature Varieties

9 
GOVERNOR
Arthur Salaco Christopher Johnson

DEPUTY GOVERNOR
Mohammed Remilekun Tejan-Cole

DIRECTORS
Sheku Siaka Magona
George Lawrence Valentine Williams
Massayeli Tham

10 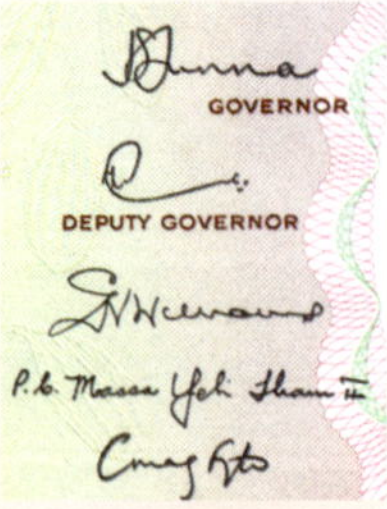
GOVERNOR
James S. A. Funna

DEPUTY GOVERNOR
Mohammed Remilekun Tejan-Cole

DIRECTORS
George Lawrence Valentine Williams
Massayeli Tham
Cecil Magbaily Fyle

11 
GOVERNOR
James S. A. Funna

DEPUTY GOVERNOR
J. T. Sarjah-Wright

12 
GOVERNOR
James S. A. Funna

DEPUTY GOVERNOR
J. T. Sarjah-Wright

DIRECTORS
George Lawrence Valentine Williams
Cecil Magbaily Fyle
P. C. Sese Mahulor Koker

	GOVERNOR	DEPUTY GOVERNOR
13	 Abdul R. Turay	 James K. E. Cole
14	 Stephen Swaray	 Yvonne N. Gibril
15	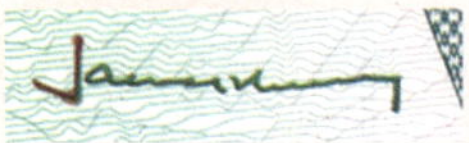 James Sanpha Koroma	 Yvonne N. Gibril
16	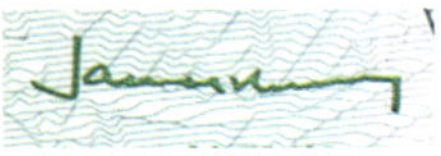 James Sanpha Koroma	 G. Melvin Tucker

BSL Signature Varieties

17
James D. Rogers — Mohamed Sanpha Fofana

18
GOVERNOR
Sheku Sambadeen Sesay
(01.07.2009 - present)

DEPUTY GOVERNOR
Andrina Rosa Coker
(06.10.2008 - present)

1964-1970 Issues

These notes replaced the West African Currency Board's notes, which ceased to be legal tender within Sierra Leone in February 1966, but could be exchanged until 1 December 1970.

BSL B1 (P1): 1 leone   VG   VF   UNC

Green. Front: Cotton Tree and Law Court building in Freetown. Back: Coat of arms; men working in alluvial diamond mine in Hangha; diamond in the rough. Solid security thread. Watermark: Lion head. Printer: *THOMAS DE LA RUE & COMPANY, LIMITED*. 150 x 72 mm.

		VG	VF	UNC
☐ a.	No date. Sig. 1. Prefix A/1 - A/6. Intro: 04.08.1964.	2.50	10	65
☐ b.	Signature 3. Prefix A/7 - A/8. Intro: 1969.	4	15	85
☐ c.	Signature 4. Prefix A/9 - A/12. Intro: 1970.	2.50	10	50
☐ as.	Diagonal red *SPECIMEN* overprint.	—	—	—

Replacement notes: Prefix Z/1.

1972-1985 Issues

BSL B2 (P2): **2 leones**   VG   VF   UNC

Red. Front: Cotton Tree and Law Court building in Freetown. Back: Coat of arms; village scene with people weaving rush mats and cooking food; date palm. Solid security thread. Watermark: Lion head. Printer: *THOMAS DE LA RUE & COMPANY, LIMITED*. 150 x 73 mm.

☐	a.	No date. Sig. 1. Prefix B/1 - B/21. Intro: 04.08.1964.	5	15	60
☐	b.	Signature 2. Prefix B/22 - B/25. Intro: 1967.	6	20	85
☐	c.	Signature 3. Prefix B/26 - B/30. Intro: 1969.	6	20	85
☐	d.	Signature 4. Prefix B/31 - B/41. Intro: 1970.	5	15	70
☐	as.	Diagonal red *SPECIMEN* overprint.	—	—	—

Replacement notes: Prefix Z/1.

BSL B3 (P3): **5 leones**   VG   VF   UNC

Purple. Front: Cotton Tree and Law Court building in Freetown. Back: Coat of arms; ships in harbor, port, and mountain; carving; tree. Solid security thread. Watermark: Lion head. Printer: *THOMAS DE LA RUE & COMPANY, LIMITED*. 158 x 80 mm.

☐	a.	No date. Signature 1. Prefix C/1. Intro: 04.08.1964.	50	200	600
☐	as1.	Diagonal red *SPECIMEN* overprint.	—	—	—
☐	as2.	Horizontal *CANCELLED* perforation.	—	—	400

Replacement notes: Prefix Z/1.

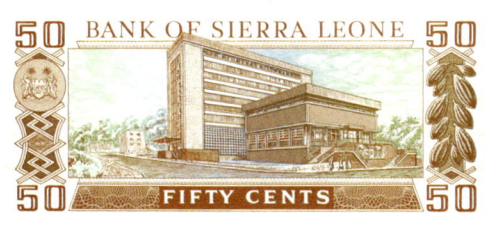

BSL B4 (P4): **50 cents**   VG   VF   UNC

Brown. Front: President Siaka P. Stevens; hibiscus flowers. Back: Coat of arms; Bank of Sierra Leone building; cocoa pods. Solid security thread. Watermark: None. Printer: *THOMAS DE LA RUE & COMPANY, LIMITED*. 140 x 64 mm.

☐	a.	No date. Sig. 5. Prefix D/1 - D/2. Intro: 19.04.1972.	1.25	5	20
☐	b.	Signature 6. Prefix D/3 - D/5. Intro: 1974.	1.25	5	20
☐	c.	1ST JULY 1979. Signature 8. Prefix D/6 - D/8.	1.25	5	20
☐	d.	1ST JULY 1981. Signature 10. Prefix D/9 - D/10.	0.50	2.50	10
☐	e.	4TH AUGUST 1984. Sig. 12. Prefix D/11 - D/16.	0.25	0.75	3
☐	as1.	Diagonal red *SPECIMEN* overprint.	—	—	—
☐	as2.	Diagonal red *SPECIMEN* and DLR oval overprints; horizontal red *SPECIMEN Nº* # ovpt at lower left; punched.	—	—	65

Replacement notes: Prefix Z/1.

BSL B5 (P5): **1 leone**   VG   VF   UNC

Green. Front: President Siaka P. Stevens. Back: Bank of Sierra Leone building; coat of arms. Solid security thread. Watermark: Lion head. Printer: *THOMAS DE LA RUE & COMPANY, LIMITED*. 150 x 70 mm.

☐	a.	19TH APRIL 1974. Signature 6. Prefix A/1 - A/7. Intro: 05.08.1974.	0.50	2	8
☐	b.	1ST JANUARY 1978. Signature 7. Prefix A/8 - A/12.	0.50	2.50	10
☐	c.	1ST MARCH 1980. Signature 9. Prefix A/13 - A/17.	0.25	1.25	5
☐	d.	1ST JULY 1981. Signature 10. Prefix A/18 - A/26.	0.25	1.25	5
☐	e.	4TH AUGUST 1984. Signature 12. Prefix A/27 - A/41.	0.25	0.75	3
☐	as.	Diagonal red *SPECIMEN* and DLR oval overprints; horizontal red *SPECIMEN Nº* # ovpt at lower left; punched.	—	—	—

Replacement notes: Prefix Z/1.

BSL B6 (P6): **2 leones**   VG   VF   UNC

Red. Front: President Siaka P. Stevens. Back: Date cluster; Bank of Sierra Leone building; coat of arms. Solid security thread. Watermark: Lion head. Printer: *THOMAS DE LA RUE & COMPANY, LIMITED*. 152 x 70 mm.

			VG	VF	UNC
☐	a.	19TH APRIL 1974. Signature 6. Prefix B/1 - B/20. Intro: 05.08.1974.	3	12	50
☐	b.	1ST JANUARY 1978. Signature 7. Prefix B/21 - B/22.	6	15	65
☐	c.	1ST JULY 1978. Signature 8. Prefix B/23 - B/27.	1.25	5	20
☐	d.	1ST JULY 1979. Signature 8. Prefix B/28 - B/31.	1.25	5	20
☐	e.	1ST MAY 1980. Signature 9. Prefix B/32 - B/37.	1.25	5	20
☐	f.	1ST JULY 1983. Signature 12. Prefix B/38 - B/69.	1.25	5	20
☐	g.	4TH AUGUST 1984. Prefix B/72 - B/104.	0.75	3	12
☐	h.	4TH AUGUST 1985. Prefix B/117 - B/160.	0.25	1	4
☐	as.	Diagonal red *SPECIMEN* and DLR oval overprints; horizontal red *SPECIMEN NO* # ovpt at lower left; punched.	—	—	—

Replacement notes: Prefix Z/1.

BSL B7 (P7): **5 leones**   VG   VF   UNC

Purple. Front: President Siaka P. Stevens; poinsettia leaves. Back: Leaves; Parliament building; coat of arms; leaves and berries of coffee plant. Solid security thread. Watermark: Lion head. Printer: *THOMAS DE LA RUE & COMPANY, LIMITED*. 162 x 75 mm.

			VG	VF	UNC
☐	a.	4TH AUGUST 1975. Signature 6. Prefix C/1.	2.50	10	40
☐	b.	1ST JULY 1978. Signature 8. Prefix C/2.	2	8	30
☐	c.	1ST MARCH 1980. Signature 9. Prefix C/3.	1	4	15
☐	d.	1ST JULY 1981. Signature 10. Prefix C/4 - C/6.	0.50	2.50	10
☐	e.	19TH APRIL 1984. Signature 12. Prefix C/8 - C/12.	0.50	2.50	10
☐	f.	4TH AUGUST 1984. Prefix C/16 - C/23.	0.50	2.50	10
☐	g.	4TH AUGUST 1985. Prefix C/27 - C/42.	0.50	2.50	10
☐	as.	Diagonal red *SPECIMEN* and DLR oval overprints; horizontal red *SPECIMEN NO* # ovpt at lower left; punched.	—	—	—

Replacement notes: Prefix Z/1.

BSL B8 (P8): **10 leones**   VG   VF UNC

Blue-gray. Front: Organization of African Unity logo; President Siaka P. Stevens; outline of Sierra Leone; map of Africa. Back: Rutile dredging; coat of arms. Solid security thread. Watermark: Lion head. Printer: *THOMAS DE LA RUE & COMPANY, LIMITED*. 160 x 77.5 mm.

☐	a.	1ST JULY 1980. Signature 9. Prefix E/1 - E/4.	1	4	15
☐	b.	19TH APRIL 1984. Signature 12. Prefix E/5 - E/9.	0.25	1	3
☐	c.	4TH AUGUST 1984. Prefix E/14 - E/19.	0.25	1	3
☐	as.	Diagonal red *SPECIMEN* and DLR oval overprints; horizontal red *SPECIMEN* N^{O} # ovpt at lower left; punched.	—	—	—

Replacement notes: Prefix Z/1.
BSL B8a was issued to mark the OAU Conference held in Freetown on 01.07.1980.

1979 Numismatic Products

Thomas De La Rue created "official presentation sets of specimen banknotes from around the world" for The Franklin Mint, a private company that mailed the sets every six weeks to subscribers from 1978 to 1979. Each set of notes with matching serial numbers originally cost $14 and came in an envelope with a numbered and dated certificate of authenticity and an index card describing the notes in detail. Based upon serial numbers observed, at least 10,440 sets were produced, and a complete collection comprises 15 sets with a total of 73 notes from 16 issuing authorities. Rarely available in the original small brown storage box, the notes are usually sold by country set, but are sometimes sold individually. Do not mistake these numismatic products for the specimen varieties listed separately, which the security printer created for its note-issuing clients.

BSL BNP1 (PCS2): **50 cents - 5 leones**   UNC

☐ a. BSL B4-B7 (4 notes) with diagonal *SPECIMEN* overprint and   35
      Maltese cross prefix. Intro: 16.04.1979.

1980 Numismatic Products

1,800 sets of notes were issued in booklets. These notes are similar to the preceding issues, but the serial numbers are printed in red, not black, and they are overprinted *COMMEMORATING THE ORGANIZATION OF AFRICAN UNITY CONFERENCE FREETOWN 1980* along with the date, *1ST JULY 1980*.

BSL BNP2 (P9-13): **50 cents - 10 leones**   UNC

☐ a. BSL B4-B8 (5 notes) with red overprint. Intro: 1980.   100

1982-1984 Issues

BSL B9 (P14): **20 leones** (<US$0.01)   VG   VF UNC

Orange. Front: Coat of arms; Cotton Tree in Freetown; President Siaka P. Stevens. Back: Two boys panning for gold or diamonds in river; palm trees. Solid security thread. Watermark: Lion head. Printer: *BRADBURY WILKINSON*. 160 x 77.5 mm.

☐	a.	24th AUGUST 1982. Signature 11. Prefix FF. 7-digit serial numbers.	2	8	30
☐	b.	24th AUGUST 1984. 7- or 8-digit serial numbers.	0.25	1	4
☐	as.	Diagonal red *SPECIMEN* overprint; punched.	—	—	110
☐	bs.	Diagonal red *SPECIMEN* overprint; punched.	—	—	100
☐	p.	No date; no signatures; no serial numbers.	—	—	—

Sierra Leone 1988-1991 Issues

1988-1991 Issues

These portrait on these notes is of Joseph Saidu Momoh, who took over the presidency from Siaka Stevens on 28 November 1985.

BSL B10 (P15): **10 leones** (<US$0.01) VG VF UNC
Blue. Front: Coat of arms; President Joseph Saidu Momoh. Back: Steer; farmer harvesting stalks. Solid security thread. Watermark: Lion head. Printer: Unknown. 160 x 77.5 mm.
    a. 27TH APRIL 1988. Signature 13. Prefix A/1- A/20. 0.25 0.50 2.25
Replacement notes: Prefix Z/1.

BSL B11 (P16): **20 leones** (<US$0.01) VG VF UNC
Orange. Front: Coat of arms; Cotton Tree in Freetown; President Joseph Saidu Momoh. Back: Two boys panning for gold or diamonds in river; palm trees. Solid security thread. Watermark: Lion head. Printer: Unknown. 160 x 77.5 mm.
    a. 27TH APRIL 1988. Signature 13. Prefix B/1 - B/19. 0.25 1 4
Replacement notes: Prefix Z/1.

BSL B12 (P17): **50 leones** (<US$0.01) VG VF UNC
Mauve and green. Front: Coat of arms; National Stadium; President Joseph Saidu Momoh. Back: Musical instruments; traditional dancers; drum. Solid security thread. Watermark: Lion head. Printer: THOMAS DE LA RUE AND COMPANY LIMITED. 160 x 77.5 mm.
    a. 27TH APRIL 1988. Signature 13. Without imprint. Prefix C/1 - C/16. 0.50 2 8
    b. 27TH APRIL 1989. With imprint. Prefix C/39 - C/45. 0.50 1.75 7
Replacement notes: Prefix Z/1.

BSL B13 (P18): **100 leones** (<US$0.05) VG VF UNC
Blue and green. Front: Port building and cargo ship; coat of arms; President Joseph Saidu Momoh. Back: Stylized man with date cluster; Bank of Sierra Leone building. Solid security thread. Watermark: Lion head. 160 x 77.5 mm.
    a. 27TH APRIL 1988. Signature 13. Printer: (TDLR). Prefix D/1 - D/5. 0.50 2 8
    b. 27TH APRIL 1989. Printer: THOMAS DE LA RUE AND COMPANY LIMITED. Prefix D/6 - D/54. 0.25 1 4
    c. 26TH SEPT 1990. Prefix D/76 - D/135. 0.25 1 4
    as. Diagonal red SPECIMEN and DLR oval overprints; horizontal red SPECIMEN Nº # ovpt at lower left; punched. — — 125
Replacement notes: Prefix Z/1.

BSL B14 (P19): **500 leones** (US$0.10)　　　　　　　　VG　VF　UNC
Brown and green. Front: Spearhead; fish; coat of arms; State House building with palm trees; President Joseph Saidu Momoh. Back: Two fishing boats in Freetown harbor; carp. Solid security thread. Watermark: Lion head. Printer: Unknown. 160 x 77.5 mm.
- a. 27TH APRIL 1991. Signature 13. Prefix E/1 - E/44.　　0.25　1　4

Replacement notes: Prefix Z/1.

1993-1996 Issues

On 29 April 1992, a military coup sent President Momoh into exile in Guinea. The chairman of the National Provisional Ruling Council took over as head of state, and subsequently banknotes were issued without Momoh's portrait.

BSL B15 (P20): **1,000 leones** (US$0.20)　　　　　　　VG　VF　UNC
Red and yellow. Front: Carving; coat of arms; Bai Bureh. Back: Telecommunications satellite dish. Solid security thread. Watermark: Lion head. Printer: *THOMAS DE LA RUE AND COMPANY LIMITED*. 160 x 77.5 mm.
- a. 4TH AUGUST 1993. Signature 14. Prefix F/1 - F/20.　　0.50　2　6.50
- b. 27TH APRIL 1996. Prefix F/27 - F/28.　　　　　　　 　0.25　1.25　5

Replacement notes: Prefix Z/1.

BSL B16 (P21): **5,000 leones** (withdrawn 14.08.2000)　　VG　VF　UNC
Blue and purple. Front: Old Fourah Bay College building in Freetown; coat of arms; Sengbe Pieh. Back: Bumbuna Dam. Solid security thread. Watermark: Lion head. Printer: *THOMAS DE LA RUE AND COMPANY LIMITED*. 160 x 77.5 mm.
- a. 4TH AUGUST 1993. Signature 14. Prefix G/1 - G/9.　　1.25　5　20
- b. 27TH APRIL 1996. Prefix G/18 - G/20.　　　　　　　　3　12　50
- as. Diagonal red *SPECIMEN* overprint.　　　　　　　　—　—　—

Replacement notes: Prefix Z/1.

In a news release dated 14 August 2000, the BSL announced that it was withdrawing from circulation the 5,000-leone denomination notes of the G17 series as a result of the proliferation of counterfeits. This move was geared towards forestalling further printing and circulation of these notes. The notes are no longer legal tender but they can be exchanged at any commercial bank or at the central bank for their full face value.

1995-2003 Issues

The 2,000-leone denomination is brand new. The 1,000- and 5,000-leone notes are similar to the preceding issues, but with different screen traps and other geometric design changes.

BSL B17 (P23): **500 leones** (US$0.10)　　　　　　　　VG　VF　UNC
Brown and green. Front: Spearhead; fish; coat of arms; State House building with palm trees; Kai Londo. Back: Two fishing boats in Freetown harbor; carp. Solid security thread. Watermark: Lion head. Printer: *THOMAS DE LA RUE LIMITED*. 160 x 77.5 mm.
- a. 27TH APRIL 1995. Signature 14. Prefix E/52 - E/80.　　FV　FV　3
- b. 15TH JULY 1998. Signature 15. Prefix E/81 - E/89.　　　FV　FV　3
- c. 1ST MARCH 2003. Signature 16. Prefix E/91 - E/97.　　FV　FV　3
- cs. Diagonal red *SPECIMEN* overprint.　　　　　　　　—　—　20

BSL B18 (P20): **1,000 leones** (US$0.20)   VG   VF   UNC

Red and yellow. Front: Carving; coat of arms; Bai Bureh. Back: Telecommunications satellite dish. Solid security thread. Watermark: Lion head. Printer: *THOMAS DE LA RUE AND COMPANY, LIMITED*. 160 x 77.5 mm.

     ☐ a.   27ᵀᴴ APRIL 1997. Signature 14. Prefix F/31 - F/35.   0.50   2   8
     ☐ b.   15ᵀᴴ JULY 1998. Signature 15. Prefix F/41 - F/43.   0.50   2   8

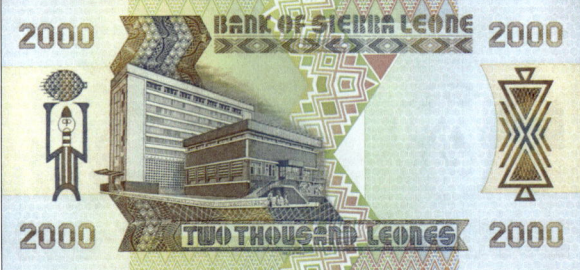

BSL B19 (P25): **2,000 leones** (US$0.45)   VG   VF   UNC

Blue and orange. Front: Port building and cargo ship; coat of arms; I.T.A. Wallace-Johnson. Back: Stylized man with date cluster; Bank of Sierra Leone building. Solid security thread. Watermark: Lion head. Printer: *DE LA RUE*. 160 x 77.5 mm.

     ☐ a.   1ˢᵀ JANUARY 2000. Signature 16. Prefix H/1 - H/9.   FV   2.50   10

BSL B20 (P21): **5,000 leones** (withdrawn 14.08.2000)   VG   VF   UNC

Blue and purple. Front: Old Fourah Bay College building in Freetown; coat of arms; Sengbe Pieh. Back: Bumbuna Dam. Solid security thread. Watermark: Lion head. Printer: *THOMAS DE LA RUE AND COMPANY LIMITED*. 160 x 77.5 mm.

     ☐ a.   27ᵀᴴ APRIL 1997. Signature 14. Prefix G/22 - G/25.   2   8   30
     ☐ b.   15ᵀᴴ JULY 1998. Signature 15. Prefix G/33.   2   8   30

Replacement notes: Prefix Z/1.

2002-2007 Issues

These notes are like the preceding issues, but with new dates, new signatures, windowed security threads, shaded watermark areas, left serial numbers vertical, and novel serial numbering. Also, the 10,000-leone note is a new denomination.

BSL B21 (P24): **1,000 leones** (withdrawn 15.08.2011)   VG   VF   UNC

Red and yellow. Front: Carving; coat of arms; Bai Bureh. Back: Telecommunications satellite dish. Windowed security thread with demetalized *BSL*. Watermark: Lion head and electrotype *BSL*. Printer: *DE LA RUE*. 160 x 77.5 mm.

     ☐ a.   1ˢᵀ FEBRUARY 2002. Signature 16. Prefix A - K.   0.25   1   4
     ☐ b.   1ˢᵀ MARCH 2003. Prefix L - T.   0.25   1.50   6
     ☐ c.   4ᵀᴴ AUGUST 2006. Signature 17.   0.25   0.75   3.50
          Watermark: Cornerstones added. Prefix U - AU.
     ☐ bs.   Diagonal red *SPECIMEN* overprint.   —   —   65

BSL B22 (P26): **2,000 leones** (withdrawn 15.08.2011)   VG   VF   UNC

Blue and orange. Front: Port building and cargo ship; double diamond foil patch; coat of arms; I.T.A. Wallace-Johnson. Back: Stylized man with date cluster; Bank of Sierra Leone building. Windowed security thread with demetalized *BSL*. Watermark: Lion head and electrotype *BSL*. Printer: *DE LA RUE*. 160 x 77.5 mm.

☐ a.	1ST FEBRUARY 2002. Signature 16. Prefix A - H.	0.50	2	7.50
☐ b.	1ST MARCH 2003. Prefix P - V.	0.50	2	7.50
☐ c.	4TH AUGUST 2006. Signature 17. Watermark: Cornerstones added. Prefix X - AX.	0.25	1	4.50

BSL B23 (P27): **5,000 leones** (withdrawn 15.08.2011)   VG   VF   UNC

Blue and purple. Front: Diamond foil patch; Old Fourah Bay College building in Freetown; coat of arms; Sengbe Pieh. Back: Bumbuna Dam. Windowed security thread with demetalized *BSL*. Watermark: Lion head and electrotype *BSL*. Printer: *DE LA RUE*. 160 x 77.5 mm.

☐ a.	1ST FEBRUARY 2002. Signature 16. Prefix A - Q.	0.50	2.50	10
☐ b.	1ST MARCH 2003. Prefix R - AB.	0.50	2.50	10
☐ c.	4TH AUGUST 2006. Signature 17. Watermark: Cornerstones added. Prefix AC - BC.	0.50	2.25	9
☐ bs.	Diagonal red *SPECIMEN* overprint.	—	—	65

BSL B24 (P29): **10,000 leones** (withdrawn 15.08.2011)   VG   VF   UNC

Blue and green. Front: Dove flying over the map of Sierra Leone; national flag; pentagon foil patch. Back: Coat of arms; Cotton Tree in Freetown. Windowed security thread with demetalized *BSL*. Watermark: Lion head and electrotype *BSL*. Printer: *DE LA RUE*. 160 x 77.5 mm.

☐ a.	4th AUGUST 2004. Signature 17. Prefix A - Q.	2	8	30
☐ b.	4th AUGUST 2007. Wmk: Cornerstones added. Prefix W - AE.	1.25	5	22

2010 Issues

According to Sheku Sambadeen Sesay, the governor of the Bank of Sierra Leone, this new family of banknotes was introduced "to step up our 'clean notes' policy while launching a new family of resized banknotes of the same design, but with enhanced security features and durability. One of the major advantages of this family of banknotes is that they will be differentiated by size, making them easily identifiable by all members of society including the blind, illiterate people and children."

BSL B25 (P30): **1,000 leones** (US$0.20)   VG   VF   UNC

Red and yellow. Front: Carving; coat of arms; Bai Bureh. Back: Telecommunications satellite dish. Windowed security thread with demetalized *BSL 1000*. Watermark: Lion head, electrotype *1000*, and Cornerstones. Printer: *DE LA RUE*. 135 x 67 mm.

☐ a.	27th APRIL 2010. Signature 18. Prefix BE - BS. Intro: 14.05.2010.	FV	FV	1.75

BSL B26 (P31): **2,000 leones** (US$0.45)　　　　VG　VF　UNC

Blue and orange. Front: Port building and cargo ship; double diamond foil patch with demetalized *BSL*; coat of arms; I.T.A. Wallace-Johnson. Back: Stylized man with date cluster; Bank of Sierra Leone building. Windowed security thread with demetalized *BSL 2000* and scrollwork. Watermark: Lion head, electrotype *2000*, and Cornerstones. Printer: *DE LA RUE*. 140 x 69 mm.

　　☐　a.　27th APRIL 2010. Signature 18. Prefix BD - CD.　　FV　FV　2.25
　　　　　Intro: 14.05.2010.

BSL B27 (P32): **5,000 leones** (US$1.15)　　　　VG　VF　UNC

Blue and purple. Front: Diamond holographic patch; Old Fourah Bay College building in Freetown; coat of arms; Sengbe Pieh. Back: Bumbuna Dam. StarChrome windowed security thread with demetalized *BSL 5000*. Watermark: Lion head, electrotype *5000*, and Cornerstones. Printer: *DE LA RUE*. 145 x 71 mm.

　　☐　a.　27th APRIL 2010. Signature 18. Prefix BF - DK.　　FV　FV　4.50
　　　　　Intro: 14.05.2010.

BSL B28 (P33): **10,000 leones** (US$2.30)　　　　VG　VF　UNC

Blue and green. Front: Dove flying over the map of Sierra Leone; national flag; holographic patch. Back: Coat of arms; Cotton Tree in Freetown. StarChrome windowed security thread with demetalized *BSL 10000*. Watermark: Lion head, electrotype *10000*, and Cornerstones. Printer: *DE LA RUE*. 150 x 73 mm.

　　☐　a.　27TH APRIL 2010. Signature 18. Prefix AG - BJ.　　FV　FV　8
　　　　　Intro: 14.05.2010.

Acknowledgements

This chapter was compiled with the generous assistance of Arigo Avbovbo, Wally Myers, Rui Manuel Palhares, Mikhail "Mike" Prizov, Andrew Roberts, Menelaos Stamatelos, Bill Stubkjaer, Christoph Thomas, Tristan Williams, Christof Zellweger, and others.

Sources

August, D. B. "Banknotes of Sierra Leone." *IBNS Journal*. Volume 20 Number 1. p.3.

Cuhaj, George S. *Standard Catalog of World Paper Money, Modern Issues, 1961-Present*. 18th edition. 2012. ISBN 978-1-4402-2956-5. Krause Publications (www.krausebooks.com), 700 East State St., Iola, WI, 54990-0001.

Symes, Peter. "The Colonial Paper Money of Sierra Leone." *IBNS Journal*. Volume 46 Number 2. p.52.

Share Your Input, Info, and Images

This catalog is believed to be complete and correct as of the time of publication. Prices and face values were last updated 2 September 2011. Please report errors or omissions so that corrections may be made. If you can more precisely identify the name or location of anything depicted on a note, please share that information. Furthermore, if you own an unlisted type or variety, please submit scans of the front and back of the note so that it can be documented. Scans should be 300 dots per inch, 100% actual size, 24-bit color, saved as *uncompressed* JPEG files, and sent to owen@banknotenews.com. Be sure to fully describe all attributes of the note which are not apparent upon visual inspection of the images alone, such as physical dimension, watermark, and security thread.

Singapore

For earlier issues, see Malaya and British Borneo.

Contents

Board of Commissioners of Currency (BCCS) 1865
Monetary Authority of Singapore (MAS) 1879

Monetary System
12.06.1967: 1 Singapore dollar (SGD) = 100 cents

Board of Commissioners of Currency

The Board of Commissioners of Currency, Singapore (BCCS) was established on 7 April 1967, by the enactment of the Currency Act of 1967.

BCCS Signature Varieties

1 — MINISTER FOR FINANCE, Lim Kim San (1965 - 16.08.1967)
2* — MINISTER FOR FINANCE, Goh Keng Swee (17.08.1967 - 1970)
3* — MINISTER FOR FINANCE, Hon Sui Sen (1970 - 14.10.1983)
4 — CHAIRMAN, Goh Keng Swee
5 — MINISTER FOR FINANCE, Richard Hu Tsu Tau (02.01.1985 - 2001)
6 — CHAIRMAN, Lee Hsien Loong (2001 - 30.11.2007)

* This signature appears on some notes with and without the red seal at right.

1967-1973 Orchid Issues

This series has nine denominations. The dominant feature is a spray of orchid in the center of the front, along with the Singapore coat of arms, a lion head watermark, and the signature of the minister for finance and the chairman of the BCCS. Different scenes of Singapore are depicted on the back of each note.

BCCS B1 (P1): **1 dollar** (US$0.80)   VG   VF   UNC
Dark blue. Front: Vanda Jenet Kaneali orchid; coat of arms. Back: Public housing apartment buildings. Solid security thread. Watermark: Lion head. Printer: *BRADBURY, WILKINSON & C? L? NEW MALDEN, SURREY, ENGLAND*. 121 x 64 mm.

		VG	VF	UNC
☐ a.	No date. Signature 1. Intro: 12.06.1967.	1.25	5	20
☐ b.	Signature 2 with red seal. Intro: 1970.	5	20	40
☐ c.	Signature 3 without red seal. Intro: 1971.	1.50	6	25
☐ d.	Signature 3 with red seal. Intro: 1972.	FV	3	12
☐ cs.	Horizontal red *SPECIMEN* overprint.	—	—	—

Replacement notes: Prefix numerator Z.

BCCS B2 (P2): **5 dollars** (US$4.15)   VG   VF   UNC
Green. Front: Vanda TMA orchid; coat of arms. Back: Small boats in Singapore river; city skyline. Solid security thread. Watermark: Lion head. Printer: *BRADBURY, WILKINSON & C? L? NEW MALDEN, SURREY, ENGLAND*. 127 x 71 mm.

		VG	VF	UNC
☐ a.	No date. Signature 1. Intro: 12.06.1967.	10	25	100
☐ b.	Sig. 2 with red seal. White background. Intro: 1970.	75	100	1,000
☐ c.	Yellow background on front.	80	225	560
☐ d.	Sig. 3 w/o red seal. White background. Intro: 1972.	15	50	200
☐ e.	Yellow background on front.	15	50	200
☐ f.	Sig. 3 with red seal. White background. Intro: 1973.	10	25	100
☐ fs.	Specimen.	—	—	450

Replacement notes: Prefix numerator Z.

BCCS B3 (P3): **10 dollars** (US$8.30)   VG   VF   UNC
Red. Front: Dendrobium Marjorie Ho "Tony Pek" orchid; coat of arms. Back: Four clasped hands; map of Singapore. Solid security thread. Watermark: Lion head. Printer: *THOMAS DE LA RUE & COMPANY, LIMITED*. 133 x 79 mm.

		VG	VF	UNC
☐ a.	No date. Signature 1. Intro: 12.06.1967.	FV	15	55
☐ b.	Signature 2 with red seal. Intro: 1970.	FV	40	120
☐ c.	Signature 3 without red seal. Intro: 1972.	FV	25	100
☐ d.	Signature 3 with red seal. Intro: 1973.	FV	20	70
☐ as.	Diagonal red *SPECIMEN* and DLR oval ovpts; horizontal red *SPECIMEN* Nº # ovpt at lower left; punched.	—	—	3,050
☐ cs.	Diagonal red *SPECIMEN* overprint; punched.	—	—	525

Replacement notes: Prefix numerator Z.

BCCS B5 (P5): **50 dollars** (US$41)   VG   VF   UNC
Blue. Front: Vanda Rothscildiana "Teo Choo Hong" orchid; coat of arms. Back: Small boats along Singapore seafront and Clifford pier. Solid security thread. Watermark: Lion head. Printer: *THOMAS DE LA RUE & COMPANY, LIMITED*. 146 x 87 mm.

		VG	VF	UNC
☐ a.	No date. Signature 1. Intro: 12.06.1967.	50	100	300
☐ b.	Signature 2 with red seal. Intro: 1970.	125	250	500
☐ c.	Signature 3 without red seal. Intro: 1972.	50	100	300
☐ d.	Signature 3 with red seal. Intro: 1973.	FV	65	130
☐ as.	Diagonal red *SPECIMEN* and DLR oval overprints; punched.	—	—	—
☐ cs.	Diagonal red *SPECIMEN* overprint; punched.	—	—	620
☐ ds.	Diagonal red *SPECIMEN* overprint; punched.	—	—	640

Replacement notes: Prefix numerator Z.

BCCS B4 (P4): **25 dollars** (US$21)   VG   VF   UNC
Brown. Front: Renanthopsis Aurora orchid; coat of arms. Back: Supreme Court building; trees. Solid security thread. Watermark: Lion head. Printer: *THOMAS DE LA RUE & COMPANY, LIMITED*. 140 x 79 mm.

		VG	VF	UNC
☐ a.	No date. Sig. 3 with red seal. Intro: 07.08.1972.	30	60	225
☐ as.	Diagonal red *SPECIMEN* overprint; punched.	—	—	2,900

Replacement notes: Prefix numerator Z.

BCCS B6 (P6): **100 dollars** (US$83)   VG   VF   UNC

Blue and mauve. Front: Cattleya orchid; coat of arms. Back: Sail boats along Singapore waterfront. Solid security thread. Watermark: Lion head. Printer: *THOMAS DE LA RUE & COMPANY, LIMITED*. 159 x 95 mm.

		VG	VF	UNC
☐	a. No date. Signature 1. Intro: 12.06.1967.	100	200	400
☐	b. Signature 2 with red seal. Intro: 1970.	125	500	1,000
☐	c. Signature 3 without red seal. Intro: 1972.	100	200	400
☐	d. Signature 3 with red seal. Intro: 1973.	100	200	400
☐	s. Specimen.	—	—	650

Replacement notes: Prefix numerator Z.

BCCS B7 (P7): **500 dollars** (US$414)   VG   VF   UNC

Green. Front: Dendrobium Shangri-La orchid; coat of arms. Back: Government building with flag on Saint Andrew's Road. Solid security thread. Watermark: Lion head. Printer: *THOMAS DE LA RUE & COMPANY, LIMITED*. 160 x 96 mm.

		VG	VF	UNC
☐	a. No date. Sig. 3 with red seal. Intro: 07.08.1972.	500	700	1,400

Replacement notes: Prefix numerator Z.

BCCS B8 (P8): **1,000 dollars** (US$828)   VG   VF   UNC

Mauve and dark gray. Front: Dendrobium Kimiyo Kondo "Chay" orchid; coat of arms. Back: Victoria Theatre and Empress Place. Solid security thread. Watermark: Lion head. Printer: *THOMAS DE LA RUE & COMPANY, LIMITED*. 159 x 95 mm.

		VG	VF	UNC
☐	a. No date. Signature 1. Intro: 12.06.1967.	FV	1,500	2,500
☐	b. Signature 2 without red seal. Intro: 1970.	FV	1,500	2,500
☐	c. Signature 3 without red seal. Intro: 1972.	FV	1,500	2,500
☐	d. Signature 3 with red seal. Intro: 1975.	FV	1,000	2,000
☐	as. Diagonal red *SPECIMEN* and DLR oval ovpts; horizontal red *SPECIMEN Nº #* ovpt at lower left; punched.	—	—	22,600

Replacement notes: Prefix numerator Z.

BCCS B9 (P8A): **10,000 dollars** (US$8,282)   VG   VF   UNC
Green. Front: Aranda Majulah orchid; coat of arms. Back: Istana (office of the president) building with flag and palm trees. Two solid security threads. Watermark: Lion head. Printer: *THOMAS DE LA RUE & COMPANY, LIMITED*. 203 x 133 mm.
☐ a.   No date. Sig. 3 with red seal. Intro: 29.01.1973.   FV   FV   14,000
Replacement notes: Prefix numerator Z.
Reproductions of this note with all-zero s/n printed on paper provided by Debden Security Printing Works were sold for US$18 in the late 1990s.

Numismatic Products

Three different collectors' sets of the Orchid series have been issued, each overprinted *SPECIMEN*, with and without holes punched in the paper. They were packaged in black leather albums with numbered certificates of authenticity.

BCCS BNP1 (PCS1): **1, 5, 10, 50, and 100 dollars**   UNC
☐ a.   77 sets issued. Signature 1. Specimens with *SPECIMEN* overprints; punched.   2,000

BCCS BNP2 (PCS2): **1, 5, 10, 50, and 100 dollars**   UNC
☐ a.   89 sets issued. Signature 3 without red seal.   2,800

BCCS BNP3 (PCS3): **1, 5, 10, 25, 50, and 100 dollars**   UNC
☐ a.   82 sets issued. Signature 3 with red seal.   2,800

1976-1980 Bird Issues

This series also has nine denominations as in the first, except that a 20-dollar note was introduced to replace the 25-dollar note of the Orchid series. The dominant feature is a bird on the left side of the front of each note. The birds depicted on the notes are known for their strength, adaptability, and independence, which the BCCS believed characterized the young Republic of Singapore with the potential of soaring to greater heights.

On the front, all notes have the Singapore coat of arms, a lion head watermark, and the signature and seal of the minister for finance and the chairman of the BCCS.

BCCS B10 (P9): **1 dollar** (US$0.80)   VG   VF   UNC
Pink and dark blue. Front: Black-naped tern bird; buildings in city skyline; coat of arms. Back: Woman with parasol; National Day parade passing government building with grandstand. Watermark: Lion head. Printer: *BRADBURY, WILKINSON & C⁰ L^D* 125 x 63 mm.
☐ a.   No date. Sig. 3 with red seal. Intro: 06.08.1976. Solid security thread.   FV   FV   3.25
☐ b.   Solid security thread with printed *SINGAPORE*.   FV   FV   3.25

BCCS B11 (P10): **5 dollars** (US$4.15)   VG   VF   UNC
Green. Front: Red-whiskered bulbul bird; buildings in city skyline; coat of arms. Back: Female dancer; skyway tram cars on cable above ships in harbor. Watermark: Lion head. Printer: *BRADBURY, WILKINSON & C⁰ L^D* 133 x 66 mm.
☐ a.   No date. Sig. 3 with red seal. Intro: 06.08.1976. Solid security thread.   FV   FV   12
☐ b.   Solid security thread with printed *SINGAPORE*.   FV   FV   12

BCCS B12 (P11): **10 dollars** (US$8.30) VG VF UNC

Red. Front: White-collared kingfisher bird; buildings in city skyline; map of Singapore; merlion as registration device; coat of arms. Back: Merlion; Garden City with high rise public housing buildings; lion. Watermark: Lion head. Printer: *THOMAS DE LA RUE & COMPANY, LIMITED*. 141 x 69 mm.

- ☐ a. No date. Sig. 3 with red seal. Intro: 06.08.1976.   FV   FV   20
Solid security thread.
- ☐ b. Solid security thread with printed *SINGAPORE*.   FV   FV   20
Intro: October 1976.

Replacement notes: Prefix numerator Z.

BCCS B13 (P12): **20 dollars** (US$17)   VG   VF   UNC

Yellow and brown. Front: Yellow-breasted sunbird; buildings in city skyline; coat of arms. Back: Female dancer; Singapore Airlines Concorde jet over Changi International Airport (SIN). Solid security thread. Watermark: Lion head. Printer: *BRADBURY, WILKINSON & Cº Lᴅ* 149 x 72 mm.

- ☐ a. No date. Sig. 3 with red seal. Intro: 06.08.1979.   FV   20   40

BCCS B14 (P13): **50 dollars** (US$41)   VG   VF   UNC

Blue. Front: White-rumped shama bird; buildings in city skyline; map of Singapore; merlion as registration device; coat of arms. Back: Merlion; school band with musical instruments on parade in front of domed government building; female dancer. Watermark: Lion head. Printer: *THOMAS DE LA RUE & COMPANY, LIMITED*. 157 x 75 mm.

- ☐ a. No date. Sig. 3 with red seal. Intro: 06.08.1976.   FV   75   150
Solid security thread.
- ☐ b. Solid security thread with printed *SINGAPORE*.   FV   60   120

Replacement notes: Prefix numerator Z.

BCCS B15 (P14): **100 dollars** (US$83)   VG   VF   UNC

Blue. Front: Blue-throated bee-eater bird; buildings in city skyline; coat of arms. Back: Various ethnic dancers. Solid security thread. Watermark: Lion head. Printer: *BRADBURY, WILKINSON & Cº Lᴅ* 165 x 78 mm.

- ☐ a. No date. Sig. 3 with red seal. Intro: 01.02.1977.   FV   125   250

BCCS B16 (P15): **500 dollars** (US$414)   VG   VF   UNC

Green. Front: Black-naped oriole bird; buildings in city skyline; map of Singapore; merlion as registration device; coat of arms. Back: Merlion; oil refinery; ships; female dancer. Solid segmented security thread with printed text. Watermark: Lion head. Printer: *THOMAS DE LA RUE & COMPANY, LIMITED*. 181 x 84 mm.

    ☐ a.   No date. Sig. 3 with red seal. Intro: 01.02.1977.   FV   500   1,000
    ☐ as.   Diagonal *SPECIMEN* overprint; punched.   —   —   —

Replacement notes: Prefix numerator Z.

BCCS B17 (P16): **1,000 dollars** (US$828)   VG   VF   UNC

Purple. Front: Brahminy Kite bird; buildings in city skyline; map of Singapore; merlion as registration device; coat of arms. Back: Merlion; crane and container ship at port; female dancer. Two solid security threads. Watermark: Lion head. Printer: *THOMAS DE LA RUE & COMPANY, LIMITED*. 197 x 90 mm.

    ☐ a.   No date. Sig. 3 with red seal. Intro: 07.08.1978.   FV   FV   1,600

Replacement notes: Prefix numerator Z.

BCCS B18 (P17): **10,000 dollars** (US$8,282)   VG   VF   UNC

Green. Front: White-bellied sea-eagle bird; buildings in city skyline; map of Singapore; merlion as registration device; coat of arms. Back: Merlion; two scenes of the Singapore River; drummer. Two solid security threads. Watermark: Lion head. Printer: *THOMAS DE LA RUE & COMPANY, LIMITED*. 203 x 133 mm.

    ☐ a.   No date. Sig. 3 with red seal. Intro: 01.02.1980.   FV   FV   11,000
    ☐ as.   Diagonal *SPECIMEN* overprint; punched.   —   —   1,500

Replacement notes: Prefix numerator Z.

1977 Numismatic Products

One type of collectors' set of the Bird series has been issued, overprinted *SPECIMEN*, with and without holes punched in the paper. 311 sets were packaged in black leather albums with numbered certificates of authenticity.

BCCS BNP4 (PCS4): **1, 5, 10, 50, and 100 dollars**   UNC

    ☐ a.   Specimens with diagonal red *SPECIMEN* overprints and three   1,500
         holes punched in all denominations except $5 and $100. Sig. 3
         with seal.

1984-1997 Ship Issues

As was the case with the previous two issues, the Ship series also has nine denominations. The denominations are similar except that the previous 20-dollar note was discontinued and a new denomination of 2 dollars was introduced. The pictorial and aesthetic themes of this series are based on maritime vessels and the modern development of Singapore. The vignettes on the front depict vessels that have plied the waters of Singapore over the centuries. The series starts with the merchant craft of bygone days, and progresses to the modern bulk carrier which is featured on the highest denomination. The series pays homage to the contribution of merchant shipping to the development of Singapore from an entrepot trading center to the busiest port in the world.

On the front, all notes have the Singapore coat of arms, a lion head watermark, and the signature and seal of the minister for finance and the chairman of the BCCS. On the front center panel are creatures from Chinese mythology. On the backs of the notes are scenes depicting Singapore's achievements in the fields of communication, housing, defense, and port management. The orchid featured on the back of all the Ship series notes is the national flower of Singapore, Vanda Miss Joaquim.

BCCS B20 (P27): **2 dollars** (US$1.65) VG VF UNC
Red and yellow. Front: Coat of arms; "Tongkang" two-masted sailboat and two smaller boats; seagull birds. Back: Vanda Miss Joaquim orchid; Chingay procession parade with dragon. Solid security thread. Watermark: Lion head. Printer: *THOMAS DE LA RUE AND COMPANY LIMITED*. 133 x 63 mm.
- a. No date. Signature 5. Intro: 28.01.1991. FV FV 2.50
- as. Diagonal red *SPECIMEN* overprint; — — 400
  horizontal red *SPECIMEN Nº* # ovpt at lower left.

Replacement notes: Prefix numerator Z.

BCCS B19 (P18): **1 dollar** (US$0.80) VG VF UNC
Blue. Front: Coat of arms; "Sha Chuan" four-masted ship; Chinese crane; Chinese carp (Cyprinus carpio) fish. Back: Vanda Miss Joaquim orchid; Sentosa satellite earth station. Solid security thread. Watermark: Lion head. Printer: *THOMAS DE LA RUE & COMPANY, LIMITED*. 125 x 63 mm.
- a. No date. Signature 4. Intro: 12.01.1987. FV FV 3
- b. Signature 5. Intro: 19.12.1988. FV FV 2
  Last 1-dollar note is serial number D/20 750000.

Replacement notes: Prefix numerator Z.
Engraving of ship on front in error in that flags on mast are blowing to stern, not bow.

BCCS B21 (P19 & P35): **5 dollars** (US$4.15) VG VF UNC
Green. Front: Coat of arms; unknown boat; Twakow boat; Chinese lion with ball; Commerson's anchovy (Stolephorus commersonii) fish. Back: Commerson's anchovy fish; Vanda Miss Joaquim orchid; PSA Container Terminal with ships and cranes. Solid security thread. Watermark: Lion head. 133 x 63 mm.
- a. No date. Signature 5. Printer: *THOMAS DE LA* FV FV 10
  RUE & COMPANY, LIMITED. Intro: 21.08.1989.
- b. Printer: *HARRISON AND SONS LIMITED*. FV FV 9
  Intro: 1997.

Replacement notes: Prefix numerator Z.

BCCS B22 (P20): **10 dollars** (US$8.30) VG VF UNC
Red. Front: Coat of arms; "Palari" barter trading sailboat; phoenix; round scad (Decapterus macrosoma) fish. Back: Round scad fish; Vanda Miss Joaquim orchid; map of Singapore; public housing buildings. Solid security thread. Watermark: Lion head. Printer: *THOMAS DE LA RUE & COMPANY, LIMITED.* 141 x 69 mm.

☐ a. No date. Signature 5. Intro: 01.03.1988.   FV FV 16

Replacement notes: Prefix numerator Z.

BCCS B23 (P22): **50 dollars** (US$41) VG VF UNC
Blue. Front: Coat of arms; "Perak" coaster boat; two Mandarin ducks; six-banded grouper (Epinephelus sexfasciatus; valenciennes) fish. Back: Six-banded grouper fish; Vanda Miss Joaquim orchid; Benjamin Sheares bridge. Watermark: Lion head. Printer: *THOMAS DE LA RUE & COMPANY, LIMITED.* 156 x 74 mm.

☐ a. No date. Signature 5. Intro: 09.03.1987.   FV FV 85
    Solid security thread.
☐ b. Windowed security thread.   FV FV 80

Replacement notes: Prefix numerator Z.

BCCS B24 (P23): **100 dollars** (US$83) VG VF UNC
Brown. Front: Coat of arms; "Chusan" passenger liner boat; Chinese crane bird; slender shad (Ilisha elongata) fish. Back: Slender shad fish; Vanda Miss Joaquim orchid; Singapore Airlines Boeing 747-300 "Big Top" jet plane above Changi International Airport (SIN). Watermark: Lion head. Printer: *THOMAS DE LA RUE & COMPANY, LIMITED.* 165 x 78 mm.

☐ a. No date. Intro: 01.08.1985.   FV FV 150
    Signature 4. Solid security thread.
☐ b. Signature 5.   FV FV 125
☐ c. Windowed security thread with demetalized   FV FV 125
    SINGAPORA $100.

Replacement notes: Prefix numerator Z.

BCCS B25 (P24): **500 dollars** (US$414) VG VF UNC
Green. Front: Coat of arms; "Neptune Sardonyx" general cargo boat; Chinese peony and butterfly; Indian mackerel (Rastrelliger kanagurta) fish. Back: Indian mackerel fish; Vanda Miss Joaquim orchid; group of men and women from the three services of the Armed Forces and the Civil Defence Force; flag and map of Singapore. Solid security thread. Watermark: Lion head. Printer: *THOMAS DE LA RUE AND COMPANY LIMITED.* 175 x 83 mm.

☐ a. No date. Signature 5. Intro: 01.03.1988.   FV FV 800

Replacement notes: Prefix numerator Z.

BCCS B26 (P25): **1,000 dollars** (US$828)   VG   VF   UNC
Purple. Front: Coat of arms; "Neptune Garnet" container ship with two container quay cranes; phoenix; polka-dot grouper (Cromileptes altivelis) fish. Back: Polka-dot grouper fish; Vanda Miss Joaquim orchid; ship repair yard. Solid security thread. Watermark: Lion head. Printer: *THOMAS DE LA RUE AND COMPANY LIMITED*. 185 x 88 mm.
- ☐ a. No date. Signature 4. Intro: 22.10.1984.   FV   FV   1,100
- ☐ b. Signature 5.   FV   FV   1,000
- ☐ as. Specimen.   —   —   —

Replacement notes: Prefix numerator Z.

1990 Commemorative Issues

Designed by artist Chua Mia Tee, this 50-dollar note was issued to commemorate the 25th anniversary of Singapore's independence. A total of 4.8 million undated notes were issued at face value for circulation. This is the first polymer note issued by Singapore.

BCCS B28 (P31): **50 dollars** (US$41)   VG   VF   UNC
Orange and red. Front: Sailing ships in harbor; Yusof Bin Ishak hologram; Vanda Miss Joaquim orchid flowers; container ship and crane; Financial District skyscraper buildings. Back: First parliament held 8TH DECEMBER 1965; Yusof Bin Ishak hologram; group of cheering people under flag and coat of arms. Watermark (shadow image): 25th anniversary logo. Printer: (NPA). 156 x 74 mm. Polymer.
- ☐ a. No date. Signature 5. Intro: 24.07.1990.   FV   FV   80

BCCS B27 (P26): **10,000 dollars** (US$8,282)   VG   VF   UNC
Red. Front: Coat of arms; "Neptune Canopus" general bulk carrier boat; Chinese dragon; white promfret (Pampus chinesis) fish. Back: White promfret fish; Vanda Miss Joaquim orchid; 1987 National Day Parade. Solid security thread. Watermark: Lion head. Printer: *THOMAS DE LA RUE AND COMPANY LIMITED*. 195 x 93 mm.
- ☐ a. No date. Signature 5. Intro: 21.08.1989.   FV   FV   9,200

Replacement notes: Prefix numerator Z.

1990 Numismatic Products

This 50-dollar note is identical to the commemorative issue except that it is overprinted in red with the date *9 AUGUST 1990*. A total of 300,000 dated notes were packaged in booklets and sold for S$55 each.

BCCS BNP5 (P30): **50 dollars** (US$41) UNC
- a. BCCS B28 with *9 AUGUST 1990* overprint in booklet. 80
- as. Horizontal red *SPECIMEN* overprint on front; horizontal red *SPECIMEN No. #* overprint on back. —

1991-1998 Issues

The public complained that the red color scheme of the 2-dollar note (BCCS B20) introduced in January 1991 was too similar to that of the 10-dollar note (BCCS B22) introduced in 1988. To reduce confusion, the 2-dollar note was made more distinctive by changing its color to purple.

BCCS B29 (P28, P34 & P37): **2 dollars** (US$1.65)   VG   VF   UNC
Purple. Front: Coat of arms; "Tongkang" two-masted sailboat and two smaller boats; seagull birds. Back: Vanda Miss Joaquim orchid; Chingay procession parade with dragon. Solid security thread. Watermark: Lion head. 133 x 63 mm.
- a. No date. Sig. 5. Printer: *THOMAS DE LA RUE AND COMPANY LIMITED*. Intro: 16.12.1991.   FV   FV   3.25
- b. Printer: *HARRISON AND SONS LIMITED*. Intro: 1997.   FV   FV   4
- c. Printer: *B A BANKNOTE*. Intro: 1998.   FV   FV   3

Replacement notes: Prefix ZZ.

1992 Numismatic Products

This legal tender 2-dollar note was issued to commemorate the 25th anniversary of the BCCS. A total of 5,000 notes were packaged with the book, *Prudence at the Helm,* and 4,000 were sold for S$60 each, the remaining copies were distributed by the BCCS. The notes are overprinted with a BCCS logo and *25 YEARS OF CURRENCY ISSUE, 1967-1992, BOARD OF COMMISSONERS* [sic] *OF CURRENCY, SINGAPORE, 12TH JUNE, 1967.*

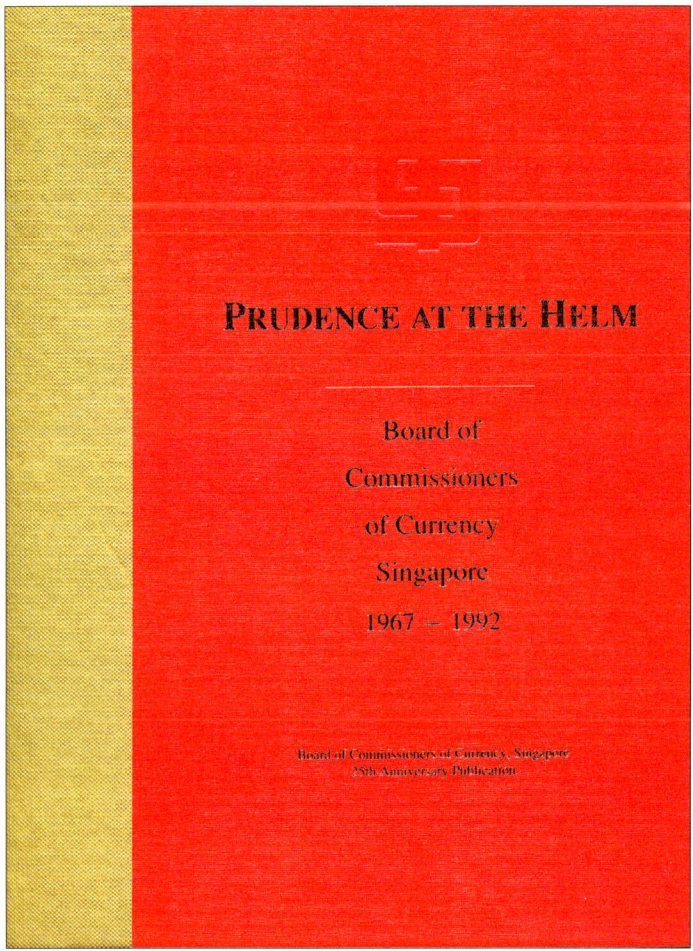

BCCS BNP6 (P29): **2 dollars** (US$1.65)   **UNC**
Purple. Front: Coat of arms; "Tongkang" two-masted sailboat and two smaller boats; seagull birds; red overprint. Back: Vanda Miss Joaquim orchid; Chingay procession parade with dragon. Solid security thread. Watermark: Lion head. Printer: *THOMAS DE LA RUE AND COMPANY LIMITED.* 133 x 63 mm.
    ☐ a.   12TH JUNE 1992. Signature 5. Intro: 29.06.1992.   400

1994 Commemorative Issues

This 2-dollar note was issued to commemorate the BCCS. Each note is overprinted with the logo of the board below the coat of arms on the left front.

BCCS B30 (P31A): **2 dollars** (US$1.65)   **VG**   **VF**   **UNC**
Purple. Front: Coat of arms; overprint; "Tongkang" two-masted sailboat and two smaller boats; seagull birds. Back: Vanda Miss Joaquim orchid; Chingay procession parade with dragon. Solid security thread. Watermark: Lion head. Printer: *THOMAS DE LA RUE AND COMPANY LIMITED.* 133 x 63 mm.
    ☐ a.   No date. Signature 5. Intro: 1994.   —   —   100

1994 Issues

This 50-dollar note is similar to BCCS B23, but the colors were changed from blue to slate gray and the security thread was changed from solid to windowed.

BCCS B31 (P32 & P36): **50 dollars** (US$41)   **VG**   **VF**   **UNC**
Slate gray. Front: Coat of arms; "Perak" coaster boat; two Mandarin ducks; six-banded grouper (Epinephelus sexfasciatus; valenciennes) fish. Back: Vanda Miss Joaquim orchid; Benjamin Sheares bridge. Watermark: Lion head. Printer: *THOMAS DE LA RUE & COMPANY, LIMITED.* 156 x 74 mm.
    ☐ a.   No date. Signature 5. Intro: 1991.   FV   FV   100
           Windowed security thread.
    ☐ b.   Windowed security thread with demetalized   FV   FV   100
           SINGAPORA $50. Intro: 1994.
Replacement notes: Prefix Z.

1996 Numismatic Products

This 25-dollar note was issued to commemorate the 25th anniversary of the Monetary Authority of Singapore. A total of 600,000 notes were sold for S$34 in a folder or S$36 in a cheque book.

BCCS BNP7 (P33): **25 dollars** (US$21) UNC
Red-brown. Front: Coat of arms; holographic patch; Monetary Authority building; lion head as registration device. Back: Lion head; financial sector skyline with Monetary Authority building; abacus; keyboard; SIMEX (Singapore International Monetary Exchange) trading floor. Solid security thread. Watermark: Lion head. Printer: Unknown. 141 x 79 mm.
    a. No date. Signature 5. Note in folder. Intro: 10.05.1996. 90
    b. Note in cheque book. 75

1999 Portrait Issues

The Portrait series was introduced by the BCCS on 9 September 1999, to usher in the new millennium. Designed by local artist Eng Siak Loy, the banknotes' fronts feature the portrait of the first president of Singapore, Encik Yusof bin Ishak. The backs contain secondary themes that are linked to his life. The series has a total of seven denominations in general circulation; the 1- and 500-dollar denominations were not carried forward from the preceding Ship series.

BCCS B32 (P38): **2 dollars** (US$1.65)   VG   VF   UNC
Purple. Front: Coat of arms; ; lion head as registration device; Kinegram holographic patch; Yusof bin Ishak. Back: Education theme; Victoria Bridge School, Old Raffles Institution at Bras Basah Road, and College of Medicine buildings; teacher lecturing to students in "borderless classroom;" lion head. Windowed security thread with demetalized *SINGAPORA $2*. Watermark: Yusof bin Ishak with electrotype braille codes. Printer: (OeBS). 126 x 63 mm.
    a. No date. Signature 5. Intro: 09.09.1999.   FV   FV   3.50
Replacement notes: Prefix ZZ.

BCCS B33 (P39): **5 dollars** (US$4.15)   VG   VF   UNC
Green. Front: Coat of arms; lion head as registration device; Kinegram holographic patch; Yusof bin Ishak. Back: Garden City; tembusu tree (Fagraea fragrans) at Singapore Botanic Gardens; Vanda Miss Joaquim flowers; skyscraper buildings; lion head. Windowed security thread with demetalized *SINGAPORA $5*. Watermark: Yusof bin Ishak with electrotype braille codes. Printer: (OeBS). 133 x 66 mm.
    a. No date. Signature 5. Intro: 09.09.1999.   FV   FV   8

BCCS B34 (P40): **10 dollars** (US$8.30)   VG   VF   UNC
Red. Front: Coat of arms; lion head as registration device; Kinegram holographic patch; Yusof bin Ishak. Back: Sports theme; jogging; tennis; soccer (football); sailing; swimming; lion head. Windowed security thread with demetalized *SINGAPORA $10*. Watermark: Yusof bin Ishak with electrotype braille codes. Printer: (OeBS). 141 x 69 mm.
   ☐   a.   No date. Signature 5. Intro: 09.09.1999.   FV   FV   14
Replacement notes: Prefix ZZ.

BCCS B35 (P41): **50 dollars** (US$41)   VG   VF   UNC
Blue. Front: Coat of arms; lion head as registration device; Kinegram holographic patch; Yusof bin Ishak. Back: Arts theme; musical instruments (Chinese pipa; Malay kompang, Indian veena, and classical violin); Chen Wen Hsi's "Gibbons Fetching the Moon from the Water;" Cheong Soo Pieng's "Drying Salted Fish;" lion head. Windowed security thread with demetalized *SINGAPORA $50*. Watermark: Yusof bin Ishak with electrotype braille codes. Printer: (OeBS). 156 x 74 mm.
   ☐   a.   No date. Signature 5. Intro: 09.09.1999.   FV   FV   90
   ☐   b.   Signature 6. Intro: March 2002.   FV   FV   90

BCCS B36 (P42): **100 dollars** (US$83)   VG   VF   UNC
Orange. Front: Coat of arms; lion head as registration device; Kinegram holographic patch; Yusof bin Ishak. Back: Youth theme; members of the Singapore Red Cross; Saint John's Ambulance Bridgade, National Police Cadet Corp officer with sword; tower of the SAFTI (Singapore Armed Forces Training Institute) Military Institute, tower with flag; lion head. Windowed security thread. Watermark: Yusof bin Ishak with electrotype braille codes. Printer: (OeBS). 162 x 77 mm.
   ☐   a.   No date. Signature 5. Intro: 09.09.1999.   FV   FV   200

BCCS B37 (P43): **1,000 dollars** (US$828)   VG   VF   UNC
Purple. Front: Coat of arms; lion head as registration device; Kinegram holographic patch; Yusof bin Ishak. Back: Government theme; Parliament House; Istana (office of the president); Old Supreme Court building; lion head. Windowed security thread. Watermark: Yusof bin Ishak with electrotype braille codes. Printer: (OeBS). 170 x 83 mm.
   ☐   a.   No date. Signature 5. Intro: 09.09.1999.   FV   FV   1,200
   ☐   as.   Diagonal *SPECIMEN* perforation.   —   —   975

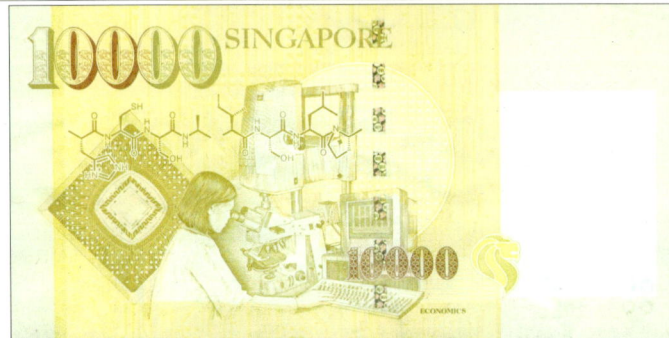

BCCS B38 (P44): **10,000 dollars** (withdrawn 01.10.2014)   VG   VF   UNC

Gold. Front: Coat of arms; lion head as registration device; Kinegram holographic patch; Yusof bin Ishak. Back: Economics theme; microprocessor silicon wafer; partial sequences of two proteins (tyrosine kinase and tyrosine phosphatease); researcher with microscope and computer; lion head. Windowed security thread. Watermark: Yusof bin Ishak with electrotype braille codes. Printer: (OeBS). 180 x 90 mm.

  ☐ a. No date. Signature 5. Intro: 09.09.1999.   FV   FV   9,000
  ☐ as. Diagonal red *SPECIMEN* overprint.   —   —   500

This note is tied with the 10,000-dollar note (BCMB B5) from Brunei for the circulating note with the highest face value in the world.

2000 Commemorative Issues

This 2-dollar note was issued to commemorate the new millennium. A total of 3 million notes were issued at face value for circulation. Like BCCS B32, but with 2000 logo instead of alphabetic serial number prefix.

BCCS B39 (P45): **2 dollars** (US$1.65)   VG   VF   UNC

Purple. Front: Coat of arms; lion head as registration device; Kinegram holographic patch; Yusof bin Ishak; red 2000 logo instead of prefix. Back: Education theme; Victoria Bridge School, Old Raffles Institution at Bras Basah Road, and College of Medicine buildings; teacher lecturing to students in "borderless classroom;" lion head. Windowed security thread with demetalized *SINGAPORA $2*. Watermark: Yusof bin Ishak with electrotype braille codes. Printer: (OeBS). 126 x 63 mm.

  ☐ a. 2000. Signature 5. Intro: 08.12.1999.   FV   FV   3

2000 Numismatic Products

BCCS BNP8 (PNL): **three 2 dollars**   UNC
  ☐ a. Three BCCS B39 notes in hardback folder.   120

2002 Numismatic Products

To commemorate the January 2002 appointment of Lee Hsien Loong as chairman of the BCCS, five thousand 50-dollar notes with his signature were paired with notes bearing matching serial numbers and signed by the outgoing chairman, Richard Hu Hsu Tau. The Lee Hsien Loong notes are overprinted with the logos of the BCCS and the MAS at right on the front.

BCCS BNP9 (PNL): **two 50 dollars** (US$83)   **UNC**
Blue. Front: Coat of arms; lion head as registration device; Kinegram holographic patch; Yusof bin Ishak. Back: Arts theme; musical instruments (Chinese pipa; Malay kompang, Indian veena, and classical violin); Chen Wen Hsi's "Gibbons Fetching the Moon from the Water;" Cheong Soo Pieng's "Drying Salted Fish;" lion head. Windowed security thread. Watermark: Yusof bin Ishak with electrotype braille codes. Printer: (OeBS). 156 x 74 mm.
    a.   No date. Signatures 5 and 6. Intro: January 2002.   500

Monetary Authority of Singapore

Prior to 1970, the various monetary functions associated with a central bank were performed by several government departments and agencies. As Singapore progressed, the demands of an increasingly complex banking and monetary environment necessitated streamlining the functions to facilitate the development of a more dynamic and coherent policy on monetary matters. Therefore, parliament passed the Monetary Authority of Singapore Act in 1970, leading to the formation of MAS on 1 January 1971. The MAS Act gave the MAS the authority to regulate all elements of monetary, banking, and financial aspects of Singapore.

On 31 March 2003, the Board of Commissioners of Currency Singapore (BCCS) merged with the Monetary Authority of Singapore (MAS), which took over the responsibility of banknote issuance.

For more information, visit www.mas.gov.sg.

MAS Signature Varieties

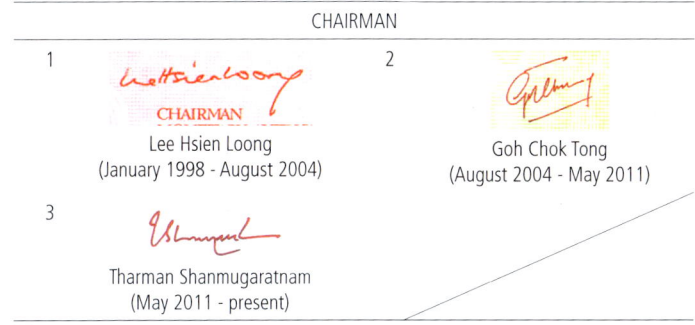

CHAIRMAN

1. Lee Hsien Loong (January 1998 - August 2004)
2. Goh Chok Tong (August 2004 - May 2011)
3. Tharman Shanmugaratnam (May 2011 - present)

2004 Issues

This polymer 10-dollar note is the first issue by the Monetary Authority of Singapore. A total of 10 million notes were issued at face value for circulation. The serial numbers for the first edition of the 10-dollar polymer note have prefixes from 0AA to 9AA, then from 0AB to 2AB.

MAS B1 (P48): **10 dollars** (US$8.30)   VG   VF   UNC
Red. Front: Coat of arms; lion head as registration device; gold lion head; purple *10*; Yusof bin Ishak. Back: Sports theme; jogging; tennis; soccer (football); sailing; swimming; lion head. Security thread shaped like Singapore island. Watermark (shadow image): Yusof bin Ishak. Printer: (NPA). 141 x 69 mm. Polymer.
    a.   No date. Signature 1. Intro: 04.05.2004.   FV   FV   15

2004 Numismatic Products

This polymer 10-dollar note commemorates the first issue of banknotes by the Monetary Authority of Singapore. A total of 10,000 notes overprinted *Commemorative First Issue by MAS* with MAS prefix were sold for S$35.

MAS BNP1 (P54): **10 dollars** (US$8.30) UNC
Red. Front: Coat of arms; lion head as registration device; gold lion head; *Commemorative First Issue by MAS* overprint; Yusof bin Ishak. Back: Sports theme; jogging; tennis; soccer (football); sailing; swimming; lion head. Security thread shaped like Singapore island. Watermark (shadow image): Yusof bin Ishak. Printer: (NPA). 141 x 69 mm. Polymer.
    ☐ a. No date. Signature 1. Intro: 04.05.2004.   100

2004-2014 Issues

These notes are like the preceding Portrait series, but reflect the new name of the issuer, the Monetary Authority of Singapore.

At some point in the late 2000s, the MAS began including symbols on the back of the notes to indicate new printings. The first issue under a given signature has no symbol. The second printing has one square; the third, two squares; the fourth, one triangle; the fifth, two triangles; the sixth, one diamond; and the seventh, two diamonds.

MAS B2 (PNL): **2 dollars** (US$1.65)   VG VF UNC
Purple. Front: Coat of arms; lion head as registration device; Kinegram holographic patch; Yusof bin Ishak. Back: Education theme; Victoria Bridge School, Old Raffles Institution at Bras Basah Road, and College of Medicine buildings; teacher lecturing to students in "borderless classroom;" lion head. Windowed security thread with demetalized *SINGAPORA $2*. Watermark: Yusof bin Ishak with electrotype braille codes. Printer: (OeBS). 126 x 63 mm.
    ☐ a. No date. Signature 1. Intro: January 2005.   FV FV 3

MAS B3 (P47): **5 dollars** (US$4.15)   VG VF UNC
Green. Front: Coat of arms; lion head as registration device; Kinegram holographic patch; Yusof bin Ishak. Back: Garden City; tembusu tree (Fagraea fragrans) at Singapore Botanic Gardens; Vanda Miss Joaquim flowers; skyscraper buildings; lion head. Windowed security thread. Watermark: Yusof bin Ishak with electrotype braille codes. Printer: (OeBS). 133 x 66 mm.
    ☐ a. No date. Signature 1. Intro: August 2004.   FV FV 7

MAS B4 (PNL): **10 dollars** (US$8.30)   VG VF UNC
Red. Front: Coat of arms; lion head as registration device; Kinegram holographic patch; brown *10*; Yusof bin Ishak. Back: Sports theme; jogging; tennis; soccer (football); sailing; swimming; lion head. Windowed security thread. Watermark: Yusof bin Ishak. Printer: (OeBS). 141 x 69 mm.
    ☐ a. No date. Signature 1. Intro: January 2005.   FV FV 13

MAS B5 (P49): **50 dollars** (US$41) VG VF UNC
Blue. Front: Coat of arms; lion head as registration device; Kinegram holographic patch; Yusof bin Ishak. Back: Arts theme; musical instruments (Chinese pipa; Malay kompang, Indian veena, and classical violin); Chen Wen Hsi's "Gibbons Fetching the Moon from the Water;" Cheong Soo Pieng's "Drying Salted Fish;" lion head. Watermark: Yusof bin Ishak with electrotype braille codes. Printer: (OeBS). 156 x 74 mm.

☐	a. No date. Signature 1. Intro: August 2004. No symbol below *ARTS* on back.	FV	FV	60
☐	b. Sig. 2. One square on back. Intro: Jan. 2010.	FV	FV	60
☐	c. Two squares on back. Intro: September 2010.	FV	FV	60
☐	d. Sig. 3. One triangle on back. Intro: July 2012.	FV	FV	60
☐	e. Two triangles on back. Intro: January 2013.	FV	FV	60
☐	f. One diamond on back. Intro: January 2014.	FV	FV	60

MAS B6 (P50): **100 dollars** (US$83) VG VF UNC
Orange. Front: Coat of arms; lion head as registration device; Kinegram holographic patch; Yusof bin Ishak. Back: Youth theme; members of the Singapore Red Cross; Saint John's Ambulance Bridgade, National Police Cadet Corp officer with sword; tower of the SAFTI (Singapore Armed Forces Training Institute) Military Institute, tower with flag; lion head. Windowed security thread. Watermark: Yusof bin Ishak with electrotype braille codes. Printer: (OeBS). 162 x 77 mm.

☐	a. No date. Signature 2. Intro: 2009. No symbol below *YOUTH* on back.	FV	FV	100
☐	b. One squares on back. Intro: November 2009.	FV	FV	100
☐	c. Two squares on back.	FV	FV	100
☐	d. Signature 3. One triangle on back. Intro: Jan.'13.	FV	FV	100
☐	e. Two triangles on back. Intro: January 2014.	FV	FV	100

MAS B7 (P51): **1,000 dollars** (US$828) VG VF UNC
Purple. Front: Coat of arms; lion head as registration device; Kinegram holographic patch; Yusof bin Ishak. Back: Government theme; Parliament House; Istana (office of the president); Old Supreme Court building; lion head. Windowed thread. Watermark: Yusof bin Ishak with electrotype braille codes. Printer: (OeBS). 170 x 83 mm.

☐	a. No date. Signature 2. Intro: 2009. No symbol below *GOVERNMENT* on back.	FV	FV	1,000
☐	b. One triangle on back.	FV	FV	1,000
☐	c. Two triangles on back.	FV	FV	1,000
☐	d. One diamond on back.	FV	FV	1,000
☐	e. Two diamonds on back. Intro: 2013.	FV	FV	1,000
☐	f. Sig. 3. One star on back. Intro: January 2014.	FV	FV	1,000

2006-2014 Polymer Issues

Apparently pleased with the public acceptance of the polymer 10-dollar note issued in 2004, MAS began issuing other denominations on polymer in 2006. These notes are similar to the paper versions of the preceding notes, but have a new signature in addition to different security features necessitated by the change in substrate.

MAS B8 (P46): 2 dollars (US$1.65)   VG   VF   UNC

Purple. Front: Coat of arms; lion head as registration device; gold lion head; Yusof bin Ishak. Back: Education theme; Victoria Bridge School, Old Raffles Institution at Bras Basah Road, and College of Medicine buildings; teacher lecturing to students in "borderless classroom;" lion head. Security thread shaped like Singapore island. Watermark (shadow image): Yusof bin Ishak. Printer: (OFSP). 126 x 63 mm. Polymer.

☐ a.	No date. Signature 2. Intro: 12.01.2006. No symbol below *EDUCATION* on back.	FV	FV	3
☐ b.	One square on back. Intro: 2009.	FV	FV	3
☐ c.	Two squares on back. Intro: 2010.	FV	FV	3
☐ d.	One triangle on back. Intro: February 2011.	FV	FV	3
☐ e.	Two triangles on back. Intro: July 2011.	FV	FV	3
☐ f.	Sig. 3. One diamond on back. Intro: 21.01.2013.	FV	FV	3

MAS B9 (PNL): 5 dollars (US$4.15)   VG   VF   UNC

Green. Front: Coat of arms; lion head as registration device; gold lion head; Yusof bin Ishak. Back: Garden City; tembusu tree (Fagraea fragrans) at Singapore Botanic Gardens; Vanda Miss Joaquim flowers; skyscraper buildings; lion head. Security thread shaped like Singapore island. Watermark (shadow image): Yusof bin Ishak. Printer: (OFSP). 133 x 66 mm. Polymer.

☐ a.	No date. Signature 2. Intro: 18.05.2007. No symbol below *GARDEN CITY* on back.	FV	FV	6
☐ b.	One square on back. Intro: November 2010.	FV	FV	6
☐ c.	Sig. 3. Two triangles on back. Intro: Jan. 2013.	FV	FV	6
☐ d.	One triangle on back. Intro: 2014.	FV	FV	6

MAS B10 (P48): 10 dollars (US$8.30)   VG   VF   UNC

Red. Front: Coat of arms; lion head as registration device; gold lion head; brown *10*; Yusof bin Ishak. Back: Sports theme; jogging; tennis; soccer (football); sailing; swimming; lion head. Security thread shaped like Singapore island. Watermark (shadow image): Yusof bin Ishak. Printer: (OFSP). 141 x 69 mm. Polymer.

☐ a.	No date. Signature 2. Intro: 01.02.2008. No symbol below *SPORTS* on back.	FV	FV	13
☐ b.	One square on back. Intro: September 2008.	FV	FV	13
☐ c.	Two squares on back. Intro: January 2009.	FV	FV	13
☐ d.	One triangle on back. Intro: October 2009.	FV	FV	13
☐ e.	Two triangles on back. Intro: May 2011.	FV	FV	13
☐ f.	One diamond on back. Intro: January 2012.	FV	FV	13
☐ g.	Two diamonds on back. Intro: January 2013.	FV	FV	13
☐ h.	One star on back. Intro: January 2014.	FV	FV	13

2007 Commemorative Issues

This 20-dollar note commemorates the 40th anniversary of the Currency Interchangeability Agreement between Brunei and Singapore. A total of 3 million notes were issued at face value for circulation. The notes were unveiled 27 June 2007, but were not available to the public until 16 July.

MAS B11 (P53): **20 dollars** (US$17)　　　　　VG　　VF　　UNC
Yellow. Front: Coat of arms; gold lion head; Dendrobium Puan Noor Aishah orchids; Yusof bin Ishak. Back: Singapore's esplanade and buildings along the city's waterfront; Singapore and Brunei coats of arms; the Sultan Omar Ali Saifuddien mosque; Royal Barge; Water Village. Security thread shaped like Singapore island. Watermark (shadow image): Yusof bin Ishak. Printer: (NPA). 149 x 72 mm. Polymer.
- ☐ a. 2007. Signature 2. Intro: 16.07.2007.　　FV　　FV　　25

2007 Numismatic Products

These notes commemorate the 40th anniversary of the Currency Interchangeability Agreement between Brunei and Singapore. A total of 12,000 overprinted sets of Singapore and Brunei notes bearing matching serial numbers and BND/SGD prefixes were sold for S$88. 10,000 sets were allocated to Singapore and the remaining 2,000 sets went to Brunei. Although the notes contained in the sets are the same, the folders are different. As a result, the Brunei sets command a premium over the Singapore sets due to their relative rarity.

MAS BNP2 (PNL): **20 ringgit** (US$17) **and 20 dollars** (US$17)　　UNC
- ☐ a. Brown *40TH Anniversary Currency Interchangeability Agreement* overprint on Brunei note and red *40th Anniversary Currency Interchangeability Agreement* overprint on Singapore note. Intro: 27.06.2007.　　200
- ☐ as. Specimen.　　—

Acknowledgements

This chapter was compiled with the generous assistance of Adwind Cheah, Donald Cleveland, Mirsad Delic, Kee Hong Boon (Tigerson), Kai Hwong, Tan Wei Jie, Bin Hee Jum, JianKuan Lee, Claudio Marana, Robert Mol, Wally Myers, Nazir Rahemtulla, George Provencal, Derrick See, Bill Stubkjaer, Vincent Tan, Donald Teo, Christoph Thomas, Tristan Williams, and others.

Sources

Boon, K. N. *Malaysia Brunei & Singapore Banknotes & Coins.* 6th edition. 2012. ISBN 978-983-43313-5-1. Trigometric Sdn.Bhd. (www.3833.com), Lot 327, Amcorp Mall, 18 Jalan Persiaran Barat, off Jalan Timur, Petaling Jaya, 46050 Selangor D.E., Malaysia.

Boon, K. N. *World Paper & Polymer Uncut Banknotes.* 1st edition. 2012. ISBN 978-983-43313-4-4. Trigometric Sdn.Bhd. (www.3833.com), Lot 327, Amcorp Mall, 18 Jalan Persiaran Barat, off Jalan Timur, Petaling Jaya, 46050 Selangor D.E., Malaysia.

Cuhaj, George S. *Standard Catalog of World Paper Money, Modern Issues, 1961-Present.* 19th edition. 2013. ISBN 978-1-4402-3571-9. Krause Publications (www.krausebooks.com), 700 East State St., Iola, WI, 54990-0001.

Eu, Peter, Ben Chiew, and Stane Straus. *World Polymer Banknotes: A Standard Reference.* 2nd edition. 2006. ISBN 983-43038-2-3. Eureka Metro, P. O. Box 30, Jalan Kelang Lama, Kuala Lumpur, 57000, Malaysia.

Krause, Thomas and Peter Bauer. *Specialized Catalogue of World Plastic Money.* 5th edition. 2009. www.polymernotes.de.

Tan, Steven. *Standard Catalogue of Malaysia Singapore Brunei Coin & Paper Money.* 18th edition. 2007. ISBN 983-9650-02-05. International Stamp & Coin Sn. Bhd., 2.4 & 2.5, Pertama Shopping Complex, 2nd Floor, Jalan Tuanku Abdul Rahman, 50100 Kaula Lumpur, Malaysia.

Odds & Ends of South East Asian Banknotes & Coins. http://clement-oddsends.blogspot.com.

Share Your Input, Info, and Images

This catalog is believed to be complete and correct as of the time of publication. Prices and face values were last updated 12 August 2011. Please report errors or omissions so that corrections may be made. If you can more precisely identify the name or location of anything depicted on a note, please share that information. Furthermore, if you own an unlisted type or variety, please submit scans of the front and back of the note so that it can be documented. Scans should be 300 dots per inch, 100% actual size, 24-bit color, saved as *uncompressed* JPEG files, and sent to owen@banknotenews.com. Be sure to fully describe all attributes of the note which are not apparent upon visual inspection of the images alone, such as physical dimension, watermark, and security thread.

Slovakia

For earlier issues, see Czechoslovakia.

Contents

Slovenský Štát (SS)	1885
Slovenská Republika (SR)	1886
Slovenská Národná Banka (SNB)	1888
Slovenská Republika (SR)	1890
Národná Banka Slovenska (NBS)	1892

Monetary System

1939: 1 Slovak koruna (SKK) = 100 halierov
1945: 1 Czechoslovak koruna (CSK) = 100 halierov
08.02.1993: 1 Slovak koruna (SKK) = 100 halierov

Slovak Months of the Year

Január (January)	Február (February)	Marec (March)
Apríl (April)	Máj (May)	Jún (June)
Júl (July)	August (August)	September (September)
Október (October)	November (November)	December (December)

After World War II, many Slovakian banknotes were sold to collectors after being cancelled with several different types of perforationorations. Technically these are not official specimens, but since they are usually sold as such, that's how they are listed in this catalog.

Slovenský Štát (Slovakia State)

1939 Provisional Issues

The Slovak koruna was the currency of the Slovak Republic from 1939 to 1945. It replaced the Czechoslovak koruna at par and was itself replaced by the reconstituted Czechoslovak koruna, again at par.

Initially, the Slovak koruna was at par with the Bohemian and Moravian koruna, with 10 korunas = 1 Reichsmark. This was changed, on 1 October 1940, to a rate of 11.62 Slovak korunas = 1 Reichsmark, with the value of the Bohemian and Moravian currency unchanged against the Reichsmark.

In 1939, Czechoslovak notes for 100, 500, and 1000 korún were issued with *SLOVENSKÝ ŠTÁT* overprinted on them for use in Slovakia.

SS B1 (P1): **100 korún** (withdrawn 01.09.1941)   VG   VF   UNC
Green. Front: Nude boy holding seedling and open book; hammer and wheel; falcon; coat of arms; red overprint; laurel leaves; Liberty wearing Phrygian cap; constitution scroll. Back: Topless woman with laurel crown and man sitting on wheat and corn; doves; cherubs supporting portrait of President Tomáš Garrigue Masaryk; open book. No security thread. Watermark: Pattern. Printer: (TB, Prague). 171 x 87 mm.

			VG	VF	UNC
☐	a.	10. ledna 1931. Intro: 06.06.1939. Prefix format X.	15	75	325
☐	b.	Prefix format Xx.	15	75	325
☐	s1.	Two horizontal *SPECIMEN* perfs, on one line.	3	12	75
☐	s2.	Two horizontal *SPECIMEN* perforations, stacked.	3	12	75
☐	s3.	Horizontal *PADĚLEK* perforation.	3	12	75

SS B2 (P2): **500 korún** (withdrawn 31.10.1945)   VG   VF   UNC
Red. Front: Coat of arms; blue overprint; WWI Czech Legionnaire with laurel crown. Back: Lion with open book; Liberty with laurel crown; child. No security thread. Watermark: None. Printer: (ABNC). 184 x 93 mm.

		VG	VF	UNC
☐	a. 2. MAJA 1929. Intro: 26.04.1939.	25	100	400
☐	s1. Two horizontal *SPECIMEN* perfs, on one line.	10	40	60
☐	s2. Two horizontal *SPECIMEN* perforations, stacked.	10	40	60
☐	s3. Horizontal *SPECIMEN* perforation.	10	40	60

SS B3 (P3): **1,000 korún** (withdrawn 17.08.1942)   VG   VF   UNC
Green, blue, and brown. Front: Rooster; nude boy kneeling beside woman with open book, archery bow, and girl leaning on shoulder; fruit and vegetables; violet overprint. Back: Fruit and vegetables; flowers; František Palacký; open book. No security thread. Watermark: Woman's head. Printer: (TB, Prague). 200 x 105 mm.

		VG	VF	UNC
☐	a. 25. KVĚTNA 1934. Intro: 26.04.1939.	100	250	750
☐	s1. Two horizontal *SPECIMEN* perfs, on one line.	7.50	30	100
☐	s2. Two horizontal *SPECIMEN* perforations, stacked; vertical *SPECIMEN* perforation.	7.50	30	100
☐	s3. Two horizontal *SPECIMEN* perfs, on one line; punched.	7.50	30	100

Slovenská Republika (Slovak Republic)

SR Signature Varieties

1   
MINISTER FINANCII (Finance Minister)
Mikuláš Pružinský

1939 Issues

These 10- and 20-koruna notes are the first notes created specifically for the Slovak Republic.

SR B1 (P4): **10 korún** (withdrawn 31.10.1945)   VG   VF   UNC
Brown and blue. Front: Coat of arms; linden leaves; priest Andrej Hlinka. Back: Linden leaves; girl. No security thread. Watermark: Pattern. Printer: (NBČM). 142 x 72 mm.

			VG	VF	UNC
☐	a.	15. SEPTEMBRA 1939. Sig. 1. Intro: 23.10.1939.	10	40	150
☐	as1.	Horizontal *SPECIMEN* perforation; non-zero s/n.	2.50	10	40
☐	as2.	Two horizontal *SPECIMEN* perforations, stacked.	2.50	10	40

SR B2 (P5): **20 korún** (withdrawn 31.10.1945)   VG   VF   UNC
Green, brown, and blue. Front: Coat of arms; priest Andrej Hlinka. Back: Shrine. No security thread. Watermark: Pattern. Printer: (NBČM). 153 x 76 mm.

			VG	VF	UNC
☐	a.	15. SEPTEMBRA 1939. Sig. 1. Intro: 09.12.1939. Dark paper.	5	25	500
☐	b.	White paper.	3	15	50
☐	as1.	Horizontal *SPECIMEN* perforation; non-zero s/n.	1	4	15
☐	as2.	Two horizontal *SPECIMEN* perforations, stacked.	1	4	15
☐	as3.	Punched.	1	4	15

1942-1943 Issues

SR B3 (P6): **10 korún** (withdrawn 31.10.1945)   VG   VF   UNC
Blue, orange, and brown. Front: Coat of arms; harp; Ludovít Štúr; leaves. Back: Table with pine cone, fir branches, bucket, carved objects, leaves, mushrooms, strawberries, and runner. No security thread. Watermark: Linden leaf and double cross pattern. Printer: *NEOGRAFIA*. 131 x 62 mm.

			VG	VF	UNC
☐	a.	20. JÚLA 1943. Signature 1. Intro: 26.10.1944.	0.50	2.50	30
☐	as1.	Horizontal *SPECIMEN* perforation; non-zero s/n.	1	4	12
☐	as2.	Two horizontal *SPECIMEN* perforations, stacked.	1	4	12

SR B4 (P7): **20 korún** (withdrawn 31.10.1945)   VG   VF   UNC
Brown and blue. Front: Coat of arms; eagle; Ján Holly; linden leaves; quill. Back: Table with cloth, double salt cellar, vase, wheat stalks, loaf of bread, knife, apple, pear, and cup. No security thread. Watermark: Linden leaf and double cross pattern. Printer: *NEOGRAFIA*. 139 x 67 mm.

			VG	VF	UNC
☐	a.	11.SEPTEMBRA 1942. Sig 1. Intro: 25.09.1943.	4	15	75
☐	as1.	Horizontal *SPECIMEN* perforation; non-zero s/n.	1.25	5	20
☐	as2.	Two horizontal *SPECIMEN* perforations, stacked.	1.25	5	20

1945 Issues

SR B5 (P8): **5 korún** (withdrawn 31.10.1945) VG VF UNC
Lilac and blue. Front: Coat of arms; girl with braided hair in bow. Back: Wheat stalks; linden leaves; pine cones; fir branches. No security thread. Watermark: None. Printer: *NEOGRAFIA UC. SPOL.* 122 x 59 mm.

☐	a.	No date. Intro: 15.02.1945.	1	5	100
☐	as1.	Horizontal *SPECIMEN* perforation; non-zero s/n.	2	7.50	30
☐	as2.	Two horizontal *SPECIMEN* perforations, stacked.	2	7.50	30

For additional notes issued by the Slovenská Republika (Slovak Republic), see 1993 Provisional Issues following the next section on Slovenská Národná Banka issues.

Slovenská Národná Banka (Slovak National Bank)

SNB Signature Varieties

1	GUVERNÉR (Governor) Imrich Karvaš	RIADITEL (Director) Martin Kollár
2	VICEGUVERNÉR (Vice Governor) Josef Fundárek	RIADITEL (Director) Julius Pazman
3	GUVERNÉR (Governor) Rudolf Kubiš	RIADITEL (Director) Martin Kollár

1940-1944 Issues

SNB B1 (P9): **50 korún** (withdrawn 31.10.1945) VG VF UNC
Violet, lilac, and light blue. Front: Two girls in Slovak national costume holding wheat stalks; flowers; coat of arms. Back: Orava castle. No security thread. Watermark: Woman's head. Printer: *GIESECKE & DEVRIENT.* 127 x 67 mm.

☐	a.	15.októbra 1940. Signature 1. Intro: 18.12.1941.	4	15	60
☐	as1.	Horizontal *SPECIMEN* perforation; non-zero s/n.	0.50	2.50	10
☐	as2.	Two horizontal *SPECIMEN* perforations, stacked.	0.50	2.50	10

SNB B2 (P9A): **50 korún** VG VF UNC
Violet, lilac, and light blue. Front: Two girls in Slovak national costume holding wheat stalks; flowers; coat of arms; *II. em.* in watermark area. Back: Orava castle. No security thread. Watermark: Pattern. Printer: *GIESECKE & DEVRIENT.* 127 x 67 mm.

☐	a.	15.októbra 1940. Signature 1. Unissued.	—	—	—

SNB B3 (P10): **100 korún** (withdrawn 31.10.1945)   VG   VF   UNC

Dark blue, brown, and green. Front: Church; Prince Pribina. Back: Grapes; wheat; book; apples; seated woman with coat of arms; gear and hammer; doves; linden leaves; fruit. No security thread. Watermark: Woman's head. Printer: *GIESECKE & DEVRIENT*. 127 x 73 mm.

		VG	VF	UNC
☐	a. 7. októbra 1940. Signature 1. Intro: 01.09.1941.	1	5	15
☐	as1. Horizontal *SPECIMEN* perforation; non-zero s/n.	0.50	1.75	7
☐	as2. Two horizontal *SPECIMEN* perforations, stacked.	0.50	1.75	7
☐	as3. Two vertical *SPECIMEN* perforations.	0.50	1.75	7

For note with adhesive stamp, see Czechoslovakia.

SNB B4 (P11): **100 korún** (withdrawn 31.10.1945)   VG   VF   UNC

Dark blue, brown, and green. Front: Church; Prince Pribina. Back: *II. Emisia* in left margin; grapes; wheat; book; apples; seated woman with coat of arms; gear and hammer; doves; linden leaves; fruit. No security thread. Watermark: Triangle pattern. Printer: *GIESECKE & DEVRIENT*. 127 x 73 mm.

		VG	VF	UNC
☐	a. 7. októbra 1940. Signature 1. Intro: 26.01.1945.	3	12	55
☐	as1. Horizontal *SPECIMEN* perforation; non-zero s/n.	0.75	3	12
☐	as2. Two horizontal *SPECIMEN* perforations, stacked.	0.75	3	12
☐	as3. Two vertical *SPECIMEN* perforations.	0.75	3	12

For note with adhesive stamp, see Czechoslovakia.

SNB B5 (P12): **500 korún** (withdrawn 31.10.1945)   VG   VF   UNC

Green. Front: Doves; coat of arms; man in national costume. Back: Mountains; scythe, wheat, and open book; fruit bowl and vase; gear, hammer, and anvil; pine trees; flowers. No security thread. Watermark: Linden leaf pattern. Printer: (NBČM). 175 x 85 mm.

		VG	VF	UNC
☐	a. 12. JÚLA 1941. Signature 2. Intro: 26.10.1944.	4	15	75
☐	as1. Horizontal *SPECIMEN* perforation; non-zero s/n.	1.50	6	25
☐	as2. Two horizontal *SPECIMEN* perfs, on one line.	1.50	6	25
☐	as3. Two vertical *SPECIMEN* perforations.	1.50	6	25

For note with adhesive stamp, see Czechoslovakia.

SNB B6 (P13): **1,000 korún** (withdrawn 31.10.1945)   VG   VF   UNC

Brown and red. Front: Coat of arms; eagle; shield; King Svatopluk I with bear rug and three sons. Back: Mosaic birds and flowers; coat of arms. No security thread. Watermark: Linden leaf pattern. Printer: (NBČM). 192 x 90 mm.

		VG	VF	UNC
☐	a. 25. NOVEMBRA 1940. Sig. 2. Intro: 17.08.1942.	5	15	60
☐	as1. Horizontal *SPECIMEN* perforation; non-zero s/n.	2.50	10	40
☐	as2. Two horizontal *SPECIMEN* perfs, on one line.	2.50	10	40
☐	as3. Four horizontal *SPECIMEN* perforations, on two lines.	2.50	10	40

SNB B7 (P14): **5,000 korún**   VG   VF   UNC

Brown, orange, and green. Front: Prince Mojmír I. Back: Fruits (apples, grapes, pears) and vegetables (potatoes, turnips, squash, pumpkin, corn, peas); coat of arms; flowers; sword and branch. No security thread. Watermark: Woman's head. Printer: *NEOGRAFIA UC. SPOL.* 203 x 96 mm.

- ☐ a.   18. decembra 1944. Signature 3. Unissued.   50   100   200
- ☐ as1. Horizontal *SPECIMEN* perforation; non-zero s/n.   2.50   10   40
- ☐ as2. Two horizontal *SPECIMEN* perfs, on one line.   2.50   10   40
- ☐ as3. Four horizontal *SPECIMEN* perforations, on two   2.50   10   40
         lines.

Slovenská Republika (Slovak Republic)

1993 Provisional Issues

At midnight on 31 December 1992, the Czechoslovak Republic bifurcated into the Czech Republic and the Slovak Republic. In 1993, the newly independent Slovakia introduced its own koruna, replacing the Czechoslovak koruna at par. Provisional banknotes were issued in denominations of 20, 50, 100, 500, and 1,000 korún by affixing stamps bearing the coat of arms of Slovakia and the denomination to Czechoslovak banknotes (P95, 96, 91b, 93, and 98, respectively).

SR B6 (P15): **20 korún** (withdrawn 30.11.1993)   VG   VF   UNC

Blue, green, and gold. Front: Open book; stars; Jan Ámos Komensky; fruit tree. Back: Flowers; Slovak alphabet; calligraphy; fruit tree growing out of open book; woman and man reading book; sun; flowers. No security thread. Watermark: Star and linden leaf pattern. Printer: *STÁTNI TISKÁRNA CENIN, PRAHA*. 140 x 67 mm.

- ☐ a.   1988. Intro: 08.02.1993.   1   4   15
- ☐ as. Horizontal *SPECIMEN* perforation; non-zero s/n.   —   —   —

SR B7 (P16): **50 korún** (withdrawn 31.10.1993)   VG   VF   UNC

Red and brown. Front: Golden eagle; Tatra mountains; Ludovít Štúr. Back: Bratislava castle; town; highway interchange; River Danube; bunch of grapes. No security thread. Watermark: Star and linden leaf pattern. Printer: *STÁTNI TISKÁRNA CENIN, PRAHA*. 144 x 67 mm.

- ☐ a.   1987. Intro: 08.02.1993.   1   4   15
- ☐ as. Horizontal *SPECIMEN* perforation; non-zero s/n.   —   —   —

THE BANKNOTE BOOK	SLOVAKIA 1993 PROVISIONAL ISSUES

SR B8 (P17): **100 korún** (withdrawn 30.11.1993) VG VF UNC
Green. Front: Factory with smokestacks; atom; man and woman farmers holding a sheaf of wheat. Back: Charles Bridge and Hradcany in Prague; coat of arms. No security thread. Watermark: Star and linden leaf. Printer: *STÁTNÍ TISKÁBNA CENIN, PRAHA*. 166 x 80 mm.

- ☐ a.   1961. Intro: 08.02.1993.   1.25   5   25
- ☐ as. Vertical *SPECIMEN* perforation; non-zero s/n.   —   —   —

SR B9 (P18): **500 korún** (withdrawn 10.01.1994) VG VF UNC
Tan and brown. Front: Coat of arms; two soldiers carrying machine guns; castle on hill; armed men. Back: Medieval shield; mountain fortress ruins in Devín. No security thread. Watermark: Star and linden leaf pattern. Printer: *ŠTÁTNA TLAČIAREN CENÍN, PRAHA* 152 x 67 mm.

- ☐ a.   1973. Intro: 08.02.1993.   4   12   50
- ☐ as. Horizontal *SPECIMEN* perforation; non-zero s/n.   —   —   —

SR B10 (P19): **1,000 korún** (withdrawn 22.10.1993) VG VF UNC
Blue. Front: Coat of arms; flowers; composer Bedřich Smetana. Back: Vyšehrad castle and Vltava River in Prague. No security thread. Watermark: Star and linden leaf pattern. Printer: *STÁTNI TISKÁRNA CENIN, PRAHA*. 156 x 67 mm.

- ☐ a.   1985. Intro: 08.02.1993.   20   75   150
- ☐ as. Horizontal *SPECIMEN* perforation; non-zero s/n.   —   —   —

Národná Banka Slovenska (National Bank of Slovakia)

The Národná Banka Slovenska (NBS) was established on 1 January 1993 by the Act of the National Council of the Slovak Republic No. 566/1992 Coll. on the National Bank of Slovakia as the independent central bank of the Slovak Republic.

For more information, visit www.nbs.sk.

NBS Signature Varieties

	(Governor)	(Executive Director)
1	Marián Tkáč (01.01.1993 - 29.07.1993)	Ján Mathes (01.01.1993 - 31.01.2007)
2	Vladimir Masár (July 1993 - July 1999)	Marián Tkáč (01.01.1993 - 11.04.1994)
3	Vladimir Masár (July 1993 - July 1999)	Ján Mathes (01.01.1993 - 31.01.2007)
4	Marian Jusko (July 1999 - December 2004)	Ján Mathes (01.01.1993 - 31.01.2007)
5	Ivan Šramko (01.01.2005 - 31.12.2009)	Ján Mathes (01.01.1993 - 31.01.2007)
6	Ivan Šramko (01.01.2005 - 31.12.2009)	Milena Korenová (01.02.2007 - 31.12.2009)

1993-2006 Issues

In late 1993, regular issue banknotes were introduced in the same denominations as the earlier provisional issues. The main motifs on the fronts of the banknotes represent important people living in the territory of the present Slovakia in various historical eras. On the backs, these motifs are complemented by places where these people lived and were active.

On each of these notes, the name of the designer (Jozef Bubák) appears in the bottom right front and the name of the engraver (Ron Beckers, Vaclav Fajt, or Jim Moore) is in the top right front. The symbols in the bottom left front are intaglio printed for the benefit of the visually impaired.

NBS B1 (P20): **20 korún** (US$0.95)   VG   VF   UNC
Green. Front: Prince Pribina. Back: 9th century coral necklace with crescent-shaped bronze locket; Nitra Castle; coat of arms. Solid security thread printed *NÁRODNÁ BANKA SLOVENSKA*. Watermark: Prince Pribina. 128 x 65 mm.

- a. 1. SEPTEMBRA 1993. Signature 1.   FV   FV   5
  Printer: *B A BANKNOTE*. Intro: 09.09.1993.
- b. 1. JÚNA 1995. Signature 3.   FV   FV   10
- c. 31. OKTÓBRA 1997.   FV   FV   2.50
- d. 1. JÚLA 1999.   FV   FV   6
- e. 31. AUGUSTA 2001. Signature 4.   FV   FV   2.50
- f. 6. SEPTEMBRA 2004.   FV   FV   2.50
  Printer: *B A INTERNATIONAL INC*.
- g. 20. OKTÓBRA 2006. Sig. 5. Printer: *PWPW S.A.*   FV   FV   2.50
- as. Horizontal *SPECIMEN* perforation; non-zero s/n.   —   —   —
- cs. Diagonal red hollow *SPECIMEN* overprint; horizontal red # ovpt at lower center on back.   —   —   —

NBS B2 (P21): **50 korún** (US$2.30)   VG   VF   UNC
Blue. Front: Saints Cyril and Method; Christian cross. Back: Medieval church in Drazovce (District of Nitra); two hands with the first seven letters of the old Slavonic alphabet, Hlaholika, between them; coat of arms. Solid security thread printed *NÁRODNÁ BANKA SLOVENSKA*. Watermark: Saint Method. 134 x 68 mm.

- a. 1. AUGUSTA 1993. Signature 1.   FV   FV   6
  Printer: *B A BANKNOTE*. Intro: 30.08.1993.
- b. 1. JÚNA 1995. Signature 3.   FV   FV   7
- c. 1. JÚLA 1999.   FV   FV   6
- d. 2. MÁJA 2002. Signature 4.   FV   FV   8
- e. 16. NOVEMBRA 2005. Sig. 5. Printer: *CBNC*.   FV   FV   4.25
- as. Horizontal *SPECIMEN* perforation; non-zero s/n.   —   —   —

NBS B3 (P22): **100 korún** (US$4.60)   VG   VF   UNC

Orange, red, and brown. Front: Madonna from the Altar of Birth in Saint Jacob´s Church in Levoca. Back: Church of Saint Jacob and city hall in Levoca; gothic stone head from the sacristy of the old church of the minorite order; coat of arms. Windowed security thread with demetalized *100 Sk*. Watermark: Madonna. Printer: *THOMAS DE LA RUE AND COMPANY LIMITED*. 140 x 71 mm.

☐ a.	1. SEPTEMBRA 1993. Sig. 1. Intro: 30.09.1993.	FV	FV	8
☐ as.	Two horizontal *SPECIMEN* perfs; non-zero s/n.	—	—	—

NBS B4 (P23): **500 korún** (US$23)   VG   VF   UNC

Brown, orange, and blue. Front: Ludovit Stur. Back: Bratislava Castle; Saint Michael´s; Gothic tower of Klarisky Church; River Danube; coat of arms. Windowed security thread with demetalized *500 Sk*. Watermark: Ludovit Stur. Printer: *THOMAS DE LA RUE AND COMPANY LIMITED*. 152 x 77 mm.

☐ a.	1. OKTÓBRA 1993. Sig. 2. Intro: 15.11.1993.	FV	FV	80
☐ as1.	Two horizontal *SPECIMEN* perforations; non-zero s/n.	—	—	—
☐ as2.	Diagonal red *SPECIMEN* overprint; horizontal red *SPECIMEN N°* # ovpt at lower left.	—	—	—

NBS B5 (P24): **1,000 korún** (US$46)   VG   VF   UNC

Purple. Front: Clergyman Andrej Hlinka. Back: Roman Catholic Church of Saint Andrew in Ruzomberok; Angels placing crown on Madonna as depicted in the church's medieval fresco; Andrej Hlinka´s mausoleum; coat of arms. Windowed security thread with demetalized *1000 Sk*. Watermark: Andrej Hlinka. Printer: *THOMAS DE LA RUE AND COMPANY LIMITED*. 158 x 80 mm.

☐ a.	1. OKTÓBRA 1993. Sig. 1. Intro: 29.10.1993.	FV	FV	100
☐ b.	1. JÚNA 1995. Signature 3.	FV	FV	100
☐ c.	1. AUGUSTA 1997.	FV	FV	100
☐ as.	Three diagonal *SPECIMEN* perfs; non-zero s/n.	—	—	—
☐ cs.	Diagonal red *SPECIMEN* overprint; horizontal red *SPECIMEN N°* # ovpt at lower left.	—	—	—

1995-2004 Issues

In 1995, the 200- and 5,000-koruna notes were issued for the first time. In 1996, the 100- and 500-koruna notes underwent subtle design changes and ink colors to better distinguish between denominations.

NBS B6 (P25 & P44): **100 korún** (US$4.60)   VG   VF   UNC

Orange, red, and brown. Front: Madonna from the Altar of Birth in Saint Jacob´s Church in Levoca. Back: Church of Saint Jacob and city hall in Levoca; gothic stone head from the sacristy of the old church of the minorite order; coat of arms. Windowed security thread with demetalized *100 Sk*. Watermark: Madonna. 140 x 71 mm.

- ☐ a. 1. JÚLA 1996. Signature 3. Printer: *THOMAS DE LA RUE AND COMPANY LIMITED*.   FV   FV   15
- ☐ b. 1. OKTÓBRA 1997.   FV   FV   15
- ☐ c. 1. JÚLA 1999. Printer: *DE LA RUE*.   FV   FV   15
- ☐ d. 10. OKTÓBRA 2001. Signature 4.   FV   FV   10
- ☐ e. 5. NOVEMBRA 2004. Printer: *PWPW S.A.*   FV   FV   10
- ☐ bs. Diagonal red *SPECIMEN* overprint; horizontal red *SPECIMEN Nº #* ovpt at lower left.   —   —   —

NBS B7 (P26): **200 korún** (US$9.20)   VG   VF   UNC

Olive green, teal blue, and purple. Front: Linguist and priest Anton Bernolak. Back: Renaissance City Tower in 18th century Trnava; coat of arms. Windowed security thread with demetalized *200 Sk*. Watermark: Anton Bernolak. Printer: *GIESCKE & DEVRIENT*. 146 x 74 mm.

- ☐ a. 1. AUGUSTA 1995. Signature 3.   FV   FV   27
- ☐ as. Two horizontal *SPECIMEN* perfs; non-zero s/n.   —   —   —

NBS B8 (P27): **500 korún** (US$23)   VG   VF   UNC

Brown, orange, and blue. Front: Ludovit Stur. Back: Bratislava Castle; Saint Michael´s; Gothic tower of Klarisky Church; River Danube; coat of arms. Windowed security thread with demetalized *500 Sk*. Watermark: Ludovit Stur. Printer: *THOMAS DE LA RUE AND COMPANY LIMITED*. 152 x 77 mm.

- ☐ a. 31. OKTÓBRA 1996. Signature 3.   FV   FV   50
- ☐ as. Specimen.   —   —   —

NBS B9 (P29): **5,000 korún** (US$230)   VG   VF   UNC

Orange, yellow, and rust. Front: Sun and moon foil patch; Milan Rastislav Stefanik. Back: Stefanik´s grave on Bradlo Hill; Great Bear constellation; pasque flower; coat of arms. Windowed security thread with demetalized *5000 Sk*. Watermark: Milan Rastislav Stefanik. Printer: *GIESCKE & DEVRIENT*. 164 x 82 mm.

- ☐ a. 3. APRILA 1995. Signature 3.   FV   FV   300
- ☐ as. Three diagonal *SPECIMEN* perforations.   —   —   —

1999-2007 Issues

These notes are like the preceding issues, but with Omron rings on both sides, stylized symbols printed in OVI at the bottom of the watermark field on the front, electrotype elements added to the watermarks, and iridescent coating on the backs of all denominations (the 5,000-koruna note dated 03.04.1995 has slightly different iridescent coating than do later issues).

NBS B11 (P31 & P46): **500 korún** (US$23)   VG   VF   UNC
Brown, orange, and blue. Front: Stylized eagle head in green-to-blue OVI; Ludovit Stur. Back: Bratislava Castle; Saint Michael´s; Gothic tower of Klarisky Church; River Danube; coat of arms. Windowed security thread with demetalized *500 Sk*. Watermark: Ludovit Stur and electrotype feather. Printer: *DE LA RUE*. 152 x 77 mm.

- a. 20 OKTÓBRA 2000. Signature 4.   FV   FV   50
- b. 10. JÚLA 2006. Signature 5.   FV   FV   50

NBS B10 (P30, P41 & P45): **200 korún** (US$9.20)   VG   VF   UNC
Olive green, teal blue, and purple. Front: Stylized lime leaves in green-to-purple/red OVI; linguist and priest Anton Bernolak. Back: Renaissance City Tower in 18th century Trnava; coat of arms. Windowed security thread with demetalized *200 Sk*. Watermark: Anton Bernolak and electrotype leaves. 146 x 74 mm.

- a. 31 MARCA 1999. Signature 3.   FV   FV   20
  Printer: *GIESCKE & DEVRIENT*.
- b. 30. AUGUSTA 2002. Signature 4.   FV   FV   20
  Printer: *FRANÇOIS-CHARLES OBERTHUR FIDUCIAIRE*.
- c. 1. JUNA 2006. Signature 5.   FV   FV   20

NBS B12 (P32, P42 & P47): **1,000 korún** (US$46)   VG   VF   UNC
Purple. Front: Stylized rose thorus in magenta-to-gold/green OVI; rose in foil triangle patch; clergyman Andrej Hlinka. Back: Roman Catholic Church of Saint Andrew in Ruzomberok; Angels placing crown on Madonna as depicted in the church's medieval fresco; Andrej Hlinka´s mausoleum; coat of arms. Windowed security thread with demetalized *1000 Sk*. Watermark: Andrej Hlinka and electrotype rose. Printer: *DE LA RUE*. 158 x 80 mm.

- a. 1 OKTÓBRA 1999. Signature 4.   FV   FV   120
- b. 10. JUNA 2002.   FV   FV   120
- c. 25. AUGUSTA 2005. Signature 5.   FV   FV   120
- d. 1. AUGUSTA 2007. Signature 6.   FV   FV   120

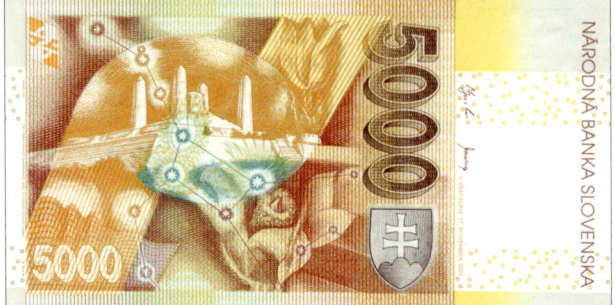

NBS B13 (P33 & P43): **5,000 korún** (US$230)   VG   VF   UNC

Orange, yellow, and rust. Front: Stylized sun and rays in gold-to-green OVI; sun and moon foil patch; crescent-shaped Kinegram; Milan Rastislav Stefanik. Back: Stefanik´s grave on Bradlo Hill; Great Bear constellation; pasque flower; coat of arms. Windowed security thread with demetalized *5000 Sk*. Watermark: Milan Rastislav Stefanik and electrotype oak leaf. 164 x 82 mm.

   ☐ a.   10. MÁJA 1999. Signature 3.   FV   FV   475
            Printer: *GIESCKE & DEVRIENT.*
   ☐ b.   17. NOVEMBRA 2003. Signature 4.   FV   FV   475
            Printer: *OESTERREICHISHE BANKNOTEN*
            UND SICHERHEITSDRUCK GMBH.

2000 Commemorative Issues

In December 1999, all seven denominations of banknotes were overprinted in foil (silver foil for all 1993 series notes and the 200-koruna note dated 1995; gold foil for the 5,000-koruna note dated 1995) with the text *ROK 2000 BIMILÉNIUM ANNO DOMINI MM* above and inside a circle of stars printed over the watermark field on the front.

NBS B14 (P34): **20 korún** (US$0.95)   VG   VF   UNC

Green. Front: *ROK 2000* overprint; Prince Pribina. Back: 9th century coral necklace with crescent-shaped bronze locket; Nitra Castle; coat of arms. Solid security thread printed *NÁRODNÁ BANKA SLOVENSKA*. Watermark: Prince Pribina. Printer: *B A BANKNOTE*. 128 x 65 mm.

   ☐ a.   1. SEPTEMBRA 1993. Signature 1.   FV   FV   4

NBS B15 (P35): **50 korún** (US$2.30)   VG   VF   UNC

Blue. Front: *ROK 2000* overprint; Saints Cyril and Method; Christian cross. Back: Medieval church in Drazovce (District of Nitra); two hands with the first seven letters of the old Slavonic alphabet, Hlaholika, between them; coat of arms. Solid security thread printed *NÁRODNÁ BANKA SLOVENSKA*. Watermark: Saints Cyril and Method. Printer: *B A BANKNOTE*. 134 x 68 mm.

   ☐ a.   1. AUGUSTA 1993. Signature 1.   FV   FV   6

NBS B16 (P36): **100 korún** (US$4.60)   VG   VF   UNC

Orange, red, and brown. Front: *ROK 2000* overprint; Madonna from the Altar of Birth in Saint Jacob´s Church in Levoca. Back: Church of Saint Jacob and city hall in Levoca; gothic stone head from the sacristy of the old church of the minorite order; coat of arms. Windowed security thread with demetalized *100 Sk*. Watermark: Madonna. Printer: *THOMAS DE LA RUE AND COMPANY LIMITED*. 140 x 71 mm.

   ☐ a.   1. SEPTEMBRA 1993. Signature 1.   FV   FV   14

NBS B17 (P37): **200 korún** (US$9.20)　　　　　VG　VF　UNC
Olive green, teal blue, and purple. Front: *ROK 2000* overprint; Linguist and priest Anton Bernolak. Back: Renaissance City Tower in 18th century Trnava; coat of arms. Windowed security thread with demetalized *200 Sk*. Watermark: Anton Bernolak. Printer: *GIESCKE & DEVRIENT*. 146 x 74 mm.
　☐ a.　1. AUGUSTA 1995. Signature 3.　　　FV　FV　20

NBS B18 (P38): **500 korún** (US$23)　　　　　VG　VF　UNC
Brown, orange, and blue. Front: *ROK 2000* overprint; Ludovit Stur. Back: Bratislava Castle; Saint Michael´s; Gothic tower of Klarisky Church; River Danube; coat of arms. Windowed security thread with demetalized *500 Sk*. Watermark: Ludovit Stur. Printer: *THOMAS DE LA RUE AND COMPANY LIMITED*. 152 x 77 mm.
　☐ a.　1. OKTÓBRA 1993. Signature 2.　　　FV　FV　60

NBS B19 (P39): **1,000 korún** (US$46)　　　　VG　VF　UNC
Purple. Front: *ROK 2000* overprint; Clergyman Andrej Hlinka. Back: Roman Catholic Church of Saint Andrew in Ruzomberok; Angels placing crown on Madonna as depicted in the church's medieval fresco; Andrej Hlinka´s mausoleum; coat of arms. Windowed security thread with demetalized *1000 Sk*. Watermark: Andrej Hlinka. Printer: *THOMAS DE LA RUE AND COMPANY LIMITED*. 158 x 80 mm.
　☐ a.　1. OKTÓBRA 1993. Signature 1.　　　FV　FV　120

NBS B20 (P40): **5,000 korún** (US$230)　　　　VG　VF　UNC
Orange, yellow, and rust. Front: *ROK 2000* overprint; sun and moon foil patch; crescent-shaped Kinegram; Milan Rastislav Stefanik. Back: Stefanik´s grave on Bradlo Hill; Great Bear constellation; pasque flower; coat of arms. Windowed security thread with demetalized *5000 Sk*. Watermark: Milan Rastislav Stefanik. Printer: *GIESCKE & DEVRIENT*. 164 x 82 mm.
　☐ a.　3. APRILA 1995. Signature 3.　　　FV　FV　500

Looking Forward

Slovakia switched its currency from the koruna to the euro on 1 January 2009, at a rate of 30.126 korún to the euro.

For later issues, see European Monetary Union.

Acknowledgements

This chapter was compiled with the generous assistance of Brent Arthurson, Stelios Constantinou, Peter Jarabek (National Bank of Slovakia), Peter Lorenc, Stanislav Májek (National Bank of Slovakia), Wally Myers, Mikhail "Mike" Prizov, Gergely Scheidl (banknoteshop@gmx.net), Bill Stubkjaer, Jan Stuller, Stanislav Suja (National Bank of Slovakia), Christoph Thomas, Frank van Tiel, Tristan Williams, Didier Wiot, Christof Zellweger, and others.

Sources

Allgood, Emanuela M. "Letters to the Editor." *IBNS Journal*. Volume 32 Number 2. p.6.

Bajer, Jan. *Papírová platidla Československa 1919 - 1993, České republiky Slovenské republiky 1993 - 2003*. 2003 edition. ISBN 80-902683-1-5.

Bartel, Helmet. "Letters to the Editor." *IBNS Journal*. Volume 37 Number 2. p.52.

Boon, K. N. *World Paper & Polymer Uncut Banknotes*. 1st edition. 2012. ISBN 978-983-43313-4-4. Trigometric Sdn.Bhd. (www.3833.com), Lot 327, Amcorp Mall, 18 Jalan Persiaran Barat, off Jalan Timur, Petaling Jaya, 46050 Selangor D.E., Malaysia.

Cuhaj, George S. *Standard Catalog of World Paper Money, General Issues, 1368-1960*. 14th edition. 2012. ISBN 978-1-4402-3090-5. Krause Publications (www.krausebooks.com), 700 East State St., Iola, WI, 54990-0001.

Cuhaj, George S. *Standard Catalog of World Paper Money, Modern Issues, 1961-Present*. 17th edition. 2011. ISBN 978-1-4402-1584-1. Krause Publications (www.krausebooks.com), 700 East State St., Iola, WI, 54990-0001.

Hessler, Gene. "Max Svabinsky: Czechoslovak Designer." *IBNS Journal*. Volume 23 Number 4. p.103.

Papierové peniaze na Slovensku v rokoch 1939 - 1945 (Paper money in Slovakia in 1939 - 1945). http://slovenskebankovky.com/doku.php

Prochaska, Fredinand. "Letters to the Editor." *IBNS Journal*. Volume 33 Number 3. p.4.

Rowder, Michal. "Letters to the Editor." *IBNS Journal*. Volume 39 Number 1. p.5.

Share Your Input, Info, and Images

This catalog is believed to be complete and correct as of the time of publication. Prices and face values were last updated 21 October 2011. Please report errors or omissions so that corrections may be made. If you can more precisely identify the name or location of anything depicted on a note, please share that information. Furthermore, if you own an unlisted type or variety, please submit scans of the front and back of the note so that it can be documented. Scans should be 300 dots per inch, 100% actual size, 24-bit color, saved as *uncompressed* JPEG files, and sent to owen@banknotenews.com. Be sure to fully describe all attributes of the note which are not apparent upon visual inspection of the images alone, such as physical dimension, watermark, and security thread.

Slovenia

For earlier issues, see Yugoslavia.

Contents

Republic of Slovenia (RS).. 1899
Banka Slovenije (BS) 1902

Monetary System
08.10.1991: 1 Slovenian tolar (SIT) = 100 stotini
01.01.2007: 1 euro (EUR) = 100 cents

Slovene Months of the Year

Januar (January)	Februar (February)	Marec (March)
April (April)	Maj (May)	Junij (June)
Julij (July)	Avgust (August)	September (September)
Oktober (October)	November (November)	December (December)

Republika Slovenija (Republic of Slovenia)

Shortly before independence and the establishment of the Slovenian National Bank, both on 25 June 1991, private individuals in Ljubljana printed notes denominated in lipa for use in Ljubljana and Maribor. These unofficial notes circulated briefly and were accepted by some businesses, but were never legal tender even though they bear the name Banka Slovenija, an institution which did not exist at the time. Following independence, parliament considered naming the nation's new currency the lipa, but chose tolar instead. After the introduction of the official tolar notes, the unofficial lipa notes ceased to circulate.

RS Signature Varieties

1	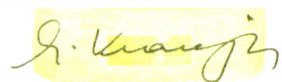 Sekretar za finance (Secretary of Finance) Marko Kranjec

1990-1992 Issues

The tolar was introduced on 8 October 1991. It replaced the 1990 convertible version of the Yugoslav dinar at par. Curiously, these notes do not bear a unit of currency, but rather, simply numerical denominations. The first banknotes were provisional payment notes all featuring Triglav, the tallest mountain in Slovenia on the front and the Duke Stone (Knežji kamen) and a Carniolan honey bee, on the back. As a general rule, the first two digits of the serial number represent the last two digits of the year of printing. However, there are a handful of notes of each variety with the wrong date caused by the serial number rolling over to the subsequent "year." All of the notes were printed by Cetis Celje in Slovenia without imprint.

One thousand specimens of each denomination were printed with diagonal *SPECIMEN* overprints and all-zero serial numbers. These should not to be confused with the specimens created by the bank specifically for resale by Educational Coin Company. These specimens bear the overprint of *VZOREC* on notes with normal serial numbers. The 200-tolar note is not available with the *VZOREC* overprint because the bank lacked sufficient supplies of this denomination.

RS B1 (P1): **1 (tolar)** (withdrawn 30.06.1993)   VG   VF   UNC
Yellow and olive green. Front: Triglav mountain peak. Back: Duke Stone; honeycomb pattern; Carniolan honey bee under denomination. No security thread. Watermark: Snowflake pattern. Printer: (Cetis Celje). 150 x 73 mm.
- a. (19)90. Signature 1. Intro: 08.10.1991. — — 1
- as1. Diagonal red *SPECIMEN* overprint. — — 45
- as2. Diagonal red *VZOREC* overprint. — — 10

Replacement notes: Prefix ZA.

RS B2 (P2): **2 (tolarjev)** (withdrawn 30.06.1993)   VG   VF   UNC
Tan and brown. Front: Triglav mountain peak. Back: Duke Stone; honeycomb pattern; Carniolan honey bee under denomination. No security thread. Watermark: Snowflake pattern. Printer: (Cetis Celje). 150 x 73 mm.
- a. (19)90. Signature 1. Intro: 08.10.1991. — — 1
- as1. Diagonal red *SPECIMEN* overprint. — — 45
- as2. Diagonal red *VZOREC* overprint. — — 10

Replacement notes: Prefix ZA.

RS B3 (P3): **5 (tolarjev)** (withdrawn 30.06.1993)   VG   VF   UNC
Pink. Front: Triglav mountain peak. Back: Duke Stone; honeycomb pattern; Carniolan honey bee under denomination. No security thread. Watermark: Snowflake pattern. Printer: (Cetis Celje). 150 x 73 mm.
- ☐ a. (19)90. Signature 1. Intro: 08.10.1991. — — 1.50
- ☐ as1. Diagonal red *SPECIMEN* overprint. — — 45
- ☐ as2. Diagonal red *VZOREC* overprint. — — 10

Replacement notes: Prefix ZA.

RS B4 (P4): **10 (tolarjev)** (withdrawn 30.06.1993)   VG   VF   UNC
Aqua. Front: Triglav mountain peak. Back: Duke Stone; honeycomb pattern; Carniolan honey bee under denomination. No security thread. Watermark: Snowflake pattern. Printer: (Cetis Celje). 150 x 73 mm.
- ☐ a. (19)90. Signature 1. Intro: 08.10.1991. — — 2.50
- ☐ as1. Diagonal red *SPECIMEN* overprint. — — 45
- ☐ as2. Diagonal red *VZOREC* overprint. — — 10

Replacement notes: Prefix ZA.

RS B5 (P5): **50 (tolarjev)** (withdrawn 30.06.1993)   VG   VF   UNC
Gray. Front: Triglav mountain peak. Back: Duke Stone; honeycomb pattern; Carniolan honey bee under denomination. No security thread. Watermark: Snowflake pattern. Printer: (Cetis Celje). 150 x 73 mm.
- ☐ a. (19)90. Signature 1. Intro: 08.10.1991. — — 2.50
- ☐ as1. Diagonal red *SPECIMEN* overprint. — — 45
- ☐ as2. Diagonal red *VZOREC* overprint. — — 10

Replacement notes: Prefix ZA.

RS B6 (P6): **100 (tolarjev)** (withdrawn 30.06.1993)   VG   VF   UNC
Orange and red. Front: Triglav mountain peak. Back: Duke Stone; honeycomb pattern; Carniolan honey bee under denomination. No security thread. Watermark: Snowflake pattern. Printer: (Cetis Celje). 150 x 73 mm.
- ☐ a. (19)90. Signature 1. Intro: 08.10.1991. — — 3.50
- ☐ as1. Diagonal red *SPECIMEN* overprint. — — 45
- ☐ as2. Diagonal red *VZOREC* overprint. — — 10

Replacement notes: Prefix ZA.

RS B7 (P7): **200 (tolarjev)** (withdrawn 30.06.1993)   VG   VF   UNC
Green. Front: Triglav mountain peak. Back: Duke Stone; honeycomb pattern; Carniolan honey bee under denomination. No security thread. Watermark: Snowflake pattern. Printer: (Cetis Celje). 150 x 73 mm.

☐	a.	(19)90. Signature 1. Intro: 08.10.1991.	—	—	90
☐	as.	Diagonal red *SPECIMEN* overprint.	—	—	45

Replacement notes: Prefix ZA.

RS B8 (P8): **500 (tolarjev)** (withdrawn 30.06.1993)   VG   VF   UNC
Purple. Front: Triglav mountain peak. Back: Duke Stone; honeycomb pattern; Carniolan honey bee under denomination. No security thread. Watermark: Snowflake pattern. Printer: (Cetis Celje). 150 x 73 mm.

☐	a.	(19)90. Signature 1. Intro: 08.10.1991.	—	—	110
☐	b.	(19)92.	—	—	225
☐	as.	Diagonal red *SPECIMEN* overprint.	—	—	45
☐	bs.	Diagonal red *VZOREC* overprint.	—	—	10

Replacement notes: Prefix ZA.

RS B9 (P9): **1,000 (tolarjev)** (withdrawn 06.11.1992)   VG   VF   UNC
Blue. Front: Triglav mountain peak. Back: Duke Stone; honeycomb pattern; Carniolan honey bee under denomination. No security thread. Printer: (Cetis Celje). 150 x 73 mm.

☐	as.	Diagonal red *SPECIMEN* overprint. No date. Signature 1. Watermark: Snowflake pattern (error). Unissued.	125	250	550
☐	b.	(19)91. Watermark: Duke Stone pattern. Intro: 08.10.1991.	75	150	300
☐	c.	(19)92.	75	150	300
☐	cs.	Diagonal red *VZOREC* overprint.	—	—	10
☐	s.	Inverted diagonal red *SPECIMEN* ovpt on back. All-zero serial number.	—	—	45

Replacement notes: Prefix ZA.
Notes dated (19)90 were printed in error with a snowflake pattern watermark. These unissued notes were destroyed, although specimens of this error are available.

RS B10 (P10): **5,000 (tolarjev)** (withdrawn 01.02.1994)   VG   VF   UNC
Lilac. Front: Triglav mountain peak. Back: Duke Stone; honeycomb pattern; Carniolan honey bee under denomination. No security thread. Watermark: Duke Stone pattern. Printer: (Cetis Celje). 150 x 73 mm.

☐	a.	(19)92. Signature 1. Intro: 27.05.1992	—	—	750
☐	as1.	Diagonal red *SPECIMEN* overprint.	—	—	45
☐	as2.	Diagonal red *VZOREC* overprint.	—	—	10

Replacement notes: Prefix ZA.

1992 Numismatic Products

Although similar in design to the 1990-1992 issues, these two unissued notes were never legal tender. One thousand sets with matching serial numbers were sold for 5,000 tolarjev each beginning on 6 May 2002.

RS BNP1 (PB1 & P9A): **0.50 & 2,000 (tolarjev)**   UNC
Front: Triglav mountain peak. Back: Duke Stone; honeycomb pattern; Carniolan honey bee under denomination. No security thread. Watermark: Snowflake (0.50) & Duke Stone pattern (2,000). Printer: (Cetis Celje). 120 x 60 mm & 150 x 73 mm.
   ☐ a. No date. Signature 1. Unissued. Intro: 06.05.2002.   225

Banka Slovenije (Bank of Slovenia)

For more information, visit www.bsi.si.

BS Signature Varieties

	GUVERNER (Governor)	LAN SVETA BANKE (Board Member)
1	France Arhar	Janez Košak
2	France Arhar	Ivan Ribnikar
3	France Arhar	Andrej Rant
4	France Arhar	Andrej Hazabent
5	France Arhar	Velimir Bole
6	France Arhar	Jurij Kleindienst
7	France Arhar	Jože Mencinger
8	France Arhar	Bogomir Kos
9	France Arhar	Marko Kranjec
10	France Arhar	Dušan Zbašnik
11	France Arhar	Samo Nu i
12	France Arhar	Darko Bohnec

BS Signature Varieties

	GUVERNER (Governor)	LAN SVETA BANKE (Board Member)
13	Mitja Gaspari (2001 - March 2007)	Leon Repovž
14	Mitja Gaspari	Janez Košak
15	Mitja Gaspari	Andrej Rant
16	Mitja Gaspari	Darko Bohnec
17	Mitja Gaspari	Samo Nu i
18	Mitja Gaspari	Božo Jašovi
19	Mitja Gaspari	Ivan Ribnikar

1992-2005 Issues

In September 1992, the first tolar banknotes were issued. The tolar banknotes feature designs by Miljenko Licul and Zvone Kosovelj, with portraits by the artist Rudi Španzel. All of the notes were printed by De La Rue, with the exception of the highest denomination, which was printed by Giesecke & Devrient. A member of the Slovenian parliament visited De La Rue in London and was presented with a set of specimens with DLR oval ovpts which was later acquired by the National Museum; this set is thought to be unique in private hands.

BS B1 (P11): **10 tolarjev** (withdrawn 01.15.2007)   VG   VF   UNC
Multicolor. Front: Quill pen; Protestant reformer and author Primož Trubar. Back: New Testament text; Ursuline Church in Ljubljana. Solid security thread printed *BANKA SLOVENIJE*. Watermark: Trubar. Printer: (TDLR). 120 x 60 mm.

- ☐ a. 15. JANUAR 1992. Sig. 4. Intro: 27.11.1992. — — 1
- ☐ as1. Diagonal red *SPECIMEN* overprint on front; diagonal red *VZOREC* overprint on back; horizontal red *SPECIMEN #* overprint at lower left on back. — — 25
- ☐ as2. Like as2, but with handwritten specimen number. — — 25
- ☐ as3. Diagonal red *SPECIMEN* and DLR oval ovpts; punched. — — —

Replacement notes: Prefix AZ.

BS B2 (P12): **20 tolarjev** (withdrawn 01.15.2007)   VG   VF   UNC
Multicolor. Front: Topographic maps; quill pen; scholar Janez Vajkard Valvasor. Back: Topographic maps; angels from Valvasor's book *The Glory of the Duchy of Carniola*. Solid security thread printed *BANKA SLOVENIJE*. Watermark: Valvasor. Printer: (TDLR). 126 x 63 mm.

☐	a.	15. JANUAR 1992. Sig. 5. Intro: 28.12.1992.	— —	1
☐	as1.	Diagonal red *SPECIMEN* overprint on front; diagonal red *VZOREC* overprint on back; horizontal red *SPECIMEN Nº #* overprint at lower left on back.	— —	25
☐	as2.	Like as2, but with handwritten specimen number.	— —	25
☐	as3.	Diagonal red *SPECIMEN* and DLR oval ovpts; punched.	— —	—

Replacement notes: Prefix AZ.

BS B3 (P13): **50 tolarjev** (withdrawn 01.15.2007)   VG   VF   UNC
Multicolor. Front: Geometric sphere; phases of moon; mathematician Jurij Vega. Back: Slovenian Academy of Sciences and Arts building in Ljubljana; solar system planets. Solid security thread printed *BANKA SLOVENIJE*. Watermark: Vega. Printer: (TDLR). 132 x 66 mm.

☐	a.	15. JANUAR 1992. Sig. 7. Intro: 19.03.1993.	— —	1.50
☐	as1.	Diagonal red *SPECIMEN* overprint on front; diagonal red *VZOREC* overprint on back; horizontal red *SPECIMEN #* overprint at lower left on back.	— —	25
☐	as2.	Like as2, but with handwritten specimen number.	— —	25
☐	as3.	Diagonal red *SPECIMEN* and DLR oval ovpts; punched.	— —	—

Replacement notes: Prefix AZ.

BS B4 (P14 & P31): **100 tolarjev** (withdrawn 01.15.2007)   VG   VF   UNC
Multicolor. Front: Paint brush; artist's palette; Impressionist painter Rihard Jakopič. Back: Jakopič's painting "The Sun;" architectural plan of the former Jakopič Pavilion in Ljubljana. Solid security thread printed *BANKA SLOVENIJE*. Watermark: Jakopič. Printer: (TDLR). 138 x 69 mm.

☐	a.	15. JANUAR 1992. Sig. 1. Intro: 30.09.1992.	— —	2.50
☐	b.	15. JANUAR 2003. Sig. 14. Intro: 12.05.2003.	— —	2.50
☐	as1.	Diagonal red *SPECIMEN* overprint on front; diagonal red *VZOREC* overprint on back; horizontal red *SPECIMEN #* overprint at lower left on back.	— —	25
☐	as2.	Like as2, but with handwritten specimen number.	— —	25
☐	as3.	Diagonal red *SPECIMEN* and DLR oval ovpts; punched.	— —	—
☐	bs.	Diagonal red *SPECIMEN* overprint on front; diagonal red *VZOREC* overprint on back; horizontal red *SPECIMEN #* overprint at lower left on back.	— —	25

Replacement notes: Prefix AZ.
For notes with 2001 and 2004 overprints, see BS B14 and BS B16, respectively.

BS B5 (P15): **200 tolarjev** (withdrawn 01.15.2007) VG VF UNC

Multicolor. Front: 17th-century organ; composer Iacobus Gallus. Back: Slovenian Philharmonic Hall building in Ljubljana; musical notations. Solid security thread printed *BANKA SLOVENIJE*. Watermark: Gallus. Printer: (TDLR). 144 x 72 mm.

☐ a.	15. JANUAR 1992. Sig. 6. Intro: 22.02.1993.	—	—	20
☐ b.	8. OKTOBER 1997. Sig. 11. Intro: 10.03.1998.	—	—	10
☐ c.	15. JANUAR 2001. Intro: 20.06.2001.	—	—	5
☐ d.	15. JANUAR 2004. Sig. 17. Intro: 02.08.2004.	—	—	5
☐ as1.	Diagonal red *SPECIMEN* overprint on front; diagonal red *VZOREC* overprint on back; horizontal red *SPECIMEN N°* # overprint at lower left on back.	—	—	25
☐ as2.	Like as2, but with handwritten specimen number.	—	—	25
☐ as3.	Diagonal red *SPECIMEN* and DLR oval ovpts; punched.	—	—	—
☐ bs1.	Diagonal red *SPECIMEN* overprint on front; diagonal red *VZOREC* overprint on back; horizontal red *SPECIMEN N°* # overprint at lower left on back.	—	—	25
☐ bs2.	Diagonal red *SPECIMEN* and DLR oval ovpts; punched.	—	—	—
☐ cs.	Diagonal red *SPECIMEN* overprint on front; diagonal red *VZOREC* overprint on back; horizontal red *SPECIMEN* # overprint at lower left on back.	—	—	25
☐ ds.	Diagonal red *SPECIMEN* overprint on front; diagonal red *VZOREC* overprint on back; horizontal red *SPECIMEN* # overprint at lower left on back.	—	—	25

Replacement notes: Prefix AZ.

BS B6 (P16): **500 tolarjev** (withdrawn 01.15.2007) VG VF UNC

Multicolor. Front: Compass; architect Jože Plečnik. Back: National and University Library building in Ljubljana; ground plan of the library. Solid security thread printed *BANKA SLOVENIJE*. Watermark: Plečnik. Printer: (TDLR). 150 x 75 mm.

☐ a.	15. JANUAR 1992. Sig. 2. Intro: 30.09.1992.	—	—	15
☐ b.	15. JANUAR 2001. Intro: 20.06.2001.	—	—	12
☐ c.	15. JANUAR 2005. Sig. 19. Intro: 20.06.2005.	—	—	9.50
☐ as1.	Diagonal red *SPECIMEN* overprint on front; diagonal red *VZOREC* overprint on back; horizontal red *SPECIMEN* # overprint at lower left on back.	—	—	25
☐ as2.	Like as2, but with handwritten specimen number.	—	—	25
☐ as3.	Diagonal red *SPECIMEN* and DLR oval ovpts; punched.	—	—	—
☐ bs.	Diagonal red *SPECIMEN* overprint on front; diagonal red *VZOREC* overprint on back; horizontal red *SPECIMEN* # overprint at lower left on back.	—	—	25
☐ cs.	Diagonal red *SPECIMEN* overprint on front; diagonal red *VZOREC* overprint on back; horizontal red *SPECIMEN* # overprint at lower left on back.	—	—	25

Replacement notes: Prefix AZ.

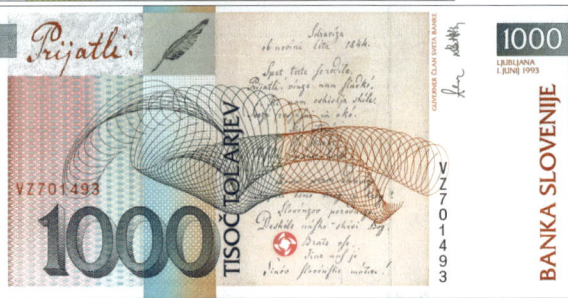

BS B7 (P17): **1,000 tolarjev** (withdrawn 01.15.2007)   VG   VF   UNC
Multicolor. Front: Prešeren signature; poet France Prešeren. Back: "Prijatli" (Friends); quill pen; text from "The Toast" (Slovenian national anthem). Solid security thread printed *BANKA SLOVENIJE*. Watermark: Prešeren. Printer: (TDLR). 156 x 78 mm.

☐	a.	15. JANUAR 1992. Sig. 3. Intro: 30.09.1992.	—	60	120
☐	as1.	Diagonal red *SPECIMEN* overprint on front; diagonal red *VZOREC* overprint on back; horizontal red *SPECIMEN #* overprint at lower left on back.	—	—	25
☐	as2.	Like as2, but with handwritten specimen number.	—	—	25
☐	as3.	Diagonal red *SPECIMEN* and DLR oval ovpts; punched.	—	—	—

Replacement notes: Prefix AZ.

BS B8 (P18, P22 & P32): **1,000 tolarjev** (withdrawn 1.15.2007)   VG   VF   UNC
Multicolor. Front: Prešeren signature; poet France Prešeren. Back: "Prijatli" (Friends); quill pen; text from "The Toast" (Slovenian national anthem). Solid security thread printed *BANKA SLOVENIJE*. Watermark: Prešeren. Printer: (TDLR). 156 x 78 mm.

☐	a.	1. JUNIJ 1993. Signature 3. Intro: 13.12.1993.	—	—	100
☐	b.	With *1000* in UV ink on back.	—	—	50
☐	c.	15. JANUAR 2000. Intro: 10.07.2000.	—	—	15
☐	d.	15. JANUAR 2003. Sig. 15. Intro: 12.05.2003.	—	—	15
☐	e.	15. JANUAR 2004. Intro: 02.08.2004.	—	—	13
☐	f.	15. JANUAR 2005. Intro: 20.06.2005.	—	—	13
☐	as1.	Diagonal red *SPECIMEN* overprint on front; diagonal red *VZOREC* overprint on back; horizontal red *SPECIMEN N° #* overprint at lower left on back.	—	—	25
☐	as2.	Like as2, but with handwritten specimen number.	—	—	25
☐	as3.	Diagonal red *SPECIMEN* and DLR oval ovpts; punched.	—	—	—
☐	cs.	Diagonal red *SPECIMEN* overprint on front; diagonal red *VZOREC* overprint on back; horizontal red *SPECIMEN #* overprint at lower left on back.	—	—	25
☐	ds.	Diagonal red *SPECIMEN* overprint on front; diagonal red *VZOREC* overprint on back; horizontal red *SPECIMEN #* overprint at lower left on back.	—	—	25
☐	es.	Diagonal red *SPECIMEN* overprint on front; diagonal red *VZOREC* overprint on back; horizontal red *SPECIMEN #* overprint at lower left on back.	—	—	25
☐	fs.	Diagonal red *SPECIMEN* overprint on front; diagonal red *VZOREC* overprint on back; horizontal red *SPECIMEN #* overprint at lower left on back.	—	—	25

Replacement notes: Prefix ZA.
Like BS B7, but modified portrait and minor color changes.
For notes with 2001 and 2004 overprints, see BS B15 and BS B17, respectively.

BS B9 (P19): **5,000 tolarjev** (withdrawn 01.15.2007)   VG   VF   UNC

Multicolor. Front: Artist's palette in silver-to-green OVI; easel; profile in silhouette; Artist Ivana Kobilca. Back: National Gallery building in Ljubljana; Robba Fountain. Solid security thread printed *BANKA SLOVENIJE*. Watermark: Kobilca. Printer: (TDLR). 156 x 78 mm.

- a. 1. JUNIJ 1993. Signature 8. Intro: 13.12.1993. — — 250
- as1. Diagonal red *SPECIMEN* overprint on front; diagonal red *VZOREC* overprint on back; horizontal red *SPECIMEN N°* # overprint at lower left on back. — — 25
- as2. Like as2, but with handwritten specimen number. — — 25
- as3. Diagonal red *SPECIMEN* and DLR oval ovpts; punched. — — —
- as4. No overprints. All-zero serial numbers. — — 700

Replacement notes: Prefix AZ.

BS B10 (P21 & P23): **5,000 tolarjev** (withdrawn 01.15.2007)   VG   VF   UNC

Multicolor. Front: Foil patch with profile and denomination; easel; profile in silhouette; Artist Ivana Kobilca. Back: National Gallery building in Ljubljana; Robba Fountain. Solid security thread printed *BANKA SLOVENIJE*. Watermark: Kobilca. Printer: (TDLR). 156 x 78 mm.

- a. 8. OKTOBER 1997. Sig. 10. Intro: 10.02.1998. Embossed *5000* starts at bottom on foil patch. — — 100
- b. Embossed *5000* starts at top on foil patch. — — 150
- c. 15. JANUAR 2000. Intro: 10.07.2000. — — 100
- as1. Diagonal red *SPECIMEN* overprint on front; diagonal red *VZOREC* overprint on back; horizontal red *SPECIMEN N°* # overprint at lower left on back. — — 100
- as2. Diagonal red *SPECIMEN* and DLR oval ovpts; punched. — — —
- cs. Diagonal red *SPECIMEN* overprint on front; diagonal red *VZOREC* overprint on back; horizontal red *SPECIMEN* # overprint at lower left on back. — — 25

Replacement notes: Prefix AZ.

Like BS B9, but with foil patch (called LIFT by TDLR) on the upper left front.

On early 5,000-tolar issues dated 1997, the *5000* embossed on the foil patch starts at the bottom and is read sideways (B10a, left), but on later issues it starts on the top and is read normally (B10b, right).

BS B11 (P33): **5,000 tolarjev** (withdrawn 01.15.2007)   VG   VF   UNC

Multicolor. Front: Artist's palette hologram; easel; profile in silhouette; Artist Ivana Kobilca. Back: National Gallery building in Ljubljana; Robba Fountain. Solid security thread and windowed thread with demetalized *BANKA SLOVENIJE*. Watermark: Kobilca. Printer: (TDLR). 156 x 78 mm.

☐	a.	15. JANUAR 2002. Sig. 13. Intro: 15.07.2002.	—	—	125
☐	b.	15. JANUAR 2004. Sig. 18. Intro: 02.08.2004.	—	—	95
☐	as.	Diagonal red *SPECIMEN* overprint on front; diagonal red *VZOREC* overprint on back; horizontal red # overprint at lower left on back.	—	—	25
☐	bs.	Diagonal red *SPECIMEN* overprint on front; diagonal red *VZOREC* overprint on back; horizontal red *SPECIMEN* # overprint at lower left on back.	—	—	25

Replacement notes: Prefix AZ.

Like BS B10, but gold foil portrait in upper left front has been replaced by a holographic artist's palette.

BS B12 (P20): **10,000 tolarjev** (withdrawn 01.15.2007)   VG   VF   UNC

Multicolor. Front: Quill pen in OVI; stage plan of the former Theatre of Ljubljana; writer Ivan Cankar. Back: Chrysanthemum; Cankar's handwriting. Solid security thread printed *BANKA SLOVENIJE*. Watermark: Cankar. Printer: (G&D). 156 x 78 mm.

☐	a.	28. JUNIJ 1994. Signature 9. Intro: 15.03.1995.	—	—	250
☐	as.	Diagonal red *SPECIMEN* overprint on front; diagonal red *VZOREC* overprint on back; horizontal red *SPECIMEN* Nº # overprint at upper left on back.			25

Replacement notes: Prefix AZ.

2001 Commemorative Issues

These notes were issued on 8 October 2001 to commemorate the tenth anniversary of the tolar. They are identical to BS B4a and BS B8c, respectively, but with spiral *BANKA SLOVENIJE 1991•2001* overprinted in gold on the watermark area at left on the front.

BS B13 (P24 & P34): **10,000 tolarjev** (withdrawn 01.15.2007)   VG   VF   UNC
Multicolor. Front: Quill pen; stage plan of the former Theatre of Ljubljana; writer Ivan Cankar. Back: Chrysanthemum; Cankar's handwriting. Holographic stripe. Solid security thread printed *BANKA SLOVENIJE*. Watermark: Cankar. Printer: (TDLR). 156 x 78 mm.

- ☐ a. 15. JANUAR 2000. Sig. 12. Intro: 19.06.2000. — — 200
- ☐ b. 15. JANUAR 2003. Signature 1. — — 125
  Iridescent blossom with *SIT* added on upper left on back. Intro: 13.10.2003.
- ☐ c. 15. JANUAR 2004. Intro: 04.04.2005. — — 115
- ☐ as. Diagonal red *SPECIMEN* overprint on front; — — 25
  diagonal red *VZOREC* overprint on back;
  horizontal red *SPECIMEN Nº #* overprint at upper left on back.
- ☐ bs. Diagonal red *SPECIMEN* overprint on front; — — 25
  diagonal red *VZOREC* overprint on back;
  horizontal red *No #* overprint at upper left on back.
- ☐ cs. Diagonal red *SPECIMEN* overprint on front; — — 25
  diagonal red *VZOREC* overprint on back;
  horizontal red *SPECIMEN Nº #* overprint at upper left on back.

Replacement notes: Prefix AZ.
Like BS B12, but with holographic stripe at right front.
For notes with 2001 and 2004 overprints, see BS BNP1 and BS B18/BNP2, respectively.

BS B14 (P25): **100 tolarjev** (withdrawn 01.15.2007)   VG   VF   UNC
Multicolor. Front: *BANKA SLOVENIJE 1991•2001* overprint; paint brush; artist's palette; Impressionist painter Rihard Jakopič. Back: Jakopič's painting "The Sun;" architectural plan of the former Jakopič Pavilion in Ljubljana. Solid security thread printed *BANKA SLOVENIJE*. Watermark: Jakopič. Printer: (TDLR). 138 x 69 mm.

- ☐ a. 15. JANUAR 1992. Sig. 1. Intro: 08.10.2001. — — 15

BS B15 (P26): **1,000 tolarjev** (withdrawn 01.15.2007)   VG   VF   UNC
Multicolor. Front: *BANKA SLOVENIJE 1991•2001* overprint; Prešeren signature; poet France Prešeren. Back: "Prijatli" (Friends); quill pen; text from "The Toast" (Slovenian national anthem). Solid security thread printed *BANKA SLOVENIJE*. Watermark: Prešeren. Printer: (TDLR). 156 x 78 mm.

- ☐ a. 15. JANUAR 2000. Sig. 3. Intro: 08.10.2001. — — 40

2001 Numismatic Products

A total of 1,000 pieces each of the preceding 100 and 1,000-tolar commemorative notes were packaged in green albums with 10,000-tolar commemoratives similarly overprinted on BS B13. The 10,000-tolar note never circulated; it was sold in sets only. The original cost of each set was 13,000 tolars.

BS BNP1 (PNL): **100, 1,000, and 10,000 tolarjev**   UNC
    ☐ a.   BS B14, B15, and overprinted B13a (3 notes) issued in dark green folder. Intro: 08.10.2001.   200

2004 Commemorative Issues

These notes commemorate the signing of Slovenia's agreement on full membership in the European Union in Athens in April 2003. They have *2004* and five stars overprinted vertically in gold to the left of the portrait on the front.

BS B16 (P28): **100 tolarjev** (withdrawn 01.15.2007)   VG   VF   UNC
Multicolor. Front: Paint brush; artist's palette; *2004* and stars overprint; Impressionist painter Rihard Jakopič. Back: Jakopič's painting "The Sun;" architectural plan of the former Jakopič Pavilion in Ljubljana. Solid security thread printed *BANKA SLOVENIJE*. Watermark: Jakopič. Printer: (TDLR). 138 x 69 mm.
    ☐ a.   15. JANUAR 2003. Sig. 14. Intro: 26.05.2003.   —   —   15

BS B17 (P29): **1,000 tolarjev** (withdrawn 01.15.2007)   VG   VF   UNC
Multicolor. Front: Prešeren signature; *2004* and stars overprint; poet France Prešeren. Back: "Prijatli" (Friends); quill pen; text from "The Toast" (Slovenian national anthem). Solid security thread printed *BANKA SLOVENIJE*. Watermark: Prešeren. Printer: (TDLR). 156 x 78 mm.
    ☐ a.   15. JANUAR 2003. Sig. 15. Intro: 26.05.2003.   —   —   30
Replacement notes: Prefix ZA.

BS B18 (P30): **10,000 tolarjev** (withdrawn 01.15.2007) VG VF UNC
Multicolor. Front: Quill pen; stage plan of the former Theatre of Ljubljana; *2004* and stars overprint; writer Ivan Cankar. Back: Chrysanthemum; Cankar's handwriting. Holographic stripe. Solid security thread printed *BANKA SLOVENIJE*. Watermark: Cankar. Printer: (TDLR). 156 x 78 mm.
☐ a. 15. JANUAR 2000. Sig. 12. Intro: 26.05.2003. — — 110

2004 Numismatic Products

A total of 500 pieces each of the preceding commemorative notes were packaged in green albums. The 100-tolar notes in these sets have prefix CC, and the other two denominations have prefix BB. The original cost of each set was 13,000 tolars.

BS BNP2 (PNL): **100, 1,000, and 10,000 tolarjev** UNC
☐ a. BS B16-B18 (3 notes) issued in dark green folder. Intro: 26.05.2003. 200

Looking Forward

On 1 January 2007, Slovenia replaced its tolar with the euro. Tolar banknotes can be exchanged for euros at the Bank of Slovenia in perpetuity.

For later issues, see European Monetary Union.

Acknowledgements

This chapter was compiled with the generous assistance of Thomas Augustsson, Mirsad Delic, Manfred Dietl jun., Peter Kelly, Majda Koren (Bank of Slovenia), Nives Kupic (Bank of Slovenia), Don Ludwig, Wally Myers, Menelaos Stamatelos, Stanko Štiblar, Sasa Stojmenovic, Stane Štraus, Bill Stubkjaer, Tristan Williams, Christof Zellweger, and others.

Sources

Cuhaj, George S. *Standard Catalog of World Paper Money, Modern Issues, 1961-Present*. 17th edition. 2011. ISBN 978-1-4402-1584-1. Krause Publications (www.krausebooks.com), 700 East State St., Iola, WI, 54990-0001.

Palairet, Michael. "Bombardment by Bank Notes: The Monetary Fallout of the Yugoslav Crisis." *IBNS Journal*. Volume 31 Number 3. p.30.

Potočnik, Andrej and Stanislav Štibler. *Denar na Slovenskem*. 1st edition. 2007. ISBN 978-961-238-853-9. Masta Trade d.o.o., Ljubljana, Slovenia.

Štraus, Stane. "Bank Notes of the Republic of Slovenia (1991 to date)." *IBNS Journal*. Volume 39 Number 1. p.9.

Viščević, Zlatko. *Coins and Banknotes of Yugoslavia, Slovenia, Croatia, Bosnia and Herzegovina, Serbia, Montenegro and Macedonia*. 2nd edition. 2011. ISBN 978-953-5689-0-3.

Share Your Input, Info, and Images

This catalog is believed to be complete and correct as of the time of publication. Prices and face values were last updated 3 June 2011. Please report errors or omissions so that corrections may be made. If you can more precisely identify the name or location of anything depicted on a note, please share that information. Furthermore, if you own an unlisted type or variety, please submit scans of the front and back of the note so that it can be documented. Scans should be 300 dots per inch, 100% actual size, 24-bit color, saved as *uncompressed* JPEG files, and sent to owen@banknotenews.com. Be sure to fully describe all attributes of the note which are not apparent upon visual inspection of the images alone, such as physical dimension, watermark, and security thread.

Solomon Islands

For earlier issues, see Australia, British Solomon Islands, and Oceania.

Contents

Solomon Islands Monetary Authority (SIMA)........ 1912
Central Bank of Solomon Islands (CBSI) 1914

Monetary System
24.10.1977: 1 Solomon Islands dollar (SBD) = 100 cents

Solomon Islands Monetary Authority

SIMA Signature Varieties

	Chairman	Member
1	John Palfrey	Jezriel Korinihona
2	Barry Longmuire	Jezriel Korinihona
3	Philip Corney	Jezriel Korinihona

1977-1981 Issues

A memorandum dated 23 April 1975 and entitled "Solomon Islands – Currency Arrangements" was drawn up as a result of moves to introduce a separate currency in Solomon Islands in line with constitutional development and movement towards self government. The Solomon Islands authorities hoped to introduce the new currency in mid-1975, however the Solomon Islands dollar was not introduced until 24 October 1977 (the Solomons became self-governing on 2 January 1976 and independence from the United Kingdom was officially achieved 7 July 1978). The Solomon Islands dollar replaced the Australian dollar at par, which was withdrawn in October 1978.

SIMA B1 (P5): **2 dollars** (US$0.30)   VG   VF   UNC
Green. Front: Birds; fish; Queen Elizabeth II. Back: Fish; men spear fishing; bird. Solid security thread. Watermark: Falcon in flight. Printer: (TDLR). 140 x 70 mm.
    a. No date. Signature 1. Intro: 24.10.1977.   0.75   2.50   10
    as. Specimen.   —   —   30
Replacement notes: Prefix Z/1.

SIMA B2 (P6): **5 dollars** (US$0.70)   VG   VF   UNC
Blue. Front: Birds; fish; Queen Elizabeth II. Back: Bird; wood carvings of sea spirit; traditional war canoes; hut on stilts; palm trees. Solid security thread. Watermark: Falcon in flight. Printer: (TDLR). 145 x 75 mm.
    a. No date. Signature 1. Intro: 24.10.1977.   2   7.50   25
    b. Signature 2.   2   7.50   25
    as. Two diagonal red *SPECIMEN* overprints.   —   —   30
    bs. Specimen.   —   —   30
Replacement notes: Prefix Z/1.

SIMA B3 (P7): **10 dollars** (US$1.40)　　　　　VG　VF　UNC
Violet and purple. Front: Birds; fish; Queen Elizabeth II. Back: Fish; woman making shell money. Solid security thread. Watermark: Falcon in flight. Printer: (TDLR). 150 x 80 mm.

- ☐ a. No date. Signature 1. Intro: 24.10.1977.　　7.50　25　100
- ☐ b. Signature 2.　　　　　　　　　　　　　　 7.50　25　100
- ☐ as. Specimen.　　　　　　　　　　　　　　　 —　 —　 30

Replacement notes: Prefix Z/1.

SIMA B4 (P8): **20 dollars** (US$2.80)　　　　　VG　VF　UNC
Brown, orange, and purple. Front: Club; fish; Queen Elizabeth II. Back: Warriors; turtle. Solid security thread. Watermark: Falcon in flight. Printer: (TDLR). 155 x 85 mm.

- ☐ a. No date. Signature 3. Intro: 24.10.1980.　　12　50　200
- ☐ as. Two diagonal red SPECIMEN overprints.　　—　 —　 30

Replacement notes: Prefix Z/1.

1977 Numismatic Products

SIMA BNP1 (PNL): **2 - 10 dollars**　　　　　　　　　　UNC
- ☐ a. SIMA B1a, B2a, and B3a (3 notes) with matching serial numbers　350
  in first day of issue stamped envelopes, in album with seven
  coins. Intro: 24.10.1977.

1979 Numismatic Products

Thomas De La Rue created "official presentation sets of specimen banknotes from around the world" for The Franklin Mint, a private company that mailed the sets every six weeks to subscribers from 1978 to 1979. Each set of notes with matching serial numbers originally cost $14 and came in an envelope with a numbered and dated certificate of authenticity and an index card describing the notes in detail. Based upon serial numbers observed, at least 10,440 sets were produced, and a complete collection comprises 15 sets with a total of 73 notes from 16 issuing authorities. Rarely available in the original small brown storage box, the notes are usually sold by country set, but are sometimes sold individually. Do not mistake these numismatic products for the specimen varieties listed separately, which the security printer created for its note-issuing clients.

SIMA BNP2 (PCS1): **2 - 10 dollars**　　　　　　　　UNC
- ☐ a. SIMA B1a, B2b, and B3b (3 notes) with diagonal SPECIMEN　25
  overprint and Maltese cross prefix. Intro: 03.07.1979.

Central Bank of Solomon Islands

Central Bank of Solomon Islands (CBSI) was established in February 1983 under the Central Bank of Solomon Islands Act 1976.

For more information, visit www.cbsi.com.sb.

CBSI Signature Varieties

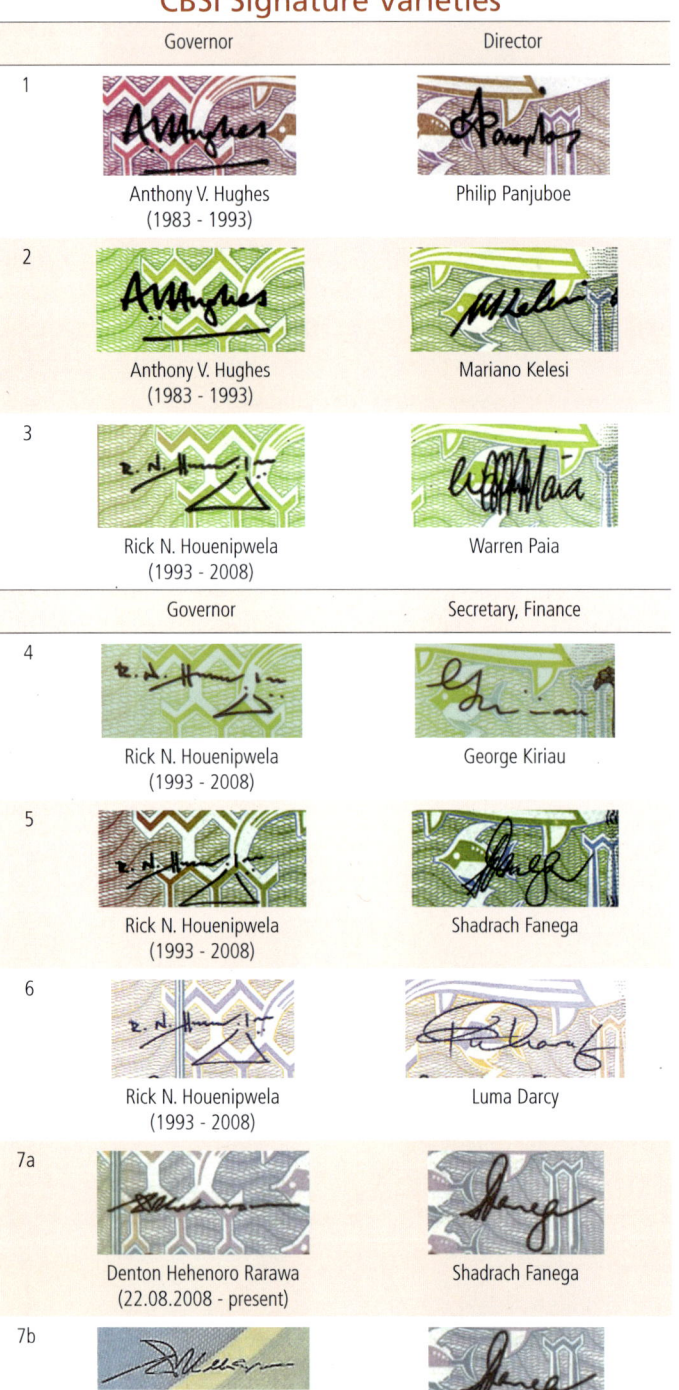

1984 Issues

These notes are like preceding issues, but with the name of the new issuer, plus new signatures and titles.

CBSI B1 (P11): **10 dollars** (US$1.40)   VG   VF   UNC
Violet and purple. Front: Birds; fish; Queen Elizabeth II. Back: Fish; woman making shell money. Solid security thread. Watermark: Falcon in flight. Printer: (TDLR). 150 x 80 mm.
    ☐ a. No date. Signature 1. Intro: 1984.   7.50   25   100
Replacement notes: Prefix Z/1.

CBSI B2 (P12): **20 dollars** (US$2.80)   VG   VF   UNC
Brown, orange, and purple. Front: Club; fish; Queen Elizabeth II. Back: Warriors; turtle. Solid security thread. Watermark: Falcon in flight. Printer: (TDLR). 155 x 85 mm.
    ☐ a. No date. Signature 1. Intro: 1984.   12   50   200
Replacement notes: Prefix Z/1.

1986 Issues

These notes are like preceding issues, but with the portrait of Queen Elizabeth II replaced by that of the coat of arms. The 50-dollar denomination is new.

CBSI B3 (P13): **2 dollars** (US$0.30)   VG   VF   UNC
Green. Front: Birds; fish; coat of arms. Back: Fish; men spear fishing; bird. Solid security thread. Watermark: Falcon in flight. Printer: (TDLR). 140 x 70 mm.
- a. No date. Signature 2. Intro: 1986.   FV   FV   2
- as. Two diagonal red *SPECIMEN* overprints.   —   —   25

Replacement notes: Prefix Y/1.

CBSI B4 (P14): **5 dollars** (US$0.70)   VG   VF   UNC
Blue. Front: Birds; fish; coat of arms. Back: Bird; wood carvings of sea spirit; traditional war canoes; hut on stilts; palm trees. Solid security thread. Watermark: Falcon in flight. Printer: (TDLR). 142 x 72 mm.
- a. No date. Signature 2. Intro: 1986.   FV   FV   5
- as. Two diagonal red *SPECIMEN* overprints.   —   —   25

Replacement notes: Prefix Y/1.

CBSI B5 (P15): **10 dollars** (US$1.40)   VG   VF   UNC
Violet and purple. Front: Birds; fish; coat of arms. Back: Fish; woman making shell money. Solid security thread. Watermark: Falcon in flight. Printer: (TDLR). 147 x 74 mm.
- a. No date. Signature 2. Intro: 1986.   FV   FV   10
- as. Two diagonal red *SPECIMEN* overprints.   —   —   10

Replacement notes: Prefix Y/1.

CBSI B6 (P16): **20 dollars** (US$2.80)   VG   VF   UNC
Brown, orange, and purple. Front: Club; fish; coat of arms. Back: Warriors; turtle. Solid security thread. Watermark: Falcon in flight. Printer: (TDLR). 154 x 77 mm.
- a. No date. Signature 2. Intro: 1986.   FV   FV   10
- as. Two diagonal red *SPECIMEN* overprints.   —   —   25

Replacement notes: Prefix Y/1.

CBSI B7 (P17): **50 dollars** (US$7)   VG   VF   UNC
Purple, green, and yellow. Front: Club; dog carvings; coat of arms. Back: Nymphalid butterflies; flowers; pot; snake; lizards; shells; plants; spear. Solid security thread. Watermark: Falcon in flight. Printer: (TDLR). 160 x 79 mm.
    ☐ a.   No date. Signature 2. Intro: 13.10.1986.   FV   FV   30
    ☐ as.   Two diagonal red *SPECIMEN* overprints.   —   —   30
Replacement notes: Prefix Y/1.

1996-1997 Issues

These notes are like the preceding issues, but they have novel serial numbers printed in two different colors, and the security thread is now demetalized with the initials of the Central Bank of Solomon Islands.

CBSI B8 (P18): **2 dollars** (US$0.30)   VG   VF   UNC
Green. Front: Stylized frigate birds; stylized porpoises and angel fish; coat of arms; decorative shell rings as registration device. Back: Shell rings; fish; men spear fishing; bird. Solid security thread with demetalized *CBSI*. Watermark: Falcon in flight. Printer: (TDLR). 140 x 70 mm.
    ☐ a.   No date. Signature 3. Intro: 1997.   FV   FV   1.75
    ☐ as.   Two diagonal red *SPECIMEN* overprints.   —   —   —
Replacement notes: Prefix X/1.

CBSI B9 (P19): **5 dollars** (US$0.70)   VG   VF   UNC
Blue. Front: Birds; fish; coat of arms. Back: Bird; wood carvings of sea spirit; traditional war canoes; hut on stilts; palm trees. Solid security thread with demetalized *CBSI*. Watermark: Falcon in flight. Printer: (TDLR). 142 x 72 mm.
    ☐ a.   No date. Signature 3. Intro: 1997.   FV   FV   3
    ☐ as.   Two diagonal red *SPECIMEN* overprints.   —   —   —
Replacement notes: Prefix X/1.

CBSI B10 (P20): **10 dollars** (US$1.40)   VG   VF   UNC
Violet and purple. Front: Birds; fish; coat of arms. Back: Fish; woman making shell money. Solid security thread with demetalized *CBSI*. Watermark: Falcon in flight. Printer: (TDLR). 147 x 74 mm.
    ☐ a.   No date. Signature 3. Intro: 1997.   FV   FV   4.25
    ☐ as.   Two diagonal red *SPECIMEN* overprints.   —   —   —
Replacement notes: Prefix X/1.

2001 Commemorative Issues

This 2-dollar note was issued to commemorate the 25th anniversary of the Central Bank of Solomon Islands. It is the first polymer note for the country, a move intended "to increase durability of the note, enhance security of the note and thereby reduce printing costs in the long run." 1.5 million notes were produced.

CBSI B11 (P21): **20 dollars** (US$2.80)   VG   VF   UNC
Brown, orange, and purple. Front: Club; fish; coat of arms. Back: Warriors; turtle. Solid security thread with demetalized *CBSI*. Watermark: Falcon in flight. Printer: (TDLR). 154 x 77 mm.
- a. No date. Signature 3. Intro: 1997.   FV   FV   9
- as. Two diagonal red *SPECIMEN* overprints.   —   —   —

Replacement notes: Prefix X/1.

CBSI B13 (P23): **2 dollars** (US$0.30)   VG   VF   UNC
Green. Front: Stylized frigate birds; Sanford pacific eagle; stylized porpoises and angel fish; coat of arms; decorative shell rings as registration device; *CBSI SILVER JUBILEE* silver overprint. Back: Shell rings; fish; men spear fishing; bird. Simulated windowed security thread with demetalized *CBSI*. Watermark (shadow image): Coat of arms and *CBSI*. Printer: (NPA). 140 x 72 mm. Polymer.
- a. (20)01. Signature 4. Intro: 21.06.2001.   FV   FV   2.25
- as. Diagonal red *SPECIMEN* overprint.   —   —   —

CBSI B12 (P22): **50 dollars** (US$7)   VG   VF   UNC
Purple, green, and yellow. Front: Club; dog carvings; coat of arms. Back: Nymphalid butterflies; flowers; pot; snake; lizards; shells; plants; spear. Solid security thread with demetalized *CBSI*. Watermark: Falcon in flight. Printer: (TDLR). 160 x 79 mm.
- a. No date. Signature 3. Intro: 1997.   FV   FV   20
- as. Two diagonal red *SPECIMEN* overprints.   —   —   —

Replacement notes: Prefix X/1.

2001 Numismatic Products

CBSI BNP1 (PNL): **2 dollars**   UNC
- a. CBSI B13 in folder.   15

2001 Issues

This 50-dollar note is like the preceding issue, but it has a flag added on front, the security thread is now windowed, the right-hand serial number is now vertical, and an electrotype *CBSI* has been added to the new watermark of a falcon head. It was the initial step taken to standardize the size of the banknotes in Solomon Islands. One million notes were produced.

CBSI B14 (P24): **50 dollars** (US$7) VG VF UNC
Purple, green, and yellow. Front: Club; flag; dog carvings; coat of arms. Back: Nymphalid butterflies; flowers; pot; snake; lizards; shells; plants; spear. Windowed security thread with demetalized *CBSI*. Watermark: Falcon head with electrotype *CBSI*. Printer: (TDLR). 162 x 72 mm.

☐ a. No date. Signature 4. Intro: June 2001. FV FV 20
☐ as. Diagonal red *SPECIMEN* overprint. — — —

2004-2011 Issues

These notes are like the preceding issues, but the national flag has been added on front, the right-hand serial number is now vertical, and—except for the 5-dollar note—the security thread is now windowed, plus an electrotype *CBSI* has been added to the watermark, along with Cornerstones. The 50-dollar note now has a hologram at right on the front, as does the new 100-dollar denomination. The bank decided to revert to printing the 2-dollar note on cotton paper in response to public complaints about the quality of the polymer note.

CBSI B15 (P25): **2 dollars** (US$0.30) VG VF UNC
Green. Front: Birds; fish; flag; coat of arms. Back: Fish; men spear fishing; bird. Windowed security thread with demetalized scroll. Watermark: Falcon head, electrotype *CBSI*, and Cornerstones. Printer: (TDLR). 142 x 72 mm.

☐ a. No date. Signature 5. Intro: 2006. FV FV 1
☐ b. Signature 7a. FV FV 1

CBSI B16 (P26): **5 dollars** (US$0.70) VG VF UNC
Blue. Front: Birds; fish; flag; coat of arms. Back: Bird; wood carvings of sea spirit; traditional war canoes; hut on stilts; palm trees. Solid security thread with demetalized *CBSI*. Watermark: Falcon in flight. Printer: (TDLR). 145 x 72 mm.

☐ a. No date. Signature 5. Intro: 2004. FV FV 2.50
☐ b. Signature 6. FV FV 2.25
☐ c. Signature 7a. FV FV 2.25

Replacement notes: Prefix X/1.

CBSI B17 (P27): **10 dollars** (US$1.40)   VG   VF   UNC

Violet and purple. Front: Birds; fish; flag; coat of arms. Back: Fish; woman making shell money. Windowed security thread with demetalized *CBSI*. Watermark: Falcon head, electrotype *CBSI*, and Cornerstones. Printer: (TDLR). 147 x 72 mm.

     ☐ a.   No date. Signature 5.   FV   FV   7.50
     ☐ b.   Signature 6. Intro: 19.08.2009.   FV   FV   7
     ☐ c.   Signature 7a.   FV   FV   7

CBSI B18 (P28): **20 dollars** (US$2.80)   VG   VF   UNC

Brown, orange, and purple. Front: Club; fish; flag; coat of arms. Back: Warriors; turtle. Solid security thread with demetalized *CBSI*. Watermark: Falcon head, electrotype *CBSI*, and Cornerstones. Printer: (TDLR). 155 x 72 mm.

     ☐ a.   No date. Signature 5. Intro: 2004.   FV   FV   10
     ☐ b.   Signature 7a.   FV   FV   9
     ☐ as.   Diagonal red *SPECIMEN* overprint.   —   —   —

CBSI B19 (P29): **50 dollars** (US$7)   VG   VF   UNC

Purple, green, and yellow. Front: Club; flag; dog carvings; coat of arms; hologram. Back: Nymphalid butterflies; flowers; pot; snake; lizards; shells; plants; spear. Windowed security thread with demetalized *CBSI*. Watermark: Falcon head, electrotype *CBSI*, and Cornerstones. Printer: (TDLR). 160 x 72 mm.

     ☐ a.   No date. Signature 5. Intro: 04.10.2007.   FV   FV   25
     ☐ b.   Signature 6.   FV   FV   20
     ☐ as.   Diagonal red *SPECIMEN* overprint.   —   —   —

Replacement notes: Prefix numerator Z.

CBSI B20 (P30): **100 dollars** (US$14)   VG   VF   UNC

Light brown, red, and peach. Front: Club; flag; bird; coconuts; coat of arms; flower; hologram. Back: Flower; palm trees; coconut harvesting; ray. Windowed security thread with demetalized design. Watermark: Falcon head, electrotype *CBSI*, and Cornerstones. Printer: (TDLR). 162 x 72 mm.

     ☐ a.   No date. Signature 5. Intro: 02.09.2006.   FV   FV   50
     ☐ b.   Signature 6.   FV   FV   40
     ☐ c.   Signature 7a.   FV   FV   40

2013 Issues

This is the first denomination in a new family to be issued over the course of the next few years.

CBSI B21 (PNL): **50 dollars** (US$7)   VG   VF   UNC
Purple, green, and yellow. Front: Basket weave designs; bird as registration device; flag; bird carvings; coat of arms. Back: Nymphalid butterflies; flowers; lizards; shells; plants; spear; bird. Optiks security thread. Watermark: Falcon head, electrotype *CBSI*, and Cornerstones. Printer: (TDLR). 160 x 72 mm.

☐ a.   No date. Signature 7b. Intro: 26.09.2013.   FV   FV   25

2013 Numismatic Products

CBSI BNP2 (PNL): **50 dollars**   UNC
☐ a.   CBSI B21 in folder.   40

Acknowledgements

This chapter was compiled with the generous assistance of Enoch Ilisia (Central Bank of Solomon Islands), Don Ludwig, Claudio Marana, Wally Myers, Paul Nahmias, Rui Manuel Palhares, Alexander Petrov, George Provencal, Andrew Randall, Gylfi Snorrason, Bill Stubkjaer, Christoph Thomas, and others.

Sources

Central Bank of Solomon Islands. *Annual Reports*. 1999-2008.

Cuhaj, George S. *Standard Catalog of World Paper Money, General Issues, 1368-1960*. 14th edition. 2012. ISBN 978-1-4402-3090-5. Krause Publications (www.krausebooks.com), 700 East State St., Iola, WI, 54990-0001.

Cuhaj, George S. *Standard Catalog of World Paper Money, Modern Issues, 1961-Present*. 17th edition. 2011. ISBN 978-1-4402-1584-1. Krause Publications (www.krausebooks.com), 700 East State St., Iola, WI, 54990-0001.

Eu, Peter and Ben Chiew. *Queen Elizabeth II*. 1st edition. 2006. ISBN 983-43038-1-5. Eureka Metro, P. O. Box 30, Jalan Kelang Lama, Kuala Lumpur, 57000, Malaysia.

Eu, Peter, Ben Chiew, and Stane Straus. *World Polymer Banknotes: A Standard Reference*. 2nd edition. 2006. ISBN 983-43038-2-3. Eureka Metro, P. O. Box 30, Jalan Kelang Lama, Kuala Lumpur, 57000, Malaysia.

Krause, Thomas and Peter Bauer. *Specialized Catalogue of World Plastic Money*. 5th edition. 2009. www.polymernotes.de.

Munoz, M. A. "Signature Varieties of the Dollar System Bank Notes of the Solomon Islands." *IBNS Journal*. Volume 30 Number 1. p.22.

Symes, Peter. "The Portraits of Queen Elizabeth II on World Bank Notes." *IBNS Journal*. Volume 44 Number 2. p.8.

Share Your Input, Info, and Images

This catalog is believed to be complete and correct as of the time of publication. Prices and face values were last updated 24 June 2011. Please report errors or omissions so that corrections may be made. If you can more precisely identify the name or location of anything depicted on a note, please share that information. Furthermore, if you own an unlisted type or variety, please submit scans of the front and back of the note so that it can be documented. Scans should be 300 dots per inch, 100% actual size, 24-bit color, saved as *uncompressed* JPEG files, and sent to owen@banknotenews.com. Be sure to fully describe all attributes of the note which are not apparent upon visual inspection of the images alone, such as physical dimension, watermark, and security thread.

Somalia

For earlier issues, see East Africa, India, and Italian Somaliland.

Contents

Banca Nazionale Somala (BNS)	1921
Somali National Bank (SNB)	1925
Central Bank of Somalia (CBS)	1926
Mogadishu Northern Forces (CBS)	1930
Puntland Region (CBS)	1931

Monetary System
1962: 1 Somali shilling (SOS) = 100 cents

Banca Nazionale Somala (National Bank of Somalia)

On 1 July 1960, the newly independent Republic of Somalia established the Banca Nazionale Somala (National Bank of Somalia) to take over the activities of Cassa per la Circulazione Monetaria della Somali and the Mogadishu branch of Banca d'Italia, which had originally opened its branch on 15 November 1920. The new bank combined central banking activities with commercial banking activities.

BNS Signature Varieties

1962 Issues

At the time of unification, the East African shilling was circulating in the former British Protectorate of Somaliland and the somalo was circulating in the former United Nations Trust Territory of Somalia. Monetary Ordinance of 6 March 1961 established the somalo as the currency for unified Somalia. Shillings could be exchanged for somali until 31 July 1961, at which time shillings were no longer legal tender. Presidential Decree No. 86 of 5 March 1962 set forth the specifications for a new series of banknotes denominated in scellini (shillings), and the new series was put into circulation on 15 December 1962. Somalo notes issued by Cassa per la Circulazione Monetaria della Somali ceased to be legal tender on 31 December 1963.

BNS B1 (P1): 5 scellini / 5 shillings
Red, green, and orange. Front: Greater kudu antelope. Back: Dhow boat. No security thread. Watermark: Leopard head. Printer: *I.PS. OFF. CARTE VALORI-ROMA*. 152 x 72 mm.

		VG	VF	UNC
a.	1962. Signature 1. Intro: 15.12.1962.	50	125	550
as1.	Diagonal red *SPECIMEN* overprint.	—	—	400
as2.	Diagonal red *SPECIMEN* overprint; diagonal *ANNULLATO* perforation.	—	—	110

BNS B2 (P2): 10 scellini / 10 shillings VG VF UNC
Green and orange. Front: Cotton plant flower. Back: Juba River, bushes, and trees. No security thread. Watermark: Leopard head. Printer: *I.P.S. OFF. CARTE VALORI-ROMA*. 152 x 72 mm.

☐	a.	1962. Signature 1. Intro: 15.12.1962.	75	150	650
☐	as.	Diagonal red *SPECIMEN* overprint.	—	—	185

BNS B3 (P3): 20 scellini / 20 shillings VG VF UNC
Burgundy, brown, and blue. Front: Bananas. Back: Trees; Banca Nazionale Somala headquarters building. No security thread. Watermark: Leopard head. Printer: *I.P.S. OFF. CARTE VALORI-ROMA*. 164 x 81 mm.

☐	a.	1962. Signature 1. Intro: 15.12.1962.	25	175	1,400
☐	as.	Diagonal red *SPECIMEN* overprint.	—	500	750

BNS B4 (P4): 100 scellini / 100 shillings VG VF UNC
Blue and red. Front: Vase; statuette; musical instrument. Back: Trees; National Assembly building in Mogadishu. No security thread. Watermark: Leopard head. Printer: *I.P.S. OFF. CARTE VALORI-ROMA*. 164 x 81 mm.

☐	a.	1962. Signature 1. Intro: 15.12.1962.	75	300	2,500
☐	as.	Diagonal red *SPECIMEN* overprint.	—	—	400

1966-1971 Issues

These notes are like the preceding issues, but they have been redesigned with new borders, a circle (not an oval) around the watermark, bolder colors, and a solid security thread that fluoresces blue under UV light. The denomination is repeated in fluorescent ink over the watermark on the 1966 issues, but not on the 1968 issues. Notes overprinted *SPECIMEN OF NO VALUE* but without perforations were likely looted from the bank during the civil war.

BNS B7 (P6, P10 & P14): **10 scellini / 10 shillings**   VG   VF   UNC
Green and orange. Front: Cotton plant flower. Back: Juba River, bushes, and trees. Solid security thread. Watermark: Leopard head. Printer: (TDLR). 152 x 72 mm.

			VG	VF	UNC
☐	a.	1966. Signature 2.	25	100	400
☐	b.	1968. Signature 3.	25	125	500
☐	c.	1971. Signature 4.	25	100	400
☐	as1.	Diagonal red *SPECIMEN* and DLR oval ovpts; horizontal red *SPECIMEN Nº #* ovpt at lower left.	—	—	225
☐	as2.	Diagonal red *SPECIMEN OF NO VALUE* ovpt; diagonal *ANNULLATO* perforation.	—	—	—
☐	as3.	Diagonal red *SPECIMEN OF NO VALUE* ovpt.	—	—	—
☐	bs2.	Diagonal red *SPECIMEN OF NO VALUE* ovpt; diagonal *ANNULLATO* perforation.	—	—	—
☐	bs3.	Diagonal red *SPECIMEN OF NO VALUE* ovpt.	—	—	—
☐	cs3.	Diagonal red *SPECIMEN OF NO VALUE* ovpt.	—	—	175

BNS B5 (P5 & P9): **5 scellini / 5 shillings**   VG   VF   UNC
Red, green, and orange. Front: Greater kudu antelope. Back: Dhow boat. Solid security thread. Watermark: Leopard head. Printer: (TDLR). 152 x 72 mm.

			VG	VF	UNC
☐	a.	1966. Signature 2.	25	110	250
☐	b.	1968. Signature 3.	50	175	350
☐	as1.	Diagonal red *SPECIMEN* and DLR oval ovpts; horizontal red *SPECIMEN Nº #* ovpt at lower left.	—	—	—
☐	as2.	Diagonal red *SPECIMEN OF NO VALUE* ovpt; diagonal *ANNULLATO* perforation.	—	—	300
☐	as3.	Diagonal red *SPECIMEN OF NO VALUE* ovpt.	—	—	—
☐	bs.	Diagonal red *SPECIMEN OF NO VALUE* ovpt; diagonal *ANNULLATO* perforation.	—	—	—

BNS B6 (P13): **5 scellini / 5 shillings**   VG   VF   UNC
Brown, blue, and orange. Front: Greater kudu antelope. Back: Dhow boat. Solid security thread. Watermark: Leopard head. Printer: (TDLR). 152 x 72 mm.

			VG	VF	UNC
☐	a.	1971. Signature 4.	50	100	400
☐	as.	Specimen.	—	—	110

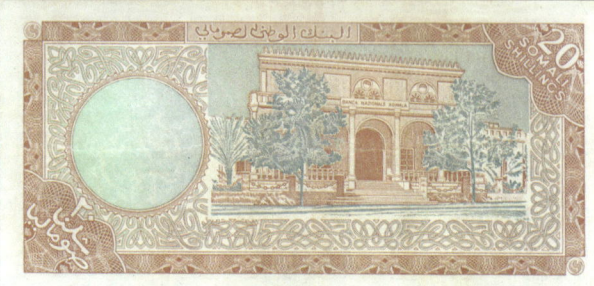

BNS B8 (P7, P11 & P15): **20 scellini / 20 shillings** VG VF UNC
Burgundy, brown, and blue. Front: Bananas. Back: Trees; Banca Nazionale Somala headquarters building. Solid security thread. Watermark: Leopard head. Printer: (TDLR). 164 x 81 mm.

			VG	VF	UNC
☐	a.	1966. Signature 2.	25	65	450
☐	b.	1968. Signature 3.	25	85	575
☐	c.	1971. Signature 4. Intro: 10.03.1972.	120	225	650
☐	as1.	Diagonal red *SPECIMEN* and DLR oval ovpts; horizontal red *SPECIMEN Nº* # ovpt at lower left.	—	—	325
☐	bs1.	Diagonal red *SPECIMEN* and DLR oval ovpts; horizontal red *SPECIMEN Nº* # ovpt at lower left.	—	—	—
☐	bs2.	Diagonal red *SPECIMEN OF NO VALUE* ovpt; diagonal *ANNULLATO* perforation.	—	—	—
☐	bs3.	Diagonal red *SPECIMEN OF NO VALUE* ovpt.	—	—	—
☐	cs3.	Diagonal *SPECIMEN OF NO VALUE* overprint.	—	—	275

BNS B9 (P8, P12 & P16): **100 scellini / 100 shillings** VG VF UNC
Blue and red. Front: Vase; statuette; musical instrument. Back: Trees; National Assembly building in Mogadishu. Solid security thread. Watermark: Leopard head. Printer: (TDLR). 164 x 81 mm.

			VG	VF	UNC
☐	a.	1966. Signature 2.	35	120	600
☐	b.	1968. Signature 3.	40	125	850
☐	c.	1971. Signature 4. Intro: 10.03.1972.	20	150	900
☐	as1.	Diagonal red *SPECIMEN* and DLR oval ovpts; horizontal red *SPECIMEN Nº* # ovpt at lower left.	—	—	525
☐	as3.	Diagonal red *SPECIMEN OF NO VALUE* ovpt.	—	—	—
☐	bs2.	Diagonal red *SPECIMEN OF NO VALUE* ovpt; diagonal *ANNULLATO* perforation.	—	—	—
☐	bs3.	Diagonal red *SPECIMEN OF NO VALUE* ovpt.	—	—	—
☐	cs3.	Diagonal red *SPECIMEN OF NO VALUE* ovpt.	—	—	375

Bankiga Qaranka Soomaaliyeed
(Somali National Bank)

SNB Signature Varieties

	TALIYAHA (President)	LACAGHAYAHA (Cashier)
1	Omar Ahmed Omar	Mohamed Dalmar

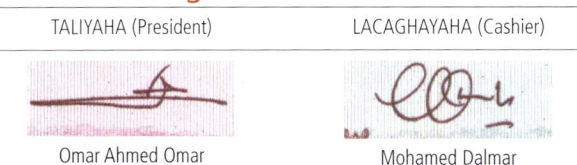

1975 Issues

SNB B1 (P17): **5 shillings** (<US$0.01)   VG   VF   UNC

Burgundy, green, and orange. Front: Coat of arms; three wildebeests/gnus and two zebras; bananas. Back: Three men harvesting bananas. Solid security thread. Watermark: Sayyīd Mohammed Abdullah Hassan. Printer: (TDLR). 152 x 72 mm.

☐ a. 1975. Signature 1.   5   15   50
☐ as1. Diagonal black *SPECIMEN* and DLR oval ovpts;   —   —   —
    horizon. black *SPECIMEN Nº* # ovpt at lower left.
☐ as2. Diagonal black *SPECIMEN OF NO VALUE* ovpt.   —   —   —

Replacement notes: Series Z001.

SNB B2 (P18): **10 shillings** (<US$0.01)   VG   VF   UNC

Green. Front: Coat of arms; minaret of Abdul Aziz mosque in Mogadishu. Back: Boat at anchor; men constructing boat on beach; fishing net. Solid security thread. Watermark: Sayyīd Mohammed Abdullah Hassan. Printer: (TDLR). 152 x 72 mm.

☐ a. 1975. Signature 1.   5   20   60
☐ as1. Diagonal red *SPECIMEN* and DLR oval ovpts;   —   —   —
    horizontal red *SPECIMEN Nº* # ovpt at lower left.
☐ as2. Diagonal red *SPECIMEN OF NO VALUE* ovpt.   —   —   —

Replacement notes: Series Z001.

SNB B3 (P19): **20 shillings** (US$0.01)   VG   VF   UNC

Brown. Front: Coat of arms; Somali National Bank headquarters building in Mogadishu; trees. Back: Cattle walking along stream; trees. Solid security thread. Watermark: Sayyīd Mohammed Abdullah Hassan. Printer: (TDLR). 165 x 80 mm.

☐ a. 1975. Signature 1.   15   50   275
☐ as1. Diagonal red *SPECIMEN* and DLR oval ovpts;   —   —   —
    horizontal red *SPECIMEN Nº* # ovpt at lower left.
☐ as2. Diagonal red *SPECIMEN OF NO VALUE* ovpt.   —   —   —

SNB B4 (P20): **100 shillings** (US$0.05)   VG   VF   UNC

Blue, green, and orange. Front: Coat of arms; woman with baby in sling, rifle in one hand, shovel and hoe in the other hand; laurels; Dagahtur (throwing stones) monument. Back: Men and women working in fruit processing factory. Solid security thread. Watermark: Sayyīd Mohammed Abdullah Hassan. Printer: (TDLR). 165 x 80 mm.

- ☐ a. 1975. Signature 1.   10   40   175
- ☐ as1. Diagonal red *SPECIMEN* and DLR oval ovpts;   —   —   —
  horizontal red *SPECIMEN N°* # ovpt at lower left.
- ☐ as2. Diagonal red *SPECIMEN OF NO VALUE* ovpt.   —   —   —

Replacement notes: Series Z001.

Bankiga Dhexe ee Soomaaliya (Central Bank of Somalia)

CBS Signature Varieties

	TALIYAHA (President)	LACAGHAYAHA (Cashier)
1	Omar Ahmed Omar	Ali Sheikh Hussein
	GUDDOOMIYAHA (Chairman)	LACAGHAYAHA (Cashier)
2	Mohamud Jama Ahmed	Barre Haji Omar
3	Mohamud Jama Ahmed	Hassan Elmi Barkhadle
4	Omar Ahmed Omar	Hassan Elmi Barkhadle
5	Mahmud Muhommad Nur	Hassan Elmi Barkhadle
6	Ali Abdi Amalow (October 1990 - Unknown)	Hassan Elmi Barkhadle

1977-1981 Issues

These notes are like the preceding issues, but with the new name of the issuer, new decrees, new dates, and new signatures. The front of the new 5-shilling note was subsequently redesigned to replace the non-native wildebeests and zebras with water buffalo.

CBS B1 (P20A): **5 shillings** (<US$0.01)   VG   VF   UNC

Burgundy, green, and orange. Front: Coat of arms; three wildebeests/gnus and two zebras; bananas. Back: Three men harvesting bananas. Solid security thread. Watermark: Sayyīd Mohammed Abdullah Hassan. Printer: Unknown. 152 x 72 mm.

☐	a. 1978. Signature 1.	5	20	60
☐	as. Diagonal black *SPECIMEN* overprint.	—	—	25

Replacement notes: Series Z001.

CBS B2 (P21): **5 shillings** (<US$0.01)   VG   VF   UNC

Burgundy, green, and orange. Front: Coat of arms; six water buffalo; bananas. Back: Three men harvesting bananas. Solid security thread. Watermark: Sayyīd Mohammed Abdullah Hassan. Printer: Unknown. 152 x 72 mm.

☐	a. 1978. Signature 1.	2	7.50	30
☐	as. Diagonal black *SPECIMEN* and DLR oval ovpts; horizon. black *SPECIMEN N°* # ovpt at lower left.	—	—	—

Replacement notes: Series Z001.

CBS B3 (P22 & P26): **10 shillings** (<US$0.01)   VG   VF   UNC

Green. Front: Coat of arms; minaret of Abdul Aziz mosque in Mogadishu. Back: Boat at anchor; men constructing boat on beach; fishing net. Solid yellow security thread. Watermark: Sayyīd Mohammed Abdullah Hassan. Printer: Unknown. 152 x 72 mm.

☐	a. 1978. Signature 1. Black serial numbers.	1	4	25
☐	b. 1980. Signature 2. Red serial numbers.	1	4	12
☐	as. Specimen.	—	—	25
☐	bs. Diagonal black *SPECIMEN* and DLR oval ovpts; horizon. black *SPECIMEN N°* # ovpt at lower left.	—	—	—

Replacement notes: Series Z001.

CBS B4 (P23, P27 & P29): **20 shillings** (US$0.01)   VG   VF   UNC

Brown. Front: Coat of arms; Somali National Bank headquarters building in Mogadishu; trees. Back: Cattle walking along stream; trees. Solid yellow security thread. Watermark: Sayyīd Mohammed Abdullah Hassan. Printer: Unknown. 165 x 80 mm.

☐	a. 1978. Signature 1. Black serial numbers.	3	12	50
☐	b. 1980. Signature 2. Red serial numbers.	2	8	35
☐	c. 1981.	5	25	110
☐	as. Specimen.	—	—	40

Replacement notes: Series Z001.

CBS B5 (P24, P28 & P30): **100 shillings** (US$0.05)   VG   VF   UNC
Blue, green, and orange. Front: Coat of arms; woman with baby in sling, rifle in one hand, shovel and hoe in the other hand; laurels; Dagahtur (throwing stones) monument. Back: Men and women working in fruit processing factory. Solid yellow security thread. Watermark: Sayyīd Mohammed Abdullah Hassan. Printer: Unknown. 165 x 80 mm.

		VG	VF	UNC
☐ a.	1978. Signature 1. Black serial numbers.	4	17	70
☐ b.	1980. Signature 2. Red serial numbers.	5	25	100
☐ c.	1981.	4	17	70
☐ as.	Specimen.	—	—	25

Replacement notes: Series Z001 and ZZ001.

1982-1983 Issues

These notes retain the basic design elements of the preceding issues, but are reduced in size. The 50-shilling note is a new denomination.

CBS B6 (P31): **5 shillings** (<US$0.01)   VG   VF   UNC
Burgundy. Front: Six water buffalo; coat of arms; star. Back: Three men harvesting bananas. No security thread. Watermark: None. Printer: Unknown. 120 x 60 mm.

		VG	VF	UNC
☐ a.	1983. Signature 3.	FV	0.50	2.50
☐ b.	1986. Signature 4.	FV	0.50	2
☐ c.	1987.	FV	0.25	1

Replacement notes: Series Z001.

CBS B7 (P32): **10 shillings** (<US$0.01)   VG   VF   UNC
Green. Front: Historic Abdul-Aziz mosque in Mogadishu; coat of arms; star. Back: Boat at anchor; men constructing boat on beach; fishing net. Solid yellow security thread. Watermark: Sayyīd Mohammed Abdullah Hassan. Printer: Unknown. 133 x 68 mm.

		VG	VF	UNC
☐ a.	1983. Signature 3.	0.25	1	4
☐ b.	1986. Signature 4.	0.25	1	4
☐ c.	1987.	0.25	1	4

Replacement notes: Series Z001.

CBS B8 (P33): **20 shillings** (US$0.01)   VG   VF   UNC
Brown. Front: Somali National Bank headquarters building in Mogadishu; coat of arms; star. Back: Cattle walking along stream; trees. Solid yellow security thread. Watermark: Sayyīd Mohammed Abdullah Hassan. Printer: Unknown. 137 x 70 mm.

		VG	VF	UNC
☐ a.	1983. Signature 3.	0.25	1.50	6
☐ b.	1986. Signature 4.	0.25	1.50	6
☐ c.	1987.	0.25	0.75	3
☐ d.	1989. Signature 5.	0.25	1	4

Replacement notes: Series Z001.

CBS B9 (P34): **50 shillings** (<US$0.05)   VG   VF   UNC

Brown, red, and green. Front: Ruins of mosque in Hamar Weyne district of Mogadishu; coat of arms; star. Back: Men and women with camels, cattle, and sheep at feeding trough. Solid yellow security thread. Watermark: Sayyīd Mohammed Abdullah Hassan. Printer: Unknown. 142 x 72 mm.

☐	a.	1983. Signature 3.	2.50	10	20
☐	b.	1986. Signature 4.	0.25	1.25	6
☐	c.	1987.	1	4	12
☐	d.	Signature 5.	0.50	2	8
☐	e.	1988.	0.50	2	8
☐	f.	1989.	0.50	2	8

Replacement notes: Series Z001.

CBS B10 (P35): **100 shillings** (US$0.05)   VG   VF   UNC

Blue, green, and orange. Front: Woman with baby in sling, rifle in one hand, shovel and hoe in the other hand; laurels; coat of arms; Dagahtur (throwing stones) monument; star. Back: Men and women working in fruit processing factory. Solid yellow security thread. Watermark: Sayyīd Mohammed Abdullah Hassan. Printer: (DLR). 148 x 74 mm.

☐	a.	1983. Signature 3.	2	8	35
☐	b.	1986. Signature 4.	0.25	1.25	5
☐	c.	1987.	0.25	1.25	5
☐	d.	Signature 5.	0.25	1.25	5
☐	e.	1988.	0.50	2.50	10
☐	f.	1989.	0.25	1.25	5
☐	as.	Diagonal black *SPECIMEN* and DLR oval ovpts; horizon. black *SPECIMEN N°* # ovpt at lower left.	—	—	—

Replacement notes: Series Z001.

1989-1996 Issues

Somalia's failing economy necessitated the issuance of these two new higher denominations. The centralized government ceased to function after the outbreak of civil war in November 1990, so notes dated 1996 are not official issues of the Central Bank of Somalia; they are unauthorized notes issued by rival warlords or local businessmen and might well be considered counterfeits.

CBS B11 (P36): **500 shillings** (US$0.30)   VG   VF   UNC

Green. Front: Fisherman repairing net; spiny lobster; coat of arms; star; fish; man poling boat. Back: Solidarity mosque in Mogadishu. Solid yellow security thread. Watermark: Sayyīd Mohammed Abdullah Hassan. Printer: (DLR). 148 x 74 mm.

☐	a.	1989. Signature 5.	FV	FV	6
☐	b.	Signature 4.	FV	FV	6
☐	c.	1990.	FV	FV	6
☐	d.	1996. Signature 6.	FV	FV	3
☐	ds.	Diagonal red *SPECIMEN* overprint; horizontal red # overprint at lower left.	—	—	—

Replacement notes: Series Z001.

SOMALIA 1991 ISSUES

CBS B12 (P37): **1,000 shillings** (US$0.60)   VG   VF   UNC
Orange, purple, and green. Front: Two women weaving baskets and mats; coat of arms. Back: City coastline; ships and buildings at port of Mogadishu. Watermark: Sayyīd Mohammed Abdullah Hassan. Printer: Unknown. 154 x 76 mm. Intaglio.

☐	a. 1990. Signature 4. Solid yellow security thread.	FV	FV	1.50
☐	b. 1996. Signature 6. Plain 6-digit serial number.	FV	FV	2
☐	c. Fancy 6-digit serial number.	FV	FV	2
☐	d. Fancy 7-digit serial number. No security thread.	FV	FV	2
☐	bs. Diagonal red *SPECIMEN* overprint; horizontal red # overprint at lower left.	—	—	275

Replacement notes: Series Z001.
For lithographed note with purple *1000* at center front, see CBS B15.

The 1,000-shilling note dated 1996 is available in plain (CBS B12b, above left) and fancy (CBS B12c, above right) serial number font varieties.

Mogadishu Northern Forces

1991 Issues

In response to the economic crisis of 1990, the government established the new Somali shilling worth 100 old shillings. Two denominations of new shilling notes were printed and delivered in late 1991, after civil war had broken out. The notes were seized by interim president Ali Mahdi Mohamed and circulated in areas under the control of his Mogadishu Northern Forces.

CBS B13 (PR1): **20 N shillings**   VG   VF   UNC
Purple, red, yellow, and green. Front: Coat of arms; man with camel; star. Back: Field workers picking cotton. Solid yellow security thread. Watermark: Sayyīd Mohammed Abdullah Hassan. Printer: Unknown. 134 x 68 mm.

☐	a. 1991. Signature 4.	0.25	0.50	1

Replacement notes: Prefix ZZ.

CBS B14 (PR2): **50 N shillings**   VG   VF   UNC
Green, brown, and blue. Front: Coat of arms; man with hand loom; star. Back: Man with donkey carrying three children. Watermark: Sayyīd Mohammed Abdullah Hassan. Printer: Unknown. 138 x 71 mm.

☐	a. 1991. Signature 4. Solid yellow security thread.	0.25	0.50	1
☐	b. Solid black security thread.	0.25	0.50	1

Puntland Region

1990 Issue

This note was printed by Pura Group in Indonesia for the administration of the Puntland region. Like the last of the authorized 1,000-shilling notes (CBS B12) issued by the Central Bank of Somalia, it is dated 1990, though it was produced and issued regionally in 1999. It can be distinguished from the authorized issue by its lithograph (not intaglio) printing, and the purple (not green) *1000* at front center.

CBS B15 (PR10): **1,000 shillings** (US$0.60)   VG   VF   UNC

Orange, purple, and green. Front: Two women weaving baskets and mats; coat of arms. Back: City coastline; ships and buildings at port of Mogadishu. No security thread. Watermark: Sayyid Mohammed Abdullah Hassan. Printer: (Pura Group, Indonesia). 154 x 76 mm. Lithographed.

☐ a. 1990. Signature 4. Intro: 1999.   0.25   0.50   1

For intaglio note with green *1000* at center front, see CBS B12.

Acknowledgements

This chapter was compiled with the generous assistance of Thomas Augustsson, Jean-Michel Engels, Chris Hall, John Miskell, Wally Myers, Luca Maria Peri, Bill Stubkjaer, Christoph Thomas, Frank van Tiel, Ludek Vostal, and others.

Sources

Augustsson, Thomas. "The Story of Somalia 20 and 50 N.Shillings." *IBNS Journal.* Volume 37 Number 3. p.40.

Cuhaj, George S. *Standard Catalog of World Paper Money, Modern Issues, 1961-Present.* 17th edition. 2011. ISBN 978-1-4402-1584-1. Krause Publications (www.krausebooks.com), 700 East State St., Iola, WI, 54990-0001.

Symes, Peter. "The Bank Notes of Somalia — Part I." *IBNS Journal.* Volume 45 Number 1. p.6.

Symes, Peter. "The Bank Notes of Somalia — Part II." *IBNS Journal.* Volume 45 Number 2. p.20.

Symes, Peter. Reference Site for Islamic Banknotes (www.islamicbanknotes.com).

Share Your Input, Info, and Images

This catalog is believed to be complete and correct as of the time of publication. Prices and face values were last updated 14 October 2011. Please report errors or omissions so that corrections may be made. If you can more precisely identify the name or location of anything depicted on a note, please share that information. Furthermore, if you own an unlisted type or variety, please submit scans of the front and back of the note so that it can be documented. Scans should be 300 dots per inch, 100% actual size, 24-bit color, saved as *uncompressed* JPEG files, and sent to owen@banknotenews.com. Be sure to fully describe all attributes of the note which are not apparent upon visual inspection of the images alone, such as physical dimension, watermark, and security thread.

Somaliland

For earlier issues, see Somalia.

Somaliland is an autonomous region in the northern part of the Somali republic (shown in its entirety above) located in the Horn of Africa. The Republic of Somaliland considers itself to be the successor state of the former British Somaliland protectorate. Having declared its own local government in Somalia on 18 May 1991, Somaliland remains unrecognized by any country or international organization.

Monetary System
18.10.1994: 1 Somaliland shilling = 100 Somali shillings (SOS)

Baanka Somaliland (Bank of Somaliland)

For more information, visit www.somalilandgov.com/bank.htm.

BOS Signature Varieties

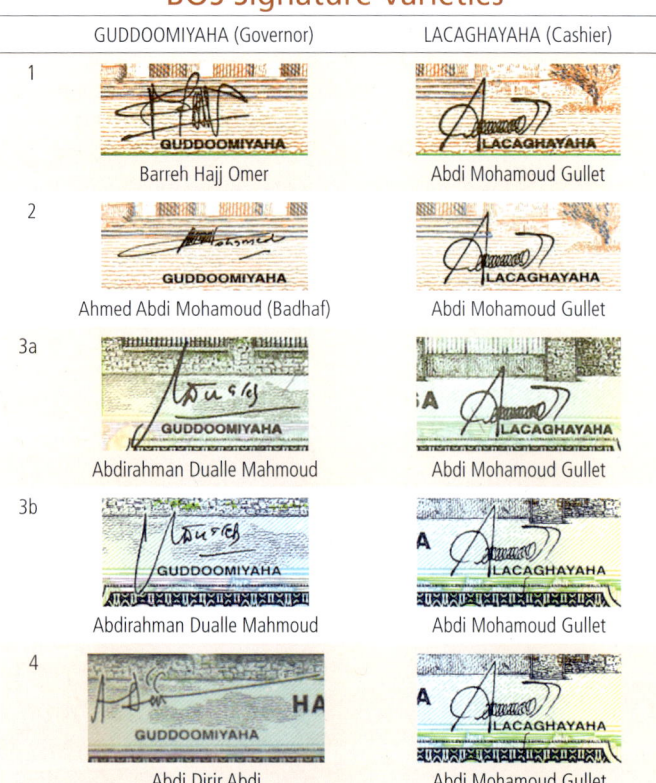

1994 Issues

These notes were first introduced on 18 October 1994, and replaced the Somali shilling (at a rate of 100 to 1), which ceased being legal tender in Somaliland after 31 January 1995. The name of the capital (Hargeysa) is printed next to the date on the front of each note.

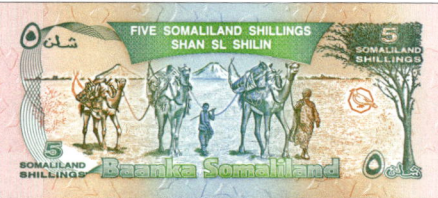

BOS B1 (P1): 5 shillings (<US$0.01) VG VF UNC
Green and brown. Front: Goodirka (former House of Representative; now Supreme Court building); male greater kudu. Back: Two nomads with three camels; twin hills of Naasa-Hablood (Somali for Girls' Breasts) near Hargeisa; tree. No security thread. Watermark: None. Printer: Unknown. 120 x 53 mm.
- a. 1994. Signature 1. Intro: 18.10.1994. — — 1
- as. Diagonal red hollow *SPECIMEN* overprint; horiz. red *SPECIMEN Nº#* overprint at lower left. — — 100

BOS B2 (P2): 10 shillings (<US$0.01) VG VF UNC
Purple and brown. Front: Goodirka (former House of Representative; now Supreme Court building); male greater kudu. Back: Two nomads with three camels; twin hills of Naasa-Hablood (Somali for Girls' Breasts) near Hargeisa; tree. No security thread. Watermark: None. Printer: Unknown. 120 x 53 mm.
- a. 1994. Signature 1. Intro: 18.10.1994. — — 1.50
- b. 1996. Signature 2. — — 1.50
- as. Diagonal red hollow *SPECIMEN* overprint; horiz. red *SPECIMEN Nº#* overprint at lower left. — — 100

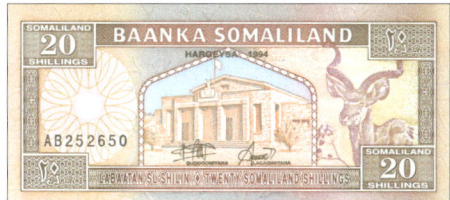

BOS B3 (P3): **20 shillings** (<US$0.01)   VG   VF   UNC
Brown. Front: Goodirka (former House of Representative; now Supreme Court building); male greater kudu. Back: Two nomads with three camels; twin hills of Naasa-Hablood (Somali for Girls' Breasts) near Hargeisa; tree. No security thread. Watermark: None. Printer: Unknown. 120 x 53 mm.

     ☐ a.   1994. Signature 1. Intro: 18.10.1994.   —   —   2
     ☐ b.   1996. Signature 2.   —   —   2
     ☐ as.   Specimen.   —   —   100

BOS B4 (P4): **50 shillings** (<US$0.01)   VG   VF   UNC
Blue and brown. Front: Goodirka (former House of Representative; now Supreme Court building); male greater kudu. Back: Two nomads with three camels; twin hills of Naasa-Hablood (Somali for Girls' Breasts) near Hargeisa; tree. No security thread. Watermark: None. Printer: Unknown. 120 x 53 mm.

     ☐ a.   1994. Signature 1. Intro: 18.10.1994.   —   —   6
     ☐ as.   Specimen.   —   —   100

BOS B5 (P5): **100 shillings** (<US$0.01)   VG   VF   UNC
Dark brown. Front: Bank of Somaliland building in Hargeisa; trees; camels. Back: Herdsmen with flock of sheep and goats on Berbera dock; ship; trucks. No security thread. Watermark: None. Printer: Unknown. 135 x 62 mm.

     ☐ a.   1994. Signature 1. Intro: 18.10.1994.   —   —   6
     ☐ b.   1996. Signature 2.   —   —   3
     ☐ c.   1999. Signature 3a.   —   —   3
     ☐ d.   2002.   —   —   3
     ☐ as.   Diagonal red *SPECIMEN* overprint.   —   —   100
     ☐ bs.   Specimen.   —   —   100

BOS B6 (P6): **500 shillings** (US$0.05)   VG   VF   UNC
Blue. Front: Bank of Somaliland building in Hargeisa; trees; camels. Back: Herdsmen with flock of sheep and goats on Berbera dock; ship; trucks. No security thread. Watermark: None. Printer: Unknown. 145 x 66 mm.

     ☐ a.   1994. Signature 1. Intro: 18.10.1994.   —   —   12
     ☐ b.   1996. Signature 2.   —   —   6
     ☐ c.   1999. Signature 3a.   —   —   6
     ☐ as.   Diagonal red *SPECIMEN* overprint.   —   —   100
     ☐ bs.   Specimen.   —   —   100

1996 Issues

This 50-shilling note is like the 1994 issue of the same denomination, but larger in size.

BOS B7 (P7): **50 shillings** (<US$0.01)   VG   VF   UNC
Blue and brown. Front: Goodirka (former House of Representative; now Supreme Court building); male greater kudu. Back: Two nomads with three camels; twin hills of Naasa-Hablood (Somali for Girls' Breasts) near Hargeisa; tree. No security thread. Watermark: None. Printer: Unknown. 130 x 58 mm.

     a.   1996. Signature 1.   —   —   2.50
     b.   Signature 2.   —   —   2.50
     c.   1999. Signature 3a.   —   —   2.50
     d.   2002.   —   —   2.50
     bs.   Diagonal red hollow *SPECIMEN* overprint; horiz. red *SPECIMEN* Nº# ovpt at lower center.   —   —   —

1996 "Gold" Commemorative Issues

Notes of the first series were overprinted *5th Anniversary of Independence 18 May 1996* and *Sanad Gurada 5ee Gobanimadda 18 May 1996* on the front in gold-colored ink. It is not known whether these notes were issued by Baanka Somaliland to circulate within Somaliland or created by an enterprising numismatic dealer for sale strictly to international collectors.

BOS B8 (P8): **5 shillings** (<US$0.01)   VG   VF   UNC
Green and brown. Front: Goodirka (former House of Representative; now Supreme Court building); male greater kudu; gold anniversary overprint. Back: Two nomads with three camels; twin hills of Naasa-Hablood (Somali for Girls' Breasts) near Hargeisa; tree. No security thread. Watermark: None. Printer: Unknown. 120 x 53 mm.

     a.   18 May 1996 over 1994. Signature 1.   —   —   2

BOS B9 (P9): **10 shillings** (<US$0.01)   VG   VF   UNC
Purple and brown. Front: Goodirka (former House of Representative; now Supreme Court building); male greater kudu; gold anniversary overprint. Back: Two nomads with three camels; twin hills of Naasa-Hablood (Somali for Girls' Breasts) near Hargeisa; tree. No security thread. Watermark: None. Printer: Unknown. 120 x 53 mm.

     a.   18 May 1996 over 1994. Signature 1.   —   —   3

BOS B10 (P10): **20 shillings** (<US$0.01)   VG   VF   UNC
Brown. Front: Goodirka (former House of Representative; now Supreme Court building); male greater kudu; gold anniversary overprint. Back: Two nomads with three camels; twin hills of Naasa-Hablood (Somali for Girls' Breasts) near Hargeisa; tree. No security thread. Watermark: None. Printer: Unknown. 120 x 53 mm.

     a.   18 May 1996 over 1994. Signature 1.   —   —   4

BOS B11 (P11): **50 shillings** (<US$0.01)   VG   VF   UNC
Blue and brown. Front: Goodirka (former House of Representative; now Supreme Court building); male greater kudu; gold anniversary overprint. Back: Two nomads with three camels; twin hills of Naasa-Hablood (Somali for Girls' Breasts) near Hargeisa; tree. No security thread. Watermark: None. Printer: Unknown. 120 x 53 mm.

     a.   18 May 1996 over 1994. Signature 1.   —   —   5
Overprinted on B4a.

BOS B12 (P11A): **50 shillings** (<US$0.01)   VG VF UNC
Blue and brown. Front: Goodirka (former House of Representative; now Supreme Court building); male greater kudu; gold anniversary overprint. Back: Two nomads with three camels; twin hills of Naasa-Hablood (Somali for Girls' Breasts) near Hargeisa; tree. No security thread. Watermark: None. Printer: Unknown. 130 x 58 mm.
    ☐ a. 18 May 1996 over 1996. Signature 1.   — — 5
Overprinted on B7a.

BOS B13 (P12): **100 shillings** (<US$0.01)   VG VF UNC
Dark brown. Front: Goodirka (former House of Representative; now Supreme Court building); trees; camels; gold anniversary overprint. Back: Herdsmen with flock of sheep and goats on Berbera dock; ship; trucks. No security thread. Watermark: None. Printer: Unknown. 135 x 62 mm.
    ☐ a. 18 May 1996 over 1994. Signature 1.   — — 8

BOS B14 (P13): **500 shillings** (<US$0.05)   VG VF UNC
Blue. Front: Goodirka (former House of Representative; now Supreme Court building); trees; camels; gold anniversary overprint. Back: Herdsmen with flock of sheep and goats on Berbera dock; ship; trucks. No security thread. Watermark: None. Printer: Unknown. 145 x 66 mm.
    ☐ a. 18 May 1996 over 1994. Signature 1.   — — 20

1996 "Silver" Commemorative Issues

Notes of the first series were overprinted *Sanad Gurada 5ee Gobanimadda 18 May 1996* on the front in silver-colored ink. It is not known whether these notes were issued by Baanka Somaliland to circulate within Somaliland or created by an enterprising numismatic dealer for sale strictly to international collectors.

BOS B15 (P14): **5 shillings** (<US$0.01)   VG VF UNC
Green and brown. Front: Goodirka (former House of Representative; now Supreme Court building); male greater kudu; silver anniversary overprint. Back: Two nomads with three camels; twin hills of Naasa-Hablood (Somali for Girls' Breasts) near Hargeisa; tree. No security thread. Watermark: None. Printer: Unknown. 120 x 53 mm.
    ☐ a. 18 May 1996 over 1994. Signature 1.   — — 2

BOS B16 (P15): **10 shillings** (<US$0.01) VG VF UNC
Purple and brown. Front: Goodirka (former House of Representative; now Supreme Court building); male greater kudu; silver anniversary overprint. Back: Two nomads with three camels; twin hills of Naasa-Hablood (Somali for Girls' Breasts) near Hargeisa; tree. No security thread. Watermark: None. Printer: Unknown. 120 x 53 mm.
    ☐ a. 18 May 1996 over 1994. Signature 1.   — — 3

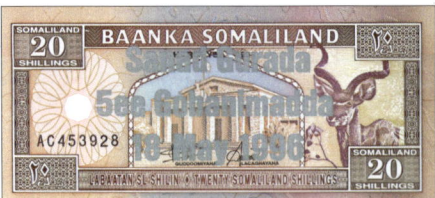

BOS B17 (P16): **20 shillings** (<US$0.01) VG VF UNC
Brown. Front: Goodirka (former House of Representative; now Supreme Court building); male greater kudu; silver anniversary overprint. Back: Two nomads with three camels; twin hills of Naasa-Hablood (Somali for Girls' Breasts) near Hargeisa; tree. No security thread. Watermark: None. Printer: Unknown. 120 x 53 mm.
    ☐ a. 18 May 1996 over 1994. Signature 1.   — — 4

BOS B18 (P17): **50 shillings** (<US$0.01) VG VF UNC
Blue and brown. Front: Goodirka (former House of Representative; now Supreme Court building); male greater kudu; silver anniversary overprint. Back: Two nomads with three camels; twin hills of Naasa-Hablood (Somali for Girls' Breasts) near Hargeisa; tree. No security thread. Watermark: None. Printer: Unknown. 120 x 53 mm.
    ☐ a. 18 May 1996 over 1994. Signature 1.   — — 5
Overprinted on B4a.

BOS B19 (P17A): **50 shillings** (<US$0.01) VG VF UNC
Blue and brown. Front: Goodirka (former House of Representative; now Supreme Court building); male greater kudu; silver anniversary overprint. Back: Two nomads with three camels; twin hills of Naasa-Hablood (Somali for Girls' Breasts) near Hargeisa; tree. No security thread. Watermark: None. Printer: Unknown. 130 x 58 mm.
    ☐ a. 18 May 1996 over 1996. Signature 1.   — — 5
    ☐ b. Signature 2.   — — 5
Overprinted on B7.

BOS B20 (P18): **100 shillings** (<US$0.01) VG VF UNC
Dark brown. Front: Bank of Somaliland building in Hargeisa; trees; camels. Back: Herdsmen with flock of sheep and goats on Berbera dock; ship; trucks. No security thread. Watermark: None. Printer: Unknown. 135 x 62 mm.
    ☐ a. 18 May 1996 over 1994. Signature 1.   — — 8

BOS B21 (P19): **500 shillings** (<US$0.05)   VG   VF   UNC
Blue. Front: Bank of Somaliland building in Hargeisa; trees; camels. Back: Herdsmen with flock of sheep and goats on Berbera dock; ship; trucks. No security thread. Watermark: None. Printer: Unknown. 145 x 66 mm.
    ☐ a. 18 May 1996 over 1994. Signature 1.   —   —   20

2002-2011 Issues

This note is like the preceding issues, but with a modified color scheme and a windowed security thread.

BOS B22 (P6): **500 shillings** (<US$0.05)   VG   VF   UNC
Blue. Front: Bank of Somaliland building in Hargeisa; trees; camels. Back: Herdsmen with flock of sheep and goats on Berbera dock; ship; trucks. Windowed security thread. Watermark: None. Printer: Unknown. 145 x 66 mm.
    ☐ a. 2002. Signature 3a. Thread at left.   —   —   6
    ☐ b. 2005.   —   —   6
    ☐ c. 2006. Thread at right with demetalized *BOS 500*.   —   —   5
    ☐ d. 2008. Signature 3b.   —   —   5
    ☐ e. 2011. Signature 4.   —   —   3
Replacement notes: Prefix ZZ.

2006 Numismatic Products

The following note was created exclusively for the numismatic market by Universal Coins in Canada and has never been legal tender within Somaliland or anywhere else. Reportedly 20,000 notes were produced, along with 1,000 specimens packaged in a booklet.

BOS BNP1 (PCS1a): **1,000 shillings**   UNC
Purple, brown, and orange. Front: Lion; girl with hood; camel holographic patch. Back: Lion; camel. No security thread. Watermark: Diagonal line pattern. Printer: Unknown. 160 x 76 mm.
    ☐ a. ٢٠٠٦ 2006.   5
        Signature: Hussein (Awil) Ali Du'aleh, MINISTER OF FINANCE.

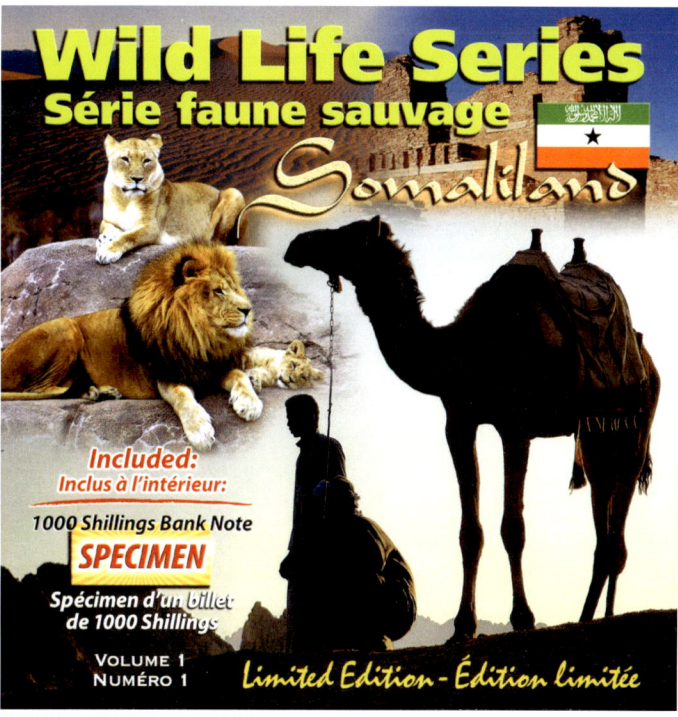

BOS BNP2 (PCS1s): **1,000 shillings**   UNC
    ☐ a. Specimen of BNP1 in folder.   6.50

2011 Issues

BOS B23 (PNL): **1,000 shillings** (US$0.10)　　　　**VG　VF　UNC**
Red. Front: Bank of Somaliland building in Hargeisa; trees; camels. Back: Herdsmen with flock of sheep and goats on Berbera dock; ship; trucks. Windowed security thread with demetalized *BOS 1000*. Watermark: None. Printer: Unknown. 145 x 66 mm.
　☐　a.　2011. Signature 4.　　　　　　　—　—　6

BOS B24 (PNL): **5,000 shillings** (US$0.50)　　　　**VG　VF　UNC**
Green. Front: Bank of Somaliland building in Hargeisa; trees; camels. Back: Three camels and three goats. Windowed security thread with demetalized *BOS 5000*. Watermark: None. Printer: Unknown. 145 x 66 mm.
　☐　a.　2011. Signature 4.　　　　　　　—　—　30

Acknowledgements

This chapter was compiled with the generous assistance of Thomas Augustsson, Pierguido Laffi, Art Levenite, John Miskell, Wally Myers, Andrew Roberts, Bill Stubkjaer, Christoph Thomas, Frank van Tiel, Dennis Zammit, and others.

Sources

Cuhaj, George S. *Standard Catalog of World Paper Money, Modern Issues, 1961-Present*. 17th edition. 2011. ISBN 978-1-4402-1584-1. Krause Publications (www.krausebooks.com), 700 East State St., Iola, WI, 54990-0001.

Symes, Peter. "The Bank Notes of Somalia—Part II." *IBNS Journal*. Volume 45 Number 2. p.20.

Symes, Peter. Reference Site for Islamic Banknotes (www.islamicbanknotes.com).

Share Your Input, Info, and Images

This catalog is believed to be complete and correct as of the time of publication. Prices and face values were last updated 3 June 2011. Please report errors or omissions so that corrections may be made. If you can more precisely identify the name or location of anything depicted on a note, please share that information. Furthermore, if you own an unlisted type or variety, please submit scans of the front and back of the note so that it can be documented. Scans should be 300 dots per inch, 100% actual size, 24-bit color, saved as *uncompressed* JPEG files, and sent to owen@banknotenews.com. Be sure to fully describe all attributes of the note which are not apparent upon visual inspection of the images alone, such as physical dimension, watermark, and security thread.

South Arabia

For earlier issues, see East Africa and India.

Monetary System
1 South Arabian dinar = 1,000 fils

South Arabian Currency Authority

The lands that would become modern Yemen had long been under the control of colonial powers. The Ottoman Empire controlled the north until 1918 and the British Empire controlled the south. Upon independence, the north was known as the Mutawakkilite Kingdom of Yemen, but in 1962, it became the Arab Republic of Yemen, while Britain's colony around the southern port of Aden joined with neighboring protectorates to form the Federation of South Arabia.

For notes issued in the north, see Arab Republic of Yemen.

On 13 October 1964, the South Arabian Currency Authority (SACA) was created by enactment of the Currency Law.

SACA Signature Varieties

	SECRETARY	(Chairman)
1	John Ashington Owen (1964 - November 1965)	Sheik Abdul Bari Ali Bazara (1964 - 1967)
2	J. L. Ireland (November 1965 - 1967)	Sheik Abdul Bari Ali Bazara (1964 - 1967)

1965-1967 Issues

These dinar notes replaced the East African shillings at an exchange rate of 1:20.

SACA B1 (P1): **250 fils** (demonetized 11.06.1996)   VG   VF   UNC
Brown. Front: Dhow boat in Aden harbor. Back: Date palm tree. Solid security thread. Watermark: Camel head. Printer: *THOMAS DE LA RUE & COMPANY, LIMITED*. 140 x 70 mm.

☐ a.	No date. Signature 1. Intro: 01.04.1965.	2	8	35
☐ b.	Signature 2.	0.75	3	14
☐ as.	Specimen.	—	—	35
☐ bs.	Diagonal red *SPECIMEN* and DLR oval overprints; red *SPECIMEN Nº #* ovpt at lower left; punched.	—	—	—
☐ p.	All-zero serial numbers; sample signatures; black *PROOF Nº #* overprint at lower left.	—	—	600

Replacement notes: Prefix Z99, Z98, and Z97.

SACA B2 (P2): **500 fils** (demonetized 11.06.1996)   VG   VF   UNC
Green. Front: Dhow boat in Aden harbor. Back: Heads of wheat; date palm tree. Solid security thread. Watermark: Camel head. Printer: *THOMAS DE LA RUE & COMPANY, LIMITED*. 146 x 83 mm.

☐ a.	No date. Signature 1. Intro: 01.04.1965.	5	22	85
☐ b.	Signature 2.	2	8	30
☐ as.	Specimen.	—	—	50
☐ bs1.	Diagonal red *SPECIMEN* and DLR oval overprints; red *SPECIMEN Nº #* ovpt at lower left; punched.	—	—	—
☐ bs2.	Horizontal *SPECIMEN OF NO VALUE* perforation.	—	—	—

Replacement notes: Prefix Z99, Z98, and Z97.

SACA B3 (P3): **1 dinar** (demonetized 11.06.1996)   VG   VF   UNC
Blue. Front: Dhow boat in Aden harbor. Back: Cotton plant; date palm tree. Solid security thread. Watermark: Camel head. Printer: *THOMAS DE LA RUE & COMPANY, LIMITED*. 152 x 89 mm.

☐	a.	No date. Signature 1. Intro: 01.04.1965.	7.50	25	150
☐	b.	Signature 2.	15	30	60
☐	as.	Specimen.	—	—	75
☐	bs.	Diagonal red *SPECIMEN* and DLR oval overprints; red *SPECIMEN N°* # ovpt at lower left; punched.	—	—	—

Replacement notes: Prefix Z99, Z98, and Z97.

SACA B4 (P4): **5 dinars** (demonetized 11.06.1996)   VG   VF   UNC
Red. Front: Dhow boat in Aden harbor. Back: Millet (sorghum); date palm tree; cotton plant. Solid security thread. Watermark: Camel head. Printer: *THOMAS DE LA RUE & COMPANY, LIMITED*. 159 x 95 mm.

☐	a.	No date. Signature 1. Intro: 01.04.1965.	18	75	350
☐	b.	Signature 2.	5	10	40
☐	as.	Specimen.	—	—	100
☐	bs.	Diagonal red *SPECIMEN* and DLR oval overprints; red *SPECIMEN N°* # ovpt at lower left; punched.	—	—	—

Replacement notes: Prefix Z99, Z98, and Z97.

SACA B5 (P5): **10 dinars** (demonetized 11.06.1996)   VG   VF   UNC
Green. Front: Dhow boat in Aden harbor. Back: Cotton plant; heads of wheat; date palm tree; ears of corn. Solid security thread. Watermark: Camel head. Printer: *THOMAS DE LA RUE & COMPANY, LIMITED*. 165 x 95 mm.
-   a.   No date. Signature 2. Intro: 01.07.1967.   35   75   200
-   bs.   Diagonal red *SPECIMEN* and DLR oval overprints;   —   —   —
       red *SPECIMEN Nº* # ovpt at lower left; punched.

Replacement notes: Prefix Z99, Z98, and Z97.

Looking Forward

On 30 November 1967, the region of South Arabia gained its independence and became known as the People's Republic of Southern Yemen. Although never the official name, people began calling the country "South Yemen," and consequently used the term "North Yemen" to refer to the Arab Republic of Yemen. Alternate forms were "Yemen (Aden)" for South Yemen and "Yemen (Sana'a)" for North Yemen, after their respective capital cities.

Following a Communist take-over in "South Yemen," on 1 December 1970 the country's name changed again, this time to the People's Democratic Republic of Yemen. On 22 May 1990, the People's Democratic Republic of Yemen united with the Arab Republic of Yemen to form the Republic of Yemen. The South Yemeni dinar was one of the two official currencies used in the Republic of Yemen until 11 June 1996.

For later issues, see Democratic Republic of Yemen.

Acknowledgements

This chapter was compiled with the generous assistance of Jean-Michel Engels, Peter Symes, Christof Zellweger, and others.

Sources

Cuhaj, George S. *Standard Catalog of World Paper Money, Modern Issues, 1961-Present*. 17th edition. 2011. ISBN 978-1-4402-1584-1. Krause Publications (www.krausebooks.com), 700 East State St., Iola, WI, 54990-0001.

Symes, Peter and Murray Hanewich and Keith Street. *The Bank Notes of Yemen*. 1997. ISBN 0-646-30063-6. Canberra, Australia.

Symes, Peter. Reference Site for Islamic Banknotes (www.islamicbanknotes.com).

Share Your Input, Info, and Images

This catalog is believed to be complete and correct as of the time of publication. Prices and face values were last updated 27 January 2012. Please report errors or omissions so that corrections may be made. If you can more precisely identify the name or location of anything depicted on a note, please share that information. Furthermore, if you own an unlisted type or variety, please submit scans of the front and back of the note so that it can be documented. Scans should be 300 dots per inch, 100% actual size, 24-bit color, saved as *uncompressed* JPEG files, and sent to owen@banknotenews.com. Be sure to fully describe all attributes of the note which are not apparent upon visual inspection of the images alone, such as physical dimension, watermark, and security thread.

(South) Korea

For earlier issues, see Korea.

Contents

Bank of Chosen (BOC) 1942
Bank of Korea (BOK) 1943

Monetary System
1945: 1 South Korean won = 100 jeon
15.02.1953: 1 South Korean hwan = 100 jeon
09.06.1962: 1 new South Korean won (KRW) = 100 jeon

Specimens are available with all-zero and normal serial number varieties. The all-zero specimens command a premium.

Block number ranges represent only confirmed notes for the variety. If you know the definitive range, please share that knowledge, or help extend the range with observed block numbers.

Bank of Chosen

The Bank of Korea was founded in July 1909. Three years later, it became the Bank of Chosen (or Bank of Joseon), which was the central bank of Korea under Japanese rule, and of South Korea under American occupation. The Bank of Chosen (BOC) issued the Korean yen from 1910 to 1945 and the won from 1945 to 1950.

1949-1950 Issues

Following Japan's defeat in World War II, in August 1945 Korea was divided into a Soviet-occupied zone north of the 38th parallel and an American-occupied zone in the south. In 1948, Korea was divided into two separate countries (the Democratic People's Republic of Korea in the north, and the Republic of Korea in the south), each with their own currencies, both called won, and both of which replaced the yen at par.

The South Korean won was subdivided into 100 jeon. The value of the South Korean won was initially pegged at a rate of 15 won to 1 US dollar, although a series of devaluations followed over the years.

On these three notes, the denomination is expressed in Hanja (logographic Chinese characters) at center.

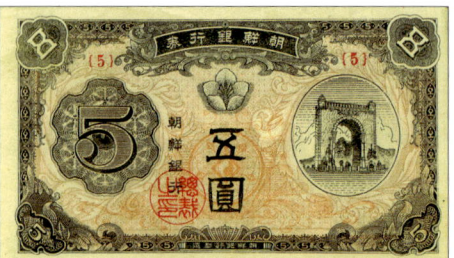

BOC B1 (P1): 5 圓 (won) (withdrawn 16.01.1953)   VG   VF   UNC
Black, orange, and lilac. Front: Bank logo (hibiscus syriacus flower); Independence Gate in Seoul. Back: Bank of Korea headquarters building in Seoul; bank logo. No security thread. Watermark: None. Printer: 造製行銀鮮朝 (Bank of Chosen). 123 x 72 mm.
     a.   No date. Block 1-5. Intro: 15.09.1949.   10   25   180
     as. Boxed red 見樣 handstamp.   —   —   500

BOC B2 (P2): 10 圓 (won) (withdrawn 16.01.1953)   VG   VF   UNC
Black, light blue, and lilac. Front: Bank logo (hibiscus syriacus flower); Independence Gate in Seoul. Back: Bank of Korea headquarters building in Seoul; bank logo. No security thread. Watermark: None. Printer: 造製行銀鮮朝 (Bank of Chosen). 130 x 74 mm.
     a.   No date. Block 15-43. Intro: 01.09.1949.   4   25   100
     as. Boxed red 見樣 handstamp.   —   —   500

BOC B3 (P3): 1,000 圓 (won)   VG   VF   UNC

Pink and light blue. Front: Bearded Yoon Shik Kim wearing hat; hibiscus syriacus flowers. Back: Hibiscus syriacus flowers. No security thread. Watermark: None. Printer: 造製社會式株刷印籍書鮮朝 (Chosen Book Printing Company). 160 x 91 mm.

- a. No date. Intro: 28.06.1950.   2.50   10   75
- as. Horizontal *SPECIMEN* perfs.   —   —   600

This note was unofficially issued by the North Korean Army during the Korean conflict.

Bank of Korea

The Bank of Korea (BOK) was established on 12 June 1950. On 26 August 1950, Bank of Chosen notes lost their legal tender status. For more information, visit www.bok.or.kr.

1949 Issues

On these three notes, the denomination is expressed in Hanja (logographic Chinese characters) at center on front, and in English on back.

Even though they bear the name Bank of Korea in English on the back, these notes were issued by the Bank of Chosen in 1949.

BOK B1 (P4): 5 chon (withdrawn 17.02.1953)   VG   VF   UNC

Red and orange. Front: Bank logo (hibiscus syriacus flower). Back: Bank logo (hibiscus syriacus flower). No security thread. Watermark: None. Printer: 造製行銀鮮朝 (Bank of Chosen). 91 x 41 mm.

- a. No date. Block 1. Intro: 15.11.1949.   4   15   60
- as. Boxed red 見樣 handstamp.   —   —   300

BOK B2 (P5): 10 chon (withdrawn 17.02.1953)   VG   VF   UNC

Brown, violet, and red. Front: Bank logo (hibiscus syriacus flower). Back: Bank logo (hibiscus syriacus flower). No security thread. Watermark: None. Printer: 造製行銀鮮朝 (Bank of Chosen). 95 x 43 mm.

- a. No date. Block 1. Intro: 15.11.1949.   10   40   150
- as. Boxed red 見樣 handstamp.   —   —   200

BOK B3 (P6): 50 chon (withdrawn 17.02.1953)   VG   VF   UNC

Blue, light green, and red. Front: Bank logo (hibiscus syriacus flower). Back: Bank logo (hibiscus syriacus flower). No security thread. Watermark: None. Printer: 造製行銀鮮朝 (Bank of Chosen). 101 x 46 mm.

- a. No date. Block 1. Intro: 15.11.1949.   10   40   175
- as. Boxed red 見樣 handstamp.   —   —   125

1950 Issues

These notes were issued during the Korean War.

BOK B4 (P7): 100 won (withdrawn 17.02.1953)   VG   VF   UNC
Olive green, light blue, and red. Front: Gwanghwamun gate to Gyeongbokgung palace in Seoul; mountain; two people. Back: Guilloche pattern. No security thread. Watermark: Character. Printer: (Bank of Korea). 158 x 78 mm.

- ☐ a. No date. Block 1-218. Intro: 22.07.1950.   1.50   6   25
- ☐ as. Vertical red 見本 overprint on front; horizontal red script *Specimen* overprint on back; punched.   —   —   650

BOK B5 (P8): 1,000 won (US$0.95) (withdrawn 17.02.1953)   VG   VF   UNC
Teal and lilac. Front: President Syngman Rhee wearing hanbok, traditional Korean dress. Back: Guilloche pattern. No security thread. Watermark: Character. 170 x 78 mm.

- ☐ a. No date. Intro: 22.07.1950.   6   25   100
  Block 1-500. Printer: (Bank of Japan).
- ☐ b. Block 501-581. Printer: (Bank of Korea).   6   25   100
- ☐ as. Vertical red 見本 overprint on front; horizontal red script *Specimen* on back.   —   —   650

1952-1953 Issues

These notes bear the year of printing expressed as the number of years since the founding of the Tan'gun dynasty. To convert to Western date format, subtract 2333 from the date printed on the front of the note.

The Korea Minting and Security Printing Corporation (KOMSCO) was founded on 1 October 1951 and is a government-owned corporation responsible for producing South Korea's coins and paper money. KOMSCO's headquarters are in Daejeon, South Korea. For more information, visit www.komsco.com.

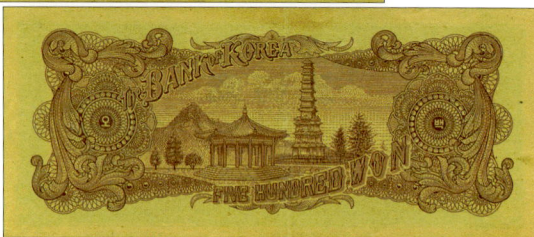

BOK B6 (P9): 500 won (withdrawn 17.02.1953)   VG   VF   UNC
Blue and brown. Front: President Syngman Rhee wearing hanbok, traditional Korean dress; bank logo (hibiscus syriacus flower). Back: Trees, mountain, and Pagoda Gongweon in Seoul. No security thread. Watermark: Character. Printer: 한국조폐공사 제조 (KOMSCO). 147 x 63 mm.

- ☐ a. 4285 (1952). Block 1-2. Intro: 10.10.1952.   5   40   275
- ☐ as. Horizontal red 見樣 overprint on front.   —   —   —

BOK B7 (P10): 1,000 won (US$0.95) (withdrawn 17.02.1953)   VG   VF   UNC
Brown, green, and teal. Front: President Syngman Rhee wearing hanbok, traditional Korean dress; bank logo (hibiscus syriacus flower). Back: Trees, mountain, and Pagoda Gongweon in Seoul. No security thread. Watermark: Character. Printer: 한국조폐공사 제조 (KOMSCO). 155 x 65 mm.

- ☐ a. 4285 (1952). Block 1-47. Intro: 10.10.1952.   2   8   35
- ☐ b. 4286 (1953). Block 48-67.   2.50   10   75
- ☐ as. Horizontal red 見樣 overprint on front.   —   —   —

1953 Hwan/Won Issues

On 15 February 1953, the South Korean won was replaced by the South Korean hwan at a rate of 100:1. These notes are denominated in hwan. However, the name of the currency appears incorrectly as "won" in English on the back, and in Hangul (원) on both sides; the currency is correctly written as "hwan" in Hanja.

The 1- and 5-hwan notes were printed in Korea from glass positives furnished by the US Bureau of Engraving and Printing. The three larger denominations were printed in the United States by Tudor Press in Boston, Massachusetts.

BOK B8 (P11): **1 hwan** (withdrawn 10.06.1962)   VG   VF   UNC
Lilac, light blue, orange, and red. Front: Guilloche pattern; laurel leaves. Back: Bank logo (hibiscus syriacus flower). No security thread. Printer: (KOMSCO). 111 x 54 mm.
- a. No date. Intro: 17.02.1953.   2   10   80
  Thin paper. Watermark: Characters. Block 1-43.
- b. Thick paper. Watermark: None. Block 43-50.   3   15   100
- as. Diagonal red *SPECIMEN* overprint on front.   —   —   —
- bs. Diagonal black *SPECIMEN* overprint on front.   —   —   —

BOK B9 (P12): **5 hwan** (withdrawn 10.06.1962)   VG   VF   UNC
Red, light blue, and orange. Front: Guilloche pattern; laurel leaves. Back: Bank logo (hibiscus syriacus flower). No security thread. Watermark: None. Printer: (KOMSCO). 111 x 54 mm.
- a. No date. Block 7-44. Intro: 17.02.1953.   2.50   10   50
- as1. Diagonal red *SPECIMEN* overprint on front.   —   —   —
- as2. Diagonal black *SPECIMEN* overprint on front.   —   —   —
- as3. Boxed red 見樣 overprint.   —   —   —

BOK B10 (P13): **10 hwan** (withdrawn 10.06.1962)   VG   VF   UNC
Blue, light blue, orange, and red. Front: Guilloche pattern; kobukson (ironclad turtle warship). Back: Bank logo (hibiscus syriacus flower). No security thread. Watermark: None. Printer: (Tudor Press). 156 x 66 mm.
- a. No date. Intro: 17.02.1953.   8   35   100
- as. Diagonal red *SPECIMEN* overprint.   —   —   500

Replacement notes: Prefix D with no suffix letter.

BOK B11 (P14): **100 hwan** (withdrawn 10.06.1962)   VG   VF   UNC
Green, light blue, orange, and red. Front: Guilloche pattern; kobukson (ironclad turtle warship). Back: Bank logo (hibiscus syriacus flower). No security thread. Watermark: None. Printer: (Tudor Press). 156 x 66 mm.
- a. No date. Intro: 17.02.1953.   10   40   200
- as. Diagonal red *SPECIMEN* overprint; horizontal black # ovpt at lower right on back.   —   —   —

Replacement notes: Prefix D with no suffix letter.

BOK B12 (P15): **1,000 hwan** (US$0.95) (withdrawn 10.06.1962)　　**VG　VF　UNC**
Brown, light blue, orange, and red. Front: Guilloche pattern; kobukson (ironclad turtle warship). Back: Bank logo (hibiscus syriacus flower). No security thread. Watermark: None. Printer: (Tudor Press). 156 x 66 mm.

☐	a. No date. Intro: 17.02.1953.	60	200	750
☐	as1. Diagonal red *SPECIMEN* overprint.	—	—	500
☐	as2. Diagonal black *SPECIMEN* overprint.	—	—	500
☐	as3. Boxed red 見樣 overprint.	—	—	500

Replacement notes: Prefix D with no suffix letter.

1953-1958 Hwan Issues

The name of the currency appears correctly as "hwan" in English on the back, as well as in Hangul (환) and Hanja on both sides.

These notes bear the year of printing expressed as the number of years since the founding of the Tan'gun dynasty. To convert to Western date format, subtract 2333 from the date printed on the front of the note.

BOK B13 (P16): **10 hwan** (withdrawn 10.06.1962)　　**VG　VF　UNC**
Black, light blue, purple, and red on buff paper. Front: Bank logo (hibiscus syriacus flower); Namdaemun (Great Southern Gateway) in Seoul. Back: Haegeumgang seaside rock formation in Geoje. No security thread. Watermark: Character. Printer: 한국조폐공사 제조 (KOMSCO). 156 x 66 mm.

☐	a. 4286 (1953). Block 1-123. Intro: 15.03.1953.	2.50	10	100
☐	as1. Diagonal red *SPECIMEN* overprint.	—	—	—
☐	as2. Vertical red 見樣券 overprint.	—	—	—

BOK B14 (P17): **10 hwan** (withdrawn 10.06.1962)　　**VG　VF　UNC**
Black, light blue, purple, and red on white paper. Front: Bank logo (hibiscus syriacus flower); Namdaemun (Great Southern Gateway) in Seoul. Back: Haegeumgang seaside rock formation in Geoje. No security thread. Watermark: Character. Printer: 한국조폐공사 제조 (KOMSCO). 156 x 66 mm.

☐	a. 4286 (1953). Block 124-143. Intro: 15.12.1953.	4	25	125
☐	b. 4287 (1954). Block 144-153.	3	20	100
☐	c. 4288 (1955). Block 154-159.	2	15	55
☐	d. 4289 (1956). Block 160-173.	1	12	50
☐	e. 4290 (1957). Block 174-187.	1	10	40
☐	f. 4291 (1958). Block 188-206.	25	50	100
☐	ds. Diagonal red *SPECIMEN* overprint.	—	—	—
☐	s. Vertical red 見樣券 overprint.	—	—	—

Like preceding issue, but on white, not buff, paper.

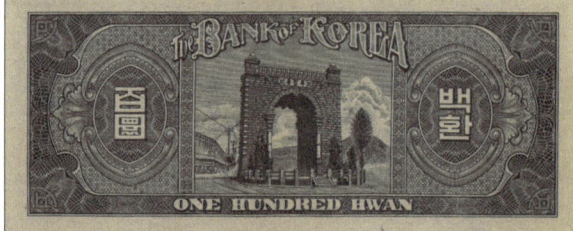

BOK B15 (P18): **100 hwan** (withdrawn 10.06.1962)　　**VG　VF　UNC**
Green, red, and orange on buff paper. Front: President Syngman Rhee wearing hanbok, traditional Korean dress; bank logo (hibiscus syriacus flower). Back: City building, telephone poles, trees, clouds, mountain, and Independence Gate in Seoul. No security thread. Watermark: Character. Printer: 한국조폐공사 제조 (KOMSCO). 156 x 66 mm.

☐	a. 4286 (1953). Block 1-5. Intro: 18.12.1953.	400	1,200	—
☐	as. Diagonal red *SPECIMEN* overprint.	—	—	—

1957-1960 Issues

These notes feature a new portrait of President Syngman Rhee wearing a jacket and tie.

BOK B16 (P19): **100 hwan** (withdrawn 10.06.1962)   VG   VF   UNC
Green, red, and orange on white paper. Front: President Syngman Rhee wearing hanbok, traditional Korean dress; bank logo (hibiscus syriacus flower). Back: City building, telephone poles, trees, clouds, mountain, and Independence Gate in Seoul. No security thread. Watermark: Character. Printer: 한국조폐공사 제조 (KOMSCO). 156 x 66 mm.

		VG	VF	UNC
☐ a.	4287 (1954). Block 6-39. Intro: 01.02.1954.	15	70	150
☐ b.	4288 (1955). Block 47-99.	20	80	160
☐ c.	4289 (1956). Block 102-129.	5	15	50
☐ as.	Diagonal red SPECIMEN overprint. Block 16.	—	—	—
☐ bs.	Diagonal red SPECIMEN overprint. Block 92.	—	—	—
☐ cs.	Diagonal red SPECIMEN overprint. Block 104.	—	—	—

Like preceding issue, but on white, not buff, paper.

BOK B18 (P21): **100 hwan** (withdrawn 10.06.1962)   VG   VF   UNC
Black, green, tan, and red. Front: Bank logo (hibiscus syriacus flower); President Syngman Rhee wearing jacket and tie. Back: Floral design. No security thread. Watermark: Character. Printer: 한국조폐공사 제조 (KOMSCO). 156 x 66 mm.

		VG	VF	UNC
☐ a.	4290 (1957). Block 1-12. Intro: 26.03.1957.	20	125	500
☐ as.	Diagonal SPECIMEN overprint; horizontal red # overprint at lower left on back.	—	—	—

BOK B17 (P20): **500 hwan** (withdrawn 10.06.1962)   VG   VF   UNC
Gray-blue, green, and brown. Front: President Syngman Rhee wearing hanbok, traditional Korean dress. Back: Guilloche patterns. No security thread. Watermark: Character. Printer: 한국조폐공사 제조 (KOMSCO). 152 x 72 mm.

		VG	VF	UNC
☐ a.	4289 (1956). Block 1-10. Intro: 26.03.1956.	40	175	500
☐ b.	4290 (1957). Block 11-13.	40	175	500
☐ as.	Diagonal red SPECIMEN overprint.	—	—	—

BOK B19 (P24): **500 hwan** (withdrawn 10.06.1962)   VG   VF   UNC
Dark green, brown, and red. Front: Bank logo (hibiscus syriacus flower); President Syngman Rhee wearing jacket and tie. Back: Guilloche pattern. No security thread. Watermark: Character. Printer: 한국조폐공사 제조 (KOMSCO). 155 x 74 mm.

		VG	VF	UNC
☐ a.	4291 (1958). Block 1-26. Intro: 15.08.1958.	75	400	4,250
☐ b.	4292 (1959). Block 28-50.	50	200	3,600
☐ as.	Diagonal SPECIMEN overprint.	—	—	—

BOK B20 (P22): **1,000 hwan** (withdrawn 10.06.1962) VG VF UNC
Purple, brown, green, blue, and red. Front: President Syngman Rhee wearing jacket and tie. Back: Bank logo (hibiscus syriacus flower). No security thread. Watermark: Character. Printer: 한국조폐공사 제조 (KOMSCO). 166 x 73 mm.

- a. 4290 (1957). Block 1-6. Intro: 26.03.1957. 100 400 1,500
- b. 4291 (1958). Block 7-15. 100 400 1,500
- c. 4292 (1959). Block 16-44. 100 400 1,500
- d. 4293 (1960). Block 45-75. 100 400 1,500
- as. Diagonal SPECIMEN overprint; horizontal red # overprint at lower right on back. — — 1,425
- cs. Diagonal SPECIMEN overprint. — — —

1958 Issues

This note was issued to celebrate Korea's liberation from Japan.

BOK B21 (P23): **50 hwan** (withdrawn 10.06.1962) VG VF UNC
Green-blue, yellow, and red. Front: Independence Gate in Seoul; bank logo (hibiscus syriacus flower). Back: Statue of standing Admiral Yi Sun-shin holding sword; kobukson (ironclad turtle warship). No security thread. Watermark: Character. Printer: 한국조폐공사 제조 (KOMSCO). 149 x 66 mm.

- a. 4291 (1958). Block 1-4. Intro: 15.08.1958. 100 400 1,800
- as. Diagonal SPECIMEN overprint. — — —

1960-1962 Issues

Following the resignation of President Syngman Rhee on 19 April 1960 due to a student uprising, the new government issued new notes without his portrait and without Chinese characters.

BOK B22 (P26): **100 hwan** (withdrawn 10.06.1962) VG VF UNC
Green, orange, and red. Front: Young boy and woman holding savings account booklet. Back: Independence Gate in Seoul. No security thread. Watermark: Character. Printer: (KOMSCO). 156 x 66 mm.

- a. 1962. Block 1-3. Intro: 16.05.1962. 50 100 2,500
- as. Horizontal red 견양 overprint on front; horizontal red SPECIMEN overprint on back. — — —

BOK B23 (P27): **500 hwan** (withdrawn 10.06.1962) VG VF UNC
Blue-green and red. Front: King Sejong the Great wearing hanbok, traditional Korean dress. Back: Bank logo (hibiscus syriacus flower); Bank of Korea headquarters building in Seoul. No security thread. Watermark: Character. Printer: (KOMSCO). 156 x 73 mm.

- a. 4294 (1961). Block 1-10. Intro: 19.04.1961. 150 600 2,000
- as. Vertical red 見樣券 overprint on front; diagonal red SPECIMEN overprint on back; horizontal red # overprint at lower right on back. — — 3,000

BOK B24 (P25): **1,000 hwan** (withdrawn 10.06.1962)   VG   VF   UNC

Black, brown, green, and red. Front: Bank logo (hibiscus syriacus flower); King Sejong the Great wearing hanbok, traditional Korean dress. Back: Laurel wreath; torch. No security thread. Watermark: Character. Printer: (KOMSCO). 166 x 73 mm.

		VG	VF	UNC
☐	a. 4293 (1960). Block 1-29. Intro: 15.08.1960.	20	80	250
☐	b. 4294 (1961). Block 30-136.	20	80	250
☐	c. 1962. Block 147-186.	20	80	250
☐	as. Horizontal red 견양 overprint on front; horizontal red *SPECIMEN* overprint on back.	—	—	—

1962 Won Issues

On 9 June 1962, the won replaced the hwan at a rate of 1:10, and became the sole legal tender on 22 March 1975, following the withdrawal of the last circulating hwan coins. At the reintroduction of the won in 1962, its value was pegged at 125 won to 1 US dollar, although a series of devaluations followed over the years until it was allowed to float on 24 December 1997.

The two jeon-denominated notes bear the year of printing expressed in Western date format at lower right on back. All of these notes bear the imprint of 한국조폐공사 제조 (Korea Minting and Security Printing Corporation), but in fact KOMSCO printed only the 10- and 50-jeon notes; all the other denominations were printed by Thomas De La Rue (TDLR) without imprint.

BOK B25 (P28): **10 jeon** (withdrawn 01.12.1980)   VG   VF   UNC

Dark blue, light blue, and red. Front: Guilloche pattern. Back: Guilloche pattern. No security thread. Watermark: Character. Printer: 한국조폐공사 제조 (KOMSCO). 90 x 50 mm.

		VG	VF	UNC
☐	a. 1962. Block 1-2. Intro: 01.12.1962.	—	0.25	1
☐	as. Horizontal red hollow 견양 overprint on front; horizontal red hollow *SPECIMEN* ovpt on back; horizontal red # overprint at lower right on back.	—	—	50

BOK B26 (P29): **50 jeon** (withdrawn 01.12.1980)   VG   VF   UNC

Black, green, red, and brown. Front: Guilloche pattern. Back: Guilloche pattern. No security thread. Watermark: Character. Printer: 한국조폐공사 제조 (KOMSCO). 90 x 50 mm.

		VG	VF	UNC
☐	a. 1962. Block 1-2. Intro: 01.12.1962.	—	0.50	1.75
☐	as. Horizontal red hollow 견양 overprint on front; horizontal red hollow *SPECIMEN* ovpt on back; horizontal red # overprint at lower right on back.	—	—	50

BOK B27 (P30): **1 won** (withdrawn 20.05.1970)   VG   VF   UNC

Violet, orange, and yellow. Front: Bank logo (hibiscus syriacus flower); guilloche pattern. Back: Guilloche pattern. No security thread. Watermark: Character. Printer: 한국조폐공사 제조 (TDLR). 94 x 50 mm.

		VG	VF	UNC
☐	a. No date. Intro: 10.06.1962. Red serial number and bank seal.	0.50	2	10
☐	b. Dark red serial number and bank seal.	—	—	—
☐	as. Horizontal red 견양 overprint on front; diagonal red *SPECIMEN* overprint on back; horizontal red # overprint at lower right on back.	—	—	150

Replacement note: Prefix ✤.

BOK B28 (P31): **5 won** (withdrawn 01.05.1969)   VG   VF   UNC

Black, green, and red. Front: Bank logo (hibiscus syriacus flower); guilloche pattern. Back: Guilloche pattern. No security thread. Watermark: Character. Printer: 한국조폐공사 제조 (TDLR). 94 x 50 mm.

		VG	VF	UNC
☐	a. No date. Intro: 10.06.1962. Red serial number and bank seal.	2	8	35
☐	b. Dark red serial number and bank seal.	—	—	—
☐	as. Horizontal red 견양 overprint on front; diagonal red *SPECIMEN* overprint on back.	—	—	—

Replacement note: Prefix ✤.

BOK B29 (P32): **10 won** (withdrawn 01.09.1967)   VG   VF   UNC

Brown, green, and red. Front: Bank logo (hibiscus syriacus flower); guilloche pattern. Back: Guilloche pattern. No security thread. Watermark: Character. Printer: 한국조폐공사 제조 (TDLR). 108 x 54 mm.

- ☐ a. No date. Intro: 10.06.1962.   8   30   100
  Red serial number and bank seal.
- ☐ b. Dark red serial number and bank seal.   —   —   —
- ☐ as. Horizontal red 견양 overprint on front;   —   —   300
  horizontal red *SPECIMEN* ovpt on back;
  horizontal red # overprint at lower right on back.
- ☐ bs. Horizontal red 견양 overprint on front;   —   —   600
  horizontal red *SPECIMEN* ovpt on back;
  horizontal red # overprint at lower right on back.

Replacement note: Prefix ✣.

BOK B31 (P36): **100 won** (withdrawn 14.02.1969)   VG   VF   UNC

Green, blue, yellow, and red. Front: Clouds, trees, mountains, and Independence Gate in Seoul; bank logo (hibiscus syriacus flower). Back: Laurel wreath; torch. No security thread. Watermark: None. Printer: 한국조폐공사 제조 (TDLR). 156 x 66 mm.

- ☐ a. No date. Intro: 10.06.1962.   15   60   230
  Red serial number and bank seal.
- ☐ b. Dark red serial number and bank seal.   —   —   —
- ☐ as. Horizontal red 견양 overprint on front;   —   XF   300
  diagonal red *SPECIMEN* overprint on back;
  horizontal red # overprint at lower right on back.

Replacement note: Prefix ✣.

BOK B30 (P34): **50 won** (withdrawn 20.05.1970)   VG   VF   UNC

Rust, blue, green, violet, and red. Front: Haegeumgang seaside rock formation in Geoje; bank logo (hibiscus syriacus flower). Back: Laurel wreath; torch. No security thread. Watermark: Character. Printer: 한국조폐공사 제조 (TDLR). 156 x 66 mm.

- ☐ a. No date. Prefix EA-ED. Intro: 10.06.1962.   35   175   400
  Red serial number and bank seal.
- ☐ b. Dark red serial number and bank seal.   —   —   —
- ☐ as. Horizontal red 견양 overprint on front;   —   XF   600
  diagonal red *SPECIMEN* overprint on back;
  horizontal red # overprint at lower right on back.

Replacement note: Prefix ✣.

BOK B32 (P37): **500 won** (withdrawn 03.02.1967)   VG   VF   UNC

Blue, green, red, and yellow. Front: Trees, clouds, and Namdaemun (Great Southern Gateway) in Seoul; bank logo (hibiscus syriacus flower). Back: Laurel wreath; torch. No security. Watermark: None. Printer: 한국조폐공사 제조 (TDLR). 156 x 66 mm.

- ☐ a. No date. Intro: 10.06.1962.   8   30   140
  Red serial number and bank seal.
- ☐ b. Dark red serial number and bank seal.   —   —   —
- ☐ as. Horizontal red hollow 견양 overprint on front;   —   —   —
  diagonal red hollow *SPECIMEN* ovpt on back;
  horizontal red # overprint at lower right on back.

Replacement note: Prefix ✣.

1962-1969 Issues

These notes feature revised designs and Western dates at lower right on back. Both of these notes were printed in Korea.

BOK B33 (P33): **10 won** (withdrawn 30.10.1973)   VG   VF   UNC
Brown, pale green, light blue, and red. Front: Cheomseongdae astronomical observatory in Gyeongju; bank logo (hibiscus syriacus flower). Back: Kobukson (ironclad turtle warship). No security thread. Watermark: Character. Printer: 한국조폐공사 제조 (KOMSCO). 140 x 63 mm.

		VG	VF	UNC
☐ a.	1962. Block 1-17. Intro: 21.09.1962.	2.50	8	50
☐ b.	1963. Block 18-30.	2.75	8.50	55
☐ c.	1964. Block 31-55.	1.50	4.50	30
☐ d.	1965. Block 56-95.	2.50	8	50
☐ e.	No date. Block 96-284. Intro: 1966.	0.25	0.50	3
☐ as.	Horizontal red 견양 overprint on front; diagonal red *SPECIMEN* overprint on back; horizontal red # overprint at lower right on back.	—	—	—
☐ cs.	Specimen.	—	—	—
☐ es.	Horizontal red *SPECIMEN* overprint.	—	—	525

BOK B34 (P35): **100 won** (withdrawn 30.10.1973)   VG   VF   UNC
Green and red. Front: Clouds, trees, and Independence Gate in Seoul. Back: Gyeonghoeru (Royal Banquet Hall) at Gyeongbokgung Palace in Seoul. No security thread. Watermark: Character. Printer: 한국조폐공사 제조 (KOMSCO). 156 x 66 mm.

		VG	VF	UNC
☐ a.	1962. Block 1-35. Intro: 01.11.1962.	15	60	250
☐ b.	1963. Block 37-174.	15	60	250
☐ c.	1964. Block 206-298.	4	25	75
☐ d.	1965. Block 308-379.	4	25	75
☐ e.	1969. Block 385-389.	6	25	75
☐ as.	Horizontal red 견양 overprint on front; diagonal red *SPECIMEN* overprint on back; horizontal red # ovpt at lower center on back.	—	350	—

Replacement notes: Serial number starts with 9.

1966-1969 Issues

All of these notes are undated. In 1965, the 100-won note was the first denomination to be printed domestically with intaglio, followed by the 500-won in 1966. The 50-won note is lithographed.

BOK B35 (P40): **50 won** (withdrawn 30.10.1973)   VG   VF   UNC
Tan, black, blue, and red. Front: Pagoda Gongweon in Seoul. Back: Hibiscus syriacus flower wreath; torch. No security thread. Watermark: Character. Printer: 한국조폐공사 제조 (KOMSCO). 149 x 64 mm.

		VG	VF	UNC
☐ a.	No date. Block 1-24. Intro: 21.03.1969.	2.50	10	40
☐ as.	Horizontal red hollow 견양 overprint on front; horizontal red hollow *SPECIMEN* ovpt on back; horizontal red # overprint at lower right on back.	—	—	—

Replacement notes: Serial number starts with 9.

BOK B36 (P38 & P38A): **100 won** (withdrawn 01.12.1980)   VG   VF   UNC
Green, blue, red, and orange. Front: King Sejong the Great wearing hanbok, traditional Korean dress. Back: Bank of Korea headquarters building in Seoul. No security thread. Watermark: Character. Printer: 한국조폐공사 제조 (KOMSCO). 156 x 66 mm.

		VG	VF	UNC
☐ a.	No date. Intro: 14.08.1965. Black 백원 on front.	0.75	2.25	10
☐ b.	Brown 백원 on front.	0.75	2.25	10
☐ c.	Red 백원 on front.	0.75	2.25	10
☐ as.	Horizontal red 견양 overprint on front; diagonal red *SPECIMEN* overprint on back; horizontal red # overprint at lower right on back.	—	—	—

Replacement notes: Serial number starts with 9.

SOUTH KOREA 1972-1975 PORTRAIT ISSUES

BOK B37 (P39): **500 won** (withdrawn 10.05.1975) VG VF UNC
Black, orange, green, violet, and red. Front: Namdaemun (Great Southern Gateway) in Seoul. Back: Fleet of kobukson (ironclad turtle warships). No security thread. Watermark: Character. Printer: 한국조폐공사 제조 (KOMSCO). 165 x 73 mm.
- ☐ a.   No date. Intro: 16.08.1966.   1   5   35
- ☐ as. Horizontal red hollow 견양 overprint on front;   —   —   —
   horizontal red hollow *SPECIMEN* ovpt on back;
   horizontal red # overprint at lower right on back.

Replacement notes: Serial number starts with 9.

1972-1975 Portrait Issues

BOK B38 (P43): **500 won** (withdrawn 12.05.1993) VG VF UNC
Blue, green, orange, and red. Front: Admiral Yi Sun-shin wearing hanbok, traditional Korean dress; kobukson (ironclad turtle warship); stylized bird. Back: Trees and Yi Sun-shin Shrine at Hyeonchungsa in Asan. No security thread. Watermark: Korean characters. Printer: 한국조폐공사 제조 (KOMSCO). 159 x 69 mm.
- ☐ a.   No date. Intro: 01.09.1973.   —   2   10
- ☐ as. Horizontal red hollow 견양 overprint on front;   —   —   —
   diagonal red hollow *SPECIMEN* ovpt on back;
   horizontal black # ovpt at lower right on back.

Replacement notes: Serial number starts with 9.

BOK B39 (P44): **1,000 won** (withdrawn 12.05.1993) VG VF UNC
Purple, green, brown, and red. Front: Hibiscus syriacus flowers; Confucian scholar Toegye Yi Hwang wearing hanbok, traditional Korean dress; bank logo (hibiscus syriacus flower). Back: Dosan Seowon Confucian academy buildings in Andong; trees. No security thread. Watermark: Hibiscus syriacus flowers. Printer: 한국조폐공사 제조 (KOMSCO). 163 x 72 mm.
- ☐ a.   No date. Intro: 14.08.1975.   —   3   12
- ☐ as. Horizontal red hollow 견양 overprint on front;   —   —   —
   diagonal red hollow *SPECIMEN* ovpt on back;
   horizontal red # overprint at lower right on back.

Replacement notes: Serial number starts with 9.

BOK B40 (P41): **5,000 won** (withdrawn 01.12.1980) VG VF UNC
Brown, olive green, and red. Front: Confucian scholar Yulgok Yi I wearing hanbok, traditional Korean dress; torch. Back: Bank of Korea headquarters building in Seoul. Solid security thread. Watermark: Yulgok Yi I. Printer: 한국조폐공사 제조 (KOMSCO). 167 x 77 mm.
- ☐ a.   No date. Intro: 01.07.1972.   8   35   175
- ☐ as. Horizontal red hollow 견양 overprint on front;   —   —   —
   diagonal red hollow *SPECIMEN* ovpt on back;
   horizontal black # ovpt at lower right on back.

Replacement notes: Serial number starts with 9.

BOK B41 (P42): **10,000 won** (withdrawn 10.11.1981)　　　　VG　VF　UNC
Brown, olive green, and red. Front: King Sejong the Great wearing hanbok, traditional Korean dress; hibiscus syriacus flowers. Back: Trees, mountains, and Geunjeongjeon (Throne Hall) at Gyeongbokgung Palace in Seoul. Solid security thread. Watermark: Head of Buddhist Goddess of Mercy. Printer: 한국조폐공사 제조 (KOMSCO). 171 x 81 mm.

☐　a.　No date. Intro: 12.06.1973.　　　　　　　　　　8　30　150
☐　as.　Horizontal red hollow 견양 overprint on front;　　—　—　—
　　　　diagonal red hollow *SPECIMEN* ovpt on back;
　　　　horizontal black # ovpt at lower right on back.

Replacement notes: Serial number starts with 9.

BOK B43 (P46): **10,000 won** (withdrawn 12.05.1993)　　　　VG　VF　UNC
Olive green, tan, and red. Front: Borugak Jagyeongnu (water clock of Borugak Pavilion); dragon; King Sejong the Great wearing hanbok, traditional Korean dress; bank logo (hibiscus syriacus flower). Back: Gyeonghoeru (Royal Banquet Hall) at Gyeongbokgung Palace in Seoul; hibiscus syriacus flowers. No security thread. Watermark: King Sejong the Great. Printer: 한국조폐공사 제조 (KOMSCO). 172 x 81 mm.

☐　a.　No date. Intro: 15.06.1979.　　　　　　　　　　—　20　35
☐　as.　Horizontal red hollow 견양 overprint on front;　　—　—　—
　　　　diagonal red hollow *SPECIMEN* ovpt on back;
　　　　horizontal red # overprint at lower right on back.

Replacement notes: Serial number starts with 9.

1977-1979 Issues

These notes feature new portraits and different vignettes.

BOK B42 (P45): **5,000 won** (withdrawn 12.05.1993)　　　　VG　VF　UNC
Brown, orange, and red. Front: Confucian scholar Yulgok Yi I wearing hanbok, traditional Korean dress; bank logo (hibiscus syriacus flower). Back: Ojukheon House buildings (birthplace of Yulgok Yi I); hibiscus syriacus flowers. No security thread. Watermark: Yulgok Yi I. Printer: 한국조폐공사 제조 (KOMSCO). 167 x 77 mm.

☐　a.　No date. Intro: 01.06.1977.　　　　　　　　　　—　8.50　25
☐　as.　Horizontal red hollow 견양 ovpt on front;　　　　—　—　1,500
　　　　diagonal red hollow *SPECIMEN* ovpt on back;
　　　　horizontal red # overprint at lower right on back.

Replacement notes: Serial number starts with 9.

1983 Issues

These notes include tactile marks below the watermark area on the front so that the sight-impaired can distinguish between denominations. They have also been reduced in size, with their heights standardized to 76 mm.

BOK B44 (P47): **1,000 won** (US$0.95)   VG   VF   UNC
Purple, green, orange, and red. Front: Tuho jar and sticks (for folk game); two stylized deer; bank logo (hibiscus syriacus flower); Confucian scholar Toegye Yi Hwang wearing hanbok, traditional Korean dress; antlered deer. Back: Antlered deer; trees and Dosan Seowon Confucian academy buildings in Andong. No security thread. Watermark: Toegye Yi Hwang. Printer: 한국조폐공사 제조 (KOMSCO). 151 x 76 mm.
- ☐ a. No date. Intro: 11.06.1983.   FV   FV   3
  Purple portrait and buildings.
- ☐ b. Brown portrait and buildings.   FV   FV   3
- ☐ as. Horizontal red hollow 견양 overprint on front;   —   —   —
  diagonal red hollow *SPECIMEN* ovpt on back;
  horizontal red # overprint at lower right on back.

Replacement notes: Serial number starts with 9.

BOK B45 (P48): **5,000 won** (US$4.70)   VG   VF   UNC
Brown, green, blue, and red. Front: Stylized bird; bank logo (hibiscus syriacus flower); Confucian scholar Yulgok Yi I wearing hanbok, traditional Korean dress; bird. Back: Bird; Ojukheon House buildings (birthplace of Yulgok Yi I). No security thread. Watermark: Yulgok Yi I. Printer: 한국조폐공사 제조 (KOMSCO). 156 x 76 mm.
- ☐ a. No date. Intro: 11.06.1983.   FV   FV   10
- ☐ as. Horizontal red hollow 견양 overprint on front;   —   —   —
  diagonal red hollow *SPECIMEN* ovpt on back;
  horizontal blue # overprint at lower right on back.

Replacement notes: Serial number starts with 9.

BOK B46 (P49): **10,000 won** (US$9.40)   VG   VF   UNC
Olive green, tan, and green. Front: Borugak Jagyeongnu (water clock of Borugak Pavilion); dragon; bank logo (hibiscus syriacus flower); King Sejong the Great wearing hanbok, traditional Korean dress. Back: Gyeonghoeru (Royal Banquet Hall) at Gyeongbokgung Palace in Seoul. No security thread. Watermark: King Sejong the Great. Printer: 한국조폐공사 제조 (KOMSCO). 161 x 76 mm.
- ☐ a. No date. Intro: 08.10.1983.   FV   FV   20
- ☐ as. Horizontal red hollow 견양 overprint on front;   —   —   —
  diagonal red hollow *SPECIMEN* ovpt on back;
  horizontal blue # overprint at lower right on back.

Replacement notes: Serial number starts with 9.

1994 Issues

This 10,000-won note is like the preceding issue, but with increased security features, including concentric green circles over the watermark area on front which create an optical interference pattern when scanned, windowed security thread, and microtext below the water clock.

BOK B47 (P50): **10,000 won** (US$9.40) VG VF UNC

Olive green, tan, and red. Front: Borugak Jagyeongnu (water clock of Borugak Pavilion); dragon; bank logo (hibiscus syriacus flower); King Sejong the Great wearing hanbok, traditional Korean dress. Back: Gyeonghoeru (Royal Banquet Hall) at Gyeongbokgung Palace in Seoul. Windowed security thread. Watermark: King Sejong the Great. Printer: 한국조폐공사 제조 (KOMSCO). 161 x 76 mm.

- ☐ a. No date. Intro: 20.01.1994.   FV   FV   17
- ☐ as. Horizontal red hollow 견양 overprint on front; diagonal red hollow *SPECIMEN* ovpt on back.   —   —   —

2000-2002 Issues

These notes are like the preceding issues, but with copyright notices including Western dates below the tactile dots for the sight-impaired at lower left front, and below the denomination at lower right back. The 5,000-won note now has a windowed security thread. The 10,000-won note has Omron rings added, and the concentric green circles over the watermark area on front have been removed.

BOK B48 (P51): **5,000 won** (US$4.70)   VG VF UNC

Brown, green, blue, and red. Front: Stylized bird; bank logo (hibiscus syriacus flower); Confucian scholar Yulgok Yi I wearing hanbok, traditional Korean dress; bird. Back: Bird; Ojukheon House buildings (birthplace of Yulgok Yi I). Windowed security thread. Watermark: Yulgok Yi I. Printer: 한국조폐공사 제조 (KOMSCO). 156 x 76 mm.

- ☐ a. 2002. Intro: 12.06.2002.   FV   FV   10
- ☐ as. Horizontal red hollow 견양 overprint on front; diagonal red hollow *SPECIMEN* ovpt on back; horizontal red # overprint at lower right on back.   —   —   —

BOK B49 (P52): **10,000 won** (US$9.40) VG VF UNC

Olive green, tan, and red. Front: Borugak Jagyeongnu (water clock of Borugak Pavilion); dragon; bank logo (hibiscus syriacus flower); King Sejong the Great wearing hanbok, traditional Korean dress. Back: Gyeonghoeru (Royal Banquet Hall) at Gyeongbokgung Palace in Seoul. Windowed security thread. Watermark: King Sejong the Great with electrotype t'aeguk (two-comma roundel). Printer: 한국조폐공사 제조 (KOMSCO). 161 x 76 mm.

☐ a. 2000. Intro: 19.06.2000.   FV FV 17
☐ as. Horizontal red hollow 견양 overpint on front; diagonal red hollow *SPECIMEN* ovpt on back; horizontal red # overprint at lower right on back. — — —

Replacement notes: Serial number starts with 9.

2006-2009 Issues

These notes have Western prefixes and serial numbers, as well as improved security features, including Omron rings on all denominations.

BOK B50 (P54): **1,000 won** (US$0.95) VG VF UNC

Blue, purple, and green. Front: T'aeguk (two-comma roundel) as registration device; mume (Japanese apricot) tree branch and blossoms; Myungryundang lecture hall building in Daegu; Confucian scholar Toegye Yi Hwang wearing hanbok, traditional Korean dress. Back: Bank logo (hibiscus syriacus flower); Gaesang junggeodo watercolor painting of landscape with mountains, trees, water, and boat; t'aeguk. Windowed security thread. Watermark: Toegye Yi Hwang and electrotype *1000*. Printer: 한국조폐공사 제조 (KOMSCO). 136 x 68 mm.

☐ a. No date. Intro: 22.01.2007.   FV FV 2
☐ as. Horizontal red 보기 overprint on front; vertical red *SPECIMEN* overprint on back; horizontal red # overprint at lower right on back. — — 550

Replacement notes: Prefix LA and serial number starts with 9.

BOK B51 (P55): **5,000 won** (US$4.70)   VG   VF   UNC

Red, yellow, green, and blue. Front: Round holographic patch; t'aeguk (two-comma roundel) as registration device; ojuk (black bamboos); Ojukheon (Mongryoungsil) building; Confucian scholar Yulgok Yi I wearing hanbok, traditional Korean dress. Back: Bank logo (hibiscus syriacus flower); swallowtail butterfly; watermelons; cockscomb flowers; katydid cricket; t'aeguk. Solid security thread with printed 한국은행 BANK OF KOREA 5000. Watermark: Yulgok Yi I and electrotype *5000*. Printer: 한국조폐공사 제조 (KOMSCO). 142 x 68 mm.

   ☐ a.   No date. Intro: 02.01.2006.   FV   FV   8
   ☐ as.   Horizontal red 보기 overprint on front;   —   —   1,500
         vertical red *SPECIMEN* overprint on back;
         horizontal red # overprint at lower right on back.

Replacement notes: Prefix LA and serial number starts with 9.

BOK B53 (P57): **50,000 won** (US$47)   VG   VF   UNC

Yellow and green. Front: T'aeguk (two-comma roundel) as registration device; tree branches; Mukpododo painting of grape leaf; berries; Chochungdo-subyeong folding screen painting of eggplant; painter and author Shin Saim-dang wearing hanbok, traditional Korean dress. Back (vertical): Poongjukdo painting of bamboo tree; Wolmaedo painting of Japanese apricot tree; t'aeguk. Holographic stripe with demetalized *BANK OF KOREA 50000*. Windowed Motion security thread. Solid security thread with printed 한국은행 BANK OF KOREA 50000. Watermark: Shin Saim-dang and electrotype *5* within pentagon. Printer: 한국조폐공사 제조 (KOMSCO). 154 x 68 mm.

   ☐ a.   No date. Intro: 23.06.2009.   FV   FV   60
   ☐ as.   Horizontal red 보기 overprint on front;   —   —   9,000
         vertical red *SPECIMEN* overprint on back;
         horizontal red # overprint at lower right on back.

Replacement notes: Prefix LA and serial number starts with 9.

BOK B52 (P56): **10,000 won** (US$9.40)   VG   VF   UNC

Green and blue. Front: Square holographic patch; t'aeguk (two-comma roundel) as registration device; Ilwolohbongdo painting of the sun, moon, and five mountain peaks; Korean text of Yongbiacheonga (Songs of Flying Dragons); King Sejong the Great wearing hanbok, traditional Korean dress. Back: Bank logo (hibiscus syriacus flower); celestial globe; star charts; modern telescope; t'aeguk. Solid security thread with printed 한국은행 BANK OF KOREA 10000. Watermark: King Sejong the Great and electrotype *10000*. Printer: 한국조폐공사 제조 (KOMSCO). 148 x 68 mm.

   ☐ a.   No date. Intro: 22.01.2007.   FV   FV   15
   ☐ as.   Horizontal red 보기 overprint on front;   —   —   3,000
         vertical red *SPECIMEN* overprint on back;
         horizontal red # overprint at lower right on back.

Replacement notes: Prefix LA and serial number starts with 9.

Bank of Korea Museum

In June 2001, the Bank of Korea Museum opened in the bank's headquarters in Seoul.

For more information, visit http://museum.bok.or.kr.

Acknowledgements

This chapter was compiled with the generous assistance of Sejin Ahn, Robert Breslin, Dwight Brown (kaydees@embarqmail.com), Jim W.-C. Chen, Isaac Chung, David F. Cieniewicz (www.banknotestore.com), Radoslaw Dlouhy, Jean-Michel Engels, Larry Hirsch (www.aworldcurrency.com), Kevin Klauss, Jaehong Lee, Braz Ferrari Lomonaco, José Fabrício Macêdo, Wally Myers, Bill Stubkjaer, Christoph Thomas, Frank van Tiel, Ludek Vostel, Tristan Williams, and others.

Sources

Boon, K. N. *World Paper & Polymer Uncut Banknotes.* 1st edition. 2012. ISBN 978-983-43313-4-4. Trigometric Sdn.Bhd. (www.3833.com), Lot 327, Amcorp Mall, 18 Jalan Persiaran Barat, off Jalan Timur, Petaling Jaya, 46050 Selangor D.E., Malaysia.

Cuhaj, George S. *Standard Catalog of World Paper Money, General Issues, 1368-1960.* 14th edition. 2012. ISBN 978-1-4402-3090-5. Krause Publications (www.krausebooks.com), 700 East State St., Iola, WI, 54990-0001.

Cuhaj, George S. *Standard Catalog of World Paper Money, Modern Issues, 1961-Present.* 18th edition. 2012. ISBN 978-1-4402-2956-5. Krause Publications (www.krausebooks.com), 700 East State St., Iola, WI, 54990-0001.

Heath, Henry B. "Personalities on the Bank Notes of Korea." *IBNS Journal.* Volume 39 Number 3. p.39.

Rodgers, Dr. Kerry and Ron Wise. "The Amazing Turtle Ships of Admiral Yi Soon-shin." *IBNS Journal.* Volume 43 Number 2. p.6.

http://ybnotes.com/gallery/KoreaSouth2.html.

Unknown. *Korean Standard Coins and Banknotes Catalogue.* 2007. Korean Coins and Banknotes Dealer Association.

Share Your Input, Info, and Images

This catalog is believed to be complete and correct as of the time of publication. Prices and face values were last updated 17 August 2012. Please report errors or omissions so that corrections may be made. If you can more precisely identify the name or location of anything depicted on a note, please share that information. Furthermore, if you own an unlisted type or variety, please submit scans of the front and back of the note so that it can be documented. Scans should be 300 dots per inch, 100% actual size, 24-bit color, saved as *uncompressed* JPEG files, and sent to owen@banknotenews.com. Be sure to fully describe all attributes of the note which are not apparent upon visual inspection of the images alone, such as physical dimension, watermark, and security thread.

South Sudan

For earlier issues, see Sudan.

Monetary System
2011: 1 South Sudanese pound (SSP) = 100 piasters

Bank of South Sudan

The Bank of South Sudan (BSS) is the central bank of South Sudan, headquartered in the capital, Juba. Established in 2005, it was a branch of the Bank of Sudan until 9 July 2011, when South Sudan seceded to become an independent republic.

BSS Signature Varieties

1		
	Governor Elijah Malok	Minister of Finance David Deng Athorbei

2011 Pound Issues

On 18 July 2011, South Sudan introduced its own banknotes, exchanging them at par for existing Sudanese pounds. The front of the South Sudan notes feature a portrait of rebel leader Dr. John Garang de Mabior, while the backs contain images of the country's culture and wealth. The notes are signed by Elijah Malok as "Governor" even though he had not been officially appointed to the position.

The security features of these notes are virtually identical; only the windowed threads are different. On the 1- and 5-pound notes, the thread is thin and silver with demetalized *BANK OF SOUTH SUDAN* and the denomination. The other notes have a wider, gold-to-green color shifting thread with demetalized *BSS* and the denomination. Otherwise, the anti-counterfeiting features common to all denominations include intaglio printing, microtext, registration devices, novel serial numbers, opalescent stripes on back with repeated denominations, UV square with denomination, and watermark John Garang with electrotype denomination and Cornerstones.

BSS B1 (P5): **1 pound** (US$0.40)   VG   VF   UNC
Green. Front: Dr. John Garang de Mabior; spear. Back: Eight giraffes. Windowed security thread with demetalized *BANK OF SOUTH SUDAN 1*. Watermark: John Garang, electrotype *1*, and Cornerstones. Printer: (TDLR). 125 x 62 mm.
    a. No date. Signature 1. Prefix AA - AE.   FV   FV   1.75
        Intro: 18.07.2011.

BSS B2 (P6): **5 pounds** (US$1.90)   VG   VF   UNC
Red. Front: Dr. John Garang de Mabior; spear. Back: Six Juba cattle. Windowed security thread with demetalized *BANK OF SOUTH SUDAN 5*. Watermark: John Garang, electrotype *5*, and Cornerstones. Printer: (TDLR). 130 x 64 mm.
    a. No date. Signature 1. Prefix AB - AH.   FV   FV   5
        Intro: 18.07.2011.

BSS B3 (P7): **10 pounds** (US$3.75)　　　　　　　　　　VG　VF　UNC
Aqua. Front: Dr. John Garang de Mabior; spear. Back: Pineapple; water buffalo. Windowed security thread with demetalized *BSS 10*. Watermark: John Garang, electrotype *10,* and Cornerstones. Printer: (TDLR). 135 x 66 mm.

 ☐ a. No date. Signature 1. Prefix AD - AE.　　　　FV　FV　10
    Intro: 18.07.2011.
 ☐ as. Diagonal red *SPECIMEN* overprint.　　　　　—　　—　120

BSS B4 (P8): **25 pounds** (US$9.35)　　　　　　　　　　VG　VF　UNC
Brown. Front: Dr. John Garang de Mabior; spear. Back: Mine shaft or oil derrick; antelope. Windowed security thread with demetalized *BSS 25*. Watermark: John Garang, electrotype *25,* and Cornerstones. Printer: (TDLR). 140 x 70 mm.

 ☐ a. No date. Signature 1. Prefix AB - AC.　　　　FV　FV　20
    Intro: 18.07.2011.
 ☐ as. Diagonal red *SPECIMEN* overprint.　　　　　—　　—　120

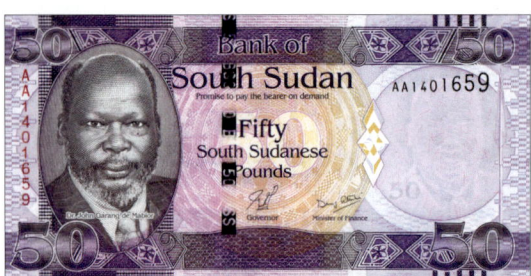

BSS B5 (P9): **50 pounds** (US$19)　　　　　　　　　　VG　VF　UNC
Purple. Front: Dr. John Garang de Mabior; spear. Back: Sorghum; four elephants. Windowed security thread with demetalized *BSS 50*. Watermark: John Garang, electrotype *50,* and Cornerstones. Printer: (TDLR). 142 x 72 mm.

 ☐ a. No date. Signature 1. Prefix AA.　　　　　FV　FV　50
    Intro: 18.07.2011.

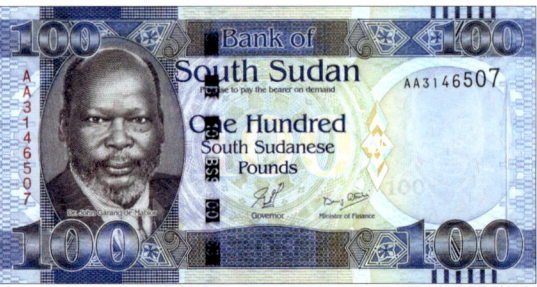

BSS B6 (P10): **100 pounds** (US$37)　　　　　　　　　VG　VF　UNC
Blue. Front: Dr. John Garang de Mabior; spear. Back: Reclining lion; waterfalls. Windowed security thread with demetalized *BSS 100*. Watermark: John Garang, electrotype *100,* and Cornerstones. Printer: (TDLR). 146 x 74 mm.

 ☐ a. No date. Signature 1. Prefix AA.　　　　　FV　FV　100
    Intro: 18.07.2011.

2011 Piaster Issues

On 19 October 2011 the Central Bank of South Sudan issued new notes in the denominations of 5, 10, and 25 piasters. These low-value notes make it possible to purchase smaller items that cost less than a pound, said Governor Kornelio Koriom. Initially a 50-piaster note was planned, but this denomination was dropped in favor of a coin.

BSS B7 (P1): 5 piasters (<US$0.05)   VG   VF   UNC
Brown, orange, and green. Front: Spear; Dr. John Garang de Mabior. Back: Two ostriches; spear. Solid security thread. Watermark: Flag pattern. Printer: (TDLR). 120 x 60 mm.
    ☐ a.   No date. Signature 1. Prefix AA.   FV   FV   7
          Intro: 19.10.2011.

BSS B8 (P2): 10 piasters (<US$0.05)   VG   VF   UNC
Green and yellow. Front: Spear; Dr. John Garang de Mabior. Back: Antelope; spear. Solid security thread. Watermark: Flag pattern. Printer: (TDLR). 120 x 60 mm.
    ☐ a.   No date. Signature 1. Prefix AB.   FV   FV   7
          Intro: 19.10.2011.

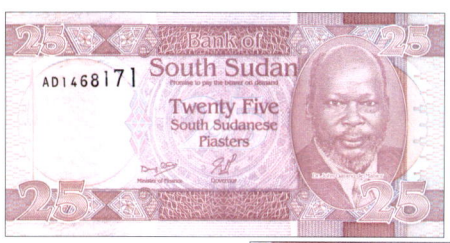

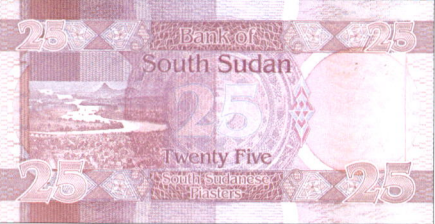

BSS B9 (P3): 25 piasters (US$0.10)   VG   VF   UNC
Violet and light blue. Front: Spear; Dr. John Garang de Mabior. Back: River; spear. Solid security thread. Watermark: Flag pattern. Printer: (TDLR). 120 x 60 mm.
    ☐ a.   No date. Signature 1. Prefix AD.   FV   FV   7
          Intro: 19.10.2011.

Looking Forward

According to a Reuters Africa article dated 16 August 2011, Elijah Malok has been replaced as the governor of the Bank of South Sudan by his former deputy, Kornelio Koriom Mayik (also reported as Cornella Koryom Mayiik). Malok's signature appears on South Sudan's first notes, so this move could lead to a new signature variety.

Acknowledgements

This chapter was compiled with the generous assistance of Murtaza Karimjee (m_abdeali@hotmail.com), Christoph Thomas, and others.

Sources

Anonymous. "South Sudan." *Exchange: The Global Magazine of De La Rue*. De La Rue, Hampshire, United Kingdom.
Cuhaj, George S. *Standard Catalog of World Paper Money, Modern Issues, 1961-Present*. 19th edition. 2013. ISBN 978-1-4402-3571-9. Krause Publications (www.krausebooks.com), 700 East State St., Iola, WI, 54990-0001.
Symes, Peter. "The Elusive Unofficial Banknotes of New Sudan." *IBNS Journal*. Volume 50 Number 1. p.27.

Share Your Input, Info, and Images

This catalog is believed to be complete and correct as of the time of publication. Prices and face values were last updated 17 November 2012. Please report errors or omissions so that corrections may be made. If you can more precisely identify the name or location of anything depicted on a note, please share that information. Furthermore, if you own an unlisted type or variety, please submit scans of the front and back of the note so that it can be documented. Scans should be 300 dots per inch, 100% actual size, 24-bit color, saved as *uncompressed* JPEG files, and sent to owen@banknotenews.com. Be sure to fully describe all attributes of the note which are not apparent upon visual inspection of the images alone, such as physical dimension, watermark, and security thread.

(South) Vietnam

For earlier issues, see French Indo-China.

Contents

National Bank of Vietnam (NBV)	1962
Bank of Vietnam (BOV)	1972
National Liberation Front (NLF)	1974

Monetary System
1953 - 02.05.1978: 1 South Vietnamese dong = 100 xu

Ngân-Hàng Quốc-Gia Việt-Nam (National Bank of Vietnam)

On 28 April 1954, France formally granted Vietnam full independence. The Geneva Accords, signed in July, established the division between Ho Chi Minh's North Vietnam and Bao Dai's South Vietnam. On 1 January 1955, the National Bank of Vietnam (Ngan Hang Quoc Gia Vietnam) assumed all central bank functions for the south, occupying the facilities of the Bank of Indochina on Quay de Belgique (renamed Chong Duong) in Saigon.

NBV Signature Varieties

1955 Issues

On 22 September 1955, the Ministry of Finance and Economic Affairs announced that notes from the Bank of Indochina and the Institut d'Emission issues for Cambodia and Laos would be exchanged for Institut d'Emission issues for Vietnam starting 30 September until 7 November. The Institut issues for Cambodia and Laos ceased to be legal tender on 7 October, and all Bank of Indochina notes lost their legal tender status on 31 October following the 15 October introduction of the first notes from the National Bank of Vietnam (NBV). The final step in the conversion process was the withdrawal of the Institut d'Emission issues for Vietnam, which took place on 8 January 1957, followed by demonetization on 18 January.

For its first decade, the issues of the National Bank of Vietnam didn't follow any obvious logical progression and don't group neatly into coherent series due to the use of several printers with disparate aesthetics and simultaneous introductions of notes of the same denominations with different designs.

NBV B1 (P11): **1 dong**   VG   VF   UNC
Gray. Front: Farmer threshing rice. Back: Farmer with pole in rice paddy. No security thread. Watermark: None. Printer: *SECURITY BANKNOTE COMPANY*. 115 x 65 mm.
- ☐ a. No date. Signature 1. Intro: 15.10.1955.   0.25   2   6
- ☐ as. Diagonal red *GIẤY MẪU* overprint; punched.   —   —   175
- ☐ p. Separate uniface front and back.   —   —   —

Replacement notes: Star control group.

NBV B2 (P12): **2 dong**   VG   VF   UNC
Purple. Front: Sail boat. Back: Palm trees, straw huts, and river. No security thread.
Watermark: None. Printer: SECURITY BANKNOTE COMPANY. 120 x 65 mm.

- a. No date. Signature 1. Intro: 15.10.1955.   0.25   1.25   3.75
- as1. Diagonal red *GIẤY MẪU* overprint;   —   —   165
  red # overprint on sail; punched.
- as2. Diagonal red *GIẤY MẪU* ovpt on uniface front;   —   —   165
  horizontal red *SPECIMEN No. US2-* # on back.
- p. Separate uniface front and back.   —   —   175

NBV B3 (P13): **5 dong**   VG   VF   UNC
Red. Front: Man with plow and water buffalo in rice paddy. Back: Tropical vegetation, river, straw hut. No security thread. Watermark: None. Printer: SECURITY BANKNOTE COMPANY. 125 x 65 mm.

- a. No date. Signature 1. Intro: 15.11.1955.   0.25   1.25   4.50
- as. Diagonal red *GIẤY MẪU* overprint; punched.   —   —   175
- p. Separate uniface front and back.   —   —   —

NBV B4 (P2): **5 dong**   VG   VF   UNC
Olive green. Front: Bird; dragons. Back: Dragons; man and water buffalo with plow in rice paddy field. No security thread. Watermark: Tiger head. Printer: (TDLR). 133 x 83 mm.

- a. No date. Signature 1. Intro: 15.11.1955.   —   —   —
  Error: Without tilde above *Y* in title at right.
- b. Corrected: With tilde above *Y* in title at right.   0.50   1.50   4.50
- as. Diagonal red *GIẤY MẪU* overprint;   —   —   150
  red # overprint on watermark oval.

NBV B5 (P3): **10 dong**   VG   VF   UNC
Red. Front: Fish; dragons. Back: Dragons; five boats at shore; trees. No security thread. Watermark: Tiger head. Printer: (TDLR). 140 x 87 mm.

- a. No date. Signature 1. Intro: 15.11.1955.   0.50   4.25   11
  Error: Without tilde above *Y* in title at right.
- b. Corrected: With tilde above *Y* in title at right.   0.50   4.25   11
- bs. Diagonal black *GIẤY MẪU* overprint;   —   —   200
  red # overprint on watermark oval.

NBV B6 (P8): **100 dong**   VG   VF   UNC
Black and green. Front: Man on modern tractor. Back: Peacock. No security thread.
Watermark: None. Printer: *ABNCo*. 155 x 66 mm.

☐	a.	No date. Signature 1. Intro: 01.11.1955.	3	12	45
☐	as1.	Two diagonal red GIẤY MẪU overprints; red # overprint near tractor; punched.	—	—	325
☐	as2.	Diagonal red SPECIMEN overprint.	—	—	325
☐	p.	Separate uniface front and back.	—	—	—

NBV B7 (P14): **200 dong** (demonetized 25.10.1958)   VG   VF   UNC
Green. Front: Soldier with rifle; palm tree; water buffalo. Back: Young girl with sheaves in field. No security thread. Watermark: None. Printer: *SECURITY BANKNOTE COMPANY*. 163 x 70 mm.

☐	a.	No date. Signature 1. Intro: 24.10.1955.	40	150	600
☐	as1.	Diagonal red GIẤY MẪU overprint.	—	—	500
☐	as2.	Diagonal red GIẤY MẪU overprint; red # overprint at upper left; punched.	—	—	500

Due to the controversy caused by its militaristic design, the bank stopped issuing this note shortly after its introduction.

NBV B8 (P14A): **200 dong**   VG   VF   UNC
Green. Front: Soldier with rifle; palm tree; water buffalo. Back: Young girl with sheaves in field. No security thread. Watermark: None. Printer: *SECURITY BANKNOTE COMPANY*. 130 x 65 mm.

☐	p.	Separate uniface front and back with horizontal red SPECIMEN overprint and 6-22-56 in border. Unissued.	—	—	1,000
☐	s.	Diagonal red GIẤY MẪU overprint.	—	—	675
☐	t1.	Color trial: Red.	—	—	2,500
☐	t2.	Color trial: Light blue.	—	—	2,500
☐	t3.	Color trial: Olive green.	—	—	2,500
☐	t4.	Color trial: Gray.	—	—	2,500
☐	t5.	Color trial: Dark blue.	—	—	2,500
☐	t6.	Color trial: Dark green.	—	—	2,500

Like NBV B7, but many decorative elements redesigned.

NBV B9 (P10): **500 dong** (demonetized 02.09.1964)   VG   VF   UNC
Blue and orange. Front: Thien Mu pagoda in Hue. Back: Guilloche pattern. No security thread. Watermark: None. Printer: (ABNC). 169 x 75 mm.

☐	a.	No date. Signature 1. Intro: 01.11.1955.	25	85	500
☐	as1.	Two diagonal red GIẤY MẪU overprints; punched.	—	—	1,200
☐	as2.	Diagonal red SPECIMEN overprint.	—	—	750
☐	p.	Separate uniface front and back.	—	—	—

1956 Issues

NBV B10 (P1): 1 dong   VG   VF   UNC
Green, yellow, and pink. Front: Ornate carved columns; temple building. Back: Trees; temple building. No security thread. Watermark: Tiger head. Printer: (BWC). 124 x 78 mm.
- a. No date. Signature 1. Intro: 02.02.1956.   0.25   1   4.25
- as. Diagonal red *GIẤY MẪU* overprint; red # overprint on watermark area; punched.   —   —   125

NBV B11 (P4): 20 dong   VG   VF   UNC
Green and red. Front: Trees; straw huts; boats; vines; bananas. Back: Water buffalo and farmers with plow in rice paddy. No security thread. Watermark: Tiger head. Printer: (BDF). 145 x 93 mm.
- a. No date. Signature 1. Intro: 29.12.1956.   3   12   55
- as. Diagonal black *GIẤY MẪU* overprint.   —   —   400

NBV B12 (P7): 50 dong   VG   VF   UNC
Purple. Front: Water buffalo and young boy. Back: Three straw bowls; two farmers with hats spreading rice to dry. No security thread. Watermark: None. Printer: *SECURITY BANKNOTE COMPANY*. 143 x 66 mm.
- a. No date. Signature 1. Intro: 29.12.1956.   3   12   45
- as. Diagonal red *GIẤY MẪU* overprint.   —   —   150
- p. Separate uniface front and back.   —   —   —

NBV B13 (P4A): 1,000 dong   VG   VF   UNC
Multicolor. Front: Old man; temple. Back: Sampan boat; young woman. No security thread. Printer: (BDF). 195 x 125 mm.
- p. Without watermark. Unissued (1955).   —   —   10,000
- s. Watermark: Woman. Horizontal black *GIẤY MẪU* overprint.   —   —   10,000

1958-1962 Issues

NBV B14 (P5): 10 dong   VG   VF   UNC
Red. Front: Woman with hat holding sheaf of rice; man with hoe over shoulder. Back: Palm trees; arched gate. No security thread. Watermark: None. Printer: *SECURITY BANKNOTE COMPANY*. 132 x 65 mm.

			VG	VF	UNC
☐	a.	No date. Signature 1. Intro: 14.01.1962.	0.50	1.25	5
☐	as.	Diagonal red *GIẤY MẪU* overprint; punched.	—	—	150
☐	p.	Separate uniface front and back.	—	—	150

NBV B15 (P6): 20 dong   VG   VF   UNC
Brown. Front: Trees; two oxen pulling cart with farmer. Back: Woman with shovel and baskets near stream. No security thread. Watermark: None. Printer: *SECURITY BANKNOTE COMPANY*. 138 x 65 mm.

			VG	VF	UNC
☐	a.	No date. Signature 1. Intro: 12.03.1962.	1.75	7	30
☐	as.	Diagonal blue *GIẤY MẪU* overprint; punched.	—	—	275
☐	p.	Separate uniface front and back.	—	—	150

NBV B16 (P18): 100 dong   VG   VF   UNC
Brown and green. Front: Dragon; National Assembly parliament (formerly the French Opera House) building in Saigon. Back: Dong Cam dam (part of the Tuy Hoa irrigation project); trees. Solid security thread. Watermark: Bamboo tree. Printer: (TDLR). 158 x 77 mm.

			VG	VF	UNC
☐	a.	No date. Sig. 1. Intro: 24.10.1960. Light brown and light green.	2.50	10	40
☐	b.	Dark brown and dark green.	2.50	10	40
☐	as1.	Diagonal red *GIẤY MẪU* overprint; punched.	—	—	300
☐	as2.	Diagonal black *GIẤY MẪU* overprint; punched.	—	—	300

NBV B17 (P9): 200 dong   VG   VF   UNC
Purple and green. Front: Peacocks; coat of arms with bamboo; National Bank of Vietnam headquarters building, cars, trees. Back: Fishing boats. No security thread. Watermark: None. Printer: *ABNCo*. 169 x 83 mm.

			VG	VF	UNC
☐	a.	No date. Signature 1. Intro: 25.10.1958.	5	15	65
☐	as.	Diagonal red *GIẤY MẪU* overprint; punched.	—	—	300
☐	p.	Separate uniface front and back.	—	—	—

NBV B18 (P6A): **500 dong** (demonetized 02.09.1964)   VG   VF   UNC
Blue and green. Front: Dragons; Norodom Palace (old French Governor-General's residence) building in Saigon. Back: Two straw huts; palm trees; water buffalos and man. Solid security thread. Watermark: Ngo Dinh Diem. Printer: (TDLR). 150 x 75 mm.

  ☐   a.   No date. Signature 2. Intro: 12.03.1962.   50   100   700
  ☐   as1. Diagonal red *GIẤY MẪU* overprint; punched.   —   —   1,000
  ☐   as2. DLR ovals.   —   —   1,000

Ngo Dinh Diem was overthrown on 1 November 1963, and assassinated the next day. This note circulated for only a short time, perhaps because it depicts his presidential palace (which was bombed in a failed 1962 coup d'etat attempt) and has the despised former president's portait as the watermark.

1964-1966 Issues

NBV B19 (P15): **1 dong**   VG   VF   UNC
Brown and orange. Front: Guilloche patterns. Back: Trees; man on modern tractor. No security thread. Watermark: Bamboo tree. Printer: (TDLR). 126 x 63 mm.

  ☐   a.   No date. Signature 2. Intro: 07.03.1964.   0.25   1   4
  ☐   as1. Diagonal red *GIẤY MẪU* overprint; punched.   —   —   1,200
  ☐   as2. DLR ovals.   —   —   1,200

NBV B20 (P16): **20 dong**   VG   VF   UNC
Green, brown, and blue. Front: Guilloche patterns. Back: Fish. Solid security thread. Watermark: Demon head. Printer: (TDLR). 144 x 70 mm.

  ☐   a.   No date. Signature 2. Intro: 08.01.1965.   0.25   1   6.25
  ☐   as. Diagonal red *GIẤY MẪU* overprint; punched.   —   —   300

NBV B21 (P17): **50 dong**   VG   VF   UNC
Purple, light blue, and orange. Front: Flowers; trellis. Back: Flowers. Solid security thread. Watermark: None. Printer: (BWC). 144 x 70 mm.

  ☐   a.   No date. Signature 3. Intro: 14.03.1966.   1   5   20
  ☐   as1. Diagonal red *GIẤY MẪU* overprint; punched.   —   —   300
  ☐   as2. Horizontal *CANCELLED* perforation.   —   —   —

NBV B22 (P19): **100 dong**   VG   VF   UNC
Red and yellow. Front: General Lê Văn Duyệt. Back: Temple and arched gate; trees. Solid security thread. Printer: (TDLR). 145 x 71 mm.

   ☐ a. No date. Signature 3. Intro: 01.11.1966.   1   10   40
         Watermark: Demon head.
   ☐ b. Watermark: Lê Văn Duyệt.   0.25   4   15
   ☐ as. DLR ovals.   —   —   500
   ☐ bs. Specimen.   —   —   500

NBV B23 (P20): **200 dong**   VG   VF   UNC
Brown and pink. Front: Emperor Nguyen Hue wearing helmet; trees. Back: Nguyen Hue with sword on rearing horse leading soldiers with spears, swords, and flag. Solid security thread. Printer: (BWC). 147 x 72 mm.

   ☐ a. No date. Signature 3. Intro: 03.01.1966.   1   14   45
         Watermark: Demon head.
   ☐ b. Watermark: Emperor Nguyen Hue.   0.25   10   25
   ☐ as. Specimen.   —   —   500
   ☐ bs. Specimen.   —   —   500
   ☐ bt. Color trial: Blue.   —   —   —

NBV B24 (P22): **500 dong**   VG   VF   UNC
Brown, yellow, and green. Front: National Museum (formerly the Musee Blanchard de la Brosse) building in Saigon. Back: Two dragons. Solid security thread. Watermark: Demon head. Printer: (TDLR). 149 x 74 mm.

   ☐ a. No date. Signature 2. Intro: 24.08.1964.   3   13   50
   ☐ as1. Diagonal red *GIẤY MẪU* overprint;   —   —   300
         horizontal red *GIẤY MẪU KHÔNG GIÁ TRI*
         overprint at upper left.
   ☐ as2. DLR ovals.   —   —   600

NBV B25 (P23): **500 dong**   VG   VF   UNC
Blue, green, and orange. Front: Grand Commander Tran Hung Dao. Back: Warships. Solid security thread. Watermark: Tran Hung Dao. Printer: (TDLR). 150 x 75 mm.

   ☐ a. No date. Signature 3. Intro: 27.07.1966.   0.75   3   15
   ☐ as. DLR ovals.   —   —   500

1969-1971 Issues

The watermark on all these notes is a portrait of Tran Hung Dao, a 13th century military Grand Commander of armies that repelled two major Mongol invasions.

NBV B26 (P24): **20 dong**   VG   VF   UNC
Red. Front: National Bank of Vietnam headquarters building. Back: Guilloche patterns. Solid security thread. Watermark: Tran Hung Dao. Printer: (BWC). 143 x 70 mm.

- ☐ a. No date. Signature 4. Intro: 15.12.1969.   0.25   1   2
- ☐ as. Diagonal red GIẤY MẪU overprint; punched.   —   —   175
- ☐ at. Color trial: Purple.   —   —   —

NBV B27 (P25): **50 dong**   VG   VF   UNC
Blue, red, and green. Front: National Bank of Vietnam headquarters building. Back: Guilloche patterns. Solid security thread. Watermark: Tran Hung Dao. Printer: (BWC). 143 x 70 mm.

- ☐ a. No date. Signature 4. Intro: 15.12.1969.   0.25   0.50   2
- ☐ as. Diagonal red GIẤY MẪU overprint; punched.   —   —   175
- ☐ at. Color trial: Olive green.   —   —   —

NBV B28 (P26): **100 dong**   VG   VF   UNC
Olive green and yellow. Front: National Bank of Vietnam headquarters building. Back: Guilloche patterns. Solid security thread. Watermark: Tran Hung Dao. Printer: (TDLR). 145 x 72 mm.

- ☐ a. No date. Signature 4. Intro: 16.02.1970.   0.25   1   5
- ☐ as1. Diagonal red GIẤY MẪU overprint; punched.   —   —   175
- ☐ as2. Diagonal red SPECIMEN and DLR oval ovpts; horizontal red SPECIMEN Nº # ovpt at lower left; punched.   —   —   865

NBV B29 (P27): **200 dong**   VG   VF   UNC
Purple and orange. Front: National Bank of Vietnam headquarters building. Back: Guilloche patterns. Solid security thread. Watermark: Tran Hung Dao. Printer: (TDLR). 143 x 70 mm.

- ☐ a. No date. Signature 4. Intro: 16.02.1970.   0.50   3   25
- ☐ as1. Diagonal red GIẤY MẪU overprint; punched.   —   —   300
- ☐ as2. Diagonal red SPECIMEN and DLR oval ovpts; horizontal red SPECIMEN Nº # ovpt at lower left; punched.   —   —   875

1972 Issues

These notes were announced on 25 August 1972, but their introduction may have been delayed until existing stocks of preceding issues were depleted. The front of all these notes depicts Independence Palace located on the site of the former presidential palace, which was severely damaged in a 1962 coup attempt. The new palace was inaugurated on 31 October 1966. The backs of these notes feature different native animals.

NBV B30 (P28): **500 dong**   VG   VF   UNC
Orange and green. Front: National Bank of Vietnam headquarters building. Back: Guilloche patterns. Solid security thread. Watermark: Tran Hung Dao. Printer: (TDLR). 152 x 76 mm.

- a. No date. Signature 4. Intro: 16.02.1970.   0.25   1.75   5
- as. Diagonal red *GIẤY MẪU* overprint; punched.   —   —   200

NBV B31 (P29): **1,000 dong**   VG   VF   UNC
Pink and turquoise. Front: National Bank of Vietnam headquarters building. Back: Guilloche patterns. Solid security thread. Watermark: Tran Hung Dao. Printer: (TDLR). 152 x 76 mm.

- a. No date. Signature 4. Intro: 29.11.1971.   0.25   1   5
- as. Diagonal red *GIẤY MẪU* overprint; punched.   —   —   250

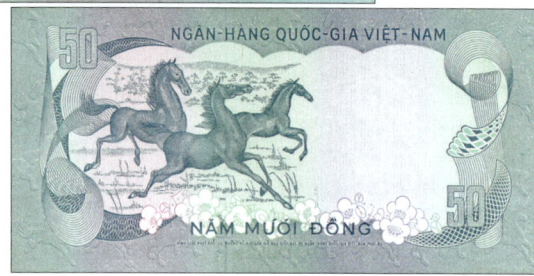

NBV B32 (P30): **50 dong**   VG   VF   UNC
Teal. Front: Independence Palace in Saigon. Back: Three horses running. Solid security thread. Watermark: Young woman. Printer: (BWC). 143 x 70 mm.

- a. No date. Signature 5. Intro: 27.08.1972.   0.25   1   4
- as. Diagonal red *GIẤY MẪU* overprint; horizontal red *GIẤY MẪU KHÔNG GIÁ TRỊ* overprint at upper left; punched.   —   —   400
- at. Color trial: Purple building.   —   —   —

NBV B33 (P31): **100 dong**   VG   VF   UNC
Green. Front: Independence Palace in Saigon. Back: Man with two water buffalo. Solid security thread. Watermark: Young woman. Printer: (BWC). 149 x 72 mm.

- a. No date. Signature 5. Intro: 27.08.1972.   0.25   1   4
- as. Diagonal red *GIẤY MẪU* overprint; horizontal red *GIẤY MẪU KHÔNG GIÁ TRỊ* overprint at upper left; punched.   —   —   400

NBV B34 (P32): **200 dong** VG VF UNC
Burgundy and green. Front: Flowers; Independence Palace in Saigon. Back: Three deer; fruit. Solid security thread. Watermark: Young woman. Printer: (TDLR). 149 x 72 mm.

- ☐ a. No date. Signature 5. Intro: 27.08.1972.   1   3   11
- ☐ as. Diagonal red *GIẤY MẪU* overprint; horizontal red *GIẤY MẪU KHÔNG GIÁ TRI* overprint at upper left.   —   —   500

NBV B35 (P33): **500 dong** VG VF UNC
Orange and olive green. Front: Flowers; Independence Palace in Saigon. Back: Tiger. Solid security thread. Watermark: Young woman. Printer: (TDLR). 153 x 75 mm.

- ☐ a. No date. Signature 5. Intro: 27.08.1972.   0.50   1.25   5
- ☐ as. Diagonal red *GIẤY MẪU* overprint; horizontal red *GIẤY MẪU KHÔNG GIÁ TRI* overprint at upper left.   —   —   500

NBV B36 (P34): **1,000 dong** VG VF UNC
Blue and green. Front: Flowers; Independence Palace in Saigon. Back: Three elephants carrying crates and drivers. Solid security thread. Watermark: Young woman. Printer: (TDLR). 153 x 75 mm.

- ☐ a. No date. Signature 5. Intro: 27.08.1972.   0.50   0.75   2
- ☐ as. Diagonal red *GIẤY MẪU* overprint; horizontal red *GIẤY MẪU KHÔNG GIÁ TRI* overprint at upper left.   —   —   500

NBV B37 (P35): **5,000 dong** VG VF UNC
Brown, gold, and red. Front: Flowers; Independence Palace in Saigon. Back: Snarling leopard. Solid security thread. Watermark: Young woman. Printer: (TDLR). 153 x 75 mm.

- ☐ a. No date. Signature 6. Unissued (1972).   50   200   825
- ☐ as. Diagonal red *GIẤY MẪU* overprint.   —   —   625

NBV B38 (P36): 10,000 dong   VG   VF   UNC
Purple and brown. Front: Flowers; Independence Palace in Saigon. Back: Water buffalo. Solid security thread. Watermark: Young woman. Printer: (TDLR). 153 x 75 mm.
- a. No date. Signature 6. Unissued (1972).   50   80   700
- as. Diagonal red *GIẤY MẪU* overprint.   —   —   750

1975 Issues

NBV B39 (P34A): 1,000 dong   VG   VF   UNC
Green and multicolor. Front: Fish; mandarin Truong Dinh. Back: Tomb of Truong Dinh in Gò Công, Tien Giang. Unknown security thread. Watermark: Young woman. Printer: (TDLR). 153 x 75 mm.
- s. Diagonal red *GIẤY MẪU* overprint.   —   —   2,200
  No date. Signature 6. Unissued (1975).

Ngân Hàng Việt-Nam (Bank of Vietnam)

1966 (1975) Issues

On 30 April 1975, President Duong Van Minh unconditionally surrendered to North Vietnamese forces and a new Provisional Revolutionary Government of South Vietnam assumed power. The notes of the now defunct National Bank of Vietnam continued to circulate until 22 September 1975, when they were exchanged at a rate of 500:1 for new issues of the Bank of Vietnam (BOV). Curiously the "new" notes were dated 1966 because they had been printed in advance of the Tet Offensive that began 31 January 1968, but had remained in storage for nearly a decade following the failure to topple South Vietnam. These new notes remained in use until the country merged with the Democratic Republic of Vietnam in 1978.

BOV B1 (P37): 10 xu   VG   VF   UNC
Brown, green, and yellow. Front: Workers with rakes and bowls drying salt in evaporating ponds. Back: Workers unloading boats of bales and large urns. No security thread. Watermark: None. Printer: Unknown. 100 x 50 mm.
- a. 1966. Intro: September 1975.   0.50   1.25   2.50
- as. Horizontal red *GIẤY MẪU* overprint;   —   —   15
  red # overprint at lower center on back.

BOV B2 (P38): 20 xu   VG   VF   UNC
Blue and orange. Front: Workers with truck harvesting rubber among trees. Back: Soldiers waving to farmers with oxen; palm trees. No security thread. Watermark: None. Printer: Unknown. 108 x 54 mm.
- a. 1966. Intro: September 1975.   0.50   1.25   3
- as. Horizontal red *GIẤY MẪU* overprint;   —   —   15
  red # overprint at lower center on back.

BOV B3 (P39): **50 xu** VG VF UNC

Brown and purple. Front: Farmers harvesting sugar cane and loading trucks. Back: Women weaving rugs. No security thread. Watermark: None. Printer: Unknown. 116 x 58 mm.

    ☐ a. 1966. Intro: September 1975.   0.50   2.50   8
    ☐ as. Horizontal red *GIẤY MẪU* overprint;   —   —   20
        red # overprint at lower center on back.

BOV B5 (P41): **2 dong** VG VF UNC

Green and blue. Front: Bridge, boats, and houseboats. Back: Farmers sharing food with soldiers with rifles, flag, and armored personnel carriers; palm trees. No security thread. Watermark: Stars and *VN* pattern. Printer: Unknown. 132 x 66 mm.

    ☐ a. 1966. Intro: September 1975.   1.50   2.50   10
    ☐ as. Horizontal red *GIẤY MẪU* overprint;   —   —   20
        red # overprint at lower center on back.

BOV B4 (P40): **1 dong** VG VF UNC

Reddish orange. Front: Palm trees; men on boats laden with fruit. Back: Farmers working in field with oxen, plow, rifles, trees, and huts. No security thread. Watermark: Stars and *VN* pattern. Printer: Unknown. 124 x 62 mm.

    ☐ a. 1966. Intro: September 1975.   1   3   10
    ☐ as. Horizontal blue *GIẤY MẪU* overprint;   —   —   20
        blue # overprint at lower center on back.

BOV B6 (P42): **5 dong** VG VF UNC

Purple. Front: Four women with spools of thread in textile factory. Back: Soldiers with rifles and flag cheering; smoldering crashed helicopters (Bell UH-1 Iroquois, Piasecki H-21 Workhorse/Shawnee, Sikorsky H-34 Choctaw). No security thread. Watermark: Stars and *VN* pattern. Printer: Unknown. 140 x 70 mm.

    ☐ a. 1966. Intro: September 1975.   1   4   15
    ☐ as. Horizontal red *GIẤY MẪU* overprint;   —   —   25
        red # overprint at lower center on back.

BOV B7 (P43): **10 dong**   VG   VF   UNC
Red. Front: House on stilts; trees; harbor with ships; steam train; three women with flowers; building. Back: Village buildings; trees; soldiers and citizens carrying flag. No security thread. Watermark: Stars and *VN* pattern. Printer: Unknown. 148 x 75 mm.
   ☐ a. 1966. Intro: September 1975.   2.50   10   40
   ☐ as. Horizontal black *GIẤY MẪU* overprint;   —   —   15
       black # overprint at lower center on back.

BOV B8 (P44): **50 dong**   VG   VF   UNC
Green and blue. Front: Workers in factories. Back: Combine harvester. No security thread. Watermark: Stars and *VN* pattern. Printer: Unknown. 156 x 79 mm.
   ☐ a. 1966. Intro: September 1975.   10   25   200
   ☐ as. Horizontal red *GIẤY MẪU* overprint;   —   —   50
       red # overprint at lower center on back.

Uy Ban Trung Uong Mat Tran Dan Toc Giai Phong Mien Nam Vietnam (Central Committee of the Popular Front for the Liberation of South Vietnam)

1966 Issues

These notes were prepared by the National Liberation Front (NLF) for issue in areas under NLF control, but the entire stock of notes was captured when the NLF headquarters in Cambodia was overrun during a 63-day joint operation between the United States and South Vietnamese which began 29 April 1970. These notes are likely produced at the same time (1966) and by the same printer as the Ngan Hang Vietnam (Bank of Vietnam) issues, and were probably also intended for introduction after the Tet Offensive.

NLF B1 (PR1): **10 xu**   VG   VF   UNC
Purple. Front: Star. Back: Star; guilloche pattern. No security thread. Watermark: None. Printer: (Unknown, China). 94 x 45 mm.
   ☐ a. No date. Unissued (1966).   0.25   1   3

NLF B2 (PR2): **20 xu**   VG   VF   UNC
Brown. Front: Star. Back: Star. No security thread. Watermark: None. Printer: (Unknown, China). 106 x 53 mm.
   ☐ a. No date. Unissued (1966).   0.25   1   5

NLF B3 (PR3): **50 xu**   VG   VF   UNC
Green. Front: Star. Back: Star; floral design. No security thread. Watermark: None. Printer: (Unknown, China). 114 x 57 mm.

☐ a. No date. Unissued (1966).   0.50   2   5

NLF B4 (PR4): **1 dong**   VG   VF   UNC
Brown. Front: Farmers harvesting grain. Back: Schoolchildren at desks with open books. No security thread. Watermark: Star pattern. Printer: (Unknown, China). 122 x 61 mm.

☐ a. No date. Unissued (1966).   1   3   10

NLF B5 (PR5): **2 dong**   VG   VF   UNC
Blue and yellow. Front: Women with backpacks hiking through forest. Back: Men in boats casting nets into river. No security thread. Watermark: Star pattern. Printer: (Unknown, China). 130 x 65 mm.

☐ a. No date. Unissued (1966).   1   5   25

NLF B6 (PR6): **5 dong**   VG   VF   UNC
Lilac. Front: Women with rifles harvesting tea in a field. Back: Women soldiers with weapons; palm trees. No security thread. Watermark: Star pattern. Printer: (Unknown, China). 140 x 69 mm.

☐ a. No date. Unissued (1966).   1.50   6   50

NLF B7 (PR7): **10 dong**   VG   VF   UNC
Green. Front: Farmers harvesting sugar cane. Back: Soldiers ambushing armored convey on road through forest. No security thread. Watermark: Star pattern. Printer: (Unknown, China). 145 x 73 mm.

☐ a. No date. Unissued (1966).   5   20   80

NLF B8 (PR8): **50 dong**   VG   VF   UNC
Orange. Front: Truck convoy. Back: Soldiers shooting down helicopters. No security thread. Watermark: Stars and *VN* pattern. Printer: (Unknown, China). 155 x 77 mm.
☐   a.   No date. Unissued (1966).   20   100   200

Looking Forward

On 3 May 1978, the currency of a unified Socialist Republic of Vietnam (SRVN) was introduced, replacing at par the notes previously issued by the Democratic Republic of Vietnam (North Vietnam), and at 0.8:1 for the 1966-dated notes issued by the Provisional Revolutionary Government in September 1975.

For later issues, see Vietnam.

Acknowledgements

This chapter was compiled with the generous assistance of Jim W. C. Chen, Compagnie Generale De Bourse (www.cgb.fr), Stephen Dowsett, Larry Hirsch (www.aworldcurrency.com), Sema Kachalo (http://art-hanoi.com), Victor M. González Miguel, Wally Myers, Bill Stubkjaer, Chris Twining (www.pagescoinsandcurrency.com), and others.

Sources

Cuhaj, George S. *Standard Catalog of World Paper Money, General Issues, 1368-1960.* 14th edition. 2012. ISBN 978-1-4402-3090-5. Krause Publications (www.krausebooks.com), 700 East State St., Iola, WI, 54990-0001.

Cuhaj, George S. *Standard Catalog of World Paper Money, Modern Issues, 1961-Present.* 18th edition. 2012. ISBN 978-1-4402-2956-5. Krause Publications (www.krausebooks.com), 700 East State St., Iola, WI, 54990-0001.

Friedman, Herbert A. "Propaganda Overprints on the Wartime Currency of Vietnam." *IBNS Journal.* Volume 26 Number 1. p.10.

Friedman, Herbert A. "Vietnam War Propaganda Notes." *IBNS Journal.* Volume 21 Number 3. p.76.

Reedy, Clyde M. "A Historical Study: Banknotes of South Vietnam." *IBNS Journal.* Volume 22 Number 2. p.35.

Share Your Input, Info, and Images

This catalog is believed to be complete and correct as of the time of publication. Prices and face values were last updated 22 June 2012. Please report errors or omissions so that corrections may be made. If you can more precisely identify the name or location of anything depicted on a note, please share that information. Furthermore, if you own an unlisted type or variety, please submit scans of the front and back of the note so that it can be documented. Scans should be 300 dots per inch, 100% actual size, 24-bit color, saved as *uncompressed* JPEG files, and sent to owen@banknotenews.com. Be sure to fully describe all attributes of the note which are not apparent upon visual inspection of the images alone, such as physical dimension, watermark, and security thread.

Sri Lanka

Ceylon Issues

In 1972, Ceylon became a republic and the official name of the country was changed to "Free, Sovereign and Independent Republic of Sri Lanka." Nonetheless, the banknotes continued to bear the name of the Central Bank of Ceylon until 1985. For notes issued prior to 1985, see Ceylon.

Monetary System

1 Sri Lankan rupee (LKR) = 100 cents

Central Bank of Sri Lanka

The Central Bank of Ceylon (CBC) was renamed the Central Bank of Sri Lanka (CBSL) in 1985.

CBSL Signature Varieties

	Finance Minister	Governor
1	 Ronald Joseph Godfrey de Mel (23.07.1977 - 18.01.1988)	 Warnasena Rasaputram (1979 - 1988)
2	 M. H. M. Naina Marikkar (10.01.1988 - 03.01.1989)	 Warnasena Rasaputram (1979 - 1988)
3	 M. H. M. Naina Marikkar (10.01.1988 - 03.01.1989)	 H. N. S. Karunatilake (1988 - 1992)
4a	 Dingiri Banda Wijetunge (18.02.1989 - 31.08.1994)	 H. N. S. Karunatilake (1988 - 1992)
4b	 Dingiri Banda Wijetunge (18.02.1989 - 31.08.1994)	 H. N. S. Karunatilake (1988 - 1992)
5	 Dingiri Banda Wijetunge (18.02.1989 - 31.08.1994)	 H. B. Dissanayaka (1992 - 1995)
6	 Chandrika Kumaranatunga (30.09.1994 - 05.12.2001)	 H. B. Dissanayaka (1992 - 1995)

CBSL Signature Varieties

	Finance Minister	Governor
7	 Chandrika Kumaranatunga (30.09.1994 - 05.12.2001)	 A. S. Jayawardana (1995 - 2004)
8	 K. Nariman Choksy (12.12.2001 - 02.04.2004)	 A. S. Jayawardana (1995 - 2004)
9	 Sarath L. B. Amunugama (14.04.2004 - 22.11.2005)	 A. S. Jayawardana (1995 - 2004)
10	 Sarath L. B. Amunugama (14.04.2004 - 22.11.2005)	 Sunil Mendis (2004 - 2006)
11	 Mahinda Rajapaksa (23.11.2005 - present)	 Sunil Mendis (2004 - 2006)
12	Mahinda Rajapaksa (23.11.2005 - present)	 Ajith Nivard Cabraal (2006 - present)

1987-1990 Issues

These notes are like the preceding issues from Ceylon, but the bank's name has been changed, there have been some minor changes to captions and designs, and the watermark now bears the heraldic lion depicted in the national flag of Sri Lanka. This new series of notes no longer contains a 5-rupee denomination.

CBSL B1 (P96): **10 rupees** (US$0.10)   VG   VF   UNC
Brown. Front: Octagon building (paththirippuwa) at Temple of the Sacred Tooth Relic in Kandy. Back: Dagoba Raja Maha Vihare (Buddhist temple) in Kelaniya. Solid security thread with printed CENTRAL BANK OF SRI LANKA. Watermark: Chinthe. Printer: BRADBURY WILKINSON. 127 x 66 mm.

	Date	Signature/Prefix	VG	VF	UNC
☐ a.	1987-01-01. Signature 1. Prefix F/1 - F/60.		0.25	0.75	3
☐ b.	1988-11-21. Signature 3. Prefix F/62 - F/69.		0.25	0.75	3
☐ c.	1989-02-21. Signature 4b. Prefix F/73 - F/120.		0.25	0.75	3
☐ d.	1990-04-05. Prefix F/121 - F/183.		0.25	0.75	3

CBSL B3 (P98): **50 rupees** (US$0.40)   VG   VF   UNC
Blue and brown. Front: Birds; Raja Maha Vihare temple in Kelaniya. Back: Flowers; headless Buddha statue at Lankatilaka Vihare shrine in Polonnaruwa. Solid security thread with printed CENTRAL BANK OF SRI LANKA. Watermark: Chinthe. Printer: BRADBURY WILKINSON. 147 x 74 mm.

| ☐ a. | 1989-02-21. Signature 4a. Prefix D/1 - D/23. | 0.75 | 2 | 8 |
| ☐ b. | 1990-04-05. Signature 4b. Prefix D/24. | 0.75 | 2 | 8 |

CBSL B2 (P97): **20 rupees** (US$0.15)   VG   VF   UNC
Purple and red. Front: Moonstone (sandakada pahana) steps at Anuradhapura. Back: Thuparama Dagoba (temple) in Anuradhapura; orchids. Solid security thread with printed CENTRAL BANK OF SRI LANKA. Watermark: Chinthe. Printer: BRADBURY WILKINSON. 137 x 70 mm.

☐ a.	1988-11-21. Signature 3. Prefix E/1 - E/5.	0.75	3	12
☐ b.	1989-02-21. Signature 4a. Prefix E/6 - E/18.	FV	1.50	5
☐ c.	1990-04-05. Signature 4b. Prefix E/20 - E/49.	FV	1.50	5

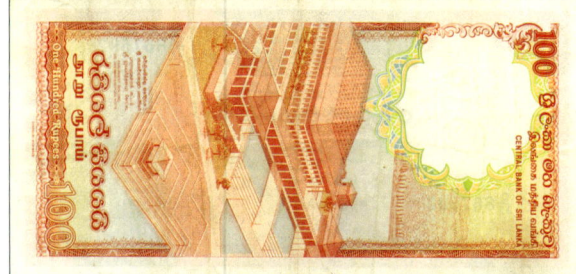

CBSL B4 (P99): **100 rupees** (US$0.75)   VG   VF   UNC
Orange and brown. Front: Animals; stone carving (korawakgala) of chinthe in Anuradhapura. Back: Parliament building in Sri Jayewardenepura-Kotte. Solid security thread with printed CENTRAL BANK OF SRI LANKA. Watermark: Chinthe. Printer: BRADBURY WILKINSON. 157 x 76 mm.

☐ a.	1987-01-01. Signature 1. Prefix C/1 - C/10.	FV	5	18
☐ b.	1988-02-01. Signature 2. Prefix C/11 - C/42.	FV	5	18
☐ c.	1989-02-21. Signature 4b. Prefix C/48 - C/52.	FV	5	18
☐ d.	1990-04-05. Prefix C/55 - C/74.	FV	5	18

1991-1994 "Heritage" Issues

These notes feature new designs and are smaller in size than the preceding notes.

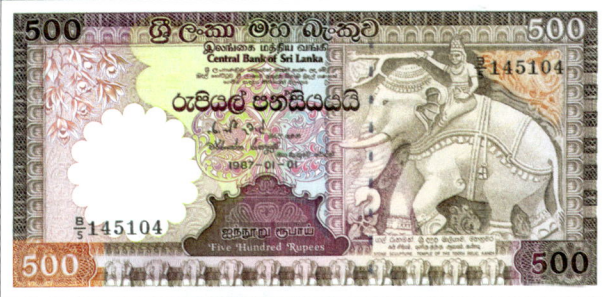

CBSL B5 (P100): **500 rupees** (US$3.85)   VG   VF   UNC

Brown and purple. Front: Stone carving (korawakgala) of elephant with rider at Temple of the Sacred Tooth Relic in Kandy. Back: Abhayagiri stupa; Anuradhapura temple. Windowed security thread. Watermark: Chinthe. Printer: *BRADBURY WILKINSON.* 167 x 79 mm.

☐	a.	1987-01-01. Signature 1. Prefix B/1 - B/5.	FV	20	75
☐	b.	1988-11-21. Signature 3. Prefix B/6 - B/8.	FV	20	75
☐	c.	1989-02-21. Signature 4a. Prefix B/9 - B/15.	FV	20	75
☐	d.	1990-04-05. Signature 4b. Prefix B/18 - B/20.	FV	20	75

CBSL B6 (P101): **1,000 rupees** (US$7.70)   VG   VF   UNC

Green. Front: Bowattena dam. Back (vertical): University of Ruhuna buildings; peacock. Windowed security thread. Watermark: Chinthe. Printer: *BRADBURY WILKINSON.* 177 x 82 mm.

☐	a.	1987-01-01. Signature 1. Prefix A/1 - A/9.	FV	15	60
☐	b.	1989-02-21. Signature 4a. Prefix A/13 - A/15.	FV	15	60
☐	c.	1990-04-05. Signature 4b. Prefix A/16 - A/18.	FV	15	60

CBSL B7 (P102): **10 rupees** (US$0.10)   VG   VF   UNC

Green and brown. Front: Chinthe sculpture in Yapahuwa. Back (vertical): Painted stork; Presidential Secretariat building in Colombo; flowers. Solid security thread with printed *CENTRAL BANK OF SRI LANKA RUPEES TEN.* Watermark: Chinthe. Printer: *THOMAS DE LA RUE AND COMPANY LIMITED.* 122 x 60 mm.

☐	a.	1991-01-01. Signature 4b. Prefix M/1 - M/15.	FV	0.50	2
☐	b.	1992-07-01. Signature 5. Prefix M/18 - M/76.	FV	0.50	2
☐	c.	1994-08-19. Signature 6. Prefix M/78 - M/146. Watermark: Electrotype sword added.	FV	0.50	1.50

Replacement notes: Prefix Z/1.

CBSL B8 (P103): **20 rupees** (US$0.15)   VG   VF   UNC

Purple and red. Front: Native devil mask (vesmuhunu). Back (vertical): Fish; two boys with hats fishing seated on poles; conch shells. Solid security thread with printed *CENTRAL BANK OF SRI LANKA RUPEES TWENTY.* Watermark: Chinthe. Printer: *THOMAS DE LA RUE AND COMPANY LIMITED.* 130 x 64 mm.

☐	a.	1991-01-01. Signature 4b. Prefix L/1 - L/18.	FV	0.75	2.50
☐	b.	1992-07-01. Signature 5. Prefix L/21 - L/26.	FV	0.75	2.50
☐	c.	1994-08-19. Signature 6. Prefix L/39.	FV	0.75	2.50

Replacement notes: Prefix Z/1.

CBSL B9 (P104): **50 rupees** (US$0.40) VG VF UNC

Blue and green. Front: Kandyan dancer with ornate headdress. Back (vertical): Butterflies; Jetavana and Thuparama stupas in Anuradhapura; shield; ornamental sword. Solid security thread with printed *CENTRAL BANK OF SRI LANKA RUPEES FIFTY*. Watermark: Chinthe. Printer: *THOMAS DE LA RUE AND COMPANY LIMITED*. 136 x 68 mm.

☐ a.	1991-01-01. Signature 4b. Prefix K/1 - K/5.	FV	1	5
☐ b.	1992-07-01. Signature 5. Prefix K/9 - K/37.	FV	1	5
☐ c.	1994-08-19. Signature 6. Prefix K/43 - K/58.	FV	1	5

Replacement notes: Prefix Z/1.

CBSL B11 (P105A): **100 rupees** (US$0.75) VG VF UNC

Orange. Front: Ornate urn. Back (vertical): Flowers; Sigiriya (Lion's Rock) castle ruins in Matale District; four women picking tea leaves; two rose-ringed parakeet birds. Solid security thread with printed *CENTRAL BANK OF SRI LANKA RUPEES ONE HUNDRED*. Watermark: Chinthe. Printer: *THOMAS DE LA RUE AND COMPANY LIMITED*. 144 x 72 mm.

☐ a.	1992-07-01. Signature 5. Prefix J/124.	FV	1.50	6

Replacement notes: Prefix Z/1.

This note is like CBSL B10, but with orange instead of brown on the back.

CBSL B10 (P105): **100 rupees** (US$0.75) VG VF UNC

Orange. Front: Ornate urn. Back (vertical): Flowers; Sigiriya (Lion's Rock) castle ruins in Matale District; four women picking tea leaves; two rose-ringed parakeet birds. Solid security thread with printed *CENTRAL BANK OF SRI LANKA RUPEES ONE HUNDRED*. Watermark: Chinthe. Printer: *THOMAS DE LA RUE AND COMPANY LIMITED*. 144 x 72 mm.

☐ a.	1991-01-01. Signature 4b. Prefix J/1. Without dot over Tamil text at left front.	FV	15	60
☐ b.	With dot over Tamil text. Prefix J/1 - J/5.	FV	2.50	30
☐ c.	1992-07-01. Signature 5. Prefix J/23 - J/46.	FV	2.50	10

Replacement notes: Prefix Z/1.

CBSL B12 (P106): **500 rupees** (US$3.85) VG VF UNC

Multicolor. Front: Kandyan dancer; two male drummers. Back (vertical): Stork-billed kingfisher with fish in beak; Ruwanwelisaya stupa and lotus stem pillars in Anuradhapura; orchids. Windowed security thread. Watermark: Chinthe. Printer: *THOMAS DE LA RUE AND COMPANY LIMITED*. 150 x 75 mm.

☐ a.	1991-01-01. Signature 4b. Prefix H/1 - H/14.	FV	15	50
☐ b.	1992-07-01. Signature 5. Prefix H/22 - H/34.	FV	15	50

Replacement notes: Prefix Z/1.

CBSL B10a (left) without dot over Tamil text at left front and B10b (right).

CBSL B13 (P107): **1,000 rupees** (US$7.70) VG VF UNC

Green. Front: Chinthe; Raja, a Sathdantha tusker elephant, carrying relic in Esala Perahera (Festival of the Tooth); elephant with mahout. Back (vertical): Lotus flowers; Octagon building (paththirippuwa) at Temple of the Sacred Tooth Relic in Kandy; two peacocks. Windowed security thread. Watermark: Chinthe. Printer: *THOMAS DE LA RUE AND COMPANY LIMITED*. 157 x 78 mm.

- ☐ a. 1991-01-01. Signature 4b. Prefix G/1 - G/4. FV FV 50
- ☐ b. 1992-07-01. Signature 5. Prefix G/7 - G/13. FV FV 50

Replacement notes: Prefix Z/1.

1995-2006 Issues

These notes are like the preceding issues, but with latent images at lower center on front.

CBSL B14 (P108 & P115): **10 rupees** (US$0.10) VG VF UNC

Green and brown. Front: Chinthe sculpture in Yapahuwa. Back (vertical): Painted stork; Presidential Secretariat building in Colombo; flowers. Solid security thread with printed *CENTRAL BANK OF SRI LANKA RUPEES TEN*. Watermark: Chinthe with electrotype sword. Printer: *THOMAS DE LA RUE AND COMPANY LIMITED*. 122 x 60 mm.

- ☐ a. 1995-11-15. Signature 7. Prefix M/147 - M/263. FV FV 1.50
- ☐ b. 2001-12-12. Signature 8. Prefix M/269 - M/346. FV FV 1
- ☐ c. 2004-04-10. Signature 9. Prefix M/347 - M/383. FV FV 1
- ☐ d. 2004-07-01. Signature 10. Prefix M/387 - M/457. FV FV 0.75
- ☐ e. 2005-11-19. Signature 11. Prefix M/462 - M/545. FV FV 0.75
- ☐ f. 2006-07-03. Signature 12. Prefix M/553 - M/581. FV FV 0.50

Replacement notes: Prefix Z/1.

CBSL B15 (P109 & P116): **20 rupees** (US$0.15) VG VF UNC

Purple and red. Front: Native devil mask (vesmuhunu). Back (vertical): Fish; two boys with hats fishing seated on poles; conch shells. Solid security thread with printed *CENTRAL BANK OF SRI LANKA RUPEES TWENTY*. Watermark: Chinthe with electrotype sword Printer: *THOMAS DE LA RUE AND COMPANY LIMITED*. 130 x 64 mm.

- ☐ a. 1995-11-15. Signature 7. Prefix L/41 - L/172. FV FV 2
- ☐ b. 2001-12-12. Signature 8. Prefix L/186 - L/257. FV FV 1.50
- ☐ c. 2004-07-01. Signature 10. Prefix L/261 - L/294. FV FV 1
- ☐ d. 2005-11-19. Signature 11. Prefix L/303 - L/364. FV FV 1
- ☐ e. 2006-07-03. Signature 12. Prefix L/367 - L/445. FV FV 0.50

Replacement notes: Prefix Z/2.

CBSL B16 (P110 & P117): **50 rupees** (US$0.40) VG VF UNC

Blue and green. Front: Kandyan dancer with ornate headdress. Back (vertical): Butterflies; Jetavana and Thuparama stupas in Anuradhapura; shield; ornamental sword. Solid security thread with printed *CENTRAL BANK OF SRI LANKA RUPEES FIFTY*. Watermark: Chinthe with electrotype sword. Printer: *THOMAS DE LA RUE AND COMPANY LIMITED*. 136 x 68 mm.

- ☐ a. 1995-11-15. Signature 7. Prefix K/64 - K/149. FV FV 3.50
- ☐ b. 2001-12-12. Signature 8. Prefix K/158 - K/184. FV FV 2
- ☐ c. 2004-04-10. Signature 9. Prefix K/190 - K/214. FV FV 2
- ☐ d. 2004-07-01. Signature 10. Prefix K/220 - K/244. FV FV 1.50
- ☐ e. 2005-11-19. Signature 11. Prefix K/245 - K/280. FV FV 1
- ☐ f. 2006-07-03. Signature 12. Prefix K/281 - K/332. FV FV 1.50

Replacement notes: Prefix Z/3.

CBSL B17 (P111 & P118): **100 rupees** (US$0.75)   VG   VF   UNC

Orange. Front: Ornate urn. Back (vertical): Flowers; Sigiriya (Lion's Rock) castle ruins in Matale District; four women picking tea leaves; two rose-ringed parakeet birds. Solid security thread with printed *CENTRAL BANK OF SRI LANKA RUPEES ONE HUNDRED*. Watermark: Chinthe with electrotype sword. Printer: *THOMAS DE LA RUE AND COMPANY LIMITED*. 144 x 72 mm.

☐	a. 1995-11-15. Signature 7. Prefix J/126 - J/225.	FV	FV	4
☐	b. 2001-12-12. Signature 8. Prefix J/237 - J/313.	FV	FV	3.50
☐	c. 2004-07-01. Signature 10. Prefix J/336 - J/379.	FV	FV	3
☐	d. 2005-11-19. Signature 11. Prefix J/391 - J/527. Intro: 22.05.2006.	FV	FV	2.50
☐	e. 2006-07-03. Signature 12. Prefix J/533 - J/565.	FV	FV	2

Replacement notes: Prefix Z/4.

CBSL B18 (P112 & P119): **500 rupees** (US$3.85)   VG   VF   UNC

Multicolor. Front: Kandyan dancer; two male drummers. Back (vertical): Stork-billed kingfisher with fish in beak; Ruwanwelisaya stupa and lotus stem pillars in Anuradhapura; orchids. Printer: *THOMAS DE LA RUE AND COMPANY LIMITED*. 150 x 75 mm.

☐	a. 1995-11-15. Signature 7. Prefix H/39 - H/70. Windowed security thread. Watermark: Chinthe with electrotype sword.	FV	FV	50
☐	b. 2001-12-12. Signature 8. Prefix H/72 - H/80. Windowed security thread with demetalized ornamental daisies pattern.	FV	FV	25
☐	c. 2004-04-10. Signature 9. Prefix H/87 - H/92.	FV	FV	15
☐	d. 2004-07-01. Signature 10. Prefix H/97 - H/109.	FV	FV	15
☐	e. 2005-11-19. Signature 11. Prefix H/112 - H/146. Red-to-green 3-mm StarChrome windowed security thread with *RS 500* and butterfly. Watermark: Cornerstones added. Intro: 17.10.2006.	FV	FV	12
☐	cs. Diagonal red *SPECIMEN* overprint; horizontal red *SPECIMEN Nº #* at lower left.	—	—	275

Replacement notes: Prefix Z/5.

CBSL B19 (P113 & P120): **1,000 rupees** (US$7.70)   VG   VF   UNC

Green. Front: Chinthe; Raja, a Sathdantha tusker elephant, carrying relic in Esala Perahera (Festival of the Tooth); elephant with mahout. Back (vertical): Lotus flowers; Octagon building (paththirippuwa) at Temple of the Sacred Tooth Relic in Kandy; two peacocks. Printer: *THOMAS DE LA RUE AND COMPANY LIMITED.* 157 x 78 mm.

- ☐ a. 1995-11-15. Signature 7. Prefix G/31 - G/102. FV FV 60
    Windowed security thread.
    Watermark: Chinthe with electrotype sword.
- ☐ b. 2001-12-12. Signature 8. Prefix G/109 - G/130. FV FV 20
    Windowed security thread with demetalized ornamental pattern.
- ☐ c. 2004-04-10. Signature 9. Prefix G/135 - G/147. FV FV 20
- ☐ d. 2004-07-01. Signature 10. Prefix G/156 - G/177. FV FV 30
- ☐ e. 2006-07-03. Signature 12. Prefix G/186 - G/245. FV FV 17
    Red-to-green 3-mm StarChrome windowed security thread with *SRI LANKA RS 1000* and butterfly. Watermark: Cornerstones added.
    Intro: 03.03.2008.

Replacement notes: Prefix Z/6.

CBSL B20 (P121): **2,000 rupees** (US$18)   VG   VF   UNC

Light rose and brown. Front: Elephant procession; Sigiriya (Lion's Rock) castle ruins in Matale District; Sesatha (ceremonial flag). Back (vertical): Sigiriya fresco. Red-to-green 4-mm StarChrome windowed security thread with demetalized *SRI LANKA RS 2000* and butterfly. Watermark: Chinthe with electrotype sword; Cornerstones. Printer: *DE LA RUE.* 164 x 82 mm.

- ☐ a. 2005-11-02. Signature 10. Prefix P1/ - P/29. FV FV 35
    Intro: 17.10.2006.
- ☐ b. 2006-07-03. Signature 12. Prefix P/32 - P/70. FV FV 30

Replacement notes: Prefix Z/7.

1998 Commemorative Issues

This 200-rupee note was issued to commemorate the 50th anniversary of independence (1948-1998). This is the first polymer banknote issued in Sri Lanka.

CBSL B21 (P114b): **200 rupees** (US$1.80) VG VF UNC

Blue and yellow. Front: Temple; scenes of "progress:" doctor and nurse representing free education and health services; woman with scythe (Gal Oya development); electrical power tower; Bandaranaike Memorial International Conference Hall; Victoria Dam (Mahaweli development project); jumbo jet and control tower at Bandaranaike International Airport (BIA); telecommunications satellite dishes; young women (Investment Promotion Zone); new parliament complex in Sri Jayewardenepura-Kotte; Colombo port and city; two couples with dove; churches and temples (unity and peace). Back: Octagon building (paththirippuwa) at Temple of the Sacred Tooth Relic in Kandy; scenes of "national heritage;" advent of Prince Vijaya; arrival of Arahant Mahinda and introduction of Buddhism; King Durugemunu builds Maha Seya; King Kasyapa build palace at Sigiriya rock; King Parakramabahu the Great constructs Sea of Parakrama; invasion by Portuguese and Dutch; conquest by British; Wariyapola Sri Sumangala Thero hauling down British flag at Kandyan convention. No security thread. Watermark: Chinthe within *200*. Printer: (NPA). 146 x 72 mm. Polymer.

    ☐ a. 1998-02-04. Signature 7. Black serial numbers.   FV   FV   5
         Prefix N/1 - N/22.
    ☐ as. Horizontal red *SPECIMEN No. #* overprint.   —   —   1,500

1998 Numismatic Products

CBSL BNP1 (P114a): **200 rupees** (US$1.75)   UNC
    ☐ a. CBSL B21 with red serial numbers in folder. Prefix N/1.   10

2009 Commemorative Issues

This 1,000-rupee note was issued to commemorate "the ushering of peace and prosperity to Sri Lanka." The theme on the front of the note is "one country and one nation in harmony, progressing towards prosperity." The back celebrates "the valiant contribution made by the nation's victorious sons and daughters of the security forces and the police."

CBSL B22 (P122): **1,000 rupees** (US$7.70) VG VF UNC

Blue, yellow, and red. Front: Ears of paddy and Punkalasa on map with rising sun behind; President Mahinda Rajapaksa with outstretched arms; flag. Back: Tank; ship; helicopter; hoisting of the national flag by members of the security forces; Mavil Aru annicut; Thoppigala rock (Baron's Cap); two jet fighters. 1.2-mm wide windowed ClearText security thread with demetalized *CBSL 1000*. Watermark: Chinthe with electrotype sword; Cornerstones. Printer: (TDLR). 157 x 78.5 mm.

    ☐ a. 2009-05-20. Signature 12. Prefix Q/1 - Q/24.   FV   FV   17
         Intro: 17.11.2009.
    ☐ as. Diagonal red *SPECIMEN* overprint;   —   —
         horizontal red *SPECIMEN Nº #* at lower left.

Replacement notes: Prefix Z/7.

2009 Numismatic Products

A limited number of commemorative 1,000-rupee notes with the first serial numbers in an folder were issued at a price of 1,500 rupees each. Furthermore, specimens were also packaged in a different folder.

CBSL BNP2 (PNL): **1,000 rupees** (US$7.70) UNC
- a. CBSL B22a with first serial numbers in folder. 30

CBSL BNP2.5 (PNL): **1,000 rupees** (US$7.70) UNC
- a. CBSL B22as in folder. 550

2010 Issues

To celebrate its 60th anniversary, the Central Bank of Sri Lanka issued a new series of banknotes on 4 February 2011. The series was designed by two Sri Lankan artists selected from an island-wide competition. The themes of the new notes are Development and Prosperity, and Sri Lankan Dancers. The fronts of the new notes bear artistic impressions of selected development projects in Sri Lanka and native birds and butterflies. The backs depict Sri Lankan traditional dancers and guard stone (muragala)s in a background of a map of Sri Lanka. This new family does not include a 10-rupee note because that denomination was replaced by a coin on 5 April 2010.

CBSL B23 (P123): **20 rupees** (US$0.15) VG VF UNC
Red and orange. Front: Baronet (Symphaedra nais) butterfly; modern Port of Colombo with ships, containers, and gantry cranes; old Port of Colombo with ship; Sri Lanka Serendib Scops Owl (Otus thilohoffmanni) bird; chinthe with sword. Back (vertical): Geta Bera drummer and Ves Netuma dancer; guard stone (muragala) with punkalasa (pot of plenty, symbol of prosperity); stylized liya vela floral motif. Solid security thread with printed *CBSL RS 20*. Watermark: Owl with electrotype *20* and Cornerstones. Printer: *DE LA RUE*. 128 x 67 mm.
- a. 2010-01-01. Signature 12. Prefix W/1 - W/154. FV FV 0.50
Intro: 04.02.2011.

Replacement notes: Prefix Z/2.

CBSL B24 (P124): **50 rupees** (US$0.40)　　　　VG　VF　UNC

Blue and green. Front: Blue Oakleaf (Kallima philarchus) butterfly; ancient stone arch railway bridge with train; old steel bridge; new concrete automobile bridge at Manampitiya; Sri Lanka dull blue flycatcher (Eumyias sordida) bird; chinthe with sword. Back (vertical): Yakbera drummer and Vadiga Patuna dancer; guard stone (muragala) with punkalasa (pot of plenty, symbol of prosperity); stylized liya vela floral motif. Solid security thread with printed *CBSL RS 50*. Watermark: Flycatcher bird with electrotype *50* and Cornerstones. Printer: *DE LA RUE*. 133 x 67 mm.

☐　a.　2010-01-01. Signature 12. Prefix V/1 - V/59.　　FV　FV　1
　　　　Intro: 04.02.2011.

Replacement notes: Prefix Z/3.

CBSL B26 (P126): **500 rupees** (US$3.85)　　　　VG　VF　UNC

Purple. Front: Ceylon indigo royal (Tajuria arida) butterfly; World Trade Center and Bank of Ceylon headquarters buildings in Colombo; ancient Buddhist temple, Lankathilaka Viharaya, in Kandy; Sri Lanka emerald-collared parakeet (Layard's Parakeet - Psittacula calthropae) bird; chinthe with sword. Back (vertical): Yak Bera drummer and Thelme Netuma dancer; Padmanidhi guard stone (muragala); stylized Dvithva liya vela floral motif. 2-mm wide red-to-green StarChrome windowed security thread with demetalized *CBSL RS 500*. Watermark: Parakeet with electrotype *500* and Cornerstones. Printer: *DE LA RUE*. 143 x 67 mm.

☐　a.　2010-01-01. Signature 12. Prefix T/1 - T/50.　　FV　FV　6
　　　　Intro: 04.02.2011.

Replacement notes: Prefix Z/4.

CBSL B25 (P125): **100 rupees** (US$0.75)　　　　VG　VF　UNC

Orange. Front: Autumn leaf (Doleschallia bisaltidae) butterfly; Laxapana waterfall; Norochcholai coal power plant; Sri Lanka orange-billed babbler (Turdoides rufescens) bird; chinthe with sword. Back (vertical): Mridangam drummer and Bharatanatyam dancer; Naga guard stone (muragala); stylized Dvithva liya vela floral motif. Solid security thread with printed *CBSL RS 100*. Watermark: Babbler bird with electrotype *100* and Cornerstones. Printer: *DE LA RUE*. 138 x 67 mm.

☐　a.　2010-01-01. Signature 12. Prefix U/1 - U/144.　FV　FV　1.50
　　　　Intro: 04.02.2011.

CBSL B27 (P127): **1,000 rupees** (US$7.70)　　　VG　VF　UNC

Green. Front: White Four Ring (Ypthima ceylonica) butterfly; old rock wall and new Ramboda Tunnel entrance; Sri Lanka hanging parrot (Loriculus beryllinus); chinthe with sword. Back (vertical): Davul Bera drummer and Malpadaya Netuma dancer; guard stone (muragala) of naga-raja holding sprouting branch and punkalasa (pot of plenty, symbol of prosperity), beneath hood of cobra heads, with Sankha and Padma at feet; stylized Dvithva liya vela floral motif. 2.5-mm wide red-to-green StarChrome windowed security thread with demetalized *CBSL RS 1000*. Watermark: Parrot with electrotype *1000* and Cornerstones. Printer: *DE LA RUE*. 148 x 67 mm.

☐　a.　2010-01-01. Signature 12. Prefix S/1 - S/86.　　FV　FV　14
　　　　Intro: 04.02.2011.

Replacement notes: Prefix Z/6.

CBSL B28 (P128): **5,000 rupees** (US$38) VG VF UNC

Gold and brown. Front: Lemon migrant (Catopsilia Pomona) butterfly; Weheragala Dam and Canyon Dam; Sri Lanka yellow-eared bulbul (Pycnonotus penicillatus) bird; chinthe with sword. Back (vertical): Guruluraksha dancer and Nagaraksha dancer; Rathnaprasadaya guard stone (muragala) of naga-raja holding sprouting branch and punkalasa (pot of plenty, symbol of prosperity), beneath hood of cobra heads, with Sankha or Padma at feet; stylized Kalpavrksha floral motif. 3-mm wide red-to-green StarChrome windowed security thread with demetalized *CBSL RS 5000*. Watermark: Bulbul bird with electrotype *5000* and Cornerstones. Printer: *DE LA RUE*. 153 x 67 mm.

    a. 2010-01-01. Signature 12. Prefix R/1 - R/25. FV FV 55
       Intro: 04.02.2011.

Replacement notes: Prefix Z/8.

2011 Numismatic Products

Sets of notes with matching serial numbers were issued at a price of 7,500 rupees each. In addition, individual notes were sold in separate folders for each denomination, priced as 150, 200, 250, 750, 1,250, and 5,500 rupees, respectively.

CBSL BNP3 (PNL): **20-5,000 rupees** UNC
    a. CBSL B23-B28 (6 notes) with matching serial numbers in folder. 85

CBSL BNP4 (PNL): **20 rupees** (US$0.15) UNC
    a. CBSL B23 in folder. 3.50

CBSL BNP5 (PNL): **50 rupees** (US$0.40) UNC
    a. CBSL B24 in folder. 5

Sri Lanka 2013 Commemorative Issues

2013 Commemorative Issues

On 15 November 2013, the Central Bank of Sri Lanka began issuing 5 million 500-rupee notes commemorating the Commonwealth Heads of Government Meeting held in Sri Lanka from 15 to 17 November 2013. The note is like the preceding issues, but with a purple CHOGM 2013 Sri Lanka logo instead of a butterfly at the lower left front, decorative artwork flanking the electrotype watermark, new date, and serial numbers from T/51 000001- T/55 1000000.

CBSL BNP6 (PNL): 100 rupees (US$0.75)		UNC
☐ a. CBSL B25 in folder.		6

CBSL BNP7 (PNL): 500 rupees (US$3.85)		UNC
☐ a. CBSL B26 in folder.		11

CBSL BNP8 (PNL): 1,000 rupees (US$7.70)		UNC
☐ a. CBSL B27 in folder.		30

CBSL BNP9 (PNL): 5,000 rupees (US$38)		UNC
☐ a. CBSL B28 in folder.		110

CBSL B29 (P129): **500 rupees** (US$3.85) VG VF UNC
Purple. Front: CHOGM 2013 Sri Lanka logo; World Trade Center and Bank of Ceylon headquarters buildings in Colombo; ancient Buddhist temple, Lankathilaka Viharaya, in Kandy; Sri Lanka emerald-collared parakeet (Layard's Parakeet - Psittacula calthropae) bird; chinthe with sword. Back (vertical): Yak Bera drummer and Thelme Netuma dancer; Padmanidhi guard stone (muragala); stylized Dvithva liya vela floral motif. 2-mm wide red-to-green StarChrome windowed security thread with demetalized *CBSL RS 500*. Watermark: Parakeet with electrotype *500* and Cornerstones. Printer: *DE LA RUE*. 143 x 67 mm.

☐ a. 2013-11-15. Signature 12. Prefix T/51 - T/55. FV FV 9
   Intro: 15.11.2013.

Replacement notes: Prefix Z/5.

2013 Numismatic Products

A limited number of commemorative notes with low serial numbers were packaged in a folder and sold at a price of 800 rupees each.

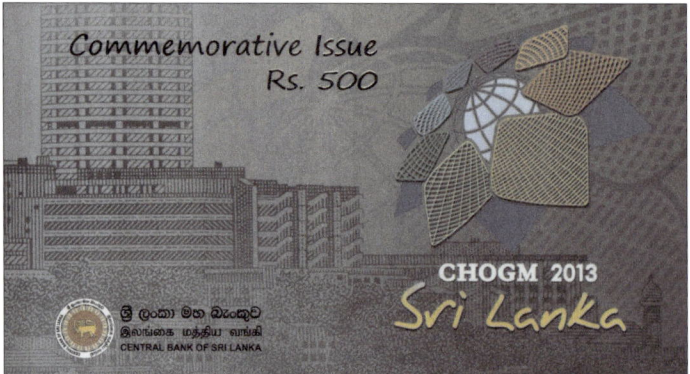

CBSL BNP10 (PNL): 500 rupees (US$3.85)		UNC
☐ a. CBSL B29a (1 note) in folder.		10

Currency Museum

The Central Bank of Sri Lanka maintains two Currency Museums. One is housed at 58, Sri Jayawardhanapura Mawatha, Rajagiriya, and the other is located at 314, Stage 1, New Town, Anuradhapura. Admission is free.

Acknowledgements

This chapter was compiled with the generous assistance of David F. Cieniewicz (www.banknotestore.com), Jean-Michel Engels, Larry Hirsch (www.aworldcurrency.com), David Hull, Kai Hwong, Mark Irwin, Jarno Komulainen, Wally Myers, P. K. Piyasena (Central Bank of Sri Lanka), George Provencal, TDS, Dilminidu Samarasekara, Menelaos Stamatelos, Bill Stubkjaer, Vincent Tan, Christoph Thomas, Frank van Tiel, Chris Twining (www.pagescoinsandcurrency.com), Ömer Yalcinkaya, and others.

Sources

Boon, K. N. *World Paper & Polymer Uncut Banknotes*. 1st edition. 2012. ISBN 978-983-43313-4-4. Trigometric Sdn.Bhd. (www.3833.com), Lot 327, Amcorp Mall, 18 Jalan Persiaran Barat, off Jalan Timur, Petaling Jaya, 46050 Selangor D.E., Malaysia.

Cuhaj, George S. *Standard Catalog of World Paper Money, Modern Issues, 1961-Present*. 20th edition. 2014. ISBN 978-1-4402-4037-9. Krause Publications (www.krausebooks.com), 700 East State St., Iola, WI, 54990-0001.

Eu, Peter and Ben Chiew. *Queen Elizabeth II*. 1st edition. 2006. ISBN 983-43038-1-5. Eureka Metro, P. O. Box 30, Jalan Kelang Lama, Kuala Lumpur, 57000, Malaysia.

Eu, Peter, Ben Chiew, and Stane Straus. *World Polymer Banknotes: A Standard Reference*. 2nd edition. 2006. ISBN 983-43038-2-3. Eureka Metro, P. O. Box 30, Jalan Kelang Lama, Kuala Lumpur, 57000, Malaysia.

Krause, Thomas and Peter Bauer. *Specialized Catalogue of World Plastic Money*. 5th edition. 2009. www.polymernotes.de.

Symes, Peter. "The Portraits of Queen Elizabeth II on World Bank Notes." *IBNS Journal*. Volume 44 Number 2. p.8.

http://coins.lakdiva.org/currency/

Share Your Input, Info, and Images

This catalog is believed to be complete and correct as of the time of publication. Prices and face values were last updated 25 July 2014. Please report errors or omissions so that corrections may be made. If you can more precisely identify the name or location of anything depicted on a note, please share that information. Furthermore, if you own an unlisted type or variety, please submit scans of the front and back of the note so that it can be documented. Scans should be 300 dots per inch, 100% actual size, 24-bit color, saved as *uncompressed* JPEG files, and sent to owen@banknotenews.com. Be sure to fully describe all attributes of the note which are not apparent upon visual inspection of the images alone, such as physical dimension, watermark, and security thread.

Straits Settlements

For earlier issues, see India.

1840-1921 Private Issues

In December 1840, the first private banks began operating in the Straits Settlements. Over the years, the following banks issued notes for use the Straits Settlements: Asiatic Banking Corporation; Chartered Bank of India, Australia & China; the Chartered Mercantile Bank of India, London & China; Hong Kong & Shanghai Banking Corporation; New Oriental Bank Corporation; North Western Bank of India; and the Union Bank of Calcutta. As private issues, these notes are not yet covered in this chapter, but may be added in the future.

Monetary System

1 Straits dollar = 100 cents

The Straits Settlements were a group of British territories located in Southeast Asia: Christmas Island, Cocos (Keeling) Islands, Dinding, Labuan, Malacca, Penang, and Singapore. Originally established in 1826 as part of the territories controlled by the British East India Company, the Straits Settlements came under direct British control as a crown colony on 1 April 1867.

Government of the Straits Settlements

From 1898, the Straits dollar was issued by the Board of Commissioners of Currency and private banks were prevented from issuing notes which they had done since 1840.

GSS Signature Varieties

Currency Commissioners

1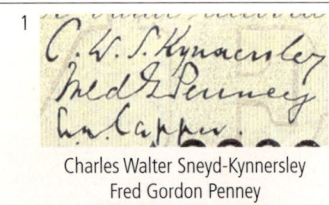
Charles Walter Sneyd-Kynnersley
Fred Gordon Penney
Alfred Houston Capper
(1898)

1.5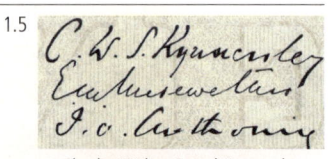
Charles Walter Sneyd-Kynnersley
Edward Marsh Merewether
James Oliver Anthonisz
(1900)

2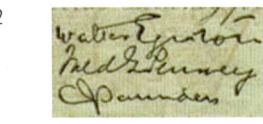
Walter Egerton
Fred Gordon Penney
Charles James Saunders
(1901)

3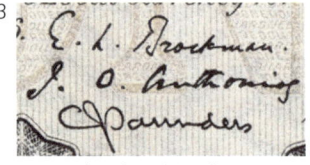
Edward Lewis Brockman
James Oliver Anthonisz
Charles James Saunders
(1906)

GSS Signature Varieties

Currency Commissioners

4
Arthur Henderson Young
James Oliver Anthonisz
David Beatty
(1909)

5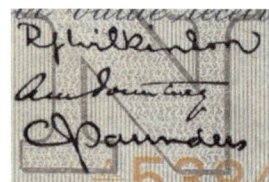
Edward Lewis Brockman
Walter Cecil Michell
Paul August Felix David
(1911)

6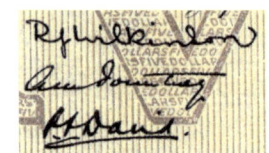
Richard James Wilkinson
Arthur Meek Pountney
Paul August Felix David
(1914)

7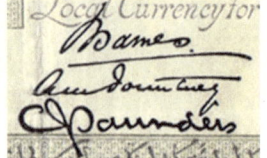
Richard James Wilkinson
Arthur Meek Pountney
Charles James Saunders
(1915)

8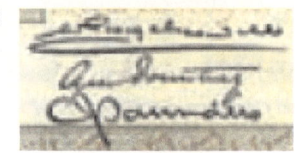
William George Maxwell
Arthur Meek Pountney
Charles James Saunders
(1916)

9
Frederick Seton James
Arthur Meek Pountney
Charles James Saunders
(1916 - 1921)

10a
Ag. Treasurer
Hayes Marriott
(1917)

10b
Ag. Treasurer
Hayes Marriott
(1917)

11
Ag. Treasurer / Treasurer
Arthur Meek Pountney
(1919 - 1920)

12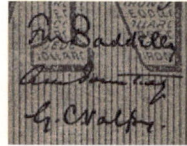
Frank Morrish Baddeley
Arthur Meek Pountney
George Cordy Valpy
(1924)

13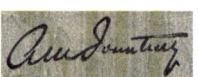
Arthur Meek Pountney
(1925)

14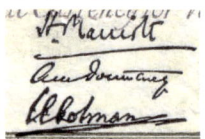
Hayes Marriott
Arthur Meek Pountney
Eugene Ernest Colman
(1925)

15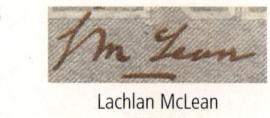
Lachlan McLean
(1927)

16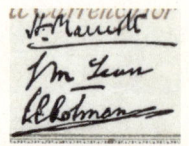
Hayes Marriott
Lachlan McLean
Eugene Ernest Colman
(1927)

GSS Signature Varieties
Currency Commissioners

17
Malcolm Bond Shelley
(1929 - 1932)

18
John Scott
Malcolm Bond Shelley
Geoffey Edmund Cator
(1930)

19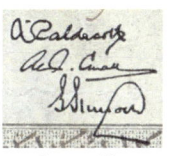
Andrew Caldecott
Alexander Sym Small
Palgrave Simpson
(1933)

20
Alexander Sym Small
(1933 - 1935)

Prefixes

In the following listings, the earliest and latest prefixes which have been verified for a given variety are listed. However, this information may be incomplete. Be advised that not all prefixes within the range shown have been verified; it's possible that the printer skipped some letters or numbers for unknown reasons.

1898-1924 Issues

Ordinance No. 4 of 1899 authorized the issuance of 1-dollar notes with a limited legal tender of 10 dollars, and the following of unlimited legal tender: 5-, 10-, 20-, 50-, and 100-dollar notes, and any multiple of 100-dollar notes. Issues of 5, 10, 50, and 100 dollars were made initially, but no 1-dollar notes were issued until 1906, and by that time they too had unlimited legal tender status. No 20-dollar notes have been confirmed.

GSS B1 (P1A): 1 dollar   Good   Fine   XF

Black. Front: Coat of arms; Chinese, English, and Malay text. Back: Tiger prowling in jungle, surrounded by four elephants and kris (daggers). No security thread. Watermark: Geometric pattern. Printer: *THOS. DE LA RUE & C° LTD LONDON*. 121 x 64 mm.

- ☐ a.   1st September 1906. Sig. 3. Prefix A/1 - A/9.   100   400   1,500
- ☐ as. Diagonal black *SPECIMEN* overprint;   —   —   —
  horizontal *CANCELLED* perforation; normal s/n.

Like subsequent issues, but without large number *1* in the underprint between the serial numbers at left and right front.

GSS B2 (P1): 1 dollar   Good   Fine   XF

Black. Front: Coat of arms; Chinese, English, and Malay text. Back: Tiger prowling in jungle, surrounded by four elephants and kris (daggers). No security thread. Watermark: Geometric pattern. Printer: *THOS. DE LA RUE & C° LTD LONDON*. 121 x 64 mm.

- ☐ a.   1st September 1906. Sig. 3. Prefix A/31 - A/41.   270   725   2,100
- ☐ as. Diagonal black *SPECIMEN* overprint;   —   —   —
  horizontal *CANCELLED* perforation; normal s/n;
  cream-colored paper.

Like preceding issues, but with large number *1* in the underprint between the serial numbers at left and right front.

GSS B3 (P1): 1 dollar   Good   Fine   XF

Black and olive green. Front: Coat of arms; Chinese, English, and Malay text. Back: Tiger prowling in jungle, surrounded by four elephants and kris (daggers). No security thread. Watermark: Geometric pattern. Printer: *THOS. DE LA RUE & C° LTD LONDON*. 121 x 64 mm.

- ☐ a.   1st September 1906. Sig. 3. Prefix A/44 - A/47.   270   725   2,100
- ☐ b.   8th June 1909. Sig. 4. Prefix A/60 - A/75.   270   600   2,100
- ☐ c.   17th March 1911. Sig. 5. Prefix A/86 - B/9.   270   600   2,100
- ☐ d.   2nd January 1914. Sig. 6. Prefix B/27.   90   200   750
- ☐ e.   4th March 1915. Sig. 7. Prefix B/34 - B/74.   90   200   750
- ☐ f.   10th July 1916. Sig. 9. Prefix B/78 - E/85.   50   175   650
- ☐ g.   20th June 1921. Prefix F/30 - G/31.   90   200   750
- ☐ h.   5th September 1924. Sig. 12. Prefix G/67 - H/50.   90   200   750
- ☐ as. Horizontal purple *SPECIMEN* ovpt at lower right;   —   —   —
  diagonal *CANCELLED* perforation; all-zero s/n.
- ☐ bs. Diagonal black *SPECIMEN* overprint;   —   —   —
  horizontal *CANCELLED* perforation; normal s/n.

Like preceding issues, but printed on reddish/pinkish paper, not cream paper.

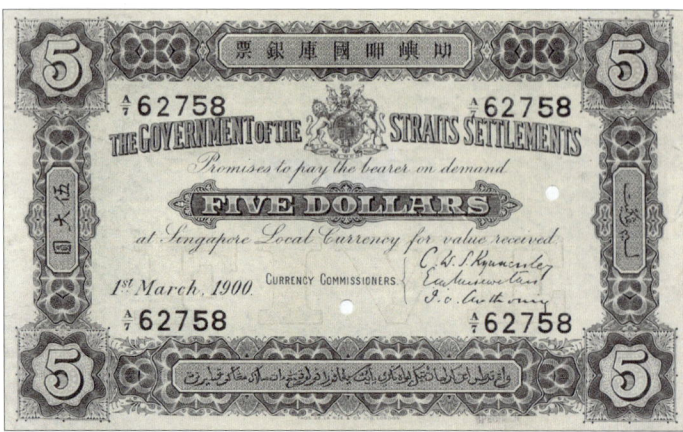

GSS B5 (P3): **5 dollars**   Good   Fine   XF

Black and purple. Front: Coat of arms; Chinese, English, and Malay text. Back: Tiger prowling in jungle, surrounded by four elephants and kris (daggers). No security thread. Watermark: Geometric pattern. Printer: *THOS. DE LA RUE & Cº LTD LONDON*. 121 x 76 mm.

- ☐ a. 1ˢᵗ February 1901. Sig. 2. Prefix B/1 - B/20.   300   1,000   2,500
- ☐ as1. Horizontal purple *SPECIMEN* ovpt at lower right; diagonal *CANCELLED* perforation; all-zero s/n.   —   —   —
- ☐ as2. Diagonal black *SPECIMEN* overprint; horizontal *CANCELLED* perforation; normal s/n.   —   —   —

Like preceding issues, but physically smaller.

GSS B4 (P2): **5 dollars**   Good   Fine   XF

Black and purple. Front: Coat of arms; Chinese, English, and Malay text. Back: Tiger prowling in jungle, surrounded by four elephants and kris (daggers). No security thread. Watermark: Geometric pattern. Printer: *THOS. DE LA RUE & Cº LTD LONDON*. 195 x 120 mm.

- ☐ a. 1ˢᵗ September 1898. Sig. 1. Prefix A/1 - A/4.   1,100   2,700   —
- ☐ b. 1ˢᵗ March 1900. Sig. 1.5. Prefix A/6 - A/7.   1,100   2,700   —
- ☐ as. Diagonal black *SPECIMEN* overprint; horizontal *CANCELLED* perforation; normal s/n.   —   —   —
- ☐ bs. Horizontal purple *SPECIMEN* ovpt at lower right; punched; all-zero s/n.   —   —   —

Like subsequent issues, but physically larger.

GSS B6 (P3): **5 dollars**   Good   Fine   XF

Black and purple. Front: Coat of arms; Chinese, English, and Malay text. Back: Tiger prowling in jungle, surrounded by four elephants and kris (daggers). No security thread. Watermark: Geometric pattern. Printer: *THOS. DE LA RUE & Cº LTD LONDON*. 121 x 76 mm.

- ☐ a. 8ᵗʰ June 1909. Sig. 4. Prefix B/26 - B/31.   300   1,000   2,500
- ☐ b. 17ᵗʰ March 1911. Sig. 5. Prefix B/36.   300   1,000   2,500
- ☐ c. 2ⁿᵈ January 1914. Sig. 6. Prefix B/38 - B/44.   300   1,000   2,500
- ☐ d. 4ᵗʰ March 1915. Sig. 7. Prefix B/52.   300   1,000   2,500
- ☐ e. 10ᵗʰ July 1916. Sig. 9. Prefix B/56 - B/97.   300   1,000   2,500
- ☐ f. 20ᵗʰ June 1921. Prefix C/5 - C/31.   300   1,000   2,500
- ☐ g. 5ᵗʰ September 1924. Sig. 12. Prefix C/39 - C/41.   300   1,000   2,500

Like preceding issues, but printed on cream-colored paper, not white paper.

In 1912 there were forgeries of 5-dollar notes on a considerable scale, most likely of the 1909 or 1911 issues.

GSS B7 (P4): 10 dollars   Good   Fine   XF

Blue and purple. Front: Coat of arms; Chinese, English, and Malay text. Back: Tiger prowling in jungle, surrounded by four elephants and kris (daggers). No security thread. Watermark: Geometric pattern. Printer: *THOS. DE LA RUE & Cº LTD LONDON*. 195 x 120 mm.

☐	a.	1st September 1898. Sig. 1. Prefix A/1 - A/2.	—	—	—
☐	b.	1st March 1900. Prefix unknown.	—	—	—
☐	c.	1st February 1901. Sig. 2. Prefix A/3 - A/7.	—	—	—
☐	d.	8th June 1909. Sig. 4. Prefix unknown.	—	—	—
☐	e.	17th March 1911. Sig. 5. Prefix A/10 - A/19.	—	—	—
☐	f.	2nd January 1914. Sig. 6. Prefix A/22 - A/25.	800	2,300	—
☐	g.	4th March 1915. Sig. 7. Prefix A/32 - A/39.	800	2,300	—
☐	h.	10th July 1916. Sig. 9. Prefix A/44 - A/78.	500	1,500	—
☐	i.	20th June 1921. Prefix A/85 - B/5.	500	1,500	—
☐	j.	5th September 1924. Sig. 12. Prefix B/12 - B/30.	500	1,500	—
☐	as.	Diagonal black *SPECIMEN* overprint; horizontal *CANCELLED* perforation; normal s/n.	—	—	—
☐	bs.	Horizontal *CANCELLED* perforation; all-zero s/n.	—	—	—
☐	ds.	Horizontal *CANCELLED* perforation; all-zero s/n.	—	—	—
☐	p.	No date; no signatures; no serial numbers; horizontal *CANCELLED* perforation.	—	—	—

GSS B8 (P4A): 50 dollars   Good   Fine   XF

Green and light brown. Front: Coat of arms; Chinese, English, and Malay text. Back: Tiger prowling in jungle, surrounded by four elephants and kris (daggers). No security thread. Watermark: Geometric pattern. Printer: *THOS. DE LA RUE & Cº LTD LONDON*. 200 x 122 mm.

☐	a.	1st September 1898. Signature 1. Unconfirmed.	—	—	—
☐	b.	1st February 1901. Signature 2. Prefix A/1 - A/2.	—	—	—
☐	bs.	Diagonal black *SPECIMEN* overprint; horizontal *CANCELLED* perforation; normal s/n.	—	—	—
☐	p.	No date; no signatures; no serial numbers.	—	—	—

GSS B9 (P4C): 100 dollars   Good   Fine   XF
Red and green. Front: Coat of arms; Chinese, English, and Malay text. Back: Tiger prowling in jungle, surrounded by four elephants and kris (daggers). No security thread. Watermark: Geometric pattern. Printer: *THOS. DE LA RUE & Cº LTD LONDON*. 200 x 122 mm.

- a. 1st September 1898. Signature 1. Prefix A/1.   —   —   —
- b. 1st February 1901. Signature 2. Prefix A/1.   —   —   —
- c. 8th August 1909. Signature 4. Prefix A/1.   —   —   —
- bs. Diagonal black *SPECIMEN* overprint; horizontal *CANCELLED* perforation; normal s/n.   —   —   —
- cs. Horizon. purple *SPECIMEN* ovpt at lower center; horizontal *CANCELLED* perforation; all-zero s/n.   —   —   —

GSS B10 (PNL): 1,000 dollars   Good   Fine   XF
Green. Front: Coat of arms; Chinese, English, and Malay text. Back: Tiger prowling in jungle, surrounded by four elephants and kris (daggers). Watermark: Geometric pattern. Printer: *THOS. DE LA RUE & Cº LTD LONDON*. 200 x 122 mm.

- a. 17th March 1911. Signature 5. Prefix A/1.   —   —   —
- as1. Diagonal purple *SPECIMEN* overprints; horizontal *CANCELLED* perforation; all-zero s/n.   —   —   —
- as2. Diagonal black *SPECIMEN* overprint; horizontal *CANCELLED* perf; s/n A/1 00001.   —   400000

1916-1933 Issues

These large uniface note have irregular deckle edges and as such dimensions may vary.

GSS B11 (PA5 & P12): **50 dollars** Good Fine XF

Purple and blue. Uniface: Tiger prowling in jungle; crowned bust of King George V; Chinese, English, and Malay text. No security thread. Watermark: Elephants and *$50 STRAITS SETTLEMENTS*. Printer: *THOMAS DE LA RUE & COMPANY LIMITED, LONDON*. 205 x 128 mm.

- ☐ a. 7th March 1916. Signature 8. Prefix B/1. — — —
- ☐ b. 1st June 1920. Signature 9. Prefix B/2. — — 95,000
- ☐ c. 24th September 1925. Sig. 14. Prefix B/3 - B/5. 1,500 4,000 15,000
- ☐ d. 1st November 1927. Sig. 16. Prefix B/6. — — —
- ☐ e. 1st October 1930. Sig. 18. Prefix B/6. — — —
- ☐ p. No date; no signatures; B/1 00000 serial number; horizontal *CANCELLED* perforation. — — —
- ☐ es. Horizontal *CANCELLED* perforation. — — —

GSS B12 (P5 & P13): **100 dollars** Good Fine XF

Red and green. Uniface: Tiger prowling in jungle; crowned bust of King George V; Chinese, English, and Malay text. No security thread. Watermark: Elephants and *$100 STRAITS SETTLEMENTS*. Printer: *THOS. DE LA RUE & C° LTD LONDON*. 205 x 128 mm.

- ☐ a. 7th March 1916. Signature 8. Prefix B/1. — 17,750 —
- ☐ b. 1st June 1920. Signature 9. Prefix B/2. — — 45,000
- ☐ c. 24th September 1925. Sig. 14. Prefix B/3 - B/4. 1,300 5,000 25,000
- ☐ d. 1st November 1927. Sig. 16. Prefix B/4. — — —
- ☐ ds. Horizontal *CANCELLED* perforation; all-zero s/n. — — —

GSS B13 (P14): **1,000 dollars** Good Fine XF

Brown and olive green. Uniface: Tiger prowling in jungle; crowned bust of King George V; Coat of arms; Chinese, English, and Malay text. No security thread. Watermark: Elephants and *$1000 STRAITS SETTLEMENTS*. Printer: *THOS. DE LA RUE & C° LTD LONDON*. 205 x 128 mm.

- ☐ a. 1st September 1919. Signature 11. Prefix B/1. — — —
- ☐ b. 24th September 1925. Sig. 14. Prefix B/2. — — —
- ☐ c. 1st October 1930. Signature 19. Prefix B/2. — — —
- ☐ d. 8th December 1933. Prefix B/3. — — —
- ☐ bs. Horizontal *CANCELLED* perforation; all-zero s/n. — — —

GSS B14 (P15): **10,000 dollars** Good Fine XF

Green and brown. Uniface: Tiger prowling in jungle; crowned bust of King George V; Coat of arms; Chinese, English, and Malay text. No security thread. Watermark: Elephants and *$10000 STRAITS SETTLEMENTS*. Printer: *THOS. DE LA RUE & C° LTD LONDON*. Unknown dimensions.

- ☐ a. 1st September 1919. Signature 11. — — —
- ☐ b. 24th September 1925. Signature 14. — — —
- ☐ c. 1st October 1930. Signature 19. — — —
- ☐ d. 8th December 1933. — — —
- ☐ s. Horizontal *CANCELLED* perforation; horizon. purple *SPECIMEN* ovpt at lower center; no date; no signatures.
- ☐ p. No date; no signatures; B/1 00000 serial number; horizontal *CANCELLED* perforation. — — —

This note did not circulate in public; it was used only for interbank transactions.

1917-1920 Emergency Issues

These notes were issued to counter the shortage of coins. Due to a sharp rise in the price of silver, the local coins became intrinsically more valuable than their face value, so the public hoarded the coins and sold them to be melted into bullion.

The 10-cent notes are dated around the crown on the back, with the day at left, the month at right, and the last two digits of the year below. Due to the large number of dates, unique variety letters have been assigned only to the three design and signature varieties.

GSS B16 (P7): **25 cents** — Good — Fine — XF
Black. Front: Coat of arms; Chinese, English, and Malay text. Back: Tiger. No security thread. Watermark: None. Printer: (Government Survey Office, Kuala Lumpur). 109 x 76 mm.

- a. No date. Signature 10b. Intro: January 1917. — 50 — 125 — 500
  Yellow underprint. Prefix C/1 - E/1.
- b. Orange underprint. Prefix J/1 - N/1. — 50 — 125 — 500

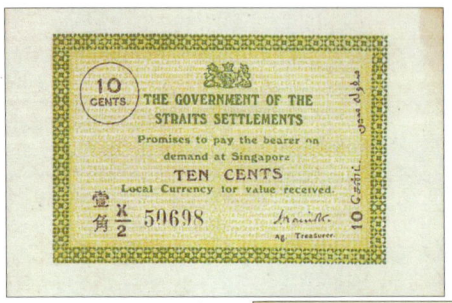

GSS B15 (P6): **10 cents** — Good — Fine — XF
Green, black, yellow, and red. Front: Coat of arms; Chinese, English, and Malay text. Back: Decorative design; central crown surrounded by encoded date. No security thread. Watermark: None. Printer: (Government Survey Office, Kuala Lumpur). 118 x 76 mm.

- a. 1.10.17. Signature 10a. — 25 — 100 — 425
  With № before serial number. Prefix O/1.
- b. 1.11.17. Without № before s/n. Prefix T/1. — 25 — 100 — 425
- b. 1.12.17. Prefix G/2. — 25 — 100 — 425
- b. 1.1.18. Prefix J/2 - K/2. — 25 — 100 — 425
- b. 1.2.18. Prefix X/2. — 25 — 100 — 425
- b. 1.3.18. Prefix F/3 - L/3. — 25 — 100 — 425
- b. 1.4.18. — 25 — 100 — 425
- b. 1.9.18. — 25 — 100 — 425
- c. 2.1.19. Signature 11. Prefix W/3 - Y/3. — 25 — 100 — 425
- c. 11.1.19. — 25 — 100 — 425
- c. 29.1.19. Prefix E/4. — 25 — 100 — 425
- c. 22.2.19. Prefix Q/4. — 25 — 100 — 425
- c. 20.3.19. Prefix X/4. — 25 — 100 — 425
- c. 8.4.19. Prefix X/4. — 25 — 100 — 425
- c. 24.4.19. — 25 — 100 — 425
- c. 12.5.19. — 25 — 100 — 425
- c. 10.6.19. Prefix K/5 - Q/5. — 25 — 100 — 425
- c. 1.7.19. — 25 — 100 — 425
- c. 22.7.19. Prefix X/5. — 25 — 100 — 425
- c. 8.8.19. Prefix A/6. — 25 — 100 — 425
- c. 23.8.19. — 25 — 100 — 425
- c. 10.9.19. — 25 — 100 — 425
- c. 1.11.19. — 25 — 100 — 425
- c. 15.1.20. Prefix N/6. — 25 — 100 — 425
- c. 2.2.20. Prefix T/6 - Q/6. — 25 — 100 — 425
- c. 5.2.20. Prefix G/7. — 25 — 100 — 425
- c. 25.2.20. Prefix T/7 - G/8. — 25 — 100 — 425
- c. 8.3.20. Prefix Q/8 - F/9. — 25 — 100 — 425
- c. 6.4.20. Prefix V/9 - L/10. — 25 — 100 — 425
- c. 1.5.20. Prefix L/10. — 25 — 100 — 425
- c. 10.6.20. — 25 — 100 — 425

1919 Emergency Issues

GSS B17 (P8): **10 cents** — Good — Fine — XF
Green, red, and light brown. Front: Coat of arms; Chinese, English, and Malay text. Back: Chinese dragon on guilloche pattern. No security thread. Watermark: None. Printer: *THOS. DE LA RUE & Cº Lᵗᵈ LONDON*. 109 x 63 mm.

- a. 14th October 1919. — 40 — 150 — 600
  Signature 11, title *Ag. Treasurer*.
  Dark red printing. Prefix A/1 - A/48.
- b. Signature 11, title *Treasurer*. — 15 — 40 — 200
  Bright red printing. Prefix A/52 - G/60.

1925-1930 Issues

GSS B18 (P9): **1 dollar**   Good   Fine   XF

Red and purple. Front: Palm trees on shore and sailboat in water; coat of arms; attap houses on stilts, palm trees, and boat; Chinese, English, and Malay text. Back: Attap houses on stilts, palm trees, and three people walking on shoreline. No security thread. Watermark: None. Printer: *THOMAS DE LA RUE & COMPANY LIMITED, LONDON*. 124 x 64 mm.

			Good	Fine	XF
☐	a.	1ST January, 1925. Signature 13. Date and signature in red. Prefix J/15 - K/7.	50	95	480
☐	b.	1ST September, 1927. Sig. 15. Prefix L/20 - M/21.	50	95	480
☐	c.	1ST January, 1929. Sig. 17. Prefix M/48 - N/41.	50	95	480
☐	d.	1ST January, 1930. Date and signature in black. Security fibers in paper. Prefix N/54 - P/72.	150	500	2,000
☐	ap.	Proof: Uniface.	—	—	1,875
☐	as.	Horizontal purple *SPECIMEN* overprint; diagonal purple *CANCELLED* overprint; horizontal *CANCELLED* perforation; low s/n.	—	—	—
☐	ds.	Horizontal purple *SPECIMEN* overprint; all-zero serial number; punched.	—	—	—
☐	t.	Color trial: Blue.	—	—	10,000

GSS B19 (P10): **5 dollars**   Good   Fine   XF

Green. Front: Coat of arms; farmer leading water buffalo carrying child, with palm trees and attap houses in background; Chinese, English, and Malay text. Back: Tiger prowling in jungle. No security thread. Watermark: Tiger head and *$5*. Printer: *THOMAS DE LA RUE & COMPANY LIMITED, LONDON*. 134 x 76 mm.

			Good	Fine	XF
☐	a.	1ST January, 1925. Signature 13. Date and signature in green. Intro: May 1926. Prefix D/1 - D/80.	200	500	1,750
☐	b.	1ST September, 1927. Sig. 15. Prefix D/90 - E/8.	200	500	1,750
☐	c.	1ST January, 1929. Sig. 17. Prefix E/17 - E/39.	200	500	1,750
☐	d.	1ST January, 1930. Date and signature in black. Prefix E/41 - E/68.	200	500	1,750
☐	ap.	Proof: Uniface; black and white.	—	—	7,000
☐	as.	Horizontal purple *SPECIMEN* overprint; diagonal purple *CANCELLED* overprint; horizontal *CANCELLED* perforation; low s/n.	—	—	—
☐	ds.	Horizontal purple *SPECIMEN* ovpt at lower right; punched; all-zero serial number.	—	—	—
☐	p.	Proof: Uniface back.	—	—	—
☐	t1.	Color trial: Brown & yellow; wmk King George V.	—	—	—
☐	t2.	Color trial: Brown & red; uniface back.	—	—	4,500

1931-1935 Issues

The preceding issues continued to circulate in parallel with these new notes, and were withdrawn only when worn out.

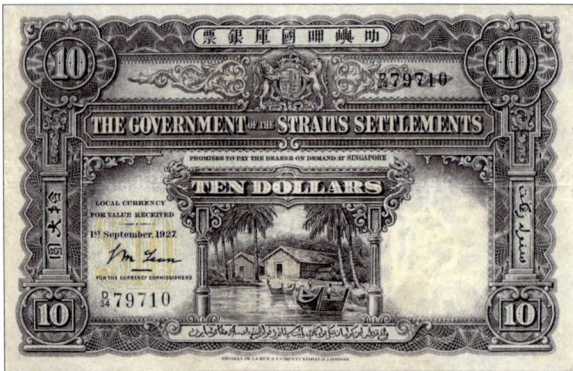

GSS B20 (P11): **10 dollars**   Good   Fine   XF

Purple and light green. Front: Palm trees and huts on shore with boats in water; coat of arms; Chinese, English, and Malay text. Back: Two-wheeled bullock cart. No security thread. Watermark: Tiger head and $10. Printer: *THOMAS DE LA RUE & COMPANY LIMITED, LONDON.* 158 x 101 mm.

		Good	Fine	XF
☐ a.	1ST January 1925. Signature 13. Intro: Nov. 1925. Prefix C/4 - C/80.	250	1,000	4,000
☐ b.	1ST September 1927. Sig. 15. Prefix D/14 - D/34.	250	1,000	4,000
☐ c.	1ST January, 1929. Sig. 17. Prefix D/64.	250	1,000	4,000
☐ d.	1ST January, 1930. Prefix D/91 - E/16.	250	1,000	4,000
☐ as.	Horizontal purple *SPECIMEN* overprint; diagonal purple *CANCELLED* overprint; horizontal *CANCELLED* perforation; low s/n.	—	—	—
☐ ds.	Horizontal purple *SPECIMEN* ovpt at right; punched; all-zero serial number.	—	—	—
☐ p.	Proof: Uniface back.	—	—	—
☐ t.	Color trial: Green & yellow; wmk King George V.	—	—	5,700

GSS B21 (P16): **1 dollar**   Good   Fine   XF

Blue. Front: King George V. Back: Britannia; tiger prowling in jungle. No security thread. Watermark: Tiger head. Printer: *BRADBURY, WILKINSON & Cº Lᵈ ENGRAVERS, NEW MALDEN, SURREY, ENGLAND.* 125 x 64 mm.

		Good	Fine	XF
☐ a.	1ST JANUARY 1931. Signature 17. Intro: August 1932. Prefix A/1 - C/3.	60	350	550
☐ b.	1ST JANUARY 1932. Prefix C/10 - C/72.	60	350	550
☐ c.	1ST JANUARY 1933. Sig. 20. Prefix D/10 - D/77.	60	350	550
☐ d.	1ST JANUARY 1934. Prefix E/7 - E/71.	60	350	550
☐ e.	1ST JANUARY 1935. Prefix F/11 - L/67.	20	30	185
☐ as.	Horizontal *CANCELLED* perforation.	—	AU	5,850
☐ es.	Horizontal *CANCELLED* perforation.	—	—	3,850
☐ t.	Color trial: Brown.	—	—	—

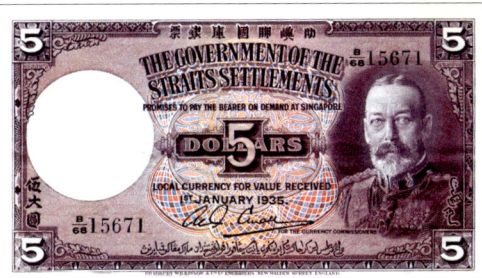

GSS B22 (P17): **5 dollars** Good Fine XF

Purple. Front: King George V. Back: Britannia; tiger prowling in jungle. No security thread. Watermark: Tiger head. Printer: *BRADBURY, WILKINSON & C° Ld ENGRAVERS, NEW MALDEN, SURREY, ENGLAND*. 135 x 76 mm.

			Good	Fine	XF
☐	a.	1ST JANUARY 1931. Signature 17. Intro: June 1933. Prefix A/1 - A/31.	125	500	900
☐	b.	1ST JANUARY 1932. Prefix A/36 - A/49.	150	600	1,000
☐	c.	1ST JANUARY 1933. Sig. 20. Prefix A/57 - A/73.	125	500	900
☐	d.	1ST JANUARY 1934. Prefix A/83 - A/95.	125	500	900
☐	e.	1ST JANUARY 1935. Prefix A/97 - B/88.	55	260	800
☐	bs1.	Horizontal *CANCELLED* perforation.	—	—	8,100
☐	bs2.	Horizontal *SPECIMEN ONLY* perf; normal s/n.	—	—	2,000
☐	es.	Horizontal *CANCELLED* perforation.	—	—	6,175
☐	t.	Color trial: Green.	—	—	—

GSS B23 (P18): **10 dollars** Good Fine XF

Green and mauve. Front: King George V. Back: Britannia; tiger prowling in jungle. No security thread. Watermark: Tiger head. Printer: *BRADBURY, WILKINSON & C° Ld ENGRAVERS, NEW MALDEN, SURREY, ENGLAND*. 161 x 89 mm.

			Good	Fine	XF
☐	a.	1ST JANUARY 1931. Signature 17. Intro: March 1932. Prefix A/6 - A/65.	125	500	2,000
☐	b.	1ST JANUARY 1932. Prefix A/66 - A/83.	125	500	2,000
☐	c.	1ST JANUARY 1933. Sig. 20. Prefix A/90 - B/4.	125	500	2,000
☐	d.	1ST JANUARY 1934. Prefix B/10 - B/46.	125	500	2,000
☐	e.	1ST JANUARY 1935. Prefix B/47 - C/38.	75	250	1,100
☐	es.	Horizontal *CANCELLED* perforation.	—	—	—
☐	t.	Color trial: Blue.	—	—	—

Looking Forward

The Straits dollar was replaced at par by the Malayan dollar in 1939. The Straits Settlements was dissolved as part of the British reorganization of its South-East Asian dependencies following the end of World War II.

For later issues, see Malaysia and Singapore.

Acknowledgements

This chapter was compiled with the generous assistance of K. N. Boon, Clement Chee, Compagnie Generale De Bourse (www.CGB.fr), Dr. Frühwald (www.auktionen-fruehwald.com), Arthur Gearing (De La Rue), Heritage Auctions (HA.com), Larry Hirsch (www.aworldcurrency.com), Michael Kovac, Sam Nakhjavani (www.foreignpapermoney.com), Mikhail "Mike" Prizov, Stack's Bowers (www.stacksbowers.com), Ludek Vostal, and others.

Sources

Anonymous. "Straits Settlements Currency Notes (from 1898 to 1935)." *IBNS Journal*. Volume 7 Number 2. p.14.

Anthonisz, J. O. *Currency Reform in the Straits Settlements*. R. W. Simpson & Co. Ltd, London.

Boon, K. N. *Malaysia Brunei & Singapore Banknotes & Coins*. 6th edition. 2012. ISBN 978-983-43313-5-1. Trigometric Sdn.Bhd. (www.3833.com), Lot 327, Amcorp Mall, 18 Jalan Persiaran Barat, off Jalan Timur, Petaling Jaya, 46050 Selangor D.E., Malaysia.

Chee, Clement. Odds & Ends of South East Asian Banknotes & Coins. http://clement-oddsends.blogspot.com.

Cuhaj, George S. *Standard Catalog of World Paper Money, General Issues, 1368-1960*. 14th edition. 2012. ISBN 978-1-4402-3090-5. Krause Publications (www.krausebooks.com), 700 East State St., Iola, WI, 54990-0001.

Tan, Steven. *Standard Catalogue of Malaysia Singapore Brunei Coin & Paper Money*. 18th edition. 2007. ISBN 983-9650-02-05. International Stamp & Coin Sn. Bhd., 2.4 & 2.5, Pertama Shopping Complex, 2nd Floor, Jalan Tuanku Abdul Rahman, 50100 Kaula Lumpur, Malaysia.

Share Your Input, Info, and Images

This catalog is believed to be complete and correct as of the time of publication. Prices and face values were last updated 10 May 2013. Please report errors or omissions so that corrections may be made. If you can more precisely identify the name or location of anything depicted on a note, please share that information. Furthermore, if you own an unlisted type or variety, please submit scans of the front and back of the note so that it can be documented. Scans should be 300 dots per inch, 100% actual size, 24-bit color, saved as *uncompressed* JPEG files, and sent to owen@banknotenews.com. Be sure to fully describe all attributes of the note which are not apparent upon visual inspection of the images alone, such as physical dimension, watermark, and security thread.

Sudan

For earlier issues, see Egypt.

Contents

Sudan Government (SG)	2001
Sudan Currency Board (SCB)	2002
Bank of Sudan (BOS)	2005
Central Bank of Sudan (CBS)	2020

Monetary System

1956: 1 Sudanese pound (SDP) = 100 piastres
1992: 1 Sudanese dinar (SDD) = 10 Sudanese pounds
10.01.2007: 1 Sudanese pound (SDG) = 100 piastres

Sudan Government

SG Signature Varieties

1	 (Minister of Finance and Economics) Hammad Tewfik	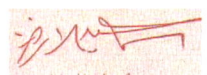 (Prime Minister) Ismail al Azhari

1955 Issues

Following the 1953 election, a series of banknotes dated (in Arabic) 6 July 1955 was prepared bearing the name of the issuer on back as *SUDAN GOVERNMENT* and the signatures of Prime Minister Ismail Al-Azhari as "Head of the Council of Ministers," and Hammad Tewfik as "Minister of Finance and Economics." However, when Abdullah Khalil was named prime minister on 4 July 1956, he demanded Waterlow & Sons destroy the 1955 notes because it would be inappropriate to issue them with Azhari's signature. The 1955 notes were not issued, and none is known to survive other than in specimen or color trial form.

Throughout this chapter, full Western dates are shown in parentheses, although only the year is reproduced in the Arabic as it appears on the actual note (omitted are the month in longhand followed by a numeral).

SG B1 (PA1): 25 piastres VG VF UNC
Red. Front: Troops with rifles. Back: Camel postman. Solid security thread. Watermark: None. Printer: *WATERLOW & SONS LIMITED, LONDON*. 120 x 65 mm.
- s1. ١٩٥٥ (06.07.1955). Signature 1. — — —
  All-zero 8-digit serial number; punched.
- s2. No date; no signature; all-zero 6-digit s/n. — — —
- s3. Signature 1 pasted onto note; handwritten s/n. — — —
- t. Color trial. — — —

SG B2 (PA2): 50 piastres VG VF UNC
Green. Front: Two elephants; trees. Back: Camel postman. Solid security thread. Watermark: None. Printer: *WATERLOW & SONS LIMITED, LONDON*. 125 x 70 mm.
- s1. ١٩٥٥ (06.07.1955). Signature 1. — — —
  All-zero 8-digit serial number; punched.
- s2. No date; no signature. — — —

SG B3 (PA3): **1 Sudanese pound** VG VF UNC
Blue. Front: Sennar dam on Blue Nile. Back: Camel postman. Solid security thread. Watermark: Three palm trees. Printer: *WATERLOW & SONS LIMITED, LONDON*. 140 x 75 mm.

☐ s1. ١٩٥٥ (06.07.1955). Signature 1. — — —
  All-zero 8-digit serial number; punched.
☐ s2. No date; no signature; all-zero 6-digit s/n. — — —
☐ t. Color trial: Purple. — — —

SG B4 (PA4): **5 Sudanese pounds** VG VF UNC
Brown. Front: Four men in dhow; palm trees. Back: Camel postman. Solid security thread. Watermark: Three palm trees. Printer: *WATERLOW & SONS LIMITED, LONDON*. 155 x 88 mm.

☐ s1. ١٩٥٥ (06.07.1955). Signature 1. — — —
  All-zero 8-digit serial number; punched.
☐ s2. No date; no signature; all-zero 6-digit s/n. — — —

SG B5 (PA5): **10 Sudanese pounds** VG VF UNC
Black and green. Front: University of Khartoum building; palm trees. Back: Camel postman. Solid security thread. Watermark: Three palm trees. Printer: *WATERLOW & SONS LIMITED, LONDON*. 169 x 88 mm.

☐ s1. ١٩٥٥ (06.07.1955). Signature 1. — — —
  All-zero 8-digit serial number; punched.
☐ s2. No date; no signature; all-zero 6-digit s/n. — — —
☐ t. Color trial: Purple and green. — — 2,000

Sudan Currency Board

SCB Signature Varieties

1	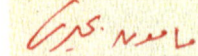	
	(Board Member)	(Chairman of the Board)
	Ibrahim Osman Ishag	Mamoun Ahmed A. Beheiry

1956 First Issues

When introduced in April 1957, the Sudanese pound replaced the Egyptian pound at par. These notes are like the preceding issues, but with a new date, new signatures, new issuer's name on back, and without the printer's imprint at lower center.

Only the 25- and 50-piastre notes are known to have been issued. The 1- and 10-pound notes are known only as color trials. The 5-pound note is unconfirmed in any form.

SCB B1 (P1B): **25 piastres** VG VF UNC
Red. Front: Troops with rifles. Back: Camel postman. No security thread. Watermark: None. Printer: (W&S). 120 x 65 mm.

☐ a. ١٩٥٦ (15.09.1956). Sig. 1. Intro: April 1957. 25 100 300
☐ as. Diagonal black *SPECIMEN* overprint; punched. — — 180

Like SCB B6, but longer third line of Arabic text at top left on front.

SCB B2 (P2B): **50 piastres** VG VF UNC
Green. Front: Two elephants; trees. Back: Camel postman. No security thread. Watermark: None. Printer: (W&S). 125 x 70 mm.

☐ a. ١٩٥٦ (15.09.1956). Sig. 1. Intro: April 1957. 50 150 600
☐ as. Diagonal red *SPECIMEN* overprint; punched. — — 550

Like SCB B7, but longer third line of Arabic text at top left on front.

SCB B3 (P3): **1 Sudanese pound** VG VF UNC
Blue. Front: Sennar dam on Blue Nile. Back: Camel postman. No security thread. Watermark: Three palm trees. Printer: (W&S). 140 x 75 mm.

☐ t. Color trial: Green. — — —
   ١٩٥٦ (15.09.1956). Signature 1. Unissued.

No image available.

SCB B4 (P4): **5 Sudanese pounds** VG VF UNC
Brown. Front: Four men in dhow; palm trees. Back: Camel postman. No security thread. Watermark: Three palm trees. Printer: (W&S). 155 x 88 mm.

☐ ١٩٥٦ (15.09.1956). Signature 1. Unconfirmed.

SCB B5 (P5): **10 Sudanese pounds** VG VF UNC
Black and green. Front: University of Khartoum building; palm trees. Back: Camel postman. No security thread. Watermark: Three palm trees. Printer: (W&S). 169 x 88 mm.

☐ t. Color trial: Brown. — — —
   ١٩٥٦ (15.09.1956). Signature 1. Unissued.

1956 Second Issues

These notes are like the preceding issues, but with solid security threads instead of planchettes, and numbers instead of letters in the prefix denominators. Although they do not bear imprints, they were printed by Thomas De La Rue, not Waterlow & Sons.

SCB B6 (P1A): 25 piastres   VG   VF   UNC
Red. Front: Troops with rifles. Back: Camel postman. Solid security thread. Watermark: None. Printer: (TDLR). 120 x 65 mm.
- ☐ a. ١٩٥٦ (15.09.1956). Sig. 1. Intro: April 1960.   5   25   250
- ☐ as. Diagonal red *CANCELLED* overprint; punched.   —   —   100

Like SCB B1, but shorter third line of Arabic text at top left on front.

SCB B8 (P3): 1 Sudanese pound   VG   VF   UNC
Blue. Front: Sennar dam on Blue Nile. Back: Camel postman. Solid security thread. Watermark: Three palm trees. Printer: (TDLR). 140 x 75 mm.
- ☐ a. ١٩٥٦ (15.09.1956). Sig. 1. Intro: April 1960.   15   75   350
- ☐ as. Diagonal red *CANCELLED* overprint; punched.   —   —   385

SCB B7 (P2A): 50 piastres   VG   VF   UNC
Green. Front: Two elephants; trees. Back: Camel postman. Solid security thread. Watermark: None. Printer: (TDLR). 125 x 70 mm.
- ☐ a. ١٩٥٦ (15.09.1956). Sig. 1. Intro: April 1960.   75   200   600
- ☐ as. Diagonal red *CANCELLED* overprint; punched.   —   —   450

Like SCB B2, but shorter third line of Arabic text at top left on front.

SCB B9 (P4): 5 Sudanese pounds   VG   VF   UNC
Brown. Front: Four men in dhow; palm trees. Back: Camel postman. Solid security thread. Watermark: Three palm trees. Printer: (TDLR). 155 x 88 mm.
- ☐ a. ١٩٥٦ (15.09.1956). Sig. 1. Intro: April 1960.   30   125   950
- ☐ as. Diagonal red *CANCELLED* overprint; punched.   —   —   250

SCB B10 (P5): 10 Sudanese pounds VG VF UNC

Black and green. Front: University of Khartoum building; palm trees. Back: Camel postman. Solid security thread. Watermark: Three palm trees. Printer: (TDLR). 169 x 88 mm.

☐	a. ١٩٥٦ (15.09.1956). Sig. 1. Intro: April 1960.	75	300	1,200
☐	as. Diagonal red *CANCELLED* overprint; punched.	—	—	650

Bank of Sudan

The Bank of Sudan Act (1959) established the bank which commenced business on 22 February 1960.

BOS Signature Varieties

1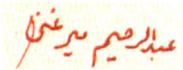
(Governor)
Mamoun Ahmed A. Beheiry
(01.12.1959 - 13.11.1963)

2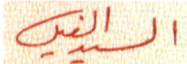
(Governor)
Elsayid Elfeel
(01.03.1964 - 13.09.1967)

3
(Governor)
Abdelrahim Mayrgani
(07.10.1967 - 16.05.1970)

4
(Chairman of the Board of Directors)
Awad Abdel Magid
(21.08.1971 -19.09.1972)

5
(Governor)
Ibrahim Mohammed Ali Nimir
(11.02.1973 - 13.02.1980)

6
(Governor)
Elsaikh Hassan Belail
(13.03.1980 - 26.05.1983)

7
(Governor)
Faroug Ibrahim Elmagbool
(26.05.1983 - 09.04.1985)

8a
(Deputy Governor)
Mahdi El Faki (large)

8b
(Governor)
Mahdi El Faki (small)

9
(Governor)
Ismail El-Misbah Mekki Hamad
(26.07.1985 - 13.10.1988)

10
(Governor)
Elshaik SidAhmed Elshaikh
(09.09.1990 - 08.07.1993)

11
(Governor)
Sabir Mohamed Hassan
(07.08.1993 - 20.04.1996)
(10.03.1998 - present)

12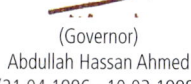
(Governor)
Abdullah Hassan Ahmed
(21.04.1996 - 10.03.1998)

1961-1968 Issues

These notes are like the preceding issues, but carry the name of the new issuer (Bank of Sudan), and on those notes with signature 3, the Arabic word for Khartoum no longer appears to the right of the date.

BOS B1 (P6): 25 piastres

Red. Front: Troops with rifles. Back: Camel postman. Solid security thread. Watermark: None. Printer: (TDLR). 120 x 65 mm.

		VG	VF	UNC
☐	a. ١٩٦٤ (13.07.1964). Signature 2.	25	100	400
☐	b. ١٩٦٦ (20.01.1966).	25	100	400
☐	c. ١٩٦٧ (25.01.1967).	10	50	250
☐	d. ١٩٦٨ (07.02.1968). Signature 3.	10	50	250
☐	as1. Four horizontal *SPECIMEN* perforations; diagonal red *CANCELLED* overprint.	—	—	100
☐	as2. Diagonal red *SPECIMEN* and DLR oval ovpts; horizontal red *SPECIMEN Nº #* ovpt at lower left; punched.	—	—	150
☐	bs. Four horizontal *SPECIMEN* perforations; diagonal red *CANCELLED* overprint.	—	—	150
☐	cs1. Four horizontal *SPECIMEN* perforations; diagonal red *CANCELLED* overprint.	—	—	100
☐	cs2. Diagonal red *SPECIMEN* and DLR oval ovpts; horizontal red *SPECIMEN Nº #* ovpt at lower left; punched.	—	—	150
☐	ds. Four horizontal *SPECIMEN* perforations; diagonal red *CANCELLED* overprint.	—	—	150
☐	p. Proof.	—	—	400

BOS B2 (P7): 50 piastres

Green. Front: Two elephants; trees. Back: Camel postman. Solid security thread. Watermark: None. Printer: (TDLR). 125 x 70 mm.

		VG	VF	UNC
☐	a. ١٩٦٤ (13.07.1964). Signature 2.	40	50	800
☐	b. ١٩٦٧ (25.01.1967).	40	155	850
☐	c. ١٩٦٨ (07.02.1968). Signature 3.	40	155	975
☐	as1. Four horizontal *SPECIMEN* perforations; diagonal red *CANCELLED* overprint.	—	—	185
☐	as2. Diagonal red *SPECIMEN* and DLR oval ovpts; horizontal red *SPECIMEN Nº #* ovpt at lower left; punched.	—	—	300
☐	bs. Horizontal *SPECIMEN OF NO VALUE* perf.	—	—	350
☐	cs. Four horizontal *SPECIMEN* perforations; diagonal red *CANCELLED* overprint.	—	—	180

BOS B3 (P8): **1 Sudanese pound**   VG   VF   UNC
Blue. Front: Sennar dam on Blue Nile. Back: Camel postman. No security thread.
Watermark: Three palm trees. Printer: (TDLR). 140 x 75 mm.

		VG	VF	UNC
☐	a. ١٩٦١ (08.04.1961). Signature 1.	8	200	400
☐	b. ١٩٦٥ (02.03.1965). Signature 2.	8	75	400
☐	c. ١٩٦٦ (20.01.1966).	6	45	300
☐	d. ١٩٦٧ (25.01.1967).	6	45	300
☐	e. ١٩٦٨ (07.02.1968). Signature 3.	5	40	275
☐	as1. Four horizontal SPECIMEN perforations; diagonal red CANCELLED overprint.	—	—	180
☐	as2. Diagonal red SPECIMEN and DLR oval ovpts; horizontal red SPECIMEN Nº # ovpt at lower left; punched.	—	—	275
☐	as3. Horizontal CANCELLED perforation.	—	—	1,200
☐	as4. Diagonal CANCELLED perforation; punched.	—	—	550
☐	cs1. Four horizontal SPECIMEN perforations; diagonal red CANCELLED overprint.	—	—	260
☐	cs2. Diagonal red SPECIMEN and DLR oval ovpts; horizontal red SPECIMEN Nº # ovpt at lower left; punched.	—	—	180
☐	ds1. Four horizontal SPECIMEN perforations; diagonal red CANCELLED overprint.	—	—	180
☐	ds2. Diagonal red SPECIMEN and DLR oval ovpts; horizontal red SPECIMEN Nº # ovpt at lower left; punched.	—	—	180
☐	es. Four horizontal SPECIMEN perforations; diagonal red CANCELLED overprint.	—	—	180

BOS B4 (P9): **5 Sudanese pounds**   VG   VF   UNC
Brown. Front: Four men in dhow; palm trees. Back: Camel postman. No security thread.
Watermark: Three palm trees. Printer: (TDLR). 155 x 88 mm.

		VG	VF	UNC
☐	a. ١٩٦٢ (17.06.1962). Signature 1.	15	150	1,200
☐	b. ١٩٦٥ (02.03.1965). Signature 2.	10	125	1,000
☐	c. ١٩٦٦ (20.01.1966).	10	100	875
☐	d. ١٩٦٧ (25.01.1967).	10	100	850
☐	e. ١٩٦٨ (07.02.1968). Signature 3.	10	100	950
☐	as1. Four horizontal SPECIMEN perforations; diagonal red CANCELLED overprint.	—	—	325
☐	as2. Diagonal red SPECIMEN and DLR oval ovpts; horizontal red SPECIMEN Nº # ovpt at lower left; punched.	—	—	325
☐	as3. Diagonal red SPECIMEN and DLR oval ovpts; horizontal red SPECIMEN Nº # ovpt at lower left; not punched.	—	—	325
☐	bs1. Four horizontal SPECIMEN perforations; diagonal red CANCELLED overprint.	—	—	250
☐	bs2. Diagonal red SPECIMEN and DLR oval ovpts; horizontal red SPECIMEN Nº # ovpt at lower left; punched.	—	—	250
☐	cs. Four horizontal SPECIMEN perforations; diagonal red CANCELLED overprint.	—	—	250
☐	ds1. Four horizontal SPECIMEN perforations; diagonal red CANCELLED overprint.	—	—	250
☐	ds2. Diagonal red SPECIMEN and DLR oval ovpts; horizontal red SPECIMEN Nº # ovpt at lower left; punched.	—	—	250
☐	es. Horizontal SPECIMEN OF NO VALUE perf.	—	—	—

1970-1980 Issues

All denominations in this family have two varieties dated 1978 in year, month (longhand), day format, all in Arabic. The first is dated 1 January 1978 and contains the word Khartoum to the right of the year (top). The second is dated 28 May 1978 without the place of issue (bottom), as is the case with all other date varieties in this family, except the initial variety from 1970.

BOS B5 (P10): 10 Sudanese pounds

Gray-black. Front: University of Khartoum building; palm trees. Back: Camel postman. Solid security thread. Watermark: Three palm trees. Printer: (TDLR). 169 x 88 mm.

		VG	VF	UNC
a.	١٩٦٤ (01.03.1964). Signature 2.	20	150	1,000
b.	١٩٦٦ (20.01.1966).	20	150	1,000
c.	١٩٦٧ (25.01.1967).	20	150	1,000
d.	١٩٦٨ (07.02.1968). Signature 3.	20	150	1,000
as1.	Four horizontal *SPECIMEN* perforations; diagonal red *CANCELLED* overprint.	—	—	200
as2.	Diagonal red *SPECIMEN* and DLR oval ovpts; horizontal red *SPECIMEN* Nº # ovpt at lower left; punched.	—	—	375
bs.	Four horizontal *SPECIMEN* perforations; diagonal red *CANCELLED* overprint.	—	—	375
cs.	Diagonal red *SPECIMEN* and DLR oval ovpts; horizontal red *SPECIMEN* Nº # ovpt at lower left; punched.	—	—	375
ds.	Four horizontal *SPECIMEN* perforations; diagonal red *CANCELLED* overprint.	—	—	325

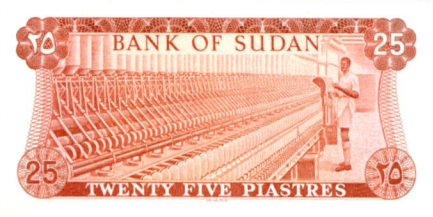

BOS B6 (P11): 25 piastres

Red. Front: Bank of Sudan headquarters building in Khartoum. Back: Man in cotton spinning factory. Solid security thread. Watermark: None. Printer: *DE LA RUE*. 120 x 60 mm.

		VG	VF	UNC
a.	١٩٧٠ (01.01.1970). Signature 3.	2	10	40
b.	١٩٧١ (30.11.1971). Signature 4.	2	10	60
c.	١٩٧٣ (01.04.1973). Signature 5.	0.75	2.50	10
d.	١٩٧٤ (27.04.1974).	0.75	2.50	10
e.	١٩٧٥ (25.01.1975).	0.75	2.50	10
f.	١٩٧٧ (07.02.1977).	0.75	2.50	10
g.	١٩٧٨ (01.01.1978).	0.75	2.50	10
h.	١٩٧٨ (28.05.1978).	0.75	2.50	10
i.	١٩٨٠ (02.01.1980).	0.75	2.50	10
as.	Four horizontal *SPECIMEN* perforations; diagonal red *CANCELLED* overprint.	—	—	—
bs.	Two diagonal red *CANCELLED* overprints.	—	—	—
cs.	Two diagonal red *CANCELLED* overprints; horizontal # perforation.			

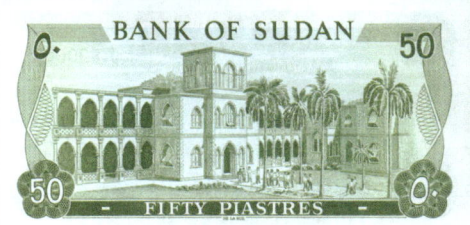

BOS B7 (P12): **50 piastres** VG VF UNC

Green. Front: Water primrose plant; Bank of Sudan headquarters building in Khartoum. Back: University of Khartoum building; palm trees. Solid security thread. Watermark: None. Printer: *DE LA RUE*. 130 x 65 mm.

		VG	VF	UNC
☐	a. ١٩٧٠ (01.01.1970). Signature 3.	5	20	85
☐	b. ١٩٧١ (30.11.1971). Signature 4.	5	20	85
☐	c. ١٩٧٣ (01.04.1973). Signature 5.	1.25	5	20
☐	d. ١٩٧٤ (27.04.1974).	1.25	5	20
☐	e. ١٩٧٥ (25.01.1975).	1.25	5	20
☐	f. ١٩٧٨ (01.01.1978).	1.25	5	20
☐	g. ١٩٧٨ (28.05.1978).	1.25	5	20
☐	h. ١٩٨٠ (02.01.1980).	1	4	15
☐	as1. Two diagonal red *CANCELLED* overprints.	—	—	—
☐	as2. Four horizontal *SPECIMEN* perforations; diagonal red *CANCELLED* overprint.	—	—	—
☐	bs. Two diagonal red *CANCELLED* overprints.	—	—	40
☐	cs. Two diagonal red *CANCELLED* overprints; horizontal # perforation.	—	—	—

BOS B8 (P13): **1 Sudanese pound** VG VF UNC

Blue. Front: Orchid flowers; Bank of Sudan headquarters building in Khartoum; orchid flowers. Back: Orchid flowers; ancient temple ruins, the Kiosk at Naqab (Naga); statue of King Taharqa with cobra crown. Solid security thread. Printer: *DE LA RUE*. 140 x 70 mm.

		VG	VF	UNC
☐	a. ١٩٧٠ (01.01.1970). Sig. 3. Wmk: Rhinoceros.	—	—	100
☐	b. ١٩٧١ (30.11.1971). Sig. 4. Wmk: Coat of arms.	5	20	85
☐	c. ١٩٧٣ (01.04.1973). Signature 5.	5	20	85
☐	d. ١٩٧٤ (27.04.1974).	2	10	30
☐	e. ١٩٧٥ (25.01.1975).	2	10	30
☐	f. ١٩٧٧ (07.02.1977).	2	10	30
☐	g. ١٩٧٨ (01.01.1978).	2	10	30
☐	h. ١٩٧٨ (28.05.1978).	2	10	30
☐	i. ١٩٨٠ (02.01.1980).	2	10	30
☐	as1. Two diagonal red *CANCELLED* overprints.	—	—	—
☐	as2. Four horizontal *SPECIMEN* perforations; diagonal red *CANCELLED* overprint.	—	—	135
☐	bs. Two diagonal red *CANCELLED* overprints.	—	—	—
☐	cs. Two diagonal red *CANCELLED* overprints; horizontal # perforation.	—	—	—

BOS B9 (P14): **5 Sudanese pounds**   VG   VF   UNC

Brown and red. Front: Cotton plants; Bank of Sudan headquarters building in Khartoum; cotton plants. Back: Ibex; cotton plants; palm trees; cattle; camels; rhinoceros; lion; elephant. Solid security thread. Printer: *DE LA RUE*. 150 x 75 mm.

			VG	VF	UNC
☐	a.	١٩٧٠ (01.01.1970). Sig. 3. Wmk: Rhinoceros.	15	50	225
☐	b.	١٩٧١ (30.11.1971). Sig. 4. Wmk: Coat of arms.	10	40	200
☐	c.	١٩٧٣ (01.04.1973). Signature 5.	10	40	200
☐	d.	١٩٧٤ (27.04.1974).	10	40	200
☐	e.	١٩٧٥ (25.01.1975).	10	40	200
☐	f.	١٩٧٧ (07.02.1977).	10	40	200
☐	g.	١٩٧٨ (01.01.1978).	10	40	200
☐	h.	١٩٧٨ (28.05.1978).	10	40	200
☐	i.	١٩٨٠ (02.01.1980).	10	40	200
☐	as1.	Four horizontal *SPECIMEN* perforations; diagonal red *CANCELLED* overprint.	—	—	100
☐	as2.	Diagonal red *SPECIMEN* and DLR oval ovpts; horizontal red *SPECIMEN* № # ovpt at lower left; punched.	—	—	—
☐	as3.	Two diagonal red *CANCELLED* overprints.	—	—	—
☐	bs.	Two diagonal red *CANCELLED* overprints.	—	—	—
☐	cs.	Two diagonal red *CANCELLED* overprints; horizontal # perforation.	—	—	—
☐	hs.	Diagonal red *SPECIMEN* and DLR oval ovpts; horizontal red *SPECIMEN* № # ovpt at lower left; punched.	—	—	—

BOS B10 (P15): **10 Sudanese pounds**   VG   VF   UNC

Purple and green. Front: Acacia plant; Bank of Sudan headquarters building in Khartoum; acacia plant. Back: Acacia plant; ships at Port Sudan loading cargo with cranes; trucks; railroad; jet plane. Solid security thread. Printer: *DE LA RUE*. 160 x 80 mm.

			VG	VF	UNC
☐	a.	١٩٧٠ (01.01.1970). Sig. 3. Wmk: Rhinoceros.	10	50	175
☐	b.	١٩٧١ (30.11.1971). Sig. 4. Wmk: Coat of arms.	8	25	100
☐	c.	١٩٧٣ (01.04.1973). Signature 5.	8	25	100
☐	d.	١٩٧٤ (27.04.1974).	8	25	100
☐	e.	١٩٧٥ (25.01.1975).	8	25	100
☐	f.	١٩٧٧ (07.02.1977).	8	25	100
☐	g.	١٩٧٨ (01.01.1978).	8	25	100
☐	h.	١٩٧٨ (28.05.1978).	8	25	100
☐	i.	١٩٨٠ (02.01.1980).	5	15	45
☐	as1.	Four horizontal *SPECIMEN* perforations; diagonal red *CANCELLED* overprint.	—	—	125
☐	as2.	Two diagonal red *CANCELLED* overprints.	—	—	—
☐	bs.	Two diagonal red *CANCELLED* overprints.	—	—	—
☐	cs.	Two diagonal red *CANCELLED* overprints; horizontal # perforation.	—	—	100
☐	is.	Diagonal red *SPECIMEN* and نموذج overprints.	—	—	—

1981 Commemorative Issue

This 20-pound note commemorates 25 years of independence and is like the regular issue note (BOS B17) of the same date, but has a circular black overprint around the watermark area on front.

BOS B11 (P22): 20 Sudanese pounds   VG   VF   UNC
Green, light blue, purple, and brown. Front: President Gaafar Nimeiry; map; *1956-1981 25th ANNIVERSARY OF INDEPENDENCE* overprint; Unity monument in Khartoum. Back: Unity monument in Khartoum; coat of arms; Presidential Palace building in Khartoum. Solid security thread. Watermark: Coat of arms. Printer: (TDLR). 160 x 80 mm.
☐ a. ١٩٨١ (01.01.1981). Signature 6.   20   85   375
☐ as1. Diagonal red *SPECIMEN* and نموذج overprints.   —   —   200

1981-1983 Issues

The front of these notes feature a portrait of Gaafar Muhammad an-Nimeiry (otherwise known as Jaafar Nimeiry, Gaafar Nimeiry or Ga'far Muhammad an-Numayri), the fifth president of Sudan, who served from 1969 to 1985.

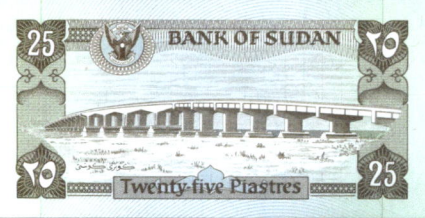

BOS B12 (P16): 25 piastres   VG   VF   UNC
Green and light blue. Front: President Gaafar Nimeiry; secretary bird with snake on map. Back: Coat of arms; Kosti railway and vehicular bridge over White Nile river. No security thread. Watermark: None. Printer: (TDLR). 120 x 60 mm.
☐ a. ١٩٨١ (01.01.1981). Signature 6.   0.25   1.50   5
☐ as. Diagonal red *SPECIMEN* and نموذج overprints.   —   —   75

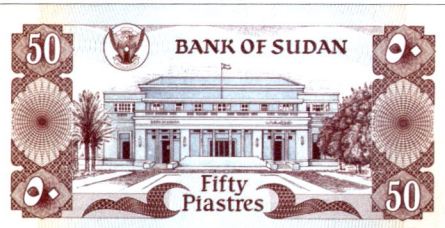

BOS B13 (P17 & P24): 50 piastres   VG   VF   UNC
Purple and brown. Front: President Gaafar Nimeiry; secretary bird with snake on map; plant. Back: Coat of arms; Bank of Sudan headquarters building in Khartoum. No security thread. Watermark: None. Printer: (TDLR). 130 x 65 mm.
☐ a. ١٩٨١ (01.01.1981). Signature 6.   0.25   1.50   8
☐ b. ١٩٨٣ (01.01.1983).   0.50   2.50   10
☐ as. Diagonal red *SPECIMEN* and نموذج overprints.   —   —   30
☐ bs. Diagonal red *SPECIMEN* and نموذج overprints.   —   —   50

SUDAN 1981-1983 ISSUES

BOS B14 (P18): **1 Sudanese pound**   VG   VF   UNC

Blue. Front: President Gaafar Nimeiry; secretary bird with snake on map; bamboo. Back: Bamboo; coat of arms; People's Assembly building in Khartoum. Solid security thread. Watermark: Coat of arms. Printer: (TDLR). 135 x 67.5 mm.

		VG	VF	UNC
☐	a. ١٩٨١ (01.01.1981). Signature 6.	2	8	30
☐	as. Diagonal red *SPECIMEN* and نموذج overprints.	—	—	175

BOS B15 (P19 & P26): **5 Sudanese pounds**   VG   VF   UNC

Green and brown. Front: President Gaafar Nimeiry; secretary bird with snake on map; plant. Back: Coat of arms; Islamic Centre mosque in Khartoum. Solid security thread. Watermark: Coat of arms. Printer: (TDLR). 143 x 71 mm.

		VG	VF	UNC
☐	a. ١٩٨١ (01.01.1981). Signature 6.	2	6	35
☐	b. ١٩٨٣ (01.01.1983).	2	6	35
☐	as. Diagonal red *SPECIMEN* and نموذج overprints.	—	—	100
☐	bs. Diagonal red *SPECIMEN* and نموذج overprints.	—	—	60

BOS B16 (P20): **10 Sudanese pounds**   VG   VF   UNC

Blue-green and orange. Front: President Gaafar Nimeiry; secretary bird with snake on map; cotton plant. Back: Cotton plant; coat of arms; Kenana Sugar Company factory near Kosti. Solid security thread. Watermark: Coat of arms. Printer: (TDLR). 153 x 76 mm.

		VG	VF	UNC
☐	a. ١٩٨١ (01.01.1981). Signature 6.	5	20	80
☐	as1. Diagonal red *SPECIMEN* and نموذج overprints.	—	—	100
☐	as2. Diagonal red *SPECIMEN* and DLR oval ovpts; horizontal red *SPECIMEN Nº #* ovpt at lower left; punched.	—	—	150

BOS B17 (P21 & P28): **20 Sudanese pounds**   VG   VF   UNC

Green, light blue, purple, and brown. Front: President Gaafar Nimeiry; map; Unity monument in Khartoum. Back: Unity monument in Khartoum; coat of arms; Presidential Palace building in Khartoum. Solid security thread. Watermark: Coat of arms. Printer: (TDLR). 160 x 80 mm.

		VG	VF	UNC
☐	a. ١٩٨١ (01.01.1981). Signature 6.	10	40	150
☐	b. ١٩٨٣ (01.01.1983).	10	40	150
☐	as. Diagonal red *SPECIMEN* and نموذج overprints.	—	—	175
☐	bs. Diagonal red *SPECIMEN* and نموذج overprints.	—	—	—

1983-1984 Issues

BOS B18 (P23): **25 piastres**   VG   VF   UNC

Red. Front: President Gaafar Nimeiry; secretary bird with snake on map. Back: Coat of arms; Kosti railway and vehicular bridge over White Nile river. No security thread. Watermark: None. Printer: (TDLR). 120 x 60 mm.

   ☐ a. ١٩٨٣ (01.01.1983). Signature 6.   0.25   0.50   3
   ☐ as. Diagonal red *SPECIMEN* and نموذج overprints.   —   —   50

BOS B19 (P25): **1 Sudanese pound**   VG   VF   UNC

Blue. Front: President Gaafar Nimeiry; secretary bird with snake on map. Back: Coat of arms; People's Assembly building in Khartoum. Solid security thread. Watermark: Coat of arms. Printer: (TDLR). 135 x 67.5 mm.

   ☐ a. ١٩٨٣ (01.01.1983). Signature 6.   0.50   2.50   10
   ☐ as. Diagonal red *SPECIMEN* and نموذج overprints.   —   —   50

Like BOS B14, but with monochrome, not two-tone, building on back surrounded by shadows.

BOS B20 (P27): **10 Sudanese pounds**   VG   VF   UNC

Purple. Front: President Gaafar Nimeiry; secretary bird with snake on map; cotton plant. Back: Cotton plant; coat of arms; Kenana Sugar Company factory near Kosti. Solid security thread. Watermark: Coat of arms. Printer: (TDLR). 152 x 76 mm.

   ☐ a. ١٩٨٣ (01.01.1983). Signature 6.   4   15   60
   ☐ as. Diagonal red *SPECIMEN* and نموذج overprints.   —   —   50

BOS B21 (P29): **50 Sudanese pounds**   VG   VF   UNC

Light green, olive green, and blue. Front: Oil refinery equipment; President Gaafar Nimeiry; seashell; wheat; flag. Back: Anchor; coat of arms; prow of a sailing ship; modern oil tanker. Solid security thread. Watermark: Coat of arms. Printer: (TDLR). 160 x 80 mm.

   ☐ a. ١٩٨٤ (25.05.1984). Signature 7.   10   40   150
   ☐ as. Diagonal red *SPECIMEN* and نموذج overprints.   —   —   100

1985-1990 Issues

BOS B22 (P30 & P37): **25 piastres**   VG   VF   UNC
Purple. Front: Two camels; map. Back: Bank of Sudan headquarters building in Khartoum. No security thread. Watermark: None. Printer: (TDLR). 120 x 60 mm.

☐ a. ١٩٨٥ (30.06.1985). Signature 8a.   —   0.50   1.75
☐ b. ١٩٨٧ (01.01.1987). Signature 9.   —   0.25   1
☐ as. Diagonal red *SPECIMEN* and نموذج overprints.   —   —   50

Replacement notes: Prefix Z/1.

BOS B23 (P31 & P38): **50 piastres**   VG   VF   UNC
Red. Front: Kissar (African lyre) and drum; map; peanut plant. Back: Bank of Sudan headquarters building in Khartoum. No security thread. Watermark: None. Printer: (TDLR). 128 x 64 mm.

☐ a. ١٩٨٥ (30.06.1985). Signature 8a.   0.25   1   4
☐ b. ١٩٨٧ (01.01.1987). Signature 9.   —   0.25   1.50
☐ as. Diagonal red *SPECIMEN* and نموذج overprints.   —   —   —
☐ bs. Diagonal red *SPECIMEN* and نموذج overprints.   —   —   25

Replacement notes: Prefix Z/11.

BOS B24 (P32 & P39): **1 Sudanese pound**   VG   VF   UNC
Blue and green. Front: Cotton plant; map; cotton plant. Back: Bank of Sudan headquarters building in Khartoum. Solid security thread. Watermark: Coat of arms. Printer: (TDLR). 136 x 68 mm.

☐ a. ١٩٨٥ (30.06.1985). Signature 8a.   0.25   0.75   3
☐ b. ١٩٨٧ (01.01.1987). Signature 9.   0.25   0.50   2
☐ as. Diagonal red *SPECIMEN* and نموذج overprints.   —   —   35
☐ bs. Diagonal red *SPECIMEN* and نموذج overprints.   —   —   30

Replacement notes: Prefix Z/21.

BOS B25 (P33 & P40): **5 Sudanese pounds**   VG   VF   UNC
Green and brown. Front: Cattle; map; plant. Back: Bank of Sudan headquarters building in Khartoum. Solid security thread. Watermark: Coat of arms. Printer: (TDLR). 144 x 72 mm.

☐ a. ١٩٨٥ (30.06.1985). Signature 8a.   2.50   10   40
☐ b. ١٩٨٧ (01.01.1987). Signature 9.   1.25   5   20
☐ c. ١٩٨٩ (March 1989). Signature 8b.   1.25   5   20
☐ d. ١٩٩٠ (January 1990).   0.50   2   8
☐ as. Diagonal red *SPECIMEN* and نموذج overprints.   —   —   —
☐ cs. Diagonal red *SPECIMEN* and نموذج overprints.   —   —   —
☐ ds. Diagonal red *SPECIMEN* and نموذج overprints.   —   —   —

Replacement notes: Prefix Z/31.

BOS B26 (P34 & P41): **10 Sudanese pounds** VG VF UNC
Brown and orange. Front: Old City Gate of Suakin; map; cotton plant. Back: Bank of Sudan headquarters building in Khartoum. Solid security thread. Watermark: Coat of arms. Printer: (TDLR). 152 x 76 mm.

		VG	VF	UNC
☐ a.	١٩٨٥ (30.06.1985). Signature 8a.	5	20	80
☐ b.	١٩٨٧ (01.01.1987). Signature 9.	2.50	10	40
☐ c.	١٩٨٩ (March 1989). Signature 8b.	2.50	10	40
☐ d.	١٩٩٠ (January 1990).	2.50	10	40
☐ as.	Diagonal red *SPECIMEN* and نموذج overprints.	—	—	—
☐ bs.	Diagonal red *SPECIMEN* and نموذج overprints.	—	—	—

Replacement notes: Prefix Z/41.

BOS B27 (P35 & P42): **20 Sudanese pounds** VG VF UNC
Green and purple. Front: Palm trees; feluka boat; map; wheat. Back: Bank of Sudan headquarters building in Khartoum. Solid security thread. Watermark: Coat of arms. Printer: (TDLR). 160 x 80 mm.

		VG	VF	UNC
☐ a.	١٩٨٥ (30.06.1985). Signature 8a.	15	50	250
☐ b.	١٩٨٧ (01.01.1987). Signature 9.	2	8	30
☐ c.	١٩٨٩ (March 1989). Signature 8b.	1.50	5	25
☐ d.	١٩٩٠ (January 1990).	1.50	5	25
☐ as.	Diagonal red *SPECIMEN* and نموذج overprints.	—	—	—
☐ bs.	Diagonal red *SPECIMEN* and نموذج overprints.	—	—	—
☐ ds.	Diagonal red *SPECIMEN* and نموذج overprints.	—	—	—

Replacement notes: Prefix Z/51.

BOS B28 (P36 & P43): **50 Sudanese pounds** VG VF UNC
Red and brown. Front: National Museum building; columns poolside; map; sword and spear. Back: Bank of Sudan headquarters building in Khartoum; tree. Solid security thread. Watermark: Coat of arms. Printer: (TDLR). 160 x 80 mm.

		VG	VF	UNC
☐ a.	١٩٨٥ (30.06.1985). Signature 8a.	5	20	275
☐ b.	١٩٨٧ (01.01.1987). Signature 9.	4	15	75
☐ c.	١٩٨٩ (March 1989). Signature 8b.	4	15	75
☐ d.	١٩٩٠ (January 1990).	4	15	75
☐ as.	Diagonal red *SPECIMEN* and نموذج overprints.	—	—	—
☐ bs.	Diagonal red *SPECIMEN* and نموذج overprints.	—	—	—
☐ ds.	Diagonal red *SPECIMEN* and نموذج overprints.	—	—	—

Replacement notes: Prefix Z/61.

BOS B29 (P44): **100 Sudanese pounds** VG VF UNC
Green. Front: Shield; University of Khartoum building; map; open book. Back: Bank of Sudan headquarters building in Khartoum; coin. Solid security thread. Watermark: Coat of arms. Printer: (TDLR). 160 x 80 mm.

		VG	VF	UNC
☐ a.	١٩٨٨ (01.01.1988). Signature 9.	1.50	5	20
☐ b.	١٩٨٩ (March 1989). Signature 8b.	—	—	1.50
☐ c.	١٩٩٠ (January 1990).	—	—	1.50
☐ bs.	Diagonal red *SPECIMEN* and نموذج overprints.	—	—	—
☐ cs.	Diagonal red *SPECIMEN* and نموذج overprints.	—	—	—

Replacement notes: Prefix Z/71.

1991-1992 Issues

These notes are like the preceding issues, but with revised color schemes.

BOS B30 (P45): **5 Sudanese pounds** — VG VF UNC
Orange, light blue, and violet. Front: Cattle; map; plant. Back: Bank of Sudan headquarters building in Khartoum. Solid security thread. Watermark: Coat of arms. Printer: (TDLR). 144 x 72 mm.

    ☐ a. ١٩٩١ (January 1991). Signature 10.   0.25   0.50   1.75
    ☐ as. Diagonal red *SPECIMEN* and نموذج overprints.   —   —   —

Replacement notes: Prefix Z/31.

BOS B31 (P46): **10 Sudanese pounds** — VG VF UNC
Brown and orange. Front: Old City Gate of Suakin; map; ear of wheat. Back: Ear of wheat; Bank of Sudan headquarters building in Khartoum. Solid security thread. Watermark: Coat of arms. Printer: (TDLR). 152 x 76 mm.

    ☐ a. ١٩٩١ (January 1991). Signature 10.   0.25   0.75   2
    ☐ as. Diagonal red *SPECIMEN* and نموذج overprints.   —   —   35

Replacement notes: Prefix Z/41.

BOS B32 (P47): **20 Sudanese pounds** — VG VF UNC
Green and purple. Front: Palm trees; feluka boat; map; wheat. Back: Bank of Sudan headquarters building in Khartoum. Solid security thread. Watermark: Coat of arms. Printer: (TDLR). 160 x 80 mm.

    ☐ a. ١٩٩١ (January 1991). Signature 10.   0.25   0.75   2.50
    ☐ as. Diagonal red *SPECIMEN* and نموذج overprints.   —   —   —

Replacement notes: Prefix Z/51.

BOS B33 (P48): **50 Sudanese pounds** — VG VF UNC
Red and brown. Front: National Museum building; columns poolside; map; sword and spear. Back: Bank of Sudan headquarters building in Khartoum; tree. Solid security thread. Watermark: Coat of arms. Printer: (TDLR). 160 x 80 mm.

    ☐ a. ١٩٩١ (January 1991). Signature 10.   0.50   1   3.50
    ☐ as. Diagonal red *SPECIMEN* and نموذج overprints.   —   —   —

Replacement notes: Prefix Z/61.

1992-2002 Issues

When introduced on 8 June 1992, the Sudanese dinar replaced the Sudanese pound at a rate of 1:10. Sudan Currency Printing Press (www.sudancurrency.com) was established in May 1994 and started production at the end of 1994. It purchases paper from Louisenthal.

BOS B34 (P49): **100 Sudanese pounds**   VG   VF   UNC
Purple and teal. Front: Shield; University of Khartoum building; map; open book. Back: Bank of Sudan headquarters building in Khartoum; coin. Solid security thread. Watermark: Coat of arms. Printer: (TDLR). 160 x 80 mm.

     ☐ a. ١٩٩١ (January 1991). Signature 10.   5   25   100
     ☐ as. Diagonal red *SPECIMEN* and نموذج overprints.   —   —   45

Replacement notes: Prefix Z/71.
Like BOS B35, but intaglio.

BOS B35 (P50): **100 Sudanese pounds**   VG   VF   UNC
Purple and teal. Front: Shield; University of Khartoum building; map; open book. Back: Bank of Sudan headquarters building in Khartoum; coin. Solid security thread. Watermark: Coat of arms. Printer: (TDLR). 160 x 80 mm.

     ☐ a. ١٩٩١ (January 1991). Signature 10.   1   2.50   5
     ☐ b. ١٩٩٢ (January 1992).   1   2.50   5
     ☐ bs. Diagonal red *SPECIMEN* and نموذج overprints.   —   —   —

Replacement notes: Prefix Z/71.
Like BOS B34, but lithograph.

BOS B36 (P51): **5 Sudanese dinars** (demonetized 01.09.2007)   VG   VF   UNC
Green and brown. Front: Tree; Presidential Palace building in Khartoum. Back: Field of millet and sunflower plants. Solid security thread printed *BANK OF SUDAN*. Watermark: Masjid Al-Nilin. Printer: (TDLR). 140 x 65 mm.

     ☐ a. ١٩٩٣ (February 1993). Signature 10.   0.25   1   2
     ☐ as. Diagonal red hollow *SPECIMEN* overprint;   —   —   20
        horizontal red *SPECIMEN* Nº # ovpt at lower left.

Replacement notes: Prefix GZ.

BOS B37 (P52): **10 Sudanese dinars** (demon. 01.09.2007)   VG   VF   UNC
Red, yellow, and purple. Front: Tree; Presidential Palace building in Khartoum. Back: Masjid Al-Nilin (Mosque of the two Niles) building in Omdurman. Solid security thread printed *BANK OF SUDAN*. Watermark: Masjid Al-Nilin. Printer: (TDLR). 140 x 65 mm.

     ☐ a. ١٩٩٣ (February 1993). Signature 10.   0.25   1   2.50
     ☐ as. Diagonal red hollow *SPECIMEN* overprint;   —   —   85
        horizontal red *SPECIMEN* Nº # ovpt at lower left.

Replacement notes: Prefix HZ.

BOS B38 (P53): **25 Sudanese dinars** (demon. 01.09.2007) VG VF UNC
Green, brown, and yellow. Front: Tree; Presidential Palace building in Khartoum. Back: Arabesque design. Solid security thread printed *BANK OF SUDAN*. Watermark: Masjid Al-Nilin. 140 x 65 mm.

☐	a.	١٩٩٢ (March 1992). Sig. 10. Fractional prefix. Printer: (TDLR). With artist's name (*DOSOUGI*) at lower right.	0.25	1	3
☐	b.	Without artist's name at lower right front.	0.25	1	3
☐	c.	Signature 11. Printer: (Sudan Currency Printing Press).	0.25	1	3
☐	bs.	Diagonal red *SPECIMEN* overprint; horizontal red *N. #* overprint at left center.	—	—	40
☐	cs.	Diagonal red hollow *SPECIMEN* overprint; horizontal red *N. #* overprint at lower left.	—	—	40

Replacement notes: Prefix IZ.

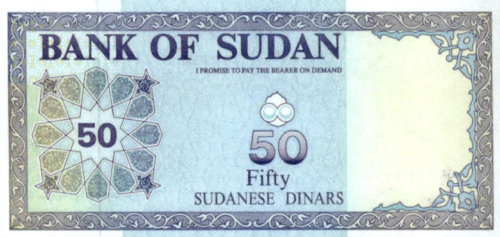

BOS B39 (P54): **50 Sudanese dinars** (demon. 01.09.2007) VG VF UNC
Light blue and purple. Front: Tree; Presidential Palace building in Khartoum. Back: Denomination in Arabesque design. Watermark: Masjid Al-Nilin. 140 x 65 mm.

☐	a.	١٩٩٢ (March 1992). Sig. 10. Fractional prefix. Printer: (TDLR). Solid security thread printed *BANK OF SUDAN*. With artist's name (*DOSOUGI*) at lower right.	1.50	5	20
☐	b.	Without artist's name at lower right front.	0.50	1.50	5
☐	c.	Signature 11.	0.50	1.50	5
☐	d.	Printer: (Sudan Currency Printing Press). 2-letter prefix (JA-JX). 7-digit serial numbers.	0.50	1.50	2.50
☐	e.	1-letter prefix (J or P). 8-digit serial numbers. Windowed security thread with demetalized *BANK OF SUDAN*.	0.50	1.50	2.50
☐	f.	2-letter prefix (PA-PO). 8-digit serial numbers.	0.50	1.50	2.50
☐	as.	Diagonal red *SPECIMEN* ovpt on front; horizontal red *N. #* overprint at lower center.	—	—	30

BOS B39 (P54): **50 Sudanese dinars** (demon. 01.09.2007) VG VF UNC
☐	bs.	Diagonal red *SPECIMEN* ovpt on front; horizontal red *N. #* overprint at lower left.	—	—	30

Replacement notes: Prefix JZ.

BOS B40 (P55): **100 Sudanese dinars** (demon. 01.09.2007) VG VF UNC
Blue, orange, green, and red. Front: Two ancient doors; tree; Presidential Palace building in Khartoum. Back: Parliament House building in Omdurman; trees. Solid security thread printed *BANK OF SUDAN*. Watermark: Masjid Al-Nilin. Printer: (Sudan Currency Printing Press). 140 x 65 mm.

☐	a.	١٩٩٤ (April 1994). Signature 11.	0.50	2	5.50
☐	as.	Diagonal red hollow *SPECIMEN* ovpt on front; horizontal red *N. #* overprint at lower left.	—	—	—

Replacement notes: Prefix KZ.

BOS B41 (P56): **100 Sudanese dinars** (demon. 01.09.2007) VG VF UNC
Orange, green, and red. Front: Two ancient doors; tree; Presidential Palace building in Khartoum. Back: Parliament House building in Omdurman; trees. Watermark: Masjid Al-Nilin. Printer: (Sudan Currency Printing Press). 140 x 65 mm.

☐	a.	١٩٩٤ (April 1994). Signature 11. 7- or 8-digit serial numbers. 1-mm windowed security thread with demetalized *BANK OF SUDAN* and Arabic text.	0.50	1.50	2.50
☐	b.	9-digit serial numbers. 2-mm windowed security thread with demetalized *B of S 100* and Arabic text.	0.50	1.50	2.50
☐	c.	8- or 9-digit serial numbers. 1-mm windowed security thread with demetalized *BANK OF SUDAN* and Arabic text.	0.50	1.50	2.50

Replacement notes: Prefix LZ.

BOS B42 (P57 & P60): **200 Sudanese dinars** (dem. 01.09.07)   VG   VF   UNC
Green and purple. Front: Wheat; Presidential Palace building in Khartoum. Back: Seal; coat of arms; building; palm trees; millet. Watermark: Masjid Al-Nilin. Printer: (Sudan Currency Printing Press). 140 x 65 mm.

- a. ١٩٩٨ (April 1998). Signature 11.   0.50   1   4
  7-digit serial numbers.
  Solid security thread with printed text.
  Planchettes.
- b. 8-digit serial numbers.   0.50   1   4
  Windowed security thread with demetalized
  BANK OF SUDAN and Arabic text.
  No planchettes.
- as. Diagonal red hollow SPECIMEN ovpt on front;   —   —   —
  horizontal red N # overprint at lower left.

BOS B43 (P58 & P61): **500 Sudanese dinars** (dem. 01.09.07)   VG   VF   UNC
Red, blue, and violet. Front: Presidential Palace building in Khartoum. Back: Seal; oil well; building; palm trees; coat of arms. Watermark: Masjid Al-Nilin. Printer: (Sudan Currency Printing Press). 140 x 65 mm.

- a. ١٩٩٨ (April 1998). Signature 11.   0.50   1.50   6
  Solid security thread with demetalized
  BANK OF SUDAN and Arabic text.
  Planchettes.
- b. Windowed security thread with demetalized   0.50   1.50   6
  BANK OF SUDAN and Arabic text.
  No planchettes.
- as. Diagonal red hollow SPECIMEN ovpt on front;   —   —   —
  horizontal red N # overprint at lower left.

BOS B44 (P59): **1,000 Sudanese dinars** (demon. 01.09.2007)   VG   VF   UNC
Green, orange, and purple. Front: Cotton flowers; Presidential Palace building in Khartoum. Back: Seal; coat of arms; building. Windowed security thread with demetalized BANK OF SUDAN and Arabic text. Watermark: Masjid Al-Nilin. Printer: (Sudan Currency Printing Press). 140 x 65 mm.

- a. ١٩٩٦ (19.05.1996).   1   3   10
  Signature 12. 7- or 8-digit serial numbers.
- b. Signature 11. 8-digit serial numbers.   1   3   10
- as. Diagonal red hollow SPECIMEN overprint;   —   —   —
  horizontal red N # overprint at lower left.

BOS B45 (P62): **2,000 Sudanese dinars** (demon. 01.09.2007)   VG   VF   UNC
Tan, red, violet, pink, and orange. Front: Presidential Palace building in Khartoum. Back: Oil well; dam; refinery equipment; Bank of Sudan headquarters building in Khartoum; coat of arms. Holographic stripe. Windowed security thread with demetalized SUDAN 2000 and Arabic text. Watermark: Masjid Al-Nilin with electrotype 2000. Printer: (G&D). 140 x 65 mm.

- a. ٢٠٠٢ (January 2002). Signature 11.   1.50   6   20
- as. Diagonal red hollow SPECIMEN ovpt on front;   —   —   60
  horizontal red N. # overprint at center left.

Replacement notes: Prefix second letter J.
This note is the first in the world to feature a copper LEAD holographic stripe.

Central Bank of Sudan

For more information, visit www.bankofsudan.org.

CBS Signature Varieties

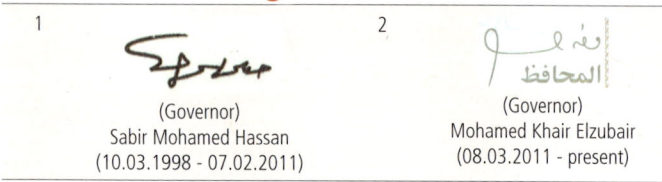

1	2
(Governor) Sabir Mohamed Hassan (10.03.1998 - 07.02.2011)	(Governor) Mohamed Khair Elzubair (08.03.2011 - present)

2006 Issues

When introduced on 10 January 2007, the second Sudanese pound replaced the Sudanese dinar at a rate of 1:100. This new currency was mandated by the 2005 Comprehensive Peace Agreement signed between the Sudanese government and the Sudan People's Liberation Movement to end the country's 21- year civil war. Deputy Governor Badr-Eddin Mahmoud said the cost to print the new currency was US$156 million.

These notes are the first in the world printed on Louisenthal's Synthec, a cotton substrate with approximately 20% synthetic fibers for greater durability. Synthec also features LongLife coating to protect the substrate from moisture and soiling.

The substrate for the 1-pound note was switched to Hybrid at some point (exact prefix range to be determined), but the printer wasn't satisfied with how the ink adhered, so Hybrid was never used on the other denominations.

BOS B46 (P63): **5,000 Sudanese dinars** (demon. 01.09.2007)   VG   VF   UNC
Pink, orange, and blue. Front: Pyramid; wheat and cotton crops; alphabet; crown; doorway; columns; Presidential Palace building in Khartoum; coat of arms. Back: Boat with sail; artifacts; Bank of Sudan headquarters building in Khartoum; coat of arms. Holographic stripe. Windowed security thread with demetalized *SUDAN 5000* and Arabic text. Watermark: Masjid Al-Nilin with electrotype *5000*. Printer: (G&D). 140 x 65 mm.

    ☐ a.   ٢٠٠٢ (January 2002). Signature 11.   —   —   20
    ☐ as. Diagonal red hollow *SPECIMEN* ovpt on front;   —   —   —
        horizontal red *№* # overprint at lower left.

Replacement notes: Prefix second letter J.

BOS B47 (P59A): **10,000 Sudanese dinars**   VG   VF   UNC
Brown and blue. Front: Presidential Palace building in Khartoum; sunflower; leaf; wheat; frond. Back: Wheat; coat of arms; water jugs; building; palm trees. Windowed security thread with demetalized *BANK OF SUDAN* and Arabic text. Watermark: Masjid Al-Nilin. Printer: (Sudan Currency Printing Press). 140 x 65 mm.

    ☐ a.   ١٩٩٦ (19.05.1996). Signature 12. Prefix NA.   —   —   —
    ☐ as. Diagonal red hollow *SPECIMEN* overprint;   —   —   600
        horizontal red *N* # overprint at lower left.

CBS B1 (P64): **1 Sudanese pound** (US$0.20)   VG   VF   UNC
Light brown. Front: Sunflower as registration device; peace theme with dove in flight above map, Central Bank of Sudan headquarters building in Khartoum, and drums; map. Back: Bank logo; two doves in flight; sunflower. 2-mm wide windowed security thread with demetalized *CBS 1 LS* and Arabic text. Watermark: Pigeon and electrotype *LS 1*. Printer: (Sudan Currency Printing Press). 139 x 64 mm.

    ☐ a.   July 9 2006. Signature 1. Intro: 10.01.2007.   FV   FV   1.50
        Printed on Synthec substrate. Blurry watermark.
    ☐ b.   Printed on Hybrid substrate. Clear watermark.   FV   FV   5
    ☐ as1. Diagonal red sans serif *SPECIMEN* and Arabic   —   —   65
        overprint on front only.
    ☐ as2. Diagonal red serif *SPECIMEN* and Arabic   —   —   65
        overprint on front only; normal serial numbers.
    ☐ as3. Diagonal red نموذج ovpt; normal serial numbers.   —   —   40

Replacement notes: Prefix second letter J.

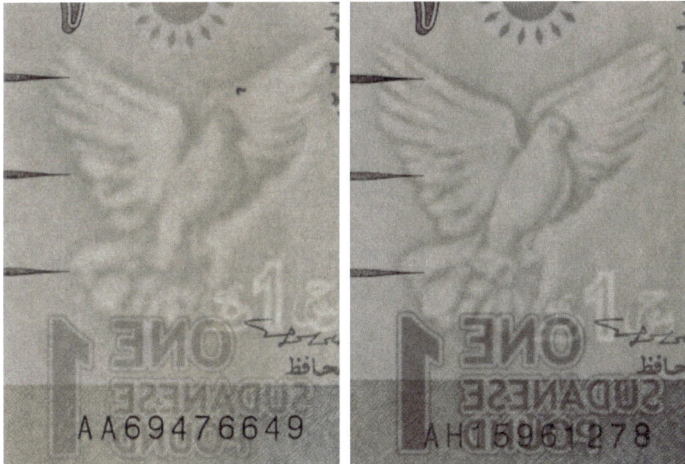

The 1-pound note printed on Synthec substrate has a blurry watermark (CBS B1a, left), whereas the watermark on the Hybrid substrate is clearly defined (B1b, right).

CBS B2 (P65): **2 Sudanese pounds** (US$0.45)　　　　VG　VF　UNC

Light blue. Front: Pottery bowl as registration device; civilization theme with bowls, plates, and vases; map. Back: Bank logo; musical instruments; pottery bowl. 2-mm wide windowed security thread with demetalized *CBOS 2 LS* and Arabic text. Watermark: Pigeon and electrotype *LS 2*. Printer: (Sudan Currency Printing Press). 144 x 64 mm.

  ☐ a. July 9 2006. Signature 1. Intro: May 2007. FV FV 2
  ☐ as. Vertical blue *SPECIMEN* stamp; — — —
     horizontal *SPECIMEN* perforation.

Replacement notes: Prefix second letter J.

CBS B3 (P66): **5 Sudanese pounds** (US$1.15)　　　　VG　VF　UNC

Pink. Front: Balance scale as registration device; future theme with modern architecture and satellite; map. Back: Bank logo; electrical tower; hydroelectric dam; solar panel; wind turbine; balance scale. 2-mm wide windowed security thread with demetalized *CBOS 5 LS* and Arabic text. Watermark: Pigeon and electrotype *LS 5*. Printer: (Sudan Currency Printing Press). 150 x 69 mm.

  ☐ a. July 9 2006. Signature 1. Intro: May 2007. FV FV 5
  ☐ as. Vertical blue *SPECIMEN* stamp; — — —
     horizontal *SPECIMEN* perforation.

Replacement notes: Prefix second letter J.

CBS B4 (P67): **10 Sudanese pounds** (US$2.30)　　　VG　VF　UNC

Violet. Front: Map as registration device; national unity theme with tree in Tabaldia, clasped hands, watusi cattle, mountains, and camel; map. Back: Bank logo; Presidential Palace building in Khartoum; map. Holographic stripe. 2-mm wide windowed security thread with demetalized *CBS 10 LS* and Arabic text. Watermark: Secretary bird and electrotype *LS 10*. Printer: (Sudan Currency Printing Press). 155 x 69 mm.

  ☐ a. July 9 2006. Signature 1. Intro: 10.01.2007. FV FV 7
  ☐ as1. Diagonal red *SPECIMEN* and Arabic overprint on — — —
     front only.
  ☐ as2. Diagonal red *SPECIMEN* overprint. — — —

Replacement notes: Prefix second letter J.

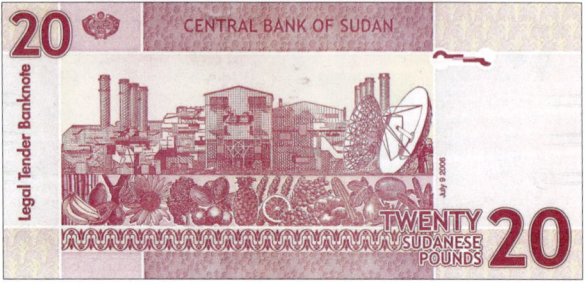

CBS B5 (P68): **20 Sudanese pounds** (US$4.55)   VG   VF   UNC

Dark red. Front: Wrench as registration device; industrial development theme with three pyramids, irrigation wheel, and oil drilling platform; map. Back: Bank logo; factory, satellite dishes, and fruit (bananas, papayas, flowers, pineapples, citrus, grapes, corn); wrench. Holographic stripe. 2-mm wide windowed security thread with demetalized *CBS 20 LS* and Arabic text. Watermark: Secretary bird and electrotype *LS 20*. Printer: (Sudan Currency Printing Press). 160 x 74 mm.

- ☐ a. July 9 2006. Signature 1. Intro: May 2007.   FV   FV   17
- ☐ as1. Vertical blue *SPECIMEN* stamp; horizontal *SPECIMEN* perforation.   —   —   —
- ☐ as2. Diagonal red *SPECIMEN* overprint; horizontal red *SPECIMEN* № # ovpt at lower left.   —   —   —

Replacement notes: Prefix second letter J.

CBS B6 (P69): **50 Sudanese pounds** (US$11)   VG   VF   UNC

Yellow, green, and brown. Front: Fish as registration device; natural resources theme with rhinoceros, elephants, ape in tree, water buffalo, zebras, and giraffe; map. Back: Bank logo; camels, goats, and cattle; fish. Holographic stripe. 2-mm wide windowed security thread with demetalized *CBS 50 LS* and Arabic text. Watermark: Secretary bird and electrotype *LS 50*. Printer: (Sudan Currency Printing Press). 165 x 74 mm.

- ☐ a. July 9 2006. Signature 1. Intro: 10.01.2007.   FV   FV   40
- ☐ as. Vertical blue *SPECIMEN* stamp; horizontal *SPECIMEN* perforation.   —   —   —

Replacement notes: Prefix second letter J.

2011 Issues

These notes were issued in response to the creation of a new currency for South Sudan after it seceded from northern Sudan on 9 July 2011. The designs are like the preceding issues, but the colors have changed, the map at upper right front has been removed, and the signature and date are new. The 1-pound note was replaced by a coin at the end of November 2011.

For notes issued in South Sudan, see South Sudan.

CBS B7 (PNL): **2 Sudanese pounds** (US$0.45)   VG   VF   UNC

Yellow, purple, and brown. Front: Sunflower as registration device; peace theme with dove in flight above map, Central Bank of Sudan headquarters building in Khartoum, and drums. Back: Bank logo; two doves in flight; sunflower. 2-mm wide windowed security thread with demetalized *CBOS 2 LS* and Arabic text. Watermark: Pigeon and electrotype *LS 1*. Printer: (Sudan Currency Printing Press). 139 x 64 mm.

- ☐ a. JUNE 2011. Signature 2. Intro: November 2011.   FV   FV   1.50

CBS B8 (PNL): **5 Sudanese pounds** (US$1.15)   VG   VF   UNC

Blue, violet, and green. Front: Balance scale as registration device; future theme with modern architecture and satellite. Back: Bank logo; electrical tower; hydroelectric dam; solar panel; wind turbine; balance scale. 2-mm wide windowed security thread with demetalized *CBOS* and Arabic text. Watermark: Pigeon and electrotype *LS 5*. Printer: (Sudan Currency Printing Press). 150 x 69 mm.

- ☐ a. JUNE 2011. Signature 2. Windowed thread on back. Intro: 24.07.2011.   FV   FV   3.50
- ☐ b. Windowed thread on front (error).   FV   FV   6.50

CBS B9 (PNL): **10 Sudanese pounds** (US$2.30)   VG   VF   UNC
Green. Front: Sorghum plant as registration device; national unity theme with tree in Tabaldia, clasped hands, mountains, and camel. Back: Bank logo; Presidential Palace building in Khartoum; sorghum plant. Holographic stripe. 2-mm wide windowed security thread with demetalized *CBS 10 LS* and Arabic text. Watermark: Secretary bird and electrotype *LS 10*. Printer: (Sudan Currency Printing Press). 155 x 69 mm.
   ☐ a.   JUNE 2011. Signature 2. Intro: 24.07.2011.   FV   FV   7
The watusi cattle of the preceding issue was removed because it is a symbol of South Sudan's western Bahar Gazal region.

CBS B11 (PNL): **50 Sudanese pounds** (US$11)   VG   VF   UNC
Gray, blue, green, and brown. Front: Fish as registration device; natural resources theme with rhinoceros, elephants, ape in tree, water buffalo, zebras, and giraffe. Back: Bank logo; camels, goats, and cattle; fish. Holographic stripe. 2-mm wide windowed security thread with demetalized *CBS 50 LS* and Arabic text. Watermark: Secretary bird and electrotype *LS 50*. Printer: (Sudan Currency Printing Press). 165 x 74 mm.
   ☐ a.   JUNE 2011. Signature 2. Intro: 24.07.2011.   FV   FV   30

CBS B10 (PNL): **20 Sudanese pounds** (US$4.55)   VG   VF   UNC
Tan, orange, and purple. Front: Wrench as registration device; industrial development theme with three pyramids, irrigation wheel, and oil drilling platform. Back: Bank logo; factory, satellite dishes, and fruit (bananas, papayas, flowers, pineapples, citrus, grapes, corn); wrench. Holographic stripe. 2-mm wide windowed security thread with demetalized *CBS 20 LS* and Arabic text. Watermark: Secretary bird and electrotype *LS 20*. Printer: (Sudan Currency Printing Press). 160 x 74 mm.
   ☐ a.   JUNE 2011. Signature 2.   FV   FV   15
           Windowed thread on back. Intro: 24.07.2011.
   ☐ b.   Windowed thread on front (error).   FV   FV   15

Acknowledgements

This chapter was compiled with the generous assistance of Khalifa Abdallatif (www.stores.ebay.com/philanote), Tom A. Adami, Bushra Ali, Thomas Augustsson, Edwin Biersteker, Randy Briggs, Jim W.-C. Chen, Don Cleveland, Jean-Michel Engels, Larry Hirsch (www.aworldcurrency.com), Michael Kovac, Claudio Marana, Dr. Ali Mehilba, Yuri Minkin (http://stores.ebay.com/yuri111), Magda A. Musa (Central Bank of Sudan), Wally Myers, Rui Manuel Palhares, Andrew Roberts, Kang Hyun Soon, Bill Stubkjaer, Christoph Thomas, and others.

Sources

Ali, Bushra El-Fatih A. *Encyclopedia of Sudan Banknotes 1856-2012*. 1st edition. 2012.

Cuhaj, George S. *Standard Catalog of World Paper Money, General Issues, 1368-1960*. 14th edition. 2012. ISBN 978-1-4402-3090-5. Krause Publications (www.krausebooks.com), 700 East State St., Iola, WI, 54990-0001.

Cuhaj, George S. *Standard Catalog of World Paper Money, Modern Issues, 1961-Present*. 19th edition. 2013. ISBN 978-1-4402-3571-9. Krause Publications (www.krausebooks.com), 700 East State St., Iola, WI, 54990-0001.

McCarthy, Michael. "Sudan's Camel Postman." *IBNS Journal*. Volume 24 Number 2. p.52.

Parr, Martin. "History of the Gordon Notes." *IBNS Journal*. Volume 12 Number 1. p.5.

Parr, Martin. "History of the Gordon Note." *IBNS Journal*. Volume 12 Number 2. p.7.

Philipson, F. "Gordon…Khartoum." *IBNS Journal*. Volume 10 Number 2. p.93.

Symes, Peter. "Sudan's Camel Postman." *IBNS Journal*. Volume 46 Number 1. p.51.

Symes, Peter. "Sudan's First Bank Notes." *IBNS Journal*. Volume 40 Number 3. p.12.

Symes, Peter. "The Bank of Sudan's Second Series." *IBNS Journal*. Volume 49 Number 3. p.39.

Symes, Peter. Reference Site for Islamic Banknotes (www.islamicbanknotes.com).

Share Your Input, Info, and Images

This catalog is believed to be complete and correct as of the time of publication. Prices and face values were last updated 8 February 2013. Please report errors or omissions so that corrections may be made. If you can more precisely identify the name or location of anything depicted on a note, please share that information. Furthermore, if you own an unlisted type or variety, please submit scans of the front and back of the note so that it can be documented. Scans should be 300 dots per inch, 100% actual size, 24-bit color, saved as *uncompressed* JPEG files, and sent to owen@banknotenews.com. Be sure to fully describe all attributes of the note which are not apparent upon visual inspection of the images alone, such as physical dimension, watermark, and security thread.

Suriname

De Surinaamsche Bank Issues

Prior to the establishment of Central Bank of Suriname in 1957, banknotes were issued by De Surinaamsche Bank. These notes will be added to this chapter in the future.

Currency Note (Muntbiljet) Issues

In Suriname, banknotes are issued by the Central Bank van Suriname by virtue of the Banking Act 1956, whereas currency notes (muntbiljet) and coins are issued by the finance ministry under the Coinage Act 1960. Currency notes will be added to this chapter in the future.

Monetary System

1 Surinamese guilder (SRG) = 100 cent
01.01.2004: 1 Surinamese dollar (SRD) = 100 cent

Dutch Months of the Year

Januari (January)	Februari (February)	Maart (March)
April (April)	Mei (May)	Juni (June)
Juli (July)	Augustus (August)	September (September)
Oktober (October)	November (November)	December (December)

Centrale Bank van Suriname (Central Bank of Suriname)

Suriname had been a Dutch colony since the 17th century, but in 1954, the Dutch placed Suriname under a system of limited self-government, with the Netherlands retaining control of defense and foreign affairs. Political self-government affected the monetary system of the country. Circulation banking by De Surinaamsche Bank, a private bank, was taken over by the Centrale Bank van Suriname (CBVS), which was founded on 1 April 1957, and headquartered in the Waterkant in Paramaribo.

For more information, visit www.cbvs.sr.

CBVS Signature Varieties

PRESIDENT

1 — R. W. Groenman (January 1957 - August 1961)

2 — Victor Max de Miranda (1963 - 1980)

3 — Jules Sedney (1980 - 1983)

4a — Hendrik "Henk" Otmar Goedschalk (1985)

4b — Hendrik "Henk" Otmar Goedschalk (1986 - 1988)

4c — Hendrik "Henk" Otmar Goedschalk (1991 - 1993)

5 — André Eugene Telting (24-mm) (1994 - 1996)

6 — Hendrik "Henk" Otmar Goedschalk (1997 - 2000)

7 — André Eugene Telting (12-mm) (2004 - September 2010)

8 — Gillmore Hoefdraad (September 2010 - present)

1957 Issues

The banknotes of De Surinaamsche Bank were gradually replaced by notes issued by the Central Bank of Suriname. These notes are denominated in guilders, expressed on the notes using the Dutch word gulden.

CBVS B1 (P111): 5 gulden (guilders) VG VF UNC
Blue and bluish-gray. Front: Woman carrying basket of fruit and vegetables on head; torch with *1957* banner. Back: Coat of arms of two native indians with bows and arrows flanking a sailing ship. No security thread. Watermark: Parrot head. Printer: *JOH. ENSCHEDÉ EN ZONEN IMP.* 152 x 66 mm.
- ☐ a.   2 JANUARI 1957. Signature 1.   25   120   250
- ☐ as. Diagonal red *SPECIMEN* ovpt; s/n Z 012345...   —   —   150

CBVS B2 (P112): 10 gulden (guilders) VG VF UNC
Reddish-orange. Front: Woman carrying basket of fruit and vegetables on head; torch with *1957* banner. Back: Coat of arms of two native indians with bows and arrows flanking a sailing ship. No security thread. Watermark: Parrot head. Printer: *JOH. ENSCHEDÉ EN ZONEN IMP.* 152 x 66 mm.
- ☐ a.   2 JANUARI 1957. Signature 1.   40   175   400
- ☐ as. Diagonal red *SPECIMEN* ovpt; s/n Z 012345...   —   —   250

CBVS B3 (P113): 25 gulden (guilders) VG VF UNC
Green and red. Front: Woman's head; fruit and vegetables; torch with *1957* banner. Back: Coat of arms of two native indians with bows and arrows flanking a sailing ship. No security thread. Watermark: Parrot head. Printer: *JOH. ENSCHEDÉ EN ZONEN IMP.* 152 x 66 mm.
- ☐ a.   2 JANUARI 1957. Signature 1.   70   300   600
- ☐ as. Diagonal red *SPECIMEN* ovpt; s/n Z 012345...   —   —   450

CBVS B4 (P114): 100 gulden (guilders) VG VF UNC
Purple and green. Front: Woman's head; fruit and vegetables; torch with *1957* banner. Back: Coat of arms of two native indians with bows and arrows flanking a sailing ship. No security thread. Watermark: Parrot head. Printer: *JOH. ENSCHEDÉ EN ZONEN IMP.* 152 x 66 mm.
- ☐ a.   2 JANUARI 1957. Signature 1.   75   375   —
- ☐ as. Diagonal red *SPECIMEN* ovpt; s/n Z 012345...   —   —   600

CBVS B5 (P115): **1,000 gulden (guilders)**　　　VG　VF　UNC

Brown and blue. Front: Woman's head; fruit and vegetables; torch with *1957* banner. Back: Coat of arms of two native indians with bows and arrows flanking a sailing ship. No security thread. Watermark: Parrot head. Printer: *JOH. ENSCHEDÉ EN ZONEN IMP.* 152 x 66 mm.

- ☐ a.　2 JANUARI 1957. Signature 1.　　　　250　1,000　—
- ☐ as.　Diagonal red *SPECIMEN* ovpt; s/n Z 012345...　—　—　700

1963 Issues

These notes are like the preceding issues, but with a new coat of arms with a shield at center. The ship on the left of the shield symbolizes the past, when slaves were brought from Africa by boat. The royal palm tree on the right of the shield symbolizes the present, and is the symbol of a just person ("The just person should blossom like a palm"). The diamond in the middle is the stylized form of the heart, the organ of love. The points of the diamond show the four directions of the wind. Inside the diamond is a five-pointed star symbolizing the five continents from which the inhabitants of Suriname migrated: Africa, America, Australia, Asia, and Europe.

CBVS B6 (P120): **5 gulden (guilders)**　　　VG　VF　UNC

Blue and bluish-gray. Front: Woman carrying basket of fruit and vegetables on head; torch with *1963* banner. Back: Coat of arms of two native indians with bows and arrows flanking a shield with sailing ship, star, and palm tree. No security thread. Watermark: Parrot head. Printer: *JOH. ENSCHEDÉ EN ZONEN IMP.* 152 x 66 mm.

- ☐ a.　1 SEPTEMBER 1963. Signature 2.　　　—　0.75　2
  2.75-mm tall serial numbers. Prefix A-F, AA-AC.
- ☐ b.　3.25-mm tall serial numbers. Prefix AC-.　—　0.50　1.50
- ☐ as.　Diagonal red *SPECIMEN* ovpt; s/n Z 012345...　—　—　—

Replacement notes: Prefix ZZ.

CBVS B7 (P121): **10 gulden (guilders)**　　　VG　VF　UNC

Reddish-orange. Front: Woman carrying basket of fruit and vegetables on head; torch with *1963* banner. Back: Coat of arms of two native indians with bows and arrows flanking a shield with sailing ship, star, and palm tree. No security thread. Watermark: Parrot head. Printer: *JOH. ENSCHEDÉ EN ZONEN IMP.* 152 x 66 mm.

- ☐ a.　1 SEPTEMBER 1963. Signature 2.　　　—　0.50　1.50
  2.75-mm tall serial numbers.
- ☐ b.　3.25-mm tall serial numbers.　　　　—　0.50　1.50
- ☐ as.　Diagonal red *SPECIMEN* ovpt; s/n Z 012345...　—　—　—

Replacement notes: Prefix ZZ.

CBVS B8 (P122): **25 gulden (guilders)**　　　VG　VF　UNC

Green and red. Front: Woman's head; fruit and vegetables; torch with *1963* banner. Back: Coat of arms of two native indians with bows and arrows flanking a shield with sailing ship, star, and palm tree. No security thread. Watermark: Parrot head. Printer: *JOH. ENSCHEDÉ EN ZONEN IMP.* 152 x 66 mm.

- ☐ a.　1 SEPTEMBER 1963. Signature 2.　　　0.50　3　10
  2.75-mm tall serial numbers.
- ☐ b.　3.25-mm tall serial numbers.　　　　0.50　3　10
- ☐ as.　Diagonal red *SPECIMEN* ovpt; s/n Z 012345...　—　—　—

Replacement notes: Prefix ZZ.

1982 Issues

Suriname achieved full independence from the Netherlands on 25 November 1975. However, the democratic government was overthrown on 25 February 1980, and the new military leaders declared a socialist republic. At front right of these notes is a depiction of "Monument van de Revolutie" (Monument of the Revolution) in Paramaribo, which commemorates the coup d'état. Unlike the two preceding families of notes, this new family did not include a 1,000-guilder denomination.

CBVS B9 (P123): **100 gulden (guilders)**   VG   VF   UNC

Purple and green. Front: Woman's head; fruit and vegetables; torch with *1963* banner. Back: Coat of arms of two native indians with bows and arrows flanking a shield with sailing ship, star, and palm tree. No security thread. Watermark: Parrot head. Printer: *JOH. ENSCHEDÉ EN ZONEN IMP.* 152 x 66 mm.

   ☐ a.   1 SEPTEMBER 1963. Signature 2.   1   5   15
   ☐ as.   Diagonal red *SPECIMEN* ovpt; s/n Z 012345…   —   —   —

Replacement notes: Prefix ZZ.

CBVS B10 (P124): **1,000 gulden (guilders)**   VG   VF   UNC

Brown and blue. Front: Woman's head; fruit and vegetables; torch with *1963* banner. Back: Coat of arms of two native indians with bows and arrows flanking a shield with sailing ship, star, and palm tree. No security thread. Watermark: Parrot head. Printer: *JOH. ENSCHEDÉ EN ZONEN IMP.* 152 x 66 mm.

   ☐ a.   1 SEPTEMBER 1963. Signature 2.   5   15   40
   ☐ as.   Diagonal red *SPECIMEN* ovpt; s/n Z 012345…   —   —   —

Replacement notes: Prefix ZZ.

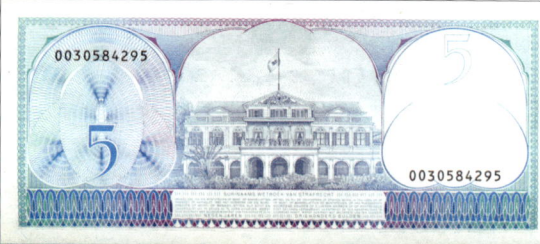

CBVS B11 (P125): **5 gulden (guilders)**   VG   VF   UNC

Blue, violet, and green. Front: Monument of five soldiers with rifles, woman with flag, and date *25 FEBRUARI 1980*. Back: Presidential palace in Paramaribo. No security thread. Watermark: Parrot head. Printer: *JOH. ENSCHEDÉ EN ZONEN IMP.* 152 x 66 mm.

   ☐ a.   1 APRIL 1982. Signature 3.   0.25   0.75   1.50

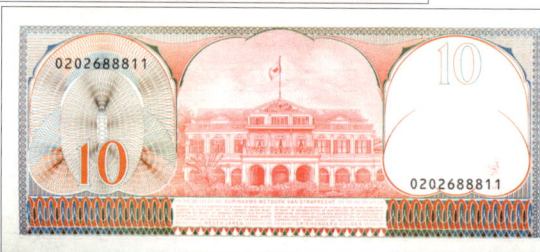

CBVS B12 (P126): **10 gulden (guilders)**   VG   VF   UNC

Red and green. Front: Monument of five soldiers with rifles, woman with flag, and date *25 FEBRUARI 1980*. Back: Presidential palace in Paramaribo. No security thread. Watermark: Parrot head. Printer: *JOH. ENSCHEDÉ EN ZONEN IMP.* 152 x 66 mm.

   ☐ a.   1 APRIL 1982. Signature 3.   0.25   0.50   1.25

CBVS B13 (P127): **25 gulden (guilders)**   VG   VF   UNC

Green, blue, and red. Front: Monument of five soldiers with rifles, woman with flag, and date *25 FEBRUARI 1980*. Back: Presidential palace in Paramaribo. No security thread. Watermark: Parrot head. Printer: *JOH. ENSCHEDÉ EN ZONEN IMP.* 152 x 66 mm.

☐ a. 1 APRIL 1982. Signature 3.   1   2.50   5
☐ b. 1 NOVEMBER 1985. Signature 4a.   —   0.50   1

CBVS B14 (P128): **100 gulden (guilders)**   VG   VF   UNC

Purple, green, and orange. Front: Monument of five soldiers with rifles, woman with flag, and date *25 FEBRUARI 1980*. Back: Presidential palace in Paramaribo. No security thread. Watermark: Parrot head. Printer: *JOH. ENSCHEDÉ EN ZONEN IMP.* 152 x 66 mm.

☐ a. 1 APRIL 1982. Signature 3.   5   10   20
☐ b. 1 NOVEMBER 1985. Signature 4a.   0.25   0.75   1.25

CBVS B15 (P129): **500 gulden (guilders)**   VG   VF   UNC

Brown, green, and red. Front: Monument of five soldiers with rifles, woman with flag, and date *25 FEBRUARI 1980*. Back: Presidential palace in Paramaribo. No security thread. Watermark: Parrot head. Printer: *JOH. ENSCHEDÉ EN ZONEN IMP.* 152 x 66 mm.

☐ a. 1 APRIL 1982. Signature 3.   1   2   7

1986-1988 Issues

The front of these notes features a portrait of Anton de Kom, a Surinamese resistance fighter and anti-colonialist author. The vignette at front right is a mirror image of the "Monument van de Revolutie" (Monument of the Revolution) in Paramaribo. This family contains all of the denominations of the preceding issues, as well as a new 250-guilder note.

CBVS B16 (P130): **5 gulden (guilders)**   VG   VF   UNC

Blue, green, and red. Front: Buildings; flags; Anton de Kom; faya lobi flowers; star; five soldiers with rifles, woman with flag. Back: Toucan on branch; hibiscus, heliconia, ginger, and faya lobi flowers; crowd listening to Anton de Kom outside his father's house, 1 February 1933. No security thread. Watermark: Toucan. Printer: *THOMAS DE LA RUE AND COMPANY LIMITED*. 150 x 72 mm.

☐ a. 1 JULI 1986. Signature 4b.   —   0.75   3
☐ b. 9 JANUARI 1988.   —   —   2

CBVS B17 (P131): **10 gulden (guilders)**   VG   VF   UNC

Red, orange, and yellow. Front: Buildings; flags; Anton de Kom; faya lobi flowers; star; five soldiers with rifles, woman with flag. Back: Toucan on branch; hibiscus, heliconia, ginger, and faya lobi flowers; crowd listening to Anton de Kom outside his father's house, 1 February 1933. No security thread. Watermark: Toucan. Printer: *THOMAS DE LA RUE AND COMPANY LIMITED*. 150 x 72 mm.

    ☐   a.   1 JULI 1986. Signature 4b.   —   1.25   10
    ☐   b.   9 JANUARI 1988.   —   —   2

CBVS B18 (P132): **25 gulden (guilders)**   VG   VF   UNC

Green, orange, and red. Front: Buildings; flags; Anton de Kom; faya lobi flowers; star; five soldiers with rifles, woman with flag. Back: Toucan on branch; hibiscus, heliconia, ginger, and faya lobi flowers; crowd listening to Anton de Kom outside his father's house, 1 February 1933. No security thread. Watermark: Toucan. Printer: *THOMAS DE LA RUE AND COMPANY LIMITED*. 150 x 72 mm.

    ☐   a.   1 JULI 1986. Signature 4b.   —   2   8
    ☐   b.   9 JANUARI 1988.   —   —   1.25

CBVS B19 (P133): **100 gulden (guilders)**   VG   VF   UNC

Purple, orange, and red. Front: Buildings; flags; Anton de Kom; faya lobi flowers; star; five soldiers with rifles, woman with flag. Back: Toucan on branch; hibiscus, heliconia, ginger, and faya lobi flowers; crowd listening to Anton de Kom outside his father's house, 1 February 1933. No security thread. Watermark: Toucan. Printer: *THOMAS DE LA RUE AND COMPANY LIMITED*. 150 x 72 mm.

    ☐   a.   1 JULI 1986. Signature 4b.   —   —   1
               Monochrome buildings. 1-letter prefix.
    ☐   b.   Two-tone buildings. 2-letter prefix.   —   —   20
    ☐   c.   9 JANUARI 1988.   —   —   1

On CBVS B19a (top), the buildings along the bottom front of the note are entirely purple, but on later issues (B19c, bottom), the ones beneath Anton de Kom's portrait are red.

CBVS B20 (P134): **250 gulden (guilders)**   VG   VF   UNC

Aqua, orange, and brown. Front: Buildings; flags; Anton de Kom; faya lobi flowers; star; five soldiers with rifles, woman with flag. Back: Toucan on branch; hibiscus, heliconia, ginger, and faya lobi flowers; crowd listening to Anton de Kom outside his father's house, 1 February 1933. No security thread. Watermark: Toucan. Printer: *THOMAS DE LA RUE AND COMPANY LIMITED*. 150 x 72 mm.

    ☐   a.   9 JANUARI 1988. Signature 4b.   —   2   4

CBVS B21 (P135): **500 gulden (guilders)** VG VF UNC

Brown, orange, green, and yellow. Front: Buildings; flags; Anton de Kom; faya lobi flowers; star; five soldiers with rifles, woman with flag. Back: Toucan on branch; hibiscus, heliconia, ginger, and faya lobi flowers; crowd listening to Anton de Kom outside his father's house, 1 February 1933. No security thread. Watermark: Toucan. Printer: *THOMAS DE LA RUE AND COMPANY LIMITED*. 150 x 72 mm.

		VG	VF	UNC
☐	a. 1 JULI 1986. Signature 4b.	20	40	80
☐	b. 9 JANUARI 1988.	—	3	6

1991-1998 Issues

Following the 1991 election of a democratic regime which failed to enforce previous price controls, Suriname experienced an intense bout of high inflation which peaked at 43 percent a month in November 1994, just short of the threshold for hyperinflation (50 percent per month). As a result, 1,000- and 2,000-guilder notes were added to this family.

CBVS B22 (P136): **5 gulden (guilders)** VG VF UNC

Blue, violet, green, and red. Front: Two logging trucks; Central Bank van Suriname headquarters building at the Waterkant in Paramaribo; hibiscus flower. Back: Toucan on branch; hibiscus flowers; two bulldozers felling trees, man wearing hardhat cutting lumber with chainsaw; coat of arms. Solid security thread. Watermark: Toucan. Printer: *THOMAS DE LA RUE AND COMPANY LIMITED*. 147 x 68 mm.

		VG	VF	UNC
☐	a. 9 JULI 1991. Signature 4c.	—	—	1
☐	b. 1 JUNI 1995. Signature 5.	—	—	1
☐	c. 1 DECEMBER 1996.	—	—	1
☐	d. 10 FEBRUARI 1998. Signature 6.	—	—	1

CBVS B23 (P137): **10 gulden (guilders)** VG VF UNC

Red, green, and orange. Front: Banana stalk; Central Bank van Suriname headquarters building at the Waterkant in Paramaribo; hibiscus flower. Back: Toucan on branch; hibiscus flowers; mechanized banana harvesting; coat of arms. Solid security thread. Watermark: Toucan. Printer: *THOMAS DE LA RUE AND COMPANY LIMITED*. 147 x 68 mm.

		VG	VF	UNC
☐	a. 9 JULI 1991. Signature 4c.	—	—	2
☐	b. 1 JUNI 1995. Signature 5.	—	—	1
☐	c. 1 DECEMBER 1996.	—	—	1
☐	d. 10 FEBRUARI 1998. Signature 6.	—	—	1

CBVS B24 (P138): **25 gulden (guilders)** VG VF UNC

Green, orange, red, and yellow. Front: Two track runners; Central Bank van Suriname headquarters building at the Waterkant in Paramaribo; hibiscus flower. Back: Toucan on branch; hibiscus flowers; 1988 Olympic gold-medalist Anthony Nesty swimming the butterfly stroke; coat of arms. Solid security thread. Watermark: Toucan. Printer: *THOMAS DE LA RUE AND COMPANY LIMITED*. 147 x 68 mm.

		VG	VF	UNC
☐	a. 9 JULI 1991. Signature 4c.	—	—	3
☐	b. 1 JUNI 1995. Signature 5.	—	—	25
☐	c. 1 DECEMBER 1996.	—	—	2
☐	d. 10 FEBRUARI 1998. Signature 6.	—	—	2

CBVS B25 (P139): **100 gulden (guilders)** VG VF UNC
Purple, yellow, red, and green. Front: Factory with smokestacks; Central Bank van Suriname headquarters building at the Waterkant in Paramaribo; hibiscus flower. Back: Toucan on branch; hibiscus flowers; hydraulic excavator loading dump truck in open-pit mine; coat of arms. Solid security thread. Watermark: Toucan. Printer: *THOMAS DE LA RUE AND COMPANY LIMITED*. 147 x 68 mm.

☐ a. 9 JULI 1991. Signature 4c. — — 5
☐ b. 10 FEBRUARI 1998. Signature 6. — — 1

CBVS B27 (P141): **1,000 gulden (guilders)** VG VF UNC
Red, black, blue, and green. Front: Combine harvester; Central Bank van Suriname headquarters building at the Waterkant in Paramaribo; hibiscus flower. Back: Toucan on branch; hibiscus flowers; combine harvester and truck in grain field; coat of arms. Solid security thread. Watermark: Toucan. Printer: *THOMAS DE LA RUE AND COMPANY LIMITED*. 147 x 68 mm.

☐ a. 1 JULI 1993. Signature 4c. — — 10
☐ b. 1 MAART 1995. Signature 5. — — 6.50

CBVS B26 (P140): **500 gulden (guilders)** VG VF UNC
Brown, blue, orange, red, and green. Front: Pumpjack; Central Bank van Suriname headquarters building at the Waterkant in Paramaribo; hibiscus flower. Back: Toucan on branch; hibiscus flowers; pumpjack and workers on drilling platform; coat of arms. Solid security thread. Watermark: Toucan. Printer: *THOMAS DE LA RUE AND COMPANY LIMITED*. 147 x 68 mm.

☐ a. 9 JULI 1991. Signature 4c. — — 15

CBVS B28 (P142): **2,000 gulden (guilders)** VG VF UNC
Violet, green, red, and yellow. Front: Two logging trucks; Central Bank van Suriname headquarters building at the Waterkant in Paramaribo; hibiscus flower. Back: Toucan on branch; hibiscus flowers; two bulldozers felling trees, man wearing hardhat cutting lumber with chainsaw; coat of arms. Solid security thread with demetalized *CBVS*. Watermark: Toucan. Printer: *THOMAS DE LA RUE AND COMPANY LIMITED*. 147 x 68 mm.

☐ a. 1 JUNI 1995. Signature 5. — — 12

1997-1999 Issues

While inflation had lessened considerably from its annual high of almost 600 percent in 1994, these large-denomination banknotes were issued to facilitate economic transactions in the later half of the decade.

CBVS B29 (P143): **5,000 gulden (guilders)**   VG   VF   UNC
Gold, purple, green, and red. Front: Gold foil toucan; Central Bank van Suriname headquarters building at the Waterkant in Paramaribo; flower. Back: Long-billed gnatwren bird on branch; coat of arms; mechanized banana harvesting; bank logo. Windowed security thread with demetalized *CBVS*. Watermark: Toucan and electrotype *CBVS*. Printer: THOMAS DE LA RUE LIMITED. 147 x 68 mm.

   a.   5 OCTOBER 1997. Signature 6.   —   —   60
   b.   1 FEBRUARI 1999.   —   —   30

CBVS B30 (P144 & P145): **10,000 gulden (guilders)**   VG   VF   UNC
Green, purple, red, and orange. Front: Gold foil parrot; Central Bank van Suriname headquarters building at the Waterkant in Paramaribo; flower. Back: Long-billed gnatwren bird on branch; coat of arms; alumina industrial complex; bank logo. Watermark: Toucan and electrotype *CBVS*. Printer: DE LA RUE. 147 x 68 mm.

   a.   5 OCTOBER 1997. Signature 6.   —   —   75
        Windowed security thread with demetalized
        CBVS. Green storage tanks on back.
   b.   Purple windowed security thread.   —   —   50
        Red storage tanks on back.

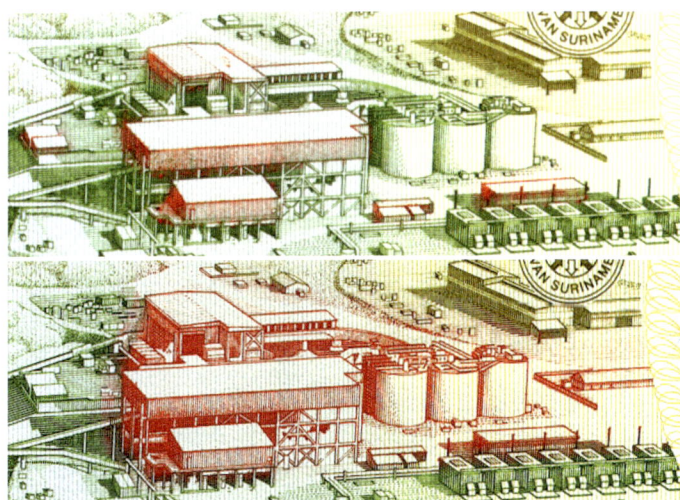

Earlier issues (B30a, top) of the 10,000-gulden note have green storage tanks on the back vignette, whereas they are red on later issues (B30b, bottom).

2000 Issues

CBVS B31 (P146): **5 gulden (guilders)**   VG   VF   UNC
Blue and multicolor. Front: Nymphalid butterflies; Campephilus rubricollis (red-necked woodpecker) bird; bat registration device; coat of arms; map; trees. Back: Bat; Central Bank van Suriname headquarters building at the Waterkant in Paramaribo; Passiflora quadrangularis (giant granadilla) flowers; bank logo. Windowed security thread with demetalized *CBVS 5*. Watermark: Bank headquarters and electrotype *CBVS*. Printer: DE LA RUE. 140 x 70 mm.

   a.   1 JANUARI 2000. Signature 6.   —   —   1.25

CBVS B32 (P147): **10 gulden (guilders)** VG VF UNC
Green, purple, and red. Front: Nymphalid butterflies; Anthracothorax viridigula (green-throated mango) bird; stag beetle registration device; coat of arms; map; trees. Back: Stag beetle; Central Bank van Suriname headquarters building at the Waterkant in Paramaribo; Guzmania lingulata (scarlet star) flowers; bank logo. Windowed security thread with demetalized *CBVS 10*. Watermark: Bank headquarters and electrotype *CBVS*. Printer: *DE LA RUE*. 140 x 70 mm.

☐ a.   1 JANUARI 2000. Signature 6.   —   —   1.50

CBVS B33 (P148): **25 gulden (guilders)** VG VF UNC
Purple, blue, red, green, and orange. Front: Nymphalid butterflies; Ramphastos tucanus (white-throated toucan) bird; praying mantis insect registration device; coat of arms; map; trees. Back: Praying mantis insect; Central Bank van Suriname headquarters building at the Waterkant in Paramaribo; Couroupita guianensis (ayahuma or cannonball tree) flowers; bank logo. Windowed security thread with demetalized *CBVS 25*. Watermark: Bank headquarters and electrotype *CBVS*. Printer: *DE LA RUE*. 140 x 70 mm.

☐ a.   1 JANUARI 2000. Signature 6.   —   —   1.75

CBVS B34 (P149): **100 gulden (guilders)** VG VF UNC
Red, violet, blue, and orange. Front: Nymphalid butterflies; Phaethornis superciliosus (long-tailed hermit) bird; chameleon registration device; coat of arms; map; trees. Back: Chameleon; Central Bank van Suriname headquarters building at the Waterkant in Paramaribo; Plumeria rubra (red frangipani) flowers; bank logo. Windowed security thread with demetalized *CBVS 100*. Watermark: Bank headquarters and electrotype *CBVS*. Printer: *DE LA RUE*. 140 x 70 mm.

☐ a.   1 JANUARI 2000. Signature 6.   —   —   6

CBVS B35 (P150): **500 gulden (guilders)** VG VF UNC
Orange, red, blue, and green. Front: Papilionid (swallowtail) butterflies; Rupicola rupicola (Guianan cock-of-the-rock) bird; lantern bug insect registration device; coat of arms; map; trees. Back: Lantern bug; Central Bank van Suriname headquarters building at the Waterkant in Paramaribo; Mandevilla splendens flowers; bank logo. Windowed security thread with demetalized *CBVS 500*. Watermark: Bank headquarters and electrotype *CBVS*. Printer: *DE LA RUE*. 140 x 70 mm.

☐ a.   1 JANUARI 2000. Signature 6.   —   —   25

CBVS B36 (P151): **1,000 gulden (guilders)**   VG   VF   UNC

Brown, olive green, orange, blue, and yellow. Front: Silver holographic patch; Onychorhynchus coronatus (royal flycatcher) bird; diving water beetle registration device; coat of arms; map; trees. Back: Diving water beetle; Central Bank van Suriname headquarters building at the Waterkant in Paramaribo; Orchidaceae violacea flowers; bank logo. Windowed security thread with demetalized *CBVS 1000*. Watermark: Bank headquarters and electrotype *CBVS*. Printer: *DE LA RUE*. 140 x 70 mm.

   ☐ a. 1 JANUARI 2000. Signature 6.   —   —   10

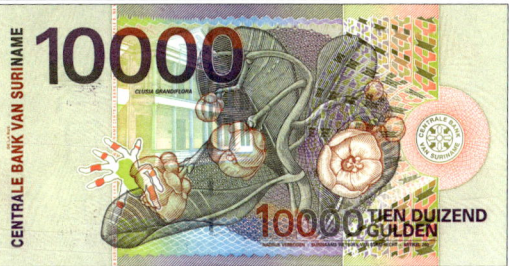

CBVS B38 (P153): **10,000 gulden (guilders)**   VG   VF   UNC

Olive green, red, purple, and blue. Front: Gold holographic patch; Spizaetus ornatus (ornate hawk-eagle) bird; tarantula spider registration device; coat of arms; map; trees. Back: Tarantula spider; Central Bank van Suriname headquarters building at the Waterkant in Paramaribo; Clusia grandiflora flowers; bank logo. Windowed security thread with demetalized *CBVS 10000*. Watermark: Bank headquarters and electrotype *CBVS*. Printer: *DE LA RUE*. 140 x 70 mm.

   ☐ a. 1 JANUARI 2000. Signature 6.   —   —   95

CBVS B37 (P152): **5,000 gulden (guilders)**   VG   VF   UNC

Yellow, blue, green, orange, and red. Front: Silver holographic patch; Aratinga solstitialis (sun conure parrot) bird; snake registration device; coat of arms; map; trees. Back: Snake; Central Bank van Suriname headquarters building at the Waterkant in Paramaribo; Oncidium papilio (psychopsis orchid) flowers; bank logo. Windowed security thread with demetalized *CBVS 5000*. Watermark: Bank headquarters and electrotype *CBVS*. Printer: *DE LA RUE*. 140 x 70 mm.

   ☐ a. 1 JANUARI 2000. Signature 6.   —   —   40

CBVS B39 (P154): **25,000 gulden (guilders)**   VG   VF   UNC

Brown, orange, red, and green. Front: Gold holographic patch; Pulsatrix perspicillata (spectacled owl) bird; frog registration device; coat of arms; map; trees. Back: Frog; Central Bank van Suriname headquarters building at the Waterkant in Paramaribo; Hymenocallis caribaea (Caribbean spiderlily) flowers; bank logo. Windowed security thread with demetalized *CBVS 25000*. Watermark: Bank headquarters and electrotype *CBVS*. Printer: *DE LA RUE*. 140 x 70 mm.

   ☐ a. 1 JANUARI 2000. Signature 6.   —   —   425

Suriname 2004-2009 Issues

2004-2009 Issues

The Surinamese dollar replaced the Surinamese guilder on 1 January 2004, with one dollar equal to 1,000 guilders, prompting the issuance of the following notes denominated in the new currency. On the notes, the currency is expressed in the singular, as is the Dutch custom.

CBVS B40 (P157): **5 dollar** (US$1.50)   VG   VF   UNC
Orange, red, brown, green, and blue. Front: Coat of arms; Central Bank van Suriname headquarters building at the Waterkant in Paramaribo; Nymphaea missouri (missouri waterlily) flower; bank logo registration device. Back: Bank logo; Cocos nucifera (coconut palm) tree; forest and rapids near Gran-Rio in Sula. Solid security thread. Watermark: Bank headquarters. Printer: (CBN). 140 x 70 mm.

   ☐ a.   1 JANUARI 2004. Signature 7.   FV   FV   5
   ☐ c.   1 APRIL 2006.   —   —   —
   ☐ b.   1 MEI 2009. Translucent band moved to back.   FV   FV   5

CBVS B41 (P158): **10 dollar** (US$3)   VG   VF   UNC
Green, purple, and brown. Front: Coat of arms; Central Bank van Suriname headquarters building at the Waterkant in Paramaribo; Zingiber spectabile (golden sceptor) flower; bank logo registration device. Back: Bank logo; Tabebuia serratifolia (yellow lapacho or yellow poui) tree; forest and Suriname river. Solid security thread. Watermark: Bank headquarters. Printer: (CBN). 140 x 70 mm.

   ☐ a.   1 JANUARI 2004. Signature 7.   FV   FV   10
   ☐ b.   1 NOVEMBER 2004.   FV   FV   10
   ☐ d.   1 APRIL 2006.   —   —   —
   ☐ c.   1 MEI 2009. Translucent band moved to back.   FV   FV   10

CBVS B42 (P159): **20 dollar** (US$6.05)   VG   VF   UNC
Blue and purple. Front: Coat of arms; Central Bank van Suriname headquarters building at the Waterkant in Paramaribo; Passiflora edulis (passion fruit) flowers; bank logo registration device. Back: Bank logo; Rhizophora mangle (red mangrove) tree; Voltzberg dome mountain with waterfalls. Solid security thread. Watermark: Bank headquarters. Printer: (CBN). 140 x 70 mm.

   ☐ a.   1 JANUARI 2004. Signature 7.   FV   FV   20
   ☐ b.   1 NOVEMBER 2004.   FV   FV   20
   ☐ d.   1 APRIL 2006.   —   —   —
   ☐ c.   1 MEI 2009. Translucent band moved to back.   FV   FV   40

CBVS B43 (P160): **50 dollar** (US$15)   VG   VF   UNC
Brown and green. Front: Coat of arms; Central Bank van Suriname headquarters building at the Waterkant in Paramaribo; bougainvillea flower; bank logo registration device. Back: Bank logo; Ceiba pentandra (Java cotton or kapok) tree; Mount Kasikasima. Solid security thread. Watermark: Bank headquarters. Printer: (CBN). 140 x 70 mm.

   ☐ a.   1 JANUARI 2004. Signature 7.   FV   FV   40
   ☐ b.   1 NOVEMBER 2004.   FV   FV   40
   ☐ c.   1 APRIL 2006.   —   —   —

CBVS B44 (P161): **100 dollar** (US$30)   VG VF UNC

Brown, red, and green. Front: Coat of arms; Central Bank van Suriname headquarters building at the Waterkant in Paramaribo; Heliconia humilis (lobster claw) flower; bank logo registration device. Back: Bank logo; Pterocarpus officinalis (dragonsblood tree) tree; Aruba-tabbetje, Marowijne rivier (tributary flowing from forest into river). Solid security thread. Watermark: Bank headquarters. Printer: (CBN). 140 x 70 mm.

- [ ] a. 1 JANUARI 2004. Signature 7. FV FV 105
- [ ] b. 1 APRIL 2006. — — —

2010-2012 Issues

These notes are like the preceding issues, but with new dates, holographic stripe at right front, electrotype *CBvS* added to the watermark, signature moved to below the serial number, serial number repositioned, bank logo as registration device, color-shifting windowed security thread, protective varnish increases durability, and reshaped denomination numerals on back.

CBVS B45 (PNL): **5 dollar** (US$1.50)   VG VF UNC

Orange, red, brown, green, and blue. Front: Coat of arms; Central Bank van Suriname headquarters building at the Waterkant in Paramaribo; Nymphaea missouri (missouri waterlily) flower; bank logo registration device. Back: Bank logo; Cocos nucifera (coconut palm) tree; forest and rapids near Gran-Rio in Sula. Holographic stripe. Windowed security thread with demetalized *SRD*. Watermark: Bank headquarters, electrotype *CBvS*, and Cornerstones. 140 x 70 mm.

- [ ] a. 1 SEPTEMBER 2010 (horizontal in red). Sig. 7. FV FV 5
      Printer: Unknown. Intro: 20.12.2010.
- [ ] b. 1 APRIL 2012 (vertical in blue). Signature 8. FV FV 5
      Printer: *Giesecke & Devrient*.

CBVS B46 (PNL): **10 dollar** (US$3)   VG VF UNC

Green, purple, and brown. Front: Coat of arms; Central Bank van Suriname headquarters building at the Waterkant in Paramaribo; Zingiber spectabile (golden sceptor) flower; bank logo registration device. Back: Bank logo; Tabebuia serratifolia (yellow lapacho or yellow poui) tree; forest and Suriname river. Holographic stripe. Windowed security thread with demetalized *SRD*. Watermark: Bank headquarters, electrotype *CBvS*, and Cornerstones. Printer: Unknown. 140 x 70 mm.

- [ ] a. 1 SEPTEMBER 2010. Sig. 7. Intro: 20.12.2010. FV FV 10

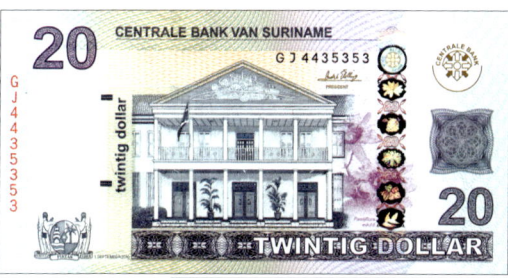

CBVS B47 (PNL): **20 dollar** (US$6.05)   VG VF UNC

Blue and purple. Front: Coat of arms; Central Bank van Suriname headquarters building at the Waterkant in Paramaribo; Passiflora edulis (passion fruit) flowers; bank logo registration device. Back: Bank logo; Rhizophora mangle (red mangrove) tree; Voltzberg dome mountain with waterfalls. Holographic stripe. Windowed security thread with demetalized *SRD*. Watermark: Bank headquarters, electrotype *CBvS*, and Cornerstones. Printer: Unknown. 140 x 70 mm.

- [ ] a. 1 SEPTEMBER 2010. Sig. 7. Intro: 22.11.2010. FV FV 20

SURINAME 2010-2012 ISSUES — THE BANKNOTE BOOK

CBVS B48 (PNL): **50 dollar** (US$15)　　　　　VG　VF　UNC
Brown and green. Front: Coat of arms; Central Bank van Suriname headquarters building at the Waterkant in Paramaribo; bougainvillea flower; bank logo registration device. Back: Bank logo; Ceiba pentandra (Java cotton or kapok) tree; Mount Kasikasima. Holographic stripe. Windowed security thread with demetalized *SRD*. Watermark: Bank headquarters, electrotype *CBvS*, and Cornerstones. Printer: Unknown. 140 x 70 mm.

☐ a.　1 SEPTEMBER 2010. Sig. 7. Intro: 22.11.2010.　　FV　FV　50

CBVS B49 (PNL): **100 dollar** (US$30)　　　　　VG　VF　UNC
Brown, red, and green. Front: Coat of arms; Central Bank van Suriname headquarters building at the Waterkant in Paramaribo; Heliconia humilis (lobster claw) flower; bank logo registration device. Back: Bank logo; Pterocarpus officinalis (dragonsblood tree) tree; Aruba-tabbetje, Marowijne rivier (tributary flowing from forest into river). Holographic stripe. Windowed security thread with demetalized *SRD*. Watermark: Bank headquarters, electrotype *CBvS*, and Cornerstones. 140 x 70 mm.

☐ a.　1 SEPTEMBER 2010 (horizontal in red). Sig. 7.　FV　FV　100
　　　Printer: Unknown. Intro: 20.12.2010.
☐ b.　1 APRIL 2012 (vertical in blue). Signature 8.　　FV　FV　100
　　　Printer: *Giesecke & Devrient*.

Acknowledgements

This chapter was compiled with the generous assistance of Thomas Augustsson, Richard Castedo (web.me.com/castedos), David F. Cieniewicz (www.banknotestore.com), Theo van Elmpt, Bill Fife, Heritage Auctions (HA.com), David Jones, Wonsik Kang, George H. LaBarre Galleries (www.glabarre.com), Henk van Lier, Claudio Marana, Frederick Martin, Wally Myers, Rafal Nogowczyk, Nazir Rahemtulla, Menelaos Stamatelos, Bill Stubkjaer, Frank van Tiel, and others.

Museum

The Numismatic Museum of the Centrale Bank van Suriname opened on 8 April 2002 and is located at the Mr. F.H.R. Lim A Postraat # 7. The museum administers, collects, studies, and presents a collection to give an overall picture of the exchange in goods, the circulation of coins, and the monetary system in Suriname from its beginning until present day. For more information, visit www.cbvs.sr/english/museum/numis-intro.htm.

Sources

Braumann, Benedikt and Sukhdev Shah. *Suriname: A Case Study of High Inflation*. International Monetary Fund. November 1999.

Cuhaj, George S. *Standard Catalog of World Paper Money, General Issues, 1368-1960*. 14th edition. 2012. ISBN 978-1-4402-3090-5. Krause Publications (www.krausebooks.com), 700 East State St., Iola, WI, 54990-0001.

Cuhaj, George S. *Standard Catalog of World Paper Money, Modern Issues, 1961-Present*. 17th edition. 2011. ISBN 978-1-4402-1584-1. Krause Publications (www.krausebooks.com), 700 East State St., Iola, WI, 54990-0001.

van Elmpt, Theo. *Surinam Paper Currency - Volume 1 - 1760 to 1957*. 1st edition. 1997. ISBN 90-801808-3-1. Elran Press Uithoorn, The Netherlands.

van Elmpt, Theo. *Surinam Paper Currency - Volume 2 - 1957 to 2000*. 1st edition. 2002. ISBN 90-801808-5-8. Elran Press Uithoorn, The Netherlands.

van Elmpt, Theo. *Surinam Paper Currency - Volume 3 - Treasury Notes 1918 to 1987*. 1st edition. 2000. ISBN 90-801808-4-x. Elran Press Uithoorn, The Netherlands.

Underwood, Richard. "Insect Images on Banknotes Part III—Security Devices." *IBNS Journal*. Volume 48 Number 1. p44.

Share Your Input, Info, and Images

This catalog is believed to be complete and correct as of the time of publication. Prices and face values were last updated 16 Dec. 2011. Please report errors or omissions so that corrections may be made. If you can more precisely identify the name or location of anything depicted on a note, please share that information. Furthermore, if you own an unlisted type or variety, please submit scans of the front and back of the note so that it can be documented. Scans should be 300 dots per inch, 100% actual size, 24-bit color, saved as *uncompressed* JPEG files, and sent to owen@banknotenews.com. Be sure to fully describe all attributes of the note which are not apparent upon visual inspection of the images alone, such as physical dimension, watermark, and security thread.

Swaziland

For earlier issues, see South Africa.

Contents

Monetary Authority of Swaziland (MAS) 2039
Central Bank of Swaziland (CBS) 2041

Monetary System
1 Swazi lilangeni (SZL) = 100 cents

Monetary Authority of Swaziland

On 22 March 1974, King Sobhuza II established the Monetary Authority of Swaziland (MAS) through The Monetary Authority of Swaziland Order of 1974. On 1 April 1974, the bank officially began its operations.

MAS Signature Varieties

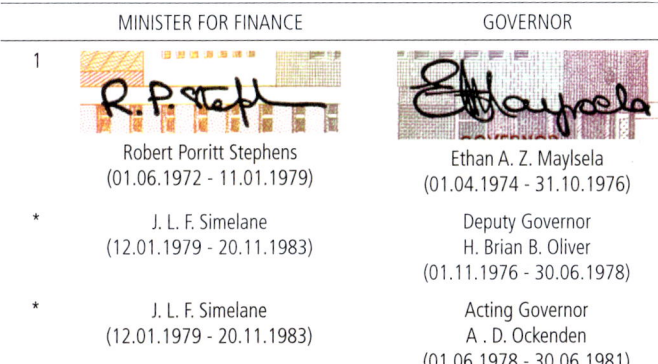

	MINISTER FOR FINANCE	GOVERNOR
1	Robert Porritt Stephens (01.06.1972 - 11.01.1979)	Ethan A. Z. Maylsela (01.04.1974 - 31.10.1976)
*	J. L. F. Simelane (12.01.1979 - 20.11.1983)	Deputy Governor H. Brian B. Oliver (01.11.1976 - 30.06.1978)
*	J. L. F. Simelane (12.01.1979 - 20.11.1983)	Acting Governor A. D. Ockenden (01.06.1978 - 30.06.1981)

* These officials are not known to have signed any notes.

1974-1978 Issues

On 6 September 1974, Independence Day, the lilangeni became legal tender throughout the nation. The Swazi lilangeni was pegged at par with the South African rand.

MAS B1 (P1): **1 lilangeni** (US$0.15)   VG   VF   UNC
Red. Front: King Sobhuza II; Parliament House building in Lobamba; lion with mask; elephant; shield (isihlangu), spears (sikhali), and staff (umgobo); staff (umgobo) with widow bird plumes. Back: Ten topless princesses taking part in the Ncwala (kingship ceremony). Solid security thread. Watermark: Shield and spears. Printer: *THOMAS DE LA RUE & COMPANY, LIMITED*. 150 x 70 mm.
   ☐ a. No date. Sig. 1. Prefix A - M. Intro: 06.09.1974.   0.25   1   4.25
   ☐ as1. Diagonal red *SPECIMEN* overprint.   —   —   65
   ☐ as2. Diagonal red *SPECIMEN* and DLR oval ovpts; horiz. black *SPECIMEN Nº #* ovpt at lower left; punched.   —   —   —

MAS B2 (P2): **2 emalangeni** (US$0.30)   VG   VF   UNC
Brown. Front: King Sobhuza II; Parliament House building in Lobamba; lion with mask; elephant; shield (isihlangu), spears (sikhali), and staff (umgobo); spear. Back: Sugar mill factory buildings. Solid security thread. Watermark: Shield and spears. Printer: *THOMAS DE LA RUE & COMPANY, LIMITED*. 150 x 70 mm.
   ☐ a. No date. Sig. 1. Prefix A - E. Intro: 06.09.1974.   0.75   3   12
   ☐ as1. Diagonal red *SPECIMEN* overprint.   —   —   65
   ☐ as2. Diagonal red *SPECIMEN* and DLR oval ovpts; horiz. black *SPECIMEN Nº #* ovpt at lower left; punched.   —   —   —

MAS B3 (P3): 5 emalangeni (US$0.75)   VG   VF   UNC
Green. Front: King Sobhuza II; Parliament House building in Lobamba; lion with mask; elephant; shield (isihlangu), spears (sikhali), and staff (umgobo); battle axe (sizeze). Back: Mantenga Falls and landscape. Solid security thread. Watermark: Shield and spears. Printer: *THOMAS DE LA RUE & COMPANY, LIMITED*. 150 x 70 mm.

☐	a. No date. Sig. 1. Prefix A – D. Intro: 06.09.1974.	2.50	10	40
☐	as1. Diagonal red *SPECIMEN* overprint.	—	—	50
☐	as2. Diagonal red *SPECIMEN* and DLR oval ovpts; horiz. black *SPECIMEN Nº* # ovpt at lower left; punched.	—	—	—

MAS B4 (P4): 10 emalangeni (US$1.50)   VG   VF   UNC
Blue. Front: King Sobhuza II; Parliament House building in Lobamba; lion with mask; elephant; shield (isihlangu), spears (sikhali), and staff (umgobo); grooved knobkerrie club (lingedla). Back: Asbestos mine buildings. Solid security thread. Watermark: Shield and spears. Printer: *THOMAS DE LA RUE & COMPANY, LIMITED*. 150 x 70 mm.

☐	a. No date. Sig. 1. Prefix A. Intro: 06.09.1974.	5	20	80
☐	as1. Diagonal red *SPECIMEN* overprint.	—	—	65
☐	as2. Diagonal red *SPECIMEN* and DLR oval ovpts; horiz. black *SPECIMEN Nº* # ovpt at lower left; punched.	—	—	—

MAS B5 (P5): 20 emalangeni (US$3)   VG   VF   UNC
Purple. Front: King Sobhuza II; Parliament House building in Lobamba; lion with mask; elephant; shield (isihlangu), spears (sikhali), and staff (umgobo); straight knobkerrie club (sishinga). Back: Pineapples; cattle; cotton; lumber on flatbed truck; citrus; corn. Solid security thread. Watermark: Shield and spears. Printer: *THOMAS DE LA RUE & COMPANY, LIMITED*. 150 x 70 mm.

☐	a. No date. Sig. 1. Prefix A. Intro: 1978.	15	50	200
☐	as1. Diagonal red *SPECIMEN* overprint.	—	—	65
☐	as2. Diagonal red *SPECIMEN* and DLR oval ovpts; horiz. black *SPECIMEN Nº* # ovpt at lower left; punched.	—	—	—

1978 Numismatic Products

Thomas De La Rue created "official presentation sets of specimen banknotes from around the world" for The Franklin Mint, a private company that mailed the sets every six weeks to subscribers from 1978 to 1979. Each set of notes with matching serial numbers originally cost $14 and came in an envelope with a numbered and dated certificate of authenticity and an index card describing the notes in detail. Based upon serial numbers observed, at least 10,440 sets were produced, and a complete collection comprises 15 sets with a total of 73 notes from 16 issuing authorities. Rarely available in the original small brown storage box, the notes are usually sold by country set, but are sometimes sold individually. Do not mistake these numismatic products for the specimen varieties listed separately, which the security printer created for its note-issuing clients.

MAS BNP1 (PCS1): 1 - 20 emalangeni   UNC

☐	a. MAS B1-B5 (5 notes) with diagonal *SPECIMEN* overprint and Maltese cross prefix. Intro: 15.09.1978.	80

Central Bank of Swaziland

The Central Bank of Swaziland (CBS) replaced the Monetary Authority of Swaziland on 18 July 1979.

For more information, visit www.centralbank.org.sz.

CBS Signature Varieties

	MINISTER FOR FINANCE	GOVERNOR
*	J. L. F. Simelane (12.01.1979 - 20.11.1983)	Deputy Governor H. Brian B. Oliver (01.11.1976 - 30.06.1978) Acting Governor: A . D. Ockenden (01.06.1978 - 30.06.1981)
1	 J. L. F. Simelane (12.01.1979 - 20.11.1983)	 H. Brian B. Oliver (01.07.1981 - 30.06.1992)
2	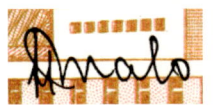 Simon Sishayi Nxumalo (21.11.1983 - 08.06.1984)	 H. Brian B. Oliver (01.07.1981 - 30.06.1992)
3	 Barnabas Sibusiso Dlamini (27.08.1984 - 05.11.1993)	 H. Brian B. Oliver (01.07.1981 - 30.06.1992)
4	 Barnabas Sibusiso Dlamini (27.08.1984 - 05.11.1993)	 James Nxumalo (01.07.1992 - 30.06.1997)
5	 Isaac Stanley Shabangu (10.11.1993 - 03.03.1995)	 James Nxumalo (01.07.1992 - 30.06.1997)
6a	 Derek von Wissel (03.03.1995 - 12.11.1996)	 James Nxumalo (01.07.1992 - 30.06.1997)
6b	 Derek von Wissel (03.03.1995 - 12.11.1996)	 James Nxumalo (01.07.1992 - 30.06.1997)
7	 Themba Masuku (12.11.1996 - 19.11.1998)	 James Nxumalo (01.07.1992 - 30.06.1997)
8a	 Themba Masuku (12.11.1996 - 19.11.1998)	Martin G. Dlamini (01.07.1997 - present)

CBS Signature Varieties

	MINISTER FOR FINANCE	GOVERNOR
8b	Themba Masuku (12.11.1996 - 19.11.1998)	Martin G. Dlamini (01.07.1997 - present)
*	J. Charmichael (20.11.1998 - 14.02.2001)	Martin G. Dlamini (01.07.1997 - present)
9a	Majozi V. Sithole (15.02.2001 - present)	Martin G. Dlamini (01.07.1997 - present)
9b	Majozi V. Sithole (15.02.2001 - present)	Martin G. Dlamini (01.07.1997 - present)

* These officials are not known to have signed any notes.

1981 Commemorative Issues

These two notes were issued to commemorate the 60th anniversary of the coronation of King Sobhuza II.

CBS B1 (P6): **10 emalangeni** (US$1.50)   VG VF UNC
Blue. Front: King Sobhuza II; Parliament House building in Lobamba; lion with mask; elephant; shield (isihlangu), spears (sikhali), and staff (umgobo); *DIAMOND JUBILEE H. M. KING SOBHUZA II 1921-1981* overprint; grooved knobkerrie club (lingedla). Back: Asbestos mine buildings. Solid security thread. Watermark: Shield and spears. Printer: *THOMAS DE LA RUE & COMPANY, LIMITED.* 150 x 70 mm.

    ☐ a. 1981. Signature 1. Prefix L - P. Intro: 1981.   25 75 300
    ☐ as. Diagonal red *SPECIMEN* overprint.   — — 175

Replacement notes: Prefix Z.

CBS B2 (P7): 20 emalangeni (US$3) VG VF UNC

Purple. Front: King Sobhuza II; Parliament House building in Lobamba; lion with mask; elephant; shield (isihlangu), spears (sikhali), and staff (umgobo); *DIAMOND JUBILEE H. M. KING SOBHUZA II 1921-1981* overprint; straight knobkerrie club (sishinga). Back: Pineapples; cattle; cotton; lumber on flatbed truck; citrus; corn. Solid security thread. Watermark: Shield and spears. Printer: *THOMAS DE LA RUE & COMPANY, LIMITED*. 150 x 70 mm.

☐ a.	1981. Signature 1. Prefix D - E. Intro: 1981.	30	90	350
☐ as.	Diagonal red *SPECIMEN* overprint.	—	—	200

Replacement notes: Prefix Z.

1982-1985 Issues

These notes are like the preceding issues, but with the new issuing authority name and new signature combinations. The 1-lilangeni denomination was dropped from this family.

CBS B3 (P8): 2 emalangeni (US$0.30) VG VF UNC

Brown. Front: King Sobhuza II; Parliament House building in Lobamba; lion with mask; elephant; shield (isihlangu), spears (sikhali), and staff (umgobo); spear. Back: Sugar mill factory buildings. Solid security thread. Watermark: Shield and spears. Printer: *THOMAS DE LA RUE & COMPANY, LIMITED*. 150 x 70 mm.

☐ a.	No date. Signature 1. Prefix F. Intro: 1983.	2	8	25
☐ b.	Signature 3. Prefix G - L. Intro: 1984.	0.25	1	4
☐ as.	Diagonal red *SPECIMEN* overprint.	—	—	65
☐ bs.	Diagonal red *SPECIMEN* overprint.	—	—	65

Replacement notes: Prefix Z.

CBS B4 (P9): 5 emalangeni (US$0.75) VG VF UNC

Green. Front: King Sobhuza II; Parliament House building in Lobamba; lion with mask; elephant; shield (isihlangu), spears (sikhali), and staff (umgobo); battle axe (sizeze). Back: Mantenga Falls and landscape. Solid security thread. Watermark: Shield and spears. Printer: *THOMAS DE LA RUE & COMPANY, LIMITED*. 150 x 70 mm.

☐ a.	No date. Signature 1. Prefix D - F. Intro: 1982.	5	20	80
☐ b.	Signature 3. Prefix H - J. Intro: 1984.	1.25	3.50	14
☐ as.	Diagonal red *SPECIMEN* overprint.	—	—	65
☐ bs.	Diagonal red *SPECIMEN* overprint.	—	—	65

Replacement notes: Prefix Z.

CBS B5 (P10): 10 emalangeni (US$1.50) VG VF UNC

Blue. Front: King Sobhuza II; Parliament House building in Lobamba; lion with mask; elephant; shield (isihlangu), spears (sikhali), and staff (umgobo); grooved knobkerrie club (lingedla). Back: Asbestos mine buildings. Solid security thread. Watermark: Shield and spears. Printer: *THOMAS DE LA RUE & COMPANY, LIMITED*. 150 x 70 mm.

☐ a.	No date. Signature 1. Prefix R - S. Intro: 1982.	10	40	150
☐ b.	Signature 2. Prefix U - V. Intro: 1984.	8	35	125
☐ c.	Signature 3. Prefix W - AB. Intro: 1985.	0.50	2.50	10
☐ as.	Diagonal red *SPECIMEN* overprint.	—	—	65
☐ bs.	Diagonal red *SPECIMEN* overprint.	—	—	65
☐ cs.	Specimen.	—	—	65

Replacement notes: Prefix Z.

CBS B6 (P11): **20 emalangeni** (US$3)   VG   VF   UNC

Purple. Front: King Sobhuza II; Parliament House building in Lobamba; lion with mask; elephant; shield (isihlangu), spears (sikhali), and staff (umgobo); straight knobkerrie club (sishinga). Back: Pineapples; cattle; cotton; lumber on flatbed truck; citrus; corn. Solid security thread. Watermark: Shield and spears. Printer: *THOMAS DE LA RUE & COMPANY, LIMITED*. 150 x 70 mm.

   ☐   a.   No date. Signature 2. Prefix E - F. Intro: 1984.   15   50   200
   ☐   b.   Signature 3. Prefix G - H. Intro: 1985.   FV   12   45
   ☐   as.   Diagonal red *SPECIMEN* overprint.   —   —   65
   ☐   bs.   Diagonal red *SPECIMEN* overprint.   —   —   65

Replacement notes: Prefix Z.

1986 Issues

The design of this 20-lilangeni notes is like the preceding issue of the same denomination, but with a portrait of King Mswati III instead of King Sobhuza II.

CBS B7 (P12): **20 emalangeni** (US$3)   VG   VF   UNC

Purple. Front: King Mswati III; Parliament House building in Lobamba; lion with mask; elephant; shield (isihlangu), spears (sikhali), and staff (umgobo); straight knobkerrie club (sishinga). Back: Pineapples; cattle; cotton; lumber on flatbed truck; citrus; corn. Solid security thread. Watermark: Shield and spears. Printer: *THOMAS DE LA RUE & COMPANY, LIMITED*. 150 x 70 mm.

   ☐   a.   No date. Signature 3. Prefix A - B. Intro: 1986.   1.25   5   20
   ☐   as.   Diagonal red *SPECIMEN* overprint.   —   —   30

1986-1987 Issues

These notes retain the color scheme of the preceding issues, but the designs have been changed and now include a portrait of King Mswati III instead of King Sobhuza II.

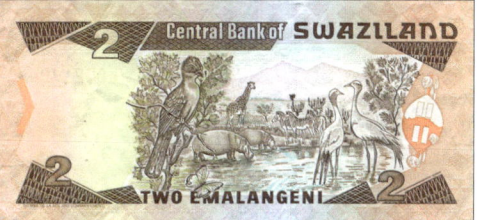

CBS B8 (P13): **2 emalangeni** (US$0.30)   VG   VF   UNC

Brown. Front: Shield and spears as registration device; King Mswati III; Parliament House building in Lobamba; coat of arms with lion and elephant flanking shield topped with crown of feathers (lidlabe); spear (umkhonto). Back: Watering hole scene with gray lourie, nymphalid butterfly, hippos, giraffe, zebras, and blue cranes. Solid security thread. Watermark: Shield and spears. Printer: *THOMAS DE LA RUE AND COMPANY, LIMITED*. 132 x 60 mm.

   ☐   a.   No date. Signature 3. Prefix A - L. Intro: 1987.   FV   1.50   7
   ☐   as.   Diagonal red *SPECIMEN* overprint.   —   —   80

Replacement notes: Prefix Z.

CBS B9 (P14): **5 emalangeni** (US$0.75)   VG   VF   UNC

Green. Front: Shield and spears as registration device; King Mswati III; Parliament House building in Lobamba; coat of arms with lion and elephant flanking shield topped with crown of feathers (lidlabe); grooved knobkerrie club (lingedla). Back: Warriors. Solid security thread. Watermark: Shield and spears. Printer: *THOMAS DE LA RUE AND COMPANY, LIMITED*. 140 x 63 mm.

   ☐   a.   No date. Signature 3. Prefix A - C. Intro: 1987.   1   3.75   15
   ☐   as.   Diagonal red *SPECIMEN* overprint.   —   —   110

Replacement notes: Prefix Z.

CBS B10 (P15): **10 emalangeni** (US$1.50)   VG   VF   UNC

Blue. Front: Shield and spears as registration device; King Mswati III; Parliament House building in Lobamba; coat of arms with lion and elephant flanking shield topped with crown of feathers (lidlabe); staff (umgobo) with widow bird plumes. Back: Bird; hydroelectric plant at Luphohlo. Solid security thread. Watermark: Shield and spears. Printer: *THOMAS DE LA RUE AND COMPANY, LIMITED*. 145 x 66 mm.

     ☐ a.   No date. Signature 3. Prefix A - E. Intro: 1986.   FV   3.50   20
     ☐ as.   Diagonal red *SPECIMEN* overprint.   —   —   110

Replacement notes: Prefix Z.

CBS B11 (P16): **20 emalangeni** (US$3)   VG   VF   UNC

Purple. Front: Shield and spears as registration device; King Mswati III; Parliament House building in Lobamba; coat of arms with lion and elephant flanking shield topped with crown of feathers (lidlabe); battle axe (sizeze). Back: Rice; corn; cotton; cattle; lumber on flatbed truck; pineapples; citrus. Solid security thread. Watermark: Shield and spears. Printer: *THOMAS DE LA RUE AND COMPANY, LIMITED*.150 x 70 mm.

     ☐ a.   No date. Signature 3. Prefix A. Intro: 1986.   7.50   30   120
     ☐ as.   Diagonal red *SPECIMEN* overprint.   —   —   110

Replacement notes: Prefix Z.

1989 Commemorative Issues

This 20-lilangeni note was issued to commemorate the 21st birthday of King Mswati III (born 19.04.1968). It is identical to CBS B11, but with a silver overprint.

CBS B12 (P17): **20 emalangeni** (US$3)   VG   VF   UNC

Purple. Front: Shield and spears as registration device; King Mswati III; Parliament House building in Lobamba; coat of arms with lion and elephant flanking shield topped with crown of feathers (lidlabe); *HIS MAJESTY KING MSWATI III 19.4.68-19.4.89* silver overprint; battle axe (sizeze). Back: Rice; corn; cotton; cattle; lumber on flatbed truck; pineapples; citrus. Solid security thread. Watermark: Shield and spears. Printer: *THOMAS DE LA RUE AND COMPANY, LIMITED*. 150 x 70 mm.

     ☐ a.   19.4.89. Signature 3. Prefix A - C.   2.50   7.50   30
     ☐ as.   Diagonal red *SPECIMEN* overprint.   —   —   160

1990-1995 Issues

The design of these notes is like the preceding issues, but with an updated portrait of King Mswati III. The 50-lilangeni denomination is new in this family.

CBS B13 (P18): **2 emalangeni** (US$0.30)   VG   VF   UNC

Brown. Front: Shield and spears as registration device; King Mswati III; Parliament House building in Lobamba; coat of arms with lion and elephant flanking shield topped with crown of feathers (lidlabe); spear (umkhonoto). Back: Watering hole scene with gray lourie, nymphalid butterfly, hippos, giraffe, zebras, and blue cranes. Solid security thread. Watermark: Shield and spears. Printer: THOMAS DE LA RUE AND COMPANY, LIMITED. 132 x 60 mm.

			VG	VF	UNC
☐	a.	No date. Signature 3. Prefix M - Q. Intro: 1992.	FV	3	12
☐	b.	Signature 5. Prefix S. Intro: 1994.	1.50	6	25
☐	as.	Diagonal red SPECIMEN overprint.	—	—	100
☐	bs.	Diagonal red SPECIMEN overprint.	—	—	100

Replacement notes: Prefix Z.

CBS B14 (P19): **5 emalangeni** (US$0.75)   VG   VF   UNC

Green. Front: Shield and spears as registration device; King Mswati III; Parliament House building in Lobamba; coat of arms with lion and elephant flanking shield topped with crown of feathers (lidlabe); knobkerrie (club). Back: Warriors. Solid security thread. Watermark: Shield and spears. Printer: THOMAS DE LA RUE AND COMPANY, LIMITED. 140 x 63 mm.

			VG	VF	UNC
☐	a.	No date. Signature 3. Prefix D - J. Intro: 1990.	FV	3	9
☐	b.	Signature 5. Prefix J - K. Intro: 1994.	3	12	50
☐	as.	Diagonal red SPECIMEN overprint.	—	—	100
☐	bs.	Diagonal red SPECIMEN overprint.	—	—	90

Replacement notes: Prefix Z.

CBS B15 (P20): **10 emalangeni** (US$1.50)   VG   VF   UNC

Blue. Front: Shield and spears as registration device; King Mswati III; Parliament House building in Lobamba; coat of arms with lion and elephant flanking shield topped with crown of feathers (lidlabe); staff (umgobo) with widow bird plumes. Back: Bird; hydroelectric plant at Luphohlo. Solid security thread. Watermark: Shield and spears. Printer: THOMAS DE LA RUE AND COMPANY, LIMITED. 145 x 66 mm.

			VG	VF	UNC
☐	a.	No date. Signature 3. Prefix J - L. Intro: 1990.	FV	7	30
☐	b.	Signature 4. Prefix N - Q. Intro: 1992.	FV	7	30
☐	as.	Diagonal red SPECIMEN overprint.	—	—	100
☐	bs.	Diagonal red SPECIMEN overprint.	—	—	100

Replacement notes: Prefix Z.

CBS B16 (P21): **20 emalangeni** (US$3)   VG   VF   UNC

Purple. Front: Shield and spears as registration device; King Mswati III; Parliament House building in Lobamba; coat of arms with lion and elephant flanking shield topped with crown of feathers (lidlabe); battle axe (sizeze). Back: Rice; corn; cotton; cattle; lumber on flatbed truck; pineapples; citrus. Solid security thread. Watermark: Shield and spears. Printer: THOMAS DE LA RUE AND COMPANY, LIMITED. 150 x 70 mm.

			VG	VF	UNC
☐	a.	No date. Signature 3. Prefix G. Intro: 1990.	5	15	60
☐	b.	Signature 4. Prefix K. Intro: 1992.	5	15	60
☐	as.	Diagonal red SPECIMEN overprint.	—	—	100
☐	bs.	Diagonal red SPECIMEN overprint.	—	—	100

Replacement notes: Prefix Z.

CBS B17 (P22): **50 emalangeni** (US$7.45)   VG   VF   UNC

Orange. Front: Shield and spears as registration device; King Mswati III; Parliament House building in Lobamba; coat of arms with lion and elephant flanking shield topped with crown of feathers (lidlabe). Back: Bank seal; Central Bank of Swaziland headquarters building. Solid security thread with printed *SWAZILAND*. Watermark: Shield and spears. Printer: *THOMAS DE LA RUE AND COMPANY, LIMITED*. 156 x 72 mm.

		VG	VF	UNC
☐ a.	No date. Signature 3. Prefix A - B. Intro: 1990.	FV	25	100
☐ b.	Signature 5. Prefix C. Intro: 1995.	25	50	200
☐ as.	Diagonal red *SPECIMEN* overprint.	—	—	90
☐ bs.	Diagonal red *SPECIMEN* overprint.	—	—	85

1995-1998 Issues

These notes are like the preceding issues, but with novel serial numbering, windowed security threads, new signatures, and new printer imprints. The 50-lilangeni denomination has a holographic stripe added at right front. The 2-lilangeni denomination was dropped and the 100-lilangeni denomination was added in this family.

CBS B18 (P23): **5 emalangeni** (US$0.75)   VG   VF   UNC

Green. Front: Shield and spears as registration device; King Mswati III; Parliament House building in Lobamba; coat of arms with lion and elephant flanking shield topped with crown of feathers (lidlabe); knobkerrie (club). Back: Warriors. Windowed security thread. Watermark: Shield and spears. Printer: *HARRISON AND SONS LIMITED*. 140 x 63 mm.

		VG	VF	UNC
☐ a.	No date. Sig. 6a. Prefix AA - AE. Intro: 1995.	FV	1.25	5
☐ as.	Diagonal red hollow *SPECIMEN* overprint; horizontal red SPECIMEN Nº # ovpt at lower left.	—	—	85

CBS B19 (P24): **10 emalangeni** (US$1.50)   VG   VF   UNC

Blue. Front: Shield and spears as registration device; King Mswati III; Parliament House building in Lobamba; coat of arms with lion and elephant flanking shield topped with crown of feathers (lidlabe); staff (umgobo) with widow bird plumes. Back: Bird; hydroelectric plant at Luphohlo. Watermark: Shield and spears. Printer: *FRANÇOIS-CHARLES OBERTHUR*. 145 x 66 mm.

		VG	VF	UNC
☐ a.	No date. Signature 6a. Prefix AA - AE. Windowed security thread. Intro: 1995.	FV	8	25
☐ b.	08.04.97. Signature 7. Prefix AG - AH.	FV	4	16
☐ c.	01.04.98. Signature 8a. Prefix AL - AO. Windowed security thread with demetalized *CENTRAL BANK OF SWAZILAND*.	FV	FV	5
☐ as.	Specimen.	—	—	85
☐ bs.	Diagonal red boxed *SPÉCIMEN* overprint.	—	—	85
☐ cs.	Diagonal red boxed *SPÉCIMEN* overprint.	—	—	85

CBS B20 (P25): **20 emalangeni** (US$3)   VG   VF   UNC

Purple. Front: Shield and spears as registration device; King Mswati III; Parliament House building in Lobamba; coat of arms with lion and elephant flanking shield topped with crown of feathers (lidlabe); battle axe (sizeze). Back: Rice; corn; cotton; cattle; lumber on flatbed truck; pineapples; citrus. Watermark: Shield and spears. Printer: *FRANÇOIS-CHARLES OBERTHUR*. 150 x 70 mm.

		VG	VF	UNC
☐ a.	No date. Signature 6a. Prefix AA - AB. Windowed security thread. Intro: 1995.	FV	7	25
☐ b.	08.04.97. Signature 7. Prefix AF - AG.	FV	10	40
☐ c.	01.04.98. Signature 8a. Prefix AK - AL. Windowed security thread with demetalized *CENTRAL BANK OF SWAZILAND*.	FV	FV	6.50
☐ as.	Diagonal red *SPECIMEN* overprint.	—	—	85
☐ bs.	Diagonal red boxed *SPÉCIMEN* overprint.	—	—	35
☐ cs.	Specimen.	—	—	85

CBS B21 (P26): **50 emalangeni** (US$7.45)   VG   VF   UNC
Orange. Front: Shield and spears as registration device; King Mswati III; Parliament House building in Lobamba; coat of arms with lion and elephant flanking shield topped with crown of feathers (lidlabe). Back: Bank seal; Central Bank of Swaziland headquarters building. Holographic stripe. Windowed security thread with demetalized *CENTRAL BANK OF SWAZILAND*. Watermark: Shield and spears. Printer: *GIESECKE & DEVRIENT - GERMANY*. 152 x 70 mm.

- ☐ a. 1.4.1995. Signature 6b. Prefix AA.   FV   10   40
- ☐ b. 1.4.1998. Signature 8b. Prefix AA - AB.   FV   FV   25
- ☐ as. Diagonal purple *SPECIMEN* overprint;   —   —   85
  horiz. purple *SPECIMEN Nº* # ovpt at lower left.
- ☐ bs. Diagonal purple *SPECIMEN* overprint;   —   —   85
  horiz. purple *SPECIMEN Nº* # ovpt at lower left.

CBS B22 (P27): **100 emalangeni** (US$15)   VG   VF   UNC
Brown. Front: Shield and spears as registration device; King Mswati III; Parliament House building in Lobamba; coat of arms with lion and elephant flanking shield topped with crown of feathers (lidlabe). Back: Bank seal; rock formation. Holographic stripe. Windowed security thread with demetalized *CENTRAL BANK OF SWAZILAND*. Watermark: Shield and spears. Printer: *GIESECKE & DEVRIENT - GERMANY*. 157 x 70 mm.

- ☐ a. 6.9.1996. Signature 6b. Prefix AA.   FV   FV   60
- ☐ as. Diagonal purple *SPECIMEN* overprint;   —   —   85
  horiz. purple *SPECIMEN Nº* # ovpt at lower left.

1998 Commemorative Issues

This first-ever 200-lilangeni note was issued to commemorate the 30th anniversary of Swaziland's independence from Britain.

CBS B23 (P28): **200 emalangeni** (US$30)   VG   VF   UNC
Green. Front: Shield and spears as registration device; King Mswati III; Parliament House building in Lobamba; coat of arms with lion and elephant flanking shield topped with crown of feathers (lidlabe); *30TH INDEPENDENCE ANNIVERSARY* text. Back: Bank seal; straw huts; overprint. Holographic stripe. Windowed security thread with demetalized *CENTRAL BANK OF SWAZILAND*. Watermark: Shield and spears. Printer: *GIESECKE & DEVRIENT - GERMANY*. 162 x 70 mm.

- ☐ a. 6.9.1998. Signature 8b. Prefix AA.   FV   FV   100
- ☐ as. Diagonal red *SPECIMEN* overprint;   —   —   85
  horizontal red *SPECIMEN Nº* # ovpt at lower left.

2001-2006 Issues

These notes are like the preceding issues, but have the text *GOD IS OUR SOURCE* added above the bank's name on the back. The 5-lilangeni denomination was dropped from this family.

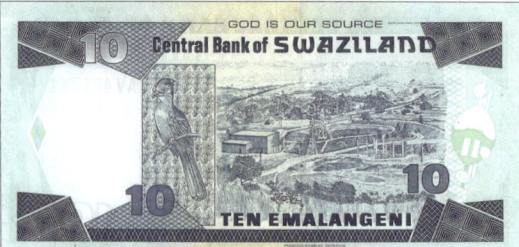

CBS B24 (P29): **10 emalangeni** (US$1.50)   VG   VF   UNC

Blue. Front: Shield and spears as registration device; King Mswati III; Parliament House building in Lobamba; coat of arms with lion and elephant flanking shield topped with crown of feathers (lidlabe); staff (umgobo) with widow bird plumes. Back: Bird; hydroelectric plant at Luphohlo. Windowed security thread with demetalized *CENTRAL BANK OF SWAZILAND*. Watermark: Shield and spears. Printer: FRANÇOIS CHARLES OBERTHUR. 145 x 66 mm.

- ☐ a. 01.04.01. Signature 9a. Prefix AP - AT.   FV   FV   4.25
- ☐ b. 01.04.04. Prefix AV - AX.   FV   FV   5
- ☐ c. 01:04:2006. Prefix BA - BI.   FV   FV   3
- ☐ bs. Diagonal red boxed *SPÉCIMEN* overprint; horizontal red # overprint at lower left.   —   —   40

CBS B25 (P30): **20 emalangeni** (US$3)   VG   VF   UNC

Purple. Front: Shield and spears as registration device; King Mswati III; Parliament House building in Lobamba; coat of arms with lion and elephant flanking shield topped with crown of feathers (lidlabe); battle axe (sizeze). Back: Rice; corn; cotton; cattle; lumber on flatbed truck; pineapples; citrus. Windowed security thread with demetalized *CENTRAL BANK OF SWAZILAND*. Watermark: Shield and spears. Printer: FRANÇOIS-CHARLES OBERTHUR. 150 x 70 mm.

- ☐ a. 01.04.01. Signature 9a. Prefix AM - AQ.   FV   FV   6
- ☐ b. 01.04.04. Prefix AR - AU.   FV   FV   6.75
- ☐ c. 01:04:2006. Prefix AW - BD.   FV   FV   5
- ☐ as. Diagonal red boxed *SPÉCIMEN* overprint.   —   —   80
- ☐ bs. Diagonal red boxed *SPÉCIMEN* overprint; horizontal red # overprint at lower left.   —   —   85

CBS B26 (P31): **50 emalangeni** (US$7.45)   VG   VF   UNC

Orange. Front: Shield and spears as registration device; King Mswati III; Parliament House building in Lobamba; coat of arms with lion and elephant flanking shield topped with crown of feathers (lidlabe). Back: Bank seal; Central Bank of Swaziland headquarters building. Holographic stripe. Windowed security thread with demetalized *CENTRAL BANK OF SWAZILAND*. Watermark: Shield and spears. Printer: GIESECKE & DEVRIENT - GERMANY. 152 x 70 mm.

- ☐ a. 1.4.2001. Signature 9b. Prefix AA - AC.   FV   FV   13
- ☐ as. Specimen.   —   —   80

CBS B27 (P32): **100 emalangeni** (US$15)   VG   VF   UNC

Brown. Front: Shield and spears as registration device; King Mswati III; Parliament House building in Lobamba; coat of arms with lion and elephant flanking shield topped with crown of feathers (lidlabe). Back: Bank seal; rock formation. Holographic stripe. Windowed security thread with demetalized *CENTRAL BANK OF SWAZILAND*. Watermark: Shield and spears. Printer: *GIESECKE & DEVRIENT - GERMANY*. 157 x 70 mm.

- a. 1.4.2001. Signature 9b. Prefix AA - AC.   FV   FV   35
- as. Diagonal purple *SPECIMEN* overprint;   —   —   80
horiz. purple *SPECIMEN Nr. #* ovpt at lower left.

2004 Commemorative Issues

This 100-lilangeni note was issued to commemorate the 30th anniversary of the founding of the Monetary Authority of Swaziland.

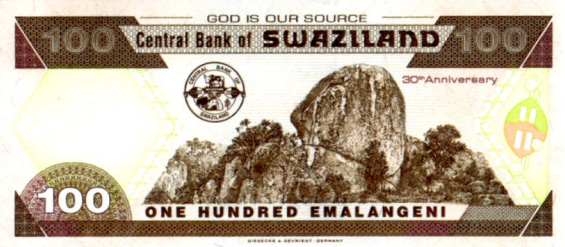

CBS B28 (P33): **100 emalangeni** (US$15)   VG   VF   UNC

Brown. Front: Shield and spears as registration device; King Mswati III; Parliament House building in Lobamba; coat of arms with lion and elephant flanking shield topped with crown of feathers (lidlabe); *30th Anniversary* text. Back: Bank seal; rock formation; *30th Anniversary* text. Holographic stripe. Windowed security thread with demetalized *CENTRAL BANK OF SWAZILAND*. Watermark: Shield and spears. Printer: *GIESECKE & DEVRIENT - GERMANY*. 157 x 70 mm.

- a. 1.4.2004. Signature 9b. Prefix AB.   FV   FV   35
- as. Diagonal red *SPECIMEN* overprint;   —   —   55
horizontal red *SPECIMEN Nr. #* ovpt at lower left.

2008 Commemorative Issues

These notes commemorate the 40th birthday of King Mswati III (born 19 April 1968) and the 40th anniversary of independence. They are the first in the world to use intaglio halftone technology, creating photo-like portraits. They are also the first notes to be printed on G&D's patented Hybrid substrate, comprised of cotton fibers sandwiched between layers of plastic for increased durability.

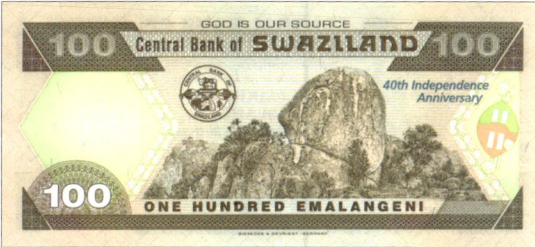

CBS B29 (P34): **100 emalangeni** (US$15)   VG   VF   UNC

Brown. Front: Shield and spears as registration device; King Mswati III; Parliament House building in Lobamba; coat of arms with lion and elephant flanking shield topped with crown of feathers (lidlabe); *The King's 40th Birthday* text. Back: Bank seal; rock formation; *40th Independence Anniversary* text. Holographic stripe. Solid security thread with demetalized *CENTRAL BANK OF SWAZILAND*. Watermark: Shield and spears. Printer: *GIESECKE & DEVRIENT - GERMANY*. 157 x 70 mm.

- a. 19.4.2008. Sig. 9b. Prefix HM. Intro: 05.09.2008.   FV   FV   30
- as. Diagonal red *SPECIMEN* overprint;   —   —   100
horizontal red *SPECIMEN Nº #* ovpt at lower left.

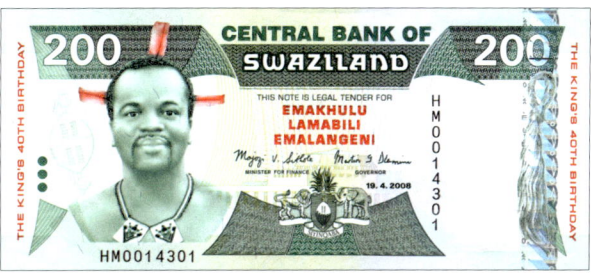

CBS B30 (P35): **200 emalangeni** (US$30)   VG   VF   UNC

Green. Front: Shield and spears as registration device; King Mswati III; Parliament House building in Lobamba; coat of arms with lion and elephant flanking shield topped with crown of feathers (lidlabe); *THE KING'S 40TH BIRTHDAY* text. Back: Bank seal; straw huts; *40TH INDEPENDENCE ANNIVERSARY* text. Holographic stripe. Solid security thread with demetalized *CENTRAL BANK OF SWAZILAND*. Watermark: Shield and spears. Printer: *GIESECKE & DEVRIENT - GERMANY*. 160 x 70 mm.

- a. 19.4.2008. Sig. 9b. Prefix HM. Intro: 05.09.2008.   FV   FV   55
- as. Diagonal red *SPECIMEN* overprint;   —   —   100
horizontal red *SPECIMEN Nº #* ovpt at lower left.

Replacement notes: Prefix HZ.

2010 Issues

On 1 November 2010, the Central Bank of Swaziland began issuing a new series of banknotes with upgraded security features. All of these notes use intaglio halftone technology and are printed on G&D's Hybrid substrate.

CBS B31 (P36): **10 emalangeni** (US$1.50)   VG   VF   UNC
Blue. Front: King Mswati III; coat of arms with lion and elephant flanking shield topped with crown of feathers (lidlabe); shield (isihlangu), spears (sikhali), and staff (umgobo). Back: Nine princesses taking part in the Ncwala (kingship ceremony); bank seal. Windowed security thread with demetalized *CENTRAL BANK OF SWAZILAND*. Watermark: King Mswati III and electrotype *10*. Printer: GIESECKE & DEVRIENT - GERMANY. 148 x 70 mm.

    ☐ a.   6.9.2010. Sig. 9b. Prefix AA. Intro: 30.06.2011.   FV   FV   3
    ☐ as.   Diagonal red *SPECIMEN* overprint;   —   —   70
            horizontal red *SPECIMEN Nº* # ovpt at lower left.

Replacement notes: Prefix AZ.

CBS B32 (P37): **20 emalangeni** (US$3)   VG   VF   UNC
Purple. Front: King Mswati III; coat of arms with lion and elephant flanking shield topped with crown of feathers (lidlabe); shield (isihlangu), spears (sikhali), and staff (umgobo). Back: Flower, corn, and pineapple; steer; refinery; bank seal. Windowed security thread with demetalized *CENTRAL BANK OF SWAZILAND*. Watermark: King Mswati III and electrotype *20*. Printer: GIESECKE & DEVRIENT - GERMANY. 151 x 70 mm.

    ☐ a.   6.9.2010. Sig. 9b. Prefix AA. Intro: 30.06.2011.   FV   FV   6
    ☐ as.   Diagonal red *SPECIMEN* overprint;   —   —   80
            horizontal red *SPECIMEN Nº* # ovpt at lower left.

CBS B33 (P38): **50 emalangeni** (US$7.45)   VG   VF   UNC
Violet. Front: King Mswati III; coat of arms with lion and elephant flanking shield topped with crown of feathers (lidlabe); green-to-blue OVI shield (isihlangu), spears (sikhali), and staff (umgobo). Back: Central Bank of Swaziland headquarters Umntsholi building in Mbabane; bank seal. Green-to-pink windowed security thread with demetalized *CENTRAL BANK OF SWAZILAND*. Watermark: King Mswati III and electrotype *50*. Printer: GIESECKE & DEVRIENT - GERMANY. 154 x 70 mm.

    ☐ a.   6.9.2010. Sig. 9b. Prefix AA. Intro: 30.06.2011.   FV   FV   15
    ☐ as.   Diagonal red *SPECIMEN* overprint;   —   —   90
            horizontal red *SPECIMEN Nº* # ovpt at lower left.

CBS B34 (P39): **100 emalangeni** (US$15)   VG   VF   UNC
Brown. Front: King Mswati III; coat of arms with lion and elephant flanking shield topped with crown of feathers (lidlabe); green-to-blue OVI shield (isihlangu), spears (sikhali), and staff (umgobo). Back: Elephant, rhinoceros, lion, flowers, and bird; bank seal. Green-to-pink windowed security thread with demetalized *CENTRAL BANK OF SWAZILAND*. Watermark: King Mswati III and electrotype *100*. Printer: GIESECKE & DEVRIENT - GERMANY. 157 x 70 mm.

    ☐ a.   6.9.2010. Sig. 9b. Prefix AA. Intro: 01.11.2010.   FV   FV   30
    ☐ as.   Diagonal red *SPECIMEN* overprint;   —   —   100
            horizontal red *SPECIMEN Nº* # ovpt at lower left.

Replacement notes: Prefix AZ.

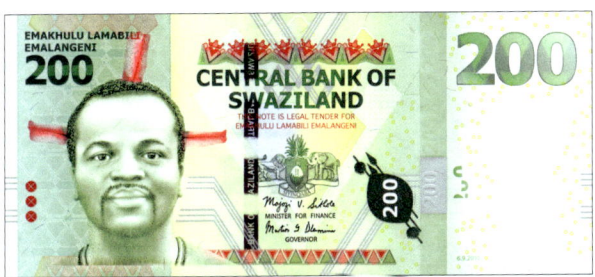

CBS B35 (P40): **200 emalangeni** (US$30) VG VF UNC

Green. Front: King Mswati III; coat of arms with lion and elephant flanking shield topped with crown of feathers (lidlabe); green-to-blue OVI shield (isihlangu), spears (sikhali), and staff (umgobo). Back: Straw huts; two goats; warrior; rock formation; bank seal. Green-to-pink windowed security thread with demetalized *CENTRAL BANK OF SWAZILAND*. Watermark: King Mswati III and electrotype *200*. Printer: *GIESECKE & DEVRIENT - GERMANY*. 160 x 70 mm.

- ☐ a. 6.9.2010. Sig. 9b. Prefix AA. Intro: 30.06.2011.   FV   FV   60
- ☐ as. Diagonal red *SPECIMEN* overprint; horizontal red *SPECIMEN N⁰ #* ovpt at lower left.   —   —   120

Acknowledgements

This chapter was compiled with the generous assistance of Thomas Augustsson, Arigo Avbovbo, Michael Boehm (Louisenthal), Jean-Michel Engels, Joseph Gerber, Murray Hanewich, Hermann Huber, Malcolm Knight (De La Rue), Thomas Krause (www.polymernotes.de), Dmitriy Litvak, Claudio Marana, Wally Myers, Leszek Porowski, Ny Andry Ranaivosolo, Andrew Roberts, TDS, Gergely Scheidl (banknoteshop@gmx.net), Bill Stubkjaer, Christoph Thomas, Andre du Toit, Christof Zellweger, and others.

Sources

Anonymous. "New 2010 series of banknotes using the Hybrid® substrate in Swaziland." *Billetaria*. April 2010. p.28.

Cuhaj, George S. *Standard Catalog of World Paper Money, Modern Issues, 1961-Present*. 18th edition. 2012. ISBN 978-1-4402-2956-5. Krause Publications (www.krausebooks.com), 700 East State St., Iola, WI, 54990-0001.

Wirz, Dr. Heinz. *Dr Heinz Wirz on the Bank Notes of SWAZILAND*. 3rd edition. 2002.

Share Your Input, Info, and Images

This catalog is believed to be complete and correct as of the time of publication. Prices and face values were last updated 10 June 2011. Please report errors or omissions so that corrections may be made. If you can more precisely identify the name or location of anything depicted on a note, please share that information. Furthermore, if you own an unlisted type or variety, please submit scans of the front and back of the note so that it can be documented. Scans should be 300 dots per inch, 100% actual size, 24-bit color, saved as *uncompressed* JPEG files, and sent to owen@banknotenews.com. Be sure to fully describe all attributes of the note which are not apparent upon visual inspection of the images alone, such as physical dimension, watermark, and security thread.

Syria

1919-1955 Issues

Earlier notes from other issuers will be added to this chapter in the future.

Monetary System

1 Syrian pound (SYP) = 100 piastres

Arabic Numbers

0	1	2	3	4	5	6	7	8	9
٠	١	٢	٣	٤	٥	٦	٧	٨	٩

Banque Centrale de Syrie (Central Bank of Syria)

The Central Bank of Syria (CBS) was established by Legislative Decree No. 87 dated 28 March 1953. The bank started its operations on 1 August 1956, with its headquarters in the city of Damascus.

For more information, visit www.banquecentrale.gov.sy.

CBS Signature Varieties

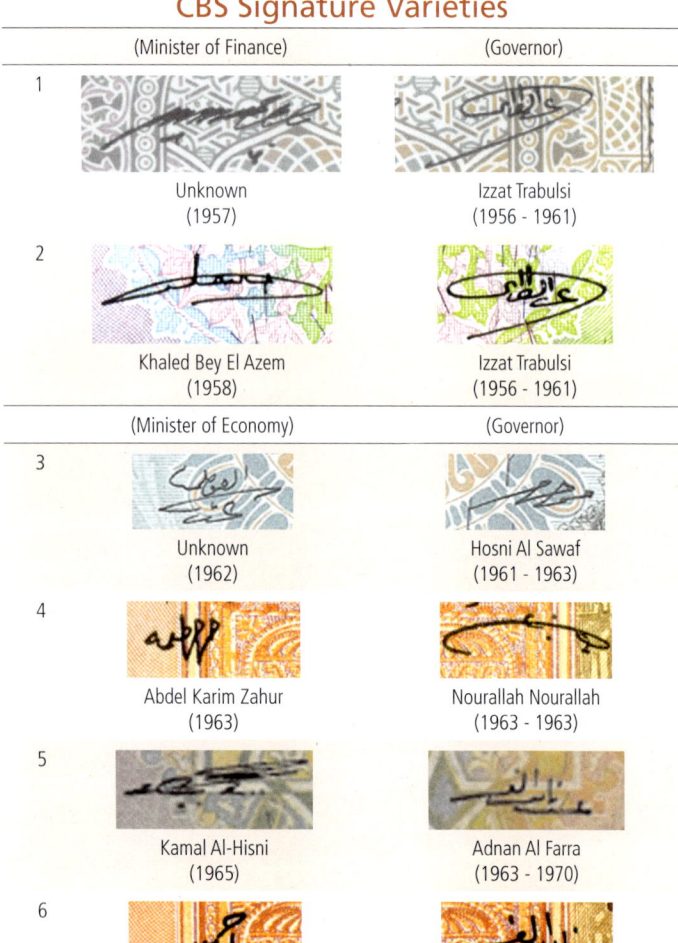

	(Minister of Finance)	(Governor)
1	Unknown (1957)	Izzat Trabulsi (1956 - 1961)
2	Khaled Bey El Azem (1958)	Izzat Trabulsi (1956 - 1961)
	(Minister of Economy)	(Governor)
3	Unknown (1962)	Hosni Al Sawaf (1961 - 1963)
4	Abdel Karim Zahur (1963)	Nourallah Nourallah (1963 - 1963)
5	Kamal Al-Hisni (1965)	Adnan Al Farra (1963 - 1970)
6	Ahmed Murad (1966 - 1967)	Adnan Al Farra (1963 - 1970)

CBS Signature Varieties

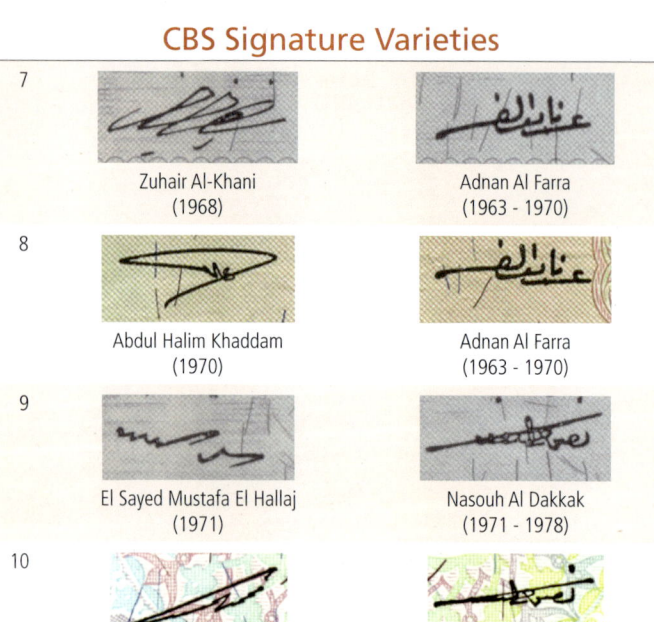

7	Zuhair Al-Khani (1968)	Adnan Al Farra (1963 - 1970)
8	Abdul Halim Khaddam (1970)	Adnan Al Farra (1963 - 1970)
9	El Sayed Mustafa El Hallaj (1971)	Nasouh Al Dakkak (1971 - 1978)
10	 Mohammad al-Imadi (1973 - 1977)	 Nasouh Al Dakkak (1971 - 1978)
11	 Mohammad al-Imadi (1978 - 1979)	 Rifaat Al Akkad (1978 - 1984)
12	 Salim Said Yasin (1982)	 Rifaat Al Akkad (1978 - 1984)
13	 Mohammad al-Imadi (1986)	Hisham Mutawalli (1984 - 1987)
14	 Mohammad al-Imadi (1988 - 1992)	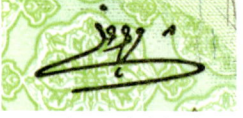 Mohammad Al Sharif (1987 - 1995)
15	 Mohammad al-Imadi (1997 - 1998)	 Mohammad Bashar Kabbarah (1995 - 2004)
16	 Mohammad Naji Al-Otri (2009)	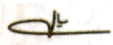 Adib Mayaleh (04.01.2005 - present)
17	 Unknown (2013)	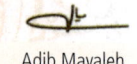 Adib Mayaleh (04.01.2005 - present)

1957-1958 Issues

The coat of arms of the Syrian Republic appears on the front of all of these notes. The arms consist of the Hawk of Qureish, which holds a shield of the national flag (in vertical form), and a scroll with the words "Syrian Arab Republic" in Arabic.

The text on the front of these notes is Arabic, and the text on the back is French.

CBS B1 (P79): **1 livre syrienne** (withdrawn 26.04.1971)   VG   VF   UNC

Brown, orange, purple, and green. Front: Coat of arms. Back: Arches, Minaret of the Bride, and Dome of the Clock in courtyard of Umayyad mosque in Damascus. Unknown security thread. Watermark: Arabian horse head. Printer: (BWC). 138 x 65 mm.

			VG	VF	UNC
☐	a.	1957. Signature 1.	15	50	200
☐	as.	Diagonal red نموذج overprint on front; diagonal red SPECIMEN overprint on back; punched.	—	—	650
☐	p.	Separate front/back monochrome proofs.	—	—	—
☐	t.	Color trial: Purple.	—	—	—

CBS B2 (P80): **5 livres syriennes** (withdrawn 26.04.1971)   VG   VF   UNC

Brown. Front: Coat of arms. Back: Entrance to Citadel of Aleppo. Unknown security thread. Watermark: Arabian horse head. Printer: (BWC). 149 x 72 mm.

			VG	VF	UNC
☐	a.	1957. Signature 1.	18	65	300
☐	as.	Diagonal red نموذج overprint on front; diagonal red SPECIMEN overprint on back; punched.	—	—	1,000
☐	p.	Separate front/back monochrome proofs.	—	—	—
☐	t.	Color trial: Blue.	—	—	—

CBS B3 (P84): **50 livres syriennes**   VG   VF   UNC

Green, purple, and blue. Front: Coat of arms. Back: Arches and trees in courtyard of Azm Palace (now Museum of Arts and Popular Traditions) in Damascus. Unknown security thread. Watermark: Arabian horse head. Printer: (BWC). 183 x 90 mm.

			VG	VF	UNC
☐	a.	1957. Signature 1.	60	275	650
☐	b.	1958. Signature 2.	60	275	650
☐	bt.	Color trial: Brown.	—	—	1,800

CBS B4 (P85): **100 livres syriennes**   VG   VF   UNC

Purple, green, orange, and blue. Front: Coat of arms. Back: Norias (waterwheels) of Hama on the Orontes River. Unknown security thread. Watermark: Arabian horse head. Printer: (BWC). 195 x 96 mm.

			VG	VF	UNC
☐	a.	1958. Signature 2.	80	350	850
☐	at.	Color trial: Gray, purple, and aqua.	—	—	—
☐	p.	Proof.	—	—	—

1958-1992 Issues

The text on the front of these notes remains Arabic, but the French of the preceding issue has been replaced by English.

The three smaller denominations were printed without imprint by Pakistan Security Printing Corporation, Pakistan, whereas the four larger denominations were printed with imprint by Johan Enschedé en Zonen, Netherlands.

CBS B5 (P86 & P93): **1 Syrian pound** (<US$0.01)   VG   VF   UNC

Brown, yellow, purple, and orange. Front: Factory worker with machinery. Back: Norias (waterwheels) of Hama on the Orontes River. No security thread. Watermark: Arabian horse head. Printer: (PSPC). 130 x 65 mm.

☐	a. 1958. Signature 2.	2	15	75
☐	b. 1963. Signature 4. No security thread.	2	8	30
☐	c. 1967. Signature 6.	2	8	30
☐	d. 1973. Signature 10.	1.50	6	25
☐	e. 1978. Signature 11. Solid security thread with printed CENTRAL BANK OF SYRIA.	0.50	1.25	5
☐	f. 1982. Signature 12.	—	—	2.50
☐	as. Diagonal red Arabic and SPECIMEN WITHOUT VALUE overprints.	—	—	375
☐	bs. Specimen.	—	—	85
☐	es. Diagonal red Arabic overprint; punched.	—	—	—

CBS B6 (P87 & P94): **5 Syrian pounds** (<US$0.05)   VG   VF   UNC

Green, orange, purple, and yellow. Front: Factory worker with machinery. Back: Entrance to Citadel of Aleppo. No security thread. Watermark: Arabian horse head. Printer: (PSPC). 142 x 69 mm.

☐	a. 1958. Signature 2.	6	20	100
☐	b. 1963. Signature 4.	5	20	75
☐	c. 1967. Signature 6.	5	20	75
☐	d. 1970. Signature 8.	5	20	75
☐	e. 1973. Signature 10.	4	15	50
☐	as. Diagonal red Arabic and SPECIMEN WITHOUT VALUE overprints.	—	—	475
☐	cs. Diagonal red Arabic and SPECIMEN WITHOUT VALUE overprints.	—	—	425

CBS B7 (P88 & P95): **10 Syrian pounds** (US$0.05)   VG   VF   UNC

Purple, yellow, blue, green, and orange. Front: Factory worker with machinery. Back: Arches, Minaret of the Bride, and Dome of the Clock in courtyard of Umayyad mosque in Damascus. Unknown security thread. Watermark: Arabian horse head. Printer: (PSPC). 142 x 70 mm.

☐	a. 1958. Signature 2.	8	30	135
☐	b. 1965. Signature 5.	8	30	100
☐	c. 1968. Signature 7.	8	30	100
☐	d. 1973. Signature 10.	8	30	100
☐	as. Diagonal red Arabic and SPECIMEN WITHOUT VALUE overprints.	—	—	600
☐	bs. Diagonal red Arabic and SPECIMEN WITHOUT VALUE overprints.	—	—	550

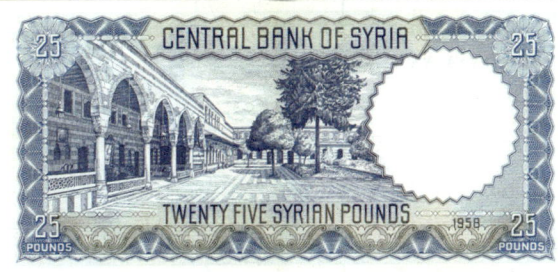

CBS B8 (P89): **25 Syrian pounds** (US$0.05) VG VF UNC
Blue, orange, and gray. Front: Two women with wicker baskets in cotton field. Back: Arches and trees in courtyard of Azm Palace (now Museum of Arts and Popular Traditions) in Damascus. Solid security thread. Watermark: Arabian horse head. Printer: *JOH. ENSCHEDE EN ZONEN. IMP.* 158 x 75 mm.

☐ a. 1958. Signature 2. 10 35 400
☐ as. Diagonal red Arabic and — — 750
   SPECIMEN WITHOUT VALUE overprints.

CBS B9 (P90): **50 Syrian pounds** (US$0.30) VG VF UNC
Orange, brown, and purple. Front: Two women with wicker baskets in cotton field. Back: Statue of seated lion; mosque of Sultan Selim in Damascus; statue of seated lion. Solid security thread. Watermark: Arabian horse head. Printer: *JOH. ENSCHEDE EN ZONEN. IMP.* 158 x 75 mm.

☐ a. 1958. Signature 2. 20 75 300
☐ as. Diagonal red Arabic and — — 825
   SPECIMEN WITHOUT VALUE overprints.

CBS B10 (P91): **100 Syrian pounds** (US$0.65) VG VF UNC
Green, brown, and blue. Front: Corinthian column; two women with wicker baskets in cotton field; Corinthian column. Back: Statue of perched eagle; ancient ruins of Hadrian's gate and row of columns in Palmyra; eagle with outstretched wings; statue of perched eagle. Solid security thread. Watermark: Arabian horse head. Printer: *JOH. ENSCHEDE EN ZONEN. IMP.* 167 x 79 mm.

☐ a. 1958. Signature 2. 20 75 300
☐ b. 1962. Signature 3. 15 60 275
☐ as. Diagonal red Arabic and — — 610
   SPECIMEN WITHOUT VALUE overprints.
☐ bs. Diagonal red Arabic and — — 575
   SPECIMEN WITHOUT VALUE overprints.

1966-1974 Issues

CBS B11 (P92 & P105): **500 Syrian pounds** (US$3.30)   VG   VF   UNC

Olive green, brown, and purple. Front: Artifacts from kingdom of Ugarit; two figures holding stalk; ivory bas-relief of winged goddess Anat suckling two princes; carved head of Ugaritic prince; two figures holding stalk. Back: Clay pot; clay pitcher adorned with antlered deer and tree; leaping ram in underprint; gold bowl decorated with hunting/animal scenes from the Temple of Baal at Ugarit; leaping ram in underprint; Ugarit alphabet on cuneiform clay tablet; clay pot. Solid security thread. Watermark: Arabian horse head. Printer: *JOH. ENSCHEDE EN ZONEN. IMP.* 179 x 85 mm.

a.	1958. Signature 2.	50	150	450
b.	1976. Signature 10. Solid security thread.	FV	20	80
c.	1979. Signature 11. Solid security thread with printed CENTRAL BANK OF SYRIA.	FV	30	120
d.	1982. Signature 12.	FV	20	80
e.	1986. Signature 13.	FV	FV	35
f.	1990. Signature 14.	FV	FV	25
g.	1992. Solid security thread.	FV	FV	35
as.	Diagonal red Arabic and *SPECIMEN WITHOUT VALUE* overprints.	—	—	1,000
bs.	Diagonal red Arabic and *SPECIMEN WITHOUT VALUE* overprints; horizontal *SPECIMEN* perforation.	—	—	750

CBS B12 (P96): **25 Syrian pounds** (US$0.05)   VG   VF   UNC

Blue, brown, orange, purple, and green. Front: Man working with modern loom. Back: Ruins of ancient Roman theater in Bosra. Solid security thread. Watermark: Arabian horse head. Printer: Unknown. 158 x 75 mm.

a.	1966. Signature 6.	20	75	250
b.	1970. Signature 8.	15	50	150
c.	1973. Signature 10.	5	15	75
t.	Color trial: Brownish-purple and green.	—	—	425

CBS B13 (P97): **50 Syrian pounds** (US$0.30)   VG   VF   UNC

Brown, green, red, blue, and orange. Front: Man wearing keffiyeh driving combine harvester in wheat field. Back: Entrance to the National Museum in Damascus. Solid security thread. Watermark: Arabian horse head. Printer: Unknown. 158 x 75 mm.

a.	1966. Signature 6.	50	150	400
b.	1970. Signature 8.	15	50	200
c.	1973. Signature 10.	5	20	80
at.	Color trial: Blue and purple.	—	—	500
bt.	Color trial: Blue and purple.	—	—	500

CBS B14 (P98): **100 Syrian pounds** (US$0.65)   VG   VF   UNC

Purple, green, orange, and red. Front: Docked cargo ship, grain elevator, and silos in port of Lattakia. Back: Hydroelectric dam; flowers in vase. Solid security thread. Watermark: Arabian horse head. Printer: Unknown. 167 x 79 mm.

			VG	VF	UNC
☐	a.	1966. Signature 6.	20	75	350
☐	b.	1968. Signature 7.	5	15	100
☐	c.	1971. Signature 9.	6	25	100
☐	d.	1974. Signature 10.	6	25	100
☐	at.	Color trial: Aqua, purple, and brown.	—	—	625

1976-1991 Issues

CBS B15 (P99): **1 Syrian pound** (<US$0.01)   VG   VF   UNC

Green, orange, and brown. Front: Dome of the Treasury in courtyard of Umayyad mosque in Damascus; man hammering decoration onto metal platter. Back: Man driving combine harvester in wheat field. Solid security thread. Watermark: Arabian horse head. Printer: Unknown. 130 x 65 mm.

			VG	VF	UNC
☐	a.	1977. Signature 10.	1.25	5	20
☐	as.	Diagonal red Arabic overprint on front; diagonal red CANCELLED overprint on back; # overprint at upper left on back; punched.	—	—	—

CBS B16 (P100): **5 Syrian pounds** (<US$0.05)   VG   VF   UNC

Green, yellow, and purple. Front: Ancient Roman theater in Bosra; 2nd-century statue of Allāt-Minerva (Athena) carrying shield, from Roman ruins in As-Suwayda. Back: Man inspecting spinning frame in factory; women picking cotton in field. Watermark: Arabian horse head. Printer: Unknown. 142 x 69 mm.

			VG	VF	UNC
☐	a.	1977. Signature 10. Solid security thread.	0.25	1.50	6
☐	b.	1978. Signature 11. Solid security thread with printed CENTRAL BANK OF SYRIA.	FV	FV	2
☐	c.	1982. Signature 12.	FV	FV	2
☐	d.	1988. Signature 14. Solid security thread.	FV	FV	2
☐	e.	1991.	FV	FV	1.50
☐	as.	Diagonal red Arabic overprint on front; diagonal red CANCELLED overprint on back; # overprint at upper left on back; punched.	—	—	—
☐	bs.	Diagonal red Arabic overprint on front; diagonal red CANCELLED overprint on back; # overprint at upper left on back; punched.	—	—	—

CBS B17 (P101): **10 Syrian pounds** (US$0.05)   VG   VF   UNC

Purple, green, and orange. Front: Arches, fountain, and trees in courtyard of Azm Palace (now Museum of Arts and Popular Traditions) in Damascus; woman dancing in traditional clothes. Back: Censer; seawater desalination plant. Watermark: Arabian horse head. Printer: Unknown. 142 x 70 mm.

			VG	VF	UNC
☐	a.	1977. Signature 10. Solid security thread.	0.50	2.50	10
☐	b.	1978. Signature 11. Solid security thread with printed CENTRAL BANK OF SYRIA.	0.50	2.50	10
☐	c.	1982. Signature 12.	FV	FV	4
☐	d.	1988. Signature 14. Solid security thread.	0.50	2.50	10
☐	e.	1991.	FV	FV	1.50
☐	bs.	Diagonal red Arabic overprint on front; diagonal red CANCELLED overprint on back; # overprint at upper left on back; punched.	—	—	—

CBS B18 (P102): **25 Syrian pounds** (US$0.05)　　VG　VF　UNC
Purple, dark blue, green, and orange. Front: Krak des Chevaliers medieval crusader castle near Homs; Sultan Saladin. Back: Central Bank of Syria headquarters building in Damascus. Watermark: Arabian horse head. Printer: (TDLR). 158 x 75 mm.

☐	a.	1977. Signature 10. Solid security thread.	FV	2.50	10
☐	b.	1978. Signature 11. Solid security thread with printed CENTRAL BANK OF SYRIA.	1	4	15
☐	c.	1982. Signature 12.	FV	2	7.50
☐	d.	1988. Signature 14. Solid security thread.	FV	2	7.50
☐	e.	1991.	FV	0.75	3
☐	bs.	Diagonal red Arabic overprint on front; diagonal red CANCELLED overprint on back; # overprint at upper left on back; punched.	—	—	—

CBS B20 (P104): **100 Syrian pounds** (US$0.65)　　VG　VF　UNC
Green, brown, yellow, blue, and pink Front: Ancient ruins of Hadrian's gate and row of columns in Palmyra; Zenobia, 3rd-century queen of the Palmyrene Empire in Roman Syria. Back: Grain elevator and silos in port of Lattakia. Watermark: Arabian horse head. Printer: Unknown. 167 x 79 mm.

☐	a.	1977. Signature 10. Solid security thread.	FV	5	35
☐	b.	1978. Signature 11. Solid security thread with printed CENTRAL BANK OF SYRIA.	5	12	30
☐	c.	1982. Signature 12.	FV	3	10
☐	d.	1990. Signature 14. Solid security thread.	FV	2	8
☐	as.	Diagonal red Arabic overprint on front; diagonal red CANCELLED overprint on back; # overprint at upper left on back; punched.	—	—	—
☐	bs.	Diagonal red Arabic overprint on front; diagonal red CANCELLED overprint on back; # overprint at upper left on back; punched.	—	—	—

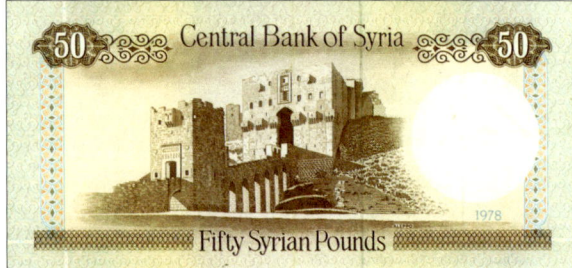

CBS B19 (P103): **50 Syrian pounds** (US$0.30)　　VG　VF　UNC
Brown, yellow, and green. Front: Hydroelectric Tabqa/al-Thawra Dam on the Euphrates River; statue of water goddess holding vase, from Sumarian ruins in Mari. Back: Entrance to Citadel of Aleppo. Watermark: Arabian horse head. Printer: Unknown. 158 x 75 mm.

☐	a.	1977. Signature 10. Solid security thread.	2.50	10	40
☐	b.	1978. Signature 11. Solid security thread with printed CENTRAL BANK OF SYRIA.	FV	4	15
☐	c.	1982. Signature 12.	FV	2	8
☐	d.	1988. Signature 14. Solid security thread.	FV	4	15
☐	e.	1991.	FV	1.50	5
☐	as.	Diagonal red Arabic overprint on front; diagonal red CANCELLED overprint on back; # overprint at upper left on back; punched.	—	—	—

1997-1998 Issues

CBS B21 (P107): **50 Syrian pounds** (US$0.30)   VG   VF   UNC
Brown, yellow, purple, red, and green. Front: Ancient chalice; coat of arms as registration device; ancient astrolabe; entrance to Citadel of Aleppo; Norias (waterwheels) of Hama on the Orontes River; ancient chalice. Back: Hanging bunch of grapes; Al-Assad National Library building in Damascus; students seated at desks, writing on tablets and paper; Abbasiyyin Stadium in Damascus; coat of arms. Windowed security thread with demetalized *CBS 50* separated by Arabic text. Watermark: Arabian horse head. Printer: Unknown. 150 x 75 mm.

     ☐ a.   1998. Signature 15.   FV   FV   3.50

CBS B22 (P108): **100 Syrian pounds** (US$0.65)   VG   VF   UNC
Blue, purple, brown, and green. Front: Ancient vase; mythological winged animal; coat of arms as registration device; ancient Roman theater in Bosra; bust of Roman Emperor Caesar Marcus Julius Philippus Augustus (Philip the Arab) from Hermitage Museum, Russia; mythological winged animal; ancient vase. Back: Branch with leaves and figs; Hejaz Railway locomotive; Hejaz Railway Station in Damascus-Kanawat; freeway interchange; coat of arms. Windowed security thread with demetalized *CBS 100* separated by Arabic text. Watermark: Arabian horse head. Printer: Unknown. 155 x 75 mm.

     ☐ a.   1998. Signature 15.   FV   FV   6

CBS B23 (P109): **200 Syrian pounds** (US$1.30)   VG   VF   UNC
Red, orange, green, blue, purple, and brown. Front: Corinthian column; coat of arms as registration device; Tomb of the Unknown Soldier in Damascus; ancient coin; equestrian statue of Sultan Saladin and soldier with sword and shield; Corinthian column. Back: Cotton plant; two women harvesting cotton in field; woman controlling spinning machine in factory; energy plant; coat of arms. Windowed security thread with demetalized *CBS 200* separated by Arabic text. Watermark: Arabian horse head. Printer: Unknown. 160 x 75 mm.

     ☐ a.   1997. Signature 15.   FV   FV   13

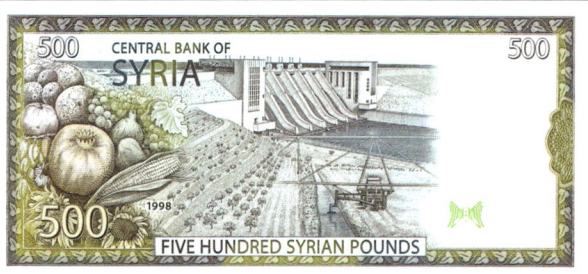

CBS B24 (P110): **500 Syrian pounds** (US$3.30)   VG   VF   UNC
Olive green, brown, green, and orange. Front: Corinthian column; crescent moon; coat of arms as registration device; palm trees, ancient ruins of Hadrian's gate, and theater in Palmyra; brooch; Zenobia, 3rd-century queen of the Palmyrene Empire in Roman Syria; Corinthian column. Back: Fruits and vegetables, including dates, gourds, figs, grapes, corn, and sunflowers; terraced hillside with trees being irrigated by tractor; hydroelectric Tabqa/al-Thawra Dam on the Euphrates River; coat of arms. Windowed security thread with demetalized *CBS 500* separated by Arabic text. Watermark: Arabian horse head. Printer: Unknown. 165 x 75 mm.

     ☐ a.   1998. Signature 15.   FV   FV   20
     ☐ b.   Small map in circle added below *SYRIA* on back.   FV   25   100

Both the 500- and 1,000-pound notes dated 1998 are available with (right) and without (left) a small map of Syria in a circle below the bank's name on back.

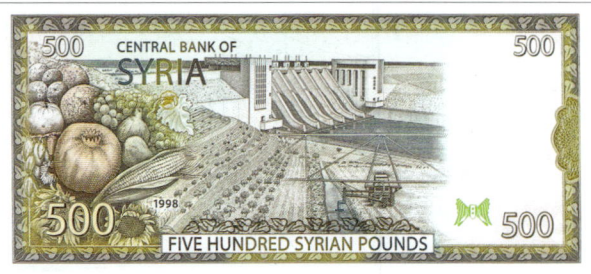

CBS B25 (PNL): **500 Syrian pounds** (US$3.30)   VG VF UNC

Olive green, brown, green, and orange. Front: Corinthian column; crescent moon; coat of arms as registration device; palm trees, ancient ruins of Hadrian's gate, and theater in Palmyra; brooch; Zenobia, 3rd-century queen of the Palmyrene Empire in Roman Syria; Corinthian column. Back: Fruits and vegetables, including dates, gourds, figs, grapes, corn, and sunflowers; terraced hillside with trees being irrigated by tractor; hydroelectric Tabqa/al-Thawra Dam on the Euphrates River; coat of arms. Windowed security thread with demetalized *CBS 500* separated by Arabic text. Watermark: Arabian horse head. Printer: Unknown. 165 x 75 mm.

☐ a. 1998. Signature 15.   FV FV 20

Like CBS B24b, but leaves added above *FIVE HUNDRED Syrian poundS* on back, and denomination added to lower right on back.

CBS B26 (P111): **1,000 Syrian pounds** (US$6.55)   VG VF UNC

Green, brown, and light blue. Front: Corinthian column; coat of arms as registration device; olive branch; Umayyad mosque in Damascus; ancient writing on cuneiform clay tablet from Ebla; ancient coin; olive branch; President Hafez al-Assad; Corinthian column. Back: Two men with drill; oil refinery; man driving combine harvester in wheat field; cargo ship; coat of arms. Windowed security thread with demetalized *CBS 1000* separated by Arabic text. Watermark: Hafez al-Assad. Printer: Unknown. 170 x 75 mm.

☐ a. 1997. Signature 15. Novel s/n at lower right.   FV FV 25
☐ b. Small map in circle added below *SYRIA* on back.   FV FV 25
☐ c. Small map removed. Normal s/n at lower right.   FV FV 20
Intro: June 2012. Printer: (Goznak).

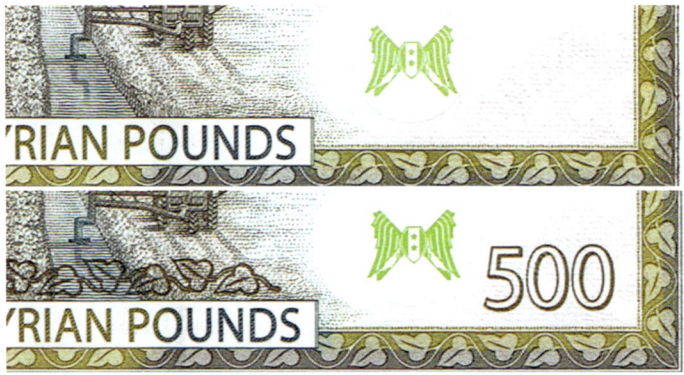

CBS B25a (bottom) is like CBS B24b (top), but with leaves added above the denomination, as well as *500* added at lower right on back.

Early 1,000-pound notes have novel numbering (CBS B26a/b, left); whereas on those notes issued in 2012, all the numbers are the same height (B26c, right).

2009 Issues

These notes were printed without imprint by Oesterreichische Banknoten- und Sicherheitsdruck, a subsidiary of Oesterreichische Nationalbank, Austria's central bank.

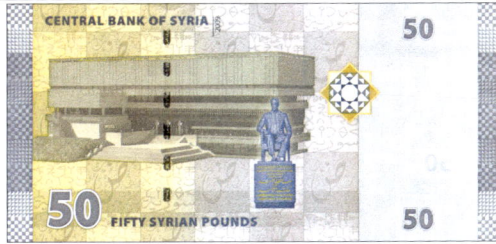

CBS B27 (P112): **50 Syrian pounds** (US$0.30)   VG   VF   UNC
Blue and tan. Front: Ugarit alphabet on cuneiform clay tablet; ancient writing on cuneiform clay tablet from Ebla. Back: Library of Hafiz Al Assad in Damascus; statue of Hafiz Al Assad. Windowed security thread with demetalized *CBS 50* and Arabic text. Watermark: Arabian horse head and electrotype *50*. Printer: (OEBS). 135 x 65 mm.
     ☐ a.   2009. Signature 16. Intro: 27.07.2010.   FV   FV   3

CBS B28 (P113): **100 Syrian pounds** (US$0.65)   VG   VF   UNC
Red and tan. Front: Ancient Roman theater and archway of main gate in Bosra. Back: Dome of the Treasury at Umayyad mosque in Damascus; Central Bank of Syria headquarters building in Damascus; ancient coin. Windowed security thread with demetalized *CBS 100* and Arabic text. Watermark: Arabian horse head and electrotype *100*. Printer: (OEBS). 140 x 65 mm.
     ☐ a.   2009. Signature 16. Intro: 27.07.2010.   FV   FV   4

CBS B29 (P114): **200 Syrian pounds** (US$1.30)   VG   VF   UNC
Tan and green. Front: Norias (waterwheels) of Hama on the Orontes River. Back: Ceiling of Temple Bel in Palmyra. Windowed security thread with demetalized *CBS 200*. Watermark: Arabian horse head and electrotype *200* and Arabic text. Printer: (OEBS). 145 x 65 mm.
     ☐ a.   2009. Signature 16. Intro: 27.07.2010.   FV   FV   7

2013 Issues

Adib Mayala, governor of the Central Bank of Syria, stated that the new 500-pound notes are made of better-quality materials "in a way to reflect the cultural and historical image of Syria and protect the banknotes from getting worn out." New 1,000-pound notes are expected to follow by September 2014.

CBS B30 (PNL): **500 Syrian pounds** (US$3.30)   VG   VF   UNC
Blue, gray, bown, red, and green. Front: Opera House (Dar Al Assad for Culture and Arts) in Damascus. Back: Four female musicians with instruments and oldest musical note. 4-mm wide windowed security thread with demetalized *SP500* and Arabic text. Watermark: Electrotype *500* and eagle coat of arms. Printer: (Goznak). 145 x 65 mm.
     ☐ a.   2013. Sig. 17. Prefix A/27. Intro: 02.07.2014.   FV   FV   10

Acknowledgements

This chapter was compiled with the generous assistance of Yaqoob Alshaer, Abdullah Beydoun (www.banknotecoins.com), Alex Bloy (http://stores.ebay.com/Hirsh-Collection), Robert Breslin, David F. Cieniewicz (www.banknotestore.com), Frank Citriniti, Coin Galleries of Oyster Bay (www.coingalleriesofoysterbay.com), Besher Ghannam (www.aleppo.tk), Murray Hanewich, Heritage Auctions (HA.com), Detlef Hilmer (detlef_hilmer@web.de), Takis Kouvatseas, Peter Mosselberger (www.banknote.ws), Wally Myers, Sam Nakhjavani (www.foreignpapermoney.com), Mikhail "Mike" Prizov, Stack's Bowers & Ponterio (www.StacksBowers.com), Menelaos Stamatelos, Bill Stubkjaer, Christoph Thomas, Gaetano Trabattoni, Christof Zellweger, and others.

Sources

Cuhaj, George S. *Standard Catalog of World Paper Money, General Issues, 1368-1960*. 14th edition. 2012. ISBN 978-1-4402-3090-5. Krause Publications (www.krausebooks.com), 700 East State St., Iola, WI, 54990-0001.

Cuhaj, George S. *Standard Catalog of World Paper Money, Modern Issues, 1961-Present*. 19th edition. 2013. ISBN 978-1-4402-3571-9. Krause Publications (www.krausebooks.com), 700 East State St., Iola, WI, 54990-0001.

Djarouehl, Adnan G. "Study and Comparison Between Standard Catalog of World Paper Money (Syrian Paper Money Section) and Encyclopedia of Syrian Paper Money." *IBNS Journal*. Volume 45 Number 3. p.6.

Eu, Peter and Ben Chiew. *Robert Kalina - The Man Behind The Euro*. 2nd edition. 2011. ISBN 978-983-44932-2-6. Eureka Metro sdn Bhd. Malaysia (www.eurekametro.my).

Heath, Henry B. "Personalities on Syrian Bank Notes." *IBNS Journal*. Volume 40 Number 3. p.20.

Salem, Farid. "The Present Bank Notes of the Middle East." *IBNS Journal*. Volume 34 Number 3. p.36.

Shneydor, N. A. "Evolving Policies in the Dating of Banknotes of the Near-East." *IBNS Journal*. Volume 53 Number 2. p.9.

Symes, Peter. Reference Site for Islamic Banknotes (www.islamicbanknotes.com).

Zellweger, Christof. "History on the Back of the Syrian 500 Pounds Note." *IBNS Journal*. Volume 36 Number 3. p.23.

Share Your Input, Info, and Images

This catalog is believed to be complete and correct as of the time of publication. Prices and face values were last updated 12 April 2013. Please report errors or omissions so that corrections may be made. If you can more precisely identify the name or location of anything depicted on a note, please share that information. Furthermore, if you own an unlisted type or variety, please submit scans of the front and back of the note so that it can be documented. Scans should be 300 dots per inch, 100% actual size, 24-bit color, saved as *uncompressed* JPEG files, and sent to owen@banknotenews.com. Be sure to fully describe all attributes of the note which are not apparent upon visual inspection of the images alone, such as physical dimension, watermark, and security thread.

Tajikistan

For earlier issues, see Russia.

Contents

National Bank of the Rep. of Tajikistan (NBRT).... 2063
National Bank of Tajikistan (NBT) 2065

Monetary System
10.05.1995: 1 Tajikistani ruble (TJR) = 100 tanga
30.10.2000: 1 Tajikistani somoni (TJS) = 100 diram

БОНКИ МИЛЛИИ ЧУМХУРИИ ТОЧИКИСТОН
(National Bank of the Republic of Tajikistan)

1994 Issues

NBRT B1 (P1): 1 ruble   VG   VF   UNC
Brown. Front: Coat of arms. Back: Majlisi Olii (Parliament) building with flag. No security thread. Watermark: Star pattern. Printer: (Goznak). 102 x 55 mm.
- a. 1994.   0.25   0.50   1
- as. Diagonal black *НАМУНА* overprint; all-zero s/n. — — —

NBRT B2 (P2): 5 rubles   VG   VF   UNC
Blue. Front: Coat of arms. Back: Majlisi Olii (Parliament) building with flag. No security thread. Watermark: Star pattern. Printer: (Goznak). 102 x 55 mm.
- a. 1994.   0.25   0.50   1
- as. Diagonal black *НАМУНА* overprint; all-zero s/n. — — —

NBRT B3 (P3): 10 rubles   VG   VF   UNC
Red. Front: Coat of arms. Back: Majlisi Olii (Parliament) building with flag. No security thread. Watermark: Star pattern. Printer: (Goznak). 102 x 55 mm.
- a. 1994.   0.25   0.50   1
- as. Diagonal black *НАМУНА* overprint; all-zero s/n. — — —

NBRT B4 (P4): 20 rubles   VG   VF   UNC
Purple. Front: Coat of arms. Back: Majlisi Olii (Parliament) building with flag. No security thread. Watermark: Star pattern. Printer: (Goznak). 102 x 55 mm.
- a. 1994.   0.25   0.50   1
- as. Diagonal black *НАМУНА* overprint; all-zero s/n. — — —

NBRT B5 (P5): 50 rubles   VG   VF   UNC
Green. Front: Coat of arms. Back: Majlisi Olii (Parliament) building with flag. No security thread. Watermark: Star pattern. Printer: (Goznak). 102 x 55 mm.
- a. 1994.   0.25   0.50   1
- as. Diagonal black *НАМУНА* overprint; all-zero s/n. — — —

NBRT B6 (P6): **100 rubles**   VG   VF   UNC
Gold. Front: Coat of arms. Back: Majlisi Olii (Parliament) building with flag. No security thread. Watermark: Star pattern. Printer: (Goznak). 120 x 60 mm.
   ☐ a.   1994.   0.25   0.50   1
   ☐ as.   Diagonal black *НАМУНА* overprint; normal s/n.   —   —   —

NBRT B7 (P7): **200 rubles**   VG   VF   UNC
Green. Front: Coat of arms. Back: Majlisi Olii (Parliament) building with flag. No security thread. Watermark: Star pattern. Printer: (Goznak). 120 x 60 mm.
   ☐ a.   1994.   0.25   0.50   1.50
   ☐ as.   Diagonal black *НАМУНА* overprint; normal s/n.   —   —   —

NBRT B8 (P8): **500 rubles**   VG   VF   UNC
Red. Front: Coat of arms. Back: Majlisi Olii (Parliament) building with flag. No security thread. Watermark: Star in wave pattern. Printer: (Goznak). 120 x 60 mm.
   ☐ a.   1994.   0.25   0.75   2.75
   ☐ as.   Diagonal black *НАМУНА* overprint; normal s/n.   —   —   —

NBRT B9 (P9): **1,000 rubles**   VG   VF   UNC
Peach. Front: Coat of arms. Back: Majlisi Olii (Parliament) building with flag. No security thread. Watermark: Star in wave pattern. Printer: (Goznak). 142 x 70 mm.
   ☐ a.   1994. Intro: 1999.   0.25   0.50   5
   ☐ as.   Diagonal black *НАМУНА* overprint; normal s/n.   —   —   —

NBRT B10 (P9A): **5,000 rubles**   VG   VF   UNC
Blue. Front: Coat of arms. Back: Majlisi Olii (Parliament) building with flag. No security thread. Watermark: Star in circle pattern. Printer: (Goznak). 142 x 70 mm.
   ☐ a.   1994. Unissued.   1.75   7   25
   ☐ as.   Diagonal black *ОБРАЗЕЦ* overprint; all-zero s/n.   —   —   —

1999 (2000) Issues

On 30 October 2000, Tajikistan introduced its new national currency, the somoni, named in honor of Ismoil Somoni (849-907), the founder of Samanids State, the first centralized state of Tajiks. The somoni replaced the Tajikistani ruble at the rate of 1 somoni = 1,000 rubles.

NBRT B11 (P9B): **10,000 rubles**   VG   VF   UNC
Pink. Front: Coat of arms. Back: Majlisi Olii (Parliament) building with flag. No security thread. Watermark: Star in circle pattern. Printer: (Goznak). 142 x 70 mm.
- a.   1994. Unissued.   2.50 10   40
- as. Diagonal black *НАМУНА* overprint; normal s/n.   —   —   —

БОНКИ МИЛЛИИ ТОЧИКИСТОН
(National Bank of Tajikistan)

For more information, visit www.nbt.tj.

NBT Signature Varieties

1	 РАИС (Chairman) Murodali Alimardon	 МУОВИНИ АВВАЛ (1st Vice-Governor) Sharif Rahimzoda
	ПРЕЗИДЕНТИ ТОЧИКИСТОН (Tajikistan President)	РАИСИ БОНКИ МИЛЛӢ (Governor)
2	Emmomali Rakhmonov	Murodali Alimardon
3	Emmomali Rakhmonov	Sharif Rahimzoda

NBT B1 (P10): **1 diram** (<US$0.01)   VG   VF   UNC
Brown. Front: Coat of arms; Sadriddin Ayni Theater and Opera House building. Back: Pamir mountains. Solid security thread printed *БМТ*. Watermark: Two mountains over rectangle (bank logo). Printer: (G&D). 110 x 60 mm.
- a.   1999. Signature 1. Intro: 30.10.2000.   FV   FV   1
- as. Diagonal red *SPECIMEN* overprint;   —   —   50
       horizontal red *SPECIMEN Nº* # ovpt at lower left.

NBT B2 (P11): **5 dirams** (US$0.01)   VG   VF   UNC
Blue. Front: Coat of arms; Culture Palace in Urunkhodjaev. Back: Sepulchre in Chiluchorchashma locality of Shahritus district. Solid security thread printed *БМТ*. Watermark: Two mountains over rectangle (bank logo). Printer: (G&D). 110 x 60 mm.
- a.   1999. Signature 1. Intro: 30.10.2000.   FV   FV   1
- as. Diagonal red *SPECIMEN* overprint;   —   —   50
       horizontal red *SPECIMEN Nº* # ovpt at lower left.

NBT B3 (P12): **20 dirams** (US$0.05)   VG   VF   UNC

Green. Front: Coat of arms; Meetings Hall of the National Bank of Tajikistan. Back: Mountain road. Solid security thread printed БМТ. Watermark: Two mountains over rectangle (bank logo). Printer: (G&D). 110 x 60 mm.

    ☐ a.   1999. Signature 1. Intro: 30.10.2000.   FV   FV   1
    ☐ as.   Diagonal red *SPECIMEN* overprint;   —   —   50
           horizontal red *SPECIMEN Nº* # ovpt at lower left.

NBT B4 (P13): **50 dirams** (US$0.10)   VG   VF   UNC

Purple. Front: Coat of arms; Ismoil Somoni horseback with shield and sword. Back: Mountain valley. Solid security thread printed БМТ. Watermark: Two mountains over rectangle (bank logo). Printer: (G&D). 110 x 60 mm.

    ☐ a.   1999. Signature 1. Intro: 30.10.2000.   FV   FV   1.25
    ☐ as.   Diagonal red *SPECIMEN* overprint;   —   —   50
           horizontal red *SPECIMEN Nº* # ovpt at lower left.

NBT B5 (P14 & P14A): **1 somoni** (US$0.20)   VG   VF   UNC

Green. Front: Coat of arms; map of Tajikistan; globe; Mirzo Tursunzoda, poet; bank logo as registration device. Back: Bank logo; National Bank of Tajikistan building; flag. Windowed security thread with demetalized БМТ. Watermark: Mirzo Tursunzoda. Printer: (G&D). 141 x 65 mm.

    ☐ a.   1999. Sig. 2. Two-tone globe. Intro: 30.10.2000.   FV   FV   1.25
    ☐ b.   Monochrome globe.   FV   FV   1.25
    ☐ as.   Diagonal red *SPECIMEN* overprint;   —   —   60
           horizontal red *SPECIMEN Nº* # ovpt at lower left.

On earlier 1-somoni notes, the globe at center front is green and orange (NBT B5a, left), but on later notes, the globe is all green (NBT B5b, right).

NBT B6 (P15): **5 somoni** (US$1.10)   VG   VF   UNC

Blue. Front: Coat of arms; desk, scroll, pen, and inkwell; Sadriddin Ayni, founder of Tajik modern literature; bank logo as registration device. Back: Bank logo; Tomb of Abuabdullo Rudaki in Panjakent district; flag. Windowed security thread with demetalized *БМТ*. Watermark: Sadriddin Ayni. Printer: (G&D). 144 x 65 mm.

- ☐ a. 1999. Signature 2.   FV   FV   4
  Central vignette in gray. Intro: 30.10.2000.
- ☐ b. Central vignette in blue. Intro: 2010.   FV   FV   4
- ☐ as. Diagonal red *SPECIMEN* overprint;   —   —   60
  horizontal red *SPECIMEN Nº #* ovpt at lower left.

On earlier 5-somoni notes, the desk, scroll, pen, and inkwell at center front are gray (NBT B6a, left), but on later notes, these items are blue (NBT B6b, right).

NBT B7 (P16): **10 somoni** (US$2.15)   VG   VF   UNC

Red, yellow, and orange. Front: Coat of arms; scroll, pen, and inkwell; Mir Said Ali Hamadoni, thinker and poet; bank logo as registration device. Back: Bank logo; Tomb of Mir Said Ali Hamadoni in Kulob town; flag. Windowed security thread with demetalized *БМТ*. Watermark: Mir Said Ali Hamadoni. Printer: (G&D). 147 x 65 mm.

- ☐ a. 1999. Signature 2. Intro: 30.10.2000.   FV   FV   6.50
- ☐ as. Diagonal red *SPECIMEN* overprint;   —   —   65
  horizontal red *SPECIMEN Nº #* ovpt at lower left.

NBT B8 (P17): **20 somoni** (US$4.30)   VG   VF   UNC

Brown. Front: Coat of arms; snake and flowers; Abuali ibn Sino (Avicenna), great scientist, encyclopaedist of the Tajik people; bank logo as registration device. Back: Bank logo; Hissar Castle; flag. Holographic stripe. Windowed security thread with demetalized *БМТ*. Watermark: Abuali ibn Sino. Printer: (G&D). 150 x 65 mm.

- ☐ a. 1999. Signature 2. Intro: 30.10.2000.   FV   FV   15
- ☐ b. Last 3-digits of s/n laser-etched into stripe.   FV   FV   15
- ☐ as. Diagonal red *SPECIMEN* overprint;   —   —   65
  horizontal red *SPECIMEN Nº #* ovpt at lower left.

On 5 March 2013, the 20-, 50-, 100-, and 200-somoni notes were issued with the last three digits of the serial number laser-etched into the adjacent holographic stripe. The original 20-somoni note (NBT B8a, left) without etching, and revised note (B8b, right) with etching.

2001 Numismatic Products

In December 2001, Moscow hosted an exhibition called the Day of Tajikistan. The National Bank of Tajikistan produced these sets of notes for the occasion.

NBT B9 (P18): **50 somoni** (US$11)   VG   VF   UNC

Blue. Front: Coat of arms; flowers and book, ТОЧИКОН; Bobojon Gafurov, scientist, politician, and statesman; bank logo as registration device. Back: Bank logo; "Sino" Chaikhana in Isfara district; flag. Holographic stripe. Windowed security thread with demetalized БМТ. Watermark: Bobojon Gafurov. Printer: (G&D). 153 x 65 mm.

- a. 1999. Signature 2. Intro: 30.10.2000.   FV   FV   30
- b. Last 3-digits of s/n laser-etched into stripe.   FV   FV   30
- as. Diagonal red SPECIMEN overprint; horizontal red SPECIMEN Nº # ovpt at lower left.   —   —   65

NBT B10 (P19): **100 somoni** (US$22)   VG   VF   UNC

Brown. Front: Coat of arms; Ismoil Somoni, founder of the first centralized state; bank logo as registration device. Back: Bank logo; Presidential Palace in Dushanbe; flag. Holographic stripe. Windowed security thread with demetalized БМТ. Watermark: Bobojon Gafurov. Printer: (G&D). 156 x 65 mm.

- a. 1999. Signature 2. Intro: 30.10.2000.   FV   FV   60
- b. Last 3-digits of s/n laser-etched into stripe.   FV   FV   60
- as. Diagonal red SPECIMEN overprint; horizontal red SPECIMEN Nº # ovpt at lower left.   —   —   70

NBT BNP1 (PNL): **1 - 10,000 rubles**   UNC
- a. NBRT B1-B11 (11 notes). Intro: December 2001.   —

NBT BNP2 (PNL): **1 diram - 100 somoni**   UNC
- a. NBT B1-B10 (10 notes). Intro: December 2001.   —

2010 Issues

NBT B11 (P20): **3 somoni** (US$0.65) VG VF UNC
Violet. Front: Coat of arms; open book with pen; Shirinsho Shotemur, hero statesman; bank logo as registration device. Back: Bank logo; Majlisi Oli (parliament) building in Dushanbe; flag. Windowed security thread with demetalized БМТ. Watermark: Shirinsho Shotemur. Printer: Unknown. 141 x 65 mm.

    a. 2010. Signature 3. Intro: 10.09.2010. FV FV 1

NBT B12 (P21): **200 somoni** (US$43) VG VF UNC
Brown and yellow. Front: Coat of arms; building with red flag; Nusratullo Makhsum, hero statesman; bank logo as registration device. Back: Bank logo; National Library building in Dushanbe; pen, inkwell, and candlestick; flag. Holographic stripe. Windowed security thread with demetalized БМТ. Watermark: Nusratullo Makhsum. Printer: Unknown. 159 x 68 mm.

    a. 2010. Signature 3. Intro: 10.09.2010. FV FV 90
    Last 3-digits of s/n laser-etched into stripe.

NBT B13 (P22): **500 somoni** (US$108) VG VF UNC
Purple and gray. Front: Coat of arms; Abuabdullo Rudaki, founder of Tajik classic literature; bank logo as registration device. Back: Bank logo; Palace of Nations in Dushanbe; flag. Holographic stripe. varifeye thread and windowed security thread with demetalized БМТ. Watermark: Abuabdullo Rudaki. Printer: (G&D). 162 x 71 mm.

    a. 2010. Signature 3. Intro: 10.09.2010. FV FV 300

1999 (2012) Issues

These notes are like the preceding issues, but with a holographic Kinegram stripe at right front, portraits shifted to the left, and smaller central vignettes.

NBT B14 (PNL): **5 somoni** (US$1.10) VG VF UNC
Blue. Front: Coat of arms; desk, scroll, pen, and inkwell; Sadriddin Ayni, founder of Tajik modern literature; bank logo as registration device. Back: Bank logo; Tomb of Abuabdullo Rudaki in Panjakent district; flag. Holographic stripe. Windowed security thread with demetalized БМТ. Watermark: Sadriddin Ayni. Printer: (G&D). 144 x 65 mm.

    a. 1999. Signature 2. Intro: 27.12.2012. FV FV 4

NBT B15 (PNL): **10 somoni** (US$2.15) VG VF UNC
Red, yellow, and orange. Front: Coat of arms; scroll, pen, and inkwell; Mir Said Ali Hamadoni, thinker and poet; bank logo as registration device. Back: Bank logo; Tomb of Mir Said Ali Hamadoni in Kulob town; flag. Holographic stripe. Windowed security thread with demetalized БМТ. Watermark: Mir Said Ali Hamadoni. Printer: (G&D). 147 x 65 mm.
☐ a. 1999. Signature 2. Intro: 27.12.2012.   FV   FV   6.50

Acknowledgements

This chapter was compiled with the generous assistance of Thomas Augustsson, Hartmut Fraunhoffer (www.banknoten.de), Mikhail Istomin, Peter Kelly, Chris Kropinski, Gianni Lorenzoli, Claudio Marana, Wally Myers, Alexander Petrov, Mikhail "Mike" Prizov, Gergely Scheidl (banknoteshop@gmx.net), Christoph Thomas, and others.

Sources

Cuhaj, George S. *Standard Catalog of World Paper Money, Modern Issues, 1961-Present*. 19th edition. 2013. ISBN 978-1-4402-3571-9. Krause Publications (www.krausebooks.com), 700 East State St., Iola, WI, 54990-0001.

Share Your Input, Info, and Images

This catalog is believed to be complete and correct as of the time of publication. Prices and face values were last updated 24 June 2011. Please report errors or omissions so that corrections may be made. If you can more precisely identify the name or location of anything depicted on a note, please share that information. Furthermore, if you own an unlisted type or variety, please submit scans of the front and back of the note so that it can be documented. Scans should be 300 dots per inch, 100% actual size, 24-bit color, saved as *uncompressed* JPEG files, and sent to owen@banknotenews.com. Be sure to fully describe all attributes of the note which are not apparent upon visual inspection of the images alone, such as physical dimension, watermark, and security thread.

Tangier

For earlier issues, see Morocco.

Contents

Servicios Municipales (SM) 2071
Junta de Servicios Municipales (JSM) 2072

Monetary System
1 franc = 100 centimes

Servicios Municipales (Municipal Services)

Tangier was made an international zone under the joint administration of Britain, France, and Spain under an international convention signed in Paris on 18 December 1923. During World War II, Spanish troops occupied Tangier on 14 June 1940, the same day Paris fell to the Germans. The Spanish regime of Francisco Franco publicly considered the occupation a temporary wartime measure. The territory was restored to its pre-war status on 11 October 1945.

The Serie A and B emergency issue notes (dated August 1941 and March 1942) were issued by Servicios Municipales (SM) whereas the Serie C notes (dated October 1942) were issued by Junta de Servicios Municipales (JSM). All text on the notes is in Spanish.

SM Signature Varieties

1941-1942 Emergency Issues

These notes have the issuer as Servicios Municipales (SM) in the design on the front of the notes as well as the text and middle signature title on the back.

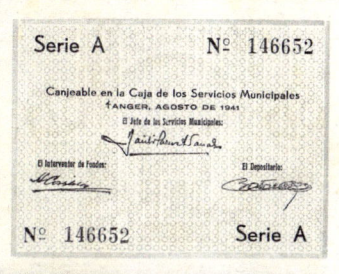

SM B1 (P1): 0.25 francos   Good   Fine   XF
Blue. Front: 5-pointed Moroccan star. Back: Serial numbers; redemption text; signatures. No security thread. Watermark: None. Printer: Unknown. 95 x 71 mm.
- a. AGOSTO DE 1941. Signature 1.   550   1,350   —
- b. MARZO 1942. Signature 2.   650   1,500   —

SM B2 (P2): 0.50 francos   Good   Fine   XF
Brown. Front: 5-pointed Moroccan star. Back: Serial numbers; redemption text; signatures. No security thread. Watermark: None. Printer: Unknown. 90 x 71 mm.
- a. AGOSTO DE 1941. Signature 1.   550   1,250   —
- b. MARZO 1942. Signature 2.   650   1,500   —

SM B3 (P3): 1 franco   Good   Fine   XF
Purple. Front: 5-pointed Moroccan star. Back: Serial numbers; redemption text; signatures. No security thread. Watermark: None. Printer: Unknown. 105 x 71 mm.
- a. AGOSTO DE 1941. Signature 1.   550   1,350   3,000
- b. MARZO 1942. Signature 2.   650   1,500   —

SM B4 (P4): 2 francos   Good   Fine   XF
Orange. Front: 5-pointed Moroccan star. Back: Serial numbers; redemption text; signatures. No security thread. Watermark: None. Printer: Unknown. 100 x 71 mm.
- a. AGOSTO DE 1941. Signature 1.   650   1,500   —
- b. MARZO 1942. Signature 2.   —   —   —

Junta de Servicios Municipales (Municipal Services Board)

The Serie C notes (dated October 1942) were issued by Junta de Servicios Municipales (JSM).

JSM Signature Varieties

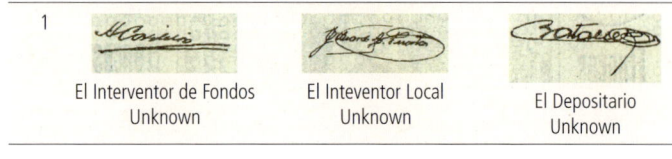

1   El Interventor de Fondos Unknown   El Inteventor Local Unknown   El Depositario Unknown

1942 Emergency Issues

These notes are like the preceding issues, but have the issuer as Junta de Servicios Municipales (JSM) in the design on the front of the notes, and have changes to the text and middle signature title on the back.

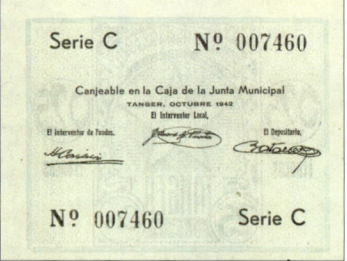

JSM B1 (P1): 0.25 francos   Good   Fine   XF
Blue. Front: 5-pointed Moroccan star. Back: Serial numbers; redemption text; signatures. No security thread. Watermark: None. Printer: Unknown. 95 x 71 mm.
- a. OCTUBRE 1942. Signature 1.   550   1,350   3,150

 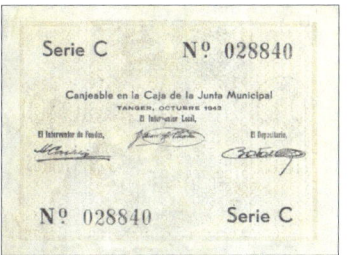

JSM B2 (P2): 0.50 francos   Good   Fine   XF
Brown. Front: 5-pointed Moroccan star. Back: Serial numbers; redemption text; signatures. No security thread. Watermark: None. Printer: Unknown. 90 x 71 mm.
    ☐ a.   OCTUBRE 1942. Signature 1.   550   1,000   —

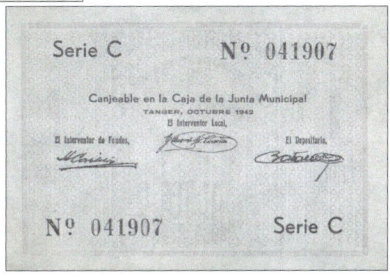

JSM B3 (P3): 1 franco   Good   Fine   XF
Purple. Front: 5-pointed Moroccan star. Back: Serial numbers; redemption text; signatures. No security thread. Watermark: None. Printer: Unknown. 105 x 71 mm.
    ☐ a.   OCTUBRE 1942. Signature 1.   550   1,350   —

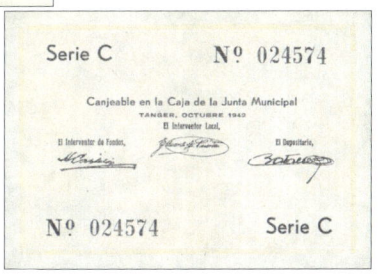

JSM B4 (P4): 2 francos   Good   Fine   XF
Orange. Front: 5-pointed Moroccan star. Back: Serial numbers; redemption text; signatures. No security thread. Watermark: None. Printer: Unknown. 100 x 71 mm.
    ☐ a.   OCTUBRE 1942. Signature 1.   650   1,500   —

Looking Forward

Tangier was restored to its pre-war status on 11 October 1945. Tangier joined with the rest of Morocco following the restoration of full sovereignty in 1956. For later issues, see Morocco.

Acknowledgements

This chapter was compiled with the generous assistance of Detlef Hilmer (detlef_hilmer@web.de), Don Ludwig, and others.

Sources

Cuhaj, George S. *Standard Catalog of World Paper Money, General Issues, 1368-1960*. 14th edition. 2012. ISBN 978-1-4402-3090-5. Krause Publications (www.krausebooks.com), 700 East State St., Iola, WI, 54990-0001.

Muszynski, Maurice and Maurice Kolsky. *Les Billets du Maghreb et du Levant*. Volume 11. 2002. Éditions Victor Gadoury, 57, rue Grimaldi, MC-98000 Monaco. ISBN 2-906602-18-3.

Share Your Input, Info, and Images

This catalog is believed to be complete and correct as of the time of publication. Prices and face values were last updated 14 June 2013. Please report errors or omissions so that corrections may be made. If you can more precisely identify the name or location of anything depicted on a note, please share that information. Furthermore, if you own an unlisted type or variety, please submit scans of the front and back of the note so that it can be documented. Scans should be 300 dots per inch, 100% actual size, 24-bit color, saved as *uncompressed* JPEG files, and sent to owen@banknotenews.com. Be sure to fully describe all attributes of the note which are not apparent upon visual inspection of the images alone, such as physical dimension, watermark, and security thread.

Tanzania

For earlier issues, see East Africa and Zanzibar.

Monetary System
1 Tanzanian shilling (TZS) = 100 senti

Bank of Tanzania

Following the decision to dissolve the East African Currency Board (EACB) and to establish separate central banks in Tanzania, Kenya, and Uganda, the Bank of Tanzania Act, 1965, was passed by the National Assembly in December 1965, and the Bank of Tanzania (BOT) was opened on 14 June 1966.

For more information, visit www.BOT-tz.org.

BOT Signature Varieties

	MINISTER FOR FINANCE or WAZIRI WA FEDHA	GOVERNOR or GAVANA
1	Amir Jamal	Edwin I. Mtei (1966 - 1974)
2	Cleopa David Msuya	Edwin I. Mtei (1966 - 1974)
3	Cleopa D. Msuya	Charles Nyirabu (1974 - 1989)
4	Amir Jamal	Charles Nyirabu (1974 - 1989)
5	Edwin I. M. Mtei	Charles Nyirabu (1974 - 1989)
6	Amir Jamal	Charles Nyirabu (1974 - 1989)
7	Cleopa David Msuya	Gilman Rutihinda (1989 - 1993)

BOT Signature Varieties

	MINISTER FOR FINANCE or WAZIRI WA FEDHA	GOVERNOR or GAVANA
8	Stephen A. Kibona	Gilman Rutihinda (1989 - 1993)
9	Ali Kigoma Malima	Gilman Rutihinda (1989 - 1993)
10	Ali Kigoma Malima	Idris M. Rashidi (1993 - 1998)
11	Jakaya Mrisho Kikwete	Idris M. Rashidi (1993 - 1998)
12	Simon Mbilinyi	Idris M. Rashidi (1993 - 1998)
13	Daniel Yona	Daudi T. S. Ballali (1998 - 08.01.2008)
14	Basil P. Mramba	Daudi T. S. Ballali (1998 - 08.01.2008)
15	Mustafa Mkulo (WAZIRI WA FEDHA)	Benno Ndulu (08.01.2008 - present)

1966 Issues

Tanzania came into being on 26 April 1964, with the merger of the mainland territory of Tanganyika—which had gained its independence from the United Kingdom in late 1961—and the former sultanate of Zanzibar, an archipelago in the Indian Ocean.

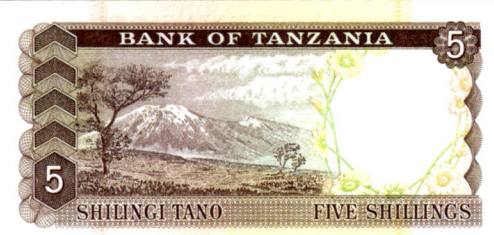

BOT B1 (P1): **5 shillings** (<US$0.01)   VG   VF   UNC

Brown. Front: Flowers; coat of arms; first president, Julius Kambarage Nyerere; palm tree. Back: Trees; Mount Kilimanjaro; clouds; flowers. Solid security thread. Watermark: Giraffe head. Printer: (TDLR). 139 x 65 mm.

☐	a.	No date. Sig. 1. Prefix A - BL. Intro: 14.06.1966.	1	4	15
☐	as.	Diagonal red *SPECIMEN* overprint.	—	—	25

Replacement notes: Prefix ZZ and ZY.

BOT B2 (P2): **10 shillings** (<US$0.01)   VG   VF   UNC

Brown. Front: Laurel leaves; coat of arms; first president, Julius Kambarage Nyerere; palm tree. Back: Drying sisal in a field; laurel leaves. Solid security thread. Watermark: Giraffe head. Printer: (TDLR). 145 x 70 mm.

☐	a.	No date. Intro: 14.06.1966. Signature 1. Prefix A - AR.	1	4	15
☐	b.	Signature 2. Prefix BL - CL.	2.50	10	40
☐	c.	Signature 3. Prefix CM - CR.	7.50	30	225
☐	d.	Signature 4. Prefix CS - DA.	0.50	2.50	10
☐	e.	Signature 5. Prefix DE - DL.	0.50	2.50	10
☐	as.	Diagonal red *SPECIMEN* overprint.	—	—	25

Replacement notes: Prefix ZZ and ZY.

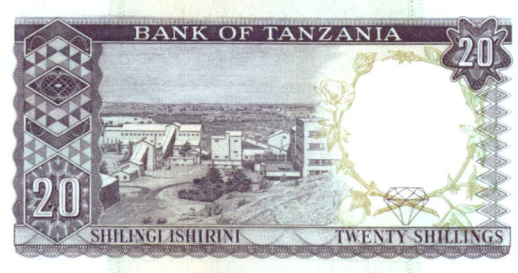

BOT B3 (P3): **20 shillings** (US$0.01)   VG   VF   UNC

Purple. Front: Flowers; coat of arms; first president, Julius Kambarage Nyerere; palm tree. Back: Mine buildings; diamond; flowers. Solid security thread. Watermark: Giraffe head. Printer: (TDLR). 149 x 76 mm.

☐	a.	No date. Intro: 14.06.1966. Signature 1. Prefix A - AV.	0.75	3	12
☐	b.	Signature 2. Prefix BA - BM.	0.75	3	12
☐	c.	Signature 3. Prefix BR - CF.	0.75	3	12
☐	d.	Signature 4. Prefix CH - CP.	0.75	3	12
☐	e.	Signature 5. Prefix CS - DB.	0.75	3	12
☐	as.	Diagonal red *SPECIMEN* overprint.	—	—	25

Replacement notes: Prefix ZZ and ZY.

BOT B4 (P4): **100 shillings** (US$0.05)   VG   VF   UNC

Red. Front: Coffee beans and leaves; coat of arms; first president, Julius Kambarage Nyerere; palm tree. Back: Cattle; Maasai herdsman with spear; coffee berries and leaves. Solid security thread. Watermark: Giraffe head. Printer: (TDLR). 156 x 83 mm.

☐	a.	No date. Sig. 1. Prefix A - E. Intro: 14.06.1966.	30	125	500
☐	as.	Diagonal red *SPECIMEN* overprint.	—	—	85

Replacement notes: Prefix ZZ and ZY.

In keeping with Nyerere's attempt to form a multi-cultural, non-racial, and non-tribalist society, the Maasai herdsman on the back of BOT B4 was replaced by wildlife on B5.

BOT B5 (P5): **100 shillings** (US$0.05)   VG   VF   UNC

Red. Front: Coffee beans and leaves; coat of arms; first president, Julius Kambarage Nyerere; palm tree. Back: Two lions in tree; three giraffes; coffee berries and leaves. Solid security thread. Watermark: Giraffe head. Printer: (TDLR). 156 x 83 mm.

- a. No date. Intro: late-1966.   25   100   400
  Signature 1. Prefix A - K.
- b. Signature 3. Prefix L - T.   20   75   300
- as. Diagonal red *SPECIMEN* and DLR oval ovpts; horizontal red *SPECIMEN Nº* # ovpt at lower left; punched.   —   —   —

Replacement notes: Prefix ZZ and ZY.

Benki Kuu Ya Tanzania (Bank of Tanzania)

1977-1978 Issues

These notes are like the first series, with an updated portrait of President Nyerere and the name of the issuing authority changed from English to Swahili *(BANK OF TANZANIA* is now *BENKI KUU YA TANZANIA)*. The signature titles also changed from English to Swahili *(MINISTER OF FINANCE* and *GOVERNOR* are now *WAZIRI WA FEDHA* and *GAVANA*, respectively). Note that signature 3 was reused after signature 6 and is therefore assigned a later variety letter.

BOT B6 (P6): **10 shillings** (<US$0.01)   VG   VF   UNC

Green. Front: Torch; coat of arms; first president, Julius Kambarage Nyerere. Back: Sculpture; Uhura (Peace) monument in Arusha; Mount Kilimanjaro; map of Tanzania with islands; torch. Solid security thread. Watermark: Giraffe head. Printer: (TDLR). 143 x 70 mm.

- a. No date. Intro: 1978.   0.75   3   12
  Signature 5. Prefix A - BU.
- b. Signature 6. Prefix CS - GA.   0.25   0.75   3
- c. Signature 3. Prefix GQ - HS.   0.25   0.75   3
- as. Diagonal red *SPECIMEN* overprint.   —   —   —
- cs. Diagonal red *SPECIMEN* and DLR oval ovpts; horizontal red *SPECIMEN Nº* # ovpt at lower left; punched.   —   —   —

Replacement notes: Prefix ZZ and ZY.

BOT B7 (P7): **20 shillings** (US$0.01)   VG   VF   UNC

Blue. Front: Torch; coat of arms; first president, Julius Kambarage Nyerere. Back: Worker with cotton knitting machine; map of Tanzania with islands; torch. Solid security thread. Watermark: Giraffe head. Printer: (TDLR). 149 x 76 mm.

- a. No date. Intro: 1978.   1.25   5   20
  Signature 5. Prefix A - BS.
- b. Signature 6. Prefix CH - FC.   0.50   2   8
- c. Signature 3. Prefix FX - FY.   0.50   2   8
- as. Diagonal red *SPECIMEN* overprint.   —   —   —

Replacement notes: Prefix ZZ and ZY.

BOT B8 (P8): **100 shillings** (US$0.05)   VG   VF   UNC

Red. Front: Torch; coat of arms; first president, Julius Kambarage Nyerere. Back: Students reading books in library; boy with hoe and girl with tool; map of Tanzania with islands; village; torch. Solid security thread. Watermark: Giraffe head. Printer: (TDLR). 156 x 83 mm.

☐	a.	No date. Intro: 1977. Signature 4. Prefix A - T.	2	8	30
☐	b.	Signature 5. Prefix Y - BN.	2	8	30
☐	c.	Signature 6. Prefix BR - GA.	1.25	5	20
☐	d.	Signature 3. Prefix GA - GL.	0.50	2.50	10
☐	as.	Diagonal red *SPECIMEN* overprint.	—	—	70

Replacement notes: Prefix ZZ and ZY.

1985 Issues

These notes caused an uproar when issued because the map on the back does not include the islands of Mafia, Pemba, and Zanzibar off the east coast of Tanzania where they belong.

BOT B9 (P9): **20 shillings** (US$0.01)   VG   VF   UNC

Purple. Front: Torch; coat of arms; first president, Julius Kambarage Nyerere. Back: Workers and machines in tire factory; map of Tanzania without islands; torch. Solid security thread. Watermark: Giraffe head. Printer: (TDLR). 140 x 70 mm.

    ☐ a. No date. Signature 3. Prefix A - CL. Intro: 1985.   0.50   2   8

Replacement notes: Prefix ZZ and ZY.

BOT B10 (P10): **50 shillings** (<US$0.05)   VG   VF   UNC

Reddish orange. Front: Torch; coat of arms; first president, Julius Kambarage Nyerere. Back: Workers making mud bricks and laying them out to dry; map of Tanzania without islands; torch. Solid security thread. Watermark: Giraffe head. Printer: (TDLR). 144 x 70 mm.

    ☐ a. No date. Signature 3. Prefix A - BB. Intro: 1985.   0.25   1.50   5

Replacement notes: Prefix ZZ and ZY.

BOT B11 (P11): **100 shillings** (US$0.05)   VG   VF   UNC

Blue, purple, and green. Front: Torch; coat of arms; first president, Julius Kambarage Nyerere. Back: University of Dar es Salaam campus buildings on Observation Hill; students in graduation procession; map of Tanzania without islands; torch. Solid security thread. Watermark: Giraffe head. Printer: (TDLR). 150 x 76 mm.

    ☐ a. No date. Signature 3. Prefix A - GM. Intro: 1985.   1   4   15

Replacement notes: Prefix ZZ and ZY.

1986 Issues

These notes are identical to the preceding issues, except on the back the word *TANZANIA* was shifted to the left so as to reveal the islands of Mafia, Pemba, and Zanzibar, which were added to the map.

On 1985 issues, *TANZANIA* covered the map (BOT B9a, left), but on 1986 issues, the name was moved and the islands of Mafia, Pemba, and Zanzibar were added (BOT B12a, right).

BOT B12 (P12): **20 shillings** (US$0.01)   VG   VF   UNC
Purple. Front: Torch; coat of arms; first president, Julius Kambarage Nyerere. Back: Workers and machines in tire factory; map of Tanzania with islands; torch. Solid security thread. Watermark: Giraffe head. Printer: (TDLR). 140 x 70 mm.
   ☐ a. No date. Sig. 3. Prefix CR - DC. Intro: 1986.   —   0.50   2
Replacement notes: Prefix ZZ and ZY.

BOT B13 (P13): **50 shillings** (<US$0.05)   VG   VF   UNC
Reddish orange. Front: Torch; coat of arms; first president, Julius Kambarage Nyerere. Back: Workers making mud bricks and laying them out to dry; map of Tanzania with islands; torch. Solid security thread. Watermark: Giraffe head. Printer: (TDLR). 144 x 70 mm.
   ☐ a. No date. Signature 3. Prefix BK - BX. Intro: 1986.   0.25   1   3.50
Replacement notes: Prefix ZZ and ZY.

BOT B14 (P14): **100 shillings** (US$0.05)   VG   VF   UNC
Blue, purple, and green. Front: Torch; coat of arms; first president, Julius Kambarage Nyerere. Back: University of Dar es Salaam campus buildings on Observation Hill; students in graduation procession; map of Tanzania with islands; torch. Solid security thread. Watermark: Giraffe head. Printer: (TDLR). 150 x 76 mm.
   ☐ a. No date. Intro: 1986.   0.50   2   8
           Signature 3. Prefix HB - NV.
   ☐ b. Signature 8. Prefix PK - QC.   0.25   1   5
Replacement notes: Prefix ZZ and ZY.

1986-1987 Issues

The portrait on the front of these notes has changed to that of Ali Hassan Mwinyi, who took office as Tanzania's second president on 5 November 1985.

BOT B15 (P15): **20 shillings** (US$0.01)   VG   VF   UNC
Purple. Front: Torch; coat of arms; second president, Ali Hassan Mwinyi. Back: Workers and machines in tire factory; map of Tanzania with islands; torch. Solid security thread. Watermark: Giraffe head. Printer: (TDLR). 140 x 70 mm.
- a. No date. Sig. 3. Prefix DG - GA. Intro: 1987.   0.25   1   4

Replacement notes: Prefix ZZ and ZY.

BOT B16 (P16): **50 shillings** (<US$0.05)   VG   VF   UNC
Reddish orange. Front: Torch; coat of arms; second president, Ali Hassan Mwinyi. Back: Workers making mud bricks and laying them out to dry; map of Tanzania with islands; torch. Solid security thread. Watermark: Giraffe head. Printer: (TDLR). 144 x 70 mm.
- a. No date. Intro: 1986.   0.50   2   8
  Signature 3. Prefix CA - CM.
- b. Signature 7. Prefix DC - DJ.   0.50   2   8

Replacement notes: Prefix ZZ and ZY.

BOT B17 (P18): **200 shillings** (US$0.15)   VG   VF   UNC
Brown, tan, and orange. Front: Torch; coat of arms; second president, Ali Hassan Mwinyi. Back: Two men in shallow water carrying fish; boats; map of Tanzania with islands; torch. Solid security thread. Watermark: Giraffe head. Printer: (TDLR). 156 x 83 mm.
- a. No date. Intro: 1986.   0.50   2.50   10
  Signature 3. Prefix AA - EB.
- b. Signature 7. Prefix EX - FZ.   1.25   5   20

Replacement notes: Prefix ZZ and ZY.

1990-1992 Issues

The 50- and 200-shilling notes are like the preceding issues, except that the portrait on the front is slightly different. New higher-denomination notes were issued for the first time to keep up with inflation which flourished under Mwinyi's administration.

BOT B18 (P19): **50 shillings** (<US$0.05)   VG   VF   UNC
Reddish orange. Front: Torch; coat of arms; second president, Ali Hassan Mwinyi. Back: Workers making mud bricks and laying them out to dry; map of Tanzania with islands; torch. Solid security thread. Watermark: Giraffe head. Printer: (TDLR). 144 x 70 mm.
- a. No date. Sig. 8. Prefix DQ - EK. Intro: 1992.   0.50   2   8
- as. Diagonal red *SPECIMEN* overprint;   —   —   —
  horizontal red *SPECIMEN* Nº # ovpt at lower left.

Replacement notes: Prefix ZZ and ZY.

Tanzania 1990-1992 Issues

BOT B19 (P20): **200 shillings** (US$0.15) VG VF UNC

Brown, tan, and orange. Front: Torch; coat of arms; second president, Ali Hassan Mwinyi. Back: Two men in shallow water carrying fish; boats; map of Tanzania with islands; torch. Solid security thread. Watermark: Giraffe head. Printer: (TDLR). 156 x 83 mm.

- ☐ a. No date. Intro: 1992. — — —
  Signature 7. Prefix unknown.
- ☐ b. Signature 8. Prefix GQ - JT. 0.50 1.50 6

Replacement notes: Prefix ZZ and ZY.

Shadows are easily seen under President Mwinyi's collar on BOT B17 (top), but are less evident on the revised portrait on BOT B19 (bottom).

BOT B20 (P21): **500 shillings** (US$0.30) VG VF UNC

Blue, pink, and orange. Front: Zebra; coat of arms; second president, Ali Hassan Mwinyi. Back: Seated woman with basket; five workers harvesting clove tree; coffee berries. Solid security thread. Watermark: Giraffe head. Printer: (TDLR). 163 x 87 mm.

- ☐ a. No date. Intro: 1992. 2.25 8.50 35
  Signature 3. Prefix AA - BR.
- ☐ b. Signature 7. Prefix BU - DE. 2 8 30
  Thread printed *BENKI KUU YA TANZANIA*.
- ☐ c. Signature 8. Prefix DM - FA. 1.25 5 20

Replacement notes: Prefix ZZ and ZY.

Clove tree harvesting is featured on the back of this note as an apology to Zanzibar and Pemba for omitting them from the map on the back of B9-11. The islands provided most of Tanzania's export earnings through tourism and cloves in the 1970s and 1980s.

BOT B21 (P22): **1,000 shillings** (US$0.60) VG VF UNC

Green, purple; and rust. Front: Two elephants; coat of arms; second president, Ali Hassan Mwinyi. Back: Factory buildings; plant; ancient carved door to People's Bank of Zanzibar. Solid security thread with printed *BENKI KUU YA TANZANIA*. Watermark: Giraffe head. Printer: (TDLR). 167 x 91 mm.

- ☐ a. No date. Signature 8. Prefix AA - BH. Intro: 1990. 2 8 30

Replacement notes: Prefix ZZ and ZY.

1993-1995 Issues

These notes are similar to the preceding issues, except their sizes have been reduced, new animals have been added at left on the front, and the backs have been simplified.

BOT B22 (P23): **50 shillings** (<US$0.05) VG VF UNC
Red and brown. Front: Grazing wildebeest; coat of arms; second president, Ali Hassan Mwinyi. Back: Workers making mud bricks and laying them out to dry. Solid security thread. Watermark: None. Printer: (TDLR). 128 x 62 mm.
    ☐ a. No date. Sig. 9. Prefix EQ - EW. Intro: 1993.   FV   FV   4
Replacement notes: Prefix ZZ and ZY.

BOT B23 (P24): **100 shillings** (US$0.05) VG VF UNC
Blue, purple, and brown. Front: Kudu; coat of arms; first president, Julius Kambarage Nyerere. Back: University of Dar es Salaam campus buildings on Observation Hill; students in graduation procession. Solid security thread. Watermark: None. Printer: (TDLR). 132 x 65 mm.
    ☐ a. No date. Signature 9. Prefix QF - QY. Intro: 1993.   0.50   1.75   7
Replacement notes: Prefix ZZ and ZY.
This note marks the 70th birthday of President Nyerere (born 13.04.1922).

BOT B24 (P25): **200 shillings** (withdrawn 30.09.2003) VG VF UNC
Brown, tan, and orange. Front: Leopard with two cubs; coat of arms; second president, Ali Hassan Mwinyi. Back: Two men in shallow water carrying fish; boats. Solid security thread. Watermark: None. Printer: (TDLR). 135 x 67 mm.
    ☐ a. No date. Intro: 25.05.1993.   0.25   1   4
           Signature 9. Prefix KM - LX.
    ☐ b. Signature 11. Prefix MD - ST.   0.25   0.75   3
    ☐ as. Diagonal red *SPECIMEN* overprint;   —   —   150
           horizontal red *SPECIMEN N^o #* ovpt at lower left.
Replacement notes: Prefix ZZ and ZY.

BOT B25 (P26): **500 shillings** (US$0.30) VG VF UNC
Purple, green, and orange. Front: Zebra; torch; coat of arms; second president, Ali Hassan Mwinyi. Back: Seated woman with basket; five workers harvesting clove tree; torch; coffee berries. Solid security thread with printed *BENKI KUU YA TANZANIA*. Watermark: Giraffe head. Printer: (TDLR). 138 x 69 mm.
    ☐ a. No date. Intro: 1993.   0.50   2.50   10
           Signature 9. Prefix FG - GT.
    ☐ b. Signature 10. Prefix HA - LH.   0.25   1.25   5
    ☐ c. Signature 11. Prefix MG - NF.   0.25   1.25   5
Replacement notes: Prefix ZZ and ZY.

BOT B26 (P27): **1,000 shillings** (US$0.60)   VG   VF   UNC

Green, brown, and red. Front: Two elephants; coat of arms; second president, Ali Hassan Mwinyi. Back: Factory buildings; plant; ancient carved door to People's Bank of Zanzibar. Solid security thread with printed *BENKI KUU YA TANZANIA*. Watermark: Giraffe head. Printer: (TDLR). 142 x 71 mm.

   ☐ a.   No date. Intro: 1993.   1   4   15
          Signature 9. Prefix BT - CU.
   ☐ b.   Signature 10. Prefix DD - GX.   0.50   2.50   10
   ☐ c.   Signature 11. Prefix HA - JK.   0.50   1.75   7

Replacement notes: Prefix ZZ and ZY.

BOT B27 (P28): **5,000 shillings** (US$3.15)   VG   VF   UNC

Brown and yellow. Front: Rhinoceros; coat of arms; second president, Ali Hassan Mwinyi. Back: Six giraffes; Mount Kilimanjaro; chest. Windowed security thread. Watermark: Giraffe head. Printer: (TDLR). 145 x 73 mm.

   ☐ a.   No date. Sig. 10. Prefix AA - BB. Intro: 1995.   FV   5   20

Replacement notes: Prefix ZZ and ZY.

BOT B28 (P29): **10,000 shillings** (US$6.30)   VG   VF   UNC

Blue and red. Front: Lion; coat of arms; second president, Ali Hassan Mwinyi. Back: Bank of Tanzania headquarters building in Dar es Salaam; House of Wonders (Beit el Ajaib) building in Zanzibar. Windowed security thread. Watermark: Giraffe head. Printer: (TDLR). 149 x 75 mm.

   ☐ a.   No date. Sig. 10. Prefix AA - BC. Intro: 1995.   FV   FV   25

Replacement notes: Prefix ZZ and ZY.

1997 Issues

Following the end of Ali Hassan Mwinyi's term as president on 23 November 1995, his portrait was replaced by an illustration of a giraffe head on the front of these new notes. To the right of the giraffe are tactile marks for the sight impaired. These notes are confirmed to have been printed by Gieseck & Devrient, which has been supplying BOT with notes since June 1996.

BOT B29 (P30): **500 shillings** (withdrawn 30.09.2003)   VG   VF   UNC

Purple, green, and orange. Front: Zebra; torch; coat of arms; giraffe head. Back: Seated woman with basket; five workers harvesting clove tree; torch; coffee berries. Solid security thread with printed *BENKI KUU YA TANZANIA*. Watermark: Giraffe head. Printer: (G&D). 138 x 69 mm.

   ☐ a.   No date. Signature 12. Prefix AC - GQ.   0.25   0.75   3
          Intro: 10.03.1997.

BOT B30 (P31): **1,000 shillings** (withdrawn 30.09.2003)   VG   VF   UNC

Green, brown, and red. Front: Two elephants; coat of arms; giraffe head. Back: Factory buildings; plant; ancient carved door to People's Bank of Zanzibar. Solid security thread with printed *BENKI KUU YA TANZANIA*. Watermark: Giraffe head. Printer: (G&D). 142 x 71 mm.

    ☐ a.   No date. Signature 12. Prefix BD - BR.   0.50   1.50   6
            Intro: 10.03.1997.

BOT B31 (P32): **5,000 shillings** (withdrawn 30.09.2003)   VG   VF   UNC

Brown and yellow. Front: Rhinoceros; coat of arms; giraffe head. Back: Six giraffes; Mount Kilimanjaro; chest. Windowed security thread with demetalized *BOT 5000*. Watermark: Giraffe head. Printer: (G&D). 145 x 73 mm.

    ☐ a.   No date. Signature 12. Prefix CA - CP.   1.25   5   20
            Intro: 10.03.1997.

BOT B32 (P33): **10,000 shillings** (withdrawn 30.09.2003)   VG   VF   UNC

Purple and red. Front: Lion; coat of arms; giraffe head. Back: Bank of Tanzania headquarters building in Dar es Salaam; House of Wonders (Beit el Ajaib) building in Zanzibar. Holographic stripe. Windowed security thread with demetalized *BOT 10000*. Watermark: Giraffe head. Printer: (G&D). 149 x 75 mm.

    ☐ a.   No date. Signature 12. Prefix DA - DM.   1.50   6   25
            Intro: 10.03.1997.
    ☐ as.   Diagonal red *SPECIMEN* overprint;   —   —   175
            horizontal red *SPECIMEN N°* # ovpt at lower left.

2000 Issues

BOT B33 (P34): **1,000 shillings** (US$0.60)   VG   VF   UNC

Green, brown, and red. Front: Two elephants; coat of arms; first president, Julius Kambarage Nyerere. Back: Factory buildings; plant; ancient carved door to People's Bank of Zanzibar. Solid security thread with printed *BENKI KUU YA TANZANIA*. Watermark: Giraffe head. Printer: (G&D). 142 x 71 mm.

    ☐ a.   No date. Sig. 13. Prefix FB - HR. Intro: 2000.   FV   1.25   5.25

2003-2009 Issues

These notes have the bank name in Swahili on the front and English on the back. Though they bear no printed dates, the windowed security thread is demetalized with the year of introduction. The notes feature an array of Giesecke & Devrient's latest security elements, such as LEAD holographic stripes, green-to-purple STEP elements, PEAK anti-copy elements, Iriodin iridescent stripes, electrotype watermarks, registration devices, latent images, microprinting, windowed security threads with demetalized text, novel serial numbers with fluorescent ink, and tactile marks for the sight-impaired.

BOT B34 (P35): **500 shillings** (US$0.30)   VG   VF   UNC
Green. Front: Coat of arms; Cape Buffalo; trees. Back: Sail boats; University of Dar es Salaam central hall building; snake coiled around stick. Windowed security thread with demetalized *BOT 2003*. Watermark: Giraffe head with electrotype *500*. Printer: (G&D). 130 x 63 mm.

- [ ] a. No date. Signature 14. Prefix AB - CX.   FV   FV   1.50
         Intro: 03.02.2003.

Replacement notes: Prefix BZ.
Later issues have been observed with a varnish coating.

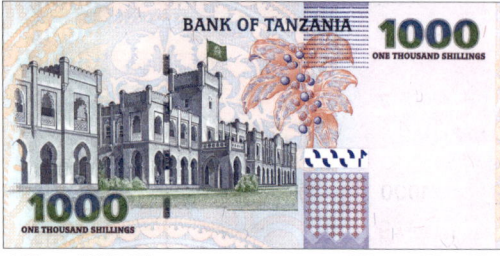

BOT B35 (P36): **1,000 shillings** (US$0.60)   VG   VF   UNC
Purple. Front: Coat of arms; first president, Julius Kambarage Nyerere; Bismarck Rock in Mwanza Harbor. Back: State House (Ikulu) building with flag in Dar Es Salaam; plant. Holographic stripe. Windowed security thread with demetalized *BOT 2003*. Watermark: Giraffe head with electrotype *1000*. Printer: (G&D). 135 x 66 mm.

- [ ] a. No date. Signature 14. Prefix AA - BG.   FV   FV   2
         Intro: 03.02.2003.
- [ ] b. Nyerere's shirt buttoned on "masculine" side.   FV   FV   2
         Prefix BP - DU. Intro: 08.08.2006.

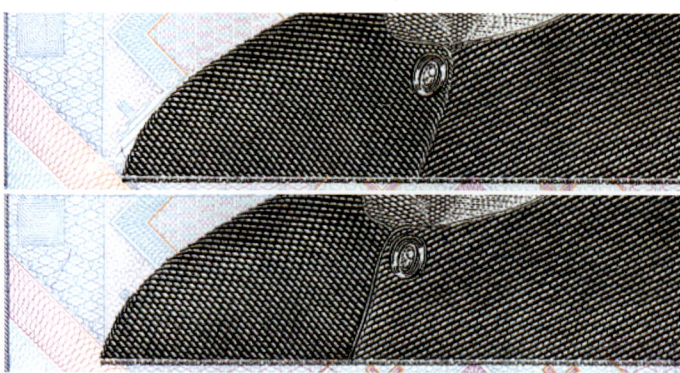

Shirt buttoned incorrectly on BOT B35a (top), and on "masculine" side on BOT B35b (bottom).

BOT B36 (P37): **2,000 shillings** (US$1.25) VG VF UNC

Tan and brown. Front: Coat of arms; Mount Kilimanjaro; lion. Back: Old Omani Arab Fort (Ngome Kongwe) in Zanzibar's Stone Town; carved block. Holographic stripe. Windowed security thread with demetalized *BOT 2003*. Watermark: Giraffe head with electrotype *2000*. Printer: (G&D). 140 x 69 mm.

- a. No date. Intro: 03.02.2003.   FV FV 5
  Signature 14. Prefix AA - BQ.
- b. Signature 15. Prefix CE - CM. Intro: 2009.   FV FV 5

BOT B37 (P38): **5,000 shillings** (US$3.15) VG VF UNC

Purple. Front: Coat of arms; balancing rocks; black rhinoceros. Back: House of Wonders (Beit el Ajaib) building in Zanzibar; mining machinery. Holographic stripe. Windowed security thread with demetalized *BOT 2003*. Watermark: Giraffe head with electrotype *5000*. Printer: (G&D). 145 x 72 mm.

- a. No date. Signature 14. Prefix AA - CF.   FV FV 8.50
  Intro: 03.02.2003.

BOT B38 (P39): **10,000 shillings** (US$6.30) VG VF UNC

Red and yellow. Front: Coat of arms; elephants. Back: Bank of Tanzania headquarters building in Dar es Salaam; water fountain; flowers. Holographic stripe. Windowed security thread with demetalized *BOT 2003*. Watermark: Giraffe head with electrotype *10000*. Printer: (G&D). 150 x 75 mm.

- a. No date. Signature 14. Prefix AA - CH.   FV FV 17
  Intro: 03.02.2003.

2011 Issues

According to an article in The Citizen dated 10 March 2011, Bank of Tanzania has refuted rumors it was withdrawing this new family of notes introduced on 1 January. Apparently there were widespread complaints that the new notes are of inferior quality compared to the older notes. The bank insists the notes are of good quality and has no plans to withdraw them from circulation.

BOT B39 (P40): **500 shillings** (US$0.30) VG VF UNC

Green. Front: Coat of arms; Sheikh Abeid Amani Karume. Back: Snake coiled around stick; University of Dar es Salaam central hall building; graduating students wearing caps and gowns. giraffe. Motion windowed security thread. Watermark: Julius Kambarage Nyerere with electrotype *500*. Printer: (Crane). 120 x 60 mm.

- a. No date. Signature 15. Prefix AD - CN.   FV FV 1.50
  Intro: 01.01.2011.

Replacement notes: Prefix ZZ.

BOT B40 (P41): **1,000 shillings** (US$0.60) VG VF UNC
Blue. Front: Coat of arms; first president, Julius Kambarage Nyerere; Bismarck Rock in Mwanza Harbor; holographic patch. Back: Coffee plant; State House (Ikulu) building with flag in Dar Es Salaam. Windowed security thread with demetalized *BOT 2010*. Watermark: Julius Kambarage Nyerere with electrotype *1000* and Cornerstones. Printer: (TDLR). 125 x 65 mm.

☐ a. No date. Signature 15. Prefix AA - AQ. FV FV 1.25
Intro: 01.01.2011.
Replacement notes: Prefix Z.

BOT B41 (P42): **2,000 shillings** (US$1.25) VG VF UNC
Tan and brown. Front: Coat of arms; lion. Back: Palm trees; old Omani Arab Fort (Ngome Kongwe) in Zanzibar's Stone Town; carved block; diamond-shaped Spark patch with giraffe head. Motion windowed security thread. Watermark: Julius Kambarage Nyerere with electrotype *2000*. Printer: (Crane). 130 x 66 mm.

☐ a. No date. Signature 15. Prefix AA - CB. FV FV 2.25
Intro: 01.01.2011.

BOT B42 (P43): **5,000 shillings** (US$3.15) VG VF UNC
Purple. Front: Coat of arms; plant; black rhinoceros. Back: Mining machinery; rough and cut diamonds; diamond-shaped Spark patch with giraffe head. Motion windowed security thread. Watermark: Julius Kambarage Nyerere with electrotype *5000*. Printer: (Crane). 135 x 67 mm.

☐ a. No date. Signature 15. Prefix AA - BU. FV FV 10
Intro: 01.01.2011.
Replacement notes: Prefix ZZ.

BOT B43 (P44): **10,000 shillings** (US$6.30) VG VF UNC
Red and yellow. Front: Coat of arms; elephant. Back: Flowers; Bank of Tanzania headquarters building in Dar es Salaam; diamond-shaped Spark patch with giraffe head. Motion windowed security thread. Watermark: Julius Kambarage Nyerere with electrotype *10000*. Printer: (Crane). 140 x 68 mm.

☐ a. No date. Signature 15. Prefix AA - BW. FV FV 13
Intro: 01.01.2011.
Replacement notes: Prefix ZZ.

Looking Forward

- On 1 July 2010, the East African Community (www.eac.int)—Burundi, Kenya, Rwanda, Tanzania, and Uganda—launched the EAC Common Market for goods, labor, and capital within the region, with the goals of a common currency (the East African shilling) by 2012, and full political federation in 2015. The common currency has yet to come to pass.
- According to an article on DailyNews dated 1 March 2012, the Bank of Tanzania plans to replace 500-shilling notes with coins.

Acknowledgements

This chapter was compiled with the generous assistance of Murtaza Abdeali, Thomas Augustsson, Arigo Avbovbo, Aleksey Avdeev, Arthur Gearing (De La Rue), Chris Hall, Murray Hanewich, Jørgen S. Jørgensen, Kuchimwa Jurango (Bank of Tanzania), Wally Myers, Jose Manuel Peso, Nazir Rahemtulla, Nicholas Reynolds, Andrew Roberts, Bill Stubkjaer, Christoph Thomas, Frank van Tiel, Christof Zellweger, and others.

Sources

Boon, K. N. *World Paper & Polymer Uncut Banknotes*. 1st edition. 2012. ISBN 978-983-43313-4-4. Trigometric Sdn.Bhd. (www.3833.com), Lot 327, Amcorp Mall, 18 Jalan Persiaran Barat, off Jalan Timur, Petaling Jaya, 46050 Selangor D.E., Malaysia.

Cuhaj, George S. *Standard Catalog of World Paper Money, Modern Issues, 1961-Present*. 18th edition. 2012. ISBN 978-1-4402-2956-5. Krause Publications (www.krausebooks.com), 700 East State St., Iola, WI, 54990-0001.

Remick, Jerry. "Republic of Kenya Issues First Banknote." *IBNS Journal*. Volume 6 Number 3. p.17.

Share Your Input, Info, and Images

This catalog is believed to be complete and correct as of the time of publication. Prices and face values were last updated 1 July 2011. Please report errors or omissions so that corrections may be made. If you can more precisely identify the name or location of anything depicted on a note, please share that information. Furthermore, if you own an unlisted type or variety, please submit scans of the front and back of the note so that it can be documented. Scans should be 300 dots per inch, 100% actual size, 24-bit color, saved as *uncompressed* JPEG files, and sent to owen@banknotenews.com. Be sure to fully describe all attributes of the note which are not apparent upon visual inspection of the images alone, such as physical dimension, watermark, and security thread.

Tonga

Government of Tonga Issues

Prior to the establishment of the National Reserve Bank of Tonga, notes were issued by the Government of Tonga. These notes will be added to this chapter in the future.

Monetary System
1 Tongan pa'anga (TOP) = 100 seniti

National Reserve Bank of Tonga

On 3 November 1988, the Legislative Assembly approved the National Reserve Bank of Tonga Act. The NRBT started its operations on 1 July 1989.

For more information, visit www.reservebank.to.

NRBT Signature Varieties

	PALEMIA 'O TONGA (Prime Minister)	MINISTA PA 'ANGA (Minister of Finance)
1	 Tu'i Pelehake (1965 – 22.08.1991)	 J. Cecil Cocker (1982 - 1991)
2	 Baron Vaea von Houma (22.08.1991 – 2000)	 J. Cecil Cocker (1982 - 1991)
3	Baron Vaea von Houma (22.08.1991 – 2000)	 K. Tutoatasi Fakafanua (1991 - 2000)
4	 'Ulukalala Lavaka Ata (03.01.2000 - 11.02.2006)	K. Tutoatasi Fakafanua (1991 - 2000)
5	 'Ulukalala Lavaka Ata (03.01.2000 - 11.02.2006)	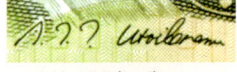 Siosiua T. T. 'Utoikamanu (2001 - 2008)
6	 Feleti Vaka'uta Sevele (30.03.2006 - 22.12.2010)	 'Otenifi Afu'alo Matoto (2008 - 2010)
*	Siale 'Ataongo Kaho, Lord Tu'ivakano (22.12.2010 - present)	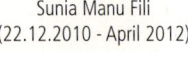 Sunia Manu Fili (22.12.2010 - April 2012)
7	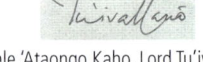 Siale 'Ataongo Kaho, Lord Tu'ivakano (22.12.2010 - present)	 Lisiate 'Aloveita 'Akolo (April 2012 - present)

* This official is not known to have signed any notes.

1989 Commemorative Issue

This 20-pa'anga note commemorates the inauguration of the National Reserve Bank of Tonga, and contains circular overprints to that effect on the watermark areas on front (Tongan) and back (English).

NRBT B1 (P30): 20 pa'anga　　　　　　　　VG　VF　UNC
Brown and orange. Front: King Taufa'ahau Tupou IV; coat of arms. Back: Tonga Development Bank building. Solid security thread. Watermark: King Taufa'ahau Tupou IV. Printer: (TDLR). 150 x 70 mm.
- ☐ a.　1 JULY 1989. Signature 1. Prefix C/1.　　—　—　60
- ☐ as.　Diagonal red *SPECIMEN* overprint.　　—　—　70

1992 Issues

These notes are like the preceding issues, but with the new name of the issuer, no dates, and the denominations with a simple dollar sign instead of T$.

NRBT B2 (P25): 1 pa'anga　　　　　　　　VG　VF　UNC
Green and blue. Front: Coat of arms; King Taufa'ahau Tupou IV. Back: Vava'u Harbor; palm trees; village. Solid security thread. Watermark: None. Printer: (TDLR). 150 x 70 mm.
- ☐ a.　No date. Signature 1. Prefix C/1. Intro: 1992.　　—　—　10

NRBT B3 (P26): 2 pa'anga VG VF UNC
Red and brown. Front: Coat of arms; King Taufa'ahau Tupou IV. Back: Four women making tapa cloth with fibers of mulberry tree; hut; palm trees. Solid security thread. Watermark: None. Printer: (TDLR). 150 x 70 mm.
    ☐ a. No date. Signature 1. Prefix C/1. Intro: 1992. — — 15

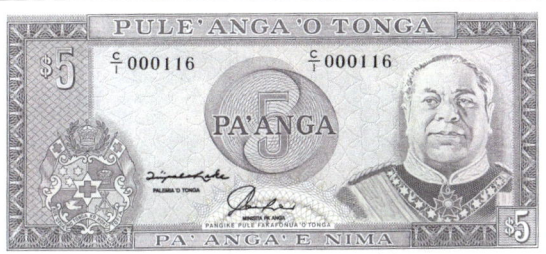

NRBT B4 (P27): 5 pa'anga VG VF UNC
Purple. Front: Coat of arms; King Taufa'ahau Tupou IV. Back: Ha'amonga stone gateway. Solid security thread. Watermark: None. Printer: (TDLR). 150 x 70 mm.
    ☐ a. No date. Signature 1. Prefix C/1. Intro: 1992. — — 25

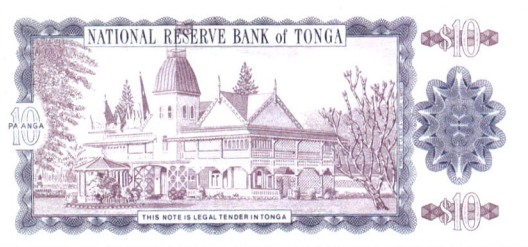

NRBT B5 (P28): 10 pa'anga VG VF UNC
Dark blue and purple. Front: Coat of arms; King Taufa'ahau Tupou IV. Back: Royal Palace. Solid security thread. Watermark: None. Printer: (TDLR). 150 x 70 mm.
    ☐ a. No date. Signature 1. Prefix C/1. Intro: 1992. — — 40
    ☐ b. Signature 2. — — 40

1992-2006 Issues

With these notes, the design of the front of all denominations is standardized along the lines of the preceding 20- and 50-pa'anga notes.

NRBT B6 (P31): 1 pa'anga VG VF UNC
Green. Front: King Taufa'ahau Tupou IV; coat of arms. Back: Vava'u Harbor; palm trees; village. Solid security thread. Watermark: King Taufa'ahau Tupou IV. Printer: *THOMAS DE LA RUE AND COMPANY LIMITED*. 150 x 70 mm.
    ☐ a. No date. Intro: 1995. — — 8
        Signature 2. Prefix C/1 - C/2.
    ☐ b. Signature 3. Prefix C/2 - C/3. — — 5
    ☐ c. Signature 4. Prefix C/3. — — 5
    ☐ d. Signature 5. Prefix C/4. — — 4

NRBT B7 (P32): **2 pa'anga**   VG   VF   UNC

Red. Front: King Taufa'ahau Tupou IV; coat of arms. Back: Four women making tapa cloth with fibers of mulberry tree; hut; palm trees. Solid security thread. Watermark: King Taufa'ahau Tupou IV. Printer: *THOMAS DE LA RUE AND COMPANY LIMITED*. 150 x 70 mm.

- ☐ a. No date. Intro: 1995.   —   —   12
  Signature 2. Prefix C/1 - C/2.
- ☐ b. Signature 3. Prefix C/2.   —   —   10
- ☐ c. Signature 4. Prefix C/2 - C/3.   —   —   10
- ☐ d. Signature 5. Prefix C/3 - C/4.   —   —   10
- ☐ as. Diagonal red *SPECIMEN* overprint.   —   —   —

NRBT B8 (P33): **5 pa'anga**   VG   VF   UNC

Purple. Front: King Taufa'ahau Tupou IV; coat of arms. Back: Ha'amonga stone gateway. Solid security thread. Watermark: King Taufa'ahau Tupou IV. Printer: *THOMAS DE LA RUE AND COMPANY LIMITED*. 150 x 70 mm.

- ☐ a. No date. Intro: 30.06.1995.   —   —   15
  Signature 2. Prefix C/1.
- ☐ b. Signature 3.   —   —   12
- ☐ c. Signature 5. Prefix C/2.   —   —   12
- ☐ as. Diagonal red *SPECIMEN* overprint.   —   —   —

NRBT B9 (P34): **10 pa'anga**   VG   VF   UNC

Blue. Front: King Taufa'ahau Tupou IV; coat of arms. Back: Royal Palace. Solid security thread. Watermark: King Taufa'ahau Tupou IV. Printer: *THOMAS DE LA RUE AND COMPANY LIMITED*. 150 x 70 mm.

- ☐ a. No date. Intro: 1995.   —   —   20
  Signature 2. Prefix C/1 - C/2.
- ☐ b. Signature 4. Prefix C/3.   —   —   20
- ☐ c. Signature 5. Prefix C/3 - C/4.   —   —   15
- ☐ as. Diagonal red *SPECIMEN* overprint.   —   —   —

NRBT B10 (P29 & P35): **20 pa'anga**   VG   VF   UNC

Brown and orange. Front: King Taufa'ahau Tupou IV; coat of arms. Back: Tonga Development Bank building. Solid security thread. Watermark: King Taufa'ahau Tupou IV. Printer: (TDLR). 150 x 70 mm.

- ☐ a1. No date. Signature 2. Prefix C/1. Intro: 1992.   —   —   25
  Two six-pointed star with cross in UV ink.
- ☐ a2. *20* in rectangle added to left of portrait in UV ink.   —   —   25
- ☐ b. Signature 4. Prefix C/2.   —   —   45
- ☐ c. Signature 5. Prefix C/2 - C/3.   —   —   25
- ☐ a1s. Diagonal red *SPECIMEN* overprint.   —   —   200

NRBT B11 (P36): **50 pa'anga** VG VF UNC

Green, yellow, and brown. Front: King Taufa'ahau Tupou IV; coat of arms. Back: Sail boats; ship; Vava'u Harbor; palm trees; village buildings. Solid security thread. Watermark: King Taufa'ahau Tupou IV. Printer: (TDLR). 150 x 70 mm.

☐ a. No date. Signature 5. Prefix A/1. Intro: 2000. — — 70

2008-2009 Issues

On 21 January 2009, the National Reserve Bank of Tonga issued newly designed banknotes in the denominations of 1, 2, 5, 10, 20, and 50 pa'anga. The new notes replace the image of King Taufa'ahau Tupou IV with that of the reigning King George Tupou V. The watermark is of King Tupou V with electrotype *NRBT*. On the $1-$5 notes, the 1.4-mm wide windowed security thread is demetalized *NRBT*. Larger denominations have a 2.0-mm wide red-to-green thread with demetalized *NRBT*. Older notes remain legal tender, but will be phased out over time.

NRBT B12 (P37): **1 pa'anga** (US$0.60) VG VF UNC

Green. Front: King George Tupou V. Back: Whale leaping out of water; medallion. 1.4-mm windowed security thread with demetalized *NRBT*. Watermark: King Tupou, electrotype *NRBT*, and Cornerstones. Printer: (TDLR). 150 x 70 mm.

☐ a. No date. Intro: 21.01.2009. FV FV 4
Signature 6. Prefix A.
☐ b. Signature 7. Prefix B. FV FV 4

Replacement notes: Prefix Z.

NRBT B13 (P38): **2 pa'anga** (US$1.15) VG VF UNC

Light red. Front: King George Tupou V. Back: Children studying outside school building; two men playing rugby; medallion. 1.4-mm windowed security thread with demetalized *NRBT*. Watermark: King Tupou, electrotype *NRBT*, and Cornerstones. Printer: (TDLR). 150 x 70 mm.

☐ a. No date. Intro: 21.01.2009. FV FV 6
Signature 6. Prefix A.
☐ b. Signature 7. FV FV 6

NRBT B14 (P39): **5 pa'anga** (US$2.90) VG VF UNC

Purple. Front: King George Tupou V. Back: Langi; medallion. 1.4-mm windowed security thread with demetalized *NRBT*. Watermark: King Tupou, electrotype *NRBT*, and Cornerstones. Printer: (TDLR). 150 x 70 mm.

☐ a. No date. Intro: 21.01.2009. FV FV 10
Signature 6. Prefix A.
☐ b. Signature 7. FV FV 10

NRBT B15 (P40): **10 pa'anga** (US$5.80)   VG   VF   UNC
Blue. Front: King George Tupou V. Back: Royal tomb; medallion. 2.0-mm red-to-green windowed security thread with demetalized *NRBT*. Watermark: King Tupou, electrotype *NRBT*, and Cornerstones. Printer: (TDLR). 150 x 70 mm.
   ☐ a.   No date. Intro: 21.01.2009.   FV   FV   15
          Signature 6. Prefix A.
   ☐ b.   Signature 7. Prefix B.   FV   FV   15

NRBT B17 (P42): **50 pa'anga** (US$29)   VG   VF   UNC
Light green and yellow. Front: King George Tupou V. Back: Royal Palace building; medallion. 2.0-mm red-to-green windowed security thread with demetalized *NRBT*. Watermark: King Tupou, electrotype *NRBT*, and Cornerstones. Printer: (TDLR). 150 x 70 mm.
   ☐ a.   No date. Signature 6. Prefix A. Intro: 21.01.2009.   FV   FV   75

NRBT B16 (P41): **20 pa'anga** (US$12)   VG   VF   UNC
Brown. Front: King George Tupou V. Back: NRBT building; medallion. 2.0-mm red-to-green windowed security thread with demetalized *NRBT*. Watermark: King Tupou, electrotype *NRBT*, and Cornerstones. Printer: (TDLR). 150 x 70 mm.
   ☐ a.   No date. Sig. 6. Prefix A - B. Intro: 21.01.2009.   FV   FV   30
Replacement notes: Prefix Z.

NRBT B18 (P43): **100 pa'anga** (US$58)   VG   VF   UNC
Cherry red and white. Front: King George Tupou V. Back: Vava'u Harbor; medallion. Optiks security thread. Watermark: King Tupou, electrotype *NRBT*, and Cornerstones. Printer: (TDLR). 150 x 70 mm.
   ☐ a.   No date. Signature 6. Prefix A. Intro: 30.07.2008.   FV   FV   150

2009 Numismatic Products

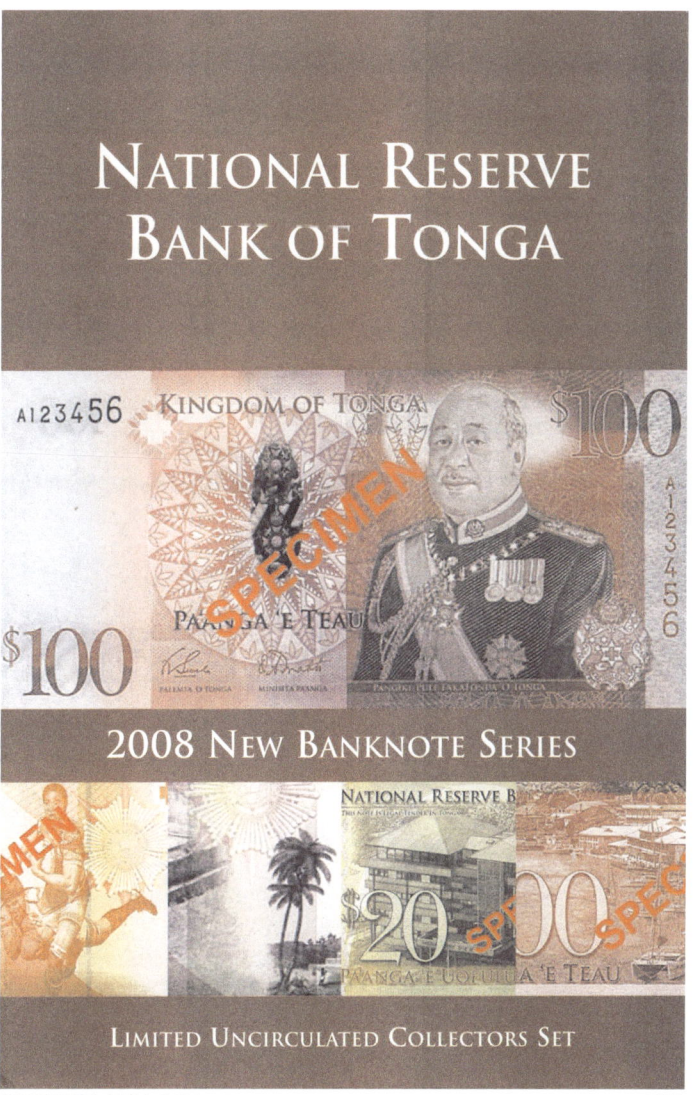

NRBT BNP1 (PNL): 1-100 pa'anga — UNC
- a. NRBT B12-B18 (7 notes) with matching serial numbers in tri-fold album. Intro: May 2009. — 370

Acknowledgements

This chapter was compiled with the generous assistance of Sejin Ahn, Thomas Augustsson, William Barrett, David F. Cieniewicz, Arthur Gearing (De La Rue), Merjim Groen, Detlef Hilmer (detlef_hilmer@web.de), Larry Hirsch (www.aworldcurrency.com), Charles Hunt (www.tongannotes.info), Don Ludwig, Claudio Marana, Wally Myers, Sam Nakhjavani (www.foreignpapermoney.com), George Provencal, TDS, Bill Stubkjaer, Christoph Thomas, Frank van Tiel, and others.

Buying Banknotes

The National Reserve Bank of Tonga sells uncirculated notes to the public. For more information, write nrbt@reservebank.to.

Sources

Anonymous. Annual Reports. National Reserve Bank of Tonga.

Cuhaj, George S. *Standard Catalog of World Paper Money, General Issues, 1368-1960*. 14th edition. 2012. ISBN 978-1-4402-3090-5. Krause Publications (www.krausebooks.com), 700 East State St., Iola, WI, 54990-0001.

Cuhaj, George S. *Standard Catalog of World Paper Money, Modern Issues, 1961-Present*. 19th edition. 2013. ISBN 978-1-4402-3571-9. Krause Publications (www.krausebooks.com), 700 East State St., Iola, WI, 54990-0001.

Eu, Peter, Ben Chiew, and Stane Straus. *World Polymer Banknotes: A Standard Reference*. 2nd edition. 2006. ISBN: 983-43038-2-3. Eureka Metro, P. O. Box 30, Jalan Kelang Lama, Kuala Lumpur, 57000, Malaysia.

Hunt, Charles. Tongan Notes web site: www.tongannotes.info

Krause, Thomas and Peter Bauer. *Specialized Catalogue of World Plastic Money*. 5th edition. 2009. www.polymernotes.de.

http://en.wikipedia.org/wiki/Prime_Minister_of_Tonga

Share Your Input, Info, and Images

This catalog is believed to be complete and correct as of the time of publication. Prices and face values were last updated 6 September 2013. Please report errors or omissions so that corrections may be made. If you can more precisely identify the name or location of anything depicted on a note, please share that information. Furthermore, if you own an unlisted type or variety, please submit scans of the front and back of the note so that it can be documented. Scans should be 300 dots per inch, 100% actual size, 24-bit color, saved as *uncompressed* JPEG files, and sent to owen@banknotenews.com. Be sure to fully describe all attributes of the note which are not apparent upon visual inspection of the images alone, such as physical dimension, watermark, and security thread.

Trans-Dniester

For earlier issues, see Russia.

Contents

Trans-Dniester Bank (TDB).................................. 2094
Trans-Dniester Republican Bank (TDRB).............. 2101

Trans-Dniester—also known as Transnistria, Transdniestria, and Pridnestrovie—is a disputed region in southeastern Europe. Since its declaration of independence on 2 September 1990, it has been governed by the unrecognized Pridnestrovskaya Moldavskaya Respublica (PMR), which claims the left bank of the river Dniester and the city of Bendery within the former Moldavian SSR. The modern Republic of Moldova did not recognize the secession, leading to a brief war in 1992. Although a cease-fire agreement has held since then, the territory's political status remains unresolved: *de jure* part of Moldova, Trans-Dniester is *de facto* independent. It is organized as a presidential republic, with its own government, parliament, military, police, postal system, and currency. Its authorities have adopted a constitution, flag, national anthem, and a coat of arms.

Monetary System

July 1993: 1 Trans-Dniester ruble = 1 Russian ruble
22.08.1994: 1 Trans-Dniester coupon ruble = 1,000 T-D rubles
01.01.2001: 1 "new" T-D ruble = 1,000,000 T-D coupon rubles

ПРИДНЕСТРОВСКИЙ БАНК
(Trans-Dniester Bank)

On 22 December 1992, the Supreme Council of Trans-Dniester Moldavian Republic decreed to establish the Trans-Dniester Bank (TDB).

TDB Signature Varieties

1 — ПРЕДСЕДАТЕЛЬ (Governor)
Vyacheslav Zagryatskiy

1961-1992 (1994) Provisional Issues

Soviet banknotes were used in the Trans-Dniester Moldavian Republic after its formation in 1990. When the former Soviet republics began issuing their own currencies, Trans-Dniester was flooded with Soviet rubles. In an attempt to protect its financial system, in July 1993 the government bought used Goznak-printed Soviet and Russian notes dated 1961-1992 which it modified in Trans-Dniester by adhering stamps bearing the image of General Alexander Vasilyevich Suvorov, founder of Tiraspol, Trans-Dniester's capital. These stamped notes replaced unstamped Soviet and Russian notes at par. It is thought that most uncirculated notes bearing these stickers were created after 1994 specifically for collectors.

TDB B1 (P1): **10 rubles** (demonetized 01.12.1994) VG VF UNC
Reddish brown. Front: Coat of arms; Vladimir Ilyich Lenin; green Alexander Suvorov sticker. Back: Denomination. No security thread. Watermark: Star pattern. Printer: (Goznak). 121 x 62 mm.
☐ a. 1961. Intro: 24.01.1994.   1   2   4

TDB B2 (P2): **10 rubles** (demonetized 01.12.1994) VG VF UNC
Reddish brown. Front: Coat of arms; Vladimir Ilyich Lenin; green Alexander Suvorov sticker. Back: Denomination. No security thread. Watermark: Star pattern. Printer: (Goznak). 125 x 61 mm.
☐ a. 1991. Intro: 24.01.1994.   1   2   4

TDB B3 (P3): **25 rubles** (demonetized 01.12.1994) VG VF UNC
Purple. Front: Vladimir Ilyich Lenin; coat of arms; red Alexander Suvorov sticker. Back: Denomination. No security thread. Watermark: Star pattern. Printer: (Goznak). 121 x 62 mm.
☐ a. 1961. Intro: 24.01.1994.   0.25   0.75   3.50

TDB B4 (P4): **50 rubles** (demonetized 01.12.1994)   VG   VF   UNC
Green and brown. Front: Vladimir Ilyich Lenin; coat of arms; red Alexander Suvorov sticker. Back: Kremlin building. No security thread. Watermark: Lenin. Printer: (Goznak). 144 x 70 mm.
  ☐   a.   1991. Intro: 24.01.1994.   2   6   12

TDB B5 (P5): **50 rubles** (demonetized 01.12.1994)   VG   VF   UNC
Green and brown. Front: Vladimir Ilyich Lenin; coat of arms; red Alexander Suvorov sticker. Back: Kremlin building. No security thread. Watermark: Star in wave pattern. Printer: (Goznak). 142 x 70 mm.
  ☐   a.   1992. Intro: 24.01.1994.   1   3   8

TDB B6 (P6): **100 rubles** (demonetized 01.12.1994)   VG   VF   UNC
Brown, blue, and tan. Front: Vladimir Ilyich Lenin; coat of arms; black Alexander Suvorov sticker. Back: Kremlin tower building. No security thread. Watermark: Lenin. Printer: (Goznak). 143 x 70 mm.
  ☐   a.   1991. Intro: 24.01.1994.   3   6   12

TDB B7 (P7): **100 rubles** (demonetized 01.12.1994)   VG   VF   UNC
Brown, blue, and tan. Front: Vladimir Ilyich Lenin; coat of arms; black Alexander Suvorov sticker on guilloché. Back: Kremlin tower building. No security thread. Watermark: Star pattern. Printer: (Goznak). 139 x 70 mm.
  ☐   a.   1991. Intro: 24.01.1994.   0.50   1.50   5.50

TDB B8 (P8): **200 rubles** (demonetized 01.12.1994)   VG   VF   UNC
Brown and green. Front: Vladimir Ilyich Lenin; coat of arms; green Alexander Suvorov sticker. Back: Kremlin building. Solid security thread printed ГОСБАНК СССР. Watermark: Lenin. Printer: (Goznak). 145 x 70 mm.
☐   a.   1991. Intro: 24.01.1994.   5   10   30

TDB B10 (P10): **500 rubles** (demonetized 01.12.1994)   VG   VF   UNC
Red and purple. Front: Vladimir Ilyich Lenin; coat of arms; blue Alexander Suvorov sticker. Back: Kremlin building. Solid security thread printed ГОСБАНК СССР. Watermark: Lenin. Printer: (Goznak). 145 x 70 mm.
☐   a.   1991. Intro: 24.01.1994.   8   20   40

TDB B9 (P9): **200 rubles** (demonetized 01.12.1994)   VG   VF   UNC
Brown and green. Front: Vladimir Ilyich Lenin; coat of arms; green Alexander Suvorov sticker. Back: Kremlin building. No security thread. Watermark: Star in wave pattern. Printer: (Goznak). 145 x 70 mm.
☐   a.   1992. Intro: 24.01.1994.   1   3   6

TDB B11 (P11): **500 rubles** (demonetized 01.12.1994)   VG   VF   UNC
Red and purple. Front: Vladimir Ilyich Lenin; coat of arms; blue Alexander Suvorov sticker. Back: Kremlin building. No security thread. Watermark: Star pattern. Printer: (Goznak). 145 x 70 mm.
☐   a.   1992. Intro: 24.01.1994.   0.25   1.50   5.50

TDB B12 (P12): **1,000 rubles** (demonetized 01.12.1994)   VG   VF   UNC
Brown and blue. Front: Vladimir Ilyich Lenin; coat of arms; violet Alexander Suvorov sticker. Back: Kremlin building. Solid security thread printed ГОСБАНК СССР. Watermark: Lenin. Printer: (Goznak). 145 x 70 mm.
    a. 1991. Intro: 24.01.1994.   8   20   50

TDB B13 (P13): **1,000 rubles** (demonetized 01.12.1994)   VG   VF   UNC
Brown and blue. Front: Vladimir Ilyich Lenin; coat of arms; violet Alexander Suvorov sticker. Back: Kremlin building. No security thread. Watermark: Star pattern. Printer: (Goznak). 145 x 70 mm.
    a. 1992. Intro: 24.01.1994.   0.50   2.50   10

TDB B14 (P14): **5,000 rubles** (demonetized 01.12.1994)   VG   VF   UNC
Light blue. Front: St. Basil's Cathedral; brown Alexander Suvorov sticker. Back: Kremlin building. No security thread. Watermark: Star pattern. Printer: (Goznak). 145 x 70 mm.
    a. 1992. Sig.: Georgui Matiukhin. Intro: 24.01.1994.   1   2   6

TDB B15 (P14A): **5,000 rubles** (demonetized 01.12.1994)   VG   VF   UNC
Light blue. Front: Coat of arms; Kremlin Spasski tower; brown Alexander Suvorov sticker. Back: Denomination. No security thread. Watermark: Star pattern. Printer: (Goznak). 114 x 57 mm.
    a. 1961. Intro: June 1994.   1   2   4

TDB B16 (P14B): **5,000 rubles** (demonetized 01.12.1994)   VG   VF   UNC
Light blue. Front: Coat of arms; Kremlin Spasski tower; brown Alexander Suvorov sticker. Back: Denomination. No security thread. Watermark: Star in wave pattern. Printer: (Goznak). 114 x 57 mm.
    a. 1991. Intro: June 1994.   1   2   5

TDB B17 (P15): **10,000 rubles** (demonetized 01.12.1994) VG VF UNC
Brown, black, and red. Front: Kremlin dome with tricolor flag; purple Alexander Suvorov sticker. Back: Kremlin buildings. No security thread. Watermark: Kremlin. Printer: (Goznak). 145 x 70 mm.
☐ a. 1992. Intro: 24.01.1994. 1 2 5

1993-1994 Issues

On 22 August 1994, the provisional issues were replaced by coupon ruble (КУПОН РУБЛЕЙ) notes at a rate of 1 to 1,000 "old" rubles.

Be aware that stamps bearing a map of Trans-Dniester have been affixed to TDB B18-20 by unknown sources. These are unauthorized fantasy notes.

TDB B18 (P16): **1 coupon ruble** VG VF UNC
Green. Front: Alexander Suvorov. Back: Parliament building. No security thread. Watermark: Block pattern. Printer: (Goznak). 125 x 58 mm.
☐ a. 1994. Intro: September 1994. 0.25 0.50 1

TDB B19 (P17): **5 coupon rubles** VG VF UNC
Blue. Front: Alexander Suvorov. Back: Parliament building. No security thread. Watermark: Block pattern. Printer: (Goznak). 125 x 58 mm.
☐ a. 1994. Intro: September 1994. 0.25 0.50 1
For note with hologram, see TDB B29.

TDB B20 (P18): **10 coupon rubles** VG VF UNC
Red-violet. Front: Alexander Suvorov. Back: Parliament building. No security thread. Watermark: Block pattern. Printer: (Goznak). 125 x 58 mm.
☐ a. 1994. Intro: September 1994. 0.25 0.50 1

TDB B21 (P19): **50 coupon rubles** VG VF UNC
Green. Front: Alexander Suvorov equestrian statue in Tiraspol. Back: Parliament building. No security thread. Watermark: Block pattern. Printer: (Goznak). 125 x 58 mm.
☐ a. 1993. Intro: 22.08.1994. 0.25 0.50 1

TDB B22 (P20): **100 coupon rubles** VG VF UNC
Tan. Front: Alexander Suvorov equestrian statue in Tiraspol. Back: Parliament building. No security thread. Watermark: Block pattern. Printer: (Goznak). 125 x 58 mm.
☐ a. 1993. Intro: 22.08.1994.   0.25 0.50 1.25

TDB B23 (P21): **200 coupon rubles** VG VF UNC
Red-violet. Front: Alexander Suvorov equestrian statue in Tiraspol. Back: Parliament building. No security thread. Watermark: Block pattern. Printer: (Goznak). 125 x 58 mm.
☐ a. 1993. Intro: 22.08.1994.   0.25 0.50 1.50

TDB B24 (P22): **500 coupon rubles** VG VF UNC
Blue. Front: Alexander Suvorov equestrian statue in Tiraspol. Back: Parliament building. No security thread. Watermark: Block pattern. Printer: (Goznak). 125 x 58 mm.
☐ a. 1993. Intro: 22.08.1994.   0.25 0.50 1.50

TDB B25 (P23): **1,000 coupon rubles** VG VF UNC
Purple. Front: Alexander Suvorov equestrian statue in Tiraspol. Back: Parliament building. No security thread. Watermark: Block pattern. Printer: (Goznak). 125 x 58 mm.
☐ a. 1993. Intro: 22.08.1994.   0.50 0.75 3

TDB B26 (P24): **5,000 coupon rubles** VG VF UNC
Green. Front: Alexander Suvorov equestrian statue in Tiraspol. Back: Parliament building. No security thread. Watermark: Block pattern. Printer: (Goznak). 125 x 58 mm.
☐ a. 1993. Intro: 1995.   0.50 0.75 3.75

1994-1995 Provisional Issues

Hyperinflation had eroded the value of the coupon ruble to the point where the bank was preparing to reform its currency, but was forced to prematurely introduce two new notes, both of which are printed as though they are denominated in rubles, but in actuality they are coupon rubles.

TDB B27 (P26): **1,000 (coupon) rubles** VG VF UNC
Purple. Front: Alexander Suvorov. Back: Parliament building. Solid security thread. Watermark: None. Printer: Former DDR Staatsdruckerei. 129 x 58 mm.
   ☐ a. 1994. Intro: June 1995.   0.50   2.50   10

TDB B28 (P28): **50,000 (coupon) rubles** VG VF UNC
Brown. Front: Bohdan Khmelnytsky. Back: Taras Shevchenko statue; drama and comedy theater building. Solid security thread. Watermark: None. Printer: Former DDR Staatsdruckerei. 129 x 62 mm.
   ☐ a. 1995. Signature 1. Intro: April 1996.   1   3   12
   ☐ as. Diagonal red *ОБРАЗЕЦ* overprint; horizontal red *SPECIMEN Nº* # ovpt at lower left.   —   —   25

1994 (1996) Provisional Issues

Due to cash shortages, the bank reused old 5-coupon ruble notes by overprinting them in Tiraspol with a crude hologram containing its new value of 50,000 coupon rubles.

TDB B29 (P27): **50,000 (coupon) rubles** VG VF UNC
Blue. Front: Hologram of equestrian statue in Tiraspol and *50000*; Alexander Suvorov. Back: Parliament building. No security thread. Watermark: Block pattern. Printer: (Goznak). 125 x 58 mm.
   ☐ a. 1994. Intro: June 1996.   0.25   0.75   3
Overprinted on TDB B19.

1996-1998 Provisional Issues

In August 1996, old 1-, 5-, and 10-coupon ruble notes (TDB B18-20) were overprinted in Tiraspol with higher denominations to keep pace with inflation.

TDB B30 (P29): **10,000 coupon rubles** VG VF UNC
Green. Front: Overprint; Alexander Suvorov. Back: Parliament building. No security thread. Watermark: Block pattern. Printer: (Goznak). 125 x 58 mm.
   ☐ a. 1996. Intro: August 1996.   0.25   0.50   1

TDB B31 (P29A): **10,000 coupon rubles** VG VF UNC
Green. Front: Overprint; Alexander Suvorov. Back: Overprint; Parliament building. No security thread. Watermark: Block pattern. Printer: (Goznak). 125 x 58 mm.
☐ a. 1998. 0.25 0.50 1

TDB B32 (P30): **50,000 coupon rubles** VG VF UNC
Blue. Front: Overprint; Alexander Suvorov. Back: Overprint; Parliament building. No security thread. Watermark: Block pattern. Printer: (Goznak). 125 x 58 mm.
☐ a. 1996. Intro: August 1996. 0.25 0.75 2.50

TDB B33 (P31): **100,000 coupon rubles** VG VF UNC
Red-violet. Front: Overprint; Alexander Suvorov. Back: Overprint; Parliament building. No security thread. Watermark: Block pattern. Printer: (Goznak). 125 x 58 mm.
☐ a. 1996. Intro: August 1996. 0.25 0.75 3

TDB B34 (P33): **500,000 coupon rubles** VG VF UNC
Purple. Front: Alexander Suvorov equestrian statue in Tiraspol. Back: Silhouette of equestrian statue; Parliament building. No security thread. Watermark: Looped pattern. Printer: (Goznak). 125 x 58 mm.
☐ a. 1997. Intro: June 1997. 1 3 12

ПРИДНЕСТРОВСКИЙ РЕСПУБЛИКАНСКИЙ БАНК (Trans-Dniester Republican Bank)

For more information, visit http://cbpmr.net.

2000-2004 Issues

At the start of 2001, old coupon rubles were exchanged for new rubles at the ratio of 1,000,000:1.

TDRB B1 (P34): **1 ruble** (US$0.10) VG VF UNC
Brown. Front: Alexander Suvorov. Back: Kitskansky Bridgehead Memorial Complex. Solid security thread. Watermark: None. Printer: (Trans-Dniester). 129 x 56 mm.
☐ a. 2000. 0.25 0.50 1
☐ as. Diagonal red ОБРАЗЕЦ overprint. — — 1

TDRB B2 (P35): **5 rubles** (US$0.60) VG VF UNC
Blue. Front: Alexander Suvorov. Back: KVINT Distillery administrative building. Solid security thread. Watermark: None. Printer: (Trans-Dniester). 129 x 56 mm.
☐ a. 2000.   FV   FV   2
☐ as. Diagonal red ОБРАЗЕЦ overprint.   —   —   3

TDRB B3 (P36): **10 rubles** (US$1.20) VG VF UNC
Brown. Front: Alexander Suvorov. Back: Novo-Nyametsky monastery. Solid security thread. Watermark: None. Printer: (Trans-Dniester). 129 x 56 mm.
☐ a. 2000.   FV   FV   2.75
☐ as. Diagonal red ОБРАЗЕЦ overprint.   —   —   5

TDRB B4 (P37): **25 rubles** (US$2.95) VG VF UNC
Red. Front: Alexander Suvorov. Back: Bendery fortress; memorial to Russian warriors. Solid security thread. Watermark: None. Printer: (Trans-Dniester). 129 x 56 mm.
☐ a. 2000.   FV   FV   10
☐ as. Diagonal red ОБРАЗЕЦ overprint.   —   —   10

TDRB B5 (P38): **50 rubles** (US$5.90) VG VF UNC
Green. Front: Poet Taras Shevchenko. Back: Parliament building. Solid security thread. Watermark: None. Printer: (Trans-Dniester). 129 x 60 mm.
☐ a. 2000.   FV   FV   15
☐ as. Diagonal red ОБРАЗЕЦ overprint.   —   —   25

TDRB B6 (P39): **100 rubles** (US$12) VG VF UNC
Violet. Front: Prince Dmitry Kantemir. Back: Cathedral of Christmas in Tiraspol. Solid security thread. Watermark: None. Printer: (Trans-Dniester). 129 x 60 mm.
☐ a. 2000.   FV   FV   30
☐ as. Diagonal red ОБРАЗЕЦ overprint.   —   —   50

TDRB B7 (P40): **200 rubles** (US$24)   VG   VF   UNC
Brown. Front: Count Petr Rumiantsev-Zadunaiskiy. Back: Battle of Gross-Egersdorf. Windowed security thread. Watermark: Petr Rumiantsev-Zadunaiskiy with electrotype *ПРБ*. Printer: (Trans-Dniester). 135 x 64 mm.

☐	a.	2004. Prefix AA. Error in text on front.	FV	FV	45
☐	b.	Prefix AB-. Corrected text.	FV	FV	45
☐	c.	2004 МОДИФИКАЦИЯ (modified) 2012. 4.5-mm wide security thread. Intro: 15.01.2013.	FV	FV	45
☐	as.	Diagonal red *ОБРАЗЕЦ* overprint.	—	—	25
☐	cs.	Diagonal red *ОБРАЗЕЦ* overprint.	—	—	25

TDRB B8 (P41): **500 rubles** (US$59)   VG   VF   UNC
Green. Front: Empress Catherine the Second. Back: Fortress of Tiraspol; Empress's Decree. Windowed security thread. Watermark: Empress Catherine with electrotype *ПРБ*. Printer: (Trans-Dniester). 140 x 68 mm.

☐	a.	2004. Prefix AA. Error in text on front.	FV	FV	100
☐	b.	Prefix AB-. Corrected text.	FV	FV	100
☐	c.	2004 МОДИФИКАЦИЯ (modified) 2012. 4.5-mm wide security thread. Intro: 2014.	FV	FV	100
☐	as.	Diagonal red *ОБРАЗЕЦ* overprint.	—	—	45
☐	cs.	Diagonal red *ОБРАЗЕЦ* overprint.	—	—	45

TDRB B7a (top) with error in text on front, and TDRB B7b (bottom) with corrected text.

2004 Numismatic Products

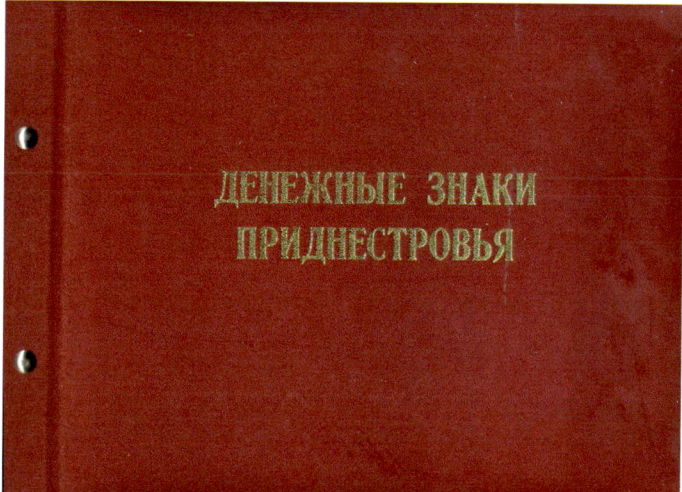

TDRB BNP1 (PNL): **1-5,000 rubles**   UNC
☐ a. TDB B21-B28, TDB B31-34, and TDRB B1-B8 specimens (20 notes) in red album.   —

2007-2012 Issues

On 22 December 2007, the Trans-Dniester Republican Bank issued a new series of banknotes. The new notes feature the same people and places as the old notes, but the images have been modified to extend to the border. Furthermore, anti-counterfeiting features have been enhanced with the inclusion of a windowed security thread on all denominations. The existing 200- and 500-rubles notes will not be issued as part of this series as they already contain sophisticated security features. Both the new and old series will circulate without restrictions.

TDRB B9 (P42): **1 ruble** (US$0.10)   VG   VF   UNC
Brown. Front: Alexander Suvorov. Back: Kitskansky Bridgehead memorial complex. Watermark: Alexander Suvorov with electrotype *ПРБ*. Printer: (Trans-Dniester). 129 x 56 mm.

☐	a.	2007. Intro: 22.12.2007. Windowed security thread.	FV FV	1
☐	b.	2007 МОДИФИКАЦИЯ (modified) 2012. Winged security thread. Intro: 15.01.2013.	FV FV	1
☐	as.	Diagonal red *ОБРАЗЕЦ* overprint.	— —	5
☐	bs.	Diagonal red *ОБРАЗЕЦ* overprint.	— —	5

The original notes issued in 2007 have traditional windowed security threads (TDRB B9a, left), whereas modified notes issued in 2012 have "winged" security threads (B9b, right).

TDRB B10 (P43): **5 rubles** (US$0.60)   VG   VF   UNC
Blue. Front: Alexander Suvorov. Back: KVINT Distillery administrative building. Windowed security thread. Watermark: Alexander Suvorov with electrotype *ПРБ*. Printer: (Trans-Dniester). 129 x 56 mm.

☐	a.	2007. Intro: 22.12.2007.	FV FV	1.50
☐	b.	2007 МОДИФИКАЦИЯ (modified) 2012. Winged security thread. Intro: 30.05.2014.	FV FV	1.50
☐	as.	Diagonal red *ОБРАЗЕЦ* overprint.	— —	5
☐	bs.	Diagonal red *ОБРАЗЕЦ* overprint.	— —	5

TDRB B11 (P44): **10 rubles** (US$1.20)   VG   VF   UNC
Brown and green. Front: Alexander Suvorov. Back: Novo-Nyametsky monastery. Windowed security thread. Watermark: Alexander Suvorov with electrotype *ПРБ*. Printer: (Trans-Dniester). 129 x 56 mm.

☐	a.	2007. Intro: 22.12.2007.	FV FV	2.75
☐	b.	2007 МОДИФИКАЦИЯ (modified) 2012. Winged security thread.	FV FV	2.75
☐	as.	Diagonal red *ОБРАЗЕЦ* overprint.	— —	5
☐	bs.	Diagonal red *ОБРАЗЕЦ* overprint.	— —	5

TDRB B12 (P45): **25 rubles** (US$2.95)   VG   VF   UNC

Red. Front: Alexander Suvorov; Alexander Suvorov equestrian statue in Tiraspol. Back: Bendery fortress; memorial to Russian warriors. Windowed security thread. Watermark: Empress Catherine with electrotype ПРБ. Printer: (Trans-Dniester). 129 x 56 mm.

			VG	VF	UNC
☐	a.	2007. Intro: 22.12.2007.	FV	FV	6
☐	b.	2007 МОДИФИКАЦИЯ (modified) 2012. 4.5-mm wide security thread. Intro: 11.12.2013.	FV	FV	6
☐	as.	Diagonal red ОБРАЗЕЦ overprint.	—	—	10
☐	bs.	Diagonal red ОБРАЗЕЦ overprint.	—	—	10

TDRB B13 (P46): **50 rubles** (US$5.90)   VG   VF   UNC

Green. Front: Poet Taras Shevchenko. Back: Parliament building. Windowed security thread. Watermark: Petr Rumiantsev-Zadunaiskiy with electrotype ПРБ. Printer: (Trans-Dniester). 129 x 60 mm.

			VG	VF	UNC
☐	a.	2007. Intro: 22.12.2007.	FV	FV	12
☐	b.	2007 МОДИФИКАЦИЯ (modified) 2012. 4.5-mm wide security thread. Intro: 15.01.2013.	FV	FV	12
☐	as.	Diagonal red ОБРАЗЕЦ overprint.	—	—	25
☐	bs.	Diagonal red ОБРАЗЕЦ overprint.	—	—	25

The original notes issued in 2007 have traditional windowed security threads (TDRB B13a, left), whereas modified notes issued in 2013 have 4.5-mm wide security threads (B13b, right). The 25-, 100-, and 200-ruble notes were also modified in 2013 with the wide threads.

TDRB B14 (P47): **100 rubles** (US$12) VG VF UNC
Violet. Front: Prince Dmitry Kantemir. Back: Cathedral of Christmas in Tiraspol. Windowed security thread. Watermark: Petr Rumiantsev-Zadunaiskiy with electrotype *ПРБ*. Printer: (Trans-Dniester). 129 x 60 mm.

☐	a. 2007. Intro: 22.12.2007.	FV	FV	22
☐	b. 2007 МОДИФИКАЦИЯ (modified) 2012. 4.5-mm wide security thread. Intro: 11.12.2013.	FV	FV	22
☐	as. Diagonal red *ОБРАЗЕЦ* overprint.	—	—	50
☐	bs. Diagonal red *ОБРАЗЕЦ* overprint.	—	—	50

2009 Numismatic Products

On 18 August 2009, the Trans-Dniester Republican Bank introduced a 10-ruble banknote commemorating 15 years of national currency. 1,000 copies of the note were sold in a folder.

TDRB BNP2 (PNL): **10 rubles** (US$1.20) UNC
Brown and green. Front: Alexander Suvorov; bank initials on watermark area. Back: Trans-Dniester Republican Bank headquarters building in Tiraspol. Windowed security thread. Watermark: Alexander Suvorov with electrotype *ПРБ*. Printer: (Trans-Dniester). 129 x 56 mm.

☐	a. 2009. Intro: 18.08.2009.	40
☐	as. Diagonal red *ОБРАЗЕЦ* overprint.	95

2014 Composite Coins

On 22 August 2014, the Trans-Dniester Republican Bank issued new 1-, 3-, 5-, and 10-ruble coins which replace the low-denomination banknotes (TDRB B9-B11, respectively). These "coins" are made of an unspecified composite material and have ultraviolet and infrared security elements. Because they bear images taken from the notes which they replace and are unusual, they are illustrated below as curiosities, but they are not considered banknotes and hence not assigned catalog numbers.

2014 Numismatic Products

On 22 August 2014, the Trans-Dniester Republican Bank issued 1-, 5-, 10-, and 25-ruble banknotes commemorating 20 years of national currency. 2,020 copies of each denomination were sold in folders. The notes are like the regular issues of 2012, but with a commemorative rosette over the watermark area at lower right front.

TDRB BNP3 (PNL): **1 ruble** (US$0.10)   **UNC**
Brown. Front: Alexander Suvorov. Back: Kitskansky Bridgehead memorial complex. Winged security thread. Watermark: Alexander Suvorov with electrotype *ПРБ*. Printer: (Trans-Dniester). 129 x 56 mm.
    ☐ a. 2007 МОДИФИКАЦИЯ (modified) 2012.   —   —
         Intro: 22.08.2014.

TDRB BNP4 (PNL): **5 rubles** (US$0.60)   **UNC**
Blue. Front: Alexander Suvorov. Back: KVINT Distillery administrative building. Windowed security thread. Winged security thread. Watermark: Alexander Suvorov with electrotype *ПРБ*. Printer: (Trans-Dniester). 129 x 56 mm.
    ☐ a. 2007 МОДИФИКАЦИЯ (modified) 2012.   —   —
         Intro: 22.08.2014.

TDRB BNP5 (PNL): **10 rubles** (US$1.20)   **UNC**
Brown and green. Front: Alexander Suvorov. Back: Novo-Nyametsky monastery. Winged security thread. Watermark: Alexander Suvorov with electrotype *ПРБ*. Printer: (Trans-Dniester). 129 x 56 mm.
    ☐ a. 2007 МОДИФИКАЦИЯ (modified) 2012.   —   —
         Intro: 22.08.2014.

TDRB BNP6 (PNL): **25 rubles** (US$2.95) UNC
Red. Front: Alexander Suvorov; Alexander Suvorov equestrian statue in Tiraspol. Back: Bendery fortress; memorial to Russian warriors. 4.5-mm wide windowed security thread. Watermark: Empress Catherine with electrotype ПРБ. Printer: (Trans-Dniester). 129 x 56 mm.

- a. 2007 МОДИФИКАЦИЯ (modified) 2012. — — —
Intro: 22.08.2014.

Acknowledgements

This chapter was compiled with the generous assistance of Thomas Augustsson, Daniele Paolo Dreoni, Hartmut Fraunhoffer (www.banknoten.de), Mikhail Istomin, Chris Kessler (Trans-Dniester Republican Bank), Vladimir Kozin (myworld.ebay.com/transnistriabanknotes), George Provencal, Gergely Scheidl (banknoteshop@gmx.net), Bill Stubkjaer, Christoph Thomas, Vadim Tislenko, Dmitry Zagorenko, and others.

Sources

Anonymous. "Transnistria Currency Notes." *IBNS Journal*. Volume 20 Number 3/4. p.68.

Augustsson, Thomas. "Bank Notes of PMR–The Transdiestr Moldavian Republic." *IBNS Journal*. Volume 37 Number 4. p.21.

Cuhaj, George S. *Standard Catalog of World Paper Money, Modern Issues, 1961-Present*. 17th edition. 2011. ISBN 978-1-4402-1584-1. Krause Publications (www.krausebooks.com), 700 East State St., Iola, WI, 54990-0001.

Istomin, Mikhail. "Transdniester Moldavian Republic." *IBNS Journal*. Volume 34 Number 1. p.29.

Share Your Input, Info, and Images

This catalog is believed to be complete and correct as of the time of publication. Prices and face values were last updated 1 July 2011. Please report errors or omissions so that corrections may be made. If you can more precisely identify the name or location of anything depicted on a note, please share that information. Furthermore, if you own an unlisted type or variety, please submit scans of the front and back of the note so that it can be documented. Scans should be 300 dots per inch, 100% actual size, 24-bit color, saved as *uncompressed* JPEG files, and sent to owen@banknotenews.com. Be sure to fully describe all attributes of the note which are not apparent upon visual inspection of the images alone, such as physical dimension, watermark, and security thread.

Trinidad and Tobago

Contents

Government of Trinidad and Tobago (GTT).......... 2109
Central Bank of Trinidad and Tobago (CBTT)....... 2113

Monetary System
1898: 1 Trinidad and Tobago dollar = 4 shillings 2 pence
1935: 1 Trinidad and Tobago dollar = 1 British W. Indies dollar
1951: British Caribbean Territories dollar
1964: 1 Trinidad and Tobago dollar (TTD) = 100 cents

Government of Trinidad and Tobago

In 1904, the Government of Trinidad and Tobago (GTT) passed the Currency Notes Ordinance, establishing the Board of Commissioners of Currency with the right to issue banknotes in denominations of 1, 2, and 1,000 dollars, in exchange for gold or silver coins previously issued.

GTT Signature Varieties
Commissioners of Currency

1  Hugh Charles Clifford | Denis Slyne | William Colebrook Lynch Dyett

2  Samuel William Knaggs | Denis Slyne | Adam Smith

3  Thomas Alexander Vans Best | John Tordeff Hewetson | William Louis Joseph Kernahan

4  Wilfred Edward Francis Jackson | Henry Barclay Walcott | William Louis Joseph Kernahan

5    Selwyn McGregor Grier | Herbert Laurence Bayles | William Louis Joseph Kernahan

6    Selwyn McGregor Grier | Errol Lionel dos Santos | Courtney Cornwall George

7    Alfred Wallace Seymour | Errol Lionel dos Santos | Courtney Cornwall George

GTT Signature Varieties
Commissioners of Currency

8    John Huggins | Errol Lionel dos Santos | Courtney Cornwall George

9 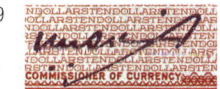   Andrew Barkworth Wright | Errol Lionel dos Santos | Courtney Cornwall George

10   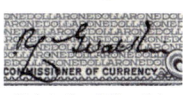 Andrew Barkworth Wright | Algar Ronald Ward Robertson | Ralph Lloyd Gwatkin

11    Louis Nathaniel Blache-Fraser | Algar Ronald Ward Robertson | Ralph Lloyd Gwatkin

1905-1926 Issues

GTT B1 (P1b/c): 1 dollar (demonetized 02.01.1955) | **Good** | **Fine** | **XF**

Blue. Front: Blue vignette of landing of Columbus; coat of arms. Back: Mountain with sailing ship. No security thread. Watermark: Diamond pattern. 177 x 82 mm.

☐	a.	1st April, 1905. Signature 1. Printer: (TDLR). Prefix with horizontal bar. Prefix A/1 - A/16.	275	500	1,600
☐	b.	Prefix without horizontal bar. Prefix A/25 - A/33.	200	400	1,200
☐	c.	1st January, 1924. Sig. 3. Prefix A/42 - A/45. Printer: *THOS. DE LA RUE & CO LTD LONDON*.	75	300	800
☐	d.	1st March, 1926. Signature 4. Prefix A/50 - A/51.	75	500	800
☐	as.	No overprint; all-zero serial numbers; black vignette and coat of arms on front.	—	—	—
☐	p.	Proof. No date; no signatures; no serial numbers.	—	—	—

GTT B2 (P2b): **2 dollars** (demonetized 02.01.1955)   Good   Fine   XF
Red and green. Front: Sailing ship in harbor; palm tree with sailing ship. Back: Cocoa field; coat of arms; cane field. No security thread. Watermark: Unknown. Printer: *THOS. DE LA RUE & CO LTD LONDON*. 174 x 90 mm.

☐ a.   1st April, 1905. Signature 1. Prefix A/1 - A/2.   —   —   —
☐ as.   Horizontal red *SPECIMEN* stamp.   —   —   5,000

Like subsequent issues, but green, not red, banner and vignettes on front.

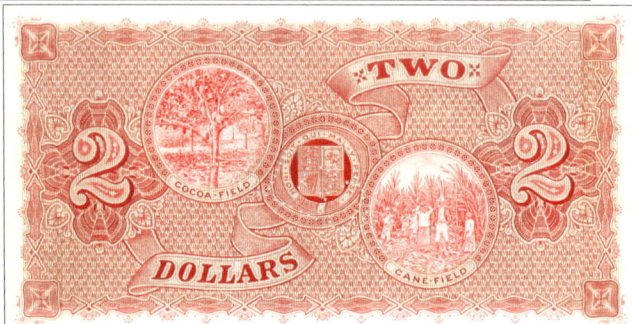

GTT B3 (P2a): **2 dollars** (demonetized 02.01.1955)   Good   Fine   XF
Red. Front: Sailing ship in harbor; palm tree with sailing ship. Back: Cocoa field; coat of arms; cane field. No security thread. Watermark: Unknown. Printer: *THOS. DE LA RUE & CO LTD LONDON*. 174 x 90 mm.

☐ a.   1st April, 1905. Signature 1.   200   700   2,500
       Prefix with horizontal bar. Prefix A/4 - A/8.
☐ b.   Prefix without horizontal bar. Prefix A/10.   200   700   2,500
☐ as.   Diagonal *CANCELLED* perforation.   —   —   —
☐ p.   Proof. No date; no signatures; no serial numbers.   —   —   —

Like preceding issues, but red, not green, banner and vignettes on front.

GTT B4 (P2E): **1,000 dollars**   Good   Fine   XF
Green. Front: Athena wearing helmet; coat of arms. Back: Cherubs flanking sailing ship in harbor. No security thread. Watermark: Unknown. Printer: *THOS. DE LA RUE & CO LTD LONDON*. 190 x 120 mm.

☐ p.   Horizontal *CANCELLED* perforation;   —   —   12,000
       no date; no signatures; no serial numbers.
☐ s1.   Horizontal *CANCELLED* perforation;   —   —   —
       horizontal purple *SPECIMEN* stamp;
       1st January 1914. Signature 2.
☐ s2.   1st April 1914. Signature 1.   —   —   —
       Uniface front/back.

1929-1934 Issues

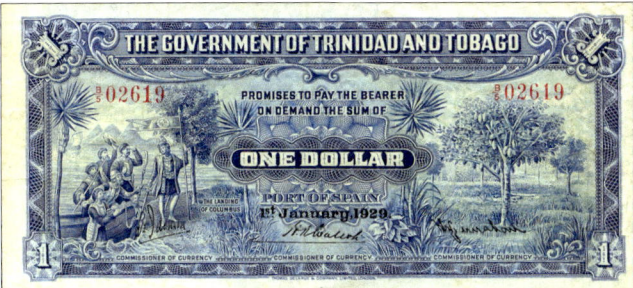

GTT B5 (P3): 1 dollar (demonetized 02.01.1955)   Good   Fine   XF
Blue. Front: Landing of Columbus; cocoa trees. Back: Mountain with sailing ship. No security thread. Watermark: Pineapple pattern. Printer: *THOMAS DE LA RUE & COMPANY LIMITED, LONDON*. 172 x 78 mm.

☐	a.	1st January,1929. Signature 4. Prefix B/1 - B/13.	250	1,000	4,000
☐	b.	1st January,1932. Signature 5. Prefix B/14 - B/24.	250	1,000	4,000
☐	as.	Horizontal red *SPECIMEN* stamp.	—	UNC	1,100

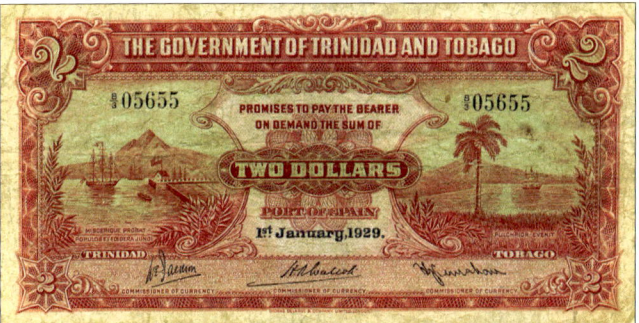

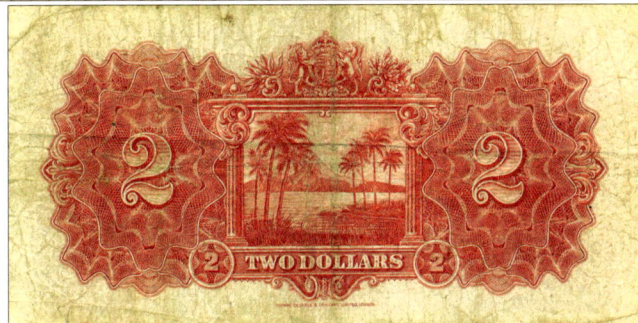

GTT B6 (P4): 2 dollars (demonetized 02.01.1955)   Good   Fine   XF
Red. Front: Sailing ship in harbor; palm tree with sailing ship. Back: Palm trees, harbor, and mountain. No security thread. Watermark: Unknown. Printer: *THOMAS DE LA RUE & COMPANY LIMITED, LONDON*. 172 x 78 mm.

☐	a.	1st January,1929. Signature 4. Prefix B/1 - B/5.	—	—	—
☐	b.	1st May,1934. Signature 6. Prefix B/9.	—	—	—
☐	p.	Proof: Uniface.	—	AU	575
☐	as.	No overprint; no perforation; all-zero s/n.	—	—	—

1935-1949 Issues

The Government Currency Authority (in accordance with the Currency Notes Ordinance, Ch. 35, No. 6) took over the function of issuing notes in the 1930s.

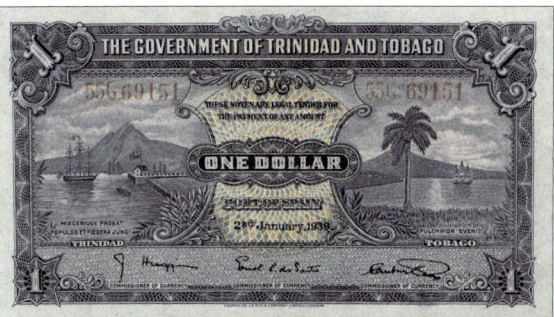

GTT B7 (P5): 1 dollar (demonetized 02.01.1955)   Good   Fine   XF
Blue and yellow. Front: Sailing ship and mountain; palm tree and sailing ship. Back: Coat of arms. No security thread. Watermark: *TRINIDAD*. Printer: *THOMAS DE LA RUE & COMPANY LIMITED, LONDON*. 152 x 82 mm.

☐	a1.	1st September,1935. Signature 7. Fractional prefix. Prefix C/2 - C/7.	15	50	200
☐	a2.	Number letter prefix. Prefix 16C - 23C.	15	50	200
☐	b.	2nd January,1939. Signature 8. Prefix 26C - 10D.	2	8	35
☐	c.	1st May,1942. Signature 9. Prefix 11D - 29D.	2	8	35
☐	d.	1st January,1943. Prefix 33D - 69D.	6	25	100
☐	e.	1st. JULY, 1948. Signature 10. Prefix 70D - 80D.	3	12	50
☐	f.	1st July,1949. Signature 11. Prefix 85D - 97D.	4	15	65
☐	bs.	Horizontal *CANCELLED* perforation.	—	—	—
☐	cs.	Horizontal *CANCELLED* perforation.	—	—	—
☐	ds.	Horizontal *CANCELLED* perforation.	—	—	—

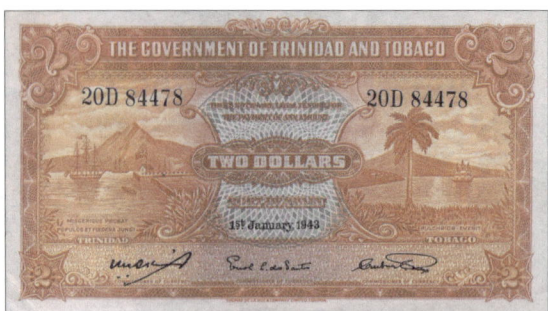

GTT B8 (P6 & P8): **2 dollars** (demonetized 02.01.1955)   Good   Fine   XF
Red and green. Front: Sailing ship and mountain; palm tree and sailing ship. Back: Coat of arms. No security thread. Watermark: *TRINIDAD*. Printer: *THOMAS DE LA RUE & COMPANY LIMITED, LONDON*. 152 x 82 mm.

			Good	Fine	XF
☐	a1.	1st September, 1935. Signature 7. Fractional prefix. Prefix C/1 – C/2.	25	75	260
☐	a2.	Number letter prefix. Prefix 6C.	25	75	260
☐	b.	2nd January, 1939. Signature 8. Prefix 8C – 5D.	25	100	250
☐	c.	1st May, 1942. Signature 9. Prefix 6D – 15D.	10	40	265
☐	d.	1st January, 1943. Prefix 17D – 27D.	10	40	265
☐	e.	1st July, 1949. Signature 11. Prefix 30D.	—	—	—
☐	bs.	Horizontal *CANCELLED* perforation.	—	—	—
☐	ds.	Horizontal *CANCELLED* perforation.	—	—	—

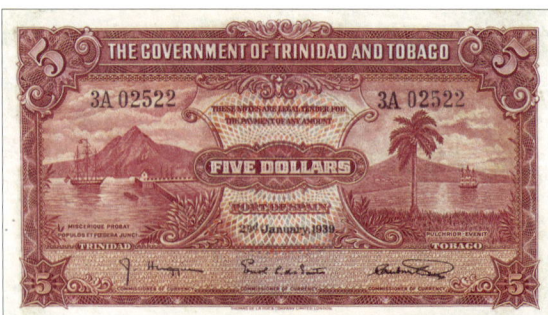

GTT B9 (P7): **5 dollars** (demonetized 02.01.1955)   Good   Fine   XF
Purple. Front: Sailing ship and mountain; palm tree and sailing ship. Back: Coat of arms. No security thread. Watermark: *TRINIDAD*. Printer: *THOMAS DE LA RUE & COMPANY LIMITED, LONDON*. 152 x 82 mm.

			Good	Fine	XF
☐	a.	1st September, 1935. Signature 7. Unconfirmed.	—	—	—
☐	b.	2nd January, 1939. Signature 8. Prefix 1A – 23A.	25	100	400
☐	c.	1st May, 1942. Signature 9. Prefix 27A – 37A.	50	200	800
☐	p.	Proof.	—	—	—
☐	cs.	Horizontal *CANCELLED* perforation.	—	—	—

GTT B10 (P9): **10 dollars** (demonetized 02.01.1955)   Good   Fine   XF
Reddish brown. Front: Sailing ship and mountain; palm tree and sailing ship. Back: Coat of arms. No security thread. Watermark: Unknown. Printer: *THOMAS DE LA RUE & COMPANY LIMITED, LONDON*. 152 x 82 mm.

			Good	Fine	XF
☐	a.	2nd January, 1939. Signature 8. Prefix 1A.	100	400	—
☐	b.	1st May, 1942. Signature 9. Prefix 3A – 8A.	75	275	650
☐	p.	Proof.	—	—	—
☐	s.	Diagonal black *SPECIMEN* and DLR oval ovpts; horizontal black *SPECIMEN OF NO VALUE* ovpt at upper left; no date; no signatures; no s/n.	—	—	—
☐	t.	Color trial: Red. No date; no signatures.	—	UNC	1,100

GTT B11 (P10): **20 dollars** (demonetized 02.01.1955)   Good   Fine   XF
Green. Front: Sailing ship and mountain; palm tree and sailing ship. Back: Coat of arms. No security thread. Watermark: Unknown. Printer: *THOMAS DE LA RUE & COMPANY LIMITED, LONDON*. 152 x 82 mm.

			Good	Fine	XF
☐	a.	1st May, 1942. Signature 9. Prefix 1A – 2A.	450	550	1,000
☐	b.	1st January, 1943. Prefix 4A – 7A.	450	1,000	3,000
☐	as.	Horizontal *CANCELLED* perforation.	—	—	825
☐	bs.	Horizontal *CANCELLED* perforation.	—	—	825

GTT B12 (PNL): **100 dollars**   Good   Fine   XF

Olive green. Front: Sailing ship and mountain; palm tree and sailing ship. Back: Coat of arms. No security thread. Watermark: Unknown. Printer: *THOMAS DE LA RUE & COMPANY LIMITED, LONDON.* 152 x 82 mm.

- ☐ p. Proof.   —   —   —
- ☐ s. Specimen: 1st January, 1943. Signature 9.   —   UNC   3,500

1951-1964 Issues

The Government Currency Authority was replaced (in accordance with the Currency Notes Ordinance, Ch 35 No 2) by the British Caribbean Currency Board (BCCB). In keeping with its mandate to manage a unified decimal system of currency for all British colonies of the Eastern Caribbean (Antigua, Barbados, Dominica, Grenada, Monsterrat, St Kitts, St Lucia, St Vincent, and Trinidad and Tobago) as well as mainland British Guiana, the BCCB issued its first currency notes on 15 August 1951.

See British Caribbean Territories.

Central Bank of Trinidad and Tobago

Trinidad and Tobago became independent on 31 August 1962 and as such became solely responsible for its economic development and other national objectives. Thus, the existing central monetary authority, the British Caribbean Currency Board, could not provide the government with the monetary instruments necessary to implement the economic policies being undertaken since it was not structured to serve an independent country.

The Central Bank of Trinidad and Tobago (CBTT) was established in December 1964 under the provisions of the Central Bank Act 1964. Act No. 23 of 1964 gave the Central Bank "the sole right to issue notes and coins in Trinidad and Tobago." The Central Bank's first act was to issue new designs of currency on 14 December 1964 just two days after the proclamation of the Central Bank Act.

For more information, visit www.central-bank.org.tt.

CBTT Signature Varieties

Governor

1   John F. Pierce (1964 - 1966)

2  Alexander N. McLeod (1966 - 1969)

3   Victor E. Bruce (1969 - 1984)

4  Euric A. Bobb (1984 - 1988)

5  William G. Demas (1988 - 1992)

6  T. Ainsworth Harewood (1992 - 1997)

7  Winston Dookeran (1997 - 2002)

8  Ewart S. Williams (17.07.2002 - 12.07.2012)

9  Jwala Rambarran (13.07.2012 - present)

1964 Issues

All of these notes feature the coat of arms at left and a portrait of Queen Elizabeth II at center. On the back the bank's headquarters is depicted at center, with various local economic activities represented in vignettes at upper right.

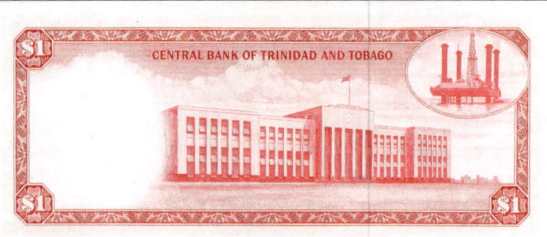

CBTT B1 (P26): **1 dollar** (US$0.15)   VG   VF   UNC

Red. Front: Coat of arms; Queen Elizabeth II. Back: Old Central Bank building in Port of Spain; off-shore oil platform. Solid security thread. Watermark: Bird of paradise. Printer: (BWC). 155 x 66 mm.

			VG	VF	UNC
☐	a.	1964. Intro: 14.12.1964. Signature 1. Prefix A - Q.	5	20	80
☐	b.	Signature 2. Prefix R - W.	5	20	70
☐	c.	Fractional prefix. Prefix A/1 - X/1.	5	20	70
☐	d.	Signature 3. Prefix B/2 - P/4.	2	8	35
☐	cs.	Horizontal *SPECIMEN* overprint; punched.	—	—	125
☐	dt.	Color trial: Purple.	—	—	115
☐	t.	Color trial: Purple. No signature.	—	—	115

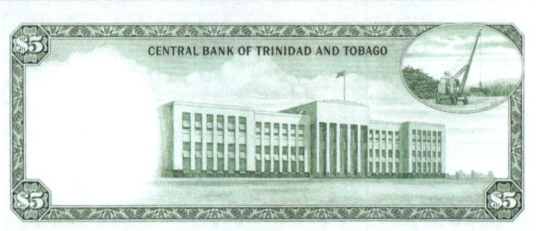

CBTT B2 (P27): **5 dollars** (US$0.80)   VG   VF   UNC

Green. Front: Coat of arms; Queen Elizabeth II. Back: Old Central Bank building in Port of Spain; crane lifting sugar cane. Solid security thread. Watermark: Bird of paradise. Printer: (BWC). 155 x 66 mm.

			VG	VF	UNC
☐	a.	1964. Intro: 14.12.1964. Signature 1. Prefix A - F.	30	125	500
☐	b.	Signature 2. Prefix G - R.	10	40	125
☐	c.	Signature 3. Prefix S - T.	5	20	85
☐	d.	Fractional prefix. Prefix J/1.	5	20	85
☐	at.	Color trial: Brown.	—	—	300
☐	cs.	Horizontal *SPECIMEN* overprint; punched.	—	—	215
☐	dt.	Color trial: Brown.	—	—	300

CBTT B3 (P28): **10 dollars** (US$1.55)   VG   VF   UNC

Brown. Front: Coat of arms; Queen Elizabeth II. Back: Old Central Bank building in Port of Spain; sugar processing plant. Solid security thread. Watermark: Bird of paradise. Printer: (BWC). 155 x 66 mm.

			VG	VF	UNC
☐	a.	1964. Intro: 14.12.1964. Signature 1. Prefix A - B.	150	600	2,400
☐	b.	Signature 2. Prefix D - H.	125	500	2,000
☐	c.	Signature 3. Prefix L - U.	40	175	550
☐	at.	Color trial: Olive green.	—	—	300
☐	cs.	Horizontal *SPECIMEN* overprint; punched.	—	—	250

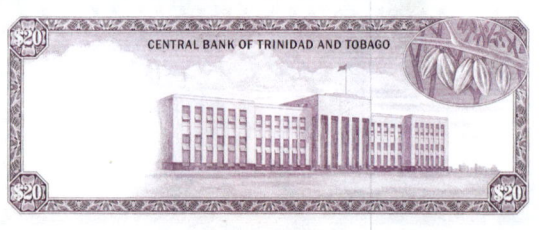

CBTT B4 (P29): **20 dollars** (US$3.15)   VG   VF   UNC

Purple. Front: Coat of arms; Queen Elizabeth II. Back: Old Central Bank building in Port of Spain; cacao pods. Solid security thread. Watermark: Bird of paradise. Printer: (BWC). 155 x 66 mm.

			VG	VF	UNC
☐	a.	1964. Intro: 14.12.1964. Signature 1. Prefix A.	75	300	1,200
☐	b.	Signature 2. Prefix K - Q.	60	250	1,000
☐	c.	Signature 3. Prefix R.	40	150	500
☐	d.	Fractional prefix. Prefix R/1 - W/1.	40	150	500
☐	at.	Color trial: Red.	—	—	300
☐	cs.	Horizontal *SPECIMEN* overprint; punched.	—	—	400

CBTT B4.5 (PNL): 100 dollars (US$16)	VG	VF	UNC

Blue. Front: Coat of arms; Queen Elizabeth II. Back: Old Central Bank building in Port of Spain; cacao pods. Solid security thread. Watermark: Bird of paradise. Printer: (BWC). 155 x 66 mm.

☐ p. Proof. 1964. Signature 1. Unissued. — — —

1977 Issues

In recognition of the country's assumption of republican status on 1 August 1976, the bank issued new notes on 6 June 1977, with depictions of local flora and fauna and scenes at left, and the coat-of-arms replacing the portrait of Queen Elizabeth II at center. The 50- and 100-dollar denominations are entirely new, but feature the same overall design.

CBTT B6 (P31): 5 dollars (US$0.80)	VG	VF	UNC

Green. Front: Branches and leaves; coat of arms. Back: Old Central Bank building in Port of Spain; crane lifting sugar cane. Solid security thread. Watermark: Bird of paradise. Printer: (BWC). 155 x 66 mm.

☐ a. 1964. Intro: 06.06.1977. Signature 3. Prefix AA - BH. FV 8 35
☐ b. Signature 4. Prefix BJ - BK. FV 15 60
☐ as. Horizontal *SPECIMEN* overprint; punched. — — —

Replacement notes: Prefix XX.

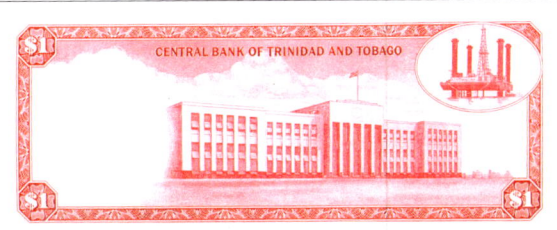

CBTT B7 (P32): 10 dollars (US$1.55)	VG	VF	UNC

Brown. Front: piping uan bird on branch; coat of arms. Back: Old Central Bank building in Port of Spain; sugar processing plant. Solid security thread. Watermark: Bird of paradise. Printer: (BWC). 155 x 66 mm.

☐ a. 1964. Sig. 3. Prefix AA - BK. Intro: 06.06.1977. — — —
☐ as. Horizontal *SPECIMEN* overprint; punched. — — 215

Replacement notes: Prefix XX.

CBTT B5 (P30): 1 dollar (US$0.15)	VG	VF	UNC

Red. Front: Two scarlet ibis birds; coat of arms. Back: Old Central Bank building in Port of Spain; off-shore oil platform. Solid security thread. Watermark: Bird of paradise. Printer: (BWC). 155 x 66 mm.

☐ a. 1964. Intro: 06.06.1977. Signature 3. Prefix AA - FA. FV FV 6.50
☐ b. Signature 4. Prefix FC - FN. FV FV 4
☐ as. Horizontal black *SPECIMEN* overprint; horizontal red *SPECIMEN OF NO VALUE* overprint at upper left; black # ovpt at upper left back; punched. — — 150

Replacement notes: Prefix XX.

CBTT B8 (P33): **20 dollars** (US$3.15) VG VF UNC

Purple. Front: Hibiscus flowers; coat of arms. Back: Old Central Bank building in Port of Spain; cacao pods. Solid security thread. Watermark: Bird of paradise. Printer: (BWC). 155 x 66 mm.

☐	a.	1964. Signature 3. Prefix AP - BX.	FV	50	80
☐	b.	Signature 4. Prefix CD.	FV	50	80
☐	bs.	Horizontal *SPECIMEN* overprint; punched.	—	—	—

Replacement notes: Prefix XX.

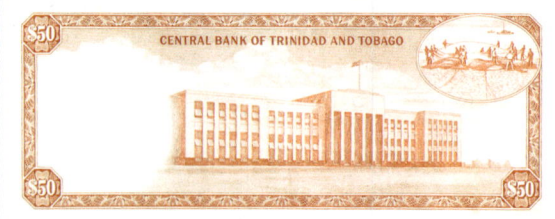

CBTT B9 (P34): **50 dollars** (demonetized 25.02.1979) VG VF UNC

Red-orange. Front: Long-billed starthroat bird; coat of arms. Back: Old Central Bank building in Port of Spain; net fishing. Solid security thread. Watermark: Bird of paradise. Printer: (BWC). 155 x 66 mm.

☐	a.	1963 [sic]. Sig. 3. Prefix AA. Intro: 06.06.1977.	20	75	350
☐	b.	1964. Prefix AC.	50	200	900
☐	bs.	Horizontal red *SPECIMEN* overprint; horizontal red *SPECIMEN OF NO VALUE* overprint at upper left; black # overprint at upper left back; punched.	—	—	325

Replacement notes: Prefix XX.

CBTT B10 (P35): **100 dollars** (US$16) VG VF UNC

Blue. Front: Branch with leaves and berries; coat of arms. Back: Old Central Bank building in Port of Spain; huts and palm trees. Solid security thread. Watermark: Bird of paradise. Printer: (BWC). 155 x 66 mm.

☐	a.	1964. Intro: 06.06.1977. Signature 3. Prefix AA - AX.	FV	30	105
☐	b.	Signature 4. Prefix AZ.	FV	80	350
☐	as.	Horizontal *SPECIMEN* overprint; punched.	—	—	—

Replacement notes: Prefix XX.

1985 Issues

These notes are like the preceding issue, but they now are issued in accordance with the Central Bank Act Chap. 79:02. Additional colors are employed to make counterfeiting more difficult. The designs on back have been revised with the new Central Bank high-rise building (part of the Eric Williams Financial Complex) and updated vignettes no longer enclosed in ovals.

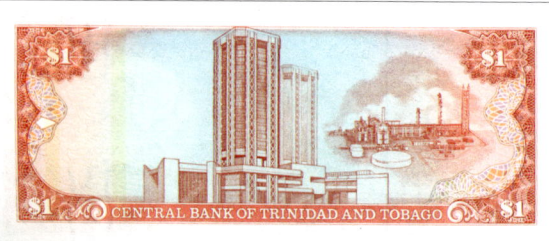

CBTT B11 (P36): **1 dollar** (US$0.15) VG VF UNC

Red. Front: Two scarlet ibis birds; coat of arms. Back: Eric Williams Financial Complex in Port of Spain; Tringen oil refinery at the Point Lisas industrial estate. Solid security thread. Watermark: Bird of paradise and *1*. Printer: (TDLR). 155 x 66 mm.

☐	a.	No date. Intro: 02.12.1985. Signature 4. Prefix AA - CD.	FV	FV	1.50
☐	b.	Signature 5. Prefix CK - EV.	FV	FV	1.50
☐	c.	Signature 6. Prefix EW - JP.	FV	FV	1.25
☐	d.	Signature 7. Prefix KK - QY.	FV	FV	1.25
☐	as.	Diagonal *SPECIMEN* overprint; punched.	—	—	150

Replacement notes: Prefix XX.

CBTT B12 (P37): **5 dollars** (US$0.80)   VG   VF   UNC

Green and blue. Front: Mot mot bird on branch; coat of arms. Back: Eric Williams Financial Complex in Port of Spain; three women at produce market with wicker baskets. Solid security thread. Watermark: Bird of paradise and *5*. Printer: (TDLR). 155 x 66 mm.

- a. No date. Intro: 02.12.1985.   FV   FV   5
  Signature 4. Prefix AA - AK.
- b. Signature 5. Prefix AU - BJ.   FV   FV   3
- c. Signature 6. Prefix BR - CN.   FV   FV   4
- d. Signature 7. Prefix CP - CT.   FV   FV   2
- as. Diagonal *SPECIMEN* overprint; punched.   —   —   150

Replacement notes: Prefix XX.

CBTT B14 (P39): **20 dollars** (US$3.15)   VG   VF   UNC

Purple and green. Front: Hummingbird drinking nectar from flower; coat of arms. Back: Eric Williams Financial Complex in Port of Spain; five steel drum musical instruments. Solid security thread. Watermark: Bird of paradise and *20*. Printer: (TDLR). 155 x 66 mm.

- a. No date. Intro: 02.12.1985.   FV   FV   15
  Signature 4. Prefix AA - AS.
- b. Signature 5. Prefix AU - CT.   FV   FV   15
- c. Signature 6. Prefix CX - EQ.   FV   FV   15
- d. Signature 7. Prefix EU - GQ.   FV   FV   15
- as. Diagonal *SPECIMEN* overprint; punched.   —   —   175

Replacement notes: Prefix XX.

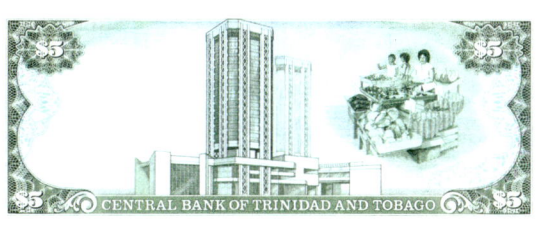

CBTT B13 (P38): **10 dollars** (US$1.55)   VG   VF   UNC

Gray and yellow. Front: Cocorico bird on branch; coat of arms. Back: Eric Williams Financial Complex in Port of Spain; gantry crane unloading containers off ship in port. Solid security thread. Watermark: Bird of paradise and *10*. Printer: (TDLR). 155 x 66 mm.

- a. No date. Intro: 02.12.1985.   FV   FV   8
  Signature 4. Prefix AA - AH.
- b. Signature 5. Prefix AT - BH.   FV   FV   8
- c. Signature 6. Prefix BG - BS.   FV   FV   8
- d. Signature 7. Prefix BW - CW.   FV   FV   8
- as. Diagonal *SPECIMEN* overprint; punched.   —   —   175

Replacement notes: Prefix XX.

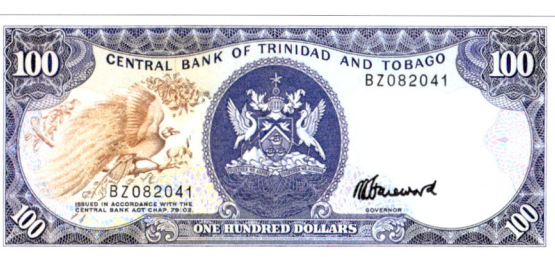

CBTT B15 (P40): **100 dollars** (US$16)   VG   VF   UNC

Blue and brown. Front: Bird of paradise on branch; coat of arms. Back: Eric Williams Financial Complex in Port of Spain; off-shore oil platform. Solid security thread. Watermark: Bird of paradise and *100*. Printer: (TDLR). 155 x 66 mm.

- a. No date. Intro: 02.12.1985.   FV   FV   150
  Signature 4. Prefix AA - AV.
- b. Signature 5. Prefix AV.   FV   FV   150
- c. Signature 6. Prefix BF - BZ.   FV   FV   150
- d. Signature 7. Prefix CE - DK.   FV   FV   150
- as. Diagonal *SPECIMEN* overprint; punched.   —   —   225
- bs. Diagonal red *SPECIMEN* and DLR oval ovpts; horizontal red *SPECIMEN Nº #* ovpt at lower left; punched.   —   —   —

Replacement notes: Prefix XX.

2002 Issues

These notes are like the preceding issues, but with design changes to accommodate enhanced security, including full-bleed colors, 2-mm wide windowed security threads, registration devices, large textured numerals, gold iridescent bands, and novel serial numbering with the vertical numbers printed in red. Notes with signature 7 use prefixes that continue from the preceding issues, but when signature 8 was adopted, the prefixes reverted back to AA.

CBTT B16 (P41): **1 dollar** (US$0.15)   VG   VF   UNC

Red. Front: Two scarlet ibis birds; coat of arms; ibis as registration device. Back: Ibis; Eric Williams Financial Complex in Port of Spain; Tringen oil refinery at the Point Lisas industrial estate. Windowed security thread with demetalized *CBTT1*. Watermark: Bird of paradise and electrotype *T&T*. Printer: (TDLR). 152.4 x 69.85 mm.

    ☐ a.   2002. Signature 8. Prefix AA - DX.   FV   FV   1

CBTT B17 (P42): **5 dollars** (US$0.80)   VG   VF   UNC

Green and blue. Front: Mot mot bird on branch; coat of arms; mot mot as registration device. Back: Mot mot; Eric Williams Financial Complex in Port of Spain; three women at produce market with wicker baskets. Windowed security thread with demetalized *CBTT5*. Watermark: Bird of paradise and electrotype *T&T*. Printer: (TDLR). 152.4 x 69.85 mm.

    ☐ a.   2002.   FV   FV   2
        Signature 7. Prefix DL - DR.
    ☐ b.   Signature 8. Prefix AA - AV.   FV   FV   2

CBTT B18 (P43): **10 dollars** (US$1.55)   VG   VF   UNC

Gray and yellow. Front: Cocorico bird on branch; coat of arms; cocorico as registration device. Back: Cocorico; Eric Williams Financial Complex in Port of Spain; gantry crane unloading containers off ship in port. Windowed security thread with demetalized *CBTT10*. Watermark: Bird of paradise and electrotype *T&T*. Printer: (TDLR). 152.4 x 69.85 mm.

    ☐ a.   2002. Signature 8. Prefix AA - AV.   FV   FV   3

CBTT B19 (P44): **20 dollars** (US$3.15)   VG   VF   UNC

Purple and green. Front: Hummingbird drinking nectar from flower; coat of arms; hummingbird as registration device; gold foil hibiscus flower. Back: Hummingbird; Eric Williams Financial Complex in Port of Spain; five steel drum musical instruments. Windowed security thread with demetalized *CBTT20*. Watermark: Bird of paradise and electrotype *T&T*. Printer: (TDLR). 152.4 x 69.85 mm.

    ☐ a.   2002.   FV   FV   5
        Signature 7. Prefix HC - JA.
    ☐ b.   Signature 8. Prefix AA - BW.   FV   FV   5

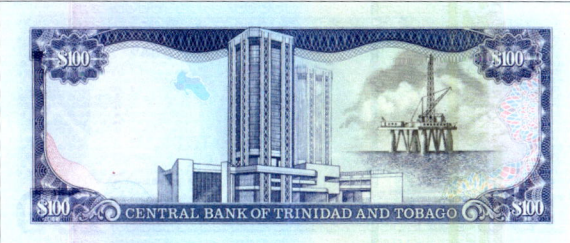

CBTT B20 (P45): **100 dollars** (US$16) VG VF UNC

Blue and brown. Front: Bird of paradise on branch; coat of arms; bird of paradise as registration device; silver shield hologram. Back: Bird of paradise; Eric Williams Financial Complex in Port of Spain; off-shore oil platform. Windowed security thread with demetalized *CBTT100*. Watermark: Bird of paradise and electrotype *T&T*. Printer: (TDLR). 152.4 x 69.85 mm.

☐ a. 2002. Signature 8. Prefix AA - BQ. FV FV 30

2006 Issues

In 2007, the bank upgraded all denominations with new security features. Instead of using the bird of paradise as the watermark on all notes, the watermarks match the birds printed on the individual notes, with the addition of Cornerstones and electrotype elements that indicate the denomination. In addition, the color of the vertical serial number at right is now blue, not red.

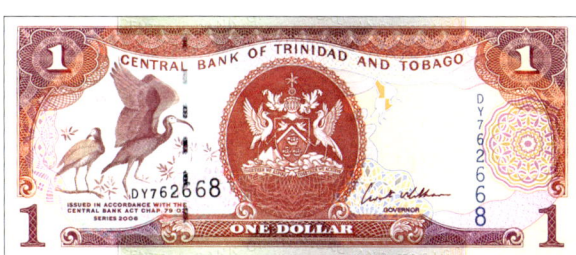

CBTT B21 (P46): **1 dollar** (US$0.15) VG VF UNC

Red. Front: Two scarlet ibis birds; coat of arms; ibis as registration device. Back: Ibis; Eric Williams Financial Complex in Port of Spain; Tringen oil refinery at the Point Lisas industrial estate. 1.2-mm wide windowed security thread with demetalized *CBTT1*. Watermark: Scarlet ibis bird, electrotype *TT1*, and Cornerstones. Printer: (TDLR). 152.4 x 69.85 mm.

☐ a. 2006. Sig. 8. Prefix DY - LN. Intro: 26.02.2007. FV FV 1

CBTT B22 (P47): **5 dollars** (US$0.80) VG VF UNC

Green and blue. Front: Mot mot bird on branch; coat of arms; mot mot as registration device. Back: Mot mot; Eric Williams Financial Complex in Port of Spain; three women at produce market with wicker baskets. Windowed security thread with demetalized *CBTT5*. Watermark: Mot mot bird, electrotype *TT5*, and Cornerstones. Printer: (TDLR). 152.4 x 69.85 mm.

☐ a. 2006. Sig. 8. Prefix AZ - CE. Intro: 26.02.2007. FV FV 2

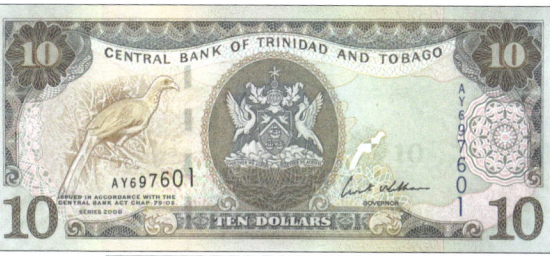

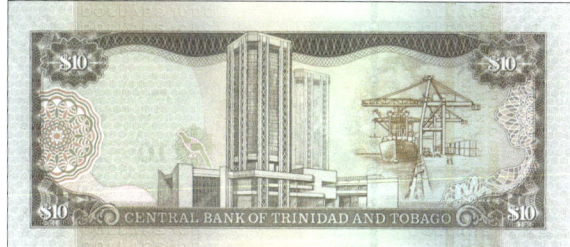

CBTT B23 (P48): **10 dollars** (US$1.55) VG VF UNC

Gray and yellow. Front: Cocorico bird on branch; coat of arms; cocorico as registration device. Back: Cocorico; Eric Williams Financial Complex in Port of Spain; gantry crane unloading containers off ship in port. Windowed security thread with demetalized *CBTT10*. Watermark: Cocorico bird, electrotype *10*, and Cornerstones. Printer: (TDLR). 152.4 x 69.85 mm.

☐ a. 2006. Sig. 8. Prefix AX - BS. Intro: 13.11.2007. FV FV 3.50

2009 Commemorative Issues

This 100-dollar note commemorates the Commonwealth Heads of Government Meeting (CHOGM) that was held 27-29 November in the capital, Port of Spain.

CBTT B24 (P49): **20 dollars** (US$3.15)   VG   VF   UNC
Purple and green. Front: Hummingbird drinking nectar from flower; coat of arms; hummingbird as registration device; gold foil hibiscus flower. Back: Hummingbird; Eric Williams Financial Complex in Port of Spain; five steel drum musical instruments. Windowed security thread with demetalized *CBTT20*. Watermark: Hummingbird, electrotype *20*, and Cornerstones. Printer: (TDLR). 152.4 x 69.85 mm.
     ☐ a.   2006. Sig. 8. Prefix CK - EZ. Intro: 13.11.2007.   FV   FV   6

CBTT B26 (P52): **100 dollars** (US$16)   VG   VF   UNC
Blue and brown. Front: Bird of paradise on branch; brown *60 YEARS OF THE COMMONWEALTH 1949-2009* overprint around coat of arms; bird of paradise as registration device; silver shield hologram; CHOGM logo. Back: CHOGM logo; city buildings; bird of paradise; Port-of-Spain International Waterfront Centre; Carnival sun; off-shore oil platform. Windowed security thread with demetalized *CBTT100*. Watermark: Bird of paradise, electrotype *100*, and Cornerstones. Printer: (TDLR). 152.4 x 69.85 mm.
     ☐ a.   Series 2006; 2009 on overprint. Signature 8.   FV   FV   40
               Prefix AA.

CBTT B25 (P51): **100 dollars** (US$16)   VG   VF   UNC
Blue and brown. Front: Bird of paradise on branch; coat of arms; bird of paradise as registration device; silver shield hologram. Back: Bird of paradise; Eric Williams Financial Complex in Port of Spain; off-shore oil platform. Windowed security thread with demetalized *CBTT100*. Watermark: Bird of paradise, electrotype *100*, and Cornerstones. Printer: (TDLR). 152.4 x 69.85 mm.
     ☐ a.   2006. Sig. 8. Prefix BY - FU. Intro: 13.11.2007.   FV   FV   25

2012 Commemorative Issues

On 20 June 2012, the Central Bank of Trinidad and Tobago unveiled this 50-dollar note commemorating the nation's 50th independence anniversary. "A limited number of notes" carry the following red text around the coat of arms at center front: *CELEBRATING 50 YEARS OF INDEPENDENCE 1962-2012*. The commemorative notes with overprint and regular issue notes without overprint are both legal tender, and entered circulation at face value in August 2012.

CBTT B27 (P53): **50 dollars** (US$8)   VG   VF   UNC
Gold and olive green. Front: Red-capped cardinal bird on branch; red *CELEBRATING 50 YEARS OF INDEPENDENCE 1962-2012* overprint around coat of arms; red-capped cardinal as registration device; Depth Image holographic patch. Back: Red-capped cardinal; Eric Williams Financial Complex in Port of Spain; Red House (Parliament building). 2-mm wide windowed security thread with demetalized *CBTT50*. Watermark: Red-capped cardinal, electrotype *50*, and Cornerstones. Printer: (TDLR). 152.4 x 69.85 mm.

    a.   Series 2006; 2012 on overprint. Signature 8.   FV   FV   20
         Prefix AD. Intro: August 2012.
    as.   Diagonal red *SPECIMEN* overprint.   —   —   —

2006 (2012-2014) Issues

The 50-dollar note is identical to the commemorative (CBTT B27), but without the red overprint text around the coat of arms. This was the first note issued in a new family revised by the addition of raised horizontal bars at upper left and right front to assist the visually impaired distinguish between denominations.

CBTT B29 (PNL): **1 dollar** (US$0.15)   VG   VF   UNC
Red. Front: Two scarlet ibis birds; coat of arms; ibis as registration device. Back: Ibis; Eric Williams Financial Complex in Port of Spain; Tringen oil refinery at the Point Lisas industrial estate. 1.2-mm wide windowed security thread with demetalized *CBTT1*. Watermark: Scarlet ibis bird, electrotype *TT1*, and Cornerstones. Printer: (TDLR). 152.4 x 69.85 mm.

    a.   2006. Sig. 9. Prefix MA - MK. Intro: Nov. 2013.   FV   FV   1

No image available.
CBTT B30 (PNL): **5 dollars** (US$0.80)   VG   VF   UNC
Green and blue. Front: Mot mot bird on branch; coat of arms; mot mot as registration device. Back: Mot mot; Eric Williams Financial Complex in Port of Spain; three women at produce market with wicker baskets. Windowed security thread with demetalized *CBTT5*. Watermark: Mot mot bird, electrotype *TT5*, and Cornerstones. Printer: (TDLR). 152.4 x 69.85 mm.

    a.   2006. Expected new issue.   FV   FV   2

No image available.
CBTT B31 (PNL): **10 dollars** (US$1.55)   VG   VF   UNC
Gray and yellow. Front: Cocorico bird on branch; coat of arms; cocorico as registration device. Back: Cocorico; Eric Williams Financial Complex in Port of Spain; gantry crane unloading containers off ship in port. Windowed security thread with demetalized *CBTT10*. Watermark: Cocorico bird, electrotype *10*, and Cornerstones. Printer: (TDLR). 152.4 x 69.85 mm.

    a.   2006. Expected new issue.   FV   FV   3.50

CBTT B32 (PNL): **20 dollars** (US$3.15)　　　　VG　VF　UNC

Purple and green. Front: Hummingbird drinking nectar from flower; coat of arms; hummingbird as registration device; gold foil hibiscus flower. Back: Hummingbird; Eric Williams Financial Complex in Port of Spain; five steel drum musical instruments. Windowed security thread with demetalized *CBTT20*. Watermark: Hummingbird, electrotype *20*, and Cornerstones. Printer: (TDLR). 152.4 x 69.85 mm.

☐　a.　2006. Signature 9. Prefix HD.　　　FV　FV　6

CBTT B33 (PNL): **100 dollars** (US$16)　　　　VG　VF　UNC

Blue and brown. Front: Bird of paradise on branch; coat of arms; bird of paradise as registration device; silver shield hologram. Back: Bird of paradise; Eric Williams Financial Complex in Port of Spain; off-shore oil platform. Windowed security thread with demetalized *CBTT100*. Watermark: Bird of paradise, electrotype *100*, and Cornerstones. Printer: (TDLR). 152.4 x 69.85 mm.

☐　a.　2006. Signature 9. Prefix JJ. Intro: March 2014.　　FV　FV　25

CBTT B28 (P50): **50 dollars** (US$8)　　　　VG　VF　UNC

Gold and olive green. Front: Red-capped cardinal bird on branch; coat of arms; red-capped cardinal as registration device; Depth Image holographic patch. Back: Red-capped cardinal; Eric Williams Financial Complex in Port of Spain; Red House (Parliament building). 2-mm wide windowed security thread with demetalized *CBTT50*. Watermark: Red-capped cardinal, electrotype *50*, and Cornerstones. Printer: (TDLR). 152.4 x 69.85 mm.

☐　a.　2006. Signature 8. Prefix AF. Intro: August 2012.　　FV　FV　20
Like CBTT B27, but without overprint around coat of arms.

Money Museum

The Central Bank Money Museum opened at the bank's Independence Square headquarters in Port of Spain on 3 December 2004 to celebrate the bank's 40th anniversary. It is open to the public Tuesdays to Fridays from 10 am to 2 pm.

Acknowledgements

This chapter was compiled with the generous assistance of Wendy D'Arbasie (Central Bank of Trinidad and Tobago), Tony Ball, Robert Bethea, Simon Biddlestone, Martin Burger, David Burns, Manuel Rodriguez Cassanello (stores.ebay.com/numiscondor-world-banknotes), Adwind Cheah Lee Sun, Donald Cleveland, Compagnie Generale De Bourse (www.cgb.fr), Dieter Eheim (www.papermoneyandcoins.net), Arthur Gearing (De La Rue), Madis Gerbasevskis, Ian Gradon (www.worldnotes.co.uk), Ronny Hick, Don Ludwig, Troy MacDonald (www.themonetaryman.com), Robert Mol, Sean Morrison, Wally Myers, Mikhail "Mike" Prizov, TDS, Gergely Scheidl (banknoteshop@gmx.net), Stack's Bowers & Ponterio (www.stacksbowers.com), Bill Stubkjaer, Frank van Tiel, Ludek Vostal, Russell Waller, and others.

Sources

Buczacki, Jerry. "The Currency Notes of Queen Elizabeth II." *IBNS Journal*. Volume 17 Number 2. p.61.

Cleveland, Donald. "Right on the Money. The story behind the banknote: Trinidad and Tobago's $100." *IBNS Journal*. Volume 46 Number 1. p.56.

Cuhaj, George S. *Standard Catalog of World Paper Money, General Issues, 1368-1960*. 14th edition. 2012. ISBN 978-1-4402-3090-5. Krause Publications (www.krausebooks.com), 700 East State St., Iola, WI, 54990-0001.

Cuhaj, George S. *Standard Catalog of World Paper Money, Modern Issues, 1961-Present*. 20th edition. 2014. ISBN 978-1-4402-4037-9. Krause Publications (www.krausebooks.com), 700 East State St., Iola, WI, 54990-0001.

Eu, Peter and Ben Chiew. *Queen Elizabeth II*. 1st edition. 2006. ISBN 983-43038-1-5. Eureka Metro, P. O. Box 30, Jalan Kelang Lama, Kuala Lumpur, 57000, Malaysia.

Kemp, Brian. "British West Indies." *IBNS Journal*. Volume 15 Number 1. p.13.

Salem, Farid. "Trinidad and Tobago from the Currency Board to the Central Bank." *IBNS Journal*. Volume 41 Number 2. p.18.

Symes, Peter. "The Portraits of Queen Elizabeth II on World Bank Notes." *IBNS Journal*. Volume 44 Number 2. p.8.

Share Your Input, Info, and Images

This catalog is believed to be complete and correct as of the time of publication. Prices and face values were last updated 2 March 2012. Please report errors or omissions so that corrections may be made. If you can more precisely identify the name or location of anything depicted on a note, please share that information. Furthermore, if you own an unlisted type or variety, please submit scans of the front and back of the note so that it can be documented. Scans should be 300 dots per inch, 100% actual size, 24-bit color, saved as *uncompressed* JPEG files, and sent to owen@banknotenews.com. Be sure to fully describe all attributes of the note which are not apparent upon visual inspection of the images alone, such as physical dimension, watermark, and security thread.

Tunisia

Earlier Issues

Prior to the establishment of the Banque Centrale de Tunisie in 1958, banknotes were issued by Dar-el-Mal in 1846, Régence de Tunis from 1918 to 1943, Banque de l'Algérie from 1904 to 1945, and Banque de l'Algérie et de la Tunisie from 1946 to 1954. These issues will be added to this chapter in the future.

Monetary System

1 Tunisian riyal = 16 kharub
1891: 1 Tunisian franc = 100 centimes
1958: 1 Tunisian dinar (TND) = 1,000 millim

Banque Centrale de Tunisie (Central Bank of Tunisia)

On 20 March 1956, Tunisia achieved independence from France. On 19 September 1958, the Banque Centrale de Tunisie (BCT) was created by the enactment of Act n° 58-90. On 3 November 1958, the bank began its activity with the establishment of the Tunisian dinar as a unit of account, replacing the Tunisian franc at a rate of 1:1,000.

For more information, visit www.bct.gov.tn.

BCT Signature Varieties

	(General Manager)	(Governor)
1	 Mansour Moalla (30.09.1958 - 27.05.1961)	 Hédi Amara Nouira (30.09.1958 - 09.11.1970)
2	 Ali Zouaoui (27.05.1961 - 10.11.1970)	 Hédi Amara Nouira (30.09.1958 - 09.11.1970)
3	 Mohamed Bousbia (12.03.1971 - 12.07.1980)	 Ali Zouaoui (10.11.1970 - 18.02.1972)

	(Sub-Governor)	(Governor)
4	Tahar Sioud (01.08.1980 - 31.12.1987)	 Mohamed Ghenima (04.03.1972 - 07.05.1980)

BCT Signature Varieties

*		Moncef Belkhodja (12.07.1980 - 14.03.1986)
5	 Tahar Sioud (01.08.1980 - 31.12.1987)	 Mohamed Skhiri (15.03.1986 - 26.10.1987)
*	Abdelmajid Frej (29.08.1991 - 21.06.1992)	Ismail Khelil (27.10.1987 - 02.03.1990)
	(Vice-Governor)	(Governor)
6	 Abdelmoumen Souayah (22.06.1992 - 21.10.1996)	 Mohamed El Béji Hamda (03.03.1990 - 22.01.2001)
7	 Mohamed Daouas (30.10.1996 - 22.01.2001)	Mohamed El Béji Hamda (03.03.1990 - 22.01.2001)
*		Mohamed Daouas (23.01.2001 - 13.01.2004)
8a	 Hédi Zar (03.08.2004 - 28.02.2010)	 Taoufik Baccar (14.01.2004 - 16.01.2011)
8b	 Hédi Zar (03.08.2004 - 28.02.2010)	Taoufik Baccar (14.01.2004 - 16.01.2011)
9	Brahim Saada	 Mustapha Kamel Nabli (17.01.2011 - 27.06.2012)
10	Mohamed Rekik	Chedly Ayari

* This official is not known to have signed any notes.

1958 Issues

These notes feature a portrait of Habib Bourguiba, who became the first president of the independent Tunisian republic on 25 July 1957. These notes were issued on 3 November 1958. On 30 December 1958, the Tunisian dinar was disconnected from the French franc and the country withdrew from the franc zone.

According to salesman Alexi Napier, as quoted in *The Highest Perfection: A History of De La Rue*, Tunisia originally ordered all of its new notes from Bradbury, Wilkinson & Co., but Thomas De La Rue convinced Taiev Slin, the Tunisian ambassador to England, to give half the order to TDLR. For several years the note printing was split between BWC and TDLR, until eventually the latter got the whole business. Ultimately BWC was acquired by TDLR in 1986.

BCT B1 (P57): **1/2 dinar** (demonetized 01.10.1968)   VG   VF   UNC
Purple and light green. Front: President Habib Bourguiba; Great Mosque of Kirouan (aka Mosque of Uqba). Back: Temple of Jupiter ruins in Dougga; coat of arms. No security thread. Watermark: Coat of arms. Printer: (TDLR). 138 x 75 mm
- a. No date. Signature 1. Intro: 03.11.1958.   15   65   250
- as1. Diagonal red *SPECIMEN* and DLR oval ovpts; horizon. red *SPECIMEN No. #* ovpt at lower left.   —   —   —
- as2. Diagonal red *SPECIMEN* overprint; punched.   —   —   —

BCT B2 (P58): **1 dinar** (demonetized 01.10.1968)   VG   VF   UNC
Green and light blue. Front: President Habib Bourguiba; branches with fruit; farmer riding mechanical plow. Back: Ben Mitir dam. No security thread. Watermark: Coat of arms. Printer: (BWC). 150 x 84 mm.
- a. No date. Signature 1. Intro: 03.11.1958.   8   30   325
- as1. Diagonal red *SPECIMEN* overprint.   —   —   —
- as2. Diagonal red *SPECIMEN* overprint; punched.   —   —   —

BCT B3 (P59): **5 dinars** (demonetized 28.05.1962)   VG   VF   UNC
Brown and green Front: Bridge over Mellegue River; President Habib Bourguiba. Back: Interior columns of Great Mosque of Kairouan; coat of arms; branch with fruit. No security thread. Watermark: Coat of arms. Printer: (BWC). 164 x 93 mm.
- a. No date. Signature 1. Intro: 03.11.1958.   15   50   350
- as1. Diagonal red *SPECIMEN* overprint.   —   —   —
- as2. Diagonal red *SPECIMEN* overprint; punched.   —   —   —

1960 Issues

This note is like preceding issues, but with the denomination in the front corners expressed in Western, not Arabic, numerals.

BCT B4 (P60): **5 dinars** (demonetized 28.05.1962)   VG   VF   UNC
Brown and light green Front: Bridge over Mellegue River; President Habib Bourguiba. Back: Interior columns of Great Mosque of Kairouan; coat of arms; branch with fruit. No security thread. Watermark: Coat of arms. Printer: (BWC). 164 x 93 mm.

    a.   1-11-1960. Signature 1.   20   75   350
    as.   Diagonal red *SPECIMEN* overprint; punched.   —   —   —

1962 Issues

This note is like preceding issues, but the color has been changed.

BCT B5 (P61): **5 dinars** (demonetized 01.10.1968)   VG   VF   UNC
Blue, light green, and pink. Front: Bridge over Mellegue River; President Habib Bourguiba. Back: Interior columns of Great Mosque of Kairouan; coat of arms; branch with fruit. No security thread. Watermark: Coat of arms. Printer: (BWC). 164 x 93 mm.

    a.   20-3-1962. Signature 2.   30   120   400
    as.   Diagonal red *SPECIMEN* overprint; punched.   —   —   500

1965-1969 Issues

BCT B6 (P62): **1/2 dinar** (demonetized 01.01.1982)   VG   VF   UNC
Blue, yellow, orange, and green. Front: President Habib Bourguiba; Bourguiba mosque in Monastir. Back: Mosaic (from the Monastir Museum collection) of flowers, fish, men with scales, and ancient boat. No security thread. Watermark: Habib Bourguiba. Printer: (TDLR). 146 x 75 mm.

    a.   1-6-1965. Signature 2. Intro: 03.06.1966.   8   30   200
    as.   Diagonal red *SPECIMEN* overprint; punched.   —   —   100

BCT B7 (P63): **1 dinar** (demonetized 01.01.1982)   VG   VF   UNC

Black, violet, blue, green, and brown. Front: Phosphoric acid plant in Sfax; President Habib Bourguiba. Back: Mosaic of Neptune and four horses; shells. No security thread. Watermark: Habib Bourguiba. Printer: (TDLR). 155 x 80 mm.

- a. 1-6-1965. Signature 2. Intro: 03.06.1966.   8   30   250
- as1. Diagonal red SPECIMEN overprint; punched.   —   —   250
- as2. Diagonal red SPECIMEN and DLR oval ovpts; horizontal red SPECIMEN Nº # ovpt at lower left; punched.   —   —   —

BCT B8 (P64): **5 dinars** (demonetized 01.01.1982)   VG   VF   UNC

Crimson, green, brown, yellow, red, and blue. Front: Sadiki College buildings in Tunis; President Habib Bourguiba. Back: Mosaic of wreathes of fruits and leaves surrounding Roman woman's head; Triumphal Arch of the Tetrarchy in Sbeitla; mosaic wreathes surrounding sun. No security thread. Watermark: Habib Bourguiba. Printer: (TDLR). 165 x 85 mm.

- a. 1-6-1965. Signature 2. Intro: 03.06.1966.   10   50   300
- as1. Diagonal red SPECIMEN overprint; punched.   —   —   100
- as2. Diagonal red SPECIMEN and DLR oval ovpts; horizontal red SPECIMEN Nº # ovpt at lower left; punched.   —   —   600

BCT B9 (P65): **10 dinars** (demonetized 01.01.1995)   VG   VF   UNC

Brown, aqua, green, and pink. Front: Oil refinery; President Habib Bourguiba. Back: Palm trees, horse, and oasis at Gabes. Solid security thread. Watermark: Habib Bourguiba. Printer: Unknown. 182 x 95 mm.

- a. 1-6-1969. Signature 2. Intro: 02.01.1970.   6   25   100
- as. Diagonal SPECIMEN perforation.   —   —   100

1972 Issues

BCT B10 (P66): **1/2 dinar** (demonetized 01.01.1995)   VG   VF   UNC

Brown, tan, and green. Front: Harbor at Goulette; President Habib Bourguiba. Back: Buildings in city of Tunis. Solid security thread with printed Arabic text. Watermark: Habib Bourguiba. Printer: *DE LA RUE*. 140 x 70 mm.

- a. 3-8-1972. Signature 3. Into: 21.03.1973.   1   5   20
- as1. Diagonal red SPECIMEN overprint.   —   —   150
- as2. Diagonal red SPECIMEN and DLR oval ovpts; horizontal red SPECIMEN Nº # ovpt at lower left; punched.   —   —   —

Replacement notes: Prefix numerator AR.

1973 Issues

BCT B11 (P67): **1 dinar** (demonetized 01.01.1995)   VG   VF   UNC

Violet and blue. Front: Fort in Monastir; President Habib Bourguiba. Back: Medina minaret in Tunis; Berber woman. Solid security thread with printed Arabic text. Watermark: Habib Bourguiba. Printer: *DE LA RUE*. 150 x 75 mm.

	a.	3-8-1972. Signature 3. Intro: 21.03.1973.	1.50	6	25
	as1.	Diagonal red *SPECIMEN* overprint.	—	—	150
	as2.	Diagonal red *SPECIMEN* and DLR oval ovpts; horizontal red *SPECIMEN №* # ovpt at lower left; punched.	—	—	—

BCT B12 (P68): **5 dinars** (demonetized 01.01.1995)   VG   VF   UNC

Green and brown. Front: National Stadium in Tunis; President Habib Bourguiba. Back: Ruins of Roman amphitheater in El Djem; prickly pear cacti. Solid security thread with printed Arabic text. Watermark: Habib Bourguiba. Printer: *DE LA RUE*. 162 x 81 mm.

	a.	3-8-1972. Signature 3. Intro: 21.03.1973	4	15	50
	as.	Diagonal red *SPECIMEN* overprint.	—	—	40

Replacement notes: Prefix numerator CR.

1973 Issues

BCT B13 (P69): **1/2 dinar** (demonetized 01.01.1995)   VG   VF   UNC

Green, black, blue and orange. Front: Palm trees; man plowing with camel; President Habib Bourguiba; four modern combines harvesting in field. Back: Sail boat on Bay of Tunis; sheep; tractor; tree with bird; olive branch; bowl of fruit; date palm trees; fish; branch with fruit. Solid security thread with printed Arabic text. Watermark: Habib Bourguiba. Printer: (TDLR). 142 x 71 mm.

	a.	1973-10-15. Signature 3. Intro: 21.08.1978.	0.50	2	8
	as.	Diagonal red *SPECIMEN* overprint.	—	—	—

Replacement notes: Prefix numerator AR.

BCT B14 (P70): **1 dinar** (demonetized 01.01.1995)   VG   VF   UNC

Blue, green, and violet. Front: President Habib Bourguiba; oil refinery. Back: Agricultural processing plant; man with mechanical lathe; woman with sewing machine; man carving wooden decoration; woman weaving rug; man welding; bridge. Solid security thread with printed Arabic text. Watermark: Habib Bourguiba. Printer: (TDLR). 151 x 75 mm.

	a.	1973-10-15. Signature 3. Intro: 21.08.1978	1	4	12
	as.	Diagonal red *SPECIMEN* overprint.	—	—	—

Replacement notes: Prefix numerator BR.

1980 Issues

BCT B15 (P71): **5 dinars** (demonetized 31.12.2003) VG VF UNC
Brown, yellow, orange, and green. Front: Medina in Sousse; President Habib Bourguiba; three row boats along shore. Back: Palm trees; buildings; mosaics; minaret; camels in archway; column; metal gate; ancient coin of Carthage with male head; domed mosque; modern buildings; archways. Solid security thread with printed Arabic text. Watermark: Habib Bourguiba. Printer: (TDLR). 162 x 81 mm.

☐ a. 1973-10-15. Signature 3. Intro: 04.06.1979. 4 15 50
☐ as. Diagonal red *SPECIMEN* overprint. — — —

Replacement notes: Prefix numerator CR.

BCT B16 (P72): **10 dinars** (demonetized 01.01.1995) VG VF UNC
Orange, purple, and green. Front: President Habib Bourguiba; mine equipment and buildings. Back: Columns; drummer; mythical flying woman/horse; camel caravan; train; tree; students studying with books; ship; palm trees; drummers. Solid security thread with printed Arabic text. Watermark: Habib Bourguiba. Printer: (TDLR). 170 x 85 mm.

☐ a. 1973-10-15. Signature 3. Intro: 21.08.1978. 5 20 65
☐ as. Diagonal red *SPECIMEN* overprint. — — —

BCT B17 (P74): **1 dinar** (demonetized 01.01.1996) VG VF UNC
Reddish brown and olive green. Front: Ruins of Roman theatre in Carthage; President Habib Bourguiba. Back: Seaside village buildings of Korbous (Qurbus) on Cape Bon. Solid security thread. Watermark: Habib Bourguiba. Printer: Unknown. 151 x 75 mm.

☐ a. 1980-10-15. Signature 4. Intro: 16.10.1984. 0.50 2 8
☐ as. Diagonal red *SPECIMEN* overprint; horizontal red *SPECIMEN N°* # ovpt at lower left; punched. — — —

BCT B18 (P75): **5 dinars** (demonetized 31.12.2003) VG VF UNC
Yellow, green, red and brown. Front: Ezzitouna mosque in Tunis; President Habib Bourguiba. Back: Ruins of Roman Temple of Water in Zaghouan. Solid security thread with printed Arabic text. Watermark: Habib Bourguiba. Printer: Unknown. 162 x 81 mm.

☐ a. 1980-10-15. Signature 4. Intro: 26.05.1986. 2 8 35
☐ as. Diagonal red *SPECIMEN* overprint. — — —

Replacement notes: Prefix numerator CR.

1983 Issues

BCT B19 (P76): 10 dinars (demonetized 31.12.2003)   VG   VF   UNC
Green and brown. Front: President Habib Bourguiba; Sadiki College buildings in Tunis. Back: Nebhana dam. Solid security thread with printed Arabic text. Watermark: Habib Bourguiba. Printer: Unknown. 170 x 85 mm.
   ☐ a.   1980-10-15. Signature 4. Intro: 23.01.1984.   5   20   60
   ☐ as.   Diagonal red *SPECIMEN* overprint.   —   —   —
Replacement notes: Prefix numerator DR.

BCT B21 (P79): 5 dinars (demonetized 31.12.2003)   VG   VF   UNC
Purple and brown. Front: President Habib Bourguiba; palm trees along traditional oasis irrigation canal with camel. Back: El Aroussia dam. Solid security thread. Watermark: Habib Bourguiba. Printer: Unknown. 162 x 81 mm.
   ☐ a.   1983-11-3. Signature 4. Intro: 15.02.1989.   2   8   30
   ☐ as.   Diagonal red *SPECIMEN* overprint; horizontal red *SPECIMEN* Nº # ovpt at lower left; punched.   —   —   —

BCT B20 (P77): 20 dinars (demonetized 31.12.2008)   VG   VF   UNC
Green, brown, and blue. Front: Ruins of El Djem Roman amphitheater; President Habib Bourguiba. Back: Boats in fishing port at Monastir; Medina at Sousse. Solid security thread. Watermark: Habib Bourguiba. Printer: Unknown. 181 x 90 mm.
   ☐ a.   1980-10-15. Signature 4. Intro: 26.12.1984.   8   25   75
   ☐ as.   Diagonal red *SPECIMEN* overprint; horizontal red *SPECIMEN* Nº # ovpt at lower left; punched.   —   —   —

BCT B22 (P80): 10 dinars (demonetized 31.12.2003)   VG   VF   UNC
Blue, violet, and green. Front: Men in factory pressing olive oil, President Habib Bourguiba; Ashtart offshore oil rigs. Back: Traditional money changer, seated with coins and basket; Central Bank headquarters building in Tunis; Arches of Bab El Khadhra. Solid security thread. Watermark: Habib Bourguiba. Printer: Unknown. 170 x 85 mm.
   ☐ a.   1983-11-3. Signature 4. Intro: 26.05.1988.   4   15   60
   ☐ as.   Diagonal red *SPECIMEN* overprint.   —   —   —

BCT B23 (P81): **20 dinars** (demonetized 31.12.2003)   VG   VF   UNC

Green, blue, and purple. Front: President Habib Bourguiba; Central Bank buildings in Sfax. Back: El Kantaoui resort and marina in Sousse. Solid security thread. Watermark: Habib Bourguiba. Printer: Unknown. 180 x 90 mm.

- ☐ a.   1983-11-3. Signature 4. Intro: 15.02.1989.   5   20   70
- ☐ as.   Diagonal red *SPECIMEN* overprint;
horizontal red *SPECIMEN* № # ovpt at lower left;
punched.   —   —   —

1986 Issues

BCT B24 (P84): **10 dinars** (US$6.40)   VG   VF   UNC

Brown and green. Front: President Habib Bourguiba; olive presses, groves, and branch. Back: Ashtart oil platform in Gulf of Gabès. Solid security thread. Watermark: Habib Bourguiba. Printer: Unknown. 170 x 85 mm.

- ☐ a.   1986-3-20. Signature 5. Intro: 15-2-1989.   FV   FV   35
- ☐ as.   Diagonal red *SPECIMEN* overprint;
horizontal red *SPECIMEN* № # ovpt at lower left;
punched.   —   —   —

1992-1997 Commemorative Issues

On 7 November 1987, Prime Minister Zine El Abidine Ben Ali, in a coup d'état, declared President Habib Bourguiba impeached on medical grounds and constitutionally replaced him as president. These notes were originally issued to commemorate the anniversary of the overthrow of Bourguiba, which explains the prominence of the date 7 November 1987 on the back of these notes.

BCT B25 (P86): **5 dinars** (US$3.20)   VG   VF   UNC

Green. Front: Olive branch; Carthaginian general, Hannibal wearing helmet; ancient Punic port. Back: Sailing ship; antelope; flamingo; oil refinery; sea fish mosaic. Solid security thread with demetalized *5 DINARS*. Watermark: Carthaginian general, Hannibal. Printer: Unknown. 137 x 70 mm.

- ☐ a.   93-11-7. Signature 6. Intro: 21.09.1992.   FV   10   30
- ☐ as.   Diagonal red *SPECIMEN* overprint.   —   —   —

BCT B26 (P87): **10 dinars** (US$6.40)   VG   VF   UNC

Blue, green, purple, and orange. Front: Islamic philosopher, Abd-Alrahman Ibn Khaidoun; street view of Ibn Khaidoun's home. Back: Open book dated *7 NOVEMBRE 1987*, with *OUVERTURE DEMOCRATIE ETAT DE DROIT* (Beginning of Democracy and State of Rights) in French and Arabic. Solid security thread with demetalized *10 DINARS*. Watermark: Ibn Khaidoun. Printer: Unknown. 145 x 73 mm.

- ☐ a.   1994-11-7. Signature 6. Intro: 08.11.1994.   FV   FV   25
- ☐ as.   Diagonal red *SPECIMEN* overprint;
horizontal red *SPECIMEN* № # ovpt above date.   —   —   —

BCT B27 (P87A): **10 dinars** (US$6.40)   VG   VF   UNC
Brown, yellow, and green. Front: Islamic philosopher, Abd-Alrahman Ibn Khaidoun; street view of Ibn Khaidoun's home. Back: Open book dated *7 NOVEMBRE 1987*, with *OUVERTURE DEMOCRATIE ETAT DE DROIT* (Beginning of Democracy and State of Rights) in French and Arabic. Solid security thread with demetalized *10 DINARS*. Watermark: Ibn Khaidoun. Printer: Unknown. 145 x 73 mm.

☐ a. 1994-11-7. Signature 6. Intro: 2005.   FV   FV   25
☐ as. Diagonal red *SPECIMEN* overprint.   —   —   —

BCT B28 (P88): **20 dinars** (demonetized 31.12.2017)   VG   VF   UNC
Purple, blue, yellow, and green. Front: Mosque of Sidi Mehrez in Tunis Medina; Kheireddine Ettounsi with sword on horse; entrance to Palace of the Chamber of Deputies. Back: Tram; factory worker; large 7 with flag; crescent moon and star; dove; buildings; palm trees; sail boat; man carrying basket of olive branches on his back. 3-mm wide segmented foil stripe. Solid security thread with demetalized *20 DINARS*. Watermark: Portrait of Ettounsi. Printer: Unknown. 153 x 76 mm.

☐ a. 1992-11-7. Signature 6. Intro: 09.11.1992.   —   10   25
☐ as. Diagonal red boxed *SPÉCIMEN* overprint; vertical *SPECIMEN* perforation; horizontal red # ovpt on right watermark area.   —   —   —

BCT B29 (P89): **30 dinars** (demonetized 31.12.2017)   VG   VF   UNC
Orange, green, brown, and blue. Front: Stalk of wheat; ancient columns; modern bridge; highway interchange; Science Institute, planetarium; poet Aboul El Kacem Chebbi. Back: Crescent moon and star with dove logo of "26-26 Program of Solidarity;" two girls drinking from fountain; farmers in field; irrigation towers; sheep; woman weaving rug on loom. 5-mm wide segmented foil stripe. Solid security thread with demetalized *30 D BCT*. Watermark: Aboul El Kacem Chebbi. Printer: Unknown. 161 x 79 mm.

☐ a. 1997-11-7. Signature 7. Intro: 10.11.1997.   —   30   40
☐ as. Diagonal red *SPECIMEN* overprint.   —   —   —

2005-2008 Issues

BCT B30 (P92): **5 dinars** (US$3.20)   VG   VF   UNC
Green. Front: Olive branch; Carthaginian general, Hannibal wearing helmet; ancient Punic port. Back: Sailing ship; antelope; flamingo; oil refinery; sea fish mosaic. Windowed security thread with demetalized *5 DINARS*. Watermark: Carthaginian general, Hannibal, electrotype *5*, and Cornerstones. Printer: (TDLR). 137 x 70 mm.

☐ a. 2008. Signature 8b. Intro: 22.06.2009.   FV   FV   8
Replacement notes: Prefix numerator CR.
Like the preceding issue, but with new date, new signatures, vertical serial number at right, windowed security thread, Omron rings, more durable paper, elements for the sight-impaired, UV printing, and electrotype 5 and Cornerstones added to the watermark.

2011 Issues

These notes were issued following the ouster of President Zine El Abidine Ben Ali on 14 January 2011, the first of several political upheavals resulting from the revolutionary movements known collectively as the Arab Spring.

BCT B31 (P90): **10 dinars** (US$6.40) VG VF UNC

Light blue, peach, and yellow. Front: El Abidine mosque in Carthage; arabesque design; ornamental 7; Élissa fondatrice de Carthage (Élissa, founder of Carthage). Back: The capitol (Roman temple ruins) in Dougga; satellite dish. Holographic stripe. Windowed security thread with demetalized *10 DINARS BCT*. Watermark: Élissa and electrotype *10*. Printer: Unknown. 145 x 73 mm.

    ☐ a.   2005-11-7. Signature 8a. Intro: 08.11.2005.   FV   FV   12

BCT B32 (P91): **50 dinars** (demonetized 31.12.2017) VG VF UNC

Green, purple, and orange. Front: La Cite de la Culture (The City of Culture) building; scholar Ibn Rachiq. Back: Rades-La Goulette suspension bridge over canal; planes and jetways at Zine El Abidine Ben Ali Enfidha Airport terminal. Holographic stripe. Windowed security thread with demetalized *50 DINARS BCT*. Watermark: Ibn Rachiq and electrotype *50*. Printer: (OT). 167 x 80 mm.

    ☐ a.   2008 ７ رَبِـﻣفـﻮْن (2008.11.07). Signature 8a.   —   —   65
           Intro: 25.07.2009.
    ☐ as. Diagonal red boxed *SPECIMEN* overprint.   —   —   100

Commemorates the 25th anniversary of the Republic and the bank's 21st anniversary.

BCT B33 (P93): **20 dinars** (US$13) VG VF UNC

Red, blue, and yellow. Front: Ksar Ouled Soltane fortified granary in Tataouine district; Kheireddine Ettounsi with sword on horse. Back: L'ecole Sadiki (Sadiki College) building in Tunis. Holographic stripe. Windowed security thread with demetalized *20 DINARS BCT*. Watermark: Olive tree with electrotype *20*. Printer: (OT). 153 x 76 mm.

    ☐ a.   2011-3-20. Signature 9. Intro: 20.10.2011.   FV   FV   20
    ☐ as. Diagonal red boxed *SPECIMEN* overprint.   —   —   —

BCT B34 (P94): **50 dinars** (US$32) VG VF UNC

Green, blue, and orange. Front: Musée de la Monnaie (Currency Museum) building in Tunis; scholar Ibn Rachiq. Back: Place Gouvernement la Kasbah, central square in Tunis. Holographic stripe. Windowed security thread with demetalized *50 DINARS BCT*. Watermark: Olive tree and electrotype *50*. Printer: (OT). 158 x 79 mm.

    ☐ a.   2011-3-20. Signature 9. Intro: 03.11.2011.   FV   FV   60

2013 Issues

These notes were issued per decree 1223 of 2013. Also, per decree 1224 of 2013, Tunisia withdrew 5-dinar notes dated 1993 and 2008, as well as 10-dinar notes dated 1986, 1994, and 2005.

Acknowledgements

This chapter was compiled with the generous assistance of Mohamed Arfaoui (Central Bank of Tunisia), Thomas Augustsson, Donald Cleveland, Compagnie Generale De Bourse (www.CGB.fr), Steve Cox, Jean-Michel Engels, Heritage Auctions (HA.com), Detlef Hilmer (detlef_hilmer@web.de), Max Keller, Dave Mills (www.frenchbanknotes.com), Wally Myers, Thomas Neldner, George Provencal, TDS, Bill Stubkjaer, Jan Stuller, David White, and others.

Sources

Cleveland, Don. "Queen Elissa, Founder of Carthage – Right on the Money." *IBNS Journal*. Volume 49 Number 4. p.55.

Cuhaj, George S. *Standard Catalog of World Paper Money, General Issues, 1368-1960*. 14th edition. 2012. ISBN 978-1-4402-3090-5. Krause Publications (www.krausebooks.com), 700 East State St., Iola, WI, 54990-0001.

Cuhaj, George S. *Standard Catalog of World Paper Money, Modern Issues, 1961-Present*. 19th edition. 2013. ISBN 978-1-4402-3571-9. Krause Publications (www.krausebooks.com), 700 East State St., Iola, WI, 54990-0001.

Heath, Henry B. "The Bank Notes Of Tunisia." *IBNS Journal*. Volume 42 Number 2. p.42.

MacKenzie, Kenneth M. "Banknotes from Ottoman Tunisia." *IBNS Journal*. Volume 26 Number 2. p.48.

Muszynski, Maurice and Maurice Kolsky. *Les Billets du Maghreb et du Levant*. Volume 11. 2002. Éditions Victor Gadoury, 57, rue Grimaldi, MC-98000 Monaco. ISBN 2-906602-18-3.

Pugh, Peter. *The Highest Perfection: A History of De La Rue*. 2011. ISBN 978-184831-335-4. Icon Books Ltd. 39-41 North Road, London, N7 9DP.

Schwan, Fred. "Why I Collect Independent Tunisia." *IBNS Journal*. Volume 37 Number 2. p.44.

Shneydor, N. A. "Evolving Policies in the Dating of Banknotes of the Near-East." *IBNS Journal*. Volume 53 Number 2. p.9.

Share Your Input, Info, and Images

This catalog is believed to be complete and correct as of the time of publication. Prices and face values were last updated 22 March 2013. Please report errors or omissions so that corrections may be made. If you can more precisely identify the name or location of anything depicted on a note, please share that information. Furthermore, if you own an unlisted type or variety, please submit scans of the front and back of the note so that it can be documented. Scans should be 300 dots per inch, 100% actual size, 24-bit color, saved as *uncompressed* JPEG files, and sent to owen@banknotenews.com. Be sure to fully describe all attributes of the note which are not apparent upon visual inspection of the images alone, such as physical dimension, watermark, and security thread.

BCT B36 (PNL): **5 dinars** (US$3.20) — VG VF UNC
Green. Front: City of Carthage; Carthaginian general, Hannibal wearing helmet. Back: Carthaginian ships. Holographic stripe with Hannibal, Carthaginian ship, and crescent moon and star. Windowed green-to-gold security thread with demetalized *5 DINARS* and design. Watermark: Olive tree, electrotype *5*, and Cornerstones. Printer: Unknown. 143 x 73 mm.

   ☐ a.   2013-3-20. Signature 10. Intro: 17.03.2014.   FV   FV   6

BCT B35 (PNL): **10 dinars** (US$6.40) — VG VF UNC
Light blue and yellow. Front: Poet, Aboul El Kacem Chebbi. Back: Arches of Medesa Bacchia school in Tunis. Holographic stripe with Aboul El Kacem Chebbi, quill, and crescent moon and star. Windowed security thread with demetalized *10 DINARS* and design. Watermark: Olive tree and electrotype *10*. Printer: Unknown. 148 x 73 mm.

   ☐ a.   2013-3-20. Signature 10. Intro: 28.11.2013.   FV   FV   12

Turkey

For earlier issues, see Ottoman Empire.

Contents

Ministry of Finance (MOF) 2135
Türkiye Cümhuriyet Merkez Bankası (TCMB) 2138

Monetary System

1923: 1 Turkish lira (TRL) = 100 kuruş
01.01.2005: 1 new Turkish lira (TRY) = 100 kuruş
01.01.2009: 1 Turkish lira = 100 kuruş

Turkish Months of the Year

Ocak (January)	Şubat (February)	Mart (March)
Nisan (April)	Mayıs (May)	Haziran (June)
Temmuz (July)	Ağustos (August)	Eylül (September)
Ekim (October)	Kasım (November)	Aralık (December)

Ministry of Finance

The Republic of Turkey was established in 1922 and officially proclaimed on 29 October 1923. The currency of the Ottoman Empire issued during World War I was withdrawn from circulation on 4 December 1927 and lost its value on 4 September 1928.

MOF Signature Varieties

1	
	Mustafa Abdülhalik Renda

1926 Issues

The Turkish text in Arabic transcript on the front of these notes indicates that they were issued by the Ministry of Finance for the Republic of Turkey pursuant to law 701 of 30 Kanunuevvel 1341 (12 January 1926). They were printed by Thomas de la Rue in England at a cost of 88,000 pounds sterling, and were issued on 5 December 1927.

MOF B1 (P119): **1 livre turque** (demonetized 25.04.1949) VG VF UNC
Green. Front: Parliament building with flag; farmer plowing field with team of oxen; Citadel of Ankara. Back: Prime Ministry building. No security thread. Watermark: Mustafa Kemal Atatürk. Printer: *THOMAS DE LA RUE & COMPANY, LIMITED, LONDRES*. 166 x 90 mm.

☐ a. ١٣٤١ (SH1341/1926). Signature 1.   100   500   1,500
   Série 1 - 20, 22 - 41. Intro: 05.12.1927.
☐ as. Red DLR oval ovpt on back; no s/n; punched.   —   —   500
☐ at. Color trial: Orange; uniface front only.   —   XF   1,100

Replacement notes: Série 21, 42.

MOF B2 (P120): **5 livres turques** (demonetized 14.10.1947) Good Fine XF
Blue. Front: Bounding gray wolf; star; Citadel of Ankara; men, car, and House of Parliament. Back: Stone bridge over Ankara Çayı river with ducks; town of Ankara on hillside. No security thread. Watermark: Mustafa Kemal Atatürk. Printer: *THOMAS DE LA RUE & COMPANY, LIMITED, LONDRES*. 170 x 94 mm.

☐ a. ١٣٤١ (SH1341/1926). Signature 1. Série 1 - 20.   300   750   1,500
   Intro: 05.12.1927.
☐ ap. Proof.   —   —   2,000
☐ as. Red DLR oval ovpt on back; no s/n; punched.   —   —   750
☐ at. Color trial: Purple; uniface front and back.   —   —   4,000

MOF B3 (P121): **10 livres turques** (demonetized 15.05.1948) Good Fine XF
Purple, yellow, and red. Front: Bounding gray wolf; star; Citadel of Ankara. Back: Citadel of Ankara; shephard with flock; trees; stone bridge. No security thread. Watermark: Mustafa Kemal Atatürk. Printer: *THOMAS DE LA RUE & COMPANY, LIMITED, LONDRES*. 175 x 99 mm.

- ☐ a. ١٣٤١ (SH1341/1926). Signature 1. Série 1 - 18. Intro: 05.12.1927. 500 1,000 2,500
- ☐ ap. Proof. — — 2,000
- ☐ as. Red DLR oval ovpt on back; no s/n; punched. — — 1,000
- ☐ at. Color trial: Orange; uniface front and back. — — 2,800

MOF B4 (P122): **50 livres turques** (demonetized 31.03.1948) Good Fine XF
Brown. Front: Mustafa Kemal Atatürk. Back: Black rock looming over town of Afyon. No security thread. Watermark: Arabic text. Printer: *THOMAS DE LA RUE & COMPANY, LIMITED, LONDRES*. 185 x 108 mm.

- ☐ a. ١٣٤١ (SH1341/1926). Signature 1. Série 1 - 11. Intro: 05.12.1927. 800 1,300 3,800
- ☐ as. Red DLR oval ovpt on back; no s/n; punched. — — 1,500
- ☐ at1. Color trial: Yellow-brown; uniface front only. Back signed by designer, Ali Sami Boyar. — — 2,000
- ☐ at2. Color trial: Lilac and light green underprint. — — 2,000

MOF B5 (PNL): **100 livres turques** VG VF UNC
Dark green-gray, blue-red. Front: Mustafa Kemal Atatürk. Back: Handsigned by designer, Ali Sami Boyar. No security thread. Watermark: Arabic text. Printer: *THOMAS DE LA RUE & COMPANY, LIMITED, LONDRES*. 189 x 112 mm.

- ☐ p. Proof. ١٣٤١ (SH1341/1926). Unissued. — — 5,000

MOF B6 (P123): **100 livres turques** (demonetized 29.02.1948)   **Good   Fine   XF**
Green and yellow. Front: Mustafa Kemal Atatürk. Back: Ankara town buildings; stone bridge over river. No security thread. Watermark: Arabic text. Printer: *THOMAS DE LA RUE & COMPANY, LIMITED, LONDRES.* 189 x 112 mm.

☐	a.	١٣٤١ (SH1341/1926). Signature 1. Série 1 - 11. Intro: 05.12.1927.	1,500	3,000 15,000
☐	as.	Red DLR oval ovpt on back; no s/n; punched.	—	— 2,000
☐	at1.	Color trial: Purple, lavender-green underprint with straight diagonal lines; uniface front only.	—	— 5,000
☐	at2.	Color trial: Purple, green-yellow underprint with wavy diagonal lines; uniface front only.	—	— 5,000
☐	at3.	Color trial: Dark gray-green, green-yellow underprint with straight diagonal lines; uniface front only.	—	— 5,000

MOF B7 (P124): **500 livres turques** (demonetized 15.06.1949)   **Good   Fine   XF**
Brown and yellow. Front: Gök Medrese in Amasya; Mustafa Kemal Atatürk. Back: Town of Sivas with buildings, trees, and mountain. No security thread. Watermark: Arabic text. Printer: *THOMAS DE LA RUE & COMPANY, LIMITED, LONDRES.* 194 x 120 mm.

☐	a.	١٣٤١ (SH1341/1926). Signature 1. Série 1 - 8. Intro: 05.12.1927.	20,000	— —
☐	as.	Red DLR oval ovpt on back; no s/n; punched.	—	— 2,500
☐	at1.	Color trial: Reddish brown, red-green underprint; uniface front only. Back signed by designer, Ali Sami Boyar.	—	— 3,500
☐	at2.	Color trial: Blue and light green underprint; uniface front only.	—	— 5,500

Türkiye Cümhuriyet Merkez Bankası (Central Bank of Turkey)

For more information, visit www.tcmb.gov.tr.

MOF B8 (P125): **1,000 livres turques** (demon. 14.06.1949)   VG   VF   UNC
Blue. Front: Mustafa Kemal Atatürk. Back: Railroad tracks through Geyve strait; town of Sakarya in distance with minarets. No security thread. Watermark: Arabic text. Printer: *THOMAS DE LA RUE & COMPANY, LIMITED, LONDRES*. 201 x 124 mm.

☐	a.	١٣٤١ (SH1341/1926). Signature 1. Série 1 - 16. Intro: 05.12.1927.	—	—
☐	as.	Red DLR oval ovpt on back; no s/n; punched.	—	3,000
☐	at1.	Color trial: Yellow-green underprint; uniface front only. Front signed by designer, Ali Sami Boyar.	—	4,000
☐	at2.	Color trial: Green; uniface front only.	—	5,500

TCMB Signature Varieties

	UMUM MÜDÜR (General Manager)	UMUM MÜDÜR MUAVİNİ (Assistant General Manager)	
1	 Selahattin Çam (09.06.1931 - 21.03.1938)	H. Bedirgil	
2	 Selahattin Çam (09.06.1931 - 21.03.1938)	Said Erda	
3	 A. Kemal Zaim Sunel (21.03.1938 - 09.03.1949)	Said Erda	
4	 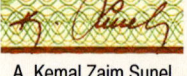 A. Kemal Zaim Sunel (21.03.1938 - 09.03.1949)	 Nedim Ersun	

	UMUM MÜDÜR	UMUM MÜDÜR MUAVİNİ	VEZNE VE EMİSYON MÜDÜRÜ (Cashier's & Issue Mgr.)
5	 A. Kemal Zaim Sunel (21.03.1938-09.03.1949)	Nedim Ersun	Fethi Aktan
6	 A. Kemal Zaim Sunel (21.03.1938-09.03.1949)	 Nedim Ersun	 EMİSYON VE VEZNE MÜDÜRÜ (Issue & Cashier's Mgr.) Kamil Kıbrıslı
7	  A. Kemal Zaim Sunel (21.03.1938-09.03.1949)	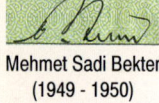 Mehmet Sadi Bekter (1949 - 1950)	Kamil Kıbrıslı
8	 Osman Nuri Göver (13.04.1951-28.05.1953)	 Reşat Aksan	 Kamil Kıbrıslı

#	Signature	Name	Signature	Name
9		Mustafa Nail Gidel (20.07.1953-16.07.1960) / Emir Sencer / Kamil Kıbrıslı		
10		Mustafa Nail Gidel (20.07.1953-16.07.1960) / Fikri Diker / Ekrem Sungar		
11		Mustafa Nail Gidel (20.07.1953-16.07.1960) / Fikri Diker / Kamil Kıbrıslı		
12		Mustafa Nail Gidel (20.07.1953-16.07.1960) / Fikret Sözer / Ekrem Sungar		
13		Fikri Diker / Emin Ali Serim / Kamil Kıbrıslı		
14		UMUM MÜDÜR (General Manager) İbrahim Münir Mostar (23.11.1960-28.08.1962) / UMUM MÜDÜR MUAVİNİ (Asst. General Manager) Emin Ali Serim / EMİSYON DAİRESİ REİSİ (Head of Issue Dept.) Kamil Kıbrıslı		
15		İbrahim Münir Mostar (23.11.1960-28.08.1962) / Necati Oktay / Yahya Arslaner		

	GENEL MÜDÜR (General Manager)	GENEL MÜDÜR MUAVİNİ (Asst. General Manager)	EMİSYON VE VEZNE MÜDÜRÜ (Issue & Cashier's Mgr.)
16	Ziyaettin Kayla (28.06.1963-13.01.1966)	Emin Ali Serim	Yahya Arslaner
17	Mehmet Naim Talu (14.07.1967-11.12.1971)	Nevzat Alptürk	Rıza Uygurer

	BAŞKAN (Governor)	BAŞKAN YARDIMCISI (Vice Governor)
18	Mehmet Naim Talu (14.07.1967 - 11.12.1971)	Nevzat Alptürk
19	Mehmet Naim Talu (14.07.1967 - 11.12.1971)	Memduh Güpgüpoğlu

20 — Memduh Güpgüpoğlu (25.07.1972 - 09.01.1975) / Numan Aksoy
21 — Memduh Güpgüpoğlu (25.07.1972 - 09.01.1975) / Yahya Arslaner
22 — Memduh Güpgüpoğlu (25.07.1972 - 09.01.1975) / Naci Tibet
23 — Numan Aksoy / Yahya Arslaner
24 — Cafer Tayyar Sadıklar (26.06.1976 - 18.09.1978) / Naci Tibet
25 — Cafer Tayyar Sadıklar (26.06.1976 - 18.09.1978) / Osman Şıklar
26 — İsmail Hakkı Aydınoğlu (21.10.1978 - 10.01.1981) / Tanju Polatkan
27 — İsmail Hakkı Aydınoğlu (21.10.1978 - 10.01.1981) / Vural Günal
28 — Osman Şıklar (12.01.1981 - 04.01.1984) / Yavuz Canevi
29 — Osman Şıklar (12.01.1981 - 04.01.1984) / İbrahim Kurt
30 — Osman Şıklar (12.01.1981 - 04.01.1984) / Ruhi Haseski

#	Signature (left)	Signature (right)	Name
55			Durmuş Yılmaz (18.04.2006 - 13.04.2011) / Mehmet Yörükoğlu
56			Erdem Başçı (19.04.2011 - present) / Mehmet Yörükoğlu
57			Erdem Başçı (19.04.2011 - present) / Necati Şahin
58			Erdem Başçı (19.04.2011 - present) / Murat Çetinkaya
59			Erdem Başçı (19.04.2011 - present) / Turalay Kenç

1930 Latin Alphabet Proofs

A new Turkish alphabet—derived from the Latin alphabet—was adopted on 1 November 1928. After this reform, the Central Bank of Turkey revised the preceding Ministry of Finance designs with the new alphabet, but these notes were never issued. Based upon the terms of office of the signatories (Selahattin Çam and what appears to be H. Bedirgil), these proofs were likely created after 1931. To date only the 50- and 1,000-Türk lirası denominations have surfaced in proof form; it's not known if other "Latin Alphabet" denominations exist.

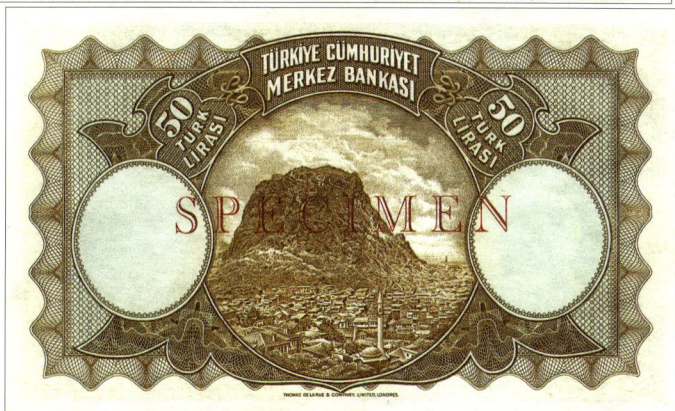

TCMB B1 (PNL): **50 Türk lirası**   VG   VF   UNC
Brown and yellow. Front: Gate with towers; Mustafa Kemal Atatürk. Back: Black rock looming over town of Afyon. No security thread. Watermark: Mustafa Kemal Atatürk. Printer: *THOMAS DE LA RUE & COMPANY, LIMITED, LONDRES*. 196 x 119 mm.

☐ p1. Proof: 11 HAZİRAN 1930. Signature 1. Seri 1. — — 5,000
    Red hollow *SPECIMEN* ovpt. Unissued.
☐ p2. Proof: Horizontal *CANCELLED* perf. Unissued. — — 1,800

1930 (1937-1939) Atatürk Bowtie Issues

TCMB B2 (PNL): **1,000 Türk lirası**　　　　　　　　　　VG　VF　UNC
Blue. Front: Mustafa Kemal Atatürk. Back: Railroad tracks through Geyve strait; town of Sakarya in distance with minarets. No security thread. Watermark: Mustafa Kemal Atatürk. Printer: *THOMAS DE LA RUE & COMPANY, LIMITED, LONDRES*. 200 x 122 mm.

　　☐ p.　Proof: 11 HAZİRAN 1930. Signature 1. Seri 1.　—　—　15,000
　　　　　Unissued.

TCMB B3 (PNL): **1 Türk lirası**　　　　　　　　　　　VG　VF　UNC
Green. Front: Mustafa Kemal Atatürk. Back: Trees; State Art and Sculpture Museum building in Ankara. No security thread. Watermark: Mustafa Kemal Atatürk. Printer: *THOMAS DE LA RUE & COMPANY, LIMITED, LONDRES*. 125 x 64 mm.

　　☐ p1.　11 HAZİRAN 1930. Signature 3. Seri D20.　—　—　1,800
　　　　　Proof: Green. Unissued.
　　☐ p2.　Proof: Orange. Unissued.　　　　　　　　　—　—　1,800
　　☐ p3.　Proof: Red. Unissued.　　　　　　　　　　—　—　1,800

TCMB B4 (P126): **2 1/2 Türk lirası** (demonetized 15.07.1962)　VG　VF　UNC
Olive green. Front: Mustafa Kemal Atatürk. Back: The Republic Monument in Ulus Square in Old Ankara (bronze equestrian statue of Mustafa Kemal Atatürk and WWI soldiers by Austrian sculptor Heinrich Krippel). No security thread. Watermark: Mustafa Kemal Atatürk. Printer: *THOMAS DE LA RUE & COY, LTD, LONDRES ANGLETERRE*. 145 x 65 mm.

　　☐ a.　11 HAZİRAN 1930. Signature 2. Seri A - C.　80　250　1,200
　　　　　Intro: 25.04.1939.
　　☐ as1.　Diagonal *SPECIMEN* perforation;　　　　—　—　500
　　　　　large red *X* overprint on back.
　　☐ as2.　Horizontal *CANCELLED* perforation.　　—　—　500
　　☐ as3.　Diagonal red hollow *SPECIMEN* and black DLR　—　—　500
　　　　　oval overprints; horizontal red *SPECIMEN No. #*
　　　　　ovpt at lower left.

TCMB B5 (P127): **5 Türk lirası** (demonetized 11.11.1962) VG VF UNC
Blue and green. Front: Mustafa Kemal Atatürk. Back: Security Monument (two bronze soliders with rifles) in Ankara's Güvenpark by Austrian architect Clemens Holzmeister and Austrian sculptors Anton Hanak and Josef Thorak. No security thread. Watermark: Mustafa Kemal Atatürk. Printer: *THOMAS DE LA RUE & COY, LTD, LONDRES ANGLETERRE*. 155 x 70 mm.

- ☐ a. 11 HAZİRAN 1930. Signature 2. Seri A - F. Intro: 15.10.1937. 150 350 1,500
- ☐ as1. Diagonal *SPECIMEN* perforation. — 300 750
- ☐ as2. Handwritten *SPECIMEN No.* # at lower left; punched. — — 750

TCMB B6 (P128): **10 Türk lirası** (demonetized 03.06.1962) VG VF UNC
Brick red. Front: Mustafa Kemal Atatürk. Back: Citadel of Ankara. No security thread. Watermark: Mustafa Kemal Atatürk. Printer: *THOMAS DE LA RUE & COY, LTD, LONDRES ANGLETERRE*. 165 x 75 mm.

- ☐ a. 11 HAZİRAN 1930. Signature 2. Seri A - G. Intro: 16.05.1938. 300 1,200 5,000
- ☐ as. Specimen. — — 900

TCMB B7 (P129): **50 Türk lirası** (demonetized 03.06.1962) VG VF UNC
Purple. Front: Mustafa Kemal Atatürk. Back: Tree; farmhouse; corral; Angora goats; mountain. No security thread. Watermark: Mustafa Kemal Atatürk. Printer: *THOMAS DE LA RUE & COY, LTD, LONDRES ANGLETERRE*. 175 x 80 mm.

- ☐ a. 11 HAZİRAN 1930. Signature 2. Seri A - D. Intro: 01.04.1938. 750 1,500 7,500
- ☐ as1. Diagonal *SPECIMEN* perforation; large red *X* overprint on back. — — 1,200
- ☐ as2. Horizontal *CANCELLED* perforation. — — 1,000
- ☐ as3. Diagonal red hollow *SPECIMEN* overprint; horizon. red *SPECIMEN No.* # ovpt at lower left. — — 1,000

TCMB B8 (P130): **100 Türk lirası** (demonetized 16.10.1962) VG VF UNC
Brown. Front: Mustafa Kemal Atatürk. Back: Ship passing through The Dardanelles; fortress ruins. No security thread. Watermark: Mustafa Kemal Atatürk. Printer: *THOMAS DE LA RUE & COY, LTD, LONDRES ANGLETERRE*. 185 x 85 mm.

- ☐ a. 11 HAZİRAN 1930. Signature 2. Seri A - C. Intro: 01.03.1938. 2,000 5,000 —
- ☐ as. Handwritten *SPECIMEN No.* # at lower left; punched. — — 1,500

1930 (1940-1947) İnönü Necktie Issues

Following the death of Mustafa Kemal Atatürk on 10 November 1938, İsmet İnönü became president. His portrait replaced that of Atatürk on all new banknotes, beginning with the 500- and 1,000- Türk lirası notes introduced on 18 November 1940.

TCMB B9 (P131): **500 Türk lirası** (demonetized 25.04.1956)   VG   VF   UNC
Olive green. Front: Mustafa Kemal Atatürk. Back: Roumeli Hissar castle on the Bosporus. No security thread. Watermark: Mustafa Kemal Atatürk. Printer: *THOMAS DE LA RUE & COY, LTD, LONDRES ANGLETERRE*. 195 x 90 mm.
- ☐ a. 11 HAZİRAN 1930. Signature 3. Seri A - D.   4,000   8,500   —
  Intro: 15.06.1939.
- ☐ as. Diagonal red hollow *SPECIMEN* and DLR   —   —   2,200
  oval overprints on front only; horizontal red
  SPECIMEN No. # overprint at lower left.

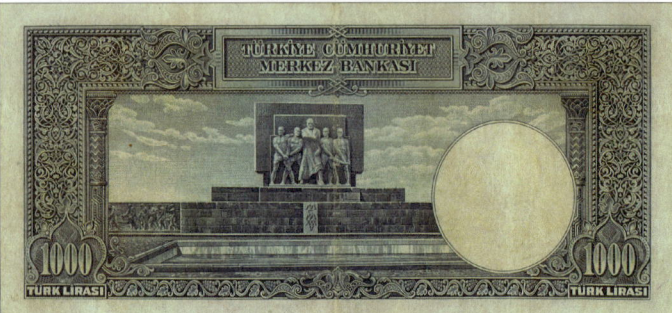

TCMB B10 (P132): **1,000 Türk lirası** (demonetized 25.04.1956)   VG   VF   UNC
Blue. Front: Mustafa Kemal Atatürk. Back: Security Monument (five men) in Ankara's Güvenpark by Austrian architect Clemens Holzmeister and Austrian sculptors Anton Hanak and Josef Thorak. No security thread. Watermark: Mustafa Kemal Atatürk. Printer: *THOMAS DE LA RUE & COY, LTD, LONDRES ANGLETERRE*. 205 x 95 mm.
- ☐ a. 11 HAZİRAN 1930. Signature 3. Seri A - B.   10,000   —   —
  Intro: 15.06.1939.
- ☐ as. Diagonal black hollow *SPECIMEN* and DLR   —   —   2,500
  oval overprints on front only; horizontal black
  SPECIMEN No. # overprint at lower left.

TCMB B11 (P133): **50 kuruş**   VG   VF   UNC
Brown and lilac. Front: İsmet İnönü wearing necktie. Back: Trees; State Art and Sculpture Museum building in Ankara. No security thread. Watermark: İsmet İnönü. Printer: *BRADBURY, WILKINSON & Cº Lᴅ NEW MALDEN, SURREY, ENGLAND*. 125 x 55 mm.
- ☐ a. 11 HAZİRAN 1930. Signature 3. Seri A - C.   15   60   100
  Seri C notes command 100x premium. Unissued.

BWC printed 40 million notes and shipped them to Turkey on the British vessel SS City of Roubaix, which was sunk at Piraeus, Greece on 16 April 1941 by German warplanes. The notes washed up on the beach and were collected by the public. Upon learning of the incident, the Turkish Prime Ministry issued a decree abolishing their validity. The Greeks returned the remainder of the notes recovered from the sunken ship to the Republic of Turkey. These notes were sent to the SEKA Paper Factory to be recycled.

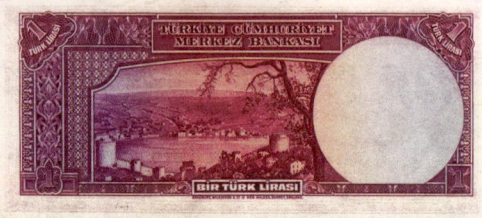

TCMB B12 (P135): **1 Türk lirası** (demonetized 02.08.1957)   VG   VF   UNC
Purple. Front: İsmet İnönü wearing necktie. Back: Roumeli Hissar castle on the Bosporus in Istanbul. No security thread. Watermark: İsmet İnönü. Printer: *BRADBURY, WILKINSON & Cº Lᴅ NEW MALDEN, SURREY, ENGLAND*. 135 x 60 mm.
- ☐ a. 11 HAZİRAN 1930. Signature 4. Seri A - B.   50   100   400
  Intro: 25.04.1942.
- ☐ as. Diagonal *GEÇMEZ* perforation;   —   —   500
  large red *X* overprint on back.
- ☐ at. Color trial: Green.   —   —   700

TCMB B13 (P140): **2 1/2 Türk lirası** (demonetized 15.07.1962)   VG   VF   UNC
Violet, brown, and yellow. Front: İsmet İnönü wearing necktie. Back: Trees; State Art and Sculpture Museum building in Ankara. Solid security thread. Watermark: İsmet İnönü. Printer: *BRADBURY, WILKINSON & C⁰ L^D NEW MALDEN, SURREY, ENGLAND*. 145 x 65 mm.

- ☐ a. 11 HAZİRAN 1930. Signature 6. Seri A - B. Intro: 27.03.1947.   100   200   450
- ☐ at. Color trial: Green.   —   —   500

Cumhuriyet in bank name spelled without umlaut over first u.

TCMB B14 (P147): **10 Türk lirası** (demonetized 02.06.1962)   VG   VF   UNC
Red. Front: İsmet İnönü wearing necktie. Back: Fountain of Ahmed III in front of the Imperial Gate of Topkapı Palace in Istanbul. No security thread. Watermark: None. Printer: *AMERICAN BANK NOTE COMPANY*. 165 x 75 mm.

- ☐ a. 11 HAZİRAN 1930. Signature 4. Seri H - R. Intro: 17.02.1947.   150   450   1,800
- ☐ as. Diagonal dark blue SPECIMEN overprint; punched.   —   —   250

TCMB B15 (P136): **50 Türk lirası**   VG   VF   UNC
Purple. Front: İsmet İnönü wearing necktie. Back: Tree; farmhouse; corral; Angora goats; mountain. No security thread. Watermark: İsmet İnönü. Printer: *THOMAS DE LA RUE & COY, LTD, LONDRES ANGLETERRE*. 176 x 79 mm.

- ☐ a. 11 HAZİRAN 1930. Signature 3. Unissued.   —   —   —
- ☐ as. Diagonal red hollow SPECIMEN overprint; horizon. red SPECIMEN No. # ovpt at lower left.   —   —   3,000

Of the four million 50-Türk lirası notes printed by TDLR, 126,000 were destroyed in an air attack on London on 11 September 1940 during WWII. The remaining notes were safely delivered to the Central Bank of Turkey, which decided not to issue them. These notes (along with the 50-kuruş and 100-Türk lirası notes retrieved from the sunken SS City of Roubaix) were destroyed on 15 May 1955 at the SEKA Paper Factory.

TCMB B16 (P142): **50 Türk lirası** (demonetized 01.12.1961)   VG   VF   UNC
Purple. Front: İsmet İnönü wearing necktie. Back: Angora goats. No security thread. Watermark: None. Printer: *AMERICAN BANK NOTE COMPANY*. 175 x 80 mm.

- ☐ a. 11 HAZİRAN 1930. Signature 4. Seri N - Z. Intro: 25.04.1942.   300   1,200   4,500
- ☐ as. Diagonal red SPECIMEN overprint; punched.   —   —   450

TCMB B17 (P137): **100 Türk lirası**   VG   VF   UNC
Brown. Front: İsmet İnönü wearing necktie. Back: Ship passing through The Dardanelles; fortress ruins. No security thread. Watermark: İsmet İnönü. Printer: *THOMAS DE LA RUE & COY, LTD, LONDRES ANGLETERRE*. 188 x 85 mm.

- ☐ a.   11 HAZİRAN 1930. Signature 3. Unissued.   —   —   —
- ☐ as.   Diagonal red hollow *SPECIMEN* and DLR oval overprints; horizontal red *SPECIMEN No.* # ovpt at lower left.   —   —   2,000

These 100-Türk lirası notes were on the SS City of Roubaix when it was sunk. Notes that escaped confiscation were introduced by Greek and non-Muslim tradesmen and put into circulation in eastern provinces where the means of communication were poor. The variety of notes confused the public who were not in a position to be able to tell if they were legitimate or not. These notes exchanged hands among the public unofficially. Up through 1945, the government in Ankara had great difficult withdrawing these notes from circulation.

TCMB B18 (P138): **500 Türk lirası** (demonetized 25.04.1956)   VG   VF   UNC
Green. Front: İsmet İnönü wearing necktie. Back: Roumeli Hissar castle on the Bosporus in Istanbul. No security thread. Watermark: İsmet İnönü. Printer: *THOMAS DE LA RUE & COY, LTD, LONDRES ANGLETERRE*. 195 x 90 mm.

- ☐ a.   11 HAZİRAN 1930. Signature 3. Seri E - H. Intro: 18.11.1940.   2,500   —   —
- ☐ as.   Diagonal red hollow *SPECIMEN* and DLR oval overprints; horizontal red *SPECIMEN No.* # ovpt at lower left.   —   —   2,500

TCMB B19 (PNL): **500 Türk lirası on 10 Türk lirası**   VG   VF   UNC
Red. Front: İsmet İnönü wearing necktie. Back: Fountain of Ahmed III in front of the Imperial Gate of Topkapı Palace in Istanbul. No security thread. Watermark: None. Printer: *AMERICAN BANK NOTE COMPANY*. 165 x 75 mm.

- ☐ s.   Specimen. 11 HAZİRAN 1930. Sig. 4. Unissued.   —   —   5,000

Overprinted on TCMB B14.

TCMB B20 (P139): **1,000 Türk lirası** (demonetized 25.04.1956)   VG   VF   UNC
Blue. Front: İsmet İnönü wearing necktie. Back: Security Monument (five men) in Ankara's Güvenpark by Austrian architect Clemens Holzmeister and Austrian sculptors Anton Hanak and Josef Thorak. No security thread. Watermark: İsmet İnönü. Printer: *THOMAS DE LA RUE & COY, LTD, LONDRES ANGLETERRE*. 205 x 95 mm.

- ☐ a.   11 HAZİRAN 1930. Signature 3. Seri C - D.   8,000   —   —
    Intro: 18.11.1940.
- ☐ as. Diagonal black hollow *SPECIMEN* and DLR oval   —   —   3,300
    overprints; horizontal black *SPECIMEN No. #*
    ovpt at lower left.

1930 (1942-1947) İnönü Bowtie Issues

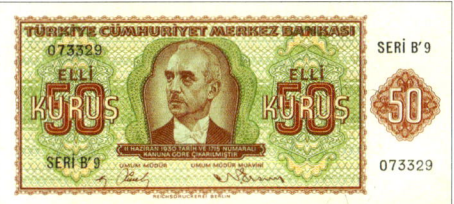

TCMB B21 (P134): **50 kuruş** (demonetized 02.08.1957)   VG   VF   UNC
Brown, green, and yellow. Front: İsmet İnönü wearing bowtie. Back: Tree, house, former bank headquarters building in Ankara, and automobile. No security thread. Watermark: None. Printer: *REICHSDRUCKEREI BERLIN*. 125 x 55 mm.

- ☐ a.   11 HAZİRAN 1930. Signature 4. Seri A - C.   75   180   1,500
    Intro: 26.06.1944.
- ☐ as1. Vertical *MUSTER* perforation.   —   —   750
- ☐ as2. Diagonal red *SPECIMEN* overprint.   —   XF   800
- ☐ r.   Remainder: No serial numbers.   —   —   —

TCMB B22 (PNL): **5 Türk lirası**   VG   VF   UNC
Purple. Front: İsmet İnönü wearing bowtie. Back: Unknown. No security thread. Watermark: Unknown. Printer: *MAARIF MATBAASI*. 139 x 56 mm.

- ☐ a.   11 HAZİRAN 1930. Signature 4. Seri D.   —   —   —
    Unissued.

TCMB B23 (P141): **10 Türk lirası** (demonetized 01.04.1960)   VG   VF   UNC
Brown and reddish-brown. Front: İsmet İnönü wearing bowtie. Back: Three village women in local costumes. No security thread. Watermark: Pattern. Printer: *REICHSDRUCKEREI BERLIN*. 155 x 65 mm.

- ☐ a.   11 HAZİRAN 1930. Signature 4. Seri A - E.   200   500   4,000
    Intro: 15.01.1942.
- ☐ as. Diagonal red *SPECIMEN* overprint.   —   —   1,000

TCMB B24 (P148): **10 Türk lirası** (demonetized 02.06.1962)   VG   VF   UNC
Brown. Front: İsmet İnönü wearing bowtie. Back: Fountain of Ahmed III in front of the Imperial Gate of Topkapı Palace in Istanbul. No security thread. Watermark: None. Printer: *AMERICAN BANK NOTE COMPANY*. 165 x 75 mm.

- ☐ a.   11 HAZİRAN 1930. Signature 4. Seri A - E.   150   450   4,000
    Intro: 19.09.1948.
- ☐ as1. Diagonal red *SPECIMEN* overprint; punched.   —   —   300
- ☐ as2. Diagonal red *GEÇMEZ* overprint; punched.   —   —   300

TCMB B25 (P142A): **50 Türk lirası**   VG   VF   UNC
Purple. Front: İsmet İnönü wearing bowtie. Back: Angora goats. No security thread. Watermark: None. Printer: *AMERICAN BANK NOTE COMPANY*. 177 x 80 mm.

☐	s1.	Diagonal red *SPECIMEN* overprint; punched. Signature 4. Seri E. Unissued.	— —	500
☐	s2.	Diagonal red *GEÇMEZ* overprint; punched.	— —	450
☐	p.	Uniface proofs.	— —	400

TCMB B26 (P143): **50 Türk lirası** (demonetized 01.12.1961)   VG   VF   UNC
Blue. Front: İsmet İnönü wearing bowtie. Back: Angora goats. No security thread. Watermark: None. Printer: *AMERICAN BANK NOTE COMPANY*. 177 x 80 mm.

☐	a.	11 HAZİRAN 1930. Signature 4. Seri A - D. Intro: 17.02.1947.	300	1,300	4,500
☐	as.	Diagonal red *SPECIMEN* overprint; punched.	—	—	400

TCMB B27 (P144): **100 Türk lirası** (demonetized 09.08.1948)   VG   VF   UNC
Brown. Front: İsmet İnönü wearing bowtie. Back: Young girl with bunch of grapes. No security thread. Watermark: Pattern. Printer: *REICHSDRUCKEREI BERLIN*. 175 x 75 mm.

☐	a.	11 HAZİRAN 1930. Sig. 4. Intro: 18.08.1942. With imprint. Seri A - B.	150	500	2,000
☐	b.	Without imprint. Seri C - J.	150	500	2,200
☐	r.	Remainder without serial numbers.	—	—	—
☐	as.	Vertical *MUSTER* perforation.	—	—	1,000

TCMB B28 (P149): **100 Türk lirası** (demonetized 10.10.1962)   VG   VF   UNC
Green. Front: İsmet İnönü wearing bowtie. Back: Roumeli Hissar castle on the Bosporus in Istanbul; ship. No security thread. Watermark: None. Printer: *AMERICAN BANK NOTE COMPANY*. 181 x 83 mm.

☐	a.	11 HAZİRAN 1930. Signature 7. Seri K - O. Intro: 18.07.1947.	250	750	4,000
☐	as.	Two diagonal red *SPECIMEN* ovpts; punched.	—	—	500
☐	p.	Uniface front proof.	—	—	—

Cumhuriyet in bank name spelled without umlaut over first u.

1930 (1951-1971) Atatürk Bowtie Issues

With the exception of TCMB B50, all of these notes bear the 1930 law date. For the easiest identification of the many different color varieties, consult the series ranges.

TCMB B29 (P145): **500 Türk lirası** (demonetized 15.04.1963)   VG   VF   UNC
Olive green. Front: İsmet İnönü wearing bowtie. Back: Students at the Technical School in Ankara with machine tools on factory floor. No security thread. Watermark: None. Printer: *AMERICAN BANK NOTE COMPANY*. 185 x 85 mm.

- ☐ a. 11 HAZİRAN 1930. Signature 5. Seri A - C.   1,000   3,500   10,000
  Intro: 24.04.1946.
- ☐ as. Two diagonal red SPECIMEN ovpts; punched.   —   —   1,300
- ☐ p. Separate uniface front/back proofs in black.   —   —   —

TCMB B30 (P146): **1,000 Türk lirası** (demonetized 15.04.1963)   VG   VF   UNC
Blue. Front: İsmet İnönü wearing bowtie. Back: Scouts with bugles. No security thread. Watermark: None. Printer: *AMERICAN BANK NOTE COMPANY*. 195 x 95 mm.

- ☐ a. 11 HAZİRAN 1930. Signature 5. Seri A - C.   15,000   —   —
  Intro: 24.04.1946.
- ☐ as. Diagonal red SPECIMEN overprint; punched.   —   —   1,500
- ☐ p. Uniface front proof.   —   —   —

TCMB B31 (P150): **2 1/2 Türk lirası** (demonetized 20.10.1976)   VG   VF   UNC
Purple. Front: Mustafa Kemal Atatürk. Back (purple): Bank headquarters building in Ankara. Solid security thread. Watermark: Mustafa Kemal Atatürk. Printer: *THOMAS DE LA RUE & CO. LTD*. 145 x 65 mm.

- ☐ a. 11 HAZİRAN 1930. Signature 8. Seri A - J.   50   250   1,500
  Intro: 15.07.1952.
- ☐ as. Diagonal red hollow SPECIMEN overprint;   —   —   500
  horiz. black SPECIMEN No. # ovpt at lower left.

TCMB B32 (P151): **2 1/2 Türk lirası** (demonetized 20.10.1976)   VG   VF   UNC
Purple. Front: Mustafa Kemal Atatürk. Back (brown): Bank headquarters building in Ankara. Solid security thread. Watermark: Mustafa Kemal Atatürk. Printer: *THOMAS DE LA RUE & CO. LTD*. 145 x 65 mm.

- ☐ a. 11 HAZİRAN 1930. Signature 9. Seri K - U.   25   75   500
  Intro: 01.01.1955.
- ☐ as1. Diagonal red GEÇMEZ overprint; punched.   —   —   400
- ☐ as2. Black DLR oval overprints;   —   —   400
  horiz. black SPECIMEN No. # ovpt at lower left.

TCMB B33 (P152): **2 1/2 Türk lirası** (demonetized 20.10.1976) VG VF UNC
Purple. Front: Mustafa Kemal Atatürk. Back (red): Bank headquarters building in Ankara. Solid security thread. Watermark: Mustafa Kemal Atatürk. Printer: *THOMAS DE LA RUE & CO. LTD.* 145 x 65 mm.

- ☐ a. 11 HAZİRAN 1930. Signature 10. Seri Ü - Z. Intro: 01.07.1957. — 25 90 150
- ☐ as1. Diagonal red *GEÇMEZ* overprint on front; diagonal black *GEÇMEZ* overprint on back; punched. — — 400
- ☐ as2. Diagonal black *SPECIMEN* and DLR oval ovpts; horiz. black *SPECIMEN No. #* ovpt at lower left; punched. — — 400
- ☐ as3. Diagonal black DLR oval ovpts; horiz. black *SPECIMEN No. #* ovpt at lower left; punched. — — 400

TCMB B34 (P153): **2 1/2 Türk lirası** (demonetized 20.10.1976) VG VF UNC
Purple. Front: Mustafa Kemal Atatürk. Back (green): Bank headquarters building in Ankara. Solid security thread. Watermark: Mustafa Kemal Atatürk. Printer: *THOMAS DE LA RUE & CO. LTD.* 145 x 65 mm.

- ☐ a. 11 HAZİRAN 1930. Signature 11. Seri A - B. Intro: 02.02.1960. — 20 75 400
- ☐ as1. Diagonal red *NUMUNEDIR GEÇMEZ* overprint; punched. — — 400
- ☐ as2. Diagonal red *SPECIMEN* and DLR oval ovpts; horiz. red *SPECIMEN No. #* ovpt at lower left; punched. — — 400

TCMB B35 (P154): **5 Türk lirası** (demonetized 08.01.1978) VG VF UNC
Blue. Front: Mustafa Kemal Atatürk. Back (blue): Three women with wicker baskets filled with hazelnuts. Solid security thread. Watermark: Mustafa Kemal Atatürk. Printer: *BRADBURY, WILKINSON & C⁰ L^D NEW MALDEN, SURREY, ENGLAND.* 150 x 68 mm.

- ☐ a. 11 HAZİRAN 1930. Signature 8. Seri A - D. Intro: 10.11.1952. — 50 180 1,200
- ☐ as. Diagonal red *GEÇMEZ* overprint; horizontal *CANCELLED* perforation. — — XF 200
- ☐ at. Color trial: Purple. — — 450

TCMB B36 (P155): **5 Türk lirası** (demonetized 08.01.1978) VG VF UNC
Blue. Front: Mustafa Kemal Atatürk. Back (green): Three women with wicker baskets filled with hazelnuts. Solid security thread. Watermark: Mustafa Kemal Atatürk. Printer: *BRADBURY, WILKINSON & C⁰ L^D NEW MALDEN, SURREY, ENGLAND.* 150 x 68 mm.

- ☐ a. 11 HAZİRAN 1930. Signature 9. Seri E. Intro: 08.06.1959. — 60 180 1,200
- ☐ as. Diagonal red *GEÇMEZ* overprint; horizontal *CANCELLED* perforation; punched. — — 500

TCMB B37 (P173): **5 Türk lirası** (demonetized 08.01.1978)   VG   VF   UNC

Blue and orange. Front: Mustafa Kemal Atatürk. Back (blue): Three women with wicker baskets filled with hazelnuts. Solid security thread. Watermark: Mustafa Kemal Atatürk. Printer: (TCMB). 150 x 68 mm.

- ☐ a. 11 HAZİRAN 1930. Signature 13. (Seri) F - G.   20   75   350
  Intro: 25.10.1961.
- ☐ as. Horizontal red *NÜMUNEDİR GEÇMEZ* overprint on front; large red *X* overprint on back; punched.   —   —   400

TCMB B38 (P174): **5 Türk lirası** (demonetized 08.01.1978)   VG   VF   UNC

Blue. Front: Mustafa Kemal Atatürk. Back (blue): Three women with wicker baskets filled with hazelnuts. Solid security thread. Watermark: Mustafa Kemal Atatürk. Printer: (TCMB). 150 x 68 mm.

- ☐ a. 11 HAZİRAN 1930. Signature 16. (Seri) H - J.   15   50   250
  Intro: 04.01.1965.
- ☐ as. Horizontal red *SPECIMEN* overprint on front; large red *X* overprint on back; punched.   —   —   400

TCMB B39 (P156): **10 Türk lirası** (demonetized 04.07.1976)   VG   VF   UNC

Green. Front: Mustafa Kemal Atatürk. Back (green): Trees, stone bridge in Edirne over Meriç (Maritsa) river. Solid security thread. Watermark: Mustafa Kemal Atatürk. Printer: THOMAS DE LA RUE & CO. LTD. 155 x 71 mm.

- ☐ a. 11 HAZİRAN 1930. Signature 8. Seri A - J.   50   250   2,500
  Intro: 02.06.1952.
- ☐ as1. Diagonal red hollow *SPECIMEN* overprint; horiz. red *SPECIMEN No.* # ovpt at lower left.   —   —   500
- ☐ as2. Diagonal red *GEÇMEZ* overprint; punched.   —   400   —

TCMB B40 (P157): **10 Türk lirası** (demonetized 04.07.1976)   VG   VF   UNC

Green. Front: Mustafa Kemal Atatürk. Back (red): Trees, stone bridge in Edirne over Meriç (Maritsa) river. Solid security thread. Watermark: Mustafa Kemal Atatürk. Printer: THOMAS DE LA RUE & CO. LTD. 155 x 71 mm.

- ☐ a. 11 HAZİRAN 1930. Signature 8. Seri K - U.   10   100   750
  Intro: 26.10.1953.
- ☐ as1. Diagonal black hollow *SPECIMEN* overprint; horiz. red *SPECIMEN No.* # ovpt at lower left.   —   —   500
- ☐ as2. Diagonal black *GEÇMEZ* overprint; punched.   —   400   —

TCMB B41 (P158): **10 Türk lirası** (demonetized 04.07.1976) VG VF UNC
Green. Front: Mustafa Kemal Atatürk. Back (brown): Trees, stone bridge in Edirne over Meriç (Maritsa) river. Solid security thread. Watermark: Mustafa Kemal Atatürk. Printer: *THOMAS DE LA RUE & CO. LTD*. 155 x 71 mm.

- a. 11 HAZİRAN 1930. Signature 9. Seri V - Y.   100   750   4,500
  Intro: 24.03.1958.
- as. Diagonal black *GEÇMEZ* overprint; punched.   —   —   500

TCMB B43 (P160): **10 Türk lirası** (demonetized 04.07.1976) VG VF UNC
Green and pink. Front: Mustafa Kemal Atatürk. Back (red): Trees, stone bridge in Edirne over Meriç (Maritsa) river. Solid security thread. Watermark: Mustafa Kemal Atatürk. Printer: (TCMB). 155 x 71 mm.

- a. 11 HAZİRAN 1930. Signature 12. (Seri) Z.   20   60   300
  Intro: 15.05.1961.
- as. Horizontal red *NÜMUNEDİR GEÇMEZ* overprint on front; large red *X* overprint on back.   —   —   300

TCMB B42 (P159): **10 Türk lirası** (demonetized 04.07.1976) VG VF UNC
Green and pink. Front: Mustafa Kemal Atatürk. Back (green): Trees, stone bridge in Edirne over Meriç (Maritsa) river. Solid security thread. Watermark: Mustafa Kemal Atatürk. Printer: (TCMB). 155 x 71 mm.

- a. 11 HAZİRAN 1930. Signature 12. (Seri) Z.   15   50   300
  Intro: 25.04.1960.
- as. Specimen.   —   —   300

TCMB B44 (P161): **10 Türk lirası** (demonetized 04.07.1976) VG VF UNC
Green and pink. Front: Mustafa Kemal Atatürk. Back (green): Trees, stone bridge in Edirne over Meriç (Maritsa) river. Solid security thread. Watermark: Mustafa Kemal Atatürk. Printer: (TCMB). 155 x 71 mm.

- a. 11 HAZİRAN 1930. Signature 15. (Seri) A - B.   15   50   250
  Intro: 02.01.1963.
- as. Horizontal red *NÜMUNEDİR GEÇMEZ* overprint on front; large red *X* overprint on back; punched.   —   —   300

TCMB B45 (P162): **50 Türk lirası** (demonetized 07.05.1989)   VG   VF   UNC
Brown. Front: Mustafa Kemal Atatürk. Back (brown): Statue of Victory (solider with rifle) at Ulus Square in Ankara. Solid security thread. Watermark: Mustafa Kemal Atatürk. Printer: *BRADBURY, WILKINSON & C⁰ L⁰ NEW MALDEN, SURREY, ENGLAND*. 160 x 74 mm.

- ☐ a. 11 HAZİRAN 1930. Signature 8. Seri A - D.   100   500   1,000
  Intro: 01.12.1951.
- ☐ as1. Diagonal red *GEÇMEZ* overprint;   —   —   750
  horizontal *CANCELLED* perforation.
- ☐ as2. Horizontal red *SPECIMEN* overprint; punched.   —   —   550
- ☐ at. Color trial: Green.   —   —   —

TCMB B46 (P163): **50 Türk lirası** (demonetized 07.05.1989)   VG   VF   UNC
Brown. Front: Mustafa Kemal Atatürk. Back (orange): Statue of Victory (solider with rifle) at Ulus Square in Ankara. Solid security thread. Watermark: Mustafa Kemal Atatürk. Printer: *BRADBURY, WILKINSON & C⁰ L⁰ NEW MALDEN, SURREY, ENGLAND*. 160 x 74 mm.

- ☐ a. 11 HAZİRAN 1930. Signature 8. Seri E - N.   150   700   3,000
  Intro: 02.02.1953.
- ☐ as. Diagonal red *GEÇMEZ* overprint;   —   —   750
  horizontal *CANCELLED* perforation.

TCMB B47 (P164): **50 Türk lirası** (demonetized 07.05.1989)   VG   VF   UNC
Brown. Front: Mustafa Kemal Atatürk. Back (red): Statue of Victory (solider with rifle) at Ulus Square in Ankara. Solid security thread. Watermark: Mustafa Kemal Atatürk. Printer: *BRADBURY, WILKINSON & C⁰ L⁰ NEW MALDEN, SURREY, ENGLAND*. 160 x 74 mm.

- ☐ a. 11 HAZİRAN 1930. Signature 9. Seri O - S.   200   900   4,300
  Intro: 15.10.1956.
- ☐ as. Diagonal red *GEÇMEZ* overprint;   —   —   750
  horizontal *CANCELLED* perforation.

TCMB B48 (P165): **50 Türk lirası** (demonetized 07.05.1989)   VG   VF   UNC
Brown. Front: Mustafa Kemal Atatürk. Back (bluish gray): Statue of Victory (solider with rifle) at Ulus Square in Ankara. Solid security thread. Watermark: Mustafa Kemal Atatürk. Printer: *BRADBURY, WILKINSON & C⁰ L⁰ NEW MALDEN, SURREY, ENGLAND*. 160 x 74 mm.

- ☐ a. 11 HAZİRAN 1930. Signature 10. Seri T - Z.   75   150   1,500
  Intro: 01.10.1957.
- ☐ as. Diagonal red *GEÇMEZ* overprint;   —   —   600
  horizontal *CANCELLED* perforation.
- ☐ at. Color trial: Green.   —   —   375

TCMB B49 (P166): **50 Türk lirası** (demonetized 07.05.1989)   VG   VF   UNC
Brown, red, and blue. Front: Mustafa Kemal Atatürk. Back (brown): Statue of Victory (solider with rifle) at Ulus Square in Ankara. Solid security thread. Watermark: Mustafa Kemal Atatürk. Printer: (TCMB). 160 x 74 mm.

- ☐ a. 11 HAZİRAN 1930. Signature 17. (Seri) A - G.   25   200   1,000
  Intro: 15.02.1960.
- ☐ as. Horizontal red *NÜMUNEDİR GEÇMEZ* overprint on front; large red *X* overprint on back; punched.   —   —   500

TCMB B50 (P175 & P187A): **50 Türk lirası** (demon. 07.05.89)   VG   VF   UNC
Brown. Front: Mustafa Kemal Atatürk. Back: Statue of Victory (solider with rifle) at Ulus Square in Ankara. Solid security thread. Watermark: Mustafa Kemal Atatürk. Printer: (TCMB). 160 x 74 mm.

- ☐ a. 11 HAZİRAN 1930. Signature 16. (Seri) H - N.   20   75   200
  Intro: 01.06.1964.
- ☐ b. 14 OCAK 1970. Signature 18. (Seri) O - Y. Lighter portrait. Intro: 02.08.1971.   5   20   100
- ☐ as. Horizontal red *SPECIMEN* overprint on front; large red *X* overprint on back; punched.   —   —   550
- ☐ bs. Specimen.   —   —   250

Replacement notes: (Seri) Y.

TCMB B51 (P167): **100 Türk lirası** (demonetized 12.04.1986)   VG   VF   UNC
Green. Front: Mustafa Kemal Atatürk. Back (green): Trees; bridge over river in The Youth Park; Ankara fortress on hillside. Solid security thread. Watermark: Mustafa Kemal Atatürk. Printer: *BRADBURY, WILKINSON & C⁰ L⁰ NEW MALDEN, SURREY, ENGLAND*. 170 x 80 mm.

- ☐ a. 11 HAZİRAN 1930. Signature 8. Seri A - G.   100   250   2,500
  Intro: 10.10.1952.
- ☐ as. Diagonal red *GEÇMEZ* overprint; horizontal *CANCELLED* perforation.   —   —   1,000
- ☐ at. Color trial: Orange-brown.   —   —   500

TCMB B52 (P168): **100 Türk lirası** (demonetized 12.04.1986)   VG   VF   UNC
Green. Front: Mustafa Kemal Atatürk. Back (blue): Trees; bridge over river in The Youth Park; Ankara fortress on hillside. Solid security thread. Watermark: Mustafa Kemal Atatürk. Printer: *BRADBURY, WILKINSON & C⁰ L⁰ NEW MALDEN, SURREY, ENGLAND*. 170 x 80 mm.

- ☐ a. 11 HAZİRAN 1930. Signature 9. Seri H - J.   150   750   4,500
  Intro: 02.07.1956.
- ☐ as. Diagonal red *GEÇMEZ* overprint; horizontal *CANCELLED* perforation.   —   XF   400

TCMB B53 (P169): **100 Türk lirası** (demonetized 12.04.1986)   VG   VF   UNC

Green. Front: Mustafa Kemal Atatürk. Back (green): Trees; bridge over river in The Youth Park; Ankara fortress on hillside. Solid security thread. Watermark: Mustafa Kemal Atatürk. Printer: (TCMB). 170 x 80 mm.

- ☐ a. 11 HAZİRAN 1930. Signature 10. (Seri) K - P.   75   150   900
  Intro: 04.08.1958.
- ☐ as. Horizontal red NÜMUNEDİR GEÇMEZ overprint;   —   —   1,000
  punched.

This is the first bank note printed in Turkey.

TCMB B54 (P170): **500 Türk lirası** (demonetized 01.09.1986)   VG   VF   UNC

Dark brown. Front: Mustafa Kemal Atatürk. Back: Sultan Ahmet Mosque, the Obelix and the Hippodrome in Istanbul. Solid security thread. Watermark: Mustafa Kemal Atatürk. Printer: *BRADBURY, WILKINSON & C⁰ L⁰ NEW MALDEN, SURREY, ENGLAND.* 170 x 80 mm.

- ☐ a. 11 HAZİRAN 1930. Signature 8. Seri A - E.   150   1,500   3,500
  Intro: 15.04.1953.
- ☐ as. Specimen.   —   —   1,250
- ☐ at. Color trial: Green.   —   —   700

TCMB B55 (P171): **500 Türk lirası** (demonetized 01.09.1986)   VG   VF   UNC

Dark brown. Front: Mustafa Kemal Atatürk. Back: Sultan Ahmet Mosque, the Obelix and the Hippodrome in Istanbul. Solid security thread. Watermark: Mustafa Kemal Atatürk. Printer: *BRADBURY, WILKINSON & C⁰ L⁰ NEW MALDEN, SURREY, ENGLAND.* 170 x 80 mm.

- ☐ a. 11 HAZİRAN 1930. Signature 10. (Seri) F - O.   160   1,100   4,000
  Intro: 16.02.1959.
- ☐ as. Diagonal red NÜMUNEDİR GEÇMEZ overprint   —   —   1,200
  on front; large red *X* overprint on back; punched.
- ☐ at. Color trial: Green.   —   —   500

TCMB B56 (P172): **1,000 Türk lirası** (demonetized 07.05.1989)   VG   VF   UNC

Purple. Front: Mustafa Kemal Atatürk. Back: Roumeli Hissar castle on the Bosporus in Istanbul. Solid security thread. Watermark: Mustafa Kemal Atatürk. Printer: *BRADBURY, WILKINSON & C⁰ L⁰ NEW MALDEN, SURREY, ENGLAND.* 170 x 80 mm.

- ☐ a. 11 HAZİRAN 1930. Signature 8. Seri A - E.   200   350   4,500
  Intro: 15.04.1953.
- ☐ as. Diagonal red GEÇMEZ overprint.   —   —   1,500
- ☐ at. Color trial: Brown.   —   —   1,200
- ☐ p. Separate uniface front/back proofs in black.   —   —   —

1930 (1962-1969) Atatürk Bust Issues

TCMB B57 (P176): **100 Türk lirası** (demonetized 12.04.1986)   **VG**   **VF**   **UNC**
Olive green and orange. Front: Mustafa Kemal Atatürk. Back: Youth Park in Ankara. Solid security thread. Watermark: Mustafa Kemal Atatürk. Printer: (TCMB). 170 x 80 mm.
- ☐ a. 11 HAZİRAN 1930. Signature 14. (Seri) R - U, Z.   50   150   800
  Intro: 15.03.1962.
- ☐ as. Specimen.   —   —   750

TCMB B58 (P177): **100 Türk lirası** (demonetized 12.04.1986)   **VG**   **VF**   **UNC**
Olive green and blue. Front: Mustafa Kemal Atatürk. Back: Youth Park in Ankara. Solid security thread. Watermark: Mustafa Kemal Atatürk. Printer: (TCMB). 170 x 80 mm.
- ☐ a. 11 HAZİRAN 1930. Sig. 16. (Seri) V - Z, A - C.   30   100   350
  Intro: 01.10.1964.
- ☐ as. Diagonal red *SPECIMEN* overprint on front;   —   250   750
  large red *X* overprint on back; punched.

Replacement notes: (Seri) Z.

TCMB B59 (P182): **100 Türk lirası** (demonetized 12.04.1986)   **VG**   **VF**   **UNC**
Olive green, orange, and pink. Front: Mustafa Kemal Atatürk. Back: Youth Park in Ankara. Solid security thread. Watermark: Mustafa Kemal Atatürk. Printer: (TCMB). 170 x 80 mm.
- ☐ a. 11 HAZİRAN 1930. Signature 17. (Seri) D - G.   15   50   350
  Intro: 17.03.1969.
- ☐ as. Diagonal red *SPECIMEN* overprint on front;   —   —   750
  large red *X* overprint on back; punched.

TCMB B60 (P178): **500 Türk lirası** (demonetized 01.09.1986)   **VG**   **VF**   **UNC**
Brown. Front: Mustafa Kemal Atatürk. Back: Sultan Ahmet Mosque, the Obelix and the Hippodrome in Istanbul. Solid security thread. Watermark: Mustafa Kemal Atatürk. Printer: (TCMB). 170 x 80 mm.
- ☐ a. 11 HAZİRAN 1930. Signature 14. (Seri) P - T.   50   200   1,000
  Intro: 01.12.1962.
- ☐ as. Horizontal red *NÜMUNEDİR GEÇMEZ* overprint   —   —   1,000
  on front; large red *X* overprint on back; punched.

1930 and 1970 (1966-1983) Issues

TCMB B61 (P183): **500 Türk lirası** (demonetized 01.09.1986)   VG   VF   UNC
Violet. Front: Mustafa Kemal Atatürk. Back: Sultan Ahmet Mosque, the Obelix and the Hippodrome in Istanbul. Solid security thread. Watermark: Mustafa Kemal Atatürk. Printer: (TCMB). 170 x 80 mm.

☐	a.	11 HAZİRAN 1930. Signature 17. (Seri) S - Z. Intro: 03.06.1968.	25	100	500
☐	as.	Diagonal red *SPECIMEN* overprint on front; large red *X* overprint on back; punched.	—	—	1,000

TCMB B62 (P179 & P185): **5 Türk lirası** (demon. 16.05.1993)   VG   VF   UNC
Brown and purple. Front: Mustafa Kemal Atatürk. Back: Manavgat waterfall in Antalya. Solid security thread. Watermark: Mustafa Kemal Atatürk. Printer: (TCMB). 135 x 60 mm.

☐	a.	11 HAZİRAN 1930. Sig. 17. Intro: 08.01.1968. Watermark: Type A. Prefix A01 - D90, E01 - E31.	0.25	1.50	5
☐	b.	Watermark: Type B. Prefix E32 - E90, F01 - F90.	0.25	1.50	4
☐	c.	14 OCAK 1970. Signature 24. Prefix G01 - L05. Intro: 20.09.1976.	0.25	0.50	2
☐	as.	Diagonal red *SPECIMEN* overprint; punched.	—	—	200
☐	cs.	Diagonal red *SPECIMEN* overprint on front; large red *X* overprint on back.	—	—	—

Replacement notes: Prefix Z91 - Z95.

Watermark Varieties

Type A   Type B
Small watermark.   Large watermark.

TCMB B63 (P180 & P186): **10 Türk lirası** (demon. 21.09.1991)　　VG　VF　UNC
Green. Front: Mustafa Kemal Atatürk. Back: Maiden's Tower on Bosphorus in Istanbul. Solid security thread. Watermark: Mustafa Kemal Atatürk. Printer: (TCMB). 140 x 65 mm.

- ☐ a. 11 HAZİRAN 1930. Intro: 04.07.1966.　　　　　1　5　15
  Signature 17 with title *GENEL MÜDÜR V.*
  Prefix A01 - C37.
- ☐ b. Signature 17 with title *GENEL MÜDÜR.*　　　　1　4　8
  Prefix D01 - F44.
- ☐ c. 14 OCAK 1970. Signature 22. Prefix G01 - L90.　0.75　3　6
  Intro: 07.04.1975.
- ☐ as. Horizontal red *SPECIMEN* overprint;　　　　—　—　200
  red *X* overprint on back; punched.

TCMB B64 (P181 & P187): **20 Türk lirası** (demon. 21.08.1997)　　VG　VF　UNC
Light brown. Front: Mustafa Kemal Atatürk. Back: Anıtkabir (memorial tomb) of Atatürk in Ankara. Solid security thread. Watermark: Mustafa Kemal Atatürk. 143 x 65 mm.

- ☐ a. 11 HAZİRAN 1930. Sig. 16. Intro: 15.06.1966.　80　225　1,200
  Printer (TDLR). Prefix A1 - A9, B1 - B9.
- ☐ b. Printer: (TCMB). Prefix A10 - B90.　　　　　　5　15　30
- ☐ c. 14 OCAK 1970. Signature 20. Prefix C01 - E84.　1　3　6
  Intro: 24.06.1974.
- ☐ d. Signature 26. Intro: 29.08.1979.　　　　　　0.75　2　4
  Non-fluorescent serial numbers. Prefix E85-G61.
- ☐ e. Fluorescent serial numbers. Prefix G62 - H90.　1　3　6
- ☐ f. Signature 28. Prefix I01 - I90. Intro: 30.05.1983.　0.25　0.50　2
- ☐ as1. Diagonal red *NUMUNEDIR GEÇMEZ* overprint;　—　—　200
  punched.
- ☐ as2. Diagonal red *SPECIMEN* and DLR oval ovpts;　—　—　300
  horizontal red *SPECIMEN Nº #* ovpt at lower left;
  punched.

TCMB B65 (P188): **50 Türk lirası** (demonetized 21.08.1997)　VG　VF　UNC
Brown. Front: Mustafa Kemal Atatürk. Back: Marble Fountain in Topkapı Palace in Istanbul. Solid security thread. Watermark: Mustafa Kemal Atatürk. Printer: (TCMB). 160 x 71 mm.

- ☐ a. 14 OCAK 1970. Signature 23. Intro: 09.04.1976.　2　3.50　6
  Non-fluorescent serial numbers. Prefix A01 - I28.
- ☐ b. Fluorescent serial numbers. Prefix I29 - I36.　　5　15　25
- ☐ c. Signature 29. Prefix I37 - J28. Intro: 04.04.1983.　0.50　2　4
- ☐ cs. Diagonal red *SPECIMEN* overprint on front;　—　—　250
  large red *X* overprint on back; punched.

Replacement notes: Prefix Z91.

TCMB B66 (P189): **100 Türk lirası** (demonetized 05.05.1996)　VG　VF　UNC
Green and brown. Front: Mustafa Kemal Atatürk. Back: Mount Ararat in Ağrı. Watermark: Mustafa Kemal Atatürk. Printer: (TCMB). 170 x 77 mm.

- ☐ a. 14 OCAK 1970. Intro: 15.05.1972.　　　　　　5　15　30
  Sig. 18. Solid security thread. Prefix A01 - F27.
- ☐ b. Sig. 26. Solid security thread with printed *TCMB*.　2　5　10
  Non-fluorescent s/n. Prefix F28 - H70.
  Intro: 24.09.1979.
- ☐ c. Fluorescent serial numbers. Prefix H71 - I44.　　2　5　10
- ☐ d. Signature 30. Prefix J01 - J49. Intro: 20.06.1983.　2　4.50　9
- ☐ as. Specimen.　　　　　　　　　　　　　　　　—　—　250

Watermark Varieties

Type A — Large watermark. Type B — Small watermark.

TCMB B67 (P190): **500 Türk lirası** (demonetized 15.06.1994)   VG   VF   UNC
Olive green and blue. Front: Mustafa Kemal Atatürk. Back: Main Gate of Istanbul University. Solid security thread. Watermark: Mustafa Kemal Atatürk. Printer: (TCMB). 170 x 80 mm.

		VG	VF	UNC
a.	14 OCAK 1970. Sig. 19. Prefix A01 - D09. Intro: 01.09.1971.	100	300	500
b.	Sig. 21. Prefix E01 - O90. Intro: 09.09.1974.	5	15	30
as.	Diagonal red *SPECIMEN* overprint on front; large red *X* overprint on back; punched.	—	—	400

Replacement notes: Prefix Z91.

1970 (1979-1997) Issues

TCMB B69 (P192 & P193): **10 Türk lirası** (demon. 21.08.1997)   VG   VF   UNC
Olive green and pink. Front: Heads of young boy and girl; Mustafa Kemal Atatürk. Back: Atatürk receiving flowers from group of young students. Solid security thread with printed *T.C.M.B. 10 TL*. Watermark: Mustafa Kemal Atatürk. Printer: *TÜRKİYE CUMHURİYET MERKEZ BANKASI BANKNOT MATBAASI*. 122 x 55 mm.

		VG	VF	UNC
a.	14 OCAK 1970. Signature 27. Intro: 25.12.1979. Long eyelash. Prefix A01 - A54, B78 - B90, C01 - C73.	0.25	1	2
b.	Short eyelash. Prefix A55 - A90, B01 - B78, B90, C74 - C90.	0.25	1	2
c.	Signature 30. Intro: 15.11.1982. Darker printing overall. Non-fluorescent s/n. Prefix D01 - D40.	1	2.50	4
d.	Fluorescent serial numbers. Prefix D41 - E82.	0.25	1	2

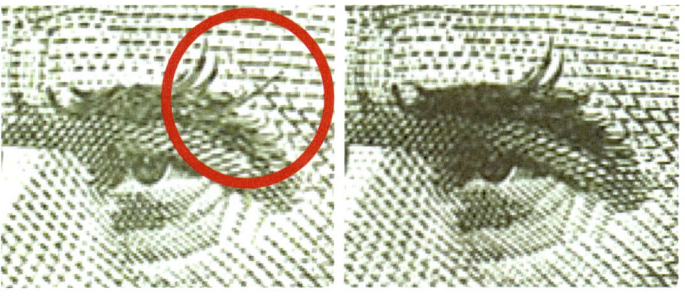

On some 10-Türk lirası notes, Mustafa Kemal Atatürk has a long eyelash (TCMB B69a, left) which is shortened on other notes (B69b, right).

TCMB B68 (P191): **1,000 Türk lirası** (demonetized 29.09.1996)   VG   VF   UNC
Violet. Front: Mustafa Kemal Atatürk. Back: Ship in river and First Bosphorus Bridge. Solid security thread with printed *TÜRKİYE CUMHURİYET MERKEZ BANKASI*. Watermark: Mustafa Kemal Atatürk. Printer: *TÜRKİYE CUMHURİYET MERKEZ BANKASI-BANKNOT MATBAASI*. 170 x 82 mm.

		VG	VF	UNC
a.	14 OCAK 1970. Signature 25. Intro: 29.05.1978. Watermark: Type A. Prefix A01 - B90.	10	20	35
b.	Watermark: Type B. Prefix C01 - C64.	20	40	60
c.	Sig. 26. Prefix C64 - E90. Intro: 17.12.1979.	5	10	20
d.	Sig. 29. Prefix F01 - F59. Intro: 10.06.1981. Non-fluorescent serial numbers.	4	8	15
e.	Fluorescent serial numbers. Prefix F60 - F90.	5	12	20

Replacement notes: Prefix Z91.

TCMB B70 (P194): **100 Türk lirası** (demonetized 21.08.1999)   VG   VF   UNC
Purple and brown. Front: Mustafa Kemal Atatürk. Back: Home of Ersoy in Ankara; Hittite fort with flag atop hill in Ankara; scroll with first two quatrains of Turkish National Anthem; poet Mehmed Akif Ersoy. Watermark: Mustafa Kemal Atatürk. Printer: (TCMB). 131 x 63 mm.

☐	a.	14 OCAK 1970. Signature 28. Intro: 26.12.1983. Solid security thread with printed *TURKIYE CUMHURIYET MERKEZ BANKASI*. Watermark: Type A. Prefix A01 - B42.	0.75	1.50	3
☐	b.	Sig. 33. Prefix C01 - E11. Intro: 17.09.1984.	0.75	1.50	3
☐	c.	Solid security thread. Watermark: Type B. Prefix E12 - F59.	0.75	1.50	3
☐	as.	Diagonal red *SPECIMEN* overprint on front; large red *X* overprint on back.	—	—	250

Watermark Varieties

Type A
Small watermark, facing right.

Type B
Large watermark, facing 3/4 right.

TCMB B71 (P195): **500 Türk lirası** (demonetized 21.08.1999)   VG   VF   UNC
Blue. Front: Mustafa Kemal Atatürk. Back: İzmir Saat Kulesi (İzmir clock tower) and palm trees in Konak Square. Watermark: Mustafa Kemal Atatürk. Printer: (TCMB). 140 x 72 mm.

☐	a.	14 OCAK 1970. Signature 30. Intro: 01.07.1983. Solid security thread with printed *TCMB*. Watermark: Type A. Prefix A01 - B90.	1	2.50	4
☐	b.	Sig. 32. Prefix C01 - C16. Intro: 21.05.1984.	0.75	1.50	3
☐	c.	Solid security thread with printed *TURKIYE CUMHURIYET MERKEZ BANKASI*. Watermark: Type B. Prefix C17 - E90.	0.75	1.50	3

Watermark Varieties

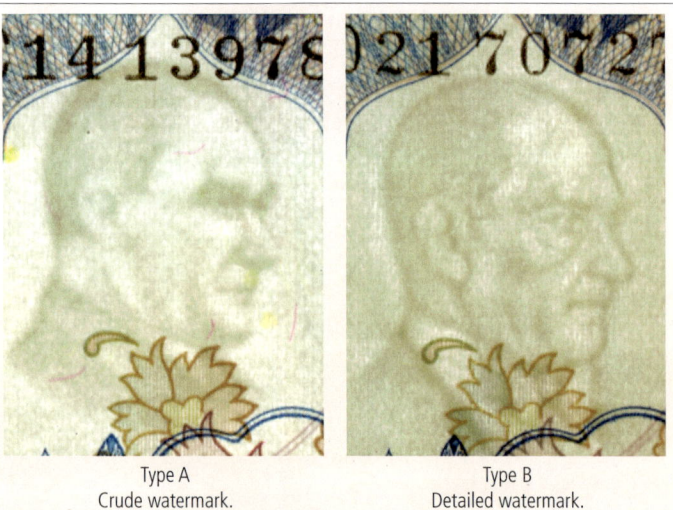

Type A
Crude watermark.

Type B
Detailed watermark.

TCMB B72 (P196): **1,000 Türk lirası** (demonetized 03.08.2002)   VG   VF   UNC

Violet. Front: Mustafa Kemal Atatürk. Back: Sailing ship in Constantinople harbor; Fatih Sultan Mehmed (The Conqueror). Solid security thread with printed *TÜRKİYE CUMHURİYET MERKEZ BANKASI*. Watermark: Mustafa Kemal Atatürk. Printer: (TCMB). 140 x 72 mm.

☐ a. 14 OCAK 1970. Sig. 31. Prefix A01 - E69. Intro: 31.03.1986.	0.75	1.50	3
☐ b. Sig. 34. Prefix F01 - J74. Intro: 19.02.1988.	0.25	1	2

TCMB B74 (P197): **5,000 Türk lirası** (demonetized 31.01.2004)   VG   VF   UNC

Brown and green. Front: Mustafa Kemal Atatürk. Back: Philosopher and mystic Mevlânâ Celaleddin-i Belhi Rumi; minaret and turquoise dome in Konya; whirling dervishes. Solid security thread with printed *TÜRKİYE CUMHURİYET MERKEZ BANKASI*. Watermark: Mustafa Kemal Atatürk. Printer: (TCMB). 146 x 72 mm.

☐ a. 14 OCAK 1970. Sig. 32. Prefix B01 - D77. Intro: 29.07.1985.	3	8	15
☐ b. Sig. 35. Prefix E01 - F29. Intro: 13.06.1988.	3	8	15

TCMB B73 (P196A): **5,000 Türk lirası** (demon. 31.01.2004)   VG   VF   UNC

Brown, orange, and blue. Front: Mustafa Kemal Atatürk. Back: Mevlânâ museum and mausoleum in Konya; philosopher and mystic Mevlânâ Celaleddin-i Belhi Rumi. Solid security thread with printed *TCMB*. Watermark: Mustafa Kemal Atatürk. Printer: *TÜRKİYE CUMHURİYET MERKEZ BANKASI BANKNOT MATBAASI*. 140 x 72 mm.

☐ a. 14 OCAK 1970. Signature 28. Prefix A01 - A57. Intro: 02.11.1981.	10	40	120
☐ b. Watermark: None (error).	150	500	2,000

TCMB B75 (P198): **5,000 Türk lirası** (demonetized 31.01.2004)   VG   VF   UNC

Brown and green. Front: Mustafa Kemal Atatürk. Back: Concrete cooling towers at coal-fired Afşin-Elbistan Termik Santralı (Afşin-Elbistan Thermal Power Plant). Solid security thread with printed *TÜRKİYE CUMHURİYET MERKEZ BANKASI*. Watermark: Mustafa Kemal Atatürk. Printer: (TCMB). 146 x 72 mm.

☐ a. 14 OCAK 1970. Signature 35. Prefix G01 - I76. Intro: 28.05.1990.	0.25	1	2

TCMB B76 (PNL): **10,000 Türk lirası** (demonetized 15.12.2005)   VG   VF   UNC
Purple and green. Front: Mustafa Kemal Atatürk. Back: Selimiye mosque and minarets in Edirne; architect Mimar Sinan. Solid security thread with printed *TÜRKİYE CUMHURİYET MERKEZ BANKASI*. Watermark: Mustafa Kemal Atatürk. Printer: (TCMB). 146 x 72 mm.

- ☐ a. 14 OCAK 1970. Signature 29. Intro: 25.10.1982.   10   40   80
  Watermark: Type A. Prefix A01 - A70.
- ☐ b. Watermark: Type B. Prefix A71 - A77.   15   50   400
- ☐ c. Sig. 31. Prefix B01 - B88. Intro: 13.04.1984.   10   20   45

Watermark Varieties

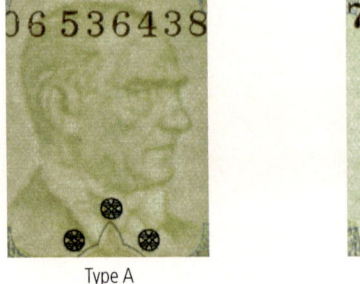 

Type A   Type B

TCMB B77 (P199): **10,000 Türk lirası** (demon. 15.12.2005)   VG   VF   UNC
Purple and green. Front: Mustafa Kemal Atatürk. Back: Selimiye mosque and minarets in Edirne; architect Mimar Sinan. Solid security thread with printed *TÜRKİYE CUMHURİYET MERKEZ BANKASI*. Watermark: Mustafa Kemal Atatürk. Printer: (TCMB). 146 x 72 mm.

- ☐ a. 14 OCAK 1970. Intro: 13.04.1984.   4   8   15
  Sig. 31. Watermark: Type A. Prefix C01 - F40.
- ☐ b. Signature 37. Intro: 24.01.1989.   1   3   6
  Watermark: Type A. Prefix G01 - H42.
- ☐ c. Watermark: Type B. Prefix H43 - H55.   10   20   30

Like TCMB B76, but with three tactile dots in watermark area on front.

Watermark Varieties

Type A   Type B

TCMB B78 (P200): **10,000 Türk lirası** (demon. 15.12.2005) VG VF UNC
Purple and green. Front: Mustafa Kemal Atatürk. Back: Selimiye mosque and minarets in Edirne; architect Mimar Sinan. Solid security thread with printed *TÜRKİYE CUMHURİYET MERKEZ BANKASI*. Watermark: Mustafa Kemal Atatürk. Printer: (TCMB). 146 x 72 mm.

☐	a.	14 OCAK 1970. Signature 37. Intro: 22.02.1993. White paper. Watermark: Type A. Prefix I01 - I80.	1	5	10
☐	b.	Yellowish paper. Wmk: Type B. Prefix I81 - K61.	5	18	25
☐	c.	Watermark: Inverted and on wrong side (some, not all, K26 and K30 prefix notes).	80	200	400
☐	as.	Diagonal red *SPECIMEN* overprint.	—	—	250

Like TCMB B77, but monochromatic main vignette on back.

TCMB B79 (P201): **20,000 Türk lirası** (demon. 09.09.2007) VG VF UNC
Claret red and violet. Front: Mustafa Kemal Atatürk. Back: Central Bank headquarters building in Ankara. Windowed security thread. Watermark: Mustafa Kemal Atatürk. Printer: (TCMB). 152 x 76 mm.

☐	a.	14 OCAK 1970. Signature 34. Intro: 09.05.1988. Reddish paper. Wmk: Type A. Prefix A01 - C49.	5	20	30
☐	b.	White paper. Wmk: Type B. Prefix C49 - F40.	1	3	6
☐	as.	Diagonal red *SPECIMEN* overprint.	—	—	250

Watermark Varieties

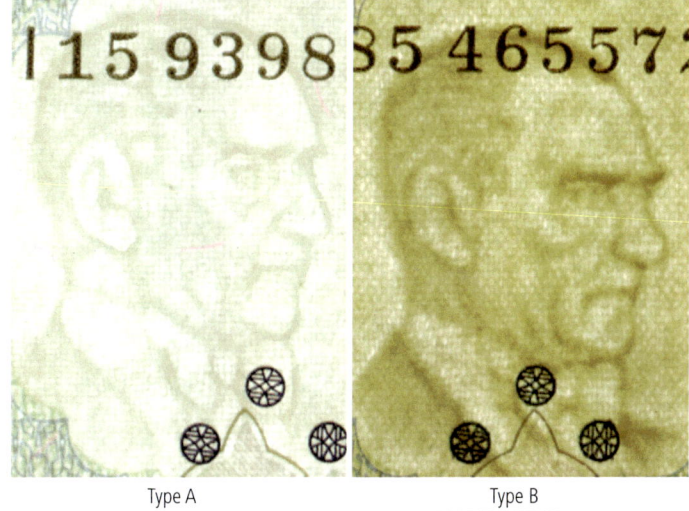

Type A · Type B

Watermark Varieties

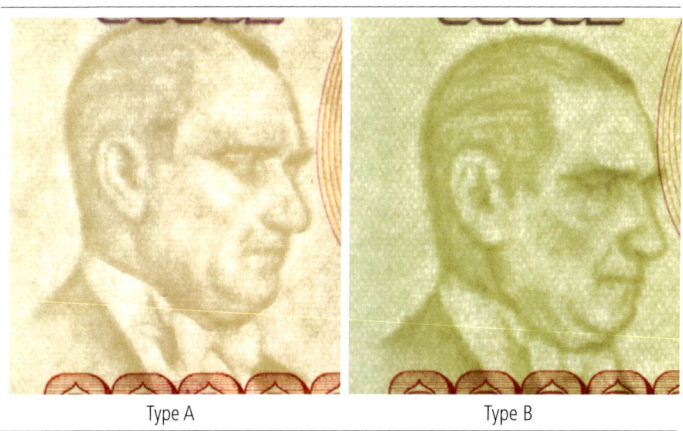

Type A · Type B

TCMB B80 (P202): **20,000 Türk lirası** (demon. 09.09.2007)   **VG**   **VF**   **UNC**
Claret red and violet. Front: Mustafa Kemal Atatürk. Back: Central Bank headquarters building in Ankara. Windowed security thread. Watermark: Mustafa Kemal Atatürk. Printer: (TCMB). 152 x 76 mm.

    ☐ a.   14 OCAK 1970. Signature 41. Prefix G01 - G82.   1   2   3
           Intro: 03.04.1995.

Like TCMB B79, but back lithographed instead of intaglio, and lighter shading.

TCMB B81 (P203): **50,000 Türk lirası** (demon. 04.11.2009)   **VG**   **VF**   **UNC**
Green. Front: Mustafa Kemal Atatürk. Back: Statue of Atatürk with man and woman holding flag and banner; Grand National Assembly Parliament building and flag in Ankara. Windowed security thread. Watermark: Mustafa Kemal Atatürk. Printer: (TCMB). 152 x 76 mm.

    ☐ a.   14 OCAK 1970. Signature 36. Prefix A01 - J44.   4   8   15
           Intro: 15.05.1989.
    ☐ as. Diagonal red *SPECIMEN* overprint.   —   —   250

Due to extremely small print run, prefix H01-H03 notes are worth up to 100x normal value.

TCMB B82 (P204): **50,000 Türk lirası** (demon. 04.11.2009)   **VG**   **VF**   **UNC**
Green. Front: Mustafa Kemal Atatürk. Back: Statue of Atatürk with man and woman holding flag and banner; Grand National Assembly Parliament building and flag in Ankara. Windowed security thread. Watermark: Mustafa Kemal Atatürk. Printer: (TCMB). 152 x 76 mm.

    ☐ a.   14 OCAK 1970. Signature 40. Prefix K01 - M84.   1   2   4
           Intro: 20.02.1995.
    ☐ as. Diagonal red *SPECIMEN* overprint.   —   —   250

Like TCMB B81, but slightly modified design on front, and reduced colors on back.

1970 (1991-2002) Issues

TCMB B83 (P205): **100,000 Türk lirası** (demon. 04.11.2011)   **VG**   **VF**   **UNC**
Brown and green. Front: Equestrian statue of Atatürk in Samsun; Mustafa Kemal Atatürk; bank logo. Back: Bank logo; Atatürk receiving flowers from group of young students. Windowed security thread with demetalized *TCMB*. Watermark: Mustafa Kemal Atatürk. Printer: (TCMB). 158 x 76 mm.

    ☐ a.   14 OCAK 1970.   10   40   70
           Sig. 37. Prefix A01 - C57. Intro: 11.11.1991.
    ☐ b.   Sig. 40. Prefix D01 - E86. Intro: 15.07.1994.   2   6   10

TCMB B84 (P206): **100,000 Türk lirası** (demon. 04.11.2011)　　VG　VF　UNC

Brown and green. Front: Equestrian statue of Atatürk in Samsun; Mustafa Kemal Atatürk; bank logo. Back: Bank logo; Atatürk receiving flowers from group of young students. Windowed security thread with demetalized *TCMB*. Watermark: Mustafa Kemal Atatürk. Printer: (TCMB). 158 x 76 mm.

- a.　14 OCAK 1970. Signature 42. Intro: 31.03.1996.　　1　2　4
  Watermark: Type A.
  Prefix F01 - G90, H86 - J79.
- b.　Watermark: Type B.　　1　2　4
  Prefix H01 - H85.
- as.　Diagonal red *SPECIMEN* overprint.　　—　—　250

Like TCMB B83, but back lithographed instead of intaglio, different coloring, and without round geometric symbol at upper right on front.

Watermark Varieties

Type A　　　　　　　　Type B
Narrow head, looking down.　　Wide head, looking forward.

TCMB B85 (P207): **250,000 Türk lirası** (demon. 01.01.2016)　　VG　VF　UNC

Blue. Front: Mustafa Kemal Atatürk; bank logo. Back: Bank logo; Kızılkule (Red Tower), harbor, and ships in Alanya. Windowed security thread with demetalized *TCMB*. Watermark: Mustafa Kemal Atatürk. Printer: (TCMB). 158 x 76 mm.

- a.　14 OCAK 1970.　　　　　　　　　　5　10　20
  Sig. 37. Prefix A01 - D25. Intro: 02.10.1992.
- b.　Sig. 40. Prefix E01 - E43. Intro: 02.10.1995.　　8　15　25
- bs.　Diagonal red *SPECIMEN* overprint.　　—　—　300

TCMB B86 (P211): **250,000 Türk lirası** (demon. 01.01.2016)　　VG　VF　UNC

Blue. Front: Mustafa Kemal Atatürk; bank logo. Back: Bank logo; Kızılkule (Red Tower), harbor, and ships in Alanya. Windowed security thread with demetalized *TCMB*. Watermark: Mustafa Kemal Atatürk. Printer: (TCMB). 158 x 76 mm.

- a.　14 OCAK 1970. Signature 45. Prefix F01 - I90.　　1　2　3
  Intro: 16.03.1998.

Like TCMB B85, but blue triangle on front, and reduced colors on back.

TCMB B87 (P208): **500,000 Türk lirası** (demon. 01.01.2016) VG VF UNC
Purple. Front: Mustafa Kemal Atatürk; bank logo. Back: Bank logo; Çanakkale Şehitleri Anıtı (Çanakkale Martyrs' Memorial) on Hisarlık Hill in Morto Bay. Windowed security thread with demetalized *TCMB*. Watermark: Mustafa Kemal Atatürk. Printer: (TCMB). 160 x 76 mm.

			VG	VF	UNC
☐	a.	14 OCAK 1970. Sig. 38. Prefix A01 - C43. Intro: 18.03.1993.	5	8	15
☐	b.	Sig. 39. Prefix D01 - D07. Intro: 16.05.1994.	50	120	200
☐	c.	Sig. 41. Prefix E01 - G81. Intro: 26.08.1994.	2	6	10
☐	as.	Diagonal red *SPECIMEN* overprint.	—	—	300
☐	cs.	Diagonal red *SPECIMEN* overprint.	—	—	300

TCMB B88 (P212): **500,000 Türk lirası** (demon. 01.01.2016) VG VF UNC
Purple. Front: Mustafa Kemal Atatürk; bank logo. Back: Bank logo; Çanakkale Şehitleri Anıtı (Çanakkale Martyrs' Memorial) on Hisarlık Hill in Morto Bay. Windowed security thread with demetalized *TCMB*. Watermark: Mustafa Kemal Atatürk. Printer: (TCMB). 160 x 76 mm.

			VG	VF	UNC
☐	a.	14 OCAK 1970. Signature 44. Intro: 10.10.1997. Watermark: Type A. Prefix H.	2	5	10
☐	b.	Watermark: Type B. Prefix H50 - H68.	2	4	8
☐	c.	Watermark: Type C. Prefix K33 - L79.	1	2	3
☐	as.	Horizontal red *SPECIMEN* overprint; horizontal red *SPECIMEN NO:* # overprint on watermark area.	—	—	300

Like TCMB B87, but without OVI square on front, and reduced colors on back.

Watermark Varieties

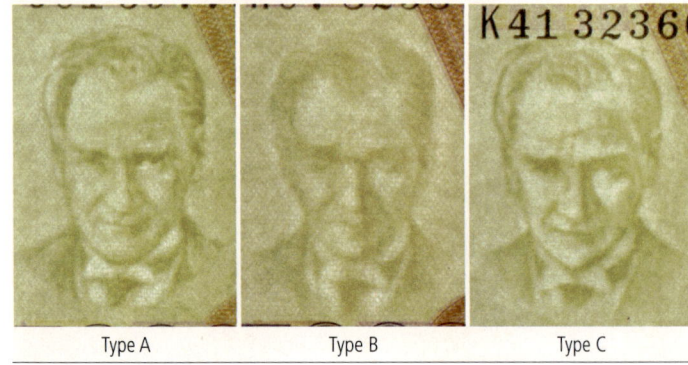

Type A Type B Type C

TCMB B89 (P209): **1,000,000 Türk lirası** (demon. 01.01.2016) VG VF UNC
Claret red and blue. Front: Mustafa Kemal Atatürk; bank logo. Back: Bank logo; Atatürk Barajı (Atatürk dam) in Şanlıurfa. Windowed security thread with demetalized *TCMB*. Watermark: Mustafa Kemal Atatürk. Printer: *TÜRKİYE CUMHURİYET MERKEZ BANKASI BANKNOT MATBAASI*. 160 x 76 mm.

- a. 14 OCAK 1970. Signature 40. Intro: 16.01.1995. Watermark: Type A. Prefix A01 - G57. 5 15 25
- b. Signature 43. Intro: 09.09.1996. Prefix H01 - H70, I34 - I90, J01 - K36, L01 - L03, L10 - N90. 2 6 12
- c. Watermark: Type B. Prefix H71 - H90, I03 - I33, K37 - K90, L04 - L09. 4 15 25
- bs. Diagonal red *SPECIMEN* overprint. — — 300

TCMB B90 (P213): **1,000,000 Türk lirası** (demon. 01.01.2016) VG VF UNC
Claret red and blue. Front: Mustafa Kemal Atatürk; bank logo. Back: Bank logo; Atatürk Barajı (Atatürk dam) in Şanlıurfa. Windowed security thread with demetalized *TCMB*. Watermark: Mustafa Kemal Atatürk. Printer: *TÜRKİYE CUMHURİYET MERKEZ BANKASI BANKNOT MATBAASI*. 160 x 76 mm.

- a. 14 OCAK 1970. Signature 48. Intro: 10.01.2002. Watermark: Type A. Prefix O01 - O74. Also prefixes P34 and S21, which have Type C watermark as well. 2 4 6
- b. Watermark: Type C. Prefix O75 - U37. 2 4 6

Like TCMB B89, but without OVI triangle on front, reduced colors and repositioned dam caption on back.

TCMB B91 (P210): **5,000,000 Türk lirası** (demon. 01.01.2016) VG VF UNC
Pastel yellow and greenish brown. Front: Map; Mustafa Kemal Atatürk; golden seal radiating beams. Back: Anıtkabir (memorial tomb) of Atatürk in Ankara; stylized flame; sculpture of three men at Road of Lions entry. Windowed security thread with demetalized *TCMB*. Watermark: Mustafa Kemal Atatürk. Printer: (TCMB). 162 x 76 mm.

- a. OCAK 1997. Signature 43. Intro: 06.01.1997. Watermark: Type A. Prefix A01 - A90, B01 - B35, C84 - K61 5 18 30
- b. Watermark: Type B. Prefix B36 - C83. 10 30 50
- c. Watermark: Type C. Prefix J15 - N16. 2 8 15
- as. Diagonal red *SPECIMEN* overprint. — — 300

TCMB B92 (P214): **10,000,000 Türk lirası** (demon. 01.01.2016) VG VF UNC
Red. Front: Crescent; Mustafa Kemal Atatürk; star; stylized flame. Back: Compass rose on modern map; 1513 dünya haritası (world map) by cartographer Piri Reis; globe; sailing ship. Windowed security thread with demetalized *TCMB*. Watermark: Mustafa Kemal Atatürk. Printer: *TÜRKİYE CUMHURİYET MERKEZ BANKASI BANKNOT MATBAASI*. 162 x 76 mm.

- a. 1999. Signature 46. Intro: 05.11.1999. Watermark: Type A. Prefix A - F40. 10 20 35
- b. Watermark: Type C. Prefix G44 - H. 8 15 25
- as. Horizontal blue *SPECIMEN* overprint; horizontal blue *SPECIMEN NO:* # overprint on watermark area. — — 300

2005 Yeni Türk Lirası Issues

On 1 January 2005, Turkey revalued its currency by removing six zeroes, thereby creating the new Turkish lira (*yeni Türk lirası*). Although these notes still carry the authorization date *14 OCAK 1970* above the signatures, the year of printing appears to the right of the printer imprint, below the portrait.

TCMB B93 (P215): **20,000,000 Türk lirası** (demon. 01.01.2016)   VG   VF   UNC
Green. Front: Dove with olive branch; bank logo; globe; Mustafa Kemal Atatürk. Back: Efes Antik Kenti - Selçuk (ancient city of Ephesus in Selçuk) ruins including columns, Library of Celsus, and Temple of Hadrian; bank logo. Windowed security thread with demetalized *TCMB*. Watermark: Mustafa Kemal Atatürk. Printer: *TÜRKİYE CUMHURİYET MERKEZ BANKASI BANKNOT MATBAASI*. 162 x 76 mm.

- a. 2001. Signature 47. Intro: 05.11.2001.   10   30   45
  Watermark: Type A. Prefix A01 - C55.
- b. Watermark: Type C. Prefix C56 - K.   8   18   30
- as. Horizontal red *SPECIMEN* overprint;   —   —   300
  horizontal red *SPECIMEN NO:* # overprint on watermark area.

TCMB B94 (P216): **1 yeni Türk lirası** (demonetized 01.01.2020)   VG   VF   UNC
Claret red and blue. Front: Mustafa Kemal Atatürk; bank logo. Back: Bank logo; Atatürk Barajı (Atatürk dam) in Şanlıurfa. Windowed security thread with demetalized *TCMB*. Watermark: Mustafa Kemal Atatürk and electrotype *1*. Printer: *TÜRKİYE CUMHURİYET MERKEZ BANKASI BANKNOT MATBAASI*. 156 x 76 mm.

- a. 2005. Signature 49. Prefix A01 - A79.   1   2   5
  Intro: 01.01.2005.

Watermark Varieties

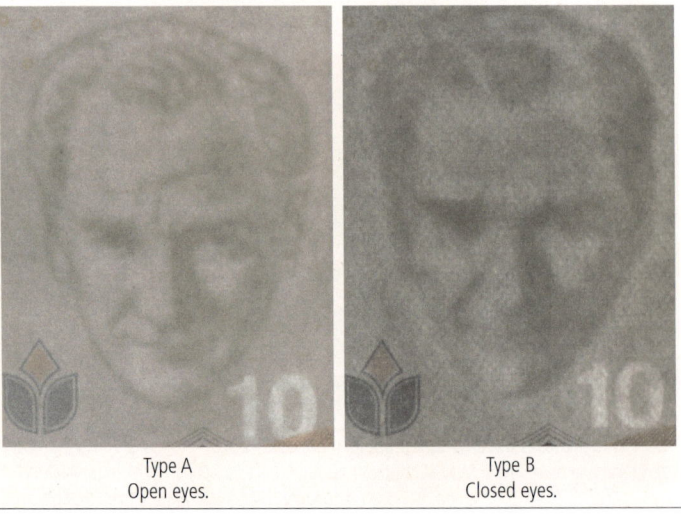

Type A — Open eyes.   Type B — Closed eyes.

All denominations except the 1-yeni Türk lirası are available with two different watermark varieties (open eyes, left; and closed eyes, right). The prefix ranges listed encompass both varieties because there is overlap and precise ranges for each is not yet known.

TCMB B95 (P217): **5 yeni Türk lirası** (demonetized 01.01.2020)   VG   VF   UNC
Pastel yellow and greenish brown. Front: Map; Mustafa Kemal Atatürk; golden seal radiating beams. Back: Anıtkabir (memorial tomb) of Atatürk in Ankara; stylized flame; sculpture of three men at Road of Lions entry. Windowed security thread with demetalized *TCMB*. Watermark: Mustafa Kemal Atatürk and electrotype *5*. Printer: *TÜRKİYE CUMHURİYET MERKEZ BANKASI BANKNOT MATBAASI*. 162 x 76 mm.

		VG	VF	UNC
☐ a.	2005. Sig. 50. Prefix A01-G90. Intro: 01.01.2005. Watermark: Type A.	3	4	8
☐ b.	Watermark: Type B.	3	4	8

TCMB B96 (P218): **10 yeni Türk lirası** (demon. 01.01.2020)   VG   VF   UNC
Red and purple. Front: Crescent; Mustafa Kemal Atatürk; star; stylized flame. Back: Compass rose on modern map; 1513 dünya haritası (world map) by cartographer Piri Reis; globe; sailing ship. Windowed security thread with demetalized *TCMB*. Watermark: Mustafa Kemal Atatürk and electrotype *10*. Printer: *TÜRKİYE CUMHURİYET MERKEZ BANKASI BANKNOT MATBAASI*. 162 x 76 mm.

		VG	VF	UNC
☐ a.	2005. Sig. 48. Prefix A01 - I90. Intro: 01.01.2005. Watermark: Type A.	5	8	15
☐ b.	Watermark: Type B.	5	8	15

TCMB B97 (P219): **20 yeni Türk lirası** (demon. 01.01.2020)   VG   VF   UNC
Green and orange. Front: Dove with olive branch; bank logo; globe; Mustafa Kemal Atatürk. Back: Efes Antik Kenti - Selçuk (ancient city of Ephesus in Selçuk) ruins including columns, Library of Celsus, and Temple of Hadrian; bank logo. Windowed security thread with demetalized *TCMB*. Watermark: Mustafa Kemal Atatürk and electrotype *20*. Printer: *TÜRKİYE CUMHURİYET MERKEZ BANKASI BANKNOT MATBAASI*. 162 x 76 mm.

		VG	VF	UNC
☐ a.	2005. Sig. 51. Prefix A01 - I90. Intro: 01.01.2005. Watermark: Type A.	10	15	25
☐ b.	Watermark: Type B.	10	15	25

TCMB B98 (P220): **50 yeni Türk lirası** (demon. 01.01.2020)   VG   VF   UNC
Orange and brown. Front: Mustafa Kemal Atatürk. Back: Rock fairy chimneys in Kapadokya (Cappadocia). Windowed security thread with demetalized *TCMB*. Watermark: Mustafa Kemal Atatürk and electrotype *50*. Printer: *TÜRKİYE CUMHURİYET MERKEZ BANKASI BANKNOT MATBAASI*. 152 x 81 mm.

		VG	VF	UNC
☐ a.	2005. Sig. 49. Prefix A01-H90. Intro: 01.01.2005. Watermark: Type A.	25	35	60
☐ b.	Watermark: Type B.	25	35	60

TCMB B99 (P221): **100 yeni Türk lirası** (demon. 01.01.2020)   VG   VF   UNC
Blue. Front: Mustafa Kemal Atatürk. Back: İshakpaşa Sarayı - Doğubayazıt (Ishak Pasha Palace in Doğubayazıt). Windowed security thread with demetalized *TCMB*. Watermark: Mustafa Kemal Atatürk and electrotype *100*. Printer: *TÜRKİYE CUMHURİYET MERKEZ BANKASI BANKNOT MATBAASI*. 158 x 81 mm.

- ☐ a. 2005. Sig. 50. Prefix A01-D90. Intro: 01.01.2005.   50   80   150
Watermark: Type A.
- ☐ b. Watermark: Type B.   50   80   150

2005 Numismatic Products

TCMB BNP1 (PNL): **1 - 100 yeni Türk lirası**   UNC
- ☐ a. TCMB B94-B99 (6 notes) with A01 prefix in folder.   300

2009 Issues

On 1 January 2009, Turkey reverted the name of the currency to the Turkish lira, necessitating the issuance of new banknotes and coins without the "new" (*yeni*) adjective. A 200-lira denomination was introduced for the first time.

TCMB B100 (P222): **5 Türk lirası** (US$2.40)   VG   VF   UNC
Tan. Front: Star; Mustafa Kemal Atatürk; star and crescent. Back: Open hands; planets; atom; double helix DNA chain; science historian Aydın Sayılı. Holographic stripe. Solid security thread with printed *TL 5*. Watermark: Mustafa Kemal Atatürk and electrotype *5*. Printer: *TÜRKİYE CUMHURİYET MERKEZ BANKASI BANKNOT MATBAASI*. 130 x 64 mm.

- ☐ a. 2009. Signature 52. Prefix A001 - A388.   FV   FV   5
Intro: 01.01.2009.

TCMB B101 (P223): **10 Türk lirası** (US$4.80)   VG   VF   UNC
Violet. Front: Star; Mustafa Kemal Atatürk; star and crescent. Back: "Arf Invariant" math equation; mathematician Cahit Arf. Holographic stripe. Solid security thread with printed *TL 10*. Watermark: Mustafa Kemal Atatürk and electrotype *10*. Printer: *TÜRKİYE CUMHURİYET MERKEZ BANKASI BANKNOT MATBAASI*. 136 x 64 mm.

- ☐ a. 2009.   FV   FV   10
Sig. 53. Prefix A002 - A150. Intro: 01.01.2009.
- ☐ b. Sig. 57. Prefix B001 - B161. Intro: 24.12.2012.   FV   FV   10

TCMB B102 (P224): **20 Türk lirası** (US$9.55)   VG   VF   UNC
Green. Front: Mustafa Kemal Atatürk. Back: Viaduct; line drawing of Gazi University Presidential Building; architect Mimar Kemaleddin. Holographic stripe. Solid security thread with printed *TL 20*. Watermark: Mustafa Kemal Atatürk and electrotype *20*. Printer: *TÜRKİYE CUMHURİYET MERKEZ BANKASI BANKNOT MATBAASI*. 142 x 68 mm.

☐ a. 2009.   FV   FV   20
     Sig. 54. Prefix A001 - A178. Intro: 01.01.2009.
☐ b. Sig. 58. Prefix B001 - B035. Intro: 24.12.2012.   FV   FV   18

TCMB B103 (P225): **50 Türk lirası** (US$24)   VG   VF   UNC
Tan. Front: Star; Mustafa Kemal Atatürk; star and crescent. Back: Flowers; books; quill in inkwell; novelist Fatma Aliye. Holographic stripe. Solid security thread with printed *TL 50*. Watermark: Mustafa Kemal Atatürk and electrotype *50*. Printer: *TÜRKİYE CUMHURİYET MERKEZ BANKASI BANKNOT MATBAASI*. 148 x 68 mm.

☐ a. 2009.   FV   FV   35
     Sig. 55. Prefix A001 - A306. Intro: 01.01.2009.
☐ b. Sig. 59. Prefix B001 - B004. Intro: 08.04.2013.   FV   FV   35

TCMB B104 (P226): **100 Türk lirası** (US$48)   VG   VF   UNC
Blue. Front: Star; Mustafa Kemal Atatürk; star and crescent. Back: Musical instruments (lute and kudüm drums); composer Itri (Buhurizade Mustafa Efendi). Holographic stripe. Solid security thread with printed *TL 100*. Watermark: Mustafa Kemal Atatürk and electrotype *100*. Printer: *TÜRKİYE CUMHURİYET MERKEZ BANKASI BANKNOT MATBAASI*. 154 x 72 mm.

☐ a. 2009.   FV   FV   80
     Sig. 53. Prefix A001 - A607. Intro: 01.01.2009.
☐ b. Sig. 57. Prefix B001 - B100. Intro: 24.12.2012.   FV   FV   70

TCMB B105 (P227): **200 Türk lirası** (US$96)   VG   VF   UNC
Purple. Front: Star; Mustafa Kemal Atatürk; star and crescent. Back: Doves; Emre's tomb; roses; *Sevelim Sevilelim* (Love and Be Loved); poet Yunus Emre. Holographic stripe. Solid security thread with printed *TL 200*. Watermark: Mustafa Kemal Atatürk and electrotype *200*. Printer: *TÜRKİYE CUMHURİYET MERKEZ BANKASI BANKNOT MATBAASI*. 160 x 72 mm.

☐ a. 2009.   FV   FV   130
     Sig. 52. Prefix A001 - A131. Intro: 01.01.2009.
☐ b. Sig. 56. Prefix B001 - B048. Intro: 08.04.2013.   FV   FV   130

2009 Numismatic Products

TCMB BNP2 (PNL): 5 - 200 Türk lirası — **UNC**
☐ a. TCMB B100-B105 (6 notes) with A001 prefix in folder. 275

2009 (2013) Issues

This 5-lira note is purple, not tan, to help distinguish it from the brown 50-lira note.

TCMB B106 (PNL): **5 Türk lirası** (US$2.40) — **VG VF UNC**
Purple. Front: Star; Mustafa Kemal Atatürk; star and crescent. Back: Open hands; planets; atom; double helix DNA chain; science historian Aydın Sayılı. Holographic stripe. Solid security thread with printed *TL 5*. Watermark: Mustafa Kemal Atatürk and electrotype *5*. Printer: *TÜRKİYE CUMHURİYET MERKEZ BANKASI BANKNOT MATBAASI*. 130 x 64 mm.
☐ a. 2009. Signature 56. Prefix B001- B212. FV FV 4.50
Intro: 08.04.2013.

Acknowledgements

This chapter was compiled with the generous assistance of Richard Bonkowski, Jim W.-C. Chen, Donald Cleveland, David F. Cieniewicz (www.banknotestore.com), Mert Erdumlu, Larry Hirsch (www.aworldcurrency.com), Don Ludwig, Robert Mol, Paul Nahmias, Adil Önder, Mikdat Ortacbayram, Menelaos Stamatelos, Bill Stubkjaer, Christoph Thomas, Kaan Uslu (www.ottomancoins.com), Tristan Williams, Ömer Yalcinkaya, and others.

Sources

Akyol, Mustafa. *ÇINARALTI KOLEKSİYON 2010*. 1st edition. 2010. ISBN 978-605-89025-0-3.

Bahadır, A. Şükrü. *PULKO, Türkiye Cumhuriyeti Kağit Para Kataloğu (Republic of Turkey Paper Money Catalogue)*. 6th edition. 2009. www.pulko.com.tr

Barlok, Cem. "New Turk Note Discovered." *IBNS Journal*. Volume 23 Number 4. p.118.

Cuhaj, George S. *Standard Catalog of World Paper Money, General Issues, 1368-1960*. 14th edition. 2012. ISBN 978-1-4402-3090-5. Krause Publications (www.krausebooks.com), 700 East State St., Iola, WI, 54990-0001.

Cuhaj, George S. *Standard Catalog of World Paper Money, Modern Issues, 1961-Present*. 20th edition. 2014. ISBN 978-1-4402-4037-9. Krause Publications (www.krausebooks.com), 700 East State St., Iola, WI, 54990-0001.

Mehilba, Dr. Ali. *Mehilba World Replacements*. 1st edition. 2013. (www.alinotes.com).

Ölçer, Cüneyt. *50 Yilin Turk Kagit Paralari (Paper Money of the Republic of Turkey)*. Turkiyie Is Bankasi, Istanbul, 1973.

Shneydor, N. A. "Evolving Policies in the Dating of Banknotes of the Near-East." *IBNS Journal*. Volume 53 Number 2. p.9.

Turkish Central Bank website: www.tcmb.gov.tr

Usla, Kaan and Ömer Yalcinkaya. "Bombs and Banknotes: The Tragic Tale of Three Turkish Notes." *IBNS Journal*. Volume 50 Number 2. p.32.

Usla, Kaan and M. Fatih Beyazit and Tuncay Kara. *Türkiye Cumhuriyeti 2012 (Turkish Republic 2012)*. 2011. ISBN 976-605-88966-2-8.

Yalcinkaya, Ömer. "New Issue of Turkish Banknotes without 'New.'" *IBNS Journal*. Volume 48 Number 1. p.66.

Yapı Kredi Kültür Sanat Yayıncılık A.Ş. *İmparatorluktan Cumhuriyete Kâğıt Paranın Öyküsü (The Odyssey of the Paper Money from the Empire to the Republic)*. 1st printing. May 2008. ISBN 978-975-08-1440-2.

www.turkishbanknotes.info

Share Your Input, Info, and Images

This catalog is believed to be complete and correct as of the time of publication. Prices and face values were last updated 8 August 2014. Please report errors or omissions so that corrections may be made. If you can more precisely identify the name or location of anything depicted on a note, please share that information. Furthermore, if you own an unlisted type or variety, please submit scans of the front and back of the note so that it can be documented. Scans should be 300 dots per inch, 100% actual size, 24-bit color, saved as *uncompressed* JPEG files, and sent to owen@banknotenews.com. Be sure to fully describe all attributes of the note which are not apparent upon visual inspection of the images alone, such as physical dimension, watermark, and security thread.

Turkmenistan

For earlier issues, see Russia.

Contents

Türkmenistanyñ Merkezi Döwlet Banky (TMDB). 2173
Türkmenistanyñ Merkezi Banky (TMB) 2175

Monetary System
27.10.1993: 1 Turkmenistani manat (TMM) = 100 tennesi
01.01.2009: 1 new manat (TMT) = 5,000 Turkmenistani manat

Türkmenistanyñ Merkezi Döwlet Banky (Central State Bank of Turkmenistan)

TMDB Signature Varieties

| 1 |  BASLYK (Head) Khudaiberdy Orazov |

1993-1995 Issues

In 1993, the Turkmenistani manat replaced the Russian ruble at the rate of 500 rubles to 1 manat.

TMDB B1 (P1): 1 manat VG VF UNC
Brown. Front: Ylymlar Akademiyasy (Academy) building; native crafts. Back: Coat of arms; Ilarslanyn Yadygarligi mausoleum building. Solid security thread. Watermark: Rearing Arabian horse. Printer: (TDLR). 120 x 60 mm.
☐ a. No date. Signature 1. Intro: 27.10.1993.   0.25 0.50 1
Replacement notes: Prefix ZZ.

TMDB B2 (P2): 5 manat VG VF UNC
Blue. Front: Sazcylyk Okuw Jayy building; carved horn. Back: Coat of arms; Abu Seyidin Yadygarligi mausoleum building. Solid security thread. Watermark: Rearing Arabian horse. Printer: (TDLR). 126 x 63 mm.
☐ a. No date. Signature 1. Intro: 27.10.1993.   0.25 0.50 1.50
Replacement notes: Prefix ZZ.

TMDB B3 (P3): 10 manat VG VF UNC
Orange. Front: Turkmenistanyn Hökümetinin Jayy building; President Saparmurat Niyazov. Back: Coat of arms; Tekesin Yadygärligi building. Solid security thread. Watermark: Rearing Arabian horse. Printer: (TDLR). 132 x 66 mm.
☐ a. No date. Signature 1. Intro: 27.10.1993.   0.25 0.50 1.75
Replacement notes: Prefix ZZ.

TMDB B4 (P4): 20 manat   VG   VF   UNC
Green. Front: Milli Kitaphana (National Library) building; President Saparmurat Niyazov.
Back: Coat of arms; Astanababa Yadygärligi building. Solid security thread. Watermark:
Rearing Arabian horse. Printer: (TDLR). 140 x 70 mm.

    a. No date. Signature 1. Intro: 27.10.1993.   0.25   1   4
    b. 1995.   0.25   1   2

Replacement notes: Prefix ZZ (B4b).

TMDB B5 (P5): 50 manat   VG   VF   UNC
Tan. Front: Urusda Wepat Bolanlara Yadygärlik; arch; President Saparmurat Niyazov.
Back: Coat of arms; Änew Metjidi mosque ruins. Solid security thread. Watermark:
Rearing Arabian horse. Printer: (TDLR). 144 x 72 mm.

    a. No date. Signature 1. Intro: 27.10.1993.   0.25   1   4
    b. 1995.   0.25   1   2

Replacement notes: Prefix ZZ (B5b).

TMDB B6 (P6): 100 manat   VG   VF   UNC
Blue. Front: Prezident Kosgi building; President Saparmurat Niyazov. Back: Coat of
arms; Soltan Sanjaryn Yadygärligi mausoleum building. Solid security thread. Watermark:
Rearing Arabian horse. Printer: (TDLR). 150 x 75 mm.

    a. No date. Signature 1. Intro: 27.10.1993.   0.50   1.50   6
    b. 1995.   0.25   1   2

Replacement notes: Prefix ZZ.

TMDB B7 (P7): 500 manat   VG   VF   UNC
Maroon. Front: Mollanepes Teatry (National Theater) building; President Saparmurat
Niyazov. Back: Coat of arms; Törebeg Hanymyn Yadygärligi mausoleum building. Solid
security thread. Watermark: Rearing Arabian horse. Printer: (TDLR). 156 x 78 mm.

    a. No date. Signature 1. Intro: 27.10.1993.   10   40   150
    b. 1995.   0.25   0.75   3

Replacement notes: Prefix ZZ.

Türkmenistanyñ Merkezi Banky (Central Bank of Turkmenistan)

For more information, visit www.cbt.tm.

TMB Signature Varieties

1. BASLYK (Head) Khudaiberdy Orazov
2. BASLYK (Head) Seitbai Kandymov (1999 - 06.05.2002)
3. PREZIDENT (President) Saparmurat Niyazov
4. BASLYK (Head) Guwanchmyrat Gyoklenow
5. BASLYK (Head) Tuvakmammet Japarov (July 2011 - January 2014)
6. BASLYK (Head) Gochmyrat Myradov (January 2014 - present)

1995-2000 Issues

These notes have the new name of the issuer. Higher denominations were needed to keep up with inflation.

TMB B1 (P8): **1,000 manat**   VG   VF   UNC
Green. Front: Prezident Kosgi building; President Saparmurat Niyazov. Back: Coat of arms. Solid security thread. Watermark: Rearing Arabian horse. Printer: (TDLR). 156 x 78 mm.
- a. 1995. Signature 1.   0.25   1   4

Replacement notes: Prefix ZZ.

TMB B2 (P9 & P12): **5,000 manat**   VG   VF   UNC
Purple. Front: Prezident Kosgi building; President Saparmurat Niyazov. Back: Coat of arms. Solid security thread. Watermark: Rearing Arabian horse. Printer: (TDLR). 156 x 78 mm.
- a. 1996. Signature 1.   0.50   2.50   10
- b. 1999. Signature 2.   0.50   2.50   10

Replacement notes: Prefix ZZ.

TMB B3 (P12): **5,000 manat**   VG   VF   UNC
Purple. Front: Prezident Kosgi building; President Saparmurat Niyazov. Back: Coat of arms. Solid security thread. Watermark: Rearing Arabian horse. Printer: (TDLR). 156 x 78 mm.
- a. 2000. Signature 2.   0.25   1   4

5,000-manat notes dated 1999 have a tilde over the N in MÜN (TMB B2b, left), whereas notes dated 2000 have a hacheck accent over the N in MÜÑ (TMB B3a, right). There are also other differences in the accents on the text below the bank's name on front and back.

TMB B4 (P10): **10,000 manat**　　　　　　　　　　　　　VG　VF　UNC
Light blue. Front: Prezident Kosgi building; President Saparmurat Niyazov. Back: Coat of arms. Solid security thread. Watermark: Rearing Arabian horse. Printer: (TDLR). 156 x 78 mm.

☐ a.　1996. Signature 1.　　　　　　　　0.50　1.75　7

1998 Issues

This note is like the preceding issue, but the coat of arms has been reduced in size on the back and moved to the left to make room for the Saparmyrat Hajy Metjidi mosque.

TMB B5 (P11): **10,000 manat**　　　　　　　　　　　　　VG　VF　UNC
Light blue. Front: Türkmenbasy Kosgi building; President Saparmurat Niyazov. Back: Coat of arms; Saparmyrat Hajy Metjidi mosque. Solid security thread. Watermark: Rearing Arabian horse. Printer: (TDLR). 156 x 78 mm.

☐ a.　1998. Signature 1.　　　　　　　　0.75　3　12

1999 Issues

This note is like the preceding issue, but the embossed rosette at upper left front has been replaced with a crescent moon and five stars in OVI, and President Niyazov's portrait has three medals added to his jacket's lapel.

TMB B6 (P13): **10,000 manat**　　　　　　　　　　　　　VG　VF　UNC
Light blue. Front: Five stars and crescent moon; Türkmenbasy Kosgi building; President Saparmurat Niyazov. Back: Coat of arms; Saparmyrat Hajy Metjidi mosque. Solid security thread. Watermark: Rearing Arabian horse. Printer: (TDLR). 156 x 78 mm.

☐ a.　1999. Signature 1.　　　　　　　　1.25　5　20

2000 Issues

This note is like the preceding issue, but the Saparmyrat Hajy Metjidi mosque on the back has been replaced by the Bitaraplyk Binasy and Ruhyyet Köşgi.

TMB B7 (P14): **10,000 manat** VG VF UNC
Light blue. Front: Five stars and crescent moon; Türkmenbasy Kosgi building; President Saparmurat Niyazov. Back: Bitaraplyk Binasy (Neutrality Arch) in Ashgabat; Ruhyyet Köşgi (Ruhyyet Palace) building; coat of arms. Solid security thread. Watermark: Rearing Arabian horse. Printer: (TDLR). 156 x 78 mm.
 ☐ a. 2000. Signature 2.   0.50 2 8
 ☐ as. Diagonal red *NUSGA* overprint. — — —

2003-2005 Issues

These notes feature a new portrait of President Niyazov, new color schemes, and a completely new design on back.

TMB B8 (P15): **10,000 manat** VG VF UNC
Green and tan. Front: Türkmenbasy Kosgi building; President Saparmurat Niyazov. Back: Ruhyyet Köşgi (Ruhyyet Palace) building; Garaşsyzlyk Binasy (Independence Monument) in Ashgabat; coat of arms. Solid security thread. Watermark: Rearing Arabian horse. Printer: (TDLR). 156 x 78 mm.
 ☐ a. 2003. Signature 3.   0.25 1.25 5
Replacement notes: Prefix ZZ.

TMB B9 (P16): **10,000 manat** VG VF UNC
Green and tan. Front: President Saparmurat Niyazov; Türkmenbasy Kosgi building. Back: Ruhyyet Köşgi (Ruhyyet Palace) building; Garaşsyzlyk Binasy (Independence Monument) in Ashgabat; coat of arms. Windowed security thread with demetalized *TMB 10000*. Watermark: Saparmurat Niyazov with electrotype signature and Cornerstones. Printer: (TDLR). 156 x 78 mm.
 ☐ a. 2005. Signature 3.   0.25 1.25 5
Replacement notes: Prefix ZZ.

2005 Issues

These notes now have a unified design and novel serial numbering, with the horizontal serial number at left in black and the vertical serial number at right in red.

TMB B10 (P17): **50 manat**   VG   VF   UNC
Purple. Front: Coat of arms; President Saparmurat Niyazov. Back: Racehorse and grandstand. Solid security thread with demetalized *TMB 50*. Watermark: Saparmurat Niyazov. Printer: (TDLR). 144 x 72 mm.
   ☐   a.   2005. Signature 3.   0.25   0.50   1
Replacement notes: Prefix ZZ.

TMB B11 (P18): **100 manat**   VG   VF   UNC
Red. Front: Coat of arms; President Saparmurat Niyazov. Back: Central bank building and coins. Solid security thread with demetalized *TMB 100*. Watermark: Saparmurat Niyazov. Printer: (TDLR). 150 x 75 mm.
   ☐   a.   2005. Signature 3.   0.25   0.50   1.50

TMB B12 (P19): **500 manat**   VG   VF   UNC
Gold. Front: Coat of arms; President Saparmurat Niyazov. Back: Jewelry. Windowed security thread with demetalized *TMB 500*. Watermark: Saparmurat Niyazov with electrotype signature and Cornerstones. Printer: (TDLR). 156 x 78 mm.
   ☐   a.   2005. Signature 3.   0.25   0.75   2

TMB B13 (P20): **1,000 manat**   VG   VF   UNC
Green. Front: Coat of arms; President Saparmurat Niyazov. Back: Presidential palace in Ashgabat. Windowed security thread with demetalized *TMB 1000*. Watermark: Saparmurat Niyazov with electrotype signature and Cornerstones. Printer: (TDLR). 156 x 78 mm.
   ☐   a.   2005. Signature 3.   0.25   0.75   3

TMB B14 (P21): **5,000 manat**   VG   VF   UNC
Blue. Front: Coat of arms; President Saparmurat Niyazov. Back: Presidential palace in Ashgabat. Windowed security thread with demetalized *TMB 5000*. Watermark: Saparmurat Niyazov with electrotype signature and Cornerstones. Printer: (TDLR). 156 x 78 mm.

  ☐ a.   2005. Signature 3.   0.25   1   4

2009 Issues

On 1 January 2009, the Central Bank of Turkmenistan issued a new series of notes printed by De La Rue, which has printed Turkmenistan currency since independence in 1991. The new notes bear images of prominent figures of the Turkmen nation and various buildings in the capital, Ashgabat. The government revalued its currency in conjunction with the introduction of the new notes. Prior to the revaluation, the official exchange rate was 5,000 manats to the US dollar, with the black market rate almost five times that. The new manat is equal to 5,000 of the "old" manat.

TMB B15 (P22): **1 manat** (US$0.35)   VG   VF   UNC
Green. Front: Map of Turkmenistan; coat of arms; Togrul Beg Türkmen. Back: Beyik Saparmyrat Türkmenbasynyň Milli Medeniyet Merkezi (National Cultural Centre of Turkmenistan) buildings; five stars and crescent moon. Solid security thread and solid security thread with demetalized *1TMB*. Watermark: Togrul Beg Türkmen; electrotype five stars, crescent moon, and *1*; Cornerstones. Printer: (TDLR). 120 x 60 mm.

  ☐ a.   2009. Signature 4. Intro: 01.01.2009.   FV   FV   2.25

TMB B16 (P23): **5 manat** (US$1.75)   VG   VF   UNC
Tan. Front: Map of Turkmenistan; coat of arms; Soltan Sansar Türkmen. Back: Buildings; Garassyzlyk Binasy and Bitaraplyk Binasy (Independence Monument and Neutrality Arch in Ashgabat); five stars and crescent moon. Solid security thread and solid security thread with demetalized *5TMB*. Watermark: Soltan Sansar Türkmen; electrotype five stars, crescent moon, and *5*; Cornerstones. Printer: (TDLR). 126 x 63 mm.

  ☐ a.   2009. Signature 4. Intro: 01.01.2009.   FV   FV   6

TMB B17 (P24): **10 manat** (US$3.50)   VG   VF   UNC
Red. Front: Map of Turkmenistan; coat of arms; Magtymguly Pyragy. Back: Türkmenistanyň Merkezi Banky (Turkmenistan central bank) headquarters building; five stars and crescent moon. Solid security thread and windowed security thread with demetalized *10 MANAT*. Watermark: Magtymguly Pyragy; electrotype five stars, crescent moon, and *10*; Cornerstones. Printer: (TDLR). 132 x 66 mm.

  ☐ a.   2009. Signature 4. Intro: 01.01.2009.   FV   FV   15

TMB B18 (P25): **20 manat** (US$7)　　　　　　　　　VG　VF　UNC

Purple. Front: Map of Turkmenistan; coat of arms; Görogly Beg Türkmen. Back: Ruhyyet Köşgi (Ruhyyet Palace) building; five stars and crescent moon. Solid security thread and windowed security thread with demetalized *20 MANAT*. Watermark: Görogly Beg Türkmen; electrotype five stars, crescent moon, and *20*; Cornerstones. Printer: (TDLR). 138 x 69 mm.

☐ a.　2009. Signature 4. Intro: 01.01.2009.　　　FV　FV　20

TMB B19 (P26): **50 manat** (US$18)　　　　　　　　VG　VF　UNC

Green. Front: Holographic patch; map of Turkmenistan; coat of arms; Gorkut Ata Türkmen. Back: Türkmenistanyň Mejlisi (Turkmenistan National Assembly in Ashkhabat) building; five stars and crescent moon. Solid security thread and windowed security thread with demetalized *50 MANAT*. Watermark: Gorkut Ata Türkmen; electrotype five stars, crescent moon, and *50*; Cornerstones. Printer: (TDLR). 144 x 72 mm.

☐ a.　2009. Signature 4. Intro: 01.01.2009.　　　FV　FV　35

TMB B20 (P27): **100 manat** (US$35)　　　　　　　VG　VF　UNC

Blue. Front: Holographic patch; map of Turkmenistan; coat of arms; Oguz Han Türkmen. Back: Prezident Köşgi (Palace of Turkmenbashi in Ashgabat) building; five stars and crescent moon. Solid security thread and windowed security thread with demetalized *100 MANAT*. Watermark: Oguz Han Türkmen; electrotype five stars, crescent moon, and *100*; Cornerstones. Printer: (TDLR). 150 x 75 mm.

☐ a.　2009. Signature 4. Intro: 01.01.2009.　　　FV　FV　70

TMB B21 (P28): **500 manat** (US$175)　　　　　　VG　VF　UNC

Orange. Front: Holographic patch; map of Turkmenistan; coat of arms; President Saparmurat Niyazov. Back: Kipchak mosque in Ashgabat; five stars and crescent moon. Solid security thread and windowed security thread with demetalized *500 MANAT*. Watermark: President Saparmurat Niyazov; electrotype five stars, crescent moon, and *500*; Cornerstones. Printer: (TDLR). 156 x 78 mm.

☐ s.　2009. Signature 4. Unissued.　　　　　　—　—　—

A specimen was prepared, but this denomination never went into production.

2012-2014 Issues

These notes are like the preceding issues, but the lower right front around the denomination numeral has been redesigned, the date and signature are new, and a pearlescent stripe has been added on back. The 10- and 20-manat notes also have SPARK patches on front, whereas the 50- and 100-manat notes have holographic stripes and wider windowed security threads.

TMB B24 (P31): **10 manat** (US$3.50)   VG   VF   UNC

Red. Front: Map of Turkmenistan; coat of arms; Magtymguly Pyragy. Back: Türkmenistanyň Merkezi Banky (Turkmenistan central bank) headquarters building; five stars and crescent moon. Solid security thread and windowed security thread with demetalized *10 MANAT*. Watermark: Magtymguly Pyragy; electrotype five stars, crescent moon, and *10*; Cornerstones. Printer: (TDLR). 132 x 66 mm.
    ☐ a. 2012. Signature 5. Intro: September 2012.   FV   FV   15

TMB B22 (P29): **1 manat** (US$0.35)   VG   VF   UNC

Green. Front: Map of Turkmenistan; coat of arms; Togrul Beg Türkmen. Back: Beyik Saparmyrat Türkmenbasynyň Milli Medeniyet Merkezi (National Cultural Centre of Turkmenistan) buildings; five stars and crescent moon. Solid security thread and solid security thread with demetalized *1TMB*. Watermark: Togrul Beg Türkmen; electrotype five stars, crescent moon, and *1*; Cornerstones. Printer: (TDLR). 120 x 60 mm.
    ☐ a. 2012. Signature 5. Intro: September 2012.   FV   FV   2.25
    ☐ b. 2014. Signature 6. Intro: 01.07.2014.   FV   FV   2.25

TMB B25 (P32): **20 manat** (US$7)   VG   VF   UNC

Purple. Front: Map of Turkmenistan; coat of arms; Görogly Beg Türkmen. Back: Ruhyyet Köşgi (Ruhyyet Palace) building; five stars and crescent moon. Solid security thread and windowed security thread with demetalized *20 MANAT*. Watermark: Görogly Beg Türkmen; electrotype five stars, crescent moon, and *20*; Cornerstones. Printer: (TDLR). 138 x 69 mm.
    ☐ a. 2012. Signature 5. Intro: September 2012.   FV   FV   20

TMB B23 (P30): **5 manat** (US$1.75)   VG   VF   UNC

Tan. Front: Map of Turkmenistan; coat of arms; Soltan Sansar Türkmen. Back: Buildings; Garassyzlyk Binasy and Bitaraplyk Binasy (Independence Monument and Neutrality Arch in Ashgabat); five stars and crescent moon. Solid security thread and solid security thread with demetalized *5TMB*. Watermark: Soltan Sansar Türkmen; electrotype five stars, crescent moon, and *5*; Cornerstones. Printer: (TDLR). 126 x 63 mm.
    ☐ a. 2012. Signature 5. Intro: September 2012.   FV   FV   6

TMB B26 (PNL): **50 manat** (US$18)   VG   VF   UNC

Green. Front: 13-mm wide holographic stripe; map of Turkmenistan; coat of arms; Gorkut Ata Türkmen. Back: Türkmenistanyň Mejlisi (Turkmenistan National Assembly in Ashkhabat) building; five stars and crescent moon. Solid security thread and windowed security thread with demetalized *50 MANAT*. Watermark: Gorkut Ata Türkmen; electrotype five stars, crescent moon, and *50*; Cornerstones. Printer: (TDLR). 144 x 72 mm.

☐   a.   2014. Signature 6. Intro: 01.07.2014.   FV   FV   35

TMB B27 (PNL): **100 manat** (US$35)   VG   VF   UNC

Blue. Front: 14-mm wide holographic stripe; map of Turkmenistan; coat of arms; Oguz Han Türkmen. Back: Prezident Köşgi (Palace of Turkmenbashi in Ashgabat) building; five stars and crescent moon. Solid security thread and windowed security thread with demetalized *100 MANAT*. Watermark: Oguz Han Türkmen; electrotype five stars, crescent moon, and *100*; Cornerstones. Printer: (TDLR). 150 x 75 mm.

☐   a.   2014. Signature 6. Intro: 01.07.2014.   FV   FV   70

Acknowledgements

This chapter was compiled with the generous assistance of Thomas Augustsson, Dmitry Litvak, Alexander Petrov, Mikhail "Mike" Prizov, Bill Stubkjaer, Dainius Tamošiūnas, Vadim Tislenko, Christof Zellweger, and others.

Sources

Cuhaj, George S. *Standard Catalog of World Paper Money, Modern Issues, 1961-Present.* 20th edition. 2014. ISBN 978-1-4402-4037-9. Krause Publications (www.krausebooks.com), 700 East State St., Iola, WI, 54990-0001.

Diaczun, Dan. "USSR—The 15 Independent Republics (1990-3): A Numismatic Overview." *IBNS Journal.* Volume 34 Number 1. p.27.

Lönnberg, Åke. "New Money." *Finance & Development.* December 2013. p.38.

Yalcinkaya, Ömer. "Who is Who on Turkmenistan's New Banknotes." *IBNS Journal.* Volume 48 Number 2. p.59.

Share Your Input, Info, and Images

This catalog is believed to be complete and correct as of the time of publication. Prices and face values were last updated 1 July 2011. Please report errors or omissions so that corrections may be made. If you can more precisely identify the name or location of anything depicted on a note, please share that information. Furthermore, if you own an unlisted type or variety, please submit scans of the front and back of the note so that it can be documented. Scans should be 300 dots per inch, 100% actual size, 24-bit color, saved as *uncompressed* JPEG files, and sent to owen@banknotenews.com. Be sure to fully describe all attributes of the note which are not apparent upon visual inspection of the images alone, such as physical dimension, watermark, and security thread.

Turks & Caicos Islands

Monetary System
1 pound = 20 shillings

The Government of the Turks & Caicos Islands

GTC Signature Varieties
DIRECTORS OF CURRENCY

1. Hugh Houston Hutchings
1913-1918

   Lindsay Lea-Smith
   1913-1918

2.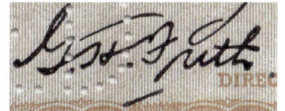
   Lindsay Lea-Smith
   1924

   Geoffrey Hammond Frith
   1924

3. Thomas G. Southby
   1928

   Geoffrey Hammond Frith
   1928

1903-1910 Issues

These notes are dated and signed by hand and originally had counterfoils at left. The dimensions in the following listings are for the issued notes without counterfoils. Based upon records in the archives at De La Rue, it appears some, if not all, of the notes were bound into booklets of 100 pieces. These notes have perforated left edges.

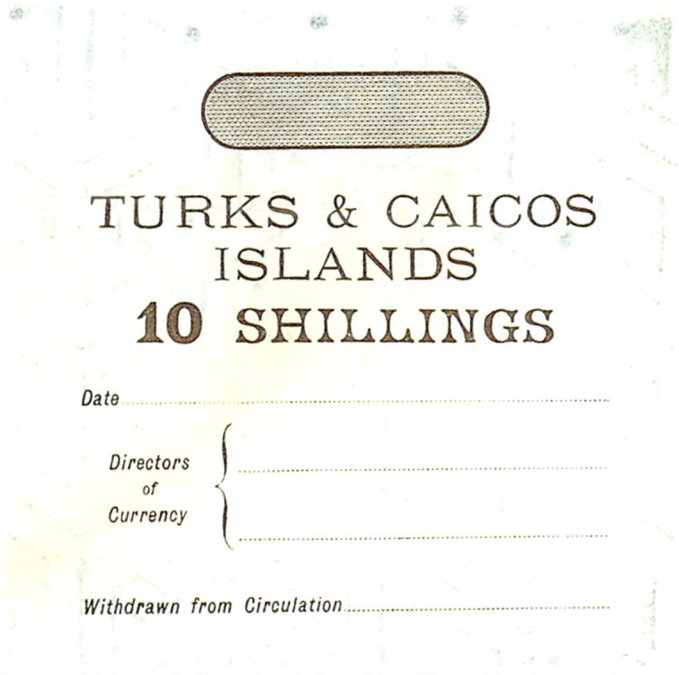

The counterfoils on earlier issues have horizontal dotted lines for Date, Directors of Currency, and Withdrawn from Circulation.

No image available
GTC B1 (PNL): **5 shillings**   Good   Fine   XF
Blue and yellow. Front (uniface): Coat of arms with sailing ship. No security thread.
Watermark: Geometric pattern. Printer: *THOMAS DE LA RUE AND COMPANY LIMITED*.
198 x 90 mm.
- a. Handwritten date and signature.   —   —   —
     Printed 07.07.1910.
     Serial numbers A/1 0001 - 01200.

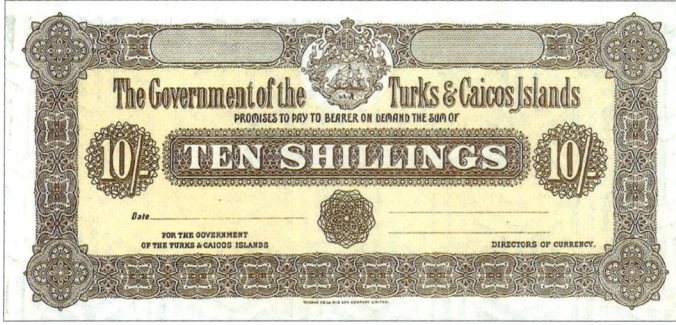

GTC B2 (PNL): **10 shillings**   Good   Fine   XF
Brown and pale brown. Front (uniface): Coat of arms with sailing ship. No security thread.
Watermark: Geometric pattern. Printer: *THOMAS DE LA RUE AND COMPANY LIMITED*.
198 x 90 mm.
- s. No date; no signatures; no serial numbers;   —   —   2,600
     with counterfoil at left.
- t. Color trial: Blue and pale brown.   —   —   5,000

GTC B3 (P3a): 1 pound   Good   Fine   XF

Red and light blue. Front (Uniface): Coat of arms with sailing ship. No security thread. Watermark: Geometric pattern. Printer: *THOMAS DE LA RUE AND COMPANY LIMITED*. 198 x 90 mm.

- ☐ a.   Handwritten date and signature. Prefix A/1. December 2nd 1903.   —   —   —
- ☐ as.   Horizontal red *CANCELLED* overprint; no date; no signatures; all-zero serial number.   —   2,000   —

GTC B4 (P2): 10 shillings   Good   Fine   XF

Brown and olive green. Front (uniface): Coat of arms with sailing ship. No security thread. Watermark: Geometric pattern. Printer: *THOMAS DE LA RUE AND COMPANY LIMITED*. 198 x 90 mm.

- ☐ a.   21st July 1913. Signature 1. Prefix A/1.   —   —   —
- ☐ b.   1st June 1924. Signature 2.   —   —   —
- ☐ as.   Horizontal *CANCELLED* perforation; with counterfoil at left.   —   20,000   —
- ☐ bs1. Two diagonal red *SPECIMEN* ovpts; normal s/n.   —   —   —
- ☐ bs2. Horizontal *CANCELLED* perforation; horizontal purple *SPECIMEN* ovpt at lower right.   —   —   —

1913-1924 Issues

These notes are like the preceding issues, but with printed dates and signatures, and vertical lines (not interlocking circles) for underprinting. Some (perhaps all) notes originally had counterfoils. Based upon records in the archives at De La Rue, it appears that at some point the notes were printed with "new sensitive inks" and "more flexible and tougher paper," though it is not known when these changes took place.

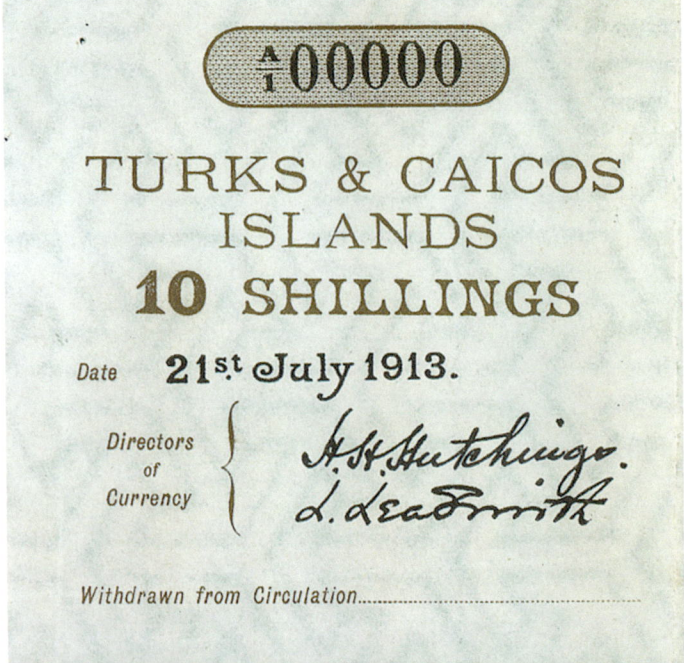

GTC B5 (P3b): 1 pound   Good   Fine   XF

Red and brown. Front (Uniface): Coat of arms with sailing ship. No security thread. Watermark: Geometric pattern. Printer: *THOMAS DE LA RUE AND COMPANY LIMITED*. 198 x 90 mm.

- ☐ a.   12th November 1918. Signature 1. Prefix A/1.   —   —   —
- ☐ b.   1st June 1924. Signature 2.   —   —   —
- ☐ bs.   Two diagonal black *SPECIMEN* overprints.   —   —   —

Like subsequent issues, but uniface.

The counterfoils on these issues have blank spaces for the printed Date and Directors of Currency, plus a horizontal dotted line for Withdrawn from Circulation.

1928 Issues

These notes are like the preceding issues, but now printed on the back with the coat of arms at center flanked by guilloche patterns.

GTC B6 (P1): 5 shillings   Good   Fine   XF
Blue and yellow. Front: Coat of arms with sailing ship. Back: Guilloche pattern; coat of arms with sailing ship. No security thread. Watermark: Geometric pattern. Printer: *THOMAS DE LA RUE AND COMPANY LIMITED*. 198 x 90 mm.

- a. 10th January 1928. Signature 3. Prefix A/1.   —   —   —
- as. Horizontal *CANCELLED* perforation;   —   —   —
  horizontal purple *SPECIMEN* ovpt at lower right.
- p. Horizontal *CANCELLED* perforation;   —   —   2,000
  no date; no signatures; no serial numbers.

GTC B7 (P4): 1 pound   Good   Fine   XF
Red and brown. Front: Coat of arms with sailing ship. Back: Guilloche pattern; coat of arms with sailing ship. No security thread. Watermark: Geometric pattern. Printer: *THOMAS DE LA RUE AND COMPANY LIMITED*. 198 x 90 mm.

- a. 10th January 1928. Signature 3. Prefix A/1.   —   —   —
- as. Horizontal *CANCELLED* perforation;   —   —   —
  horizontal purple *SPECIMEN* ovpt at lower right.

Looking Forward

For later issues, see Jamaica (1930-) and British Caribbean Territories (1950-1964).

Acknowledgements

This chapter was compiled with the generous assistance of Dr. Frühwald (www.auktionen-fruehwald.com), Arthur Gearing (De La Rue), Andrew Pattison (Spink), Mikhail "Mike" Prizov, and others.

Sources

Cuhaj, George S. *Standard Catalog of World Paper Money, General Issues, 1368-1960*. 14th edition. 2012. ISBN 978-1-4402-3090-5. Krause Publications (www.krausebooks.com), 700 East State St., Iola, WI, 54990-0001.

Narbeth, Colin. "Of Turks and Caicos Isles." *IBNS Journal*. Volume 24 Number 1. p.15.

Share Your Input, Info, and Images

This catalog is believed to be complete and correct as of the time of publication. Prices and face values were last updated 11 April 2014. Please report errors or omissions so that corrections may be made. If you can more precisely identify the name or location of anything depicted on a note, please share that information. Furthermore, if you own an unlisted type or variety, please submit scans of the front and back of the note so that it can be documented. Scans should be 300 dots per inch, 100% actual size, 24-bit color, saved as *uncompressed* JPEG files, and sent to owen@banknotenews.com. Be sure to fully describe all attributes of the note which are not apparent upon visual inspection of the images alone, such as physical dimension, watermark, and security thread.

Uganda

For earlier issues, see East Africa.

Monetary System
1966: 1 Ugandan shilling (UGS) = 100 cents
1987: 1 Ugandan shilling (UGX) = 100 cents

Bank of Uganda

The Bank of Uganda (BOU) was established on 1 July 1966 and started using its own currency on 15 August 1966 after the collapse of the East African Currency Board.

For more information, visit www.bou.or.ug.

BOU Signature Varieties

BOU Signature Varieties

	GOVERNOR	SECRETARY, TREASURY
7	Suleiman Kiggundu (1986 - 1990)	James Kahoza
8	Charles Nyonyintono Kikonyogo (1990 - 2000)	James Kahoza

	GOVERNOR	SECRETARY
9	Charles Nyonyintono Kikonyogo (1990 - 2000)	Joshua Mugyenyi
10	Charles Nyonyintono Kikonyogo (1990 - 2000)	Janet Kahirimbanyi
11	DEPUTY GOVERNOR Louis A. Kasekende (1999 - 2002)	Janet Kahirimbanyi
12	Emmanuel Tumusiime Mutebile (2001 - present)	Janet Kahirimbanyi
13	Emmanuel Tumusiime Mutebile (2001 - present)	Rweikiza Rweinamu
14	Emmanuel Tumusiime Mutebile (2001 - present)	George William Nyeko

* This official is not known to have signed any notes.

Prefixes

In the following listings, the earliest and latest prefixes which have been verified are shown. Be advised that not all prefixes within the range shown have been verified; it's possible that the printer skipped some letters for unknown reasons. Also, cross-overs (i.e. the same prefix appears on different types or varieties) exist, therefore the prefix itself can't be used as the sole determining factor in identifying a note.

1966 Issues

The Ugandan shilling replaced the East African shilling at par, although the latter was not demonetized until 1969.

BOU B1 (P1): 5 shillings   VG   VF   UNC
Blue. Front: Coat of arms. Back: Waterfall. Solid security thread. Watermark: Palm of open hand. Printer: Unknown. 146 x 80 mm.

- a. No date. Signature 1. Prefix A/1 - A/32.   0.50   1.50   6
   Intro: 15.08.1966.
- as. Diagonal red *SPECIMEN* overprint; punched.   —   —   25
- p. Proof. No signatures.   —   —   —
- t. Color trial: Purple. No signatures.   —   —   75

Replacement notes: Prefix Z/1.

BOU B2 (P2): 10 shillings   VG   VF   UNC
Brown. Front: Coat of arms. Back: Four workers picking cotton in field. Solid security thread. Watermark: Palm of open hand. Printer: Unknown. 146 x 80 mm.

- a. No date. Signature 1. Prefix A/1 - A/31.   0.50   2   7
   Intro: 15.08.1966.
- as. Diagonal red *SPECIMEN* overprint; punched.   —   —   25
- t. Color trial: Red. No signatures.   —   —   125

Replacement notes: Prefix Z/1.

BOU B3 (P3): 20 shillings   VG   VF   UNC
Purple. Front: Coat of arms. Back: Green monkey, lion and cub, Marabou stork, elephants, zebra, and impala. Solid security thread. Watermark: Palm of open hand. Printer: Unknown. 146 x 80 mm.

- a. No date. Signature 1. Prefix A/1 - A/24.   0.50   2   8
   Intro: 15.08.1966.
- as. Diagonal red *SPECIMEN* overprint; punched.   —   —   60
- t. Color trial: Green. No signatures.   —   —   250

Replacement notes: Prefix Y/1.

BOU B4 (P4 & P5): 100 shillings   VG   VF   UNC
Green. Front: Crowned crane; coat of arms; coffee plants. Back: Parliament building in Kampala. Solid security thread. Watermark: Palm of open hand. Printer: Unknown. 146 x 80 mm.

- a. No date. Sig. 1. Prefix A/1 - A/2.   50   200   800
   Intro: 15.08.1966.
- b. With *FOR BANK OF UGANDA* below *ONE HUNDRED SHILLINGS* on front. Prefix A/3 - A/8.   0.50   2   8
- as. Diagonal red *SPECIMEN* overprint.   —   —   125
- at. Color trial: Blue.   —   —   500
- bp1. No signatures; no serial numbers.   —   —   125
- bp2. With signatures and all-zero serial numbers.   —   —   125
- bs1. Diagonal red *SPECIMEN* overprint; punched.   —   —   25
- bs2. s/n range A/6 000001- 100000; dated 10.3.69.   —   —   50

Replacement notes: Prefix X/1.

1973-1977 Issues

During a military coup on 25 January 1971, army commander Idi Amin Dada seized power from President Apollo Milton Opeto Obote. Among the hundreds of thousands of people killed during Amin's 8-year dictatorship was the first governor of the Bank of Uganda, Joseph Mubiru, whose signature appeared on the first Ugandan shilling notes.

Uncirculated notes with signature 4 are available with prefixes punched, reportedly to prevent use if captured by rebels. So-called "war notes" can be easily faked, and as such aren't cataloged.

BOU B5 (P5A): **5 shillings**   VG   VF   UNC

Blue, pink, and yellow. Front: President Idi Amin in military cap and uniform; coat of arms. Back: Woman picking coffee berries. Solid security thread. Watermark: Crested crane. Printer: (TDLR). 135 x 70 mm.

☐	a.	No date. Sig. 4. Prefix A/1 - A/52. Intro: 1977.	—	0.50	2
☐	as.	Diagonal red *SPECIMEN* and DLR oval ovpts.		—	85

Replacement notes: Prefix Z/1.

BOU B6 (P6): **10 shillings**   VG   VF   UNC

Brown. Front: President Idi Amin in military cap and uniform; coat of arms. Back: Three elephants; waterfall; antelope; hippopotamus. Solid security thread. Watermark: Crested crane. Printer: Unknown. 135 x 70 mm.

☐	a.	No date. Sig. 2. Prefix A/1 - A/20. Intro: 1973.	20	75	300
☐	b.	Signature 3. Prefix A/54.	0.75	3	12
☐	c.	Signature 4. Prefix A/55 - A/76.	0.50	1.50	6
☐	as.	Diagonal red *SPECIMEN* overprint.	—	—	80

Replacement notes: Prefix Z/1.

BOU B7 (P7): **20 shillings**   VG   VF   UNC

Purple and brown. Front: President Idi Amin in military cap and uniform; coat of arms. Back: Bank of Uganda building in Kampala. Solid security thread. Watermark: Crested crane. Printer: Unknown. 140 x 73 mm.

☐	a.	No date. Sig. 2. Prefix B/1 - B/13. Intro: 1973.	25	100	400
☐	b.	Signature 3. Prefix B/18 - B/31.	5	20	80
☐	c.	Signature 4. Prefix B/36 - B/60.	0.50	1.50	6.50
☐	as.	Specimen.	—	—	90
☐	bs.	Diagonal red *SPECIMEN* overprint.	—	—	90

Replacement notes: Prefix Y/1.

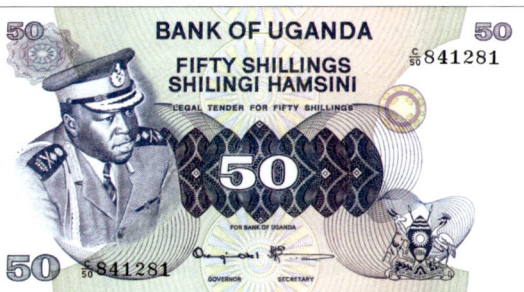

BOU B8 (P8): **50 shillings**   VG   VF   UNC

Purple and brown. Front: President Idi Amin in military cap and uniform; coat of arms. Back: Owen Falls dam and Nalubaale Power Station in Jinja. Solid security thread. Watermark: Crested crane. Printer: Unknown. 142 x 76 mm.

☐	a.	No date. Sig. 2. Prefix C/1 - C/2. Intro: 1973.	15	75	300
☐	b.	Signature 3. Prefix C/7 - C/15.	5	20	85
☐	c.	Signature 4. Prefix C/21 - C/50.	0.50	2	8
☐	as.	Specimen.	—	—	135

Replacement notes: Prefix X/1.

BOU B9 (P9): **100 shillings**   VG   VF   UNC
Green. Front: President Idi Amin in military cap and uniform; coat of arms. Back: Trees; cattle; Lake Kyoga; hills. Solid security thread. Watermark: Crested crane. Printer: Unknown. 146 x 80 mm.

   ☐ a. No date. Sig. 2. Prefix D/1 - D/3. Intro: 1973.   8   30   120
   ☐ b. Signature 3. Prefix D/4 - D/9.   6   25   100
   ☐ c. Signature 4. Prefix D/15 - D/38.   0.50   1.50   6
   ☐ as. Diagonal red *SPECIMEN* overprint.   —   —   110

Replacement notes: Prefix W/1.

1979 "Light Bank" Issues

Idi Amin fled Uganda after Kampala fell to Tanzanian forces on 11 April 1979. To expunge his memory, these notes are like the preceding issues, except that the portrait of Idi Amin on the front has been replaced with an illustration of the Bank of Uganda's headquarters building in Kampala.

All but the 5-shilling note are available in two types with different engravings of the bank building at left front. The latter engraving is distinguished from the earlier by its darker printing as well as a curved border that clearly defines the right of the vignette.

Earlier issues (BOU B11, left) are lighter than later issues (B15, right), and do not have a curved border at the right of the vignette of the bank headquarters.

BOU B10 (P10): **5 shillings**   VG   VF   UNC
Blue, pink, and yellow. Front: Bank of Uganda building in Kampala; coat of arms. Back: Woman picking coffee berries. Solid security thread. Watermark: Crested crane. Printer: Unknown. 136 x 70 mm.

   ☐ a. No date. Sig. 5. Prefix A/62 - A/90. Intro: 1979.   —   0.50   2
   ☐ as. Diagonal red *SPECIMEN* overprint.   —   —   140

Replacement notes: Prefix Z/1.

BOU B11 (P11a): **10 shillings**   VG   VF   UNC
Brown. Front: Bank of Uganda building in Kampala; coat of arms. Back: Three elephants; waterfall; antelope; hippopotamus. Solid security thread. Watermark: Crested crane. Printer: Unknown. 135 x 70 mm.

   ☐ a. No date. Sig. 5. Prefix A/104 - A/109. Intro: 1979.   0.50   2   6

Replacement notes: Prefix Z/1.

BOU B12 (P12a): **20 shillings**   VG   VF   UNC

Purple and brown. Front: Bank of Uganda building in Kampala; coat of arms. Back: Bank of Uganda building in Kampala. Solid security thread. Watermark: Crested crane. Printer: Unknown. 140 x 73 mm.

☐ a. No date. Sig. 5. Prefix B/61 - B/73. Intro: 1979.   0.50   1.75   7

Replacement notes: Prefix Y/1.

BOU B13 (P13a): **50 shillings**   VG   VF   UNC

Purple and brown. Front: Bank of Uganda building in Kampala; coat of arms. Back: Owen Falls dam and Nalubaale Power Station in Jinja. Solid security thread. Watermark: Crested crane. Printer: Unknown. 142 x 76 mm.

☐ a. No date. Sig. 5. Prefix C/51 - C/70. Intro: 1979.   6   25   100

Replacement notes: Prefix X/1.

BOU B14 (P14a): **100 shillings**   VG   VF   UNC

Green. Front: Bank of Uganda building in Kampala; coat of arms. Back: Trees; cattle; Lake Kyoga; hills. Solid security thread. Watermark: Crested crane. Printer: Unknown. 146 x 80 mm.

☐ a. No date. Sig. 5. Prefix D/40 - D/84. Intro: 1979.   6   25   100

Replacement notes: Prefix W/1.

1979 "Dark Bank" Issues

These notes are like the preceding issues, but with darker printing on the bank headquarters building as well as a curved border that clearly defines the right of the vignette.

BOU B15 (P11b): **10 shillings**   VG   VF   UNC

Brown. Front: Bank of Uganda building in Kampala; coat of arms. Back: Three elephants; waterfall; antelope; hippopotamus. Solid security thread. Watermark: Crested crane. Printer: Unknown. 135 x 70 mm.

☐ a. No date. Sig. 5. Prefix A/114 - A/139. Intro: 1979.   0.25   0.75   2.50

Replacement notes: Prefix Z/1.

BOU B16 (P12b): **20 shillings**   VG   VF   UNC

Purple and brown. Front: Bank of Uganda building in Kampala; coat of arms. Back: Bank of Uganda building in Kampala. Solid security thread. Watermark: Crested crane. Printer: Unknown. 140 x 73 mm.

☐ a. No date. Sig. 5. Prefix B/81 - B/101. Intro: 1979.   0.25   1.25   5
Replacement notes: Prefix Y/1.

BOU B17 (P13b): **50 shillings**   VG   VF   UNC

Purple and brown. Front: Bank of Uganda building in Kampala; coat of arms. Back: Owen Falls dam and Nalubaale Power Station in Jinja. Solid security thread. Watermark: Crested crane. Printer: Unknown. 142 x 76 mm.

☐ a. No date. Sig. 5. Prefix C/78 - C/132. Intro: 1979.   0.50   2   8
Replacement notes: Prefix X/1.

BOU B18 (P14b): **100 shillings**   VG   VF   UNC

Green. Front: Bank of Uganda building in Kampala; coat of arms. Back: Trees; cattle; Lake Kyoga; hills. Solid security thread. Watermark: Crested crane. Printer: Unknown. 146 x 80 mm.

☐ a. No date. Sig. 5. Prefix D/93 - D/145. Intro: 1979.   0.50   1.50   6
Replacement notes: Prefix W/1.

1982 Issues

These notes are like the preceding issues, except that the color schemes are new, and the illustration of the Bank of Uganda's headquarters on the front has been replaced with the Ugandan coat of arms on a map of Uganda. Some denominations have been observed with different sized prefixes, but a complete accounting for same has not been possible to date.

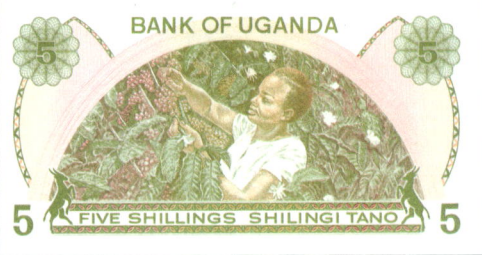

BOU B19 (P15): **5 shillings**   VG   VF   UNC

Green. Front: Coat of arms on map of Uganda; bank emblem. Back: Woman picking coffee berries. Solid security thread. Watermark: Crested crane. Printer: Unknown. 136 x 70 mm.

☐ a. No date. Sig. 6. Prefix A/1 - A/30. Intro: 1982.   —   0.50   1.50
Replacement notes: Prefix Z/1.

BOU B20 (P16): **10 shillings**   VG   VF   UNC
Purple. Front: Coat of arms on map of Uganda; bank emblem. Back: Three elephants; waterfall; antelope; hippopotamus. Solid security thread. Watermark: Crested crane. Printer: Unknown. 136 x 70 mm.

   ☐ a. No date. Sig. 6. Prefix A/1 - A/38. Intro: 1982.   —   0.50   2

Replacement notes: Prefix Z/1.

BOU B21 (P17): **20 shillings**   VG   VF   UNC
Green and red. Front: Coat of arms on map of Uganda; bank emblem. Back: Bank of Uganda building in Kampala. Solid security thread. Watermark: Crested crane. Printer: Unknown. 140 x 73 mm.

   ☐ a. No date. Sig. 6. Prefix B/1 - B/25. Intro: 1982.   0.50   2   8

Replacement notes: Prefix Y/1.

BOU B22 (P18): **50 shillings**   VG   VF   UNC
Brown. Front: Coat of arms on map of Uganda; bank emblem. Back: Owen Falls dam and Nalubaale Power Station in Jinja. Solid security thread. Watermark: Crested crane. Printer: Unknown. 142 x 76 mm.

   ☐ a. No date. Prefix C/1 - C/27. Intro: 1982.   1.25   5   20
         Sig. 6 titles *GOVERNOR* and *SECRETARY*.
   ☐ b. Sig. 6 titles *GOVERNOR* and *DEPUTY*   1   4   15
         GOVERNOR. Prefix C/31 - C/40.
   ☐ bs. Diagonal red *SPECIMEN* overprint.   —   —   —

Replacement notes: Prefix X/1.

BOU B23 (P19): **100 shillings**   VG   VF   UNC
Violet and red. Front: Coat of arms on map of Uganda; bank emblem. Back: Trees; cattle; Lake Kyoga; hills. Solid security thread. Watermark: Crested crane. Printer: Unknown. 146 x 80 mm.

   ☐ a. No date. Prefix D/1 - D/50. Intro: 1982.   0.50   2.50   10
         Sig. 6 titles *GOVERNOR* and *SECRETARY*.
   ☐ b. Sig. 6 titles *GOVERNOR* and *DEPUTY*   0.25   1.25   5
         GOVERNOR. Prefix D/57 - D/80.
   ☐ bs. Diagonal red *SPECIMEN* overprint.   —   —   —

Replacement notes: Prefix W/1.

1983-1985 Issues

These notes are like the preceding issues, except that the coat of arms on the front has been replaced with a portrait of President Apollo Milton Opeto Obote, and larger denominations have been added to this series. Milton Obote had been overthrown by Idi Amin in 1971, but regained power in 1980, after self-imposed exile in Tanzania. Some denominations have been observed with different sized prefixes, but a complete accounting for same has not been possible to date.

BOU B24 (P20): 50 shillings   VG   VF   UNC
Brown. Front: President Milton Obote; coat of arms. Back: Owen Falls dam and Nalubaale Power Station in Jinja. Solid security thread. Watermark: Palm of open hand. Printer: Unknown. 142 x 76 mm.
- a. No date. Sig. 6. Prefix C/1 - C/10. Intro: 1985.   0.25   1   4
- as. Diagonal red *SPECIMEN* overprint.   —   —   40

Replacement notes: Prefix X/1.

BOU B25 (P21): 100 shillings   VG   VF   UNC
Violet and red. Front: President Milton Obote; coat of arms. Back: Trees; cattle; Lake Kyoga; hills. Solid security thread. Watermark: Palm of open hand. Printer: Unknown. 145 x 80 mm.
- a. No date. Sig. 6. Prefix D/1 - D/9. Intro: 1985.   1.50   6   25

Replacement notes: Prefix W/1.

BOU B26 (P22): 500 shillings   VG   VF   UNC
Blue. Front: President Milton Obote; coat of arms. Back: Herd of Watusi cattle; man picking coffee berries. Solid security thread. Watermark: Palm of open hand. Printer: Unknown. 152 x 85 mm.
- a. No date. Signature 6. Intro: 1983.   0.25   1.25   5
  4.5-mm tall prefix. Prefix G/1 - G/38.
- b. 5.5-mm tall prefix. Prefix G/73 - G/78.   0.25   1.25   5
- as. Diagonal red *SPECIMEN* overprint.   —   —   45

Replacement notes: Prefix U/1.

BOU B27 (P23): 1,000 shillings   VG   VF   UNC
Red. Front: President Milton Obote; coat of arms. Back: Parliament building in Kampala. Solid security thread. Watermark: Palm of open hand. Printer: Unknown. 156 x 88 mm.
- a. No date. Signature 6. Intro: 1983.   2   8   30
  4.5-mm tall prefix. Prefix H/1 - H/22.
- b. 5.5-mm tall prefix. Prefix H/57 - H/68.   1.50   6   25
- as. Diagonal red *SPECIMEN* overprint.   —   —   60

Replacement notes: Prefix T/1.

1985-1986 Issues

On 27 July 1985, Milton Obote was overthrown in a military coup d'état. As a result, a new series of notes was issued without his portrait, reverting back to the motif of the coat of arms on a map of Uganda.

BOU B28 (P25): **500 shillings**   VG   VF   UNC
Blue. Front: Coat of arms on map of Uganda. Back: Herd of Watusi cattle; man picking coffee berries. Solid security thread. Watermark: Crested crane. Printer: Unknown. 152 x 85 mm.

     a.   1986. Signature 6. Prefix G/1 - G/9.   —   0.50   2
     as.   Diagonal red *SPECIMEN* overprint.   —   —   30

Replacement notes: Prefix U/1.

BOU B29 (P26): **1,000 shillings**   VG   VF   UNC
Red. Front: Coat of arms on map of Uganda. Back: Parliament building in Kampala. Solid security thread. Watermark: Crested crane. Printer: Unknown. 156 x 88 mm.

     a.   1986. Signature 6. Prefix H/1 - H/35.   0.25   1   3

Replacement notes: Prefix T/1.

BOU B30 (P24): **5,000 shillings**   VG   VF   UNC
Purple. Front: Coat of arms on map of Uganda. Back: Makerere University Main Hall building with clock tower. Solid security thread. Printer: Unknown. 158 x 90 mm.

     a.   1985. Sig. 6. Watermark: Palm of open hand.   2.50   10   40
        Prefix J/1 - J/10.
     b.   1986. Wmk: Crested crane. Prefix J/19 - J/78.   0.50   2   6
     as.   Diagonal red *SPECIMEN* overprint.   —   —   —
     bs.   Diagonal red *SPECIMEN* overprint.   —   —   40

Replacement notes: Prefix S/1.

1987-1998 Issues

Due to high inflation rates, the old Ugandan shilling (UGS) was replaced in 1987 by the new Ugandan shilling (UGX) at a rate of 100 to 1. These notes now have two-character prefixes instead of the fractional prefixes on preceding issues.

BOU B31 (P27): **5 shillings** (demonetized 31.12.2000)   VG   VF   UNC
Brown. Front: Coat of arms; outline of Uganda; bank emblem. Back: Crested crane; elephant; waterbuck; hippopotamus. Solid security thread. Watermark: None. Printer: THOMAS DE LA RUE AND COMPANY LIMITED. 127 x 62 mm.

     a.   1987. Signature 7. Prefix AA - CB.   —   0.50   2.50

Replacement notes: Prefix ZZ.

BOU B32 (P28): **10 shillings** (demonetized 31.12.2000)　　VG　VF　UNC
Green. Front: Coat of arms; outline of Uganda; bank emblem. Back: Coffee berries; Watusi cattle; bamboo; men fishing with net in canoe; bananas. Solid security thread. Watermark: None. Printer: *THOMAS DE LA RUE AND COMPANY LIMITED*. 131 x 64 mm.

☐ a.　1987. Signature 7. Prefix AA - BF.　　—　0.50　2.50

Replacement notes: Prefix ZZ.

BOU B33 (P29): **20 shillings** (demonetized 31.12.2000)　　VG　VF　UNC
Purple. Front: Coat of arms; outline of Uganda; bank emblem. Back: Modern buildings, including original Bank of Uganda headquarters on Kampala Road and BoU Extension facing Nile Avenue. Solid security thread. Watermark: Crested crane. 136 x 66 mm.

☐ a.　1987. Signature 7. Printer: *THOMAS DE LA RUE AND COMPANY LIMITED*. Prefix AA - BC.　　0.25　0.75　3.50
☐ b.　1988. Without imprint. Prefix BP - CG.　　—　0.50　2.50

Replacement notes: Prefix ZZ.

BOU B34 (P30): **50 shillings** (demonetized 31.12.2000)　　VG　VF　UNC
Red. Front: Coat of arms; outline of Uganda; bank emblem. Back: Parliament building in Kampala. Solid security thread. Watermark: Crested crane. 142 x 69 mm.

☐ a.　1987. Signature 7. Printer: *THOMAS DE LA RUE AND COMPANY LIMITED*. Prefix AA - EU.　　—　0.75　3
☐ b.　1988. Without imprint. Prefix EY - GK.　　—　0.50　2.50
☐ c.　1989. Prefix GM - LM.　　—　0.50　2
☐ d.　1994. Signature 9. Prefix LR - MA.　　—　0.50　1.50
☐ e.　1996. Prefix MC - ML.　　—　0.50　1.50
☐ f.　1997. Prefix MQ - NA.　　—　0.50　1.50
☐ g.　1998. Prefix NE - NM.　　—　0.50　1.50

Replacement notes: Prefix ZZ.

BOU B35 (P31): **100 shillings** (demonetized 31.12.2000)　　VG　VF　UNC
Blue. Front: Coat of arms; outline of Uganda; bank emblem. Back: High Court building with clock tower in Kampala. Solid security thread. Watermark: Crested crane. 146 x 71 mm.

☐ a.　1987. Signature 7. Printer: *THOMAS DE LA RUE AND COMPANY LIMITED*. Prefix AA - CJ.　　0.25　1　4
☐ b.　1988. Without imprint. Prefix DN - UT.　　—　0.75　3
☐ c.　1994. Signature 9. Prefix UU - VD.　　—　0.50　2
☐ d.　1996. Prefix VF - VP.　　—　0.50　2
☐ e.　1997. Prefix VQ - WK.　　0.25　1　4
☐ f.　1998. Prefix WN - WV.　　—　0.50　2

Replacement notes: Prefix ZZ.

1991 Issues

Continued inflation required the introduction of these two high-denomination notes.

BOU B36 (P32): **200 shillings** (demonetized 31.12.2000)   VG   VF   UNC
Orange and brown. Front: Coat of arms; outline of Uganda; bank emblem. Back: Worker in textile factory. Solid security thread. Watermark: Crested crane. Printer: Unknown. 151 x 74 mm.

☐	a.	1987. Signature 7. Prefix AA - BE.	—	1	4
☐	b.	1991. Signature 8. Prefix BS - CX.	—	1	4
☐	c.	1994. Signature 9. Prefix CY - DL.	—	1	3.50
☐	d.	1996. Prefix DT - EC.	—	0.75	3
☐	e.	1997. Prefix EH.	—	1.50	6
☐	f.	1998. Prefix EP.	—	0.50	2

Replacement notes: Prefix ZZ.

BOU B37 (P33): **500 shillings** (demonetized 31.12.2000)   VG   VF   UNC
Brown and purple. Front: Elephant; coat of arms; bank emblem. Back: National Independence monument in Kampala: Makerere University Main Hall building with clock tower. Solid security thread printed *BANK OF UGANDA*. Watermark: Crested crane. Printer: Unknown. 151 x 74 mm.

☐	a.	1991. Signature 8. Prefix AA - BP.	0.25	1	4
☐	b.	Signature 9. Prefix BY - CJ.	0.25	1	4.50
☐	as.	Diagonal red *SPECIMEN* overprint; horizontal red # ovpt at upper center on back.	—	—	30
☐	bs.	Diagonal red hollow *SPECIMEN* overprint; horizontal black # overprint at lower left on back.	—	—	30

Replacement notes: Prefix ZZ.

BOU B38 (P34): **1,000 shillings** (demonetized 31.12.2013)   VG   VF   UNC
Green. Front: Farmer with hoe; coat of arms; corn stalks; bank emblem. Back: Two trucks; grain silos in Jinja. Solid security thread printed *BANK OF UGANDA*. Watermark: Crested crane. Printer: Unknown. 151 x 74 mm.

☐	a.	1991. Signature 8. Prefix AA - BE.	0.50	1.50	6
☐	b.	Signature 9. Prefix BM - ET.	0.25	1	4
☐	as.	Diagonal red *SPECIMEN* overprint; horizontal red # ovpt at upper center on back.	—	—	30

Replacement notes: Prefix ZZ.

1993-1998 Issues

The two lowest denominations in this series are like the preceding issues, but the security thread is now windowed, not solid, and the vertical serial number at left front is novel format. Also, two higher denominations were issued for the first time. Beginning in 1995, the watermark of the crested crane was revised on some denominations; it's slightly smaller and with a bright white patch on the bird's cheek.

BOU B40 (P36): **1,000 shillings** (demonetized 31.12.2013)   VG   VF   UNC
Green and brown. Front: Farmer with hoe; coat of arms; corn stalks; bank emblem. Back: Two trucks; grain silos in Jinja. Windowed security thread with demetalized *1000*. Watermark: Crested crane. Printer: Unknown. 150 x 75 mm.

			VG	VF	UNC
☐	a.	1994. Signature 9. Prefix FA - GB.	0.50	2	8
☐	b.	1996. Prefix GE - GQ.	0.50	2	8
☐	c.	1998. Watermark: Revised crane. Prefix HY - JB.	0.50	2	8
☐	d.	1999. Prefix JJ - JP.	0.50	2	8

Replacement notes: Prefix ZZ.

BOU B39 (P35): **500 shillings** (demonetized 31.12.2000)   VG   VF   UNC
Brown and purple. Front: Elephant; coat of arms; bank emblem. Back: National Independence monument in Kampala: Makerere University Main Hall building with clock tower. Windowed security thread with demetalized *500*. Watermark: Crested crane. Printer: Unknown. 150 x 75 mm.

			VG	VF	UNC
☐	a.	1994. Signature 9. Prefix DK - DX.	0.50	1.50	6
☐	b.	1996. Prefix EB - EK.	0.25	1	4
☐	c.	1997. Watermark: Revised crane. Prefix EN - ET.	0.25	1	4
☐	d.	1998. Prefix EZ - FB.	0.25	1	4

Replacement notes: Prefix ZZ.

BOU B41 (P37): **5,000 shillings** (demonetized 31.12.2013)   VG   VF   UNC
Violet. Front: Lake Bunyonyi and terraces; coat of arms; leaves; bank emblem; equator monument near Masaka. Back: Railroad cars and Kaawa ferry; coffee bush. Windowed security thread with demetalized *5000*. Watermark: Crested crane. Printer: Unknown. 150 x 75 mm.

			VG	VF	UNC
☐	a.	1993. Signature 9. Prefix AA - BM.	1.25	5	20
☐	b.	1998. Watermark: Revised crane. Prefix BR - BZ.	1.25	5	20

Replacement notes: Prefix ZZ.

BOU B42 (P38): **10,000 shillings** (demonetized 31.12.2005)   VG   VF   UNC
Multicolor. Front: Musical instruments; coat of arms; crested crane holographic patch; bank emblem. Back: Owen Falls dam and Nalubaale Power Station in Jinja; kob (antelope). Windowed security thread with demetalized *10000*. Watermark: Revised crested crane. Printer: Unknown. 150 x 76 mm.

    ☐ a.   1995. Signature 9. Prefix AA - AQ.   2   8   30
    ☐ b.   1998. Prefix AX - BF.   2   8   30
Replacement notes: Prefix ZZ.

2000 Issues

Although at first glance this 1,000-shilling note looks like the preceding issues, it has a solid, not windowed security thread, and the letter *M* in *MOJA* at center front and right back is different.

BOU B43 (P39a): **1,000 shillings** (demonetized 31.12.2013)   VG   VF   UNC
Green and brown. Front: Farmer with hoe; coat of arms; corn stalks; bank emblem. Back: Two trucks; grain silos in Jinja. Solid security thread with demetalized *1000*. Watermark: Crested crane. Printer: Unknown. 150 x 75 mm.

    ☐ a.   2000. Signature 10. Prefix JR - LA.   0.50   1.25   5.25
Replacement notes: Prefix ZZ.

1999-2004 Issues

These notes are like the preceding issues, except that the windowed security thread has been replaced with a solid thread, the denomination now appears more clearly in the lower left on the front, and intaglio symbols for the partially sighted have been added to the lower right on the front. Also, a new 20,000-shilling denomination was issued for the first time.

BOU B44 (P39b & P39A): **1,000 shillings** (demon. 31.12.2013)   VG   VF   UNC
Green and brown. Front: Farmer with hoe; coat of arms; corn stalks; bank emblem. Back: Two trucks; grain silos in Jinja. Solid security thread with demetalized *1000*. Watermark: Crested crane. Printer: Unknown. 150 x 75 mm.

    ☐ a.   2001. Sig. 12. Prefix LV - NF. Intro: 10.12.2001.   FV   FV   3
    ☐ b.   2003. Prefix PD - RC.   FV   FV   3
Replacement notes: Prefix ZZ.

BOU B45 (P40 & P40A): **5,000 shillings** (demon. 31.12.2013)   VG   VF   UNC
Violet. Front: Lake Bunyonyi and terraces; silver foil leaves; coat of arms; leaves; bank emblem; equator monument near Masaka. Back: Railroad cars and Kaawa ferry; coffee bush. Solid security thread with demetalized *5000*. Watermark: Crested crane. Printer: Unknown. 150 x 75 mm.

    ☐ a.   2000. Signature 11. Prefix CA - CU.   FV   5   14
    ☐ b.   2002. Signature 12. Prefix DA - DL.   FV   FV   8.50
    ☐ as.   Diagonal red *SPECIMEN* overprint.   —   —   20

2003-2009 Issues

These notes are like the preceding issues, except all denominations now have a holographic stripe on the front. Furthermore, additional elements are intaglio printed, the cotton paper quality has been improved to increase circulation life, and a post-print coating has been applied to maintain cleanliness.

BOU B46 (P41): **10,000 shillings** (demonetized 31.12.2013)   VG   VF   UNC
Multicolor. Front: Musical instruments; coat of arms; bank emblem. Back: Owen Falls dam and Nalubaale Power Station in Jinja; kob (antelope). Holographic stripe. Solid security thread with demetalized *10000*. Watermark: Crested crane. Printer: Unknown. 156 x 76 mm.

- ☐ a. 2001. Signature 11. Prefix BG - BW.   FV   10   20
- ☐ b. 2003. Signature 12. Prefix CL - CR.   FV   10   20
- ☐ c. 2004. Prefix CV - DG.   FV   10   20

BOU B48 (P43): **1,000 shillings** (demonetized 31.12.2013)   VG   VF   UNC
Green and brown. Front: Farmer with hoe; coat of arms; corn stalks; bank emblem. Back: Two trucks; grain silos in Jinja. Holographic stripe. Solid security thread with demetalized *1000*. Watermark: Crested crane. Printer: Unknown. 150 x 75 mm.

- ☐ a. 2005. Signature 12. 6-digit s/n. Prefix SF - VY.   FV   FV   3
  Intro: 31.05.2005.
- ☐ b. 2007. Signature 13. Prefix WV - XA.   FV   FV   2.25
- ☐ c. 2008. Prefix XN - ZY.   FV   FV   2.25
- ☐ d. 2009. 7-digit serial number. Prefix B - G.   FV   FV   2.25
  Intro: 01.09.2009.
- ☐ bs. Diagonal red *SPECIMEN* overprint;   —   —   155
  horizontal red *SPECIMEN Nº #* ovpt at lower left.

Replacement notes: Prefix Z.

BOU B47 (P42): **20,000 shillings** (demonetized 31.12.2013)   VG   VF   UNC
Green. Front: Crested crane; coat of arms; bank emblem. Back: Parliament building in Kampala. Holographic stripe. Solid security thread with demetalized *20000*. Watermark: Coat of arms. Printer: Unknown. 160 x 78 mm.

- ☐ a. 1999. Signature 10. Prefix AA - AK.   FV   20   40
- ☐ b. 2002. Signature 12. Prefix AQ - AV.   FV   20   40
- ☐ as. Diagonal red hollow *SPECIMEN* overprint.   —   —   —

Replacement notes: Prefix ZA.

BOU B49 (P44): **5,000 shillings** (demonetized 31.12.2013)   **VG**   **VF**   **UNC**
Violet. Front: Lake Bunyonyi and terraces; coat of arms; leaves; bank emblem; equator monument near Masaka. Back: Railroad cars and Kaawa ferry; coffee bush. Holographic stripe. Solid security thread with demetalized *5000*. Watermark: Crested crane. Printer: Unknown. 150 x 75 mm.

- a. 2004. Sig. 12. Prefix DY - EB. Intro: 01.11.2004.   FV   FV   9
- b. 2005. Prefix EF - GB.   FV   FV   7
- c. 2008. Signature 13. Prefix GJ - HH.   FV   FV   6
- d. 2009. Prefix HL - JL.   FV   FV   6
- bs. Diagonal red hollow *SPECIMEN* overprint; horizontal red # overprint at lower left.   —   —   170

BOU B50 (P45): **10,000 shillings** (demonetized 31.12.2013)   **VG**   **VF**   **UNC**
Green and red. Front: Musical instruments; coat of arms; bank emblem. Back: Owen Falls dam and Nalubaale Power Station in Jinja; kob (antelope). Holographic stripe. Solid security thread with demetalized *10000*. Watermark: Crested crane, electrotype *10000*, and Cornerstones. Printer: (TDLR). 156 x 76 mm.

- a. 2005. Sig. 12. Prefix DN - EW. Intro: 02.01.2006.   FV   10   20
- b. 2008. Signature 13. Prefix EY - FT.   FV   FV   15
- c. 2009. Prefix FY - JR.   FV   FV   13
- as. Diagonal red *SPECIMEN* overprint; horizontal red # overprint at lower left.   —   —   195

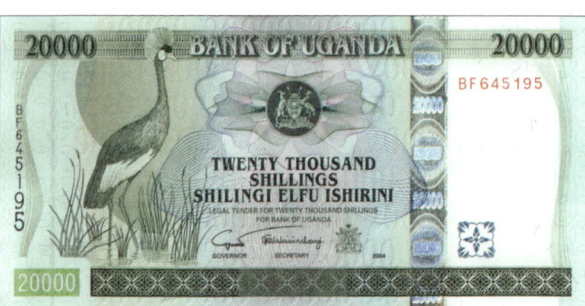

BOU B51 (P46): **20,000 shillings** (demonetized 31.12.2013)   **VG**   **VF**   **UNC**
Green. Front: Crested crane; coat of arms; bank emblem. Back: Parliament building in Kampala. Holographic stripe. Solid security thread with demetalized *20000*. Watermark: Coat of arms. Printer: Unknown. 160 x 78 mm.

- a. 2004. Sig. 12. Prefix BF. Intro: 01.11.2004.   FV   FV   35
- b. 2005. Prefix BT - CW.   FV   FV   30
- c. 2008. Signature 13. Prefix DQ - DX.   FV   FV   20
- d. 2009. Prefix EC - ER.   FV   FV   20
- bs. Diagonal red hollow *SPECIMEN* overprint; horizontal red # overprint at lower left.   —   —   205

BOU B52 (P47): **50,000 shillings** (demonetized 31.12.2013)   **VG**   **VF**   **UNC**
Brown. Front: National Independence monument in Kampala; coat of arms; bank emblem; pineapple. Back: Four workers picking cotton in field. Holographic stripe. Solid security thread with demetalized *50000*. Watermark: Coat of arms and electrotype *50000*. Printer: Unknown. 160 x 80 mm.

- a. 2003. Sig. 12. Prefix AA - BC. Intro: 01.12.2003.   FV   FV   45
- b. 2007. Signature 13. Prefix BE - BN.   FV   FV   45
- c. 2008. Prefix BS - BZ.   FV   FV   45
- as. Diagonal red *SPECIMEN* overprint; horizontal red *SPECIMEN Nº* # ovpt at lower left.   —   —   215

Replacement notes: Prefix Z.

2007 Commemorative Issues

The Bank of Uganda issued a legal tender commemorative 10,000-shilling note on 19 November, ahead of the Commonwealth Heads of Governments Meeting (CHOGM) that took place in Kampala, 23-25 November 2007.

BOU B53 (P48): **10,000 shillings** (demonetized 31.12.2013)   VG   VF   UNC
Yellow and brown. Front: CHOGM logo; coat of arms; bank emblem. Back: Owen Falls dam and Nalubaale Power Station in Jinja; two mountain gorillas. Green-to-red windowed security thread with demetalized *BOU 10000*. Watermark: Crested crane, electrotype *10000*, and Cornerstones. Printer: (TDLR). 156 x 76 mm.
- a. 2007 23-25 NOVEMBER. Sig. 13. Prefix UG.   FV   FV   20
  Intro: 19.11.2007.

2007 Numismatic Products

The first 1,500 of the commemorative 10,000-shilling notes were packaged in special folders and sold at a small premium over face value.

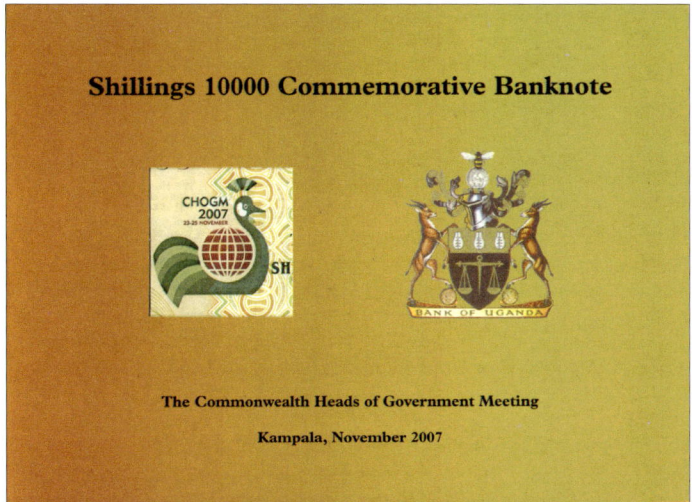

BOU BNP1 (PNL): **10,000 shillings** (US$4.15)   UNC
- a. B53 in folder. Intro: 19.11.2007.   30

2010-2011 Issues

These notes feature a harmonized banknote design that depict Uganda's rich historical, natural, and cultural heritage. They also bear improved security features. Five images appear on all the six denominations: Ugandan mat patterns, Ugandan basketry, the map of Uganda (complete with the equator line), the Independence Monument, and a profile of a man wearing Karimojong headdress. Bank of Uganda Governor Emmanuel Tumusiime Mutebile said the new notes did not constitute a currency reform, nor were they dictated by politics. The redesign, he said, was driven by the need to comply with international practices and to beat counterfeiters. "Uganda is the first country in Africa to introduce the ultra-modern security feature called SPARK," an optical security feature from SICPA first used on Kazakhstan's 5,000-tengé commemorative of 2008.

BOU B54 (P49): **1,000 shillings** (US$0.40)   VG   VF   UNC
Orange. Front: Profile of a man wearing Karimojong headdress; Nyero rock paintings in Kumi; savannah grasslands; purple-to-green OVI patch; coat of arms. Back: Profile of a man wearing Karimojong headdress; sun; map; kob (antelope); National Independence monument in Kampala. Red-to-green windowed security thread with demetalized *BOU I*. Watermark: Crested crane, electrotype *1000*, and Cornerstones. Printer: (TDLR). 131 x 64 mm.
- a. 2010. Sig. 14. Prefix AA - BC. Intro: 17.05.2010.   FV   FV   1
- as. Diagonal red *SPECIMEN* overprint;   —   —   125
  horizontal red # overprint at lower left.

Replacement notes: Prefix ZA.

Uganda 2010-2011 Issues

BOU B55 (P50): **2,000 shillings** (US$0.85) VG VF UNC

Blue. Front: Profile of a man wearing Karimojong headdress; Source of the Nile Monument in Njeru; Nile river; purple-to-green OVI patch; coat of arms. Back: Profile of a man wearing Karimojong headdress; sun; map; talapia fish; National Independence monument in Kampala. Red-to-green windowed security thread with demetalized *BOU II*. Watermark: Crested crane, electrotype *2000*, and Cornerstones. Printer: (TDLR). 135 x 66 mm.

    ☐ a. 2010. Sig. 14. Prefix AA - AP. Intro: 17.05.2010.   FV   FV   2
    ☐ as. Diagonal red *SPECIMEN* overprint;   —   —   125
           horizontal red *SPECIMEN Nº #* ovpt at lower left.

Replacement notes: Prefix ZA.

BOU B56 (P51): **5,000 shillings** (US$2.10) VG VF UNC

Green. Front: Profile of a man wearing Karimojong headdress; World War I and II memorial at Constitutional Square in Kampala; Rwenzori mountains; purple-to-green OVI patch; coat of arms. Back: Profile of a man wearing Karimojong headdress; sun; map; bird's nest; weaver birds; National Independence monument in Kampala. Red-to-green windowed security thread with demetalized *BOU V*. Watermark: Crested crane and electrotype *5000*. Printer: (TDLR). 139 x 68 mm.

    ☐ a. 2010. Sig. 14. Prefix AA - AH. Intro: 17.05.2010.   FV   FV   5
    ☐ b. 2011. Prefix AJ - AP.   FV   FV   5
    ☐ c. 2013. Prefix AS.   FV   FV   5
    ☐ as. Diagonal red hollow *SPECIMEN* overprint;   —   —   150
           horizontal red *#* overprint at lower left.

Replacement notes: Prefix ZA.

BOU B57 (P52): **10,000 shillings** (US$4.15) VG VF UNC

Purple and red. Front: Profile of a man wearing Karimojong headdress; Key to Success monument at Kyambogo University; Sipi Falls at Mount Elgon; green-to-blue SPARK patch; coat of arms; jugs. Back: Jugs; profile of a man wearing Karimojong headdress; sun; map; matoke plantains; National Independence monument in Kampala. Holographic stripe. Red-to-green windowed security thread with demetalized *BOU X*. Watermark: Crested crane and electrotype *10000*. Printer: (TDLR). 143 x 70 mm.

    ☐ a. 2010. Sig. 14. Prefix AA - AE. Intro: 17.05.2010.   FV   FV   10
    ☐ b. 2011. Prefix AG - AN.   FV   FV   10
    ☐ c. 2013. Prefix AU.   FV   FV   10
    ☐ as. Diagonal red hollow *SPECIMEN* overprint;   —   —   150
           horizontal red *#* overprint at lower left.

Replacement notes: Prefix ZA.

BOU B58 (P53): **20,000 shillings** (US$8.30) VG VF UNC

Red. Front: Profile of a man wearing Karimojong headdress; Socio Economic Growth of Kampala City monument in Centenary Park in Kampala; trees and crater lake in Ndali; green-to-blue SPARK patch; coat of arms; drums. Back: Drums; profile of a man wearing Karimojong headdress; sun; map; long-horned bull; National Independence monument in Kampala. Holographic stripe. Red-to-green windowed security thread with demetalized *BOU XX*. Watermark: Crested crane and electrotype *20000*. Printer: (TDLR). 147 x 72 mm.

    ☐ a. 2010. Sig. 14. Prefix AA - AN. Intro: 17.05.2010.   FV   FV   20
    ☐ as. Diagonal red *SPECIMEN* overprint;   —   —   175
           horizontal red *SPECIMEN Nº #* ovpt at lower left.

Replacement notes: Prefix ZA.

BOU B59 (P54): **50,000 shillings** (US$21)   VG   VF   UNC
Gold. Front: Profile of a man wearing Karimojong headdress; Stride monument of family with CHOGM flag; Bwindi Impenetrable Forest; green-to-blue SPARK patch; coat of arms; shields. Back: Shields; profile of a man wearing Karimojong headdress; sun; map; silver back mountain gorillas; National Independence monument in Kampala. Holographic stripe. Red-to-green windowed security thread with demetalized *BOU L*. Watermark: Crested crane and electrotype *50000*. Printer: (TDLR). 151 x 74 mm.

☐ a. 2010. Sig. 14. Prefix AA - AF. Intro: 17.05.2010.   FV   FV   55
☐ b. 2013. Prefix AM.   FV   FV   55
☐ as. Diagonal red *SPECIMEN* overprint; horizontal red # overprint at lower left.   —   —   180

Replacement notes: Prefix ZA.
This note was honored as the IBNS Bank Note of the Year 2010.

Looking Forward

• On 1 July 2010, the East African Community (www.eac.int)—Burundi, Kenya, Rwanda, Tanzania, and Uganda—launched the EAC Common Market for goods, labor, and capital within the region, with the goals of a common currency (the East African shilling) by 2012, and full political federation in 2015. The common currency has yet to come to pass.

• According to an article on Daily Monitor dated 30 December 2010, the Bank of Uganda used an image of a sculpture on the front of the 20,000-shilling note issued 17 May 2010 without the permission of its creator, Sylvia Nabiteeko Katende, a senior lecturer at the Margaret Trowel School of Industrial and Fine Art at Makerere University. The artist is suing the bank for over 1 billion shillings (US$430,000), claiming fraudulent use of her intellectual property. Ms Katende claims she created the sculpture, named the Socio Economic Growth of Kampala City, to commemorate the city's centenary celebrations in 2000.

• According to an UGPulse article, Governor Emmanuel Tumusiime Mutebile said the Bank of Uganda would consider introducing a 100,000-shilling banknote if inflation doesn't ease from recent levels around 30 percent. Currently the largest denomination is the 50,000-shilling note issued on 17 May 2010.

In a follow-up statement dated 11 November 2011, the Bank of Uganda clarified that it is not contemplating and has no immediate plans to introduce a 100,000-shilling note and that the bank has no intention of changing its currency structure at the moment.

Acknowledgements

This chapter was compiled with the generous assistance of Thomas Augustsson, Arigo Avbovbo, Ricardo Castedo, Murray Hanewich, Jørgen S. Jørgensen, Marie Kasule (Bank of Uganda), Marcin Lemanski, Richard Miranda, Monetary Research Institute (www.mriguide.com), Wally Myers, Nazir Rahemtulla, Ny Andry Ranaivosolo, Andrew Roberts, Gergely Scheidl (banknoteshop@gmx.net), John Silver, Bill Stubkjaer, Brian O'Sullivan, Frank van Tiel, Andre du Toit, Chris Twining (www.pagescoinsandcurrency.com), Ludek Vostal, David White, Christof Zellweger, and others.

Sources

Cuhaj, George S. *Standard Catalog of World Paper Money, Modern Issues, 1961-Present*. 18th edition. 2012. ISBN 978-1-4402-2956-5. Krause Publications (www.krausebooks.com), 700 East State St., Iola, WI, 54990-0001.

Hanewich, Murray. "Bank of Uganda: Latest Issues." *IBNS Journal*. Volume 24 Number 3. p.77.

Remick, Jerome H. "New Banknotes of the World: The Republic of Uganda Issues its First Banknotes." *IBNS Journal*. Volume 6 Number 4. p.17.

Remick, Jerry. "Republic of Kenya Issues First Banknote." *IBNS Journal*. Volume 6 Number 3. p.17.

Share Your Input, Info, and Images

This catalog is believed to be complete and correct as of the time of publication. Prices and face values were last updated 17 June 2011. Please report errors or omissions so that corrections may be made. If you can more precisely identify the name or location of anything depicted on a note, please share that information. Furthermore, if you own an unlisted type or variety, please submit scans of the front and back of the note so that it can be documented. Scans should be 300 dots per inch, 100% actual size, 24-bit color, saved as *uncompressed* JPEG files, and sent to owen@banknotenews.com. Be sure to fully describe all attributes of the note which are not apparent upon visual inspection of the images alone, such as physical dimension, watermark, and security thread.

Ukraine

Earlier Issues

With the collapse of the Russian and Austrian empires following World War I and the Russian Revolution of 1917, a Ukrainian national movement for self-determination reemerged. During 1917-1920, several separate Ukrainian states briefly emerged: the Ukrainian People's Republic, the Hetmanate, the Directorate, and the pro-Bolshevik Ukrainian Soviet Socialist Republic (or Soviet Ukraine) successively established territories in the former Russian empire.

Notes issued by the Ukrainian People's Republic, Government of Hetman Skoropadskyi, Symon Petliura Directorate, Ukrainian Soviet Socialist Republic, German Occupation Emission Bank, and Ukrainian Central Bank will be added to this chapter in the future.

Monetary System

1917-1920: 1 karbovanets = 100 kopiyok = 2 hryvni = 200 shahiv

1991-1996: 1 karbovanets (UAK) = 100 kopiyok

02.09.1996: 1 Ukrainian hryvnia (UAH) = 100 kopiyok

Національний Банк України (National Bank of Ukraine)

For more information, visit www.bank.gov.ua.

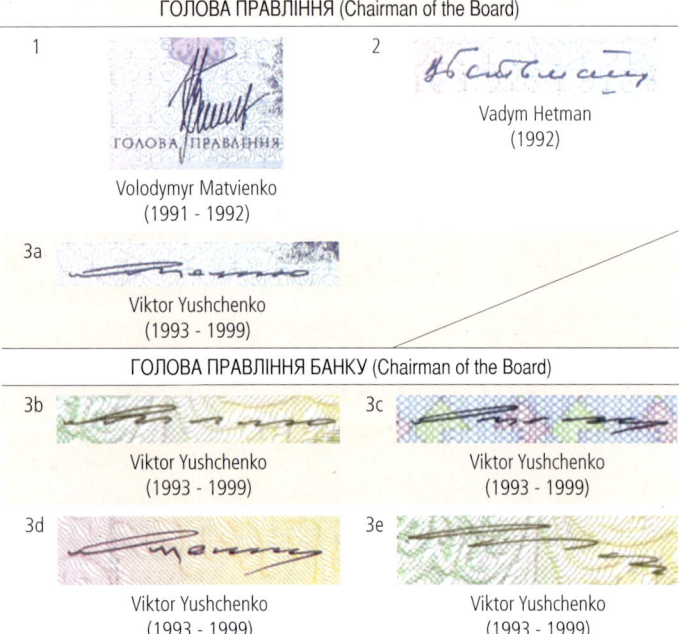

1990 Українська РСР Картка Споживача (Ukrainian SSR Consumer Card) Issues

After the new parliament adopted the Declaration of State Sovereignty of Ukraine on 16 July 1990, Russian rubles flooded into the country, buying up goods which were promptly exported. To regain control of the economy, on 1 November 1990, the Ukrainian government issued crudely printed sheets of "Ruble Support Coupons." To purchase goods other than produce, customers had to pay in rubles along with an equal number of coupons. Because they were never legal tender in and of themselves, the Ruble Support Coupons are not included in this catalog.

1991 Coupon Issues

These karbovanets-denominated notes were issued at par with the Russian ruble. Despite the word "coupon" (купон) on their face, they were legal tender in their own right and were not used the same way as the Ruble Support Coupons. All of these notes are of the same size, have the same images (a statue of Lybid, sister of the founders of Kiev, Kyi, Schek and Khoryv), and lack serial numbers and signatures. They were printed in France by Imprimerie Speciale de Banque (ISDB). All coupons were withdrawn on 16 September 1996.

The denomination printed vertically to the left of the Statue of Lybid is normally visible only under UV light, but may be visible (the above detail has been enhanced for clarity) in ordinary light on some notes (confirmed on 1, 5, and 50); these carry little, if any, premium.

NBU B1 (P81): **1 карбованець (karbovanets)** VG VF UNC

Light brown and yellow. Front: Statue of Lybid in Navodnytsky Park, Kiev. Back: Saint Sophia's Cathedral in Kiev. No security thread. Watermark: Parquet pattern. Printer: (ISDB). 105 x 53 mm.

☐	a.	1991. Intro: January 1992.	—	—	1.50
☐	as.	Horizontal *SPECIMEN* perforation.	—	—	200
☐	t.	Color trial: Orange, beige, and yellow.	—	—	200

NBU B2 (P82): **3 карбованці (karbovantsi)** VG VF UNC

Gray-green and yellow. Front: Statue of Lybid in Navodnytsky Park, Kiev. Back: Saint Sophia's Cathedral in Kiev. No security thread. Watermark: Parquet pattern. Printer: (ISDB). 105 x 53 mm.

☐	a.	1991. Intro: January 1992.	—	—	1.50
☐	as.	Horizontal *SPECIMEN* perforation.	—	—	200
☐	t.	Color trial: Dark green, brown, and yellow.	—	—	200

NBU B3 (P83): **5 карбованців (karbovantsiv)** VG VF UNC

Dark blue and yellow. Front: Statue of Lybid in Navodnytsky Park, Kiev. Back: Saint Sophia's Cathedral in Kiev. No security thread. Watermark: Parquet pattern. Printer: (ISDB). 105 x 53 mm.

☐	a.	1991. Intro: January 1992.	—	—	2
☐	as.	Horizontal *SPECIMEN* perforation.	—	—	200
☐	t.	Color trial: Blue, light blue, and yellow.	—	—	200

NBU B4 (P84): **10 карбованців (karbovantsiv)** VG VF UNC

Pink and yellow. Front: Statue of Lybid in Navodnytsky Park, Kiev. Back: Saint Sophia's Cathedral in Kiev. No security thread. Watermark: Parquet pattern. Printer: (ISDB). 105 x 53 mm.

☐	a.	1991. Intro: January 1992.	—	—	2.50
☐	as.	Horizontal *SPECIMEN* perforation.	—	—	200
☐	t.	Color trial: Red, violet, and yellow.	—	—	200

NBU B5 (P85): **25 карбованців (karbovantsiv)** VG VF UNC

Violet and yellow. Front: Statue of Lybid in Navodnytsky Park, Kiev. Back: Saint Sophia's Cathedral in Kiev. No security thread. Watermark: Parquet pattern. Printer: (ISDB). 105 x 53 mm.

☐	a.	1991. Intro: January 1992.	0.50	2	6
☐	as.	Horizontal *SPECIMEN* perforation.	—	—	200
☐	t.	Color trial: Violet, gray, and yellow.	—	—	200

NBU B6 (P86): **50 карбованців (karbovantsiv)** VG VF UNC

Green and yellow. Front: Statue of Lybid in Navodnytsky Park, Kiev. Back: Saint Sophia's Cathedral in Kiev. No security thread. Watermark: Parquet pattern. Printer: (ISDB). 105 x 53 mm.

☐	a.	1991. Intro: January 1992.	0.50	1	4
☐	as.	Horizontal *SPECIMEN* perforation.	—	—	200
☐	t.	Color trial: Green, olive, and yellow.	—	—	200

1991-1992 Coupon Issues

NBU B7 (P87): **100 карбованців (karbovantsiv)**   VG   VF   UNC
Brown and yellow. Front: Statue of Lybid in Navodnytsky Park, Kiev. Back: Saint Sophia's Cathedral in Kiev. No security thread. Watermark: Parquet pattern. Printer: (ISDB). 105 x 53 mm.
   ☐ a.   1991. Intro: January 1992.   0.50   2   8
   ☐ as.   Horizontal *SPECIMEN* perforation.   —   —   200
   ☐ t.   Color trial: Brown, violet-brown, and yellow.   —   —   200

NBU B8 (P87A): **250 карбованців (karbovantsiv)**   VG   VF   UNC
Orange. Front: Statue of Lybid in Navodnytsky Park, Kiev. Back: Saint Sophia's Cathedral in Kiev. No security thread. Watermark: Parquet pattern. Printer: (ISDB). 105 x 53 mm.
   ☐ as.   Horizontal *SPECIMEN* perforation. Unissued.   —   —   500
   ☐ t.   Color trial: Seven color varieties.   —   —   500

NBU B9 (P87B): **500 карбованців (karbovantsiv)**   VG   VF   UNC
Gray. Front: Statue of Lybid in Navodnytsky Park, Kiev. Back: Saint Sophia's Cathedral in Kiev. No security thread. Watermark: Parquet pattern. Printer: (ISDB). 105 x 53 mm.
   ☐ as.   Horizontal *SPECIMEN* perforation. Unissued.   —   —   500
   ☐ t.   Color trial: Seven color varieties.   —   —   500

1991-1992 Coupon Issues

NBU B10 (PNL): **5 карбованців (karbovantsiv)**   VG   VF   UNC
Blue, gray, and orange. Front: Statue of Lybid in Navodnytsky Park, Kiev. Back: Saint Sophia's Cathedral in Kiev. No security thread. Watermark: Parquet pattern. Printer: (TDLR). 105 x 53 mm.
   ☐ p.   Proof: 1991.   —

NBU B11 (PNL): **50 карбованців (karbovantsiv)**   VG   VF   UNC
Orange, lilac, and gray. Front: Statue of Lybid in Navodnytsky Park, Kiev. Back: Saint Sophia's Cathedral in Kiev. No security thread. Watermark: Parquet pattern. Printer: (TDLR). 105 x 53 mm.
   ☐ p.   Proof: 1991.   —

NBU B12 (PNL): **50 карбованців (karbovantsiv)**   VG   VF   UNC
Light green, lilac, and gray. Front: Statue of Lybid in Navodnytsky Park, Kiev. Back: Saint Sophia's Cathedral in Kiev. No security thread. Watermark: Parquet pattern. Printer: (TDLR). 105 x 53 mm.
   ☐ p.   Proof: 1991.   —

NBU B13 (PNL): **100 карбованців (karbovantsiv)** VG VF UNC
Blue-green, lilac, and gray. Front: Statue of Lybid in Navodnytsky Park, Kiev. Back: Saint Sophia's Cathedral in Kiev. No security thread. Watermark: Parquet pattern. Printer: (TDLR). 105 x 53 mm.
☐ p. Proof: 1991. — — —

NBU B14 (PNL): **100 карбованців (karbovantsiv)** VG VF UNC
Light green, purple, and gray. Front: Statue of Lybid in Navodnytsky Park, Kiev. Back: Saint Sophia's Cathedral in Kiev. No security thread. Watermark: Parquet pattern. Printer: (TDLR). 105 x 53 mm.
☐ p. Proof: 1991. — — —

NBU B15 (P88): **100 карбованців (karbovantsiv)** VG VF UNC
Orange, lilac, and gray. Front: Statue of Kyi, Schek, Khoryv, and Lybid in Navodnytsky Park, Kiev. Back: Saint Sophia's Cathedral in Kiev. No security thread. Watermark: Parquet pattern. Printer: (TDLR). 105 x 53 mm.
☐ a. 1992. 0.25 1 4
☐ as. Diagonal red *ЗРАЗОК* overprint. — — 30
Replacement notes: Prefix denominator 99.

NBU B16 (P89): **200 карбованців (karbovantsiv)** VG VF UNC
Brown, lilac, and gray. Front: Statue of Kyi, Schek, Khoryv, and Lybid in Navodnytsky Park, Kiev. Back: Saint Sophia's Cathedral in Kiev. No security thread. Watermark: Parquet pattern. Printer: (TDLR). 105 x 53 mm.
☐ a. 1992. 0.50 2 8
☐ as. Diagonal red *ЗРАЗОК* overprint. — — 35
Replacement notes: Prefix denominator 99.

NBU B17 (P90): **500 карбованців (karbovantsiv)** VG VF UNC
Light blue, lilac, and gray. Front: Statue of Kyi, Schek, Khoryv, and Lybid in Navodnytsky Park, Kiev. Back: Saint Sophia's Cathedral in Kiev. No security thread. Watermark: Parquet pattern. Printer: (TDLR). 105 x 53 mm.
☐ a. 1992. 1 5 15
☐ as. Diagonal red *ЗРАЗОК* overprint. — — 50
☐ t. Color trial: Olive, lilac, and gray. — — —
Replacement notes: Prefix denominator 99.

NBU B18 (P91): **1,000 карбованців (karbovantsiv)** VG VF UNC
Purple, lilac, and gray. Front: Statue of Kyi, Schek, Khoryv, and Lybid in Navodnytsky Park, Kiev. Back: Saint Sophia's Cathedral in Kiev. No security thread. Watermark: Parquet pattern. Printer: (TDLR). 105 x 53 mm.
☐ a. 1992. 0.50 2 10
☐ as. Diagonal red *ЗРАЗОК* overprint. — — 50
Replacement notes: Prefix denominator 99.

1993-1995 Coupon Issues

NBU B19 (P92): **2,000 карбованців (karbovantsiv)**   VG   VF   UNC

Blue, light blue, and gray. Front: Tryzub (trident) coat of arms as registration device; statue of Kyi, Schek, Khoryv, and Lybid in Navodnytsky Park, Kiev. Back: Saint Sophia's Cathedral in Kiev; tryzub (trident) coat of arms. No security thread. Watermark: Parquet pattern. Printer: (TDLR). 105 x 53 mm.

			VG	VF	UNC
☐	a.	1993.	0.25	1.50	6
☐	as.	Diagonal red ЗРАЗОК overprint.	—	—	50
☐	t.	Color trial: Pink, light blue, and gray.	—	—	—

Replacement notes: Prefix denominator 99.

NBU B20 (P93): **5,000 карбованців (karbovantsiv)**   VG   VF   UNC

Pink, light blue, and gray. Front: Tryzub (trident) coat of arms as registration device; statue of Kyi, Schek, Khoryv, and Lybid in Navodnytsky Park, Kiev. Back: Saint Sophia's Cathedral in Kiev; tryzub (trident) coat of arms. No security thread. Watermark: Parquet pattern. 105 x 53 mm.

			VG	VF	UNC
☐	a.	1993. Fractional prefix. Printer: (TDLR).	—	—	2
☐	b.	1995. Two-character prefix. Printer: (NBU).	—	—	2
☐	as.	Diagonal red ЗРАЗОК overprint.	—	—	50
☐	bs.	Diagonal red ЗРАЗОК overprint.	—	—	50

Replacement notes: Prefix denominator 99 (NBU B20a only).

NBU B21 (P94): **10,000 карбованців (karbovantsiv)**   VG   VF   UNC

Light green and light blue. Front: Tryzub (trident) coat of arms as registration device; statue of Vladimir the Great holding cross in Vladimirskaya Gorka Park, Kiev. Back: National Bank of Ukraine headquarters building in Kiev; tryzub (trident) coat of arms. 126 x 57 mm.

			VG	VF	UNC
☐	a.	1993. Solid security thread with printed УКРАЇНА. Wmk: Shield pattern. Fractional prefix. Printer: (TDLR).	—	—	3
☐	b.	1995. Two-character prefix. Printer: (NBU).	—	—	3
☐	c.	1996. No security thread. Wmk: Parquet pattern.	—	—	3
☐	as1.	Diagonal red ЗРАЗОК overprint.	—	—	50
☐	as2.	Diagonal red SPECIMEN - NO VALUE overprint and no serial number.	—	—	50
☐	bs.	Diagonal red ЗРАЗОК overprint.	—	—	50
☐	cs.	Diagonal red ЗРАЗОК overprint.	—	—	50

NBU B22 (P95): **20,000 карбованців (karbovantsiv)**   VG   VF   UNC

Violet and light blue. Front: Tryzub (trident) coat of arms as registration device; statue of Vladimir the Great holding cross in Vladimirskaya Gorka Park, Kiev. Back: National Bank of Ukraine headquarters building in Kiev; tryzub (trident) coat of arms. 126 x 57 mm.

			VG	VF	UNC
☐	a.	1993. Solid security thread with printed УКРАЇНА. Watermark: Shield pattern. Fractional prefix. Printer: (TDLR).	0.25	1	5
☐	b.	1994. Two-character prefix. Printer: (NBU).	0.25	1	5
☐	c.	1995.	0.25	1	5
☐	d.	1996. No security thread. Wmk: Parquet pattern.	0.25	1	5
☐	as.	Diagonal red ЗРАЗОК overprint.	—	—	50
☐	bs.	Diagonal red ЗРАЗОК overprint.	—	—	50
☐	cs.	Diagonal red ЗРАЗОК overprint.	—	—	50
☐	ds.	Diagonal red ЗРАЗОК overprint.	—	—	50

NBU B23 (P96): **50,000 карбованців (karbovantsiv)**   VG   VF   UNC

Light brown and light blue. Front: Tryzub (trident) coat of arms as registration device; statue of Vladimir the Great holding cross in Vladimirskaya Gorka Park, Kiev. Back: National Bank of Ukraine headquarters building in Kiev; tryzub (trident) coat of arms. Solid security thread with printed *УКРАЇНА*. Watermark: Shield pattern. 126 x 57 mm.

☐	a.	1993. Fractional prefix. Printer: (TDLR).	0.50	2.50	10
☐	b.	1994. Two-character prefix. Printer: (NBU).	0.25	1	4
☐	c.	1995.	0.25	1	4
☐	as.	Diagonal red *ЗРАЗОК* overprint.	—	—	40
☐	bs.	Diagonal red *ЗРАЗОК* overprint.	—	—	40
☐	cs.	Diagonal red *ЗРАЗОК* overprint.	—	—	40

NBU B24 (P97): **100,000 карбованців (karbovantsiv)**   VG   VF   UNC

Gray-green and light blue. Front: Tryzub (trident) coat of arms as registration device; statue of Vladimir the Great holding cross in Vladimirskaya Gorka Park, Kiev. Back: National Bank of Ukraine headquarters building in Kiev; tryzub (trident) coat of arms. Solid security thread with printed *УКРАЇНА*. Watermark: Shield pattern. 126 x 57 mm.

☐	a.	1993. Fractional prefix. Printer: (TDLR).	2.50	10	40
☐	b.	1994. Two-character prefix. Printer: (NBU).	0.75	3	12
☐	as.	Diagonal red *ЗРАЗОК* overprint.	—	—	40
☐	bs.	Diagonal red *ЗРАЗОК* overprint.	—	—	40

Replacement notes: Prefix denominator 99 (NBU B24a only).

NBU B25 (P98): **200,000 карбованців (karbovantsiv)**   VG   VF   UNC

Brown, light blue, and yellow. Front: Tryzub (trident) coat of arms as registration device; statue of Vladimir the Great holding cross in Vladimirskaya Gorka Park, Kiev. Back: National Opera Theatre building in Kiev; tryzub (trident) coat of arms. Solid security thread with printed *УКРАЇНА*. 126 x 57 mm.

☐	a.	1994. Watermark: Shield pattern. Fractional prefix. Printer: (TDLR).	1.25	5	20
☐	b.	Watermark: Tryzub (trident) pattern. Two-character prefix. Printer: (NBU).	1	4	15
☐	as.	Diagonal red *ЗРАЗОК* overprint.	—	—	40
☐	bs.	Diagonal red *ЗРАЗОК* overprint.	—	—	40

Replacement notes: Prefix denominator 99 (NBU B25a only).

NBU B26 (P99): **500,000 карбованців (karbovantsiv)**   VG   VF   UNC

Purple, blue, and yellow. Front: Tryzub (trident) coat of arms as registration device; statue of Vladimir the Great holding cross in Vladimirskaya Gorka Park, Kiev. Back: National Opera Theatre building in Kiev; tryzub (trident) coat of arms. Solid security thread with printed *УКРАЇНА*. Watermark: Tryzub (trident) pattern. Printer: (NBU). 126 x 57 mm.

☐	a.	1994.	1	4	15
☐	as.	Diagonal red *ЗРАЗОК* overprint.	—	—	40

NBU B27 (P100): **1,000,000 карбованців (karbovantsiv)**   VG   VF   UNC
Multicolor. Front: Tryzub (trident) coat of arms as registration device; statue of artist Taras Shevchenko in Taras Shevchenko Park, Kiev. Back: Taras Shevchenko National University building in Kiev; tryzub (trident) coat of arms. Solid security thread with printed *УКРАЇНА*. Watermark: Tryzub (trident) pattern. Printer: (NBU). 126 x 57 mm.

☐	a.	1995.	4	15	40
☐	as.	Diagonal red *ЗРАЗОК* overprint.	—	—	40

1992 Hryvnia Issues

The hryvnia replaced the karbovanets at a rate of 1:100,000 on 2 September 1996. At that time the National Bank of Ukraine issued two distinct families of notes. The notes dated 1992 were printed by the Canadian Banknote Company, whereas the notes dated 1994 (as well as undated 50- and 100-hryvnia notes) were printed by Thomas De La Rue as well as National Bank of Ukraine's new Banknote and Coin Mint in Kiev.

The watermark of the 1992-dated notes is a tryzub (trident), once the coat of arms of Vladimir the Great and now the official coat of arms of modern Ukraine.

NBU B28 (P103): **1 гривня (hryvnia) (US$0.10)**   VG   VF   UNC
Green, yellow, and purple. Front: Grand Prince of Kiev Vladimir the Great. Back: Greek columns and doorway to ruins of basilica in Chersonesos. No security thread. Watermark: Tryzub (trident) pattern. Printer: (CBNC). 135 x 70 mm.

☐	a.	1992. Signature 2. Intro: 02.09.1996.	0.25	1.50	5
☐	b.	Signature 3a.	0.25	1.50	5
☐	as.	Specimen.	—	—	—
☐	bs.	Diagonal red *ЗРАЗОК* overprint.	—	—	—

Replacement notes: Serial number begins with 9.

NBU B29 (P104): **2 гривні (hryvni) (US$0.15)**   VG   VF   UNC
Brown. Front: Grand Prince of Novgorod and Kiev Yaroslav I the Wise. Back: Saint Sophia's Cathedral in Kiev. No security thread. Watermark: Tryzub (trident) pattern. Printer: (CBNC). 135 x 70 mm.

☐	a.	1992. Signature 1. Intro: 02.09.1996.	—	2	7.50
☐	b.	Signature 2.	—	2	7.50
☐	c.	Signature 3a.	—	2	7.50
☐	as.	Specimen.	—	—	—
☐	bs.	Specimen.	—	—	—
☐	cs.	Diagonal red *ЗРАЗОК* overprint.	—	—	—

Replacement notes: Serial number begins with 9.

NBU B30 (P105): **5 гривень (hryven) (US$0.45)**   VG   VF   UNC
Blue, yellow, pink, and green. Front: Hetman Bohdan Khmelnytsky. Back: Illinska Church and bell tower in Subotiv. No security thread. Watermark: Tryzub (trident) pattern. Printer: (CBNC). 135 x 70 mm.

☐	a.	1992. Signature 1. Intro: 02.09.1996.	—	—	7
☐	b.	Signature 2.	—	—	7
☐	c.	Signature 3a.	—	—	7
☐	as.	Specimen.	—	—	—
☐	bs.	Diagonal red *ЗРАЗОК* overprint.	—	—	—
☐	cs.	Specimen.	—	—	—

Replacement notes: Serial number begins with 9.

NBU B31 (P106): **10 гривень (hryven)** (US$0.90) VG VF UNC
Violet. Front: Cossack Hetman Ivan Mazepa. Back: Kiev Pechersk Lavra (also known as the Kiev Monastery of the Caves). No security thread. Watermark: Tryzub (trident) pattern. Printer: (CBNC). 135 x 70 mm.

☐	a.	1992. Signature 2. Intro: 02.09.1996.	—	4	15
☐	b.	Signature 3a.	—	4	15
☐	as.	Specimen.	—	—	—
☐	bs.	Diagonal red *ЗРАЗОК* overprint.	—	—	—

Replacement notes: Serial number begins with 9.

NBU B32 (P107): **20 гривень (hryven)** (US$1.75) VG VF UNC
Brown, yellow, and green. Front: Writer Ivan Franko. Back: Theatre of Opera and Ballet in Lviv. No security thread. Watermark: Tryzub (trident) pattern. Printer: (CBNC). 135 x 70 mm.

☐	a.	1992. Signature 2. Intro: 02.09.1996.	2.50	10	35
☐	b.	Signature 3a.	2.50	10	35
☐	as.	Specimen.	—	—	—
☐	bs.	Diagonal red *ЗРАЗОК* overprint.	—	—	—

Replacement notes: Serial number begins with 9.

NBU B33 (P107A): **50 гривень (hryven)** (US$4.35) VG VF UNC
Red. Front: Diagonal red *ЗРАЗОК* overprint; historian Mykhailo Hrushevskyi. Back: Diagonal red *ЗРАЗОК* overprint; Verkhovna Rada (parliament building) in Kiev. No security thread. Watermark: Tryzub (trident) pattern. Printer: (CBNC). 135 x 70 mm.

☐	s.	1992. Signature 2. Unissued.	—	—	400

NBU B34 (P107B): **100 гривень (hryven)** (US$8.75) VG VF UNC
Green. Front: Diagonal red *ЗРАЗОК* overprint; poet and artist Taras Shevchenko. Back: Diagonal red *ЗРАЗОК* overprint; Verkhovna Rada (parliament building) in Kiev. No security thread. Watermark: Tryzub (trident) pattern. Printer: (CBNC). 135 x 70 mm.

☐	s.	1992. Signature 2. Unissued.	—	—	400

1994-2001 Issues

These notes depict the same people and places as the preceding issues, but have been substantially redesigned with more colors and enhanced security features. Although they are visually quite different from their predecessors, the 1-, 50-, and 100-hryvnia banknotes dated 1994 were issued at the same time as all the 1992-dated denominations: 2 September 1996.

NBU B35 (P108): **1 гривня (hryvnia)** (US$0.10)   VG   VF   UNC
Green and brown. Front: Grand Prince of Kiev Vladimir the Great. Back: Greek columns and doorway to ruins of basilica in Chersonesos. Watermark: Vladimir the Great. Printer: (NBU). 133 x 66 mm.

- a. 1994. Signature 3b. Solid security thread with printed УКРАЇНА. Intro: 02.09.1996.   FV   FV   5
- b. 1995. Signature 3e. Solid security thread with demetalized 1 ГРИВНЯ. Intro: 01.09.1997.   FV   FV   5
- as. Diagonal red ЗРАЗОК overprint.   —   —   35
- bs. Diagonal red ЗРАЗОК overprint.   —   —   35

NBU B36 (P109): **2 гривні (hryvni)** (US$0.15)   VG   VF   UNC
Brown. Front: Grand Prince of Novgorod and Kiev Yaroslav I the Wise. Back: Saint Sophia's Cathedral in Kiev. Watermark: Yaroslav I the Wise. Printer: (NBU). 133 x 66 mm.

- a1. 1995. Signature 3e. Solid security thread with demetalized УКРАЇНА. Intro: 01.09.1997.   FV   FV   5
- a2. Solid security thread with demetalized 2 ГРИВНІ.   FV   FV   5
- b. 2001. Signature 4. Intro: 06.07.2001.   FV   FV   5
- as. Diagonal red ЗРАЗОК overprint.   —   —   30
- bs. Diagonal red ЗРАЗОК overprint.   —   —   30

NBU B37 (P110): **5 гривень (hryven)** (US$0.45)   VG   VF   UNC
Blue. Front: Hetman Bohdan Khmelnytsky. Back: Illinska Church and bell tower in Subotiv. Watermark: Bohdan Khmelnytsky. 133 x 66 mm.

- a. 1994. Signature 3c. Solid security thread with printed УКРАЇНА. Printer: (TDLR). Intro: 01.09.1997.   FV   4   12
- b. 1997. Signature 3e. Solid security thread with demetalized 5 ГРИВНЬ. Printer: (NBU). Intro: 01.09.1998.   FV   4   12
- c. 2001. Signature 4. Intro: 05.03.2001.   FV   4   12
- as. Diagonal red SPECIMEN overprint.   —   —   —
- bs. Diagonal red ЗРАЗОК overprint.   —   —   —
- cs. Diagonal red ЗРАЗОК overprint.   —   —   —

Replacement notes: Prefix ЯБ (NBU B37a only).

NBU B38 (P111): **10 гривень (hryven)** (US$0.90)   VG   VF   UNC
Brown. Front: Cossack Hetman Ivan Mazepa. Back: Kiev Pechersk Lavra (also known as the Kiev Monastery of the Caves). Solid security thread with printed УКРАЇНА. Watermark: Ivan Mazepa. 133 x 66 mm.

- a. 1994. Signature 3b. Intro: 01.09.1997. 2.5-mm wide sans serif s/n. Printer: (TDLR).   2.50   10   35
- b. 2.8-mm wide serif s/n. Printer: (NBU).   2.50   10   35
- c. 2000. Signature 4. Intro: 08.11.2000.   FV   2   7
- bs. Diagonal red ЗРАЗОК overprint.   —   —   —
- cs. Diagonal red ЗРАЗОК overprint.   —   —   —

Replacement notes: Prefix ЯА (NBU B38a only).

The printers of the 10-hryvnia notes can be distinguished by the serial number fonts and width. The 2.5-mm wide sans serif serial numbers (NBU B38a, top) are printed by TDLR, whereas the 2.8-mm wide serif serial numbers (B38b, bottom) are printed in Ukraine.

NBU B39 (P112): **20 гривень (hryven)** (US$1.75) VG VF UNC

Brown, green, and purple. Front: Writer Ivan Franko. Back: Theatre of Opera and Ballet in Lviv. Windowed security thread. Watermark: Ivan Franko. Printer: (NBU). 133 x 66 mm.

    ☐ a. 1995. Signature 3c. Intro: 01.09.1997.   5   15   60
    ☐ b. 2000. Signature 4. Intro: 20.11.2000.   5   15   60
    ☐ as. Diagonal red *ЗРАЗОК* overprint.   —   —   —
    ☐ bs. Diagonal red *ЗРАЗОК* overprint.   —   —   —

NBU B40 (P113): **50 гривень (hryven)** (US$4.35) VG VF UNC

Yellow and violet. Front: Historian Mykhailo Hrushevskyi. Back: Verkhovna Rada (parliament building) in Kiev. Solid security thread with printed *УКРАЇНА*. Watermark: Mykhailo Hrushevskyi. Printer: (TDLR). 133 x 66 mm.

    ☐ a. No date. Signature 2. Intro: 02.09.1996.   FV   FV   20
    ☐ b. Signature 3d.   FV   FV   35
    ☐ x. Watermark: Taras Shevchenko.   —   —   —
    ☐ as. Diagonal red *SPECIMEN* overprint.   —   —   —
    ☐ bs. Diagonal red *SPECIMEN* overprint.   —   —   —

Replacement notes: Prefix ЯЯ.

NBU B41 (P114): **100 гривень (hryven)** (US$8.75) VG VF UNC

Rose and green. Front: Poet and artist Taras Shevchenko. Back: Rear of statue of Vladimir the Great holding cross in Vladimirskaya Gorka Park, Kiev; Saint Sophia's Cathedral in Kiev. Solid security thread with printed *УКРАЇНА*. Watermark: Taras Shevchenko. Printer: (TDLR). 133 x 66 mm.

    ☐ a. No date. Signature 2. Intro: 02.09.1996.   FV   FV   45
    ☐ b. Signature 3d.   FV   FV   45
    ☐ x. Watermark: Mykhailo Hrushevsky.   —   —   —
    ☐ as. Diagonal red *SPECIMEN* overprint.   —   —   —
    ☐ bs. Diagonal red *SPECIMEN* overprint.   —   —   —

Replacement notes: Prefix ЯЯ.

NBU B42 (P115): **200 гривень (hryven)** (US$17) VG VF UNC

Blue, orange, red, and purple. Front: Poet and writer Lesya Ukrainka; Tower of Lubart's Castle in Lutsk. Back: Tower of Lubart's Castle in Lutsk. Solid security thread with printed *УКРАЇНА*. Watermark: Lesya Ukrainka. Printer: (TDLR). 133 x 66 mm.

    ☐ a. No date. Signature 2. Intro: 22.08.2001.   FV   FV   70
    ☐ as. Diagonal red *SPECIMEN* overprint.   —   —   —

Replacement notes: Prefix ЯЯ.

1996 Numismatic Products

No image available.

NBU BNP1 (PCS1): **1 гривня (hryvnia)**   UNC   —
- a. NBU B35 with silver 2,000,000-karbovantsiv 1996 independence coin in folder.

NBU BNP2 (PNL): **1-1,000,000 карбованців (karbovantsiv)**   UNC   —
- a. Circulated and uncirculted NBU B1-B7 and B15-B27 coupon karbovanets in booklet.

2000 Numismatic Products

No image available.

NBU BNP3 (PNL): **1,000,000 карбованців (karbovantsiv)**   UNC   —
- a. NBU B27 with silver 2,000,000-karbovantsiv 1996 independence coin in folder.

2003-2013 Issues

The signatures on these notes may appear to have been issued out of order, but in fact are correct because Volodymyr Stelmakh (Signature 4) served as governor before and after Sergiy Tigipko (Signature 5).

NBU B43 (P116): **1 гривня (hryvnia)** (US$0.10)   VG   VF   UNC
Gray-green, violet, and purple. Front: Coat of arms; Grand Prince of Kiev, Vladimir the Great. Back: Bank logo; Vladimir's burg in Kiev, with walled fortifications and churches; eagle, cross, mace, ax, and sword. Solid security thread with printed 1 ГРН and trident. Watermark: Vladimir the Great and electrotype 1. Printer: (NBU). 118 x 63 mm.

- a. 2004. Signature 5. Intro: 01.12.2004.   FV   FV   4
- b. 2005. Signature 4.   FV   FV   3
- as. Diagonal red ЗРАЗОК overprint.   —   —   —

NBU B44 (P116A): **1 гривня (hryvnia)** (US$0.10)   VG   VF   UNC
Yellow and blue. Front: Coat of arms; Grand Prince of Kiev, Vladimir the Great. Back: Bank logo; Vladimir's burg in Kiev, with walled fortifications and churches; eagle, cross, mace, ax, and sword. Solid security thread with printed 1 ГРН and trident. Watermark: Vladimir the Great and electrotype hyrvnia symbol (backwards S with two horizontal bars). Printer: (NBU). 118 x 63 mm.

- a. 2006. Signature 4. Intro: 22.05.2006.   FV   FV   1.25
- b. 2011. Signature 6. Intro: 01.09.2011.   FV   FV   2.50
- as. Diagonal red ЗРАЗОК overprint; vertical red № # overprint at left front.   —   —   —

NBU B45 (P117): **2 гривні (hryvni)** (US$0.15)　　　VG　VF　UNC

Brown. Front: Coat of arms; Grand Prince of Novgorod and Kiev Yaroslav I the Wise. Back: Bank logo; Saint Sophia's Cathedral in Kiev; bowl, helmet, swords, and document. Solid security thread with printed 2 ГРН and trident. Watermark: Yaroslav I the Wise and electrotype 2. Printer: (NBU). 118 x 63 mm.

☐	a.	2004. Signature 5. Intro: 28.09.2004.	FV	FV	4
☐	b.	2005. Signature 4.	FV	FV	1.50
☐	c.	2011. Signature 6.	FV	FV	1
☐	d.	2013. Signature 7.	FV	FV	1
☐	as.	Diagonal red ЗРАЗОК overprint.	—	—	—

NBU B46 (P118): **5 гривень (hryven)** (US$0.45)　　　VG　VF　UNC

Blue, green, and red. Front: Coat of arms; Hetman Bohdan Khmelnytsky. Back: Bank logo; Illinska Church in Subotiv; quiver of arrows, bow, spears, mace, flintlock pistol, and swords. Solid security thread with printed 5 ГРН and trident. Watermark: Bohdan Khmelnytsky and electrotype 5. Printer: (NBU). 118 x 63 mm.

☐	a.	2004. Signature 5. Intro: 14.06.2004.	FV	FV	8
☐	b.	2005. Signature 4.	FV	FV	4
☐	c.	2011. Signature 6. Intro: 01.10.2011.	FV	FV	3.75
☐	d.	2013. Signature 7.	FV	FV	3.75
☐	as.	Diagonal red ЗРАЗОК overprint.	—	—	—

NBU B47 (P119): **10 гривень (hryven)** (US$0.90)　　　VG　VF　UNC

Pink. Front: Coat of arms; Cossack Hetman Ivan Mazepa. Back: Bank logo; Cathedral of the Assumption in Kiev; quill in inkwell, books, kobza, candle, and tambourine. Solid security thread with printed 10 ГРН and trident. Watermark: Ivan Mazepa and electrotype 10. Printer: (NBU). 124 x 66 mm.

☐	a.	2004. Signature 5. Intro: 01.11.2004.	FV	FV	8
☐	b.	2005. Signature 4.	FV	FV	30
☐	as.	Diagonal red ЗРАЗОК overprint.	—	—	—

Like NBU B48, but portrait and cathedral brown, not gray.

NBU B48 (P119A): **10 гривень (hryven)** (US$0.90)　　　VG　VF　UNC

Pink. Front: Coat of arms; Cossack Hetman Ivan Mazepa. Back: Bank logo; Cathedral of the Assumption in Kiev; quill in inkwell, books, kobza, candle, and tambourine. Solid security thread with printed 10 ГРН and trident. Watermark: Ivan Mazepa and electrotype 10. Printer: (NBU). 124 x 66 mm.

☐	a.	2006. Signature 4. Intro: 03.08.2006.	FV	FV	6
☐	b.	2011. Signature 6. Intro: 01.07.2011.	FV	FV	4.50
☐	c.	2013. Signature 7. Intro: 02.09.2013.	FV	FV	4.50
☐	as.	Diagonal red ЗРАЗОК overprint; vertical red № # overprint at left front.	—	—	—

Like NBU B47, but portrait and cathedral gray, not brown.

NBU B49 (P120): **20 гривень (hryven)** (US$1.75)   VG   VF   UNC

Green, blue, and brown. Front: Coat of arms; writer Ivan Franko. Back: Bank logo; Theatre of Opera and Ballet in Lviv; statue of winged woman holding fern, from roof of building. Solid security thread with printed *20 ГРН* and trident. Watermark: Ivan Franko and electrotype *20*. Printer: (NBU). 130 x 69 mm.

☐ a.	2003. Signature 5. Intro: 01.12.2003.	FV	FV	8
☐ b.	2005. Signature 4.	FV	FV	8
☐ c.	2011. Signature 6. Intro: 01.03.2012.	FV	FV	8
☐ d.	2013. Signature 7. Intro: 2014.	FV	FV	8
☐ as.	Diagonal red *ЗРАЗОК* overprint.	—	—	—

NBU B50 (P121): **50 гривень (hryven)** (US$4.35)   VG   VF   UNC

Yellow and violet. Front: Coat of arms; man on horse; Historian Mykhailo Hrushevskyi. Back: Bank logo; Verkhovna Rada (parliament building) in Kiev flanked by woman and man. Solid security thread with printed *50 ГРН* and trident. Watermark: Mykhailo Hrushevskyi and electrotype *50*. Printer: (NBU). 136 x 72 mm.

☐ a.	2004. Signature 5. Intro: 29.03.2004.	FV	FV	25
☐ b.	2005. Signature 4.	FV	FV	15
☐ c.	2011. Signature 6. Intro: 01.06.2011.	FV	FV	13
☐ d.	2013. Signature 7. Intro: 02.09.2013.	FV	FV	13
☐ e.	2014. Signature 8.	FV	FV	13
☐ as.	Diagonal red *ЗРАЗОК* overprint; vertical red *№ #* overprint at left front.	—	—	—

NBU B51 (P122): **100 гривень (hryven)** (US$8.75)   VG   VF   UNC

Olive green, burgundy, and yellow. Front: Coat of arms; painter's palette and brushes; artist Taras Shevchenko. Back: Bank logo; Chernecha mountain landscape near Chercasy; kobzar (Ukrainian bard playing the kobza) and guide boy. Solid security thread with printed *100 ГРН* and trident. Watermark: Taras Shevchenko and electrotype *100*. Printer: (NBU). 142 x 75 mm.

☐ a.	2005. Signature 4. Intro: 20.02.2006.	FV	FV	25
☐ b.	2011. Signature 6. Intro: 01.03.2012.	FV	FV	25
☐ c.	2014. Signature 8.	FV	FV	25
☐ as.	Diagonal red *ЗРАЗОК* overprint; vertical red *№ #* overprint at left front.	—	—	—

NBU B52 (P123): **200 гривень (hryven)** (US$17)   VG   VF   UNC

Pink and blue. Front: Poet and writer Lesya Ukrainka; coat of arms; building; wreath. Back: Bird; Tower of Lubart's Castle in Lutsk. Solid security thread with printed *200 ГРН* and trident. Watermark: Lesya Ukrainka and electrotype hyrvnia symbol (backwards S with two horizontal bars). Printer: (NBU). 148 x 75 mm.

☐ a.	2007. Signature 4. Intro: 28.05.2007.	FV	FV	50
☐ b.	2011. Signature 6. Intro: 01.10.2011.	FV	FV	50
☐ c.	2013. Signature 7.	FV	FV	30
☐ as.	Diagonal red *ЗРАЗОК* overprint.	—	—	—

NBU B53 (P124): **500 гривень (hryven)** (US$44)   VG   VF   UNC
Beige, brown, green, blue, and pink. Front: Violin; philosopher, poet, writer, pedagogue, and musician Hryhorii Skovoroda; coat of arms; fountain. Back: Equilateral triangle with eye at center; Mohyla Academy building in Kiev; academy seal. Solid security thread with printed *500 ГРН* and trident. Watermark: Hryhorii Skovoroda and electrotype *500*. Printer: (NBU). 154 x 75 mm.

☐ a. 2006. Signature 4. Intro: 15.09.2006.   FV   FV   85
☐ b. 2011. Signature 6. Intro: 01.12.2011.   FV   FV   85
☐ as. Diagonal red *ЗРАЗОК* overprint.   —   —   —

2011 Numismatic Products

This note commemorates the National Bank of Ukraine's 20th anniversary. It is like the note originally issued in 2004 (NBU B50), but with "НБУ 20 років" (NBU 20 years) in a green-to-gold color-shifting SPARK patch on the front, and serial numbers НБ 0000001 - 0001000 on the back. While technically legal tender, the first 200 notes were encased in acrylic and packaged in a box containing a silver version of the note; the remaining 800 notes were sold in a commemorative folder.

NBU BNP4 (PNL): **50 гривень (hryven)** (US$4.35)   UNC
Yellow and violet. Front: Coat of arms; man on horse; Historian Mykhailo Hrushevskyi. Back: Bank logo; Verkhovna Rada (parliament building) in Kiev flanked by woman and man. Solid security thread with printed *50 ГРН* and trident. Watermark: Mykhailo Hrushevskyi and electrotype *50*. Printer: (NBU). 136 x 72 mm.

☐ a. 2011. Signature 6. Intro: 05.10.2011.   250

Looking Forward

According to a Ukrainian Journal article dated 1 December 2011, the National Bank of Ukraine (NBU) has no plans to issue a 1,000-hryvnia banknote, says Viktor Zaivenko, deputy director general of the Money Circulation Department. "The NBU has no such plans. And did not have [such plans]… The NBU is not working on issuing of 1,000 hryvnia banknotes and has not even designed them… The NBU thinks that the nominal range of banknotes as of today is sufficient for the economy," Zaivenko told reporters.

Acknowledgements

This chapter was compiled with the generous assistance of Thomas Augustsson, Mahdi Bseiso, Jim W.-C. Chen, Olexandr Danishenko, Aleksey Gladkov (www.bonistika.net), Larry Hirsch (www.aworldcurrency.com), Mikhail Istomin, Peter Kelly, Dmitri Kharitonov, Mykhaylo Kharytonov (www.worldbanknotes.t15.org), Alexander Kirshankov, Thomas Krause, Pavlo Kravchuk, Igor Kvyat, Bill Stubkjaer, Christoph Thomas, Vadim Tislenko, Jacek Tylicki, Tristan Williams, Dmitry Zagorenko (http://bonistica.ru), and others.

Sources

Boon, K. N. *World Paper & Polymer Uncut Banknotes.* 1st edition. 2012. ISBN 978-983-43313-4-4. Trigometric Sdn.Bhd. (www.3833.com), Lot 327, Amcorp Mall, 18 Jalan Persiaran Barat, off Jalan Timur, Petaling Jaya, 46050 Selangor D.E., Malaysia.

Uwe Bronnert. "Where are the Millions of Rosenberg Rubles Made for Wartime Use by Germany?" *IBNS Journal.* Volume 52 Number 1. p.24.

Cuhaj, George S. *Standard Catalog of World Paper Money, General Issues, 1368-1960.* 14th edition. 2012. ISBN 978-1-4402-3090-5. Krause Publications (www.krausebooks.com), 700 East State St., Iola, WI, 54990-0001.

Cuhaj, George S. *Standard Catalog of World Paper Money, Modern Issues, 1961-Present.* 20th edition. 2014. ISBN 978-1-4402-4037-9. Krause Publications (www.krausebooks.com), 700 East State St., Iola, WI, 54990-0001.

Diaczun, Dan. "USSR-The 15 Independent Republics (1990-3): A Numismatic Overview." *IBNS Journal.* Volume 34 Number 1. p.27.

Goncharuck, William D. "Gryvna: a Handbook of Ukrainian History" *IBNS Journal.* Volume 36 Number 3. p.39.

Goncharuck, William D. "Letters to the Editor." *IBNS Journal.* Volume 35 Number 3. p.4.

Goncharuck, William D. "Ration Coupons or Ruble Support Coupons: Which is Correct?" *IBNS Journal.* Volume 33 Number 3. p.17.

Kharitonov, Dmitri. *Ukrainian Paper Money 1917-2005.* ISBN: 966-8679-03-2.

Pugh, Peter. *The Highest Perfection: A History of De La Rue.* 2011. ISBN 978-184831-335-4. Icon Books Ltd. 39-41 North Road, London, N7 9DP.

Slusarczuk, George M. J. "Letters to the Editor." *IBNS Journal.* Volume 36 Number 3. p.5.

Share Your Input, Info, and Images

This catalog is believed to be complete and correct as of the time of publication. Prices and face values were last updated 25 April 2014. Please report errors or omissions so that corrections may be made. If you can more precisely identify the name or location of anything depicted on a note, please share that information. Furthermore, if you own an unlisted type or variety, please submit scans of the front and back of the note so that it can be documented. Scans should be 300 dots per inch, 100% actual size, 24-bit color, saved as *uncompressed* JPEG files, and sent to owen@banknotenews.com. Be sure to fully describe all attributes of the note which are not apparent upon visual inspection of the images alone, such as physical dimension, watermark, and security thread.

United Arab Emirates

For earlier issues, see Bahrain, India, and Qatar & Dubai.

Contents

United Arab Emirates Currency Board (CBO) 2219
United Arab Emirates Central Bank (CBA) 2221

Monetary System
1 United Arab Emirates dirham (AED) = 100 fils

Arabic Numbers

0	1	2	3	4	5	6	7	8	9
٠	١	٢	٣	٤	٥	٦	٧	٨	٩

United Arab Emirates Currency Board

On 2 December 1971, the six emirates of Abu Dhabi, Ajman, Dubai, Fujairah, Sharjah, and Umm al-Quwain formed the United Arab Emirates (UAE), with Ras al-Khaimah joining the federation on 11 February 1972. The United Arab Emirates Currency Board (CBO) was established on 19 May 1973 under Union Law No. 2 of 1973.

CBO Signature Varieties

1
(Chairman of Currency Board)
Sheikh Hamdan bin Rashid al Maktoum

1973-1976 Issues

These dirham notes replaced the riyal banknotes of Qatar & Dubai at par, and replaced the dinar banknotes of Bahrain at a rate of 10:1, although both continued to circulate in the UAE until these currencies lost their legal tender status on 18 August 1973 and 18 November 1973, respectively.

CBO B1 (P1): 1 dirham (withdrawn)   VG   VF   UNC
Green. Front: Palm tree; caravan with man leading four camels; sama'a dhow with sail; oil derrick; outline of UAE coast; string of pearls. Back: Sparrow-hawk; fort (police headquarters building), cannons, and clock tower in Sharjah. Solid security thread. Watermark: Arabian horse head. Printer: *DE LA RUE*. 140 x 60 mm.
  ☐ a.   No date. Signature 1. Prefix ١١ - ٢١١.   15   50   100
         Intro: 20.05.1973.
  ☐ as. Specimen.   —   —   75
Replacement notes: Prefix ١٤.

CBO B2 (P2): 5 dirhams (withdrawn)   VG   VF   UNC
Purple. Front: Palm tree; caravan with man leading four camels; sama'a dhow with sail; oil derrick; outline of UAE coast; string of pearls. Back: Sparrow-hawk; fort at Bithna in Fujairah. Solid security thread. Watermark: Arabian horse head. Printer: *DE LA RUE*. 145 x 63 mm.
  ☐ a.   No date. Signature 1. Prefix ١ ب - ١٥ب.   15   60   125
         Intro: 20.05.1973.
  ☐ as. Specimen.   —   —   75
Replacement notes: Prefix ١ظ.

CBO B3 (P3): **10 dirhams** (withdrawn)   VG   VF   UNC

Gray-blue. Front: Palm tree; caravan with man leading four camels; sama'a dhow with sail; oil derrick; outline of UAE coast; string of pearls. Back: Sparrow-hawk; aerial view of Umm al-Qaiwain. Solid security thread. Watermark: Arabian horse head. Printer: *DE LA RUE*. 151 x 66 mm.

    ☐ a. No date. Signature 1. Prefix ج ١٩ - ج.   20   60   175
        Intro: 20.05.1973.
    ☐ as. Specimen.   —   —   100

CBO B4 (P4): **50 dirhams** (withdrawn)   VG   VF   UNC

Red. Front: Palm tree; caravan with man leading four camels; sama'a dhow with sail; oil derrick; outline of UAE coast; string of pearls. Back: Sparrow-hawk; sheikh's palace at Ajman. Solid security thread. Watermark: Arabian horse head. Printer: *DE LA RUE*. 163 x 72 mm.

    ☐ a. No date. Signature 1. Prefix ره - ر١.   75   300   1,000
        Intro: 20.05.1973.
    ☐ as. Specimen.   —   —   225

CBO B5 (P5): **100 dirhams** (withdrawn)   VG   VF   UNC

Green. Front: Palm tree; caravan with man leading four camels; sama'a dhow with sail; oil derrick; outline of UAE coast; string of pearls. Back: Sparrow-hawk; beached boats; city of Khorfakkan in the Emirate of Fujairah. Solid security thread. Watermark: Arabian horse head. Printer: *DE LA RUE*. 166 x 73 mm.

    ☐ a. No date. Signature 1. Prefix ١٧٥ - ١٥.   50   150   600
        Intro: 20.05.1973.
    ☐ as. Specimen.   —   —   325

CBO B6 (P6): **1,000 dirhams** (withdrawn)   VG   VF   UNC

Blue. Front: Palm tree; caravan with man leading four camels; sama'a dhow with sail; oil derrick; outline of UAE coast; string of pearls. Back: Sparrow-hawk; Fort Jahili at Al Ain; Fahidi Fort and minaret of Grand Mosque in Dubai. Solid security thread. Watermark: Arabian horse head. Printer: *DE LA RUE*. 171 x 75 mm.

    ☐ a. No date. Signature 1. Prefix وه - و١.   250   1,250   4,000
        Intro: 03.01.1976.
    ☐ as. Specimen.   —   —   750

United Arab Emirates Central Bank

Established on 10 December 1980 by Union Law No. 10 of 1980, the United Arab Emirates Central Bank (CBA) took over the duties of the United Arab Emirates Currency Board.

For more information, visit www.centralbank.ae.

CBA Signature Varieties

	(Minister of Finance)	(Chairman of Board of Directors)
1	 Sheikh Hamdan bin Rashid al Maktoum	Sheikh Suroor bin Mohamed al-Nahyan
2	 Sheikh Hamdan bin Rashid al Maktoum	 Muhammad Eid al-Muraiki
3	 Sheikh Hamdan bin Rashid al Maktoum	 Khalid Foulathi (2008 - July 2012)
4	 Sheikh Hamdan bin Rashid al Maktoum	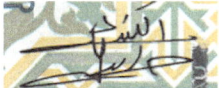 Khalifa al-Kindi (November 2012 - present)

1982 Issues

CBA B2 (P8): **10 dirhams** (withdrawn)   VG   VF   UNC
Green. Front: Coat of arms; traditional dagger (khanjar). Back: Sparrow-hawk; agricultural scene with date palm trees. Solid security thread printed *UAE*. Watermark: Sparrow-hawk head. Printer: Unknown. 147 x 62 mm.

- a. No date. Signature 1. Prefix ١/ج - ٢٢/ج.   FV   25   50
  Intro: 01.09.1982.
- as. Specimen.   —   —   50

CBA B3 (P9): **50 dirhams** (withdrawn)   VG   VF   UNC
Purple. Front: Coat of arms; oryx (antelope) head. Back: Sparrow-hawk; Fort Jahili at Al Ain. Solid security thread printed *UAE*. Watermark: Sparrow-hawk head. Printer: Unknown. 151 x 64 mm.

- a. No date. Signature 1. Prefix ١/ث - ١٠/ث.   25   75   300
  Intro: 20.11.1982.
- as. Diagonal red نموذج overprint; horizontal *SPECIMEN* perforation.   —   —   1,500

CBA B1 (P7): **5 dirhams** (withdrawn)   VG   VF   UNC
Brown. Front: Coat of arms; Blue Souk in Sharjah. Back: Sparrow-hawk; Bay of Khorfakkan in Fujairah; tower. Solid security thread printed *UAE*. Watermark: Sparrow-hawk head. Printer: Unknown. 143 x 60 mm.

- a. No date. Signature 1. Prefix ١/ح - ٣٤/ح.   FV   10   15
  Intro: 01.09.1982.
- as. Specimen.   —   —   50

CBA B4 (P10): 100 dirhams (withdrawn)   VG   VF   UNC
Red. Front: Coat of arms; Fahidi Fort in Dubai. Back: Sparrow-hawk; Trade Centre Tower in Dubai. Solid security thread printed *UAE*. Watermark: Sparrow-hawk head. Printer: Unknown. 155 x 66 mm.

- a. No date. Signature 1. Prefix ١/ت - ٢٢/ت.   30   75   300
  Intro: 20.11.1982.
- as. Specimen.   —   —   100

CBA B5 (P11): 500 dirhams (withdrawn)   VG   VF   UNC
Blue. Front: Coat of arms; sparrow-hawk head. Back: Sparrow-hawk; Jumeirah Mosque in Dubai. Solid security thread printed *UAE*. Watermark: Sparrow-hawk head. Printer: Unknown. 159 x 68 mm.

- a. No date. Signature 1. Prefix ١/ب - ١٧/ب.   300   600   1,500
  Intro: 08.12.1982.
- as. Specimen.   —   —   350

CBA B6 (PNL): 1,000 dirhams   VG   VF   UNC
Purple and brown. Front: Coat of arms; dhala, a traditional coffee pot. Back: Sparrow-hawk; Maqta' watchtower and bridge in Abu Dhabi. Solid security thread printed *UAE*. Watermark: Sparrow-hawk head. Printer: Unknown. 162 x 70 mm.

- p. Diagonal red نموذج overprint on front;   —   —   1,000
  diagonal red *SPECIMEN* overprint on back;
  horizontal *SPECIMEN* perforation; punched.
  No date. Signature 1. Prefix ١/١. Unissued.

1989-1996 Issues

Unlike the preceding issues, these notes have the year in Arabic numerals on the front and Western numerals on the back. Furthermore, the serial number is printed in Arabic and Western numerals on the front.

CBA B7 (P12): 5 dirhams (US$1.35)   VG   VF   UNC
Brown. Front: Coat of arms; Blue Souk in Sharjah. Back: Sparrow-hawk; Bay of Khorfakkan in Fujairah; tower. Solid security thread printed *UAE*. Watermark: Sparrow-hawk head. Signature 2. Printer: Unknown. 143 x 60 mm.

- a. 1993 and ١٤١٤ (AH1414). Sig. 2. Prefix 016 - 066.   3   6   13
  Intro: April 1994.
- b. 1995 and ١٤١٦ (AH1416). Prefix 086 - 326.   FV   FV   5

Replacement notes: Prefix ١/ﺣ.

CBA B8 (P13): **10 dirhams** (US$2.70)   VG   VF   UNC
Green. Front: Coat of arms; traditional dagger (khanjar). Back: Sparrow-hawk; agricultural scene with date palm trees. Solid security thread printed *UAE*. Watermark: Sparrow-hawk head. Printer: Unknown. 147 x 62 mm.

a. 1993 and ١٤١٤ (AH1414). Sig. 2. Prefix 015 - 105. Intro: April 1994.	FV	5	10
b. 1995 and ١٤١٦ (AH1416). Prefix 135 - 295.	FV	10	20

CBA B9 (P14): **50 dirhams** (US$14)   VG   VF   UNC
Purple. Front: Coat of arms; oryx (antelope) head. Back: Sparrow-hawk; Fort Jahili at Al Ain. Windowed security thread with demetalized *UAE 50*. Watermark: Oryx (antelope) head. Printer: Unknown. 151 x 64 mm.

a. 1995 and ١٤١٥ (AH1415). Signature 2. Prefix 014.	FV	35	75
b. 1996 and ١٤١٧ (AH1417). Prefix 054 - 094.	FV	30	65

CBA B10 (P15): **100 dirhams** (US$27)   VG   VF   UNC
Red. Front: Coat of arms; Fahidi Fort in Dubai. Back: Sparrow-hawk; Trade Centre Tower in Dubai. Windowed security thread with demetalized *UAE 100*. Watermark: Sparrow-hawk head. Printer: Unknown. 155 x 66 mm.

a. 1993 and ١٤١٤ (AH1414). Sig. 2. Prefix 013 - 023. Intro: April 1994.	FV	100	200
b. 1995 and ١٤١٦ (AH1416). Prefix 123 - 223.	FV	50	100

CBA B11 (P16): **200 dirhams** (US$54)   VG   VF   UNC
Brown. Front: Coat of arms; Sheikh Zayed Sports City and Judicial Department and Sharia Court buildings in Abu Dhabi. Back: Sparrow-hawk; UAE Central Bank headquarters building in Abu Dhabi. Windowed security thread. Watermark: Sparrow-hawk head. Printer: Unknown. 159 x 68 mm.

a. 1989 and ١٤١٠ (AH1410). Sig. 1. Prefix 1A - 16A. Intro: 30.11.1989.	FV	FV	120
as. Diagonal red نموذج overprint.	—	—	1,500

1997-2007 Issues

These notes are like the preceding issues, but without the large denomination over the watermark area at front left.

CBA B12 (P17): **500 dirhams** (US$136)   VG   VF   UNC

Violet. Front: Coat of arms; sparrow-hawk head. Back: Sparrow-hawk; Jumeirah Mosque in Dubai. Windowed security thread with demetalized *UAE 500*. Watermark: Sparrow-hawk head. Printer: Unknown. 159 x 68 mm.

- ☐ a. 1993 and ١٤١٤ (AH1414). Sig. 2. Prefix 063 - 133.   FV   FV   450
Intro: April 1994.

Like CBA B13, but without foil tower at left front and different colored design elements.

CBA B13 (P18): **500 dirhams** (US$136)   VG   VF   UNC

Violet. Front: Foil overprint of crenellated tower over denomination; coat of arms; sparrow-hawk head. Back: Sparrow-hawk; Jumeirah Mosque in Dubai. Windowed security thread with demetalized *UAE 500*. Watermark: Sparrow-hawk head. Printer: Unknown. 159 x 68 mm.

- ☐ a. 1996 and ١٤١٦ (AH1416). Sig. 2. Prefix 032 - 062.   FV   FV   600

Like CBA B12, but with foil tower at left front and different colored design elements.

CBA B14 (P19 & P26): **5 dirhams** (US$1.35)   VG   VF   UNC

Brown. Front: Coat of arms; Blue Souk in Sharjah. Back: Sparrow-hawk; Bay of Khorfakkan in Fujairah; tower. Solid security thread with demetalized *UAE 5*. Watermark: Sparrow-hawk head. Printer: Unknown. 143 x 60 mm.

- ☐ a. 2000 and ١٤٢٠ (AH1420). Sig. 2. Prefix 006 - 096.   FV   FV   6
- ☐ b. 2001 and ١٤٢٢ (AH1422). Prefix 116 - 366.   FV   FV   6
- ☐ c. 2004 and ١٤٢٥ (AH1425). Prefix 006 - 246.   FV   FV   5.50
Watermark: Electrotype *5* and coffee pot added.
- ☐ d. 2007 and ١٤٢٨ (AH1428). Prefix 416 - 886.   FV   FV   3.50

CBA B15 (P20 & P27): **10 dirhams** (US$2.70)   VG   VF   UNC

Green. Front: Coat of arms; traditional dagger (khanjar). Back: Sparrow-hawk; agricultural scene with date palm trees. Solid security thread with demetalized *UAE 10*. Watermark: Sparrow-hawk head. Printer: Unknown. 147 x 62 mm.

- ☐ a. 1998 and ١٤١٩ (AH1419). Sig. 2. Prefix 005 - 245.   FV   FV   7.50
- ☐ b. 2001 and ١٤٢٢ (AH1422). Prefix 285 - 395.   FV   FV   7
- ☐ c. 2004 and ١٤٢٥ (AH1425). Prefix 005 - 235.   FV   FV   7
Watermark: Electrotype *10* and coffee pot added.
- ☐ d. 2007 and ١٤٢٨ (AH1428). Prefix 355 - 895.   FV   FV   6

CBA B16 (P21 & P28): **20 dirhams** (US$5.45)　　　VG　VF　UNC

Blue. Front: Coat of arms; Dubai Creek Golf & Yacht Club building. Back: Sparrow-hawk; sama'a dhow with sail. Windowed security thread with demetalized *UAE 20*. Watermark: Sparrow-hawk head. Printer: Unknown. 150 x 63 mm.

☐ a. 1997 and ١٤١٨ (AH1418). Sig. 2. Prefix 007 -057. Intro: 06.12.1998.　FV　FV　17

☐ b. 2000 and ١٤٢٠ (AH1420). Prefix 067 - 177.　FV　FV　20

☐ c. 2007 and ١٤٢٨ (AH1428). Prefix 197 - 317. Watermark: Electrotype *20* and coffee pot added.　FV　FV　11

☐ as. Diagonal *SPECIMEN* perforation.　—　—　—

Replacement notes: Serial number starts with 957.

CBA B17 (P22): **50 dirhams** (US$14)　　　VG　VF　UNC

Purple. Front: Coat of arms; oryx (antelope) head. Back: Sparrow-hawk; Fort Jahili at Al Ain. Windowed security thread with demetalized *UAE 50*. Watermark: Sparrow-hawk head. Printer: Unknown. 151 x 64 mm.

☐ a. 1998 and ١٤١٩ (AH1419). Sig. 2. Prefix 004 - 024.　FV　FV　40

CBA B18 (P23): **100 dirhams** (US$27)　　　VG　VF　UNC

Red. Front: Coat of arms; Fahidi Fort in Dubai. Back: Sparrow-hawk; Trade Centre Tower in Dubai. Windowed security thread with demetalized *UAE 100*. Watermark: Sparrow-hawk head. Printer: Unknown. 155 x 66 mm.

☐ a. 1998 and ١٤١٩ (AH1419). Sig. 2. Prefix 003 - 053.　FV　FV　100

CBA B19 (P24): **500 dirhams** (US$136)　　　VG　VF　UNC

Violet. Front: Coat of arms; sparrow-hawk head. Back: Sparrow-hawk; Jumeirah Mosque in Dubai. Holographic stripe. Windowed security thread with demetalized *UAE 500*. Watermark: Sparrow-hawk head. Printer: Unknown. 159 x 68 mm.

☐ a. 1998 and ١٤١٩ (AH1419). Sig. 2. Prefix 002 - 052.　FV　FV　300

☐ b. 2000 and ١٤٢٠ (AH1420). Prefix 102.　FV　FV　275

CBA B20 (P25): **1,000 dirhams** (US$272) VG VF UNC

Brown. Front: Sparrow-hawk head as registration device; coat of arms; Al Hosn Palace (White Fort) in Abu Dhabi. Back: Sparrow-hawk; Abu Dhabi skyline with Corniche; sparrow-hawk head. Holographic stripe. Windowed security thread with demetalized *UAE 1000*. Watermark: Sparrow-hawk head. Printer: Unknown. 163 x 70 mm.

☐ a. 1998 and ١٤١٩ (AH1419). Sig. 2. Prefix 001 - 021. FV FV 600
Intro: 06.12.1998.
☐ b. 2000 and ١٤٢٠ (AH1420). Prefix 031 - 101. FV FV 500

2003-2008 Issues

These notes are like the preceding issues, but with electrotype denomination and coffee pot added to all watermarks, a silver foil stamp added to the 50- and 100-dirham notes, and denominations added to the holographic stripes on the 500- and 1,000-dirham notes.

CBA B21 (P29): **50 dirhams** (US$14) VG VF UNC

Purple. Front: Coat of arms; oryx (antelope) head with silver foil stamp. Back: Sparrow-hawk; Fort Jahili at Al Ain. Windowed security thread with demetalized *UAE 50*. Watermark: Sparrow-hawk head with electrotype *50* and coffee pot. Printer: Unknown. 151 x 64 mm.

☐ a. 2004 and ١٤٢٥ (AH1425). Sig. 2. Prefix 004 - 014. FV FV 40
☐ b. 2006 and ١٤٢٧ (AH1427). Prefix 114 - 184. FV FV 30
☐ c. 2008 and ١٤٢٩ (AH1429). Prefix 204 - 364. FV FV 25

CBA B22 (P30): **100 dirhams** (US$27) VG VF UNC

Red. Front: Coat of arms; Fahidi Fort in Dubai with silver foil stamp of castle tower. Back: Sparrow-hawk; Trade Centre Tower in Dubai. Windowed security thread with demetalized *UAE 100*. Watermark: Sparrow-hawk head with electrotype *100* and coffee pot. Printer: Unknown. 155 x 66 mm.

☐ a. 2003 and ١٤٢٣ (AH1423). Sig. 2. Prefix 003 - 163. FV FV 80
☐ b. 2004 and ١٤٢٥ (AH1425). Prefix 233 - 383. FV 40 85
☐ c. 2006 and ١٤٢٧ (AH1427). Prefix 613 - 643. FV FV 50

CBA B23 (P31): **200 dirhams** (US$54) VG VF UNC

Tan and gold. Front: Coat of arms; Sheikh Zayed Sports City and Judicial Department and Sharia Court buildings in Abu Dhabi. Back: Sparrow-hawk; UAE Central Bank headquarters building in Abu Dhabi. Holographic stripe with denomination. Windowed security thread. Watermark: Sparrow-hawk head with electrotype *200* and coffee pot. Printer: Unknown. 159 x 68 mm.

☐ a. 2004 and ١٤٢٥ (AH1425). Sig. 2. Prefix 008 - 088. FV FV 100
Intro: 27.05.2008.

2008-2013 Issues

These notes are like the preceding issues, but with new signatures, new dates, and the new coat of arms which was adopted on 22 March 2008.

The coat of arms on older notes has a dhow on the sparrow-hawk's chest (left), whereas on newer notes (right) there is the UAE flag surrounded by stars representing the seven emirates of the federation.

CBA B24 (P24c & P32): **500 dirhams** (US$136)   VG   VF   UNC

Violet. Front: Coat of arms; sparrow-hawk head. Back: Sparrow-hawk; Jumeirah Mosque in Dubai. Holographic stripe with denomination. Windowed security thread with demetalized *UAE 500*. Watermark: Sparrow-hawk head with electrotype *500* and coffee pot. Printer: Unknown. 159 x 68 mm.

		VG	VF	UNC
a.	2004 and ١٤٢٤ (AH1424). Sig. 2. Prefix 162 - 192.	FV	FV	400
b.	2006 and ١٤٢٧ (AH1427). Prefix 322.	FV	FV	300
c.	2008 and ١٤٢٩ (AH1429). Prefix 512 - 862.	FV	FV	250

CBA B25 (P33): **1,000 dirhams** (US$272)   VG   VF   UNC

Brown. Front: Sparrow-hawk head as registration device; coat of arms; Al Hosn Palace (White Fort) in Abu Dhabi. Back: Sparrow-hawk; Abu Dhabi skyline with Corniche; sparrow-hawk head. Holographic stripe with denomination. Windowed security thread with demetalized *UAE 1000*. Watermark: Sparrow-hawk head with electrotype *1000* and coffee pot. Printer: Unknown. 163 x 70 mm.

		VG	VF	UNC
a.	2006 and ١٤٢٧ (AH1427). Sig. 2. Prefix 131 - 181.	FV	FV	400

CBA B26 (P26): **5 dirhams** (US$1.35)   VG   VF   UNC

Brown. Front: Coat of arms; Blue Souk in Sharjah. Back: Sparrow-hawk; Bay of Khorfakkan in Fujairah; tower. Solid security thread with demetalized *UAE 5*. Watermark: Sparrow-hawk head. Printer: Unknown. 143 x 60 mm.

		VG	VF	UNC
a.	2009 and ١٤٣٠ (AH1430). Signature 3. Horizontal left serial number. Prefix 000 - 090.	FV	FV	3
b.	2013 and ١٤٣٤ (AH1434). Signature 4. Vertical left serial number. Prefix 092 - 095.	FV	FV	3

United Arab Emirates 2008-2013 Issues

CBA B27 (P27): **10 dirhams** (US$2.70) VG VF UNC

Green. Front: Coat of arms; traditional dagger (khanjar). Back: Sparrow-hawk; agricultural scene with date palm trees. Solid security thread with demetalized *UAE 10*. Watermark: Sparrow-hawk head with electrotype *10* and coffee pot. Printer: Unknown. 147 x 62 mm.

- a. 2009 and ١٤٣٠ (AH1430). Sig. 3. Prefix 000 - 003.   FV FV 5.50
- b. 2013 and ١٤٣٤ (AH1434). Sig. 4. Prefix 091. Vertical left serial number.   FV FV 5.50

CBA B28 (P28): **20 dirhams** (US$5.45) VG VF UNC

Blue. Front: Coat of arms; Dubai Creek Golf & Yacht Club building. Back: Sparrow-hawk; dhow with sail. Windowed security thread with demetalized *UAE 20*. Watermark: Sparrow-hawk head with electrotype *20* and coffee pot. Printer: Unknown. 150 x 63 mm.

- a. 2009 and ١٤٣٠ (AH1430). Sig. 3. Prefix 000 - 023.   FV FV 11
- b. 2013 and ١٤٣٤ (AH1434). Sig. 4. Prefix 024.   FV FV 11

CBA B29 (PNL): **100 dirhams** (US$27) VG VF UNC

Red. Front: Coat of arms; Fahidi Fort in Dubai with silver foil stamp of castle tower. Back: Sparrow-hawk; Trade Centre Tower in Dubai. Windowed security thread with demetalized *UAE 100*. Watermark: Sparrow-hawk head with electrotype *100* and coffee pot. Printer: Unknown. 155 x 66 mm.

- a. 2008 and ١٤٢٩ (AH1429). Sig. 3. Prefix 000 - 079.   FV FV 40

CBA B30 (P31): **200 dirhams** (US$54) VG VF UNC

Tan and gold. Front: Sparrow-hawk head as registration device; coat of arms; Sheikh Zayed Sports City and Judicial Department and Sharia Court buildings in Abu Dhabi. Back: Sparrow-hawk; UAE Central Bank headquarters building in Abu Dhabi; sparrow-hawk head. Holographic stripe with denomination. Windowed security thread. Watermark: Sparrow-hawk head with electrotype *200* and coffee pot. Printer: Unknown. 159 x 68 mm.

- a. 2008 and ١٤٢٩ (AH1429). Sig. 3. Prefix 000 - 038.   FV FV 80

CBA B31 (P33): **1,000 dirhams** (US$272)   VG   VF   UNC

Brown. Front: Sparrow-hawk head as registration device; coat of arms; Al Hosn Palace (White Fort) in Abu Dhabi. Back: Sparrow-hawk; Abu Dhabi skyline with Corniche; sparrow-hawk head. Holographic stripe with denomination. Windowed security thread with demetalized *UAE 1000*. Watermark: Sparrow-hawk head with electrotype *1000* and coffee pot. Printer: Unknown. 163 x 70 mm.

    ☐   a.   2008 and ١٤٢٩ (AH1429). Sig. 3. Prefix 000 - 024.   FV   FV   400

2011 Issues

This note is like the preceding issues, but with a 3-mm wide, color-shifting windowed security thread with demetalized *UAE 50*, and Omron rings added to front and back.

CBA B33 (P29): **50 dirhams** (US$14)   VG   VF   UNC

Purple. Front: Coat of arms; oryx (antelope) head with silver foil stamp. Back: Sparrow-hawk; Fort Jahili at Al Ain. 3-mm wide, color-shifting windowed security thread with demetalized *UAE 50*. Watermark: Sparrow-hawk head with electrotype *50* and coffee pot. Printer: Unknown. 151 x 64 mm.

    ☐   a.   2011 and ١٤٣٢ (AH1432). Sig. 3. Prefix 000 - 161.   FV   FV   25
           Intro: 23.07.2012.

This note is like the preceding issues, but with the holographic stripe at right front replaced by a varifeye thread.

CBA B32 (P32): **500 dirhams** (US$136)   VG   VF   UNC

Violet. Front: Coat of arms; sparrow-hawk head. Back: Sparrow-hawk; Jumeirah Mosque in Dubai. varifeye thread and 3-mm wide windowed security thread with demetalized *UAE 500*. Watermark: Sparrow-hawk head with electrotype *500* and coffee pot. Printer: (G&D). 159 x 68 mm.

    ☐   a.   2011 and ١٤٣٢ (AH1432). Sig. 3. Prefix 001 - 371.   FV   FV   200
           Intro: 29.11.2011.

2012 Issues

These notes are like the preceding issues, but with a 3-mm wide, magenta-to-gold color-shifting windowed security thread and green-to-blue OVI coat of arms.

CBA B34 (PNL): **100 dirhams** (US$27)   VG   VF   UNC

Red. Front: OVI coat of arms; Fahidi Fort in Dubai with silver foil stamp of castle tower. Back: Sparrow-hawk; Trade Centre Tower in Dubai. 3-mm wide windowed security thread with demetalized *UAE 100*. Watermark: Sparrow-hawk head with electrotype *100* and coffee pot. Printer: Unknown. 155 x 66 mm.

    ☐   a.   2012 and ١٤٢٩ (AH1429). Sig. 3. Prefix 112 - 115.   FV   FV   40
           Intro: 02.02.2013.

CBA B35 (P33): **1,000 dirhams** (US$272) VG VF UNC
Brown. Front: Sparrow-hawk head as registration device; OVI coat of arms; Al Hosn Palace (White Fort) in Abu Dhabi. Back: Sparrow-hawk; Abu Dhabi skyline with Corniche; sparrow-hawk head. Holographic stripe with denomination. 3-mm wide windowed security thread with demetalized *UAE 1000*. Watermark: Sparrow-hawk head with electrotype *1000* and coffee pot. Printer: Unknown. 163 x 70 mm.

 ☐ a. 2012 and ١٤٢٩ (AH1429). Sig. 3. Prefix 026 - 034. FV FV 400
   Intro: 02.02.2013.

Looking Forward

According to a GulfNews.com article dated 12 July 2014, the board of directors of the Central Bank of the UAE recently instructed that necessary actions be taken to reprint all denominations of banknotes using Braille characters so that they will be readable by the visually impaired.

Acknowledgements

This chapter was compiled with the generous assistance of Sejin Ahn, Abdullah Beydoun (beydoun_co@hotmail.com), Ricardo Castedo, Amal Mehilba, Alhousani Mohammed, David Murcek (www.themonetaryunit.com), Wally Myers, Rafal Nogowczyk, Michael Reissner, Ibrahim Salem, Amirali Somji, Bill Stubkjaer, Peter Symes, Christoph Thomas, Christof Zellweger, and others.

Sources

Cuhaj, George S. *Standard Catalog of World Paper Money, Modern Issues, 1961-Present*. 20th edition. 2014. ISBN 978-1-4402-4037-9. Krause Publications (www.krausebooks.com), 700 East State St., Iola, WI, 54990-0001.

Symes, Peter. *The Bank Notes of the United Arab Emirates*. 2004. David White, P.O. Box 95, Flinders Lane, Victoria 8009, Australia.

Symes, Peter. Reference Site for Islamic Banknotes (www.islamicbanknotes.com).

Share Your Input, Info, and Images

This catalog is believed to be complete and correct as of the time of publication. Prices and face values were last updated 3 June 2011. Please report errors or omissions so that corrections may be made. If you can more precisely identify the name or location of anything depicted on a note, please share that information. Furthermore, if you own an unlisted type or variety, please submit scans of the front and back of the note so that it can be documented. Scans should be 300 dots per inch, 100% actual size, 24-bit color, saved as *uncompressed* JPEG files, and sent to owen@banknotenews.com. Be sure to fully describe all attributes of the note which are not apparent upon visual inspection of the images alone, such as physical dimension, watermark, and security thread.

Upper Senegal and Niger

Monetary System
1 franc = 100 centimes

French Months of the Year

Janvier (January)	Février (February)	Mars (March)
Avril (April)	Mai (May)	Juin (June)
Juillet (July)	Août (August)	Septembre (September)
Octobre (October)	Novembre (November)	Décembre (December)

Gouvernement Général de l'A.O.F. - Haut-Sénégal - Niger
(General Government of French West Africa - Upper Senegal and Niger)

In 1895 France established Afrique Occidentale Française (French West Africa), a federation of eight territories: Côte d'Ivoire (Ivory Coast), Dahomey (now Benin), French Guinea, French Sudan (now Mali), Mauritania, Niger, Senegal, and Upper Volta (now Burkina Faso).

GGAO Signature Varieties

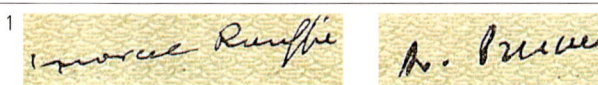

1
Le Trésorier-Payeur
(Paymaster)
Marcel Rouffle

Le Lt-Gouverneur
(Lieutenant Governor)
Louis Periquet

1917 Emergency Issues

Banque du Sénégal banknotes were in use in French West Africa until 1901 when the Banque de l'Afrique Occidentale was established and began issuing its own notes. Due to the severe shortage of coinage in the colonies due to World War I, on 11 February 1917 a special decree was passed allowing for the issuance of 50-centime, 1-franc, and 2-franc emergency notes, although not all denominations were printed for all of the colonies (for example, no 1- or 2-franc notes were issued for Upper Senegal and Niger).

The design of the emergency notes depicted a French coin corresponding to the denomination on the front, and an excerpt of the decree in French on the back. Each colony issued its own notes, distinguished by color, the name of the colony printed below *GOUVERNEMENT GÉNÉRAL DE L'A.O.F.,* and signatures of the colony's paymaster and lieutenant governor.

 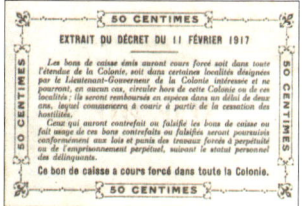

GGAO B1 (P1ct): 50 centimes — VG VF UNC
Dark brown and gray-green. Front: 50-centime coin. Back: Text. No security thread. Watermark: Laurel leaf pattern. Printer: (Imp. Chaix - Paris). 82 x 55 mm.
☐ p. 11 FÉVRIER 1917. Unissued.   750   1,500   4,200

 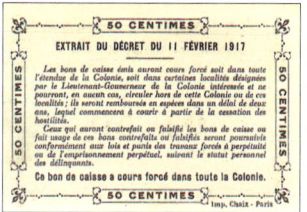

GGAO B2 (P1): 50 centimes — VG VF UNC
Brown and tan. Front: 50-centime coin. Back: Text. No security thread. Watermark: Laurel leaf pattern. Printer: *Imp. Chaix - Paris.* 82 x 55 mm.
☐ a. 11 FÉVRIER 1917. Signature 1. Intro: 1919.   1,000   2,500   6,000

Looking Forward
For later issues, see French Sudan.

Acknowledgements
This chapter was compiled with the generous assistance of Mark Irwin, Laurence Pope, and others.

Sources
Burson, Weldon. "Banknotes of Mali." *IBNS Journal.* Volume 48 Number 2. p.28.

Cuhaj, George S. *Standard Catalog of World Paper Money, General Issues, 1368-1960.* 14th edition. 2012. ISBN 978-1-4402-3090-5. Krause Publications (www.krausebooks.com), 700 East State St., Iola, WI, 54990-0001.

Share Your Input, Info, and Images
This catalog is believed to be complete and correct as of the time of publication. Prices and face values were last updated 2 August 2014. Please report errors or omissions so that corrections may be made. If you can more precisely identify the name or location of anything depicted on a note, please share that information. Furthermore, if you own an unlisted type or variety, please submit scans of the front and back of the note so that it can be documented. Scans should be 300 dots per inch, 100% actual size, 24-bit color, saved as *uncompressed* JPEG files, and sent to owen@banknotenews.com. Be sure to fully describe all attributes of the note which are not apparent upon visual inspection of the images alone, such as physical dimension, watermark, and security thread.

Uruguay

Earlier Issues

Before the establishment of the Banco Central del Uruguay, notes were issued by various organizations. These notes will be added to this chapter in the future.

Monetary System

23.06.1862: 1 uruguayan peso (UYP) = 100 centésimos
01.07.1975: 1 nuevo peso (UYN) = 1,000 pesos
01.03.1993: 1 peso uruguayo (UYU) = 1,000 nuevos pesos

Spanish Months of the Year

Enero (January)	Febrero (February)	Marzo (March)
Abril (April)	Mayo (May)	Junio (June)
Julio (July)	Agosto (August)	Septiembre (September)
Octubre (October)	Noviembre (November)	Diciembre (December)

Banco Central del Uruguay (Central Bank of Uruguay)

The Banco Central del Uruguay (BCU) was created by law 13594 of 6 July 1967 and decree on 12 September 1967. For more information, visit www.bcu.gub.uy.

BCU Signature Varieties

#	Gerente General	Secretario General	Presidente
1	 Mario Buchelli	 Juan César Pacchiotti	 Enrique V. Inglesias (1967 - 1968)
2	Mario Buchelli	Juan César Pacchiotti	 Vicepresidente Juan M. Bracco
3	 p. Gerente General Alfredo Castelli	Juan César Pacchiotti	Vicepresidente Juan M. Bracco
4	 p. Gerente General Alfredo Castelli	Juan César Pacchiotti	Enrique V. Inglesias (1967 - 1968)
5	 p. Gerente General Alfredo Castelli	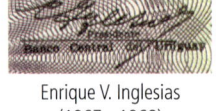 Juan César Pacchiotti	 Vicepresidente José L. Guntín Garcia

BCU Signature Varieties

#	Gerente General	Secretario General	Presidente
6	 Nilo Márquez	 Juan César Pacchiotti	 Carlos Sanguinetti (1968 - 1970)
*			Armando Malet (1970)
7	 Nilo Márquez	 Juan César Pacchiotti	 Vicepresidente José L. Guntín Garcia
8	 p. Gerente General Alfredo Castelli	 Juan César Pacchiotti	 Nilo Márquez (1970 - 1971)
9	 Co-Gerente General Walter Garrido	 Juan César Pacchiotti	 Jorge Echeverría Leunda (1971 - 1972)
10	Co-Gerente General Walter Garrido	 Juan César Pacchiotti	 Vicepresidente Raúl Acosta y Lara
11	 Co-Gerente General Walter Garrido	 Juan César Pacchiotti	 Juan Pedro Amestoy (1972 - 1973)
12	 Co-Gerente General Walter Garrido	 Juan César Pacchiotti	 Carlos Ricchi (1973 - 1974)
13	 William Rosso	 Juan César Pacchiotti	 Carlos Ricchi (1973 - 1974)
14a	 William Rosso	 Juan César Pacchiotti (with stroke)	 José Gil Díaz (1974 - 1982)
14b	William Rosso	 Juan César Pacchiotti (without stroke)	 José Gil Díaz (1974 - 1982)

BCU Signature Varieties

	Gerente General	Secretario General	Presidente
15		Juan César Pacchiotti	José Gil Díaz (1974 - 1982)
16	Carlos A. Koncke	Juan César Pacchiotti	José Gil Díaz (1974 - 1982)
17	Jorge Sambarino	Juan César Pacchiotti	José María Puppo (1982 - 1984)
18	Jorge Sambarino	Juan César Pacchiotti	Juan Carlos Protasi (1984 - 1985)
19a	Jorge Sambarino	Juan César Pacchiotti	Ricardo Pascale (1985 - 1990)
19b	Jorge Sambarino	Juan César Pacchiotti	Ricardo Pascale (1985 - 1990)
19c	Jorge Sambarino	Juan César Pacchiotti	Ricardo Pascale (1985 - 1990)
19d	Jorge Sambarino	Juan César Pacchiotti	Ricardo Pascale (1985 - 1990)
19e	Jorge Sambarino	Juan César Pacchiotti	Ricardo Pascale (1985 - 1990)
20	Juan Olascoaga	Juan César Pacchiotti	Ramón Díaz (1990 - 1993)
21	Juan Olascoaga	Aureliano Berro	Enrique Braga (1993 - 1995)

BCU Signature Varieties

	Gerente General	Secretario General	Presidente
22	Hugo Lacurcia	Aureliano Berro	Enrique Braga (1993 - 1995)
23a	Hugo Lacurcia	Aureliano Berro	Ricardo Pascale (1995)
23b	Hugo Lacurcia	Aureliano Berro	Ricardo Pascale (1995)
24a	Gualberto de León	Aureliano Berro	Humberto Capote (1995 - 2000)
24b	Gualberto de León	Aureliano Berro	Humberto Capote (1995 - 2000)
25	Gualberto de León	Aureliano Berro	César Rodríquez Batlle (2000 - 2002)
26	Gualberto de León	Aureliano Berro	Julio de Brun (2002 - 2005)
27	Gualberto de León	Aureliano Berro	Walter Cancela (2005 - 2008)
28		Aureliano Berro	Walter Cancela (2005 - 2008)
29		Aureliano Berro	Mario Bergara (2008 - 10.01.2014)
30		Elizabeth Sonia Oria	Mario Bergara (2008 - 10.01.2014)
*			Alberto Graña (10.01.2014 - present)

* This official is not known to have signed any notes.

1967 Provisional Issues

These provisional notes are from series D (dated 1939) of the previous issuer, the Banco de la República Oriental del Uruguay, but have been overprinted with Banco Central del Uruguay signature titles.

BCU B1 (P42): **10 pesos**   VG   VF   UNC
Purple. Front: Coat of arms; José Gervasio Artigas. Back: Sculptor José Belloni's monument "La Carreta" (The Ox Wagon) consisting of farmer on horseback with ox-drawn wagon in Montevideo. Solid security thread. Watermark: None. Printer: *THOMAS DE LA RUE & CO. LTD*. 147 x 73 mm.

☐ a.   2 DE ENERO DE 1939. Sig. 1. Serie D. Intro: 1967.   1.25   5   20
      Banco Central de la República below all titles.
☐ b.   *Banco Central del Uruguay* below all titles.   2.50   10   40

New signatures on P37.

BCU B2 (P42A): **50 pesos**   VG   VF   UNC
Blue and brown. Front: Coat of arms; allegorical warrior with spear wearing helmet with bull, castle tower, horse, and scales; flag in background. Back: Juan Antonio Lavalleja and soldiers with rifles and swords surrounding flag at Agraciada Beach on 19 April 1825, from Juan Manuel Blanes's painting "Juramento de los Treinta y Tres Orientales" (Oath of the 33 Easterners). Solid security thread. Watermark: José Gervasio Artigas. Printer: *THOMAS DE LA RUE & CO. LTD*. 154 x 76 mm.

☐ a.   2 DE ENERO DE 1939. Serie D. Intro: 1967.   2.50   10   40
      Signature 1.
      Banco Central del Uruguay below all titles.
☐ b.   Signature 4.   2.50   10   40
      Banco Central del Uruguay below 2 titles at right.

New signatures on P38.

BCU B3 (P43): **100 pesos**   VG   VF   UNC

Red and brown. Front: Coat of arms; allegorical woman with constitution and scales of justice. Back: Crowd of people amid flags of Brazil, Argentina, Paraguay, and UK Merchant Navy, on the promulgation of the constitution on 18 July 1830 in Plaza Matriz in front of the cabildo, Montevideo from Juan Manuel Blanes's painting, "Boceto para la Jura de la Constitución de 1830" (Sketch for Constitution Day 1830). Solid security thread. Watermark: José Gervasio Artigas. Printer: *THOMAS DE LA RUE & CO. LTD.* 162 x 80 mm.

- ☐ a. 2 DE ENERO DE 1939. Serie D. Intro: 1967.   2.50   10   45
  Signature 1.
  w/ *Banco Central del Uruguay* below all titles.
- ☐ b. w/o *Banco Central del Uruguay* below any titles.   2.50   10   45
- ☐ c. Signature 2.   2.50   10   45
  w/ *Banco Central del Uruguay* below all titles.
- ☐ d. Signature 4.   2.50   10   45
  Banco Central del Uruguay below 2 titles at right.
- ☐ e. *Banco Central del Uruguay* below all titles.   2.50   10   45
- ☐ f. Signature 5.   2.50   10   45
  Banco Central del Uruguay below 2 titles at left.
- ☐ g. Signature 6.   2.50   10   45
  Banco Central del Uruguay title below all titles.

New signatures on P39.

BCU B4 (P44): **500 pesos**   VG   VF   UNC

Green and blue. Front: Coat of arms; allegorical industrial man with airplane, gear, and factories, from José Luis Zorrilla de San Martín's painting. Back: Sheep, bull, horse, farmers with bale and sheaves of wheat, nude boy reading book to seated woman, ship and buildings in background, from Pío Collivadino's painting. Solid security thread. Watermark: José Gervasio Artigas. Printer: *THOMAS DE LA RUE & CO. LTD.* 169 x 85 mm.

- ☐ a. 2 DE ENERO DE 1939. Sig. 1. Serie D. Intro: 1967.   4   12   50
  7- or 8-digit serial number.
  Banco Central de la República below all titles.
- ☐ b. 8-digit serial number.   5   15   60
  Banco Central del Uruguay below all titles.

New signatures on P40.

BCU B5 (P45): **1,000 pesos**   VG   VF   UNC

Purple. Front: Coat of arms; José Gervasio Artigas. Back: José Gervasio Artigas on horseback overlooking cliff near water, from Carlos María Herrera's painting "Artigas en el Hervidero." Solid security thread. Watermark: José Gervasio Artigas. Printer: *THOMAS DE LA RUE & CO. LTD.* 178 x 88 mm.

- ☐ a. 2 DE ENERO DE 1939. Sig. 1. Serie D. Intro: 1967.   10   40   120
  Banco Central de la República below all titles.
- ☐ as. Horizontal *SPECIMEN OF NO VALUE* perf.   —   —   —

New signatures on P41.

1967 Issues

These are the first notes prepared specifically for the Banco Central del Uruguay. The portrait on the front of these notes is a detail taken from the painting "Artigas en la Ciudadela" (Artigas in the Citadel) by artist Juan Manuel Blanes.

BCU B6 (P46): **50 pesos**   VG   VF   UNC

Blue, violet, and green. Front: Coat of arms; José Gervasio Artigas. Back: Juan Antonio Lavalleja and soldiers with rifles and swords surrounding flag at Agraciada Beach on 19 April 1825, from Juan Manuel Blanes's painting "Juramento de los Treinta y Tres Orientales" (Oath of the 33 Easterners). Solid security thread with printed CINCUENTA. Watermark: None. Printer: THOMAS DE LA RUE & COMPANY, LIMITED. 155 x 69 mm.

☐	a.	No date. Serie A. Intro: 1967. Signature 6.	0.25	1.25	5
☐	b.	Signature 7.	0.25	1.25	5
☐	c.	Signature 11.	0.25	1	4
☐	d.	Signature 14b.	0.25	1	4
☐	s.	Diagonal red MUESTRA SIN VALOR overprint; horizontal black # overprint at lower right	—	—	60

BCU B7 (P47): **100 pesos**   VG   VF   UNC

Red, pink, and yellow. Front: Coat of arms; José Gervasio Artigas. Back: José Gervasio Artigas standing at table surrounded by standing and seated men at the 1813 Congress of Tres Cruces, from Pedro Blanes Viale's painting "Las Instrucciones del Año XIII." Solid security thread with printed CIEN. Watermark: None. Printer: THOMAS DE LA RUE & COMPANY, LIMITED. 155 x 69 mm.

☐	a.	No date. Serie A. Intro: 1967. Signature 6.	0.25	1.25	5
☐	b.	Signature 7.	0.25	1.25	5
☐	c.	Signature 8.	0.25	1.25	5
☐	d.	Signature 9.	0.25	1	4
☐	e.	Signature 11.	0.25	1	4
☐	f.	Signature 12.	0.25	1	4
☐	g.	Signature 13.	0.25	1	4
☐	h1.	Signature 14a.	0.25	1	4
☐	h2.	Signature 14b.	0.25	1	4
☐	p.	Horizontal black PROOF Nº # overprint at lower left.	—	—	35
☐	s.	Diagonal black MUESTRA SIN VALOR overprint; horizontal black No # overprint at lower right.	—	—	80

BCU B7.5 (PNL): **100 pesos**   VG   VF   UNC

Red, pink, and yellow. Front: Coat of arms; José Gervasio Artigas. Back: José Gervasio Artigas standing at table surrounded by standing and seated men at the 1813 Congress of Tres Cruces, from Pedro Blanes Viale's painting "Las Instrucciones del Año XIII." Solid security thread with printed CIEN. Watermark: None. Printer: THOMAS DE LA RUE & COMPANY, LIMITED. 155 x 69 mm.

☐	p.	Two diagonal SIN VALOR perforations; horizontal black PROOF Nº # ovpt at lower left.	—	—	—

Like BCU B7, but with issuer name as EL BANCO CENTRAL DE LA REPÚBLICA ORIENTAL DEL URUGUAY on front and back.

BCU B8 (P48): **500 pesos**   VG   VF   UNC

Green, blue, and orange. Front: José Gervasio Artigas. Back: Rincón del Bonete Hydroelectric Dam on Río Negro. Solid security thread. Watermark: Coat of arms and *500* pattern. Printer: *THOMAS DE LA RUE & COMPANY, LIMITED.* 155 x 69 mm.

			VG	VF	UNC
☐	a.	No date. Serie A. Intro: 1967. Signature 9.	0.75	3	12
☐	b.	Signature 10.	0.75	3	12
☐	c.	Signature 11.	0.50	2.50	10
☐	d.	Signature 12.	0.50	2.50	10
☐	e.	Signature 13.	0.50	2.50	10
☐	f1.	Signature 14a.	0.50	2.50	10
☐	f2.	Signature 14b.	0.50	2.50	10
☐	p.	Horizontal black *PROOF Nº #* overprint at lower left.	—	—	50
☐	s.	Diagonal red *MUESTRA SIN VALOR* overprint; horizontal black *No #* overprint at lower right.	—	—	100

BCU B8.5 (PNL): **500 pesos**   VG   VF   UNC

Green, blue, and orange. Front: José Gervasio Artigas. Back: Rincón del Bonete Hydroelectric Dam on Río Negro. Solid security thread. Watermark: Coat of arms and *500* pattern. Printer: *THOMAS DE LA RUE & COMPANY, LIMITED.* 155 x 69 mm.

☐	p.	Two diagonal *SIN VALOR* perforations; horizontal black *PROOF Nº #* ovpt at lower left.	—	—	—

Like BCU B8, but with issuer name as *EL BANCO CENTRAL DE LA REPÚBLICA ORIENTAL DEL URUGUAY* on front and back.

BCU B9 (P49): **1,000 pesos**   VG   VF   UNC

Purple and green. Front: José Gervasio Artigas. Back: Palacio Legislativo (Legistlative Palace) building in Montevideo. Solid security thread. Watermark: Coat of arms and *1000* pattern. Printer: *THOMAS DE LA RUE & COMPANY, LIMITED.* 155 x 69 mm.

			VG	VF	UNC
☐	a.	No date. Serie A. Intro: 1967. Signature 1. w/ *Banco Central del Uruguay* below all titles.	4	15	60
☐	b.	w/o *Banco Central del Uruguay* below any titles.	4	15	60
☐	c.	Signature 2.	4	15	60
☐	d.	Signature 4.	4	15	60
☐	e.	Signature 7.	4	15	60
☐	f.	Signature 8.	4	15	60
☐	g.	Signature 9.	2.50	10	40
☐	h.	Signature 10.	2.50	10	40
☐	i.	Signature 11.	2.50	10	40
☐	j.	Signature 12.	2.50	10	40
☐	k.	Signature 13.	2.50	10	40
☐	l.	Signature 14a.	2.50	10	40
☐	p.	Horizontal black *PROOF Nº #* ovpt at lower left.	—	—	40
☐	s.	Diagonal red *MUESTRA SIN VALOR* overprint; horizontal black # overprint on watermark area.	—	—	126

BCU B10 (P50): 5,000 pesos VG VF UNC

Brown and bluish-green. Front: José Gervasio Artigas. Back: Banco de la República Oriental del Uruguay headquarters building in Montevideo. Solid security thread. Watermark: Coat of arms and *5000* pattern. Printer: *THOMAS DE LA RUE & COMPANY, LIMITED*. 155 x 69 mm.

		VG	VF	UNC
☐ a.	No date. Serie A. Intro: 1967. Signature 1. w/ *Banco Central del Uruguay* below all titles.	0.75	3.50	13
☐ b.	w/o *Banco Central del Uruguay* below any titles.	0.75	3.50	13
☐ c.	Signature 3. Serie B.	0.50	2.50	10
☐ d.	Signature 5.	0.50	2.50	10
☐ e.	Signature 6.	0.50	2.50	10
☐ f.	Signature 7.	0.50	2.50	10
☐ g.	Signature 11. Serie C.	0.50	2.50	10
☐ p.	Horizontal black *PROOF Nº* # ovpt at lower left.	—	—	60
☐ s.	Diagonal red *MUESTRA SIN VALOR* overprint; horizontal black # overprint on watermark area.	—	—	60
☐ gs.	Diagonal red *SPECIMEN* and DLR oval ovpts; horizontal red *SPECIMEN Nº* # ovpt at lower left; punched.	—	—	—

BCU B10.5 (PNL): 5,000 pesos VG VF UNC

Brown and bluish-green. Front: José Gervasio Artigas. Back: Banco de la República Oriental del Uruguay headquarters building in Montevideo. Solid security thread. Watermark: Coat of arms and *5000* pattern. Printer: *THOMAS DE LA RUE & COMPANY, LIMITED*. 155 x 69 mm.

		VG	VF	UNC
☐ p.	Two diagonal *SIN VALOR* perforations; horizontal black *PROOF Nº* # ovpt at lower left.	—	—	—

Like BCU B10, but with issuer name as *EL BANCO CENTRAL DE LA REPÚBLICA ORIENTAL DEL URUGUAY* on front and back.

BCU B11 (P51): 10,000 pesos VG VF UNC

Black, green, yellow, and orange. Front: José Gervasio Artigas. Back: Palacio Estévez (Estévez Palace) in Plaza Independencia, Montevideo. Solid security thread. Watermark: Coat of arms and *10.000* pattern. Printer: *THOMAS DE LA RUE & COMPANY, LIMITED*. 155 x 69 mm.

		VG	VF	UNC
☐ a.	No date. Serie A. Intro: 1967. Signature 3.	4	12	30
☐ b.	Signature 6.	4	12	30
☐ c.	Signature 7. Serie B.	2	10	25
☐ d.	Signature 8.	2	10	25
☐ e.	Signature 9.	2	10	25
☐ s.	Diagonal black *MUESTRA SIN VALOR* overprint; horizontal black *No* # ovpt on watermark area.	—	—	150

1973-1974 Issues

The image of José Gervasio Artigas on the 10,000-peso note is from a portrait by artist José Luis Zorrilla de San Martín. This image is used on many different denominations in subsequent issues.

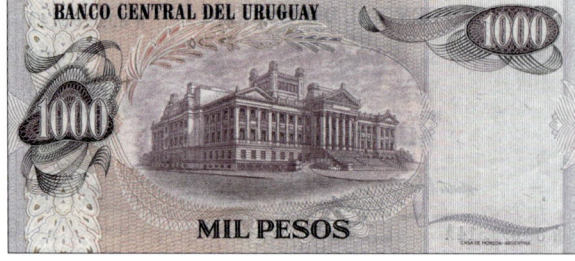

BCU B12 (P52): 1,000 pesos VG VF UNC

Purple, green, violet, red, and orange. Front: Coat of arms; José Gervasio Artigas. Back: Palacio Legislativo (Legistlative Palace) building in Montevideo. No security thread. Watermark: José Gervasio Artigas and *1000* pattern. Printer: *CASA DE MONEDA - ARGENTINA*. 155 x 69 mm.

		VG	VF	UNC
☐ a.	No date. Suffix A. Intro: 1974. Signature 12.	0.25	1	4
☐ b.	Signature 13.	0.25	1	4

Replacement notes: Prefix R.

BCU B13 (P53): **10,000 pesos** VG VF UNC

Orange, green, pink, and yellow. Front: Coat of arms; José Gervasio Artigas. Back: Palacio Estévez (Estévez Palace) in Plaza Independencia, Montevideo. Solid security thread with printed *URUGUAY*. Watermark: José Gervasio Artigas and *10.000* pattern. Printer: *THOMAS DE LA RUE & COMPANY, LIMITED*. 155 x 69 mm.

☐ a. No date. Intro: 1973. 0.75 3.50 13
  Signature 9. Serie A. 7-digit serial number.
☐ b. Signature 12. Serie B. 7- or 8-digit serial number. 0.50 2.50 10
☐ c. Signature 13. Serie C. 0.50 2.50 10
☐ as. Diagonal black *SPECIMEN* and DLR oval ovpts; — — —
  horizon. black *SPECIMEN №* # ovpt at lower left;
  punched.

Replacement notes: Serial number starts with 9.

1975 Provisional Nuevo Peso Issues

On 1 July 1975, pesos were replaced by nuevos pesos at a rate of 1,000:1 per decree law 14.316 of 16 December 1974. These notes were overprinted on preceding issues, with the exception of the 5-nuevo peso overprint on a previously unissued 5,000-peso design.

BCU B14 (P54): **0.50 nuevo peso on 500 pesos** VG VF UNC

Green, blue, and orange. Front: Black *N$0.50 LEY № 14.316* circular overprint; José Gervasio Artigas. Back: Rincon del Bonete Hydroelectric Dam on Río Negro. Solid security thread. Watermark: Coat of arms and *500* pattern. Printer: *THOMAS DE LA RUE & COMPANY LIMITED*. 155 x 69 mm.

☐ a. No date. Sig. 14b. Serie A. Intro: 01.07.1975. 0.25 1.50 6
Overprinted on BCU B8.

BCU B15 (P55): **1 nuevo peso on 1,000 pesos** VG VF UNC

Purple and green. Front: Black *N$1 LEY № 14.316* circular overprint; José Gervasio Artigas. Back: Palacio Legislativo (Legistlative Palace) building in Montevideo. Solid security thread. Watermark: Coat of arms and *1000* pattern. Printer: *THOMAS DE LA RUE & COMPANY LIMITED*. 155 x 69 mm.

☐ a. No date. Sig. 14b. Serie A. Intro: 01.07.1975. 0.25 1.50 6
Overprinted on BCU B9.

BCU B16 (P56): **1 nuevo peso on 1,000 pesos** VG VF UNC

Purple, green, violet, red, and orange. Front: Black *N$1 LEY № 14.316* circular overprint; coat of arms; José Gervasio Artigas. Back: Palacio Legislativo (Legistlative Palace) building in Montevideo. No security thread. Watermark: José Gervasio Artigas and *10.000* pattern. Printer: *CASA DE MONEDA - ARGENTINA*. 155 x 69 mm.

☐ a. No date. Sig. 13. Suffix A. Intro: 01.07.1975. 0.50 2.50 10
Overprinted on BCU B12.
Replacement notes: Prefix R.

Uruguay 1975 Issues

1975 Issues

BCU B17 (P57): **5 nuevos pesos on 5,000 pesos**　　　VG　VF　UNC

Brown and red. Front: Black *N$5 LEY № 14.316* circular overprint; coat of arms; José Gervasio Artigas. Back: Church, Banco Central del Uruguay building, and Plaza Dr. Julio C. Garcia Otero in Montevideo. No security thread Watermark: José Gervasio Artigas and *5000* pattern. Printer: *CASA DE MONEDA - ARGENTINA.* 155 x 69 mm.

　　☐　a.　No date. Sig. 14a. Serie A. Intro: 01.07.1975.　　0.25　1.50　6

Replacement notes: Prefix R.

BCU B18 (P58): **10 nuevos pesos on 10,000 pesos**　　　VG　VF　UNC

Orange, green, pink, and yellow. Front: Black *N$10 LEY № 14.316* circular overprint; coat of arms; José Gervasio Artigas. Back: Palacio Estévez (Estévez Palace) in Plaza Independencia, Montevideo. Solid security thread with printed *URUGUAY*. Watermark: José Gervasio Artigas and *10.000* pattern. Printer: *THOMAS DE LA RUE & COMPANY, LIMITED.* 155 x 69 mm.

　　☐　a.　No date. Sig. 13. Serie C. Intro: 01.07.1975.　　5　15　60

Overprinted on BCU B13.
Replacement notes: Serial number starts with 9.

BCU B19 (P59): **50 nuevos pesos** (withdrawn 31.05.1995)　VG　VF　UNC

Blue, green, orange, and yellow. Front: Coat of arms; José Gervasio Artigas. Back: Palacio Estévez (Estévez Palace) in Plaza Independencia, Montevideo. Solid security thread. Watermark: José Gervasio Artigas and *N$50* pattern. Printer: *THOMAS DE LA RUE & COMPANY, LIMITED.* 159 x 74 mm.

　　☐　a.　No date. Sig. 14a. Serie A. Intro: 16.12.1975.　　2.50　10　50
　　☐　as.　Diagonal black *SPECIMEN* and DLR oval ovpts;　—　—　—
　　　　　horizon. black *SPECIMEN №* # ovpt at lower left;
　　　　　punched.

Replacement notes: Serial number starts with 9.

BCU B20 (P60): **100 nuevos pesos** (withdrawn 31.05.1995)　VG　VF　UNC

Green, orange, blue, pink and purple. Front: Coat of arms; José Gervasio Artigas. Back: Palacio Estévez (Estévez Palace) in Plaza Independencia, Montevideo. Solid security thread. Watermark: José Gervasio Artigas and *N$100* pattern. Printer: *THOMAS DE LA RUE & COMPANY, LIMITED.* 159 x 74 mm.

　　☐　a.　No date. Sig. 14a. Serie A. Intro: 25.11.1975.　　10　20　80

Replacement notes: Serial number starts with 9.

1978-1987 Issues

The 50- and 100-nuevo peso notes are like the preceding issues, but without the *PAGARÁ AL PORTADOR Y A LA VISTA* (payable to bearer on sight) clause below the coat of arms.

BCU B21 (P61): **50 nuevos pesos** (withdrawn 31.05.1995)   VG   VF   UNC
Blue, green, orange, and yellow. Front: Coat of arms; José Gervasio Artigas. Back: Palacio Estévez (Estévez Palace) in Plaza Independencia, Montevideo. Solid security thread with printed *URUGUAY*. Watermark: José Gervasio Artigas and *N$50* pattern. Printer: THOMAS DE LA RUE & COMPANY, LIMITED. 159 x 74 mm.

- a. No date.   —   0.75   2.50
  Signature 15. Serie B. Intro: 07.02.1979.
- b. Signature 16. Serie C. Intro: 04.06.1980.   —   0.75   2.50
- c. Signature 15. Serie D. Intro: 23.12.1982.   —   0.50   2
- d. Signature 19a. Serie E. Intro: 1985.   —   0.50   2
- as. Diagonal black *MUESTRA SIN VALOR* overprint;   —   —   —
  horizontal black # overprint on watermark area.

Replacement notes: Serial number starts with 9.

BCU B22 (P62): **100 nuevos pesos** (withdrawn 31.05.1995)   VG   VF   UNC
Green, orange, blue, pink and purple. Front: Coat of arms; José Gervasio Artigas. Back: Palacio Estévez (Estévez Palace) in Plaza Independencia, Montevideo. Solid security thread with printed *URUGUAY*. Watermark: José Gervasio Artigas and *N$100* pattern. Printer: THOMAS DE LA RUE & COMPANY, LIMITED. 159 x 74 mm.

- a. No date.   0.25   1.25   5
  Sig. 15. Serie B. Intro: 08.03.1978. 7-digit s/n.
- b. Signature 16. Serie C. Intro: 05.12.1979.   0.25   1.25   5
- c. Serie D. Intro: 04.05.1981. 7- or 8-digit s/n.   0.25   1   4
- d. Sig. 18. Serie E. Intro: 02.05.1985. 7-digit s/n.   0.25   1   4
- e. Signature 19a. Serie F. Intro: 1986.   0.25   1   4
- as. Diagonal black *MUESTRA SIN VALOR* overprint;   —   —   —
  horizontal black # overprint on watermark area.

Replacement notes: Serial number starts with 9.

BCU B23 (P63): **500 nuevos pesos** (withdrawn 31.05.1995)   VG   VF   UNC
Red, purple, and green. Front: Coat of arms; José Gervasio Artigas. Back: Palacio Estévez (Estévez Palace) in Plaza Independencia, Montevideo. Solid security thread with printed *URUGUAY*. Watermark: José Gervasio Artigas and *N$500* pattern. Printer: THOMAS DE LA RUE & COMPANY, LIMITED. 159 x 74 mm.

- a. No date.   0.50   2.50   10
  Signature 15. Serie A. Intro: June 1978.
- b. Signature 16. Serie B. Intro: 28.06.1984.   0.50   2.50   10
- c. Signature 19a. Serie C. Intro: 11.09.1985.   0.50   2   8
- as. Diagonal black *MUESTRA SIN VALOR* overprint;   —   —   100
  horizontal black # overprint on watermark area.

Replacement notes: Serial number starts with 9.

BCU B24 (P64): **1,000 nuevos pesos** (withdrawn 01.03.2003) VG VF UNC
Purple, blue, and orange. Front: Coat of arms; José Gervasio Artigas. Back: Palacio Estévez (Estévez Palace) in Plaza Independencia, Montevideo. Solid security thread with printed *URUGUAY*. Watermark: José Gervasio Artigas and *N$1000* pattern. Printer: *THOMAS DE LA RUE & COMPANY, LIMITED*. 159 x 74 mm.

- ☐ a. No date. 5 15 50
  Signature 15. Serie A. Intro: 20.06.1978.
  7-digit serial numbers.
- ☐ b. Signature 16. Serie B. Intro: 29.11.1980. 2.50 10 40
  7- or 8-digit serial numbers.
- ☐ as. Diagonal black *MUESTRA SIN VALOR* overprint; — — 100
  horizontal black # overprint on watermark area.

Replacement notes: Serial number starts with 9.

1987-1992 Issues

These notes are like the preceding issues, but with simulated watermarks printed with lithography at left front.

BCU B25 (P61A): **50 nuevos pesos** (withdrawn 31.05.1995) VG VF UNC
Blue, green, orange, and yellow. Front: Coat of arms; José Gervasio Artigas. Back: Palacio Estévez (Estévez Palace) in Plaza Independencia, Montevideo. Solid security thread with printed *URUGUAY*. Simulated watermark: José Gervasio Artigas. Printer: *THOMAS DE LA RUE & COMPANY, LIMITED*. 159 x 74 mm.

- ☐ a. No date. 0.25 0.75 3
  Signature 19b. Serie F. Intro: 1988.
- ☐ b. Signature 19d. Serie G. Intro: 1989. 0.25 0.75 3

Replacement notes: Serial number starts with 9.

BCU B26 (P62A): **100 nuevos pesos** (withdrawn 31.05.1995) VG VF UNC
Green, orange, blue, pink and purple. Front: Coat of arms; José Gervasio Artigas. Back: Palacio Estévez (Estévez Palace) in Plaza Independencia, Montevideo. Solid security thread with printed *URUGUAY*. Simulated watermark: José Gervasio Artigas. Printer: *THOMAS DE LA RUE & COMPANY, LIMITED*. 159 x 74 mm.

- ☐ a. No date. Signature 19d. Serie G. Intro: 1987. 0.25 1 4

Replacement notes: Serial number starts with 9.

BCU B27 (P63A): **500 nuevos pesos** (withdrawn 31.05.1995) VG VF UNC
Red, purple, and green. Front: Coat of arms; José Gervasio Artigas. Back: Palacio Estévez (Estévez Palace) in Plaza Independencia, Montevideo. Solid security thread with printed *URUGUAY*. Simulated watermark: José Gervasio Artigas. Printer: *THOMAS DE LA RUE & COMPANY, LIMITED*. 159 x 74 mm.

- ☐ a. No date. Signature 19d. Serie D. Intro: 1990. 0.25 1.50 6

Replacement notes: Serial number starts with 9.

BCU B28 (P64A): **1,000 nuevos pesos** (withdrawn 01.03.2003)   VG   VF   UNC

Purple, blue, and orange. Front: Coat of arms; José Gervasio Artigas. Back: Palacio Estévez (Estévez Palace) in Plaza Independencia, Montevideo. Solid security thread with printed *URUGUAY*. Simulated watermark: José Gervasio Artigas. Printer: *THOMAS DE LA RUE & COMPANY, LIMITED*. 159 x 74 mm.

- ☐ a. No date. Signature 19d.   0.50   2   8
  Serie C. Intro: 1991.
- ☐ b. Serie D. Intro: 1992.   0.50   2   8

Replacement notes: Serial number starts with 9.

1983-1990 Issues

BCU B29 (P66): **200 nuevos pesos** (withdrawn 31.05.1995)   VG   VF   UNC

Teal; brown, and green. Front: Quill and scroll; coat of arms; José Enrique Rodó. Back: Sculptor José Belloni's monument to José Enrique Rodó in Parque Rodó, Montevideo. Solid security thread with printed *URUGUAY*. Watermark: José Gervasio Artigas. Printer: *CICCONE S.A.* 159 x 74 mm.

- ☐ a. 1986. Signature 19e. Serie A.   0.25   1.25   5
- ☐ as. Horizontal red *SIN VALOR* overprint;   —   —   —
  horizontal black # overprint on watermark area.

Replacement notes: Serie A-R.

BCU B30 (P65): **5,000 nuevos pesos** (withdrawn 01.03.2003)   VG   VF   UNC

Reddish brown, dark brown, blue, and green. Front: Coat of arms; Brigadier General Juan Antonio Lavalleja in military uniform; scales and rising sun underprint pattern. Back: Quill; crowd of people amid flags of Brazil, Argentina, Paraguay, and UK Merchant Navy, on the promulgation of the constitution on 18 July 1830 in Plaza Matriz in front of the cabildo, Montevideo. Solid security thread with printed *URUGUAY*. Watermark: José Gervasio Artigas. Printer: *THOMAS DE LA RUE AND COMPANY, LIMITED*. 159 x 74 mm.

- ☐ a. 18 DE JULIO 1980.   0.50   2.50   10
  Signature 17. Serie A. Intro: 1983. 7-digit s/n.
- ☐ b. Signature 19a. Serie B. Intro: 1985.   0.50   2.50   10
- ☐ c. Signature 19b. Serie C. Intro: 1987. 8-digit s/n.   0.50   2.50   10
- ☐ as. Diagonal black *MUESTRA SIN VALOR* overprint;   —   —   100
  horizontal black # overprint on watermark area.
- ☐ cs. Diagonal black *MUESTRA SIN VALOR* overprint;   —   —   100
  horizontal black # overprint on watermark area.

Replacement notes: Serial number starts with 9.

URUGUAY 1989-1992 ISSUES

1989-1992 Issues

These notes honor people who made significant contributions to Uruguayan culture.

BCU B31 (P67): **10,000 nuevos pesos** (withdrawn 01.03.2003) VG VF UNC
Blue, brown, purple, orange, and green. Front: Flag and trees in Plaza de la Democracia (Democracy Square), Montevideo. Back: Coats of arms for Uruguay's 19 departments (Artigas, Canelones, Cerro Largo, Colonia, Durazno, Flores, Florida, Lavallega, Maldonado, Montevideo, Paysandú, Río Nego, Rivera, Rocha, Salto, San José, Soriano Tacuarembó, and Treinta y Tres). Solid security thread with printed *URUGUAY*. Watermark: José Gervasio Artigas. Printer: *AMERICAN BANK NOTE COMPANY*. 159 x 74 mm.

- a. No date. 10 30 125
  Signature 17. Serie A. Intro: 1987.
  7-digit serial numbers.
- b. Signature 19c. Serie B. Intro: 1988. 2 8 30
  7- or 8-digit serial numbers.
- c. Signature 19c. Serie C. Intro: 1990. 2 8 30
  7- or 8-digit serial numbers.
- as1. Diagonal red *MUESTRA SIN VALOR* overprint; — — 1,250
  punched; with gold bar overprints.
- as2. Diagonal red *MUESTRA SIN VALOR* overprint; — — 1,250
  punched; without gold bar overprints.
- bs. Specimen. — — 1,250

The Serie A 10,000-nuevo peso notes were printed with the caption *Plaza de la Nacionaldad Oriental Monumento a la Bandera* at lower left and *DECRETO-LEY Nº14.316* at upper right. Prior to issuance, the military government was replaced by an elected civil administration which overprinted the notes with gold bars to obscure the caption and law designation. The Serie B and C notes do not have the overprints, and the caption is printed *Plaza de la Democracia Monumento a la Bandera*.

BCU B32 (P67A): **1,000 nuevos pesos** VG VF UNC
Purple, orange, green, and brown. Front: Coat of arms; laurels, sheet music, harp, and horn as registration device; Eduardo Fabini. Back: Alegoria Musical (musical allegory music) consisting of seated nude male playing pan flute; laurels, sheet music, harp, and horn. Solid security thread with printed *URUGUAY*. Watermark: José Gervasio Artigas. Printer: *THOMAS DE LA RUE AND COMPANY LIMITED*. 159 x 74 mm.

- a. 1989. Signature 19d. Serie A. Unissued. — — 20
  Diagonal blue, green, or red *NO EMITIDO* ovpt;
  normal serial number.
- as. Diagonal black *MUESTRA SIN VALOR* overprint; — — —
  horizontal black # overprint on watermark area.

BCU B33 (P68): **2,000 nuevos pesos** (withdrawn 01.03.2003) VG VF UNC
Orange, purple, brown, red, blue, and green. Front: Coat of arms; laurels, scroll, and artist's palette as registration device; Juan Manuel Blanes. Back: El Altar de la Patria (Alter of the Homeland), consisting of allegorical woman standing with staff, leaning on monument with flag and scales; laurels, scroll, and artist's palette. Solid security thread with printed *URUGUAY*. Watermark: José Gervasio Artigas. Printer: *THOMAS DE LA RUE AND COMPANY LIMITED*. 159 x 74 mm.

- a. 1989. Signature 19d. Serie A. Intro: 30.05.1990. 0.50 2 8
- as. Diagonal black *MUESTRA SIN VALOR* overprint; — — —
  horizontal black # overprint on watermark area.

Replacement notes: Serial number starts with 9.

BCU B34 (P68A): **5,000 nuevos pesos**   VG   VF   UNC
Brown, purple, green, and orange. Front: Coat of arms; laurels, scroll, and artist's palette as registration device; Pedro Figari. Back: Baile Antiguo (Old Dance), consisting of women and men in ballroom with chandeliers; laurels, scroll, and artist's palette. Solid security thread with printed *URUGUAY*. Watermark: José Gervasio Artigas. Printer: *THOMAS DE LA RUE AND COMPANY LIMITED*. 159 x 74 mm.

- a. 1989. Signature 19d. Serie A. Unissued.   —   —   20
  Diagonal blue, green, or red *NO EMITIDO* ovpt; normal serial number.
- as. Diagonal black *MUESTRA SIN VALOR* overprint;   —   —   —
  horizontal black # overprint on watermark area.

BCU B35 (P68B): **10,000 nuevos pesos**   VG   VF   UNC
Blue, purple, red, and green. Front: Coat of arms; laurels, open book, and rising sun as registration device; Alfredo Vásquez Acevedo. Back: Universidad de la República (University of the Republic) building in Montevideo; laurels, open book, and rising sun. Windowed security thread with printed *URUGUAY*. Watermark: José Gervasio Artigas. Printer: *THOMAS DE LA RUE AND COMPANY LIMITED*. 159 x 74 mm.

- a. 1989. Signature 19d. Serie A. Unissued.   —   —   20
  Diagonal blue, green, or red *NO EMITIDO* ovpt; normal serial number.
- as. Diagonal black *MUESTRA SIN VALOR* overprint;   —   —   —
  horizontal black # overprint on watermark area.

BCU B36 (P69): **20,000 nuevos pesos** (withdrawn 01.03.2003)   VG   VF   UNC
Green, purple, and red. Front: Coat of arms; laurels, ink well, quill, and scroll as registration device; Juan Zorrilla de San Martín. Back: Alegoria de la Leyenda Patria (allegory of The Patriot Legend) consisting of a flying bare-breasted angel; laurels, ink well, quill, and scroll as registration device. Windowed security thread with printed *URUGUAY*. Watermark: José Gervasio Artigas. Printer: *THOMAS DE LA RUE AND COMPANY LIMITED*. 159 x 74 mm.

- a. 1989. Signature 19d. Serie A. Intro: 13.03.1990.   1   4   15
- b. 1991. Signature 20.   1   4   15
- as. Diagonal black *MUESTRA SIN VALOR* overprint;   —   —   125
  horizontal black # overprint on watermark area.

Replacement notes: Serial number starts with 9.

BCU B37 (P70): **50,000 nuevos pesos**   VG   VF   UNC
Red, blue, green, and orange. Front: Coat of arms; laurels, open book, and rising sun as registration device; José Pedro Varela. Back: Monumento a José Pedro Varela in Montevideo; laurels, ink well, quill, and scroll as registration device. Windowed security thread with printed *URUGUAY*. Watermark: José Gervasio Artigas. Printer: *THOMAS DE LA RUE AND COMPANY LIMITED*. 159 x 74 mm.

- a. 1989. Signature 19d. Serie A. Intro: 30.04.1990.   1.50   5   20
- b. 1991. Signature 20.   1.50   5   20
- as. Diagonal black *MUESTRA SIN VALOR* overprint;   —   —   —
  horizontal black # overprint on watermark area.

Replacement notes: Serial number starts with 9.

BCU B38 (P71): **100,000 nuevos pesos** (withdrawn 01.03.03)   VG   VF   UNC
Purple, orange, green, and brown. Front: Coat of arms; laurels, sheet music, harp, and horn as registration device; Eduardo Fabini. Back: Alegoria Musical (musical allegory) consisting of seated nude male playing pan flute; laurels, sheet music, harp, and horn. Windowed security thread with printed *URUGUAY*. Watermark: José Gervasio Artigas. Printer: *THOMAS DE LA RUE AND COMPANY LIMITED*. 159 x 74 mm.

- ☐ a. 1991. Signature 20. Serie A. Intro: 30.11.1991.   2   8   30
- ☐ as. Diagonal black *MUESTRA SIN VALOR* overprint; —   —   —
horizontal black # overprint at lower left.

Replacement notes: Serial number starts with 9.

BCU B39 (P72): **200,000 nuevos pesos** (withdrawn 01.03.03)   VG   VF   UNC
Brown, purple, green, and orange. Front: Coat of arms; laurels, scroll, and artist's palette as registration device; Pedro Figari. Back: Baile Antiguo (Old Dance), consisting of women and men in ballroom with chandeliers; laurels, scroll, and artist's palette. Windowed security thread with printed *URUGUAY*. Watermark: José Gervasio Artigas. Printer: *THOMAS DE LA RUE AND COMPANY LIMITED*. 159 x 74 mm.

- ☐ a. 1992. Signature 20. Serie A.   2.50   10   40
- ☐ as. Diagonal black *MUESTRA SIN VALOR* overprint; —   —   —
horizontal black # overprint on watermark area.

Replacement notes: Serial number starts with 9.

BCU B40 (P73): **500,000 nuevos pesos**   VG   VF   UNC
Blue, purple, red, and green. Front: Coat of arms; laurels, open book, and rising sun as registration device; Alfredo Vásquez Acevedo. Back: Universidad de la República (University of the Republic) building in Montevideo; laurels, open book, and rising sun. Windowed security thread with printed *URUGUAY*. Watermark: José Gervasio Artigas. Printer: *THOMAS DE LA RUE AND COMPANY LIMITED*. 159 x 74 mm.

- ☐ a. 1992. Signature 20. Serie A. Intro: 01.03.1993.   5   15   60
- ☐ as. Diagonal black *MUESTRA SIN VALOR* overprint; —   —   —
horizontal black # overprint on watermark area.

Replacement notes: Serial number starts with 9.

1989-1992 Numismatic Products

The bank packaged the six issued notes of the 1989-1992 family in a booklet along with three unissued notes in denominations of 1,000, 5,000, and 10,000 nuevos pesos. All of the notes have normal serial numbers, and the unissued ones are overprinted *NO EMITIDO* in either blue, green, or red on the front only. These lower denominations were presumably unissued due to inflation making them impractical for economic use, but their designs were repurposed for higher denominations.

BCB BNP1 (PNL): **1,000 - 500,000 nuevos pesos**   UNC
- ☐ a. B32 - B40 (9 notes). —
Diagonal blue *NO EMITIDO* overprints on the 3 unissued notes.
- ☐ b. Diagonal green *NO EMITIDO* overprints on the 3 unissued notes. —
- ☐ c. Diagonal red *NO EMITIDO* overprints on the 3 unissued notes. —

1995-1997 Peso Uruguayo Issues

On 1 March 1993, nuevos pesos were replaced by pesos uruguayos at a rate of 1,000:1. These notes are like preceding issues, but denominated in the new currency.

BCU B41 (P73A): **5 pesos uruguayos** (US$0.25) VG VF UNC
Reddish brown, dark brown, blue, and green. Front: Coat of arms; Brigadier General Juan Antonio Lavalleja in military uniform; scales and rising sun underprint pattern. Back: Quill; crowd of people amid flags of Brazil, Argentina, Paraguay, and UK Merchant Navy, on the promulgation of the constitution on 18 July 1830 in Plaza Matriz in front of the cabildo, Montevideo. Solid security thread with printed *URUGUAY*. Watermark: José Gervasio Artigas. Printer: (TDLR). 159 x 74 mm.
- a. No date. Sig. 24b. Serie A. Intro: 22.12.1997.   1   4   12
- as. Diagonal red *MUESTRA SIN VALOR* overprint;   —   —   —
  horizontal red # overprint at lower left.

Replacement notes: Serial number starts with 9.

BCU B42 (P73B): **10 pesos uruguayos** (US$0.45) VG VF UNC
Blue, brown, purple, orange, and green. Front: Flag and trees in Plaza de la Democracia (Democracy Square), Montevideo. Back: Coats of arms for Uruguay's 19 departments (Artigas, Canelones, Cerro Largo, Colonia, Durazno, Flores, Florida, Lavallega, Maldonado, Montevideo, Paysandú, Río Nego, Rivera, Rocha, Salto, San José, Soriano Tacuarembó, and Treinta y Tres). Windowed security thread. Watermark: José Gervasio Artigas. Printer: *GIESECKE & DEVRIENT*. 159 x 74 mm.
- a. No date.   1   4   12
  Signature 23a. Serie A. Intro: 29.11.1995.
  With *DECRETO-LEY N°14.316* (error).
- b. Signature 24a. Serie B. Intro: 1997.   1   4   12
  Without law overprint (corrected).
- as. Diagonal red *MUESTRA SIN VALOR* overprint;   —   —   —
  horizontal red # overprint at lower left back.

Replacement notes: Serial number starts with 9.

1998-2011 Issues

Over the course of more than a decade, several different printers produced the various denominations with changes to the dates, signatures, imprints, security features, and screen traps, although the basic designs remained the same across the series.

BCU B43 (P80): **5 pesos uruguayos** (US$0.25)   VG   VF   UNC
Brown, orange, blue, and green. Front: Coat of arms; laurels, artist's palette, pencils, cube, ball, and pyramid as registration device; Joaquín Torres García. Back: Pintura Constructiva 1943 (Constructive picture); laurels, artist's palette, pencils, cube, ball, and pyramid. Windowed security thread. Watermark: José Gervasio Artigas. Printer: *DE LA RUE*. 159 x 74 mm.

- ☐ a. 1998. Signature 24b. Serie A. Intro: 04.08.1999.   FV   FV   3
- ☐ as. Diagonal red *MUESTRA SIN VALOR* overprint; horizontal red # overprint at lower left.   —   —   —

Replacement notes: Serial number starts with 9.

BCU B44 (P81): **10 pesos uruguayos** (US$0.45)   VG   VF   UNC
Red, purple, and green. Front: Coat of arms; laurels and open book as registration device; Eduardo Acevedo Vasquez. Back: Facultad de Agronomia (Agriculture building) at University of the Republic, Montevideo; laurels and open book. Windowed security thread. Watermark: José Gervasio Artigas. Printer: *DE LA RUE*. 159 x 74 mm.

- ☐ a. 1998. Signature 24b. Serie A. Intro: 26.04.1999.   FV   FV   4
- ☐ as. Diagonal red *MUESTRA SIN VALOR* overprint; horizontal red # overprint at lower left.   —   —   —

Replacement notes: Serial number starts with 9.

BCU B45 (P74, P83, P83A, P86): **20 pesos urug.** (US$0.90)   VG   VF   UNC
Green, purple, and red. Front: Coat of arms; laurels, ink well, quill, and scroll as registration device; Juan Zorrilla de San Martín. Back: Alegoria de la Leyenda Patria (allegory of The Patriot Legend) consisting of a flying bare-breasted angel; laurels, ink well, quill, and scroll as registration device. 159 x 74 mm.

- ☐ a. 1994. Signature 21. Serie A. Intro: 22.02.1995. Windowed security thread. Watermark: José Gervasio Artigas. Printer: *THOMAS DE LA RUE AND COMPANY LIMITED*.   FV   5   15
- ☐ b. 1997. Signature 24b. Serie B.   FV   5   15
- ☐ c. 2000. Signature 25. Serie C.   FV   FV   6
- ☐ d. 2003. Signature 26. Serie D. Printer: *FRANÇOIS-CHARLES OBERTHUR FIDUCIAIRE*.   FV   FV   6
- ☐ e. 2008. Signature 28. Serie E. No security thread. Watermark: Juan Zorrilla de San Martín and electrotype *Veinte*. Different screen trap patterns.   FV   FV   5
- ☐ f. 2011. Signature 30. Serie F. Different screen trap patterns. Printer: *DE LA RUE*.   FV   FV   5
- ☐ as. Diagonal *SPECIMEN* perforation; vertical black # overprint on watermark area.   —   —   —
- ☐ cs. Diagonal red *MUESTRA SIN VALOR* overprint; horizontal red # overprint at lower left.   —   —   75

Replacement notes: Serial number starts with 9.

BCU B46 (P75, P84 & P87): **50 pesos uruguayos** (US$2.25)   VG   VF   UNC

Red, blue, green, and orange. Front: Coat of arms; laurels, open book, and rising sun as registration device; José Pedro Varela. Back: Monumento a José Pedro Varela in Montevideo; laurels, ink well, quill, and scroll as registration device. 159 x 74 mm.

- ☐ a. 1994. Signature 21. Serie A. Intro: 05.09.1995.   FV   FV   15
  Windowed security thread. Watermark: José Gervasio Artigas.
  Printer: *THOMAS DE LA RUE AND COMPANY LIMITED.*
- ☐ b. 2000. Signature 25. Serie B.   FV   FV   10
- ☐ c. 2003. Signature 26. Serie C.   FV   FV   10
  Printer: *FRANÇOIS-CHARLES OBERTHUR FIDUCIAIRE.*
- ☐ d. 2008. Signature 28. Serie D.   FV   FV   8
  No security thread. Watermark: José Pedro Varela and electrotype *Cincuenta*. Different screen trap patterns.
- ☐ e. 2011. Signature 30. Serie E.   FV   FV   7
  Printer: *DE LA RUE.* Different screen trap patterns.
- ☐ as. Diagonal *SPECIMEN* perforation;   —   —   —
  vertical black # overprint on watermark area.
- ☐ bs. Diagonal red *MUESTRA SIN VALOR* overprint;   —   —   75
  horizontal red # overprint at lower left.

Replacement notes: Serial number starts with 9.

BCU B47 (P76, P85 & P88): **100 pesos uruguayos** (US$4.50)   VG   VF   UNC

Purple, orange, green, and brown. Front: Coat of arms; laurels, sheet music, harp, and horn as registration device; Eduardo Fabini. Back: Alegoria Musical (musical allegory) consisting of seated nude male playing pan flute; laurels, sheet music, harp, and horn. 159 x 74 mm.

- ☐ a. 1994. Signature 21. Serie A. Intro: 10.08.1995.   FV   FV   20
  Windowed security thread. Watermark: José Gervasio Artigas.
  Printer: *THOMAS DE LA RUE AND COMPANY LIMITED.*
- ☐ b. 1997. Signature 24b. Serie B.   FV   FV   15
- ☐ c. 2000. Signature 25. Serie C.   FV   FV   15
- ☐ d. 2003. Signature 26. Serie D.   FV   FV   15
  Printer: *FRANÇOIS-CHARLES OBERTHUR FIDUCIAIRE.*
- ☐ e. 2006. Signature 28. Serie D.   FV   FV   15
  Printer: *Giesecke & Devrient.*
- ☐ f. 2008. Serie E.   FV   FV   15
  Wide windowed security thread with demetalized *URUGUAY*. Watermark: Eduardo Fabini and electrotype *Cien*.
- ☐ g. 2011. Signature 30. Serie F.   FV   FV   12
  Printer: *DE LA RUE.* Intro: 11.01.2011.
- ☐ as. Diagonal *SPECIMEN* perforation;   —   —   —
  vertical black # overprint on watermark area.

Replacement notes: Serial number starts with 9.

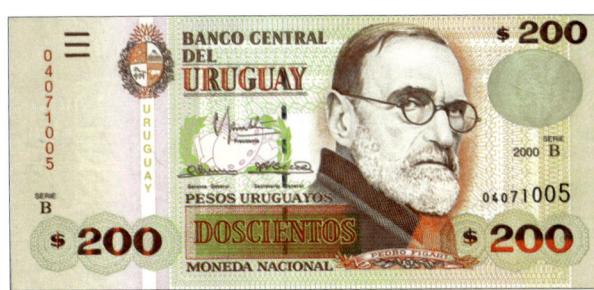

BCU B48 (P77 & P89): **200 pesos uruguayos** (US$9.05)   VG   VF   UNC

Brown, purple, green, and orange. Front: Coat of arms; laurels, scroll, and artist's palette as registration device; Pedro Figari. Back: Baile Antiguo (Old Dance), consisting of women and men in ballroom with chandeliers; laurels, scroll, and artist's palette. 159 x 74 mm.

- ☐ a. 1995. Signature 23b. Serie A. Intro: 23.10.1995.   FV   FV   50
  1-mm wide windowed security thread with demetalized *URUGUAY*. Watermark: José Gervasio Artigas and electrotype *Artigas*.
  Printer: *THOMAS DE LA RUE AND COMPANY LIMITED*.
- ☐ b. 2000. Signature 25. Serie B.   FV   FV   25
- ☐ c. 2006. Signature 27. Serie C. Intro: Nov. 2006.   FV   FV   20
  Watermark: Pedro Figari and electrotype *Doscientos*. Notes coated in varnish.
  Printer: *FRANÇOIS-CHARLES OBERTHUR FIDUCIAIRE*.
- ☐ d. 2009. Signature 29. Serie D.   FV   FV   20
  Printer: *OBERTHUR TECHNOLOGIES*.
  Different screen trap patterns.
- ☐ e. 2011. Signature 30. Serie E.   FV   FV   20
  2-mm wide windowed security thread with demetalized *URUGUAY*.
  Printer: *DE LA RUE*.
  Different screen trap patterns.
- ☐ as. Diagonal *SPECIMEN* perforation;   —   —   75
  vertical black # overprint on watermark area.
- ☐ bs. Diagonal red *MUESTRA SIN VALOR* overprint;   —   —   75
  horizontal red # overprint at lower left.

Replacement notes: Serial number starts with 9.

BCU B49 (P78, P82, P90): **500 pesos uruguayos** (US$23)   VG   VF   UNC

Blue, purple, red, and green. Front: Coat of arms; laurels, open book, and rising sun as registration device; Alfredo Vásquez Acevedo. Back: Universidad de la República (University of the Republic) building in Montevideo; laurels, open book, and rising sun. 1-mm wide windowed security thread with demetalized *URUGUAY*. 159 x 74 mm.

- ☐ a. 1994. Signature 21. Serie A. Intro: 13.06.1995.   FV   FV   80
  Watermark: José Gervasio Artigas.
  Printer: *THOMAS DE LA RUE AND COMPANY LIMITED*.
- ☐ b. 1999. Signature 24b. Serie B.   FV   FV   60
  Printer: *FRANÇOIS-CHARLES OBERTHUR FIDUCIAIRE*.
- ☐ c. 2006. Signature 27. Serie C. Intro: Nov. 2006.   FV   FV   40
  Watermark: Alfredo Vásquez Acevedo and electrotype *Quinientos*. Notes coated in varnish.
  Printer: *FRANÇOIS-CHARLES OBERTHUR FIDUCIAIRE*.
- ☐ d. 2009. Signature 29. Serie D.   FV   FV   40
  Printer: *OBERTHUR TECHNOLOGIES*.
  Different screen trap patterns.
- ☐ as. Diagonal *SPECIMEN* perforation;   —   —
  vertical black # overprint on watermark area.

Replacement notes: Serial number starts with 9.

BCU B50 (P79 & P91): **1,000 pesos uruguayos** (US$45) VG VF UNC
Green, grown, pink, and blue. Front: Coat of arms; laurels and vase as registration device; Juana de Ibarbourou. Back: Eight books (Chico Carlo, Raiz salvaje, El Cantaro Fresco, Perdida, Las Lenguas de diamante, Loores de Nuestra Señora, Estampas de la Biblia, and La rosa de los vientos); La Palma de Juana palm tree monument in Montevideo; laurels and vase. 159 x 74 mm.

- ☐ a. 1995. Signature 23b. Serie A. Intro: 15.04.1996. FV FV 120
  1-mm wide windowed security thread with demetalized *URUGUAY*. Watermark: Juana de Ibarbourou and electrotype *Artigas*.
  Printer: *THOMAS DE LA RUE AND COMPANY LIMITED*.
- ☐ b. 2004. Signature 26. Serie B. FV FV 110
  Printer: *DE LA RUE*.
- ☐ c. 2008. Signature 28. Serie C. FV FV 80
  4-mm wide holographic windowed security thread with demetalized *BCU 1000*. Watermark: Juana de Ibarbourou and electrotype *Mil*.
  Printer: *Giesecke & Devrient*.
- ☐ d. 2011. Signature 30. Serie D. FV FV 80
  Printer: *OBERTHUR TECHNOLOGIES*.
  Different screen trap patterns.
- ☐ as. Diagonal *SPECIMEN* perforation; — — 120
  vertical black # overprint on watermark area.

Replacement notes: Serial number starts with 9 or Z.

BCU B51 (P92): **2,000 pesos uruguayos** (US$90) VG VF UNC
Black, yellow, purple, and blue. Front: Coat of arms; laurels, buff-necked ibis (Theristicus caudatus) bird, and microscope as registration device; Dámaso Antonio Larrañaga. Back: Biblioteca Nacional 26 de Mayo de 1816 (National Library 26 May 1816); laurels, buff-necked ibis (Theristicus caudatus) bird, and microscope. Holographic stripe. Windowed security thread with demetalized *URUGUAY*. Watermark: José Gervasio Artigas and electrotype *Artigas*. Printer: *Giesecke & Devrient*. 159 x 74 mm.

- ☐ a. 2003. Signature 26. Serie A. Intro: 01.10.2003. — — 140
- ☐ as. Diagonal red *MUESTRA SIN VALOR* overprint; — — —
  horizontal red *SPECIMEN Nº* # ovpt at lower left.

2014 Issues

This note is like preceding issues, but has so many new and different security features with a slightly revised design that it warrants a new type listing.

BCU B52 (PNL): **500 pesos uruguayos** (US$23) VG VF UNC
Blue, purple, red, and green. Front: Denomination as registration device; coat of arms; laurels, open book, and rising sun as registration device; Alfredo Vásquez Acevedo; map of Uruguay as SPARK patch. Back: Universidad de la República (University of the Republic) building in Montevideo; laurels, open book, and rising sun. Holographic windowed security thread. Watermark: Alfredo Vásquez Acevedo and electrotype *Quinientos* and *500* stacked three times. Printer: *OBERTHUR TECHNOLOGIES*. 159 x 74 mm.

- ☐ a. 2014. Signature 30. Serie E. Intro: 08.05.2014. FV FV 40

Numismatic Museum

The Banco Central del Uruguay maintains a free numismatic museum on the mezzanine of its headquarters in Ciudad Vieja, Montevideo.

Acknowledgements

This chapter was compiled with the generous assistance of Sejin Ahn, Gustavo Fernández Artigas, Daniel Bena, David F. Cieniewicz (www.banknotestore.com), Compagnie Generale De Bourse (www.CGB.fr), Donald Cleveland, Alberto Fochi, Heritage Auctions (HA.com), Larry Hirsch (www.aworldcurrency.com), Takis Kouvatseas, Thomas Krause, Diego Torres Manzoni (Banco Central del Uruguay), Dave Mills (www.frenchbanknotes.com), Robert Mol, Wally Myers, Numismatica Cameroni, Shibu Paul (www.ebanknoteshop.com), George Provencal, Gergely Scheidl (banknoteshop@gmx.net), Rodrigo Spano, Bill Stubkjaer, Christoph Thomas, Frank van Tiel, Ludek Vostal, and others.

Sources

Allo, Alfredo. *Billetaria*. "The Banco Central del Uruguay's experience with varnished banknotes." Issue 6. October 2009.

Álvarez, Waldemar. *Variantes en los Billetes del B.R.O.U. 1896 - 1967*.

Banco Central del Uruguay. *Los Billetes de Banco Oficiales del Uruguay 1896 - 1989*. 1989. Monetvideo, Uruguay.

Cuhaj, George S. *Standard Catalog of World Paper Money, General Issues, 1368-1960*. 14th edition. 2012. ISBN 978-1-4402-3090-5. Krause Publications (www.krausebooks.com), 700 East State St., Iola, WI, 54990-0001.

Cuhaj, George S. *Standard Catalog of World Paper Money, Modern Issues, 1961-Present*. 19th edition. 2013. ISBN 978-1-4402-3571-9. Krause Publications (www.krausebooks.com), 700 East State St., Iola, WI, 54990-0001.

Rotondaro, Claudio. *Catálogo Especializado Billetes del Uruguay. Banco Central del Uruguay 1967-2010*. 1st edition. August 2010. ISBN 978-9974-98-097-6. Montevideo, Uruguay.

Share Your Input, Info, and Images

This catalog is believed to be complete and correct as of the time of publication. Prices and face values were last updated 14 February 2014. Please report errors or omissions so that corrections may be made. If you can more precisely identify the name or location of anything depicted on a note, please share that information. Furthermore, if you own an unlisted type or variety, please submit scans of the front and back of the note so that it can be documented. Scans should be 300 dots per inch, 100% actual size, 24-bit color, saved as *uncompressed* JPEG files, and sent to owen@banknotenews.com. Be sure to fully describe all attributes of the note which are not apparent upon visual inspection of the images alone, such as physical dimension, watermark, and security thread.

Uzbekistan

For earlier issues, see Russia.

Contents

Bank of Uzbekistan (BOU) 2253
Central Bank of Uzbekistan Republic (CBU) 2256

1918-1920 Emirate of Bukhara Issues

From 1918 until 1920, the Emirate of Bukhara issued an assortment of crudely produced banknotes denominated in tenga. While the Emirate of Bukhara was located within the borders of modern-day Uzbekistan, it was a distinctly separate country that existed from 1785 to 1920.

For information on these notes, see Emirate of Bukhara.

1924-1991 Soviet Issues

On 27 October 1924, the Uzbek Soviet Socialist Republic was created as part of the Soviet Union. On 31 August 1991, Uzbekistan declared independence.

For information on the Soviet notes used in Uzbekistan during this period, see Russia.

1993 Ruble Control Coupon Issues

Following the break-up of the Soviet Union, Uzbekistan issued sheets of control coupons in various denominations which were used in conjunction with Soviet rubles. As these are not banknotes, they are not covered in this catalog.

Monetary System

15.11.1993: 1 Uzbekistani som = 1 Russian ruble
01.07.1994: 1 Uzbekistani som (UZS) = 1,000 old som

ЎЗБЕКИСТОН ДАВЛАТ БАНКИ
(Bank of Uzbekistan)

1992 Issues

On 15 November 1993, Uzbekistan replaced the Soviet ruble at par with the som (also transliterated as som, and written in Cyrillic as сўм on all notes), the Uzbek word for ruble, meaning "pure." These notes were printed by Harrison & Sons, United Kingdom.

BOU B1 (P61): **1 сўм (som)**   VG   VF   UNC
Orange, blue, and gray. Front: Coat of arms. Back: Sher-Dor Madrasah of the Registan in Samarkand. No security thread. Watermark: Cotton boll and flower pattern. Printer: (H&S). 122 x 60 mm.
- a. 1992. s/n at lower left. Intro: 15.11.1993. — 0.25 1.25
- b. Serial number at upper left. — 0.25 1.25
- as. Diagonal red hollow HAMYHA overprint. — — 25

BOU B2 (P62): **3 сўм (som)**   VG   VF   UNC
Orange, blue, and green. Front: Coat of arms. Back: Sher-Dor Madrasah of the Registan in Samarkand. No security thread. Watermark: Cotton boll and flower pattern. Printer: (H&S). 122 x 60 mm.
- a. 1992. Intro: 15.11.1993. — 0.25 1.25
- as. Diagonal red hollow HAMYHA overprint. — — 25

BOU B3 (P63): **5 сўм (som)**   VG   VF   UNC

Orange, blue, and purple. Front: Coat of arms. Back: Sher-Dor Madrasah of the Registan in Samarkand. No security thread. Watermark: Cotton boll and flower pattern. Printer: (H&S). 122 x 60 mm.

- ☐ a. 1992. Intro: 15.11.1993.   —   0.25   1
  3.2-mm tall serial numbers.
- ☐ b. 3.6-mm tall serial numbers.   —   0.25   1
- ☐ as. Diagonal red hollow *HAMYHA* overprint.   —   —   25

Replacement notes: Prefix E*.

BOU B5 (P65): **25 сўм (som)**   VG   VF   UNC

Orange, blue, and green. Front: Coat of arms. Back: Sher-Dor Madrasah of the Registan in Samarkand. No security thread. Watermark: Cotton boll and flower pattern. Printer: (H&S). 122 x 60 mm.

- ☐ a. 1992. Intro: 15.11.1993.   0.25   0.50   1.50
  3.4-mm tall serial numbers.
- ☐ b. 4.2-mm tall serial numbers.   0.25   0.50   1.50
- ☐ as. Diagonal red hollow *HAMYHA* overprint.   —   —   25

BOU B4 (P64): **10 сўм (som)**   VG   VF   UNC

Orange, blue, and red. Front: Coat of arms. Back: Sher-Dor Madrasah of the Registan in Samarkand. No security thread. Watermark: Cotton boll and flower pattern. Printer: (H&S). 122 x 60 mm.

- ☐ a. 1992. Intro: 15.11.1993.   —   0.25   1
  3.4-mm tall serial numbers.
- ☐ b. 3.8-mm tall serial numbers.   —   0.25   1
- ☐ as. Diagonal red hollow *HAMYHA* overprint.   —   —   25

BOU B6 (P66): **50 сўм (som)**   VG   VF   UNC

Orange, blue, and pink. Front: Coat of arms. Back: Sher-Dor Madrasah of the Registan in Samarkand. No security thread. Watermark: Cotton boll and flower. Printer: (H&S). 145 x 70 mm.

- ☐ a. 1992. Intro: 15.11.1993.   2   8   30
- ☐ as. Diagonal red hollow *HAMYHA* overprint.   —   —   25

Replacement notes: Prefix H*.

BOU B7 (P67): **100 сўм (som)**　　　　　　　　　　　VG　VF　UNC

Orange, blue, and brown. Front: Coat of arms. Back: Sher-Dor Madrasah of the Registan in Samarkand. No security thread. Watermark: Cotton boll and flower. Printer: (H&S). 145 x 70 mm.

☐ a. 1992. Intro: 15.11.1993.　　　　　　　　　0.25　1　3
☐ as. Diagonal red hollow *HAMYHA* overprint.　—　—　25

BOU B8 (P68): **200 сўм (som)**　　　　　　　　　　　VG　VF　UNC

Orange, blue, and purple. Front: Coat of arms. Back: Sher-Dor Madrasah of the Registan in Samarkand. No security thread. Watermark: Cotton boll and flower. Printer: (H&S). 145 x 70 mm.

☐ a. 1992. Intro: 15.11.1993.　　　　　　　　　1.25　5　20
☐ as. Diagonal red hollow *HAMYHA* overprint.　—　—　25

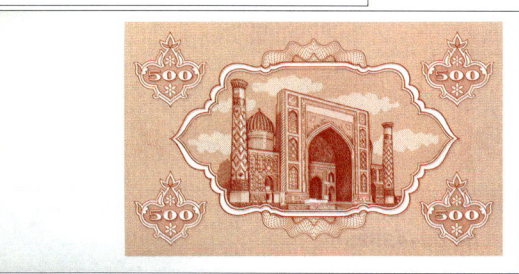

BOU B9 (P69): **500 сўм (som)**　　　　　　　　　　　VG　VF　UNC

Orange and blue. Front: Coat of arms. Back: Sher-Dor Madrasah of the Registan in Samarkand. No security thread. Watermark: Cotton boll and flower. Printer: (H&S). 145 x 70 mm.

☐ a. 1992. Intro: 15.11.1993.　　　　　　　　　2　8　30
　　Ink-jet serial numbers.
☐ b. Letterpress serial numbers.　　　　　　　0.50　2.50　10
☐ as. Diagonal red hollow *HAMYHA* overprint.　—　—　25

The ink-jet serial numbers (BOU B9a, left) on early 500-som notes are larger than the letterpress serial numbers (BOU B9b, right) used later.

BOU B10 (P70): **1,000 сўм (som)**　　　　　　　　　VG　VF　UNC

Violet, green, and brown. Front: Coat of arms. Back: Sher-Dor Madrasah of the Registan in Samarkand. No security thread. Watermark: Cotton boll and flower. Printer: (H&S). 145 x 70 mm.

☐ a. 1992. Intro: 15.11.1993.　　　　　　　　　6　25　100
　　Prefix larger than serial numbers.
☐ b. Prefix same size as serial numbers.　　　0.25　1.25　5

ЎЗБЕКИСТОН РЕСПУБЛИКАСИ МАРКАЗИЙ БАНКИ
(Central Bank of Uzbekistan Republic)

In accordance with Article 122 of the Constitution and Article 11 of the Law "On foundations of state independence of Uzbekistan," as well as the decision of the Supreme Council of the Republic of Uzbekistan dated 3 September 1993 No. 952-XII on the territory of the Republic of Uzbekistan from 1 July 1994 introduced by the national currency som, which is the sole legal tender on the territory of the Republic of Uzbekistan.

For more information, visit www.cbu.uz.

1994 Unissued Proofs

BOU B11 (P71): **5,000 сўм (som)**   VG   VF   UNC
Violet, green, and blue. Front: Coat of arms. Back: Sher-Dor Madrasah of the Registan in Samarkand. No security thread. Watermark: Cotton boll and flower. Printer: (H&S). 145 x 70 mm.

		VG	VF	UNC
☐ a.	1992. Intro: 15.11.1993. 3.7-mm tall serial numbers.	0.25	1.25	5
☐ b.	3.0-mm tall serial numbers.	2	8	30

CBU B1 (PNL): **10 сўм (som)**   VG   VF   UNC
Green, purple, and yellow. Front: Coat of arms. Back: Unknown. Unknown security thread. Watermark: Unknown. Printer: Unknown. 120 x 62 mm.

☐ p.   Proof: 1994. Unissued.   —   —   —

BOU B12 (P72): **10,000 сўм (som)**   VG   VF   UNC
Violet, green, and red. Front: Coat of arms. Back: Sher-Dor Madrasah of the Registan in Samarkand. No security thread. Watermark: Cotton boll and flower. Printer: (H&S). 145 x 70 mm.

		VG	VF	UNC
☐ a.	1992. Intro: 15.11.1993. Crude watermark. 3.5-mm tall serial numbers.	1	4	18
☐ b.	Refined watermark.	0.25	1.25	5
☐ c.	Crude watermark. 3.0-mm tall serial numbers.	1	4	18
☐ d.	Refined watermark.	0.25	1.25	5

CBU B2 (PNL): **25 сўм (som)**   VG   VF   UNC
Brown, blue, and green. Front: Coat of arms. Back: Kazi-Zadé Rumi mausoleum in the Shakhi-Zinda necropolis in Samarkand. Solid security thread. Watermark: Star pattern. Printer: Unknown. 120 x 62 mm.

☐ p.   Proof: 1994. Unissued.   —   —   150

On some 10,000-som notes (BOU B12), the watermark is crude, but on others, the watermark is refined.

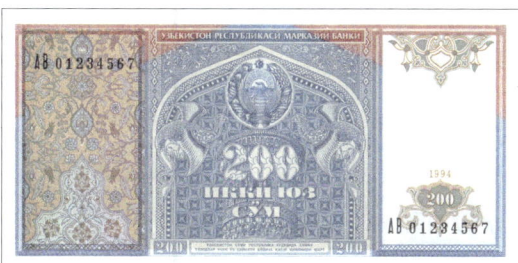

CBU B2.5 (PNL): **200 сўм (som)**   VG   VF   UNC
Blue. Front: Cotton boll and flower pattern; phoenix carrying sheep; coat of arms; ornately carved stone column. Back: Trees; monument in Alisher Navoi National Park in Tashkent. Solid security thread with demetalized ЎЗБЕКИСТОН. Watermark: Coat of arms. Printer: Unknown. 144 x 68 mm.

    ☐   p.   Proof: 1994. Unissued.   —   —   —

1994 Issues

On 1 July 1994, a second som was introduced at a rate of 1 new som = 1,000 old som. These notes are produced locally by a government printing plant in Tashkent, using equipment supplied by Harrison & Sons, which explains the contradiction between the Cyrillic text on the notes and the Latin text used for the serial number prefixes.

CBU B3 (P73): **1 сўм (som)** (<US$0.01)   VG   VF   UNC
Green and orange. Front: Coat of arms. Back: Tree; Academic Bolshoi Theater, Alisher Navoi in Tashkent; water fountain. Solid security thread. Watermark: Star pattern. Printer: (Uzbekistan). 120 x 60 mm.

    ☐   a.   1994. Intaglio. Intro: 01.07.1994.   FV   FV   2
    ☐   b.   Lithographed.   FV   FV   1.25
    ☐   as.   Diagonal red hollow НАМУНА overprint.   —   —   100

CBU B4 (P74): **3 сўм (som)** (<US$0.01)   VG   VF   UNC
Red, green, and orange. Front: Coat of arms; flowers. Back: Chashma Ayub mausoleum in Bukhara; tree. Solid security thread. Watermark: Star pattern. Printer: (Uzbekistan). 120 x 60 mm.

    ☐   a.   1994. Intaglio. Intro: 01.07.1994.   FV   FV   1
    ☐   b.   Lithographed.   FV   FV   1
    ☐   as.   Diagonal red hollow НАМУНА overprint.   —   —   —
Replacement notes: Prefix ZZ.

CBU B5 (P75): **5 сўм (som)** (<US$0.01)   VG   VF   UNC
Blue. Front: Cotton boll and flower pattern; phoenix carrying sheep; coat of arms; ornately carved stone column. Back: Trees; monument in Alisher Navoi National Park in Tashkent. Solid security thread with demetalized ЎЗБЕКИСТОН. Watermark: Coat of arms. Printer: (Uzbekistan). 144 x 68 mm.

    ☐   a.   1994. Intro: 01.07.1994.   FV   FV   1
    ☐   as.   Diagonal red hollow НАМУНА overprint.   —   —   —
Replacement notes: Prefix ZZ.

Uzbekistan 1994 Issues

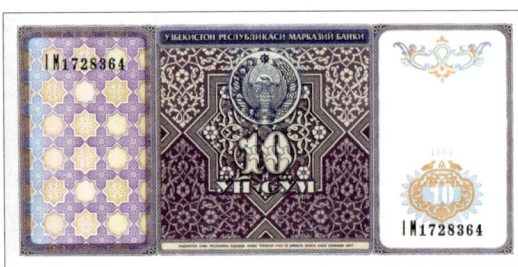

CBU B6 (P76): **10 сўм (som)** (<US$0.01) VG VF UNC

Purple and blue. Front: Tile patterns; coat of arms. Back: Guri Emir mausoleum in Samarkand. Solid security thread with demetalized *ЎЗБЕКИСТОН*. Watermark: Coat of arms. Printer: (Uzbekistan). 144 x 68 mm.

    ☐ a. 1994. Intro: 01.07.1994.   FV   FV   1
    ☐ as. Diagonal red hollow *НАМУНА* overprint.   —   —   —

Replacement notes: Prefix ZZ.

CBU B7 (P77): **25 сўм (som)** (US$0.01) VG VF UNC

Dark blue and brown. Front: Tile patterns; coat of arms. Back: Kazi-Zadé Rumi mausoleum in the Shakhi-Zinda necropolis in Samarkand. Solid security thread with demetalized *ЎЗБЕКИСТОН*. Watermark: Coat of arms. Printer: (Uzbekistan). 144 x 68 mm.

    ☐ a. 1994. Intro: 01.07.1994.   FV   FV   1.75
    ☐ as. Diagonal red hollow *НАМУНА* overprint.   —   —   —

Replacement notes: Prefix ZZ.

CBU B8 (P78): **50 сўм (som)** (<US$0.05) VG VF UNC

Brown and orange. Front: Tile patterns; coat of arms. Back: Ulugh Beg Madrasah, Tilya-Kori Madrasah, and Sher-Dor Madrasah of the Registan in Samarkand. Solid security thread with demetalized *ЎЗБЕКИСТОН*. Watermark: Coat of arms. Printer: (Uzbekistan). 144 x 68 mm.

    ☐ a. 1994. Intro: 01.07.1994.   FV   FV   1.50
    ☐ as. Diagonal red hollow *НАМУНА* overprint.   —   —   —

Replacement notes: Prefix ZZ.

CBU B9 (P79): **100 сўм (som)** (US$0.05) VG VF UNC

Purple and light blue. Front: Peacocks; Scythian torque; coat of arms. Back: Palace of Friendship of Peoples building in Tashkent. Solid security thread with demetalized *ЎЗБЕКИСТОН*. Watermark: Coat of arms. Printer: (Uzbekistan). 144 x 68 mm.

    ☐ a. 1994. Intro: 01.07.1994.   FV   FV   1.50
    ☐ as. Diagonal red hollow *НАМУНА* overprint.   —   —   —

Replacement notes: Prefix ZZ.

CBU B10 (P80): **200 сўм (som)** (US$0.10)　　　　VG　VF　UNC

Green, blue, and yellow. Front: Coat of arms. Back: Stylized lion and sun from the façade of Sher-Dor Madrasah of the Registan in Samarkand. Solid security thread with demetalized *ЎЗБЕКИСТОН*. Watermark: Coat of arms. Printer: (Uzbekistan). 144 x 77 mm.

☐ a.　1997. Intro: Spring 1997.　　　　FV　FV　2
☐ as.　Diagonal red hollow *HAMYHA* overprint.　—　—　—

Replacement notes: Prefix ZZ.

CBU B11 (P81): **500 сўм (som)** (US$0.30)　　　　VG　VF　UNC

Red, green, and yellow. Front: Coat of arms. Back: Equestrian monument of Emir Temur in Tashkent. Solid security thread with demetalized *ЎЗБЕКИСТОН*. Watermark: Coat of arms. Printer: (Uzbekistan). 144 x 77 mm.

☐ a.　1999. Intro: 01.06.2000.　　　　FV　FV　4
☐ as.　Diagonal red hollow *HAMYHA* overprint.　—　—　—

Replacement notes: Prefix ZZ.

CBU B12 (P82): **1,000 сўм (som)** (US$0.55)　　　　VG　VF　UNC

Brown, purple, and green. Front: Coat of arms. Back: Emir Temur museum building in Tashkent. Solid security thread with demetalized *ЎЗБЕКИСТОН*. Watermark: Coat of arms and *1000*. Printer: (Uzbekistan). 144 x 77 mm.

☐ a.　2001.　　　　FV　FV　5
　　　Microtext at top front ends w/ *KA* in *MARKAZIY*.
☐ b.　Microtext at top front ends with *B* in *BANKI*.　FV　FV　5
☐ c.　Microtext at top front ends with *Y* in *MARKAZIY*.　FV　FV　5
☐ as.　Diagonal red hollow *HAMYHA* overprint.　—　—　—

Replacement notes: Prefix ZZ.

O'ZBEKISTON RESPUBLIKASI MARKAZIY BANKI
(Central Bank of Uzbekistan Republic)

2013 Issues

Since 1940, the Uzbek language has been written in Cyrillic script, but following the break-up of the Soviet Union, Latin script has been officially re-introduced. This is the first note on which Latin script is used.

CBU B13 (PNL): **5,000 so'm (som)** (US$2.35) VG VF UNC
Green, blue, and brown. Front: Coat of arms. Back: Oliy Majlis parliament building in Tashkent. Windowed security thread with demetalized *UZB*. Watermark: Coat of arms and eletrotype *5000*. Printer: (Uzbekistan). 144 x 77 mm.
☐ a. 2013. Intro: 01.07.2013. FV FV 10

Acknowledgements

This chapter was compiled with the generous assistance of Thomas Augustsson, Aleksey Avdeev, Jim W.-C. Chen, David F. Cieniewicz (www.banknotestore.com), Paul Cook, Chris Hall, Heritage Auctions (HA.com), Mikhail Istomin, Peter Kelly, Robert Mol, Wally Myers, Jaime Sanz, Menelaos Stamatelos, Christoph Thomas, Tristan Williams (www.banknoteexpress.com), Ömer Yalcinkaya (stores.ebay.com/omer-yalcinkaya-store), and others.

Sources

Cuhaj, George S. *Standard Catalog of World Paper Money, General Issues, 1368-1960*. 14th edition. 2012. ISBN 978-1-4402-3090-5. Krause Publications (www.krausebooks.com), 700 East State St., Iola, WI, 54990-0001.

Cuhaj, George S. *Standard Catalog of World Paper Money, Modern Issues, 1961-Present*. 17th edition. 2011. ISBN 978-1-4402-1584-1. Krause Publications (www.krausebooks.com), 700 East State St., Iola, WI, 54990-0001.

Litvak, Dmitriy and Alexander Kuznetsov. "The Last Emir of Noble Bukhara and His Money." *IBNS Journal*. Volume 50 Number 3. p. 22.

Share Your Input, Info, and Images

This catalog is believed to be complete and correct as of the time of publication. Prices and face values were last updated 9 December 2011. Please report errors or omissions so that corrections may be made. If you can more precisely identify the name or location of anything depicted on a note, please share that information. Furthermore, if you own an unlisted type or variety, please submit scans of the front and back of the note so that it can be documented. Scans should be 300 dots per inch, 100% actual size, 24-bit color, saved as *uncompressed* JPEG files, and sent to owen@banknotenews.com. Be sure to fully describe all attributes of the note which are not apparent upon visual inspection of the images alone, such as physical dimension, watermark, and security thread.

Vanuatu

For earlier issues, see Australia and New Hebrides.

Contents

Central Bank of Vanuatu (CBV) 2261
Reserve Bank of Vanuatu (RBV) 2262

Monetary System
01.01.1981: 1 Vanuatu vatu (VUV) = 1 New Hebrides franc

Banque Centrale de Vanuatu (Central Bank of Vanuatu)

Five months after the birth of the nation in 1980, Vanuatu's parliament approved the Central Bank Act, establishing the Central Bank of Vanuatu (CBV), an institution owned by the government. The bank began operations on 1 January 1981, when it took over the relevant assets and liabilities of the Institute d'Emission. On that date, the New Hebrides franc was renamed the vatu (Bislama for "stone"). A month later, the bank began making arrangements for the design and production of the new vatu currency which would replace the New Hebrides francs and Australian dollars then in circulation (from 1966 to 1973, the New Hebrides franc was pegged to the Australian dollar at a rate of 100 francs = 1 dollar; local residents still sometimes refer to a notional dollar equal to 100 vatu). Meanwhile, the Banque de l'Indochine et de Suez was appointed to act as the Central Bank of Vanuatu's agent to issue currency, which commenced on 22 March 1982.

CBV Signature Varieties

1982 Issues

In 1982, the first series of notes consisted of denominations of 100, 500, and 1,000 vatu, all available undated in issued and specimen varieties. While each note has its own clearly distinguishable color scheme, all three notes share a similar front design of the country's coat of arms: a Melanesian chief standing holding a spear, above a banner which reads *Long God yumi stanap* (pidgin English for "In God we stand").

CBV B1 (P1): **100 vatu** (US$1.05)   VG   VF   UNC
Green, pink, and yellow. Front: Melanesian chief standing holding a spear. Back: Herd of cattle grazing beneath a canopy of coconut trees. Solid security thread. Watermark: Melanesian male head. Printer: *BRADBURY, WILKINSON & Co. Ld. NEW MALDEN, SURREY, ENGLAND*. 130 x 65 mm.
     ☐ a. No date. Sig. 1. Prefix AA, BB. Intro: 22.03.1982.   FV   1.50   5.50
     ☐ as. Diagonal red *SPECIMEN* overprint;   —   —   200
         punched or unpunched.

CBV B2 (P2): **500 vatu** (US$5.20)   VG   VF   UNC
Red, orange, and yellow. Front: Melanesian chief standing holding a spear. Back: Three statues; two male drummers; shield. Solid security thread. Watermark: Melanesian male head. Printer: *BRADBURY, WILKINSON & Co. Ld. NEW MALDEN, SURREY, ENGLAND*. 140 x 70 mm.
     ☐ a. No date. Signature 1. Prefix AA. Intro: 22.03.1982.   FV   FV   12
     ☐ as. Diagonal red *SPECIMEN* overprint;   —   —   165
         punched or unpunched.

VANUATU 1989 ISSUES

CBV B3 (P3): **1,000 vatu** (US$10)   VG   VF   UNC

Mauve, green, and blue. Front: Melanesian chief standing holding a spear. Back: Three statues; map; three males with boat. Solid security thread. Watermark: Melanesian male head. Printer: *BRADBURY, WILKINSON & Co. Ld. NEW MALDEN, SURREY, ENGLAND.* 150 x 75 mm.

- a. No date. Sig. 1. Prefix AA, BB. Intro: 22.03.1982.   FV   15   60
- as. Diagonal red *SPECIMEN* overprint;   —   —   425
  punched or unpunched.

1989 Issues

In 1989, the bank issued the following 5,000-vatu note. The signatures and titles both changed. In addition to the security features of the 1982 series, this new denomination has microprinting of *BANQUE CENTRALE DE VANUATU* (without spaces) repeated along the bottom front, and an arrowhead registration device.

CBV B4 (P4): **5,000 vatu** (US$52)   VG   VF   UNC

Brown, purple, and green. Front: Melanesian chief standing holding a spear. Back: Cruise ship; Naghol "land diving;" four cattle. Solid security thread. Watermark: Melanesian male head. Printer: *THOMAS DE LA RUE AND COMPANY LIMITED*. 160 x 80 mm.

- a. No date. Signature 2. Prefix AA. Intro: 1989.   FV   FV   110
- as. Diagonal red *SPECIMEN* overprint;   —   —   400
  punched or unpunched.

Banque de Reserve de Vanuatu (Reserve Bank of Vanuatu)

In May 1989, parliament approved an amendment to the Central Bank of Vanuatu Act, creating the Reserve Bank of Vanuatu (RBV) with greater authority over and responsibilities for the supervision and regulation of Vanuatu's banking system.

For more information, visit www.rbv.gov.vu.

RBV Signature Varieties

	GOVERNOR	MINISTER OF FINANCE
1	Franklyn Kere (1988 - 1992)	Sela Molisa (1987 - 1991)
*	Jayant Virani (1992 - 1993)	
2	Sampson Ngwele (1993 - 1998)	Willie Jimmy Tapagararua
*	Andrew Kausiama (1998 - 2003)	
3	Odo Tevi (2003 - October 2013)	Moana Carcasse Kalosil (28.07.2004 - 14.11.2005)
4	Odo Tevi (2003 - October 2013)	Willie Jimmy Tapagararua
5a	Odo Tevi (2003 - October 2013)	Sela Molisa (2002 - 2004) (2008 - 2010)
5b	Odo Tevi (2003 - October 2013)	Sela Molisa (2002 - 2004) (2008 - 2010)
6	Simeon M. Athy (October 2013 - present)	Maki Simelum (May 2013 - present)

* These officials are not known to have signed any notes.

1993-2006 Issues

In 1993, undated 500- and 1,000-vatu notes were issued with the new Reserve Bank of Vanuatu name. The 100-vatu denomination was dropped (according to the 2000 annual report, "since 1999, the VT100 bill has been out of print to be replaced by the VT100 coin"). These notes are almost identical to the ones they replaced, except they were printed by Thomas De La Rue and Company Limited, with imprint, and the signatures and titles changed. The security features are identical to those of the 1982 issues.

RBV B2 (P6): **1,000 vatu** (US$10)   VG   VF   UNC
Mauve, green, and blue. Front: Melanesian chief standing holding a spear. Back: Three statues; map; three males with boat. Solid security thread. Watermark: Melanesian male head. Printer: *THOMAS DE LA RUE AND COMPANY LIMITED*. 150 x 75 mm.

☐ a. No date. Sig. 1. Prefix BB, CC, DD. Intro: 1993.   FV   FV   25
☐ as. Diagonal red *SPECIMEN* overprint;   —   —   275
     punched or unpunched.

RBV B1 (P5): **500 vatu** (US$5.20)   VG   VF   UNC
Red, orange, and yellow. Front: Melanesian chief standing holding a spear. Back: Three statues; two male drummers; shield. 140 x 70 mm.

☐ a. No date. Signature 1. Solid security thread.   FV   FV   14
     Watermark: Melanesian male head.
     Printer: *THOMAS DE LA RUE AND COMPANY*
     LIMITED. Prefix AA, BB. Intro: 1993.
☐ b. Sig. 3. Windowed thread with demetalized *VT500*.   FV   FV   14
     Watermark: Cornerstones added.
     Printer: *DE LA RUE*. Prefix BB, CC. Intro: 2006.
☐ c. Signature 5a. Prefix CC, DD. Intro: 2010.   FV   FV   14
☐ as. Diagonal red *SPECIMEN* overprint;   —   —   160
     punched or unpunched.

1995-2007 Issues

In 1995, the first 200-vatu denomination was issued as an undated note, printed by Thomas De La Rue Limited (with vertical imprint along front left). The signatures differ from those on the 1993 notes. This is the first note to feature a vertical novel serial number at right in addition to the traditional horizontal number at left center.

In addition to the security features of the 1982 series, the new note featured microprinting of *BANQUE DE RESERVE DE VANUATU* (without spaces) repeated along the bottom front, a spiral registration device, and the denomination, arms, and serial numbers printed in ink that fluoresces green under ultraviolet (UV) light.

RBV B3 (P8): **200 vatu** (US$2.10)   VG   VF   UNC

Purple and violet. Front: Melanesian chief standing holding a spear. Back: Traditional parliament; "United In Peace We Progress" statue of husband, boy, woman, and infant girl in Port Vila. 135 x 68 mm.

☐ a.	No date. Signature 2. Solid security thread. Watermark: Melanesian male head. Printer: *THOMAS DE LA RUE LIMITED*. Prefix AA, BB. Intro: 1995.	FV	FV	5
☐ b.	Sig. 4. Windowed thread with demetalized *VT200*. Wmk: Cornerstones and electrotype spiral added. Printer: *DE LA RUE*. Prefix BB, CC. Intro: 2007.	FV	FV	5
☐ c.	Signature 5a. Prefix CC, DD.	FV	FV	5
☐ as.	Diagonal red *SPECIMEN* overprint.	—	—	200

1995 "15 Years of Independence" Commemorative Issues

This 200-vatu note commemorating 15 years of independence is identical to RBV B3, but with a black overprint (in French, Bislama, and English) on the watermark area on front. Two thousand notes were issued.

RBV B4 (P9): **200 vatu** (US$2.10)   VG   VF   UNC

Purple and violet. Front: 1980-1995 commemorative overprint; Melanesian chief standing holding a spear. Back: Traditional parliament; "United In Peace We Progress" statue of husband, boy, woman, and infant girl in Port Vila. Solid security thread. Watermark: Melanesian male head. Printer: *THOMAS DE LA RUE LIMITED*. 135 x 68 mm.

☐ a.	1995. Signature 2. Prefix AA.	FV	FV	12

2002-2009 Issues

In 2002, the bank issued a revised 1,000-vatu note featuring a vertical novel serial number at right in addition to the traditional horizontal number at left center. It differs from the 1,000-vatu note of 1993 in that the printer imprint has been shortened to *DE LA RUE* and appears at lower left, and the guilloche patterns at either side of the front have been removed.

In addition to the security features of the 1993 issue, the new notes featured microprinting of *BANQUE DE RESERVE DE VANUATU* (without spaces) repeated along the bottom front, a spiral registration device, and the denomination, arms, and serial numbers printed in ink that fluoresces green under ultraviolet (UV) light.

RBV B5 (P10): **1,000 vatu** (US$10)   VG   VF   UNC

Mauve, green, and blue. Front: Melanesian chief standing holding a spear. Back: Three statues; map; three males with boat. Solid security thread. Watermark: Melanesian male head. Printer: *DE LA RUE*. 150 x 75 mm.

☐ a.	No date. Signature 1. Prefix DD, EE. Intro: 2002.	FV	FV	20
☐ b.	Signature 3. Prefix FF, GG. Intro: July 2005.	FV	FV	20
☐ c.	Signature 5a. Prefix GG, JJ, KK, LL. Intro: 2009.	FV	FV	20

2005 Issues

In 2005, a new 5,000-vatu note was introduced which appears identical to the 1989 issue, except the printer imprint was shortened to *DE LA RUE* and the issuer is the Reserve Bank of Vanuatu.

RBV B6 (P7 & P12): **5,000 vatu** (US$52)   VG   VF   UNC

Brown, purple, and green. Front: Melanesian chief standing holding a spear. Back: Cruise ship; Naghol "land diving;" four cattle. Solid security thread. Watermark: Melanesian male head. Printer: *DE LA RUE*. 160 x 80 mm.

☐ a.	No date. CBV sig. 2. Prefix AA. Intro: May 2005.	FV	FV	100
☐ b.	RBV signature 5a. Prefix BB. Intro: 2006.	FV	FV	75

Oddly, RBV B6a bears a Central Bank signature but the issuer is the Reserve Bank.

2005 "25 Years of Independence" Commemorative Issues

This 1,000-vatu note commemorating 25 years of independence is like RBV B5, but with a circular seal overprint (in French, Bislama, and English) on the watermark area on front, as well as the special prefix XXV. Fifty thousand notes were issued.

RBV B7 (P11): **1,000 vatu** (US$10)   VG   VF   UNC
Mauve, green, and blue. Front: 25 year silver jubilee commemorative logo; Melanesian chief standing holding a spear. Back: Three statues; map; three males with boat. Solid security thread. Watermark: Melanesian male head. Printer: *DE LA RUE*. 150 x 75 mm.
     ☐ a. No date. Signature 3. Prefix XXV. Intro: July 2005.   FV   FV   25

2010-2014 Issues

The Reserve Bank of Vanuatu began issuing a new series of banknotes beginning with a polymer 10,000-vatu note introduced on 28 July 2010, coinciding with the 30th anniversary of independence. This is the largest denomination in the country. Governor Odo Tevi stated, "The existing note series has come under a lot of pressure over the years, particularly with regard to the lifespan and counterfeiting challenges. It is apparent that in recent years most countries in our region have modernized their currency, therefore it is considered appropriate that in the 30th year of independence, the Reserve Bank of Vanuatu takes steps to introduce a new modernized series of vatu banknotes." The new note carries the theme of telecommunication to reflect the recent liberalization of Vanuatu's telecoms market.

On 9 June 2014, the Reserve Bank of Vanuatu introduced three new notes produced by Oberthur Fiduciare (France) on polymer substrate from Innovia (Australia) to increase longevity and reduce counterfeiting. The notes denominated in 200, 1,000, and 2,000 vatu represent family, agriculture, and flora and fauna, respectively. Notes denominated in 500 and 5,000 vatu are planned for introduction within two to three years.

The first two digits of the serial number represent the last two digits of the year of printing.

RBV B9 (PNL): **200 vatu** (US$2.10)   VG   VF   UNC
Pink, brown, blue, and green. Front: Conch shell; waterway; Melanesian chief standing holding a spear; map of Vanuatu islands. Back: Map of Vanuatu islands; family of five seated outside house with palm trees; conch shell. No security thread. Watermark: None. Printer: *OBERTHUR FIDUCIAIRE*. 130 x 65 mm. Polymer.
     ☐ a. (20)14. Signature 6. Prefix AA. Intro: 09.06.2014.   FV   FV   6

RBV B10 (PNL): **500 vatu** (US$5.10)   VG   VF   UNC
Purple, red, blue, and green. Front: Conch shell; waterway; Melanesian chief standing holding a spear; map of Vanuatu islands. Back: Unknown. No security thread. Watermark: None. Printer: Unknown. 135 x 65 mm. Polymer.
     ☐ a. Expected new issue (2016-2017).   —   —   —

RBV B11 (PNL): **1,000 vatu** (US$10)   VG   VF   UNC

Brown, purple, blue, and green. Front: Conch shell; waterway; Melanesian chief standing holding a spear; map of Vanuatu islands. Back: Map of Vanuatu islands; flower; four farmers with crops; rancher riding horse among cattle with palm trees; conch shell. No security thread. Watermark: None. Printer: *OBERTHUR FIDUCIAIRE*. 140 x 65 mm. Polymer.

   ☐   a.   (20)14. Signature 6. Prefix AA. Intro: 09.06.2014.   FV   FV   25

RBV B12 (PNL): **2,000 vatu** (US$21)   VG   VF   UNC

Green, blue, orange, and brown. Front: Conch shell; waterway; Melanesian chief standing holding a spear; map of Vanuatu islands. Back: Map of Vanuatu islands; flower; three birds, tree, and waterfall; conch shell. No security thread. Watermark: None. Printer: *OBERTHUR FIDUCIAIRE*. 145 x 65 mm. Polymer.

   ☐   a.   (20)14. Signature 6. Prefix AA. Intro: 09.06.2014.   FV   FV   55

RBV B13 (PNL): **5,000 vatu** (US$52)   VG   VF   UNC

Orange, yellow, blue, and green. Front: Conch shell; waterway; Melanesian chief standing holding a spear; map of Vanuatu islands. Back: Unknown. No security thread. Watermark: None. Printer: Unknown. 150 x 65 mm. Polymer.

   ☐   a.   Expected new issue (2016-2017).   —   —   —

RBV B8 (P13): **10,000 vatu** (US$105)   VG   VF   UNC

Blue. Front: Conch shell; islands; Melanesian chief standing holding a spear; map. Back: Mask; statues; two male drummers; post office building with palm trees in Port Vila; satellite dishes. No security thread. Watermark: None. Printer: (NPA). 155 x 65 mm. Polymer.

   ☐   a.   (20)10. Signature 5b. Prefix AA. Intro: 28.07.2010.   FV   FV   200

2010 Numismatic Products

The first 100 (serial numbers AA 10 000001 to AA 10 000100) 10,000-vatu notes were handsigned by the governor and the minister of finance, packaged in a folder, and sold for 15,000 vatu each.

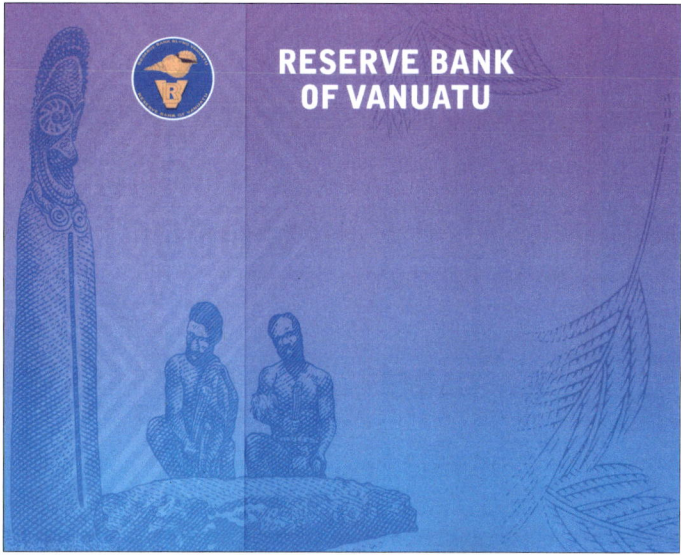
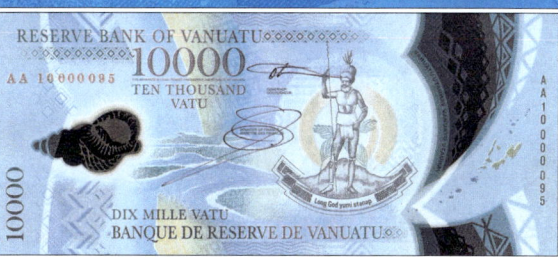

RBV BNP1 (PNL): **10,000 vatu** (US$105)   UNC

   ☐   a.   Hand-signed RBV B8a in folder.   —

Acknowledgements

This chapter was compiled with the generous assistance of Thomas Augustsson, Ricardo Castedo, Donald Cleveland, Krassy Dimitrov, Hartmut Fraunhoffer (www.banknoten.de), Marco Hass, Ronny Hick, Kai Hwong, Mark Irwin, Takis Kouvatseas, James Luke (Reserve Bank of Vanuatu), Michael Morris (www.morrismoney.com), Leszek Porowski, Gergely Scheidl (banknoteshop@gmx.net), Bill Stubkjaer, Christoph Thomas, Chris Twining (www.pagescoinsandcurrency.com), David White, Trevor Wilkin (www.polymernotes.com), Christof Zellweger, and others.

Sources

Angleviel, Frédéric. *Premier essai de nomenclature numismatique de la République du Vanuatu (ex Nouvelles-Hebrides)*.

Boon, K. N. *World Paper & Polymer Uncut Banknotes.* 1st edition. 2012. ISBN 978-983-43313-4-4. Trigometric Sdn.Bhd. (www.3833.com), Lot 327, Amcorp Mall, 18 Jalan Persiaran Barat, off Jalan Timur, Petaling Jaya, 46050 Selangor D.E., Malaysia.

Cuhaj, George S. *Standard Catalog of World Paper Money, Modern Issues, 1961-Present*. 20th edition. 2014. ISBN 978-1-4402-4037-9. Krause Publications (www.krausebooks.com), 700 East State St., Iola, WI, 54990-0001.

Share Your Input, Info, and Images

This catalog is believed to be complete and correct as of the time of publication. Prices and face values were last updated 21 July 2014. Please report errors or omissions so that corrections may be made. If you can more precisely identify the name or location of anything depicted on a note, please share that information. Furthermore, if you own an unlisted type or variety, please submit scans of the front and back of the note so that it can be documented. Scans should be 300 dots per inch, 100% actual size, 24-bit color, saved as *uncompressed* JPEG files, and sent to owen@banknotenews.com. Be sure to fully describe all attributes of the note which are not apparent upon visual inspection of the images alone, such as physical dimension, watermark, and security thread.

Vietnam

For earlier issues, see French Indo-China.

Earlier Issues

Prior to the establishment of the Ngân hàng Nhà nước Việt Nam (State Bank of Vietnam), notes were issued by the Giấy bạc Việt Nam and the Ngân hàng Quốc gia Việt Nam (National Bank of Vietnam). These notes will be added to this chapter in the future.

Monetary System

1 Vietnamese dong (VNC) = 10 hào = 100 xu
14.09.1985: 1 Vietnamese dong (VND) = 10 VNC

Ngân hàng Nhà nước Việt Nam (State Bank of Vietnam)

On 21 January 1960, the National Bank of Vietnam was renamed as the State Bank of Vietnam (SBV), in accordance with the 1946 Constitution of the Democratic Republic of Vietnam. For more information, visit www.sbv.gov.vn.

1964-1975 Issues

SBV B1 (P75): **2 xu** (withdrawn 02.05.1978)   VG   VF   UNC
Brown, green, and purple. Front: Coat of arms. Back: Ornate design. No security thread. Watermark: None. Printer: (Ministry of Finance). 83 x 41 mm.

a.	No date. Intro: 1964.	4	15	75
as.	Specimen.	—	—	200

SBV B2 (P76): **5 xu**   VG   VF   UNC
Purple. Front: Coat of arms. Back: Ornate design. No security thread. Printer: (Ministry of Finance). 90 x 41 mm.

a.	1975. Watermark: 15-mm star pattern.	0.50	2.50	10
b.	Watermark: 30-mm radiant star.	0.50	2.50	10
s.	Horizontal red hollow *MẪU BAC* ovpt on front; vertical black # ovpt on back. Watermark: None.	—	—	10

SBV B3 (P77): **1 hao**   VG   VF   UNC
Orange, purple, and blue. Front: Coat of arms. Back: Kneeling farmer feeding four pigs at trough. No security thread. Printer: (Ministry of Finance). 103 x 57 mm.

a.	1972. Watermark: 15-mm star pattern.	1.50	5	20
b.	Watermark: 32-mm encircled star pattern.	1.50	5	20
c.	Watermark: None.	1.50	5	20
s.	Horizontal blue hollow *MẪU BAC* overprint. Watermark: None.	—	—	15

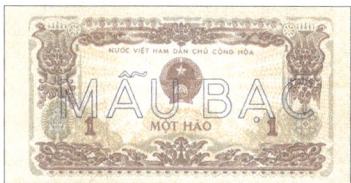

SBV B4 (P77A): **1 hao**   VG   VF   UNC
Brownish-red, olive green, and orange. Front: Coat of arms. Back: Kneeling farmer feeding four pigs at trough. No security thread. Watermark: Flower. Printer: (Ministry of Finance). 95 x 48 mm.

s.	1972. Horizontal blue hollow *MẪU BAC* ovpt. Unissued.	—	—	25

Like SBV B3, but reduced size.

SBV B5 (P78): **2 hao**   VG   VF   UNC
Green, black, and orange. Front: Coat of arms. Back: Woman and man with packs on their backs spraying rice fields. No security thread. Watermark: Flower pattern. Printer: (Ministry of Finance). 99 x 48 mm.

a.	1975.	0.75	3	12
as.	Horizontal red hollow *MẪU BAC* stamp; vertical black # ovpt at right; normal s/n.	—	—	15

SBV B6 (P74A): **20 dong**   VG   VF   UNC
Green, red, blue, and orange. Front: Ho Chi Minh; coat of arms. Back: Tractors pulling plows in wheat field. No security thread. Watermark: Geometric pattern. Printer: (Shanghai Banknote Printing Factory, China). 140 x 70 mm.
   ☐ a.   1969. Unissued.   —   —   350

1976 Issues

On 2 July 1976, the Democratic Republic of Vietnam in the north united with the Provisional Revolutionary Government of the Republic of South Vietnam as the Socialist Republic of Vietnam. In the following listings, the abbreviation NBPP is used for the National Banknote Printing Plant in Hanoi, a subsidiary of the State Bank of Vietnam.

SBV B7 (P79): **5 hao** (withdrawn 14.09.1985)   VG   VF   UNC
Purple, green, tan, and light blue. Front: Coat of arms. Back: Coconut palm trees along banks of river with three canoes. No security thread. Watermark: Flower pattern. Printer: (NBPP). 107 x 54 mm.
   ☐ a.   1976. Intro: 25.04.1978.   0.25   1   4

SBV B8 (P80): **1 dong** (withdrawn 14.09.1985)   VG   VF   UNC
Brown, orange, and light green. Front: Coat of arms. Back: Factory with smokestack. No security thread. Watermark: Flower pattern. Printer: (NBPP). 116 x 58 mm.
   ☐ a.   1976. Intro: 25.04.1978.   0.25   1   4.25

SBV B9 (P81): **5 dong** (withdrawn 14.09.1985)   VG   VF   UNC
Blue, green, orange, and purple. Front: Coat of arms. Back: Two women on shore with baskets of fish; large fishing boats in harbor. No security thread. Printer: (NBPP). 125 x 62 mm.
   ☐ a.   1976. Block letters at left, serial number at right.   —   0.50   2
         Watermark: Flower. Intro: 25.04.1978.
   ☐ b.   Block letters and s/n together. Watermark: None.   —   0.50   2

SBV B10 (P82): **10 dong** (withdrawn 14.09.1985)   VG   VF   UNC
Brown and purple. Front: Coat of arms. Back: Elephants and tractors stacking logs in forest clearing. No security thread. Watermark: None. Printer: (NBPP). 131 x 66 mm.
   ☐ a.   1976. Intro: 25.04.1978.   0.50   1.50   6

1980-1981 Issues

SBV B11 (P83): **20 dong** (withdrawn 14.09.1985) **VG VF UNC**
Blue and green. Front: Coat of arms; Ho Chi Minh. Back: Two tractors alongside dam. Solid security thread. Watermark: None. Printer: (NBPP). 140 x 70 mm.
- a. 1976. Intro: 25.04.1978.   0.75   3   12

SBV B12 (P84): **50 dong** (withdrawn 14.09.1985) **VG VF UNC**
Red and orange. Front: Coat of arms; five-pointed star; Ho Chi Minh. Back: Steam shovel excavators and dump trucks at open pit mine. Solid security thread. Watermark: None. Printer: (NBPP). 152 x 75 mm.
- a. 1976. Intro: 25.04.1978.   0.50   2.50   10
     Plain wide serial number font.
- b. Bold narrow serial number font.   0.50   2.50   10

The 50-dong note has plain wide (SBV B12a, left) and bold narrow (B12b, right) serial number varieties.

SBV B13 (P85): **2 dong** (withdrawn 14.09.1985) **VG VF UNC**
Blackish-brown, green, light blue, and red. Front: Coat of arms. Back: Buildings alongside river with boats and bridge. No security thread. Watermark: Flower pattern. Printer: (NBPP and USSR). 115 x 58 mm.
- a. 1980. Intro: 1981.   —   0.25   1.25
- as. Diagonal red hollow *SPECIMEN* overprint.   —   —   20

SBV B14 (P86): **10 dong** (withdrawn 14.09.1985) **VG VF UNC**
Brown, olive green, yellow, light blue, and red. Front: Coat of arms. Back: Ho Chi Minh's stilt house in Hanoi. No security thread. Watermark: Flower pattern. Printer: (NBPP and USSR). 130 x 65 mm.
- a. 1980. Intro: 1981.   0.25   1   4
- as. Specimen.   —   —   15

1985 Issues

On 14 September 1985, Vietnam revalued its currency at a rate of 10 "old" dong to 1 "new" dong.

SBV B15 (P87): **30 dong** (withdrawn 14.09.1985) VG VF UNC
Violet, tan, and green. Front: Coat of arms; Ho Chi Minh. Back: Crane and ship at dock with warehouses, buildings, trees, and tower. No security thread. Printer: (NBPP and USSR). 142 x 70 mm.

    ☐ a. 1981. Intro: 1981. 2.50 10 40
        4-mm tall serial numbers. Watermark: Flower.
    ☐ b. 3-mm tall serial numbers. Watermark: None. 1 4 15
    ☐ as1. Diagonal red hollow *MẪU* overprint. — — 40
    ☐ as2. *SPECIMEN* overprint. — — 25

SBV B16 (P88): **100 dong** (withdrawn 14.09.1985) VG VF UNC
Brown, purple, blue, and olive green. Front: Coat of arms; Ho Chi Minh. Back: Boats among Ha Long Bay rock formations. Solid security thread. Watermark: Ho Chi Minh. Printer: (NBPP and USSR). 160 x 80 mm.

    ☐ a. 1980. Intro: 1981. 0.75 3 12
        4.0-mm tall serif font serial number. Intro: 1981.
    ☐ b. 3.25-mm tall sans serif font serial number. 0.50 2 8
    ☐ as. Specimen. — — 30

SBV B17 (P89): **5 hao** (withdrawn 1987) VG VF UNC
Violet and light blue. Front: Flag Tower of Hanoi; coat of arms. Back: Ornate design. No security thread. Watermark: None. Printer: (NBPP). 100 x 50 mm.

    ☐ a. 1985. Intro: 14.09.1985. 0.25 1.50 6
    ☐ as. Diagonal red *SPECIMEN* overprint. — — 15

SBV B18 (P90): **1 dong** (withdrawn 1987) VG VF UNC
Blue, aqua, orange, and purple. Front: Flag Tower of Hanoi; coat of arms. Back: Boats among Ha Long Bay rock formations. No security thread. Watermark: Flower pattern. Printer: (NBPP). 115 x 55 mm.

    ☐ a. 1985. Intro: 14.09.1985. — 0.50 2
    ☐ as. Diagonal red *SPECIMEN* overprint. — — 10

SBV B19 (P91): **2 dong** (withdrawn 1987) VG VF UNC
Purple, orange, green, blue, and yellow. Front: Flag Tower of Hanoi; coat of arms. Back: Several boats moored together offshore. No security thread. Watermark: Flower pattern. Printer: (NBPP). 115 x 55 mm.

    ☐ a. 1985. Intro: 14.09.1985. 0.25 1 4
    ☐ as. Diagonal red *SPECIMEN* overprint. — — 10

SBV B20 (P92): **5 dong** (withdrawn 1987)   VG   VF   UNC

Green, light blue, and red. Front: Flag Tower of Hanoi; coat of arms. Back: Trestle bridge over river with boats at anchor. No security thread. Watermark: Flower pattern. Printer: (NBPP). 128 x 64 mm.

☐	a. 1985. Intro: 14.09.1985.	—	—	0.50
☐	as. Diagonal red *SPECIMEN* overprint.	—	—	10

SBV B22 (P94): **20 dong** (withdrawn 1987)   VG   VF   UNC

Purple, burgundy, green, blue, orange, and brown. Front: Coat of arms; Ho Chi Minh. Back: Trees and One Pillar Pagoda in Hanoi. No security thread. Watermark: Flower pattern. Printer: (NBPP). 128 x 64 mm.

☐	a. 1985. Intro: 14.09.1985.	0.25	1.25	5
☐	as. Diagonal red *SPECIMEN* overprint.	—	—	10

SBV B21 (P93): **10 dong** (withdrawn 1987)   VG   VF   UNC

Reddish-brown, pink, green, and blue. Front: Flag Tower of Hanoi; coat of arms. Back: Temple of the Jade Mountain, trees, and Huc Bridge over Hoàn Kiếm Lake (Lake of the Returned Sword) in Hanoi. No security thread. Watermark: Flower pattern. Printer: (NBPP). 128 x 64 mm.

☐	a. 1985. Intro: 14.09.1985.	0.25	1	4
☐	as. Diagonal red *SPECIMEN* overprint.	—	—	10

SBV B23 (P95): **30 dong** (withdrawn 1987)   VG   VF   UNC

Blue, orange, violet, green, and yellow. Front: Coat of arms; Ho Chi Minh. Back: Large, low-lying building with clock tower. No security thread. Watermark: Flower pattern. Printer: (NBPP and USSR). 150 x 75 mm.

☐	a. 1985. Intro: 14.09.1985.	0.50	2	8
☐	as. Diagonal red *SPECIMEN* overprint.	—	—	15

VIETNAM 1985 Issues

SBV B24 (P96): **50 dong** (withdrawn 1987)   VG   VF   UNC
Green, brown, orange, and violet. Front: Coat of arms; Ho Chi Minh. Back: Thac Ba Hydropower Plant and reservoir on Chay River in Yen Binh district, Yen Bai province. No security thread. Watermark: Flower pattern. Printer: (NBPP). 150 x 75 mm.
- a. 1985. Intro: 14.09.1985.   0.25   1   4
- as. Diagonal red *SPECIMEN* overprint.   —   —   12

SBV B25 (P97): **50 dong** (withdrawn 1990)   VG   VF   UNC
Blue, orange, violet, red, and yellow. Front: Coat of arms; Ho Chi Minh. Back: Thang Loing Bridge with automobiles crossing the Red River north of Hanoi. No security thread. Watermark: Flower pattern. Printer: (NBPP). 150 x 75 mm.
- a. 1985. Intro: 1987.   0.25   1.25   5
- as. Diagonal red *SPECIMEN* overprint.   —   —   15

SBV B26 (P98): **100 dong** (withdrawn 1992)   VG   VF   UNC
Brown, green, yellow, and pink. Front: Coat of arms; Ho Chi Minh. Back: Factory with smokestack; men and women planting rice in paddy with water buffalo pulling plow and tractors; train. No security thread. Watermark: Ho Chi Minh. Printer: (NBPP). 157 x 78 mm.
- a. 1985. Intro: 14.09.1985.   0.75   3   12
- as. Diagonal red *SPECIMEN* overprint.   —   —   20

SBV B27 (P99): **500 dong** (withdrawn 1988)   VG   VF   UNC
Red, light blue, light purple, and yellow. Front: Coat of arms; Ho Chi Minh. Back: Bim Son cement plant. No security thread. Watermark: Ho Chi Minh. Printer: (NBPP). 160 x 78 mm.
- a. 1985. Intro: 14.09.1985.   1   4   15
- as. Diagonal red *SPECIMEN* overprint.   —   —   20

1987-1988 Issues

SBV B28 (P100): **200 dong** (withdrawn 16.12.2003)   VG   VF   UNC
Brown, orange, and light blue. Front: Coat of arms; Ho Chi Minh. Back: Workers in field with tractor. No security thread. Watermark: Flower pattern. Printer: (NBPP). 132 x 66 mm.

☐	a.	1987. Intro: 30.09.1987.	—	0.25	1
		30-mm wide prefix and serial number.			
☐	b.	27-mm wide prefix and serial number.	0.25	1	4
☐	as.	Specimen.	—	—	15

SBV B29 (P101): **500 dong** (withdrawn 16.12.2003)   VG   VF   UNC
Reddish-brown, blue, purple, and tan. Front: Coat of arms; five-pointed star pattern; Ho Chi Minh. Back: Cranes, trucks, and ships at dock in Hai Phong Port. No security thread. Watermark: Flower pattern. Printer: (NBPP). 130 x 65 mm.

☐	a.	1988. Intro: 15.08.1989.	—	0.25	1
		30-mm wide prefix and serial number.			
☐	b.	25-mm wide prefix and serial number.	1	3	5
☐	as.	Diagonal blue *SPECIMEN* overprint.	—	—	20

SBV B30 (P102): **1,000 dong** (withdrawn 19.10.1989)   VG   VF   UNC
Brown, green, yellow, and light blue. Front: Coat of arms; Ho Chi Minh. Back: Power shovel excavators and dump truck at open pit mine. No security thread. Watermark: Ho Chi Minh. Printer: (NBPP). 135 x 65 mm.

☐	a.	1987. Intro: 04.03.1988.	1.25	5	20
☐	as.	Specimen.	—	—	15

SBV B31 (P103): **2,000 dong** (withdrawn 19.10.1989)   VG   VF   UNC
Purple, green, orange, and pink. Front: Coat of arms; Ho Chi Minh. Back: Electrical pylons, buildings, and smokestack at Pha Lai thermo power plant in Chí Linh District, Hai Durong Province. No security thread. Watermark: Ho Chi Minh. Printer: (NBPP). 135 x 65 mm.

☐	a.	1987. Intro: 04.03.1988.	1.50	6	25
☐	as.	Diagonal red *SPECIMEN* overprint.	—	—	20

Vietnam 1988-1991 Issues

SBV B32 (P104): **5,000 dong** (withdrawn 14.01.1993)   VG   VF   UNC
Blue, brown, green, and pink. Front: Coat of arms; Ho Chi Minh. Back: Three off-shore oil rigs. No security thread. Watermark: Ho Chi Minh. Printer: (NBPP). 135 x 65 mm.

☐ a.	1987. Intro: 04.03.1988.	1	2	8
☐ as.	Specimen.	—	—	15

1988-1991 Issues

SBV B33 (P105): **100 dong** (withdrawn 1996)   VG   VF   UNC
Brown, green, orange, and light blue. Front: Coat of arms. Back: Pho Minh Tower in Nam Dinh. No security thread. Watermark: Flower pattern. Printer: (NBPP). 120 x 60 mm.

☐ a.	1991. Intro: 02.05.1992.	—	0.25	1
	33-mm wide prefix and serial number.			
☐ b.	25-mm wide prefix and serial number.	—	0.25	1
☐ bs1.	Diagonal red *TIẾN MẪU* overprint.	—	—	20
☐ bs2.	Diagonal red *SPECIMEN* overprint.	—	—	20

SBV B34 (P106): **1,000 dong** (withdrawn 16.12.2003)   VG   VF   UNC
Purple, green, yellow, and light blue. Front: Coat of arms; Ho Chi Minh. Back: Mahout riding elephant dragging felled tree in forest. No security thread. Watermark: Flower pattern. Printer: (NBPP). 135 x 65 mm.

☐ a.	1988. Intro: 20.10.1989.	—	0.25	1
	33-mm wide prefix and serial number.			
☐ b.	27-mm wide prefix and serial number.	1	3	5
☐ as.	Diagonal blue *Tiến Mẫu* overprint.	—	—	35
☐ bs.	Diagonal red *SPECIMEN* overprint.	—	—	15

SBV B35 (P107): **2,000 dong** (withdrawn 16.12.2003)   VG   VF   UNC
Pink, purple, green, and light blue. Front: Coat of arms; Ho Chi Minh. Back: Four female workers in textile factory. No security thread. Watermark: Flower pattern. Printer: (NBPP). 135 x 65 mm.

☐ a.	1988. Intro: 20.10.1989.	0.25	0.50	2
	33-mm wide prefix and serial number.			
☐ b.	25-mm wide prefix and serial number.	—	0.25	1
☐ as.	Diagonal red *SPECIMEN* overprint on front; diagonal red *TIẾN MẪU* overprint on back.	—	—	35
☐ bs.	Diagonal red *TIẾN MẪU* overprint on front; diagonal red *SPECIMEN* overprint on back.	—	—	25

SBV B36 (P108): **5,000 dong** (withdrawn 16.12.2003)   VG   VF   UNC

Blue, green, yellow, purple, and brown. Front: Coat of arms; Ho Chi Minh. Back: Electrical pylons, power lines, and crane at Tri An Dam hydroelectric power plant on the Đong Nai River in Vinh Cuu, Đong Nai. No security thread. Watermark: None. Printer: (NBPP). 135 x 65 mm.

☐ a. 1991. Intro: 15.01.1993.   0.25   0.50   2
☐ as. Diagonal red *SPECIMEN* overprint.   —   —   15

SBV B38 (P110): **20,000 dong** (withdrawn 01.01.2013)   VG   VF   UNC

Blue, green, and purple. Front: Coat of arms; Ho Chi Minh. Back: Five workers in canning factory. No security thread. Watermark: Ho Chi Minh. Printer: (NBPP). 140 x 69 mm.

☐ a. 1991. Intro: 02.03.1993.   0.25   1   4
☐ as. Diagonal red *SPECIMEN* overprint.   —   —   20

SBV B37 (P109): **10,000 dong** (withdrawn 01.01.2013)   VG   VF   UNC

Red, green, orange, and purple. Front: Coat of arms; Ho Chi Minh. Back: Three boats sailing among Ha Long Bay rock formations. No security thread. Watermark: Ho Chi Minh. Printer: (NBPP). 140 x 69 mm.

☐ a. 1990. Intro: 04.05.1992.   1   4   15
☐ as. Diagonal red *SPECIMEN* overprint.   —   —   15

SBV B39 (P111): **50,000 dong**   VG   VF   UNC

Green, light blue, and yellow. Front: Coat of arms; Ho Chi Minh. Back: Ships and building at Nha Rong Wharf. No security thread. Watermark: Ho Chi Minh. Printer: (NBPP). 140 x 69 mm.

☐ a. 1990. Intro: 15.10.1993.   1.25   5   20
☐ as. Diagonal red *SPECIMEN* overprint.   —   —   30

1992-2002 Bearer Check Issues

From 1992 to 2002, the State Bank of Vietnam issued more than 65 bearer checks in denominations of 100,000 dong, 500,000 dong, 1,000,000 dong, and 5,000,000 dong, each with completely different designs and dates of expiration, but all measuring 180 x 90 mm and marked on back *NGÂN PHIẾU THANH TOÁN* (state bank settlement check). Because these checks are not banknotes and were not legal tender, they are not included in this catalog.

1993-1994 Issues

SBV B40 (P115): **10,000 dong** (withdrawn 01.01.2013) VG VF UNC
Red, green, orange, and purple. Front: Coat of arms; Ho Chi Minh. Back: Three boats sailing among Ha Long Bay rock formations. No security thread. Watermark: Ho Chi Minh. Printer: (NBPP). 140 x 69 mm.
    a. 1993. Intro: 15.10.1994.   0.25 1 4
    as. Diagonal black *SPECIMEN* overprint. — — 25
Like SBV B37, but with registration device and modified underprint around coat of arms.

SBV B41 (P116): **50,000 dong** VG VF UNC
Green, light blue, and yellow. Front: Coat of arms; Ho Chi Minh. Back: Ships and building at Nha Rong Wharf. No security thread. Watermark: Ho Chi Minh. Printer: (NBPP). 140 x 69 mm.
    a. 1994. Intro: 15.10.1994.   FV FV 8
    as. Diagonal red *SPECIMEN* overprint;
        horizontal red # overprint at upper right. — — 25
Like SBV B39, but modified underprint and portrait.

SBV B42 (P117): **100,000 dong** VG VF UNC
Brown, purple, orange, and blue. Front: Coat of arms; Ho Chi Minh. Back: Ho Chi Minh's stilt house in Hanoi. Solid security thread with demetalized *100000 NHNNVN*. Watermark: Ho Chi Minh. Printer: (NBPP). 145 x 70 mm.
    a. 1994. Intro: 01.09.2000.   FV FV 20
    as. Diagonal red *SPECIMEN* overprint; — — 25
        horizontal red # overprint at upper right.

2001 Numismatic Products

This 50-dong note was issued to commemorate the 50th anniversary of national banking in Vietnam.

SBV BNP1 (P118): **50 dong** (<US$0.01)   UNC
Purple, pink, orange, and green. Front: Vietnamese bronze drum; Ho Chi Minh. Back: State Bank of Vietnam headquarters building in Hanoi. No security thread. Watermark: None. Printer: (NPA and NBPP). 166 x 82 mm. Polymer.
- a. 2001. Signature: SBV President Lê Đức Thúy.   40
- as. Specimen.   —

All notes bear prefix NH for Ngân Hàng (bank).

2003-2014 Polymer Issues

The first two digits of the serial number represent the last two digits of the year of printing. Initially the 50,000 and 500,000-dong notes were printed by Note Printing Australia in Melbourne, but eventually all of the polymer notes were printed by the National Banknote Printing Plant in Hanoi under a technology transfer and training arrangement with PolyTeQ Services.

SBV B43 (P119): **10,000 dong** (US$0.50)   VG   VF   UNC
Yellow, brown, and green. Front: Coat of arms; Ho Chi Minh. Back: Off-shore oil rigs. No security thread. Watermark: One Pillar Pagoda in Hanoi. Printer: (NPA and NBPP). 132 x 60 mm. Polymer.

		VG	VF	UNC
a.	(20)06. Intro: 30.08.2006.	FV	FV	5
b.	(20)07.	FV	FV	5
c.	(20)08.	FV	FV	5
d.	(20)09.	FV	FV	4
e.	(20)10.	FV	FV	3
f.	(20)11.	FV	FV	3
g.	(20)13.	FV	FV	3
h.	(20)14.	FV	FV	3
s.	Diagonal red SPECIMEN overprint on front; horizontal black # overprint at upper right; diagonal red TIẾN MẪU overprint on back.	—	—	25

The denomination printed vertically at right front lacks a period after the first zero to indicate "thousands" as is the custom in Vietnamese numbering (it should be 10.000) and is technically an error, but was issued nonetheless.

SBV B44 (P120): **20,000 dong** (US$1)　　　　　　VG　VF　UNC

Blue, pink, and green. Front: Coat of arms; Ho Chi Minh. Back: Japanese covered bridge over Thu Bon river in Hoi An, Quang Nam province. No security thread. Watermark: Ho Chi Minh and stylized flower. Printer: (NPA and NBPP). 136 x 65 mm. Polymer.

☐	a.	(20)06. Intro: 17.05.2006.	FV	FV	7
☐	b.	(20)07.	FV	FV	7
☐	c.	(20)08.	FV	FV	7
☐	d.	(20)09.	FV	FV	5
☐	e.	(20)12.	FV	FV	4
☐	s.	Diagonal red SPECIMEN overprint on front; horizontal red # overprint at upper right; diagonal red TIẾN MẪU overprint on back.	—	—	35

SBV B45 (P121): **50,000 dong** (US$2.35)　　　　VG　VF　UNC

Pink, red, yellow, and light blue. Front: Coat of arms; stylized flower; Ho Chi Minh. Back: Pagodas and trees in Hue. Simulated solid security thread with demetalized *50000*. Watermark: Ho Chi Minh and *VN*. Printer: (NPA and NBPP). 140 x 65 mm. Polymer.

☐	a.	(20)03. Intro: 17.12.2003.	FV	FV	10
☐	b.	(20)04.	FV	FV	10
☐	c.	(20)05.	FV	FV	10
☐	d.	(20)06.	FV	FV	10
☐	e.	(20)09.	FV	FV	9
☐	f.	(20)11.	FV	FV	8
☐	g.	(20)12.	FV	FV	7
☐	s.	Diagonal blue SPECIMEN overprint on front; horizontal blue # overprint at upper right.	—	—	45

SBV B46 (P122): **100,000 dong** (US$4.75)　　　VG　VF　UNC

Green, orange, and purple. Front: Coat of arms; Ho Chi Minh. Back: Van Mieu (Temple of Literature) and Quoc Tu Giam (Imperial Academy) in Hanoi. No security thread. Watermark: Ho Chi Minh and stylized flower. Printer: (NPA and NBPP). 144 x 65 mm. Polymer.

☐	a.	(20)04. Intro: 01.09.2004.	FV	FV	8
☐	b.	(20)05.	FV	FV	10
☐	c.	(20)06.	FV	FV	12
☐	d.	(20)08.	FV	FV	15
☐	e.	(20)10.	FV	FV	15
☐	f.	(20)11.	FV	FV	10
☐	g.	(20)12.	FV	FV	10
☐	h.	(20)13.	FV	FV	10
☐	s.	Diagonal red SPECIMEN overprint on front; horizontal red # overprint at upper right; diagonal red TIẾN MẪU overprint on back.	—	—	55

In the microprinting at lower left on the front of the 100,000-dong note the denomination is spelled out in numerals, however there is a zero missing from the second full set of numerals. This error has been confirmed on all dates of SBV B46.

SBV B47 (P123): **200,000 dong** (US$9.50) VG VF UNC
Orange, red, green, and purple. Front: Coat of arms; Ho Chi Minh. Back: Boat among Ha Long Bay rock formations. No security thread. Watermark: Ho Chi Minh. Printer: (NPA and NBPP). 148 x 65 mm. Polymer.

			VG	VF	UNC
☐	a.	(20)06. Intro: 30.08.2006.	FV	FV	30
☐	b.	(20)07.	FV	FV	30
☐	c.	(20)09.	FV	FV	20
☐	d.	(20)10.	FV	FV	20
☐	e.	(20)11.	FV	FV	18
☐	f.	(20)13.	FV	FV	18
☐	s.	Diagonal blue *SPECIMEN* overprint on front; horizontal red # overprint at upper right; diagonal blue *TIẾN MẪU* overprint on back.	—	—	65

SBV B48 (P124): **500,000 dong** (US$24) VG VF UNC
Green, orange, purple, and blue. Front: Coat of arms; Ho Chi Minh. Back: Ho Chi Minh's birthplace amid trees in Kim Lien village. No security thread. Watermark: Ho Chi Minh. Printer: (NPA and NBPP). 152 x 65 mm. Polymer.

			VG	VF	UNC
☐	a.	(20)03. Intro: 17.12.2003.	FV	FV	40
☐	b.	(20)04.	FV	FV	60
☐	c.	(20)05.	FV	FV	60
☐	d.	(20)06.	FV	FV	60
☐	e.	(20)08.	FV	FV	55
☐	f.	(20)09.	FV	FV	55
☐	g.	(20)10.	FV	FV	55
☐	h.	(20)11.	FV	FV	40
☐	i.	(20)12.	FV	FV	40
☐	s.	Diagonal red *SPECIMEN* overprint on front; horizontal red # overprint at upper right.	—	—	70

Acknowledgements

This chapter was compiled with the generous assistance of Alfredo Arce, Jim W.-C. Chen, Jean-Michel Engels, Torsten Fuhlendorf, Duong Do Hoang, Victor Manuel Gonzalez Miguel, Bill Stubkjacr, Ryan Vuong, Tristan Williams, and others.

Sources

Bohora, Anil. "Vietnamese Bearer Checks." *IBNS Journal*. Volume 47 Number 1. p.19.

Cuhaj, George S. *Standard Catalog of World Paper Money, General Issues, 1368-1960*. 14th edition. 2012. ISBN 978-1-4402-3090-5. Krause Publications (www.krausebooks.com), 700 East State St., Iola, WI, 54990-0001.

Cuhaj, George S. *Standard Catalog of World Paper Money, Modern Issues, 1961-Present*. 19th edition. 2013. ISBN 978-1-4402-3571-9. Krause Publications (www.krausebooks.com), 700 East State St., Iola, WI, 54990-0001.

Valota, Massimiliano. *Vietnam Coins and Papermoney*. 2013.

Yi, Yin (editor). *Contemporary China's Banknote Printing & Minting for Foreign Countries*. March 2000. ISBN 7-5049-2116-5. China Financial Publishing House.

http://muabantien.com/2do/vnch-phat-hanh-lan-1-nam-1955

Share Your Input, Info, and Images

This catalog is believed to be complete and correct as of the time of publication. Prices and face values were last updated 24 January 2014. Please report errors or omissions so that corrections may be made. If you can more precisely identify the name or location of anything depicted on a note, please share that information. Furthermore, if you own an unlisted type or variety, please submit scans of the front and back of the note so that it can be documented. Scans should be 300 dots per inch, 100% actual size, 24-bit color, saved as *uncompressed* JPEG files, and sent to owen@banknotenews.com. Be sure to fully describe all attributes of the note which are not apparent upon visual inspection of the images alone, such as physical dimension, watermark, and security thread.

Yemen

For earlier issues, see Arab Republic of Yemen and Democratic Republic of Yemen.

Monetary System

1 South Yemeni dinar (YDD) = 1,000 fils
1 North Yemeni rial = 40 buqshas
01.04.1995: 1 Yemeni rial (YER) = 100 fils

Arabic Numbers

0	1	2	3	4	5	6	7	8	9
٠	١	٢	٣	٤	٥	٦	٧	٨	٩

Central Bank of Yemen

The Central Bank of Yemen (CBY) was established on 27 July 1971, with its headquarters in Sana'a, the capital of the Arab Republic of Yemen. The Central Bank of Yemen absorbed the functions of the Yemen Currency Board. When the Arab Republic of Yemen ("North Yemen") and the Democratic Republic of Yemen ("South Yemen") united on 22 May 1990 to form the Republic of Yemen, the north's Central Bank of Yemen merged with the south's Bank of Yemen, and the joint venture continued to use the name Central Bank of Yemen.

For simplicity's sake, all Central Bank of Yemen notes are included in the Yemen chapter, even though the earlier issues circulated exclusively in the Arab Republic of Yemen.

For more information, visit www.centralbank.gov.ye.

CBY Signature Varieties

1973-1985 Issues

CBY B1 (P11): **1 rial** (<US$0.01)   VG   VF   UNC
Green. Front: Al Baqlilyah mosque in Sana'a. Back: Coffee plants; mountains. Solid security thread. Watermark: Coat of arms. Printer: Unknown. 125 x 65 mm.

☐	a.	No date. Signature 1. Intro: 15.07.1973.	0.50	2	8
☐	b.	Signature 3.	0.50	2	8
☐	bs.	Diagonal red نموذج overprint on front; diagonal red SPECIMEN ovpt on back; punched.	—	—	100
☐	t.	Color trial.	—	—	—

Like CBY B8a, but 4-mm tall s/n and "indented" underprint on watermark area on front.

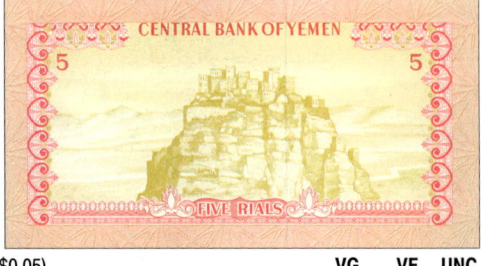

CBY B2 (P12): **5 rial** (<US$0.05)   VG   VF   UNC
Red. Front: Buildings in Wadi Du'an. Back: Buildings on Beit al Midie hill. Solid security thread. Watermark: Coat of arms. Printer: Unknown. 130 x 67.5 mm.

☐	a.	No date. Signature 1. Intro: 15.07.1973.	0.50	2	8
☐	as.	Specimen.	—	—	—
☐	t.	Color trial: Dark Blue.	—	—	—

CBY B3 (P13): **10 rials** (US$0.05)   VG   VF   UNC
Blue-green. Front: Bronze head of King Dhamer Ali. Back: Republican Palace in Sana'a. Solid security thread. Watermark: Coat of arms. Printer: Unknown. 135 x 70 mm.

☐	a.	No date. Signature 1. Intro: 15.07.1973.	0.25	1.50	6
☐	b.	Signature 3. Intro: 15.04.1985.	0.25	1.50	6
☐	as1.	Diagonal red نموذج overprint on front; diagonal red *SPECIMEN* ovpt on back; punched.	—	—	375
☐	as2.	Diagonal red *SPECIMEN* overprint on front; diagonal red *SPECIMEN* ovpt on back; punched.	—	—	350
☐	bs.	Diagonal red نموذج overprint on front; diagonal red *SPECIMEN* ovpt on back; punched.	—	—	325
☐	t.	Color trial: Purple.	—	—	—

CBY B4 (P14): **20 rials** (US$0.10)   VG   VF   UNC
Purple. Front: Marble sculpture of seated figure with grapes. Back: Terraced mountainside. Solid security thread. Watermark: Coat of arms. Printer: Unknown. 145 x 72.5 mm.

☐	a.	No date. Signature 1. Intro: 15.09.1973.	0.75	2.50	10
☐	as.	Diagonal red نموذج overprint on front; diagonal red *SPECIMEN* ovpt on back; punched.	—	—	—
☐	t.	Color trial.	—	—	—

CBY B5 (P15): **50 rials** (US$0.25)   VG   VF   UNC
Olive green. Front: Bronze statue of standing Ma'adkarib. Back: Bab al Yemen (main gate of Sana'a). Solid security thread. Watermark: Coat of arms. Printer: Unknown. 150 x 75 mm.

☐	a.	No date. Signature 1. Intro: 15.08.1973.	0.75	2.50	10
☐	b.	Signature 3.	0.25	0.75	3
☐	as.	Diagonal red نموذج overprint on front; diagonal red *SPECIMEN* ovpt on back; punched.	—	—	—
☐	bs.	Diagonal red نموذج overprint on front; diagonal red *SPECIMEN* ovpt on back; punched.	—	—	—

CBY B6 (P16): **100 rials** (US$0.45)   VG   VF   UNC
Purple. Front: Marble sculpture of cherub atop griffin. Back: Skyline of Ta'izz. Solid security thread. Watermark: Coat of arms. Printer: Unknown. 150 x 75 mm.

☐	a.	No date. Signature 1. Intro: 01.03.1976.	2.50	10	50
☐	as.	Diagonal red نموذج overprint on front; diagonal red *SPECIMEN* ovpt on back; punched.	—	—	350

1979 Issues

CBY B7 (P21): **100 rials** (US$0.45)   VG   VF   UNC
Red-violet. Front: Al Ashrafiya mosque in Ta'izz. Back: Skyline of Sana'a with minarets and mountains. Solid security thread. Watermark: Coat of arms. Printer: Unknown. 151 x 76 mm.
- ☐ a. No date. Signature 2. Intro: 15.05.1979.   0.25   1.25   5
- ☐ as. Diagonal red *SPECIMEN* overprint.   —   —   300

Replacement notes: Prefix ١/غ.

1981-1991 Issues

CBY B8 (P16B): **1 rial** (<US$0.01)   VG   VF   UNC
Olive green. Front: Al Baqliyah mosque in Sana'a. Back: Coffee plants; mountains. Solid security thread. Watermark: Coat of arms. Printer: Unknown. 125 x 66 mm.
- ☐ a. No date. Signature 3. Intro: 05.09.1983.   —   0.25   1.50

Replacement notes: Prefix ١/غ.
Like CBY B1b, but 3-mm tall s/n and "raised" underprint on watermark area on front.

CBY B9 (P17): **5 rials** (<US$0.05)   VG   VF   UNC
Red. Front: Dhahr al Dahab. Back: Fortress Qal'at al Qahir on hill in Ta'izz. Solid security thread. Watermark: Coat of arms. Printer: Unknown. 131 x 68 mm.
- ☐ a. No date. Signature 1. Intro: 10.05.1981.   0.25   1.25   5
- ☐ b. Signature 3. Varieties with and without fluorescent serial numbers. Intro: 1983.   0.25   1.25   5
- ☐ c. Signature 4. Intro: 1991.   —   0.25   1.25
- ☐ cs. Diagonal red *SPECIMEN* overprint.   —   —   250

Replacement notes: Prefix ١/غ or ١/غغ.

CBY B10 (P18): **10 rials** (US$0.05)   VG   VF   UNC
Blue. Front: Village of Thulla. Back: Al Baqiliyah mosque. Solid security thread. Watermark: Coat of arms. Printer: Unknown. 136 x 70 mm.
- ☐ a. No date. Signature 1. Intro: 10.05.1981.   0.25   1.25   5
- ☐ b. Signature 3. Varieties with and without fluorescent serial numbers. Intro: 1983.   —   0.50   2.50

Replacement notes: Prefix ١/غ or ١/غغ.

CBY B11 (P19): **20 rials** (US$0.10)　　　　　　VG　VF　UNC

Purple. Front: Marble sculpture of seated figure with grapes. Back: Skyline of Sana'a with minarets and dome. Solid security thread. Watermark: Coat of arms. Printer: Unknown. 146 x 73 mm.

		VG	VF	UNC
☐ a.	No date. Signature 3. Intro: 05.09.1983.	0.50	1.75	6
☐ b.	Signature 4. Intro: 04.12.1986.	0.25	0.75	3
☐ c.	Bank panel on back with underprint of vertical lines.	0.25	0.75	3
☐ as.	Diagonal red نموذج overprint on front; diagonal red SPECIMEN ovpt on back; punched.	—	—	—
☐ cs.	Diagonal red SPECIMEN overprint.	—	—	250

Replacement notes: Prefix ع/١.

CBY B12 (P21A): **100 rials** (US$0.45)　　　　　　VG　VF　UNC

Purple. Front: Marble sculpture of cherub atop griffin. Back: Central Bank of Yemen headquarters building in Sana'a. Solid security thread. Watermark: Coat of arms. Printer: Unknown. 151 x 76 mm.

		VG	VF	UNC
☐ a.	No date. Signature 3. Intro: 15.08.1984.	0.50	1.75	6
☐ as.	Specimen.	—	—	—

Replacement notes: Prefix ع/١.

The bank panel on the back of earlier 20-rial issues was solid (CBY B11a/b, top), but on later issues vertical lines are apparent in the underprint (CBY B11c, bottom).

1990-1997 Issues

The Arab Republic of Yemen and the Democratic Republic of Yemen united on 22 May 1990 to form the Republic of Yemen. Both the dinar and the rial circulated in the unified Republic of Yemen until 11 June 1996 at an exchange rate of 1:26. Following unification, captions were added to identify some design elements which may have been unfamiliar to all citizens.

CBY B13 (P23): **10 rials** (US$0.05)   VG   VF   UNC
Blue. Front: Al Baqilyah mosque. Back: Ma'rib Dam; coffee berries on branch. Solid security thread. Printer: (FCOF). 136 x 70 mm.
    ☐ a. No date. Signature 4.   FV   FV   1
           One-letter prefix numerator. Intro: 01.05.1990.
           Watermark: Coat of arms with stars in flags.
    ☐ b. Two-letter prefix numerator. Intro: 26.06.1990.   FV   FV   1
           Watermark: Coat of arms without stars in flags.
    ☐ bs. Diagonal red نموذج overprint on front;   —   —   200
           horizontal red *SPECIMEN Nº #* ovpt at lower left;
           diagonal red *SPECIMEN* overprint on back.
Replacement notes: Prefix اى/١.
Like CBY B14, but without denomination and Arabic caption at lower right on back.

CBY B14 (P24): **10 rials** (US$0.05)   VG   VF   UNC
Blue. Front: Al Baqilyah mosque. Back: Ma'rib Dam; coffee berries on branch; with Arabic caption at lower right. Solid security thread. Watermark: Coat of arms. Printer: (FCOF). 136 x 70 mm.
    ☐ a. No date. Signature 4. Intro: March 1993.   FV   FV   1.50
Replacement notes: Prefix اى/١.
Like CBY B13, but with denomination and Arabic caption at lower right on back.

CBY B15 (P26a): **20 rials** (US$0.10)   VG   VF   UNC
Brown. Front: Marble sculpture of seated figure with grapes. Back: Buildings in Sana'a. Solid security thread. Watermark: Coat of arms with stars in flags. Printer: (TDLR). 147 x 74 mm.
    ☐ a. No date. Signature 4. Intro: 01.05.1990.   FV   1   4
Like CBY B16, but without shading around name of bank at top center on front.

While there are other more subtle differences in the engravings between the issues, the Arabic name of the bank is on a clear multicolored background on earlier 20-rial notes (CBY B15, top), but thin horizontal shading was added on later notes (CBY B16, bottom).

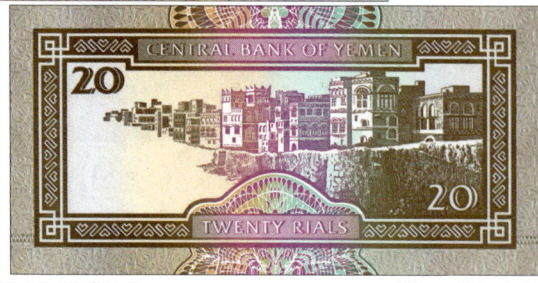

CBY B16 (P26b): **20 rials** (US$0.10)   VG   VF   UNC
Brown. Front: Marble sculpture of seated figure with grapes. Back: Buildings in Sana'a. Solid security thread. Watermark: Coat of arms without stars in flags. Printer: (TDLR). 147 x 74 mm.
    ☐ a. No date. Signature 4. Intro: 26.06.1990.   FV   1   4
Replacement notes: Prefix بى/١.
Like CBY B15, but with shading around name of bank at top center on front.

CBY B17 (P25): **20 rials** (US$0.10) VG VF UNC

Brown. Front: Marble sculpture of seated figure with grapes. Back: Modern ships and dhow boat in Aden harbor. Solid security thread. Watermark: Coat of arms without stars in flags. Printer: (G&D). 145 x 73 mm.

☐ a. No date. Signature 4. Intro: 1995. FV 0.50 2

Replacement notes: Prefix ١/ب‎غ.
The back was changed for a more equitable representation of north/south scenes.

CBY B18 (P27): **50 rials** (US$0.25) VG VF UNC

Brown. Front: Bronze statue of standing Ma'adkarib. Back: Buildings in Shibam. Solid security thread. Watermark: Coat of arms. Printer: (TDLR). 151 x 74 mm.

☐ a. No date. Signature 4. Intro: 10.02.1993. FV FV 1.25

Replacement notes: Prefix ١/ج‎.
Like CBY B19, but without Arabic caption at lower left on back.

CBY B19 (P27A): **50 rials** (US$0.25) VG VF UNC

Brown. Front: Bronze statue of standing Ma'adkarib. Back: Buildings in Shibam; Arabic caption at lower left. Solid security thread. Watermark: Coat of arms. Printer: (TDLR). 151 x 74 mm.

☐ a. No date. Signature 4. FV FV 1
☐ b. Signature 5. FV FV 1

Replacement notes: Prefix ١/ج‎.
Like CBY B18, but with Arabic caption at lower left on back.

CBY B20 (P28): **100 rials** (US$0.45) VG VF UNC

Violet. Front: Ancient water culvert in Aden. Back: Buildings in Sana'a with minaret and mountains. Solid security thread. Watermark: Coat of arms. Printer: (TDLR). 151 x 75 mm.

☐ a. No date. Signature 4. Intro: May 1993. FV FV 1.50
☐ b. Wmk: Feathers under eagle's wings end in triangles. FV FV 1.50
☐ c. Signature 5. FV FV 1.50
☐ as. Diagonal red نموذج overprint on front; diagonal red *SPECIMEN* ovpt on back; punched. — — 100
☐ bs. Diagonal red نموذج overprint on front; diagonal red *SPECIMEN* ovpt on back; punched. — — 200

Replacement notes: Prefix ١/ب‎غ.

YEMEN 1998-2001 ISSUES

1998-2001 Issues

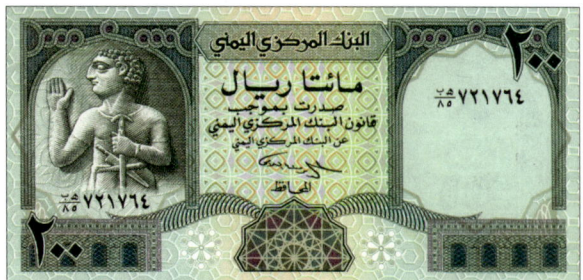

CBY B21 (P29): **200 rials** (US$0.90)   VG   VF   UNC

Green. Front: Alabaster sculpture of man with knife and sword, found in tomb at al-Jubah. Back: Mukalla harbor with boats. Solid security thread. Watermark: Coat of arms. Printer: (TDLR). 156 x 75 mm.

     a. No date. Signature 5. Intro: 11.03.1996.   FV   FV   3
     as. Diagonal red نموذج overprint on front;   —   —   350
         diagonal red SPECIMEN overprint on back.

Replacement notes: Prefix ١/غو.

CBY B22 (P30): **500 rials** (US$2.30)   VG   VF   UNC

Blue-violet. Front: Central Bank of Yemen headquarters building in Sana'a. Back: Pillars and ruins of the Bara'an temple near Ma'rib. Windowed security thread with demetalized Arabic text. Watermark: Coat of arms. Printer: (FCOF). 156 x 80 mm.

     a. No date. Signature 5. Intro: 15.02.1997.   FV   FV   9

Replacement notes: Prefix ١/وغ.

CBY B23 (P31): **500 rials** (US$2.30)   VG   VF   UNC

Blue. Front: Palace on the Rock at Wadi Dahr. Back: Al Muhdar mosque in Tarim, Hadramaut. Holographic stripe. Windowed security thread with demetalized Arabic text. Watermark: Coat of arms. Printer: Unknown. 155 x 80 mm.

     a. ٢٠٠١/١٤٢٢ (2001/AH1422). Signature 6.   FV   FV   9
         Intro: 2001.
     as. Diagonal red نموذج overprint on front;   —   —   255
         red # overprint at lower right;
         diagonal red SPECIMEN overprint on back.

Replacement notes: Prefix denominator ٩٩.

CBY B24 (P32): **1,000 rials** (US$4.60)   VG   VF   UNC

Pink and green. Front: Kathiri Sultan's palace in Seiyun, Hadramaut. Back: Bab al Yemen (main gate of Sana'a). Holographic stripe. Windowed security thread with demetalized Arabic text. Watermark: Coat of arms. Printer: Unknown. 157 x 85 mm.

     a. No date. Signature 6. Intro: 20.09.1998.   FV   FV   13
     as. Diagonal red نموذج overprint on front;   —   300   —
         red # overprint at lower right;
         diagonal red SPECIMEN overprint on back.

2004-2007 Issues

This 500-rial note is like the preceding issue, but the serial number now appears to the left of the revised holographic stripe. The 1,000-rial note is like the preceding issue, too, but it features a different color scheme.

CBY B25 (P34): **500 rials** (US$2.30)   VG   VF   UNC
Blue. Front: Palace on the Rock at Wadi Dahr. Back: Al Muhdar mosque in Tarim, Hadramaut. Holographic stripe. Windowed security thread with demetalized Arabic text. Watermark: Coat of arms. Printer: Unknown. 155 x 80 mm.
- a. ٢٠٠٧/١٤٢٨ (2007/AH1428). Signature 6.   FV   FV   6.50

CBY B26 (P33): **1,000 rials** (US$4.60)   VG   VF   UNC
Brown and green. Front: Sultan's palace in Seiyun, Hadramaut. Back: Bab al Yemen (main gate of Sana'a). Holographic stripe. Windowed security thread with demetalized Arabic text. Watermark: Coat of arms. Printer: Unknown. 156 x 83 mm.
- a. ٢٠٠٤/١٤٢٤ (2004/AH1424). Signature 6.   FV   FV   15
- b. ٢٠٠٦/١٤٢٧ (2006/AH1427).   FV   FV   10

Replacement notes: Prefix denomination ٩٩.

2009-2012 Issues

The 1,000-rial note is like the preceding issue, but with a holographic thread instead of a stripe, a revised registration device, blind embossing, and vertical *1000* in microperf.

CBY B27 (P35): **250 rials** (US$1.15)   VG   VF   UNC
Tan, blue, and red. Front: Al-Saleh mosque in Sana'a. Back: Mukalla Khor waterway in port city of Al Mukalla; buildings; bridges; mountains; Indian Ocean. Holographic security thread with demetalized ٢٥٠. Watermark: Coat of arms and electrotype ٢٥٠. Printer: (Goznak). 159 x 75 mm.
- a. ٢٠٠٩/١٤٣٠ (2009/AH1430). Signature 6.   FV   FV   2.50
  Intro: 14.11.2009.

This note is the first in the world to use Goznak's Visual Formed Image security thread.

CBY B28 (P36): **1,000 rials** (US$4.60)   VG   VF   UNC
Yellow and green. Front: Sultan's palace in Seiyun, Hadramaut. Back: Bab al Yemen (main gate of Sana'a). Holographic security thread with demetalized ١٠٠٠. Watermark: Coat of arms and electrotype ١٠٠٠. Printer: (Goznak). 156 x 83 mm.
- a. ٢٠٠٩/١٤٣٠ (2009/AH1430). Signature 6.   FV   FV   13
  Intro: August 2010.
- b. ٢٠١٢/١٤٣٣ (2012/AH1433). Intro: 12.10.2012.   FV   FV   13

Acknowledgements

This chapter was compiled with the generous assistance of Jim W.-C. Chen, Jean-Michel Engels, Murray Hanewich, Robert Mol, Manuel Rui Palhares, Luca Maria Peri, Hani Rida (http://sababanknotes.6te.net), TDS, Menelaos Stamatelos, Bill Stubkjaer, Peter Symes, Christoph Thomas, Christof Zellweger, and others.

Sources

Anonymous. "Yemen Provides Launch Pad for New Features." *Currency News.* November 2009. Volume 7 Number 11. p.10.

Cuhaj, George S. *Standard Catalog of World Paper Money, Modern Issues, 1961-Present.* 19th edition. 2013. ISBN 978-1-4402-3571-9. Krause Publications (www.krausebooks.com), 700 East State St., Iola, WI, 54990-0001.

Symes, Peter and Murray Hanewich and Keith Street. *The Bank Notes of Yemen.* 1997. ISBN 0-646-30063-6. Canberra, Australia.

Symes, Peter. Reference Site for Islamic Banknotes (www.islamicbanknotes.com).

Share Your Input, Info, and Images

This catalog is believed to be complete and correct as of the time of publication. Prices and face values were last updated 27 January 2012. Please report errors or omissions so that corrections may be made. If you can more precisely identify the name or location of anything depicted on a note, please share that information. Furthermore, if you own an unlisted type or variety, please submit scans of the front and back of the note so that it can be documented. Scans should be 300 dots per inch, 100% actual size, 24-bit color, saved as *uncompressed* JPEG files, and sent to owen@banknotenews.com. Be sure to fully describe all attributes of the note which are not apparent upon visual inspection of the images alone, such as physical dimension, watermark, and security thread.

Zaïre

For earlier issues, see Democratic Republic of the Congo.

Monetary System

23.07.1967: 1 Zairean zaïre (ZRZ) = 100 makuta
01.10.1993: 1 Zairean nouveau zaïre (ZRN) = 3 million zaïre
July 1998: 1 Congelese franc (CDF) = 100,000 nouveaux zaïres

Banque du Zaïre (Bank of Zaïre)

Following the change in the name of the country from the Republique du Congo to Zaïre on 27 October 1971, the Banque Nationale du Congo changed its name to the Banque Nationale du Zaïre under Service Order No. 218, 4 November 1971. A correction made by Service Order No. 219, 25 November 1971 changed the name to Banque du Zaïre (BDZ).

BDZ Signature Varieties

LE GOUVERNEUR (Governor)

1. Jules Fontaine Sambwa Pida N'Bagui (15.09.1970 - 10.08.1977)
2. Charles Bofossa W'Ambea Nkoso (19.08.1977 - 06.03.1979)
3. Jules Croy Emony Mondange (06.03.1979 - 27.08.1980)
4. Jules Fontaine Sambwa Pida N'Bagui (27.08.1980 - 12.04.1985)
5. Pierre Pay Pay wa Syakassighe (12.04.1985 - 30.03.1991)
6. John Gualberto Nyembo Shabani (30.03.1991 - 02.04.1993)
7. Joseph Buhendwa Bwa Mushaba (02.04.1993 - 01.02.1994)
8. Godefroid Ndiang Kabul (01.02.1994 - 25.11.1994)
9. Patrice Djamboleka Loma (16.01.1995 - 17.05.1997)

1972-1978 Issues

BDZ B1 (P16): **50 makuta**

Red. Front: Coat of arms; Mobutu Sésé Seko in civilian clothes; leopard. Back: Bank initials; native man and men fishing with nets. Solid security thread. Watermark: Mobutu Sésé Seko. Printer: *GIESECKE & DEVRIENT MUNICH*. 155 x 75 mm.

		VG	VF	UNC
a.	30 • 6 • 1973. Signature 1.	2	8	35
b.	4 • 10 • 1974.	2	8	35
c.	4 • 10 • 1975.	2	8	35
d.	24 • 6 • 1976.	2.50	10	40
e.	24 • 6 • 1977.	2.50	10	40
f.	20 • 5 • 1978. Signature 2.	1.50	7.50	25
as.	Diagonal red *SPECIMEN* overprint.	—	—	25

Replacement notes: Suffix Z.

BDZ B2 (P18): **1 zaïre**   VG   VF   UNC

Brown. Front: Coat of arms; Mobutu Sésé Seko in civilian clothes with toque; leopard. Back: Bank initials; elephant tusks; smokestack; pyramid. Solid security thread. Watermark: Mobutu Sésé Seko. Printer: *GIESECKE & DEVRIENT MUNICH*. 160 x 80 mm. Intaglio.

			VG	VF	UNC
☐	a.	15 • 3 • 1972. Signature 1.	1	4	15
☐	b.	27 • 10 • 1974.	1	4	15
☐	c.	20 • 5 • 1975.	1	4	15
☐	d.	27 • 10 • 1975.	1	4	15
☐	e.	27 • 10 • 1976.	1	4	15
☐	f.	27 • 10 • 1977. Signature 2.	0.75	2.50	10
☐	as.	Diagonal red *SPECIMEN* overprint.	—	—	45

Replacement notes: Suffix Z.

BDZ B4 (P21 & PR3): **5 zaïres**   VG   VF   UNC

Green. Front: Coat of arms; Mobutu Sésé Seko in civilian clothes; leopard. Back: Bank initials; carving of seated woman; Inga I hydroelectric dam on Congo River. Solid security thread printed *REPUBLIQUE DU ZAIRE*. Watermark: Mobutu Sésé Seko. Printer: *GIESECKE & DEVRIENT MUNICH*. 172 x 85 mm.

			VG	VF	UNC
☐	a.	30 • 11 • 1974. Signature 1. Suffix B.	2.50	10	40
☐	b.	30 • 6 • 1975. Unconfirmed.	—	—	—
☐	c.	24 • 11 • 1975. Suffix C.	2.50	10	40
☐	d.	24 • 11 • 1976. Suffix C - D.	2.50	10	40
☐	e.	24 • 11 • 1977. Signature 2. Suffix E - L.	1	2	5
☐	as.	Diagonal red *SPECIMEN* overprint.	—	—	65

Replacement notes: Suffix Z.

Also available as a regional issue with circular handstamp around the coat of arms at center.

BDZ B3 (P20): **5 zaïres**   VG   VF   UNC

Green. Front: Coat of arms; Mobutu Sésé Seko in civilian clothes; leopard. Back: Bank initials; carving of seated woman; Inga I hydroelectric dam on Congo River. Solid security thread. Watermark: Mobutu Sésé Seko. Printer: *GIESECKE & DEVRIENT MUNICH*. 172 x 85 mm.

			VG	VF	UNC
☐	a.	24 • 11 • 1972. Signature 1. Suffix A.	15	50	200
☐	p.	Separate front and back uniface proofs.	—	—	20

Replacement notes: Suffix Z.

1979-1981 Issues

These notes are like the preceding issues, but the two lowest denominations are now printed with lithograph instead of intaglio, the 5- and 10-zaïre notes have new colors, and the 50-zaïre denomination is entirely new.

BDZ B5 (P23 & PR4): **10 zaïres**　　　　　　　　VG　VF　UNC

Blue. Front: Coat of arms; Mobutu Sésé Seko in uniform; leopard. Back: Bank initials; shield depicting arm with hand holding torch. Solid security thread printed *REPUBLIQUE DU ZAIRE*. Watermark: Mobutu Sésé Seko. Printer: *GIESECKE & DEVRIENT MUNICH*. 180 x 90 mm.

- ☐ a.　30 • 6 • 1972. Signature 1. Suffix A - B.　　4　15　70
- ☐ b.　22 • 6 • 1974. Suffix B.　　　　　　　　　　4　15　70
- ☐ c.　30 • 6 • 1975. Suffix B - C.　　　　　　　　4　15　70
- ☐ d.　30 • 6 • 1976. Suffix C - D.　　　　　　　　4　15　70
- ☐ e.　27 • 10 • 1976. Unconfirmed.　　　　　　　—　—　—
- ☐ f.　27 • 10 • 1977. Signature 2. Suffix D - G.　0.75　2.50　10
- ☐ as.　Diagonal red *SPECIMEN* overprint.　　　　—　—　85

Replacement notes: Suffix Z.
Also available as a regional issue with circular handstamp around the coat of arms at center.

BDZ B6 (P17): **50 makuta**　　　　　　　　　　VG　VF　UNC

Red. Front: Coat of arms; Mobutu Sésé Seko in civilian clothes; leopard. Back: Bank initials; native man; men fishing with nets. Solid security thread. Watermark: Mobutu Sésé Seko. Printer: *GIESECKE & DEVRIENT MUNICH*. 150 x 75 mm. Lithographed.

- ☐ a.　24 • 11 • 1979. Signature 3.　　0.25　0.75　2.75
- ☐ b.　14 • 10 • 1980. Signature 1.　　0.25　0.75　2.75

Replacement notes: Suffix Z.

BDZ B7 (P19): **1 zaïre**　　　　　　　　　　　VG　VF　UNC

Brown. Front: Coat of arms; Mobutu Sésé Seko in civilian clothes with toque; leopard. Back: Bank initials; elephant tusks; smokestack; pyramid. Solid security thread. Watermark: Mobutu Sésé Seko. Printer: *GIESECKE & DEVRIENT MUNICH*. 160 x 80 mm. Lithographed.

- ☐ a.　22 • 10 • 1979. Signature 3.　　0.25　0.75　3.25
- ☐ b.　27 • 10 • 1980. Signature 1.　　0.25　1　4
- ☐ c.　20 • 5 • 1981.　　　　　　　　　0.25　1　4

Replacement notes: Suffix Z.

BDZ B8 (P22): **5 zaïres**   VG   VF   UNC

Blue. Front: Coat of arms; Mobutu Sésé Seko in civilian clothes with toque; leopard. Back: Bank initials; carving of seated woman; Inga I hydroelectric dam on Congo River. Solid security thread printed *REPUBLIQUE DU ZAIRE*. Watermark: Mobutu Sésé Seko. Printer: *GIESECKE & DEVRIENT MUNICH*. 170 x 85 mm.

- ☐ a. 20 • 5 • 1979. Signature 3. Suffix A - X.   0.50   2   8
- ☐ b. 27 • 10 • 1980. Signature 1. Suffix B - H.   0.50   1.25   5
- ☐ as. Diagonal red *SPECIMEN* overprint.   —   —   15

Replacement notes: Suffix Z.

BDZ B9 (P24): **10 zaïres**   VG   VF   UNC

Green. Front: Coat of arms; Mobutu Sésé Seko in uniform; leopard. Back: Bank initials; shield depicting arm with hand holding torch. Solid security thread printed *REPUBLIQUE DU ZAIRE*. Watermark: Mobutu Sésé Seko. Printer: *GIESECKE & DEVRIENT MUNICH*. 180 x 90 mm.

- ☐ a. 24 • 6 • 1979. Signature 3. Suffix A - N.   1.25   5   20
- ☐ b. 4 • 1 • 1981. Signature 1. Suffix Q - U.   1.25   5   20
- ☐ as. Diagonal red *SPECIMEN* overprint.   —   —   20

Replacement notes: Suffix Z.

BDZ B10 (P25): **50 zaïres**   VG   VF   UNC

Red. Front: Coat of arms; Mobutu Sésé Seko in civilian clothes with toque; leopard. Back: Bank initials; coat of arms. Solid security thread printed *REPUBLIQUE DU ZAIRE*. Watermark: Mobutu Sésé Seko. Printer: *GIESECKE & DEVRIENT MUNICH*. 190 x 95 mm.

- ☐ a. 4 • 2 • 1980. Signature 3.   2.50   10   40
- ☐ b. 24 • 11 • 1980. Signature 1.   5   20   80
- ☐ as. Diagonal red *SPECIMEN* overprint.   —   —   30
- ☐ p. Uniface proof.   —   —   1,000

Replacement notes: Suffix Z.

1982-1985 Issues

These notes were the first issues printed by the Hôtel des Monnaies in Zaïre, which was established under the technical direction of Giesecke & Devrient, which continued to print notes in Germany (and secretly in Burma) because the state-run operation lacked the capacity to keep up with the ever-increasing demand caused by high inflation.

BDZ B13 (P28): **50 zaïres**   VG   VF   UNC
Red. Front: Leopard; Mobutu Sésé Seko in civilian clothes with toque; coat of arms.
Back: Bank initials; five men on platform fishing with nets; fish. Solid security thread printed *REPUBLIQUE DU ZAIRE*. Watermark: Mobutu Sésé Seko. Printer: *GIESECKE & DEVRIENT MUNICH*. 145 x 69 mm.
- ☐ a. 24 • 11 • 1982. Signature 4.   1   4   16
- ☐ b. 24 • 6 • 1985. Signature 5.   0.50   2.50   10
- ☐ as. Diagonal red *SPECIMEN* overprint.   —   —   50
- ☐ bs. Diagonal red *SPECIMEN* overprint;   —   —   30
     horizontal red *SPECIMEN* # ovpt at lower left.

Replacement notes: Suffix Z.

BDZ B11 (P26 & P26A): **5 zaïres**   VG   VF   UNC
Blue. Front: Leopard; Mobutu Sésé Seko in civilian clothes with toque; coat of arms.
Back: Bank initials; Inga I hydroelectric dam on Congo River. Solid security thread printed *REPUBLIQUE DU ZAIRE*. Watermark: Mobutu Sésé Seko. 134 x 64 mm.
- ☐ a. 17 • 11 • 1982. Signature 4.   0.25   1.75   6
     Printer: *GIESECKE & DEVRIENT MUNICH*.
- ☐ b. 24 • 11 • 1985. Signature 5.   —   0.25   1
     Printer: *HOTEL DES MONNAIES-ZAÏRE*.
- ☐ as. Diagonal red *SPECIMEN* overprint.   —   —   85

Replacement notes: Suffix Z.

BDZ B14 (P29): **100 zaïres**   VG   VF   UNC
Orange. Front: Leopard; Mobutu Sésé Seko in civilian clothes with toque; coat of arms.
Back: Bank initials; Bank of Zaïre building. Solid security thread printed *REPUBLIQUE DU ZAIRE*. Watermark: Mobutu Sésé Seko. Printer: *GIESECKE & DEVRIENT MUNICH*. 149 x 73 mm.
- ☐ a. 30 • 6 • 1983. Signature 4.   2   8   25
- ☐ b. 30 • 6 • 1985. Signature 5.   0.25   1.25   5
- ☐ as. Diagonal red *SPECIMEN* overprint.   —   —   20
- ☐ bs. Diagonal red *SPECIMEN* overprint;   —   —   50
     horizontal red *SPECIMEN* # ovpt at lower left.

Replacement notes: Suffix Z.

BDZ B12 (P27 & P27A): **10 zaïres**   VG   VF   UNC
Green. Front: Leopard; Mobutu Sésé Seko in civilian clothes with toque; coat of arms. Back: Bank initials; arm with hand holding torch. Solid security thread printed *REPUBLIQUE DU ZAIRE*. Watermark: Mobutu Sésé Seko. 139 x 66 mm.
- ☐ a. 27 • 10 • 1982. Signature 4.   0.50   2   8
     Printer: *GIESECKE & DEVRIENT MUNICH*.
- ☐ b. 27 • 10 • 1985. Signature 5.   0.25   0.50   2.50
     Printer: *HOTEL DES MONNAIES-ZAÏRE*.
- ☐ as. Diagonal red *SPECIMEN* overprint.   —   —   50

Replacement notes: Suffix Z.

BDZ B15 (P30): 500 zaïres   VG   VF   UNC

Purple. Front: Leopard; Mobutu Sésé Seko in uniform with cap; coat of arms. Back: Bank initials; OEBK (Organization Équipage Banana-Kinshasa) suspension bridge (aka Pont Maréchal) over the Congo River at port Matadi, with tanker underneath. Solid security thread printed *REPUBLIQUE DU ZAIRE*. Watermark: Mobutu Sésé Seko. Printer: *GIESECKE & DEVRIENT MUNICH*. 154 x 76 mm.

- ☐ a. 14 • 10 • 1984. Signature 4.   5   20   80
- ☐ b. 14 • 10 • 1985. Signature 5.   0.50   2   8
- ☐ as. Diagonal red *SPECIMEN* overprint; horizontal red *SPECIMEN N⁰* # ovpt at lower left.   —   —   50
- ☐ bs. Diagonal red *SPECIMEN* overprint; horizontal red *SPECIMEN Nr.* # ovpt at lower left.   —   —   100

Replacement notes: Suffix Z.

BDZ B16 (P31): 1,000 zaïres   VG   VF   UNC

Green. Front: Leopard; Mobutu Sésé Seko in uniform with cap; coat of arms. Back: Bank initials; Palais du Peuple (Palace of the People) building and fountain in Kinshasa. Solid security thread printed *REPUBLIQUE DU ZAIRE*. Watermark: Mobutu Sésé Seko. Printer: *GIESECKE & DEVRIENT MUNICH*. 160 x 80 mm.

- ☐ a. 24 • 11 • 1985. Signature 5.   0.50   2   8
- ☐ as. Diagonal red *SPECIMEN* overprint; horizontal red *SPECIMEN N⁰* # ovpt at lower left.   —   —   40

Replacement notes: Suffix Z.

1988-1993 Issues

BDZ B17 (P32): 50 zaïres   VG   VF   UNC

Green. Front: Leopard; Mobutu Sésé Seko in uniform with cap; coat of arms. Back: Five men on platform fishing with nets; fish; bank initials. Solid security thread printed *REPUBLIQUE DU ZAIRE*. Watermark: Mobutu Sésé Seko. Printer: *HOTEL DES MONNAIES-ZAÏRE*. 129 x 61 mm.

- ☐ a. 30 • 6 • 1988. Signature 5.   —   0.25   1
- ☐ as. Diagonal red *SPECIMEN* overprint.   —   —   15

Replacement notes: Suffix Z.

BDZ B18 (P33): 100 zaïres   VG   VF   UNC

Purple. Front: Leopard; Mobutu Sésé Seko in uniform with cap; coat of arms. Back: Bank of Zaïre building; bank initials. Solid security thread printed *REPUBLIQUE DU ZAIRE*. Watermark: Mobutu Sésé Seko. Printer: *HOTEL DES MONNAIES-ZAÏRE*. 134 x 64 mm.

- ☐ a. 14 • 10 •1988. Signature 5.   0.25 0.75   3
- ☐ as. Diagonal red *SPECIMEN* overprint.   —   —   10

Replacement notes: Suffix Z.

BDZ B19 (P34): **500 zaïres**   VG   VF   UNC

Red. Front: Leopard; Mobutu Sésé Seko in uniform with cap; coat of arms. Back: OEBK (Organization Équipage Banana-Kinshasa) suspension bridge (aka Pont Maréchal) over the Congo River at port Matadi, with tanker underneath; bank initials. Solid security thread printed *REPUBLIQUE DU ZAIRE*. Watermark: Mobutu Sésé Seko. Printer: *HOTEL DES MONNAIES-ZAÏRE*. 139 x 67 mm.

   ☐ a.   24 • 6 • 1989. Signature 5.   0.25   1   4
   ☐ as.   Diagonal red *SPECIMEN* overprint.   —   —   10

Replacement notes: Suffix Z.

BDZ B20 (P35): **1,000 zaïres**   VG   VF   UNC

Purple. Front: Leopard; Mobutu Sésé Seko in uniform with cap; coat of arms. Back: Palais du Peuple (Palace of the People) building and fountain in Kinshasa; bank initials. Solid security thread printed *REPUBLIQUE DU ZAIRE*. Watermark: Mobutu Sésé Seko. Printer: *HOTEL DES MONNAIES-ZAÏRE*. 144 x 70 mm.

   ☐ a.   24.11.1989. Signature 5.   0.50   5   20
   ☐ as.   Diagonal red *SPECIMEN* overprint;   —   —   75
       horizontal red *SPECIMEN Nº* # ovpt at lower left.

Replacement notes: Suffix Z.

BDZ B21 (P36): **2,000 zaïres**   VG   VF   UNC

Red. Front: Leopard; Mobutu Sésé Seko in uniform with cap; coat of arms. Back: Men on platform fishing with nets; carving of seated woman; bank initials. Solid security thread printed *REPUBLIQUE DU ZAIRE*. Watermark: Mobutu Sésé Seko. Printer: *HOTEL DES MONNAIES-ZAÏRE*. 123 x 58 mm.

   ☐ a.   1 • 10 • 1991. Signature 6.   0.25   0.75   2.25
   ☐ as.   Diagonal red *SPECIMEN* overprint;   —   —   10
       horizontal red *SPECIMEN Nº* # ovpt at center left.

Replacement notes: Suffix Z.

BDZ B22 (P37): **5,000 zaïres**   VG   VF   UNC

Green. Front: Leopard; Mobutu Sésé Seko in uniform with cap; coat of arms. Back: Smokestack; pyramids; elephant tusks; bank initials. Solid security thread. Watermark: Mobutu Sésé Seko. Printer: *GIESECKE & DEVRIENT MUNICH*. 152 x 72 mm.

   ☐ a.   20 • 5 • 1988. Signature 5.   15   50   150
       Gold diamond to right of Mobutu Sésé Seko's ear.
   ☐ b.   Green diamond to right of Mobutu Sésé Seko's ear.   0.50   2   8
   ☐ as.   Diagonal red *SPECIMEN* overprint;   —   —   12
       horizontal red *SPECIMEN Nº* # ovpt at lower left.

Replacement notes: Suffix Z.

BDZ B22a (left) with gold diamond and BDZ B22b (right) with green diamond.

BDZ B23 (P38): **10,000 zaïres** VG VF UNC
Brown. Front: Leopard; Mobutu Sésé Seko in uniform with cap; coat of arms. Back: Banque du Zaire buildings with plaza; bank initials. Solid blue-yellow-red security thread printed *REPUBLIQUE DU ZAIRE*. Watermark: Mobutu Sésé Seko. Printer: *GIESECKE & DEVRIENT MUNICH*. 154 x 76 mm.

☐ a.   24 • 11 • 1989. Signature 5.   0.25   1.50   6
☐ as. Diagonal red *SPECIMEN* overprint;   —   —   10
       horizontal red *SPECIMEN Nº* # ovpt at lower left.

Replacement notes: Suffix Z.

BDZ B24 (P39): **20,000 zaïres** VG VF UNC
Pink and blue. Front: Leopard; Mobutu Sésé Seko in uniform with cap; coat of arms. Back: Bank of Zaïre building; bank initials. Solid security thread printed *REPUBLIQUE DU ZAIRE*. Watermark: Mobutu Sésé Seko. Printer: *HOTEL DES MONNAIES-ZAÏRE*. 139 x 67 mm.

☐ a.   1 • 7 • 1991. Signature 6.   0.25   0.75   3
☐ as. Diagonal red *SPECIMEN* overprint;   —   —   15
       horizontal red *SPECIMEN Nº* # ovpt at center left.

Replacement notes: Suffix Z.

BDZ B25 (P40): **50,000 zaïres** VG VF UNC
Brown. Front: Leopard; Mobutu Sésé Seko in uniform with cap; coat of arms. Back: Four Western gorillas; bank initials. Windowed security thread with demetalized *REPUBLIQUE DU ZAIRE*. Watermark: Mobutu Sésé Seko. Printer: *GIESECKE & DEVRIENT MUNICH*. 160 x 80 mm.

☐ a.   24 • 4 • 1991. Signature 5. Prefix J and JA.   0.75   2.50   10
☐ as. Diagonal red *SPECIMEN* overprint;   —   —   12
       horizontal red *SPECIMEN Nº* # ovpt at lower left.

Replacement notes: Suffix Z.

BDZ B26 (P41): **100,000 zaïres** VG VF UNC
Olive green. Front: Leopard; Mobutu Sésé Seko in uniform with cap; coat of arms. Back: Palais de la Nation (Palace of the Nation) building in Kinshasa; bank initials. Windowed security thread with demetalized *REPUBLIQUE DU ZAIRE*. Watermark: Mobutu Sésé Seko. Printer: *GIESECKE & DEVRIENT MUNICH*. 160 x 80 mm.

☐ a.   4 • 1 • 1992. Signature 6. Prefix K and KA.   0.25   1.25   5
☐ as. Diagonal red *SPECIMEN* overprint;   —   —   14
       horizontal red *SPECIMEN Nº* # ovpt at lower left.

Replacement notes: Suffix Z.

BDZ B27 (P42): **200,000 zaïres**　　　　　　　VG　VF　UNC

Blue. Front: Leopard; Mobutu Sésé Seko in uniform with cap; coat of arms. Back: Palais du Peuple (Palace of the People) building and fountain in Kinshasa; bank initials. Solid security thread with printed *REPUBLIQUE DU ZAIRE*. Watermark: Mobutu Sésé Seko. Printer: *HOTEL DES MONNAIES-ZAÏRE*. 144 x 70 mm.

- ☐ a.　1 • 3 • 1992. Signature 6.　　　　　　　　0.25　0.75　3
- ☐ as.　Diagonal red *SPECIMEN* overprint;　　　—　—　15
　　　 horizontal red *SPECIMEN Nº* # ovpt at center left.

Replacement notes: Suffix Z.

BDZ B28 (P43): **500,000 zaïres**　　　　　　　VG　VF　UNC

Orange. Front: Leopard; Mobutu Sésé Seko in uniform with cap; coat of arms. Back: Inga I hydroelectric dam on Congo River; bank initials. Windowed security thread with demetalized *REPUBLIQUE DU ZAIRE*. Watermark: Mobutu Sésé Seko. Printer: *GIESECKE & DEVRIENT MUNICH*. 160 x 78 mm.

- ☐ a.　15 • 3 • 1992. Signature 6. Prefix L and LA.　0.50　1.25　6
- ☐ as.　Diagonal red *SPECIMEN* overprint.　　　—　—　10

Replacement notes: Suffix Z.

BDZ B29 (P44 & P45): **1,000,000 zaïres**　　　VG　VF　UNC

Red. Front: Leopard; Mobutu Sésé Seko in uniform with cap; coat of arms. Back: OEBK (Organization Équipage Banana-Kinshasa) suspension bridge (aka Pont Maréchal) over the Congo River at port Matadi, with tanker underneath; bank initials. Windowed security thread with demetalized *REPUBLIQUE DU ZAIRE*. Watermark: Mobutu Sésé Seko. 160 x 80 mm.

- ☐ a.　31 • 7 • 1992. Signature 6. Prefix M and MA.　0.75　3　12
　　　 Printer: *GIESECKE & DEVRIENT MUNICH*.
- ☐ b.　15 • 3 • 1993. Prefix MB.　　　　　　　　0.75　3　12
　　　 Printer: *HOTEL DES MONNAIES-ZAÏRE*.
- ☐ c.　17 • 5 • 1993. Signature 7.　　　　　　　　0.50　1.25　5
- ☐ d.　30 • 6 • 1993.　　　　　　　　　　　　　0.50　1.25　5
- ☐ as.　Diagonal red *SPECIMEN* overprint;　　　—　—　15
　　　 horizontal red # ovpt at lower left.
- ☐ bs.　Diagonal red *SPECIMEN* overprint;　　　—　—　12
　　　 horizontal red *SPECIMEN Nº* # ovpt at center left.
- ☐ cs.　Diagonal red *SPECIMEN* overprint;　　　—　—　12
　　　 horizontal red *SPECIMEN* # ovpt at center left.

Replacement notes: Suffix Z.

1993-1994 Nouveau Zaïre Issues

With inflation estimated at 3,000% in 1993, the Banque du Zaïre revalued its currency at a rate of one nouveau zaïre to three million zaïre.

From 1993-1994, several denominations were inappropriately printed by Ciccone Calcográfica in Argentina, though they bore the imprint of Hotel des Monnaies. These notes entered circulation without the official authorization or knowledge of the Banque du Zaïre. As a result, it's possible to find notes of the same denomination and date from different printers with identical serial numbers.

BDZ B30 (P46): **5,000,000 zaïres** VG VF UNC
Brown. Front: Leopard; Mobutu Sésé Seko in uniform with cap; coat of arms. Back: Elephant tusks; smokestack; pyramids; bank initials. Windowed security thread with demetalized *REPUBLIQUE DU ZAIRE*. Watermark: Mobutu Sésé Seko. Printer: *HARRISON & SONS LIMITED*. 164 x 80 mm.

- a. 1 • 10 • 1992. Signature 6.   0.50   1.75   7
- as. Diagonal red *SPECIMEN* overprint;   —   —   20
  horizontal red # ovpt at lower left.

Replacement notes: Suffix Z.

This note was not immediately accepted as legal tender for several weeks following its introduction in some parts of the country (notably in the north-east), and in other parts of the country it was accepted for only part of its value. One reason for this mistrust was a grammatical error in the French number on the note, which reads *cinq millions zaïres* instead of *cinq millions de zaïres*.

BDZ B31 (P47): **1 nouveau likuta** VG VF UNC
Brown. Front: Leopard; Mobutu Sésé Seko in uniform with cap. Back: Independence Monument; coat of arms; bank initials. Solid security thread with demetalized *REPUBLIQUE DU ZAIRE*. Watermark: None. Printer: *GIESECKE & DEVRIENT MUNICH*. 124 x 58 mm.

- a. 24 • 6 • 1993. Signature 7.   0.25   0.50   1.50
- as. Diagonal red *SPECIMEN* overprint;   —   —   10
  horizontal red *SPECIMEN N°* # ovpt at lower left.

Replacement notes: Suffix Z.

BDZ B32 (P48): **5 nouveaux makuta** VG VF UNC
Blue-green. Front: Leopard; Mobutu Sésé Seko in uniform with cap. Back: Independence Monument; coat of arms; bank initials. Solid security thread with demetalized *REPUBLIQUE DU ZAIRE*. Watermark: None. Printer: *GIESECKE & DEVRIENT MUNICH*. 124 x 58 mm.

- a. 24 • 6 • 1993. Signature 7.   —   0.25   1
- as. Diagonal red *SPECIMEN* overprint;   —   —   10
  horizontal red *SPECIMEN N°* # ovpt at lower left.

Replacement notes: Suffix Z.

BDZ B33 (P49): **10 nouveaux makuta**   VG   VF   UNC
Green. Front: Leopard; Mobutu Sésé Seko in uniform with cap; coat of arms. Back: Elephant tusks; smokestack; pyramids; bank initials. No security thread. Watermark: Mobutu Sésé Seko. Printer: *HOTEL DES MONNAIES-ZAÏRE* (Ciccone Calcográfica, Argentina). 158 x 79 mm.
☐ a. 24 • 6 • 1993. Signature 7.   —   0.25   1
Replacement notes: Suffix Z.

BDZ B34 (P51): **50 nouveaux makuta**   VG   VF   UNC
Orange. Front: Leopard; Mobutu Sésé Seko in uniform with cap; coat of arms. Back: Native man and men fishing with nets; bank initials. No security thread. Watermark: Mobutu Sésé Seko. Printer: *HOTEL DES MONNAIES-ZAÏRE* (Ciccone Calcográfica, Argentina). 158 x 79 mm.
☐ a. 24 • 6 • 1993. Signature 7.   —   0.25   1
Replacement notes: Suffix Z.

BDZ B35 (P52): **1 nouveau zaïre**   VG   VF   UNC
Violet. Front: Leopard; Mobutu Sésé Seko in uniform with cap; coat of arms. Back: Banque du Zaïre building; bank initials. Windowed security thread with demetalized *REPUBLIQUE DU ZAIRE*. Watermark: Mobutu Sésé Seko. Printer: *GIESECKE & DEVRIENT MUNICH*. 160 x 80 mm.
☐ a. 24 • 6 • 1993. Signature 7.   —   0.25   1
☐ as. Diagonal red *SPECIMEN* overprint.   —   —   10
Replacement notes: Suffix Z.

BDZ B36 (P53): **5 nouveaux zaïres**   VG   VF   UNC
Brown. Front: Leopard; Mobutu Sésé Seko in uniform with cap; coat of arms. Back: Palais de la Nation (Palace of the Nation) building in Kinshasa; bank initials. Windowed security thread with demetalized *REPUBLIQUE DU ZAIRE*. Watermark: Mobutu Sésé Seko. Printer: *GIESECKE & DEVRIENT MUNICH*. 160 x 80 mm.
☐ a. 24 • 6 • 1993. Signature 7.   —   0.25   1
☐ b. Signature 8.   0.25   1   4
☐ as. Diagonal red *SPECIMEN* overprint;   —   —   12
      horizontal red *SPECIMEN N°* # ovpt at lower left.
Replacement notes: Suffix Z.

BDZ B37 (P54 & P55): **10 nouveaux zaïres** VG VF UNC

Light green. Front: Leopard; Mobutu Sésé Seko in uniform with cap; coat of arms. Back: Palais du Peuple (Palace of the People) building and fountain in Kinshasa; bank initials. Windowed security thread with demetalized *REPUBLIQUE DU ZAIRE*. Watermark: Mobutu Sésé Seko. 160 x 80 mm.

☐ a. 24 • 6 • 1993. Signature 7. — 0.50 2
    Printer: *GIESECKE & DEVRIENT MUNICH*.
☐ b. Printer: *HOTEL DES MONNAIES-ZAÏRE* (Ciccone — 0.25 1.25
    Calcográfica, Argentina).
☐ as. Diagonal red *SPECIMEN* overprint; — — 10
    horizontal red *SPECIMEN Nº* # ovpt at lower left.

Replacement notes: Suffix Z.

BDZ B39 (P57): **50 nouveaux zaïres** VG VF UNC

Red. Front: Leopard; Mobutu Sésé Seko in uniform with cap; coat of arms. Back: Inga I hydroelectric dam on Congo River; bank initials. No security thread. Watermark: Mobutu Sésé Seko. Printer: *HOTEL DES MONNAIES-ZAÏRE* (Ciccone Calcográfica, Argentina). 160 x 80 mm.

☐ a. 24 • 6 • 1993. Signature 7. 0.25 0.75 3.50

Replacement notes: Suffix Z.

BDZ B38 (P56): **20 nouveaux zaïres** VG VF UNC

Blue, brown, and green. Front: Leopard; Mobutu Sésé Seko in uniform with cap; coat of arms. Back: Palais du Peuple (Palace of the People) building and fountain in Kinshasa; bank initials. No security thread. Watermark: Mobutu Sésé Seko. Printer: *HOTEL DES MONNAIES-ZAÏRE* (Ciccone Calcográfica, Argentina). 160 x 80 mm.

☐ a. 24 • 6 • 1993. Signature 7. 0.25 0.75 3.50

Replacement notes: Suffix Z.

BDZ B40 (P59): **50 nouveaux zaïres** VG VF UNC

Red. Front: Leopard; Mobutu Sésé Seko in uniform with cap; coat of arms. Back: Inga I hydroelectric dam on Congo River; bank initials. Windowed security thread with demetalized *REPUBLIQUE DU ZAIRE*. Watermark: Mobutu Sésé Seko. Printer: *HOTEL DES MONNAIES-ZAÏRE*. 160 x 80 mm.

☐ a. 15 • 2 • 1994. Signature 8. 0.75 2.50 20
☐ as. Diagonal red *SPECIMEN* overprint; — — 10
    horizontal red *SPECIMEN Nº* # ovpt at center left.

Replacement notes: Suffix Z.
Like B39, but lithographed (not intaglio), windowed thread, and color changes on back.

BDZ B41 (P58, P58A & P60): **100 nouveaux zaïres**   VG   VF   UNC

Purple. Front: Leopard; Mobutu Sésé Seko in uniform with cap; coat of arms. Back: OEBK (Organization Équipage Banana-Kinshasa) suspension bridge (aka Pont Maréchal) over the Congo River at port Matadi, with tanker underneath; bank initials. Windowed security thread with demetalized *REPUBLIQUE DU ZAIRE*. Watermark: Mobutu Sésé Seko. 160 x 80 mm.

- ☐ a. 24 • 6 • 1993. Signature 7.   0.25   1.25   6
  Printer: *GIESECKE & DEVRIENT MUNICH*.
- ☐ b. Printer: *HOTEL DES MONNAIES-ZAÏRE*.   1.25   5   10
- ☐ c. 15 • 2 • 1994. Signature 8.   0.25   1.25   6
  Printer: *GIESECKE & DEVRIENT MUNICH*.
- ☐ d. Printer: *HOTEL DES MONNAIES-ZAÏRE*.   0.25   1.25   6
- ☐ as. Diagonal red *SPECIMEN* overprint;   —   —   12
  horizontal red *SPECIMEN Nº* # ovpt at lower left.

Replacement notes: Suffix Z.

BDZ B42 (P61 & P62): **200 nouveaux zaïres**   VG   VF   UNC

Olive green. Front: Leopard; Mobutu Sésé Seko in uniform with cap; coat of arms. Back: Men fishing with nets from wooden structure; bank initials. Windowed security thread with demetalized *REPUBLIQUE DU ZAIRE*. Watermark: Mobutu Sésé Seko. 160 x 80 mm.

- ☐ a. 15 • 2 • 1994. Signature 8.   —   0.50   2
  Printer: *HOTEL DES MONNAIES-ZAÏRE*.
- ☐ b. Printer: *GIESECKE & DEVRIENT MUNICH*.   —   0.75   3
- ☐ as. Diagonal red *SPECIMEN* overprint;   —   —   10
  horizontal red *SPECIMEN Nº* # ovpt at center left.
- ☐ bs. Diagonal red *SPECIMEN* overprint;   —   —   —
  horizontal red *SPECIMEN Nr.* # ovpt at lower left.

Replacement notes: Suffix Z.

BDZ B43 (P63 & P64 & P64A): **500 nouveaux zaïres** VG VF UNC

Dark olive green. Front: Leopard; Mobutu Sésé Seko in uniform with cap; coat of arms. Back: Banque du Zaire buildings with plaza; bank initials. Windowed security thread with demetalized *REPUBLIQUE DU ZAIRE*. Watermark: Mobutu Sésé Seko. 160 x 80 mm.

- a. 15 • 2 • 1994. Signature 8. — 0.50 2
    Printer: *HOTEL DES MONNAIES-ZAÏRE*.
- b. Printer: *GIESECKE & DEVRIENT MUNICH*. — 0.50 2
- c. Printer: *HOTEL DES MONNAIES-ZAÏRE* 0.25 0.75 2.50
    (Ciccone Calcográfica, Argentina). Prefix X and XA.
- bs. Diagonal red *SPECIMEN* overprint; — — —
    horizontal red *SPECIMEN N°* # ovpt at lower left.
- cs. Diagonal red *SPECIMEN* overprint; — — —
    horizontal red *SPECIMEN N°* # ovpt at center left.

Replacement notes: Suffix Z.

1995-1996 Issues

BDZ B44 (P65): **500 nouveaux zaïres** VG VF UNC

Blue. Front: Bank initials as registration device; leopard; Mobutu Sésé Seko in uniform with cap; coat of arms. Back: Denomination; bank initials. Wide windowed security thread. Thin windowed security thread with demetalized *REPUBLIQUE DU ZAIRE*. Watermark: Mobutu Sésé Seko. Printer: *HOTEL DES MONNAIES-ZAÏRE*. 160 x 74 mm.

- a. 30 • 1 • 1995. Signature 9. — 0.50 2.50
- as. Diagonal red *SPECIMEN* overprint; — — 10
    horizontal red *SPECIMEN N°* # ovpt at center left.

Replacement notes: Suffix Z.

BDZ B45 (P66 & P67): **1,000 nouveaux zaïres** VG VF UNC

Olive green. Front: Bank initials as registration device; leopard; Mobutu Sésé Seko in uniform with cap; coat of arms. Back: Denomination; bank initials. Wide windowed security thread. Thin windowed security thread with demetalized *REPUBLIQUE DU ZAIRE*. Watermark: Mobutu Sésé Seko. 160 x 74 mm.

- a. 30 • 1 • 1995. Signature 9. 0.25 1 4
    Printer: *GIESECKE & DEVRIENT MUNICH*.
- b. Printer: *HOTEL DES MONNAIES-ZAÏRE*. — 1.25 5
- as. Diagonal red *SPECIMEN* overprint; — — 12
    horizontal red *SPECIMEN N°* # ovpt at lower left.

Replacement notes: Suffix Z.

BDZ B46 (P68 & P69): **5,000 nouveaux zaïres** VG VF UNC

Rust. Front: Bank initials as registration device; leopard; Mobutu Sésé Seko in uniform with cap; coat of arms. Back: Denomination; bank initials. Wide windowed security thread. Thin windowed security thread with demetalized *REPUBLIQUE DU ZAIRE*. Watermark: Mobutu Sésé Seko. 160 x 74 mm.

- a. 30 • 1 • 1995. Signature 9. 0.75 2.50 10
    Printer: *GIESECKE & DEVRIENT MUNICH*.
- b. Printer: *HOTEL DES MONNAIES-ZAÏRE*. 0.25 0.75 3
- as. Diagonal red *SPECIMEN* overprint; — — 12
    horizontal red *SPECIMEN N°* # ovpt at lower left.

Replacement notes: Suffix Z.

BDZ B47 (P70 & P71): **10,000 nouveaux zaïres**　　　　**VG　VF　UNC**

Blue. Front: Bank initials as registration device; leopard; Mobutu Sésé Seko in uniform with cap; coat of arms. Back: Denomination; bank initials. Holographic stripe. Windowed security thread with demetalized *REPUBLIQUE DU ZAIRE*. Watermark: Mobutu Sésé Seko. 160 x 74 mm.

- ☐ a.　30 • 1 • 1995. Signature 9.　　　　　　　　0.25　1.25　6
　　　Printer: *GIESECKE & DEVRIENT MUNICH*.
- ☐ b.　Printer: *HOTEL DES MONNAIES-ZAÏRE*.　　0.25　1.25　6
- ☐ as.　Diagonal red *SPECIMEN* overprint;　　　　—　—　12
　　　horizontal red *SPECIMEN Nº #* ovpt at lower left.

Replacement notes: Suffix Z.

BDZ B48 (P72 & P73): **20,000 nouveaux zaïres**　　　　**VG　VF　UNC**

Brown. Front: Bank initials as registration device; leopard; Mobutu Sésé Seko in uniform with cap; coat of arms. Back: Denomination; bank initials. Holographic stripe. Windowed security thread with demetalized *REPUBLIQUE DU ZAIRE*. Watermark: Mobutu Sésé Seko. 160 x 74 mm.

- ☐ a.　30 • 1 • 1996. Signature 9.　　　　　　　　0.50　1.50　7
　　　Printer: *GIESECKE & DEVRIENT MUNICH*.
- ☐ b.　Printer: *HOTEL DES MONNAIES-ZAÏRE*.　　0.50　1.50　7
- ☐ as.　Diagonal red *SPECIMEN* overprint;　　　　—　—　12
　　　horizontal red *SPECIMEN Nº #* ovpt at lower left.

Replacement notes: Suffix Z.

BDZ B49 (P74 & P75): **50,000 nouveaux zaïres**　　　　**VG　VF　UNC**

Purple. Front: Bank initials as registration device; leopard; Mobutu Sésé Seko in uniform with cap; coat of arms. Back: Denomination; bank initials. Holographic stripe. Windowed security thread with demetalized *REPUBLIQUE DU ZAIRE*. Watermark: Mobutu Sésé Seko. 160 x 74 mm.

- ☐ a.　30 • 1 • 1996. Signature 9.　　　　　　　　0.75　3　12
　　　Printer: *GIESECKE & DEVRIENT MUNICH*.
- ☐ b.　Printer: *HOTEL DES MONNAIES-ZAÏRE*.　　0.75　3　12
- ☐ as.　Diagonal red *SPECIMEN* overprint;　　　　—　—　12
　　　horizontal red *SPECIMEN Nº #* ovpt at lower left.

Replacement notes: Suffix Z.

BDZ B50 (P76 & P77): **100,000 nouveaux zaïres**　　　　**VG　VF　UNC**

Orange. Front: Bank initials as registration device; leopard; Mobutu Sésé Seko in uniform with cap; coat of arms. Back: Denomination; bank initials. Holographic stripe. Windowed security thread with demetalized *REPUBLIQUE DU ZAIRE*. Watermark: Mobutu Sésé Seko. 160 x 74 mm.

- ☐ a.　30 • 6 • 1996. Signature 9.　　　　　　　　0.50　1.50　6
　　　Printer: *GIESECKE & DEVRIENT MUNICH*.
- ☐ b.　Printer: *HOTEL DES MONNAIES-ZAÏRE*.　　0.50　2　8
- ☐ as.　Diagonal red *SPECIMEN* overprint;　　　　—　—　15
　　　horizontal red *SPECIMEN Nº #* ovpt at lower left.

Replacement notes: Suffix Z.

BDZ B51 (P77A): **100,000 nouveaux zaïres**　　　　　　VG　VF　UNC
Blue-green. Front: Bank initials as registration device; leopard; Mobutu Sésé Seko in uniform with cap; coat of arms. Back: Denomination; bank initials. Holographic stripe. Windowed security thread with demetalized *REPUBLIQUE DU ZAIRE*. Watermark: Mobutu Sésé Seko. Printer: *HOTEL DES MONNAIES-ZAÏRE*. 160 x 74 mm.

☐　a.　30 • 6 • 1996. Signature 9.　　　　　　　　　　1　4　15
　　　Holographic stripe with *BZ* (correct).
☐　b.　Holographic stripe with backwards *B* in *BZ* (error).　1　4　15
☐　as.　Diagonal red *SPECIMEN* overprint;　　　　　—　—　25
　　　horizontal red *SPECIMEN Nº* ovpt at center left
　　　(without running specimen number).

Replacement notes: Suffix Z.

 On some notes, the *B* in the holographic stripe is backwards (BDZ B51b, right) even though all other text on the stripe has the correct orientation (B51a, left). This error has been confirmed on BDZ B52b as well.

BDZ B52 (P78): **500,000 nouveaux zaïres**　　　　　　VG　VF　UNC
Light green. Front: Bank initials and fish as registration devices; Mobutu Sésé Seko in uniform with cap; coat of arms. Back: Map; four people in canoe with produce; fish; bank initials. Holographic stripe. Windowed security thread with demetalized *REPUBLIQUE DU ZAIRE*. Watermark: Mobutu Sésé Seko. Printer: *GIESECKE & DEVRIENT MUNICH*. 160 x 74 mm.

☐　a.　25 • 10 • 1996. Signature 9.　　　　　　　　0.50　2　8
　　　Holographic stripe with *BZ* (correct).
☐　b.　Holographic stripe with backwards *B* in *BZ* (error).　0.50　2　8
☐　as.　Diagonal red *SPECIMEN* overprint;　　　　　—　—　20
　　　horizontal red *SPECIMEN Nº* # ovpt at lower left.

Replacement notes: Suffix Z.

BDZ B53 (P79): **1,000,000 nouveaux zaïres**　　　　　VG　VF　UNC
Light violet. Front: Bank initials and diamonds as registration devices; Mobutu Sésé Seko in uniform with cap; coat of arms. Back: Map; mine; diamond; bank initials. Holographic stripe. Windowed security thread with demetalized *REPUBLIQUE DU ZAIRE*. Watermark: Mobutu Sésé Seko. Printer: *GIESECKE & DEVRIENT MUNICH*. 160 x 74 mm.

☐　a.　25 • 10 • 1996. Signature 9.　　　　　　　　0.75　2.25　9
☐　as.　Diagonal red *SPECIMEN* overprint;　　　　　—　—　15
　　　horizontal red *SPECIMEN Nº* # ovpt at lower left.

Replacement notes: Suffix Z.

Looking Forward

With the regime change of 17 May 1997, Zaïre reverted to the Democratic Republic of the Congo, and the Bank of Zaïre changed its name to the Banque Centrale du Congo.

For later issues, see Congo Democratic Republic.

Acknowledgements

This chapter was compiled with the generous assistance of Thomas Augustsson, Arigo Avbovbo, Federico Antonio, Jim W.-C. Chen, Kristian Chiduch (www.worldbanknotes.de), Donald Cleveland, Vincent Deprêtre (vdepretre@wanadoo.fr), Richard Miranda, Alexander Petrov, Andrew Roberts, Bill Stubkjaer, Richard Sutherland, Christoph Thomas, Tristan Williams, Christof Zellweger, and others.

Sources

Bender, Klaus W. *Moneymakers: The Secret World of Banknote Printing.* 1st edition. 2006. ISBN 3-527-50236-X. Wiley (www.wiley.com).

Cuhaj, George S. *Standard Catalog of World Paper Money, Modern Issues, 1961-Present.* 19th edition. 2013. ISBN 978-1-4402-3571-9. Krause Publications (www.krausebooks.com), 700 East State St., Iola, WI, 54990-0001.

Yandesa Mavuzi, Martin. *Numismatique des Monnaies du Congo.* 2010. Brussels, Belgium.

Share Your Input, Info, and Images

This catalog is believed to be complete and correct as of the time of publication. Prices and face values were last updated 3 June 2011. Please report errors or omissions so that corrections may be made. If you can more precisely identify the name or location of anything depicted on a note, please share that information. Furthermore, if you own an unlisted type or variety, please submit scans of the front and back of the note so that it can be documented. Scans should be 300 dots per inch, 100% actual size, 24-bit color, saved as *uncompressed* JPEG files, and sent to owen@banknotenews.com. Be sure to fully describe all attributes of the note which are not apparent upon visual inspection of the images alone, such as physical dimension, watermark, and security thread.

Zambia

For earlier issues, see Rhodesia & Nyasaland.

Monetary System
1964: 1 Zambian pound = 20 shillings
16.01.1968: 1 Zambian kwacha (ZMK) = 100 ngwee
01.01.2013: 1 Zambian kwacha (ZMW) = 1,000 ZMK

Bank of Zambia

The Bank of Zambia (BOZ) was established to take over from the Bank of Northern Rhodesia on 7 August 1964, although its Act was not passed until June 1965. The Bank of Northern Rhodesia was itself constituted from the Lusaka branch of the Bank of Rhodesia and Nyasaland after it broke up together with the Federation of Rhodesia and Nyasaland on 31 December 1963.

For more information, visit www.boz.zm.

BOZ Signature Varieties

GOVERNOR

1. Richard C.H. Hallett (1964 - 1967)
2. Justin B. Zulu (1967 - 1970)
3. Valentine S. Musakanya (1970 - 1972)
4. Bitwell R. Kuwani (1972 - 1976, 1981-1984)
5. Luke J. Mwanashiku (1976 - 1981)
6. David A. R. Phiri (1984 - 1986)
7. Leonard S. Chivuno (1986 - 1987)
8. Francis X. Nkhoma (1987 - 1989)
9. Jacques A. Bussiere (1990 - 1992)
10. Dominic Mulaisho (1992 - 1995)
11. Jacob Mwanza (1995 - 2002)
12. Caleb M. Fundanga (2002 - 2011)
13. Michael M. Gondwe (2011 - present)

1963 Issues

This unissued 1-pound proof is available in several varieties, in different color schemes, with and without punches, dummy date, sample signature, and serial number.

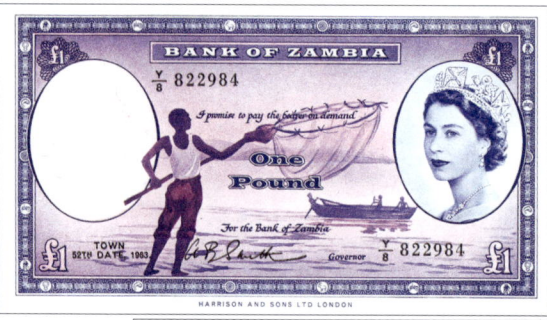

BOZ BA1 (PA1): 1 pound   VG   VF   UNC
Front: Fisherman with net on shore; two people in boat; Queen Elizabeth II. Back: Ross's Turaco bird on branch. Solid security thread. Watermark: Lion head. Printer: *HARRISON AND SONS LTD LONDON*. 150 x 82 mm.
- p1. Purple and blue. 52ᵀᴴ DATE, 1963.   —   2,500   5,800
  Signature A. B. Smith. Unissued.
- p2. Purple and pink. No date.   —   —   5,800
  No signature. Unissued.

1964 Issues

In 1964, the Bank of Zambia issued three notes in the denominations of 10 shillings, 1 pound, and 5 pounds, reflecting the nation's British colonial past and maintaining the same colors and general designs of the notes issued by the Bank of Rhodesia and Nyasaland. Although there are over 70 indigenous languages spoken in Zambia, the official language is English, as evidenced by its use on all notes past and present.

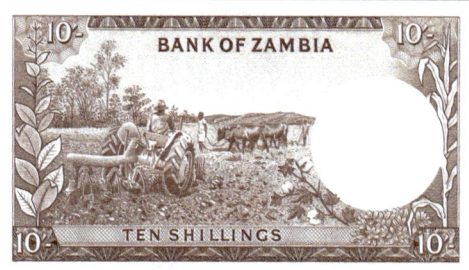

BOZ B1 (P1): **10 shillings**　　　　　　　　　VG　VF　UNC
Brown. Front: Coat of arms; chaplin's barbet (tricholaema) bird on branch. Back: Man plowing field with tractor; tobacco; cotton; corn. Solid security thread. Watermark: Wildebeest head. Printer: *THOMAS DE LA RUE & COMPANY LIMITED*. 134 x 75 mm.

☐ a.　No date. Sig. 1. Prefix A/1 - A/5. Intro: 1964.　　75　125　425
☐ as.　Horizontal *CANCELLED* perforation.　　—　—　300

BOZ B2 (P2): **1 pound**　　　　　　　　　　VG　VF　UNC
Green. Front: Coat of arms; black-cheeked lovebird on branch. Back: Copper mine. Solid security thread. Watermark: Wildebeest head. Printer: *THOMAS DE LA RUE & COMPANY LIMITED*. 150 x 82 mm.

☐ a.　No date. Sig. 1. Prefix B/1 - B/13. Intro: 1964.　　100　200　900
☐ as.　Horizontal *CANCELLED* perforation.　　—　—　325

BOZ B3 (P3): **5 pounds**　　　　　　　　　　VG　VF　UNC
Blue. Front: Coat of arms; wildebeest. Back: Victoria Falls. Solid security thread. Watermark: Wildebeest head. Printer: *THOMAS DE LA RUE & COMPANY LIMITED*. 159 x 88 mm.

☐ a.　No date. Sig. 1. Prefix C/1 - C/3. Intro: 1964.　　100　1,000　2,500
☐ as1. Horizontal *CANCELLED* perforation.　　—　—　800
☐ as2. Diagonal red *SPECIMEN* and DLR oval ovpts; horizontal red *SPECIMEN Nº* # ovpt at lower left; signature punched.　　—　—　1,500

1968 Issues

The Currency Act of 1967 replaced the Zambian pound, shilling, pence currency for new kwacha and ngwee currency. Thus on 16 January 1968, the Zambian pound was replaced by the kwacha with the new official rate equal to one half the old unit, or US$1. The 5-pound note became 10 kwacha, the 1-pound note 2 kwacha, the 10-shilling note 1 kwacha, and a new 50-ngwee note was introduced to correspond to the old 5 shillings. At the same time, the currency was decimalized.

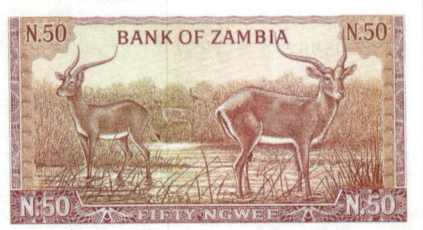

BOZ B4 (P4): **50 ngwee** (demonetized 31.12.2015)   VG   VF   UNC
Red. Front: Coat of arms; President Kenneth Kaunda. Back: Two antelopes. Solid security thread. Watermark: Kenneth Kaunda. Printer: *THOMAS DE LA RUE & COMPANY LIMITED*. 121 x 67 mm.
☐ a. No date. Sig. 2. 1/A - 5/A. Prefix Intro: 1968.   5   30   80

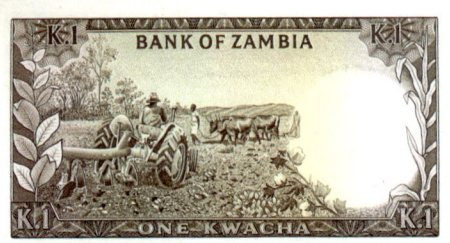

BOZ B5 (P5): **1 kwacha** (demonetized 31.12.2015)   VG   VF   UNC
Brown. Front: Coat of arms; President Kenneth Kaunda. Back: Man plowing field with tractor; tobacco; cotton; corn. Solid security thread. Watermark: Kenneth Kaunda. Printer: *THOMAS DE LA RUE & COMPANY LIMITED*. 130 x 70 mm.
☐ a. No date. Sig. 2. Prefix 1/B - 13/B. Intro: 1968.   5   40   100

BOZ B6 (P6): **2 kwacha** (demonetized 31.12.2015)   VG   VF   UNC
Green. Front: Coat of arms; President Kenneth Kaunda. Back: Copper mine. Solid security thread. Watermark: Kenneth Kaunda. Printer: *THOMAS DE LA RUE & COMPANY LIMITED*. 136 x 73 mm.
☐ a. No date. Sig. 2. Prefix 1/C - 31/C. Intro: 1968.   10   50   150

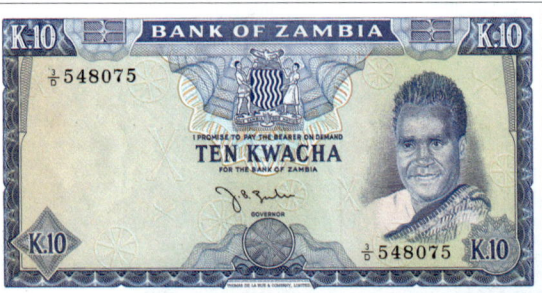
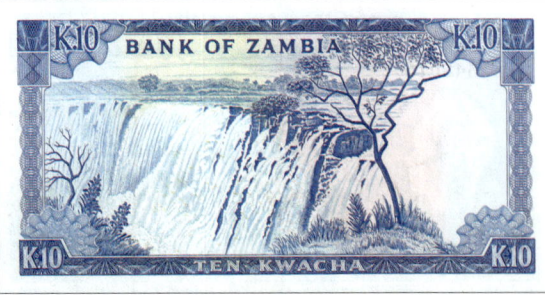

BOZ B7 (P7): **10 kwacha** (demonetized 31.12.2015)   VG   VF   UNC
Blue. Front: Coat of arms; President Kenneth Kaunda. Back: Victoria Falls. Solid security thread. Watermark: Kenneth Kaunda. Printer: *THOMAS DE LA RUE & COMPANY LIMITED*. 152 x 79 mm.
☐ a. No date. Sig. 2. Prefix 1/D - 7/D. Intro: 1968.   200   400   850

BOZ B8 (P8): **20 kwacha** (demonetized 31.12.2015) VG   VF   UNC
Purple. Front: Coat of arms; President Kenneth Kaunda. Back: National Assembly building in Lusaka. Solid security thread. Watermark: Kenneth Kaunda. Printer: *THOMAS DE LA RUE & COMPANY LIMITED*. 160 x 82 mm.
- ☐ a.   No date. Signature 2. Prefix 1/E. Intro: 1968.   50   200   950
- ☐ as. Specimen: No overprints; punched.   —   —   225

1969 Issues

These notes are like the preceding issues, except that they lack the dot in the denominations printed in the corners.

BOZ B9 (P9): **50 ngwee** (demonetized 31.12.2015) VG   VF   UNC
Red. Front: Coat of arms; President Kenneth Kaunda. Back: Two antelopes. Solid security thread. Watermark: Kenneth Kaunda. Printer: *THOMAS DE LA RUE & COMPANY LIMITED*. 121 x 67 mm.
- ☐ a.   No date. Intro: 1969.   30   60   120
           Signature 3. Prefix 7/A - 12/A.
- ☐ b.   Signature 4. Prefix 13/A - 15/A.   5   20   40
- ☐ bs. Diagonal red *SPECIMEN* overprint.   —   —   150

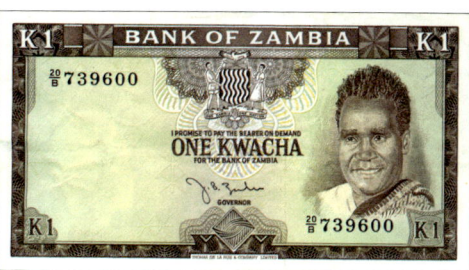

BOZ B10 (P10): **1 kwacha** (demonetized 31.12.2015) VG   VF   UNC
Brown. Front: Coat of arms; President Kenneth Kaunda. Back: Man plowing field with tractor; tobacco; cotton; corn. Solid security thread. Watermark: Kenneth Kaunda. Printer: *THOMAS DE LA RUE & COMPANY LIMITED*. 130 x 70 mm.
- ☐ a.   No date. Intro: 1969.   15   50   240
           Signature 2. Prefix 17/B - 20/B.
- ☐ b.   Signature 3. Prefix 21/B - 26/B.   10   25   75

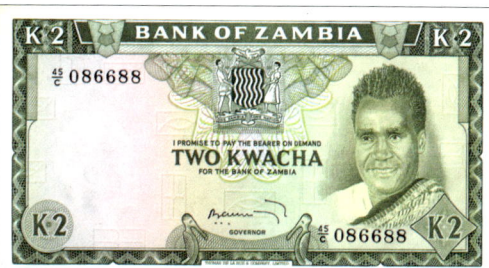

BOZ B11 (P11): **2 kwacha** (demonetized 31.12.2015) VG   VF   UNC
Green. Front: Coat of arms; President Kenneth Kaunda. Back: Copper mine. Solid security thread. Watermark: Kenneth Kaunda. Printer: *THOMAS DE LA RUE & COMPANY LIMITED*. 137 x 72 mm.
- ☐ a.   No date. Intro: 1969.   15   50   200
           Signature 2. Prefix 36/C.
- ☐ b.   Signature 3. Prefix unknown.   15   50   200
- ☐ c.   Signature 4. Prefix 40/C - 49/C.   5   25   160
- ☐ cs. Diagonal red *SPECIMEN* overprint.   —   —   200

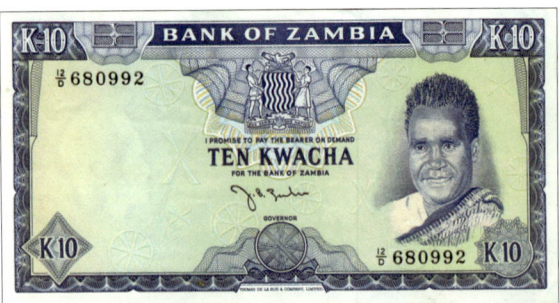

BOZ B12 (P12): **10 kwacha** (demonetized 31.12.2015)   VG   VF   UNC
Blue. Front: Coat of arms; President Kenneth Kaunda. Back: Victoria Falls. Solid security thread. Watermark: Kenneth Kaunda. Printer: *THOMAS DE LA RUE & COMPANY LIMITED*. 154 x 80 mm.

     ☐ a.   No date. Intro: 1969.   20   75   350
           Signature 2. Prefix 10/D - 12/D.
     ☐ b.   Signature 3. Prefix 13/D - 16/D.   25   150   600
     ☐ c.   Signature 4. Prefix 17/D - 18/D.   15   75   300
     ☐ bs. Diagonal red *SPECIMEN* overprint.   —   —   225

Replacement notes: Prefix 1/W.

BOZ B13 (P13): **20 kwacha** (demonetized 31.12.2015)   VG   VF   UNC
Purple. Front: Ancestral totem; coat of arms; President Kenneth Kaunda. Back: National Assembly building in Lusaka. Solid security thread. Watermark: Kenneth Kaunda. Printer: *THOMAS DE LA RUE & COMPANY LIMITED*. 160 x 82 mm.

     ☐ a.   No date. Intro: 1969.   25   150   600
           Signature 2. Prefix 1/E.
     ☐ b.   Signature 3. Prefix 1/E - 2/E.   50   200   800
     ☐ c.   Signature 4. Prefix 2/E - 6/E.   10   25   100
     ☐ cs. Diagonal red *SPECIMEN* and DLR oval ovpts;   —   —   120
           horizontal red *SPECIMEN* Nº # ovpt at lower left.

Replacement notes: Prefix 1/V.

1973 Issues

The 50-ngwee note's color was changed to eliminate the confusion that appeared to exist between it and the new 5-kwacha notes.

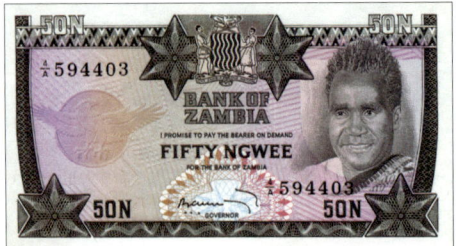

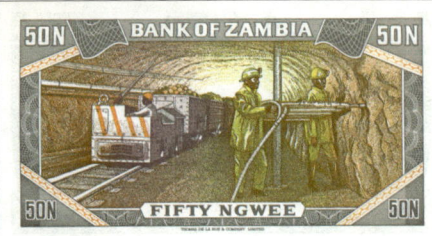

BOZ B14 (P14): **50 ngwee** (demonetized 31.12.2015)   VG   VF   UNC
Black and lilac. Front: Fish eagle; coat of arms; President Kenneth Kaunda. Back: Trams and drillers in underground mine. Solid security thread. Watermark: Kenneth Kaunda. Printer: *THOMAS DE LA RUE & COMPANY LIMITED*. 122 x 67 mm.

     ☐ a.   No date. Signature 4. Prefix 1/A - 16/A.   1   5   20
           Intro: April 1973.

Replacement notes: Prefix 1/Z.

BOZ B15 (P15): **5 kwacha** (demonetized 31.12.2015)   VG   VF   UNC
Red-rust. Front: Coat of arms; President Kenneth Kaunda. Back: School building; children. Solid security thread. Watermark: Kenneth Kaunda. Printer: *THOMAS DE LA RUE & COMPANY LIMITED*. 146 x 72 mm.

     ☐ a.   No date. Signature 4. Prefix 1/F - 9/F. Intro: 1973.   25   100   400
     ☐ as. Diagonal red *SPECIMEN* overprint.   —   —   130

Replacement notes: Prefix U.

1972 Commemorative Issues

This 1-kwacha note was issued on 13 December 1972, to commemorate the advent of the One Party Participatory Democracy, thereby celebrating the birth of the Second Republic.

BOZ B16 (P16): **1 kwacha** (demonetized 31.12.2015)   VG   VF   UNC
Orange. Front: Coat of arms; President Kenneth Kaunda. Back: Man signing document; crowd following man with torch. Solid security thread. Watermark: Kenneth Kaunda. Printer: *THOMAS DE LA RUE & COMPANY LIMITED*. 130 x 70 mm.
- a. No date. Signature 4. Prefix 1/B - 8/B. Intro: 13.12.1972.   2.50   10   40
- as. Diagonal red *SPECIMEN* overprint.   —   —   60

1974 Issues

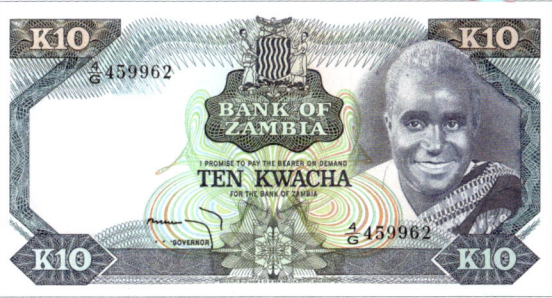

BOZ B17 (P17): **10 kwacha** (demonetized 31.12.2015)   VG   VF   UNC
Blue. Front: Coat of arms; President Kenneth Kaunda. Back: Victoria Falls. Solid security thread. Watermark: Kenneth Kaunda. Printer: *BRADBURY, WILKINSON & CO LD NEW MALDEN, SURREY, ENGLAND*. 152 x 79 mm.
- a. No date. Sig. 4. Prefix 1/G - 4/G. Intro: 1974.   20   100   350
- as. Specimen.   —   —   180

Replacement notes: Prefix W.

BOZ B18 (P18): **20 kwacha** (demonetized 31.12.2015)   VG   VF   UNC
Purple. Front: Coat of arms; President Kenneth Kaunda. Back: National Assembly building in Lusaka. Solid security thread. Watermark: Kenneth Kaunda. Printer: *BRADBURY, WILKINSON & CO LD NEW MALDEN, SURREY, ENGLAND*. 160 x 81 mm.
- a. No date. Sig. 4. Prefix 1/H - 4/H. Intro: 1974.   25   100   300
- as. Specimen.   —   —   225

Replacement notes: Prefix V.

1974-1976 Issues

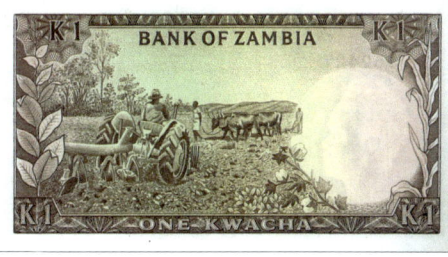

BOZ B19 (P19): **1 kwacha** (demonetized 31.12.2015)   VG   VF   UNC
Brown. Front: Coat of arms; President Kenneth Kaunda. Back: Man plowing field with tractor; tobacco; cotton; corn. Solid security thread. Watermark: Kenneth Kaunda. Printer: *THOMAS DE LA RUE & COMPANY LIMITED*. 129 x 70 mm.
- a. No date. Sig. 5. Prefix 9/B - 28/B. Intro: 1976.   1.50   6   25
- as. Diagonal red *SPECIMEN* overprint.   —   —   30

Replacement notes: Prefix Y.

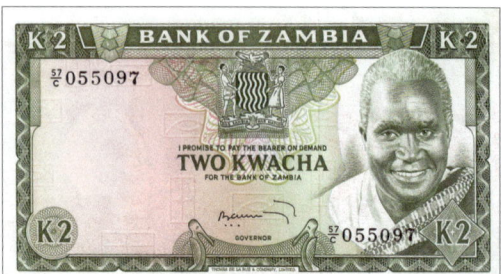

BOZ B20 (P20): **2 kwacha** (demonetized 31.12.2015)   VG   VF   UNC
Green. Front: Coat of arms; President Kenneth Kaunda. Back: Copper mine. Solid security thread. Watermark: Kenneth Kaunda. Printer: *THOMAS DE LA RUE & COMPANY LIMITED*. 138 x 72 mm.
  ☐ a. No date. Sig. 4. Prefix 52/C - 70/C. Intro: 1974.   3   10   45
  ☐ as. Specimen.   —   —   30
Replacement notes: Prefix X.

BOZ B21 (P21): **5 kwacha** (demonetized 31.12.2015)   VG   VF   UNC
Red-rust. Front: Coat of arms; President Kenneth Kaunda. Back: School building; children. Solid security thread. Watermark: Kenneth Kaunda. Printer: *THOMAS DE LA RUE & COMPANY LIMITED*. 146 x 72 mm.
  ☐ a. No date. Sig. 5. Prefix 10/F - 18/F. Intro: 1976.   5   20   70
  ☐ as. Specimen.   —   —   55
Replacement notes: Prefix U.

BOZ B22 (P22): **10 kwacha** (demonetized 31.12.2015)   VG   VF   UNC
Blue. Front: Coat of arms; President Kenneth Kaunda. Back: Victoria Falls. Solid security thread. Watermark: Kenneth Kaunda. Printer: *THOMAS DE LA RUE & COMPANY LIMITED*. 154 x 80 mm.
  ☐ a. No date. Sig. 5. Prefix 1/D - 23/D. Intro: 1976.   10   30   120
  ☐ as. Diagonal red *SPECIMEN* overprint.   —   —   350
Replacement notes: Prefix W.

No image available.
BOZ B23 (P22A): **20 kwacha** (demonetized 31.12.2015)   VG   VF   UNC
Purple. Front: Ancestral totem; coat of arms; President Kenneth Kaunda. Back: National Assembly building in Lusaka. Solid security thread. Watermark: Kenneth Kaunda. Printer: *THOMAS DE LA RUE & COMPANY LIMITED*. 160 x 81 mm.
  ☐ s. No date. Signature 5. Unissued.   —   —   —

1980-1986 Issues

BOZ B24 (P23): **1 kwacha** (demonetized 31.12.2015)   VG   VF   UNC
Pink. Front: Fish eagle; flower; coat of arms; President Kenneth Kaunda. Back: Workers picking cotton. Solid security thread. Watermark: Kenneth Kaunda. Printer: *THOMAS DE LA RUE & COMPANY, LIMITED*. 129 x 66 mm.

- a. No date. Intro: 1980. — 1.50 6
  Signature 5. Prefix 1/A - 62/A.
- b. Signature 7. Prefix 63/A - 78/A. — — 2
- as. Diagonal red *SPECIMEN* overprint. — — 40
- bs. Diagonal red *SPECIMEN* overprint. — — 40

Replacement notes: Prefix denominator Z.

BOZ B25 (P24): **2 kwacha** (demonetized 31.12.2015)   VG   VF   UNC
Olive green. Front: Fish eagle; flowers; coat of arms; President Kenneth Kaunda. Back: Teacher and student with pens and open book; school building; tree. Solid security thread. Watermark: Kenneth Kaunda. Printer: *THOMAS DE LA RUE & COMPANY, LIMITED*. 134 x 68 mm.

- a. No date. Intro: 1980. — 1 5
  Signature 5. Prefix 1/B - 36/B.
- b. Signature 6. Prefix 41/B - 62/B. — — 1.50
- c. Signature 7. Prefix 66/B - 88/B. — — 0.25
- as. Diagonal red *SPECIMEN* overprint. — — 40
- bs. Diagonal red *SPECIMEN* overprint. — — 40
- cs. Diagonal red *SPECIMEN* overprint. — — 40

Replacement notes: Prefix denominator Z.

BOZ B26 (P25): **5 kwacha** (demonetized 31.12.2015)   VG   VF   UNC
Brown. Front: Fish eagle; flowers; coat of arms; President Kenneth Kaunda. Back: Emblem with bird, fish, face; hydroelectric dam. Solid security thread. Watermark: Kenneth Kaunda. Printer: *THOMAS DE LA RUE & COMPANY, LIMITED*. 140 x 70 mm.

- a. No date. Intro: 1980. 1 2 10
  Signature 5. Prefix 1/C - 14/C.
- b. Signature 4. Prefix 18/C - 23/C. 2 8 40
- c. Signature 6. Prefix 29/C - 30/C. — — 1.50
- d. Signature 7. Prefix 39/C - 46/C. — — 0.50
- bs. Diagonal red *SPECIMEN* overprint. — — 40
- cs. Diagonal red *SPECIMEN* overprint. — — 40

Replacement notes: Prefix denominator Z.

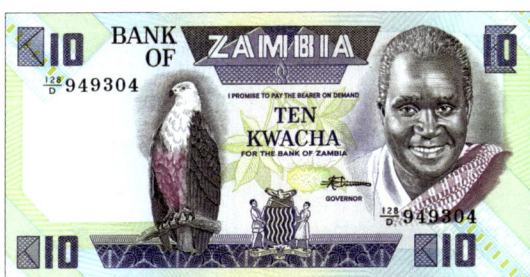

BOZ B27 (P26): **10 kwacha** (demonetized 31.12.2015)   VG   VF   UNC
Blue. Front: Fish eagle; flowers; coat of arms; President Kenneth Kaunda. Back: Bank of Zambia building. Solid security thread. Watermark: Kenneth Kaunda. Printer: *THOMAS DE LA RUE & COMPANY, LIMITED*. 145 x 70 mm.

- a. No date. Intro: 1980. 2.50 10 45
  Signature 5. Prefix 1/D - 24/D.
- b. Signature 4 in black. Prefix 27/D - 29/D. 5 25 100
- c. Signature 4 in blue. Prefix 32/D - 48/D. 4 20 85
- d. Signature 6. Prefix 52/D - 101/D. 1 5 15
- e. Signature 7. Prefix 118/D - 128/D. — — 1.50
- as1. Diagonal red *SPECIMEN* overprint. — — 40
- as2. Diagonal red *SPECIMEN* and DLR oval ovpts, signature punched. — — 40
- bs. Diagonal red *SPECIMEN* overprint. — — 40
- ds. Diagonal red *SPECIMEN* overprint. — — 40

Replacement notes: Prefix denominator Z.

ZAMBIA 1989 ISSUES

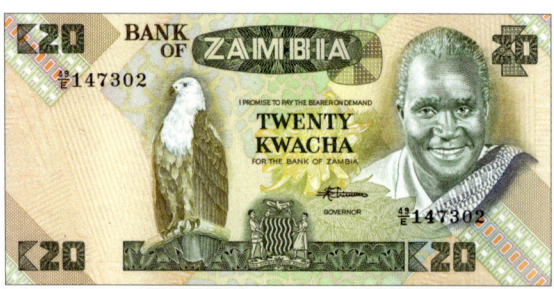

BOZ B28 (P27): **20 kwacha** (demonetized 31.12.2015) VG VF UNC

Green. Front: Fish eagle; flowers; coat of arms; President Kenneth Kaunda. Back: Woman with basket on head. Solid security thread. Watermark: Kenneth Kaunda. Printer: *THOMAS DE LA RUE & COMPANY, LIMITED*. 150 x 72 mm.

- a. No date. Intro: 1980. 4 15 60
  Signature 5. Prefix 1/E - 6/E.
- b. Signature 4 in black. Prefix 9/E - 10/E. 5 20 120
- c. Signature 4 in dark green. Prefix 14/E - 17/E. 5 20 85
- d. Signature 6. Prefix 19/E - 35/E. 1 5 20
- e. Signature 7. Prefix 45/E - 49/E. — — 2.50
- as. Diagonal red *SPECIMEN* overprint. — — 60
- bs. Diagonal red *SPECIMEN* overprint. — — 60
- ds. Diagonal red *SPECIMEN* overprint. — — 60

Replacement notes: Prefix denominator Z.

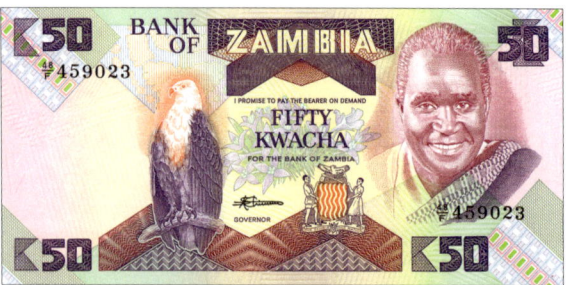

BOZ B29 (P28): **50 kwacha** (Demonetized 31.12.2015) VG VF UNC

Purple. Front: Fish eagle; flowers; coat of arms; President Kenneth Kaunda. Back: Freedom Statue in Lusaka; building. Solid security thread. Watermark: Kenneth Kaunda. Printer: *THOMAS DE LA RUE AND COMPANY LIMITED*. 155 x 74 mm.

- a. No date. Sig. 7. Prefix 1/F - 60/F. Intro: 1986. — — 0.50
- as. Diagonal red *SPECIMEN* overprint. — — 60

Replacement notes: Prefix denominator Z.

1989 Issues

BOZ B30 (P29): **2 kwacha** (demonetized 31.12.2015) VG VF UNC

Olive green. Front: Fish eagle; coat of arms; butterfly; President Kenneth Kaunda. Back: Hand holding torch; rhino head; Freedom Statue in Lusaka; corn field; primitive tool. Solid security thread. Watermark: Kenneth Kaunda. Printer: Unknown. 134 x 68 mm.

- a. No date. Sig. 8. Prefix A/1 - A/D. Intro: 1989. 0.25 1 5
- as. Diagonal red *SPECIMEN* overprint. — — 70

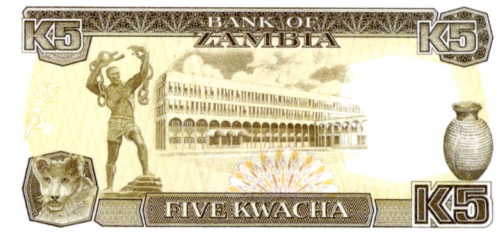

BOZ B31 (P30): **5 kwacha** (demonetized 31.12.2015) VG VF UNC

Brown. Front: Fish eagle; coat of arms; butterfly; President Kenneth Kaunda. Back: Hand holding torch; lion cub head; Freedom Statue in Lusaka; building; container. Solid security thread. Watermark: Kenneth Kaunda. Printer: (H&S). 140 x 70 mm.

- a. No date. Sig. 8. Prefix A/A - A/C. Intro: 1989. — — 1.50
- as. Diagonal red *SPECIMEN* overprint. — — 50

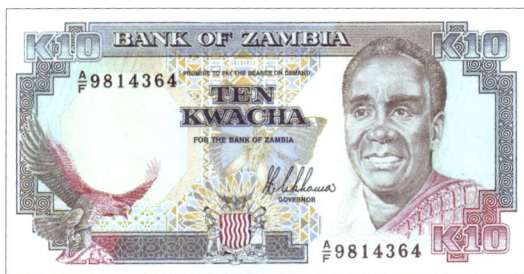

BOZ B32 (P31): **10 kwacha** (demonetized 31.12.2015)　　VG　VF　UNC
Blue. Front: Fish eagle; coat of arms; butterfly; President Kenneth Kaunda. Back: Hand holding torch; giraffe head; Freedom Statue in Lusaka; building; carving of male head. Solid security thread. Watermark: Kenneth Kaunda. Printer: (H&S). 142 x 72 mm.

- ☐ a. No date. Intro: 1989. — — 1.50
  Signature 8. Prefix A/A - A/F.
- ☐ b. Signature 9. Prefix A/F - A/G. — — 0.50
- ☐ as. Diagonal red *SPECIMEN* overprint. — — 40
- ☐ bs. Diagonal red *SPECIMEN* overprint. — — 40

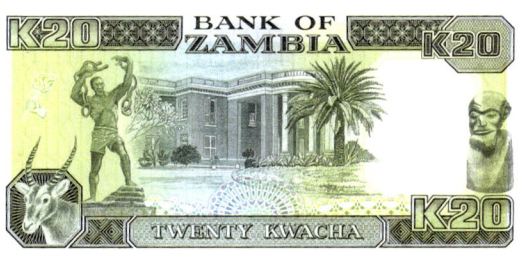

BOZ B33 (P32): **20 kwacha** (demonetized 31.12.2015)　　VG　VF　UNC
Green. Front: Fish eagle; coat of arms; butterfly; President Kenneth Kaunda. Back: Hand holding torch; dama gazelle head; Freedom Statue in Lusaka; building with palm tree; carving of male head. Solid security thread. Watermark: Kenneth Kaunda. Printer: Unknown. 150 x 73 mm.

- ☐ a. No date. Intro: 1989. 0.50 1 5
  Signature 8. Prefix A/A - A/F.
- ☐ b. Signature 9. Prefix A/F - A/H. — — 0.50
- ☐ as. Diagonal red *SPECIMEN* overprint. — — 80
- ☐ bs. Diagonal red *SPECIMEN* overprint. — — 60

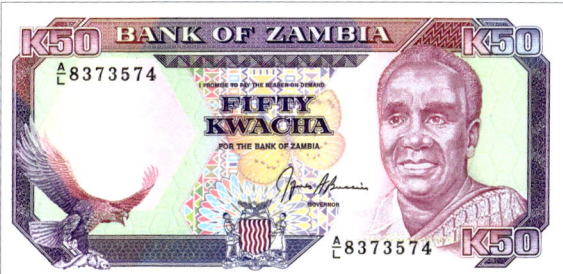

BOZ B34 (P33): **50 kwacha** (demonetized 31.12.2015)　　VG　VF　UNC
Red-violet and purple. Front: Fish eagle; coat of arms; butterfly; President Kenneth Kaunda. Back: Hand holding torch; zebra head; Freedom Statue in Lusaka; men working in factory; carving of topless female. Solid security thread. Watermark: Kenneth Kaunda. Printer: Unknown. 155 x 74 mm.

- ☐ a. No date. Intro: 1989. 0.75 6 30
  Signature 8. Prefix A/A - A/H.
- ☐ b. Signature 9. Prefix A/J - A/S. 2.50 10 35
- ☐ as. Diagonal red *SPECIMEN* overprint. — — 60

1991 Issues

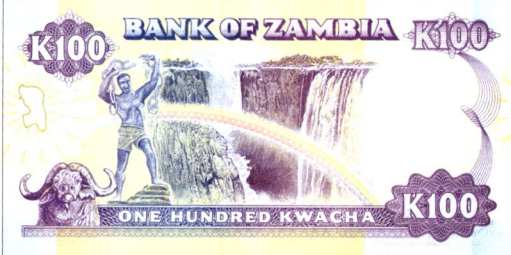

BOZ B35 (P34): **100 kwacha** (demonetized 31.12.2015)　　VG　VF　UNC
Purple. Front: Fish eagle; coat of arms; palm trees; President Kenneth Kaunda; hand holding torch. Back: Water buffalo head; Freedom Statue in Lusaka; Victoria Falls; rainbow. Windowed security thread. Watermark: Kenneth Kaunda. Printer: Unknown. 141 x 70 mm.

- ☐ a. No date. Signature 9. Prefix AA - AD. Intro: 1991. — — 0.75
- ☐ as1. Diagonal red *SPECIMEN* overprint. — — 50
- ☐ as2. Diagonal red *SPECIMEN* overprint; — — 50
  horizontal black # ovpt below s/n at lower right.

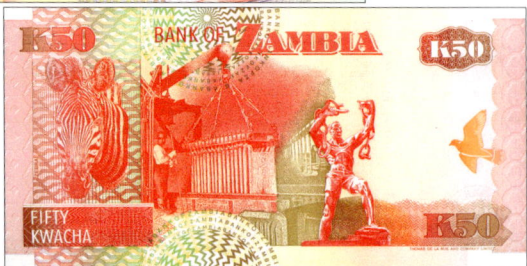

BOZ B36 (P35): **500 kwacha** (demonetized 31.12.2015)   VG   VF   UNC

Purple. Front: Fish eagle; coat of arms; baobab tree; President Kenneth Kaunda; hand holding torch. Back: Elephant; Freedom Statue in Lusaka; five women picking cotton in field with trees. Windowed security thread. Watermark: Kenneth Kaunda. Printer: Unknown. 140 x 70 mm.

☐	a.	No date. Signature 9. Prefix AA - AD. Intro: 1991.	—	—	4
☐	as.	Diagonal red *SPECIMEN* overprint.	—	—	60

BOZ B38 (P37): **50 kwacha** (demonetized 31.12.2015)   VG   VF   UNC

Red. Front: Coat of arms; tree; fish eagle perched on branch. Back: Zebra head; copper refining at Nkana mine; Freedom Statue in Lusaka. Solid security thread. Watermark: Fish eagle. 140 x 70 mm.

☐	a.	1992. Signature 10. Printer: *THOMAS DE LA RUE AND COMPANY LIMITED*. Prefix B/A - B/C.	—	—	1.50
☐	b.	Signature 11. Prefix B/D - B/H.	—	—	1.50
☐	c.	2001. Prefix B/H - B/K.	—	—	2
☐	d.	2003. Signature 12. Prefix B/K - B/L.	—	—	1
☐	e.	Printer: *SABN*. Prefix BA/03 - BE/03.	—	—	1
☐	f.	2006. Prefix BE/03 - BF/03.	—	—	0.50
☐	g.	2007. Prefix BF/03 - BJ/03.	—	—	1
☐	h.	2008. Printer: *DE LA RUE*. Prefix BJ/03 - BQ/03.	—	—	0.50
☐	i.	2009. Prefix BS/03 - BX/03.	—	—	0.50
☐	j.	2010. Prefix BY/03.	—	—	0.50
☐	as.	Diagonal red *SPECIMEN* overprint.	—	—	40

Replacement notes: Prefix denominator X.

1992-2011 Issues

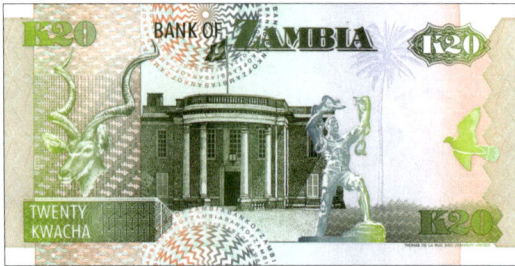

BOZ B37 (P36): **20 kwacha** (demonetized 31.12.2015)   VG   VF   UNC

Green. Front: Coat of arms; dove; tree; fish eagle perched on branch. Back: Kudu antelope; State House building with flag in Lusaka; Freedom Statue in Lusaka; palm tree. Solid security thread. Watermark: Fish eagle. Printer: *THOMAS DE LA RUE AND COMPANY LIMITED*. 142 x 70 mm.

☐	a.	1992. Signature 10. Prefix A/A - A/C.	—	—	1
☐	b.	Signature 11. Prefix A/C - A/G.	—	—	1
☐	as.	Diagonal red *SPECIMEN* overprint.	—	—	40

Replacement notes: Prefix denominator X.

BOZ B39 (P38): **100 kwacha** (demonetized 31.12.2015)   VG   VF   UNC

Red. Front: Coat of arms; palm trees with coconuts; fish eagle perched on branch. Back: Water buffalo head; Victoria Falls; Freedom Statue in Lusaka. Solid security thread. Watermark: Fish eagle. 141 x 70 mm.

☐	a.	1992. Signature 10. Printer: *THOMAS DE LA RUE AND COMPANY LIMITED*. Prefix C/A - C/P.	—	—	5
☐	b.	1992. Signature 11. Prefix C/P - C/Z.	—	—	1.50
☐	c.	2001. Prefix D/A - D/F.	—	—	3.50
☐	d.	2003. Signature 12. Prefix D/F.	—	—	1.50
☐	e.	Printer: *SABN*. Prefix CA/03 - CD/03.	—	—	4
☐	f.	2005. Prefix CE/03 - CF/03.	—	—	1
☐	g.	2006. Printer: *FRANÇOIS-CHARLES OBERTHUR FIDUCIAIRE*. Prefix CF/03 - CN/03.	—	—	0.25
☐	h.	2008. Printer: *DE LA RUE*. Prefix CO/03 - CT/03.	—	—	1
☐	i.	2009. Prefix CU/03 - CZ/03.	—	—	1
☐	j.	2010. Prefix KA/03.	—	—	0.25
☐	k.	2011. Printer: *Giesecke & Devrient*. Prefix KH/03 - KI/03.	—	—	0.50
☐	as.	Diagonal red *SPECIMEN* overprint.	—	—	40

Replacement notes: Prefix denominator X.

BOZ B40 (P39): **500 kwacha** (demonetized 31.12.2015)   VG   VF   UNC

Brown. Front: Coat of arms; dove; baobab tree; fish eagle perched on branch. Back: Elephant; workers picking cotton; Freedom Statue in Lusaka. Windowed security thread. Watermark: Fish eagle. Printer: *THOMAS DE LA RUE AND COMPANY LIMITED*. 140 x 70 mm.

☐	a.	1992. Signature 10. Prefix D/A - D/W.	—	—	5
☐	b.	Signature 11. Prefix D/W - E/E.	—	—	5
☐	c.	2001. Prefix E/E - E/H.	—	—	5
☐	d.	2003. Signature 12. Prefix E/H - E/J.	—	—	5
☐	as.	Diagonal red *SPECIMEN* overprint.	—	—	40
☐	bs.	Diagonal red *SPECIMEN* overprint.	—	—	—

Replacement notes: Prefix denominator X.

BOZ B40.5 (PNL): **1,000 kwacha**   VG   VF   UNC

Blue. Front (uniface): Coat of arms; dove; jacaranda tree; fish eagle perched on branch. No security thread. Watermark: None. Printer: (TDLR). 140 x 70 mm.

☐	a.	1992. Signature 10. Unissued.	—	—	—

BOZ B41 (P40): **1,000 kwacha** (demonetized 31.12.2015)   VG   VF   UNC

Red-violet. Front: Coat of arms; dove; jacaranda tree; fish eagle perched on branch. Back: Aardvark; man on tractor in sorghum field; Freedom Statue in Lusaka. Windowed security thread with demetalized *BOZ 1000*. Watermark: Fish eagle. Printer: THOMAS DE LA RUE AND COMPANY LIMITED. 145 x 70 mm.

    ☐ a. 1992. Signature 11. Prefix E/A - E/J. Intro: 1996.   —   —   6
    ☐ b. 2001. Prefix E/K - E/M.   —   —   6
    ☐ c. 2003. Signature 12. Prefix E/M - E/N.   —   —   2.50
    ☐ as. Diagonal red *SPECIMEN* overprint.   —   —   40

Replacement notes: Prefix denominator X.

BOZ B42 (P41): **5,000 kwacha** (demonetized 31.12.2015)   VG   VF   UNC

Purple. Front: Coat of arms; dove; murera/acacia/mopani tree; fish eagle perched on branch. Back: Lion head; root cassave plant and leaves; Freedom Statue in Lusaka. Windowed security thread with demetalized *BOZ 5000*. Watermark: Fish eagle. Printer: THOMAS DE LA RUE AND COMPANY LIMITED. 145 x 70 mm.

    ☐ a. 1992. Signature 11. Prefix F/A - F/E. Intro: 1996.   —   —   15
    ☐ b. 2001. Prefix F/G - F/J.   —   —   7
    ☐ as. Diagonal red *SPECIMEN* overprint.   —   —   40

Replacement notes: Prefix denominator X.

BOZ B43 (P42): **10,000 kwacha** (demonetized 31.12.2015)   VG   VF   UNC

Aqua. Front: Coat of arms; dove; musuku tree; fish eagle perched on branch. Back: Porcupine; workers harvesting rice paddy; Freedom Statue in Lusaka. Windowed security thread with demetalized *BOZ 10000*. Watermark: Fish eagle. Printer: THOMAS DE LA RUE AND COMPANY LIMITED. 145 x 70 mm.

    ☐ a. 1992. Signature 11. Prefix G/A - G/E. Intro: 1996.   —   —   25
    ☐ as. Diagonal red *SPECIMEN* overprint.   —   —   50

Replacement notes: Prefix denominator X.

2001-2003 Issues

This note is like the preceding issue, but with the latent image at lower left front replaced by a fish eagle patch facing left.

BOZ B44 (P42): **10,000 kwacha** (demonetized 31.12.2015)   VG   VF   UNC

Aqua. Front: Coat of arms; dove; holographic fish eagle patch facing left; musuku tree; fish eagle perched on branch. Back: Porcupine; workers harvesting rice paddy; Freedom Statue in Lusaka. Windowed security thread with demetalized *BOZ 10000*. Watermark: Fish eagle. Printer: THOMAS DE LA RUE AND COMPANY LIMITED. 146 x 69 mm.

    ☐ a. 2001. Signature 11. Prefix G/E - G/H.   —   —   25
    ☐ b. 2003. Signature 12. Prefix G/H - G/J.   —   —   25

Replacement notes: Prefix denominator X.
See BOZ B48 for this note dated 2003 with fish eagle patch facing right.

2003-2012 Issues

These notes are similar to the preceding issues, but with smaller zeros on all corner denominations above 500 kwacha, and with an electrotype denomination added to the watermark.

The two low-denomination polymer banknotes were withdrawn the day after their initial release because the serial numbers could be rubbed off easily. As many as 9,000 defective notes were issued before the problem was discovered. In November 2003, both notes were reissued with the same date but a modified ink formula. These new polymer notes were subsequently found to fade prematurely, forcing the printer to absorb the cost of replacing unfit notes.

BOZ B45 (P43): **500 kwacha** (demonetized 31.12.2015)   VG   VF   UNC
Brown. Front: Coat of arms; dove; baobab tree; fish eagle perched on branch. Back: Elephant; workers picking cotton; Freedom Statue in Lusaka. Watermark: Fish eagle. 140 x 70 mm. Polymer.

☐ a.	2003. Signature 12. Printer: *CANADIAN BANK NOTE COMPANY, LIMITED*. Prefix DA/03. Intro: 26.09.2003.	—	—	15
☐ b.	Second printing. Serial number doesn't wear off. Prefix DB/03 - DC/03. Intro: 03.11.2003.	—	—	2
☐ c.	2004. *BANK OF ZAMBIA* in different colors. Prefix DC/03 - DD/03.	—	—	2
☐ d.	2005. Prefix DD/03 - DG/03.	—	—	1.50
☐ e.	2006. Prefix DG/03 - DJ/30.	—	—	1.50
☐ f.	2008. Printer: *SABN*. Prefix DJ/03 - DM/30.	—	—	1
☐ g.	2009. Prefix DN/03 - DP/03.	—	—	0.50
☐ h.	2011. Printer: *Giesecke & Devrient*. Prefix DR/03 - DV/03.	—	—	0.50
☐ as.	Diagonal red hollow *SPECIMEN* overprint; horizontal black # overprint at lower left.	—	—	50

Replacement notes: Prefix denominator X.

BOZ B46 (P44): **1,000 kwacha** (demonetized 31.12.2015)   VG   VF   UNC
Red-violet. Front: Coat of arms; dove; jacaranda tree; fish eagle perched on branch. Back: Aardvark; man on tractor in sorghum field; Freedom Statue in Lusaka. Watermark: Fish eagle. 140 x 70 mm. Polymer.

☐ a.	2003. Signature 12. Printer: *CANADIAN BANK NOTE COMPANY, LIMITED*. Prefix EA/03. Intro: 26.09.2003.	—	—	20
☐ b.	Second printing. Serial number doesn't wear off. Prefix EA/03 - EC/03. Intro: 10.11.2003.	—	—	3.50
☐ c.	2004. *BANK OF ZAMBIA* in different colors. Prefix EC/03 - ED/03.	—	—	3
☐ d.	2005. Prefix ED/03 - EF/03.	—	—	1.50
☐ e.	2006. Prefix EF/03 - EH/03.	—	—	1.50
☐ f.	2008. Printer: *SABN*. Prefix EH/03 - EL/03.	—	—	1
☐ g.	2009. Prefix EL/03 - EO/03.	—	—	1
☐ h.	2011. Printer: *Giesecke & Devrient*. Prefix E0/03 - ES/03.	—	—	0.50
☐ i.	2012. Prefix EV/03.	—	—	15
☐ as.	Diagonal red hollow *SPECIMEN* overprint; horizontal black # overprint at lower left.	—	—	40
☐ cs.	Diagonal red hollow *SPECIMEN* overprint; horizontal red # overprint at lower left back.	—	—	250

Replacement notes: Prefix denominator X.

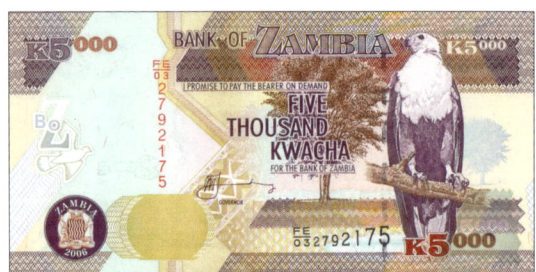

BOZ B47 (P45): **5,000 kwacha** (demonetized 31.12.2015)　　VG　VF　UNC

Purple. Front: Coat of arms; dove; murera/acacia/mopani tree; fish eagle perched on branch. Back: Lion head; root cassave plant and leaves; Freedom Statue in Lusaka. Windowed security thread with demetalized *BOZ 5000*. Watermark: Fish eagle, electrotype *5000* plus fish eagle, and Cornerstones. 145 x 70 mm.

- ☐ a. 2003. Signature 12. Printer: *DE LA RUE*. — — 4
  Prefix FA/03 - FB/03.
- ☐ b. 2005. Prefix FB/03 - FD/03. — — 4
- ☐ c. 2006. Prefix FE/03. — — 4
- ☐ d. 2008. Prefix FF/03 - FG/03. — — 3
- ☐ e. 2009. Prefix FH/03. — — 3
- ☐ f. 2010. Prefix FJ/03 - FL/03. — — 3
- ☐ g. 2011. Printer: *Giesecke & Devrient*. — — 2
  Prefix FL/03 - FM/03.
- ☐ h. 2012. Prefix FN/03. — — 4.50

Replacement notes: Prefix denominator X.

BOZ B49 (P47): **20,000 kwacha** (demonetized 31.12.2015)　　VG　VF　UNC

Orange. Front: Coat of arms; dove; holographic patch; mukwa tree; fish eagle perched on branch. Back: Black lechwe (kobus leche) antelope; men working pneumatic drill in mine; Freedom Statue in Lusaka. Windowed security thread with demetalized *BOZ 20000*. Watermark: Fish eagle, electrotype *20000* plus fish eagle, and Cornerstones. 145 x 70 mm.

- ☐ a. 2003. Signature 12. Printer: *DE LA RUE*. — — 25
  Prefix HA/03 - HB/03.
- ☐ b. 2005. Prefix HC/03 - HE/03. — — 25
- ☐ c. 2006. Prefix HE/03 - HF/03. — — 17
- ☐ d. 2008. Prefix HF/03 - HG/03. — — 12
- ☐ e. 2009. Prefix HG/03 - HH/03. — — 17
- ☐ f. 2010. Prefix HJ/03 - HL/03. — — 15
- ☐ g. 2011. Printer: *Giesecke & Devrient*. — — 12
  Prefix HL/03 - HN/03.
- ☐ h. 2012. Prefix HO/03. — — 12
- ☐ s. Specimen. — — 50

Replacement notes: Prefix denominator X.

BOZ B48 (P46): **10,000 kwacha** (demonetized 31.12.2015)　　VG　VF　UNC

Aqua. Front: Coat of arms; dove; holographic fish eagle patch facing right; musuku tree; fish eagle perched on branch. Back: Porcupine; workers harvesting rice paddy; Freedom Statue in Lusaka. Windowed security thread with demetalized *BOZ 10000*. Watermark: Fish eagle, electrotype *10000* plus fish eagle, and Cornerstones. Printer: *DE LA RUE*. 145 x 70 mm.

- ☐ a. 2003. Signature 12. Prefix GA/03 - GB/03. — — 10
- ☐ b. 2005. Prefix GB/03 - GC/03. — — 10
- ☐ c. 2006. Prefix GC/03 - GD/03. — — 10
- ☐ d. 2007. Prefix GE/03 - GF/03. — — 10

Replacement notes: Prefix denominator X.
See B44 for this note dated 2003 with fish eagle patch facing left.

BOZ B50 (P48): **50,000 kwacha** (demonetized 31.12.2015)   VG   VF   UNC
Blue. Front: Coat of arms; dove; holographic patch; fig tree in Kabwe; fish eagle perched on branch. Back: Leopard; Bank of Zambia building; Freedom Statue in Lusaka. Windowed security thread with demetalized *BOZ 50000*. Watermark: Fish eagle, electrotype *50000* plus fish eagle, and Cornerstones. 145 x 70 mm.

- ☐ a. 2003. Signature 12. Printer: *DE LA RUE*. — — 35
  Prefix JA/03.
- ☐ b. 2006. Prefix JB/03 - JC/03. — — 25
- ☐ c. 2007. Prefix JC/03. — — 25
- ☐ d. 2008. Prefix JD/03 - JE/03. — — 25
- ☐ e. 2009. Prefix JE/03 - JF/03. — — 25
- ☐ f. 2010. Prefix JF/03 - JH/03. — — 25
- ☐ g. 2011. Printer: *Giesecke & Devrient*. — — 25
  Prefix JH/03 - JK/03.
- ☐ h. 2012. Prefix JK/03 - JL/03. — — 15
- ☐ s. Specimen. — — 50

Replacement notes: Prefix denominator X.

2008-2012 Issues

This note is like B48, but instead of a holographic patch in the shape of a fish eagle head, an entire fish eagle is represented in a bright silver demetalized holographic LEAD (longlasting economical anticopy device) at left center on the front. Furthermore, the denomination at top right on the back is printed in copper-to-green OVI.

BOZ B51 (P46): **10,000 kwacha** (demonetized 31.12.2015)   VG   VF   UNC
Aqua. Front: Coat of arms; dove; fish eagle; musuku tree; fish eagle perched on branch. Back: Porcupine; workers harvesting rice paddy; Freedom Statue in Lusaka. Holographic LEAD stripe. Windowed security thread with demetalized *BOZ 10000*. Watermark: Fish eagle and electrotype *10000* plus fish eagle. Printer: *Giesecke & Devrient*. 145 x 70 mm.

- ☐ a. 2008. Signature 12. Prefix GF/03 - GJ/03. — — 6
  Intro: June 2008.
- ☐ b. 2009. Prefix GJ/03 - GL/03. — — 6
- ☐ c. 2011. Prefix GL/03 - GN/03. — — 6
- ☐ d. 2012. Prefix GN/03 - GO/03. — — 6

Replacement notes: Prefix denominator X.

2012-2013 Rebased Kwacha Issues

On 1 January 2013, Zambia revalued its currency by removing three zeros from all denominations of the kwacha. Old notes ceased to be legal tender as of 30 June 2013, but may be exchanged at the Bank of Zambia until 31 December 2015, after which time they will be demonetized.

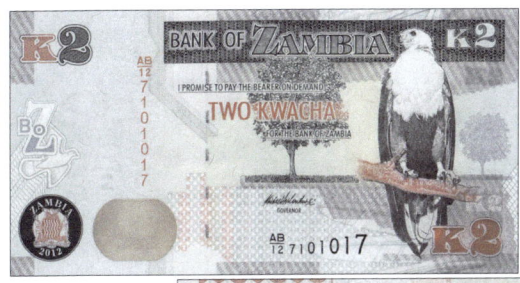

BOZ B52 (P49): **2 kwacha** (US$0.35)   VG   VF   UNC
Gray. Front: Coat of arms; dove; trees; fish eagle perched on branch. Back: Roan antelope; two woman with baskets and produce; Freedom Statue in Lusaka. Windowed security thread with demetalized *BOZ 2*. Watermark: Fish eagle and electrotype *2* plus fish eagle. Printer: *Giesecke & Devrient*. 140 x 70 mm.

- ☐ a. 2012. Signature 13. Prefix AA/12 - AC/12. FV FV 1
  Intro: 01.01.2013.
- ☐ b. 2013. Prefix AH/12. FV FV 1

Replacement notes: Prefix denominator X.

ZAMBIA 2012-2013 Rebased Kwacha Issues

BOZ B53 (P50): **5 kwacha** (US$0.80) VG VF UNC

Purple. Front: Coat of arms; dove; murera/acacia/mopani tree; fish eagle perched on branch. Back: Lion head; root cassave plant and leaves; Freedom Statue in Lusaka. Windowed security thread with demetalized *BOZ 5*. Watermark: Fish eagle and electrotype *5* plus fish eagle. Printer: *Giesecke & Devrient*. 140 x 70 mm.

☐ a. 2012. Signature 13. Prefix BA/12 - BD/12. FV FV 1.50
Intro: 01.01.2013.
☐ b. 2013. Prefix BE/12. FV FV 1.50

Replacement notes: Prefix BA/X2.

BOZ B54 (P51): **10 kwacha** (US$1.65) VG VF UNC

Aqua. Front: Coat of arms; dove; musuku tree; fish eagle perched on branch. Back: Porcupine; workers harvesting rice paddy; Freedom Statue in Lusaka. Holographic LEAD stripe. Windowed security thread with demetalized *BOZ 10*. Watermark: Fish eagle and electrotype *10* plus fish eagle. Printer: *Giesecke & Devrient*. 145 x 70 mm.

☐ a. 2012. Signature 13. Prefix CA/12 - CC/12. FV FV 3
Intro: 01.01.2013.
☐ b. 2013. Prefix CF/12. FV FV 3

BOZ B55 (P52): **20 kwacha** (US$3.30) VG VF UNC

Brown. Front: Coat of arms; dove; mukwa tree; fish eagle perched on branch. Back: Black lechwe (kobus leche) antelope; men working pneumatic drill in mine; Freedom Statue in Lusaka. Holographic LEAD stripe. Windowed security thread. Watermark: Fish eagle and electrotype *20* plus fish eagle. Printer: *Giesecke & Devrient*. 145 x 70 mm.

☐ a. 2012. Sig. 13. Prefix DA/12. Intro: 01.01.2013. FV FV 5
☐ b. 2013. Prefix DG/12. FV FV 5

BOZ B56 (P53): **50 kwacha** (US$8.20) VG VF UNC

Blue. Front: Coat of arms; dove; fish eagle; fig tree in Kabwe; fish eagle perched on branch. Back: Leopard; Bank of Zambia building; Freedom Statue in Lusaka. Holographic LEAD stripe. Windowed security thread. Watermark: Fish eagle and electrotype *50* plus fish eagle. Printer: *Giesecke & Devrient*. 145 x 70 mm.

☐ a. 2012. Signature 13. Prefix EA/12 - ED/12. FV FV 15
Intro: 01.01.2013.

BOZ B57 (P54): **100 kwacha** (US$16)   VG   VF   UNC

Olive green. Front: Coat of arms; dove; fish eagle; musuku tree; fish eagle perched on branch. Back: Buffalo; National Assembly of Zambia building; Freedom Statue in Lusaka. Holographic LEAD stripe. Windowed security thread. Watermark: Fish eagle and electrotype *100* plus fish eagle. Printer: *Giesecke & Devrient*. 145 x 70 mm.

☐ a. 2012. Signature 13. Prefix FA/12 - FC/12.   FV   FV   35
       Intro: 01.01.2013.
☐ b. 2013. Prefix FC/12.   FV   FV   35

Looking Forward

According to an article on LusakaTimes dated 8 August 2014, the Bank of Zambia will honor all heads of state—President Sata, Dr Kenneth Kaunda, late Dr Frederick Chiluba, late Dr Levy Mwanawasa, and Mr Rupiah Banda—by incorporating their portraits on a commemorative banknote to be issued in October this year, as part of the golden jubilee celebrations to be held on 24 October 2014.

Acknowledgements

This chapter was compiled with the generous assistance of Sejin Ahn, Brent Arthurson, Thomas Augustsson, Jim W.-C. Chen, Garry Craig, Eastgate Universal Stamps and Coins (eastgate.coins@gmail.com), Chris Hall, Mark Irwin, Manjunath P. Iyer, Vygandas Kadzys, Thomas Krause, Claudio Marana, David Murcek (www.themonetaryunit.com), Wally Myers, Jim O'Connell III, Nazir Rahemtulla, Andrew Roberts, Gergely Scheidl, Steffen Simon, Jeremey Steinberg (www.banknotes-steinberg.com), Bill Stubkjaer, Christoph Thomas, Ömer Yalcinkaya (omeryk@yahoo.com), Christof Zellweger, and others.

Sources

Cuhaj, George S. *Standard Catalog of World Paper Money, Modern Issues, 1961-Present*. 20th edition. 2014. ISBN 978-1-4402-4037-9. Krause Publications (www.krausebooks.com), 700 East State St., Iola, WI, 54990-0001.

Eu, Peter, Ben Chiew, and Stane Straus. *World Polymer Banknotes: A Standard Reference*. 2nd edition. 2006. ISBN 983-43038-2-3. Eureka Metro, P. O. Box 30, Jalan Kelang Lama, Kuala Lumpur, 57000, Malaysia.

Krause, Thomas and Peter Bauer. *Specialized Catalogue of World Plastic Money*. 5th edition. 2009. www.polymernotes.de.

Share Your Input, Info, and Images

This catalog is believed to be complete and correct as of the time of publication. Prices and face values were last updated 22 June 2014. Please report errors or omissions so that corrections may be made. If you can more precisely identify the name or location of anything depicted on a note, please share that information. Furthermore, if you own an unlisted type or variety, please submit scans of the front and back of the note so that it can be documented. Scans should be 300 dots per inch, 100% actual size, 24-bit color, saved as *uncompressed* JPEG files, and sent to owen@banknotenews.com. Be sure to fully describe all attributes of the note which are not apparent upon visual inspection of the images alone, such as physical dimension, watermark, and security thread.

Zanzibar

Monetary System
1908: 1 Zanzibar rupee = 100 cents

The Zanzibar Government

Zanzibar is currently a semi-autonomous part of Tanzania. The Zanzibar archipelago in the Indian Ocean consists of numerous small islands and two large ones: Unguja (the main island, informally referred to as Zanzibar), and Pemba. Portuguese explorers gained control of the region during the 15th century, followed by the Omanis in the 18th century. In 1890, Zanzibar became a British protectorate, and subsequently the Zanzibar Government (ZG) issued local banknotes.

ZG Signature Varieties

	Signature (left)	Signature (right)
1	Financial Member of Council — Charles Edmond Akers	Treasurer — James Corbett Davis
2a	Chief Secretary — John Houston Sinclair	Treasurer — James Corbett Davis
2b	Chief Secretary — John Houston Sinclair	Treasurer — James Corbett Davis
3	Chief Secretary — Richard Hayes Crofton	Treasurer — Norman Blakiston Cox

1908-1928 Issues

All of these uniface notes depict an Arab dhow boat at left and workers harvesting a clove tree at right, symbolizing the importance of sea trade and agriculture on the island nation of Zanzibar, once the top clove producer and exporter in the world.

ZG B1 (P1): **1 rupee** (demonetized 1936) Good Fine XF
Blue, green, and orange. Uniface: Dhow boat on water; nine workers harvesting clove tree with rudimentary ladder. No security thread. Watermark: None. Printer: *THOS DE LA RUE & C⁰ L^TD LONDON*. 122 x 70 mm.

- ☐ a. 1ST September 1920. Signature 2b. 3,500 11,500 —

ZG B2 (P2): **5 rupees** (demonetized 1936) Good Fine XF
Brown, black, and green. Uniface: Dhow boat on water; nine workers harvesting clove tree with rudimentary ladder. No security thread. Watermark: None. Printer: *Waterlow & Sons, Ld London Wall, London*. 180 x 110 mm.

- ☐ a. JANUARY 1ST 1908. Signature 1. 4,750 15,500 —
- ☐ b. 1ST AUGUST, 1916. Signature 2a. 5,000 17,000 —
  Financial Member of Council title blacked out, *Chief Secretary* title added by handstamp.
- ☐ c. *Chief Secretary* title printed. 4,000 14,000 —
- ☐ d. 1ST FEBRUARY, 1928. Signature 3. 4,500 15,000 —
- ☐ ap. No overprint; no serial numbers; punched. — — —
- ☐ dp. Proof. — — —

ZG B3 (P3): **10 rupees** (demonetized 1936) Good Fine XF
Red and green. Uniface: Dhow boat on water; nine workers harvesting clove tree with rudimentary ladder. No security thread. Watermark: None. Printer: *Waterlow & Sons, Ld London Wall, London*. 180 x 110 mm.

- ☐ a. JANUARY 1ST 1908. Signature 1. 9,000 22,500 —
- ☐ b. 1ST AUGUST, 1916. Signature 2a. 7,500 18,500 —
- ☐ c. 1ST FEBRUARY, 1928. Signature 3. 8,000 20,000 —
- ☐ ap. No overprint; no serial numbers; punched. — — —
- ☐ cp. Proof. — — —

ZG B4 (P4): **20 rupees** (demonetized 1936)　　　　Good　Fine　XF

Green, lilac, and orange. Uniface: Dhow boat on water; nine workers harvesting clove tree with rudimentary ladder. No security thread. Watermark: None. Printer: *Waterlow & Sons, L*^{d} *London Wall, London*. 180 x 110 mm.

- ☐ a.　January 1ST 1908. Signature 1.　—　—　—
- ☐ b.　1ST August, 1916. Signature 2a.　—　—　60,000
- ☐ c.　1ST February, 1928. Signature 3.　—　—　—
- ☐ ap.　No overprint; no serial numbers; punched.　—　—　—
- ☐ bp.　Proof.　—　—　—
- ☐ cp.　Proof.　—　—　—
- ☐ at1.　Color trial: Lilac brown, pink, and green. Two diagonal red *SPECIMEN* overprints; blue *WATERLOW & SONS* circle ovpt; punched.　—　—　—
- ☐ at2.　Color trial: Lilac brown, pink, and green. Horizontal red *SPECIMEN NO VALUE* overprint; horizontal black *SPECIMEN NOTE, WATERLOW AND SONS LTD.* ovpt at upper left; punched.
- ☐ ct.　Color trial: Lilac brown, pink, and green.　—　—　20,000

ZG B5 (P5): **50 rupees** (demonetized 1936)　　　　Good　Fine　XF

Brown. Uniface: Dhow boat on water; nine workers harvesting clove tree with rudimentary ladder. No security thread. Watermark: None. Printer: *Waterlow & Sons, L*^{d} *London Wall, London*. 180 x 110 mm.

- ☐ a.　1ST August, 1916. Signature 2a.　—　—　—
- ☐ ap.　No overprint; no serial numbers.　—　—　—

ZG B6 (P6): **100 rupees** (demonetized 1936)　　　　Good　Fine　XF

Blue and pink. Uniface: Dhow boat on water; nine workers harvesting clove tree with rudimentary ladder. No security thread. Watermark: None. Printer: *Waterlow & Sons, L*^{d} *London Wall, London*. 180 x 110 mm.

- ☐ a.　January 1ST 1908. Signature 1.　—　—　—
- ☐ b.　1ST August, 1916. Signature 2a.　—　—　—
- ☐ ap.　No overprint; no serial numbers; punched.　—　—　—
- ☐ bp.　Proof.　—　—　—

ZG B7 (P7): **500 rupees** (demonetized 1936)　　　　Good　Fine　XF

Black. Uniface: Dhow boat on water; nine workers harvesting clove tree with rudimentary ladder. No security thread. Watermark: None. Printer: *Waterlow & Sons, L*^{d} *London Wall, London*. 180 x 110 mm.

- ☐ a.　1ST August, 1916. Signature 2a.　—　—　—
- ☐ b.　1ST September, 1920.　—　—　—
- ☐ ap.　No overprint; no serial numbers; punched.　—　—　—
- ☐ bs.　No overprint; all-zero serial numbers.　—　—　—

1908 Numismatic Products

In 2011, Spink auctioned the following presentation album containing uniface proofs of the 5, 10, 20, and 100 rupee notes, all dated January 1ST 1908.

		UNC
ZG BNP1 (PNL): **5 - 100 rupees**		
☐ a. ZG B2ap, B3ap, B4ap, and B6ap (4 notes) in leather album.		240,000

Looking Forward

In 1936, all Zanzibar rupee notes were withdrawn, demonetized, and replaced with shilling notes of the East African Currency Board. For later issues, see East Africa and Tanzania.

Acknowledgements

This chapter was compiled with the generous assistance of Keith Allen, David Burns, Gene Hessler, Wally Myers, Ibrahim Salem, Stack's Bowers & Ponterio (www.StacksBowers.com), Ludek Vostal, and others.

Sources

Cuhaj, George S. *Standard Catalog of World Paper Money, General Issues, 1368-1960*. 14th edition. 2012. ISBN 978-1-4402-3090-5. Krause Publications (www.krausebooks.com), 700 East State St., Iola, WI, 54990-0001.

Hessler, Gene. "The Paper Money (and Coins) of Zanzibar." *IBNS Journal*. Volume 38 Number 3. p.6.

Muszynski, Maurice. "L'aristocratie du papier-monnaie: Zanzibar." *PM Magazine*. Number 1. Novembre 1990. p.4.

Share Your Input, Info, and Images

This catalog is believed to be complete and correct as of the time of publication. Prices and face values were last updated 29 June 2012. Please report errors or omissions so that corrections may be made. If you can more precisely identify the name or location of anything depicted on a note, please share that information. Furthermore, if you own an unlisted type or variety, please submit scans of the front and back of the note so that it can be documented. Scans should be 300 dots per inch, 100% actual size, 24-bit color, saved as *uncompressed* JPEG files, and sent to owen@banknotenews.com. Be sure to fully describe all attributes of the note which are not apparent upon visual inspection of the images alone, such as physical dimension, watermark, and security thread.

Zimbabwe

For earlier issues, see Rhodesia.

Contents

Reserve Bank of Zimbabwe (RBZ) 2329
Cargill Cotton Group (CC) 2354

Monetary System
- 1980: 1 Zimbabean dollar (ZWD) = 100 cents
- 01.08.2006: 1 dollar (ZWN) = 1,000 ZWD dollars
- 01.08.2008: 1 dollar (ZWR) = 10,000,000,000 ZWN dollars
- 02.02.2009: 1 dollar (ZWL) = 1,000,000,000,000 ZWR dollars

Reserve Bank of Zimbabwe

The Reserve Bank of Zimbabwe (RBZ) has its origins in the Bank of Rhodesia and Nyasaland which was created in March 1956 as a central bank for the Federation of Rhodesia and Nyasaland. The Reserve Bank was the successor to the Central African Currency Board, which had the sole right to issue currency.

The German security printer Giesecke & Devrient (G&D) is known to have been the primary supplier of paper substrate for the Reserve Bank of Zimbabwe's banknotes, but halted shipments on 1 July 2008, due to international pressure following a controversial presidential run-off election in Zimbabwe. Most notes were printed at Fidelity Printers and Refiners in Harare, though they do not carry an imprint.

For more information, visit www.rbz.co.zw.

RBZ Signature Varieties

1. Desmond C. Crough (1976 - 1983)
2. Kombo J. Moyana (1983 - 1993)
3. Leonard L. Tsumba (August 1993 - 31.07.2003)
4. Acting Governor Charles Chikaura (August 2003 - November 2003)
5. Gideon Gono (November 2003 - present)

RBZ Watermark Varieties

Type A — Zimbabwe bird in profile short neck
Type B — Zimbabwe bird 3/4 view medium neck
Type C — Zimbabwe bird 3/4 view long neck

1980-1994 Issues

The first notes of the Reserve Bank of Zimbabwe were dated 1980 to mark the nation's independence from the United Kingdom, though they were not issued until 1981 (the Z$20 was issued in 1982). Notes denominated in Rhodesian dollars were exchanged at par for new Zimbabwean-dollar notes once the Reserve Bank of Zimbabwe took over the functions of the former Reserve Bank of Rhodesia. The first series of banknotes ranged from Z$2 to Z$20, and were initially signed by Desmond C. Crough, the last governor of the Reserve Bank of Rhodesia. Additionally, they bore the name of the capital next to the date on the front; first Salisbury, then renamed Harare on 18 April 1982.

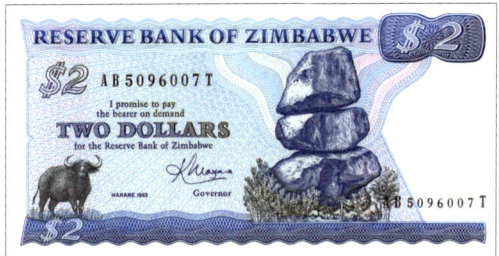

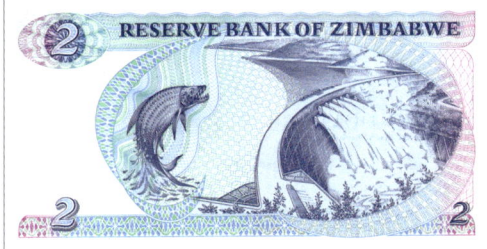

RBZ B1 (P1): **2 dollars** (demonetized 21.08.2006)   VG   VF   UNC
Blue. Front: Water buffalo; Chiremba balancing rocks in Epworth. Back: Tigerfish; Kariba Dam on Zambezi River. Solid security thread. Watermark: Zimbabwe bird. Printer: (FPZ). 134 x 69 mm.

		VG	VF	UNC
☐ a.	1980. Salisbury. Signature 1. Watermark: Type A. Intro: 15.07.1981.	1	4	17
☐ b.	1983. Harare. Signature 2.	—	1	3
☐ c.	1994. Signature 3.	—	—	6
☐ d.	Watermark: Type B.	—	—	30
☐ as.	Diagonal *SPECIMEN* perforation.	—	—	—
☐ bs.	Vertical *SPECIMEN* perforation.	—	—	—

Replacement notes: Prefix AW.

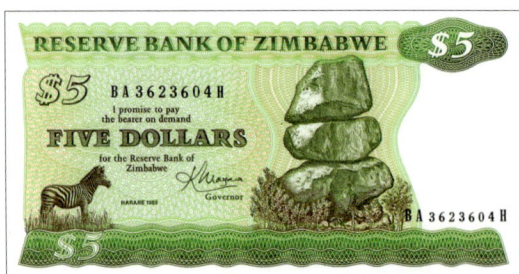

RBZ B2 (P2): **5 dollars** (demonetized 21.08.2006)   VG   VF   UNC
Green. Front: Zebra; Chiremba balancing rocks in Epworth. Back: Village huts; two women pounding maize with poles. Solid security thread. Watermark: Zimbabwe bird. Printer: (FPZ). 141 x 72 mm.

☐	a.	1980. Salisbury. Signature 1. Watermark: Type A. Intro: 14.10.1981.	2	8	30
☐	b.	1982. Harare.	5	10	25
☐	c.	1983. Signature 2.	1	2.50	9
☐	d.	1994. Signature 3.	—	—	16
☐	e.	Watermark: Type B.	—	—	15
☐	as.	Vertical *SPECIMEN* perforation.	—	—	—

Replacement notes: Prefix BW.

RBZ B3 (P3): **10 dollars** (demonetized 21.08.2006)   VG   VF   UNC
Red. Front: Sable antelope; Chiremba balancing rocks in Epworth. Back: Freedom Flame monument; Harare buildings. Solid security thread. Watermark: Zimbabwe bird Type A. Printer: (FPZ). 147 x 77 mm.

☐	a.	1980. Salisbury. Signature 1. Intro: 15.04.1981.	5	25	125
☐	b.	1982. Salisbury (error).	5	25	125
☐	c.	1982. Harare.	5	25	125
☐	d.	1983. Signature 2.	4	10	25
☐	e.	1994. Signature 3.	4	10	25
☐	as.	Diagonal *SPECIMEN* perforation.	—	—	—

Replacement notes: Prefix CW.

RBZ B4 (P4): **20 dollars** (demonetized 21.08.2006)   VG   VF   UNC
Blue and black. Front: Giraffe; Chiremba balancing rocks in Epworth. Back: Elephant; Victoria Falls. Solid security thread. Watermark: Zimbabwe bird Type A. Printer: (FPZ). 152 x 80 mm.

☐	a.	1980. Salisbury. Signature 1. Intro: 14.04.1982.	5	20	70
☐	b.	1982.	50	150	600
☐	c.	1983. Harare. Signature 2.	2	6	25
☐	d.	1994. Signature 3.	—	—	20

Replacement notes: Prefix DW.

1994-2004 Issues

In 1994, the RBZ began issuing a new series of notes with the introduction of a Z$50 note, followed by a Z$100 note the next year. Other denominations from the first series were re-issued in 1997 with the new design, with the exception of the Z$2 note, which was replaced by a coin. As inflation raged, ever higher denominations were required. The Z$500 note was issued in 2001, followed by the Z$1,000 note in 2003. For the most part, replacement note prefixes are transpositions of the first regular note prefixes used for each denomination.

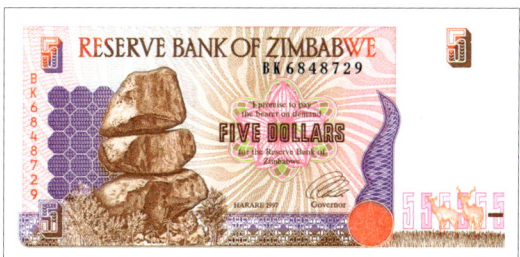
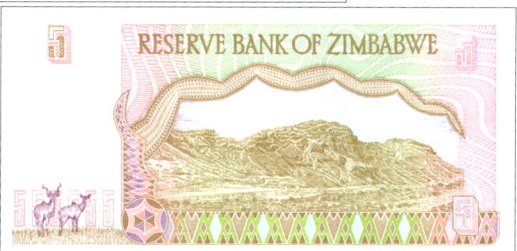

RBZ B5 (P5): **5 dollars** (demonetized 21.08.2006) VG VF UNC
Brown and purple. Front: Chiremba balancing rocks in Epworth; royal dissotis flower; two kudu. Back: Mount Nyangani; two kudu. Solid security thread with demetalized *RBZ 5*. Watermark: Zimbabwe bird Type C. Printer: (FPZ). 139 x 68 mm.
- a. 1997. Signature 3. Light brown back (lithograph; prefix BA-BL). — 1 2
- b. Dark brown back (intaglio; prefix BM-). Intro: 1998. — 1 2
- as. Diagonal red *SPECIMEN* overprint. — — —

Replacement notes: Prefix AB.

RBZ B7 (P7): **20 dollars** (demonetized 21.08.2006) VG VF UNC
Blue and purple. Front: Chiremba balancing rocks in Epworth; roadsider flower; water buffaloes. Back: Water buffaloes; Victoria Falls. Solid security thread with demetalized *RBZ 20*. Watermark: Zimbabwe bird Type C. Printer: (FPZ). 145 x 72 mm.
- a. 1997. Signature 3. — — 3
- as. Diagonal red *SPECIMEN* overprint. — — —

Replacement notes: Prefix AD.

RBZ B6 (P6): **10 dollars** (demonetized 21.08.2006) VG VF UNC
Brown and green. Front: Chiremba balancing rocks in Epworth; sabi star flower; sable antelopes. Back: Sable antelopes; Chilojo Cliffs with birds. Solid security thread with demetalized *RBZ 10*. Watermark: Zimbabwe bird Type C. Printer: (FPZ). 142 x 70 mm.
- a. 1997. Signature 3. — — 1
- as. Diagonal red *SPECIMEN* overprint. — — —

Replacement notes: Prefix AC.

RBZ B8 (P8): **50 dollars** (demonetized 21.08.2006) VG VF UNC
Brown and green. Front: Chiremba balancing rocks in Epworth; flame lily flower; rhinoceros. Back: Rhinoceros; Great Zimbabwe ruins; Zimbabwe bird. Solid security thread with demetalized *RBZ 50*. Watermark: Zimbabwe bird Type C. Printer: (FPZ). 148 x 74 mm.
- a. 1994. Signature 3. — — 2.50
- as. Diagonal red *SPECIMEN* overprint. — — —

Replacement notes: Prefix AE.

RBZ B9 (P9): **100 dollars** (demonetized 21.08.2006) VG VF UNC
Brown and purple. Front: Chiremba balancing rocks in Epworth; protea flower; elephants. Back: Elephants; Kariba Dam on Zambezi River. Solid security thread with demetalized *RBZ 100*. Watermark: Zimbabwe bird Type C. Printer: (FPZ). 152 x 75 mm.
    ☐ a. 1995. Signature 3. — — 2.50
    ☐ as. Diagonal red *SPECIMEN* overprint. — — —
Replacement notes: Prefix AF.

RBZ B10 (P10): **500 dollars** (demonetized 21.08.2006) VG VF UNC
Red and yellow. Front: Chiremba balancing rocks in Epworth; bitter apple flower; two zebras. Back: Two zebras; Hwange thermal power station smokestacks and cooling towers. Solid security thread with demetalized *RBZ 500*. Holographic stripe. Watermark: Zimbabwe bird Type C and electrotype *500*. Printer: (FPZ). 155 x 78 mm.
    ☐ a. 2001. Signature 3. — — 3.50
    ☐ as. Diagonal black *SPECIMEN* overprint. — — —
Replacement notes: Prefix AP.

RBZ B11 (P11): **500 dollars** (demonetized 21.08.2006) VG VF UNC
Brown and gray. Front: Chiremba balancing rocks in Epworth; bitter apple flower; two zebras. Back: Two zebras; Hwange thermal power station smokestacks and cooling towers. Solid security thread with demetalized *RBZ 500*. Watermark: Zimbabwe bird Type C and electrotype *500*. Printer: (FPZ). 155 x 78 mm.
    ☐ a. 2001. Signature 3. Intro: 2003. — — 2.50
    ☐ b. 2004. Signature 5. — — 2.50
    ☐ as. Diagonal red *SPECIMEN* overprint. — — —
Replacement notes: Prefix TA and TB, respectively.

RBZ B12 (P12): **1,000 dollars** (demonetized 21.08.2006) VG VF UNC
Blue and gray. Front: Chiremba balancing rocks in Epworth; bauheinia flower; giraffes. Back: Giraffes; elephants. Holographic stripe. Solid security thread with demetalized *RBZ 1000*. Watermark: Zimbabwe bird Type C and electrotype *1000*. 153 x 77 mm.
    ☐ a. 2003. Signature 3. Printer: (G&D). Prefix WA-WM. — — 4
    ☐ b. Printer: (FPZ). Prefix WN-WU. — — 4
    ☐ as. Diagonal red *SPECIMEN* overprint. — — —
Replacement notes: Prefix AW.

Serial numbers printed by G&D (RBZ B12a, left) and printed by FPZ (RBZ B12b, right).

2003 Travellers Cheque Issues

To keep up with escalating prices due to inflation, the RBZ issued travellers cheques in 2003, with six denominations from Z$1,000 to Z$100,000. Intended for use by the general public, they proved unpopular because identification was required to obtain and redeem these cheques. Since they had to be signed at the time of redemption, they could be used only once by the bearer. In the listings which follow, the uncirculated prices are for unused cheques without signatures or bank cancellation stamps on either side.

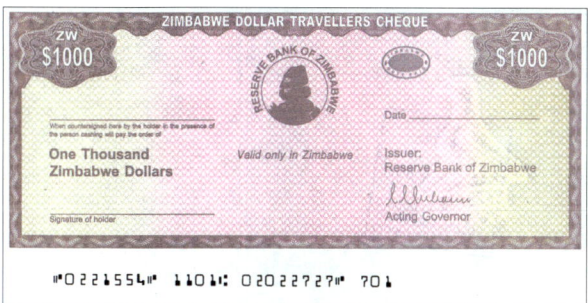

RBZ B13 (P15): **1,000 dollars** (demonetized 21.08.2006) VG VF UNC
Gray. Front: RBZ logo. Back: Wave pattern. Solid security thread. Watermark: Zimbabwe bird Type A. Printer: (FPZ). 160 x 80 mm.
- a. No date. Signature 4. Intro: 2003. — — 250
- as. Diagonal red *SPECIMEN* overprint. — — —

RBZ B14 (P16): **5,000 dollars** (demonetized 21.08.2006) VG VF UNC
Red. Front: RBZ logo. Back: Wave pattern. Solid security thread. Watermark: Zimbabwe bird Type A. Printer: (FPZ). 160 x 80 mm.
- a. No date. Signature 4. Intro: 2003. — — 250
- as. Diagonal red *SPECIMEN* overprint. — — —

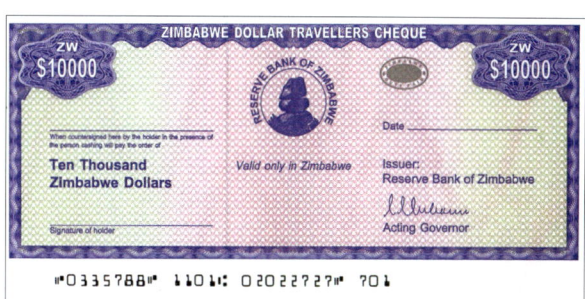

RBZ B15 (P17): **10,000 dollars** (demonetized 21.08.2006) VG VF UNC
Purple. Front: RBZ logo. Back: Wave pattern. Solid security thread. Watermark: Zimbabwe bird Type A. Printer: (FPZ). 160 x 80 mm.
- a. No date. Signature 4. Intro: 2003. — — 250
- as. Diagonal red *SPECIMEN* overprint. — — —

RBZ B16 (P18): **20,000 dollars** (demonetized 21.08.2006) VG VF UNC
Green. Front: RBZ logo. Back: Wave pattern. Solid security thread. Watermark: Zimbabwe bird Type A. Printer: (FPZ). 160 x 80 mm.
- a. No date. Signature 4. Intro: 2003. — — 250
- as. Diagonal red *SPECIMEN* overprint. — — —

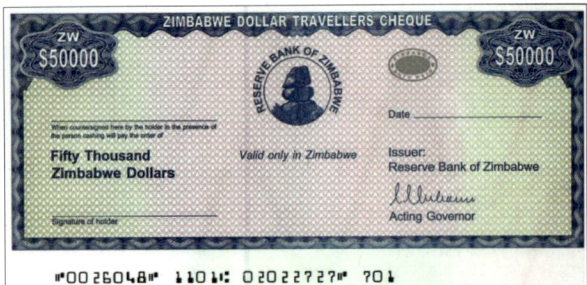

2003 Bearer Cheque Issues

Bearer cheques are promissory notes that function like banknotes, without the need for signatures or identification, which was the case with the preceding travellers cheques. Although these bearer cheques had a limited period of validity printed on their fronts, in practice they did not expire and remained valid until the monetary reform of 1 August 2006. They were printed on paper partially printed with the design of the Z$50 (RBZ B8).

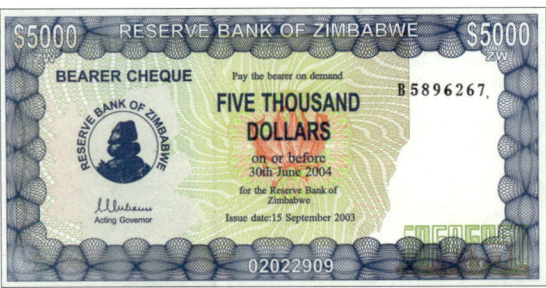

RBZ B19 (P21): **5,000 dollars** (demonetized 21.08.2006)   VG   VF   UNC
Blue. Front: RBZ logo; flame lily flower; rhinoceros. Back: Wave pattern. Watermark: Zimbabwe bird Type C. Printer: (FPZ). 148 x 74 mm.
- ☐ a. 15 September 2003. Expires 31st January 2004.   25   60   200
  Signature 4.
  Solid security thread with demetalized *RBZ 50*.
- ☐ b. Expires 30th June 2004.   —   15   60
- ☐ c. 1st December 2003. Expires 31st December   —   2.50   10
  2004. Signature 5 w/o name above title.
  Solid security thread with demetalized *RBZ*.
  Watermark: Electrotype *RBZ* added.
- ☐ d. Signature 5 with *Dr G Gono* above title.   —   5   30
- ☐ e. Expires 31st December 2005.   —   1.25   5
- ☐ bs. Diagonal red *SPECIMEN* overprint.   —   —   200

Replacement notes: Prefix ZA, ZB, ZC, and ZD.

RBZ B17 (P19): **50,000 dollars** (demonetized 21.08.2006)   VG   VF   UNC
Dark blue. Front: RBZ logo. Back: Wave pattern. Solid security thread. Watermark: Zimbabwe bird Type A. Printer: (FPZ). 160 x 80 mm.
- ☐ a. No date. Signature 4. Intro: 2003.   —   —   450
- ☐ as. Diagonal red *SPECIMEN* overprint.   —   —   —

RBZ B18 (P20): **100,000 dollars** (demonetized 21.08.2006)   VG   VF   UNC
Brown. Front: RBZ logo. Back: Wave pattern. Solid security thread. Watermark: Zimbabwe bird Type A. Printer: (FPZ). 160 x 80 mm.
- ☐ a. No date. Signature 4. Intro: 2003.   —   —   600
- ☐ as. Diagonal red *SPECIMEN* overprint.   —   —   —

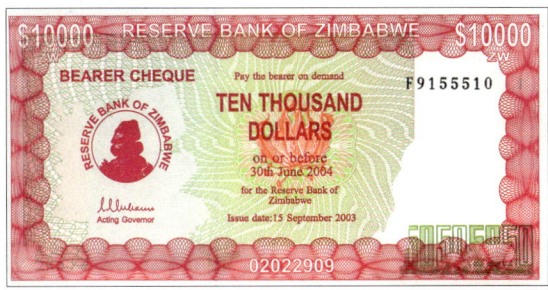

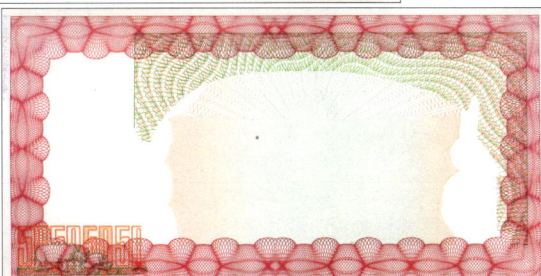

RBZ B20 (P22): **10,000 dollars** (demonetized 21.08.2006)   VG   VF   UNC
Red. Front: RBZ logo; flame lily flower; rhinoceros. Back: Wave pattern. Watermark: Zimbabwe bird Type C. Printer: (FPZ). 148 x 74 mm.

- ☐ a. 15 September 2003. Expires 31st January 2004.   25   60   200
     Signature 4.
     Solid security thread with demetalized *RBZ 50*.
- ☐ b. Expires 30th June 2004.   —   20   75
- ☐ c. 1st December 2003. Expires 31st December   —   —   10
     2004. Signature 5 w/o name above title.
     Solid security thread with demetalized *RBZ*.
     Watermark: Electrotype *RBZ* added.
- ☐ d. Signature 5 with *Dr G Gono* above title.   —   —   30
- ☐ e. Expires 31st December 2005.   —   —   9
- ☐ bs. Diagonal red *SPECIMEN* overprint.   —   —   200

Replacement notes: Prefix ZE, ZF, ZG, and ZH.

RBZ B21 (P23): **20,000 dollars** (demonetized 21.08.2006)   VG   VF   UNC
Brown. Front: RBZ logo; flame lily flower; rhinoceros. Back: Wave pattern. Watermark: Zimbabwe bird Type C. Printer: (FPZ). 148 x 74 mm.

- ☐ a. 15 September 2003. Expires 31st January 2004.   25   60   200
     Signature 4.
     Solid security thread with demetalized *RBZ 50*.
- ☐ b. Expires 30th June 2004.   —   15   60
- ☐ c. 1st December 2003. Expires 31st December   40   150   600
     2004. Signature 5 w/o name above title. Solid
     security thread with demetalized *RBZ*.
- ☐ d. Watermark: Electrotype *RBZ* added.   —   10   50
- ☐ e. Signature 5 with *Dr G Gono* above title.   —   —   35
- ☐ f. Expires 31st December 2005.   —   —   0.50
- ☐ bs. Diagonal red *SPECIMEN* overprint.   —   —   —

Replacement notes: Prefix ZJ, ZK, ZL, and ZM.

2005-2006 Bearer Cheque Issues

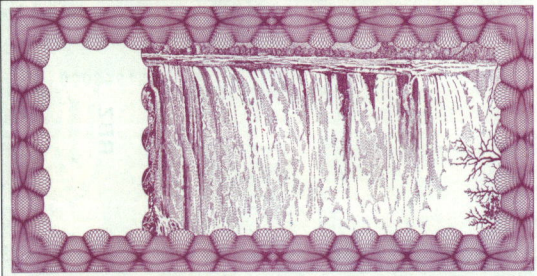

RBZ B22 (P28, P29 & P30): **50,000 dollars** (dem. 21.08.2006)   VG   VF   UNC

Purple. Front: RBZ logo; flame lily flower. Back: Victoria Falls. Solid security thread with demetalized *RBZ*. Watermark: Zimbabwe bird Type C and electrotype *RBZ*. 148 x 75 mm.

- ☐ a. 1st October 2005. Expires 31st December 2006.   2.50   10   60
  Signature 5. Printer: (FPZ). Intro: August 2006.
- ☐ b. 1st February 2006. Expires 31st December 2006.   —   —   2.50
- ☐ c. Different serial number font. Printer: (G&D).   —   —   2.50
- ☐ bs. Diagonal red *SPECIMEN* overprint.   —   —   —

Replacement notes: Prefix ZA, ZB, and CZ, respectively.

AA2814161 CF0596629

RBZ B22a/b (left) Serial numbers printed by FPZ and B22c (right) printed by G&D.

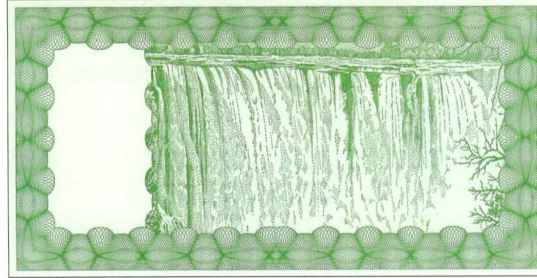

RBZ B23 (P31 & P32): **100,000 dollars** (demon. 21.08.2006)   VG   VF   UNC

Green. Front: RBZ logo; flame lily flower. Back: Victoria Falls. Solid security thread with demetalized *RBZ*. Watermark: Zimbabwe bird Type C and electrotype *RBZ*. Printer: (FPZ). 148 x 74 mm.

- ☐ a. 1st October 2005. Expires 31st December 2006.   3.50   15   50
  Signature 5. Intro: August 2006.
- ☐ b. 1st June 2006.   —   —   7
- ☐ bs. Diagonal red *SPECIMEN* overprint.   —   —   —

Replacement notes: Prefix ZA and ZB, respectively.

2006-2008 Bearer Cheque Issues

On 1 August 2006, the RBZ initiated Operation Sunrise, which lopped off three zeros from the old Zimbabwe dollar, though the name of the currency did not change. All old banknotes and bearer cheques subsequently expired on 21 August 2006. On 17 September 2006, RBZ Governor Gideon Gono declared, "10 trillion is still out there and it has become manure."

Old banknotes and bearer cheques were replaced by new bearer cheques from 1 cent to Z$100,000, which share similar front design elements of the Reserve Bank of Zimbabwe logo and signature of Dr. G. Gono, Governor at left. The new notes are distinguished primarily by different color schemes, printed denominations, and back designs. Due to paper shortages, the denomination used as the electrotype watermark on many of the notes does not match the printed denomination. This is intentional and these notes are not considered errors.

The value of the new dollar continued to fall, leading the RBZ to issue bearer cheques in ever-larger denominations, from Z$5,000 to Z$500 million.

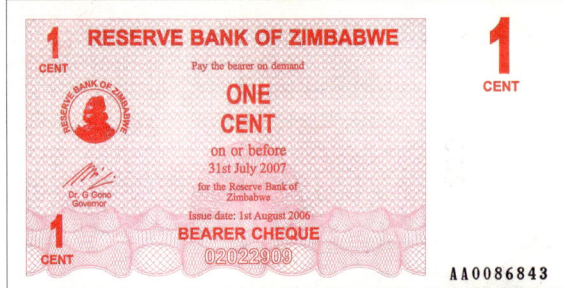

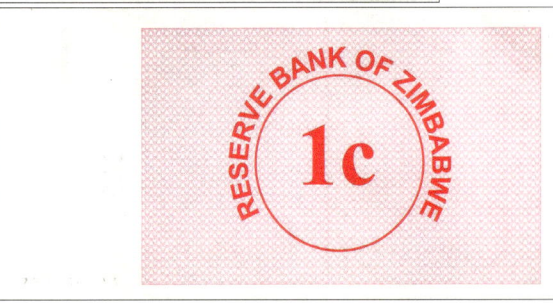

RBZ B24 (P33): **1 cent**   VG   VF   UNC

Red. Front: RBZ logo. Back: Denomination in circle. Solid security thread with demetalized *RBZ 500* [sic]. Watermark: Zimbabwe bird Type C and electrotype *500* [sic]. Printer: (FPZ). 154 x 78 mm.

- ☐ a. 1st August 2006. Signature 5.   —   —   1.50
- ☐ as. Diagonal red *SPECIMEN* overprint.   —   —   —

Replacement notes: Prefix ZA.

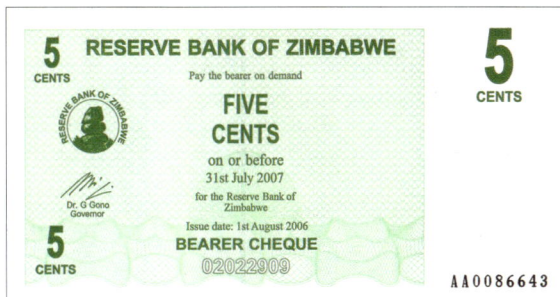
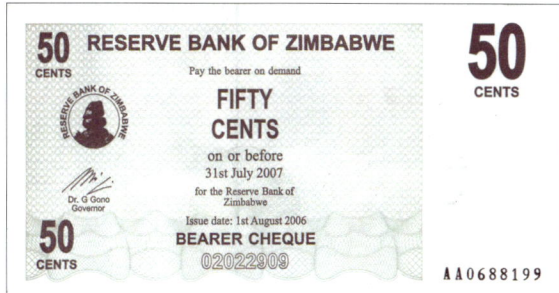

RBZ B25 (P34): **5 cents**   VG   VF   UNC
Green. Front: RBZ logo. Back: Denomination in circle. Solid security thread with demetalized *RBZ 500* [sic]. Watermark: Zimbabwe bird Type C and electrotype *500* [sic]. Printer: (FPZ). 154 x 78 mm.
    ☐ a. 1st August 2006. Signature 5.   —   —   1
    ☐ as. Diagonal red *SPECIMEN* overprint.   —   —   —
Replacement notes: Prefix ZA.

RBZ B27 (P36): **50 cents**   VG   VF   UNC
Black. Front: RBZ logo. Back: Denomination in circle. Solid security thread with demetalized *RBZ 500* [sic]. Watermark: Zimbabwe bird Type C and electrotype *500* [sic]. Printer: (FPZ). 154 x 78 mm.
    ☐ a. 1st August 2006. Signature 5.   —   —   1.50
    ☐ as. Diagonal red *SPECIMEN* overprint.   —   —   —
Replacement notes: Prefix ZA.

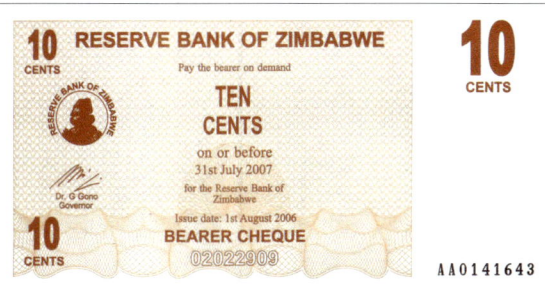
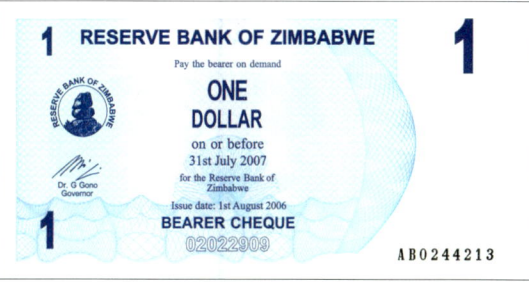

RBZ B26 (P35): **10 cents**   VG   VF   UNC
Brown. Front: RBZ logo. Back: Denomination in circle. Solid security thread with demetalized *RBZ 500* [sic]. Watermark: Zimbabwe bird Type C and electrotype *500* [sic]. Printer: (FPZ). 154 x 78 mm.
    ☐ a. 1st August 2006. Signature 5.   —   —   1
    ☐ as. Diagonal red *SPECIMEN* overprint.   —   —   —
Replacement notes: Prefix ZA.

RBZ B28 (P37): **1 dollar**   VG   VF   UNC
Blue. Front: RBZ logo. Back: Village huts; two women pounding maize with poles. Solid security thread with demetalized *RBZ*. Watermark: Zimbabwe bird Type C and electrotype *RBZ*. Printer: (FPZ). 148 x 74 mm.
    ☐ a. 1st August 2006. Signature 5.   —   —   1
    ☐ as. Diagonal red *SPECIMEN* overprint.   —   —   —
Replacement notes: Prefix ZA.

RBZ B29 (P38): **5 dollars**   VG   VF   UNC
Brown and green. Front: RBZ logo. Back: Freedom Flame monument; Harare buildings. Solid security thread with demetalized *RBZ*. Watermark: Zimbabwe bird Type C and electrotype *RBZ*. Printer: (FPZ). 148 x 74 mm.
   ☐ a.   1st August 2006. Signature 5.   —   —   1
   ☐ as. Diagonal red *SPECIMEN* overprint.   —   —   —
Replacement notes: Prefix ZA.

RBZ B31 (P40): **20 dollars**   VG   VF   UNC
Brown. Front: RBZ logo. Back: Victoria Falls. Solid security thread with demetalized *RBZ*. Watermark: Zimbabwe bird Type C and electrotype *RBZ*. Printer: (FPZ). 148 x 74 mm.
   ☐ a.   1st August 2006. Signature 5.   —   —   0.75
   ☐ as. Diagonal red *SPECIMEN* overprint.   —   —   —
Replacement notes: Prefix ZA.

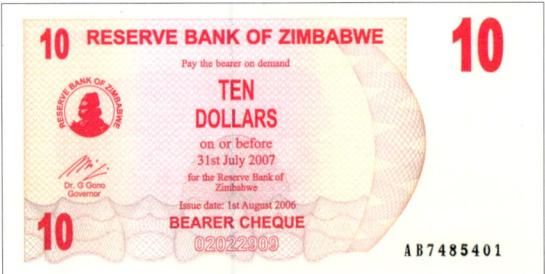

RBZ B30 (P39): **10 dollars**   VG   VF   UNC
Red. Front: RBZ logo. Back: Village huts; two women pounding maize with poles. Solid security thread with demetalized *RBZ*. Watermark: Zimbabwe bird Type C and electrotype *RBZ*. Printer: (FPZ). 148 x 74 mm.
   ☐ a.   1st August 2006. Signature 5.   —   —   0.75
   ☐ as. Diagonal red *SPECIMEN* overprint.   —   —   —
Replacement notes: Prefix ZA.

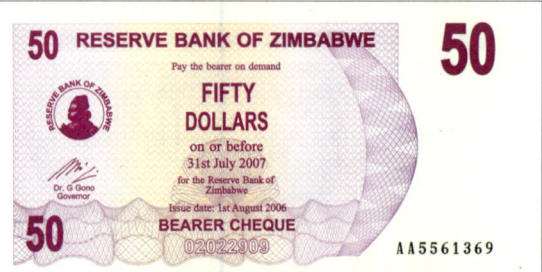

RBZ B32 (P41): **50 dollars**   VG   VF   UNC
Purple. Front: RBZ logo. Back: Victoria Falls. Solid security thread with demetalized *RBZ*. Watermark: Zimbabwe bird Type C and electrotype *RBZ*. Printer: (FPZ). 148 x 74 mm.
   ☐ a.   1st August 2006. Signature 5.   —   —   1
   ☐ as. Diagonal red *SPECIMEN* overprint.   —   —   —
Replacement notes: Prefix ZA.

RBZ B33 (P42): **100 dollars**　　　　　　　　　　　　VG　VF　UNC
Green. Front: RBZ logo. Back: Mount Nyangani. Solid security thread with demetalized *RBZ*. Watermark: Zimbabwe bird Type C and electrotype *RBZ*. Printer: (FPZ). 148 x 74 mm.
　　☐ a.　1st August 2006. Signature 5.　　　　　　　—　—　1
　　☐ as.　Diagonal red *SPECIMEN* overprint.　　　　—　—　—
Replacement notes: Prefix ZA.

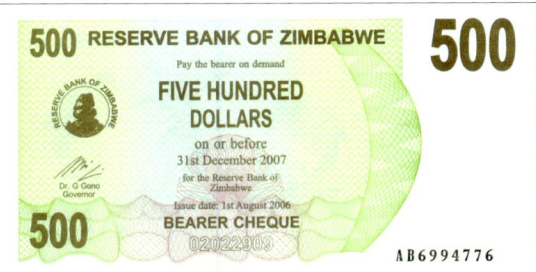

RBZ B34 (P43): **500 dollars**　　　　　　　　　　　　VG　VF　UNC
Olive green. Front: RBZ logo. Back: Tigerfish; Kariba Dam on Zambezi River. Solid security thread with demetalized *RBZ*. Watermark: Zimbabwe bird Type C and electrotype *RBZ*. Printer: (FPZ). 148 x 74 mm.
　　☐ a.　1st August 2006. Signature 5.　　　　　　　—　—　1
　　☐ as.　Diagonal red *SPECIMEN* overprint.　　　　—　—　—
Replacement notes: Prefix ZA.

RBZ B35 (P44): **1,000 dollars**　　　　　　　　　　　VG　VF　UNC
Brown. Front: RBZ logo. Back: Mount Nyangani. Solid security thread with demetalized *RBZ*. Watermark: Zimbabwe bird Type C and electrotype *RBZ*. Printer: (FPZ). 148 x 74 mm.
　　☐ a.　1st August 2006. Signature 5.　　　　　　　—　—　1
　　☐ as.　Diagonal red *SPECIMEN* overprint.　　　　—　—　—
Replacement notes: Prefix ZA.

RBZ B36 (P45): **5,000 dollars**　　　　　　　　　　　VG　VF　UNC
Blue. Front: RBZ logo. Back: Kariba Dam on Zambezi River. Solid security thread with demetalized *RBZ*. Watermark: Zimbabwe bird Type C and electrotype *RBZ*. Printer: (FPZ). 148 x 74 mm.
　　☐ a.　1st February 2007. Signature 5.　　　　　　—　—　3
　　☐ as.　Diagonal red *SPECIMEN* overprint.　　　　—　—　—
Replacement notes: Prefix ZA.

RBZ B37 (P46): **10,000 dollars**   VG   VF   UNC

Violet. Front: RBZ logo. Back: Great Zimbabwe ruins. Solid security thread with demetalized *RBZ*. Watermark: Zimbabwe bird Type C and electrotype *RBZ*. Printer: (FPZ). 148 x 74 mm.

    ☐ a.   1st August 2006. Signature 5.   —   —   30
           Denomination without space: *10000* (prefix AA).
    ☐ b.   Denomination with space: *10 000* (prefix AB-AN).   —   —   6
    ☐ as.   Diagonal red *SPECIMEN* overprint.   —   —   —

Replacement notes: Prefixes ZA and ZB.

RBZ B37a (left) without space to denote thousands and B37b (right) with space.

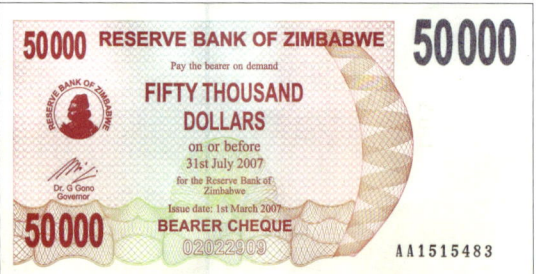

RBZ B38 (P47): **50,000 dollars**   VG   VF   UNC

Red and brown. Front: RBZ logo. Back: Elephant; Victoria Falls. Solid security thread with demetalized *RBZ*. Watermark: Zimbabwe bird Type C and electrotype *RBZ*. Printer: (FPZ). 148 x 74 mm.

    ☐ a.   1st March 2007. Signature 5.   —   —   7.50
    ☐ as.   Diagonal red *SPECIMEN* overprint.   —   —   —

Replacement notes: Prefix ZA.

RBZ B39 (P48): **100,000 dollars**   VG   VF   UNC

Teal. Front: RBZ logo. Back: Great Zimbabwe ruins. Solid security thread with demetalized *RBZ*. Watermark: Zimbabwe bird Type C and electrotype *RBZ*. Printer: (FPZ). 148 x 74 mm.

    ☐ a.   1st August 2006. Signature 5.   —   —   35
           Denomination without space: *100000*.
    ☐ b   Denomination with space: *100 000*.   —   —   4.50
    ☐ as.   Diagonal red *SPECIMEN* overprint.   —   —   —

Replacement notes: Prefix ZA.

RBZ B40 (P49): **200,000 dollars**   VG   VF   UNC

Brown. Front: RBZ logo. Back: Hwange thermal power station smokestacks and cooling towers. Solid security thread with demetalized *RBZ*. Watermark: Zimbabwe bird Type C and electrotype *RBZ*. Printer: (FPZ). 148 x 74 mm.

    ☐ a.   1st July 2007. Signature 5.   —   —   1.50
    ☐ as.   Diagonal red *SPECIMEN* overprint.   —   —   —

Replacement notes: Prefix ZA.

RBZ B41 (P50): **250,000 dollars** VG VF UNC
Green and brown. Front: RBZ logo. Back: Great Zimbabwe ruins. Solid security thread with demetalized *RBZ*. Watermark: Zimbabwe bird Type C and electrotype *RBZ*. Printer: (FPZ). 148 x 74 mm.
☐ a. 20th December 2007. Signature 5. — — 15
Replacement notes: Prefix ZA.

RBZ B42 (P51): **500,000 dollars** VG VF UNC
Green. Front: RBZ logo. Back: Three elephants. Solid security thread with demetalized *RBZ*. Watermark: Zimbabwe bird Type C and electrotype *RBZ*. Printer: (FPZ). 148 x 74 mm.
☐ a. 1st July 2007. Signature 5. — — 3.50
Replacement notes: Prefix ZA.

RBZ B43 (P52): **750,000 dollars** VG VF UNC
Purple. Front: RBZ logo. Back: Elephant and Victoria Falls. Holographic stripe. Solid security thread with demetalized *RBZ 1000* [sic]. Watermark: Zimbabwe bird Type C and electrotype *1000* [sic]. Printer: (FPZ). 152.5 x 77.5 mm.
☐ a. 31st December 2007. Signature 5. — — 1
Replacement notes: Prefix ZA.
This note uses paper left over from B12b, hence its larger size and electrotype *1000*.

RBZ B44 (P53): **1,000,000 dollars** VG VF UNC
Brown. Front: RBZ logo. Back: Village huts; two women pounding maize with poles. Solid security thread with demetalized *RBZ*. Watermark: Zimbabwe bird Type C and electrotype *RBZ*. Printer: (FPZ). 148 x 74 mm.
☐ a. 1st January 2008. Signature 5. — — 3
Replacement notes: Prefix ZA.

RBZ B45 (P54): **5,000,000 dollars** VG VF UNC
Blue. Front: RBZ logo. Back: Mount Nyangani. Solid security thread with demetalized *RBZ*. Watermark: Zimbabwe bird Type C and electrotype *RBZ*. Printer: (FPZ). 148 x 74 mm.

    ☐ a. 1st January 2008. Signature 5. — — 10
    ☐ as. Horizontal *SPECIMEN* perforation. — —

Replacement notes: Prefix ZA.

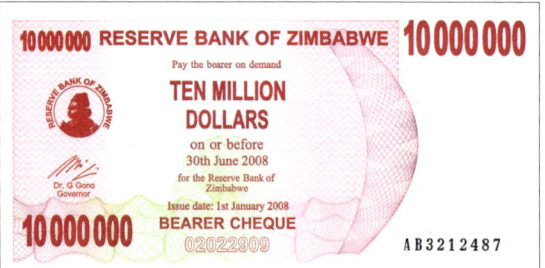

RBZ B46 (P55): **10,000,000 dollars** VG VF UNC
Red. Front: RBZ logo. Back: Tigerfish, Kariba Dam on Zambezi River, and reservoir. Solid security thread with demetalized *RBZ*. Watermark: Zimbabwe bird Type C and electrotype *RBZ*. 148 x 74 mm.

    ☐ a. 1st January 2008. Signature 5. Prefixes AA-CA. — — 30
           Printer: (FPZ).
    ☐ b. Different serial number font. Prefixes DA-DC. — — 6
           Printer: (G&D).
    ☐ as. Horizontal *SPECIMEN* perforation. — —

Replacement notes: Prefix ZA and ZE, respectively.

AB3212487 DA2878929

RBZ B46a (left) Serial numbers printed by FPZ and B46b (right) printed by G&D.

RBZ B47 (P56): **25,000,000 dollars** VG VF UNC
Green. Front: RBZ logo. Back: Freedom Flame monument and Harare buildings. Solid security thread with demetalized *RBZ 500* [sic]. Watermark: Zimbabwe bird Type C and electrotype *500* [sic]. Printer: (FPZ). 154 x 78 mm.

    ☐ a. 2nd April 2008. Signature 5. — — 2

Replacement notes: Prefix ZA.
Printed on paper used for B11, hence the wrong denomination on thread and watermark.

RBZ B48 (P57): **50,000,000 dollars** VG VF UNC
Purple. Front: RBZ logo. Back: Three elephants. Solid security thread with demetalized *RBZ*. Watermark: Zimbabwe bird Type C and electrotype *RBZ*. Printer: (FPZ). 148 x 74 mm.

    ☐ a. 2nd April 2008. Signature 5. — — 1

Replacement notes: Prefix ZA.

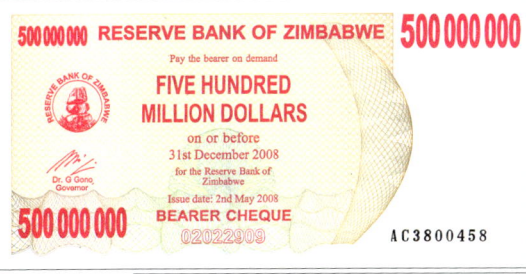

RBZ B49 (P58): **100,000,000 dollars**   VG   VF   UNC
Green. Front: RBZ logo. Back: Village huts; two women pounding maize with poles. Solid security thread with demetalized *RBZ*. Watermark: Zimbabwe bird Type C and electrotype *RBZ*. Printer: (FPZ). 148 x 74 mm.
☐ a. 2nd May 2008. Signature 5.   —   —   2.50
Replacement notes: Prefix ZA.

RBZ B51 (P60): **500,000,000 dollars**   VG   VF   UNC
Red. Front: RBZ logo. Back: Tigerfish; Kariba Dam on Zambezi River. Solid security thread with demetalized *RBZ*. Watermark: Zimbabwe bird Type C and electrotype *RBZ*. Printer: (FPZ). 148 x 74 mm.
☐ a. 2nd May 2008. Signature 5.   —   —   0.75
Replacement notes: Prefix ZA.

2008 Special Agro-Cheque Issues

Special agro-cheques were originally intended for the exclusive use of Zimbabwean farmers, although they found their way into regular commerce as prices continued to rise. The erroneous abbreviation of "agricultural" was caught too late to correct and the notes were issued anyway.

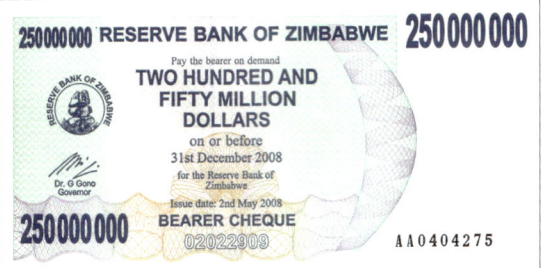

RBZ B50 (P59): **250,000,000 dollars**   VG   VF   UNC
Blue. Front: RBZ logo. Back: Elephant; Victoria Falls. Solid security thread with demetalized *RBZ*. Watermark: Zimbabwe bird Type C and electrotype *RBZ*. Printer: (FPZ). 148 x 74 mm.
☐ a. 2nd May 2008. Signature 5.   —   —   3
Replacement notes: Prefix ZA.

RBZ B52 (P61): **5,000,000,000 dollars**   VG   VF   UNC
Purple. Front: RBZ logo; denomination; giraffes. Back: Giraffes; grain silos. Solid security thread with demetalized *RBZ*. Watermark: Zimbabwe bird Type C and electrotype *RBZ*. Printer: (FPZ). 148 x 74 mm.
☐ a. 15th May 2008. Expires 31st December 2008.   —   —   1
       Signature 5.
Replacement notes: Prefix ZA.

RBZ B53 (P62): **25,000,000,000 dollars**   VG   VF   UNC
Green. Front: RBZ logo; denomination; giraffes. Back: Giraffes; grain silos. Solid security thread with demetalized *RBZ 500* [sic]. Watermark: Zimbabwe bird Type C and electrotype *500* [sic]. Printer: (FPZ). 154 x 78 mm.
    ☐ a. 15th May 2008. Expires 31st December 2008. — — 2.50
        Signature 5.
Replacement notes: Prefix ZA.

RBZ B54 (P63): **50,000,000,000 dollars**   VG   VF   UNC
Brown. Front: RBZ logo; denomination; giraffes. Back: Giraffes; grain silos. Solid security thread with demetalized *RBZ*. Watermark: Zimbabwe bird Type C and electrotype *RBZ*. Printer: (FPZ). 148 x 74 mm.
    ☐ a. 15th May 2008. Expires 31st December 2008. — — 3
        Signature 5.
Replacement notes: Prefix ZA.

RBZ B55 (P64): **100,000,000,000 dollars**   VG   VF   UNC
Blue. Front: RBZ logo; denomination; giraffes. Back: Giraffes; grain silos. Solid security thread with demetalized *RBZ*. Watermark: Zimbabwe bird Type C and electrotype *RBZ*. Printer: (FPZ). 148 x 74 mm.
    ☐ a. 1st July 2008. Expires 31st December 2008. — — 3
        Signature 5.
Replacement notes: Prefix ZA.

2007-2008 Issues

On 1 August 2008, in an effort to simplify calculations in economic transactions, the Reserve Bank of Zimbabwe revalued its currency, striking ten zeros from the old Zimbabwe dollar. The move came just a week after the introduction of a 100 billion-dollar special agro-cheque—not enough to buy a loaf of bread—which became worth ten dollars under the new system. Concurrent with the revaluation, a new series of banknotes was also issued, and old coins were also reintroduced after years of obsolescence. The new notes circulated with the older bearer cheques and special agro-cheques, which remained legal tender until 31 January 2009, instead of 31 December 2008, the expiration date printed on the bearer cheques.

RBZ B56 (P65): **1 dollar** VG VF UNC
Violet. Front: Chiremba balancing rocks in Epworth. Back: Victoria Falls; water buffalo. Windowed security thread with demetalized *RBZ 1*. Watermark: Zimbabwe bird Type C and electrotype *1*. Printer: (G&D). 134 x 68 mm.

☐ a. 2007. Signature 5. Intro: 01.08.2008. — — 0.25

Replacement notes: Prefix ZA.

RBZ B58 (P67): **10 dollars** VG VF UNC
Green. Front: Chiremba balancing rocks in Epworth. Back: Farmer plowing field on mechanical tractor; three grain silos. Windowed security thread with demetalized *RBZ 10*. Watermark: Zimbabwe bird Type C and electrotype *10*. Printer: (G&D). 142 x 70 mm.

☐ a. 2007. Signature 5. Intro: 01.08.2008. — — 2

Replacement notes: Prefix ZA.

RBZ B57 (P66): **5 dollars** VG VF UNC
Brown. Front: Chiremba balancing rocks in Epworth. Back: Dam; elephant. Windowed security thread with demetalized *RBZ 5*. Watermark: Zimbabwe bird Type C and electrotype *5*. Printer: (G&D). 138 x 68 mm.

☐ a. 2007. Signature 5. Intro: 01.08.2008. — — 1

Replacement notes: Prefix ZA.

RBZ B59 (P68): **20 dollars** VG VF UNC
Red. Front: Chiremba balancing rocks in Epworth. Back: Tailings pile; miner with jackhammer. Windowed security thread with demetalized *RBZ 20*. Watermark: Zimbabwe bird Type C and electrotype *20*. Printer: (G&D). 145 x 72 mm.

☐ a. 2007. Signature 5. Intro: 01.08.2008. — — 2

Replacement notes: Prefix ZA.

RBZ B60 (P69): **100 dollars**　　　　　　　　　　　VG　VF　UNC
Blue. Front: Chiremba balancing rocks in Epworth. Back: Aloe excelsa trees; Great Zimbabwe ruins. Windowed security thread with demetalized *RBZ 100* and balancing rocks hologram. Watermark: Zimbabwe bird Type C and electrotype *100*. Printer: (G&D). 149 x 74 mm.
　　☐　a.　2007. Signature 5. Intro: 01.08.2008.　　　—　—　1
Replacement notes: Prefix ZA.

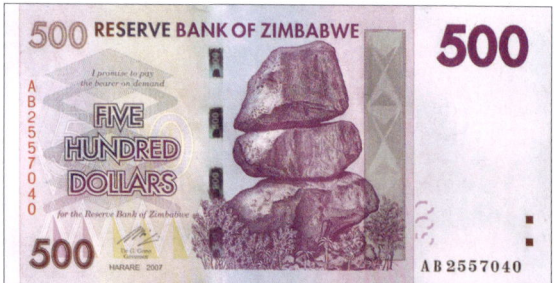

RBZ B61 (P70): **500 dollars**　　　　　　　　　　　VG　VF　UNC
Purple. Front: Chiremba balancing rocks in Epworth. Back: Workers milking cows; cattle. Windowed security thread with demetalized *RBZ 500* and balancing rocks hologram. Watermark: Zimbabwe bird Type C and electrotype *500*. Printer: (G&D). 150 x 75 mm.
　　☐　a.　2007. Signature 5. Intro: 01.08.2008.　　　—　—　4
Replacement notes: Prefix ZA.

RBZ B62 (P71): **1,000 dollars**　　　　　　　　　　VG　VF　UNC
Gold. Front: Chiremba balancing rocks in Epworth. Back: Parliament House and Reserve Bank of Zimbabwe headquarters. Windowed security thread with demetalized *RBZ 1000* and balancing rocks hologram. Watermark: Zimbabwe bird Type C and electrotype *1000*. Printer: (FPZ). 153 x 76 mm.
　　☐　a.　2007. Signature 5. Intro: 17.09.08　　　—　—　1
Replacement notes: Prefix ZA.

On 29 September 2008, less than two months after revaluing its currency and issuing a new series of notes in which the highest denomination was 1,000 dollars, Zimbabwe issued 10,000- and 20,000-dollar notes. These notes were printed locally by Fidelity Printers and Refiners in Harare. The 10,000-dollar appears to be printed on paper originally supplied by Giesecke & Devrient for use on 1,000-dollar notes, as evidenced by the fact that the electrotype watermark is 1000 and does not match the denominations printed on the note. The 20,000-dollar note lacks a security thread and watermark and is thought to be printed on paper from Art Corporation in Kadoma. The substrate consists of local cotton and contains UV planchettes, but lacks polymer coatings, pressure rolling, and polishing. Its vulnerability to counterfeiting resulted in some merchants refusing payments with the new notes.

RBZ B63 (P72): **10,000 dollars** VG VF UNC
Brown. Front: Chiremba balancing rocks in Epworth. Back: Harvester; tractor. Windowed security thread with demetalized *RBZ 1000* [sic] and balancing rocks hologram. Watermark: Zimbabwe bird Type C and electrotype *1000* [sic]. Printer: (FPZ). 153 x 76 mm.
- ☐ a. 2008. Signature 5. Intro: 29.09.2008. — — 18

Replacement notes: Prefix ZA.

RBZ B64 (P73): **20,000 dollars** VG VF UNC
Brown. Front: Chiremba balancing rocks in Epworth; Zimbabwe bird in OVI. Back: Victoria Falls; Kariba Dam on Zambezi River. 7-mm wide iridescent stripe with repeating *RBZ*. No security thread. Watermark: None. Printer: (FPZ). 148 x 74 mm.
- ☐ a. 2008. Signature 5. Intro: 29.09.2008. Plain paper. — — 9
- ☐ b. Horizontally lined paper. — — 9

Replacement notes: Prefix ZA.

RBZ B65 (P74): **50,000 dollars** VG VF UNC
Green. Front: Chiremba balancing rocks in Epworth; Zimbabwe bird in OVI. Back: Farmer plowing field on mechanical tractor; miner with jackhammer. 7-mm wide iridescent stripe with repeating *RBZ*. No security thread. Watermark: None. Printer: (FPZ). 148 x 74 mm.
- ☐ a. 2008. Signature 5. Intro: 13.10.2008. Plain paper. — — 6
- ☐ b. Horizontally lined paper. — — 6

Replacement notes: Prefix ZA.

RBZ B66 (P75): **100,000 dollars** VG VF UNC
Purple. Front: Chiremba balancing rocks in Epworth; stylized grains and cow in underprint; Zimbabwe bird in OVI. Back: Water buffalo; elephant. 7-mm wide iridescent stripe with repeating *RBZ*. No security thread. Watermark: None. Printer: (FPZ). 148 x 74 mm.
- ☐ a. 2008. Signature 5. Intro: 05.11.2008. — — 1

RBZ B67 (P76): **500,000 dollars**   VG   VF   UNC

Green. Front: Chiremba balancing rocks in Epworth; stylized grains and cow in underprint; Zimbabwe bird in OVI. Back: Aloe excelsa trees; workers milking cows. 7-mm wide iridescent stripe with repeating *RBZ*. No security thread. Watermark: None. Printer: (FPZ). 148 x 74 mm.

- ☐ a. 2008. Signature 5. Intro: 05.11.2008.   —   —   1
       Plain paper.
- ☐ b. Horizontally lined paper.   —   —   1

Replacement notes: Prefix ZA.

RBZ B68 (P77): **1,000,000 dollars**   VG   VF   UNC

Blue. Front: Chiremba balancing rocks in Epworth; stylized grains and cow in underprint; Zimbabwe bird in OVI. Back: Great Zimbabwe ruins; cattle. Windowed security thread with demetalized *RBZ 1000* [sic] and balancing rocks hologram. Watermark: Zimbabwe bird Type C and electrotype *1000* [sic]. Printer: (FPZ). 153 x 76 mm.

- ☐ a. 2008. Signature 5. Intro: 05.11.2008.   —   —   1

RBZ B69 (P78): **10,000,000 dollars**   VG   VF   UNC

Blue. Front: Chiremba balancing rocks in Epworth; stylized grains and cow in underprint; Zimbabwe bird in OVI. Back: Unknown buildings; Great Zimbabwe ruins. 3-mm gold-to-green OVI stripe with repeating *RBZ*. No security thread. Watermark: None. Printer: (FPZ). 148 x 74 mm.

- ☐ a. 2008. Signature 5. Intro: 04.12.2008.   —   —   4

RBZ B70 (P79): **50,000,000 dollars**   VG   VF   UNC

Green Front: Chiremba balancing rocks in Epworth; stylized grains and cow in underprint; Zimbabwe bird in OVI. Back: Water buffalo; Great Zimbabwe ruins. 7-mm wide iridescent stripe with repeating *RBZ*. No security thread. Watermark: None. Printer: (FPZ). 148 x 74 mm.

- ☐ a. 2008. Signature 5. Intro: 04.12.2008.   —   —   1
       Iridescent stripe with all dark diamonds.
- ☐ b. Stripe with alternating light/dark diamonds.   —   —   1

Replacement notes: Prefix ZA.

There are two varieties of the iridescent stripe on RBZ B70 (shown here horizontally): On some notes all the diamonds are dark with light lettering (B70a, left), whereas on other notes the diamonds and lettering alternate between light/dark (B70b, right).

RBZ B71 (P80): **100,000,000 dollars**   VG   VF   UNC
Red. Front: Chiremba balancing rocks in Epworth; stylized grains and cow in underprint; Zimbabwe bird in OVI. Back: Grain silos. 7-mm wide iridescent stripe with repeating *RBZ*. No security thread. Watermark: None. Printer: (FPZ). 148 x 74 mm.
   ☐ a.   2008. Signature 5. Intro: 04.12.2008.   —   —   2.50
Replacement notes: Prefix ZA.

RBZ B72 (P81): **200,000,000 dollars**   VG   VF   UNC
Brown. Front: Chiremba balancing rocks in Epworth; stylized grains and cow in underprint; Zimbabwe bird in OVI. Back: Parliament building; Heroes' Acre. 7-mm wide iridescent stripe with repeating *RBZ*. No security thread. Watermark: None. Printer: (FPZ). 148 x 74 mm.
   ☐ a.   2008. Signature 5. Intro: 12.12.2008.   —   —   1
Replacement notes: Prefix ZA.

RBZ B73 (P82): **500,000,000 dollars**   VG   VF   UNC
Purple. Front: Chiremba balancing rocks in Epworth; stylized grains and cow in underprint; Zimbabwe bird in OVI. Back: Workers milking cows; miner with jackhammer. 3-mm gold-to-green OVI stripe with repeating *RBZ*. No security thread. Watermark: None. Printer: (FPZ). 148 x 74 mm.
   ☐ a.   2008. Signature 5. Intro: 12.12.2008.   —   —   1

RBZ B74 (P83): **1,000,000,000 dollars**   VG   VF   UNC
Green. Front: Chiremba balancing rocks in Epworth; stylized grains and cow in underprint; Zimbabwe bird in OVI. Back: Aloe excelsa trees; elephant. 3-mm gold-to-green OVI stripe with repeating *RBZ*. No security thread. Watermark: None. Printer: (FPZ). 148 x 74 mm.
   ☐ a.   2008. Signature 5. Intro: 19.12.2008.   —   —   1
Replacement notes: Prefix ZA.

RBZ B75 (P84): **5,000,000,000 dollars** VG VF UNC
Brown and purple. Front: Chiremba balancing rocks in Epworth; stylized grains and cow in underprint; Zimbabwe bird in OVI. Back: Farmer plowing field on mechanical tractor; workers milking cows. 3-mm gold-to-green OVI stripe with repeating *RBZ*. No security thread. Watermark: None. Printer: (FPZ). 148 x 74 mm.
☐ a. 2008. Signature 5. Intro: 19.12.2008.   —   —   1
Replacement notes: Prefix ZA.

RBZ B77 (P86): **20,000,000,000 dollars** VG VF UNC
Green. Front: Chiremba balancing rocks in Epworth; stylized grains and cow in underprint; Zimbabwe bird in OVI. Back: Great Zimbabwe ruins; aloe excelsa trees. 3-mm gold-to-green OVI stripe with repeating *RBZ*. No security thread. Watermark: None. Printer: (FPZ). 148 x 74 mm.
☐ a. 2008. Signature 5. Intro: 09.01.2009.   —   —   1
Replacement notes: Prefix ZA.

RBZ B76 (P85): **10,000,000,000 dollars** VG VF UNC
Purple. Front: Chiremba balancing rocks in Epworth; stylized grains and cow in underprint; Zimbabwe bird in OVI. Back: Kariba dam; miner with jackhammer. 3-mm gold-to-green OVI stripe with repeating *RBZ*. No security thread. Watermark: None. Printer: (FPZ). 148 x 74 mm.
☐ a. 2008. Signature 5. Intro: 19.12.2008.   —   —   1
Replacement notes: Prefix ZA.

RBZ B78 (P87): **50,000,000,000 dollars** VG VF UNC
Brown. Front: Chiremba balancing rocks in Epworth; stylized grains and cow in underprint; Zimbabwe bird in OVI. Back: Great Zimbabwe ruins; RBZ headquarters building. 3-mm gold-to-green OVI stripe with repeating *RBZ*. No security thread. Watermark: None. Printer: (FPZ). 148 x 74 mm.
☐ a. 2008. Signature 5. Intro: 09.01.2009.   —   —   1.50
Replacement notes: Prefix ZA.

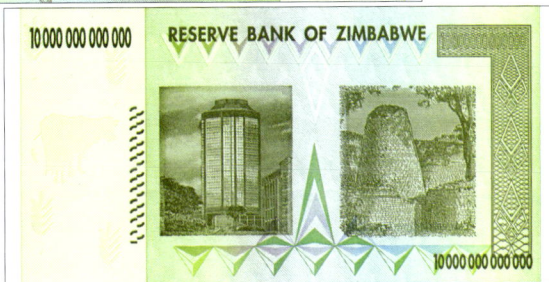

RBZ B79 (P88): **10,000,000,000,000 dollars** VG VF UNC
Green Front: Chiremba balancing rocks in Epworth; stylized grains and cow in underprint; Zimbabwe bird in OVI. Back: RBZ headquarters building; Great Zimbabwe ruins. 3-mm gold-to-green OVI stripe with repeating *RBZ*. No security thread. Watermark: None. Printer: (FPZ). 148 x 74 mm.
☐ a. 2008. Signature 5. Intro: 16.01.2009.   —   —   1.50
Replacement notes: Prefix ZA.

RBZ B80 (P89): **20,000,000,000,000 dollars** VG VF UNC
Red. Front: Chiremba balancing rocks in Epworth; stylized grains and cow in underprint; Zimbabwe bird in OVI. Back: Miner with jackhammer; GMB grain silos. 3-mm gold-to-green OVI stripe with repeating *RBZ*. No security thread. Watermark: None. Printer: (FPZ). 148 x 74 mm.
☐ a. 2008. Signature 5. Intro: 16.01.2009.   —   —   4
Replacement notes: Prefix ZA.

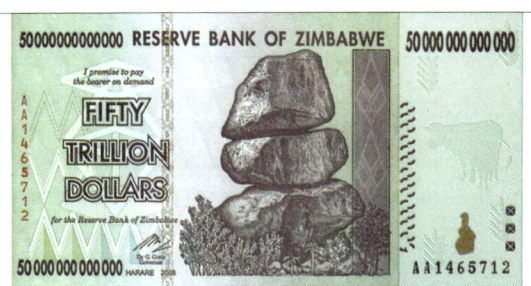

RBZ B81 (P90): **50,000,000,000,000 dollars** VG VF UNC
Green. Front: Chiremba balancing rocks in Epworth; stylized grains and cow in underprint; Zimbabwe bird in OVI. Back: Kariba dam; elephant. 3-mm gold-to-green OVI stripe with repeating *RBZ*. No security thread. Watermark: None. Printer: (FPZ). 148 x 74 mm.
☐ a. 2008. Signature 5. Intro: 16.01.2009.   —   —   1
Replacement notes: Prefix ZA.

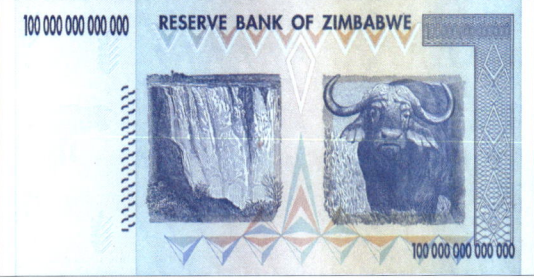

RBZ B82 (P91): **100,000,000,000,000 dollars** VG VF UNC
Blue. Front: Chiremba balancing rocks in Epworth; stylized grains and cow in underprint; Zimbabwe bird in OVI. Back: Victoria Falls; water buffalo. 3-mm gold-to-green OVI stripe with repeating *RBZ*. No security thread. Watermark: None. Printer: (FPZ). 148 x 74 mm.
☐ a. 2008. Signature 5. Intro: 16.01.2009.   —   —   8.50
Replacement notes: Prefix ZA.

2009 Issues

According to a BBC News report dated 29 January 2009, while delivering the annual budget to parliament, acting Finance Minister Patrick Chinamasa announced, "In line with the prevailing practices by the general public, [the] government is therefore allowing the use of multiple foreign currencies for business transactions alongside the Zimbabwean dollar." Previously only licensed businesses could accept foreign currencies, although it was common practice in the black market.

According to a report in The Zimbabwe Times dated 2 February 2009, Gideon Gono, governor of the Reserve Bank of Zimbabwe, said that Fidelity Printers could churn out only two million notes per day, an amount insufficient to meet the public's demand for currency. Nonetheless, the country announced that it was yet again revaluing the dollar, this time by removing 12 zeros. That meant the highest denomination in the "old" money, Z$100 trillion, would now equal to Z$100. New notes were available in denominations of 1, 5, 10, 20, 50, 100, and 500 dollars. They all feature a color-shift stripe with RBZ, a color-shift Zimbabwe bird, and chevrons as registration devices. The older notes circulated in parallel until 30 June 2009.

RBZ B83 (P92): **1 dollar**   VG   VF   UNC
Light blue. Front: Chiremba balancing rocks in Epworth; stylized grains and livestock in underprint; Zimbabwe bird in OVI. Back: Village huts; two women pounding maize with poles. 3-mm iridescent stripe with repeating *RBZ*. No security thread. Watermark: None. Printer: (FPZ). 148 x 74 mm.
 ☐ a. 2009. Signature 5. Intro: 02.02.2009. — — 1
 ☐ as. Diagonal *SPECIMEN* perforation. — — —
Replacement notes: Prefix ZA.

RBZ B84 (P93): **5 dollars**   VG   VF   UNC
Tan and green. Front: Chiremba balancing rocks in Epworth; stylized grains and livestock in underprint; Zimbabwe bird in OVI. Back: Tigerfish; Kariba Dam on Zambezi River. 3-mm iridescent stripe with repeating *RBZ*. No security thread. Watermark: None. Printer: (FPZ). 148 x 74 mm.
 ☐ a. 2009. Signature 5. Intro: 02.02.2009. — — 0.50
 ☐ as. Diagonal *SPECIMEN* perforation. — — —
Replacement notes: Prefix ZA.

RBZ B85 (P94): **10 dollars**   VG   VF   UNC
Red and tan. Front: Chiremba balancing rocks in Epworth; stylized grains and livestock in underprint; Zimbabwe bird in OVI. Back: Great Zimbabwe ruins. 3-mm iridescent stripe with repeating *RBZ*. No security thread. Watermark: None. Printer: (FPZ). 148 x 74 mm.
 ☐ a. 2009. Signature 5. Intro: 02.02.2009. — — 0;75
 ☐ as. Diagonal *SPECIMEN* perforation. — — —
Replacement notes: Prefix ZA.

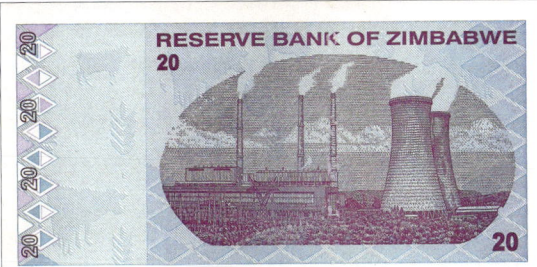

RBZ B86 (P95): **20 dollars**   VG   VF   UNC

Purple and light blue. Front: Chiremba balancing rocks in Epworth; stylized grains and livestock in underprint; Zimbabwe bird in OVI. Back: Hwange thermal power station smokestacks and cooling towers. 3-mm iridescent stripe with repeating *RBZ*. No security thread. Watermark: None. Printer: (FPZ). 148 x 74 mm.

    ☐ a. 2009. Signature 5. Intro: 02.02.2009.   —   —   0.75
    ☐ as. Diagonal *SPECIMEN* perforation.   —   —   —

Replacement notes: Prefix ZA.

RBZ B88 (P97): **100 dollars**   VG   VF   UNC

Brown. Front: Chiremba balancing rocks in Epworth; stylized grains and livestock in underprint; Zimbabwe bird in OVI. Back: Freedom Flame monument; Harare buildings. 3-mm iridescent stripe with repeating *RBZ*. No security thread. Watermark: None. Printer: (FPZ). 148 x 74 mm.

    ☐ a. 2009. Signature 5. Intro: 02.02.2009.   —   —   1
    ☐ as. Diagonal *SPECIMEN* perforation.   —   —   —

Replacement notes: Prefix ZA.

RBZ B87 (P96): **50 dollars**   VG   VF   UNC

Violet. Front: Chiremba balancing rocks in Epworth; stylized grains and livestock in underprint; Zimbabwe bird in OVI. Back: Hwange thermal power station smokestacks and cooling towers. 3-mm iridescent stripe with repeating *RBZ*. No security thread. Watermark: None. Printer: (FPZ). 148 x 74 mm.

    ☐ a. 2009. Signature 5. Intro: 02.02.2009.   —   —   2
    ☐ as. Diagonal *SPECIMEN* perforation.   —   —   —

Replacement notes: Prefix ZA.

RBZ B89 (P98): **500 dollars**   VG   VF   UNC

Green. Front: Chiremba balancing rocks in Epworth; stylized grains and livestock in underprint; Zimbabwe bird in OVI. Back: Three elephants. 3-mm iridescent stripe with repeating *RBZ*. No security thread. Watermark: None. Printer: (FPZ). 148 x 74 mm.

    ☐ a. 2009. Signature 5. Intro: 02.02.2009.   —   —   2
    ☐ as. Diagonal *SPECIMEN* perforation.   —   —   —

Replacement notes: Prefix ZA.

Cargill Cotton Group

The Cargill Cotton Group is a private company doing business in Zimbabwe.

CC Signature Varieties

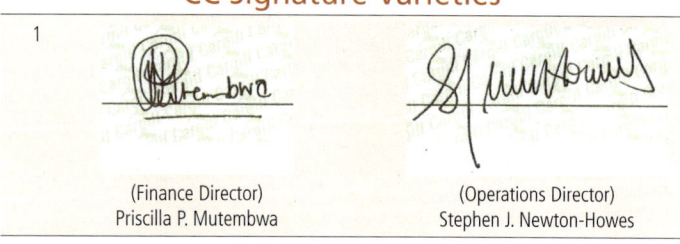

1

(Finance Director)
Priscilla P. Mutembwa

(Operations Director)
Stephen J. Newton-Howes

2003 Bearer Cheque Issues

In May 2003, the Cargill Cotton Group issued bearer cheques authorized by the RBZ. These were valid for a period of six months. By the end of 2003, 85% of them had been redeemed.

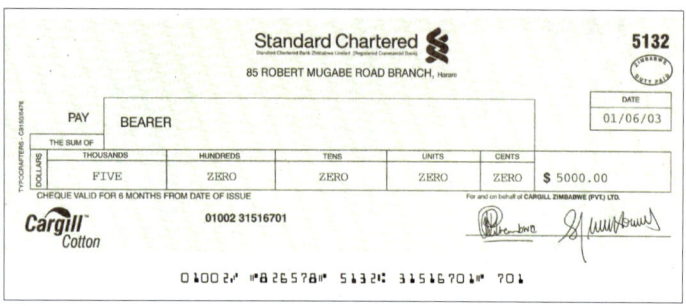

CC B1 (P13): **5,000 dollars** (demonetized 21.08.2006) VG VF UNC
Light green. Uniface: Standard Chartered logo and Cargill Cotton logo. No security thread. Watermark: *Cotton plant*. Printer: TYPOCRAFTERS. 220 x 92 mm.
   ☐ a. 01/06/03. Signature 1.   10 35 150
   ☐ b. 01/09/03.   13 45 175

CC B2 (P14): **10,000 dollars** (demonetized 21.08.2006) VG VF UNC
Blue. Uniface: Standard Chartered logo and Cargill Cotton logo. No security thread. Watermark: *Cotton plant*. Printer: TYPOCRAFTERS. 220 x 92 mm.
   ☐ a. 01/05/03. Signature 1.   15 65 250
         PAY TO ORDER OF BEARER.
   ☐ b. PAY BEARER.   15 75 300
   ☐ c. 01/09/03.   15 75 300

2004 Bearer Cheque Issues

In April 2004, the Cargill Cotton Group issued a new series of bearer cheques authorized by the RBZ.

CC B3 (P24): **10,000 dollars** (demonetized 21.08.2006) VG VF UNC
Light blue. Uniface: Standard Chartered logo and Cargill Cotton logo. No security thread. Watermark: *Citation*. Printer: TYPOCRAFTERS. 205 x 92 mm.
   ☐ a. 01 APRIL 2004. Signature 1.   7.50 20 75

CC B4 (P25): **20,000 dollars** (demonetized 21.08.2006) VG VF UNC
Light green. Uniface: Standard Chartered logo and Cargill Cotton logo. No security thread. Watermark: *Citation*. Printer: TYPOCRAFTERS. 205 x 92 mm.
   ☐ a. 01 APRIL 2004. Signature 1.   10 35 125

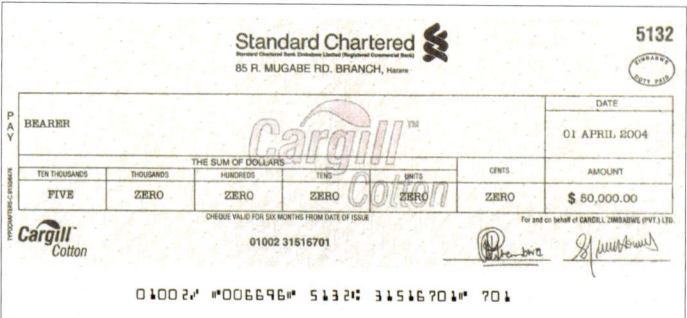

CC B5 (P26): **50,000 dollars** (demonetized 21.08.2006) VG VF UNC
Orange. Uniface: Standard Chartered logo and Cargill Cotton logo. No security thread. Watermark: *Citation*. Printer: TYPOCRAFTERS. 205 x 92 mm.
   ☐ a. 01 APRIL 2004. Signature 1.   20 65 200

CC B6 (P27): 100,000 dollars (demonetized 21.08.2006)   VG   VF   UNC
Red. Uniface: Standard Chartered logo and Cargill Cotton logo. No security thread.
Watermark: *Citation*. Printer: *TYPOCRAFTERS*. 205 x 92 mm.

☐ a. 01 APRIL 2004. Signature 1.   25   85   250

Looking Forward

According to a BBC News article dated 12 April 2009, Zimbabwe has suspended the use of the Zimbabwe dollar for at least a year following the legalization of foreign currencies (most notably the United States dollar and South African rand). "There was nothing to support the value of the Zimbabwean dollar," admitted Economic Planning Minister Elton Mangoma. The use of foreign currency has been allowed since January to combat the hyper-inflation that quickly devastated the value of all Zimbabwean dollar-denominated notes. The state-controlled Sunday Mail newspaper said the unity government of Mugabe and opposition leader Morgan Tsvangirai decided the Zimbabwe dollar should only be reintroduced when industrial output reaches about 60 percent of capacity from the current 20 percent average.

Acknowledgements

This chapter was compiled with the generous assistance of Thomas Augustsson, Nick Brice, Ricardo Castedo, Jim W.-C. Chen, Garry Craig, Mirsad Delic, Victor Hasson, Mike Hughes, Mark Irwin, Dave Kenney, Steve Milner, Wally Myers, Andrew Roberts, Bill Stubkjaer, Christoph Thomas, Tristan Williams, Didier Wiot, Christof Zellweger, and others.

Sources

Cuhaj, George S. *Standard Catalog of World Paper Money, Modern Issues, 1961-Present*. 17th edition. 2011. ISBN 978-1-4402-1584-1. Krause Publications (www.krausebooks.com), 700 East State St., Iola, WI, 54990-0001.

Milner, Steve. *Rhodesia-Zimbabwe Banknotes Newsletters*.

Share Your Input, Info, and Images

This catalog is believed to be complete and correct as of the time of publication. Prices and face values were last updated 15 July 2014. Please report errors or omissions so that corrections may be made. If you can more precisely identify the name or location of anything depicted on a note, please share that information. Furthermore, if you own an unlisted type or variety, please submit scans of the front and back of the note so that it can be documented. Scans should be 300 dots per inch, 100% actual size, 24-bit color, saved as *uncompressed* JPEG files, and sent to owen@banknotenews.com. Be sure to fully describe all attributes of the note which are not apparent upon visual inspection of the images alone, such as physical dimension, watermark, and security thread.